Honolulu Stories

Honolulu Stories

VOICES OF THE TOWN THROUGH THE YEARS

two centuries of writing

Honolulu Stories extends thanks
and appreciation for support from:

Honolulu Stories

VOICES OF THE TOWN THROUGH THE YEARS

two centuries of writing

Edited by

Gavan Daws and Bennett Hymer

Mutual Publishing

Library of Congress Cataloging-in-Publication Data

Honolulu stories : voices of the town through the years : two centuries of writing / edited by Gavan Daws and Bennett Hymer.
    p. cm.
  ISBN 1-56647-851-0 (alk. paper) -- ISBN 1-56647-843-X
(pbk. : alk. paper)
  1. Honolulu (Hawaii)--Literary collections. 2. Hawaii--Literary
collections. 3. American literature--Hawaii--Honolulu. I. Daws,
Gavan. II. Hymer, Bennett.
PS571.H3H66 2008
810.8"09969--dc22

                          2007047815

Hardcover ISBN-10: 1-56647-851-0
        ISBN-13: 978-1-56647-851-9
Softcover ISBN-10: 1-56647-843-X
        ISBN-13: 978-1-56647-843-4

Cover image courtesy of the Mark Twain Project
Bancroft Library, University of California, Berkeley
Design by Emily R. Lee
Cover Design by Cynthia Wessendorf

First Printing, April 2008

Mutual Publishing, LLC
1215 Center Street, Suite 210
Honolulu, Hawai'i 96816
Ph: 808-732-1709 / Fax: 808-734-4094
E-mail: info@mutualpublishing.com
www.mutualpublishing.com

Printed in Taiwan

Contents

THE NINETEENTH CENTURY

THE PLANTATION

TO THE TOWN

ON THE BEACH AT WAIKĪKĪ

THE WORLD TURNING

LOCAL

ON THE BEACH AT WAIKĪKĪ ONE MORE TIME

DISLOCATED

THE STREETS OF THE CITY

TO BE HAWAIIAN

AROUND THE ISLAND

PRIVATE PASSION

THIS IS PARADISE

THE WAY WE LIVE NOW

EPILOGUE

LIST OF ILLUSTRATIONS

ACKNOWLEDGMENTS

Honolulu Stories is well over a thousand pages. Thanks are due on every page.

First, to contributors, more than two hundred-fifty of them. Many are no longer with us; we thank their families, their estates, and the archivists and librarians who have preserved their words. And we thank the living for their willingness to allow their individual work to be woven into the big story of life in Honolulu that this book tells.

There are nine languages in the book, with translations. Language by language, we have many people to thank for invaluable guidance and assistance. Hawaiian: Kawika Eyre; Eddie and Myrna Kamae; Davianna McGregor; Ka'upena Wong; special thanks to Bob Stauffer of Ulukau, the Hawaiian Electronic Library; extra special thanks to Puakea Nogelmeier. Japanese: Calvin Kuniyuki; John Stephan; Elaine Takamiya; Brian Niiya of the Japanese Cultural Center of Hawai'i; extra special thanks to Tatsumi Hayashi and Shigeyuki Yoshitake. Chinese: Wing Tek Lum. Korean: Kil Cha; Hui Suk Kim; Kim Yung-Hee; Gary Pak; Michael Pettid; Hyeran Seo; special thanks to Yong-ho Choe, for access to the poems of Yi Hong-gi. Ilocano: Aurelio S. Agcaoili; Deanna Espinas; Ruth Mabanglo; Pacita Cabulera Saludes of GUMIL; extra special thanks to Virgilio Menor Felipe. Portuguese: special thanks to Edgar Knowlton, and to Jeanne Kahanaoi for access to the poems of Manuel Jesus Coito. Spanish: special thanks to Austin Dias for access to the poems of Carlos Mario Fraticelli. Samoan: John Mayer; Vita Tanielu. Pidgin: Derek Bickerton; Lee A. Tonouchi; special thanks to Sarah Roberts.

Librarians, archivists, and curators in Honolulu were extremely helpful in all sorts of ways. We thank De Soto Brown, Bernice P. Bishop Museum; Christel Collins, Mānoa Public Library; Stu Dawrs, Pacific Collection, Hamilton Library, University of Hawai'i; Barbara Dunn, Hawaiian Historical Society; Cynthia Oshiro, University of Hawai'i Center for Oral History; Kanani Reppun, Hawaii Mission Children's Society; Susan Shaner, Carol Silva, and Jason Achiu, Hawai'i State Archives; extra special thanks to Karen Peacock, Head of Special Collections and Pacific Curator, Hamilton Library, University of Hawai'i.

We called upon institutions at a distance for help in arranging reproduction of manuscript pages. We thank Natalie Russell, Huntington Library, Art Collections and Botanical Gardens; Neda Salem, Mark Twain Project, University of California, Berkeley; Natalia Sciarini, Beinecke Rare Book and Manuscript Library, Yale University; Susan Snyder, Bancroft Library, University of California, Berkeley; Thomas J. Wood, Special Collections, University of Illinois at Springfield.

We thank people who have a care for literary and artistic life, here in Hawai'i, on the mainland, and beyond, organizationally and individually: Gaye Chan of Downwind Productions; Jo Chapman of Lannan Foundation; Eric Chock, Darrell Lum, and Joy

Kobayashi Cintron of *Bamboo Ridge*; Jon De Mello and Leah Bernstein of Mountain Apple Records; Pat Matsueda and Frank Stewart of *Mānoa*; Susan Schultz of *Tinfish*; Harry Wong III of Kumu Kahua Theatre; Lois-Ann Yamanaka, Melvin Spencer III, and Lindsay Furuya of *Na'au*; Libby Young of the Star Poets program; Wanda Adams; John Berger; Elliot S. Blair; Betty Bushnell; Kiana Davenport; Keith Emmons; Kimo Gerald; Jack Gillmar; Francine du Plessix Gray; Lesa Griffith; James R. Harstad; Patrick Hennessey; Craig Howes; Martha Hunt Huie; John Jansson; Juris Jurjevics; Dennis Kawaharada; Don Lee; Mark Lutwak; Barry Menikoff; William and Paula Merwin; Melodee Metzger; James Mohr; Frank and Jan Morgan; Laura Ruby; Bruce Schauble; Linda Spalding; Stephen Sumida; Steve Taksler; Paul Theroux; Eric Weyenberg; Carol Wilcox; Y York; David Zmijewski. Special thanks to Sue Cowing; Thomas Farber; Richard Hamasaki. And specialized thanks to Fred Hemmings, who knows about surfboards in history.

We thank the people who read and evaluated the first version of *Honolulu Stories*: Jody Helfund; David Hershinow; Lavonne Leong; Naomi Long; Mindy Pennybacker; Ryan Senaga.

We thank the willing workers at Mutual Publishing: Richard Ahn; Jane Gillespie; Karen Lofstron; Cynthia Lowe; Sean Nagamatsu; Maureen O'Connor; Nicole Sakai; Pamela Simon; Rebecca Widder; extra special thanks to Emily R. Lee and Dawn Sueoka.

And we thank our significant others, Gay Wong and Carolyn Daws.

NOTES ON THE TEXT

Making a book out of hundreds of thousands of words in nine languages, put on paper in various ways over the course of two hundred years, can have complications.

Especially with Hawaiian. For example, you will see the same Hawaiian word spelled in different ways in different places. This is because there have been many changes in usage over time.

One of the main changes is that present-day practice is to indicate pronunciation, and sometimes meaning, by what are called diacritical marks: the *'okina*, a glottal stop, as in Hawai'i, and the *kahakō*, a macron, which is used for lengthening or stressing a vowel, as in Waikīkī.

In the selections, everything Hawaiian appears as it was written at the time, with or without diacriticals (and/or hyphens between syllables). As for what we have written ourselves, in the introduction and elsewhere, we follow present-day practice. But when we write about something that got its name early and was written without diacriticals, and is still around today, with diacriticals, we take note of that. For example, in 1907 it was the University of Hawaii; since the mid-1990s, it has become the University of Hawai'i.

There is also the question of whether to italicize Hawaiian words. Arguments are made for and against. Is Hawaiian a foreign language in Hawai'i? If it is, do you italicize? What about words that have been pretty much fully taken into English? Hula or *hula*, aloha or *aloha*? In the selections, as with diacriticals, everything is the way it was in the original. In our own writing, we have tried to make commonsense decisions.

Still on spelling. If a word in a selection was misspelled, we leave it that way. Jack London (or his printer) misspelled *malihini*, the Hawaiian word for stranger, newcomer or guest, as malahini. That is how it stays. This goes for all languages, not just Hawaiian. John Dominis Holt, one of the most cultivated of Hawaiians (or his printer) misspelled the name of the great seventeenth-century French letter writer as Madame de Sevigne, though the accepted spelling is Sévigny. Proofreading for print over the decades has not been immaculate—"tenderally," "dispair," and many more. So it goes. And there are writings by schoolkids in which the misspellings are part of the charm. So *that* goes.

Concerning translations: when we use a translation that is already in print, the source is listed in the bibliography. When we have had translations specially done, the name of the translator is given. Note that all new translations are "free"—that is to say, in poetry they do not necessarily follow form and meter; in prose, they do not try to replicate cadence; they concentrate on rendering meaning.

Among the nine languages in the book, pidgin is a special case. It is a language of its own, certified by scholars, who gave it a name of its own, Hawaii Creole English. Should we have supplied translations? We decided against. Anybody who lives in Hawai'i has no trouble with pidgin on the page. People reading the book elsewhere can handle pidgin as they would when they come across any regional version of English that is unfamiliar to them. (For noting, reading pidgin aloud can be an interesting way of understanding what is being said.)

Another matter: author biographies. No problem with well-known writers like Mark Twain or Robert Louis Stevenson. With living authors, wherever possible, we got them to draft their own bios—within a necessarily strict word limit, because we had so many names and lives to accommodate. This left others, in great numbers, their work very much worth including, but with little or no trace remaining of their lives—their names writ in water. We have done the best we could, trying to track the dead, and sending out all-points bulletins for the living, among literary organizations, community groups, alumni associations, everywhere we could think of—with very variable outcomes. We regret the overall inconsistency.

On a related point: permissions. No problem with well-known authors in print with major publishers. Much more of a practical difficulty with authors who may have published very little, maybe decades ago, in places that have no current knowledge of them. Again, we have done the very best we could. Many more times than we were happy with, we came up dry, and then we had to decide whether to take the chance and publish. We have kept complete records of efforts made. We would greatly appreciate hearing from anyone with information on particular cases that would help us get things perfectly squared away for any future editions.

INTRODUCTION

"It takes a great deal of history to make a little literature."

The great writer Henry James said that. He never came within an ocean of Hawai'i, but he got it right about Honolulu.

History first. Honolulu's written record goes back not much more than two centuries. The earliest words put on paper about the place date from 1793, when the Hawaiian Islands had been on the map of the world for only fifteen years and were still not charted in detail. William Brown, a merchant ship captain in the northwest America fur trade, also a seller of guns, was coasting the south shore of O'ahu, one of the eight inhabited islands in the archipelago, when he sighted the entrance to a harbor. The harbor turned out to be deep enough for Western ships. It was the making of a little town, which became known as Honolulu. Decade by decade, modern history washed in on the tides and piled up around the waterfront, and the town grew into a city. Literature came along, in its own time (the Hawaiians killed William Brown, but nobody wrote a story about it).

For at least a thousand years before Brown—possibly much longer— Hawaiians had been living by the harbor; on the shores to the east and west, from Waikīkī to Wai'anae; and in the upland valleys of Nu'uanu and Mānoa and Pālolo and Kalihi and Moanalua and Hālawa.

The history of the Hawaiians—the story they told about themselves— was set in their small islands, the most remote and isolated in the world, set in *ka moana nui o Kanaloa*, the god Kanaloa's expansive sea, the huge ocean that the world calls the Pacific. Earth, sea and sky, sun, moon and stars—for the Hawaiians, this was the universe. They did not have towns and cities. And they did not have writing; theirs was an oral culture. They told and retold their story among themselves, remembering, reconstructing, imagining, calling upon the gods who created all life to reassure them that the story was true. And everything in the Hawaiians' story, from creation to the living moment, was carried by the spoken word—words passed on, generation after generation, through the centuries, not by being written down but memorized, words that were performed, chanted, sometimes to drumming and dancing: the *hula* was Hawaiian storytelling.

Only after pen and ink, and then the printing press, came to Honolulu on Western ships was the Hawaiian language put in writing and set in type. And that is how in the nineteenth century the stories of the Hawaiians were preserved not only in memory but on paper as well—in their own rich poetic language, and in English, the great language of the big world, as the history of the Hawaiians became part of the history of the big world.

Henry James, following up on his thought about history and literature, said that "a complex social machinery" was needed to set a writer in motion. James was talking about imaginative writing, not nonfiction. In *Honolulu Stories*, all the stories are imaginative—close to three hundred-fifty of them, in nine languages, with translations, telling the tale of the town through the years, in nineteenth, twentieth, and twenty-first-century ways: short fiction, excerpts from novels, scenes from plays, musicals and operas, poems, chants, song lyrics, cartoons, standup comedy, and slam.

History, continued. By the 1820s, there was complex social machinery grinding away in Honolulu. The town was growing into a busy whaling port—raucous, rising to riotous. It was also a missionary outpost of a severe kind of Christianity, American Protestant, New England Calvinist. Now, in one square mile around the waterfront, two conflicting sets of Western social machinery were colliding and clashing. Wherever the Hawaiians of Honolulu walked, they were stepping out into new kinds of life traffic, and they had to look both ways.

Stories were written in English about this, dime novels on one side, pious tales with a moral on the other; but none of them were by people who were in Honolulu at the time they were writing about, seeing things for themselves.

Herman Melville saw for himself, in 1843. He had jumped ship from a whaler in the South Seas. He spent time on the loose in the Marquesas Islands, and a different kind of time in Tahiti, in the calabooza, a relaxed straw hut jail. After that, he made his way to Honolulu. He did some clerking, worked as a pin setter in a bowling alley, and then shipped out as a deckhand, back home to the east coast of the United States, where he wrote a novel, *Typee*. It made him a literary celebrity, amazing to Americans for having lived among savages.

Some years after Melville published his sixth book, *Moby Dick*, in New York, a Hawaiian in Honolulu composed a chant about the masts of all the ships in the harbor—*Ka Ulu Lā'au o Kai*, forest trees of the sea. The chant got written down on paper, but the name of the composer did not; like so many Hawaiians, he was left anonymous.

In 1866, Samuel Langhorne Clemens came to Honolulu from California, by steamer, the latest thing. He was a working journalist, writing letters for publication in a Sacramento newspaper, under the name Mark Twain. He stayed a few months. His look at the town and its people, and his travels around the islands, gave him material for a humorous lecture about Hawaiians, "Our Fellow Savages," that he delivered back on the American main-

land, to big audiences and great applause, close to a hundred times. It helped
to make him famous. For years, Hawai'i was in his mind. He said he was
working on a novel set there, with a part-Hawaiian who lived in Honolulu as
the main character. He wrote letters saying he had finished the book. But he
never brought it to press. Instead, he published *Huckleberry Finn*—which, in
any considered overview of the annals of history and literature, looks to have
been the better career move. The manuscript of his Hawai'i novel disappeared, except for a dozen and a half pages, never published; one of the fragments is in print here for the first time, along with the evidence of Twain's
handwriting.

The Honolulu that Twain saw and wrote about was the capital city of
the Hawaiian kingdom, an independent nation, but a tiny one. In the age
of Western imperialism it was insecure, under threat from the colonizing
powers in the Pacific—Britain, France, and then the United States. Warships were often in the harbor at Honolulu, with their cannons trained on
the town.

Foreign ships came with another kind of deathdealing. All through the
nineteenth century, Honolulu was the port of entry for lethal diseases of
the big world: smallpox, cholera, tuberculosis, influenza, measles, whooping
cough, mumps, scarlet fever, syphilis and gonorrhea, bubonic plague, leprosy. Epidemics killed thousands upon thousands of Hawaiians. There were
mass graves lying just below the surface of the town. There still are—history
in skulls and bones. And there were heartbreak voices on the wind. "*E aha 'ia
ana 'o Hawai'i, I nei ma'i 'o ka lepela?*—What will become of Hawai'i? What
will leprosy do to our land?" This was the last known chant of Ka'ehu, who
was rounded up at gunpoint as leprous and shipped away to die in exile at the
quarantine settlement of Kalaupapa on the island of Moloka'i.

While Hawaiians were dying, Honolulu was doing well. By the 1880s,
the town was making good money from plantation agriculture, exporting
sugar to the United States, and later pineapples, grown on land controlled
by big businesses—capitalism in the tropics. The crops were planted and
cultivated and harvested by contract labor shipped in from China, coolies,
working with shovels and hoes and cane knives, long days and years of sweltering in the sun; and then Japanese in large numbers, with an admixture of
Portuguese, a sprinkling of Norwegians, Germans, Scots, Austrians, Ital-
ians, Swedes, Greeks, Okinawans, and a few South Sea Islanders.

So Honolulu late in the nineteenth century had many skin colors to
show: Polynesian brown; Western white, mostly American; some black
among the Portuguese from Madeira and the Azores; and Asian yellow. A
babel of tongues on the streets, and more men than women, by an order of
magnitude—complex social machinery for a town of twenty thousand.

Away in the middle of the vast Pacific, baking in the heat of tropical latitudes, as distant from the cities of the continents as any place on earth—Honolulu could not have been farther out of the mainstream of civilization. Still, after its own fashion, the town was up-to-date, and not entirely unsophisticated. By the 1830s, it had newspapers, one in Hawaiian, 1834, even before the first one in English, 1836. A bowling alley, 1837. Public education, 1840. Daguerreotype cameras, 1845. A theater, 1847. Piped water, 1848. By 1854, brick buildings, a brewery, and a performance of opera. Gas light, 1857. And, from the mid-1850s, a Western royal court, with a Hawaiian king and queen, an English butler and a French chef, soirées, protocol, bowing from the waist, polite conversation, Paris gowns featuring décolletage, flirtatious fan play on hot nights, and waltzing. In 1864, a daily paper in Hawaiian. Horse-drawn omnibuses, 1868. Bookstores, 1869. A royal band with a first-class German bandmaster, 1872. A national museum, 1875. A library and reading room, 1879. Telephones, 1880. In 1882, a Social Science Association, "to give special attention to the consideration of various topics as these affect the general welfare of society." In 1883, a Chinese-language paper and an English-language daily. A Portuguese-language paper in 1885. And the beginnings of electric lighting.

This was the town that Robert Louis Stevenson saw. He came to Honolulu in 1889. He was the most famous novelist of his time in the English language, the author of *Treasure Island* and *Dr. Jekyll and Mr. Hyde.* He did not stay long. He was traveling for his health, which was desperately bad, looking for a climate that might help keep him alive. He eventually found it in Samoa. At Waikīkī, he sat under a banyan tree with a young Hawaiian princess, Victoria Kawēkiu Ka'iulani Lunalilo Kalaninuiahilapalapa, and wrote a poem for her in her red plush album. His mother, who was traveling with him, made a fair copy.

In 1891, the Hawaiian Historical Society was founded in Honolulu. Its membership was close to one hundred percent white. The first annual meeting was in December, 1892. A month later, there came a shocking grinding of the gears of history. In January, 1893, the Hawaiian monarchy was overthrown, in a bloodless armed revolution on the streets of the town, engineered by white men, led by descendants of the American Protestant missionaries. A good number of the historical society's members were active in the overthrow. The society did not meet again until the next year, and it did not take historical note of the revolution; the papers that were given in 1894 were about one of the kings of Hawai'i, three decades and four rulers in the past.

Then, in 1898, the United States annexed Hawai'i. There were triumphal novels written about this by Americans, and chants of loss and dispossession composed by Hawaiians, sorrowful and enraged: *"Paulele oe i ka mikanele, Aihue aina makakeleawe*—You put your trust in missionaries, A brazen bunch of land thieves . . . ".

Hawaiian kings and queens were history. In the Territory of Hawaii, in the new American century, sugar was king. More and more labor was shipped in through Honolulu harbor to work the plantations of rural O'ahu and the outer islands: more Japanese, then Koreans, Puerto Ricans, Spanish, and Filipinos in great numbers—at least ten non-English speakers for every one English speaker, and rising, meaning more and more babel on the streets of the town, Hawaiian now just one tongue among many, a minority language.

In plantation Hawai'i, alien field workers were the lowest of the low, not seriously counted as human, just as units of work, or inventory. But among themselves they were creating a literature of the place, in the languages and the writing traditions of their homelands: Japanese *haiku*, a form that went back more than two hundred years; *tanka*, twelve hundred years; Korean *ch'ironsi*, done in brush strokes; Spanish *décima* and Portuguese *fado*, copied out with steel-nibbed pens.

At the same time, more and more of the complex social machinery of America was being activated in Honolulu: modernity. The first automobile, 1899; the first auto theft, 1900; and in 1906 the first fatal accident. In 1900, a symphony orchestra. The first big hotel at Waikīkī, the Moana, 1901. The first movie house, 1906. A rudimentary university college, for agriculture, 1907. The first airplane flight over the town, 1910.

In 1913, a sensitive young British poet named Rupert Brooke spent some days at the Moana. Brooke fitted the description of a tourist; he had done a lot of traveling, and could make comparisons, from the Pyramids to Cannes to Canada. He found Honolulu dreadfully American. But there were exotic things too. In Brooke's "Waikiki," the *'ukulele* appeared in a sonnet for the first time in the world history of poetry. It was a small musical instrument, developed in Hawai'i, with a light sound, made by four strings, strummed over a wooden body. Brooke spelled it *eukaleli*, and the way he wrote it up, the chords were a "thrill and cry" that "stabbed with pain the night's brown savagery"—which was certainly exotic enough to be going on with.

Being exotic was the big selling point for tourism. Within two years of Brooke and the eukaleli, tourist-oriented sweet brown maidens were turning up in songs written in Honolulu, homegrown. "On the Beach at Waikiki" developed into an export commodity. It was a great hit in the Hawaiian pavilion at the Panama-Pacific International Exposition in San Francisco in 1915, with a sensational stageful of sweet brown maiden hula girls. From there, it went nationwide. At a time before commercial radio or widespread recorded music, it traveled all the way across country to the east coast in a matter of months, no stopping it–a big transcontinental sheet music seller. By the end of the year it had reached New York; and in the last week in December, Honolulu was on the Broadway stage in not one but two musicals opening within days of each other: Jerome Kern's *Very Good Eddie* and Irving Berlin's *Stop!Look!Listen!* More than any other song, "On the Beach at Waikiki" was responsible for a nationwide "Hawaiian" music craze–rinky-dink ricky-ticky Tin Pan Alley melodies and Hawaiianola hoola-ma-boola yaaka-hula-hickey-doola jinga-bula-jing-jing doo-wacka-doo yacki-hacki-wicki-wacki-woo kicky-koo-kicky-koo words.

Another literary tourist in those years was Jack London. He visited Hawai'i before Rupert Brooke, and again after. The first time, in 1907, he sailed to Honolulu from San Francisco on his own yacht. He stayed in the islands for months. He came back in 1915, and again in 1916. London was world-famous for his muscular writing—*White Fang* and *The Call of the Wild*. He liked Waikīkī. He spent a lot of time on the beach there with his wife, Charmian, who looked exceptionally good in a bathing suit, and he paddled out into the breaking waves on a long redwood surfboard. He was the first celebrated writer to put surfing in short stories.

W. Somerset Maugham was as famous as Jack London, as famous as anyone writing in English. He stopped at Honolulu on a world tour in 1916. He missed London by three months. Not that they would have had much in common—Maugham was not American; rather, he was British, distinctly not muscular, decidedly not a surfer, and he did not have a wife; his traveling companion was a young man. While he was in town, the vice squad happened to be cleaning out a big brothel district by the harbor, Iwilei. In the spirit of writerly curiosity, Maugham toured the whorehouse streets and took notes. When he left Honolulu, on a steamer for Samoa, a white woman from Iwilei was on board too, run out of town. Maugham put her in a short story, "Rain." He used her real name, Sadie Thompson, and in his story she ruined a Protestant missionary. "Rain" became famous. It was made into a Broadway play, and three Hollywood movies as well, starring, in order, Gloria Swanson, Joan Crawford, and Rita Hayworth—glamorous missionary ruiners, 1928-1953.

In 1920, another famous Englishman came to Honolulu, on a British battleship, in peace: Edward Albert Christian George Andrew Patrick David, Duke of Cornwall, Prince of Wales, heir to the British throne, who later gave up being Edward VIII, King of Great Britain, Ireland, the British Dominions Beyond the Seas, and Emperor of India, in favor of society life with an American woman, a double divorcee. The young prince was photographed at Waikīkī, pale-skinned in the hot Hawaiian sun, posed in a bathing suit—racy stuff for a British royal in the direct line of descent from Queen Victoria. (His father, the king, wrote him a stiffly disapproving letter about exhibiting himself.) The suit, or what was said to be the suit, was acquired by a private collector in Honolulu, who displayed it in his home, on a mannequin body, spotlit; but no one wrote a story about that.

In 1927, the Honolulu Academy of Arts opened. In the same year (and two years before a burlesque house), the Royal Hawaiian Hotel was completed, ready for business on the beach at Waikīkī—a Spanish-Moorish pink palace, looking like an extravagance of sculpted sugary confectionery. It was built on land that used to be a playground of the old high chiefs; the white owners co-opted the rank of "royal" from this piece of the history of the Hawaiians. On the hotel's first night, a Hawaiian performed a *mele inoa* for it, the kind of traditional name chant that used to be composed in honor of high chiefs. Twelve hundred invited guests sat down to dinner. All of them were white. They were served by Oriental waiters and entertained by Hawaiian dancers and chanters in a pageant directed by Princess Abigail Wahīka'ahu'ula Campbell Kawānanakoa, a niece by marriage of the last two monarchs of the Hawaiian kingdom, David La'amea Kamanakapu'u Māhinulani Nālo'iaehuokalani Lumialani Kalākaua and his sister, Lydia Kamaka'eha Ka'ōlaniali'i Neweweli'i Lili'uokalani. Princess Abigail was the first person to register at the hotel, but she did not stay the night.

Songs were written about the Royal. It was a five-star resort, catering exclusively to the highest of the high-class tourist trade. From San Francisco to Honolulu, the high-class tourists had four or five magic days and nights on the blue Pacific aboard a luxury cruise ship of the Matson Navigation Company. The richest women in the world booked top-dollar top-deck suites, with their playboy traveling companions. Movie stars came to the Royal that way: Mary Pickford and Douglas Fairbanks, Gilbert Roland, Norma Talmadge, Al Jolson, Ruby Keeler, Bing Crosby, Dorothy Lamour, Clark Gable. And Shirley Temple, the biggest box-office attraction in Hollywood—the biggest child star ever, worldwide. In 1935, at the age of six, going on seven, she danced a little-girl hula to "On the Beach at Waikiki" in the movie *Curly Top*, grass-skirted down to the ankle, and above the waist topless except for a lei. (In 1937, another Hollywood celebrity danced a hula to "On the Beach at Waikiki"—Minnie Mouse, in a Disney cartoon, *Hawaiian Holiday*, also topless, as she always was, except for a lei.) On the hotel's beach, contessas and maharajahs lounged in deck chairs, alongside the conspicuously consuming offspring of robber barons, Rockefellers, DuPonts, Fords. And when the first president of the United States to visit Hawai'i, Franklin Delano Roosevelt, came to Honolulu in 1934, the Royal was where he stayed.

A different kind of famous personage around Waikīkī was Charlie Chan. He was a detective in the Honolulu police force, made up by an American writer, Earl Derr Biggers, who spent some time in town, though not much. Charlie was Chinese, built like a Buddha. He had a full home life—a house on a hill overlooking the city, and a wife and eleven children, starting with Number One Son. On the job, Charlie proceeded in stately fashion, wearing a dark suit, unsweating in the Honolulu heat. He did not make sudden Oriental martial arts moves, or quick-draw revolvers of heavy caliber. When he spoke, which was not all that often, it was in fortune-cookie English. Who could fathom Charlie's Mysterious East thought processes? Nobody: he was inscrutable. But he was the one who solved the most baffling crimes in town. He deserved the grateful thanks of Honolulu.

Charlie Chan, the alliterative Chinaman—when he was in the movies for the first time, in 1926, the actor was a Japanese; and then, in dozens more films in the Thirties, Forties and Fifties, he was played by four white men in a row.

In 1935, while Charlie was big in Hollywood, the celebrated aviatrix Amelia Earhart sailed to Honolulu from California on the Matson liner S.S. *Lurline,* bringing her own plane with her, a Lockheed Vega, and then flew back solo to Oakland, a first across the Pacific in that direction. The next year, 1936, Pan American World Airways started its Clipper seaplane service from the west coast, averaging twenty hours in the air between San Francisco and Honolulu, touching down in Keʻehi Lagoon, a mile or so west of the business district. Don Blanding, the poet laureate of Waikīkī, flew Pan Am.

Honolulu was still exotic, a faraway place with a strange-sounding name, and the town was written about like that—Blanding, who was a great booster of tourism, made a specialty of it, for more than thirty years. But the big world was closing in, meaning geopolitics.

Hawaiʻi was the strategic spearhead of the United States in the Pacific-Asian hemisphere. The island of Oʻahu had military airfields, a marine base, and a big army barracks, Schofield, all within twenty miles or so of Honolulu—and, closer still to town, Pearl Harbor, the home port of the Pacific fleet, opened up by massive dredging of coral reefs so that battleships and aircraft carriers could anchor there in numbers. By 1940, there were more than thirty thousand men in uniform on Oʻahu, by 1941 nearly fifty thousand—a serviceman for every eight civilians.

The evening of December 6, 1941, was like every other Saturday night in Honolulu in those years—soldiers and sailors on twenty-four-hour passes, swarming all over the Chinatown bars and dance halls and tattoo parlors and souvenir shops (your photo with an authentic hula girl, cheap), and jamming the sidewalks outside the mass-production assembly-line brothels on Hotel Street.

The next morning, Sunday, December 7, just before eight o'clock—day of rest, hangover time—Japanese fighter planes and bombers came with the rising sun and attacked Pearl Harbor. World War II in the Pacific started seven miles from downtown Honolulu.

The town went under martial law—blackouts, bomb shelters, gas masks, food rationing, Japanese families fearful of being rounded up and interned. There were stories written about all this, and about local girls dancing with white servicemen on a dare.

In less than four years of war in the Pacific, the head count of men from the mainland United States who passed through Honolulu in uniform rose to millions. For the Hotel Street brothels, it was a gold rush. Sadie Thompson missed the bonanza by twenty-five years. Another hooker, a big busty blonde who had washed up in town from Hollywood, hit the peak and then some. In William Bradford Huie's novel, *The Revolt of Mamie Stover*, Mamie had a vision: servicemen, shiploads and shiploads and more shiploads of them, an endless supply of insatiable demand. She did her sums, counted the zeros on the bottom line, and turned herself into the Henry Ford of harlotry, the first Four-Bed Woman in history, with a brilliantly efficient high-volume business plan: Three Dollars for Three Minutes with any of the other girls, Five Dollars for Five Minutes with Mamie.

One of the soldiers who knew Hotel Street well was James Jones. The day Pearl Harbor was bombed, he was a private first class at Schofield Barracks. When the war moved away into the western Pacific, he found time to take two courses at the University of Hawaii, American literature and composition. It cost him five dollars a credit hour—a rate per minute multiples lower than Mamie Stover's. Jones's return on investment was a long novel, written after the war, about the miserable beaten-down life of enlisted men at Schofield. Jones was 29 when *From Here to Eternity* was published in New York, with fanfare, in February, 1951. The book was Number 1 on bestseller lists for months. It won the National Book Award. It went on to sell millions, and was made into a Hollywood movie in 1953, starring Burt Lancaster as Milt Warden, the alpha male career first sergeant, Montgomery Clift as the doomed inarticulate romantic bugler Robert E. Lee Prewitt, and Frank Sinatra as skinny little Private Angelo Maggio, who got on the wrong side of the military police and wound up in the dreadful Schofield post stockade. The movie won eight Oscars.

For thousands of local boys who had never been off the islands, the war was a revelation. They traveled to the American mainland, and from there to Europe, the far side of the world. They fought the Germans; they saw Paris; they slept with Italian signorinas; and after all that, life was never the same for them. There was a play, *Reunion*, written soon after the war by Bessie Toishigawa, a student at the University of Hawaii, about Takashi, Miyo, Shige, Masa, and the Duke coming back to Honolulu and finding their home town to be nothing but smalltime.

The war ended in 1945. The next great grinding of the gears of history was in 1959, when Hawai'i, which had been an American territory since 1900, became the Fiftieth State.

Within weeks of the formal declaration of statehood, James Michener published a novel called *Hawaii*: perfect timing. He wrote it in Honolulu. It was the biggest piece of fiction ever about the islands—in size, close to a thousand pages and half a million words, and in sales, two hundred thousand in the first two months, top of the national best seller lists nine weeks after publication, then Number 1 for 48 weeks, the longest for any novel from the Forties to the Nineties, seven million copies sold by the mid-1980s, and continuing. When it was made into a movie, in the mid-Sixties, on O'ahu, it was a big-budget Hollywood production, with more Hawaiian extras (or locals passing for Hawaiians) than even Elvis Presley's *Blue Hawaii*. Max Von Sydow, who was Swedish, played a New England Protestant missionary with a Scandinavian accent, and Julie Andrews, an Englishwoman, played his wife with a British accent.

Michener had a concept of the history of Hawai'i, his own version of complex social machinery: people of many different colors mingling over the generations to produce a new kind of human being, the Golden Men.

It was pretty to think so. But in Edward Sakamoto's play, *A'ala Park*, set right at the moment of statehood, men were not golden, and neither was life. Down at the slummiest end of Hotel Street, Manny, Bear, Jojo, Uji, Champ, and Cabral were stuck like ants in spit.

After *Hawaii* was published, Michener got a look at Honolulu that was less than golden. He was minded to buy a house in town. He could afford the best, meaning the highest-priced, and the best high-priced address was Kāhala Avenue, on the beach east of Waikīkī. But—consternation—he was blackballed. It was on account of his wife. She was Japanese, born in the United States of immigrant parents. At the start of World War II, she and her family had been interned as enemy aliens, in California, at Santa Anita racetrack, in the stables. Kāhala Avenue was a higher class of housing—so high-class that the big landowner, Bishop Estate, a Christian charitable trust based on the old Hawaiian royal lands, had restrictive covenants on the legal deeds to the big homes: whites only. The Micheners took off for Pennsylvania, and Michener was quoted in the national press saying that there was more race prejudice in Hawai'i than in Bucks County. The Honolulu morning paper, the *Advertiser*, was outraged. Michener "accepted Hawaii's hospitality, Hawaii's favors, and its information. He ate at Hawaii's table, he praised Hawaii, he reveled in his eminence, and then, after leaving, he spat from afar." No one in town wrote a story about this.

From the early eighteen-hundreds, forward into the American century, and then on into the years of statehood, the history of Honolulu was turned into literature. Some of the writing about the town was done on the fly, in the moment. Some of it looked back years and decades from the twentieth century—historical fiction; and some of the Hawaiian writers harked back much farther, to a time before writing, the time of the old chiefs and the old gods.

Some of the writing became famous. But the famous writers were all from somewhere else. They came and went. None of them stayed in Honolulu for long. Some were famous already when they came: Stevenson, London, Maugham, Michener; some got famous after they left: Melville, Twain. And none of them were famous for what they wrote specifically about Honolulu, except James Jones and William Bradford Huie. Huie's novel about Mamie Stover sold well enough to be made into a movie in 1953, starring Jane Russell, cast for her cantilevered bustline, measuring up to Mamie's. Huie wrote a sequel set after the war, *Hotel Mamie Stover*, in which Mamie dreamed up a sexy resort for tourists—but not on Hotel Street, on the island of Maui. Huie wrote twenty other books that sold thirty million copies, but they were not about Hawai'i, and he did not write them in Hawai'i. James Jones wrote *From Here to Eternity* on the mainland, with his war years behind him. He only came back to Honolulu once, in 1973, transiting from Vietnam, where he was writing about that war for the *New York Times*. He could not get a room at the Royal Hawaiian; it was full. He stayed at the Sheraton next door. He hired a car for a drive around town, and out to Schofield. A public relations officer showed him the new army. Jones was moved to be back where he had been young, but he could not find his twenty-year-old self, and after a few days he was gone.

The historical fact was that Honolulu had never been a literary city of its own making. The town never had a community of sharp intelligence like, say, Concord, Massachusetts, in the middle of the nineteenth century, or a café culture of ideas like Vienna at the turn of the twentieth. It had no Bloomsbury like London, no Greenwich Village or Algonquin Round Table like New York. And it had nothing like Paris. Take, for example, the literary and artistic salon of Natalie Barney, first at Neuilly, on the outskirts of the city, with wine and cultivated talk, Isadora Duncan dancing in gauze and Mata Hari riding horseback through the garden next to naked, and then, for the next fifty years, in town, on the Left Bank. Somerset Maugham came to Barney's *pavillon* at 20 Rue Jacob. So did everybody else who was anybody in literature, all the way from Colette to Edna St. Vincent Millay to Truman Capote. Barney's salon was on Fridays. At Gertrude Stein's, a few blocks away, it was Saturday nights. On the walls at 27 Rue de Fleurus were Picassos, Cézannes, Gauguins, Renoirs, and Matisses; and, sitting and talking and drinking, with the paintings all around—Picasso himself, and everyone from Guillaume Apollinaire to Ezra Pound to Cecil Beaton to Ernest Hemingway.

To conceive of a salon, launch it, get it established, and maintain its cachet—all this took money. And more than money, a special talent, indispensable: the ability to assemble and calibrate and control the complex social machinery of creative minds and temperaments.

First, of course, catch your creative minds. For Honolulu, that was a threshold problem. The town was small. Dozens of American cities were bigger—Akron, Omaha, Tulsa, Grand Rapids, to name a few—and places like those, at that size, were not famous for their salons. On top of which, the Hawaiian Islands were more than two thousand miles from San Francisco, five thousand from New York, and half the world away from Paris and London. Not surprising, then, that in Honolulu it could be a long time between drinks with literary lions and modern masters.

On top of that again, Honolulu being what it was, its society people did not turn their gaze towards salon life anyway. The town had big houses and big money. But the money was business money, sugar money, and none of it was more than a couple of generations old. On top of that yet again, Honolulu money was missionary-descended, Protestant-capitalist. Overall, this kind of wealth did not buy an aptitude or an appetite for the arts, or for the life of the mind, and it was not invested in freedom of the spirit.

To be sure, there were the rich people who started the Honolulu Symphony and the Academy of Arts (where the founder's collection was in fact remarkable, and various in its choices—including an excellent Gauguin, some Whistler prints, Rembrandt etchings, elegant Japanese screens, pottery of the Yi dynasty, the golden age of Korean ceramics, and a superlative eleventh-century Chinese Quanyin). There were the thoughtful people who formed the Social Science Association and the University Club, and there were a few professors willing to take trouble over students who wanted to write. But there was no Mabel Dodge, rich with family money, shedding a husband in favor of collecting interesting people at the Greenwich Village end of Fifth Avenue–modernist artists, intellectuals, radicals. No Nancy Cunard, the rich daughter of a Sir and Lady, with her Corrupt Coterie on Fitzroy Place in London—bored by Edward, Prince of Wales, and later, at La Chapelle-Réanville in Normandy, fiercely active in left-wing causes, running a small press that published experimental poetry, sleeping with three Nobel Prize winners in literature, any number of avant-garde creatives, and a black jazz musician. No Lady Ottoline Morrell of Bloomsbury and thereabouts, also rich and titled, tall, dressed in orange chiffon, dancing the can-can with Walter Sickert, a talented artist who painted prostitutes, and who had three wives and a number of lovers, not to mention a strange connection with a strange British prince of the royal blood. And no Marie-Laure de Noailles, of Clos Saint-Bernard in Hyères and Place des États-Unis in Paris, tall and titled too, a vicomtesse, great-great-great-granddaughter of the Marquis de Sade, rich enough to indulge any and all of her outré tastes, serially or simultaneously, a *connaisseur* of beautiful young bodies of various sexual persuasions, a mover and shaker among surrealist artists and writers—Salvador Dalí, Man Ray, Luis Buñuel, Jean Cocteau—painted by Balthus and Picasso (to whom she suggested an artistic romp in bed: "You'll be Goya and I'll be the Duchess of Alba,") compulsively excessive socially, with a delight in conversational shock ("Men who love Proust have short penises, don't you think?").

Hawai'i was on the far side of the earth from all that, and Honolulu's white society was the human antipodes. It did not go in for *la vie de bohème*, high or low, or for writing about it. It was polite society.

In a town that was so small, society was very small: "We live in each others' laps." Of course there were scandals, and of course the scandals were gossiped about: "We live in each others' lapses." But scandals were not written about as stories. Take the case of the extremely wealthy businessman, a recidivist womanizer, who was banished by his wife from their big house at Diamond Head, to live in marital exile (though not in sexual solitude) in the extremely well-appointed stables on the property. Everybody who was anybody in town knew that story. Edith Wharton might have liked it; Dorothy Parker certainly would have, not to mention Anita Loos. But in Honolulu, nobody wrote about it. Much less would anybody have written about another tale told on the quiet in society circles: that one of the biggest landed estates around Honolulu, dating from the nineteenth century—thousands of acres, worth hundreds of millions in twentieth-century dollars—was the gift of a Hawaiian chiefess to a white American man of good Protestant family, for what could baldly be described as stud services. Interracial sex in rich high places, lust beating out the Bible in a steamy exotic setting—this was hot stuff. True or not, fact or urban legend, it was perfect for historical fiction. But no one ever wrote the story.

On the surface in Honolulu, where appearances were kept assiduously shined so as to reflect respectability, and deeper down too, white society life was bourgeois-decorous, provincial-colonial—a weekly round of visiting back and forth, with white gloves and engraved calling cards, at big houses where Hawaiian or Chinese yardboys manicured the lawns, and silent kimono-clad Japanese maids with downcast eyes offered food on silver trays. There were set days for calling in set parts of town, Waikīkī on Mondays, Nuʻuanu on Wednesdays. And then weekends in the country, with the same people as on weekdays in town.

Town or country, everything about white Honolulu had its place, and everything was in its place. Everybody who was anybody was known and accounted for. Seldom was heard an imaginative word. Even less often was one written.

Henry James, in England, always on the alert for imaginative words, saw a distressing contrast between the beauty of the great old country houses and the dull philistine persons who owned them. Rich and illiterate, Virginia Stephen called those persons, on her way to becoming Virginia Woolf. Leave out the age of the houses, and she and James could have been talking about Honolulu.

As for twentieth-century Hawaiian high society life in Honolulu, it was a mix of Western and residual-traditional, with its own particular protocols and cultural rules about genealogy, rank, and status; but it did not go in for cultivating written literature.

To find something Hawaiian that would match the sophistication of a salon, it would be necessary to go back centuries before writing, to the courts of the high chiefs of traditional times, the *aliʻi nui*. They were warriors; they came to rule by way of bloody battle; the gods gave them their power; and they demanded human sacrifices. Between wars, in peace, they were aristocrats with a reverence for poetic utterance. Their Hawaiian language in its fullness was rich in nuances, and hidden meanings called *kaona*. And the *aliʻi nui* had a passion for performance. Among their retainers were chanters and dancers, honoring ritual and serving art. Some performances were reserved exclusively to the high chiefs: great creation chants like the *Kumulipo* were recited only in their presence, and always had to be done entire, thousands of lines, faultlessly memorized. Other chants and dances were for public enjoyment: *mele pai aliʻi*, celebrating the chiefs; *mele pana*, in honor of places; *mele hoʻoipoipo*, love songs, stories rich in feeling and fine phrasing and metaphor.

Once the Hawaiian language and the English language came into contact, there was two-way traffic in written words. The American Protestant missionaries worked with Hawaiian scholars to translate the Bible into Hawaiian, and they developed a Hawaiian-English dictionary. The missionaries were strong for public education, in Hawaiian. And Hawaiians had an appetite for language stored on paper. The Protestant mission press put out more than a hundred million printed pages by the late 1850s; and there were the Hawaiian-language newspapers, nearly a hundred of them before the end of the nineteenth century, scores of millions of words over the decades. By the 1860s, literacy rates among Hawaiian commoners were higher than among Americans or Englishmen.

King Kalākaua, who came to the throne in 1874, was a cultivated man. He was the first reigning monarch in the history of the world to travel around the world. Along the way, he spoke in several languages. At home, he published a book of Hawaiian legends and myths, in English; and he wrote songs—Western music, Hawaiian words, including the words to the national anthem, "Hawaii Ponoi." His sister, Queen Liliʻuokalani, who succeeded him in 1891—the last monarch—was especially gifted musically, and prolific: she wrote more than a hundred-fifty songs. When the monarchy was overthrown in 1893, Liliʻuokalani was not just deposed, she was imprisoned for months in an upstairs room in ʻIolani Palace on King Street in Honolulu, forbidden to go outside in daylight, so as to keep her out of sight of her people. In confinement, she wrote songs, in Hawaiian, including a prayer of forgiveness for the white men who conspired treasonably to bring down the kingdom; and another of her prison occupations was translating the *Kumulipo* into English.

Many Hawaiian commoners, too, were eloquent on the written page—notable storytellers, like Kahikina Kelekona. He was part-white. His name in English was John Graves Munn Sheldon. He published in Hawaiian, in full imaginative command of the language. Even in translation, his words flow. He was a literary artist.

In the 1890s, with annexation by the United States coming closer and closer, seen and welcomed among Americans in Hawaiʻi as Manifest Destiny—the inevitable triumph of a superior race—American English was the language of dominance. Hawaiian was the language of a people in defeat and despair, and it was despair at its deepest, because the Hawaiians were disappearing. Decade by decade, introduced diseases had been killing them off. Early in the nineteenth century, before Honolulu was anything much, the population of the Hawaiian Islands—numbers unknown, but certainly some hundreds of thousands—would have been ten or fifteen or even twenty times bigger than the population of the city of Boston, in Massachusetts, where the Protestant mission to Hawai'i was headquartered. By the end of the nineteenth century, when Honolulu was a small city, all the pure-blooded Hawaiians left on earth—thirty thousand at the most—added up to less than a third of the population of the Massachusetts town of Fall River.

Along with the terrible fact of depopulation, the Hawaiian language and the culture that it carried were devalued more and more by the ruling whites, to the point of being despised.

After the revolution of 1893, things went beyond despising. In 1896, a law was passed mandating English as the only language of instruction in schools. The law was aimed not just at Hawaiian, but at all other non-English languages as well, including Chinese and Japanese. The net of it was that English, and only English, was to rule.

For Hawaiian children, the new law meant that in the classroom—and outside in the schoolyard too—it was illegal for them to speak their parents' native tongue, the language of their land.

Nothing could stop Hawaiians speaking Hawaiian at home, among themselves. But the prospect was that the Hawaiians as a people might well go extinct, and their language would die with them—and in the mind of many whites, this passage into silence would not necessarily be something to mourn.

In 1934, Gertrude Stein, after more than thirty years in Europe, mostly in Paris, went back to the United States. When she was young, she had lived in California, in Oakland. The town was part of her history, but seeing it again did not move her. "There is," she said, succinctly, "no there there."

This could never have been said about Honolulu. There was always plenty of *there* there. The city might not have been a great literary community, a temple precinct of high culture; but it had its own distinctive look and feel and taste and sound and smell, and there was all kinds of writing being done about the place—less and less in Hawaiian, but more and more in other languages. Immigrant cultural societies were keeping homeland tongues alive; the school law of 1896 did not kill them off. The Chinese and Korean and Portuguese newspapers published poetry. There were Japanese *haiku* clubs, the first one started in 1901 by Hankuro Ishikuri, pen name Yakko-no-yakko, a plantation laborer at 'Ewa, in west O'ahu; another in 1908, in Pālama, a mixed district a couple of miles from downtown Honolulu; in 1909, a literary magazine; in 1913, a *tanka* club; in 1927, another *haiku* club, at a Waipi'o pineapple plantation. There were many others; and by the 1920s, books of *haiku* and *tanka* were being published in Honolulu—from then on, dozens over the years.

A sign of changing times: young Japanese and Chinese born in Hawai'i were writing and publishing stories and poems in English, in high school magazines and yearbooks. In 1928, students at the University of Hawaii started a literary annual, *The Hawaii Quill Magazine*. It had serious intentions. And by the mid-1930s, a professor of English was teaching a class in playwriting.

English louder and louder in the ear, Asian and European voices being heard, Hawaiian fading—and, at the same time, out of the babel of all the different tongues in the islands, there came another way of speaking: pidgin.

At first, pidgin was Hawaiian speakers and English speakers trying to make themselves understandable to each other, with most of the words in Hawaiian. Then, in plantation time, it was Hawaiian speakers, English speakers, and speakers of Cantonese Chinese, Japanese, Portuguese, and later, Korean, Spanish, and Tagalog, Visayan and Ilocano, the languages of Filipino laborers—all needing to be able to talk to each other on the job. Pidgin was the working language of the plantations, and the street language of Honolulu.

At the start, pidgin was a second language for everyone. In time, it became a first language. The shift was in two stages. Children born in Hawai'i to immigrant parents might speak their parents' language at home, and pidgin among their various friends outside the house. A generation on, when those Hawai'i-born children grew up and had families of their own, they spoke pidgin to their children at home, and those children grew up speaking pidgin as a first language.

By the 1920s and 1930s, pidgin had become the natural way of speaking for ordinary people. There were different varieties of it, district by district in Honolulu, and on the outer islands, depending on the particular ethnic mix here or there. And the ethnic mix was more and more mixed: by the 1930s, one in four marriages was across ethnic lines; by 1945, closer to one in three.

Pidgin kept developing, taking in words and structures from English and Hawaiian and the immigrant languages, until it evolved into a language in its own right. Scholars gave it the name of Hawaii Creole English. On the street it was always just pidgin.

Pidgin started out spoken. Very little of it was put on paper in the first half of the nineteenth century. More in the second half; but still it was not used in extended writing, to carry a whole story. Except in one special circumstance—in criminal trials, where pidgin on the witness stand was taken down by court reporters. In Honolulu, the longest and most complicated stories in pidgin were told by accused murderers, adulterers, thieves, brawlers, and assorted other defendants. Those stories could be very exciting, with lots of plot; and some were highly imaginative. But they were written down as sworn testimony, supposed to be true—that is to say, non-fiction—and so, unfortunately, they do not have a place in *Honolulu Stories*.

The social machinery of pidgin was complex. It was the language of local people, the great majority of them non-white, and in the American Territory of Hawaii this branded it. Speaking pidgin marked the speaker just as surely as skin color did.

Pidgin struck respectable white ears as lowlife, distasteful, even offensive, amounting to comprehensively un-white-American—which made it insupportable, intolerable. So, just as there had been a late-nineteenth-century white American war against the Hawaiian language, there was an early-twentieth-century white American war against pidgin.

In Honolulu, people who could afford to, especially whites, sent their children to private schools to keep them from being contaminated by pidgin. In the 1920s, special English Standard schools were set up in the public education system. These schools existed to teach proper speaking and proper writing—meaning proper American speaking and writing. Central Grammar School was English Standard central. There were any number of pidgin ways to flunk the entrance test: wrong vocabulary, wrong sentence construction, wrong subject-verb agreement, wrong tense, wrong singulars and plurals, wrong stress on syllables, wrong vowel sounds, wrong cadence. Or just wrong attitude would do it.

The net of it was that, in the workings of the complex social machinery of Hawai'i, to be a pidgin speaker was to be branded as not properly American, not suitable to rise in American life—or even unfit to rise. That rankled, and it rankles to this day.

Still, pidgin never went away. It refused to. It stayed, and it got on the printed page. By the early part of the twentieth century, when the Hawaiian language, spoken and written, might have looked to be headed toward extinction, pidgin-speaking characters were turning up in short stories written in English. By the mid-1930s, one-act plays in pidgin were being written by students at the University of Hawaii (with stage directions in English). And in the second half of the century—when Hawai'i was a state of the union, officially conclusively Americanized—more stories than ever, and plays and poems and songs, were being written and performed in pidgin.

Nothing could kill off pidgin—not even James Michener's butchery of it in *Hawaii*, which in the judgment of local writers was murder, or at the very least involuntary manslaughter, either way a crime.

"It takes a great deal of history to make a little literature."

The simplest possible definition of human history is: change over time affecting people. Going by that definition, a great deal of Honolulu's history was made in the second half of the twentieth century, with literature following in its own time and its own way.

The town kept growing, nonstop, at a rate far faster than the national average. More and more people, more and more change. And more and more of Honolulu was mainstream American-brand. In 1949, a drive-in theater. TV, 1952. The first freeway, 1953. Then, in 1959, to go with statehood, a shopping center at Ala Moana, close by Waikīkī, advertising itself as not just the biggest in Honolulu but the biggest in the world. Highrises, higher and higher, especially in Waikīkī, but in other parts of town too. Suburban sprawl, meaning commuter culture. And in 1968, the first McDonalds, followed by many more, with drive-thrus.

The year of statehood, 1959, was also the year the first commercial passenger jets flew into Honolulu International Airport. Now flight time from the west coast of the mainland was only five hours, all the difference in the world from twenty hours on the Pan Am Clipper, thirteen on the postwar propeller passenger planes. This was the beginning of mass tourism—a quarter of a million arrivals in 1959, by the mid-1960s a million a year, by the mid-1970s three million, rising decade by decade to four, five, six million, multiples of the local population. Millions and millions took the Pearl Harbor package tour—history repeating itself, first as tragedy, then as a visitor attraction for all that sunburned humanity in aloha shirts.

Waikīkī was tourism central, and there was a lot of new local writing about it. But, decades on from Don Blanding, what was being put on paper about the beach of all beaches was not dreamy stuff anymore, summoning up those sweet Hawaiian voices singing softly at sunset to the throb of the exotic *ʻukulele*. Now there was often a sharp, sour edge to the words—dissonance.

Famous writers kept coming and going.

In the Vietnam years, Joan Didion vacationed in Honolulu, and the town turned up in her novel *Democracy*. Her cold hyper-intelligent neurasthenic style was quite unmodulated by her having been warm in Waikīkī.

When Paul Theroux came to live on Oʻahu in 1990, he had written thirty books, about places all around the world. He kept traveling, scores of thousands of miles, and wrote a dozen more books. His one novel set locally was

Hotel Honolulu, about a no-star place in Waikīkī. Theroux's hotel, his characters, and his story line would have disqualified him from being considered for the Hawaii Visitors and Convention Bureau seal of approval—but then he was not looking for the approval of the Visitors and Convention Bureau.

Hunter S. Thompson came to Honolulu in 1980, on the pretext of reporting on the big marathon that was run annually through the streets of the town and some of its better suburbs, including Kāhala. He took off for the Kona Coast of the island of Hawaiʻi, rampaged around there, and wrote *The Curse of Lono* in pharmacologically overdriven prose. Back again in Honolulu in 2003, he was staying at the five-star Kahala Mandarin Oriental, at the high end of the pricy avenue where James Michener had been blackballed from buying a house. Late one night, Thompson, executing a sharp turn at the mini-bar, fell and broke two bones in his left leg. He set off a high-decibel hullabaloo of threats of lawsuits, then had himself specially airlifted back to the mainland. When he killed himself in 2005, his wish was to be cremated and have his ashes shot from a cannon. He got his wish. Nobody in Honolulu wrote a story about him.

Writers who were invited to visit Honolulu were, by and large, more sedate than Thompson (as, to be sure, were 99.999 percent of all human beings). A few names: John Ashbery, Margaret Atwood, Sia Fiegel, Mei-mei Berssenbrugge, Robert Bly, Tomas Tranströmer, Albert Wendt, Makoto Ooka, William Stafford, Thomas Farber, Jane Shore, James Wright, Galway Kinnell, Adrienne Rich, Gary Snyder, Michael Ondaatje. They were classified at the University of Hawaii as Major Writers (which by definition relegated local writers to Minor). Some of them gave readings; some taught; some did both. Some wrote about Honolulu; most did not. They flew in and flew out. The local writers had a name for them: "747 poets."

Historically, a great deal of the writing done by people who actually lived in Honolulu was about Honolulu: the *there* of the town. This kind of writing was very settled in place—it came out of growing up local, in "small kid time," then going out into the world, but not very far, living in familiar places among familiar faces, degrees of separation very few, following customary ways—marrying the known, surfing, working on the car, going fishing with friends, getting the kids off to school, watching the big game on TV. Lots of relax time, barefoot, beer in the cooler and plenty to eat. Quiet pleasures, modest satisfactions. Not a great deal of high excitement. No overwhelming rushes of blood to the head. Disagreements, perhaps, and some of them serious, within families, between generations, across ethnic lines, though next to never about ideas, and, by national standards, mostly low-key—maybe harsh words and raised voices, but very few violent confrontations, except perhaps arising from a hypertrophied lifelong attachment to high school football.

In the larger view, there was no great yearning after broader horizons in life, no great expectation of radical change. During the Fifties, scarcely a beatnik could have been found in Honolulu. Very few bookstores, either, and they were a long way from City Lights in San Francisco; Allen Ginsberg's *Howl* was howled on the far side of the curve of the earth, out of hearing.

But after statehood, with new and different mainland things being unloaded on the town, dumptrucks of them, nonstop, more and more of local writing came to be about disruption and dislocation. The Sixties in Honolulu turned out to be like the Sixties on the mainland, only in another time zone. Hippies; wild ideas; sex 'n drugs 'n rock'n'roll; long hair; *Hair*, with a local cast showing bare skin; and on New Year's Day, 1969, months before Woodstock, a big counterculture festival in the crater of Diamond Head—music and marijuana. And Vietnam. The military had never gone away from Hawai'i, because geopolitics never went away. In the early 1950s, it was the Korean War. Then, in the 1960s and early 1970s, hundreds of thousands of servicemen were staged through Honolulu on their way to Vietnam. Some of them came back seriously troubled in their hearts and minds. There were stories written about this.

The rate of change kept accelerating. From the Eighties to the end of the century, the years flashed by in what seemed like jump cuts—just blink, and nothing was the way it used to be.

Honolulu at the start of the new millennium was close to twenty times bigger than it had been in 1900—now it was one of the dozen largest municipalities in the United States, with half the people on the streets not born in Hawai'i. Tourists were up to seven million. Waikīkī was one of the most densely populated districts in the world. In the low-rent parts of town there were new populations: Samoans and Micronesians and Southeast Asians. The city and its suburbs and ex-urbs had more cars per mile of road than anywhere in America—SUVs and Lexuses and Chevy pickups and Toyotas and stretch limos and Hummers and junkers; jammed freeways, gas the highest-cost in the country, road rage rampant. Gangs. Guns. Domestic abuse. Graffiti. Teenagers in school with tattoos and body piercings and video-game attention spans and a text messaging habit, and attitude. Mall rats. Auditions for "American Idol." WiFi. A proliferation of latte drinkers, fully accessorized with cell phones and iPods. Strip bars by the dozen; ecstasy the nightclub drug of choice; and Hawai'i climbing to the top of the world rankings for crystal methamphetamine: Honolulu on ice.

In the real world, the world of work, the cost of living was fearsome, with a high percentage of locals having to take on two or even three jobs to keep a roof over their family's heads. At the lowest end of life prospects, Honolulu had thousands of homeless, many of them in the parks and on the beaches—this in the capital city of the state with the highest percentage of millionaires in the nation: gated communities, and people with nowhere to sleep pushing shopping carts along the streets, their lives in a tangle of plastic bags—First World and Third World in plain sight of each other, under the American flag. Hawai'i also had one of the very lowest rates of voter participation in the country, as miserable as the most benighted Southern states, meaning as bad as anywhere in the developed world; and the city and county of Honolulu, with three quarters of the state's population, had the great majority of the non-voters. Along with that, going by national figures, Honolulu was in the bottom ten of fifty big cities for community volunteering. Also by national figures, Hawai'i was one of the top ten states for property crime, Number 1 for larceny, and most of the thieves were in Honolulu.

Among the best and brightest of the local young, a tide was running, away from home, toward the mainland—a brain drain. And, very noticeably, Hawaiians were taking off, by the thousands, heading for the west coast and Las Vegas. Still, the city kept growing, with household waste piling up at ten times the rate of population increase, and lawyers metastasizing; ads for attorneys in the yellow pages of the Honolulu phone book were up 1500 percent since statehood. And not only all of the above, but the biggest registered poetry slam on earth was happening in Honolulu, at a club in Waikīkī, once a month, on a Thursday night, drawing crowds of more than six hundred, with a website, www.hawaiislam.com.

At Pearl Harbor, there were huge submarines armed with nuclear warheads. In any World War III, Honolulu would be seven miles from Ground Zero.

And in town, every so often, during excavations for the latest multi-million-dollar condominium apartment building, or when trenches were gouged in roads to repair water and sewer pipes overstressed to bursting, the bulldozers growled and brought up Hawaiian bones in their jaws.

This was the modern history of Honolulu. In such times, in such a place, what might local literature be—literature generated locally, by locals?

To start with, was there really any such thing as Local Literature? Over the years, this kind of big question had not been thought about very much. People in Honolulu just wrote what they wrote the way they wrote at the time they wrote it. Beyond that, not a great deal of attention was paid.

As late as the late Sixties, in literature courses at the University of Hawaii, the writers prescribed for study were Western White—no Asians or Africans or Latin Americans, let alone anyone local. The professors were almost all the same color as the writers, and were mostly from somewhere else.

Then, in 1974, the Hawaii Literary Arts Council was formed, publicly funded, and it began making an annual award. The first recipient was O. A. Bushnell, who wrote historical novels set in Hawai'i.

In 1978, a conference about writing was organized in Honolulu—a sign of critical thinking. It was called "Talk Story," a pidgin phrase. The subtitle was "Our Voices in Literature and Song, Hawaii's Ethnic American Writers' Conference." Talk Story, Our Voices, Ethnic American Writers: together, these spelled Local. The conference sessions drew hundreds—a sign of the times.

The next year, there was a followup gathering on the island of Hawai'i. And the year after that, 1980, in Honolulu again, in the big auditorium at the state capitol, a week-long conference was held, called "Writers of Hawaii." Five authors were discussed, an evening for each. There was ethnic and literary variety among them. O.A. Bushnell, the historical novelist, born in Honolulu, was part-Portuguese, part-Italian, part-Norwegian. John Dominis Holt, also born in Honolulu, was a fiction writer, essayist and poet, a mix of Hawaiian, Tahitian, English, New England missionary American, Spanish, and Corsican; he wrote in English and pidgin, out of a mindset that was fervently Hawaiian. Milton Murayama was local-Japanese, born on Maui, living in San Francisco, but publishing mostly in Honolulu; the people in his fiction were mostly local-Japanese, and they mostly thought local and spoke pidgin. Aldyth Morris, a mainland white who had lived in Honolulu for fifty years, wrote plays about historical characters, including Queen Lili'uokalani and Robert Louis Stevenson. Maxine Hong Kingston was Chinese-American, from Stockton, California; she lived on O'ahu for seventeen years, teaching, at a drop-in school, a business college, high schools, then the University of Hawaii, and writing. Her first book, *The Woman Warrior*, published in New York by Knopf in 1976, was a national bestseller, the only one to come from Honolulu since James Michener's *Hawaii*. Her next book, *China Men*, published in 1980, the year of the Writers of Hawaii conference, won the National Book Award. Some of Kingston's China men were plantation workers on O'ahu.

The writer who spoke most directly to the big basic issue of local literature was Bushnell, and the issue was simply this: if locals did not set the terms for writing about their own place, then outsiders would.

Outsiders had, and still did. Twenty years after the publication of *Hawaii*, the specter of Michener's huge book hovered. How could local writers get out from under that giant shadow? And what would be their place in the sun?

Taking things from the top—how should local writers see themselves and their work in relation to other writing, essentially meaning mainland American writing? Was it a matter of assimilating to established national standards, essentially meaning the standards of New York publishing? In other words, should Honolulu writers try to be just like the big time, only smaller?

Or was it better to think of local writing as regional—like, for example, writing from the American South? Mark Twain had a Southern inflection, and it had not stopped him from getting a national reputation, a world reputation, a historic reputation. The same for William Faulkner: he lived in Oxford, Mississippi, population less than ten thousand, and wrote about somewhere called Yoknapatawpha County, and he won the Nobel Prize. But then, if Hawai'i was a region, what was it a region of? Mainland America? Or the Pacific?

Then again, consider literary locals, all kinds. Were they to be defined as a single family, one blanket category—Ethnic Writers? Or did they come in different species, to be distinguished from each other, and then ranked— best of breed, best in show? And who would be judging the show?

Looking just at local-Asians: were they a variety of Asian-Americans, or something different, of their own distinct kind, Hawai'i-Asian? This came up at the Talk Story conference, where it turned out that local-Asian writers and mainland-Asian writers present by invitation saw themselves not as blood brothers and sisters but as distinct tribes, not necessarily congenial: put them in the same room and there could be bristling.

Taking a different tack altogether—should local writers relate to national and regional writing standards not by assimilating but by resisting? If so, what would local resistance writing be like in style and substance? And who would it be written for and read by, besides other local resistance writers—and how many of those would there be?

Finally, if being local was all-important, why be in the least concerned about what happened with writing and publishing in any other place? It ought to be fulfillment enough, creatively and every other way, to be read and known and applauded in two Honolulu zipcodes, famous among friends.

As in literature, so in life at large. Among locals generally, there was a matching range of attitudes to the big world, essentially meaning mainland America. Embrace everything about it. Or take some things and reject others. Or resist, turn deliberately away, face the mainland front-on only to throw stones at it. Or—just let all that go by, not make a big thing out of it one way or another.

Locally, literature itself was not a big thing. In fact, looked at diagnostically, it was stunted. As a real-world matter, there was no possibility of making a living at it in Honolulu. O. A. Bushnell talked about a vicious circle: not enough readers, meaning not enough of a market for publishers, meaning not enough of an opening for writers. The net of it was that not much local literature got into print, and the small stack of pages was almost all in publications that were shoestring, or not even shoestring—shoeless, barefoot.

Little periodicals came and went. A few managed to last. The one that established the most significant presence for local writing, and made the best sustained case for it, was *Bamboo Ridge*, which started publishing in 1979.

The founders, Eric Chock and Darrell Lum, were as local as could be: born and raised in Honolulu, public school kids, classmates from first grade through twelfth, growing up nowhere near Kāhala Avenue.

What they wanted to do with *Bamboo Ridge* was to encourage and cultivate and propagate a locally generated literature that did not start from the assumption that local things were by their nature inferior to mainland things. So—a literature that would affirm its own worth, on its own terms. The writers would be people born in Hawai'i or with strong ties to the place, writing mostly about Hawai'i. And this literature would make its affirmation by drawing on a common local history, a shared local past.

Bamboo Ridge wanted local literature to be in local language. Which raised, yet again, the question of pidgin.

The English Standard schools had been discontinued; they stopped taking in new first-grade students in 1947, and the last classes graduated in 1960. Pidgin simply outtalked the educational establishment, and went its own way for the rest of the century, alive and well on the street, in the little magazines—and in standup comedy. The alltime hall-of-fame live performer of pidgin was Rap Reiplinger. He was a genius at it, so funny he could make people snort beer through their nose and fall off their chair laughing. He was local, part-Hawaiian, and his masterpiece was about Honolulu and the big world—a mainland tourist in a Waikīkī hotel, on the phone to a local kitchen worker, trying to get room service. Reiplinger did both voices: the tourist, Fogarty, articulating his order—cheeseburger de luxe, french fries, and a thick chocolate malt—slowly, clearly, again and again, in baffled and increasingly exasperated Standard American English, to a minimum-wage pidgin speaker, an outstandingly witless local female, who kept repeating this strange white name with elaborate hospitality-industry-entry-level-crosscultural-job-training courtesy—Mister Frogtree—and who had a hundred blithe oblivious ways of not delivering even minimum service.

Mister Frogtree never did get his cheeseburger de luxe; he ended up hanging up.

Everybody could laugh at tourists, and everybody did. Then there was the question of locals laughing at each other—which was a different matter. Another standup comedian, Frank De Lima, made this his life's work. He was Portuguese, also Hawaiian, Irish, Chinese, English, Spanish, and Scottish, and he poked goodtempered fun at himself in pidgin for that–and at everyone else for being what they were. Everybody laughed with him. De Lima never wanted his jokes to hurt, and they never did.

Local ethnic humor was like ethnic humor everywhere: it was all about stereotypes. Local stereotypes had names, and the names had history. For example, in 1959, when Hawai'i became a state of the union, local people with slant eyes were still called Orientals. That had not changed since Charlie Chan. Everybody used the word: Orientals called each other Orientals, and everybody else called them that. If they were identified more specifically, it was as Japanese or Chinese or Korean—just the one word, not as hyphenate-Americans. "Asian-American" came later, out of the Sixties, the decade nationally of civil rights, after which correct terminology was prescribed for all kinds of people and all kinds of circumstances. Sex turned into Gender, Race turned into Ethnicity, and in Honolulu the old Oriental went into a slow fade. But Asian-American never took on locally, except among academics and activists. Around town, a Japanese was still a Japanese; Chinese and Koreans and Filipinos were still just that; and nobody thought anything of it one way or the other.

And, correctness or no, there were local nicknames that stuck. Buddhahead or Rice Eye for Japanese (Kotonk for mainland Japanese; and for people carrying Japan-Japanese attitudes, Bobora, meaning a pumpkin-head with no feel for local customs). Pakē for Chinese, from the Hawaiian *pakakē* or *kīpakakē*, meaning gibberish (and Kachink for mainland Chinese). Manong or Pinoy or Book-Book or Flip for Filipinos (FBI for full-blooded Ilocano). Yobo for Koreans. Portagee or Pocho or Babooze for Portuguese. Borinki for Puerto Ricans. Solē for Samoans. FOB for recent immigrants, fresh off the boat. Yellow-skinned people acting white were Bananas; for brown-skinned people it was Coconuts; for Filipinos it was Cano, short for Americano.

Then there were the mixes: Hawaiian mix, Japanese mix, Chinese mix, Portuguese mix, local mix, and so on. Mixes were all *hapa*, pidgin for half—used very approximately, because everybody kept on marrying everybody else, so that every generation got more and more mixed. By the Sixties, about one in three locals was a mix, and the mixes were of all ethnic fractions, from a half all the way to one-sixteenth or one-thirty-second, and of all skin tones. Miss Hawaii was often a mix of mixes, referred to as Cosmopolitan. In the American state of Hawai'i, the United States census form did not come close to fitting human reality.

More names. A male local mix with some Hawaiian, a man who was what he was, a pidgin speaker with zero ambition to work in an airconditioned office, wearing shiny shoes and pants with a sharp crease—this was a *moke*, or a *blallah*, a pidgin brother; his sister in blood and attitude was a *tita*. A black was a *pōpolo*, Hawaiian for the black nightshade, a weed with black berries. And a white was a *haole*, Hawaiian for stranger or foreigner. Along the way through the nineteenth century, any kind of foreigner was a *haole*, including Asian plantation workers. By the twentieth century, haole had turned white, and it stayed that way. If a local came on white, other locals would say he was acting haolefied, and this was not a compliment. Haole could have an adjective attached: coast haole or mainland haole for one from out of town, local haole for one born in Hawai'i and more or less fitting in with local ways—able, for example, to talk pidgin, turn it on and off. And, depending on circumstance and attitude, other adjectives were applicable: dumb haole, or f——— haole. There were local folk customs associated with the word—in the public schools, an annual Kill Haole Day, ritually celebrated; and at Christmas in Honolulu, the singing of a festive carol, "Deck the halls with balls of haoles, Fa la la la la, Fa la la la."

Some of these less than flattering local names got into *Bamboo Ridge*, but not all, and not all that often. It looked as if there was a quiet agreement on this kind of thing, not to go too far in print. That was typical of local life: do not push beyond a certain point, never take things to extremes, go along to get along.

In literature, this was true not just of naming. Local writing did not take it to the limit in any direction, any human dimension. The old Hawaiian ways of storytelling had much more emotional range, and much more poetry in the language of emotions. On the modern local written page, by contrast, there were very few full-out bursts of joy, very few shrieks from doomed souls. And in between ecstasy and anguish, a lot of other tonalities were missing.

In fact, whole areas of local life were hardly written about. There were next to no stories about upper middle-class social life, especially among haoles. Or business life. Or life in the professions. Or the life of the mind. Or life in the arts. Or the life of politics and all its overlaps and interlocks with the life of the law and the life of crime. Or lives of mystery, life plots that were labyrinthine. Or lives of stubborn refusal, or outright rebellion, or mad dashes for escape. Or lives driven by fatal passion or obsession. Or stories about what went on behind closed bedroom doors: the little sex that got on the printed page was mostly by women, and mostly in poetry, making it a particular kind of minority literature.

Overall, local writing did not come on loud; it shied away from engaging big ideas and taking on big issues; it stopped short of going outside itself or getting above itself. All of which was built into being local.

Another kind of self-limiting was in criticism. There was a local pidgin phrase: "No talk stink." This rule was generally observed concerning literature. There might be a dirty literary look from across a room, "stink eye," and it might be returned; and there might be badmouthing over a beer, in the absence of the person being badmouthed; but in print, in writing by local writers about other local writers, seldom was heard a discouraging word.

It took a mainland writer to talk stink out loud about local writing. Frank Chin, a Chinese-American playwright and novelist from California, was invited to the Talk Story conference in 1978. He was a guest from out of town, but he did not feel constrained by any protocol of hospitality in the land of aloha; he was a Kachink, and he spoke right up. "Is pidgin," he wanted to know, "really a language exclusive to the stupid of Hawaii? Is it a matter of prejudice, skill or inadequacy of vision that the writers championing the virtues of Hawaiian pidgin cannot make the language work complexities, communicate intelligence, perform magic?"

This did not stop locals writing in pidgin. Twenty-five years on from Chin, there was more pidgin in print than ever. *Bamboo Ridge* published a lot of it; Darrell Lum, the co-founder, was a master of the voice. An illustrated book called *Pidgin to Da Max* was a longrunning local bestseller. There were major scholarly studies of Hawai'i Creole English; and there were even pedagogical defenses of the use of pidgin in the school classroom, not just as spoken by students, but by teachers too.

In 2005, a pidgin dictionary was published in Honolulu. The compiler was Lee A. Tonouchi. He called his work *Da Kine Dictionary*, and it was the ultimate in local. He put out a call, people wrote in, and they got their definitions published—with their names, and the high school they went to, and the year they graduated. There were not many dictionaries like that.

Tonouchi had a name for himself—Da Pidgin Guerrilla. He was on a mission: to get pidgin accepted and recognized at its true worth, as a first language—and not only that, but the only language anyone could ever need. No more looking down on pidgin as a mark of local inferiority; for Tonouchi, pidgin was capable of taking its speakers anywhere they wanted to go in life anywhere in the world. He walked the walk and he talked the talk. He wore baggies and a cap on backwards. He spoke pidgin, taught at a community college in pidgin, co-edited a pidgin literary magazine, *Hybolics*, and wrote in pidgin—pidgin everything, not just his short stories and poems, but book reviews, movie reviews, restaurant reviews, emails, a letter canceling his insurance, an essay on pidgin, in pidgin, published in *College English*, the journal of the National Council of Teachers of English, among articles about rhetoric, critical theory, creative writing theory, reading theory, literacy, pedagogy. And he wrote a grant application to the Ford Foundation in pidgin. It got him flown to New York for a conference, where he talked story in pidgin.

Tonouchi spoke pidgin where no pidgin speaker had spoken it before. But what about pidgin on the page, written to be published? Its point of origin was local, absolutely; Hawai'i was the only place it could have come from. But where could it go from there? What if it was so local that it could not be understood anywhere else? This raised the eternal prickly question of getting into print on the mainland. If no one on the mainland could read pidgin, no one would go into a bookstore and pay money for a book of it—and so why would any mainland publisher ever bother with it? It was hard enough for mainland ethnic writers to get published in their own voice. Where did that leave local writers writing in a local voice?

Which raised yet another question: what if a local writer wanted to try to get published on the mainland and was willing to take the edge off pidgin, or strike it altogether? Was that selling out? What was the price of the ride?

It was not just a matter of pidgin, either. Even local writers who used standard English had trouble getting into print on the mainland. Short stories might turn up in literary periodicals here and there; a few were anthologized in collections of Asian-American writing; and a book of poetry might be published by a small press or a university press—but only rarely. As for the mainstream book business, basically meaning New York: in the second half of the twentieth century, imaginative books about Hawai'i by local writers—novels, collections of short stories, or poetry—were picked up at the rate of only one every four or five years.

For whatever it might signify, almost all of these books were by women. And a majority of those women (including Susanna Moore, Kiana Davenport, Sylvia Watanabe, Kathleen Tyau, Allegra Goodman, and Kaui Hart Hemmings) had left Hawai'i for the mainland, often first chance, right out of high school or college.

Here was the eternal vexation, the very bane of existence: viewed from the perspective of sophisticated mainland awareness, Hawai'i was remote, detached, isolated—and worse off than just being out of town, pretty much completely out of mind. An illustration: in 1976, the *New Yorker*, the ultimate magazine for literary style in the capital city of American publishing, and top of the line as well for its witty cartooning, brought out an issue that had a colored map of the United States on the cover. The map became famous. It was drawn by Saul Steinberg. He lived in New York, and you could tell it was a smart New Yorker's mental map by the fact that about eighty percent of the area of the nation was taken up by the West Side of Manhattan. As for the other twenty percent, it was negligible, derisory: west of the Hudson River, all the way to the west coast, there was next to nothing human—not even purple mountain majesties or amber waves of grain. West farther yet from California were China and Russia, featureless manifestations, barely imaginable, on the cusp of falling off the edge of the world, and Japan, one-dimensional, pimple-sized. In between America and Asia, the Pacific—a profound insult to the vision of a shining sea, just a perfunctory little strip of flat washed-out blue. And no Hawai'i at all.

Lois-Ann Yamanaka was absolutely local—Japanese, born on Moloka'i, one of the outer islands, population less than five thousand; raised in Pāhala, a very small out-of-the-way rural plantation town on the island of Hawai'i; coming to Honolulu to go to college. In 1993, Bamboo Ridge Press published a book of her poetry, *Saturday Night at the Pahala Theatre*. It got more notice around Honolulu than any poetry book ever, in fact more than any local book ever. It won the local Elliot Cades Award for Literature. It also won the literature award of the Association of Asian American Studies, a national academic organization with members in Hawai'i. And on the national open literary market, so to speak, it won a highly prestigious award, the Pushcart Prize. That made Yamanaka, as a writer from Hawai'i, unique on the mainland, because her poetry was all pidgin.

In 1996, Yamanaka's first novel, *Wild Meat and the Bully Burgers*, which was loaded with extremely salty pidgin dialogue, was published in New York by Farrar Straus Giroux, as literary an imprint as there was in the mainstream book business, with a list of authors that included twenty Pulitzer Prize winners, sixteen National Book Critics Circle Award winners, twenty-five National Book Award winners, and twenty-one Nobel Prize winners.

Wild Meat and the Bully Burgers was nominated for the Association for Asian American Studies literary award, which would have made it two in a row there for Yamanaka. But some of the academics had been offended by things in *Saturday Night at the Pahala Theatre*, and it was decided to make no award that year.

Then, in 1997, another novel by Yamanaka came out, *Blu's Hanging*, published by the same New York house, and this was where things got really tangled, for Yamanaka herself, and for ethnic literature in Hawai'i and in the United States generally.

The literature committee of the Association for Asian American Studies picked *Blu's Hanging* for the 1998 award—three nominations in a row for Yamanaka, the first successful, the second a problematical wash, and now this third one.

The association's 1998 national meeting was in Honolulu, at a hotel in Waikīkī, with almost five hundred members registered. When the award to Yamanaka was announced, some dozens of people stood up in protest. They were wearing black armbands. They turned their backs and bowed their heads.

What generated this demonstration was not any concern over the literary quality of Yamanaka's work. It was that in *Saturday Night at the Pahala Theatre*, and again in *Blu's Hanging*, Yamanaka had Filipinos being sexual predators, going after children. Sexual predation itself was not the issue. Rather, here was a writer of one local ethnic group—Japanese—nationally published, reviewed, and rewarded, talking the worst kind of stink about another local ethnic group—Filipinos. This was what the demonstration was about: cultural politics, identity politics.

The protesters, and their supporters at the University of Hawai'i, in the local community, and on the mainland, saw Yamanaka's treatment of Filipinos, a low-status ethnic group in Hawai'i, as intolerably offensive, coming as it did from someone who was Japanese, a member of a higher-status ethnic group that was built into the power structure. In this way of looking at things, all Filipinos were oppressed, and all Japanese were oppressors; Yamanaka, the individual Japanese writer, embodied all oppressor Japanese, and the individual Filipino characters in her work embodied all oppressed Filipinos.

As matter of observable readable fact, Yamanaka the Japanese writer had some nasty members of her own ethnic group in *Blu's Hanging*, and they could hardly be ranked as belonging to the oppressor power structure in Hawai'i: a dope-smoking father who was cruel to his kids and could not even keep them in clothes; a woman who starved dogs to death in cages in her basement; an old man who exposed himself. But at the Asian American Studies conference, no one stood up wearing a black armband to protest an offense to all Japanese; and any offense to Japanese was not seen as offsetting or diluting or excusing an offense to Filipinos.

Yamanaka had other R- or X-rated undesirable ethnic characters in her books, in fact a wide range of them: not only those bad Japanese in *Blu's Hanging* but unregenerately gay Japanese boys; Portagee pig hunters, barely housebroken; some very local schoolyard tormentors; a haole pervert holding a twenty-dollar bill between his teeth. So Yamanaka was an equal-opportunity offender. But at the Asian American Studies conference, only Filipinos rated a show of black armbands.

The demonstration blew the formal session of the meeting apart. The officers and the board resigned on the spot. Argument kept up until the last hours of the conference, when a secret ballot vote was taken on whether to strip Yamanaka of her award. About 165 ballots were counted. The vote carried, easily.

This episode raised big issues: the role of artists in society, their rights and responsibilities; the place of literature in life; freedom of expression; censorship and self-censorship—and political correctness.

In multiethnic, multicultural Hawai'i, in mid-1998, in a room filled mostly with ethnic-minority academics—Asian-Americans, local and mainland—political correctness beat freedom of expression.

Nationally as well as locally, a lot of argumentative ink was spilled over the rights or wrongs of Yamanaka and her writing. In the literary history of Honolulu, there had never been anything like it; but nobody in Honolulu wrote a story about it.

Four months after Yamanaka had her Asian American Studies award taken away in Honolulu, she got a major award from a mainland organization, the Lannan Foundation, a richly endowed philanthropy dedicated to cultural freedom, diversity, and creativity, whose mission was to support the creation of exceptional poetry and prose written originally in the English language, and to honor writers whose work reflected and changed understanding of the world.

The Lannan appreciation of Yamanaka read: "Ms. Yamanaka, who writes in Hawaiian Creole English, a language stigmatized by its association with the immigrant class, has said, 'I am devoted to telling stories the way I have experienced them—cultural identity and linguistic identity being skin and flesh to my body.'"

Lannan was open to honoring writers of all kinds and colors from all over the English-speaking world, and at home in the United States too—including Native Americans, African-Americans, and Asian-Americans. For one, Frank Chin, who talked stink about pidgin at the Talk Story conference in Honolulu in 1978 (and who also said in print that Maxine Hong Kingston was a bold fake who only restated a white racist stereotype about Chinese) got a Lannan award in 1992. (Sidebar: Chin and Kingston each separately supported Yamanaka in the Asian American Studies argument.) Another Hawai'i connection: the poet W. S. Merwin, who had lived and written in Hawai'i since 1975, and whose awards included the Pulitzer Prize, the National Book Award, and the Gold Medal in Poetry of the American Academy of Arts and Letters, got a Lannan award in 2004. And in 1998, Yamanaka's Lannan year, an award in the same category as hers went to J. M. Coetzee, who five years later won the Nobel Prize in Literature.

In 2000, Yamanaka received the Hawai'i Award for Literature. There were no black armbands. As of 2007, no Filipino writer had received the award.

In Hawai'i, the people with the longest history were the Hawaiians. Their Polynesian ancestors were the discoverers of the islands, the first settlers. So Hawaiians had the most to reflect upon: an ancient time stretching all the way back to creation; centuries of undisturbed isolation, a way of living that was theirs alone; and then, in two hundred years of exposure to the big world, devastation—loss of life and land and language and hope.

When Hawaiians came to write, they wrote about all this: a golden age, sacred time, and then dispossession, discrimination, victimization, poverty, rage. Their literature came out of their history, the way all local literature did.

At different times in the Hawaiians' history with the world, they had been named and written about by others in different ways. Noble savages, briefly. Then ignoble savages. Primitive children who needed to be led in the paths of Christian righteousness. Then, because they strayed or wanted to go back to where they had been, ungrateful heathens. Later, they were indolent natives, not willing to work, incapable of governing themselves. And then they were racially inferior beings, barely human, unfit to survive. That was in the nineteenth century. In the twentieth: likeable enough, but shiftless, unproductive, unwilling to improve themselves. At best, tame packaged fake-exotic entertainment for tourists. The word *kanaka*, as spoken by non-Hawaiians, was all-purpose; it could be uttered in any tone of voice, from tolerant to condescending to scornful and dismissive.

Then, beginning in the Sixties and rising in the Seventies, there was a revival of Hawaiian culture—language, music, dance—and an upsurge of political activity. This became known as the Hawaiian Renaissance. It came at a globalizing time in history, when indigenous cultures worldwide were in dire straits—for many, things were looking terminal. In the midst of this, a resurgence of high intensity and broad scope like the Hawaiian Renaissance was notable.

Somewhat strangely, this most Hawaiian of movements never had a Hawaiian-language name. That did not matter. It kept gaining strength in the Eighties, and was full-blown by the Nineties. In January, 1993, at the hundredth anniversary of the overthrow of the Hawaiian monarchy, ten thousand Hawaiians marched through the streets of Honolulu to the grounds of 'Iolani Palace, to hear prayers and chants and political speeches calling for the return of sovereignty to Hawai'i as an independent nation.

Now the most radical (or most fundamentalist) Hawaiians were rejecting being called Hawaiian-Americans, or Americans at all. They began calling themselves Native Hawaiians, or *Kanaka Maoli*, basically meaning real people.

That was history. In literature, the question was: who could claim to write authentically about Hawai'i? For Haunani-Kay Trask, the answer was: only Native Hawaiians.

Trask was a University of Hawai'i professor, a driving force in the founding of a Center for Hawaiian Studies (another product of the Renaissance). She was a public intellectual, often on local TV news and in the Honolulu papers, a prolific writer of polemic, and a published poet.

Trask was part-haole, part-Hawaiian, and it was the Hawaiian part that mattered to her. The way she saw things, the history of Hawai'i ever since the first whites, and most especially since the Protestant missionaries, was one catastrophe after another for Hawaiians, through the nineteenth century to annexation, all the way to the present. Trask spoke the word *missionary* as a curse across time.

She did not stop there. In the full sweep and force of her rage at what had happened to Hawaiians in their native land, she labeled the Asian contract labor immigrants of the nineteenth century and their descendants born in Hawai'i as invaders and usurpers along with the haoles—*settlers*, another curse across time.

Fourth-generation Chinese or Japanese of Trask's own time might call themselves "local," but according to Trask, this did not entitle them to claim that they could speak or write authentically about Hawai'i. When they drew upon the plantation past, this was false nostalgia for something they themselves never experienced; and to celebrate pidgin was false in the same way, nothing but a gloss for the absence of authentic sounds and authentic voices. *Bamboo Ridge* was neocolonial (another curse word). Local Asians and haoles, battling for hegemony in literature, were suffocating the indigenous. Non-Hawaiians who learned Hawaiian well enough to compose in the language were trespassers on sacred ground. Only the indigenous could properly claim the place, the land, the voice, the story. Whatever anyone other than Native Hawaiians wrote about Hawai'i amounted to identity theft.

With Trask, the personal and the cultural were political. She was a native-born United States citizen—born, as a matter of fact, on the mainland, in California—but she publicly refused to consider herself an American: she was a Native Hawaiian, and she took it upon herself to speak for all Hawaiians, as Native Hawaiians. At the same time, she never renounced her United States citizenship (as some Native Hawaiians did, defying any kind of American government authority, state or federal, including courts of law); and when she traveled internationally, which was not infrequently, it was on her American passport. But her way of declaring an identity was to stand on Hawaiian soil, turn her back on America, and face the South Pacific, Polynesia, where the first Hawaiians came from. And in her global projection of herself—the way she set herself to be seen in the wider world—she was a woman of color, an indigenous person embodying and speaking for a culture battling extinction, writing for her own survival and the survival of her people. She wrote and published in English.

For intellectual authority, Trask, the tenured radical, drew upon academic theory generated in the scholarly world beyond Hawai'i—postcolonial political and cultural studies. For another kind of authority, she called up the Hawaiian side of her genealogy, which she recited at the start of a paper she gave at an academic conference, in English.

What it came down to for Trask was that authenticity was in the blood, and the only authentic blood in Hawai'i was Native Hawaiian.

In the local marking of contested literary terrain, this was a big reorientation, amounting to a different mental map projection entirely—a shift from locals against haoles to Hawaiians against everyone else.

There were stories to be written about this.

At a book festival in Honolulu in 2006, a Hawaiian—a Native Hawaiian—gave it as his loudly stated opinion that anyone who was not Hawaiian should not be allowed (his word) to write about Hawai'i. This raised some questions. First, he said it not in Hawaiian, but in English—in, to be precise, a Hawai'i Creole English accent. Second, he said it at a book fair. As a matter of historical fact, English and writing and books were not native to Hawai'i. So—from the opposite side of the cultural looking glass, would it be allowable, in the twenty-first century, in Honolulu, Hawai'i, USA, to say that Hawaiians should not be allowed to speak English, or write books—or to write at all?

And, in 2006, what was a Native Hawaiian? Close to a quarter of a million people in Hawai'i had some Hawaiian blood, one in five of the total population; but only a few hundred were of pure blood. All the rest were part-Hawaiian; and, population-wide, the other parts were from every other kind of blood in Hawai'i, in varying proportions, in many cases adding up to more than fifty percent—so that in any individual part-Hawaiian body, the quantum of Hawaiian blood could well be a minority, all the way down to one-sixteenth or one-thirty-second.

Which raised questions. Was someone who was only one-sixteenth or one-thirty-second Hawaiian a Native Hawaiian, first and only? That is to say, should minority blood rule—even the tiniest minority? If so, might this be a mirror image of the bad old mainland-American race-prejudice thinking in which a single drop of black blood was enough to brand and stigmatize a human being and subject him or her to dreadful discrimination?

And—a real puzzler—if a single drop of Hawaiian blood was enough to make a person affirmatively and exclusively a Native Hawaiian, did a single drop of Asian blood make a person Asian? Did a single drop of haole blood make a person a haole? And if a person had a drop of each blood (as many people in Hawai'i did), then what was that person?

And—whatever the Hawaiian blood quantum, what was authentic Hawaiian cultural behavior? At an event at 'Iolani Palace marking Statehood Day, 2006, there were reports of dissident Native Hawaiians, on Harley Davidsons, with bullhorns.

There could be stories written about all this, but there were not.

In published local literature in the latter part of the twentieth century, writing by Hawaiians was underrepresented.

Before the late Seventies—before the time of the Talk Story conference and the founding of *Bamboo Ridge*—authors in collections of imaginative writing about Hawai'i were almost all in the well-known category of White Males, many of them Dead. From the turn of the Eighties, anthologies were ethnically more various. Bamboo Ridge Press did one called *Growing Up Local*, which was mostly local-Asian, with only bit parts for haoles. *The Best of Bamboo Ridge* was, again, mostly local-Asian. *Small Kid Time* and *Born Pidgin* were all-children, including some with Hawaiian names, but few haoles. *Poetry Hawaii* and *Passages to the Dream Shore* were grownup, and heavier on haoles, but with very few Hawaiians. *Mālama: Hawaiian Land and Water* focused on Hawaiian issues, but not all the writers were Hawaiian. *The Quietest Singing* was all-Hawai'i Award for Literature recipients. *Island Fire* had children and adults, and it was ethnically inclusive. *Best of Honolulu Fiction* was multi-ethnic. So were two annual all-children competetive collections, *Write On, HEA!* and *Star Poets Journal*. There were a number of single-ethnic-group collections. *Paké*, all-Chinese. *Yobo*, and *Hawai Sisim 100-Yŏn: One Hundred Years of Korean Poetry in Hawaii*, all-Korean. A Filipino group, GUMIL, published several collections in Ilocano; *Timek Dagiti Agtutubo: Voices of the Youth* was all-Filipino schoolchildren, writing in English. *Tātou Tusi Tala* was all-Samoan, in Samoan and English. There was no comparable modern all-Japanese anthology. And no all-male one. There was an all-female-all-ethnic one, *Wahine o Hawaii*, edited by a Hawaiian man, who regretted that more Hawaiian women did not contribute.

Between the start of the Seventies and the turn of the century, things went from a time when there was supposed to be no such animal as local literature, to a time when a course in the English department at the University of Hawai'i was titled not Literature of Hawai'i but Literatures, plural. The professor who taught the course had a local-Japanese last name; in 1998 she had been one of the most vehement voices arguing that Lois-Ann Yamanaka's Asian American Studies award should be taken away for Japanese cruelty to Filipinos.

As Eric Chock of *Bamboo Ridge* said, it had turned out to be hard to clear a space in which literature and ethnicity could be building terrain rather than contesting it.

The first all-Hawaiian anthology, *Ho'omānoa*, was published in 1989; and it was the only one, except for an all-Hawaiian issue of the university student magazine, *Hawai'i Review*, the same year.

Nine years later, in 1998, the first all-Hawaiian literary periodical, *'Ōiwi*, brought out its first issue. To be published in *'Ōiwi*, a writer had to have some Hawaiian blood. Other than that, the cultural rules were not strict. *'Ōiwi* ran poetry and prose, fiction and non-fiction, in English, pidgin, and Hawaiian; and it allowed its writers latitude in the way they rendered the Hawaiian language—whether they italicized Hawaiian words or not (the question being whether Hawaiian was to be regarded as a foreign language in Hawai'i); whether they used hyphens and diacritical marks to indicate pronunciation and meaning; and whether they supplied translations or glossaries.

Each issue of *'Ōiwi* included transcripts of discussions among the members of the editorial group. These exchanges added up to the most serious consideration in print of what a Hawaiian literature of Hawai'i might be. The conversations were mostly in English, with some pidgin, and occasional phrases in Hawaiian.

What the twenty-first-century Hawaiian literature of Hawai'i would actually turn out to be like remained to be seen. But clearly, dating from the Hawaiian Renaissance, there was a great deal happening with the Hawaiian language, amounting to history in the making.

At a state constitutional convention in 1978—the year of Talk Story, when the Renaissance was gathering strength—Hawaiian was designated an official language along with English. In the 1980s, state-funded immersion schools were started; Hawaiian parents who wanted to could have their children educated in Hawaiian as a first language, learning everything in Hawaiian, including things like science and mathematics, advancing year by year all the way through high school. In the University of Hawai'i system, enrollments in Hawaiian language courses in the Nineties were multiples higher than they had been in the Fifties and Sixties. Windward Community College on O'ahu had its own traditional hula chant; there were not many colleges like that. In 1992, a measure was approved in the state legislature calling for correct spelling of Hawaiian words, with diacritical marks, in official state and county documents. There was a privately-funded Hawaiian national bibliography, 1780-1900, four big volumes, more than five thousand items.

The net of it was that more concentrated energy was being put into the Hawaiian language than into all the other languages that had ever been spoken and written down in Hawai'i. Looked at globally, this was something exceptional. Worldwide, at the beginning of the twenty-first century, out of seven thousand minority and indigenous languages, most were endangered, more than half of them at risk of disappearing. As a matter of historical fact, a language was going extinct somewhere on earth every couple of weeks, a rate of extinction comparable to that of plants or animals. In the face of this global exterminating plague, the Hawaiian language was not only showing resistance but was gathering strength.

Part of this strong showing had to do with Information Age technology—the computer, the Internet, and the WorldWide Web. There were three Hawaiian terms for the computer: *kamepiula*, a rendering of the English sounds; *lolo uila* or *lolouila*, electric brain; *mākini ho'onohonoho 'ikena*, machine that organizes knowledge. There was a Hawaiian term for the WorldWide Web: *punaewele puni honua*, network around the world. There was a Hawaiian pronunciation website. There was Hawaiian word processing software, for getting the diacriticals right. And there was an online project, ulukau.org, with the longterm aim of putting up on the Web everything that had survived in print in Hawaiian: basic Hawaiian historical documents and books, and all the Hawaiian-language newspapers, from the first one in Honolulu in 1834—by 2007, more than a billion words, with many more to come. Ulukau.org was the busiest indigenous language website in the United States, logging more than six hundred thousand hits a month.

At the beginning of the twenty-first century, the most advanced Western information technology was making it unprecedentedly possible for the Hawaiian past to be recovered in the Hawaiian language.

The computer, the Internet, and the WorldWide Web were set to make another big historic difference in local literature generally: opening up access to publication.

A lot of the literary cultural battles in Honolulu really came down to the issue of getting published, which could be defined as making it past gatekeepers to a place of recognition in a desirable territory that was very limited in extent—starting with who got invited to join a writers' group and who did not, whose work got read and passed around, whose name came to the attention of editors, winding up with who got into print, where, when, or at all; and whether writers who did not get published were being marginalized, condemned to voicelessness, for reasons of oppressive cultural politics.

In an interesting passage of history and literature, *Bamboo Ridge* took a lot of lumps over this. The periodical had started out in 1979 as the designated place for multiethnic, multicultural local writing, opening up new literary territory; and it was seen as eminently—indisputably—worthy of praise for its pioneering efforts and its continuing labors. But after fifteen years or so, meaning by the mid-1990s, *Bamboo Ridge* was coming under local attack from many directions for being exclusionist, essentially closed to anyone except a certain narrowly defined cohort of local-Asians who wrote in a certain narrowly defined style, out of a certain narrowly defined mindset. The negative rap went even further, with the charge that *Bamboo Ridge's* version of localism was inturned, ingrown, to the point of being defensively-aggressively-know-nothing—such that anyone wanting to write any other way, especially a way that might sound like mainstream writing, betraying a possible interest in getting published on the mainland, would be targeted for stink talk by *Bamboo Ridge* people.

On this kind of issue, any number of positions could be and were taken, any number of cases argued. But by the turn of the twenty-first century, it was all looking more and more like a teapot tempest, a very small one, with the lid of the pot being held down tight—and pointlessly.

In the age of the WorldWide Web, what did squabbles over local publishing turf and territory count for? Less than nothing—because in cyberspace there were no gatekeepers, and the Web was virtually infinite in capacity. A couple of clicks, and anyone, anywhere, could be online, to read anything or to write anything. Anyone could start an online literary magazine, at next to no cost in dollars, just sweat equity. For that matter, publishing on the Web did not even depend on the existence of online magazines. Anybody could put their own writing up on the Web, all by themselves, on their own website: every writer his own publisher. Any literary critic had the whole blogosphere to be critical in. And any poet or chanter or songwriter or standup comic could do a podcast, or use a cell phone to make a performance video, and upload it to YouTube or MySpace, where every one of the billion-plus people on earth with an internet connection could watch it. Or not.

On the WorldWide Web, literature from anywhere can go anywhere. Time and place and distance are virtually abolished. But issues remain. All cultures are local somewhere. And it is not just time zones and distances that separate them—there are differences as well, things that have to be interpreted, things that may or may not be translatable. So: in a globalizing world, what does being local mean? What is being local worth?

Those are twenty-first-century questions. Back again to history and literature. The literature of Honolulu, from its beginnings to now, has been produced largely–and pretty directly–from history. Imaginative writing about the town can readily be cross-referenced with people and places and happenings in recognizable periods of time. So the literature of the town could be seen as social history, just without footnotes.

Could be. But it is not really to be depended upon in that way. "Novels arise out of the shortcomings of history." Friedrich von Hardenberg, known as Novalis, said this, in German, at the end of the eighteenth century, and it is a good positive thing to say about literature; it puts imaginative writing up on high ground, with a lot of room to move around in.

Novalis also said, "All memory is present." But the imaginative literature of Honolulu has obvious, even glaring, shortcomings as history. There are any number of invented characters interfering in real events, and people with real names doing imaginary deeds. Anachronisms too: carnations before carnations were introduced; the smell of Korean cooking long before there were Koreans; one king put in a story at the time of another king—many things like that, large and small.

And there are distortions—as in the novel *Two Gentlemen of Hawaii*, by Seward W. Hopkins, published in New York in 1894, the year after the revolution that overthrew the Hawaiian monarchy. Hopkins was a white American. His gentlemen of Hawaiʻi are white Americans too. As for his late-nineteenth-century Honolulu Hawaiians, they may be wearing the shirts and trousers of civilization, but they are not gentlemen—no, under the skin they are still savages. In their blind savage rage at the overthrow, they revert to anthropologically inaccurate primitive blood-thirstiness. They kidnap a well-brought-up young white American woman named Winnie. They perform savage ceremonies over her quivering body, chanting gibberish, doing grotesque dances, sacrificing a goat; and if the gallant white gentlemen had not come to her rescue (nobly putting their own lives in great peril), those savage Hawaiians would have savagely thrown Winnie into a fiery erupting volcano—on a Hawaiian island where, as a matter of historical geological fact, volcanoes have been extinct for more than a million years.

The moral of that story is: read the stories in *Honolulu Stories* for what they are—works of the imagination, with all kinds of imaginations working in all kinds of ways.

So—here are the stories, more than three hundred-fifty of them. For *Honolulu Stories*, as many pieces of writing of as many different kinds as possible were gathered, and then selections were made—all that could be fitted between one set of covers.

The book does not have a dog in any of the local fights about cultural turf and territory. No wagons are circled; nothing is pinned up on the page as a target, or cordoned off to be defended. The only line drawn between inclusion and exclusion is the one marking off the town of Honolulu and its island from the rest of Hawai'i: if a story is about another place, it is for another book.

Some of these Honolulu stories are famous beyond Hawai'i. Some are local classics, anthologized before. Some come from chapbooks or broadsides, published in tiny editions. Others are from out-of-print books and magazines long gone. There are words from nineteenth-century newspapers; song lyrics from old sheet music; voices transcribed from CDs; words downloaded from the Web. A good many have not been sighted in public until now: words that come from manuscripts in libraries and archives, some catalogued, some not; and handwritten words of poetry from sheets of paper brittle with age, found in a small house out in the country (with rottweilers in the yard). There could be a book of stories about finding the stories.

And another book about the writers. Every story has its own writer's story for background. There are pig shooters and cockfighters putting pen to paper. Plantation workers. Political exiles. Civil servants. A night-time poet in a mom and pop store. Another poet who lived in a piano crate. World travelers, people just passing through, and Hawaiians whose lineage goes back a thousand years. Undesirable aliens and alienated citizens. Divorcees. A disinherited rich kid. A grownup wild child, a girl. A boy crippled at fourteen in a diving accident, warehoused in a home for aged indigents until he escaped at twenty-one, having written stories to stay sane. A young man whose father bought up all the copies of his son's book and trashed them. A ninety-year old woman, the widow of a Buddhist priest, still writing *tanka*. Children of every school age, from second grade through twelfth. A man jailed for looking at child pornography on his computer. All the genders, male, female, both, undecided. All ethnicities, all the mixes. People of all aspirations and attitudes. Those who dress for business success. Those who wear their cap backwards. Those who do not trim their beards, and those whose hair is gone. People of elegant utterance. People of a crude turn of speech. People who give big screams. People who have heard the sounds of silence. People who have no story except their own story. People with inchoate yearnings, who do not know what they want, just that they *want*. People who have lost their bearings, who search outward and inward, backward and forward and sideways, and cannot find their path. People who went into the big world to discover themselves, and left their story behind. People who have never been away from home and who have been themselves all along—who are comfortable with the place where they live and comfortable with their story, content to be who they are where they are.

Each and every one, the storytellers speak for themselves. If they contradict each other, very well, then, they contradict each other. They contain multitudes. They and their stories are all pages in the book of life.

The Nineteenth Century

The harbor . . . Chiefs and commoners . . . Missionaries, whalermen and merchants . . . A run-down grog shop . . . Herman Melville the pin setter . . . Mark Twain the traveling journalist . . . The messenger came in secret . . . The gifts of civilization . . . Diseases and the chants of death . . . Take him to Sand Island . . . An orphanage for Hawaiian girls . . . Flashing red fires . . . Five-petaled flowers . . . Robert Louis Stevenson at Waikīkī . . . The songs of Liliʻuokalani . . . When the bells pealed forth their signal . . . A strange, fascinating horrible scene . . . The night ride of a princess . . . The end of kings and queens . . .

KA NUPEPA KUOKOA!

KE KILOHANA POOKELA NO KA LAHUI HAWAII.

BUKE IV. HELU 25.   HONOLULU, IUNE 22, 1865.   NA HELU A PAU 186.

"KA NUPEPA KUOKOA,"

I kela Poahakein Poaha.

$2.00 no na mahina he
UMIKUMAMALUA,
$1.00 no na mahina eono,
ME KA HOOKAA MUA MAI.

KA "NUPEPA KUOKOA,"

Is published in Honolulu

EVERY THURSDAY.

$2.00 per annum, or $1.00 per six
months, in advance.

S. KUPANEA.
J. W. KEAWEHUNAHALA.

Loio!   Loio!

HUA ALISKU, HUA KUKUI.

MA KE KUAI!

HALE PAI KII.

"A NUPEPA KUOKOA"

KUOKOA HUMUHUMUIA.

Umi Kala

Na Buke i Pai ia e ka Papa Hawaii.

Ka Nupepa Kuokon.

KE KAAO O ASIMEDA!

HELU 4.

I waahia naloko ao o ka Buke Moolelo o Geheriona.)

ANO KEIA MEA, IKE AE LA O Asimeda ua ohi pau pu ka make-
make o pau loa makou o Cinigamalaina no io i oni, a he mea
hiki ole hoi ia i ke nei ke pane hou ae, no keia, waiho aku la o Asimeda i
olelo hoopomaikai imua o Cinigamalaina penei:—

KA MOOLELO.
—O—
HAWAII NEI.
HELU 2.

No ne Kaapuni Makaikai i na wahi Kaulana a me na Kupua, a me na li'li Ka-
puu mai Hawaii a Niihau.

Samuel Mānaiakalani Kamakau

from KA NUPEPA KUOKOA

U a lohe ia ma o Makuakaumana la, na wahi kaulana; a ua hele mai au
e ike maka. O Kou ke awa, o Mamala ka nuku, o Pakaka ka heiau, o
Puowaina kahi puhi kanaka. O Hekili ka imu pikao o na'lii pio i ke kaua. O
Kewalo kahi lumalumai o na kauwa i ke Kanawai o Kekaihehee. O Honolulu
ke Ahupuaa. He aina oluolu, a maikai, e huli ana i ka aoao Hema; he momona ka nui o ka aina. He wai kahe, a he waipuna, ka wai e hoomau ai i na
loi kalo, a e hoopuni ai i ke Kulanakauhale. O ka ua kukalahale ka ua mau; ka
ua kiowao noho mai iuka, kilihehe no i ka pua kamakahala.

I had heard of famous place of Oʻahu from Makuakaʻūmana and came to see
them for myself. Kou was the harbor, Māmala the entrance, Pākākā the *heiau*. Pū-o-waina was the place where men were burned, *puhi kanaka*; Hekili
was the oven, *imu pīkaʻo*, where chiefs captured in war were parched. Kewalo
was the place where the *kauwā* were held under water to drown according to
the Kānāwai Kaihehe'e.

Honolulu was the *ahupuaʻa*, a good and pleasant land that faced to the
south. Most of it was fertile land with running water and springs that constantly irrigated the pond fields that surrounded the clusters of houses. The
customary rain was the Kūkala-hale; the Kiʻowao rain came down from the
uplands, drenching the blossoming plants.

TRANSLATED BY MARY KAWENA PUKUI

SAMUEL MĀNAIAKALANI KAMAKAU (1815-1876) *was one of the most prominent native
Hawaiian scholars of the nineteenth century. He collected and published his research on the
history and traditions of his people. He was also District Judge of Wailuku, Maui, and served
in the legislature representing Maui and Oʻahu. His series on Hawaiian history and culture
appeared in the weekly Hawaiian language newspapers* Ke Au Okoa *and* Ka Nupepa Kuokoa
from 1866 to 1871.

Charles Martin Newell

from KALANI OF OAHU

E arly in the afternoon the foremost vessels of the fleet passed Koko point, and skirted Kona's fertile shore, where the wind became light, and it was approaching night when they passed Diamond Head, and coasted just without the long line of gigantic breakers abreast of Waikiki. Every canoe feeding out their hoarded morsel to Moa-alii as they passed his caverned home under the reef-bed in front of the great *Heiau* built in the mouth of the Manoa valley beyond.

Here first Kupule saw her new Oahu home, peering out from among its great king-palms and large bread-fruit trees, far up the beautiful vale of Nuuanu, than which nothing is more charming in all the Hawaiian world. While the evening was approaching, and they were coasting along the unbroken surf, stretching from Leahi (Diamond Head) to the harbor's mouth, Kalani pointed out his seaside palace, seen in the midst of the great cocoanut grove at Waikiki.

To the right of the palm trees rose the massive walls of the great *heiau*, with its temples and towers, and sacrificial places within; where in the terrible Kapu Kane, thousands of human offerings were sacrificed in the service of Pele and Moa-alii.

To the left of Waikiki glowed Puawai—the Punch Bowl mountain—in the setting sun, looming like a monstrous storm-billow dropped in unbroken grandeur upon the plain. Where its frowning battlement of jutting rocks, and turret peaks of gray lava, overlooked the town, was now flung to the breeze a yellow tapa flag, to signal the approach of the King.

On sped the fleet with the soft-blowing trades, clinging to the white line of coral reef, and keeping just without its roaring, floundering breakers, whose crests were now gilded like oriental domes by the dying day. Kalani's heart was made glad as he passed countless scenes of happy boyhood days, while he pointed out to his blushing bride elect his fair kingdom of Oahu; his royal palace of Nuuanu—the barbaric home of a long line of warrior kings.

Here luxuriant nature seemed to have completed a grateful task of love. Grouping together in the fair Nuuanu vale her utmost beauties for a kingly home. Here flourished every fruitful tree and prolific vine, and grew the greenest grasses and the rarest flowers, with heaped-up rugged mountains to overlook and overawe the completed whole.

A wide-mouthed valley, blue-marged by the sea, and blue-rimmed by the distant sky; narrowing downward from the far skyward hills, where the mountain gateway of the dizzy Pali opens above the sea into the sky beyond. Green with the ceaseless perennity of a thousand varying hues, the Nuuanu expands as it descends in easy slopes down to the reef-barred harbor of Honolulu.

The green lawns of the valley are only separated by a coral sand-beach from ocean's rarest madreporic sea, wherein the thousands of sun-swarthed children swim, from the hour of birth to the octogenarian days of decrepitude. Here the youth of adolescent age, whether *wahine* or *kane*, may dive in playful pastime for the gaudy shells, the rare-hued corals, and the opulent pearls. Here they fish from the inner reef-edge, whether for pleasure or profit, with never a doubt of abundant pastime for the children, or of readily accorded sufficiency to the lazy housewife's demand.

Crowning a palm-clad knoll upon the east side of the valley, Kalani had already pointed out the vine-covered palace of his sires. About its numerous outbuildings were fine old bread-fruit trees, with their dark green foliage, looming stately and grand among the more graceful palms, the gnarled pandana and the symmetrical Kukui trees.

To the east of the palace rose the frowning Punch Bowl, a grass-grown crater, brooding over its ancient days of fiery splendor now long gone by. Back of this towers Tantulus, overlooking the Punch Bowl, and densely tree-clad to his top. Beyond all rises grand old Waolani, the nearest approach to Kea and Loa that Oahu can show.

Just back of the busy palace knoll uprose a higher hill, sacred to the gods, and tabooed with the utmost rigor for the use of priest and king; its whole rounded crest and sloping sides were clothed with a dense grove of orange trees, ever, as now, presenting a countless abundance of blossoms and fruit the whole year round.

On the very apex of this sacred hill there leaps up a charming natural fountain, emerging from out a mound of vine-covered rocks, jetting forth from a clear, never-failing spring, and running the zigzag course of a mountain brook down the valley to the sea. From out the cool, crystal waters of this grass-grown, flower-verged fountain, it is said that many mystic and unearthly sights have been disclosed, in divine answer to priestly oblation and royal prayers. It is the *Kiowai o' Pele* (fountain of Pele) sacred to the gods.

This sacred grove has been the holy of holies of a long line of noble kings. A tabooed resort where the reigning monarch has sought for solitude during the various phases of the midnight moon, when interceding with the gods for divine aid during contemplated wars.

Here also came the cruel Alii Kapu—the tabu chief—when his king was depressed in body or mind, with the fear of death upon him, and in the belief that some sorcerous enemy was praying him to death—a current belief of the time. Here came the great High Priest, and after fasting and prayer, would necessarily discover in the fountain the treacherous visage of the wicked *Kilo*, who was secretly praying his king to death. And when thus discovered, it was a natural sequence that the body of the impious sorcerer should be needed as a victim in the next *Kapu Kane*, proclaimed for the good of the state at the sick king's command.

Above and beyond all these lesser hill-tops arises another, where leaps a wild cascade down the rocky declivity, emerging from a densely wooded glen above, ravined and craggy with jutting rocks tumbled from the mountain by the earthquake shocks in years gone by. Below the wild cascade and the noisy stream, the waters broaden out into a mountain mere, and end in a wide, smooth waterfall, where the western orbs of night and day glass their seven prismatic hues in rainbow sheen or Luna glory. While in the windless waters of the tiny mere, the jagged peak of Waolani may mirror his rugged beauties with every eastern sun.

From another little lakelet, skirting the foot of the palace knoll, flowed the murmuring mountain stream valleyward, in eager haste to the sea. And because of the dislike for fresh water, of the fastidious polypi, who reared the great coral reefs, the Oahuans are indebted to this stream of Nuuanu for their novel and beautiful harbor of Honolulu, or Fairhaven.

True, it was the work of centuries for this little stream; but small means, with constant application, may tear a mountain from its base. And no better illustration can be shown of what may be accomplished by small things than this work of the Nuuanu brook, in excavating a roomy harbor, and an outlet, through the great reef-bed, though the sea-girt shore was defended by the inrolling avalanche of its ponderous breakers.

Not only is the harbor novel and compact, but the anchorage is made a safe one by the deep, tenacious alluvium deposit made by the stream while working patiently at its subterraneous excavation, and making its subsequent assaults to pierce through the barrier reef-bed, making a commercial gateway to the sea.

CHARLES MARTIN NEWELL (1823-1900) *was born in Concord, Massachusetts. At fifteen, he went to sea as a cabin boy on a whaler. He rose to captain, with a reputation for giving his crew good medical care and for letting them read books from his big personal library. While captaining the* Alice *in the Pacific, he had to put down a mutiny. One grievance of the mutineers was that when they returned books in bad condition, he refused to let them borrow any more. Newell practiced medicine in Boston from 1860 to 1898. He published novels under the name of Captain Robert Barnacle.*

Albertine Loomis
from GRAPES OF CANAAN

From the deck of the *Thaddeus* in the early morning of April 14, the family watched the gray land of Oahu emerge off the starboard bow, saw jutting promontories take shape and hailed the long-awaited Diamond Hill, guardian of Waikiki Bay.

The sun rose astern to sharpen the features of the island and brighten its colors. There were the cocoanut groves and the curve of sandy beach, where the bathers sported. There was the line of white breakers, marking the reef; there were the steep mountains and the deep-grooved valleys—just as Supercargo James Hunnewell had described them so often.

There, presently, was Honolulu harbor, as fair a haven as the Pacific boasts, shielded seaward by a wall of coral and landward by the Koolau range, though winds still came boisterous through the gap at the Pali. There in the sunlight swirling white mists encircled gray peaks and caressed green hillsides, and streams danced down through a tangle of *kukui, pandanus, koa* and giant ferns.

And there on the treeless flats, amid coarse *pili* grass and gray coral-dust, slouched Honolulu village—some three hundred straw huts, as frowsy as last season's haycock. On the point, the stone-faced mud walls of a fort rose high above the low dwellings. Mounting sixty guns and flaunting the Hawaiian colors—a Union Jack in the upper quarter with a field of horizontal red and white stripes—it seemed to defy foreigners to try any nonsense in this harbor.

Outside the reef the *Thaddeus* dropped anchor and sent its boat ashore to announce that—despite wind, weather and the devil—God had got around Cape Horn.

At the fort Hiram Bingham, abetted by Captain Blanchard, inquired for Boki, the governor of Oahu. But Boki was not at home. He had gone, said the second in command, to another part of the island, and who could tell when he might return? Let the *haoles* talk, if they were in such haste, with Don Marin, the interpreter.

The Spaniard, Don Francisco Paulo di Marin, had been thirty years in the Islands—so long that in 1820 there were few who could remember Honolulu without his luxurious garden and his fine, fat cattle. Before Kamehameha conquered Oahu, Marin had come from Andalusia, bringing animals, seeds and vines. He had introduced the damask rose and the cotton tree, the grape, the tamarind and the prickly pear—which he pruned into hedges. He had imported horses, mules, doves and English hares. He made wine and butter, salted beef to supply the ships and sold his lemons, oranges and pineapples; but he would allow no seeds or roots outside his own garden and no animals beyond his own acres. At his plantation behind the village, in Nuuanu valley, he received the Americans graciously, served them some of his excellent wine and, agreeing that salvation was urgent business, dispatched two messengers on horseback to bring the absent Boki home.

Meanwhile the port master, having collected his fees, sent a fleet of towing canoes to bring the *Thaddeus* into the harbor, for only if wind and tide were exceptionally favorable could a vessel sail through the gap in the reef. Presently ropes tautened, brown paddlers bent to their task, the pilot chanted his orders, and the brig moved through the narrow channel to her berth near the fort.

By his fast-sailing vessel, the *Neo*, the king had sent a message to Governor Boki: "This is my command. Furnish the *haoles* with land and houses and with provisions. Let them dwell in Honolulu for one year, if they do not make any trouble."

The governor was a brother of Kalanimoku, younger and less able than the premier, but as eager to stand well with white men. So when he returned to the fort and heard what the king's messenger had to say, Boki went on board the American vessel to greet the company of teachers. Tall, athletic and tipsy, he grinned like a genial death's head—for, to show his grief when Kamehameha died, he had had his front teeth knocked out with a chisel. He instructed Marin to speak his *aloha*, but he was in no mood, it seemed, to talk of houses.

When, in turn, the brethren called at his palace within the fort, Boki gave them presents of breadfruit and taro. But a residence for their families and a place to store their goods—all that, he said airily, could wait.

Even so, the men of the Mission were not without resources. In Boston the old sandalwood trader Captain Winship had offered the use of his house in Honolulu. He knew how things would be at the Islands, what delays and exasperations the brethren would encounter there, and so he had given Hiram Bingham a note to Don Marin, asking him to unlock the house for the missionaries. When word of Winship's generosity had made the rounds in Honolulu, the American merchant William Navarro offered a small building in his yard. Someone suggested the Lewis place, Captain Isaiah Lewis having gone to the Spanish Main. William Babcock, agent for Marshall & Wildes, said there was room in his storehouse for things not immediately to be unpacked.

About houses, then, Boki could take his own Hawaiian time. But he did send *kanakas* to help set the Mission on shore. They casually hoisted trunks to their skinny shoulders and rolled hogsheads along the beach, paying no heed to Hiram Bingham's orders or Daniel Chamberlain's frantic gestures, treating it all as a merry pastime. A four-wheeled handcart captured their fancy. Two of them seized it by the tongue and capered toward the fort; others dumped their burdens in the sand and followed till a too-sharp turn around a palm tree ended the joy-ride.

Not until all the goods had been landed were the women lowered overside and rowed to the shore. With as much dignity as if to "meeting" they walked beside their husbands through Honolulu village. Past the grogshops and the traders' houses the little procession moved, and in it the first white women to set foot on Oahu. A throng of natives, growing larger each moment, trailed behind, and chattered incessantly. Some bold ones pressed close, plucked at sleeves and peered under bonnets.

"A-i-oe-oe," one laughed, and the rest took it up like a refrain.

"They are saying your faces are small and set far in, and that you have long necks," Honolii explained.

"Long necks. Long necks," the natives kept shouting; but it was not in derision, only in wonder at the strangeness of these newcomers. And Longnecks they were called for many a year.

The houses smelled of dust and dry grass like a haymow. The windowless walls crawled with vermin. Mice scampered across the dirt floors. In the dark rooms, where capering *kanakas* had deposited them, were the boxed and bundled goods with which the Mission family must now equip their homes, the chaos out of which they must bring a New England order.

They were not dismayed. Though they were teachers and preachers, they had worked with their hands, too, and knew what it meant to rope up bedsteads, to assemble a cookstove, to build a table or a bench out of lumber that had been a crate. The men shed their jackets and pried off lids, brushed walls, repaired thatch, carried in rushes for the floor and wood for the fire. The women put on their oldest dresses and got down on their knees to scrub.

The farm tools had gone into Captain Babcock's storehouse in the governor's yard. Later, if Boki gave the Mission some land and Don Marin was willing to lend his oxen, Daniel Chamberlain would bring out the plow and the harrow. The printing press had gone in, too, and the boxes that held the types and paper, along with most of the books and slates and the maps and globes to be used one day in their schoolroom. In patience they must possess their souls, doing first those simple things that could be done by word of mouth in a tongue they knew but ill. And Elisha, the printer, must be the most patient of all.

By Sunday, four days after they had moved ashore, they were ready to hold public worship in the main room of Captain Lewis' house. Let native nobles or foreign traders come—and some did—the Mission was ready to receive them in order and peace.

Among the whites were Oliver Holmes, long of Honolulu but once of
Plymouth, Massachusetts; Jack Woodland, a refugee from Botany Bay; and
mannerly James Hunnewell, supercargo of the *Thaddeus*. Of natives there
were Boki, with his fly-brushing, fan-wielding train, and a petty chief or so.
After the service began and the word got around that the Longnecks were
making a strange *pulepule*, the yard filled up with commoners, who vied for
places at the door.

What amazed them most, it seemed, was the hymn singing. Despite the
rhythmic accent of Tamoree's bass viol, the staid harmonies were unlike any
chant Hawaii knew. When the white men bowed in prayer, covering their
faces with their hands, Honolii tip-toed about with finger on lips and whispered, "*Kapu!*" to those who spoke or moved. And when the sermon began,
he translated a little at a time.

"Behold I bring you good tidings." On earth let there be peace and good
will. It was the command of the one true *Akua* that they live together—brown
and white, kings, chiefs and commoners, whether from the windward islands
or the leeward—loving one another like brothers. Never again should they
take up their spears to kill in behalf of this chief or that, but should use them
to cut dead branches from trees, that the bananas and breadfruit might be
plentiful for all.

Harsh and inconvenient as life was in Honolulu, it was not lonely for the
Mission family. There was warmth in the welcome of their fellow-*haoles*, of
whatever faith or country. White neighbors named Babcock, Elwell, Warren, Navarro, Holmes and Harbottle made gifts of rice, beans, soap and
flour from their imported stores, yams and melons from their garden plots.
Don Marin sent a woven basket heaped with fruit and a jug of wine. Captain
William Pigot and his partner Mr. Green invited the strangers to a "friendly
cup of tea" at their establishment; and the next day, having learned that the
dishes brought out in the *Thaddeus* had been ground to rubble, they presented the Mission with a full set of brown-and-white china.

But still the native life swirled around them, alien, high-pitched and
bizarre. All through the soft, warm nights there came from the fort the
hourly clang of an iron bell and the raucous heathen shout that meant "All's
well." By day, even after Boki had tabued the yards, native hordes peered
through the palings and goggled at the American cookstove. Honolii, listening to their prattle, said they were curious about the women's work.
Cooking in Hawaii was a man's job; only cloth-making a wife's. Though
they dressed like chiefs—with flowing robes and fancy hairdress—these
haole women were always busy; they never lounged or fondled pets or
played cards.

On the dusty plain the discredited priests of the old religion went about scolding like shrews. If the people had not overthrown the idols and ceased their prayers and offerings, the old men said, there would have been rain. Now it would be dry forever. The streams would fail; the *taro* would die and the people would starve. Then sudden showers fell, and even the children mocked the false prophets, pointing at them with skinny fingers.

One morning a petty chief slipped into the yard, stole four of the precious new plates and made off amid great clamor. When the culprit had been captured, Boki turned him over to the Mission. Usually in Hawaii, the governor explained, one dealt with a thief by going to his house and taking something in return for the stolen goods. If the Longnecks did not want to do that, let them punish the fellow some other way. They could beat him or brand him or shave off his hair—anything so long as they did not kill him with their prayers. The family smiled at that until they saw a former priest and his wahine led in irons toward the governor's, accused of praying a woman to death. . . .

Meanwhile there was work to do. The Longnecks did not stay in their tabued inclosures, waiting for sinners to come and hear their gospel. Back of the fort, where Honolulu stretched southeastward among the marshes and fishponds, they sought out the poor and the wretched. Here was the village slum. Into houses but waist-high—dark, filthy, flea-ridden, without so much as a wooden bowl or a woven mat—native families crept at nightfall to sleep, close-packed, on the hard, rush-strewn earth under dusty, tattered *tapas*. Their pigs and dogs and ducks—if they were lucky enough to have any animals—huddled with them; and the places grew foul with excrement.

Daytimes the people lived outside. The strong ones frolicked in the surf or bowled on the plain or hung about the *haole* part of the village to beg or steal. But there were some so ill or indolent that they only lounged in the shade of their shacks—fly-nipped and scabby with an itch that was too common to be noticed. If there was food, they ate whenever hunger impelled, plunging their dirty fingers into the sour, fermenting contents of the common calabash. But there was never an abundance, and often nothing at all. No wonder, then, that their skins hung on their protruding bones like drying fish nets on the rocks.

For the blind and the aged, the sick and the insane, the Hawaiians showed no pity; they taunted them and drove them away, left them to starve or buried them alive in pit or stone-pile. They mated so casually, killed so calmly their unwanted infants, gave away so readily their children to other households that those who had come from America to "save" them thought at first they had no hearts at all.

But the men and women of the Mission held certain truths to be self-evident. And their creed, so annoying to many both here and in their own land, taught that the vilest and the humblest had the right to know and to choose. To these, as well as to overfed princes and dowagers they must reveal the eternal truth. So they followed the paths that wound intricately among the fishponds—royal ponds, from which a hungry commoner could draw a single mullet only at risk of his miserable life or his shrunken limb—and talked with the people, or tried to.

They were misunderstood—these Longnecks. Their prayers terrified; their clothes aroused envy; their homilies stirred resentment. But they persisted. One of the sisters took a dropsical, sore-covered orphan home to nurse it. Hiram Bingham dressed an ulcerated lip or gave a fellow some salve for his blistering rash.

All of them, as they came and went, spoke softly and smiled. They did not rub noses in the Hawaiian manner but held out their white, unblemished hands to grasp the scaly ones of their brown neighbors in *aloha*. Gradually, though they made little of the spoken words, the people began to see meaning in the quiet, trustful friendliness of the newcomers. And those of the Mission discovered hearts in the commoners. . . .

The printing press was still in Captain Babcock's storehouse. It would have been foolish to go to press with an imperfect orthography, more than foolish to print Bible passages so badly rendered that they promised earthly riches when they meant to proffer heavenly. So the printing waited, and the only schoolbooks at the Mission were Webster's speller and the English Bible.

The brethren had once hoped Providence would open a way for them to confer with the British missionaries in the Society Islands, where the work of reducing Polynesian speech to writing had been in progress for many years. When Kaumualii, about to send his brig *Becket* to Tahiti on a trading voyage, had offered free passage to two Longnecks, it had looked for a little while as if Hiram Bingham and one of his colleagues would talk face to face with the Englishmen, hear their advice and get samples of their publications. But when Kaumualii was carried captive to Oahu that fine prospect faded. By the end of 1821 the men of the Mission knew they must work things out alone.

Though there were still sharp differences among them about the interchangeable consonants, they settled tentatively on a Hawaiian alphabet of seventeen English letters and agreed that the time had come to start printing.

Elisha hired four natives to haul the press to the Mission yard in the handcart. Steadying the precious "engine" as he walked alongside, he thought of Uzzah, stricken because he touched the Ark of the Covenant "when the oxen shook it." He could not blame Uzzah; he knew how the young Israelite must have felt.

The thatched house in Missionary Row where the Chamberlains had lived was to be the printing office. There the press and the boxes of accessories and parcels of type were deposited. Elisha unwrapped and distributed his two fonts into the cases. It was good to know that his fingers still found their way unerringly to the compartments. A wonderful thing, this memory of muscles and nerves, so tenacious that, once fixed, a skill was scarcely diminished by the lapse of time. It was two and a half years since he had done such a job at Bemis'.

On a Saturday early in the new year, he began to set type for page one of the Elementary Lessons, afterward called the *pi-a-pa*. On Monday, January 7, when he was ready to strike off the first copies, he summoned the family to share the great event.

The high chief Keeaumoku, brother of Kaahumanu, was in Honolulu that day. "Have you called on the Longnecks since they have lived in a wooden house?" Kalanimoku asked him. Keeaumoku had not, but the idea of such a visit pleased him. So the governor of Maui joined the group that had assembled to watch the first printing in Hawaii.

Elisha locked up the form and lifted it into place. Then he swabbed on the ink and pressed the paper over the besmeared type. A gentle push and the frisket rolled under the platen. Now all was in readiness for the final triumphant act—a pull of the lever and the impression indelibly made.

Elisha looked at Keeaumoku, whose eyes had followed every move. "You pull?" he asked, indicating the lever.

"Me pull," Keeaumoku agreed, all smiles. He seemed afraid to release the handle once he had swung it, but at last he retreated a step and watched Elisha strip off the sheet, wondrously speckled with *a*'s and *k*'s and *l*'s and *o*'s.

"*Maikai*," said Keeaumoku.

ALBERTINE LOOMIS (1895-1985) *was the great-granddaughter of Elisha Loomis, the Protestant missionary who brought the first printing press to Hawai'i in 1820. A Michigan English teacher, she moved to Honolulu in 1959. Among her books are* Grapes of Canaan *and* For Whom Are the Stars.

Ruth Eleanor McKee

from THE LORD'S ANOINTED

S he rose and stood in the doorway, staring out across the rocky plain
toward the deep blue, glass-smooth sea, noting sails against the horizon
and hoping that if it were another whaling vessel the seamen would keep
away from the mission. Watch the orphans as diligently as they could, the
lure of a swaggering sailor with bright beads or a few yards of gaudy calico
to dangle before an acquisitive girl on the verge of womanhood was sure
to overwhelm superimposed notions of propriety. The last whaling ship in
port had cost them two girls, who now were wont to stroll past the walled-
in missionary settlement wrapped in the bright calico, the fruit of their sin,
strutting by to flaunt their ill-gotten gains before the frankly envious gaze
of their erstwhile fellows. Constancy smiled, thinking of the drunken sailor
who reeled into the mission enclosure one night, loudly calling for rum, to
be sent away with a Bible in his hand, his jaw fallen with astonishment. But
too many of the whalers saw fit to hang over the wall and jeer at the missionaries, shouting rude obscenities to embarrass the pious. . . .

Constancy went into the smaller of the two rooms in her house and began
making up the four-poster bed which Boki's wife, Liliha, had given her in
a moment of generosity. Liliha had it from a trader. When the bedroom
was put to rights Constancy found the orphans gathered about the long
table in the next room, ready for school. From the large house rose the
strains of "Rock of Ages," sung in Hawaiian. Mrs. Bingham's school had
begun. Constancy went to the rude cupboard Jonathan had made for her and
took down a pile of papers on which were printed the first simple lessons
in the Christian faith. She held up one and then another to the class. The
orphans shouted in singsong Hawaiian:
"I cannot see God, but God can see me.
"In the beginning God created the heavens and the earth.
"Jehovah is in heaven, and He is everywhere.
"Jehovah sees everything that I do.
"Jesus Christ, the good son of God, died for our sins.
"We must pray for Jehovah and love His word.
"God loves good men, and good men love God."
Then those who knew the texts by heart rose and, with hands twisting
calico skirts or folded placidly over stomach, chanted them triumphantly.
This much of the day's work over, they took pencils and odd bits of paper
and painstakingly wrote their names, the alphabet, both in printing and in
script, and while a few of the more advanced carefully wrote out the Lord's

Prayer in Hawaiian, the slower or younger children wrote out the lesson they had just been parroting. Constancy moved back and forth among them, guiding a faltering hand, reproving a careless pupil whose lines zigzagged too much or whose work showed smudges and erasures, praising a neat piece of work when she found one. Next they sang a hymn. Then little rolls of calico were brought forth from the cupboard and distributed among the orphans. The little rolls were cut in odd pieces, which, fitted together, made drawers, that the orphans might go their way in decency. The longer the children sewed, the filthier grew the garments. They stabbed themselves accidentally with their needles and their mates by intention, whereupon a loud outcry was made. Constancy sat facing them, plying her own needle in the fine linen her mother had given her before the departure of the *Thaddeus*. She made countless tiny tucks with the smallest of stitches.

RUTH ELEANOR MCKEE, *born in 1903, was a staff member at the Library of Hawaii for ten years. A poet and novelist, she is the author of* Storm Point; The Lord's Anointed; Three Daughters; *and* After A Hundred Years. *She worked as a United States Foreign Service officer, and writer for the War Relocation Authority.*

Author Unknown
"KA ULU LĀ'AU O KAI"

E 'ike auane'i 'oe
I ka ulu lā'au o kai,
Kai aloha na'u o Māmala,
Kai a'oa'o me ke aloha.

O ka home a'e o Lē'ahi,
Oni ana Pu'u-loa i ke kai,
Loa ke ki'ina a ke aloha.

E kau paha i ka palapala,
Polo'ai aku iāia,
E waiho aku a ho'i mai,
E maliu mai 'oe e ka hoa.
A hiki mai 'oe, pono au.

Ha'ina 'ia mai ka puana
I ka ulu lā'au ma kai.

"FOREST TREES OF THE SEA"

I have seen in my heart
That sea of forest trees
Of tall-masted ships returning
To Honolulu's harbor of Māmala,
Making every sea-murmur a word—
Māmala's murmur of unresting love.

Love's home is Diamond Head.
Love's shelter is where Pearl Harbor hills reach out to sea.
Love's gaze is keen and long.

Perhaps I should write a letter.
Perhaps I should show my love by asking his:
Come back, dear love, bring ease to me,
Comfort my mind.

For you I sing my song
Of forest trees on the unresting sea.

TRANSLATED BY MARY KAWENA PUKUI

William H. Thomes
from A WHALEMAN'S ADVENTURES
IN THE SANDWICH ISLANDS AND CALIFORNIA

We were at the extreme southerly end of the island, and near some village—that was evident. The question was, would the natives make us prisoners and send us to Honolulu, or keep us? It would take a canoe two days to reach Honolulu, against wind and tide, and we rather thought that the Sally would not wait so long to hear from us. Jack was in favor of launching the boat and starting for some other island; but to that proposition Will and Jake were opposed, and I did not like it; so we voted that down in short time. Jake proposed that we should go fishing, and fill the boat with fish, and offer them to the natives as a bribe; but as there was only one line, and that Jake wanted to use, the plan was not adopted, to the intense disgust of my colored friend, who retired from the conference, and went to sleep. We were about to do the same thing, and wait for events, when, looking up, I saw some thirty natives, armed with clubs and hatchets, winding round the base of the hill, and advancing towards us; and following them were about fifty women, all dressed alike, but not all young and handsome.

Our first impression upon seeing the natives was to take to our heels; for we could not help remembering that on some of the islands white men had been eaten, and esteemed a luxury. But I assured the men that I thought there was no danger, and that if any one was to be eaten it would be me, on account of my tender years. Therefore we maintained our position, and awaited the approach of the natives, who advanced in solemn silence, an old white-haired man at the head of the delegation; and from the deference which his followers paid him, I supposed that he was a chief.

"Look at dat old woman," said Jake. "She got her eye on dis child, and I tink dat she mean to eat me for sure."

"Be quiet," I said. "The old man is going to speak."

The procession halted about eight fathoms from us.

"*Ouri miti kanaka*," said the chief.

"What in thunder does he mean by that?" Jack cried.

"Speak English," I said, advancing a few steps towards the chief.

The chief consulted with one of his counsellors, and presently a young fellow stepped forward, and the people raised a murmur, as much as to say, "Now you will see something."

"Say," cried the young fellow, with an oratorical flourish of his hands and a smiling face.

The crowd took up the cry, and all shouted, "Say," and then they laughed. People don't laugh when they contemplate eating human beings. My hopes of a peaceable settlement revived.

"Say," shouted the young man, and then he stopped.

"Say," repeated the natives, and crowded closer around us.

"That makes twice you've said it," muttered Jack.

"Say, where come, hey?" the young kanaka continued, and his friends all shouted, "Ha, ha—*houri, houri*," and then nodded their heads numerous times.

I pointed in the direction of the water. The women clapped their hands.

"Say, when come?" asked the interpreter.

"This morning," I answered.

I must have said something witty in those two words, for the natives repeated them, with every variety of intonation, and then, forgetful of their fears, crowded around us without much ceremony.

"Say, what do?" said the interpreter.

"Stay here," I answered.

As soon as the young kanaka had repeated the words to the chief, and the latter to the people, there was an immense amount of talking. The old veteran dug his fist into the side of his interpreter, and the latter once more opened fire.

"Say, where boat?" he asked.

I pointed to the beach, and the chief intimated that we would confer a favor if we would lead the way and show where the boat was concealed. I led the party, followed by the young ladies, who seemed to think that they had some claim upon me, in consequence of first discovery. We continued on until we reached the beach, and tore away the brush-wood which we had piled around the boat. Then there was a shout, and the old women howled louder than all the rest.

"Ugh," grunted the chief; and his eyes brightened as they fell upon the hatchets, knives, and harpoons which the boat contained. I took a hatchet and knife, and handed them to the chief, and the old man spoke a few words to the interpreter.

"Say," said the latter, "this him?" pointing to the articles.

"Yes, all for him," I replied.

When this was known there went up a shout, and the young ladies crowded around me. The chief slipped the hatchet in the bosom of his shirt, and put the knife in a belt which he wore around his waist. The rest of the natives looked wishful; so we gave to one a harpoon and to another a lance, until the whole stock was exhausted. One hatchet I kept, and a knife I gave to the interpreter, which pleased him so intensely that he muttered his thanks in such a mixture of broken English and kanaka lingo, that there was no understanding him.

Then the chief pointed in the direction of the village, and the interpreter said, "Come," and we started, the women clustering around us and manifesting many tokens of kindness; and the chief did not evince any desire to rebuke such conduct. A ten minutes' walk brought us to the village, which contained about sixty huts, and were nestled in a valley that was surrounded by cocoa-nut trees, and orange and banana trees, the fruit on them hanging ripe, and large quantities on the ground, having dropped off, and were lying uncared for. Near each hut was a patch of cultivated land, on which were growing yams, potatoes, and other vegetables, and before each door was a brood of chickens and a few ducks. The houses were thatched to keep out the wet, and looked neat and comfortable.

We went directly to the chief's house; the inside of which we found furnished with a raised platform, covered with a bullock's hide, and seemed intended for a bedstead. Around the walls were spears, paddles, and sharks' teeth, and also a few sperm whale teeth; the latter evidently highly prized from the manner in which they were polished. There was no floor, but the earth was beaten smooth, and even polished, with constant use. There were no chairs, but, as a substitute, grass mats were spread in various parts of the room; and to these the chief pointed, and motioned for us to make ourselves at home. We squatted down, and the natives followed suit, in the open air, however, as no one but a young lady, whose attentions I was disposed to suffer without rebuke, followed us into the house. The young girl lounged on the bed, and looked at us, and laughed, and then she said something to the chief, and he laughed, and then we all laughed. The interpreter suddenly made his appearance, and after a short confab with the chief, asked,—

"You eat?"

And he placed his hands upon his stomach, and made his mouth move fearfully.

"By golly," cried Jake, "he mean dat he like to eat us. Dat old man got his eye on me. But I's tough, and he find out dat he better take de younger ones."

"But you'll be first," I suggested. "They always reserve the delicate ones for the last."

Jake's eyes began to grow large. To add to the negro's terrors, the chief, at that moment, laid his hand upon a spear, and looked unusually grave.

"Look ahere," cried the colored sailor; "I don't stand dat. I's a 'Merican sailor, and will fight like de debil afore I let you eat me."

"Be quiet, you fool, and don't cry out till you is roasting," said Jack.

"It's all berry well to say be quiet; but I won't be quiet when dey is calculating how much fat I'se got on my ribs."

If we had any doubts on the subject of cannibalism of the natives, they were happily dissipated by the entrance of two old women, who brought in stewed yams and fish, a boiled chicken, and a large basket of fruit; and as the food was set before us, the chief intimated that we were to make a meal, and the outside barbarians laughed and encouraged us when they saw that we had good appetites; but after we had finished our first course, the young lady—whom I had supposed to be the chief's daughter, and whom I called "Lilly," not on account of her white skin, however, but because she was tall and graceful—seated herself by my side, and pealed an orange for me, and insisted that I should eat it. I was not hungry, but I would have swallowed that orange if it had burst me. Then she stripped the skin from a banana, and offered me that; and I took it, and squeezed her hand while her father was not looking. I think that I should have killed myself if Jack, who was a little jealous on account of my popularity, had not said,—

"They're stuffing Pepper to get him fat. He'll be the fust one they'll eat."

I didn't believe him, but still the remark made an impression upon me, and I refused to eat the next delicate bit of fruit which was offered by Lilly, much to her regret.

She had a most bewitching method of tempting me with oranges, and smiling when I refused. I thought that she appeared to take pride in my acquaintance, and I am sure that I felt proud of her notice; and for a while I forgot Julia, Jenny, home and everything but the pleasure of leading a sort of vagabond life on the island, doing as I pleased, and accountable to no one. There was no need of wealth to find happiness where I was. The sea yielded up its treasures to supply the natives with food—on the land, fruit was in season through the year without cost or price.

After the chief had seen that we were not inclined to eat more, he motioned for us to rise, and started for the door; but Lilly stopped him, and spoke eagerly for a few seconds. I saw the chief cast his eyes upon me, and therefore I suppose that the conversation was regarding my welfare. He nodded his head, and called the interpreter to explain; which that grinning individual did in a brief manner.

"You, here," he said, and intimated that I was to remain.

My companions were motioned towards the door; and as they went they had some few words of encouragement for me.

"Good by, Pepper," they said. "If the old fellow eats you, we hope you'll lay hard on his stomach, and give him the nightmare."

"The same to you," I responded; and off they went, the chief leading and the crowd following, as before.

I felt a little lonely at thus being separated from my companions, but I rightly imagined that it was only to find them quarters during their stay in the village, and that no harm would come to them or to me while we were apart. My friend Lilly remained behind, and intimated that I might lie on the frame and go to sleep if I wished, and I liked the idea, for the heat began to grow oppressive. I filled my pipe, but before lighting it considered it would only be proper to express my gratitude to the young lady. As I knew no heathen method of. doing so, I thought that I would try the civilized. Therefore, while the young lady was watching my motions with much curiosity, I advanced, and put my arm around her waist, and kissed her before she could recover from her surprise; the next moment I got a clip on the ear that rather startled me; and before I could account for it, the young lady ran from the house laughing, as though she had perpetrated a good joke, and knew how to appreciate it. I lay down upon the bench and smoked, and went to sleep; I dreamed that I had been elected chief of the village, that I had married Lilly, and was to be tattooed with all the ceremonies.

WILLIAM H. THOMES, *born in Maine in 1824, worked as a reporter for the* Boston Daily Times. *In 1848, he went west to gold-rush California. From there, he took ship to Hawai'i, and spent several months in Honolulu. He wrote novels set in California, the Pacific, and Australia, including* The Bushrangers; The Belle of Australia; The Gold Hunters' Adventures; A Slaver's Adventures on Land and Sea; *and* A Whaleman's Adventures in the Sandwich Islands and California.

Herman Melville
from TYPEE

L ook at Honolulu, the metropolis of the Sandwich Islands!—A community of disinterested merchants, and devoted self-exiled heralds of the Cross, located on the very spot that twenty years ago was defiled by the presence of idolatry. What a subject for an eloquent Bible-meeting orator! Nor has such an opportunity for a display of missionary rhetoric been allowed to pass by unimproved!—But when these philanthropists send us such glowing accounts of one half of their labors, why does their modesty restrain them from publishing the other half of the good they have wrought?—Not until I visited Honolulu was I aware of the fact that the small remnant of the natives had been civilized into draught horses, and evangelized into beasts of burden. But so it is. They have been literally broken into the traces, and are harnessed to the vehicles of their spiritual instructors like so many dumb brutes!

Among a multitude of similar exhibitions that I saw, I shall never forget a robust, red-faced, and very lady-like personage, a missionary's spouse, who day after day for months together took her regular airings in a little go-cart drawn by two of the islanders, one an old grey-headed man, and the other a rogueish stripling, both being, with the exception of the fig-leaf, as naked as when they were born. Over a level piece of ground this pair of draught bipeds would go with a shambling, unsightly trot, the youngster hanging back all the time like a knowing horse, while the old hack plodded on and did all the work.

Rattling along through the streets of the town in this stylish equipage, the lady looks about her as magnificently as any queen driving in state to her coronation. A sudden elevation, and a sandy road, however, soon disturb her serenity. The small wheels become imbedded in the loose soil,—the old stager stands tugging and sweating, while the young one frisks about and does nothing; not an inch does the chariot budge. Will the tender-hearted lady, who has left friends and home for the good of the souls of the poor heathen, will she think a little about their bodies and get out, and ease the wretched old man until the ascent is mounted? Not she; she could not dream of it. To be sure, she used to think nothing of driving the cows to pasture on the old farm in New England; but times have changed since then. So she retains her seat and bawls out, "Hookee! Hookee!" (pull, pull.) The old gentleman, frightened at the sound, labors away harder than ever; and the younger one makes a great show of straining himself, but takes care to keep one eye on his mistress, in order to know when to dodge out of harm's way. At last the good lady loses all patience;

"Hookee! Hookee!" and rap goes the heavy handle of her huge fan over the naked skull of the old savage; while the young one shies to the side and keeps beyond its range. "Hookee! Hookee!" again she cries—"Hookee tata kanaka!" (pull strong, men,)—but all in vain, and she is obliged in the end to dismount and, sad necessity! actually to walk to the top of the hill.

At the town where this paragon of humility resides, is a spacious and elegant American chapel, where divine service is regularly performed. Twice every Sabbath towards the close of the exercises may be seen a score or two of little wagons ranged along the railing in front of the edifice, with two squalid native footmen in the livery of nakedness standing by each, and waiting for the dismission of the congregation to draw their superiors home.

Lest the slightest misconception should arise from anything thrown out in this chapter, or indeed in any other part of the volume, let me here observe, that against the cause of missions in the abstract no Christian can possibly be opposed: it is in truth a just and holy cause. But if the great end proposed by it be spiritual, the agency employed to accomplish that end is purely earthly; and, although the object in view be the achievement of much good, that agency may nevertheless be productive of evil. In short, missionary undertaking, however it may be blessed of Heaven, is in itself but human; and subject, like everything else, to errors and abuses.

Herman Melville
from OMOO

I t is well worthy remark here, that every evidence of civilization among the South Sea Islands, directly pertains to foreigners; though the fact of such evidence existing at all, is usually urged as a proof of the elevated condition of the natives. Thus, at Honolulu, the capital of the Sandwich Islands, there are fine dwelling-houses, several hotels, and barbershops, ay, even billiard-rooms; but all these are owned and used, be it observed, by whites. There are tailors, and blacksmiths, and carpenters also; but not one of them is a native.

HERMAN MELVILLE (1819-1891) *went to sea at an early age. His experiences on a whaling ship in the Pacific yielded the novels* Typee *and* Omoo, *which made him famous. His masterpiece,* Moby Dick, *sold hardly any copies on publication, and nothing he wrote after that was considered of public interest. In the latter part of his life, he worked for nineteen years in obscurity in the customs service in New York, and when he died, the* New York Times *got his name wrong. A century and more after his death, he is recognized as one of the greatest American writers.*

Kiana Davenport

from SHARK DIALOGUES

D ust was everywhere in Honolulu, it even furred the porcelain plates of
royalty. Foreigners joked about meals with the "Kanaka King," how
clumsy native footmen pouring wine would stumble, wiping grit from their
eyes. Even the wine had a gritty texture. Near the docks—a treeless clutter
of filthy, grim warehouses, grogshops, and unpaved roads—dust lay so heavy
in the air *haole* wore handkerchiefs over their faces like bandits, folks went
about coughing and sneezing. Still, the town was becoming the business
center of the islands, gathering place of traders and merchants. Establishment of a Hudson Bay Company agency there in 1834 was transforming
Honolulu into a major seaport of the Pacific.

Within two weeks of their arrival, Mathys and Kelonikoa sold a black
pearl to a precious-gems dealer from France, and Mathys began building a
modest house away from downtown Honolulu. Since foreigners couldn't
own land, the property was leased. But that law would soon change, enabling
Mathys to slowly accumulate thousands of acres.

In the early 1840s, wealth was being accumulated overnight in Honolulu—human cargo smuggled in from the Orient as cheap labor, opium
packed in champagne bottles, rare jade and gold slipped past immigration
authorities. No one inquired about the source of Mathys's income, no one
cared. When he leased livery stables on King Street, he paid in cash. Kelonikoa sold another pearl and he bought a caulking business: "SHIP CARPEN-
TERS, PREPARED TO DO ALL KINDS OF WORK IN OUR LINE."

Anticipating a boom in population, within three years he enlarged his
livery stables. Besides saddle horses and teams, he now offered ". . . SUR-
RIES, BUGGIES, AND PHAETONS," appealing to a growing carriage
trade. He and Kelonikoa were naturalized, swore allegiance to the king, and
as Honolulu grew into a premier port town of saloons and brothels, one day
Mathys leased a run-down grogshop catty-corner from his carriage business,
naming it the Bay Horse Saloon. He promptly petitioned the Minister of the
Interior for a liquor license, and directed all his energies toward gutting and
resurrecting the saloon.

In 1848, King Kamehameha III went into deep depression, mourning
the death of his beloved sister and mistress, Nahienaena. Drinking exces-
sively, he let himself be persuaded by white merchants and ex-missionaries
to "abolish feudalism and make land-rights equal." Ambitious *haole* needed
security in land tenure for their growing plantations. Under the terms of
the *Great Mahele*, or Land Division, Kamehameha III gave up the rights to
much of his former property, keeping certain estates as crown lands. High

chiefs received one and a half million acres, which they began to sell, lease or foolishly give away. For the rest, locals and foreigners alike, they could buy lots in fee simple from the rest of the islands' acreage. Foreign residents were the first to take advantage of the "reform."

Mathys's second house, built of precious lumber, was a graceful two-story on several dozen acres he now owned. It boasted wraparound *lānai* on each floor so high-ceilinged rooms had access to cooling tradewinds. Other houses were stingily and hastily put together, crowded upon one another. But Kelonikoa demanded a house surrounded by beauty and fragrance—frangipani, ginger, pīkake—sweeping lawns, and the privacy of great shade trees.

Even with such luxuries, she lacked peace of mind, for she saw how increasingly hard it was for native Hawaiians to buy simple plots of land. One day her cook asked Mathys to explain registration papers she and her husband had to complete, and the deadlines by which certain claims had to be filed. The woman could read and write English, but terminology in the forms was so entangled and complex even Mathys could not translate it. Kelonikoa saw it was a ploy, a way to discourage natives from buying land, which left more land available for *haole*. She saw how increasingly they were marrying Hawaiian women of great land-holding families, building up enormous tracts of land for white descendants.

As work progressed on his saloon, Mathys imported special steer hides from Spain for stools and booths, and a fine mahogany bar with hunt scenes carved in Canton, shipped to Honolulu in two parts. The day it was assembled and installed, most of Honolulu stopped at the intersection of Hotel and Bethel, ogling his extravaganza. Until now, saloons had been mere dives in Honolulu, troughs for sailors and brawlers. Mathys wanted a place that attracted wealthy merchants, traders and bankers in three-piece suits and Argosy suspenders, high-steppers sporting canes, in silk Stetsons and straw bowlers.

The Bay Horse slowly acquired cachet. A back room for the rowdies with its own bar and cheap spirits was separated, by a thick mahogany door, from the heavily wood-paneled, mirrored front room resembling a gentleman's club, with even a looking glass foyer where merchants hung their hats, arranged their cravats and gold watch chains. The king and his regents arrived in carriages and phaetons, suited and coiffed like Englishmen. Diplomats came, and merchants. And one night while the skin of Mathys's three-year-old son erupted in red circles, a Yank named Herman Melville declared the Bay Horse Saloon odiously pretentious and departed, leaving his whiskey untouched.

For days, Kelonikoa and Mathys prayed over their firstborn, watching the virus destroy him. While hundreds of feverish measle victims flung themselves into the sea, Mathys dragged a doctor into the house at gunpoint. He vaccinated the child, even as it died. All night, Kelonikoa sat massaging her son's big toe, calling *"Ho'i hou! Ho'i hou!"* *Come back, come back.* For Polynesians believed the dead were often undecided, and that the last of life hung back in the big toe.

She stood dry-eyed as they buried her son behind the house. But one night, feeling her sudden absence, Mathys woke. He found her in her sleeping sarong out on the lawn, digging her son up with her hands. In moonlight she and Mathys struggled, the shrouded little corpse pulled back and forth between them. Finally, he relented, let her wrap the child in *hāpu'u* leaves soaked in saliva of wild boar, old-time preservatives, which were then wrapped in soft *kukui*-cured skins of mynah, then the softest linen stained with eucalyptus, aloe and jasmine. For months they slept with the little mummy between them absorbing their grief and wilderness.

"Auwē, auwē!" the servants cried. "Mastah, Missus, come *pupule*! More bettah make anot'er *keiki*."

Finally, when Kelonikoa felt a stirring in her womb, she let Mathys return the small mummy to its grave.

Rejuvenated by the promise of another child, he returned to his businesses with vigor. In the back room of the Bay Horse, desperate Russian, British, and French seaman pawned "baubles" from the Orient, things they didn't know the value of. Delicate antiques of heavy silver from Macao, real carved gold from Siam, precious jade artifacts. In the front room, Mathys discreetly offered his treasures, one bauble at a time, to merchant princes for wives and mistresses.

In time, it was rumored he could procure anything for a price, the robes of an emperor, a crown. His saloon became so popular, his businesses so prosperous, he was invited to join the new Pacific Club, exclusively for *haole*. The day of his induction, he arrived at the club in a new gilded phaeton with matching steeds.

Kelonikoa watched and listened. She was intelligent, learning proper English from Portia Rule, a renegade Boston missionary's wife, constantly stirring up trouble, pushing for legislation to make school attendance for native children compulsory through age fourteen. Patiently, she tried to impress upon Hawaiians the danger of their Mother Tongue dying out.

"Loss of one's language is the first step toward extinction," she warned. "Your children are learning English and history from Christian textbooks. You must keep up Hawaiian conversations at home."

Kelonikoa suspected that most *haole* didn't want natives educated. They wanted to keep them in the fields, and as house servants. She told her cooks and gardeners they were free to look for more dignified work.

She would even help them. They wept and pleaded. House and yard work were all they knew.

"Then, I promise you," she said. "Your children will not be servants in someone else's home. I will help you send them to school."

One day she looked at her four-year-old son, felt the next child stirring within, and turned to Portia Rule. "What of my children who are half-castes? Will they be servants, too?"

The woman answered carefully. "Your husband is successful. Your children will be privileged. If you are lucky, one of them, just one, will try to help their people."

She advised Kelonikoa to read newspapers diligently, to listen to gossip in the streets, so she would understand how rapidly Hawai'i was changing, how radically rich and poor classes were growing. In 1853, there was no middle class. White traders and merchants were becoming millionaires in Honolulu, while behind his back they called the king "Imperial Nigger, His *Kanaka* Highness."

"There is something more heinous than bigotry," Portia Rule warned. "If your people are not careful, disease will wipe them out completely."

In 1778 when Captain Cook had "discovered" Hawai'i, the native population was nearly a million. By 1850 it was under sixty thousand. Until Cook arrived, Hawaiians had been the most isolated people in the world, and so had not built up a strong immune system. But through ingenious, rigid systems of hygiene, they had remained fiercely strong and healthy. By now, trading and whaling ships from around the world had spread syphilis, measles, typhoid, whooping cough, and worse. Quarantine laws requiring health inspectors for visiting ships had come too late.

As if in response to Portia's warning, one day a brig out of San Francisco docked in Honolulu flying a yellow flag. A sailor aboard was dying of smallpox. The crew was allowed ashore, vaccinated and quarantined, but local girls made love to them through fences, and within days, two Hawaiians collapsed. Families were quarantined, clothes and houses burned. A call for general vaccinations came too late. Within months two thousand natives were dead.

Hour after hour, Kelonikoa fed her second-born shark-fin soup, a fish known to have powerful *mana*. Still, life leaked from his delicate grotto of bones. A yellow flag hung in their doorway, and two fresh graves were dug behind their house, the second one for the child Kelonikoa was carrying when a vaccination shot left her feverish, vomiting for days. The perfectly formed fetus fell out of her, blue and hard as stone.

Inconsolable, she would not let Mathys near her. He found release in alcohol, weeping and wailing as wagons trundled by filled with corrupting corpses, noses running with worms. When they ran out of burying space, drivers stacked bodies like lumber, set them afire in fields. Soon pyramids dotted the landscape, black corpses charred into sitting-up or flying postures like monstrous acrobats. For months, Honolulu was a plague-struck town from the Middle Ages, fires of contaminated shacks blistering the night, the taste of death like soot. Floating corpses blanketed the harbor, so it looked like one huge carcass. Dogs ran in packs like gypsies, carrying limbs dug up from shallow mounds. For weeks, Mathys slept with a cocked rifle beside his childrens' graves.

One day he learned that a *haole* port official had been bribed for $1,000, allowing the pox ship from San Francisco into the harbor. In broad daylight, Mathys walked into the official's house with a rifle and cutlass, shot him through the heart, decapitated him in one swoop, stuck the head on a pole and carried it through the streets. People tore the body to shreds, flung the shreds to dancing dogs. In three years, twelve thousand native Hawaiians would die.

Kelonikoa lost her sense of speech, became a Bedouin of the valleys, wandering from village to village, wherever people mourned their dead, silently mourning with them. One night Mathys looked down from their mahogany four-poster and found her squatting wide-eyed like a madwoman. Her wrists were running blood, and with her blood she had written on the walls . . . MY DEAD CHILDREN . . . MY FATHER'S CURSE ON ME . . . He slid down beside her, gathered her to him, talking softly, explaining how loss of her presence, her love, would be greater to him than that of any child. He was nothing without her, all the sorrow, and magic, and beauty of his world was contained within her. If she went insane, or died, he would follow. Silently, she pointed to the sea.

Every day thereafter, Mathys took her to a secluded beach away from polluted harbors. There she removed her clothes, corset, underthings, and floated naked in leaping waves, mothersounds, heart thump of her ancestral home. One day she sang out in Tahitian as a school of dolphin sailed in, curious and playful, chattering in funny click-tongue. Mathys watched paralyzed as she slid onto the back of a dolphin, riding in lazy circles, the thing soaring so high his wife was sometimes airborne. Day after day the dolphins came, soaring her toward slow healing.

One day, a whale appeared on the horizon, crying out repeatedly. Mathys stared at Kelonikoa's corset lying on the sand. From the framework of the thing, the stays of wrecked whalebone, something emanated, a cry. He lunged to his feet, afraid he'd lost his mind. Kelonikoa waved as the whale moved in, singing a mournful song, almost a call. The corset responded again, a distinguishable bleating. Mathys drew his gun, aimed it at the corset. The whale, still calling, swam closer to shore.

Song of the humpback, mind of the sperm. His memory cells jostled, a joy-less comprehension. He dropped the gun, gingerly lifted the corset, and carried it into the surf, where waves washed it out toward the mother whale. Almost tenderly, she flipped the corset onto her back, and in mournful, pip-ing song, swam off. For reasons he could not discern, Mathys began to sob.

His wife turned in the shallows, held out her arms, and spoke her first words to him in months. "Come . . . into . . . me."

KIANA DAVENPORT *is of Native Hawaiian and Anglo-American descent. Her bestselling novels,* Shark Dialogues; Song of the Exile; *and* House of Many Gods, *have been translated into fourteen languages. Her short stories have won numerous O. Henry awards, Pushcart Prizes, and the Best American Short Story Award, 2000. She has been a Bunting Fellow at Harvard, Visiting Writer at Wesleyan University, and recipient of a National Endowment for the Arts grant, and the Elliot Cades Award for Literature. She lives in New York City and Hawai'i.*

Mark Twain

MANUSCRIPT FRAGMENT

"He **is**!—I feel it here!—he is praying me to death!"

These last words he shouted; the priests heard, and came running to him, exclaiming—

"What is it?—what has befallen the King?"

The monarch sunk helpless upon a stool, and said in a despairing voice—

"An enemy has stolen my spittoon!"

Puna feigned a [fair] good degree of surprise and horror; the other priests fairly reeled under the shock of a genuine consternation. The first of these to recover himself flew to a great tom-tom and struck three deep booming notes from it. Before the last one was done sounding, a multitude of excited priests came pouring into the royal enclosure from a neighbor-ing great temple, and with them a hurrying host of [word illegible] native soldiers from the royal barracks.

Puna commanded silence, and said:

"Search—search everywhere; leave no spot unvisited, for a woful disaster has befallen this land—an enemy has [befallen] stolen the King's spittoon!"

The multitude were stricken with horror. From lip to lip flew the one exclamation: "An enemy has stolen the royal spittoon—it is ornamented with the teeth of the royal ancestry—he will pray the King to death!"

huge fists. "He _is_! — I feel it here! — he is praying me to death!"

These last words he shouted; the priests heard, & came running to him, exclaiming —

"What is it? — what has befallen the King?"

The monarch sunk helpless upon a stool, & said in a despairing voice —

"An enemy has stolen my spittoon!"

Puma feigned a good degree of surprise & horror; the other priests fairly reeled under the shock of a genuine consternation. The first of these to recover himself flew to a great tom-tom & struck three

Then the crowd melted apart and the search began.

And still the ghastly news sped from mouth to mouth—outside the enclosure—along the outskirts of the village—into the village itself. Then a sudden paralysis fell upon the joyous throngs of idlers, there; the laughter suddenly ceased; and the singing, the dancing, the racing; and the swimmers ceased from swimming and splashing, and stood half immersed, and turned to bronze. Each individual looked his neighbor vacantly in the face and murmured—

"The King's spittoon stolen! The [King's] day of sorrow is come, desolation and disaster are upon us!"

MARK TWAIN (1835-1910) *was the pen name of Samuel Langhorne Clemens. Among his books are* The Innocents Abroad; A Connecticut Yankee in King Arthur's Court; The Adventures of Tom Sawyer; *and* The Adventures of Huckleberry Finn—*a landmark in bringing an authentic American voice into literature. Twain's visit to Hawai'i in 1866 produced this description, quoted hundreds of times:* "The loveliest fleet of islands that lies anchored in any ocean."

O. A. Bushnell

from KA'A'AWA

T he messenger came in secret, in the shadows of evening, without runners to cry the way or guards to show who sent him. Quietly, as a friend or neighbor might, he rode into the yard of my country house at Makiki, in the hills above Honolulu, where we had fled from the sickness which was afflicting the people in the town.

We were sitting on the front verandah, my wife and I, with our daughters and sons. The cooking-fires had been put out, the lamps were not yet lighted, and we were talking of little things while we watched the colors changing in the sky above, upon the earth and the sea below. Red the sky had been, from its eastern arch beyond Diamond Head to its western arch beyond the mountains of Wai'anae, red the color of blood, the color sacred to the great gods of old. Yet even as we exclaimed over the beauty of the heavens we gave no thought to the ancient gods or to the Jehovah who has taken their place. In our Christian household, we did not abide in fear either of the gods of our ancestors or of Him whose power is proclaimed in the glory of the firmament.

No. We were happy then, laughing at the game Daniel, our youngest son, was playing for our pleasure. Like a ship's captain he stood at the porch railing, holding a long curved piece of sugarcane to his eye as a mariner holds a telescope. "Red at night, sailor's delight," he was telling us with a big voice, in words learned from his father, "red in the morning, sailors take warning." And we were laughing because the little fellow was so comical, with his telescope pointing to the ground rather than to the horizon, and because of our contentment each with the other, when Paliku came into the yard.

I did not know it was he, for my eyes are somewhat weak with aging, and the sky's brightness did not help them to see clearly. But, as is proper with a hospitable man, I went at once to greet him.

"Good evening," I called in English, thinking he was a foreigner coming up from town to see me on business. The error was a natural one. He was dressed in a black suit, he had a tall hat upon his head and black boots upon his feet. Furthermore, evening is the time when foreigners make their visits, whereas Hawaiians come early in the day, the earlier the better, so they can partake of at least two meals as guests before they must go home again—if they go home. This is but one of the many differences between natives and foreigners. Some say that it is the difference between an open hand and a closed purse, but I do not think this is the reason, for I have found most foreigners to be generous enough in other ways.

"Good evening," he answered in our native speech as he dismounted. "Paliku is here, Paliku of 'Ewa."

While my mind wondered what this stranger could want with me, my tongue did its duty, my arm invited him to the house. "Welcome, Paliku of 'Ewa. Come in, come in. You have traveled far to find me."

"No," he said firmly, "we will talk here. This place is safer." Coming close, he showed me the back of his left hand. Written in black ink upon the brown skin were three words: Kauikeaouli, Ka Mo'i: Kauikeaouli, the King.

"You understand?" asked Paliku.

Recognizing the writing of the King's own hand—how many times I have seen it—I bowed, as much to it as to the messenger. "And what does my King wish of me?" I whispered, starting to tremble. Not for two years had I seen His Majesty, not for five years had he spoken a word to me. For five years I had thought I was out of grace with him, no longer of use to him. And now, suddenly, as fast as a shark appears beside a wounded swimmer, did he rise up out of the past to worry me. A man has the right to tremble when he sees the gape of a shark.

"He wishes to talk with you. Tonight. He is at 'Ainahau in Waikiki. I will take you to him." Even as he spoke the King's messenger was removing the sacred writing from his skin, with spit and sweat and the rubbing of fingers. In the days of the great Kamehameha, father to Kauikeaouli, I was thinking, this herald would have been killed for such an act. So upset had he made me, so stupid for the moment, that I did not remember how, in those days before the missionaries came from America, neither Kamehameha nor any man of our race could put his name down in writing.

I am not a warrior, alas, not a man of bravery. I do not think I am entirely a coward, but no matter. I am indeed a man of great imagination: at that moment I could almost feel this shark's teeth scraping against my rib cage, where the heart is, and the liver. "Now?" I asked, trying to make my voice sound like a grown man's. "Alas, alas! And what have I done, that he calls me to meet him in the dark of night?" Like a sailor in a foreign port when constables approach, I strove to remember what crime I might have committed, what offense against the King or his laws. No crimes could I recall, and only the paltriest of sins. And these were committed so seldom, with Maria in our house in Palama! Surely he wasn't calling me to account for her?

The summoners of kings must learn very early how they deliver fright along with their messages. Paliku of 'Ewa, a just man at heart if not an affable one, quieted me. "Would he tell me this?—But do not fear. Your friend is with him: the Prince Liholiho."

"Alex is there?—Ahh, then I have no fear." Paliku knew what everyone in Hawai'i Nei must know: that Alex is like a firstborn son to me, who attended him during the years of his childhood. And like a foster-father does he regard me. How, then, could I remain afraid? I ceased to tremble, my voice box was no longer tight around the sounds it made. "Come in, and rest a while. My wife will fix you a cup of tea, while I change my clothes." And now, entering into my mind, pushing fear aside, came curiosity. What does the King want with me?

"No," said Paliku, this man of stubbornness. "I shall wait here. Tell no one where you go. And do not put on the clothes you would wear to the Palace."

I heard him in amazement. "You talk like a man who has no wife! How can I just go away from here—like a wisp of black smoke drifting in a dark night?"

He waved my problem away impatiently. "Tell your wife what all husbands tell their wives when they must go from home in the night. Tell her that you are called away on business. Tell her that you are needed at a meeting. Tell her that you are called to the bedside of a friend who is sick."

"Chah!" I grumbled as I hurried back to the house. It is easy for him to talk so smoothly. But no other man can have a wife like mine. A mountain of suspicion is she, this green-eyed woman to whom I am wed. How can I tell her such a story, even if it is the truth? The last time I was late for supper she tracked me to the house in Kewalo where I thought I was dallying safely with

Abigail Moepono. Such a screaming of women, such a rending of clothing and shattering of furniture I never want to hear again. And my crooked arm: in cold weather it still pains me where the bones were not set aright. "Next time I will break your head," she said grimly, as she took me in her carriage to Dr. Newcomb, for him to fix my arm. But he, poor man, to fortify himself against his awe of her, drank so much of the whiskey which was meant to sustain me, that neither of us noticed how ill-set the bones were.

There they waited, all of them, sitting, standing, reclining, hanging from the porch rail, expecting me to explain this mysterious visitor: four daughters, five sons, and one wife, the bosom of my family. Ten pairs of eyes turned upon me, questioning as judges in a courthouse. Ten pairs of big ears, pricked up like the ears of jackasses. I loved my family, as a good father should, but they were too much with me, up there in the hills of Makiki. Once again I wished I were still a carefree sailor, drunk in a faraway port, not yet a bounden husband, not yet the parent of so many inquisitive children. *Niele, niele* they were, every one of them, I fretted, not willing to admit that they came by this talent naturally.

"Mama," I began, putting a hesitant foot upon the first step of the stairs, looking up at her with my most innocent face.—O Lord! What shall I tell her? How can I find a reasonable excuse?—But no new thought came to my aid. Remembering Paliku's lies, I used one of them whole. "Dear . . . It is a message from Noah Mahoe.—You remember Noah?—He is taken with the sickness." Just in time I recalled the name of this latest of the new plagues the foreigners have brought among us. "You know: the influenza. He asks that I come to see him—to help him with the making of a will, perhaps. I must go . . . "

She did not believe me. I knew she did not. I could tell by the set of those lips, by the steadiness of that gaze as she looked down at me, and weighed my words, and threw them away, like rubbish. While she measured me, one of the boys asked another, his eyes as rounded as a Frenchman's: "Who is this Noah Mahoe? Do we know him?" "Yes," said my wife, still looking straight through me, "he is a good friend of your father's." A very honorable woman is my wife. She does not tell untruths. The children asked no more questions. Putting her plump hands upon the rail of the porch, she raised herself up. Massive as a cliff garbed in a Mother Hubbard, she stood above me, a thin and scrawny pole of bamboo, waiting to be crushed by the flow of her anger. "If you are needed," she said quietly, "then you must go. I will help you to make ready."

A very remarkable woman is she, a true aristocrat in manner as she is in blood. She it was, not I, who remembered to tell Abel, our oldest son, to saddle Papa's horse, who sent Elisabeta to fetch a clean shirt from the clothes-press, who reminded me to put on my shoes, helped me to don my black alpaca coat. She it was who tied my neck-cloth in a comely bow when, nervous as a racing pony, I stood on the verandah while, one after the other, each of our children gave me a farewell kiss upon the cheek. And she it was who said, when she kissed me goodbye, "Do not hurry home. The making of wills can take much time. I shall not wait up for you." Then, with a gentle pat, she turned me toward the stairs.

Aye, unsettled though I was that evening, I remembered to be proud of her, and grateful for her care. Love of the flesh between us has long since ended, as she has grown older and heavier, and as I, in the way of men who are neither priests nor missionaries, have sought my comforting in other beds. But affection still abides. And respect. Of all the women who are mothers to my children, she is the one who is the best mother.

She has never told this to me, but I think that in virtuousness she is trying to live down the reputation of her family for loose living and harlotry and mischievous sleeping. "The Forrests of Kealakekua: so easily are they felled" is a saying about that notorious clan which is well known throughout the islands of this Kingdom, from Ni'ihau to Hawai'i.

Yet about Rebekah Nihoa, wife to Hiram Nihoa, nothing evil can be said. And with this I am well content. For this is the way things should be, is it not?

Soft and gray was the light of evening when Paliku and I left my family, calling their goodbyes to me. At the gate, after I put up the wooden poles which shut out roaming cows and horses from our yard, he turned to the east, toward Punahou, not to the south, toward Kaka'ako. At Kaka'ako the long causeway begins that leads across the swamps between Honolulu and Waikiki.

"Ho, Paliku," I called, checking my mount. "Here is the way to Kaka'ako." I had in mind not only the best road to Waikiki but also the pretense of going to Noah Mahoe's house, which is not reached by riding toward Punahou.

"And do I not know this?" he said. "Tonight we take a shorter way."

"Through the swamps?" I cried, not wanting to believe him.

"Be quiet!" he barked. "And hurry!"

Never, since I have become a grown man, has anyone spoken to me so rudely. When I drew up beside him he growled, "Would you tell the whole city where we are going?"

Inasmuch as my house sits half a furlong inside its yard, and my nearest neighbors are half a mile away, I thought Paliku was being more officious than reasonable. Nonetheless, I kept my peace, not being a man who holds grievances. Who am I to know where big ears may be listening and big eyes may be watching? And besides, I remembered the lesson every Hawaiian learns when he is very young: "Kick down, not up," our elders teach us, which is to say, do not question a chief or the servant of a chief who has a higher rank than your own. My excitable father, alas, did not heed these wise words. Because he questioned in anger the right of Kahanaumaika'i, tax collector of the great Kamehameha, to take away our biggest sow, he died a young man, before I could know him—offered up in sacrifice he was, along with the sow, that time Kamehameha with his mighty army and vast fleet of canoes was gathering for the second time on O'ahu to invade Kaua'i. I, who have ever been soft with my answers, I hope to die a very old man, in my very own bed.

With Paliku, also, meekness softened wrath. "Do you not worry," he said after a few minutes. "I know the way, even in the dark of night." These were the last words he spoke during that terrible ride. No doubt he was a troubled man, as servants of kings often are.

Out of regard for my brittle bones, he set our mounts an easy pace. For a while I tried to enjoy the last traces of the evening's loveliness, the excitement of my adventure, putting off in these my worries about Mo'ili'ili's swamps and the King's intentions. To our left the valley of wide Manoa opened up, the high tops of its mountains hung with clouds. "As springs in the sky are the clouds of Manoa," says an old chant, and I believe it. Almost never does sunlight touch the uplands in that place of rains and waterfalls. People can not live there, because of the lung fever such wetness causes; and wild cattle, the learned say, have grown webbed feet, like ducks, to keep them from sinking in the mud.

At the mouth of the valley, still distant from us across the plain, like stars lying upon the ground, twinkled the lights of the American missionaries' children's school at Punahou. Only there, with water flowing forth from the precious spring, or along the banks of streams issuing from the valleys, or in Mo'ili'ili's swamps, can people live, can they make Honolulu's earth yield them food for their bellies. Everywhere else upon this long plain of Kona, from Punchbowl to Koko Head, is only dust or sparse grass, cropped by horses and cattle which find no other forage. If trees grew here once upon a time, they were cut down for firewood long ago, by adzes of stone or by axes of steel.

And then the darkness was complete. But Paliku knew the way. After we had cantered for about half an hour, he slowed to a walk. We came to clumps of bushes, small shrubs, more like shadows standing up than things of stems and leaves. This sharp-eyed Paliku: his spirit-guardian must be 'Iole the rat. In a place I could not have found at midday he turned to the right, toward the distant seashore. My obedient horse followed, deaf to my moans. Trusting to him, I let the reins fall loose, thanking first Jehovah, then Kane, Ku, Lono, and Kanaloa, the four great gods, and the forty lesser gods, and the four hundred, the four thousand, the forty thousand, the four hundred thousand little gods, that my Spanish saddle had a pommel I could clutch in my tight hands. From either side came the sounds of water, of flowing, gurgling, sighing water, yearning to embrace me when, with a single misstep, my horse and I would be thrown into the swamp, to sink in its mud and drown. Frogs croaked, night birds screeched, my stomach burned, my teeth chattered, and on we plodded in the dark. Miserable, dizzy, I clung to my pommel like a shipwrecked sailor to a spar, calling on all the spirit-guardians in my family's line to help me in this journeying through the ink sack of a squid.

How could they not hear the clamor I raised? In their mercy they sent Mahina to comfort me. Out from behind the wall of Manoa's clouds she came forth for a long moment. Not yet in her full glory, she was like a pale cowry shell, or a China bowl, tipped in the heavens, to pour the rains of Ka'ele upon Manoa below. But the moment was enough.

Just before the clouds covered her kind face again, she revealed to me a gift from the greatest gods: there, growing out of the earth beside the path, was a whole clump of *ki* plants. Swiftly I reached out and pulled from their stalk a handful of the long cool leaves. According to custom I should have tucked one of these leaves into my trousers, to protect the sacred organs of generation wherein lies my *mana* and that of my line. But I did not have time to follow the ancient law, and I hoped that Kane would not mind if I thrust the leaf under the bosom of my shirt. From other leaves I fashioned wreaths to place around my wrists, forehead, and shoulders. The last two leaves I tied together, to make a *lei* for the horse. With such protection, the evil spirits, the demons in mud and water, those malicious beings from the other world who bring accident and sickness and sudden death, could not touch me or cause me harm. Nor could the great gods punish me for being a proudful traveler when I bore the amulets which asked their favor. Ahh, it is a good thing for a man to have about him the things of old, to give him comfort in times of jeopardy.

As I became more confident in the care of the gods, the ordinary things of earth, with which the gods do not bother themselves, began to afflict me. I itched, where the underdrawers we must wear these days were all bunched up, where the horse's flanks rubbed against the woolen trousers covering my legs. And the mosquitoes! A new kind of demon are they, another present from our generous foreigners. In my youth we did not have mosquitoes in Hawai'i Nei, nor scorpions, centipedes, cockroaches, or frogs. But now they are everywhere, like foreigners, poking their long noses or their sharp tails into every place, making their loud noises, beyond chasing out because they are so many. Sour as David Malo used to be, when he protested against foreigners at the Council of the Chiefs, I rode along, wishing I struck at foreigners as I slapped at mosquitoes.

And another thing!—Oh, how the anger in me swelled.—Why am I riding like this, through the swamps of Mo'ili'ili, in the dark of night? In peril to my health, if not to my very life? Were I at home now, comfortable in my parlor, I would be reading a good book, or dozing in a soft chair, thinking of a softer bed. In the dining room, seated around the big table beneath the bright whale-oil lamps, my children would be studying their school books, my wife would be sewing while she kept them at their lessons. As I thought of them, my four pretty daughters, my five handsome sons, my good and devoted wife—ahh, I longed to be with them again, I vowed I would be a better father and husband when I returned.

If I returned.—Ah, ah, I sighed again. What does the King want of me? This was the greatest worry. I skirted about it, running around it as a hunting dog runs around on a mountainside, sniffing for the scent of boar.—And why is His Majesty staying out there in Waikiki, when he has a fine palace in Honolulu to do business in? Why doesn't he—

"No, no, I take that back," I mumbled, touching my *ki* leaves as a Papist would finger his beads. *Kick down, not up.*—Needing a safer target, I found it in something utterly useless: "What is this Waikiki?" I addressed the air, full of swamp stinks and harmful vapors. "A sandspit bestuck with coconut palms and bedaubed with bird dung. A shoal of coral, caught between the vomit of the sea and the muck of Mo'ili'ili."

Really, the gods are very patient, long-suffering indeed. There I was, tongue clacking inside my head, hands waving in the dark, thinking mean thoughts about everything and everyone, yet expecting only the kindest of treatment from both gods and men. A little breeze, perchance the very least of the littlest gods, was sent to warn me: lifting a bit of the frayed *lei* upon my shoulders, it tickled my ear. All right, I yielded. I understand, I shall be careful.

No doubt at one time, when Honolulu did not exist, before these foreigners came in their sailing ships and found the harbor of Kou for an anchorage, perhaps then this Waikiki was an important place, the home of O'ahu's kings. But now, with half of O'ahu's people dead in their graves, with almost all the surviving half clustered around the wharves and warehouses, the grogshops and whorehouses of Honolulu, Waikiki too is dead. It will never amount to anything. A breeding place for mosquitoes and frogs and rats it may be, but of no use to people. They do not come here anymore, to swim or to ride their long boards in the waters of the sea, as we did when I was a youth. Forbidden by the missionaries are these disportings in the sea because they are heathen pastimes, and because the nakedness of swimmers is an invitation to sins of the flesh, is an anathema. Alas, alas! Such narrow minds, such dirty thoughts, those Christians have. I can not remember being more lustful when I swam naked than I have been since I was girded about with clothing and armored with commandments. And what is sin, anyway?—

Cha! As peevish as a man trapped in an outhouse without leaf, shirttail, or piece of paper, I endured, swatting at mosquitoes, snapping at stinging thoughts. What a marvel is a man, that he should survive despite the gods' annoyance! Perhaps he lives because the gods hope that, with time, he will learn to be forbearing. Just as, in their patience, they have tried to teach me to be forbearing. Not wisdom do they ask, certainly not silence.—I should choke to death if they did.—Only kindness, from a man to other men, from a man to his gods: this is all they wish.

As we moved farther from the mountains the clouds were left behind, and Mahina lighted up the rest of our way. To the left, a dark battlement, rose Diamond Head. The narrow path underfoot widened to become a muddy road. The wild bulrushes, the swamp weeds, fell behind and watery plantations of taro took their place. On little islands raised above the level of the mud, clusters of thatched huts, domes of trees, barking dogs, gave proof that we were coming again into the world of people. Straight ahead the glow of fires showed, a beacon in the desert of night. Soon I could see the flickering torches, the plumed crowns of palms in the coconut grove where kings reside when they wish to be undisturbed. Mingling with the sweet scent of burning candlenuts came the stronger smells of seaweed, of the salty ocean.

With a suddenness that surprised not only me, we reached the end of our journey. A startled guard, naked as a farmer in his taro patch, ran toward us, shouting "Stand!—Who comes here?" From behind the stakes topped with globes of white *kapa* which mark the boundaries of a royal *kapu* other guards appeared. Some were naked, some wore the loincloth, none was clad in the uniform all are forced to wear in town. In the shadows under the trees, upon outspread mats, women sat up to see who interrupted their pleasures of love.—O you of the worrying mind, I smiled to myself. It has not changed, this Waikiki . . .

Paliku stopped his horse, lifted a hand to halt mine. "Be easy," he called to the sentry, "Paliku of 'Ewa is here. Returning as I departed, by the quiet path of Mo'ili'ili."

"Ah, it is you," said the guard, beckoning him in. "Then welcome back from your little ride. You were not gone for long." As we moved forward into the light he burst out laughing. A most unsoldierly man is he, I was thinking, and is this the proper manner for a guard to the King? "Wait a moment," he bawled. "And who is this *kahuna* coming here with you? Have you plucked him from out of the swamp, perhaps?" Then I knew why he laughed. The loud-mouthed gossipmonger! May his stones shrivel in their bag, may moths be his seed! Many of the soldiers, who only a moment before were returning to their mats, gathered around, teeth and eyes flashing, fingers pointing at me, at the leafy *lei* I had forgotten to remove. "*E!* He is a jungle on horseback," said one. "Nah, nah, a parrot is he," said another, "a bird of many colors." "A *kahuna 'ana'ana*, beyond doubt," jeered still another. "Old man, what sorcery do you make tonight?" "*E, womanless one,*" shouted a fourth at a companion, thereby changing his laughter to frowns, "ask him to make a love-potion for to end your lonely days and nights."

A *kahuna*, indeed! They knew as well as I did, how the law of this Christian land forbids the practice of the evil arts of sorcery and even the kinder rites of magic for the sake of love. Feeling like a fool, I could do nothing but scowl at them, miserable as only an older man can be when he is taunted by the young. Something is wrong with the young men and women of today. When I was a youth, we had more respect for our elders. Never would we have mocked an old man or an old woman, never would we have dared to laugh at a *kahuna 'ana'ana*. But the young folk of today: alas for them. No wonder the nation is wasting away, no wonder we are beset with troubles from far and near.

Keeping my peace, I strove to keep my dignity. I intended nothing else, but I could mark the instant when dread entered among my tormenters. "*Auwe!*" wailed one, as he backed away, no longer laughing. "Forgive," murmured others, "forgive us." In the flick of a fly whisk they were gone, slinking away to the darkness under the trees. All of them went save one, the womanless youth who was in need of a love-potion. "Great is your *mana*," he proclaimed loudly, taking the bridle reins from my hand. Somewhat pleased with this effect—I think it must be the first reward for silence I have ever won—I looked toward Paliku, to share a little smile with him. But he did not see it, he was hurrying forward to help me from my horse.

"Now will we go to the house of the King," he said, when I stood upon the ground. While we walked along the path I removed the *ki* leaves. Not daring to throw them into the bushes, I tucked them into my shirt, where the other one lay warm against my belly. Cool they were, for a few moments, soothing against the place where my heart was beginning to quicken. The same dread which had quieted the jeering soldiers was stirring now in me. For greatest of all among the gods on earth are the Kamehameha. Very great is their *mana*, burning is their *kapu*. And deep, profound, was my fear of the King.

O. A. BUSHNELL (1913-2002) *was born in Honolulu of Portuguese-Italian-Norwegian background. He was a microbiologist by profession. At forty-three, he published the first of his five historical novels, all set in Hawai'i:* The Return of Lono; *followed by* Molokai; Kaaawa; The Stone of Kannon; *and* The Water of Kane. *His last book,* The Gifts of Civilization, *published when he was eighty, was a summation of his half-century of research and thought about the impact of disease on the people of Hawai'i. Bushnell was a respected participant in formative discussions of the development of a distinctively local voice in writing, and in 1974 was the first recipient of the Hawaii Award for Literature.*

David Malo
"HE INOA AHI NŌ KA-LĀ-KAUA"

He Inoa Ahi nō Ka-lā-kaua
Lamalama i Maka-pu'u ke ahi o Hilo.
Hanohano molale ke ahi o Ka-wai-hoa.
'Oaka 'ōni'o 'ula kāo'o ke ahi i Wai-'alae.
Ho'oluehu iluna ke ahi o Lē'ahi.
Ho'onohonoho i muliwa'a ke ahi o Ka-imu-kī.
Me he uahi koai'e la ke ahi o Wai'ahila.
Noho hiehie ke ahi i pu'u o Mānoa.
Oni e kele i luna ke ahi o 'Uala-ka'a.
A me he 'ahi la ke ahi o Kalu'-āhole.
Me he maka-ihu-wa'a la ke ahi o Helu-moa.
Me he moa-lawakea la ke ahi o Kālia.
Me he pāpahi lei la ke ahi o Ka-wai-a-Ha'o.

'O mai ke 'Li'i nona ia inoa ahi!

Kauluwela i Pū-o-waina ke ahi hō'ike inoa,
Uluwehiwehi ke ahi ho'okele Hawai'i.
Heaha la ia ka pāni'o o ke ahi? O ka Helu 'Elua.
Pū-'ulu hōkū-lani ke ahi o Mālia-ka-malu.
A ma'amau pinepine ke ahi o Kawa.
'Alua 'ole ke ahi o Moana-lua.

I puʻupuʻua ke ahi ka mauʻu nēnē.
Kaʻi haʻaheo ke ahi puoko ʻula i ka moana.
ʻĀnuenue pipiʻo lua i ka lewa ke ahi o ke kaona.

ʻO mai ke ʼLiʻi nona ia inoa ahi!

Me he papa-kōnane la ke ahi o Alanui Pāpū.
Ahu kīnohinohi ke ahi i Alanui Aliʻi.
Me he pōnaha mahina la ke ahi o Hale Aliʻi.
Ku me he ʻanuʻu la ke ahi o ka pahu hae.
Wela kuʻu ʻāina i ke ahi o ʻIhi-kapu-lani.

ʻO mai ke ʼLiʻi nona ia inoa ahi!

"FIRE CHANT FOR KING KALĀKAUA"

Torchlight of Hilo lighted his way to Maka-puʻu.
Now Ka-wai-hoa's royal fire burns clear in the Oʻahu night.
A throng of red flashing fires of Wai-ʻalae swirl in the air.
Lē'ahi's fire scatters to the stars.
Coals banked at sterns of canoes glow in Ka-imu-kī's dusky fires.
Smoky fire of Waʻahila rises like scent of acacia, aroma of love.
A chieftain pillar of proud fire stands on a Mānoa hillside.
Springing fire of ʻUala-kaʻa embraces the sky.
Gleam of *ʻahi*, fish of yellow flame, shines in the fire of Kaluʻ-
    āhole.
Fire of Helu-moa shows phosphorescent, a mirage at sea.
White cock, head of white cock lifted in darkness, is fire of Kālia.
A great Aliʻi, fire of Ka-wai-a-Haʻo, stands wreathed in purest
    light.

Answer us, O Chief, whose fire chant we sing!

Intense fire spells out his name on Punchbowl Hill.
He is the Helmsman—*Ka Mōʻī*—revealed in flame and rockets'
    glare.
What is that portal of friendly lamplight? Fire Company
    Number Two.
Blessed fires of Mary of Peace shine like a congregation of stars.
Fire of constancy is the fire of Kawa, unwavering fire.

Bonfires of Moana-lua burn unmatched for wild display.
Banks of nēnē-grass one after another burst into blaze.
So proud warriors tread by torchlight, their marching mirrored
    in the sea.
That double rainbow arching the sky is the reflected fire of the
    town.

Answer us, O Chief, whose fire chant we sing!

A checkered *kōnane*-board is Fort Street on fire.
Gay calico prints are the fires decorating King.
The fire at the Palace shines in a circle, a full moon.
Like a tower atop an ancient temple is the fire-ringed flagpole.
So lives my land heated everywhere by the sacred
    kapu-fire of 'Ihi-kapu-lani.

Answer us, O Chief, whose fire chant we sing!

TRANSLATED BY MARY KAWENA PUKUI

DAVID MALO *composed this chant in 1874, at the moment when King Kalākaua was about to take the throne as the seventh ruler of the Hawaiian kingdom. Malo, an assistant editor on a bilingual newspaper in Honolulu,* Nuhou, *had accompanied Kalākaua on a celebratory tour of the islands. Back in Honolulu, Malo got the chant into print within hours.*

———————————•◦•———————————

O. A. Bushnell

from MOLOKAI

With the Prime Minister of the Realm to present me, I went to ask the King for a boon.

Silent in his open carriage we sat, the Premier and I, as we were driven across the muddy plaza which kept the Government Buildings of Hawaii at their distance from the opulent pile of Kalakaua's new palace. I was silent because, after months of unrelieved disappointment in my research, I was discouraged and, I must admit, hurt in my pride. My hurt made me defensive; and, suspecting laughter and sneers from my associates in medicine in Honolulu, I hid behind a wall of reserve.

My companion was quiet because he did not like the errand on which we were going. "This is a strange thing to ask for," he had said once again, just before we set out for the palace. "And I am not at all sure you'll get it." He disliked asking the King for anything he was not certain the King would readily grant: many years of pleasing whimsical majesty had made him sensitive to the King's humors. With all his power he himself could have granted me in an instant the favor I sought. But "No, I cannot do it. I will not," he maintained, as stubborn as a goat. Only after I threatened to go alone to the King did he finally consent to call with me upon his master.

I looked at him, the unbelievable man who was my sponsor, my guide, my employer, and, I was beginning to suspect, my enemy. Long and lean and elegant, he lounged in his corner, his legs crossed at the knee to accommodate them in the well of the carriage. His eyes were closed against the brilliance of the tropic day; he appeared to be dozing in the shadow of his silk hat. One thin-fingered hand resting lightly on his breast kept the soft white beard from blowing about his face. The other hand, pallid and empty, lay upon the seat of the barouche. He carried no portfolio or sheaf of papers or any sign of his office. The patrician head, with its piercing eyes and long curved nose and aureole of white hair, held everything he needed to know in his tireless mind. In any country on earth this man would have been outstanding. But in the Kingdom of Hawaii, surrounded as he was by natives only a generation removed from savagery, or by white men stamped with the dullness of their Calvinism, his virtuosity made him conspicuous and, in consequence, somewhat ridiculous.

Who else but Walter Murray Gibson could have been the Prime Minister of the Nation, Minister of Foreign Affairs, Minister of the Interior, President of the Board of Health, President of the Board of Education, holder of a dozen other lesser offices, all at one and the same time? The "one-man Privy Council" he was called in Honolulu, by some in admiration, by most in execration. Equal to any task the King put to him, insatiable in his ambition to serve both the King and himself, Gibson gradually had supplanted most of the members of the Government. By the time I arrived in Honolulu, Kalakaua, it was being said, was having no difficulty in filling any vacancy in his kingdom "with a good man": he simply named Walter Murray Gibson to the post. As owner and editor of the *Pacific Commercial Advertiser*, the Government's newspaper, and as the richest white man in the kingdom, Gibson extended his power to those parts of the islands which were not under his control as a member of the Privy Council. But, in the *opera buffa* Kingdom of Hawaii, this factotum, this busybody, held one other office of supreme importance which outweighed all of the others together: he was Master of the King's Revels as well, and in this way he completed his domination over the King and the kingdom. The man was a mountebank as well as an opportunist.

To confirm my opinion of him, the elongated figure opened one glittering eye. Of astonishing brightness and blueness, it examined me, upright in my corner. It winked slowly, insolently, at me. "Sun's bad for the eyes, you know," the oracle murmured. A faint smile played about the thin lips, implying that my head as well as my eyes were in danger of the August sun. Then the eye was closed, the smile vanished, and he appeared to doze again. But I knew the clever mind was not idle: behind the closed eyelids that agile brain was juggling a dozen different schemes. He might be a mountebank, but he was no fool.

Fretted by his jeering—he could make me feel so small, so much like a child!—I turned away from him. He was right, however: the glare from my white uniform was blinding, and the sola topi I wore did nothing to protect my eyes from the reflected sunlight. I must make a note, I reminded myself, respectfully to inform the *Gesundheitsamt* at home that the uniform they designed so carefully in Berlin had its limitations in the sunny lands where it was used. It was a handsome uniform, high at the collar, slim at the waist, and I was proud to be seen in it. But perhaps—I hesitated over the proper wording of my memorandum—perhaps some other color than white might be more practical? I would offer it as a suggestion, with the correct degree of diffidence, of course, when I reached home next spring. With a sudden longing for Berlin welling up within me, I looked beyond the blur of my uniform to the dirty alien world beyond the carriage.

We were being driven along King Street, the shabby main road of Honolulu. On our left the naked statue of Kamehameha, the barbarian first king of Hawaii, leaned upon its spear, lifting its right hand like a beggar to the spendthrift successor who lived in the new palace across the street. On our right stretched the high coral wall which enclosed the great square of the palace grounds. Eight feet high, a solid rampart of hewn reef-rock, it was interrupted once upon each side, where a wide gateway permitted access to the palace. Above the wall the crowns of exotic trees, with names unknown and unknowable to me, tossed and bowed in the wind from the mountains. The pendulous leaves, unaccountably greedy for sun in this land of sun, glistened as though they had been freshly washed in a rain of oil. They were all so lush, so foreign, those trees. I didn't like them. I prefer the more restrained, the more symmetrical vegetation of my northern homeland.

Because ours was not a visit of state, we were driven past the Kauikeaouli Gate on King Street, its wrought-iron barrier closed, the two native sentries, drowsing in their narrow sentinel boxes, not even noticing our passing. We were required to go halfway around the wall, to the Kinau Gate on Richards Street, before we could turn into the palace yard.

In the meantime I was free to vent my irritation upon Kalakaua's folly. What a crazy thing it was, to be set down in that miserable dirty town, on that windswept island, in the middle of that vast and monstrous sea! A rococo concoction of stone and wood and glass, it rose like a Frenchman's wedding cake, tier upon tier, beyond the barricade of wall and the jungle of trees. Newly finished, it gleamed and sparkled like a parvenu bedecked with both true diamonds and jewels of paste. It might possibly have been at home in Florence, or in Paris, with its colonnades and balconies, its florid Corinthian pillars, its square towers and mounting turrets with their mansard roofs; but there, in a setting of fantastic vegetation and acres of vivid green grass, against a backdrop of violent mountains and brilliant blue sky, it was blatant and vulgar. Like everything else in the tawdry town, it was ridiculous. It had no right to be there.

It was like Honolulu, raw, presumptuous, and false. Honolulu had no right to be there either. I had summed it up very well, when I wrote my first impressions of it to Luise, waiting for me in Berlin:

> A village so new that it has no history, it sprawls like a pimpled adolescent beside the dirty pond its people call a harbor. The earth upon which it lies is raw and naked, not yet clothed either with buildings or with verdure. Here, for the first time, a street is forming, following the aimless path of a pig. There, upon the surrounding waterless plains, no tree has ever grown, and on the nearby foothills only the scrawny striving grass has managed to gain a hold. Palaces of princes spring from coral reefs, where the stinking seaweed has not had time to dry; and between them clapboard cottages and grogshops and churches—so many churches!—are rising to milch the commoners. I do not like this place, and I shall not be happy until I leave it, on my way home to kiss your hands again.

Nine months of hard work in the primitive place did not lead me to soften my opinion of it. *Mein Gott!* I could no longer deny it: I hated the place!

No sentries barred our way at Kinau Gate, and I looked about with interest as we drove into the enclosure. This was my first visit to the palace. I had not been honored with an invitation since soon after my arrival, when I was served with a bid to attend a Court Ball. I could spare no time for dancing, busy as I was with my research, and I did not even bother to send my regrets to Their Sable Majesties. I supposed they were pouting still, for no further claims were made upon my time.

Ahead of us, at the center of the vast yard, was the flamboyant structure itself. To our left, tucked away in a bower of trees, squatted a low frame building, with latticed verandas and the comforts of a dwelling place. This was "The Bungalow," where Kalakaua spent much of his time, even now when his fancy palace was built, and where, it was rumored, many of the revels were held at which my lolling companion presided so efficiently. To our right, less obscured by vegetation, was the octagonal pavilion where Kalakaua's private band played in concert to please the Court. The pavilion, as every visitor to Honolulu is soon informed, is a relic of the ceremonies of the King's coronation. He had been King for ten years already at the time of his crowning. After his ridiculous Royal Progress around the world, and his discovery of the pomp and splendor which the world's great rulers enjoy, he came home determined to have a palace and a coronation of his own. And—protests from his government, the poverty of his people, the foolish extravagance of it all, notwithstanding—he was given his coronation when the palace was finished. It is common knowledge that Mr. Gibson owes his power, and the enjoyment of the King's favor, to his parliamentary skill, which forced both palace and coronation upon the country without the King's having to lift a finger to acquire them for himself.

The coachman called to his horses, flicking at them with the reins. They quickened their pace as we drove along the short *allée*, between rows of young royal palms. The fanciful edifice, its towers soaring above our heads, its kingly standards flying bravely in the wind to announce that His Majesty was in residence, impressed me in spite of myself. Ornate, impossible as it was in this setting, it did have an airy sort of grace about it to save it from being a complete fraud. I was forced to admit that there are worse examples of architecture and of princely taste in London, even in Berlin. As for Birmingham, the city of my birth and of my youth—ach! the less I thought of its monstrous smoky ugliness the happier I would be. I do not think of it as home, any more, or of the sinister merchant prince in it who is my father. I do not intend to go back to Birmingham again, ever. Berlin, in the new German Empire: that is where I belong.

As we rolled smartly toward the grand staircase of the palace, the Prime Minister rearranged himself in more decorous order. The long legs were uncrossed, the narrow feet with their toothpick-toed shoes were placed on the floor, the slouching torso imperceptibly stiffened and straightened, the head rose above the folded carriage top, and, when we drew up with a flourish, amid a great stir of native footmen running down the cascade of stairs to greet us, there he was beside me, erect and composed, the very model of the dignified statesman. Oh what a rogue he was! I all but laughed in his face. Somehow, the knowledge of him, a rascal in power, combined with my sense of expectancy to lighten my humor. I shrugged. If this is the way the kingdom is managed, why should I try to change it? I was almost free of care and light of heart when we stepped from the carriage.

In the distance, as we began our ascent of the palace stairs, the bells of Kawaiahao Church were ringing the hour of eleven. . . .

The voice of the Prime Minister assumed an official tone, he drew his lank form into something resembling attention. "Good morning, Your Majesty." Then, more suavely, "Sire, may I present to you Doctor Arnold Newman, a member of my staff in the Board of Health." Again I bowed low before the King of Hawaii.

"Good morning, Your Excellency. Welcome, Doctor Newman. I have wanted to have a chat with you." The voice was soft, cultured, almost feminine in its languor. "Do come into the Sitting Room, where we can be comfortable." With a plump hand he indicated the farther end of the large room extending from the head of the staircase. His manners were impeccable.

We were moving off at his suggestion when from the room beyond the open door we heard a woman's voice. "Kawika . . . Please shut the door." The request was followed by an unmistakable sniffle.

"Yes, my dear. I'm sorry—I forgot." With surprising speed for one of his portliness, he closed the busy door, then returned to shepherd us into the sitting room.

"How is Her Majesty this morning? Is she ill?" inquired the Prime Minister, all solicitude. With my lesson in palace geography thus driven home, and with the Queen's dominion so evidently established for me, I should have had the grace to blush at the naughtiness of my thoughts about who had lain behind that mystifying door. But, alas, I have weaknesses, as have other men, and I did not profit by the lesson.

"Oh, she is quite well, thank you.—We've just had an unhappy parting with one of her Ladies-in-Waiting.—Malie, you know.—We were bidding her good-by. She's having to leave us . . ." The soft voice paused frequently in our progress, as we rounded settees and tables and potted plants in our course toward the cluster of chairs where he wanted to seat us. Passing under a large skylight designed, in a naive conceit, in the form of a crown, we skirted an enormous round table made of the same orange wood used so liberally in the walls of the palace. Neatly arranged on the table were stacks of foreign magazines, piles of foreign newspapers, all of them in English: *The Times* of London, the *New York Herald*, the *Edinburgh Review*, the *Atlantic Monthly*. As I saw the familiar names I wondered how well those publications were read. The dog-eared copies of *Punch*, lying among the pristine monthly reviews, gave me my answer.

"Here we are. Let us sit down. Doctor Newman, please, here.—Walter, you here.—The Queen is very unhappy about losing her. A lovely girl, you know. Very lovely." He stopped the disjointed talk while he eased himself into his chair. Only when he was installed in it did we seat ourselves.

I had seen him before, of course, but only at a distance, riding in his carriage, and this was my first view of him at close range. Dressed in a loose navy-blue sack coat and comfortably baggy white linen trousers, he looked heavier than he actually was. The slowness with which he walked, the frequent pauses for breath, the occasional fits of asthmatic gasping, all indicated a certain discomfort of the body. Sitting as portly men so often must, on the edge of his chair, with his feet set firm upon the floor, his rounded belly filling the space between his legs, he rested his arms upon the rails of the chair, letting his hands hang limp.

"Please be at ease," he said to me, perched stiffly on the edge of my seat. "We have no ceremony here." The First Minister of the country needed no such encouragement: his long bony body was already settled in his usual posture, with the legs crossed at the knees, almost on a level with his head.

From a table beside him the King lifted a carved wooden box. "A cigar, Doctor?" "Thank you, sir. I do not smoke."

"Walter?" As with all *kanakas*, he had difficulty in pronouncing his r's. The Premier's name, as he said it, sounded like "Waltah." Mine, inevitably, was "Doctah." This softening of the harsher letters of our English words makes the language gentle and fluid when the Hawaiians speak it.

While they lighted their cigars, filling the quiet air with blue smoke and the stench of tobacco, I examined His Hawaiian Majesty with a physician's discernment. His wide face was sallow: the color beneath the brown skin was not a healthy one. Too much easeful living, not enough exercise, was too simple a diagnosis to make. Something else—a sluggish liver? an overtaxed heart?—would need to account for the pallor, the puffiness about the eyes. The jet-black curls of his Dundrearys and the full, flowing mustachios were still untouched with gray, as were the waves of glossy hair combed back from his high forehead. But the great brown eyes, which in *kanakas* are so often the most attractive of their features, in him were weary and puzzled, as though, despite his rank, he had been rebuffed by fate and had known little but sorrow. Bloodshot and heavy-lidded, they frequently strayed from me or from Gibson, while we talked, and always they came back to rest upon us with a suggestion of surprise at finding us still there.

But the Prime Minister was not inhibited in the least by the royal vacancy. "Your Majesty," he began at once. "Doctor Newman, as you know, came at my invitation to make some inquiries upon leprosy as it is found in these Your Islands." It is characteristic of Gibson that, for his vanity's sake, he must squeeze every ounce of credit out of every one of his creditable actions.

The King's gaze turned upon me for a moment, he nodded his awareness of the self-evident fact.

The eyes of people fascinate me: I am so sensitive to them, and to the revelations they can make of the person who wears them, that they are almost an obsession with me. I look first at them, in my estimation of people, placing much faith in the signs I read in their eyes for the judgment I make of them. I was still a boy when I discovered this power, and discovered also the distressing corollary to it, that through these unguarded windows could perceive, even without the guidance of words, the nature of a mind and the anguish of a heart.

The eyes of Kalakaua were like those of a dissolute bull, jaded of his servicing, and I expected little in the way of thought to issue from the unoccupied mansion of his mind.

"Since his arrival last November," continued Mr. Gibson, "he has been pursuing his investigations with great devotion and most commendable vigor. I can vouch for this, for I have seen him working, at all hours, when less diligent folk were taking their rest." Here he rewarded me for my months of labor with a regal nod of his own and a frosty sort of smile.

"But," he hastened on, before I could grow warm in the sunshine of his approbation, certainly before the King (if he had conceived the thought) could ask him how he could know all this about me when he was noted more for his relaxations than for his diligence, "despite his efforts, and despite the most scientific of approaches to the problems of the disease, he has not yet succeeded in discovering the answer to some of the most profound—if not the most pressing—of the questions he came here to investigate." The orator in him was taking hold. The full flatulent phrases were beginning to roll, the long-fingered hands to wave. If he were not stopped soon, the King and I would be in danger of hearing an hour's flowery disquisition upon the evils of leprosy in Hawaii, in Polynesia, in the whole Orient and Occident, and of Mr. Gibson's efforts to exterminate it, single-handed, at home and abroad. The old humbug! But how could I stop him?

"He has examined, with his microscope, and by technical procedures wondrous to behold, preparations from the skin, the pus, the blood, the internal organs, yea, from the very urine and excrement of lepers, and from their food, their garments, their possessions—" He stopped for breath, choked on his verbosity. "And in all of these, Your Majesty, he has found, with his microscope, the tiny little germs, each about one thousandth the size of the eye of a louse, the devilish little bacilli, which the foremost medical scientists of Europe say are the cause of this scourge of leprosy."

Kalakaua Rex, mouth slack, eyes dull, was unhappy. I was sure that he did not understand a word of his Prime Minister's learned lecture and was merely offended by its catalogue of intimacies. In his hand the cigar hung forgotten, a thin wisp of smoke rising from it in an unwavering path.

"He has attempted," the clarion trump of the Educator went on, "in the approved manner of his fellow scientists, to grow these foul microbes in captivity, in foodstuffs, or artificial soils, prepared for the purpose from meat and eggs and blood, from fish and vegetables and even from our native poi." Here, the Mentor's proficiency as a lecturer in bacteriology being sorely tried, he broke off suddenly. I glared at him, wishing he would choke or shut up.

"He has attempted to cause leprosy in animals, by introducing into their healthy systems some of the nefarious microbes which he has descried lurking in the purulent sores of lepers, by transferring to these animals some of the diseased flesh of lepers. For this purpose he has used dogs, cats, pigs, chickens, rabbits, mice, pigeons, a monkey—even animals but recently introduced into Your Kingdom, Sire, guinea pigs from South America."

The King looked ill. This is not an uncommon effect upon people hearing for the first time of the work a bacteriologist must do.

"In all these efforts, and in others it were tedious to mention," intoned the Prime Minister, "he has failed to achieve his grand purpose—" How he drew out that word failed, dwelling on it, dragging it out, prolonging the sound of it with lingering affection, as though it were a word his tongue had fallen in love with and was unwilling to release into the air beyond the reach of his lips. But with my frown of disapproval at this turn in the flow of his discourse, he hurried on. "—that of growing the germs of leprosy in his artificial soils, or in the animals he has subjected to his experimentation. Now he wants to—"

The clever fiend! In my very presence he was maligning me and my work. Before I was given a chance to utter a word he was undermining the purpose of my call upon the King.

"Your Majesty! Permit me to speak." The bull-eyed gaze turned upon me. Without waiting for more permission than that, I rushed on, fighting to hold my anger in check. "Mr. Gibson does not say—I hope because he does not *know*—that exactly this same failure to grow the leprosy organism in experimental animals or in artificial soils has been the sole fruit of all investigations of leprosy in Europe. This failure is one of the most baffling of all the puzzles relating to this strange disease. This failure is *exactly* the reason why I came to Hawaii, all the way from Berlin, to make my studies here." How could I make him understand, this benighted man, this king of ignoramuses, so far removed from learning and from science, with its amazing discoveries and its astonishing revelations? I could only plunge on, sitting forward on the edge of my chair as though to prevent the Premier from reaching the King's mind before I could.

"The question of the *cause* of leprosy is the most essential part of my investigations here. It is the most subtle and delicate of my tasks, because upon the answer to this question depends all else. Until we know with certainty what the cause of leprosy is, we cannot with certainty know what the disease is. When I have proved its cause, then will we be aided in the detection of the disease, in our understanding of the manner in which it is spread from old victims to new, in our discovery of medicines with which to treat it."

In my eagerness to make myself clear to him, I laid my hand for a moment upon the sacrosanct arm. "Your Majesty. I am not yet discouraged. My work has only begun. The results of all the work I have done until now are not valueless, even though they have not been as successful as I hoped. Nor do they mean that my work must come to an end. On the contrary, they must act as a stimulus to further research. I must continue my investigations until I prove beyond a doubt what the cause of leprosy is."

"And how do you propose to do this, sir," asked Mr. Gibson coldly, "if all the work you and these other investigators have done has met with this—this absence of success?"

Patiently I answered him, more certain now of my hold upon my temper. "No one who has not tried this kind of modern research is able to judge of its many disappointments, its dependency upon apparently insignificant particulars, and"—I thought I might as well insert an innuendo of my own about his damned obstructive and inefficient Board of Health—"and the difficulties which crowd upon one when one is working outside of his accustomed laboratory with its intelligent assistants and its never-failing supply of the equipment he needs." I wished these critics I of my work could see my splendid laboratory in Berlin, in the Imperial Bureau of Health. Compared with it my dusty hut in the Leprosy Hospital in Honolulu was less than a German peasant's pigsty.

The President of the Board of Health grinned, knowing well what I was getting at. "You are straying from the point, Doctor. I repeat: how will you—or anyone—prove the cause of leprosy?" The sneer was the insult of a politician, offered to all scientists, not only to myself. Eagerly I took up the challenge, for now we were on familiar ground for me. Not for nothing was I a pupil of Doctor Koch.

"By following a set of rules, sir, laid down by my respected teacher, Doctor Robert Koch." I turned to the King, wondering if he would be able to follow me in the logic of discovery. He appeared to be half asleep, his mouth open, his eyes partly closed, the breath so audible between the thick lips that it sounded like snoring. Gibson, the old fox, could understand me perfectly well, I knew. His years as President of the Board of Health, coupled with his own quick intelligence, had made him sufficiently familiar with all of the new theories about disease.

He could devote his money and his labor, as well as the nation's, to the safeguarding of the Hawaiian people; he alone of all the officers of all the Boards of Health throughout the world, had the foresight to invite an investigating bacteriologist to come to his country from the font of bacteriology in Berlin. And yet, now when I was here, a member of his staff, doing my very best to solve the problems I had been invited to Hawaii to work upon, I was finding him impatient, obstructive, far from the intelligent and co-operative statesman whom I had expected to find in Honolulu when in Berlin I read his enlightened letters to Doctor Koch. This disappointment in my expectations of him baffled me.

But now, while I pondered how to explain Koch's Postulates to the King, Gibson did not bother to hinder me or to help me. A malicious glint in his eye, he left me to myself, while he puffed easily on his cigar. Hopefully I addressed myself to the King.

"In order to prove that a specific bacterium is the cause of a disease, the bacteriologist must first show that this bacterium is present in every case of the disease. Then he must take a specimen from the diseased body of such a case, and from it he must grow the suspect germs in an artificial medium." I spoke slowly, patiently, precisely, as though I were explaining something to a student. But even these simplifications of a complicated subject seemed to be too difficult for the dullard who sat opposite me.

"He must grow these germs in what is called 'a pure culture'—that is to say, in a growth in which all of the germs are of one kind, unmixed, or uncontaminated, as we say, with living microbes of any other kind. This is not always easy to do—"

"An understatement," snorted Mr. Gibson, "if ever I heard one."

"But it is possible to do so," I flared back, "and there are ways of doing it. When this pure culture has been obtained, a portion of it must be introduced into a healthy experimental animal. The animal, of course, must be of a kind which can show visible response to the germs being studied. The germs must cause the animal to show responses—we call them symptoms—which are identical with those shown in natural cases of the disease, or which are similar to them, at least."

I was treading on thin ice here, because of course laboratory animals do not show the same symptoms as humans do. But I did not want to make my explanations too complicated for the mind of the monarch who read *Punch*, and I skipped lightly past one of the chief pitfalls in the proving of Doctor Koch's Postulates.

"As a last step in the proof," I went on, feeling defeat before the battle was done, "the bacteria must be grown again in pure culture from the animal which received them. And they must be shown to be the same kind of bacteria as those which were cultivated in the first place from the original cases of the disease. Only when all of this has been done, and redone, beyond all doubting and all possibility of error, can the bacteriologist say with certainty that he has proved the etiology of a disease." Finished at last with my exposition, I sat back, exhausted. Why had I bothered? My plea was lost for lack of a listener.

His Majesty stirred, opening his heavy-lidded eyes. Panting with the effort, he reached into a pocket of his jacket for a handkerchief, into which he coughed delicately. Now the mountain labors, now let us observe the mouse of which it will be delivered.

The kerchief was applied gently to the royal forehead, to the kingly cheeks, to the pink palms of the soft moist hands. I watched in fascination, wondering how long fatuous ignorance could pretend to be learned deliberation. At last the royal lips parted for speech.

"How interesting.—How fascinating must be this microscopic world in which you work.—Is that how Doctor Koch established the cause of tuberculosis?"

I could scarcely believe my ears. I was expecting a belch. The gentle voice went on, to complete my routing. "I have read of your teacher's investigations with great interest, Doctor—although with somewhat deficient comprehension."

I could not find a word to say. Not daring to look at Mr. Gibson, who would know full well the extent of my surprise, I sat there, watching the King restore his handkerchief to its place in his pocket.

"More recently I have followed in the foreign press his studies in Egypt, about the cholera. Fortunately, the cholera is not one of our problems of health here—at least not at the present time.—We enjoy so many importations from the great world beyond our horizons, however, that it too will undoubtedly join our list before many more years have passed."

Unhurried, for he was accustomed to being listened to, he continued. "But we do have the leprosy in Hawaii Nei, and it is a terrible problem. A terrible thing. Perhaps our worst.—Would you believe it, Doctor Newman? When I was a lad there were no lepers in these islands. I was about ten years old when the first case of the leprosy in a Hawaiian was discovered—by old Doctor Baldwin, of Lahaina, I believe. He was a friend of the chiefs, this first leper, and the husband of Queen Emma's mother. I knew him well. Naea was his name.

"In twenty years there were so many lepers among my people—some say a thousand, some say two thousand—that the King of the time felt it necessary to ask his Legislature to pass an act providing for the segregation of the lepers. That is when our Settlement at Kalaupapa began.

"Today, after twenty more years—who knows?" He lifted a hand, opened it to show its emptiness. "Who knows how many lepers there are among my people, or whether this cruel isolation of them at Kalaupapa does the nation any good—any good at all? Who can say? Not Mr. Gibson's Board of Health. Not, if I have heard you aright, your learned self." Though I searched for it, there was no sarcasm in the mellow voice.

"But we are interested in finding out, Doctor. Our hearts are full of sorrow over this blight which has fallen upon the nation. And we are trying to combat it with all the means at our disposal. We have built hospitals, we have called in physicians, we have tried treatments new and old, brought in from the ends of the earth. This little nation, Doctor, devotes a greater portion of its income to the care of lepers and to the combatting of the disease than does any nation on earth."

"Sire, this is why I came to your islands."

"Yes, Doctor Newman, and we are grateful for your help in this discouraging conflict. It continues to be one-sided, with all of the victories going still to the enemy. But I hope that soon there will be a change in our fortunes. The foul plague cannot always win."

"And the first triumph against it will be achieved when someone shows what the cause of the disease is. I am hoping that this proof will be achieved here, and that I shall be the one to do it."

"Bravo!" applauded my employer from the depths of his chair. "A most laudable service—if only it can be rendered."

"What do you want in nine months?" I snarled. "Cause, cure,—and immortality?"

His complacency was unshaken. He laughed good-naturedly. "Any one of these would be enough. Give us the first two, and you may keep the third."

"I've told you that I've just begun upon my work. These things take time"—I hated the high pitch of earnestness creeping into my throat, the nervous hurrying which made me sound peevish when I wanted only to be explicit—"and more time, more facilities, more help, more of *everything*, are what I need to bring it to a successful conclusion."

"Ah, yes, the guinea pig."

"I thought that you were unsuccessful with the guinea pigs," said the King, turning from Mr. Gibson to me.

"He is being facetious, sir. He knows very well that I would not bother you with a request for guinea pigs."

"What is it, then, that you wish from me?"

And there we were, thus suddenly, and thus slowly, in the most round-about fashion, at the purpose of my call upon the King. The ease with which he invited it combined with the sensibleness of his conversation to make me state my request of him blandly, as one scientist speaking to another.

"One of your subjects, Sire. A murderer condemned to die."

"One of my people?—But why?"

"I want to experiment upon him, Sire. To see if I can give him leprosy."

Ka-'ehu

"MELE A KA-'EHU KA HAKU MELE"

E aha 'ia ana o Hawai'i
I nei ma'i o ka lēpela,
Ma'i ho'okae a ka lehulehu
A ka 'ili 'ula'ula 'ili ke 'oke'o?

'Ano 'e mai ana nā hoa hui
Like 'ole ka pilina mamua.
He 'āhiu ke 'ike mai,
Ne'e a kāhi 'e noho mai,
Kuhikuhi mai ho'i ka lima,
He ma'i Pākē kō 'iā 'la.

Kūlou au a hō'oiā'i'o,
Komo ka hilahila i ka houpo.
Lohe ana kauka aupuni,
Ho'oūna ke koa māka'i.
Hopuhopu 'ia mai kohu moa,
Alaka'i i ke ala kohu pipi.
Ku ana imua o ka Papa Ola,
Papa ola 'ole o nei ma'i.
Ki'ei wale mai nā kauka,
Hālō ma'ō, ma'ane'i,

Kuhi a'e na lima i Lē'ahi,
"Hele 'oe ma Kalawao."

Lālau nā koa Aupuni,
Halihali iā kai ka uwapo.
Ho'īli nā pio a pau,
Ka luahi i ka ma'i lēpela.
Hiki ke aloha kaumaha nō
I ka 'ike 'ole i ka 'ohana.
Ka waimaka ho'i ka 'elo'elo,
Ho'opulu i ka pāpālina.
Pau ka 'ikena i ka 'āina
I ka wehiwehi o ke kaona.

Hao wikiwiki iā lilo ho'i,
Kū ka huelo i ke kia mua,
E nonoho lua 'o *Keoni Pulu*,
Kīpū i ka hoe mahope,
Ho'ohū ka helena o ke kai,
A he pipi'i wale mai nō.
'Ike iā Moloka'i mamua
Ua pōwehiwehi i ka noe.

Ha'ina mai ka puana
Nō nei ma'i o ka lēpela.

"SONG OF THE CHANTER KA-'EHU"

What will become of Hawai'i?
What will leprosy do to our land—
Disease of the despised, dreaded alike
By white or brown or darker-skinned?
Strange when a man's neighbors
Become less than acquaintances.
Seeing me they drew away.
They moved to sit elsewhere, whispering,
And a friend pointed a finger:
"He is a leper."
I bowed my head.
I knew it was true.
In my heart I hugged my shame.

Word reached the medical authorities.
The doctors sent the military to fetch us.

We were caught like chickens, like cattle herded
Along roadway and country lane.
Then they paraded us before the Board of Health
But there was no health in that Board for such as we.
Examining doctors eyed us, squinted this way and that.
More fingers pointed Diamond Head way:
"You go to Kala-wao!"
Again the militia took over.
Soldiers escorted us to the wharf for farewell.
Prisoners, we were marched aboard,
Victims of leprosy, branded for exile.
Abandoned, cut off from family and dear ones,
We were left alone with our grief, with our love.
Rain of tears streamed from leper eyes.
Leper cheeks glistened with raindrops in the sun.
Never again would we look upon this land of ours,
This lovely harbor town.
Quickly the sails were hoisted.
Ropes dangled from the foremast,
Tails of wild animals writhing,
Whipping in the channel breeze.
The *John Bull* drew anchor.
In the stern the rudder turned.
So sailed we forth to dim Moloka'i Island,
Enshrouded in fog.
So ends my song and this refrain.
What will leprosy do to my people?
What will become of our land?

TRANSLATED BY MARY KAWENA PUKUI

KA-'EHU *was a composer, chanter, and hula master, who could compose a chant, set it to music, and perform it within an hour. He was a skilled and productive writer and a keen observer of daily life. He was active during the reigns of Kamehameha V, Lunalilo, and Kalākaua. He contracted Hansen's Disease (leprosy), and died at the quarantine settlement at Kalaupapa on Moloka'i.*

Maxine Hong Kingston

from CHINA MEN

"Right now," said the agent, "we're offering free passage, free food, free clothing, and housing. In fact, we're advancing you six dollars. Here. See. I have six dollars right here. Here, Grandma. We'll let Po Po hold it; she can return it to me if she wants to. Couldn't you use six dollars before you've even begun to work? You repay it with just six weeks' work. After six weeks, clear profit. Figure it out. You're joining us at a lucky time. The pay just went up again. You're getting an instant raise. We need every kind of labor. You inexperienced kids can be house servants for two dollars a month. Now, once you secure this fine job, you'll want to protect it, right? You're thinking, What if I get to the Sandalwood Mountains, and they fire me? Well, listen to this. We can't fire you. We protect you against firing. We can't fire you because you sign this three-year contract, and for more protection, this five-year contract." "Mm," said the family. "Of course, there'll be some hardships, but that's life, isn't it? You'll be traveling with a shipload of fellow Chinese, with whom you'll be sharing free housing. You'll have people to discuss things with. We're giving you a dormitory just like going to college. And did you know that the Sandalwood Mountains are very close to the Gold Mountain? You get free passage as far as the Sandalwood Mountains, where you can stay as long as you want, and you invest a little of your profits in passage to California. You'll get there before the Gold Rush is over. Why, in Hawai'i, you're already halfway there. Figure: You start with nothing. You already have six dollars' advance. Three years from today, home with riches."

Impressed by the agent's homely dialect, his suit, his title, and his philosophic bent, Bak Goong muttered what Confucius taught on the occasion of breaking a promise to his captors, "'Heaven doesn't hear an oath which is forced on one,'" and made his X.

He told his family that he would be back in three years. . . .

The Chinese who had sailed before him had painted a sea bird on the side of the ship, which protected it from storms. His first free moment he lowered himself on a rope and painted eyes on the bow. He tied poles and lines to the rails and caught fish. The ocean was a bowl with horizon all around. Lucky to be a crewman.

He met all manner of men, broad faced and sharp faced Han Men, tall dark ones, white ones, little ones like the Japanese. One group spoke the language so queerly that he laughed out loud. He imitated their *thl* sound blown out of the mouth with big, airy cheeks and spit. "One, two, three, returning to the various separate bodies of flesh and bone. "How not to take pain? How to have no pain?" "Be able," he said. "Be capable." "Capable." Opium was merely a rest from constant pain. He said the answer aloud, put it into words, repeated it, "Be capable," to remember it for use later when these unwordable feelings were gone. "I am a capable man. An able man," he said, and did feel a touch of dreariness at this mundane answer. He wrapped himself in his quilt and patted his money belt to feel his sugar cane contract crackle. "No pain. Don't give pain. Don't take pain." He did not smoke opium again on the journey because he did not want to become an addict or to spend money.

After three months at sea, *Bak Goong smelled in the wind a sweetness like a goddess visiting* whenever the hatches and doors opened in the right combinations, the men below *also* smelled *it* ~~a sweetness that was like a goddess visiting.~~ "It's sandal-wood," *Bak Goong* said, *looking for land on the horizon* ~~they~~ ~~It was not an incense smoke, not a smell like Hong Kong, the Fragrant Port, but the wild raw smell of new land.~~ The ~~statues and~~ *smell of the* chests and boxes *he had used back home, the statues* made of sandalwood, the castenets and fans, the incenses and powders had ~~enticed them~~ *inspired him to come* here. Chinese had followed that essence to India, where it grew in phoenix-shaped roots in the caves of lions, and to Persia, where it congeal*ed* in the Eastern Ocean as a cicada. And they ~~had~~ followed it home here.

One day ~~the doors stayed open, and~~ *Bak Goong opened the hatches for* the men *below, who* stumbled through the hallways and up ladders to the topdeck, where they blinked in the sunlight. A demon from shore counted and *four*." Sputtering and spitting as he shouted out the *four*, which has that *thl*, he called out the rhythm for lifting and hauling. "Do you come from near our village?" a man from the *thl* village asked. "Yes, I also come from the *Four* Districts," said Bak Goong. He mimicked men with staccato consonants and a lone northerner who spoke a soft dialect like English, and he would have talked to the Englishmen too except that he could not hear their sliding, slippery little voices out of the fronts of their pursed mouths. "Their asses must be as tight as their mouths," he said out loud right in front of them.

The Chinese passengers were locked belowdeck though they were not planning to escape. Their fresh air was the whiff and stir when crewmen exchanged the food buckets for the vomit and shit buckets. Some men brought their pigs, which slept under the bottom bunks. The beds looked like stacks of coffins in a death house. "Here we are," said Bak Goong, who had to sleep in this hold too, "emigrating with our pigs our only family."

He gave advice to the boys who were away from their mothers for the first time. "You'll be a rich man in three years," he said. "Three years is forever for a kid, but for a man in his thirties like me, the years pass too quickly. Don't you notice how one year passes faster than the last? The first year abroad will be the worst; then we'll wish that time would slow up for our lives to last longer." (He talked about time as going from up to down, last week being the "upper week" and next week the "lower week," time a sort of ladder that one descends.)

"Be quiet, Dog Vomit," somebody hollered. "Shut up and let me sleep."

"Don't say 'vomit,'" somebody else groaned.

"Try laughing," said Bak Goong. "I'll bet you can't laugh and vomit at the same time." Laugh is another word that has the combination in that queer dialect. "And as for the dark," he advised the children, "it makes the room feel larger, doesn't it?"

"Tobacco shit stops the seasickness," said an opium smoker, who passed his pipe.

"No, no, shit cures colds, not seasickness."

"Let's try it for seasickness."

"Your mother's cunt. You make this room smoky, and I'll throw up all over you."

The berths, come to think of it, were also stacked like beds in an opium house. "Is opium bitter?" asked Bak Goong. "It's not addicting if you just try it once, right?" The tempted men had a discussion on exactly which pipe—the twelfth? the hundredth?—addicted, and how often—once a week? five times a day? once a month?—constituted addiction. "It takes two years of smoking three times a day to learn the opium habit," an addict said confidently.

So Bak Goong gave a tobacco shit man some money and smoked. The silver and wooden water pipes gurgled like rivers; the bowl pipes drew airily. Bak Goong leaned against the wall, and the meaning of life and time and what he was doing on this ship all became clear to him; even his vomity feeling fell into its place in the scheme of the universe. . . .

After three months at sea, Bak Goong smelled in the wind a sweetness like a goddess visiting. Whenever the hatches and doors opened in the right combinations, the men below also smelled it. "It's sandalwood," Bak Goong said, looking for land on the horizon. The smell of boxes and chests of drawers, statues, castanets and fans, incenses and powders must have inspired him to come here. Chinese had followed that essence to India, where sandalwood grew in phoenix-shaped roots in the caves of lions, and to Persia, where it congealed in the Eastern Ocean as a cicada. And now they followed to its home here.

One day Bak Goong opened the hatches for the men below, who stumbled through the passageways and up ladders to the topdeck, where they blinked in the sunlight. A demon from shore counted and recounted the China Men. There were three or four fewer live ones than when they began the journey. The demon strung a tab about each neck. Bak Goong climbed down to the longboat, past the weeds that had grown like skirts on the ship's sides.

On shore among crates, burlap bags, barrels, haystacks, they waited for their bosses, some of whom were China Men. The men with no papers signed anything that was handed them; most made a cross like the ideograph *ten*; "The Word Ten," they called their signatures. A pair of horses, which delighted Bak Goong, pulled a wagon to the dock, but only a few workers rode to those fields close enough to Honolulu to be reached by roads. Bak Goong's group was to walk, led by a demon boss on a horse. He bade good-byes to friends he had made on the ship. Walking after rolling on the sea confused his legs, but with his seabag across his back, he edged quickly to the front of the group. He buffered himself in case the demon used his whip on men.

They walked out of the town and up a mountain road so narrow that the demon dismounted and led the horse. The trail led upward among banana trees. Bak Goong ate bananas to his heart's content, throwing away the peels instead of scraping their insides and eating the fibers; there were that many bananas, hands of them, overripe fruit rotting on the ground. He ate fruit and nuts he had never seen before. And mangos like in China. He wished he could give his wife some. With a handful of rice a day, he could live here without working. Five-petaled flowers spun from the trees, pink stars, white stars, yellow stars, striped red and white stars. At one beautiful spot, white trumpet flowers hung above his head like hats. He walked on ground royally carpeted with jacaranda. When the sun became hot, a tall rain fell and made two rainbows across the sky, the colors of the top one in the opposite order of the bottom one. "Aiya," said the men. "Beautiful. Beautiful." "Is that a good omen or a bad omen?" "How does it happen?" "It has to be a good omen." The rainbows moved ahead of them. Before they became too wet, the rain stopped; the sun and breeze dried them. Bak Goong memorized all this to tell his wife.

He sucked in deep breaths of the Sandalwood Mountain air, and let it fly out in a song, which reached up to the rims of volcanoes and down to the edge of the water. His song lifted and fell with the air, which seemed to breathe warmly through his body and through the rocks. The clouds and frigate birds made the currents visible, and the leaves were loud. If he did not walk heavy seated and heavy thighed like a warrior, he would float away, snuggle into the wind, and let it slide him down to the ocean, let it make a kite, a frigate bird, a butterfly of him. He would dive head first off the mountain, glide into the airstreams thick with smells, and curve into the ocean. From this mountaintop, ocean before him and behind him, he saw the size of the island. He sang like the heroes in stories about wanderers and exiles, poets and monks and monkeys, and princes and kings out for walks. His arias unfurled and rose in wide, wide arcs.

The men passed a hutment of grass shacks with long yellow thatch weathered and fine, rippling and ruffling in the breeze like the hair of blonde ladies. Roofs had fallen, and the frames showed like bones. The doorways were empty. They did not see brown people come and go.

They descended another side of the mountain and walked along the sea all day, and at last came to the place where they were to work. They had arrived in the middle of the workday, and were to start at once. There was no farm, no sugarcane ready to tend. It was their job to hack a farm out of the wilderness, which they were to level from the ocean to the mountain.

MAXINE HONG KINGSTON *was born in 1940 and is the author of the following books:* The Woman Warrior: Memoirs of a Girlhood Among Ghosts; China Men; Hawai'i One Summer; Tripmaster Monkey: His Fake Book; To Be the Poet; *and* The Fifth Book of Peace. *She is editor of the anthologies* The Literature of California *and* Veterans of War, Veterans of Peace.

Herbert K. K. Chun
"PA-KE"

you speak of shadows
and I dream of journeys—

an old ship, iron and rusted
plates. Chinese workers for sugar
plantations. I move among
broken sandals and jade-
colored bile. once a week,
they wash the hold. the water
slides across the deck, over yellow
bodies. it clings to the rusted hull.

from the vats
of cooking rice, the steam
rises in the twilight. we gather
near the warmth with our wooden
bowls. the brown rice
is over-cooked. burnt rice
scraped for those at the end
of the line. someone says every man
who can walk off the ship in Hawai'i
is worth five dollars. there are no more
men, only hollow trees. hunger,
a sparrow, flutters
among the branching bones, taking each
grain of rice. it sings and its voice
enchants the twilight
into a shadowed sigh.

Ling Wan has died. I helped
throw him into the sea. his
feet were cold and stiff. his
toenails were black. I wear his
sandals. I keep his last
words. they are,
"do not let me die."

the island, a broken piece
of jade, rises with the dawn.
and the deck is full of wandering
eyes. behind me is
Fan Wei, whose sickness covers
him with sweat, as though
he had been
laboring instead of eating
rats. gone is the pain
in my legs, where the skin
is raw from scratching at sores
as I slept. now we smile
into each other's faces. soon,
soon . . .

I push my way off the ship.
I do not limp but walk
onto the dock. a man passes
and taps me on the shoulder
with a stick. I am
number nine. I throw my bowl
into the sea. too soon
I have need for another.

the night on this island
also sighs. I have journeyed far,
thinking that I had left
nothing behind.

HERBERT K. K. CHUN *was born in Honolulu in 1955 and has remained a lifelong resident of Hawai'i. He is a fourth-generation Chinese American; his great-grandparents arrived in Hawai'i in the mid-1800s. He has an MA in English from San Francisco State University and a BA from the University of Hawai'i. His work has been published in* Hawai'i Review; Bamboo Ridge; *and* Tradewinds.

Author Unknown

from A ROMANCE

W hen Nyama and his wife arrived at the hotel they saw a man standing by the door. It was a tall man with a dark brown complexion. He wore a blue suit adorned with rows of polished brass buttons, and a felt helmet on his head, he carried a club in his belt. He was a policeman.

Nyama looked at the giant with interest; the giant returned the gaze. As our hero was passing the door he stretched out his great hand and seized him by the coat collar.

"You come with me. I arrest you," he said in a manner which showed that he was ready to take his prisoner bodily, willynilly.

Faza gave a cry and clung to her husband's neck, "What does he say? what does the creature want? oh, my dear!"

"What do you mean," demanded Nyama, "you are mistaken. What do you arrest me for?"

"You run away; you stop work. Pretty soon you find out wasamatta."

Nyama put both his arms around Faza and tried to reassure her. "Don't be alarmed, my dear; is all a mistake. It will soon be all right. Don't cry! I have not done anything to be arrested for. I'll soon be back. I must go with this policeman, but I will be back in an hour. Go up stairs and wait for me. Be a brave girl now," and he kissed her tenderally and pulled away her arms from his neck, and pushed her gently away.

"All right," he said to the policeman, and they went.

Faza ran wildly up the stairs, and bursting into their room, threw herself, face down, upon the bed and sobbed aloud. It seemed to her that the sun had gone out and all was darkness and dispair.

Nyama went with the policeman to a dingy little office down by the wharves among the forest of masts. A dusty looking iron-grey man sat behind a battered desk.

When Nyama stood before him he did not look up, but continued his writing. After a minute Nyama became impatient and asked:

"Do you know why this fellow has brought me here? I can soon clear myself of any charge against me, and I will make somebody pay for this."

The man behind the desk paid no the slightest heed but wrote serenely on. The policeman stood in the door.

Nyama looked out of the dusty cobwebbed window for a few minutes, he was getting angry. "Now, look here!" he cried, "this is a damned outrage. I will have satisfaction for this. It don't become a gentleman to be kept waiting by a little, scribbling vice, deputy, assistant clerk."

Even this produced no effect on the man. So Nyama gnashed his teeth and dropped into a chair and waited.

At the expiration of half an hour the official arose, put away his books and papers, shut and locked his desk and put on his coat and hat, then he spoke: "Are you No. 3781? Name Nyama?" he asked.

"My name is Nyama, but I am not a convict, nor a package of merchandise that I have a number," replied the young man.

"You came with the last lot of Japanese didn't you?"

"Yes, but—" began Nyama.

"Take him to Sand Island," broke in the official, speaking to the policeman, and walked out of the door and away.

The policeman motioned to his prisoner to follow, and led the way to the wharf. The sun was low and shone in their faces as they looked toward the sea. Sea and sky were on fire with the reflected light of the setting sun. The policeman motioned to a row boat lying by the wharf with the stalwart oarsman sleeping in the bottom.

They climbed into the boat and aroused the drowsy owner, who after some conversation with the policeman, put his oars in the oarlocks and pulled slowly out toward the setting sun. After a while there appeared a black line against the fiery horizon, and then widened as they approached till they saw a long, low, dark building like barracks, standing on a sand bar just a little above the water level. The boat came alongside a rude structure of old boards and the policeman told Nyama to get out.

He stood on the rude wharf and watched the receding boat, looking long at the bay, the city half hid in tropic foliage and the purple mountain beyond.

At last he turned and strode toward the buildings. Little fire were burning before the doors which turned out to be little camp fires over which many Japanese were boiling the rice for their evening meal.

Here were all the excursionists who had come on the pleasure trip to Bowowee, sitting on the sand or bits of board or lying on their red and blue blankets, eating plain boiled rice from tin plates and talking.

Nyama addressed one of these groups. They had been on the bar for ten days; they did not have enough to eat and it was cold at night; they thought they would be released tomorrow. That was all the news with them; but when they learned that Nyama had come from the city, he was soon surrounded by a crowd of eager questioners, anxious to hear about Bowowee and their prospects for making a fortune.

He could tell them but little and escaped as soon as possible. Going into one of the houses he found it empty, but for the shelves on the walls which were evidently occupied as beds. From some came snores, from others sighs and groans. Remembering that the sand outside was wet, Nyama climbed on one of the board-shelves, and lying on his back gave himself up to gloomy speculations. Here he passed the night, dressed in his best suit of clothes without a blanket, turning over and about on the hard surface, cold stiff and disconsolate. This was his introduction to the reverse side of life in the Paradise of the Pacific.

Now this same evening the Chief Supervisor of Japanese Immigration came to call at the hotel. He knocked at the door of Nyama's room, and not waiting long for an answer walked in. Faza still lying on the bed her body convulsed with grief. He put his hand on one of the small kid shoes that showed below her white dress, and giving a little pull said:

"Come now, don't cry so, your husband is all safe, get up and I will tell you all about it."

Faza sat up and pushed back her disheveled hair and wipe her swolen eyes with her handkerchief.

"Where is he?" she demanded, "why don't he come back?"

The supervisor sat down on the edge of the bed and put his arm around the slender corset-compressed waist. Faza sprang up and stood at bay staring at him and ready to run away.

"What are you scared about?" said the supervisor. "I won't hurt you. You are very handsome now. Come and give me a kiss; nobody is looking. If you don't, I won't tell you about Nyama. He might have to stay in prison for five years."

"Oh, please sir, don't mock me," cried the girl, "but tell me about my husband."

"Well," he said, "Nyama was arrested because he and all the Japanese that come here through the government are under contract to work in the cane-field for a term of five years. Any one who undertakes to work can not change his mind and refuse to carry out his contract, if he attempts to he is arrested and sent back to work.

"Nyama have no right to come on shore. He will have to go to Bowowee Island and serve in the cane field for five years. When I heard he was arrested I was sorry; but I cannot help him. I came at once to see you. I can save you from all trouble. You cannot go into the rough hard life on a plantation. I will give you a nice little cottage, furnish it beautifully for you, make it a lovely little nest for my pretty pet. I will come and see you every day so you will never get lonesome.

The supervisor had watched Faza closely during this speech, who when she heard that Nyama must go to another island covered her face with her hands and sobbed again. "I will go with my husband. Tell me where is," she said.

The supervisor went up to her and caught her wrists in his hands and pushing her hands away from her face and down behind her, lifted her in his arms. Faza struggled desperately and remonstrated so loudly that he was compelled to release her. "You are very foolish," he said, "but I will see you again," and he left the room.

She thought now only of how to find Nyama. She wanted to go to him, and go with him wherever their evil star might lead. She did not know a word of English and it was already dark. She was afraid to go out. She must wait till morning.

Having reached this conclusion, she applied some cold water to her face and combed out her long hair, then she took off her shoes and then her dress.

She was unfastening her corset when a sharp knocking came at the door. Hastily, thrusting the offending article into a drawer and pulling her dress up over her shoulders again, she opened the door. It was Moromoto of the steamship, looking fresh and dandified as usual.

"My goodness," he exclaimed, "what in the world is the matter?"

Faza explained not quite steady as to her voice, her hair flowing all around her. As she spoke the young officer looked with growing admiration. Her white feet showed under the white dress as she sat on the edge of the bed and the unbuttoned dress suggested how easily it might come off, and gave glimpses of white skin and scarcely concealed the plump, round breast. The thought flashed through the young man's mind; the fire ran through his veins; every muscle and nerve began to beat and tingle. He felt the fierce glow, the imperative impulse of animal love, the desire of the wild beast to forcibly take possession of the object of its passion and to overcome opposition with tooth and claw. He thought, if Nyama were dead Faza would belong to him. The idea was fascinating. Perhaps he would never get out of Jail, and then—Faza stopped speaking. He had not heard the last of her story. He started.

"I know you will help us, sir Moromoto," she concluded, "you have been so kind," and she looked up at him appealingly and smiled a little. It was maddening; he lifted his hands—and thrust them in his pockets. "Yes," he said shortly, "I will see what can be done," and left the room.

He was glad to get out into the cool air, out of the warm bedroom and its strange temptation. He took a deep breath and wondered at his infatuation. But the vision of the beautiful girl, setting in dishabille on the edge of her bed still followed him.

He felt ashamed of his treachery, resolved to do all in his power for his friend and if he was really gone—Faza. He went to the police station and did not find him there. He went to the Supervisor's Office, it was closed. He went to the Japanese Consulate. The Consul was out, but the clerk directed him to his residence.

When he found it, he was told that the consul was out at a grand reception given by the King of Bowowee. So he went back to his ship without having accomplished anything.

Next morning he again called on the supervisor. That official told him that men could not to break their contracts, that Nyama had been assigned to work on a plantation at Hardrow, Bowowee. "But," he added graciously, "the women are not under contract and I can find a position for his wife here in town. She had better not attempt to go with her husband."

Moromoto went to the Consulate. The consul wore glasses and seemed very haughty, but when Moromoto introduced himself, listened patiently to the whole story and at the end of it said he would see what could be done. He went to the telephone and after securing the connection called: "Is that you, Mr. Dives? Oh! all right. I want to speak to you about a young countryman of mine. He has been sent to work on your plantation at Hardrow. He is a man of good family, educated, speaks English. It was a kind of a mistake coming as an immigrant, did not understand the conditions. Well, can you give him some light work, clerical work.—In the store?—Yes, I don't think he would make trouble, all right. Thanks. Good-bye.

"Mr. Dives, the owner of the plantation at Hardrow, says he can give your friend work in the store, as a clerk and interpreter," said the consul turning to Moromoto. "He will send a letter by the same boat to his manager."

"Sir" said the young officer, "We are greatly indebted to you—." "Not at all" interrupted the consul, I am glad to serve you. Mr. Dives is an excellent gentleman. You can depend on his word. I think your friend goes on the steamer this afternoon. His wife can join him at the wharf."

Moromoto again expressed his thanks and bowed himself out. He did not know whether to be glad or sorry, but he knew his duty. So he went to the hotel to tell Faza. He found her sitting on the veranda dressed in a pale blue Japanese gown. It was a rare sight to see her sad face brighten at the good news.

He did not tarry beyond his errand and promising to come for her in the afternoon.

Faza began at once to pack their effects in the trunk and two valises they had purchased at Yokohama. When Moromoto came she was quite ready. He had paid the hotel bill. She never thought of it. The baggage was put in a hack and they drove down to the water front.

There were two great pens fenced off on the wharf. There was a gate and by the gate a kind of box or office. Two men sat in the window of the box; one was a foreigner and one a Japanese.

The pens were full of Japanese immigrants. The interpreter called out a name from the book before him. The owner of the name crowded to the gate and was let out. He passed along a row of policemen and as he passed the window the interpreter gave him a large paper. He then went on into the next pen which was alongside a small steamer.

Faza and Moromoto stood by the luggage and watched the stream of people file past. They waited some time; at last Faza cried out, "Oh there he is!" Sure enough Nyama strode out, head down, hands in his pockets, looking dejected but full of wrath. He went up to the office window, his eyes flashed, he was about to speak. He heard a little cry—"Oh Nyama" and his wife was hanging on his neck. He gently took her arms away. "Not in public," he said.

"Oh, Nyama," she said "It is all right I am going with you. Your friend Moromoto did it all, you will have money and everything, oh I'm so glad!"

The interpreter interrupted them—"Here take your contract," he said, "and go on through that gate." "Go on the boat," said the man in the box, "send the wahine around the other way; we don't want to get them mixed."

Faza drew back and joined Moromoto. They went around to the other side of the second pen, there was a gangway to go on board of the steamer. They went on board. He sent a waiter for the luggage. The immigrants were going into the hold. They saw Nyama go in with others.

"Oh! Let me go down to him," said Faza. "No" the escort said, "I will go down and bring him up." He descended a narrow stair way; at the bottom he found Nyama bent on coming up but prevented by a man who guarded the way. There was a lively altercation, but the man was immoveable. He would let no Jap go on deck. So the officer had to return and tell the little woman on deck that she must go below to see her husband. They went down and Faza went in, but the man stopped Moromoto.

"You better not go in if you don't want to go along. I might not know you from a Jap when you wanted to go out. No Jap leaves this steerage."

Moromoto pressed a little package into her hand "give that to Nyama. I will see if I can get you out of this place," he said, and left her.

She saw Nyama sitting on a fishkeg not far from the door. She ran to him and laughing and crying told him what had happened since he had been arrested. Nyama listened sullenly and gravely. She held on to his hand. It was so nice to be near the dear fellow; she would not let him go. After a little he told her to sit down on the keg.

"Oh, there is only one. You sit down—I will sit on your lap," said the lady with a blush and a persuasive smile. Every body will be looking," he replied smiling back and squeezing her hand. "I am not tired," and he put his hands on her shoulders and gently forced her to sit down. How delightful was the thrill of his touch!

"Oh yes," she exclaimed, "here is a package for you, Moromoto just gave me."

He took it and unwrapped the several papers and at last came to a nest of coin—five twenty-dollar gold pieces.

"Well, what a fellow! he knows I would not take his money—but it might be useful for you, dear I think I have about fifty dollars left,—I suppose I will not get any more from my father. Well, I will pay it back to him."

They talked on and on absorbed in each other. The steerage was rapidly filling up with people, dirty and tired from their long journey, carrying their blankets and cooking utensils. Still they kept coming. Many were reading and discussing the "contract" they had received. At last there was barely standing room. Suddenly the hole in the ship's side was shut and it was almost dark.

AUTHOR UNKNOWN. *"A Romance" was a long-running serial that appeared irregularly in the Honolulu newspaper* Ka Leo o ka Lahui *in the early 1890s. Three of the paper's four pages were in Hawaiian, one in English. "A Romance" is from the English-language page. Early episodes were by "Uncle Beke;" later ones were by "Anonymous." This episode is from the Anonymous period.*

Elma T. Cabral
"THE IRRESISTIBLE HENRIQUE"

Angelina's tired eyes followed the last boatload of baggage approaching the ship. The well chiseled profile of a head silhouetted against the feeble light of dusk caught her attention. All eyes turned to watch the figure climb the ship's ladder as nimbly as a cat. A gust of wind caught the girl's overskirt and lifted her on to the ship's deck. She was very young,—a *solteira*, perhaps.

Angelina would not be distracted from her purpose. She spied a large familiar basket being hoisted to the bow of the ship. She held her breath as it descended too quickly with a loud thump. *"Minha louca!"* she cried unable too suppress her anxiety. Then she sat heavily on her little basket of personal luggage. It was too late to fret over the broken china which had been a family heirloom. She untied her bonnet and bared her face to the wind. How it soothed her aching eyes! She could hear the wind catch the sails as the ship moved out of Funchal Bay.

She was glad she had made the decision to join her father in the "Sandwich Isles" where he enjoyed a comfortable living as a harness maker. It was good to leave sorrow and adversity behind her and it was good she deluded herself, to leave Henrique, her god-child. His unconventional behavior had been frowned upon by the austere matriarchs of the elite neighborhood where her life had been in constant turmoil since the absence of her late husband's firm hand. The Army would discipline him and she was relieved that he had been conscripted. But she would miss worrying about him, she admitted, facing reality, for Henrique had given purpose to her void existence as a widow.

Memorable episodes flashed across her mind as she lay tossing on the hard bunk which would serve as her bed for five long months. A soothing voice accompanied by a familiar guitar sounded from afar and acted as a sedative to Angelina. She could not escape this haunting voice and she was glad of it.

A knock on her cabin door frightened her into consciousness and a man's voice called out to her in the early dawn. The ship's steward asked her to come out on deck. He directed her to the hold of the ship where she waited breathlessly until he held the lamp over a handsome head bent over a guitar. "*Meu Henrique!*" she cried embracing him fondly. An unruly lock fell over his forehead and the upturned corners of his irresistible mouth broke into a shameless grin. "But how did you get here?" she asked.

"I was born to be a musician not a soldier," he answered. "Besides I have no taste for Africa. Gabriella, *meu amore*, smuggled me to Madeira. We saw you leave on the rowboat and I called out but you didn't hear me. I recognized your large basket and I emptied it of its contents. The darkness was kind to me as was Gabriella who accompanied me on board."

Now Angelina was resigned to the realization that she could never escape Henrique. "We will put him ashore in a few days at the Azores," the steward announced, trying to look stern.

"*Nao,*" Angelina cried. "My father, he 'ave business *no* Sanwich. He pay money, you wait, please," she pleaded in the faltering English that she had learned from the English patrons of her husband's hotel. The steward hesitated, then relented and led Henrique to the deck for chores, and then reported the incident to the captain.

The unrestrained romance between Henrique and Gabriella gave zest to the long dull voyage with its many privations, especially for the immigrants who had been contracted to work on the sugar plantations. Both Angelina and Gabriella had fared better than the plantation workers as they were private passengers. When the card games lagged, Gabriella charmed the men with the enchanting ballads she had sung so well in Lisbon to the accompaniment of Henrique's vibrant *viola*—sometimes she would entertain them with a dance of pursuit she had taught Henrique. She would don her favorite costume with the low fringed shawl collar and wide circular shirt cuffed with a straight band which opened into a wide umbrella, as she turned, revealing well molded underpinnings, too slender for Portuguese standards. Henrique would follow her every mood. *"Volta!"* the musicians would call. The couple clicked their fingers twisting and turning their lithe bodies as only young dancers can.

"Linda faticeira!" one of the men was heard to exclaim in admiration of her dark beauty which she had inherited from her Moorish ancestors who had held Portugal in captivity for so many years.

"What is she doing on this ship unchaperoned?" some of the women gossiped like jealous fish wives. Whispered rumours spread into greater proportions in spite of Angelina's efforts in Gabriella's behalf. "She comes from a family of *fadistas* who make their living as entertainers," she explained. "Their standards of behavior are unlike ours. When she sings she dramatizes the characters she is portraying with feeling. She will join her aunt, a *curadeira*, who makes a good living by enhancing her therapeutic treatments with fortune telling."

Gabriella was quick to sense the women's disapproval of her and she vindicated herself by retaliation. She sang a seductive *fado* in a minor key with her dark sultry eyes half-closed directing her subtle remarks to her more susceptible male targets who responded with quickening breaths as though they had been victimitized. Then as the tension soared high she rose abruptly and leaving her admirers panting she muttered coyly to Henrique, "I am trembling with cold." This was his cue to follow her to the stern of the ship.

"You enchanting witch!" he repeated crushing her in his arms. "You were a seething volcano a minute ago. Now you say you are cold! Your bewitching *fados* become you in the tavern but they are unsavory to this small group of conventional women. You will have to live with them for a long spell," Henrique chided her.

"I am unaccustomed to singing into the eyes of tigresses intent on tearing me to shreds," she sulked. "Women are not seen in the taverns of Lisbon and that is as it should be." When she saw the corners of Henrique's irresistible mouth break into an amused grin she replaced his unruly lock and kissed him on his forehead.

After five weary months they glided into Honolulu Harbor. Rosa do Canto and Francisco de Lima were there to greet them. Francisco was surprised to see Henrique with Angelina. She told him how Henrique had stowed away in her basket and the old man chuckled.

"And how do you propose to pay for your passage?" Francisco prodded, fondling his beard.

"Com os dentos," Henrique joked pointing to his fine set of teeth.

"He can work for you as an apprentice," Angelina suggested.

Soon after his arrival Francisco ordered Henrique to deliver a harness to Kalika. "He owns the taro patches in the valley. You will have no trouble finding him," he explained.

Henrique hung his guitar on the pummel of his saddle and started up the winding road. He arrived at noon and Hawaiians were huddled around a mango tree practicing on their newly acquired *rajaos* which they called the taro patch fiddle. Henrique dismounted and in no time he joined them with his *viola*. He readily won their admiration and with little coaxing he sang the ballads of his homeland.

"Welakahau!" they shouted loudly in wild acclaim. He asked for Kalika and a plump young girl offered to take him to her father. Lehua showed him a little instrument she called the ukulele. "Ukulele?" Henrique repeated quizzically. "In Madeira we call him *braginha*," he revealed. Lehua struggled to say the word and she ended up giggling hysterically. "Sometimes we call him *machete*," he added and she repeated it with little effort. Lehua's natural uninhibited charm fascinated Henrique and his visits to the valley became more frequent. She taught him the language and songs of her people and he was an apt scholar. She told him that she was descended from a long line of ancient hula dancers who came from Haena and that she was being chosen by King Kalakaua to become a member of his hula troupe. The king had adopted the ukulele as the new accompaniment o the hula. The court dancers would be personally trained by him. Then Lehua would lay her curly head in his lap while he serenaded her with his Portuguese songs.

Sometimes Henrique was asked to join a group of musicians led by a Portugese ukulele maker to play for the King. He discarded Gabriella for his newly found *wahine*, much to Angelina's anxiety.

"Gabriella is getting thin," she remarked one day to Henrique.

"She should eat poi instead of *milho*," he answered apathetically, "Lehua is *una mulher perfeita*," he added, describing her generously padded torso. "She does not frustrate me as does Gabriella. She gives freely of her love and she delights me with her good humor."

"Be cautious with those native girls," Francisco warned him. "Their acts are influenced by *kahunas*, the most deadly kind of *cobrante* for which our *faticeiras* have no antidote. Sometimes it is fatal!"

It was Lehua's birthday and everyone had been invited to her luau including Tia Rosa and Gabriella. Tia Rosa had won the family's esteem when she prescribed an effective cough syrup she had made from watercress juice and honey for old Tutu. Lehua had become a frequent patron upon learning of Tia Rosa's skill at fortune telling.

"Where did you put my ring?" Henrique asked his god mother on the eve of the luau. "I can't recall," Angelina answered suspecting his motive. Henrique was a dashing figure in his embroidered bolero and red sash. Gabriella also wore her favorite costume and they made a handsome pair. Their elders tried to stimulate conversation between them with little success.

Having been acclimated to the Hawaiian foods Henrique indulged in their delicacies with delight. *"Come o porkinho"* he encouraged his elders, dunking a fat piece of pork into the poi. *"Consola!"* he drooled, licking his sticky fingers.

"Many a neighborhood dog disappears preceding a luau," Francisco joked solemnly in his native tongue. "Heaven knows the origin of this *porkinho!"*

"O que nao mata emgorda," Henrique answered, disregarding the old man's distasteful revelation. ("What doesn't kill you will fatten you.")

As the festivities advanced Henrique and Gabriella were called upon to do their native dance. While the Hawaiians sat transfixed with a curious delight, Angelina perceived their that movements were mechanical and their eyes lacked their usual fire.

Lehua performed one of her most seductive hulas with unsurpassing grace and charm. Gabriella saw a new gleam in Henrique's eyes. Lehua invited a young man wearing a shark's tooth necklace to join her.

"There go my grandmother's teeth!" Francisco quipped giving those who understood the language a hearty chuckle as the necklace was brought to their attention. Henrique sat entranced by Lehua's fascination. When she called him to join her, he obliged charmingly, mimicking her and adding a *volta* now and then to delight his audience.

"It is a vulgar dance." Gabriella remarked at the conclusion of the hula.

"They are a happy fun-loving people," Francisco replied, "and our Henrique has won their hearts. That boy is irresistible!" Angelina was glad that she had misplaced Henrique's ring.

That night Henrique became ill and he grew progressively worse. "That native drink must have contained a *kahuna*," Angelina said.

"Perhaps my dog story is taking effect," her father chuckled.

"We shall see," Angelina replied as she prepared the test for *cobrante*. She poured water into a saucer. Then she let a drop of oil fall into the water. The drop remained intact! "It is as I thought," she exclaimed in alarm.

Henrique's discomfort increased the next morning when the neighborhood pigs were led from their sties squealing and grunting. It was the first pre-Christmas event. They were given wine to dull their senses and the noise decreased. The operation was done skillfully and quickly. The fat was saved for lard, the blood and some of the meat for sausage and the rest of the meat for pickling. It was cut into chunks and put in large mason jars to marinate in a vinegar sauce with red peppers, garlic, bayleaf, cloves, and salt until Christmas morning when *Carne da vinho ailho* would grace their breakfast table.

The women spent the day preparing *bulo de mel*, a delicious honey cake with fruit and spices including pepper. Enormous sponge cakes were baked as well as *braoas* and *rosquilhas*, Portugese sugar cookies. *Tramocos* were boiled for hours, after which they were drained and left under a dripping faucet for five days. Salt would be added to the water before the lupins were ready to eat. Angelina prepared a generous supply of these goodies so that there would be enough left over for *O Dia De Reis*, the last day of the holiday festivities.

Henrique did not rally and much to his reluctance he had to submit to Tia Rosa's treatments. She massaged his abdomen with oil and applying cabbage leaves she bound him tightly, reciting prayers as she worked. When he fell into a deep sleep she searched for a clue. The unruly brown lock had been cut!

Angelina found an unmistakable black curl among his belongings, which she gave to the practitioner. "With evidence such as I have and with the help of my cards I am confident that my *cobrante* will overpower the *kahuna*," she said. "As for that little brown witch, I shall take care of her when she comes for a reading," she added tying her brightly colored kerchief on her head.

As soon as Henrique was able he mounted his horse and rode to the valley. Lehua did not seem happy to see him and her behavior was elusive. He offered her a little token which one gives to someone he esteems in his homeland. When she saw the little crisp roasted pig's tail tied with a ribbon she thought he was playing a joke on her. "*Pupule boy!*" she said, laying it aside.

Henrique was hurt. "This is a token of my love for you," he explained with appropriate gestures.

"*Auwe!*" she replied, ignoring his remarks. My *Pake* boy bring me *hum lum*, my *Kanaka* boy bring me *opihi*, you *Pokiki* boy bring me pig tail!" She sniffed at it approvingly and commenced to chew on it muttering, "*He ono.*"

"I was very sick, Lehua," he reminded her. She was not concerned and neither would she respond to his manifestations of endearment.

"Pretty soon I make long trip with Kalakaua hula troupe," she boasted. I dance for *alii*. My fortune card say I marry rich man. He give me rich present—not pig tail! *Pilau!*" she teased spitting out the tiny bones and rumpling his hair.

Henrique would take no more and pushing her aside he galloped away furiously while Lehua giggled. Never had he been spurned thus before. "I should have given her *una torcedo dos orelhas*," he reflected, regretting that he had suppressed an impulse to twist her ears.

"Henrique is in such a depression," Angelina remarked to her father. "His *viola* remains in its case and his mouth droops."

"Never have I seen him work more quietly and diligently," he answered. "He has lost his taste for Hawaiian music. *Ill levou o sabao!*" he chuckled, twisting the lobe of his ear. The "soft soap" was a favorite expression associated with "being jilted."

"Tia Rosa's *cobrante* has triumphed over the *kahuna*," Angelina exclaimed joyously.

Henrique helped Angelina unpack the precious little figurines that would adorn their *lapinha*. When she unwrapped the last figure a head rolled off. "Baltazar!" Henrique cried remorsefully. Baltazar was a favorite childhood character who filled the boots of good children with gifts on Christmas morning. The little wiseman had withstood many generations and he aroused nostalgia. Angelina brushed a tear from her cheek as she attempted to mend him.

Henrique brought in a large rock for the grotto which he placed on the tiered table. The *Meniho do Jesus*, the center of interest was placed on the top of the rock. Wisemen bearing gifts stood at the foot of the babe. Sheep, cows and chickens were arranged around the cradle. The shepherds with their sheep were placed at the top of the table. Then came the chicken vendors and the milk men. A village band played at a little bandstand. A procession wound its way up the lower slopes of the rock. Little earthen pots of wheat and maize having been sown on the eighth of December mingled around the figures. Lovely ferns and maiden hair were banked at the back of the rock making a delightful contrast to the dark background.

On Christmas Eve tiny cakes, crab apples, oranges and chestnuts would be placed around the figures for the children. Little colored oil lamps would be lit before the shrine and left until the 6th of January, The Day of Kings.

After midnight mass on Christmas Eve, Gabriella and Tia Rosa stopped at Angelina's for chicken soup. Henrique was unusually quiet and shy. Gabriella appeared to be cold but she suffered in silence. Angelina managed to take Tia Rosa, her ally aside to tell her of her success.

It was the eve of the *Dia de Reis* and Angelina could hear the musicians approaching her home. The group was armed with brooms as it was their custom to go from house to house during this week literally to "sweep out the cupboards." Bottles would be emptied and the remains of the cake eaten. They were dressed in their carnival attire with masks. If only Henrique could be persuaded to join them, Angelina mused. As yet there was no sign of reconciliation and he chose to remain in solitary confinement.

The revelers were now at her door and they sang;

Vamos cantare os reis,
A porta dos nossos vizinhos;
"Se nao tenho nada pra me dare,
Dame o rabinho do porkinho!"

(Let us sing of the Kings,
At the door of our neighbors;
"If you have nothing to give me,
Give me a roasted pig's tail!")

The next stanza was sung by a familiar feminine voice;

Vamos cantare os reis,
A porta dos nossos vizinhos;
"Dame un coupinho de vinho,
Porque eu estou tremendo com frio!"

(Let us sing of the Kings,
At the door of our neighbors;
"Give me a glass of wine,
For I am trembling with cold.")

This familiar cue lured Henrique to the doorway and the corners of his mouth curled once more as he removed her mask and drew Gabriella into the house holding on tightly to her cold eager hands.

"I am sufficiently warm," she winced. While the revelers "swept out the cupboards" the lovers composed verses to add to their collection of songs of the Kings.

The last *bulo de mel* was cut and Gabriella was given the first piece.

"My gold crown!" she cried, as she bit into a hard shiny object.

"Meu anel!" Henrique shouted gleefully as he took his long lost ring from her hand and placed it on her finger. The last bottle of wine was poured for a betrothal toast.

"That was a clever trick, Angelina," Henrique whispered to her after the wine was drunk. Angelina looked baffled and stood speechless, oblivious to his remarks.

"Ah, now I remember where I hid your ring," she blurted, erasing the frown from her forehead. "In the flour can on the top shelf!" . . .

ELMA T. CABRAL, *born in 1909, was educated at the Territorial Normal School in Honolulu and University of Hawaii Teachers College. She was an elementary school and special education teacher. She directed the Kapālama Puppeteers, and wrote Portuguese folklore stories and articles for* Paradise of the Pacific; HONOLULU *Magazine; the* Honolulu Advertiser; *the* Honolulu Star-Bulletin; *and* School Arts, *a national magazine. She wrote a children's book,* Awapuhi, *an original story about how the ginger got its name.*

J. A. Owen

from OUR HONOLULU BOYS

Y ou need not suppose that this Honolulu is a perfect paradise. In fact I once heard a little boy call it Horrible-lulu. Sometimes it is so hot there that it makes both big and little children ill-tempered, and so tired that they are a weariness to themselves and to each other; and though there are no snakes, there are centipedes and scorpions, for which people have to be on the look-out.

A very favourite resting-place of the ugly, many-legged centipede, is the nice cool, damp sponge which you use for your bath. So you see there are unpleasant things to be on the watch against everywhere, both inside and outside of us. That very stream which seemed so delightful, and down which the boys could sail their little boats, was a great source of trouble sometimes, as you will presently hear.

It was seven o'clock in the morning; the boys had just finished breakfast and were eager to begin what to them would be the pleasantest part of the day. At nine o'clock Fred generally went to school, but to-day he had a holiday, because it was his birthday. He was very happy, his father had given him a first-rate tricycle which had three wheels under a body like a horse's, fitted with a neat little leather saddle. It was the first of the kind, just imported from the United States, and when Mr. Anderson went out to try it with him, on the smooth valley road, quite a crowd of admiring natives and Chinamen gathered round them. Ever so many of the families living near had to wait for their breakfast in consequence; for in the Sandwich Islands the natives can get their living so easily that they consider they do you a great kindness by working for you for twelve and even twenty shillings a week.

Besides this tricycle, Fred had a splendid scrap-book from his mother, which she had filled for him, so quietly and privately, that not one of the boys had seen it till that morning. And his two uncles had given him a boat which he could sail down the garden stream, and even in the quiet waters of the sea, inside the coral-reef; also a gorgeous Chinese kite, with a tail longer than that of the wildest dragon they ever painted; and Wing Sing was to be allowed to help him to fly it, when his cooking operations for the day would give him time.

The boys knew he was sure to have a good time with them, for all the big Chinamen love to fly kites; it seems to be a part of their celestial propensities.

"Come on, boys!" cried Fred, when he was tired of the first attempts at riding his tricycle; "let us go and try the boat; and, Mamma, may Keoina leave his work and come and help us?"

"Keoina is not in the garden, nor doing any work," said Ernest; "he's gone to be married. I heard him tell Uncle Will this morning he was; and he asked him if he would give him a new paper collar to put on to go in, and Uncle Will laughed, and asked him if that was all he wanted."

Becky, the sewing woman, offered to go. She was a good-natured, round-faced native, who had been trained at one of the Mission schools, but who, nevertheless, loved better to play in the sun, even with little boys, than to work; but Ernest said disdainfully, "We don't want you; you're only a woman, and don't know anything about boats."

The stream was very full and lively that day; it had been raining heavily up in the mountains during the night.

"Take care, boys," said Mamma; "and Fred, be sure and look after little George and Johnnie. Remember, too, that it is tabu (or taboo, as some write the word), to go over to the other side of the stream."

This tabu, which means a thing forbidden, was a great grief to the boys. They had no little sisters; and over the fence, which was on the opposite bank of the narrow stream, was a beautiful garden, kept by a Portuguese nursery-man, named Antone, who had three very lively and talkative little girls, with bright brown eyes and curly hair. Every morning these three would come to the fence and look out for the boys, often putting their hands through the rails with pieces of pine-apple or cocoa-nut cake to tempt them over. Once or twice Fred and Ernest had got into sad trouble by first springing across the stream, and then creeping through a hole in the same fence, in order to have a game in the next garden. The little girls were not naughty children, but the bank on the other side was narrow and steep, and there was a great danger of falling back into the water, after jumping across it. The two younger boys were never allowed to go near it without their nurse; but today she was so busy helping Mamma to get things ready for the birthday party which was to come off in the afternoon, that Johnnie and George were entrusted to Fred, who was generally a very careful boy, and proud of having charge of the two little ones.

The boat sailed splendidly, the stream was quick and the water smooth; the only tedious part of the fun was that when it got down to the end of their garden it had to be taken up and carried back to start on another voyage down; and they were always so eager to have it on the water again that they made themselves very hot with running.

"Don't let us sail it any more here," said Ernest at last; "we know it does it all right, so let us wait till father can take us down to the wharf, and out in the boat inside the reef; it will be jolly to sail about after it."

Author Unknown

"CHING CHONG AND HIS HANA"

1.

There was a kanaka in Oahu did dwell,
Who had for a daughter a monstrous fat gal;
With a very big income of poi and kukui,
And there was a young Pake she loved nuinui.

2.

The old makuakane was down on the match,
Because the young Pake had no kalo patch,
And he told her in case she did anything rash
She shouldn't eat poi out of his calabash.

3.

Now as Hana was pounding some kalo one day
Her makuakane came up to her and thus he did say
Go dress yourself Hana in bright turkey red,
I've selected a kane and you shall be wed.

4.

O makua makua do you think I'm a greeny
I'll never consent to be that man's wahine
And even a luau I'll gladly give o'er
I'm bound to be single and that is pau loa.

5.

Hele oe cried makua don't be so unruly
Oe kaikamahine nui loa no pupule
I'll give all my waiwai to some other keiki,
If you don't wed this kane and that wikiwiki.

6.

Now as Ching Chong was walking Nuuanu around
He found his poor Hana sitting dead on the ground,
With a calabash of poi lying by her side
And a palapala stating by poison she died.

7.

Then Ching Chong he blubbered and called her is Ducky,
Auwe auwe oh why did you make.

He kissed her cold corpse akolu times o'er,
Then finished the poi and died crying fer more.

8.
Then the coroner came with his twelve haole men
And seated themselves on those two corpses then;
They set there all night and the whole of next day,
Then rendered a verdict which read maipake.

9.
At twelve the next night near a coacoanut tree;
Makua, Ching Chong and his Hana did see;
He took them for messengers from the old scratch,
And drowned himself in his own kalo patch.

10.
All you kaikamahine's who've heard this sad song
About the aloha of Hana and Chong.
Take care your makua's are never huhu,
Or you will certainly meet pilikia likepu.

Author Unknown

"MAKALAPUA"

Eia mai au 'o Makala-pua
Hō'alo i ka ihu o ka Lanakila

O ke ku'e a ka hao ka i Kūwili
I ka ihona 'olu iho a 'o Hālawa

Ua lawa ka 'ikena i ke awa lau
Iā 'Ewa i ka i'a hāmau leo

Ua pua ka uwahi a i Manana
Aweawe i ke kula a 'o Waipi'o

I kai ho'i au o Honouliuli
Ahuwale ke ko'a a 'o Polea

Haʻina ʻia mai ana ka puana
O Liliʻuokalani nō he inoa

"MAKALAPUA"

Here am I, Makalapua
Going where the Lanakila points

The piston works at Kūwili
Then down the gentle grade to Hālawa

Satisfying is the sight of the locks
Of ʻEwa (land) of the "silent fish"

The smoke rises at Manana
Goes over the plain of Waipiʻo

I go down to Honouliuli
There the coral beds of Polea are exposed

This ends my song of praise
In honor of Liliʻuokalani

TRANSLATED BY PUAKEA NOGELMEIER

Lydia Kamakaʻeha Kaʻōlanialiʻi Neweweliʻi Liliʻuokalani
"KA WILIWILIWAI"

E ka wiliwiliwai
Koʻiawe i ka laʻi
A he aha kāu hana
E naue mālie nei?

hui
Ei nei, ei nei, e poahi mai nei
Āhea, āhea ʻoe kāohi mai?
Oki pau ʻo ia ala
Ua ninihi ka lawena
Kuʻu iki iho ʻoe
I inu aku wau

"O WHIRLEY WATER"

O whirley water
Gentle rain shower on the move
What do you think you're up to
Circling, twirling so quietly

chorus:
There! Yea yea coming up! As you revolve
Will you, will you hold still?

Amazing the way you take over
Irresistible
Come, slow down a little
So I can take a drink

TRANSLATED BY PUAKEA NOGELMEIER

LYDIA KAMAKA'EHA KA'ŌLANIALI'I NEWEWELI'I LILI'UOKALANI (1838-1917) *was the eighth and last ruler of the Hawaiian kingdom. Highly influential in the musical culture of her people, she was a talented instrumentalist and composer, writing lyrics in Hawaiian, set to Western melody and harmony. Many of her songs were published during her lifetime; more than 150 survive; a good number have been recorded and are performed today, including "Aloha Oe."*

Pamela Ball

from THE FLOATING CITY

S hrieking evangelicals beat tin drums and lit fires in small black kettles that were meant to represent hell. Young children crouched down and threw geckos and centipedes into the flames, and watched closely as the creatures disappeared in a wiggling flash of smoke, while above them the evangelists, tendons jumproping across their necks, remained blind to the actual hell expanding at their feet.

Eva was amazed by the beauty of the women, and how so many of them were streetwalkers. She'd never before seen salvation and prostitution in such close proximity.

What did she feel? Free. She was a stranger walking down a strange street in a town no one could find her in. Everything that had hurt her was left behind, on the other side of the world.

She carried a newspaper with an advertisement for a room for rent. By mistake, she arrived at a home for retired sailors, a dilapidated cottage with a tin roof and ferns growing out of the rain gutter.

Tomas sat on the lanai with a rooster on his lap. He told her the rooster's name before he said his own. "Lucky," he said, holding up the bird that was strangely calm in his hands. "Since no one has eaten him yet," he added with a toothless smile.

Eva held out her newspaper and showed him where she had circled the advertisement.

He cleared his throat. "I never knew reading," he apologized. "Tell me what it says."

A single woman with rooms to rent to women.

"Ah, that's Lehua. Next door. Let's see. Women only, and no Americans."

"I'm not American," Eva said. "I'm Norwegian."

He stood up and the bird fluttered to the ground. "I never took you for an American," he assured her.

She found the path through the hedge and met Lehua, a Hawaiian woman whose smile lifted the edges of her mouth like Aladdin's lamp.

There was an orphanage for Hawaiian girls across the street, and old whalers next door with a pet rooster. There was the Widow, locally famous for outliving all her husbands and winning the orchid show every year for the last twenty-two years, and a shamisen player who made enough racket to drive away the living as well as the dead. There was Lehua, who was half out of her mind with grief and opium, and for the first time in her life, Eva fit right in.

Or so it seemed at the time. Now everything had changed, as if she'd fallen asleep in one country and woken up in another.

Outside the brothels, the bamboo cages were haphazardly stacked against the walls. The cages were crowded with birds and small animals, some noisy with fear, others struck dumb with lassitude or ill health. A birdcage filled with mynahs was placed just above the cage of a mongoose, ensuring a complete frenzy. On the sidewalk, a chimpanzee's small hands shot through the bars of the cage to grab hold of Eva's skirt as she passed by. The brothel owner smiled at her shocked reaction, and with the tip of his boot he prodded the cage a little farther into the street.

It reminded her of Tomas's story of the whale who lifted its back out of the sea and was mistaken for an island. He hadn't told the girls from the orphanage the rest of the story. The sailor's anchors caught like hooks under the flesh of the whale, and they lit fires to cook dinner. When the whale felt the heat of the fire, it dove down and dragged the sailors and their anchored ships after it.

Along this street the fires had all been lit.

She passed a streetcorner missionary, a thin man wearing a shiny coat and a pair of boots for a man twice his size. "It's in the air," he proclaimed, "Honolulu is rampant with wickedness."

He shook his finger at her purple skirt, her loose hair, glaring down with a face as mottled as the inside of a biscuit, and she sensed that the evil he'd previously attached to the air of Honolulu had now found a new target.

As she came closer to Edward's office, the street widened. Alongside the road, small trees were planted in measured intervals and picket fences skirted the tidy lawns of the missionaries.

Their grand houses were the sort that as a child Eva had imagined herself living in one day, before she knew how wildly unsuitable her family was, with their gypsy colored clothes, their reputation on them like a smell they could not wash away.

But what of the luxury of these houses, the true cost of the chandeliers that trembled around the Horn, the wood that was carried out of the forests of the Philippines on an old man's back, the tablecloths that sent an Irish lacemaker into blindness? Eva rejected that world. Edward was embracing it.

When she'd first moved to Honolulu, she'd noticed Edward in a bar one night. She watched him cheating at cards and getting away with it. He looked up, saw Eva watching him closely, winked, and sent a drink her way.

At that time, he was a bartender, and also a procurer. He arranged for his customers to have whatever they could afford to pay for. Opium, prostitutes, gambling. Since then, he'd moved into politics, claiming that it was the same game, dressed up in finer clothing.

His office was at the end of a row of modest wooden buildings. An older woman sat against the wall on a small lauhala mat spread over the dirt. Eva recognized her as the woman who moved her produce up and down the street, seeking the coolness of shade. Today she had four lilikois for sale. Why only four? Eva crouched down and picked out the yellowest fruit and paid the woman.

Edward's outer room was empty except for a row of benches and broken umbrellas leaning against the wall. She knocked on the door to his office and without asking who it was, he told her to wait.

She sat down on a bench against the wall, willing herself to appear at ease. Trouble was as easy to smell as poverty, and Edward wanted nothing to do with either.

Eventually, the door to his office opened and a woman with a florid face and disheveled hair walked past Eva, pretending not to see her.

Edward was at his desk, busy copying figures into a ledger. Seeing that it was Eva, he set down his pen and regarded her fondly.

"Edward," she said. "You will never change."

"I hope not," he answered happily.

"Who is she?"

He held his finger to his lips and they both laughed.

"I miss you, Eva," he said suddenly.

Eva smiled. "Yes, I can see that. You appear miserable."

She set the lilikoi down on his desk. "Here, this is for you."

He picked it up. "How thoughtful of you. What is it?"

"It's a lilikoi, Edward. A fruit with lots of seeds. Makes a delicious juice."

"Ah, I see. You realize that you are supporting the woman who begs outside my office."

"She's not begging, Edward. She's selling fruit."

"Sure she is. So, how are things with you? How is Lehua? Still smoking opium?"

"Not at all," she lied.

"No?"

"Hasn't touched it in weeks. And yourself, Edward. How is the political life?"

"Good, but at the same time very peculiar. The politicians here? They'd think this country was paradise if they could just figure out how to get rid of the Hawaiians."

"That's disgusting."

"It is, isn't it? I've never seen anything like it." He shrugged. "Do you have any idea, Eva, how many young daughters these missionary politicians have? And all of them looking for husbands. White husbands, mind you. Only haoles. No Hawaiians need apply."

"And you are ingratiating yourself."

"I certainly hope to. You may find them disgusting, but Eva, think of how powerful they are. Think of the money."

Eva nodded. She had.

"They control more of this country than you think." He shook his head. "They even call themselves Hawaiians now. It's insidious." He laughed and pulled a cigar from his pocket.

She preferred Edward back when he was a gambler, a cardsharp who would lift money from the pocket of a sleeping drunk and buy a round of drinks for the house. To her, it was still more honest than politics.

"But I am not here just to visit, Edward."

He pretended to be surprised. "No? Eva, I hate to bring up old business, but I should remind you that you still haven't paid me back from the last time."

"Well, yes. But you know my business is seasonal."

Edward smiled, enjoying her discomfort. "Is it, now?"

"You have my word that I'll pay you back."

"Yes, that's my fear. I have your word. Not much to go on."

"How is business, Edward?"

"Unfortunately, these are slow times for me as well."

Eva sighed. "You always do something peculiar with your neck when you're lying—did you know that, Edward? I can't quite say what it is. Your Adam's apple moves about too much."

"Do I?" He laughed, placing his hand over his throat. "I'll have to watch that."

"Lehua has promised to include me in the Queen's weekly card games. It will help tremendously. I'm sure to find many new clients there."

"What the Queen needs isn't a fortuneteller or a card game. She needs an army. This government has tied her hands behind her back, and they're still scared of her."

"They should be," Eva answered.

"They are spreading the worst sort of rumors about Lili'uokalani. They're even saying that . . . "

Eva held up her hand. "I don't want to hear rumors," she interrupted. "They say whatever they think furthers their cause. It only makes them appear stupider than before."

"Don't underestimate them, Eva." He set his cigar in the ashtray. "You realize that things are heating up. Be careful which side you're standing on."

"I don't stand on either side, Edward, and neither do you."

"True enough. We might be the only two people in Honolulu who aren't pretending that this country belongs to us. But enough of all that. What's on your mind?"

"Edward, we've helped each other out quite a few times in the past," Eva began.

"Not always successfully," he answered, but he was smiling.

"No," she agreed, "not always."

"You got caught, didn't you? What has happened, Eva?"

"Nothing, really. I mean, I've done nothing. There is a situation, though."

"A situation."

"There are lists of the dead, aren't there?"

"Yes, the police would have that information."

Eva waved that idea aside. "I don't want to involve the police."

"Always a good policy."

"The other day I went fishing, down along the coast. And I found a body."

"A body?"

"A man. Washed in from the sea." Eva paused. If she told Edward that the man had been strangled, he wouldn't help her at all. Not for murder. "He was a young man," she continued, "or maybe middle-aged. Mostly Hawaiian, but perhaps a little Chinese. He had long black hair. He was handsome," she added, surprising herself.

"A handsome dead man, really?" He leaned forward, interested. "If he was Chinese, what rights he has are negligible. In this town, if you find a dead man you'd better pick his race carefully."

"Edward, you sound like one of them."

"I do, don't I? It starts to rub off on you. But why should a dead Chinese man concern you?"

"I don't know. He just does." She couldn't tell Edward that there might be a reward, because he'd try to claim it for himself.

"Was there anything on the body? Anything in his pockets?"

"I didn't look."

He raised his eyebrows in disbelief, knowing she'd never let an opportunity like that pass by.

"So, another drowned man," he shrugged. "Someone who drank too much or smoked too much opium and fell into the sea."

"Yes, it appeared that way at first. But when I took the police to where I'd left the body, it was no longer there."

"So who cares about a missing body?"

"Generally, no one does, at least in this town."

"So why not drop it? Or is there something else?"

"Well, yes. The policeman came to my house the next day. A follow-up visit, I suppose. Except that there was another person with him."

"Eva. Just tell me what happened."

"The other man was a politician." She told him about the policeman and the politician coming to her home. All of it except the jade necklace.

"Why would a politician be involved?"

She shrugged. "I don't know."

Edward stood up and moved to the window. "Unless," he finally said, "the dead man was a Royalist. In which case it could be murder. No wonder they're paying attention to you." He sounded worried, and she knew he wouldn't help her if it would hurt his career.

"I don't know who the politician was, he didn't give his name," she lied.

"What did he look like?"

"A haole man with skin like a jellyfish." That much was true, at least.

"Sounds charming. Do you remember what party he was with?"

Eva shook her head. There were more political parties than she could keep track of.

"This sounds like trouble," he warned.

Eva was suddenly exasperated. "I did not kill the man, Edward, I just found him."

He leaned forward, placing his hands on the desk. "Does it matter? You are connected."

"No, I am not. They want me to be connected, which is what I don't understand." She paused. This was the moment for Edward to offer to help. But why should he? "Edward, couldn't you ask a few discreet questions, try to find out something?"

He gestured towards his papers. "As you can see, I'm quite busy. Tell you what, when I find the time, I'll look into it."

She sighed. The cautious Edward had taken over. It was probably better not to ask about boat fares. That would have to wait for a more opportune moment.

"This town is heating up," he said, motioning her towards the door.

"You repeat yourself, Edward. And I think you worry too much."

"And you clearly don't worry enough."

On the street Eva saw a prostitute she knew well, a woman who had been one of her steadiest customers until the birth of her son. You know what your future is now, Eva had told her at their last meeting. The woman assured Eva that she would not be long in the business, which was what all the prostitutes said, but often they were supporting entire families and couldn't afford to quit.

Today she proudly held her palms apart to show how much her baby had grown. As they hugged goodbye, Eva felt the bones in the woman's back, knowing that the venereal disease that had already taken so many Hawaiian women was now claiming her as well.

An uneasy feeling came over Eva. She turned and looked back at Edward's office.

He was standing in the doorway watching her, and when their eyes met he nodded slightly before ducking back into his office. She realized that he wasn't worried for himself, he was worried for her.

PAMELA BALL *was born and raised on Oʻahu. Her novels are* Lava *and* The Floating City; *her other books include* The Power of Creative Dreaming *and* The Great Book of Spells. *She lives with her family in Tallahassee, Florida.*

Alfred R. Calhoun

from KOHALA OF HAWAII

T here were guards all along the road to the racetrack; but vigilant though these men were, they could not prevent the silent, swarming spies of the Queen from watching and reporting on their movements.

To-night there was less secrecy than heretofore. Both sides felt that the time for action had come, and that the next twenty-four hours would settle whether Hawaii was to be free or to remain under the arbitrary dominion of a monarch who, of her own volition, or through the ill-advised influence of some of her ministers, had chosen to ignore the rights of her foreign-born subjects and to trample under foot the accepted constitution of all her people.

To Kohala, who kept by Colonel Loring's side, it seemed as if the young leader had entirely changed his character since they rode into the darkness from the Hawaiian Hotel.

Ordinarily, Colonel Loring was the embodiment of courtesy; indeed, he was distinguished for his easy, graceful manners and the entire calm and self-possession of his bearing; but while the latter had not left him, he was now quick and peremptory in his manner. His voice had in it a ring that insured obedience, and his every act told of a brain-directed energy that stirred his men and filled them with confidence, for soldiers, in or on the eve of action, ever admire a commander who can command.

Kohala expected that the colonel would form his men into companies and march them directly down on the arsenal and storm it, if it were not at once surrendered; but in this he was disappointed.

Through a swarm of orderlies who stood ready to do his bidding the colonel assembled all his subordinate officers, and, as in the darkness he called each man by name, he gave him his special orders and saw before he retired that he understood them without fear of mistake.

As each subordinate was given instructions and told where he must assemble his men in the city, and what he was to do when the bells pealed forth their signal, he started off promptly to enforce the command.

In less than half an hour after their reaching the rendezvous, so perfect had been all the preliminaries, the organized troops, in small bodies and by different routes, were marching into the city.

"Now we are ready," said the colonel to Kohala, "let us ride back."

"But there are only a few men with us," said Kohala, as he looked about at the half-dozen silent, mounted men who remained behind.

"We have all we need now," said the colonel, calmly; "when we need more, depend on it they will be forthcoming."

They turned back to the city, the glow of whose lamps looked blood-red on the lowering clouds.

The other horsemen fell in behind, but not a word was spoken. The time for talk was past, and the hour for action had come.

The horsemen halted in a churchyard back of the palace and not a pistol-shot from the Hawaiian Hotel. Here all dismounted, and they found men awaiting to hold their horses.

"Keep by my side, Kohala," said Colonel Luring, as a man came up with a dark-lantern and asked:

"Are you ready to go up, sir?"

"I am," said the colonel; "lead the way, Phipps."

The man with the lantern unlocked the church door, and, when the colonel, Kohala and the two men who were to act as a signal corps had entered, the door was closed again and the slide of the lantern thrown back, so as to show the winding stairs leading up to the steeple and belfry.

The steeple ended in a tower in which hung a bell, and as soon as the party reached the little platform at the end of the last stairs the light was hidden again.

Kohala looked over the rail, and the gas lamps and electric lights revealed the city at his feet. By the glare of the lamps before the Parliament House he could see the heroic gold and bronze statue of his famed ancestor, King Kamehameha, and his heart was stirred to emulation of that great chieftain's deeds.

The palace seemed to be wrapped in darkness; even the two lamps at the great entrance gate burned with a duller glow than usual.

The Hawaiian Hotel was, in contrast with its stygian surroundings, fairly ablaze with light, and Kohala could see the silhouettelike figures of men moving swiftly across the illuminated spaces.

Down by the piers and out in the harbor he saw the colored lights that marked the port and starboard sides of warships and merchant ships at anchor; and far out beyond all these he saw the phosphorescent glow of the breakers on the barrier reef and he heard the incessant and rhythmic booming that followed their recession and advance.

After this survey he faced to the north. In that direction lay the Punch Bowl, from which the expected signal was to come, and in which direction every face was turned.

But absorbing though the situation was, Kohala could not remain indifferent, even under such circumstances, to the one object that he could not banish from his mind. Soldiers on the battlefield, with the thunder of guns and the crimson carnage of death about them, have been carried in imagination back to the days of their boyhood, when they gathered wild flowers in the woods or followed the droning wild bee to her hive; but there was nothing so startlingly psychological in the thoughts of Kohala.

"If it were day," so he reasoned, "I could see the cottage where she lives." She was to him so bright, so self-luminous, that he felt pained to think that she must be in darkness, for he could not see the glimmer of a light in or about the place where she lived.

From his reverie—and in love reveries time flies fast and unnoticed—he was roused by the low hum of the voices about him, and he heard Colonel Loring saying to the man with the dark-lantern:

"Phipps, have you a watch?"

"Yes, sir," was the reply.

"Step down where the light cannot be seen and let me know what time it is."

Phipps descended the steps some distance, a flash of light came up and vanished, then he reappeared and said:

"It is just half-past eleven, sir."

"Another long half-hour to wait," said a man beside the colonel.

"Have patience," was the young soldier's laughing response. "You may have more to do than you can well attend to before the night is over."

"Ay, faith," said Phipps, who spoke with the accent of an Irishman, "and it may be that the man who'll live to see daylight may find himself dead."

Another man was about to speak, but checked himself, for suddenly a light flashed out from the dome of the palace and it lit up the standard of Hawaii.

This was unusual, for it had been the custom to lower the flag with the sunset gun, and Colonel Loring was more than ever confident that the Queen's adherents were on the alert, and that the hour for action had come.

Following the appearance of the flag above the palace a cheer, or, rather, a shrill yell, came up from the streets, and the pounding of galloping hoofs could be heard.

At this juncture a man, who had made his way up the dark stairs, found Colonel Loring and said:

"I am ordered to report, sir, that there is a great crowd of natives gathering about the palace."

"We must expect that. How about the arsenal?" asked the colonel.

"There is no change there, sir."

"Very well. Report to our friends to stand ready for the signal. They will hear it and see it within ten minutes."

The man crept down again, and the quick fall of his feet was still echoing in the steeple when an exclamation burst from the men whose faces had been peering northward for what seemed to them an interminable time.

"They've lit the beacon!" cried one.

From the head of the Punch Bowl a fountain of flame leaped into the sky, transforming the picturesque hilt into a volcano, as it had been of old.

"Make ready the rockets, Phipps," said the colonel, his voice as calm as if there were no crisis at hand.

"All ready, sir," was the response.

Higher and higher rose the flames from the crest of the Punch Bowl, and again the shrill cheer came up from the direction of the palace.

"It's gone again!" cried a number of men, unable to suppress their excitement, for the fountain of flame died out as suddenly as it had appeared.

"Have the matches ready, Phipps."

"Ready they are, sir."

A few seconds of intense darkness over the Punch Bowl, then, like a pencil of light drawn swiftly against the black background of the night, a rocket rose up toward the lowering clouds, curved gracefully downward, then exploded, and was followed by a shower of globes, red, white and blue.

Two more rockets followed in quick succession. Then Phipps, under the colonel's orders, struck a match, and three rockets, with scarcely an interval of time between their appearance, shot up from the belfry and exploded directly over the palace.

"The bell, Phipps!"

The bell began to clang at once. A deep, hoarse cheer rang up from the streets. From tower and steeple other bells clanged out the alarm, and down by the shore there was seen a flash, followed by the ominous booming of a gun.

"Now for the arsenal! Keep close beside me, Kohala!" said the colonel, as, with lantern held high above his head, for there was no longer need for disguise, he led the way to the ground, while the bell kept up its clanging as if it had gone mad or was being rung by a madman.

"Keep the horses here; we shall not need them at present," said the colonel, to the men waiting below.

There was no excitement in his voice and no sign of nervousness in his manner, yet Kohala, who kept close to his side as he ran for the arsenal, could see by the light of the lamps past which they dashed that there was an awful, an unconquerable earnestness in the young soldier's face.

There was not a policeman to be seen. At the sight of the rockets from the steeple and the first clanging of the bells the bravest of them had vanished.

Bugle calls and hoarse commands down the side streets where the volunteers had been impatiently waiting, the quick tramp, as of trained soldiers, the galloping of orderlies and the frightened cries of women and children in the houses, told that the revolution, so long dreaded by the people of Honolulu, had come.

Colonel Loring took a position near the arsenal, but Kohala noticed that, since leaving the steeple, he had not issued an order, nor was there any occasion for his doing so. His orders were given in advance, and so perfect were all the details that his subordinates promptly marched their men to the places that had been assigned them, and there halted till they should hear the bugles sound for the assault on the arsenal.

Although the Queen's adherents had long been expecting this very thing it came upon them with all the force of a surprise, for their work was checked in its very inception by Colonel Loring's signal corps.

Had the beacon been permitted to burn on the hill for twenty-minutes, as its designers intended, the native force and the foreigners who took the side of the Queen would have rallied at the palace and marched at once on the arsenal. But the extinguishing of the light and the red glare of the rockets, with the answering rockets from the steeple, and the clanging of the bells, with the sudden movement of large bodies of armed men along the streets, had a most demoralizing effect on the men who, but one short hour before, were so confident of success that they expected to see every objectionable American on the warship *Boston* the following morning.

With his drawn sword grasped firmly in his right hand Colonel Loring, now reasonably well assured that he was master of the situation, advanced to the main door of the arsenal and knocked for admission.

After waiting long enough for a response without receiving any, he rapped again, saying, at the same time:

"Open at once, or I shall break in the door."

"Who is there?" asked a man in the voice of a native.

"I!" was the response.

"Who are you?"

"Colonel Arthur Loring, of the Provisional Army."

"I know no such man nor no such army."

"Then you had better make our acquaintance. Come, my man, I am in no mood for parleying."

"But I was placed here with my men to protect the Queen's property," said the man.

"There is no longer a Queen in Honolulu," answered the colonel.

"Where is Her Majesty?"

"There is no such person as Her Majesty. Will you open?" and the colonel beat on the door with the hilt of his sword, while a dozen brawny men appeared with a beam which they proposed to use as a battering ram.

"Hold up! we surrender!" cried the man from within.

Following this, lights were seen inside the building, the massive door was opened and the native soldiers and a number of natives with a few white men, all armed, came out, one at a time, and by the light of the improvised torches of Loring's men they laid down their weapons and were placed under guard.

Again a bugle sounded, and the company that had been detailed to take charge of the arsenal after its surrender marched in while the others fell into line like veterans, and, with the colonel at their head, advanced quickly toward the palace, not many hundred yards away.

There was no longer a guard before the entrance. The lights were extinguished in the great hall, and a timid Chinese gardener met the colonel at the steps and said:

"The Queen, she not here."

"Where is she?" asked the colonel.

"She go way."

"Where to?"

"Me not know," whined the man.

"Go up," said the colonel, to one of his men, "and take down the flag of Hawaii."

ALFRED R. CALHOUN *was born in Kentucky in 1844. He fought for the Union in the Civil War. He wrote short stories and novels, based on a plan he devised for plotting, which enabled him to turn out books at high speed. He dedicated* Kohala of Hawaii *to King Kalākaua.*

Seward W. Hopkins

from TWO GENTLEMEN OF HAWAII

"**H**ave you heard anything?" I asked, anxiously.

"Not definite. I received word from a scout, just a few minutes ago, that a band of natives were encamped at the extreme end of the valley, and were performing some of their old-time deviltries—idols, sacrifices and all that. There is going to be a great dance tonight, and a sacrifice offered to the goddess Pele, or some other heathen deity, to obtain help in restoring the queen. We will take a file of soldiers and witness that affair, and see who is to be sacrificed. The daughter of a Portuguese sailor is missing, and a French girl who was a servant in the family of Mr. Seldon. The fanatics must have one of these or Winnie. Whoever it is, we will save her."

With about twenty soldiers we started off up the Nuuanu Valley. We travelled as rapidly as our horses could carry us. The soldiers were mounted on horses from a livery stable, the popular idea among those who saw us start off being that we were a scouting party looking for hidden enemies.

At the end, or rather, the beginning of the Nuuanu Valley, it opens out into a wide plain bordered by forests. It was moonlight when we reached the place. Not a living thing, human or beast, could be seen.

"We will leave our horses here in charge of four men, and go through the woods to Lake Maliwai," said Gordon.

Cautiously we made our way through the trees. We wanted to surprise the camp.

"There they are," whispered a soldier, pointing to an opening in the thick growth of bushes and trees around us. Through it we could see a camp, on the border of the lake.

Stealthily we took our position to watch.

We looked upon a strange, fascinating, horrible scene.

A group of natives, probably two hundred in all, sat or squatted upon their haunches, in a large semicircle, in the center of which burned a fire. On either side of the fire was a hideous idol or heathen god. These gods, while still holding a mysterious power in the minds of the older natives, had of late been seldom seen. There may have been, perhaps, fifty or a hundred of them in Honolulu, but they were closely guarded by their possessors. These horrible extravaganzas in wood and lava-stone were supposed to be omnipotent.

Under the unusual excitement that had existed so long in Hawaii, all the old superstitions were revived, and the natives descended to their former level of idolaters and stone-worshipers.

"Keep quiet," said Gordon, to the soldiers. "Let us watch them."

There were men, women and a few children. But little clothing was worn. The fanaticism under which they were working had discarded clothes.

The entire crowd were putting their bodies through various methodical contortions, all in unison, and they chanted a weird, solemn dirge that had not been heard in Oahu for many years before.

One, a high-priest, stood out before them, painted and adorned most hideously, and led the ceremonies with contortions and chantings more violent and weird than the others. His long brown arm would outstretch toward a portion of the semicircle, and that section of it would throw themselves upon the ground and beat themselves, calling aloud the name of Liliuokalani. It was evidently an invocation to the gods to restore the queen.

The priest made a detour of the worshiping line, touching first one then another upon the head, all the while emitting horrible cries, groans, shrieks, to the chant they kept up constantly. Those so touched arose and followed him, throwing their arms about, rolling their eyes and mimicking their leader, and, if possible, outdoing him in awful noises. Gradually this procession increased and the excitement of the crowd increased also. The leader struck into a wild, fantastic dance, and those following took it up. Then they who still remained in the semicircle beat the air with their hands, smote their palms together and emitted strange cries.

Larger and larger grew the circle and fiercer grew their passion.

Suddenly, the dancing column having grown to over half the number of worshipers, it came to a pause. The followers of the priest stood trembling, quaking with excitement, their feverish thirst for religious extremes shown in their bloodshot eyes and panting bosoms.

Apart from them was a tent. To this tent the priest danced slowly, his worshipers keeping up the chant and standing expectantly, as if something desirable were to come.

The priest emerged from the tent, carrying a small white kid.

He took up his old position near the fire, and facing his horde of fanatics, he chanted solemnly over the kid. Then, putting it on the ground, he drew a knife across its throat, catching in a cup the blood that flowed from the stricken innocent. The kid gave a bleat and fell over—dead.

Now the fervor was at its highest.

The priest took the cup of blood, and dipping his finger into it, anointed his followers on the forehead, as he danced along the line. They howled, shrieked and groaned most horribly. The women, losing all control of themselves and casting aside their reserve, threw themselves out from the circle and performed wonderful feats of writhing, twisting and suggestive contortions.

All the time the subject of their chant, the sole idea in their shrieks and cries, was the restoration of Queen Liliuokalani. The sacrifice to the gods was to propitiate them and make them smile upon the deposed queen. I felt a sensation of chilly horror when I looked at these fanatics. If their bloodletting sacrifices stopped short of human blood it would be a gratifying surprise, so ferocious did they look.

The dance began again, more fervid than before.

The priest stooped down and picked up the dead kid.

He chanted a prayer, and threw the carcass on the fire, saying as he did so: "This is but the offering before the feast," and kept on his way. The smell of roasted flesh filled the air, and seemed to enhance the ardor of the fanatics.

Again the dancing procession stopped, and again the priest waltzed off toward the tent. This time he took another with him.

They were in the tent some few minutes, and then emerged, carrying between them a burden. This burden was covered by a large white cloth, but it seemed to be a human body on a litter.

Now there was a surprise for us. Behind the two natives walked Captain Pericles Jobbs, solemn, stern-looking, dressed in the uniform of the rank he had once held.

"Jobbs!" whispered Gordon. "What can it mean?"

"St!" I said. "We will soon see."

The priest and his helper were greeted with louder chants than ever. They laid down their burden and the priest commenced the dance again.

The crowd were now insane with their consuming passion. They filled the air with cries of Liliuokalani. Jobbs stood stolidly looking on, but even in his eyes there was a look of insanity.

The priest waved his long knife in the air and exhorted his followers to further efforts in dancing. This was necessary, for some were even now dropping from exhaustion.

Then the fierce-looking priest made several passes over the covered body, and, stooping down, raised the cloth and flung it aside.

"Great Heavens!" ejaculated Gordon, seizing his sword.

"Can it be Winnie?" I cried, my throat parched and my tongue almost refusing to act. "See! He will kill her!"

"Forward, men!" shouted Gordon. "No life there is sacred but the girl's!"

A soldier stopped, raised his rifle and took aim.

We could not reach the priest before he had committed his act. He turned and saw us. With a fierce cry he made a sweep downward with his cruel knife, his face working with passion.

"Fire!" shouted Gordon, forging ahead.

SEWARD W. HOPKINS *is the author of* Two Gentlemen of Hawaii *and* In the China Sea.

Ellen Blackmar Maxwell
from THREE OLD MAIDS IN HAWAII

O n the veranda stood one whom Belinda at once thought the knightliest man she had ever seen. His presence seemed to enlarge the veranda and give the cottage the dignity of a mansion. He was bidding some people goodbye, so the driver drove around the circle in front of the cottage that the other carriage might pass out.

"It is a face and figure to choose for the head of a great undertaking, providing the undertaking be worthy," said Belinda to Rose in an undertone, influenced at once in favor of a government which had such a leader.

The president stood waiting in the midst of palms and ferns, flecked with sunlight which filtered through the trees and gave a bright touch to the picture framed by the veranda. As they descended from the carriage and mounted the steps he bent his head in kindly courtesy and greeted them as though having found old friends. . . .

The long, hard work on the new constitution was over, and the day was at hand when it was to be promulgated and the republic proclaimed. Island-born white men side by side with kanakas, American-born white men and half-whites, all had worked in a common effort to evolve a form of government necessarily more or less an oligarchy, which should cover every distinct element of the varied communities of the various islands. It had been difficult to do this and also to provide for every exigency of a little nation liable any moment to be taken under the protection of its foster-mother, or to fall into the maw of the power which, like the grave, is not satisfied, but ever cries, "Give, give," or to be overpowered by an influx of orientals and sink quickly into an Asiatic colony.

They had found it difficult, and many had concluded that only the wisdom of all the ages could handle such a problem satisfactorily, and daily, yea, hourly, while the constitution was in the process of formation, had prayers gone up to the Source of all wisdom, invoking help to arrive at just and righteous conclusions.

Now the work was finished, and, true to the conserved spirit of "'76" in these hardy and stanch people, the old Independence Day was chosen for its adoption.

The morning dawned in gladness to many, in anxious fear to some, and in depression to others. But the morning itself, all joyous, came flinging rich color, bright sunshine, and fresh odors down upon the islands. The waves murmured a glad orison on the Reef, the trade winds sounded a solemn anthem down the valleys and through all the trees, and the banks of white clouds which ever rest above the horizon seemed to have washed and made themselves new in the ocean spray, so white they gleamed in the sun; and the golden shower tree swung its long sprays of solidified sunshine in the wind as though ringing golden bells of joy for the pleasure of existence and in honor of the day.

The passing observer would have said there was not a hint of anything save absolute joyousness in all the island; but there were shadows; the very presence of all this light and joy told this.

Among the people who had stood fearlessly for right and truth there were women who feared for their husbands and sons, and those who feared for their lovers, but not one who would have held back an instant, even though she had thought a bullet would come out of the crowd and find the heart of the man she loved.

It was a tense, terrible time, and yet it was borne with sweet smiles and kindly courtesy from Republican to Royalist and from Royalist to Republican.

Notwithstanding the kahuna's prophecy of death and the fact that there were men who had sworn to take his life before the republic was born, the president had slept well.

He had not sought the high office; he belonged to the people; and if for the rights of the people it became necessary that his life be ended, it would make no difference.

The red dog, as the kahuna had foretold, was found dead at daybreak on the steps of the church. There was no mark on him by which the manner of his death could be told, and the doors of the church stood wide open; but the sun shone bravely over the town, which was literally covered and hidden by red, white, and blue bunting, and on Washington's portrait, a little more wooden than ever, which looked down from a large building on the crowd that was beginning to throng the streets. The wind flapped the bunting on stores and houses and on, the men of war, decorated not for the independence of Hawaii but for the independence of the mother States, and brought faint snatches of music from scattered bands here and there through the town. At eight o'clock the people were massed in front of the palace, where the president's gray head, towering above the crowd on the steps, was the center of all interest as he read the constitution and proclaimed the republic, which for good and sufficient reasons had been chosen by the people as the form of government for the future.

The strong, clear voice carried the message down on the waiting air into the hearts of the people, who, whether white or olive or brown or darker brown, had only one attitude toward the one who stood before them, the attitude of reverence for the man, reverence for his message, and belief in the new republic which he was proclaiming. Later doubt and fear might come, but in his presence there was naught of them.

Ah, now is the time for the bullet to come out of the crowd, or soon it will be too late, and the republic will exist. Does the hand falter, or is the bullet only one of the many vagaries of the kahunas?

But it comes not, and the handsome, open-faced native member of the convention repeats in Hawaiian what has been read in English; then with uplifted hand the strong voice of the president calls: "God save the Republic!" and then comes a cheer from the crowd as of one voice; not a wild cheer of triumph, not a threatening, vindictive cheer, but a solemn ring of voices as in a fervent and great amen to an invocation. Now there is a salute of twenty-one guns and the playing by the band of the national air of Hawaii.

After the oath of office was administered by the chief justice the people thronged up the steps to give their hands in friendship and sympathy to the man who stood as their chosen ruler.

There were tears in many eyes—in the eyes of men whose hands had been in the breast of their coats as the proclamation had been given, ready to avenge the bullet if it came; in the eyes of women who were as ready as their husbands to defend the republic; gentle men and gentle women, quiet, meek-eyed, God-fearing and neighbor-loving, but made of the same stern stuff that fought out their rights in the days of '76.

"New occasions teach new duties;" they had learned them well, though in pain and sorrow.

"Once to every man and nation comes the moment to decide."

It had come, this moment, and their homes, their lives, their honor, all were at stake; they had chosen, and by their choice they would abide, ay, even unto death. That hour the former queen, sitting quietly in her house, knew that the bullet had not come and the republic was born and lived; knew that the "Mene, Mene, Tekel, Upharsin" of the old monarchy had been written, the monarchy of which she still, had she had nineteenth-century instincts, would have been constitutional queen. More, she knew it was indelibly written, and not to be erased by new plans in accordance with the age, and, hardest of all to bear, she knew that it had been written by herself.

The throng, having grasped the hand that was in future to lead them, poured into the palace that they might take the oath not to do anything calculated to overthrow the new order.

When white and dark had thus declared their loyalty, all dispersed as quietly as from a morning service at church. Some drove through the streets and along the water front for a prolonged view of the decorations, which Rose said were "more Fourth of Julyish than anything she had ever seen before, for there was a perfect delirium of stars and stripes." Others went quickly to the wharf, where launches waited to take them to the American man of war from whence they were to view boat and swimming races. Still others hurried away to a draped pavilion in the park where the American minister, assisted by Americans and Hawaiians, was to celebrate the day as became the envoy of his country.

There were orations and music, and all was bright and gay; and the American atmosphere, always the breath of life to Belinda, made her glad. It was refreshing to her to be in a place where it was good form to celebrate the old wornout Fourth. It was refreshing and comforting, after the Anglomania in America itself, to be in a place where America was a name to conjure with; to be where no nation on earth was thought to be so fine, so grand, so true, so right as America, and where people lived in hopes, if not eventually of being a part of the greatest big nation, at least of making their own the greatest little nation on the globe.

It occurred to Belinda, who loved the American flag and firmly believed it would bring the millennium to any country over which it floated, that if anarchists and iconoclasts were to increase in numbers and power in America that nation might in future times be forced to refer to this little Hawaii in order to learn what her original principles were, to see what the rock was like on which Columbia had built.

The orators of the day were all that could be asked; there were free lunches inside a tent for dignitaries, and outside for the crowd, where the kanaka drank lemonade with as much satisfaction as though he was under the old *régime*. Adventurers were there, too, and ate sandwiches and drank lemonade, thinking it was a pretty good government to be against.

The Portuguese husband was also there with his numerous family, and bought candies in moderation for them of the Chinese sweet vender, and let his daughter take a turn in the dance on the platform, and thanked God for comfort and peace.

Here, too, was the Jap, in his best coat and smiles, taking his saki later, as the German did his beer, down town. . . .

ELLEN BLACKMAR MAXWELL *was born in Kansas in 1851. She wrote two novels about missionary life in India, where she evangelized with her husband. Widowed, she came to Hawai'i for a few months on a publisher's commission to write about the place, and the result was* Three Old Maids in Hawaii.

Sally-Jo Keala-o-Ānuenue Bowman
from NĀ KOA

C racker followed Jack along the back way to Waikīkī. They kept their horses at a walk. At Kapi'olani Park, white buildings and fencing gleamed sharper than the high moon. From the dark beyond the buildings, five other horsemen joined them, and a dozen men followed on foot. At the beach junction Cracker saw two bands of men coming up Waikīkī Road.

The army was forming! The Queen's secret army! At last he would be fighting on the right side. He thought of the night he had seen the Queen at Washington Place, of hearing her piano music drift through the open window. He thought of all Sammy and Lehua and Jack had told him, how the sugarmen had stolen Hawai'i. Now he felt big, strong. And proud, to stand for the kingdom.

The pointed peak of Diamond Head at the end of Waikīkī towered flat and black and sharp-edged. He and Jack had climbed it, twice. It was as dry as Punchbowl, its steep outer slopes sliced by ravines.

They rode closer and closer to Diamond Head, until, at its foot, they could no longer see the top. Their destination sat in the shadow of the peak: a secret weapons depot. A place he had not been told of until just now—Bertelmann's. Jack said Bertelmann was not quite so important as Wilcox and Nowlein, but he was one of the leaders the *Pacific Commercial Advertiser* called "half-castes." It didn't sound nice, Cracker thought.

In twos and threes, men carried rifles in and out of Bertelmann's sprawling house. A lamp glowed through the front downstairs window and Cracker saw furniture, a piano, and two guitars hanging on the wall. Two men stood leaning over a table.

Jack motioned to dismount and they led the horses around the house and tied them to coconut trees on the beach side. Beyond the yard, Cracker saw surf breaking, frothing white in the moonlight. He and Jack joined dozens of men in a large canoe shed. They had moved the outriggers out onto the grass to make room for cases of rifles, which they were now cleaning. The sharp, metallic clatter of actions being tested drowned out any sound of the night surf.

Cracker followed Jack's lead and joined the labor. Talk was that the men would be ready in about two hours, then they would march for Honolulu, picking up forces along the way at other secret stations, other homes that had volunteered to hide weapons. By the time they reached town at daylight, they should be 600 strong. Six hundred! More than enough to occupy all the government buildings. The troops that had backed the overthrow had numbered less than 200.

The lantern hanging from the top beam in the canoe shed sputtered. Smoke curled under the leaf-thatched roof, its oily stink mixing with the cleaner smell of solvent rubbed over rifle barrels. The lamp flickered its last and went out.

"Eh!" A Hawaiian nudged Cracker. "Haole boy. Try go inside, get one can kerosene."

Cracker knocked on the back door. No answer, though he could hear voices. He stepped into the entryway and peered into a large kitchen. He wished someone would come. It didn't feel right, barging into Bertelmann's house without someone answering the door. After long minutes, a man strode to the sink and began to work the pump handle.

"'Scuse me," Cracker said.

The man looked up. "Eh, I never went see you. You like?" He held out a glass of water.

"They sent me for kerosene. The lamp in the shed is out."

"Come-come." The man led the way through the kitchen, down a hall-way that smelled of new wood, and into the front room, where three men sat around the table.

"Henry," the man said. "Where you get—"

The front door slammed open and the door-way filled with enormous uniformed figures.

"Police!" one of them shouted.

The first two moved farther into the room and Cracker stared into the black hole of a gun barrel.

"Search warrant! No one move!" The police fanned into the room, scanning it with their revolvers.

Like the rest of the royalists, Cracker froze. All he could hear were the sergeant's boot heels on the wood floor.

Outside, a shot cracked. Then another. Then a volley. Inside and out, the air burst with shouting, running, the zip of bullets flying, the ominous thump of lead shattering wood.

And the icy jingle of breaking glass. Cracker's face stung and he put his hands to his cheeks. The wetness smeared red in his palms. Another shot rang through the broken window and the top part of one of his legs turned into a rolling wall of pain.

Cracker fell into the shards of glass. Boots and bare feet ran over him and he choked on gunsmoke and his own blood.

SALLY-JO KEALA-O-ĀNUENUE BOWMAN *was born in Honolulu in 1940. A Kamehameha Schools graduate and holder of BA and MS degrees in journalism, she taught writing for twenty years at the University of Oregon. Her essays, poems, and magazine articles on Hawaiian topics have won writing awards in Hawai'i and the Pacific Northwest.* Nā Koa: The Warriors *is her first novel. She also is the co-author of* No Footprints in the Sand: A Memoir of Kalaupapa.

S. Pinao
"HOOHUIAINA PALA KA MAIA"

Auhea wale oe kahi Palaama,
Hoohuiaina pala ka maia,

Hapapa hewa ana ou maiuu,
I ka pahu hinuhinu a Paleka,

E kala no au i aku ai,
He aloha aina na Hawaii;

Pehea mai nei kahi Kakina,
O ka moo nihoawa hoowalewale;

Ua like pu oe me Satana,
Kepolo nui o ke ao nei,

Auhea wale oe e Kawainui
Ua paa ko maka i ke kepau,

Paulele oe i ka mikanele,
Aihue aina makakeleawe,

He keu oe a ke aloha ole,
I ka hae aloha a o Hawaii nei,

Ka makou ia kalokalo nei
E mau Hawaii la i ka pono;

Hainaia mai ana ka puana,
Hoohuiaina pala ka maia.

"ANNEXATION IS RIPE BANANAS"

Listen up, O Palaama
Annexation is ripe bananas

Your claws grope in vain
For the glistening box Paleka offers

Long ago I proclaimed
That the Hawaiians are patriots

What about that old Thurston
That deceitful and poisonous snake

You are a peer of Satan himself
Greatest devil of the world

And what of you, Kawainui
Your eyes seem to be glued shut

You put your trust in missionaries
A brazen bunch of land thieves

You are completely lacking affection
For the beloved flag of our Hawai'i

This, then, is our constant prayer
That justice will keep Hawai'i steadfast

The story is made known in the telling
Annexation is ripe bananas

TRANSLATED BY PUAKEA NOGELMEIER

Lydia Kamaka'eha Ka'ōlaniali'i Neweweli'i Lili'uokalani
"QUEEN'S PRAYER"

'O kou aloha nō
Aia i ka Lani
A 'o kou 'oia'i'o
He hemolele ho'i

Ko'u noho mihi 'ana
A pa'ahao 'ia
'O 'oe ku'u lama
Kou nani, ko'u ko'o

Mai nānā 'ino'ino
Nā hewa o kānaka
Akā e huikala
A ma'ema'e nō

No laila e ke Haku
Ma lalo o kou 'ēheu

LILIUOKALANI'S
PRAYER AND SERENADE

Composed by

Her Majesty

DURING HER
IMPRISONMENT
BY THE
REP.
Gov! of Hawaii.

Sung with Great Success

BY THE

Royal Hawaiian

GLEE CLUB

ON

ITS TOUR OF

THE WORLD.

WASHINGTON, D.C.
PUBLISHED BY SANDERS & STAYMAN, 1327 F STREET.

Courtesy of Bernice P. Bishop Museum.

Ko mākou maluhia
A mau loa aku nō
'Āmene

"QUEEN'S PRAYER"

Oh Lord thy loving mercy
Is high as the heavens
It tells us of thy truth
And 'tis filled with holiness

Whilst humbly meditating
Within these walls imprisoned
Thou art my light, my haven
Thy glory my support

Oh look not on their failings
Nor on the sins of men
Forgive with loving kindness
That we might be made pure

For Thy grace I beseech thee
Bring us 'neath thy protection
And peace will be our portion
Now and forevermore
Amen

TRANSLATED BY PUAKEA NOGELMEIER

Robert Louis Stevenson

"TO PRINCESS KAIULANI"

Forth from her land to mine she goes,
The island maid, the island rose,
Light of heart and bright of face:
The daughter of a double race.
Her islands here, in southern sun,
Shall mourn their Kaiulani gone,
And I, in her dear banyan shade,
Look vainly for my little maid.

But our Scots islands far away
Shall glitter with unwonted day,
And cast for once their tempests by
To smile in Kaiulani's eye.

Written in April to Kaiulani in the April of her age; and at Waikīkī, within easy walk of Kaiulani's banyan! When she comes to my land and her father's, and the rain beats upon the window (as I fear it will), let her look at this page; it will be like a weed gathered and pressed at home; and she will remember her own islands, and the shadow of the mighty tree; and she will hear the peacocks screaming in the dusk and the wind blowing in the palms; and she will think of her father sitting there alone. —R.L.S.

ROBERT LOUIS STEVENSON (1850-1894) *is the celebrated author of* Treasure Island; Kidnapped; *The Strange Case of Dr. Jekyll and Mr. Hyde;* and *The Ebb Tide, among many other works. He was chronically ill, and spent much of his adult life traveling for his health. He came to Hawai'i on a chartered yacht in 1889. He dined and drank with King Kalākaua, visited the leprosy settlement at Kalaupapa on Moloka'i, and passed pleasant hours with Princess Ka'iulani at her family home in Waikīkī. His last years were spent in Samoa. He is buried high on a mountain there.*

Miss Piper

13

3

To Princess Kaiulani

Forth from her land to mine she goes
The island maid, the island rose,
Light of heart and bright of face:
The daughter of a double race.

Her islands here, in southern sun,
Shall mourn their Kaiulani gone
And I, in her dear banyan shade,
Look vainly for my little maid.

But our Scots islands far away
Shall glitter with unwonted day
And cast for once their tempests by
To smile in Kaiulani's eye

John Dominis Holt
"PRINCESS OF THE NIGHT RIDES"

Riding at full gallop through the darkened streets offered a powerful sense of freedom—of utter release from the mundane, the common, the plodding. Scented air, cooling wind, and unrevealing darkness combined deliciously to fill her spirit with a moment's relief from a sustained and gnawing melancholy. A shadow of emptiness—of a massive ennui—had settled upon the princess's life. The regimen of training at the schools in England, befitting an heir to a throne; the august watchfulness and stately admonitions of Mr. Harrington Thorpe, her guardian abroad, offered little now to subdue an enormous restlessness—an increasing wildness of heart.

Time and again recently, she had taken her little mare, Damozel, on nocturnal galloping sprees through the night-lit, silent streets of Honolulu. The mare was a tangible link with England—a horse of Arabian strain, given her by an admirer. She had brought the splendid animal across the world's two great oceans and the whole stretch of North America—from east to west—to her home in the Islands of Hawaii. "What a beautiful horse! She will ride in our parades! What a spirited animal, as befitting the Princess Victoria Kaiulani as her garden at Waikiki!" some of her people had said. Now, one of her greatest pleasures was to ride into the night when it was cool. After spending seven long years in the wintry temperatures of Northern Europe, she found the languid tropical air of her island birthplace almost intolerable. It was a luxurious joy to ride in the sunless dark of the night.

Rumor of her nightly riding excursions had spread through the town. The sophisticated foreigner smiled and passed off the rides laconically as just another expression of aristocratic eccentricity. The native whites, who had recently seized the government from the princess's aunt, interpreted her behavior as another proof of monarchical decay. Caustically, they might say: "How unlady-like! It's something a common native would do—if they dared to go out at night! Is it any wonder we took the government out of their hands?" Her own people awoke with the sound of galloping hooves, and, knowing instantly the mount and its rider, they grieved. Theirs was the knowledge of kinship; and their concern was from the heart. They were of one thought: "She is troubled! Our princess grieves for Hawaii!" Their lament was: "Aloha ino o kau wahine alii pio, pua ui loa ka aina!"

Her father, an aging Scot, now given over to much brooding and silence, looked upon these nightly rides with an unyielding disapproval. They were at variance with the dream of perfection he had nurtured for his daughter from the moment of her birth. They were irascible, aberrant—befitting the hoyden or irresponsible half-witted empresses, but not the stately young woman, the Milo Venus in her beauty, whom he had sired and sent to his mighty England to be rigorously trained within "the royal set" for the role of leadership. Some "sensible" people agreed with her father. The incredible beauty of the princess, her intellect and refinement, combined, they said, to make the spectacle of her furious night rides a thing of strangeness.

But no one made light of these erratic nightly excursions—not even the foreigner with his knowing and sly appraisal—for in them there was an element of regal fatality. They contained a heavy and uncomfortable reality; they were unexpected and strange—perhaps even ghostly, like the schools of red fish that had swarmed into the quiet waters of Honolulu Harbor a few weeks before the last king of Hawaii, her mother's brother, "Uncle David," had died. The night rides exacted their toll of response from listening ears. Some grieved; some smarted with the prick of guilt; some made cynical allusion to "royal decadence" and the like. Everyone reacted.

Giving into the demands of a towering will, the princess galloped in the darkness and let the cooling winds of night bring passing comfort to her tormented body. "I find the heat more oppressive than the annexationists," she wrote her aunt, the ex-queen, who was in Washington. "My body is covered with rash, and I sometimes find it difficult to breathe. I ride at night, on occasion, to Nuuanu. The trade winds are lively there, and give me the only relief I've known from the oppressive heat. I guess I am no longer a native Hawaiian in this respect; my body is at odds with the warm air of the tropics."

In the subdued and balmy darkness of another island night, she was riding once more on the narrow road leading from Waikiki into the sleepdrenched town of Honolulu. Words and images tumbled in her thoughts, like waves breaking one upon the other at Kaalawai. She had brought the mare out of a hard gallop and subdued her, chafing, into a walk. The animal breathed hard. "Easy, Damozel, easy! We both needed that sprint!"

Memory of the tall Guards officer filled a corner of her mind. Had she loved him? She could not be certain. Had he loved her? An infatuation perhaps—nothing more. Their paths had been officially separated by edicts over which they had no control: one took him to India, and the other brought her home to the islands in the Pacific. The little mare had remained a bond with the Guards officer. It was his parting gift to her. The mare snorted and breathed in deep gasps to recapture her wind from the hard, fast spurt of a moment ago. "Easy, Damozel! Easy! It's this clammy air, this heat. You would run five times as far in England and not be gasping so to catch your breath!" England! The cool, foggy air and its green downs, the forests and castles, the clever people of her acquaintance, were a fixed part of her now. "How can we forget England, eh, Damozel?" But Captain Beautemps? What about him? He is far away now—only a figment in a large assortment of memories.

The mare started at a falling branch, swept down by the winds of the night, "Easy, Damozel," she whispered solicitously. "Nothing to be afraid of! No one can see us now! No one!" The horse was calmed, but kept an attitude of alertness.

"Thank God for Koa," she murmured as though the mare was another person. She saw Koa standing on the lanai at Ainapua, strong, gentle, and abiding. He was a prince—he was Hawaiian. And he had spent a single frigid winter in England, pursuing, he had told her, the subject of political economy at the University of London. They had met only once in England. They had met often as children in Hawaii. She summoned the image of her father. Why is he so against Koa? Bearded, his body starting to bend now and his face assuming the gaunt lines of age, her father had grown formidable in his demonstrations of disapproval. In connection with Koa, it was expressed mostly by silence, and occasionally, by faintly suggested criticisms. Koa was not business-minded enough! He ought to be, as he was poor! Koa was not serious enough in matters of government! He ought to be, in order to fight the missionary opposition! These views were expressed during long sessions at table where talk had, at times, flared into loud outbursts.

The effect upon both father and daughter became, every day, more apparent. Scarcely a night passed without an argument. The talk in these exchanges had narrowed down to a single subject. Tonight it had been of particular vehemence. They had both exceeded the usual limits in the taking of wines. This had spurred on their words:

"What are you doing with your life? You are throwing it away!"

"Does it matter, Father? Does it really matter?"

"Indeed, it does! Why do you ride at night? It is quite mad! It is dangerous! There are whispers about it all over the town!"

"By whom, and why? Do you think I care? I have harmed no one in my rides at night! Not a soul!"

It would have been unthinkable in England to ride out this way at night. For one thing, it would be too cold most of the time. "I tried, Damozel. I tried very hard in England to make the best of my opportunity. It was not always easy, as you might know, you Arab of England!" She patted the horse's neck affectionately and was answered with a soft snort. "Perhaps I was away too long—too, too long! Those dreadful last three years! They were a vigil! We wandered aimlessly from one continental spa to another, my tiresome, hired companions and I. My father, bless his heart, joined me in the last year while we waited for the haole revolutionists here to sanction my return. Those were bitter days. . . . and now . . . ?" She cast her eyes to the heavens. "Can I forgive? Should I forgive? They say one cannot live without forgiving."

A few days before this, she had written her friend, the Marquise de Cre-cy, who lived near Combray in France: "Last week some Americans came to my house and knocked rather violently at the door and when they had stated their cause, they wished to know if it would be permissable for the EX-prin-cess to have her picture taken with them. Oh will they never leave us alone? They have taken everything away from us and it seems there is left but little, and that little our very life itself. We live now in such a semi-retired way that people wonder if we even exist anymore. I, too, wonder, and to what purpose?" She patted Damozel's arching, graceful Arabian neck again.

How sweet and cool the air was; how marvelous a sedative the night and its shadows. "Sweet creature—sweet, sweet creature!" She murmured out of love for her mount. "Father keeps the illusion that I am still the languid, big-eyed child of fourteen who left here nine years ago. I have changed—I am a woman! I have been exposed to the graces and wiles of the world. Why does he cling to his illusion? I've given up mine—why can't he?" A transformation had, indeed, taken place. It had changed the shy, sweet girl into a statuesque, graceful, and beautiful woman of twenty-three. She had grown as hard as some men in her thinking during the critical year past—the year of her return from the courts of Europe. Each day, she seemed to grow more unyielding in her views.

They were now approaching King Street and Waikiki Road. A bright moon lighted cloudless skies and earth alike. The trees cast huge shadows on the roadway, and the pungent odor of island vegetation reminded her again that Honolulu was truly a large garden where plants and blossoms—pampered in palaces of glass or in the private conservatories of Europe and America—flourished all over the town in a luxuriant, natural state of growth. Her own gardens at Waikiki had become a treasured entanglement of exotic flora.

The smell of an island night! The sea, the cooling trade winds, and veg-etation combined to make a pervasive fragrance in the air. She inhaled the sweetness with sensual pleasure. How I love the night-time perfumes of Ha-waiian flowers, she thought. The compelling perfumes of some island flowers were released only after dark. These alone would have been enough to bring her out on gallops, night after night. In the long, northern, odorless nights of the winters spent abroad, she would sometimes dream of walking in gar-dens richly fragrant with blossoms of frangipani, pak lan, pikaki, or aglaia; or dream that she was riding in damp woodlands where mokihana and maile grew, causing the air to be so perfumed as to tantalize one's very being.

On King Street there were roadside lamps at each corner, throwing off a pale yellow light. Her thoughts returned to something she had said during dinner tonight: "It is a strange feeling, Father, to come home after living so many years abroad. I feel like a fish out of the water. I learned to speak French fluently. I speak some German and Italian, and Spanish. I can read proficiently in all these languages. Do you know that there is scarcely any opportunity to use them here? In Europe I could use them continually." She had paused to garner more thoughts after her father had said, rather gruffly under his breath, that she was talking nonsense; that many foreigners landed on these shores; and that from time to time she could have plenty of opportunity to speak French, Italian, or German. He reminded her there was a large colony of Germans in the islands. "And, besides," he had added "it's time you brushed up on your native tongue. Your people expect you to speak Hawaiian." She had! She had "brushed up" on the language of her mother's people. She was becoming more proficient every day in saying particular phrases—even forming sentences. But it was difficult. The native tongue was so full of idioms; its best usage was richly metaphoric, a kind of poetry. How she hoped she might win more understanding from this aging, unhappy man! In mentioning the foreign languages she had learned, she wanted merely to make the point that much of what she had learned abroad was quite irrelevant to living in the islands in the role she now must occupy. How easy it would be if her difficulties could be solved by her speaking Hawaiian fluently!

"Why are you so restless?" her father had asked abruptly, while she searched for words to say something that might give him comfort. His blunt interrogation had dissolved the moment of slight compassion she had felt and had made her say quite angrily: "There are many reasons for my restlessness, but I loathe discussing them again. It seems to me that for ages now, we've talked about little else. I ask you to allow me the privilege of my thoughts—of my own feelings. They are best kept private. I have my horses, my dogs, and the peacocks! Nanny here, and the animals are all the company I want most of the time—except for Koa. He understands more than anyone else my plight. He understands, and he says very little."

Nanny MacDougall, an elderly Scotswoman, her former nurse, now a companion, had listened to these heartbreaking deliberations night after night, a third figure at the great table that once had known abundant hospitality. For long periods now, it offered its burden of fare to only the three people sitting in tense anticipation at its oval boundaries. In her present state of mind, the princess had refused to ask dinner guests to Ainapua; and her father had grown indifferent, even hostile, to most people of the town.

"I have hoped, I have dreamed of your success in life," she remembered the old man saying wistfully, even calmly—spent, for a moment, of the anger that had possessed him a moment ago. "And now you do nothing but waste your time with Koa and the Stevenson girls, talking bitterly about the haoles here."

And he had recalled to her—not for the first time, either—the scene at the wharf when he had gone to welcome her home after the long years she had spent away. What a figure of stately beauty she had been! The wharf had been crowded with flower-bedecked Hawaiians who had come to pay respect to the beautiful young woman, whom some could remember as a shy, wide-eyed, pensive girl who had left her islands to journey across two oceans and a continent nine years earlier when she was only fourteen. The old man had enjoyed a silent triumph on this occasion. His daughter had appeared, that day, to be the very image of regal womanhood. Her courtly nods and bows, her restraint of movement, her fine speech, her well-pitched voice that was displayed as she met various people or as she responded to the loud alohas of the crowd, had illustrated this. Oh how proud, how glowing his spirit had been on that day!

The old man's spoken reverie had softened her. She had smiled and said that it had been one of the happiest days of her life. Then she had remembered his reference to Prince Kealiikoa and the Stevenson girls. "Why shouldn't we talk about the haoles, Father? They took our government away from us," she had said with a bitter laugh. "Besides," she had continued without relaxing her bitterness, "they are so unctiously censorious! You would think everyone here should scrape and bow to their wishes. What ungrateful people they are! My Hawaiian ancestors were extremely kind to the ancestors of those people when they came here! And their thanks was to be cruelly critical of everything Hawaiians believed in. How ungrateful and how disrespectful!"

Recollection of this last fragment of the talk at dinner made her restive. She loosened her grip on the reins and urged Damozel into a slow trot; but soon she brought the horse again to a walk. She disliked converting annoyance into a physical act. "Good girl, Damozel! Good, good girl! You are indeed an Arab princess!" One could love animals inordinately, she thought.

Quite suddenly she became conscious of a smell from the sea. The delicious fragrance calmed her. South winds, having disturbed the tides and currents, causing seaweed to be torn from the coral reef, blew the piquant fragrance to the shore. She was on King Street, quite far from the sea, riding toward town, yet the air was heavy with the smell of li-poa. The smell of limu li-poa was unmistakable—like no other. Li-poa! It was primordial, indigenous—a dry and full-flavored seaweed. Rough seas had torn the frizzy yellowish strands from their pinions on the coral and washed them to the shore. Having lived in Waikiki through all her childhood years, the princess knew well the smell of li-poa.

Limu li-poa! How could one forget words attached to such a fragrance? The senses were a powerful influence on the fabric of memory. Other seaweed names were more elusive—they were not easily etched into memory; but they were charmingly descriptive: hulu-hulu aina (a hairy seaweed), aala-ula (a piquant one), or limu ele-ele (green and silky) which the Hawaiians ate with beef stew.

"Easy, Damozel! Smell the limu, you English Arab! Smell the limu!"

The prolonged winters in England had not numbed all the senses that related her to the earlier years when her mother and certain retainers had repeated the spoken lore of her Polynesian ancestors. She had not forgotten the familiar sounds—the words tossed from ancient lips so musically and with such intrinsic veneration for the age-old textures of legend and epic. In spite of certain maneuvers from her earliest childhood to remove her from native speech and influences, living circumstances had interceded and made their imprint on her mind. How could she forget the somber talk of aged retainers, or the joyous exclamations of the younger fold, or the soft exchanges of conversation between her mother, Aunt Lydia, and Uncle David.

Mountain ranges and waterfalls, flowers—gaudy and fragrant—the mountain ferns, towering spreading trees as primordially indigenous as her mother's ancestors bore the beautiful names of the language. Fish and land animals, the sky, or a vista from the dizzy heights of a cliff, the burnished earth of volcanic craters . . . the sad, lingering sounds of death-wailing, the small pastel-colored native birds, the roster of native gods and goddesses . . . there were words in the music of the native tongue to describe by name all of these.

She could remember most of them. The smell of ginger flowers recalled awapuhi: the primitive half-wail and half-chant of grief-showing recalled the unforgettable kani-kau. The names of massive, brown ancestors—some of them as descriptively individual as the names given mountains, the sea, and the heavens: Keohokalole, Keawe-heulu, Kekaulike, Kamanawa, or Kapaakea—these she did not forget. Old Kali, the devoted butler at Ainapua, had ingrained them into her memory, giving her expert and furtive instruction when Nanny MacDougall or her father were not close by. Kali, with the gift that some Hawaiians have for genealogical remembrance, could recite the names of the princess's ancestors, going many generations into the past.

These names were in the heart—they brought up the sounds of words and a shower of associations from the deepest recesses of memory. They were the roots of ancestry and race, of one part of her. She could not forget them. They were a part of her in a more classic setting, in a romantic backward-looking way. She associated them with what she knew of indigenous times—the times of feather-cloaked chiefs, their impressive height so dramatized by tall feather-covered helmets—some of whom could still be seen along lonely mountain ridges or deep in hidden valleys.

But this poetic view of the language had not created her a Hawaiian in the contemporary sense. She could not join her people in the margins of their present world, one made of telephones, locomotives, banks, concrete and brick buildings, and heavily populated city slums for masses of her people. I cannot speak to them in our native tongue, she thought bitterly. I am, therefore, a Hawaiian only to the extent that intellect and imagination link me romantically to the past. How cruel! How confusing life can be, when you think of all these things. "Yes, Damozel, yes! It is all quite confusing, but we cannot wish such things out of their places in the mind. We are doomed to think of them—to make sense of them!"

Tea and cakes, refined elocution, the restrained niceties of genteel deportment, the charm of a delicate ball dress, the waltz, the comforting camaraderie of county fairs, the elegance of Adam and Temple drawing rooms with their Hepplewhite and Sheraton furnishings or the fashionable grace of Sir Joshua's or Gainsborough's ladies, had captured her fancy, too, and she would not soon erase them from memory or from the very core of her being. They, too, were a part of the complex fabric of heritage and culture.

But they were only a part. The other part of her drew its substance from aboriginal Polynesian sources; and of this she was fully conscious. Urgings and promptings from the archetype repository fashioned some of her impulses—some of her feelings—which no amount of intellection could destroy.

The princess had not realized until her return from the long years abroad that two great streams of influence gave fierce battle within her for supremacy over feelings and thoughts. The temptation to plunge headlong into the vast comforting arms of nature—made the less resistible by endless sunshine, fragrant trade wind breezes, and the delicious purity of her island waters—continually haunted her splendid body.

There had been Captain Beautemps. Now there was Koa. "Koa, Kealiikoa! How beautiful even his name! The Noble Soldier!" How handsome he was, and how the grace of the Polynesian showed in his walk, his voice, his manner. "Shake your head, little Arab princess, I know you agree," she said to her horse, and laughed. Oh how comforting the night was, how pleasantly neutral was the less obvious physical completeness of things in the darkness. *Do I love Koa?* In truth she could not answer this. She admired him; she respected him. "I am two people," she said to herself and Damozel, "I am a house divided!" At times she would have joined the women in their squidding, spear fishing or gathering limu in the shallows of Ala Moana and Waikiki. In the coverings of her stately gowns, she watched them at these pursuits in the sea, jealous to be as anonymous and free as they. Everything she did was held under the scrutiny of watching eyes, and talked about. So innocent a thing as gathering limu or fishing would have lifted eyebrows. "She is going native, returning to the old ways," the watchful, anxious, critical ones would say.

At other times, perhaps, as she remembered reading the letters of Madame de Sevigne, or the Journal of the Duchess of Newcastle, squidding and fishing in the native way would have repulsed her; for civilization had also made its claims on her, and, laying claims to her education and knowledge, she would have been called "pretentious," "uppity!" A soft, decorative non-entity was what some desired her to be. Actually, she was two people, and in this was the seed of her torment. *Who am I? What am I?* she had asked herself with a monotonous regularity.

She had gathered together a narrow circle of friends, mostly half- whites like herself, and retreated to the cottage at Ainapua. It had been an elaborate child's playhouse, built especially for her. It was lost now among thickets of palms with exotic and cumbersome names. Her father had altered the cottage, made it larger, and refurbished it to celebrate her return from England. Here she could retire with her friends and be herself. They would sing and talk, though for some reason she was never at ease. "My handful of friends are very kind to me—and they understand to some extent. They certainly have greater understanding than my father, and they try to make me feel at home again in Hawaii. I appreciate their solicitations, and I try to shake off those influences eight years of living in Europe has etched on my soul which interfere with my feeling at home in Hawaii," she had written her close friend, the Honorable Hermione Paget, now the Marchioness of Tindale. She had earnestly devoted herself to knowing what it meant to be a Hawaiian again. Koa had told her: "You are so English, Victoria! So stiff and formal! And your words come out in freshets, full of brilliance and keenness. You leave us far behind!" Why does he say such a thing? It is too candid, too intimate! "But, Koa," she had answered, almost sternly, "I am Hawaiian, and I'm proud of the fact!" He had said nothing, and looked at her gently as they walked in the garden, followed by the peafowl and the dogs.

Days on end, she had walked the luxuriant gardens of the estate at Waikiki, followed by her mother's peacocks and the greyhounds that she had brought from England—committed forever now to fulfill their days in warmer air, amidst palms and ferns rather than in the cool dark woods of England. Days of walking along the twisting, softly curling pathways of the famous gardens, restraining tears, erasing thoughts, flashing irrelevancies into consciousness to blot out painful memory. Days of walking to escape the shadows gathering in her mind; to elude the pounding thrusts of ennui and the sense of defeat that was so great she had to constantly warn herself against giving in to despair.

Both the bitches she had brought from England had whelped; there was now a small army of greyhounds at Ainapua who were constantly in attendance during these walks in the garden. When Koa was not there, Nanny MacDougall would sometimes join her. A wily psychologist, Nanny had used these more reflective and poignant moments to influence the princess away from the elegiac direction her thoughts had taken. "Think, my dear, of

Marie Antoinette, or Mary of the Scots! They lost their heads!" Although the old nurse's rather melodramatic offering of consolation had amused Victoria, she had felt grateful for it.

Perversely, darkness and its balmy air could somehow ease the parasitic draw of melancholy. She let herself feel, again and again, the peaceful neutrality of night as she rode the Arabian mare along King Street. She walked the horse for several blocks before urging her into a gallop again. Before they reached the Palace and Aliiolani Hale, she turned Damozel toward Punchbowl Street. She had vowed never to enter the Palace again. It had become a source of pain even to drive by the stylish domicile, converted as it was into an office building, where the bearded, pale-eyed president of the so-called republic and his staff had their offices. There were too many associations with her girlhood at the sight of the square colonnaded building that resembled some of the newer villas she had seen in Europe. She eased the little mare into a trot when they reached Vineyard Street, several blocks above the Palace, and turned left into the darkness.

Then she remembered more words her father had spoken. Stubbornly, they crowded her thoughts. "Your people need you now, more than ever, my dear! They need a symbol of leadership, even if the government and the throne are lost. You fit the specifications. You have been trained for this," her father had said.

"To fit into the role of a royal has-been? This is all that is left, Father? I am only the former heiress apparent to the Hawaiian throne. Should I assume this role, and conduct myself accordingly—as a tractable has-been?"

"This house, this garden, I have raised them from the mud flats to create a home befitting a princess," her father had said with a sadness. "You can be the reigning lady of the land—without the throne. I will leave money enough—enough for you to be completely independent!"

"Will money dispel loneliness? After the years of study and travel, of cautious and extensive training to command as mine the things of civilization—the theater, the music, the wit and cleverness of educated people—do you think I can easily come back here to melt wistfully into the role you specify for me? To queen it over a little circle of shopkeeper's wives, or the handful of wellborn Hawaiians and hapa-haoles who are already as broken in spirit and demoralized as I? Please, Father, allow me the privacy of my bitterness—my own sense of futility!"

"This is weakness! You are being self-indulgent! Your warrior ancestors and the bold Scots from whom you descend through me would growl with rage to hear you talk this romantic nonsense. No, Victoria, no! You have a life here of great importance. You still live in the hearts of your people us their princess—as Aunt Lydia is still their queen!"

"This is lofty talk, Father, but does it really provide the answer for me? With the risk of being repetitive and dull—even sentimental—I might say again, you are destroying what happiness I might have by taking so critical an attitude of Koa. First of all, you were critical of Captain Beautemps!"

"He would not have made a suitable husband here."

"Why not? You married Mother—weren't you a suitable husband here?"

"It was different. I had lived here for many years before I married your mother. We were both close to the scene. Captain Beautemps would have come here uninitiated. He would not have known how to take things."

She had wanted to say some harsh cruel thing about her father's present attitude toward Prince Kealiikoa, but she had suppressed it. Words seemed quite valueless at that moment. Damozel shied as a prowling cat streaked across the road in front of them.

"What about Adam Pierce? He's a fine young man!" her father had demanded. Recalling this statement at the moment the horse shied, the princess was nearly thrown. "Yes, Father, absolutely to your specifications!" As she struggled to keep her seat, the words tumbled into her mind. "A perfect match, on your terms, now! He has a promising future in business, and with my assets to pump life into his efforts at accumulating money, he could become quite rich someday!" Her father's reaction had been to send up a barrage of questions. Where had his daughter learned to think so vulgarly? When had the delicacy of the girlhood mind turned to take this direction of manlike awareness—of intensive knowing? "You talk at times like a man!" he had said accusingly.

He had had her trained to rule! Was this a man's mind? She had been trained to lead and plan for her people. Some of the world's great rulers had been women. Was it a man's mind that was required to rule a nation, to deal with rulers of other nations? What about the great Queen Elizabeth? Maria Theresa? Catherine of Russia? Man's mind? "I have been taught to think, Father—to use intellect as an instrument of survival in specific circumstances. I was trained to rule someday as a queen. That destiny has been taken from me. So now, intellect becomes ironically the instrument of my distress, my doom! What else can I be now but a soured malcontent?"

"You can be a woman, and a princess! A living symbol of the chiefs of old!"

Then he had taken another approach in the effort to penetrate the hard surface of her present thinking, and he asked: "Just what are your intentions with Prince Koa? I've watched you when he has come here. You seem quite indifferent—even bored. Perhaps you really do share my feelings that marrying him would be a mistake. You are rich, and he is not. You are a sophisticated, intelligent woman of superior training. He is just a good-natured island boy!"

"So Prince Kealiikoa is 'just a good-natured island boy,' and I am neither fish nor fowl—neither queen, nor just another citizen. I am ex-officio heiress apparent to the little throne here! I am now, to put it rather bluntly, a walking anachronism!" Again, the unwomanly words, not becoming the rare and delicate flower that had been enshrined in her father's mind before her return from England! Her words had thrust deep, and, knowing this, she had gone on: "Prince Koa is a good friend, and certain things about me he understands. He is kind, and he has warmth. I cannot see now where marriage is the issue!"

"What about children?" her father countered.

"Please, Father, be a little merciful! I haven't the heart to bear children who might suffer what I've had to endure for the past five years. Our wanderings abroad!" she had said almost savagely. "For more than three years, we were kept away from here by the people who seized the throne. They were afraid that I, of all people, would foment trouble! My presence might bring on a revolution, they said. I cannot forget the anguish of those years, the terrible longing to be here where I was born, and had a place! And now, the humiliation and dishonor of having to be stared at as a royal has-been. Children! Such a thing is in God's hands. My own thoughts on the matter are quite harsh and conclusive!"

"You seem to have no aim in life—no desire for some established end," her father had said. "You seem to be sleepwalking most of the time. Are you so tired of life already?" It was as though no word of her outpouring of the truth of her plight had penetrated to her father. He had accepted all her losses—why couldn't she? "No, Victoria, no! You can have a good life here. You have a place of endearment in the hearts of your people!"

"Yes, Father, I can be an object of sentiment—perhaps even an object of pity. Remember the official portrait that was made in London before I left? I was in my soft, silken, primrose-yellow gown. Worth, who dressed all the royal ladies of Europe, designed it for me to wear to the ball given by the Prince of Wales and Alexandra. Let the people have that picture to soothe their broken hearts. It's as much as I have. And, anyway, it is a fine photograph!"

The words were harsh, rasping, and, in some respects, she knew they were unbecoming. Koa, too, had said to her only the other day: "You talk and think like a man! Sometimes I can't follow you!" She had failed to make her father understand that his view of her was a romantic idealization. Would it be the same with Koa? Her true self was locked in her most private thoughts and feelings. These she could not share with anyone.

Sometimes only a thin thread of music came into her mind— something from a chorale or a mass—she knew not which. And other times she heard the sounds of marching armies; and she would say, *Fight! Fight! Take up arms, people of Hawaii!* At other times she heard again the deep but fragile voice of the old Queen at Windsor saying: "You are a pretty child, my dear, and you are my namesake. What a pretty child you are, indeed!"

In her reflections, she would try to sort out the facts—remove her own feelings from influencing what she could make of the holocaust that had ended Hawaiian Monarchy and ushered in what was now a fait accompli: annexation to the United States. She questioned Koa, her father, and one or two older women of their set, about what had happened in 1893. They said one thing or another, but restively indicated their distaste for the subject. "It's all over now. Let us be at peace with ourselves and the new order," was her father's favorite reply.

The accusations aimed at her uncle, the now-deceased Kalakaua Rex, and at the ex-Queen—were they true? Could Uncle David have been so profligate, so comic in his maneuvers? Could Aunt Lydia have been so stubborn, so inept in her rule, as they had reported? *They!* She thought accusingly of the handful of whites who now controlled the economic life of the islands, who had been the main force behind the destruction of the Hawaiian throne. How I loathe them—the shoddy ingrates! They speak of democracy! I have read their constitution—the one created for the Republic of Hawaii. It is more authoritarian and reactionary than any that existed here before. It is a monument of blue-stocking arrogance! They destroy a monarchy that was benign and one that provided them with all their opportunities to get rich. They take control of the government, and create an oligarchy, and make laws far less generous to the peoples of this land. They even took the vote away from most Hawaiians by establishing property qualifications which could not be met. We were landless and without money. Most of us lived in poverty in our own homeland.

They would say that, as whites, they had a distaste for living in our beautiful islands and being ruled by dark-skinned people. That is something they will never admit, for they are so unctious! So cruelly vindictive! They are the kind of haoles that have gone out all over the world and enslaved people who do not have white skins.

The ex-princess sedulously avoided confronting these people. Their mealy-mouthed expressions of goodwill were insincere, revolting! These were her legacy of thought, for no one had told her, to any informative degree, just what had happened in 1893—not even Koa. Her knowledge of the details was scant. The ex-Queen, Liliuokalani, one of the chief, characters of the tragedy, was absent from Honolulu at the time of Victoria's return. In letters from Washington, her Aunt Lydia advised she would learn of the trouble of 1893 in a book the ex-Queen was writing, one in which she hoped to relate in detail the events of the overthrow from her own point of view. Her father, not wanting to burden his daughter—his precious flower of regal womanhood—had come forth with the most peremptory statements about the upheaval which had ended Hawaiian sovereignty. There seemed to be a conspiracy at large in the islands to spare Victoria the full story of her aunt's dethronement.

"You must act with restraint now, my daughter. You must be cautious and discreet," her father once had said a few days after her return from England. "Your trip to Washington with Mr. Thorpe to plead the cause of the monarchy didn't set well with the conquerors. They will watch your every move!"

"I made the trip to Washington when I was seventeen, because I felt it was my business to plead for the cause of our government. These are *our* islands. *Our* people have ruled over them for centuries. Why shouldn't I have gone to Washington to plead for the cause of monarchy?"

Yes, and letters and news items had appeared frequently in newspapers, making shabby attempts to humiliate her—to force upon her in a crude schoolboyish way an acceptance of things as they were—after she had paid the official visit to Washington with Mr. Thorpe. She had laughed heartily at the inept phrasing, the downright vulgarity, exhibited in the newspaper bits, which she had received in letters from Nanny MacDougall. They had reflected such provincialism and such ignorance—really! Had graciousness and style already begun to depart from the island scene? she had thought after receiving one envelope full of clippings.

From the miasma of thoughts that went back to the past, as she rode tonight, one memory called forth the image of a pale emaciated face. It belonged to a tall wraith of a man who wore his hair carelessly tossed and long. He was so thin, so pale. Day after day, in the weeks before she left for England, he had come to Ainapua to talk with her father. Having settled comfortably into the large fan-backed chairs on the verandah, they had talked. Some meaning of the words had escaped her; yet enough was understood to know that the famous man of letters and her father exchanged ideas on the subject of local politics. There was an intensity in their words, a jarring note of alarm. A certain faction was asking for changes in the government; and, every day, attacks had been made publicly and privately upon the King. Poor Uncle David—he was not a gifted statesman, but he was able! He worked as hard as anyone in the government! Why had they judged him so harshly, called him those awful names, and cast aspersions, of all things, on his parentage? All this had happened so long ago. It belonged to another dimension of her consciousness—a time when she was innocent and fourteen. At the time, she could only feel in her child's heart a sense of alarm—an elusive and delicately poised sense of alarm which children feel when they overhear some things adults say. The talk of the gifted visitor and her father was sprinkled with words like "annexation" and "manifest destiny," "white supremacy" and "ungrateful haoles."

Some words the gifted man had written her when she left Hawaii stayed fast in her memory over the years. She easily recalled: "When she comes to my land, her father's, and the rain beats upon the window (as I fear it will), let her look at this page: it will be like a weed, gathered and pressed at home; and she will remember her own islands, and the shadow of the mighty trees; and she will hear the peacocks screaming in the dusk and the wind blowing in the palms; and she will think of her father sitting there alone."

Uncertainty, and a cool and relentless sense of outrage at what had happened in Hawaii during her absence, made her loath to see or speak to some who had formerly been friends. It hurt all the more to ignore them as carriages passed on the roadways, or they met in someone's drawing room, because they were so familiar. She was fourteen when she had left Hawaii—an age when the memory of those one has known for a lifetime is forever etched in the tissues of remembrance. In public, these feelings of outrage were particularly tormenting as she could not exhibit vexation when on view to the world.

And so she had ridden on, in wild galloping spurts that would be reduced to slow trotting and then to a walk. On Vineyard Street, Victoria on her Arabian mare passed the house in which she had made her royal entrance into the world. It was occupied now by a rich Hawaiian grande dame and her four half-white daughters of extraordinary beauty. It was a lovely house with a square turret in the middle, looming above the porte cochere. She remembered going up to the turret with Kali to hang the Hawaiian flag from a white pole that shot out at an angle. Her father had built the larger house at Ainapua before her mother's death. They had been living there a number of years before Victoria was sent to England. She loved the house, and paid its darkened form a long, respectful, studious look as she rode by, remembering that her mother had planted some of the trees that now had reached great height and swayed above in the darkness.

After crossing Queen Emma Street, she saw the mansion of the old Princess Deborah, which now had been converted into a public high school. Princess Deborah had deeded the land at Waikiki to Victoria on the day she was born. Had Deborah known wild defiance; and had she known heartache and the vitiating sting of defeat? It would have been impossible. No one—no one at all—had told Deborah that there were do's and do not's, that there was this restraint or that restraint to be exercised. She had moved through life with the instinctual force and wisdom of an elephant. She had torn from the cake of life large hunks for herself, and swallowed them triumphantly. A flash of recollection brought forth the memory of superbly-gowned women and courtly men dancing long into the night. Their laughter and talk now filled Victoria's ears, and she smiled. Nothing could have stopped the massive chiefess from enjoying life—except death, itself, which had visited her mercifully before the predatory ones had seized the throne. She was so bent on pleasure, and wise and strong, as well.

But the old Princess Deborah had left no children to continue the family line. Her heir, a cousin, had also died childless, leaving the great house to the restrained New Englander she had married. It seemed to be a condition of Hawaiian royalty in these times to be quite childless. Victoria's own aunt, the ex-Queen, was without issue, as was the Dowager Queen Kapiolani. The Princess Harieta Nahienaena, the daughter of the great Kamehameha, had died childless at twenty-two, surrendering to heartbreak and debauchery. The Princess Victoria Kamamalu had died at twenty-six, also childless and victim of a similar capitulation.

Why had all this happened? Why? she asked herself with vehemence. What had happened to her race that its most patrician representatives could no longer reproduce themselves? A melancholy fact that pointed up the irrefutable, disheartening specter of decline among her people. In the old days, royal children were numerous. She let a sigh escape. The mare picked up her ears. "It's nothing, Damozel, nothing! I am only thinking about some tragic facts." Why? She could no more erase consciousness of these sad losses than she could wishfully change the color of her dark brown eyes. She had been trained to think; to ponder; to evaluate.

After this, she had trotted Damozel up Fort Street, oppressed and heavy under the weight of the nostalgic interlude. I must stop giving in to these depressing looks backward that every landmark readily summons to my mind.

Near School Street, surrounded by spreading gardens, the house of a rich and prominent part-white family came into view. She thought of the dark-eyed, dark-haired children, who lived here—somewhat overdressed, somewhat overprotected, and idealized—as she had been. Would they ever know her torment and her sense of loss? Or would time and the ruthless propensity of the life force change the order of things and create, from future circumstances, a world better suited for these children to grow up in? Hauteur and fashion belonged to their parents. They had held a firm and glamorous place at the social peak of the kingdom. They owned land and cattle, carriages and beautiful horses. Was this enough? Was it enough to have incomparable physical beauty, to be clothed in splendid uniforms and gorgeous holokus; to own lands, carriages, and fine horses? Was it enough to walk with astonishing dignity; to breed an unyielding pride that separated them sharply from all other people?

"Pride goeth before the fall!" She had heard this oft repeated in Victorian England—and here! Was this stiff pride that was so common to aristocratic Hawaiians and part-Hawaiians a natural thing or was it bravado—a system of defense against any encroachment of white supremacy attitudes upon their lives? "White supremacy!" she growled at the darkened air.

This was really the basis of her father's dislike of Koa. She was now quite certain of this. Her father could marry a native and beget a child; he was a man! White men could marry native women; never the reverse. With her education and travels, her father perhaps saw her as a white woman—certainly she had been trained like one. "Oh, Koa, Koa," she whispered. "Oh, Koa!"

She patted the mare's beautifully arching neck to gain reassurance. The little horse snorted sympathetically. After they passed Kuakini Road, the fleet animal broke into a canter, and then a full gallop, as though an intuitive communication existed between herself and her mistress. The princess wanted at that moment to force Damozel into a furious gallop. But there had been no need to dig the heels of her boots into the mare's flanks; nor had it been necessary to work her into the chase with the usual verbal encouragements. Without being urged in the slightest, Damozel flew up the ascending road that narrowed perceptibly as it meandered more deeply into the valley.

Rain began to fall as they entered the lonely stretch above Hanaiakamalama. It was not a heavy rain—more like a thickened mist, and it did not discourage the princess and her horse. They flew on, to the furthermost reaches of the valley. The area was heavily wooded and unspoiled by habitations.

At Mamalahoa the frizzy mist turned into rain—a heavy, cold, upper Nuuanu rain. Still the beauteous rider and the dappled mare galloped on. How luxuriant were the smells here! Wild nature—unspoiled, unexpurgated; budding and leafing, flowering and ripening; decaying leaves, twigs, blooms in brown masses formed thick layers of compost under shrub and tree; kukui trees and ferns—pulu, pala palai, ho-io made the more fragrant with the fall of rain—grew in profusion here. The ferns were another link with the deep past. They had been celebrated, time and again, in the ancient meles, the epics of classic Hawaii which were preserved by people remembering them word for word. She reined Damozel to a stop. She studied the world around her—even in the rain and mist it was breathtaking.

This was Koa's world. It was his favorite place to come on rides. A mystical calm would come over his face when they rode, as they sometimes did, to this point in the valley. He would recite pieces of the ancient chants and translate them. He would become a chief of the old days, surveying his domain. Within this romantic framework, his eyes shining, his face aglow with hope, he seemed so far away—drawn back deep into a time of simplicity and calm that was far, far out of her reach. But tonight it was her world as well. It belonged to her as well as to Koa. The beating rain, primordial fragrances, and the clean wind chased away the specters of sorrow. She felt a surge of pure delight fill her being. She was freed from the heat of anger and outrage, from the dread feelings of doubt and confusion that had so relentlessly plagued her recent existence.

The mare's delicate feet found comfortable grooves between the rounded paving stones—her gait was even: a fast walk.

The smells. The shadows. The dripping foliage, How glorious is this island world of Hawaii nei, the princess mused. And here in the upper woodlands the Wa'o Kuahiwi. Nuuanu—it is our world—it does not belong to the foreigners. Without warning, the stately, cool and rigidly controlled Victoria began to cry. She sobbed in the shameless, earthy way of a chiefess of old in moments of sorrow. The horse responded with nervous reflexes of her neck and shoulder muscles.

"It's all right Damozel," she cried out, "I need to cry—I have not cried since we returned." The tears gushed out and little rivulets ran down her cheeks to the sides of her mouth. The salty moisture of her grief mixed with the sweetness of rain drops pelting her face. She felt relief well up as she let the tears escape the confines of her famously beautiful eyes.

At first the sound of the drums was barely audible. Gradually, it grew louder.

Damozel reared, nearly throwing her. The frenzied horse snorted wildly and reared again and then once again—what on earth is happening to you—you English Arab?

The horse sidled first to one side of the roadway then another—the drum beats became louder.

"What is happening?" she screamed and then called out, "Koa. O, Koa where are you? Something is happening here which I cannot understand."

The moon broke through clouds rushing over Nuuanu Valley toward the sea. The rain had stopped. The winds blew away in other directions. It had stopped raining. Now she could hear the dry, hollow sound of gourds and calabashes striking one another. In a moment it was clear. She was at the fringe of what she had heard described by her mother's retainers as huakai no ka po. These were the marchers of the night. The dead of old Hawaii who marched on the night of Kane, po Kane, on treks to revels or to sacred rituals.

"Po Kane!" she said under her breath. "What shall I do?" Pale yellow circles of light were approaching, the flickering kukui torches reflecting the procession at the head of which were the proud chiefs of old in splendid cloaks of red and yellow feathers. Alongside them their massive chiefesses, adorned with golden feather leis and other exquisite personal decoration. All wore the lei niho palaoa, the carved whale tooth held upright by hundreds of strands of braided human hair. Warriors and retainers and the kahunas in white tapa draped at an angle across their shoulders accompanied the chiefs, followed by women and children in the simpler garb of farmers and fishermen, bearing gourd and calabash containers.

She was dazed now and blindly accepting the scene. It would not be erased. "I will let happen what will. Whatever it is," she groaned, feeling a pang of fear enter her stomach like a dagger's thrust. Koa had told her of these Nuuanu night marches. He had heard and seen them. His mother, the Princess Kekaulike, was famed for her knowledge of the old lore. Her retainers had passed on some of this wisdom of the ancient culture to Prince David, her eldest son.

The marchers were surely the Oahu alii slain by the dreaded Kahekili of Maui. She recalled the image of this king—a man seven feet tall, one half of his body tattooed in black squares to terrorize his foes in battle. He turned his eyelids inside out with the use of bamboo slits; yet he was famed among his people as a poet and philosopher. The father of the great Kamehameha. A strange man. Why did he devote so many years of his life to the destruction of Oahu's culture—covetous of its attainments and bountiful wealth? He had practically succeeded in decimating the highest-ranking families of Oahu. She shuddered remembering their bones—Elani's, Kanamanu's, Kalaki's, Pupuka's, set up in the dread House of Bones in Moanalua.

"They march on the night of Kane. They march in this valley—in all the valleys," Koa had told her one day as they rode to the pali. He had not dreamed she would ride here alone at night.

The mare grew more skittish. She trembled. Her graceful legs were hardly able to move because of the trembling.

"Go on girl," Victoria urged. "Go on—we won't be stopped by this—it's all right. I know what is happening."

It was then she starkly realized that the entire procession walked a foot or two above the ground. Her spirit froze. Her skin was now a lava waste of lumps brought on by fear. She reined in the Arab.

I shall wait.

Unexpectedly, two chiefs broke the ranks of the procession and stood silently, confronting her. She rose in her saddle. Sat stiffly in defiance.

"He wahine alii Hawaii—owau nei—" she shouted.

"Keiki hua owau—Kepookalani, Aikanaka, Kamanawa, Kamaekalani, Kameeiamoku, Kamehameha nui—" she shouted all the names of ancestors she could remember.

One name came through the mist of time. She had remembered somewhere in her genealogy a marriage to the royal house of Oahu.

"Kaneikaiwilani" she said with authoritative firmness—remembering he was of the royal house of Oahu who married her great-ancestress Queen Keakealani. Victoria came down from the sacred Princess Kalanikauleleiaiwi, a daughter of that union.

The chiefs stood in silence. Two of the kahunas approached and commanded. "Leave her alone. She is one of ours. Leave her alone and continue the march." They waved their carved sticks with dog-tail brushes in the direction of the Princess.

For a few moments she seemed to be unconscious. When she awakened the marchers were gone; their drum beats could no longer be heard. The horse stood quietly now and the wind returned. "On we go, you nervous little creature of the desert sands. How do you like what we have just seen? Do such miraculous things take place in Arabia? Certainly not Beretania where they drink all that tea!"

They proceeded at a fast walk.

When she reached the Pali, she dismounted, walked to the edge of the cliff, and gazed into the vast darkness below. The wind was blowing with particular force. It sent huge swirls of fog and rain billowing over the famous precipice, making it impossible for her to loiter at the edge. She remembered lines from the great epic *Pele and Hiiaka*. This had been her goal for the night; and she had reached it. There was no further significance to her being here alone and at such an unprecedented hour. The common belief that certain timeless supernatural essences were the masters of the Pali at midnight and the early morning hours had not inhibited her desire to come here. And now some lines of the beautiful Pele and Hiiaka saga came to her. Hiiaka, the graceful and beautiful younger sister of the volcanic goddess, who alone among Pele's sister's offered to make the strenuous journey from Hawaii to Kauai to induce handsome Prince Lohiau to return with her and be joined in love to Pele.

How splendidly and beautifully had Hiiaka sung of the beauties of the Koolau, the windward side of Oahu. The hula dancers of Victoria's mother, Likelike, were noted for their performances of this saga. It had made her Uncle David jealous that his younger sister had been able from her youthful training in Kealakekua to be so steeped in the ancient lore she could inspire her chanters and dancers to perform with near perfection.

She remembered a fragment:

Ino Koolau, e, ino Koolau!

Ai kena i ka ua o Koolau!

Half-smiling she whispered, "How far away I've gone from all of this my birthright. How far—I ka puolo waimaka o ka onihi ke kulu iho nei, e."

My eyes a bundle of tears,

Are full to overflowing.

The words soothed. She stopped crying. She stood at the edge of the famous cliff and lifted her arms to the sky, to the towering mountain above her—Lanihuli—Heavens turned upside down. The rain and wind had stopped again. In the distance Kualoa, Moku-lii and the bastion walls of the Koolau Range were all visible in the moonlight. Willful perversity had started her riding in the dark; and on this particular night it had carried her here, far from the comfortable boundaries of her estate at Waikiki; "Papa and Wakea my progenitors I am here—I am yours," she cried out loudly.

She felt a glorious surge of freedom—of being at peace with everything. Arbitrary restraints, the ponderous burden of position and responsibility—the whole struggle of being at odds with life in the land of her birth—all suddenly dissolved, leaving her weary and confused spirit refreshed and cleansed. She mounted her horse, and started upon the long, wet ride home.

Victoria recalled words from the great Kumulipo chant of creation—the words Uncle David and her mother and Aunt Lydia had been at times so frantic in their efforts to remember.

"Darkness of the sun, darkness of the night. Nothing but night. O ka lipo o ka la, o ka lipo o ka po—po wali ho-i." She chanted the words—first in English and then in Hawaiian on the ride back to Waikiki.

It was almost dawn when the servants and Nanny MacDougall heard the clatter of Damozel's hooves on the main drive. It was drizzling in Waikiki. Her father had slept through the hub-bub resulting from the sight of her return. She was drenched and tired—so was the mare—from the long ride, the exposure to the rains. A chill and fever had already begun to exact a toll on her strong young body. She had fallen on the verandah near the heavy front doors, and it was there that Nanny and Kali found her. In two week's time, she would be dead.

JOHN DOMINIS HOLT (1919-1993) *is the author of* Waimea Summer; Princess of the Night Rides and Other Tales; Kaulana Na Pua; *and* Recollections. *His essay "On Being Hawaiian" helped launch the Hawaiian Renaissance. He received the Hawaii Award for Literature in 1985.*

Kahikina Kelekona

"HE HAAWINA PAHAOHAO"

I ka wehe'na kaiao o kekahi kakahiaka poniponi o ke Kau io Makalapua i kunewa iho la, ua haalele aku la au i ko'u wahi punee hiolani o kauhale, a niauhele mai la na kapuai wawae ma ke ala hoeu e kamoe pololei ana a loaa aku ke alapii aoao e poai nei i ke apo kilupuniu o na kiekiena o ka papu kupua o Puowaina. Na ka hoope hoolu a ke ahe palanehe o kehau huihui i hooni ae i na maawe o ko'u mau olona a me na aakoko, a eleu aku la ka niau ana, a aole no i li'uwale ka manawa, hoea aku la au i ka mole kiekie o ke alahele, a hoonanea iho la ma kahi o ke kahua i noho home ia ai e "Kalola," kekahi o na olohe pu-kuniahi kukiai o ia puu no na makahiki lehulehu iloko o ke au noho'na i hala aku maluna o na eheu ahai o ke aho o ka manawa.

I ko'u noho hooluolu ana iho ma ia wahi, akahi no a wehewehe kaiao, e uhi ana no ke kapa noe lihau i kona mau lihilihi hoomau maluna o na hiohiona o ko kakou kapitala o ka Ua Kukalahale, a me he 'la, o ka hapanui o na kini, aia no iloko o ka poli hoonanea kulipolipo o ke kamaeu Niolopua kahi i hiolani ai. Alawa ae la ko'u mau maka i hope, o ke opu kukilakila mai no a Konahuanui, me he la e kaena mai ana no i ka ui o kana punua i ka nuku lihipali o Nuuanu. Aui ae hoi ma ka hulina akau, o ke kamoe waiho kalae mai no hoi a ke kuahiwi Kaala, me he 'la e oni ae ana no e au i ke kailipo kai oehuehu e kaunu pu ai. Huli au a hui me Leahi i ke kukulu hema, o kana ku hiehie oniole no iloko o na oehukai me kona kukui onohimaka o ke awa hoolulu iloko o ka palekana, e awihi poloai aku ana i ona mau kini alokai no ke ala i ka nuku o Mamala, ka punana e hoomaha ai ka luhi o na ale kawaha hanupanupa. Kilohi hoonanea aku la ka ike a ko'u mau onohimaka a makaleho aku la.

A ano li'u wale ka manawa o ko'u noho hoohihi ana i keia mau hiona hoohialaai, aia hoi, ua lohe aku la ko'u mau pahukani i ka pa palanehe malie ana mai o kekahi mau mapuna leo kohu hanehane, a aui ae la au me ke ano pahaohao, a kau koke aku la ka ike a ko'u mau maka maluna o kekahi mau aka-ku o kekahi mau kino e noho kokoke mai ana ma kuu aoao. Nana pono aku la au, a hoomaopopo iho la he mau hapauea ko'u mau hoa noho o ia iu meha iloko o ia liula wanaao. He kane a he wahine, e luhe kawelu ana na oho lauoho hina keokeo maluna iho o na kipoohiwi o ka hapauea wahine a kamoe malie aku la mahope o kona kua, a e paani malie ana ke ahekehau me kona mau mole aweawe, a he leihulu mamo ke poaipuni ana i kona a-i. Ike aku la no hoi au ua uhi paapu ia no hoi ke poo o ka hapauea kane me na omaka hina, a ua luhe iho la a kau pono maluna o ka hokua me na kipoohiwi, a e kawelu ana kona hu'e umiumi loloa maluna o kona umauma palahalaha, a he lei ilima ke ohu ana a puni kona a-i.

A oiai au e nana aku nei me ka piha kahaha-e nalu ana i ke ano o keia mau haawina kamahao a'u e hoomaopopo aku nei, lohe aku la ko'u mau pahukani i ka pa-e ana mai o ko laua mau leo nahenahe i wili'a me na maawe o ka hanehane a ua hoomaka mai la au e omo i ka laua mau kukai-olelo, a ua hoohihi aku la au me ka hoohialaai no ka ono kuhikuhi a me ka momona kohu waiu me ka meli, a oia no ka'u e hoiloli ae nei i na hoomanao ana, a penei ka'u mau mapuna olelo i lohe aku ai.

"Auhea oe e kuu wahine, ke hoomaopopo aku la no oe i kahi i ku ai o kahi pupupu halepili o kaua, me ka moe o na wahi lo'i ai a kaua ma na aoao, me ka ulu mahiehie o na wahi pu-a ko," i ui ninau mai ai ka hapauea kane i ka hapauea wahine.

"O ka ninau mai auanei kau e ke kane a he hoomaopopo aku kahi o'u. O ka ko'u mau onohimaka ia e imi hele nei aole o ke'a mai o ka naele 'hihi kauno'a hihi i Mana' ka hoi ka ua mea o ka huikau. Ua pii mai nei a ua ko-kolo mai nei o Ainahou a eia iluna o kumupali kahi i pinana ai, a ke niau la ka pii'na iluna lilo o Ualakaa a aia i ka piko panepoo o Konahuanui, o ka hoea paha koe i ka lewaluna o na ao polohiwa a Kane."

"Ae; he oiaio kau e ka wahine. Ke ike ala no au e like me kou ike; aka, ina nae hoi oe e hoihoi aku i kou haupu i hope a hapai malie mai i na hoomanao o na la—ae-oia—e hoomaopopo aku ana no auanei oe i na helehelena a pau o ka aina e like me ia i ko kaua manawa e noho ana iluna o ko kaua wahi kahua home akahai me ka oluolu a me ka lawa pono i na mea a pau e palekana ai ka noho'na. Ke hoomaopopo nei au i na mea a pau e like no me ko ka manawa a kaua i haalele iho ai i keia noho'na ma ko'u hoomanao ana ae. Ke ike aku nei no au i kahi pa holoholona puaa a kaua, a me he la o na wahi kinana moa no kela au e ke-ke mau ai o na kakahiaka nui. Ke ike nei no au i kauhale o Ioane ma, me ko Kaaiahua ma, a me ka halepili nui aku no hoi o Kamealoha mahope mai o kahi o Ailuene a loaa aku kauhale o Naone e huli ana i Pauoa. A mamua pono ae nei hoi, ke ike aku nei au i ko Kamakau mau kauhale, a me ka hale i ke kihi kahi a Kepoikai me kona mau hoa loea kanawai e luana ai me Koii, Keawehunahala, Kalaaukane, Komoikehuehu, Kimona Kaai, Ka-makini a me na 'Lii no hoi me Kapaakea ma a lehulehu wale aku. Ke ike aku nei no au i ka ulu wehiwehi maikai o ka ai o kaupapaloi me na pukoula, ka maia a me ka papaia hoonani hoohoihoi manaolana ma na kuauna uliuli i ka mauu manienie. Ke ike aku nei no au i ke kui pua ilima o kamaliiwahine a ke lohe aku nei no hoi i na hene aka a na keiki kane hoohenoheno hookolohe. A e like no me ka laukanaka o ia mau la, pela no au e ike aku nei i ka laupa'i o na kane, na wahine a me na kamalii o ko kaua ewe ponoi e haiamu muimuia ana ma o a maanei me ko lakou mau kino nunui mohaha a me na helehelena hoihoi waipahe o ka ui olakino maikai. Ke ike aku nei au i kahi poe aia i kuauna kahi i waele ai, e kanu huli ana kahi poe a e kahu ai ana hoi kahi. O na wahine, aia nui i kahawai kahi i haha opae ai me ka oopu, hoi ae no a me na wahi aoluau, holu iho kahi iniki inamona he kani hoi ia o ka muka."

Ua loihi ko'u hoolohe ana aku i keia mau mamala olelo me ko'u nanea hoohialaai i ke kuhikuhi makolukolu, a lohe aku la nae au i ka pane ana ae a ka hapauea luahine me ka i ana ae: "Auhea oe e ua kane nei, ke kamailio mai nei oe a ke hoihoi io ia mai nei ko'u mau hoomanao, a me he 'la, e like me kou ike aku ia mau mea a pau iloko iho o kou noonoo, pela pu no me a'u, ke ike nei au, me he 'la ua kaikai hope ia aku nei a hoea hou ia mau la maikai a oluolu o ka noho ana, a ke kulu nei ko'u mau waimaka me ke aloha i ka ike moakaka aku me ka lelae i na mea a pau au i kamailio mai nei."

No'u iho, he mea e ke kamahao lua ole o ka lohe ana aku i keia mau ku-kaiolelo mawaena o keia mau luaui hapauea, a he mea e no hoi ka hoopiha ia o ko'u noonoo me na haawina like ole o ke kahaha, a ua hoomaopopo iho la au i ka hekau ana iho o kekahi mau haawina o ke kauhola eehia maluna o ko'u kino, a nalu iho la o loko me na hoohuahualau e ninole ae ana—"heaha la hoi ke ano o keia mau haawina kupaianaha, a heaha la ka puana a ka moe?" He mea maopopo loa, iloko o na makahiki lehulehu i aui hope aku la maluna o na eheu o ke au hala hope o ka manawa, he oiaio loa a oia maoli no ke kulana o ka aina a me ka noho'na o na kupa oiwi. A ia'u e noonoo a e hoomanao pu ana ia mau mea, ua pili ano e wale iho la no ko'u mau maka, aole no nae i liuliu, ua kaakaa hou ae la, a i ko'u nana ana aku, aia hoi, ike hou aku la au i ua mau hapauea nei, aole nae me ko laua mau aahu a'u i ike mua aku ai, aka, ua olohelohe iho la ko laua mau kino, a he malo poaaha wale no ke kaei ana i ka puhaka o kahi elemakule a he wahi pa-u olona wale iho no hoi ko kahi luahine, a ma kahi o na lei a'u i ike mua aku ai, ua hoomaopopo aku la au, ua malo a mimino ae la ka lei ilima a ua helelei aku la hoi na hulu o ka leihulu. Ike pu aku la no hoi au i ke kulou o na poo o ua mau hapauea nei, a ia manawa au i lohe hou aku ai i ka pa-e ana mai o ko laua mau leo hanehane me na huaolelo piha naauaua. Lohe aku la no au i ka pane ana ae o ka hapauea kane i ka i ana aku i kona hoa:

"Aloha no paha kaua, aloha no hoi na kini, a aloha no hoi ka aina. Nana aku nei no hoi kaua i ka loa me ka laula, mai ka piko a i ka papaku o lalo, a hoomaopopo aku nei no hoi i na mea a pau i kamaaina i ka ike a ko kaua mau maka, o ka uhipaapu koke ae nei no ka hoi ia o ka noe kupouli, a i ka mao ana ae la, auwe no ka hoi e, ke hoomaopopo aku nei au, e like me ka nalo ana aku la o kela noe, pela no i nalo pu aku la na helehelena a pau o ka aina o ke au i hala a kaua i ike mua aku nei, a ano, ke ike nei au ua loli a ano e loa. Ua nalohia loa aku la na wahi pupupu kauhale o kakou a ua nalo pu aku la me na wahi kaupapaloi, a o na kini lehulehu o na ewe a kaua i ike mua aku nei, aole lakou, a o ka'u e hoomaopopo aku nei, he lehulehu a kinikini wale o na kauhale a he poe okoa wale no ka'u e ike aku nei, he poe malihini a'u i ike ole mamua. Ke ui aku nei ko'u mau maka i ka akau a me ka hema, i ka hikina a me ke komohana, he ano okoa wale no ka'u mau mea e ike nei. O ke kahua ihikapu o na 'Lii ua pau ka hie a me ke kapu, a o ka hae kalaunu aole ia, he hae kahakahana okoa loa ia a'u e ike aku nei. Ma kahi i ku ai o kauhale o Kaupena ma, eia la he mau hale ano okoa loa ia a'u e ike aku nei, a he poe kanaka lauoho huelo ia e nonoho mai la. A mauka ae hoi, he ano kanaka poupou pahaahaa ia e holoke mai la ma kahi i ku ai o ko Kaomea ma kauhale. A ke ike nei au ke lalama mai nei iluna o kipapali he puulu kauhale aole a ka'e mai, ua hele a pihakuineki i kanaka ilikea namu palale, a ua kohu auna kao ka hoi keiki e naholo ae la. Ea, auhea oe e ka wahine, ke hoohewahewa nei au i neia mau mea a pau, me he'la, ke kuailo ia mai nei kau mau olelo i hoopuka mai nei, i ko ike ana aku nei i ka pii mai o Ainahou a i iluna o kumupali kahi i pinana ai a hoea iluna o Ualakaa laua o Konahuanui. Aloha no paha kaua. O ka hele mai nei ka hoi ia o ka nele i na hiona kamaaina o ka aina a i ka nalohia loa, eia la he okoa ka aina a he malihini na kupa e nonoho aihookano mai nei. Ke kamaaina nei ka malihini a malihini hoi kaua na kamaaina, a ke ulakolako kuonoono mai la lakou la, a ke kuewa olohelohe nei hoi kaua."

Ia manawa au i lohe aku ai i ko laua mau leo hanehane o ke kaniuhu naauaua, puliki ae la laua ia laua iho, a me ka malie loa, niau palanehe aku la ko laua mau kino akaku a nalowale e like me ka nalowale ana'ku o kekahi punohu uwahi imua o ka welelau o ke ahe makani, a meha laiku iho la na mea a pau. Ku ae la au iluna me ka hoomaloeloe i ko'u mau ami mauluulu, a oia no ko'u manawa i lohe maopopo aku ai i ke ke'u ana iho o ka leo puua o ka alae, kaalo ae la he manu pueo ma ko'u alo a hu aku la ka puaa i kumupali. Hoholo ae la ke kunahihi a puni ko'u kino, kuku ae la ko'u mau oho lauoho me ka maneo ano e o ko'u puniu, a ooi pololei aku la ko'u mau lihilihi maka me ko'u pihoihoi a piha eehia nui me ka naka haalulu o ko'u mau kuli.

Me keia mau haawina ano e i kauhola iho la maluna o'u, me ko'u piha uluku nui me na mahele o ka hoopahaohao, ua ui hou ae la ko'u mau maka i ke komohana, a haule aku la ka ike moakaka a ko'u mau onohi maluna o ke Kia Hoomanao o Kamehameha Na'i Aupuni, a lohe aku la ko'u mau pepeiao i kekahi leo nui kohu nakolo hekili e lawe pololei ia mai ana mai ke kahua mai a uа Kia Hoomanao nei e kuha'o kukila kaukaweli nei i keia mau mamala olelo a'u e lohe e mau nei a e hoomanao mau nei me ka eehia nui, penei:

"Ua na'i au mai Hawaii o Keawe a Kauai o Mano; ua hilo pilipaa ia e a'u na maawe a milo hookahi na Moku; ua pahola aku au i ke aloha Ahuula o ka onipaa lokahi a hookahi ewe; ua kamoe au i ke kahua a ua ku ka hale o ka palekana; ua kuahaua au i "Mamalahoe" kanawai e moe ai ka elemakule, ka luahine a me ke keiki ma ke ala; a waiho iho au ia mau pono na na mamo a ka I, ka Mahi, ka Palena a me ka Palalaui i makolekole ai na ili i ka maka o ka ihe laumeki; he Mahiole hooilina ia na ke 'Lii i waiho iho ai i na makaainana e malama pilipaa i ke kapu; a ua poni au i ka lei anuenue pi'o i ka lewa me na opuu momi—"ua mau ke ea o ka aina i ka pono;" aka, e o'u io, e o'u koko a e o'u iwi mai ka po mai, ke nana aku nei au aole oukou; o kuu lei a'u i kui ai, i hilo ai, i milo ai a i na'i ai i wehi kuleana paa no oukou e a'u mau mamo ua eheu a na ka malihini e lei haaheo nei, a ke hooho mai nei ka leo o ka hane-hane kupinai e kalahea ana—"Ua lilo ke ea o ka aina i ka hewa!""

Kuailo ia mai?

"AN AMAZING REVELATION"

At the crack of dawn one lavender morning during this last Spring season, I left my comfortable divan at the house and my feet made their way along the path aiming directly for the rising trail that spirals up to the side of the circular bowl created by the peaks of the enchanted fortress of

Pūowaina. The gentle wash of the cold dew stirred the fibers of my muscles and nerves, enlivening my progress, and in no time, I arrived at the steep base of the pathway, resting for a bit at that place inhabited by "Kalola," one of the fine cannons that have stood guard over this hill for so many years, throughout the era that has been swept away on the wings of time.

As I was relaxing there, dawn having just unfolded with a blanket of mist spreading its vaporous lace across the features of our capital, home of the Kūkalahale Rain, it seemed that most of the city's multitudes were still in the deep embrace of that mystical spirit of sleep, Niolopua. My eyes turned back and saw the majestic rise of Konahuanui, seemingly boasting about the beauty of where it nestles, there at the uppermost tips of the cliffs in Nuʻuanu. Sweeping to the north side, there, unobstructed, lay Mount Kaʻala, as though emerging ready to swim out into the dark, blustery sea, therein to take its delight. I turned and met up with Lēʻahi to the south, standing steadfast amid the spray of the sea, the lights of its eyes pointing to the safety of the harbor, winking hither and yon to its seafaring friends to show the pathway into the mouth of Mālama Bay, that nest of respite from the rigors of the gaping sea billows. My gaze was held fast, delighted in the vista my eyes beheld.

And after a short time sitting there, enjoying these entrancing features, my ears perceived the subtle presence of faint, ghostly voices, so I turned in surprise, and my glance fell upon the spectral vision of persons sitting quite nearby at my side. Peering down, I recognized that my companions in that lonely, dawn-lit lofty reach were an elderly couple, a man and woman, with silvery white hair flowing over the old lady's shoulders and down her back, a breeze toying with its strands, and a golden mamo-feather lei encircling her throat. The old man's head was covered with gray locks which draped over the back of his neck and shoulders, and his long, bushy beard hung down on his broad chest, an adorning lei of ʻilima blossoms lying around his neck.

While I was watching, stunned at the nature of these amazing happenings that I was seeing, my ears made out the soft sound of their voices, laced as they were with a ghostly quality, and I began to absorb their conversation. I was entranced, feasting on the rich flavor and honey-like sweetness, which makes me quite emotional to recall, for the discussion I heard is as follows.

"O my dear wife, do you recognize the spot where our humble thatched cottage stood, the irrigated taro terraces along its sides, and the lush clumps of cane?" asked the elderly gentleman of his old wife.

"Well, as long as you pose the question, husband, I will certainly try. My eyes search all over, yet there's nothing but an abundance of weeds, in utter confusion, 'tangled like kaunoʻa vines, as ensnaring as the mirages of Mānā.'

'Āinahou, 'New land,' that was dredged from the harbor, has clambered and crawled all the way up here to the base of the cliff, from whence it has risen and moved on up, overtaking 'Ualaka'a and even the top of Konahuanui, eventually to reach the sky itself, where the dark clouds of Kāne dwell."

"Yes, you're right, wife. I see what you see, but if you will delve into your memory and bring up your recollections of the days of our comfortable life, you will then recognize all the features of the land as it was when we lived on our modest and pleasant homestead, with enough of everything to provide a safe existence. In my mind's eye, I can make out everything just as it was when we left that life. I can see our pig pen, and it's as though the hens are still there that you would shoo away in the early morning. I see the home of Ioane and his family, and Ka'aiāhua's, and the great thatched home of Kamealoha behind that of 'Ailuene, where you'd reach the houses of Nāone as you turn toward Pauoa Valley. Right here before us, I can make out Kamakau's house compounds, and the house at the corner where Kepo'ikai and and his legal expert friends, Ko'i'i, Keawehunahala, Kalā'aukāne, Komoikeehuehu, Kimona Kā'ai, and Kamakini would relax, along with the chiefs, like Kapa'akea and so many others. I can see the lush growth of the taro in the flooded terraces, the clumps of red sugar cane, banana, and papaya adorning and adding an interesting diversity to the terrace banks, lush and green with mānienie grass. I see the girls stringing 'ilima blossoms and hear the teasing laughter of the boys, bothering them in their friendly way. Just like the large population then, I see an abundance of men, women and children of our own race, coming together and gathering here and there, with their large, ample bodies and gentle, intelligent features, glowing in the beauty of fine health. I can also see people on the taro-field banks, weeding and planting taro shoots, while others tend the fires. The women are by the stream, where they are catching shrimps and goby fish to bring back and put with some taro leaves and a pinch of kukui relish, which will truly make the lips smack with delight."

I listened for a long time to these stains of dialogue, fully engaged in the rich fullness of the conversation, but then I heard the old woman give this response:

"Listen, husband, here you are talking away, and my memories are stirred, as though what you are seeing there in your thoughts is here in mine, and I see it, as if time had marched backward and we had arrived again at those good times and that comfortable life, and my tears flow at the clear vision of all those things you've described."

To me, the amazing reality of listening to the discussions between these old timers was incredible, as my mind was filled with such feelings of wonder. I could tell that an eerie physical sensation was coming over me, and my insides were roiling with an insidious feeling of weakness—"what is the manner of these strange feelings, and what does this revelation mean?" Clearly, during countless years that had flown by on the wings of time, the land and the lifestyle of the native people had remained steadfast and true. But while I was considering and reflecting on that thought, it seemed my eyes closed for just a moment, and on opening again, when I looked, I could still see those oldsters, not, however, in the garb I'd seen them in before, for their bodies were now exposed, with only a rough scrap of bark cloth drawn about the loins of the old man and a narrow piece of pounded olonā fiber as a skirt for the old lady; the garlands that they had worn were now ruined, the 'ilima flowers dried and shriveled, the feathers fallen loose from their cord. I noticed that their heads now hung down, and then I heard again the sound of their wraithlike voices, filled with words of sorrow. I listened to the old man as he spoke to his companion:

"Alas, it seems, for you and I, and alas for the people, and, too, for the land. As we look over the length and breadth of the land, from top to bottom, and see all the things that are familiar to our sight, it seems that all is covered up by a gloomy haze, and once it clears, what a pity, I can see that, just as that haziness faded away, so did all the features of the land from the past that you and I had just seen, and now, I see that it is changed and so very strange. Our house compounds are gone, and so are the taro terraces; the multitude of our brethren who were just here are no more, and yet I can make out a great multitude of houses of very different people, strangers that I've never seen before. My eyes sweep from north to south, east to west, and all that I see is different. The sacred grounds of the chiefs have lost their nobility and sanctity, and the crown flag is no more; a completely new, striped flag is there instead. Where Ka'upena's house stood, there are buildings different from any I've seen, and pig-tailed people are living in them. Upland a ways, there are short, chubby folk running about where the house of Ka'ōmea's family stood. Scattered atop the ridge, I see a great cluster of houses, filled to overflowing with white-skinned people, chattering in a slurred language, their children running about like goats. Listen, wife, I'm overwhelmed by all of this, for it seems that all of what you said has come to be, about you seeing the rise of 'Āinahou, climbing up over the cliff base to reach the top of 'Ulaka'a and Konahuanui. Woe, it seems, for us. There will soon be no familiar features of the land at all, and once those are gone, the land will be completely different and strangers will be the proud residents. The strangers are becoming the local natives, while you and I, natives, are strangers, guests, and those people are becoming quite comfortable and wealthy, while you and I wander as nearly naked vagabonds."

At that point, as I listened to these ghostly voices expressing their sorrowful laments, the two of them embraced each other and their ethereal bodies quietly slipped away, disappearing completely like a puff of smoke in a breeze, leaving everything completely quiet and still. I stood up and stretched my stiff joints, whereupon I recognized the choking cry of the ʻalae bird, as an owl swept by before me and a pig grunted at the base of the cliff. A weakness spread throughout my body, my hair stood on end, my scalp developed an odd tingle my eyelashes stood out in excitement and an eerie sensation made my knees quake.

With all of these odd feelings that had come upon me, being completely overwhelmed with the strangeness of it all, my eyes looked to the west and beheld the statue of Kamehameha the Conqueror, and my ears heard a great, booming voice, like thunder, coming from where that statue stands, and with an intimidating and majestic voice, it uttered these words, which I can still hear and continue to recall with awe:

"I was victorious in conquest from Hawaiʻi, the realm of Chief Keawe, all the way to Kauaʻi, land of Chief Manokalanipō; I entwined each of the threads into a single united cord of islands; I spread out the regal feather cape of love for steadfast unity and togetherness as a single people; I laid down the foundation where a secure home came to stand; I proclaimed the "Māmalahoe" Law, under which old men, women and children would find safety upon any path; and I left those things for the descendants of the ʻĪ, the Mahi, the Palena, and the Palalauʻī clans who had suffered the wounds of the barbed spears of war; it was like a regal helmet left as a legacy by the chief for his people, who together would care for its sanctity; I consecrated the garland of the arching rainbow in the sky with those pearl-like words—"the life of the land is perpetuated in righteousness;" however, O people of my own flesh and blood, O kin of mine who share an ancestry from ancient time, when I look to find you, you are not there; the precious lei that I strung together, twisted, entwined, and strove to create as a permanent adornment and privilege for all of you, my descendants, has taken wing and has become the proud decoration of strangers, and now a ghostly and echoing voice resounds, crying out—"The life of the land is lost through wrongdoing!"

Is this, then, the answer?

TRANSLATED BY PUAKEA NOGELMEIER

KAHIKINA KELEKONA (JOHN GRAVES MUNN SHELDON) (1844-1914) *was the son of Hannah Hoolaikahiluonalani Munn and Henry Lawrence Sheldon, a newspaper editor. John was the editor of the newspapers* Ka Elele Poakolu *and* Hawaii Holomua. *He wrote the story of Kaluaikoolau in 1906 as well as the biography of Joseph Nawahi. He was married twice and had fourteen children.*

The Plantation

A new world ... Asian faces, Asian muscles ... I would like to present myself for Hawaii ... With a bundle on my back ... Myself, a contracted farmer ... Picture brides ... She could not read her English name ... Hot sun, bitter cane ... The knee joints of the sugarcane stalks ... Chopping as if cutting arms and legs ... A lizard darting through the leaves ... They're nothing but animals ... Where is home?

Yoshiko Matsuda

UNTITLED

Unmei wa
Hone wo gaichi ni
Uzumubeku
Sokoku wo ideshi
Ippo ni arishi

My destiny—
It was the first step
Out of the motherland
To bury my bones
In the foreign land

TRANSLATED BY JIRO NAKANO

YOSHIKO MATSUDA *was born in 1900 in Aki, Kōchi-ken, Japan. She came to Hawai'i in 1924 with her husband, the Reverend Ryugen Matsuda, a Buddhist priest. She was a member of* tanka*-writing clubs in Hilo, Hawai'i; Honolulu; and on Maui; and founded the Odamaki Tanka Honolulu Branch. She wrote thousands of* tanka *poems and received the Hawai'i Award for Literature in 1990.*

Marie M. Hara

from "THE HONEYMOON HOTEL, 1895"

The Immigration Station was a formidable building with intricate wooden decorations all over its multi-leveled roofs and windows. It could be mistaken for a temple, except that it was hardly Japanese in feeling. After the long ship voyage every detail of life on shore took her eager interest. Life here was such a novelty, just as people promised it would be. To think of it, within a season's time she had seen both the city of Hiroshima and now, Honolulu. Remarkable. And here there were no seasons. Curious. She had thought about the persistent heat while they passed long hours in quarantine.

They had to wait endlessly. Sectioned off separately for more medical questions, then lined up all together, and finally seated in a row on a polished bench, each of the women clung to the arm of a shipboard friend. Chika and she sat tensely that way for two hours of fretful anticipation.

Her name was called. When Yamamoto-san stepped out of the group of men to claim her as his wife, Sono saw his face from the vantage of her lowered head through half-closed eyes. She had to compose herself. He looked too old! The photograph she kept in her kimono depicted a smooth-shaven young man. The Yamamoto person who stood at the desk appeared to be at least forty years old and bearded heavily. Sono felt her lower lip quiver and Chika's reassuring clutch growing tighter on her now tingling arm.

So that was how he had managed to trick the family. Certainly people had forewarned them in Hiroshima that the Hawaii men were desperate in their desire to establish families. But Yamamoto-san was known to her uncle. Shouldn't he have prevented such an awkward match, knowing the man's true age? Sono was so obliged to Uncle, indeed, everyone was, for his support through the difficult years. But not to have guided her, when he must have known the true circumstances, his elderly friend's trickery. Yamamoto-san looked even older than her uncle when he moved about so cautiously, talking to the foreigners.

Her mind raced through scattered images, connecting her confusion with memories of her seated family, noisily discussing Sono's marriage, and her life faraway in Hawaii. Unconcerned by the bustle of activity around the bench, she brooded in turmoil. It was Chika who timed the little push forward when the stranger turned to face her.

Sono managed, somehow, to bow and maintain a calm demeanor, while she mentally totaled his positive attributes. He did seem to be clean, prosperous and kindly. He was polite. He smiled. Truly as hard as leaving with him was saying goodbye to Chika when all the papers had been signed, all the questions answered, and all the officials signaled them outward.

For some reason the man called Miura, Seinosuke, who was Chika's husband, was not present. There must have been a delay in his traveling from another island. Without her having to ask, Yamamoto-san promised to check on Chika's situation tomorrow. She looked very unhappy, but she smiled graciously as she bid them farewell, the humiliated Chika, a lonely kimono-clad figure left waiting on the long bench. The other girls hurried off or looked away, not wanting to injure her further with their obvious pity.

When Sono walked out of the building, following Yamamoto-san to the wagon, she had no idea where they would be going. The horse-drawn vehicle, more an open air cart, carried a number of the couples past the waterfront to a three-story brick and wood building. She could not read the English name on the sign in front of the hotel. She had stayed in an inn only once before and this could not be the same. Once in, she noticed with relief that the clerks and maids were Japanese. A tiny lobby with large chairs and sofas quickly filled up with a dozen couples and the women's large willow trunks and cloth bundles. She saw that the other girls, like herself, seemed self-conscious and subdued. Only Kono-san and her sister, Kumi-san, continued to whisper and chatter as usual. Very rudely they discussed someone whose face, it seemed, took on the appearance of "a dog when it laughs out loud." In the silence around them, smiles materialized on the faces of silent listeners. Sono did not appreciate the joke; for all she knew, they were discussing one of their own husbands.

When the manager of the hotel appeared in the main doorway, however, it became obvious that he was the one. Beaming at the company, his lip curled upward in a cock-eyed manner. No one looked more like a smiling dog, Sono considered, than this slightly balding man. Suppose he had been Yamamoto-san. Sono inhaled deeply. There was a new mood of jocularity in the room; the group grew noisy.

Slowly they were being taken upstairs to their rooms. While Yamamoto-san talked with the manager at the desk, Sono gently adjusted the obi around her waist and pressed her perspiring face with a handkerchief which she had tucked away in her sleeve. A slowly growing numbness seemed to spread into her shoulders, causing her to sit up straighter and compose her features into a stern expressionlessness.

Looking surreptitiously at the other couples, she noted with fleeting envy that Tome-san was matched with a vigorous farmer. Sleepy-eyed Tome was no beauty, even as Sono assumed she herself was ordinary in looks. On ship the other women found themselves in idle agreement that Chika was the most attractive, a "born beauty." What an unlucky fate she had found in this place.

In an instant Yamamoto was leading Sono up to the little room over the street. He seemed to prance eagerly up the flights of steps.

"Leave the luggage," he counseled. "They will bring it up later."

But all of her possessions were in the *kori*. What would she have to change into, if delivery were delayed? What if someone was a thief? Frowning, Sono said nothing.

In silence they sat on the zabuton pillows set out on the grassmat flooring. No table, no tea service, nothing but a tall chair, a lamp and a small window which drew a hazy light into the opposite end of the room, gave the space its details.

Presently her husband spoke, looking directly at her face with an appraising curiosity that embarrassed her. He asked questions about their families in Hiroshima, the crops, and the voyage across the Pacific. She answered each evenly.

"It is to be hoped, Sono-san, that you will be at home here in Hawaii."
He cleared his throat and watched her face. Yamamoto-san seemed uneasy
and did not continue.

MARIE M. HARA, *born during World War II, is the author of* Bananaheart and Other Stories
and co-editor of Intersecting Circles: the Voices of Hapa Women in Poetry and Prose. *As an
assistant professor of English at the University of Hawai'i, she teaches composition, literature,
and creative writing classes. One of the organizers of the Talk Story Conferences, Hara continues efforts toward building literary publishing in Hawai'i through Bamboo Ridge Press.*

Chan E. Park

from IN 1903, PAK HŬNGBO WENT TO HAWAI'I

*(The stage is bare, except two platforms for the Korean musicians on the right and the
Hawaiian chanters on the left. Screen in rear for slide projection of the changing scenery throughout. Another screen to the right for English subtitles for songs in Korean.
Lights dim. In the dark, Korean wind and percussion play salp'uri tunes, then strings
join. Light gradually goes up on two Korean musicians playing on the platform on the
right. Music accelerates, from medium chungmori, to syncopated chajinmori, climaxes
to frenzied hwimori, then winds down to chungmori rhythmic cycle.)*

Spoken: To their new homes in the plantation,
            Koreans brought their stories.

Sung: "*Aigo*, Older Brother!
            You tell your younger brother to get out,
            Where am I to go?
            In this viciously cold winter,
            Where and how may I survive?
            Shall I enter Chiri Mountain,
            Or starve to death on the way?"

            "Stupid! Do I have to tell you where to go?
            Save your breath and go!"

(Slide: Snowing on Paektusan Mountain)

Spoken: Hŭngbo wanders through eight provinces,
            Looking for a place to settle.

At this time, Japan was intensifying its colonial grip on Korea.
Many farmlands were being taken,
Many Koreans were being displaced,
Many crossed the borders to the Manchurian wasteland.

Sung:

Chorus: *Arirang, arirang, arariyo.*
     I go over the Arirang Hill.

1. With a bundle on my back, I go over the Arirang Hill.
2. Father, Mother, hurry, they say the soil in North Kando is good.
3. Grabbing my aching heart, I go over Paektusan Hill.

Chorus: *Ariari sŭrisŭri arariyo.*
     I go over the Arirang Hill

1. Who took my jade soil, and left me a beggar's gourd?
2. Enemy, enemy, my enemy, he with the gun is my enemy.
3. He who argues well went to court, and he who works well went to grave.

Spoken: At a schoolyard in Inch'ŏn,
     Hŭngbo chances upon an announcement that reads:

(In the Korean traditional style of book recitation)
"Looking for healthy, well mannered people." That's me!
"Salary is fifteen dollars a month.
Work ten hours per day, Sunday off." Hm!
"Housing and medical will be taken care of by the plantation owner. Education is free, and the children can learn English."

"English? Not Confucian classics?
Well, beggars can't be too choosy, sign me on."

Pak Hŭngbo and one hundred one fellow Koreans boarded a ship called *Genkai Maru.*
The ship sails out to the Pacific.

Sung: *(Chinyang)*

To the middle of the water, the ship sails.
Endless blue sea, majestic waves.

Chorus: *Ŏgiya, ŏgiya,ŏhŏ—giya, ŏgiya.*

White duckweeds bloom on the shore,
Seagulls fly up the red reed hill.

Chorus: *Ŏgiya, ŏgiya, ŏhŏ—giya, ŏgiya.*

Out from the estuary of Han River,
Geese circle the harbor in bidding farewell.

(Chungmori)

Chorus: *Ŏgiya-ch'a, Ŏgiya-ch'a!*

Set the sail to the gentle wind, weigh the anchor!
Seagulls, high up, frolic through the clouds.

Chorus: *Ŏgiya-ch'a, Ŏgiya-ch'a!*

Boundless water, endless sea,
Where are we headed?

(Chajinmori)

Chorus: *Ŏgiya-dwiyŏ-ch'a, ŏgiya-dwiyŏ-ch'a!*
         Ehehehe ŏgiya-dwiyŏ—ŏhŏ,
         Ŏŏŏŏ-ŏya, ŏ-hŏgiya . . .

(Overlaps with a Hawaiian chant.)

(Slide: Black-and-white photo of the old Honolulu Harbor)

All: *Ya! Hawai-da!* (Wow! This is Hawai'i)

(Local children greet the newcomers with leis.)

All: *Ige muŏyŏ? P'ulmokkŏri-ya? Naemsae ch'aam chotta!*
     (What's this? Grass necklace? Smells good!)

CHAN E. PARK, *born in Chinhae, Korea, in 1951, received her PhD from the University of Hawai'i at Mānoa, and is currently associate professor of Korean language, literature, and performance studies at Ohio State University. Her specialization is the research and performance of* p'ansori, *Korean story-singing—its performance in transnational contexts in particular, and the related oral narrative/lyrical/dramatic traditions and their places in the shaping of modern Korean drama. She publishes and performs nationally and transnationally.*

Hong-gi Yi
"호놀루루에 도착해서"

항해한지 27일만에 호놀루루에 도착해
이민국에서 문답을 잘 하였다.

솟아오른 산 아래에는 천 개의 집이 둘러져 있고
배가 밀집해서 있는 배 머리 옆에는 큰 시장이 즐비하더라.

섬은 이루되 항상 봄이고 나비가 노는 곳이며
나라 이름은 합중국에 잡종의 얼굴이 섞여있다.

나는 팔려 온 농부로서 자유가 없고
노로 배를 저어서 푸른 파도와 흰구름이 맞닿아 있는 바다
를 지나갈 뿐이다.

"THE FIRST IMPRESSION OF HONOLULU"

After twenty-seven days of voyage and arriving in Honolulu,
I gave the right answer at immigration.

Thousands of houses are surrounded by a soaring mountain.
A big market opens to the harbor where ships standing close
together are at anchor.

Here is the island, where spring is all year round, and butterflies
flutter from flower to flower.
The name of this country is "the Mixed States," and the hybrid
faces of its freely mingling people suggest this.

But myself, a sold farmer, I have no freedom;
I am just rowing a boat in the sea where blue waves and white
clouds touch each other.

TRANSLATED BY HYERAN SEO

HONG-GI YI (1877-1974) *was born in Hwanghae Province in North Korea and emigrated to Hawai'i in 1904. He worked on sugar plantations on Kaua'i and the island of Hawai'i before moving to Honolulu in 1941. A committed nationalist, he wrote poems throughout his life in Hawai'i that expressed his anger and frustration at the tragic fate his homeland was experiencing under Japanese colonial rule. His unpublished autobiographical poems are written in the classical Sino-Korean.*

Cathy Song

"PICTURE BRIDE"

She was a year younger
than I,
twenty-three when she left Korea.
Did she simply close
the door of her father's house
and walk away. And
was it a long way
through the tailor shops of Pusan
to the wharf where the boat
waited to take her to an island
whose name she had
only recently learned,
on whose shore
a man waited,
turning her photograph
to the light when the lanterns
in the camp outside
Waialua Sugar Mill were lit
and the inside of his room
grew luminous
from the wings of moths
migrating out of the cane stalks?
What things did my grandmother
take with her? And when
she arrived to look
into the face of the stranger
who was her husband,
thirteen years older than she,
did she politely untie
the silk bow of her jacket,
her tent-shaped dress
filling with the dry wind
that blew from the surrounding fields
where the men were burning the cane?

CATHY SONG *was born in Honolulu in 1955. She is the author of* Picture Bride; Frameless Windows, Squares of Light; School Figures; *and* The Land of Bliss. *A fifth collection of poetry,* Cloud Moving Hands, *was published in the fall of 2007.*

Virgilio Menor Felipe

from HAWAI'I: A PILIPINO DREAM

I stayed to help through with the last farming. Then one morning in No-biyembre after the harvest, I saddled my young eskoro fathered by the old one from Cagayan. As soon as I landed on top, I heeled the horse. It took off to a trot and I adjusted my tabungaw. As we went through the baetan, I heeled 'em again and pulled on the reins so we bounced to a double-trot. Ay, it was a beautiful horse. It danced and trotted and galloped in the wind so smooth like swimming through the air in a dream. It was such a nice ride to Laoag town next to the river.

I rode west on the street of Rizal that was lined for a block with the stores of the Chinese. I hear there are many Indians now too, selling cloths. Yes, they must have a lot of threads with all that cloth they wrap around their heads. We used to think that they had headaches all the time, or maybe cold heads. Hehehe!

I galloped the horse across an open field west of the marketplace then let it trot straight toward the municipio. The recruiter's office for Hawai'i was directly behind. I hear it is now a dispensary of the Red Cross. There was no free clinic then.

The agent was just coming down the steps when I halted my horse in front of the recruiter's office. He was a fellow Filipino but a Hawaiiano.

"Where are you going?" he asked.

"I would like to present myself for Hawai'i, Apo," I answered as I came down from my horse.

"Wait, I'll go see if I can get you a place on the next load." He turned back up into the door and when he came out again he had a paper in his hand. "Come up, so we can fill in the forms." He waved, so I went in.

"You write?" he asked.

"No," I lied, so he filled in the paper for me.

"Come back Monday for the doctor to check you up!" The Hawaiiano recruiter patted me on the back. "When you come, bring twenty-five, and I'll make sure of your papers for a place." He said, shaking my hand.

It was like that. "Tip" is what we call it here, but that is our custom to pasoksok, slip some for a favor.

For the check-up with the doctor, there were so many of us, so young and at the peak of our strength. The Hawaiiano stood at the door with a big cigar. "Give me five!" he shouted, and men went in by fives.

When I went in, ay, that doctor with glasses looked at my asshole, squeezed my balls with a smile and made me cough, then he pressed my tongue with a stick and peeked down my throat using a flashlight, then into my nose, my ears, and my eyes. He checked my heart, my ribs, my stomach, my knees, my feet, and my teeth—like a horse, everything! Same like checking up a car, no? I guess it was to see if I was in good condition. Hehehe!

This was my first time I had ever been checked up in the ass like that by another person. The doctor was Haole. He was a big man, and wore khaki pants with the white shirt. "Komosta boy, atta boy!" he kept on saying. I was all smiles, of course, because I wanted to be taken.

But I thought I wasn't going to be taken because in my group I was the skinniest although the tallest. They told us skinnies to step back one, and let the huskies through the back of the room. Then the agent came in smiling, telling us, "You are taken!" And we almost shouted for joy. He gave us our tickets. "Don't lose them. Come back next Monday morning, before seven o'clock, to take the truck to Currimao."

I was so happy! With a great big smile I stopped by a cantina for a halo-halo, cold sweet fruit refreshment. It cost me two centavos, but I gave the girl a nickel. Ay, money was very dear in those days.

When I got home, I was really happy. Elias was there. I threw him my tabungaw. "It's yours now!" I said, and we raced up the stairs. I was laughing so much I jumped to the top in two steps! But when we got inside they were all crying. They were so sad to see me go.

VIRGILIO MENOR FELIPE, *son of '46 sakada, Nicolas, was born in Laoag, Philippines, and came to Hawai'i at age twelve. He attended Waialua, Castle, and Kailua high schools, graduated from the University of Hawai'i, and helped found the Ethnic Studies Department and Operation Manong, now the Office of Multicultural Student Services. He has taught at the University of Hawai'i and the University of California at Berkeley. He is the author of* Hawai'i: A Pilipino Dream, *and has three children, Nicole, Steve, and Pikake.*

Albert Ross

from A SUGAR PRINCESS

'I tell you it's the same thing as slavery!' said a passenger named Hicks, hailing from Kalamazoo. 'Those Japs and Chinamen are brought out under what is called a three years' contract, and during that time they are driven into the field with black-snake whips, sick or well, and treated like dogs. Although legally they can be made to work but ten hours a day, the clocks are kept to please their masters, and they often put in more than twelve. As soon as the country is fully annexed to the United States there'll be an end to this business.'

'I should have thought the people would have foreseen that and fought annexation,' suggested a young man from Connecticut.

'If we hadn't taken them pretty soon, the Japanese Government would,' said Hicks. 'They would have attacked the place to secure justice for the Japs abused there and held on, just as England and Germany have done in similar cases.'

'The Japanese—pooh!' interrupted a gentleman from New York City. 'What do they amount to?'

'Amount to?' repeated Hicks, indignantly. 'Do you ask what a nation of forty million people amounts to, with one of the biggest navies in the world? They'd have taken the island so quick it would make your head swim, if Uncle Sam hadn't forestalled them. The Hawaiian Government didn't own a ship, a fort or a full regiment of soldiers.'

The New Yorker disdained to reply. It is often as effective to assume that air, in the eyes of those who listen, as to bring forward the most conclusive arguments. The passengers were led to believe that the New Yorker could have annihilated Mr. Hicks if he had been willing to enter into a wrangle with that hot-headed person.

Rev. Mr. Lovejoy did not disdain to spend a part of his time in the smoking-room or to indulge in an occasional cigar there. He smoked solemnly and slowly, as befitted his cloth, and his presence certainly had a restraining influence on the things said around him.

'If you will permit me a word,' he ventured, to Mr. Hicks, 'I think you do an unintentional injustice to the sugar-planters. I have spent some time there and have found no such condition as you describe.'

'In what respect?' demanded Hicks, fiercely.

'About the men being driven to work with whips, for one thing,' was the mild reply. 'I do not say it is never done, but I saw no evidence of it. And as to the hours the labourers work, most of them carry nickel watches, and are very quick to notice when their day has expired.'

To this Mr. Hicks responded, warmly that he had his information from good sources, and believed it to be true.

'I think if you will look thoroughly into the matter,' said Mr. Lovejoy, gently, 'you will find that these benighted heathen are brought to a Christian land by gentlemen of character, who defray their passage out of their own pockets; that they receive several times as much pay as they would earn at home at the same work; that nothing is required of them except to keep an agreement which they fully understood before leaving their own country; and that most of them manage, during the time they remain, to lay up a goodly amount of money, with which many go into business and amass small fortunes.'

The conversation was interesting all who sat about the room, and every eye was turned toward Mr. Hicks when his turn came to speak.

'What is done with a labourer who refuses to work?' he demanded. 'Tell me that!'

'He is taken before a judge and given his choice of carrying out the agreement he made when his fare was paid from Japan, or of going to jail.'

'Exactly. Ex-actly!' said Mr. Hicks. 'Now if that don't make a slave of him, I'd like to know what would. It is contrary to the laws of the United States to enforce labour by contract, and the moment we get full possession of the country every working man will be free to quit his employment if he pleases.'

Mr. Lovejoy asked quietly if Mr. Hicks thought it would be honest for a man who had accepted money to cross the Pacific to refuse to carry out his agreement—and for a Christian nation to abet him in the act.

'Christian nation!' repeated Hicks, with scorn. 'Who says America is a Christian nation? What *is* a Christian nation anyway? One that helps a lot of money-grabbers to swindle coolies out of the value of their labour? The missionaries came to Hawaii and stole the land from the Kanakas; and now their sons are making themselves millionaires by bringing poor Japs and Chinese over to work for half the wages a white man would require. I've no patience to talk with you!'

The indignant speaker flounced out of the room with his concluding words, as if he required the entire width of the deck to contain himself. The clergyman puffed his cigar peacefully in silence, not appearing in the least disturbed. Mr. Latham, who had remained silent till now, leaned over to ask if the reverend champion of the sugar-growers had any knowledge of the various plantations and of the best place to invest capital.

'I couldn't say, really,' was the answer he received, 'what is the best purchase just now. But I think the "Never" is paying about five per cent.'

'Only five per cent!' Mr. Latham's jaw dropped.

'That's sixty per cent, a year. They reckon these plantation stocks by their monthly dividends. You will have to pay about four hundred dollars or so a share, which will reduce your net returns to fifteen per cent. per annum. It's not quite what they ought to pay, but we shouldn't think of this matter from the pecuniary side altogether. What gratifies me is the glorious opportunity these poor heathen have to learn true religion and see it exemplified in the lives of their employers. Who can doubt that the time they spend among such refining influences will ultimately have a great effect in destroying the superstitions and idolatries of Japan and China?'

A young man named Selover, who was secretary of the Y.M.C.A. in his town in Iowa, inquired if much attention was given to instructing the labourers in religious matters.

'Why,' was the somewhat hesitating reply, 'there are churches which they can attend, and some missions. They can learn the true path if they wish to.'

'I trust there are no saloons or anything of that sort?'

'There are, I am sorry to say, a very few in some of the larger places. High licence prevails in Honolulu, for instance. It is a serious question, where so many sailors come ashore, men from the warships and that sort of thing. There's not much drunkenness though, as a rule, and the places have to close early.'

Mr. Lovejoy resumed a book he had been reading, and another passenger essayed to furnish Mr. Latham with a little more information.

'I would advise subscribing to the new ventures that are being put on the market,' he said. 'The average assessment is two dollars a month on each share. Even house servants and cabmen have become rich by subscribing for these shares and selling out again. You see the Hawaiians have several advantages over other countries. Not only is their soil exceptionally fertile, but their product is admitted to the United States free of duty, thus putting two cents a pound into the pockets of the producers. I've heard of plantations that are good for eight hundred dollars' worth of sugar per acre in a single crop. With annexation that's pretty sure to hold. Old Van Steuben' (the speaker looked cautiously around to note that Billy had left the room again) 'came to Honolulu a beggar boy, and now he's worth—the Lord only knows how much! And there's Millenham and Waterman and the Snookses and the Castletons, all made millionaires within the last five years.'

The Y.M.C.A. secretary from Iowa walked out on the deck, somewhat troubled in his mind. A text of Scripture kept vibrating in his brain, 'Seek ye first the kingdom of God and His righteousness.' He hoped these planters had done that before they realised so fully the succeeding words, 'and all these things shall be added unto you.'

It comforted him, however, to know that Rev. Mr. Lovejoy, the benevolent-looking clergyman, had looked into the matter, and was quite satisfied with the treatment accorded to the labourers in these remarkably productive vineyards.

ALBERT ROSS *is the pseudonym of Linn Boyd Porter (1851-1916). Born in Massachusetts, he worked in the newspaper business, and for thirteen years owned and edited the* Cambridge Chronicle. *He wrote novels and escape fiction.*

Genny Lim

from BITTER CANE

Storm over Oahu. Kakuku sugar cane plantation. A weary, middle-aged Chinese traveller, wearing white and a cootie hat, enters carrying a wrapped bundle. His movements should be stylized and suggestive of another world. He stops, listens and puts down his bundle.

LAU HING *(attentively)*: Listen to that. Sounds like it's never going to stop. Hear it hammering down the tin roofs? Drilling through cracks, dripping down walls, filling empty tins on the floor? Yu-chiang, the master of floods, remembers our sins. *(Miming)* Sometimes he cups the ocean in his hands and hurls a tidal wave! *(Howling of wind)* Hear him growling? *(Pauses.)* There's nothing more lonely than the sound of wind and rain. But once it stops, you're back in the fields, knuckling under the sun. Just when you think you'll collapse, you look up and there she'll be, the Cane Witch. Smiling at you from behind high stalks; long black hair shining, naked brown arms beckoning you. You blink your eyes twice to see if you're dreaming and she sighs. You don't know where she came from or who she is but you want her. You want her so bad you can feel your heart trembling. You chase her through row after row of cane till you're breathless. When you finally catch up to her, she spins around and looks at you. Her two dark eyes are caverns. You reach to enter, but a stabbing pain pierces your heart and she disappears. There's no trace of her. All you see is a lizard darting through the leaves. And the faint smell of pikake. *(Woman's laughter and sound of rain. LAU HING crosses downstage left where he remains for the rest of the play. Light goes up on a wooden shack room with a vanity, a bed and a few feminine, Victorian articles. The set should be evocative, not realistic. On the bed LI-TAI is giggling as KAM SU tickles her.)*

KAM: Teach me!

LI-TAI: I'm not Hawaiian.

KAM *(lifting her camisole)*: Then you need exposure. *(Kisses her navel.)*

LI-TAI *(sighing)*: Piko.

KAM *(tickling)*: Piko, piko, piko!

LI-TAI: Diu-mao-gwai!

KAM: Who you calling a drunk?

LI-TAI *(puts out her palm in a no-nonsense manner)*: My money?

(KAM irritably picks up a fifth of whiskey from her dresser and takes several snorts. She grabs it from him and puts it back.)

KAM: Pay day is Saturday. I'll pay you then.

LI-TAI: What do you think I am? You pay me now!

KAM: I got one year left on my contract. *(Digs into his pocket and hands her several coins.)* One more lousy year. Then I'm free.

LI-TAI *(looks at the coins with disgust)*: Fifty cents! Is that all you got?

KAM: Have a heart, Li-Tai. I came all this way in the storm!

LI-TAI: And you can go back in it!

KAM: Please . . .

LI-TAI: You wouldn't do this to a haole woman!

KAM: Just this once. I'm begging you!

LI-TAI: *Jawk-gee!* Do you think you're catching a pig?

KAM: As a countryman!

LI-TAI *(throws the coins on the floor in anger)*: Get out!

KAM: You think you so high and mighty? You think you too good for me, huh? Well I'll tell you something. You and that *pake luna* are nothing but a pair of blood-sucking leeches!

LI-TAI: You are dirt! *(She slaps him. He grabs her violently, forces her onto the bed, grabbing her bound feet. She struggles helplessly underneath him.)*

KAM *(aroused)*: Crippled woman, where can you go? You have no feet—only petals for toes. *(She spits at him. He twists her ankles. She clenches her teeth in pain.)* You can only submit! *(He bites the tip of her foot as if it was a delicacy.)* Like fish out of water, you see?

(She struggles free and in a frenzy, gathers his coins and flings them at him.)

LI-TAI: Take your crumbs and get out!

KAM: Why spit on your own kind? You think you're better than me?

LI-TAI: Shit is better than you. *(Hysterically)* Get out! Get out!

KAM *(pointing his finger)*: One day, you'll be sorry. *(He exits, slamming the door violently. She takes his shirt, opens the door, and flings it out. We hear him yell from outside.)* Pake snake! Mercenary whore!

LI-TAI *(screaming)*: Fook will kill you if you ever come back here!

(She slams the door shut, leaning against it with eyes shut. She takes big gulps from the whiskey bottle. She goes slowly to the bed, sits, then lights the opium lamp on the bedside table and prepares the pipe. She takes deep tokes. The drug has an almost immediate calming effect on her. She picks up a cricket cage from her bed table and studies it with intense fascination. The room fills with smoke and the crescendo of rain, then the sound of a cane worker singing:

> Hawaii, Hawaii
> so far, far from home,
> Hawaii, Hawaii
> My bones ache and my heart breaks,
> thinking about the one I left behind.

(The light fades on LI-TAI and comes up on KAM in the field, holding a machete and singing:

Hawaii, Hawaii
so far, far from home,
For every cane I cut, there are a thousand more,
with so many days to pay.
Hawaii, Hawaii
Don't let me die of misery,
don't bury me under the cane fields.

(*LAU HING watches him silently from a distance. KAM wipes his brow with his sleeve, then hacks the stalks with vengeance.*)

KAM: Goddam sonavabitches! (*Throws his whole body into cutting motion.*) Take that! (*Again striking*) And that, son-a-va-bitch!

(*FOOK MING, a foreman, enters with a new worker.*)

FOOK (*to KAM*): Less mouth, more action! (*Indicating newcomer*) I want you to teach this boy to cut cane. Make sure he doesn't cut the stalks too high. I want the stubs nice and low. Show him the right way. Stack them straight. No sloppy piles. No cheating. I got eyes. We have to lop this field by Saturday—otherwise, overtime.

KAM: No overtime! Our contract says no overtime Sunday!

FOOK: I'm boss here! If I say you work, you work. If I say you work overtime, you work overtime. Understand?

KAM (*stubbornly*): I understand the contract.

FOOK: Well, now, I wouldn't want to violate your contract. If you don't like working Sundays, you can work nights.

KAM: No dinner, no work!

FOOK: No work, no pay! You got that, Chinaboy? (*Waits for a response.*) Now get back to work. That's what we pay you for. (*Exits. KAM takes the machete and lands it with force.*)

KAM: You haole lap-dog! (*Strikes.*) Profit from the blood of your countrymen! (*Strikes.*) Traitor for the white devils! (*Strikes.*) Bastard! (*To Wing*) Back up! Look out for flying splinters. You might lose an eye or nose! You want to learn how to cut cane, boy? This is how we cut. Nice and deep. Down to the bone. They want the juice in that stalk. Don't let it run to the ground. The bottom's where the vein's at. Easy. Nice and sweet for the mill to grind. If you can cut one, you can cut eight! Just think of each cane stalk as Fook Ming's skinny neck . . . Aiii-ee-eee!!! (*A final angry blow.*)

(*Fadeout.*)

GENNY LIM *is a native San Franciscan poet–vocalist, performer, director, playwright, and edu-cator. Her award–winning play,* Paper Angels, *was broadcast on American Playhouse in 1985. She is the author of two collections of poetry and co–author of* Island: Poetry and History of Chinese Immigrants on Angel Island, 1910-1940. *She has appeared at numerous jazz festivals throughout the country: San Francisco, San Diego, Chicago, Houston, Berkeley, and San Jose.*

Maxine Hong Kingston

from CHINA MEN

T he men who had come earlier also said that the plantation had a rule that they not talk at work, but this rule was so absurd, he thought he must have misheard tones.

He lay down out in the open. The sights of the day unreeled behind his eyelids—the ocean jumping with silver daggers, fronds shredding in wind, twin rainbows, spinning flowers, the gray mass of the maze tree like all the roads of many lives. How was he to marvel adequately, voiceless? He needed to cast his voice out to catch ideas. I wasn't born to be silent like a monk, he thought, then promptly said. "If I knew I had to take a vow of silence," he added, "I would have shaved off my hair and become a monk. Apparently we've taken a vow of chastity too. Nothing but roosters in this flock."

The next morning at 5 a.m., he was again standing before the fist of trees. The dimness of shapes gave the coming day many possibilities until the sun delineated the pleached trees, the mountains, and another day of toil. He worked for that day and the next and the next without saying anything, but got angry, chopping as if cutting arms and legs. He withstood the hours; he did the work well, but the rule of silence wrought him up whenever a demon rode by. He wanted to talk about how he sawed through trunks and the interlocked branches held the trees upright. He suddenly had all kinds of things to say. He wanted to tell the men who worked beside him about the rewards to look forward to, for example, chewing cane for breakfast; the fibers would clean their teeth like a toothbrush. "You go out on the road to find adventure," he wanted to say, "and what do you find but another farm where the same things happen day after day. Work. Work. Work. Eat. Eat. Eat. Shit and piss. Sleep. Work. Work." He axed a limb at each word. "Actually, I like being bored," he would have said. "Nothing bad is happening, no useless excitement." He wanted to discuss mutes and kings who rip out tongues by the roots.

And one day—he could not help it—he sang about the black mountains reddening and how mighty was the sun that shone on him in this enchanted forest and on his family in China. The sweep of the ocean was so wide, he watched the sun rise and set in it. In the heat of noon, he wished he could shoot out the sun, like Prince I, who dropped nine suns with his bow and arrows. The demons paid his singing no mind. They must have thought he was singing a traditional song when he was really commenting and planning.

"I've solved the talking," he sang to his fellow workers. "If that demon whips me, I'll catch the whip and yank him off his horse, crack his head like a coconut. In an emergency a human being can do miracles—fly, swim, lift mountains, throw them. Oh, a man is capable of great feats of speed and strength."

There was a bang or crack next to his ear. The demon was recoiling his whip. "Shut up, Paké." He heard distinct syllables out of the white demon's moving mouth. "Shut up. Go work. Chinaman, go work. You stay go work. Shut up." He caught every word, which surprised him so much, he forgot to grab the whip. He labored on, muttering, "Shut up. Shut up, you." He found a cut on his shoulder.

The men tried burning instead of cutting the trees. They set fires in the red heat of the sun. Bak Goong felt the fire was the same as his anger; his anger was this size and this red. But only the dead branches and leaves burned. Cutting the burned trees, the men became sooted black. To make them work faster, the demons had a trick of telling the slowest man that he was sick and had to take the day off without pay.

On their own time, after 5 p.m., the workers built two huts for bunkhouses, each with wooden beds laid head to foot one above another like the shelves on ships. They arranged gourds and vines, buckets, and hats on the verandas, which they kept adding to the huts. Bak Goong wove a hammock, and it was as comfortable as his mother's lap.

At the very end of the day, the men exchanged remedies. They scraped one another's backs with spoons to get rid of rheumatism and arthritis. For heat sickness they scraped necks with the edge of a coin cooled in water, the square hole in the middle of the coin giving a good grip. They slapped the insides of one another's elbows and knees, where tiredness collects. They soaked cuts and sores, and rubbed bruises with tobacco and whiskey. Some exercised, and Bak Goong learned some kung fu movements and also some ways of breathing that would strengthen his body and sharpen his brain. They nursed runaways who had escaped from other work camps. Bak Goong showed his scarring shoulder and said, "I will talk again. Listen for me." Boys put rocks under their pillows to stop crying at night. Several people not from the same village believed in "passing fear over fire," which means lifting one who has been badly frightenend and passing him over a fire. Some "passed rice over hearts" and some "over heads." Everybody thought that his way of doing things was the way all Chinese were supposed to do them.

Bak Goong worried that he had overlooked a trick clause in his contract and that he would not be paid at all, this was some kind of a slave labor camp. But pay day came. When the demon handed him his money Bak Goong counted it in front of him in Chinese and in business ("pidgin") English. He came out short. "Too little," he complained, holding up his fingers. "Too little bit money. Are you trying to catch a pig?" he asked, which meant to cheat, to take advantage of a greedy person.

The paymaster demon said, "Shut up, you. You shut up," clapping a hand over his own mouth several times. Bak Goong had been fined for talking. And sick men had been docked for every day they had been lying lazy in bed. Those who had not recovered from crossing the ocean got an accounting of how much they owed for food and lodging plus passage. The strong workers had money subtracted for broken tools.

The men cursed as they reckoned their pay. "Dead man." "Rotten corpse afloat." "Corpse on the roadside." "Hunchback with a turtle on his back," that is "Cuckold." "Your mother's ass." "Your mother's cunt." "They take my piss and shit away from me to feed their fields. Take my shit." "Eat my shit and piss. Drink piss, white monster. Eat shit." Bak Goong turned his ass at the pig catcher demon's face. He was finding out that the dollar a week wasn't the minimum wage but the maximum to strive for, that hoeing paid less than other jobs. The China Man accountant told him their wages were reduced until the plantation made a bigger profit. If Bak Goong did not give any dinner parties, did not drink or smoke or gamble, he would bring home maybe a hundred dollars after three years. The big talk about a thousand dollars must have been about men who came home old to die after scrimping for thirty years and more.

One day, like a knight rescuing a princess, Bak Goong broke clear through the thicket. Then he yoked bullocks, which had longer horns than his water buffalo, to the stumps and yanked them out. But the Hawaiians quit rather than help pull the boulders out of the earth. The remaining workers plowed around groups of big rocks in the middle of the fields. They were the first human beings to dig into this part of the island and see the meat and bones of the red earth. After rain, the mud ran like blood. The maze tree and woodrose sprouted behind the plows.

A team of six men including Bak Goong was sent to a plantation farther up the coast where cane already stood like a green army; the tassels were called "arrows." On the same day as he cleared land, he cut cane twice as tall as a man. The cane and rice growers were trying out the seasons. The workers stripped the long leaves like shucking corn. Dust shook loose, and they breathed it even through their kerchiefs. They cut the stalks close to the ground. The new men tasted the cane in which the sap was running warm. They cut the tips beneath the top three nodes for seed cane. There were seeds in the arrows, but it was faster to plant the nodes. The men seemed small and few wading among the sticky mounds.

The wagoners, who had a good job, drove the cane to the sugar mill on a route along the sea. It was crushed into molasses and boiled into sugar, for which the world was developing an insatiable hunger as for opium.

Bak Goong and his team brought the seed cane and a few bottles of rum back. The land was ready to be sown. They bagged the slips in squares of cloth tied over their shoulders. Flinging the seed cane into ditches, Bak Goong wanted to sing like a farmer in an opera. When his bag was empty, he stepped into the furrow and turned the seed cane so the nodes were to the sides, nodes on either side of the stick like an animal's eyes. He filled the trenches and patted the pregnant earth.

The work changed from watering season to hoeing season. He weeded the ivy that wrapped and would choke the young cane, the ratoons. The vines pulled like rubber. Using a short hoe, he knelt to uproot them, and carried the weeds to the fires at the ends of the rows else they take root where they fell. He worked even in the rain lest he lose money. Then there was a stripping season when he peeled the plants so they would use their strength to make sugar instead of leaves.

The next harvest, the men invented a burning season when they set the cane on fire to burn off the outer leaves instead of stripping by hand. They chose a dry and moderately windy day. Like a savage, Bak Goong ran with brands, torching the cane along the border. During the night watches, fires like furry red beasts lurked and occasionally roared into the black sky, showing it endless, nothing illuminated but smoke as high as the flames climbed. In the day the smoke curled like white snakes in the directions of the winds. Demons in white suits walked gingerly inspecting the char. Then there was clearing and planting, the hoeing, and harvest, and the planting season again. . . .

He woke one morning and felt a yang wind blow too hot through his body. He forced himself to sit up, not to be left behind among the sick, who were one-third of the workers. He rolled out of bed, stood, and fell. The healthier men were heading out into the humid day. He pulled himself up and dropped into his bunk. Asleep, again and again he seemed to jump out of bed, run sluggishly about gathering his clothes and tools, run through thick air in search of the fields, hear the demon boss in wait for him saying, "Late. You late, Paké," only to wake up and find that nothing had been done, no shoes put on, no breakfast eaten. He slept while the gecko lizards tsked-tsked-tsked at his sloth. He slept while a mushroom grew in a corner of the hut. His garden did not cajole him out of bed.

Each time he awoke, he was lying among the sick men, some breathing with clogged lungs like his, some doubled up holding their stomachs, cripples soaking their limbs. A few men looked bodily healthy but did not move. Somebody seemed to be piling dry leaves near the door and lighting them.

In his fever, he yearned so hard for his family that he felt he appeared in China. He reached out his arms and said, "Wife. Wife, I'm home." But she said, "What are you doing here? What are you doing here without the money? Moneyless and bodiless, you better go back to the Sandalwood Mountains. Go back and pick up your money and your body. Go back where you belong. Go now." He tried to talk to her, but his tongue was heavy and his throat blocked. He awoke certain that he had to cure himself by talking whenever he pleased.

Yin, the cool, was returning a little. Raindrops plunked loudly on the banana and ti leaves. It was what the Hawaiians called a cane-tapping rain. He chuckled with the geckos, their fingers and toes spread like little suctioning stars on the walls and ceilings, where they waited to flick at bugs. They were so sly playing dead, but through their translucent skins he saw their blue hearts beating and their organs swallowing. He shouted to make them leap to the ground. When they hid, he heard their clucking and chuckling. He had learned to recognize some of them individually. He told the sick men around him, "You can't die because then your poor wife will miss you, your family will go hungry awaiting your pay, and your mother will be uncertain forever what became of you. If there were only yourself, you would have the luxury of dying. Uncles and Brothers, I have diagnosed our illness. It is a congestion from not talking. What we have to do is talk and talk."

He lurched out to the rain barrel, poured water down his back and splashed it on his face. His wife would have scolded him for drinking cold water, a Sandalwood Mountain habit he was acquiring. He was carrying water to the sicker men when a demon galloped toward him, boss and horse both with cavernous nostrils wide open. Bak Goong turned toward the fields. The demon pushed sick men out the door. He pulled a boy by the hair. Bak Goong could tell he was saying, "Aha! I caught you malingering, you fake, lazy, sneaky chinaman." He pointed the whip toward the cane. "Go work, Paké, No stay sick." The demons had changed their rules again, no longer sending stragglers back to the huts. Bak Goong put his left arm around the stalks and leaned his face and body against them while his right arm swung at the feet of the cane. He neither sang nor spoke. Unhealthily, he wet handkerchiefs and plastered them on his head. . . .

The next day the men plowed, working purposefully, but they dug a circle instead of straight furrows. They dug a wide hole. They threw down their tools and flopped on the ground with their faces over the edge of the hole and their legs like wheel spokes.

"Hello down there in China!" they shouted. "Hello, Mother." "Hello, my heart and my liver."

"I miss you." "What are you doing right now?" "Happy birthday. Happy birthday for last year too."

"I've been working hard for you, and I hate it."

"Sometimes I forget my family and go to clubs. I drink all night." "I lost all the money again." "I've become an opium addict." "I don't even look Chinese any more." "I'm sorry I ate it all by myself."

". . . and I fell to my knees at the sight of twenty waterfalls." "I saw only one sandalwood tree."

They said any kind of thing. "Blonde demoness." "Polynesian demoness."

"I'm coming home by and by." "I'm not coming home." "I'm staying here in the Sandalwood Mountains."

"I want to be home," Bak Goong said.

"I'm bringing her home," said Bak Sook Goong.

They had dug an ear into the world, and were telling the earth their secrets.

"I want home," Bak Goong yelled, pressed against the soil, and smelling the earth. "I want my home," the men yelled together. "I want home. Home. Home. Home. Home."

Talked out, they buried their words, planted them. "Like cats covering shit," they laughed.

"That wasn't a custom," said Bak Goong. "We made it up. We can make up customs because we're the founding ancestors of this place."

They made such a noise that the demons could have come charging upon them and the hole fill with the sounds of battle. But the demons hid, the China Men so riled up, who knows what they were up to?

From the day of the shout party, Bak Goong talked and sang at his work, and did not get sent to the punishment fields. In cutting season, the demons no longer accompanied the knife-wielding China Men into deep cane.

Soon the new green shoots would rise, and when in two years the cane grew gold tassels, what stories the wind would tell.

Yong Ho Kim
"하와이 자탕수수밭"

김영호

하와이 와이파후 농장
사탕수수나무 잎새 사이
바람소리가 거문고 산조다.

뚝 뚝 수수나무의 무릎뼈를 꺾고
삭신을 부러뜨리는 칼바람

옛 조선농부들의
눈물 머금은 탄식소리가 차다.

인고의 옛 시대 마른 강물처럼 누웠는데
아직도 목을 길게 빼고
고향쪽 뜬구름에 눈길을 주고 서있는
우리 조상의 몸들 - 사탕수수나무

둥 둥 조선의 황소울음 우는 북소리에
줄기마다 오장육부를 비틀며
거문고 자진머리로 운다.

"HAWAI SAT'ANGSUSU PAT"

At the plantation in Waipahu Hawaii,
Between the leaves on sugarcane stalks,
The sound of the wind is a rhythm on a *kŏmungo*.

Crack, crack! The knee joints of the sugarcane stalks belch out
Sinew and joints snapping in the knife wind;
The flowing tears and cold sounds of lament gush forth from
The farmers of old Chosŏn.

While the endurance of yore lies as a dried riverbed,
Yet with their necks craned,
Standing with their eyes on the clouds floating toward their
hometown
Our ancestor's bodies—sugarcane stalks.

Boom, boom! In the sound of a drum, like the cries of a
Chosŏn bull,
Wrenching the innards of every stalk
The *kŏmungo* howls an even faster rhythm.

TRANSLATED BY MICHAEL J. PETTID AND KIL CHA

YONG HO KIM (1912-1973) *graduated from Meiji University Law School in 1941 and a year later completed a degree in mass communication there. He worked as a reporter for the Sunman News Agency, and as chief editor of "Freedom Literature" from 1956 to 1958. In 1958, he became a professor of Korean Literature at Dankook University, and in 1973, the university gave him an honorary doctorate.*

Shelley Ayame Nishimura Ota
from UPON THEIR SHOULDERS

B reakfast was invariably a leisurely and pleasant family gathering in the Merle mansion, as the laborers and surrounding community called the plantation manager's house. Perched on the top of the hill, almost in the center of the plantation, and gleaming in the clear island, it was the most conspicuous landmark in all the valley. A broad lanai encircled the house, shading the first floor from the direct rays of the noonday sun, and verdant mailee entwined itself about the lanai pillars, imparting to the house a green, fresh fragrance. Perched on the hill, it was a guardian of its own safety, and from the widow's walk on the second story a clear view of the valley could be commanded.

On this April morning Claude Merle, immaculate in a white linen suit and fragrant with the scent of his favorite pine cologne, sat at the dining-room table scowling over a report that his head luna had just brought him. Breezes ruffled the shimmering curtains of silk that fell to the polished koa floor, and lauhala rugs muffled the footsteps.

The room was hung with portraits of King Kamehameha, King Kalakaua, and Queen Liliokalani. It was high-ceilinged and paneled in sandalwood. On the monkeypod sideboard reposed a family heirloom, a magnificent koa tray engraved with the Hawaiian coat of arms.

Merle's daughter Clara and wife Beatrice drank their coffee and looked questioningly at each other.

"These dogs," Merle muttered, his thin lips drawn into a tight line. "They don't know when they are well off."

Beatrice hastily put her cup down and said soothingly, "Now, dear. They are very foolish to grumble. Lord knows they have enough to be thankful for, with their lodgings provided, their fuel wood, and their medical care." Her round face, framed with black curls, beamed at him complacently. She was a woman of thirty, with large good-natured features inherited from her Hawaiian forebears.

It was her own personal fortune, an inheritance from one of her people, an alii that had built the Hillstone Sugar Plantation. She had met the tall, slim-waisted, light-haired Merle at an afternoon reception at the Royal Palace. Her laughing, roving eyes intrigued him. He smiled at her, and in the next moment he was asking her to dance.

Merle, the only son of a Southern planter family, had returned from the Civil War to find his mother dying and the plantation rank and desolate. Embittered by the death of his mother and hostile to the forces of Reconstruction, the succeeding years found him moving slowly westward, living by his wits and searching for the opportunity to sink his roots into the soil in the manner he regarded as his birthright.

And here in Honolulu, now a thriving island port, swollen with millions in sugar profits as the result of the Reciprocity Treaty of 1876, hostesses clamored for men with charming manners and witty conversation and Merle found a ready entree. He was an immediate success, for his tongue was glib and soothing, and he knew how to light a glow in the eyes of the women and attract the men who occupied positions of honor and wealth in the city.

Beatrice, the lighthearted and spoiled child of an island chieftain, was flattered by the attentions of Merle, proud that she should be singled out by the idol of Honolulu's society. Carefully he began to woo her, for he knew that if he could win her he would find the end of his quest—a rich wife who would submit her property to his managing and who would accept his word as final authority. His conquest was swift, and within two months they were married in the Hawaiian Church on Main Street where Beatrice had been christened.

Claude Merle envisioned a sugar empire of his own making. With Beatrice's money he bought a sugar plantation that had gone bankrupt, and with an iron-willed determination made it a profitable undertaking. He was a lone wolf in his speculations, having little to do with other planters. By vigorously exploiting his workers, cunningly increasing his holdings, he became the autocrat of an island empire.

He had foreseen the need of a cheap and plentiful supply of laborers to cultivate the sugar cane. In co-operation with His Majesty's government, he brought in the Chinese to work his plantation, only to have them leave for less arduous jobs as storekeepers and merchants in the city. And now the Japanese had been recruited to take the place of the Chinese, but they were showing not only the restless pattern of their predecessors but a stubborn tendency to resist efforts to subdue them to voiceless submission.

Hamako, a pretty Japanese girl of eighteen, silently flitted about the koa breakfast table in her long, flowing kimono, serving the morning Kona coffee and the hot muffins. Merle, in spite of the disturbing news, looked appraisingly at the virgin freshness of the slim girl. His eyes lingered on the swelling of the round, firm breasts above the obi.

Beatrice winked at him impudently, having noticed his absorbed interest in the maid. More than once she had caught him kissing the servant girls. But she, with the tolerant ways of the Hawaiians, laughed over his escapades. Among her people it had been a token of hospitality for a husband to lend his wife to a guest. Certainly, if for no other reason, a master had a right to her inferiors.

"My dear," Beatrice interrupted, smiling, "your coffee is getting cold."

Claude, abashed for a moment, turned his gaze upon his wife and smiled faintly. "Those dogs," he snarled, harking back to the report. "They let their pregnant wives work in the fields up to the last minute just to get an extra dollar." He buttered his muffin savagely. "Then the mothers lug their kids around on their backs all day while they work in the fields. Bah! They're nothing but animals. They even mate in the fields and they breed just like rabbits." He drank down his coffee in one long gulp.

"You would think they would be grateful for what you've done for them, Papa," airily put in Clara. Her blue eyes had the same calculating look as her father's. She was the image of Merle, having inherited his light coloring and handsome features.

Pleased at his daughter's remarks, Merle nodded emphatically. "That's just it. They don't like this and they don't like that. They don't know when they are well off. What do they think they are? You would almost think they were the haoles, the way they talk of their rights!"

Claude accepted a third cup of coffee and his thoughts returned to the Japanese girl. He wondered what this girl would be like. He moistened his lips in anticipation, felt his hands sliding over her slender waist and caressing the soft, smooth thighs. Suddenly he got up. "Well, I've got work to do." He dropped his eyes and started for the study.

Beatrice called after him, "Oh, honey, we may be home late tonight. Clara and I are going to Honolulu. Clara simply has to have a new dress for the party."

Claude turned and smiled. "That's right, I had forgotten you were going today. Take care of yourself."

She threw him a kiss. "Don't work too hard." She winked.

In his spacious study, paneled in aromatic sandalwood, Merle sat his koa desk and began checking reports of sugar-cane production from the various fields, but his mind was not on his work. Then he picked up a proposed plan for destroying the damaging sugar borer, dropped it, and looked at a new irrigation scheme. There was a frown between his deep-set blue eyes. Strangely, this morning he could not concentrate.

A light breeze, almost silken in its touch, came in softly through the open windows. The hot sultriness of the previous days had been broken by a heavy rainstorm during the night. No mosquitoes or flies buzzed in the air.

Resting his chin in his hand, he looked out of the window. Down in the valley the newly acquired plantation engine was drawing a string of tiny cars loaded with sugar cane to the mill. In the thick, ripe fields men armed with long knives were cutting down the stalks, and close behind them Japanese women laborers were picking up the stalks of fallen cane and loading them on the cars.

Claude nodded in satisfaction at the busy, humming scene. His eyes followed the thick smoke issuing out of the stacks of the mill. Suddenly he frowned and pursed his lips. If only he could keep the laborers in their places! And sugar remained at its present high level. His eyes became cold and calculating as he thought of the potential profits.

Then he became aware of the soft breeze on his face, and his thoughts swung back to the Japanese girl. Why not? He had the house to himself this morning, and for once he wouldn't have to be furtive or alert for discovery. Through her he'd show the rats down on the plantation who was master. He reached over and pulled the tasseled cord that summoned the maid.

Quietly she entered the room on *tabi*-clad feet. As she stood waiting for his orders, her head slightly bent, he saw the slender neck, the faint throbbing of the vein on the forehead, the smooth complexion, and the peachlike bloom of her cheeks. For a moment he faltered. "Water," he said briskly, glancing at the papers on his desk.

She returned with a glass of water, placed it on the koa desk, and waited to be dismissed. He stood up and motioned her to come closer. His left arm clasped her while his right feverishly hunted for an opening in her kimono.

Passively she submitted to his embrace, neither accepting nor rejecting—for deep within her were the ingrained teachings of obedience developed through the centuries of Japanese subjection of women. She was paralyzed with fear but to resist would bring the censure of her parents who needed her scanty wages.

SHELLY AYAME NISHIMURA OTA (1911-1987) *was born in Waiākea, now known as Hilo, on the island of Hawai'i. She was the youngest daughter of Shikazo Nishimura, co-founder of Suisan Company, Ltd. A graduate of the University of Hawaii, she married Robert Kazuo Ota, M.D., and in 1939, they moved to Milwaukee, Wisconsin. Her novel* Upon Their Shoulders *was published in 1951. It was recognized by the National Endowment for the Arts, under a literary grant, in 2004.*

Peter C. T. Li

"A FIRE IN THE FIELDS"

The wooden fence around Mei's two room plantation house on the Kalihiwai Sugar Plantation was faded and gray with years of water stains etched on its splintered panes. The rusty hinges of the gate creaked like the delicate sounds of crying as she opened it and walked into her yard.

"You did good, Mei," her husband, Hung, said. "Everything going be fine now. We not going get trouble from dah luna now."

"Think so?" Mei asked. The wooden steps gave a little as she walked up to the front door. A small hexagon shaped Taoist mirror used to ward off evil spirits shook above the doorway, reflecting only darkness as though it had lost its protective powers against ill fortunes.

"No worry. I know what best fo' us," Hung said.

"I lie fo' you tonight only cuz you my husband, you know," Mei said.

"Whatevahs, you wen do dah right thing fo' everybody."

She stared at Hung under the starlit night, his sunburned face dark against his red palaka shirt. "Not fo' Mrs. Oshiro and her daughtah," she said.

"Mei, you Chinese or what?" Hung said. "What is one Japanese girl compared to dah entire Chinese camp?" They entered the house and he slammed the door shut behind them and lit the oil lamp on the square table at the center of the living room. The numerous Chinese calligraphies and paintings on the wall danced to life as the light cast benevolent shadows around the confined room.

"One too much already," Mei said. "Dah luna was wrong to do that to her."

"Eh, listen," Hung said and pounded his fist on the table. The shadows on the wall flickered then disappeared for a moment. "Remember where you wen come from. If not fo' me, you still going be in Canton walking knee high in mud in dah rice paddies and raising chicken fo' your stupid family."

Mei's mind raced randomly with no will of her own as her husband scolded her. She was feeling the same emotions of worthlessness now as she had when she first married him eight years ago as a picture bride from China. She was only sixteen at the time and he was twenty eight. He was the eldest son of the Wong family and worked as a hāpai ko man for the plantation, and she had been forced to marry him against her will. She had thought things would change between the both of them and that Hung would come to care for her like a true wife—one that had married out of love. But things had not changed, and at moments like now, she had doubts about their relationship and felt things had gotten worse over the years. There was nothing she could do to try and make things better. She just listened to his words and said nothing. There was nothing she could say.

"No stare at me li'dat!" he told her. "Go boil dah water fo' take a bath. I tired."

The blocks of wood cracked and popped in the stone stove behind the plantation house as Mei scooped water into an iron pot from the large wooden barrel next to the stove. The mid January air was cool and the heat from the fire felt good and refreshed her with strength. Sounds of crickets and geckos spoke to one another and sang songs only the night understood. Mei felt at peace.

"Hi, Mei," she heard Onnei yell from a window at the house next door. "How the meeting wen go tonight at Takeda Cafe?"

Mei walked over to her small vegetable garden beneath Onnei's bedroom window. "I nevah wen say not'tin."

Onnei leaned out the window. "Nah, fo' real you nevah wen say not'tin. You must wen say something," she said.

"I wen tell them I was at home wit Hung wen they wen find dah Japanese girl in dah field," Mei said.

"Why you wen do that fo'?" Onnei asked. "Why you wen lie?"

"I had to listen to Hung. He say that if I wen tell'um that I wen see dah luna rape dah girl, dah plantation own'nahs going make pilikia for him and everybody else. Hung no like me bring trouble for him and his friends."

"Why you listen fo'? You know bet'tah than that," Onnei said.

"You know why," Mei said. She bent down and plucked one of the bug eaten leaves off a bunch of choi sum. The tiny yellow flowers of the leafy green Chinese vegetable glowed like jewels in the soil.

"This not China," Onnei said. "Was me, I go tell'um everything and help Mrs. Oshiro and her daughtah. I no care what my husband think. He only like go fishing and drinking all dah time. Men, they all the same, no mat'tah back in China or ovah hea. Hung no different, I tell you. Only want face from everybody and be one big man on dah plantation."

"He not that way. He tell me he know what best fo' dah both of us," Mei said.

"You know what, Mei? Stop letting him treat you like one stupid woman. No let him boss you around just because he wen bring you to Hawai'i."

"What you mean?" Mei waited for Onnei's reply but there was a sudden commotion in Onnei's house. Mei heard Onnei's son screaming something desperate.

"What's going on?" Mei asked.

"I think you bet'tah go back inside your house and get Hung," Onnei said.

"Why? Something wrong?"

"That Japanese girl you saw, Yumiko, she wen go kill herself. They found her hanging on a mango tree in Mrs. Oshiro's back yard. She probably wen do that wen everybody was ovah at Takeda's tonight. Poor girl."

Mei went bone white as the blood drained from her limbs to her stomach. She felt like throwing up. "No. No can be. Why? Why she wen go do that?"

Mei did not hear Onnei's last few words as she went spinning to the ground and banged her head on the rocks that surrounded the choi sum patch. "Mei!" Onnei cried. She left her house and ran out to Mei's yard.

"Onnei," Mei said from the ground. "Why she do that? Was my fault, my fault. . . . "

Mei felt the life drain from her body as she lay there with the side of her head bleeding. Images of a hundred faces with a thousand laughters and tears flashed through her mind in pulses. She heard and felt every single vision pulling her away, robbing her of control over her mind and body, like the dragging of a dying corpse. They told her truths and lies about who she was and how she should behave. They showed her the happiness she had had with her five brothers and three sisters in their small village in China. They recalled the horror she'd felt when the Ching Dynasty was overthrown and everything was in chaos, her family broken and lost in the birth of a new China. It was a China that Mei had had to escape from. It was a China where she became a picture bride.

"This is a picture of your future husband from Hawai'i, the land of the Sandalwood Mountains," Mei's father had told her. She remembered it clearly now. "And when you marry, you must listen and be good and not let your husband and our family lose face. Causing the loss of respect is the worst thing you can do."

"Ah bah! Ah bah!" Mei called out to her father as his image faded away and was replaced by Yumiko's as she passed her in the field.

Luna Williams was there also. He was dragging the kicking and punching Yumiko into the sugar canes. "Help me, help me!" Yumiko screamed as the two of them disappeared and visions of Mrs. Oshiro begging on the floor of the Takeda Cafe appeared. "Help my Yumiko, help her please, no lie, tell them what you wen see," she cried. Mei wanted to, but her husband was there. "I love you. No say not'tin. You my wife," Hung said to her. Then all the voices yelled at Mei at once. "No say not' tin. You liar. Help Yumiko. You are a Chinese wife. You must obey. Don't let our family lose face. This is your husband. I love you. No say not'tin. No say not'tin." Mei fought for her sanity and screamed as loud as she could. But the images and voices kept coming faster and louder into Mei's mind like a thousand firecrackers going off in a kaleidoscope of blurred madness. Mei screamed to fight back. Fought to hold back the pain. There was nothing Mei wanted more now, even for a brief moment, except for empty blackness and silence. Then it stopped.

"Mei going be okay?" she heard Hung ask the doctor.

"It's not serious. She should be fine. Have her rest a while," the doctor said. He wore a white shirt and a gray pinstripe vest with a black ribbon tie.

"Hung," Mei said from her bed. She felt the pounding of her head as she watched Hung speak to the doctor with Onnei standing next to him. A slight breeze blew the window curtains and the morning Pacific sun broke through into the small room and warmed her face and eased her pain.

"Thanks," Hung said. He shook the doctor's hand and walked him out of the bedroom.

"Onnei," Mei called out. She lifted her hand and reached for Onnei's layered cotton work dress that protected all hoe hana women from the razor edges of sugar cane leaves.

Onnei walked over to the straw mat lined bed. "How you feeling?" she asked.

"My head so'ah. What wen happen?"

"You wen go faint last night and wen sleep until now."

"Yumiko," Mei cried. She remembered what had happened the night before.

"It's okay." Onnei held Mei's hand and gave her a hug as she stroked Mei's black hair.

Hung returned to the bedroom. "You okay?"

"Was my fault," Mei said. "Yumiko wen die cuz I nevah wen say not'tin fo' help her."

"Was not your fault," Hung said.

Mei began to cry. "How you can say that? Yumiko wen die. Her mahdah wen ask me fo' help and I nevah wen help."

"But you not dah one wen hang her. She wen do that by herself," he said.

There was a knock on the Wong's front door. "Godfunnit," Hung said. "I go see who at dah door."

Mei lay motionless and watched the wet vision of her husband leave the room. "Onnei, who you think at dah door?" Mei asked. "What if that's Mrs. Oshiro? How I going tell her that I nevah wen say not'tin cuz Hung no like trouble? How I going tell her that saving face for him was more important than Yumiko's life?"

"Mei, we friends, right? I tell you something now. Go tell Mrs. Oshiro the truth. Tell'um what you wen see. Never mind what Hung wen say. Do'um fo' youself."

"Onnei, I dunno."

Hung came back into the room and pointed at a woman behind him. "This Mrs. Bickman."

"Hello, Mrs. Wong." Mrs. Bickman's hair was blond and she wore a tan dress with little white cross shaped prints. Her hair was tied up in a bun and she stood about a head taller than Hung. "I'm with the Hawai'i Sugar Planters' Association. I'm here to investigate what happened two days ago. May I ask you some questions?"

Mei stared at Hung and back at Mrs. Bickman again. "Guess so."

"As you may already know. The workers here at Kalihiwai have accused Mr. Williams of raping one of the women workers. I got a letter from a Mr. Takeda that said you saw everything that happened. Is this true?"

Onnei gave Mei a little push on the arm. "Go tell'um," Onnei whispered.

Mei looked up at Onnei. She saw Hung watching Onnei and then quickly turned to Mrs. Bickman. "She nevah wen see anything," he said. "We already wen tell'um."

"I am aware of that, Mr. Wong. But I need to verify your wife's story for the meeting tomorrow."

"What meeting?" Mei asked.

"The HSPA and the owner of the plantation are having a meeting tomorrow night in front of the sugar mill to settle complaints between the workers and the plantation concerning Mr. Williams. If he is found guilty, the HSPA will bring in the authorities and have him arrested."

"So you need Mei to tell you what she saw?" Onnei asked.

"Shud'dup Onnei," Hung said. "She nevah wen see not'tin."

"Why you no let Mei tell the truth?" Onnei said. "Why she gotta lie fo' you?"

Mei grabbed Onnei's hand and looked her in the eyes. "Onnei, please," she said.

"What?" Onnei yelled. "It's dah truth. No let Hung boss you anymore."

"If you my friend, quiet okay?"

Hung picked up the small Buddha from the sandalwood dresser carved with Chinese mountains and clouds, and pointed it at Onnei. "Eh, Mei, tell your friend shud'dup before I put this in her big mouth."

Mrs. Bickman stopped Hung's arm in mid air. "Is she telling the truth, Mr. Wong?"

"I dunno what that crazy woman is talking about. And if you get sense, you bet'tah not listen to her. She lōlō, like old crazy Mr. Chang up dah street. She just like make trouble."

Onnei pointed her finger at Hung and waved it like a pistol. "He dah one wen go lie. Mei wen see everything and he no like her tell. Mei, go tell'um you was deah dah ot'dah day." Onnei nudged Mei's side. "Tell Mrs. Bickman you wen see everything."

"Please, I no can," Mei said. "Just stop it, okay?"

"Mei, I'm warning you!" Hung yelled. "Tell your friend shud'dup." He pushed Mrs. Bickman aside.

"Come on Mei, tell'um," Onnei repeated.

Hung threw the little Buddha across the room at Onnei, but it missed and shattered against the wall next to the bedroom window. Ceramic fragments exploded onto Onnei's foot.

"You dah lōlō!" Onnei yelled. "Mei, how you can protect one selfish guy like that? He no care about you."

"That's enough, Mr. Wong," said Mrs. Bickman. She grabbed onto Hung's shirt sleeve as he tried to rush towards Onnei. "Leave this room now or I'll get one of the luna to drag you out."

"Why. This my house. You dah one gotta leave."

"I'm warning you, Mr. Wong."

Hung pounded the wall and then stomped out of the room. There were sounds of furniture crashing into one another and against the walls of the living room. When he became tired, he yelled profanities and cursed everyone in the house and then slammed the front door shut and left.

"I need to speak to Mei alone," Mrs. Bickman told Onnei. "Could you wait outside please."

"Yeah, sure." As Onnei looked at Mei, she tilted her head a little to one side and made her brows rise and her eyes widen. "Tell Mrs. Bickman everything," she said through clenched teeth and narrowed lips.

Mrs. Bickman closed the bedroom door and then looked at Mei. "Now, tell me everything that happened."

"I no can."

"Why? Your husband is not here now."

"You no understand. I just cannot. Hung going lose face."

"Lose face? What?"

"He going lose honor if I make trouble for him."

"That's silly," Mrs. Bickman said. "If you don't tell what you saw, Mr. Williams is going to get away with what he did?"

"Not silly. You no understand. I really no can."

"Look, if you tell them tomorrow what you saw, you'll be giving your husband face."

"No, no face," Mei replied. "You not Chinese. You no understand. I just going bring him trouble."

"You're right. I don't understand you people. A girl hung herself because Mr. Williams raped her and all you care about is your husband's respect?"

"No, I care Yumiko too," Mei said.

"Then tell everyone what you saw."

Mei did not reply. She turned away from Mrs. Bickman and stared blankly out the window. She wanted to tell Mrs. Bickman what she knew.

She wanted to tell everyone. But she could not do it for the sake of fulfilling the promises of marriage to honor and respecting the wishes of her husband. If Hung didn't want her to do something, then she wouldn't. If she was to be a good Chinese wife, then things must be this way. It was how things were traditionally. But Mei was beginning to feel trapped and wished that it wasn't. "Sorry," she said.

"I see," Mrs. Bickman said. "But please consider what I have said. Tell everyone tomorrow what you saw."

Mei watched Mrs. Bickman open the door and leave the room. "Onnei!" she yelled.

There was no answer. Mei lay in her bed for a long time and thought about Mrs. Oshiro and Yumiko, about Mr. Williams, but most of all about her marriage with Hung. Was it worth it? Was the imagined honor of a man she'd been forced to marry and did not love so important that a life could be traded for it? Was Onnei right? Was her husband selfish? Did he care about her as much as she thinks she did about him? At times Mei felt more like a servant than a wife. But she was a picture bride and she owed Hung for the life she had now. The rules of marriage would be simple if she wasn't. The answers would be simple—she would tell everyone the truth. But she was a Chinese picture bride, and little would change that and her feelings of being trapped in traditional marital obedience with no independence of her own. With no will of her own.

Mei lay in her bed until the noon sun rose and the heat of the afternoon mixed with the cool trade winds from the West to stroke her to sleep. For those brief moments Mei found escape and peace away from the plantation. Away from everyone she knew. But most of all, away from Hung, and his insistent command for her to lie.

It was night when Mei heard the front door slam shut and saw the lamp light in the living room glow bright. Mei could see a dark shadow move across the living room wall like a black serpent slithering and searching for its prey. Furniture crashed about and Mei could see her husband stumble over a fallen chair. She lit the lamp on the night stand next to her bed as Hung entered the room. The orange glow of the light revealed his drunken red face and he seem almost demonic. "What you looking at?" he yelled. The alcoholic spit from his mouth sprayed like venom.

Mei felt paralyzed in her bed and didn't know how to respond. "You wen go drinking?" she asked.

"What if I did. All cuz of you." Hung took a couple of steps but stumbled to his knees. "Why you no listen fo'? Why you gotta get diarrhea mouth and tell Onnei you saw it?"

"I sorry. Dah thing just came out wen I wen talk to her after it happened."

"Now I going get all kine trouble from dah luna."

"I nevah know you no like me say not'tin. How I going know?"

Hung pulled himself up and stood next to the bed. "Everybody at the plantation blames me for dah extra work and hassles that the luna all giving them. Now they all no like talk to me and give me stink eye. And your friend Onnei, she going around telling everybody stink stuff about me. Telling them I boss you around cuz I marry you from China." Hung slapped his palm through the air in front of him. "I like slap her."

"Sorry, Hung," Mei said. "I go ovah and tell her stop it." Mei sat up and planted her foot on the floor in front of Hung.

"Too late already," Hung snapped. "It's all your fault." He slapped Mei hard in the face and sent her flying onto her side, back into the bed.

Mei felt the pain cut through her face and saw the blood from her nose splatter onto the embroidered sheet. "Hung. No. Please. I sorry." She began to cry.

Hung moved closer. "It's always your fault."

Mei climbed to the other side of the bed. "Stay away," she warned. The blood from her nose dripped over her lips. She could taste its sweetness. "Get out or I going yell."

"You not'tin but bad luck fo' me," he said. "Even heaven punish me because of you. All these years we marry and you no can even make me one son. What kind wife you. You think you so good. You broken that what I think."

Mei picked up a piece of the shattered Buddha that Hung had broken earlier and pointed it at him. "Move away, I like go out." Mei walked towards the door and Hung moved in front of her. She could smell the alcohol from his sweating body.

"You know, your fah'dah wen marry you off fo' dah money," Hung said. "That mean you mine. Not because I wen marry you, but because I bought you. So you bet'tah listen to me because I know what best fo' you."

"Onnei was right," she said. "You only care about yourself. Know what best fo' me. You only know what best fo' you. I going tell'um everything tomorrow," she said.

"You bet'tah not. Remember where you came from. You one picture bride. I own you!"

"I going tell'um everything," She turned and ran for the front door and heard Hung fall to the floor behind her.

Mei ran out of the house towards Onnei's house. "Onnei, Onnei," she called as she pounded on Onnei's door.

The door opened and a crack of light lit Mei's bruised face. "What wen happen?" Onnei cried. She pulled Mei inside. "How come you bleeding?"

"Hung, Hung," she repeated with broken breaths. "He wen hit me."

"Why he do dat fo'?"

Mei began to cry. "He wen come home all drunk and mad."

"Look up," Onnei said. She wiped the blood off of Mei's face. "What you going do now?"

"I don't know Onnei, I don't know."

The workers at the Kalihiwai Plantation had been arriving steadily back to the sugar mill since pau hana time, when the labor train returned from the field and the mill whistle blew at four thirty in the afternoon. The yard in front of the sugar mill was now nearly filled. A number of workers that had come late climbed up onto crates, wagons, trees, and whatever else they could find that would provide them with a good perch to view from.

Mrs. Oshiro and Mr. Takeda sat on the front row of a couple of makeshift wooden benches next to a long picnic table. Mr. McCorduck, the plantation owner, and Mrs. Bickman with two other representatives from the HSPA sat behind the table. Meanwhile Mei and her husband sat next to one another on the second bench. Neither of them spoke a word to the other, nor did they look each other in the eye. They sat like the strangers they had been when they were first married and listened to Luna Williams as he gave his side of the story.

"I wasn't on that side of the field that afternoon," Luna Williams said. The afternoon sun had changed his red hair to orange and it made him look like a six foot tall match stick as he stood in front of the officials. "Just ask Robert Barlow from the Filipino camp. He'll tell you that I was with him fishing down by the landing."

"But Mrs. Oshiro insists that her daughter was raped by you," Mrs. Bickman said.

"Where's your proof that I did? Barlow will tell you I didn't." Luna Williams smiled and heard the plantation workers behind him go into a commotion.

"But we have proof," she said. "According to Mrs. Oshiro, Mrs. Wong saw you in the field with Yumiko that afternoon."

Luna Williams gave Mei a cold gaze.

"Mrs. Wong, stand up and come over here," the man next to Mrs. Bickman said.

Mei stood up and began to walk towards the table, but Hung caught her hand and stopped her. "Let go," she said.

"I sorry Mei," Hung whispered. "I was drunk and nevah wen know what I was doing last night. I promise I nevah going hit you again. Remember we husband and wife. Remember I love you."

Mei pulled her arms back. "I no like be your wife anymore. I no like be your picture bride," she said. She broke away from Hung's grasp and stood in front of the table.

"Mrs. Wong," said Mrs. Bickman. "Mrs. Oshiro and Mr. Takeda said you were in the field at the time Yumiko was raped. We have a witness here that said you carried some sugar cane to a wagon that was nearby a little before Yumiko saw you. Is this true? Were you on that side of the field?"

Mei stared at Mrs. Bickman but made no response. Her fingers were shaking. She rolled the ruffles of her skirt between her fingers and squeezed them and felt the crisscross texture of the cotton. She turned and looked at the crowd behind her, then at Hung, then at Mrs. Bickman.

"Mrs. Wong, were you on that side of the field or not the other day?" asked Mr. McCorduck loudly. His white shirt and fedora hat glowed under the crimson dusk sky.

"Yes," Mei answered. She looked at Hung and he was motionless except for his lips which parted slowly as if to say no.

"Did you see Yumiko in the field?" Mrs. Bickman asked.

"Yes."

"Did you see Mr. Williams that afternoon?"

Mei hesitated. "I did."

The talk in the crowd grew louder and everyone became restless. Torches were lit and the darkening sugar mill burst into a dance of light as the godlike shadows of the officials were etched onto the wall behind them.

"Quiet down, please," commanded the HSPA representative next to Mrs. Bickman.

The crowd grew silent, and there were only scattered comments.

"On that afternoon you were in the field," Mrs. Bickman asked. "Did you see Mr. Williams drag Yumiko into the canes then rape her?"

Mei opened her mouth a little as though to speak. She stopped. Her lips slightly parted. She turned and looked at Hung one more time. "I don't know," Mei answered in a broken voice.

"What do you mean, you don't know?"

Mei turned again and saw Hung staring back at her. She felt she owed Hung a part of herself regardless of how he had treated her. Despite whether it was the right or wrong thing to do, she felt a debt owed must be paid, and she was going to pay Hung for all the good he had done for her. Not because Hung was her husband, not because she was his wife, but because she was simply herself, Mei.

"Did you or didn't you?"

"I don't know."

"Did you see Yumiko being raped."

"No. No, I nevah!" Mei cried out, then she dropped to her knees. She began to cry like someone trying to hold back a great pain. "I nevah wen see not'tin."

"Are you sure? Are you absolutely sure?" Mrs. Bickman asked one last time.

"Yes, yes. I sure. So please, please no bahdah me anymore," Mei implored the HSPA officials in front of her. Her face was stained with red dirt as she tried to wipe the tears from her eyes. She heard everyone yell profanities at her. They didn't understand. She had to lie one last time. Not for Hung. But for herself.

Mrs. Oshiro charged from the bench. "How can you hang my daughtah a second time?" she screamed. She kicked Mei in the stomach and started pounding Mei's back with her fist until Mr. Takeda pulled her back to the bench.

Mei saw Hung get up and run over to her. She felt his arms lift her and knew it was the last time they would touch as husband and wife. Mei had decided she was no longer going to be his picture bride. She had lied to the officials to pay the debt she owed Hung. To her, he was now someone who had helped her escape China. Not someone to obey. Or to save face for. Or to love.

"Everything going be fine now," Hung said. "They not going bahdah us anymore. Our life going be back normal." He brushed Mei's hair aside and off her face.

"Let me go," Mei said. "Things not going be same. I not going be your wife anymore."

"Why you wen lie to them den?"

Tears began to flow out of Mei's eyes again.

"Right now you don't know what you saying," Hung said. "We talk about it la'tah, when you mo' calm."

"I know what I saying." She pushed him. "Things all different now."

"Where you going go? Back to China? They going laugh at you. You going be one disgrace. Picture bride running away back home. Nobody going take you. Not deah. Not hea."

Mei turned without saying another word and started to walk away.

"You wait, you going come back to me. No mo' place fo' you to go. You no can leave. I like see you try. You mine."

Mei heard Hung laugh as she pushed her way through the crowd of workers. Hung was right. There was no place for her to go, and divorce was unrealistic in a Chinese picture bride marriage. She wanted to cry, but had no more tears. She had chose to walk this path of independence that she had discovered for herself. And though she had little left of what her life was before this entire incident, she felt no regrets. The only thing she had left was her life and one last debt. It was time to pay Yumiko.

Mei watched the plantation workers go into an uproar as Mr. McCorduck and the HSPA officials announced there was no case against Luna Williams. She saw Mr. McCorduck, Mrs. Bickman, and the rest of the HSPA officials disappear quickly into the safety of the sugar mill as a mob of angry workers chased after them. The workers wanted justice, and they wanted it now, as did Mei.

Mr. Takeda, Mrs. Oshiro and a group of Japanese workers armed themselves with several torches and began to hunt after Luna Williams. Meanwhile other workers caught up in the anger and rage wanted the sugar fields burned as payment for the injustice done against Yumiko.

"Mrs. Oshiro and Mr. Takeda them going to burn Luna Williams and the sugar field," yelled Onnei after she broke away from an angry mob marching past Mei. "We bet'tah go quick before the luna come back with guns."

"Which way Mrs. Oshiro them wen go?" Mei asked.

"They went to dah west fields."

"*Doh je,*" Mei said as she thanked Onnei in Cantonese for a last time. Without saying another word, Mei turned away from Onnei and ran. She fought her way through the rushing mob and headed for the cane fields on the west side of the plantation. By the time Mei reached the field, it was already burning.

"Mrs. Oshiro!" Mei called into the dense gray smoke that guarded the flames. "Mrs. Oshiro where you stay?" Mei tried to listen for voices, but all she heard was the thunder of exploding cane stalks as the fire burned its way across the field.

Charred remains were snapping to the left and right of her as they fell to the ground. The smoke from the burning leaves rubbed against her eyes, irritating them, teasing them to close with tears. She dodged one of the hot cane, but the razor edged leaves from another cut her arm. The hot air numbed her wound and she ignored the pain. Suddenly, something burst out of the smoke. It pushed her to the ground. Mei felt the heat from the heavy object. It was too large to be sugar cane. It was Luna Williams.

"Quiet or I'll break your neck," he snarled. The blood on his burnt arm trickled down his hands.

Mei felt his hand cover her mouth. The mix of smoke and salty sweat on his fingers choked her and she bit them.

"Dammit," he cried, and he slapped her across the face.

"I saw you here the ot'dah day," Mei told him. "I saw you rape Yumiko."

"You should have told them back at the mill," he said. "Get up, you're gonna be my way out of here." Luna Williams stood up and then pulled Mei up by the hair.

Mei tried kicking Luna Williams to try and free herself, but he punched her in the head and she went crashing to the ground. She felt her eye lid split and the warm blood flow down her face.

"Try that again and . . . . "

Suddenly, Luna William's body crashed down on Mei and smashed her into the ground a second time. Mei opened her eyes and looked up. Mrs. Oshiro stood above the both of them. Her eyes were wide and red as the reflection of the fire in them grew brighter. She wielded a hoe in her hands. The blade, chipped and worn from years of cane cutting, now dripped with blood. "He wen kill my Yumiko," Mrs. Oshiro said. "I going take revenge for my Yumiko."

"No!" Mei said. She pushed Luna Williams off and stood up. "They going put you in jail if you do. Who going visit Yumiko's grave if you in jail?"

Luna Williams tried to get up. The blood on his ripped back had soaked through his torn shirt.

Mrs. Oshiro began to cry and raised the hoe into the air, its curved blade a shadow against the glowing smoke. "I kill him, Mrs. Wong. I kill him. Don't let him get away anymore."

"Stop!" Mei grabbed the hoe and pulled it away from Mrs. Oshiro.

"He die, he die," Mrs. Oshiro repeated, as if in a vengeful, hypnotic trance as she watched Luna Williams get up onto his knees.

Mei held the hoe tight in her hands. *It was her decision.* She raised the blade high into the air. *Not her husband Hung's.* And drove the hoe down. *She wasn't going to be trapped anymore.* The air snapped against the crackling sounds of exploding echoes and the blade ripped through flesh and bone as if they were sugar cane. *She had found the path to her freedom.* She thought of her parents, her brothers and sisters, her husband, Hung, and finally, Yumiko. Mei said nothing. Her face showed no emotion. She had found peace.

Luna Williams' body dropped in front of Mrs. Oshiro as an offering. It convulsed like a headless chicken reluctant to become the object of retribution. Mrs. Oshiro screamed as Luna Williams' head rolled across the ground and onto her foot. His eyes and mouth were open in a permanent silent scream as his head was drenched in a pool of sacrificial blood.

Mei dropped to the ground, her hands still holding onto the hoe. "Go home, Mrs. Oshiro, before dah fire comes."

"Why you—"

"For your daughtah," Mei said. "For Yumiko."

Mei watched Mrs. Oshiro run towards town as the flames grew red, orange, yellow, then white behind her. The fire and smoke grew stronger with each cane it consumed and seemed to have a life of its own. The fire in the field swirled like a thousand spirits ascending to heaven in the midst of destruction. Purifying and vindicating the land, the field, and all the pains it held. Mei saw the beauty of the fire come and felt the warmth of the flames bathe her as she embraced them. She was truly free now. A picture bride no more.

PETER C.T. LI *is an artist, fiction writer, and poet. He is the Chief Technology Officer at ICE Systems, Inc., where he designs and develops innovative scalable enterprise-wide B2B solutions and other incredibly cool stuff. When not preoccupied with skateboarding, his PS3, and all of life's other wonderful distractions, he hangs out with his Gen-Y wife, Wendy; i-Gen girls, Aeryn and Gillian; and his microchipped tabby, Eevee.*

Ruth Eleanor McKee

from AFTER A HUNDRED YEARS

They went up two steps, across a narrow *lanai* and through a screen door into a square box of an office. A big, powerfully built man with shaggy eyebrows, tilted back in a swivel chair behind the ugly golden oak desk, was roaring genially at a dapper little clergyman whose head rose to a curious peak of baldness, "Graham, you're up against a stone wall. You better stick to the ladies and the kids, and forget about the prostitutes—Oh!" perceiving the new arrivals. "Glad to see you, Williams! This our new man?" He shook hands with them both.

Peter nodded to the clergyman and perfunctorily introduced Hal. Mr. Graham twirled his hat in his hands, his mouth compressed, his scanty brows drawn together. "We'll continue our discussion at some other time, Mr. Grimes!" he said severely and took himself off.

Peter raised an eyebrow. "Been getting under the rector's skin?" he queried when the starting of an engine outside told him the visitor was out of earshot.

Grimes waved the two to seats and snorted. "Damned fool's wanting me to run the prostitutes off the plantation—thinks they're corrupting the morals of the laborers. Hell! We make 'em show their cards every Monday morning—what more can we do? What's he think all these blokes in the camps are going to do? Take the Filipinos, for instance—about eight percent of 'em are married. What're the rest of them going to do with their free time? Play tiddly winks? Take up crocheting? I ask you! What's more, he says Mrs. Smythe-Saunders and Mrs. Richard Adams and a few of the other old sisters in his church are making a campaign against vice on the plantations."

Peter shouted, "They are, are they! Well, well, well!" He winked at Hal. "You remember I told you how some of our best families owned those houses down around Nuuanu and School? Well, these old girls own two or three apiece, and the dear old souls don't dream that they've got a beam to get out of their own eyes when they go out hunting for motes to extract. Never you mind, Grimes. I think I'll have to make a little call on both of those *wahines* and tell them gently but firmly some of the facts of life. Can't have them taking the simple pleasures of the poor away from our laborers, by God!"

Hal's shoulders shook. "My God—what a country you've got here!"

Grimes grinned sardonically at him. "Yeah, sure." He whirled his chair toward Peter. "The Japanese are all back here. They don't know how to stage a strike. Children! Puling babies is what they are. Some bozo in Japan sends out word for them to call a strike, Carrington. So, being the most obliging race on earth, they strike, but so considerately and gently nobody'd ever have known it if they hadn't up and told us how just half of them were striking so that the other half could keep on getting wages and support the strikers. They right up and said as much. I got in about a dozen Filipinos that were new on the payroll, and the strikers got nervous. When I thought they were nervous enough, I told their friends to round 'em up and then I gave 'em a swell speech. I tell you I made 'em a speech that'd wring tears from a water buffalo, all about how they let the plantation down, and I reminded 'em what big bonuses they'd be getting this year with sugar so high, and it didn't seem right for them to cheat themselves out of their just dues, and I reminded them of the plantation Christmas tree and free medical care and what not, and, by God, the lot of them were just about crying on my shoulder by the end of it. So I said they could all come back just like before—*this* time, but next time they did such a thing—*pau!*"

Peter chuckled appreciatively. "I'd like to have heard that speech! Have to do any baby-kissing?"

"Hell, no!" said Grimes disgustedly. "Now how's for us showing Mr. Carrington the works, Williams? Or did you want to talk anything else over?"

"Guess not. The strike was the main thing. Start with the mill, shall we?"

Grimes objected: "Better to start from the field—show him step by step."

They drove up to the edge of a field where the young cane grew in parallel lines, rising and falling with the slope of the land. Gangs of laborers bent over their hoes. To Hal it seemed an endless task to clear areas of such dimension by hand labor.

Questioned on the point, Grimes shrugged. "No way been figured out to do away with it. Any machine that would get the weeds would take along the cane. These men may not be over-bright, but they can tell the difference between a weed and a cane shoot—for a dollar a day—and as long as a *luna* keeps an eye on them. That's what we pay these fellows on horseback for. Hey! Oliveira!" He roared, beckoning to the nearest of the men on horseback.

Hal noticed that the young overseer's shirt clung damply to his back and that perspiration beaded his forehead. If a person felt the heat at this season to that extent just riding around on horseback, pondered Hal, what must it be like for the poor devils tackling the weeds beneath the hot sun. At the same time he realized humorously that he was not expected to grapple weeds in person, that he was to have at least the dignity of luna-dom.

Grimes introduced them and said, "Oliveira will show you the ropes when you come on. You'll really step into his shoes. He's graduating to cutting. Next step up in the game. Good fella, Oliveira!" He struck the *luna* a thundering blow of good fellowship that made the horse shy.

They made a whirlwind tour of the mill that left Hal dizzy with intense heat, swirling belts, the hum of colossal machinery, and the vile smell of the molasses. He was also impressed with the efficiency of the operation that transformed green cane into brown sugar. He trailed along after Grimes and Peter, following the sugar cane from the point where great pronged belts scraped the cane from the cars into a pit. He saw the rush of the cane through the knives of rollers that left it cut in short lengths to be carried along through the grinders, massive steel rollers that turned the cane into a peculiarly filthy looking mess that went into enormous tanks to be treated with lime. Then it passed on to great heaters where the heavy sludge was precipitated, leaving a clear amber-colored liquid on top that went on to other gigantic tanks called multiple evaporators, thence into vacuum pans and into centrifugals where it was spun off into crystals that resembled a miniature snow storm. Eventually, after hurrying up and down long flights of ladderlike stairs to see the processes carried on at the different levels of the factory, the men arrived on the first floor where a mechanical chute opened to drop one-hundred-pound lots of the brown sugar into bags held by a man, who, the bag filled and the door of the chute snapped shut, passed the bag to a Japanese woman seated at a sewing machine and sewing up one bag at just the right speed to be ready for the next.

"How'd you like to do twelve hours of that a day, Carrington?" Grimes grinned.

"Lord!" Hal, regarding the monotony and the precision of the gestures of these workers, restrained a shudder. "Twelve hours!"

"Well," Grimes relented, "they get caught up every now and then, and can lay off for a half hour or so, till a new load arrives. Not an easy job though. Doesn't last all year, however. We harvest from April to September. Rest of the time there's nothing doing in the factory. Refining's left to Crockett—up on the coast. It's cheaper to send the stuff up there. The H.S.P.A. finances the refinery there. What say we knock off for lunch? I'll go along with you to the club. You can take Carrington up to the laboratory this afternoon."

After the luncheon at the plantation clubhouse where most of the unmarried skilled workers had their meals, they went to the office. There Hal met the heads of the various departments, was shown the filing system, drawers of cards arranged by number and showing a record of the exact work done by each laborer. Hal, studying one of the cards, suddenly looked at it more closely.

"Do these people just have numbers?" he asked in surprise. "How do you know which name belongs to which number?"

Grimes shrugged his massive shoulders. "We don't. Every man is given a bango, a little disk with a number on it that he wears on his watch or around his neck on a string. He's a number to us—easier to work with large numbers of men that way. He just shows his bango when he collects his pay or needs admittance to the hospital. It might be a good idea to have their names, or a name file, too. When any of the Johnnies from the police or the social service gang come around and ask for Kim Wong Lum, say, it's hard to lay hands on him, but nobody's gotten around to doing it yet."

Carlo Mario Fraticelli
"YO ME VOY DE ESTE LUGAR"

1
Siento dejar por detrás
a mis queridos amigos;
pero ellos son testigos
de toda mi adversidad.
Sería mi voluntad
con ellos poder estar;
pero por no presenciar
todo lo que aquí he sufrido,
triste, solo y abatido,
me voy de este lugar.

2
Después que aquí trabajé
veinte años constantemente,
yo me encuentro en el presente

más mal que cuando empecé.
Aquí fue que malgasté
mi vida en un batallar,
laborando por pasar
una vejez descansada.
Hoy con mi alma atrofiada,
yo me voy de este lugar.

3
Aquí fue donde elgí
una afable compañera,
y otra que también lo era.
También aquí la perdí.
Yo nada me divertí;
muy poco pude gozar.
Yo nunca podré olvidar
todo lo que aquí he perdido.
Hoy de todos me despido;
yo me voy de este lugar.

4
Aquí viven en mi ausencia
cinco hijos por la muerte;
y otros por mi mala suerte
huyeron de mi presencia.
Al verme ya en decadencia,
se trataron de alejar
para más no lamentar.
Y ver si cambia mi suerte
antes que venga la muerte,
yo me voy de este lugar.

"I AM LEAVING THIS PLACE"

1
I regret leaving my dear friends
behind; but they are witnesses
of all my adversity. To be able to
be with them would be my wish;
but in order not to witness all
that I have suffered here, sad

alone and dejected, I am leaving
this place.

2

After working here continually
for twenty years, I find myself
at the present time worse off
than when I began. Here was
where I wasted my life in a
struggle, working in order to
spend a tranquil old-age. Today
with my soul atrophied, I am
leaving this place.

3

Here was where I chose a nice
companion, and another who
was also like that. Here I also
lost her. I did not enjoy myself
at all; I managed to enjoy very
little. I will never be able to
forget all that I have lost here.
Today I say good-bye to every
one; I am leaving this place.

4

Here in my absence five
deceased children remain;
and due to my bad luck others
have run away from my
presence. Upon seeing me
in decline, they tried to move
away in order to lament no
more. And to see if my luck
changes before death comes,
I am leaving this place.

TRANSLATED BY AUSTIN DIAS

CARLO MARIO FRATICELLI (1863-1945) *arrived in Hawai'i with the first wave of Hawaii Sugar Producers Association-recruited sugar workers from Puerto Rico (1900-1901). He came from a landowning family and studied medicine in Paris: a most unusual immigrant laborer. He was a respected leader in the Puerto Rican community who wrote many* décimas, *the Spanish national folkloric poetic form.*

Author Unknown

"PUA MANA NŌ"

I

I Kahiki au i ka 'imi dālā,
Dālā pohō. A holo au ma ka 'ō koholā,
Koholā lalau.
Ua pau ku'u moku i kāhi kenekoa,
Ua pau ku'u moku i kāhi kenekoa.
Ho'i mai au he pua mana nō,
Ho'i mai au he pua mana nō.

II

I Ke-kaha au i ka ma'au'auwā,
I ka ma'au 'auwā.
Puehu ka lepo, welawela ka lā,
Welawela ka lā.
Ua pau ku'u pono i ka luna 'auhau,
Ua pau ku'u pono i ka luna 'auhau.
Ho'i mai au he pua mana nō,
Ho'i mai au he pua mana nō.

III

Nonoke au i ka mahi kō,
I ka mahi kō.
Ua 'eha ke kua, kakahe ka hou,
Pohō, pohō.
A 'ai'ē au i ka hale kū'ai,
A 'ai'ē au i ka hale kū'ai.
A noho ho'i he pua mana nō,
A noho ho'i he pua mana nō.

IV

A ha'alele au i ka 'imi dālā,
Dālā pohō.
E noho nō e hana ma ka lā,
Ka 'ai o ka lā.
Iā ha'i ka waiwai e luhi ai,
Iā ha'i ka waiwai e luhi ai.
E noho au he pua mana nō,
E noho au he pua mana nō.

"SURE A POOR MAN"

I

I went to a foreign land to work for money,
    Wasted money.
Then I went to harpoon whales,
    Worthless whales.
My ship soon belonged to a senator,
My ship soon belonged to a senator.
I came home a poor man,
I came home a poor man.

II

In Ke-kaha I worked as a peddler,
    A peddler was I.
The dust blew up, the sun scorched,
    The sun did scorch and burn.
The tax collector took all my gain,
The tax collector took all my gain.
I came home a poor man,
I came home a poor man.

III

I labored on a sugar plantation,
    Growing sugarcane.
My back ached, my sweat poured,
    All for nothing.
I fell in debt to the plantation store,
I fell in debt to the plantation store.
And remained a poor man,
And remained a poor man.

IV

I decided to quit working for money,
    Money to lose.
Far better work day by day,
    Grow my own daily food.
No more laboring so others get rich,
No more laboring so others get rich.
Just go on being a poor man,
Just go on being a poor man.

TRANSLATED BY MARY KAWENA PUKUI

To The
Town

The sun shines on the immigrant ... He spoke of the plantation as he spoke of death ... Half the top bunk is his ... Hard work and education ... Yoshio was interested in growing things ... Cowboy movies, opium deals and automobiles ... Intent on some celestial goal ... I like ride my surf board ... No make noise ... Some kind stink eye she give ... The King Street tram ... and Baby Street ... Home is here ...

Ellen Blackmar Maxwell

from THREE OLD MAIDS IN HAWAII

After lunch the three were sitting on the lanai, behind a drapery of blooming vines, watching the moving panorama in the street, and in it reading many tales. Belinda had the four daily papers in her hand, and glanced alternately at them and at the street. The daily papers of any place were the keys with which Belinda unlocked the doors leading to vast treasures of knowledge.

A group of Chinamen first caught their attention. They were in holiday dress and manner, their own national dress being modified by white straw sailor hats, set well back on their heads, and by American-made leather shoes. Behind them was a Portuguese gardener with a big bunch of carnations in one hand and a note in the other; then came a carriage full of tourists, and behind them a native man on a pony well laden with bags, evidently starting for some country district. Then came Japanese sailors from a man-of-war; then more Chinese. Back of them, laughing and chattering, were two or three full-breasted native women in straw hats and the Mother Hubbard style of dress, called holoku, with trains which they held well up, displaying bare fat feet and ankles. Then came a bright-faced, quick-moving little Japanese woman in a dress made of old-time pink calico; across from her were a Japanese woman and child in kimonos. Then there was a clatter of hoofs and a swift rush past of half a dozen ponies carrying large, stout native women in holokus, riding, as nearly all women, both white and black, ride in the islands, astride; then came a meat wagon, driven by an American; then an express wagon heaped up with trunks; then in her surrey a wide-awake woman of New England type going out to see some friends, having a white-faced, hollow-chested, coughing man from California on the back seat, whom she, *en passant*, was giving a drive for the cheering of his soul as well as the health of his body. Now came a German nurse leading home from school blue-eyed, round-faced little girls; then a Chinaman in pigtail and purple blouse, driving a carriage on the back seat of which was another Chinaman without visible pigtail and in American dress; then business men or perhaps members of the advisory council driven by an Irish coachman; then an American lady, in empire dress or modified holoku, going home from market with pineapples, celery, and the tops of other vegetables peeping out from the box of her buggy. Then another lady in a buggy nodding to the first as she drove quickly by, telling her to remember the committee meeting in the afternoon.

"Ah," sighed Belinda, as their words floated up, "who would have thought committees grew here? It breaks up the peace of mind I was about to enjoy, but at least I shall have no telegrams, no telephone messages, and no letters for fifteen days.

At this moment the Portuguese maid entered, asking for Miss Melrose, saying she was wanted at the telephone. The maid looked surprised at the laugh with which her words were greeted. As Judith followed her out Rose said:

"No telephone messages? and pray what did you think all those wires were for?" pointing to the poles that outlined the street and the ribbon of innumerable wires at their tops.

Belinda answered with another sigh:

"I had not noticed them. I believe there is no spot on earth where that fiend of unrest comes not."

Wing Tek Lum

"THE BUTCHER"

"There are many joys in living here,
And just to see it through is something gained."
—T'ao Ch'ien

Half of the top bunk is his,
that is he takes the night shift
sharing it with a late night short order cook
who cares for nothing,
not even a sweet bed to call his own.
The butcher does not have much more,
just what he wears or is in his pockets
and what he has saved in his small tin trunk
sealed and scented with camphor—
a second set of clothes and shoes
for festival days and funerals,
his ID papers, an IOU and a little cash,
a stack of letters, two or three photographs
and two or three clippings,
a pressed flower,
and a gold chain for the watch he once wore.
The room is small and spare

littered near the windowsill with cigarette butts
where his cousin, the oldtimer, always sits
reading the daily papers
or a broadside on revolution in the old country.
His cousin who occupies the lower bunk
never likes to go out
and with the bathroom down the hall
and the bar and grill on the ground floor
delivering dinner up to him
at the same time every night
it seems like he never does.
But the butcher loves the streets
or where the streets may take him.
Often he dines at the family clubhouse
bringing vegetables or a small fish from the docks
to share with those who have come in
from the country or another island
and need a place to stay
and fellow members and relatives to chat with.
Many remain after dinner to play dominoes or cards
but the butcher just watches
preferring to exchange a bit of lore or gossip
with the families who drop by
to pray to the Great Aunt in the front hall.
Whenever an opera troupe or an orator comes to town
the butcher is sure to attend.
Fire or flood relief drives
can consume his spare time,
and if a clansman dies
he will join in the collection.
When he returns to his room
the butcher sleeps soundly without dreams
in spite of the after work rehearsals
of the music society next door.
At dawn he awakes to the rooster crows
that punctuate each back courtyard and alleyway.
For breakfast he lingers over
his usual freshly-squeezed orange juice
and rice with ham
at the corner coffee shop;
it is named after an ancient palace

and he tells the counterman with a smile
that this is as close to one
as he would ever choose to get.
As he leaves, the cashier often goes over
the almanac predictions for the day.
The butcher has never believed in destiny
but is too polite to say so;
he waits until he is out of sight
before he shrugs his shoulders.
On his way to work he passes an old banyan
where he recalls on an earlier morning
in the slanting sunlight
he saw a woman with a thin nose
and hair as pale as lightning
who looked like a girl
he might have married.
The owner opening up his store
always nods to him with deference.
The first customers arrive
as they set out the barbeque loin and roast
pork
on hangers near the chopping block
that the owner will man.
The owner also collects the cash
leaving the butcher to work the second block
which is reserved for raw meat.
With his fat cleaver
he chops, carves, slices, minces, and trims.
Soon he is surrounded
by curly intestines and lumps of tongue,
the glutinous feet, slabs of spareribs,
pork chop, pork loin, pork butt,
pork belly, kidney and liver.
He sells to the big restaurant facing the river,
the temple next to the chicken coops,
a few wives carrying their children,
the grocery store owner, the bald tailor,
and the letter writer who never stops talking.
Sometimes the kerosene peddler will curse
him
for leaving too much fat.

Sometimes the barber will bring over
a can of soy bean milk as a gift.
He sharpens his knife when business is slow.
He remembers the sage's admonition
that to preserve a blade
the cook must seek the play
between the joints in the bones.

WING TEK LUM *is a Honolulu businessman and poet. His first collection of poetry,* Expounding the Doubtful Points, *was published by Bamboo Ridge Press in 1987.*

Linda Ching Sledge

from A MAP OF PARADISE

T he servant girl turned the steaming platter so that the head of the fish pointed at her master, Merchant Li. A naked play for Liang Mo's affections, his wife, Mei Yuk, observed, by a lowly bond maid who aspired to the rank of minor wife. Such snares had been laid for Liang Mo before. The man's taste in women was insufferably common. That small miscalculation would cost the girl dearly, for if Liang Mo's attention turned in her direction, Mei Yuk would sell her to the oldest and poorest vendor among the fish stalls, as she had others who had labored in her husband's bed and in her kitchen.

A wife of a certain age, Mei Yuk believed, had to be ever on guard against rivals, to be ruthless in maintaining her place. And her place, though nothing to compare with the luxuries she had known in China, was this block of ramshackle shops, vendors' stalls, and tenement houses in the crowded Chinatown quarter called Tin Can Alley over which she ruled as *Tai Tai*, matriarch of the wealthiest family enterprise in the islands.

Mei Yuk glanced surreptitiously at her epicene husband, sweating as he always did from the effort of eating. Did Liang Mo know how zealously she guarded their good name and her role as *Tai Tai* of his house? The week before, she had heard the news that her husband's former concubine had dropped a child. Years after fleeing their house in China, the woman had washed ashore on these islands like ocean-borne offal. For six months Mei Yuk had contemplated the movements of her former rival from afar: Rulan was seen strolling through Chinatown with a fat Hawaiian woman, buying fish or breadfruit or fresh poi from the stalls owned by the very family she had betrayed. In fury and fascination, Mei Yuk watched Rulan the way a hungry cat studies the movement of a bird perched just beyond reach. She had waited for the inattention, the small change in behavior that would carry the bird within the swipe of her claws and bring to an end that old feud once and for all.

Liang Mo dipped his chopsticks into the watery sauce and touched them to his tongue: cheap oil again, he concluded unhappily. A peasant meal, cooked by calloused peasant hands that could not even brew a proper cup of tea. Mei Yuk, at least, shared with him the memory of being rich, so rich that one had a servant for chopping vegetables, another for carrying hot water, and another for massaging one's feet. For that bond, and for other services Mei Yuk rendered to his family, he kept her as *Tai Tai* long after the beauty had faded and his passion had cooled. It was a fair exchange: his favor for her cleverness at trade. And if he slept with a lowly servant girl, Mei Yuk did not lose what she did not value.

Why then, he wondered, did Mei Yuk force her household to eat like paupers, when the family's accounts showed profits in every venture and the stalls owned by the Lis were stocked with delicacies sent at great cost from China—dried oysters, rice noodles spun into billowing translucent threads, sharks' fins, bears' paws, red dates to tame a fiery dish and to cool the blood. He pulled a handkerchief from his sleeve and mopped his damp forehead. He had always suffered an excess of heat, and that imbalance of elements made him languish in the sweltering, mosquito-ridden atmosphere of wharfside Honolulu. He decided that he had not eaten well since his Second Lady had left his house and his bed years ago. That lady, Rulan, had known the medical properties of food and could brew soups to cure a fever or stir a jaded appetite or relieve the pangs of overindulgence. That lady's unexpected appearance in the islands was a stroke of fortune. He had decided to take her back, to forgive her insult to his name, if she could restore balance to his household and lessen the influence of this harridan who usurped the part of a man.

Hiding his ill-humor under an exaggerated show of politeness, Merchant Li broke off the tender flesh behind the gills with his chopsticks and put it on his wife's plate. Mei Yuk raised it absentmindedly to her lips. She now preferred business to the pleasures of the moment—music or food or conversation. She even insisted on making their daughter, Lily, their only surviving child, take her meals with the bond maid in the kitchen, so the two of them could talk earnings and rents as they ate.

"Husband," Mei Yuk chided, "the accounts for the contract laborers are settled. If we adjust the numbers, we can claim new losses because some men perished on the voyage and some were turned away by the barbarian doctor because of disease." The servant girl returned with a fresh pot of tea, and they lapsed into silence. Liang Mo studied the girl's plump figure as if she were another dish set before him.

Although she had fled from him years ago, Rulan was still by contract his possession under Chinese law, as much part of the family's inventory as the field hands aboard the *Mei Foo*. Lian Mo doubted that the Hawaiian courts would interfere with his prior claims on Rulan: Hawaiians and *haoles* never interfered in matters between Chinese. For even if Rulan sued for release, the courts, dominated by the powerful sugar lobby, were bound to favor master rather than servant. Rescinding a labor contract made in China could throw the planter's own lucrative contracts with immigrant laborers into question. No, law was not a problem. Releasing Rulan from the white devil's protection posed a greater complication . . . and of course there was the monumental obstacle in the person of his wife. He suspected that Mei Yuk, whose network of spies was as extensive as his, had known earlier than he when Rulan had set foot in the islands and was intent on some secret mischief. She never could abide a rival.

"You are dreaming again," Mei Yuk scolded.

"Only about how we made love in the garden at my father's house. Have you grown so old that you forget young joys?" he added sullenly.

"Your *old* wife forgets nothing," Mei Yuk snapped, her pinched face clouding over with resentment. "I remember that in the same year our son wrote his first eight-legged essay, we sent his body back to Kwangtung to be buried. I remember our daughters' graves in the garden. I remember how old I have grown sacrificing for this family!" Impatiently, she ordered the bond maid to clear the table, and when the girl proved too slow, Mei Yuk threw her papers over the piles of fish bones and puddles of tea. "Here," she said to her husband with white-hot hatred. "You finish the accounts. I am old and useless."

Mei Yuk waited in the dark for Liang Mo, a habit of hers after a row, for he was a soft man who hated quarreling. Yet Liang Mo did not slip into her bed to beg forgiveness, as he always had before.

LINDA CHING SLEDGE, *PhD, was born in Honolulu and is Professor Emerita of English at Westchester Community College, State University of New York. She is the author of three books, two of them novels based on her family and set in nineteenth-century China and Hawai'i:* Empire of Heaven, *for which she won the B.Dalton/Barnes & Noble Discover Great New Writers Award; and* A Map of Paradise. *Her books have been translated into nine languages. She lives in Pleasantville, New York, with her husband, an editor at* Readers Digest.

Rae Soares

Of course, the people which participated in things of this sort are dead now, and so is nearly every one which ever knew anything about the matter, but occasionally you will run across an old Hawaiian whose memory you can always refresh by showing him a bit of silver, and then you will hear tales of the days when smuggling opium into Honolulu was a common practise.

There are some who will tell you that the blocks on the sidewalk on the right hand side of Alakea street were taken from the holds of smugglers. Nothing so very astonishing, only, in the middle of these blocks the initiated found a can of opium. Parties would contract for a load of Chinese stone and the unsuspecting Customs man would pass the ship which brought it. But when the stones were safely carried away, this same Customs man would have been astonished, could he have seen a man remove a layer from a block and take out from the cavity a can.

He would have been further astounded could he have seen what the can contained.

Ah Pung had contracted for such a load of stone and was anxiously awaiting the arrival of the ship bearing it.

Smuggling opium was getting to be a risky proposition and in view of the alarming number of captures which the government had made and the large amount of fines which it had collected from those whom it captured, Ah Pung made a mental resolve, as he walked down to the Pilot House to ask if the *Fanny* had been sighted, that with the sale of this load, his part in this illegal business terminated.

The *Fanny* was making an unusually slow passage, and many were the conjectures placed upon her delay.

"Bet you she's got a load of opium this trip," said one old sea dog to a group of his companions.

"Your bet is safe," was the reply from the youngest of the number, "she had a load of it last trip. My opinion on her delay is this: Her captain's got the wind that somethin' is blowing wrong and he's not going to risk his cargo and his ship by coming in, unless the coast is clear.

"Old Captain Mitchell is too crafty a sea dog to be caught napping. He's been engaged in this smuggling business for over twenty years. Used to smuggle wines from Portugal into Boston Harbor at one time, and then, when he found the job getting pretty hot, he took his ship when no body was looking, and went into smuggling opium. I was first mate under him two trips ago, and I know.

"I'll bet you," he said suddenly to the first speaker, "I'll bet you that this old Chink has got the cargo on board the *Fanny* this time."

The group fixed its eyes on Ah Pung who was nervously watching a customs officer who, from time to time, was scanning the horizon with his glass.

Hearing what the mate said, Ah Pung turned to them and said, "Yes, me got calgo on boad the *Flanny*. Too muchee building stone this trip. Got big contlact make floo' for lice thleshing, up Waiau."

A number of the sailors nodded as if they accepted the Chinaman's story, but the mate smiled. "That's all right, John; don't need to worry about us, you pig-tailed heathen. I know very well what's inside them stones, but if you can land them without that chap nabbing you, you'll have my sincerest admiration. I tell you," he said lowering his voice, "you'd better get some kind of a signal out to the *Fanny* telling her not to land those stones at the wharf."

The Chinaman looked the mate over carefully and then, as if satisfied with his examination, he said, "My lice schooner captain he sick. You number one sailor; you take my boat to Waiau now."

Roberts understood the ruse and got up smiling from his box and went over to Ah Pung's rice schooner. The sails were hoisted and the little schooner bounded out of the harbor. Instead of turning to his right, to where Waiau lay, Roberts steered the schooner in the direction of Diamond Head.

In response to the Chinaman's inquiring look Roberts said, "That government schooner is out some where. We'll have to find out where before we can do anything."

The schooner was skimming along at a good clip when Ah Pung's excited eyes saw another schooner bearing down upon them.

"No," Roberts said after looking the new comer over, "that's not the *Fanny*; that's the customs' schooner. Well, we'll make for Waiau."

Carefully swinging her around, he started back to town but was hailed with the cry, "Ship ahoy!"

"The *Moi Wahine*," was the reply.

"Haul hard until we come up to you," was the order.

Roberts had the one sailor on board haul down the sails and awaited the coming of the customs boat.

"What are you doing?" he was asked.

"Merely trying this boat."

"What for?"

"Want to buy her."

"What made you turn around when you saw us?"

"Didn't see you until after I started to come back."

The officer seemed appeased and he ordered his own sail up. Roberts followed suit and turning to the captain he said, "I'll race you back to the harbor for a drink all around."

"That's to find out who has the faster boat," he muttered to himself.

"All right, let her go," he shouted and both boats fairly flew, cutting the water with clean, sharp strokes as they sped along.

Roberts put on all the sail he had; the customs' man did the same and gained rapidly.

"Whew," muttered Roberts, "not much of a chance for us, Ah Pung, if we were in a pinch now. But wait a moment, I'll fix him." He veered slightly to the left and took advantage of a sudden puff of wind. That was all the *Moi Wahine* needed; her masts fairly groaned under the spread of canvas and soon the customs man was out of sight.

"I understand her now," Roberts said, "I'll guarantee to beat anything in these waters. But let's go to Waiau. I want to see what kind of a harbor they have there."

"Nothing decent," was his verdict. "Catch us here easy. I have it," he said finally, "there's Ford's Island off there," jerking his thumb in the direction of the island, "that'll help us alright. Now let's go back to the harbor and get those drinks the captain owes us."

The captain was found pouring a drink from a demijohn in his office. "It's on me," he called as Roberts passed by. He entered and took the mug which the captain filled for him.

"By the way," he asked, "what were you doing out by Diamond Head this afternoon?"

"Looking for the *Fanny*. I can't imagine what's become of the boat."

"What's so wonderful on the *Fanny* that makes you so anxious to meet her?"

"Opium."

"What do you intend to do?"

"Do? Nothing now. Wait until she gets into the harbor and then nab the man that her cargo is assigned to."

"But supposing he manages to land the cargo before the boat roaches the harbor, then what?"

"Take a mighty smart man to skin me, old fellow. Fill up your mug, I see it's empty."

"Here's to the *Fanny*; may she make port safely."

The captain looked at Roberts in mild surprise but he drank the toast and added, "May she make port safely and give her cargo up to the government."

Roberts left the room and found Ah Pung waiting for him.

"You come my house eat," he said.

The invitation was accepted and Roberts was soon at Ah Pung's home. It was a pretentious dwelling, for Ah Pung had money. He, had married a Hawaiian woman who possessed a large quantity of land. A part of this her husband had sold to enable him to buy opium, and after the second trip, he was counted a rich man.

Ah Pung had a daughter. Though dark-skinned, Kealoha was fair to behold. She had inherited her mother's Hawaiian beauty; and her only Chinese characteristic shown from her eyes.

Sam Roberts was a roving sort of a fellow. Many were the girls who would have gladly married him "back East," but be would have none of them. Tonight, as he sat on the floor, which formed Ah Pung's dining table, by the side of pretty Kealoha, he thought he had never seen any Hawaiian or any other maiden look so lovely.

Around her head she had a *lei* of red carnations, and another of *ilima* hung around her neck. Lost in the contemplation of so lovely a vision, Roberts failed to do justice to the excellent meal which Au Pung had provided.

When dinner was over, Au Pang led his guest out to the lanai and together they planned their campaign.

"You help me, I help you," said Ah Pung.

"Yes, I help you, but what do I get out of this business?"

Au Pung had noticed the effect which Kealoha had produced upon Roberts and with a crafty smile he answered, "You help me, make me win, I give you Kealoha."

"But suppose she won't have me?"

"Kealoha have anybody I tell her have," was the Chinaman's response.

"The stake is well worth the risk," Roberts muttered. "I make the old Chink win."

Kealoha came out with her guitar and in the short twilight, she sang several plaintive Hawaiian melodies. Then she suddenly arose and went into the house.

Roberts got up from his chair and said, "Let's go out to Diamond Head. I have an idea that the *Fanny* is somewhere around there."

They went to the wharf and rousing the sailor aboard the *Moi Wahine*, the sails were raised and in the calm moonlight they sped away to Diamond Head. When they were in full sight of the light house, Roberts saw a green light flash out over the water from a large black mass which was blacker than the darkness around it. The green light was followed by two red ones, and then by a white one. Roberts returned the signal and sailed for the spot.

"Ship ahoy!" he called softly.

"The *Fanny*," was the response. "Who are you?"

"The *Moi Wahine*. Don't attempt to land at Honolulu. Customs' men are on to you. They were looking for you yesterday."

The *Fanny's* captain laughed. "What would you advise, Roberts?"

"Go to Pearl Harbor instead. Nobody has seen you. The old fellow up there is asleep and we can get up to Pearl Harbor with this wind before daybreak. Once there, you can remain in hiding 'til night. Then I'll come and transfer your cargo into the *Moi Wahine*."

Capt. Mitchell favored the plan and with the *Moi Wahine* in the lead, the two schooners sailed to Pearl Harbor, where the *Fanny* was anchored. The *Moi Wahine* was sailed back to town and moored at her usual place.

"Nobody will be the wiser, old chap," he said to Ah Pung. "We'll stay at home today and tonight the opium will be brought back. Let the stones stay in the hold until the next night, then we'll bring them to your house, a few at a time. Then, Ah Pung, I'll claim my reward."

Au Pung nodded and invited Sam in to spend the day at his house.

After breakfast he followed Kealoha into the yard, and watched her make a *lei*.

They were silent for a while when Kealoha asked, "You'll help my father land his opium?"

"Yes," he replied.

"How much money will you get for the job?"

"No money at all; my dear, I get *you*."

"You get me?"

"Yes, your father has promised to let me marry you if I succeed in landing the opium so that the customs men won't know."

"Can you do it?"

"Dead easy."

"But if I don't want to marry you?"

"But you will," he said smilingly.

"But I won't," she returned firmly. "Do you think I sell myself or let my father sell me for a load of opium. No, sir! What's more, I am to marry Kea."

"Don't you love your father?"

"Yes, very much."

"Then do you want to see him go to jail?"

"No."

"Well, if I say the word, I'll get him into jail."

Kealoha burst into tears. "You white men are so cruel," she sobbed out in Hawaiian. "Not content with defrauding us out of our lands, you wish to keep us from marrying one another."

Roberts bit his lips. He disliked to see woman in tears. He took her hands in his and said gently, "Kealoha, listen to me."

She raised her head and with brimming eyes looked him full in the face.

"Kealoha," he said, "couldn't you learn to love me?"

She shook her head.

"Do you love Kea?"

"Yes," she said softly.

"Then, Kealoha, I am not the man to cross the love path of another man." He was silent for a moment then he continued: "I love you as I have never loved before. You say you love your father. For your sake, dear heart, I'll not betray him. Go, tell your father, that I have given my permission for you to marry Kea tonight. Go."

Kealoha threw her head upon his shoulder and sobbed out her thanks. Then raising her pretty face to his, she pressed a kiss on his lips and left him to himself.

Dora Broadbent

"THE THRIFT STAMP BUYER"

"Pape', Advertisa. Pape', suh," shouted the little brown boy, and the tall, busy-looking man stopped with a smile to get a newspaper from the bright-eyed Japanese boy.

This was Nagai, the boy who had come out from Japan with his mother, three years ago. He had been selling papers every afternoon since September, when school started.

One day as he hurried from the printing office to his post at the Young Hotel entrance, he noticed the big heading of one of the articles especially. "Thrift Stamp Campaign to Start. Help win the War by Saving and Buying Thrift Stamps," it read.

Nagai wondered, mildly, what thrift stamps were and read this over again during his spare moments.

The next day as he settled down by the entrance, he noticed a big picture on the glass window of the lobby. He went up to it and read it. There was a picture of a boy, about his age, and a little girl, each holding the hand of an army officer. On the top was "Help Him by Saving and Serving. Buy U.S. War Saving Stamps."

War Savings Stamps! Nagai searched his papers for information and found another notice about these stamps. He spelled out the long words and read it through this time. It explained the whole thing and Nagai understood it all except that he could not see how four dollars and thirteen cents could make five dollars in 1923. But it must be true, he thought, if the paper said so.

He dug his hand down into his pocket. He had over a dollar here and with the three dollars he had at home, saved from his scanty spending money, he had enough to buy all sixteen of the stamps. But then, he thought, these were not for poor people like him.

Just then a curly-headed Portuguese newsboy dashed around the corner and flew up to Nagai. All his papers were gone and in his hand was a yellow envelope with much printing on it.

"Nagai, see wat I got," he panted excitedly as he pulled a folded card out of the envelope and showed it full of small green stamps. "See dees stamps. Das a War Saving stamps, I tell you. I buy for quarter one stamp and one man he see I buy dees stamp and he geeve me four dollars for feenish these card. See now I buy all dees stamps. Tomorrow I go Post-office. I make change for one big stamp. You see, boy, 1918 I get five dollars, I reech you see!" and he was off, homeward bound, to exalt with his family over his luck.

Nagai stood staring after him for a while and then gathered his papers for returning them to the office. He walked rather slowly home, jingling the money in his pocket. Tomorrow he would buy his whole War Savings Certificate.

Next day he was up earlier than usual and got out his little bank. With his key he opened it and poured the three dollars into his hand. It was a good deal of money. Just think what it might buy. He could get some fine marbles and be the envy of all his school-mates. He might get a new top. But then he thought of Joe Fernando. He had been prouder of his War Stamp than of all the agates he had ever owned. So once for all Nagai decided to buy the stamp.

That afternoon he went to the post-office, gave up his precious money and bought a card like Joe's, only with one big green stamp in the corner.

That night he went home silently elated, and hardly able to wait to pull it out of his shirt and show it to her.

She was puzzled at first. Then as he explained, her expression changed until finally Nagai stopped and asked her what was wrong.

"Wat'sa matter you," she said, with a frown. "Me give you money, eh. Me tink so you keep dis money. By-mby you buy any kind you like, hat, shoes, any-kind. Wat'sa matter you buy dis kind. No good!"

Nagai explained quickly that in 1923 he would get five dollars back for this. But 1923 was the dim and distant future to Nagai's mother, and he went to bed that night, feeling that the buying of the stamp was all wrong after all.

The next morning he went to school feeling out of sorts with himself, a different boy from the Nagai of the afternoon before.

The bell rang and Nagai marched in with the rest of the children, and then sitting down at his desk in the back of the room, stared morosely at the offending man. So he did not see the tall man in the grey suit come into the room, and go up to the platform before the class. In fact Nagai knew nothing, till he heard a strange voice saying to the children, "You know that America has gone to war now. The men from America will be getting shot over there like the English and French soldiers. Now, these Thrift Stamps are here so that you can buy them and give a little money to help our soldiers. I have spoken to several classes already," he said. "Not a person in any of them had bought one yet. Of course, it is very early yet; but if there is any one in this room who has one, I should like him to come up here on the platform with me so everyone can see him."

There was no stir. The gentleman was beginning to look disappointed, when Nagai, deep crimson under his tan, rose from his seat and with the heretofore scorned certificate in his hand, walked shakily up to the platform.

There, as in a dream, the big man shook his hand, told him he was proud of him and made the whole class give three cheers for Nagai. And he gave Nagai *another whole stamp* to put on his card.

That evening a very excited boy showed the second big stamp, and told the story to a mother who listened, proudly, this time.

DORA BROADBENT *wrote this story in 1915, when she was a student at Punahou School in Honolulu.*

———————•◦•———————

Pam Chun

from THE MONEY DRAGON

The day after his father left for China, Tat-Tung stood at the window of his office overlooking King Street, the heart of Hawai'i's Chinatown. His eyes caressed the angular lines of the new motorcars as they maneuvered around the horse wagons in clouds of dust. Their engines gave off an efficient sound, the sound of serious movement.

On the way home, he stopped and admired the gleam of paint and chrome. He asked their drivers, "How fast can you go? How much fuel? How about care and maintenance? How do you drive it?"

The first time he rode in a motorcar he hung on tightly, grasping the sides of his seat. His friends sped down Queen Street to the wharf. A policeman yelled at them to slow down. Then they drove out toward the country, past farmers bent in half in the rice fields, children waving in front of small country stores, and the mute faces of plantation workers.

When he came home, his normally serene face was flushed. His crisp white shirt and tie were dusted with dirt. "Extraordinary, extraordinary," was all he could say. His mind was moving ahead, absorbing the experience and integrating it into future possibilities.

Most of the roadways within Honolulu were reasonably flat with the wear of horse wagons. As the number of motorcars increased, being the latest status symbol of the wealthy and privileged, the city smoothed more roads.

One afternoon, Tat-Tung hummed merrily down the stairs of his office. "Ah Wang," he called. He motioned his brother outside, evading the crowds of customers yelling orders to their clerks. The two stood on the sidewalk piled with bags of feed, rice, and vegetables. The air was rich with the smell of horses, the fresh ocean breeze from Honolulu Harbor a block away, and the occasional lei worn by passersby carrying jute and lauhala shopping bags.

"Look out there, Ah Wang. Motorcars. What do you think?" Tat-Tung pointed to the motorcars in the street.

"Those noisy things. A novelty for the rich," Ah Wang dismissed with a wave of his hand. This was a grand gesture, patterned after his father's.

"The future, Ah Wang," insisted the enthused Tat-Tung.

"Humph. Playthings."

"We should buy one of those," Tat-Tung pointed as a gleaming Model-T Ford sped by, narrowly missing a horse wagon. He laughed at the wide eyes and gritted teeth of the motorcar driver, who obviously didn't think he was going to make it past the horse. The wagon's driver now stood and shook his fist at the motorcar racing away at twenty miles an hour.

"You crazy! What for?" his brother asked incredulously.

"Look, a horse you have to feed. It needs a stable and a man to take care of it. If a horse is sick or lame, we have to get a veterinarian, right?"

Ah Wang nodded. Everyone knew you had to take good care of your horses if you expected them to carry loads all day, like they did.

"If we use a motorcar, we don't need a stable or a man to take care of it. We just park it."

"Baba will never go for the idea. It's too new. He has his own way of doing things. He doesn't like change."

"No hay to buy."

"Humph. A passing fad."

"Goes five times as fast. Finish all deliveries same day. We'll teach Ah Chung to drive and make him our delivery man. Also, think of the modern image it will create: 'L. Ah Leong Store delivers by motorcar.' Everyone will want to buy from us so we can drive to their store or house and deliver from our motorcar. Gives them plenty face."

Tat-Tung was inspired as he created his vision. The image of the L. Ah Leong motorcar deliveries speeding through Honolulu driven by the Lau sons was a modern view offering speed and efficiency for their customers. It could set them a step ahead of the other enterprises in town.

True, there were limits to these machines. They broke down occasionally. If an excited driver ran them off the road, they would not get right back on the path the way a horse would. They could only travel on reasonably flat roads, and definitely not through mud after a tropical storm. A bumpy road could pop a wheel or twist an axle. In the country, one could send a horse out to graze in the open land. A motorcar driver had to make sure he had a sufficient fuel supply.

Ah Wang knew his brother had researched this decision. "What will Baba say?"

"I'll talk to him when he gets back from China."

Tat-Tung had already checked out the feasibility of buying a motorcar for the store deliveries. He confirmed the size and model he needed, then put the word out through his network of friends. He negotiated a deal for $200 for a used Model-T with a modified delivery bed large enough to handle the volume currently managed by the horse wagons.

The steamer bringing L. Ah Leong was sighted by the lookout at Diamond Head. The whistle from the Hawaiian Electric Company blew, announcing its impending arrival.

Tat-Tung drove down to the dock at Honolulu Harbor and joined the quickly gathering crowd already excited by the heart-thumping marches of The Royal Hawaiian Band.

The steamer tooted. The crowd cheered. When the boat docked, the greetings of friends and relatives charged the atmosphere with kisses and screams, for the Hawaiians loved the sound of their welcoming songs and the press of human hugs. Jubilant waves from the passengers met with screams of "Aloha" from the lei-bedecked greeters on the dock.

Tat-Tung, dressed nattily in a crisp white shirt, wide flowered tie, and neatly pressed slacks, leaned boldly against the motorcar. It was polished to a gleaming black sheen, reflecting the Hawaiian sun in flashing radiance. The thirty-year-old merchant acknowledged the admiring glances of the disembarking passengers and visitors who crowded the port on Boat Day. The men salivated over the dashing vehicle. The ladies oohed.

"Look at that new machine."

"Expensive, isn't it?"

"He must be some rich guy."

Tat-Tung chuckled to himself. He couldn't wait to see his father's reaction.

Soon enough, L. Ah Leong, in no-nonsense work shoes, walked down the gangplank followed by five porters bent in half under the weight of his trunks. The sixty-four-year-old merchant had packed away his elegant Chinese clothes, his long banker's coats of dai fong chau silk, and black pigskin-soled satin shoes in reverse appliqué. Since Hawai'i meant business, he now wore thick cotton trousers and a well-mended jacket that Wong Shee had laundered, starched, and ironed. As expected, he was the first Chinese to get through Immigration.

Tat-Tung greeted him. Then the two walked out to the street.

"And how was your voyage, Baba?"

"Ships are going faster nowadays. Only took two weeks to get here. Saves time. See the weight I gained? Second wife Ho Shee and Fifth wife Wong Shee insisted on serving me all my favorite foods. Your Eighth brother Lau Chen is married now. The District Governor of Kwang Tung came to his wedding banquet. We served two thousand friends and relatives! Unfortunately, the warlords are gaining more power in the cities and it cost me much silver to convince them to leave my lands alone. They're still fighting among themselves."

Tat-Tung hmm'd and nodded. He said business was good. When the men reached the car, Tat-Tung instructed the porters; he pointed to the arrangement he wanted for the trunks in the back of the motorcar. He ignored the stunned look on his father's face.

Ah Leong walked closer, paused, then paced slowly to the front of the motorcar. He paused, then walked around to the back. He looked at his son, then back at the gleaming machine. He exploded, "Hah, what's this?"

"Your new motorcar," Tat-Tung replied calmly. He motioned his father up to the passenger seat with a gallant sweep of his arm. "Get in."

Ah Leong bellowed. "Where's the horses?"

"I sold them. Come on, let's go."

"What? You sold my horses? You spent my money?"

Tat-Tung tipped the porters. They dashed back to the ship to avoid the old merchant's legendary temper.

"Baba, we bought this motorcar secondhand. An excellent deal. No need for horses, so we sold them."

Ah Leong stared rigidly at his son.

"It makes good business sense," Tat-Tung continued. "This car doesn't need anyone to take care of it. We don't need a stable man to brush its coat every night and make sure it has hay and water. We just park it. There is no need to buy it food. We fill it with gasoline. The motorcar is so fast we will beat up the competition. Get in. I'll show you how it works. Give me your hand."

Ignoring his son's assistance, Ah Leong heaved his body into the passenger's seat. He turned around to see all his trunks firmly in place. His son had tied them down in exactly the same way they tied down loads in the delivery wagon.

The motorcar gave Ah Leong a new perspective. He observed the way people stared in admiration and the looks of respect they gave him when Tat-Tung started up the motorcar and pulled away from the curb. He could even see, reflected on the hood, the clouds floating against a turquoise sky. Best of all, he no longer saw Honolulu from behind the trotting rump of a horse, but from behind an efficiently churning engine.

"See how people are watching you?" his son shouted over the humming chug. "Business picked up since we started motorcar deliveries. We can do more deliveries per day than with the horse wagon. Drive all day long without having to change to a fresh horse. At night, I drive it home and park in the side yard of our house. In the morning, I drive to the store for the next day's deliveries." A glance at father's expression told him the old merchant was considering this analysis.

"Going home first?" Tat-Tung asked.

"Course not."

Ah Leong watched the heads that turned his way. People stared at him in the passenger seat of the gleaming motorcar. What did his son say? They were doing more business now because people wanted others to see they were receiving their deliveries via motorcar? Via the modern L. Ah Leong Store motorcar? Ah, the focus on business and greater profits from his First son who thinks like a Chinese and a haole.

Tat-Tung drove his father up to the front of the store. Sons and workers dashed out to greet him and unload the trunks.

"Hey, Ah Leong," his cronies called when they saw him alight. They ran over from their businesses, waving their greetings. "How was your trip? What's the news from the village? Rode back in this new thing, huh? Can you give us a ride?"

As friends crowded around his father, Tat-Tung directed the workers to unload the trunks into the warehouse until his father unpacked and gave his instructions. In the meantime, the old man was enjoying the adulation of his colleagues. Some took turns climbing into the driver's seat to get a feel for the wheel. Others ogled the engine.

That evening, Tat-Tung drove his father home to the mansion with the wide lanai.

There was a serious frown on the old merchant's face. He looked at his son and nodded. His son nodded back. Ah Leong slowly got out of the vehicle. He ran his fingers over the shiny polished chrome. From the shadows of the lanai, he watched his son and the motorcar chug down the road in the darkness.

PAM CHUN is a novelist who first learned about Ah Leong and her family relationship to him from former U.S. Senator Hiram L. Fong. Born and raised in Hawai'i, she attended Punahou School and the University of Hawai'i and graduated with honors from the University of California at Berkeley. She lives in Alameda County, California.

Lloyd Stone

"PICTURE OF A CHINESE GARDENER DRIVING A MODEL 'T' FORD THROUGH HEAVY TRAFFIC"

Intent on some celestial goal (perhaps
It is his lettuce bed that needs another
Soaking) Buddha glides through traffic as
An eagle's wing cleaves stratosphere.

                             His face,
A moon of pleasant thought (perhaps his onion
Bed that newly springs with tender shoots
Out of the earth inspires the smile) looks neither
To the right nor left, but wisely passes
On to other vistas, leaving in
His wake a maelstrom of grinding brakes
And curses.

             And high above the firmament
The sun revolves through vast unpeopled spaces,
Too.

LLOYD STONE (1912-1993) was a poet, artist, and musician. He published a number of books of poetry in the 1940s.

Manuel Jesus Coito

"JOGO—MESSINHA"

Este mundo é de enganos
N'elle habita malfeitores,
N'elle ha monstros e tyrannos,
Negreiros e inquizidores;
Uns furtam para viver,
Outros vendem irmãos seus,
Esquecem-se que hão-de morrer,
Até se esquecem que ha Deus.

O vicio, vicio maldito
Que existe n'esta cidade,
É qual chuva de granito
Que cae da immencidade;
Éo jogo de chi-fá,
Seven-Eleven, e outros mais,
É tudo quanto mau ha
N'esses covis infernaes.

Pelos baixos arredores
Por esses antros immundos . . .
Encontram-se os jogadores
Esses miseros, vagabundos;
Que a lei assassinando,
Faltando ao seu dever,
O pão aos filhos roubando
No jogo de Lucifer . . .

São malandros por sentença,
Assim se pode chamar,
É o que senso comum pensa
E não ha que duvidar;
Se a lei bem castigasse
Com toda a força e rigor,
Talvez o jogo acabasse
E fosse a cousa melhor.

Vergonha, vergonha infinda
Alem da crise que ha;

Jogam patricios, ainda
Ao seven-eleven e chi-fá;
É uma miseria terrivel,
São uns vicios deshumanos,
E que gente incorrigivel
Vergonha dos Lusitanos.

Alem da grande desgraça
Que causa a jogatina.
Ainda existe outra trapassa
Que arrasta para a ruina;
Vem a sêr: as mesinheiras,
Curandeiras e impostoras,
Do alheio papadeiras
Perversas, falças doutoras.

Umas com livros de sonhos,
D'elles fazem advinhações,
Inventando assim infronhos
Para desgraça e perdiçiões;
E fazendo-se tão biatas,
Sendo hypocritas, falsas,
Teem do demo as patas . . .
Vestem do Judas as calsas.

Amalgamando derriços . . .
As cuscuvilheiras, malignas,
Dizem que fazem feitiços
Com palavrinhas divinas,
Quem não as venéra e afague
Essas cróas de virtude?
Bem empregado azurrague
Até pol-as no ataude . . .

Isto de jogos ee sórtes,
De sonhos e advinhações,
São feridas, chagas, córtes
Que magôam os corações;
Mal hajam os covis sombrios,
Antros de fatalidade,
Morram do jogo os vadios
Para bern da humanidade . . .

"GAMBLING—FOLK MEDICINE"

This world is full of deceit.
In it dwell evil-doers.
In it are monsters and tyrants,
Slave-traders and inquisitors;
Some steal in order to live,
Others sell their brothers,
They forget that they will die.
They even forget there exists God.

Oh vice, accursed vice,
Which runs wild in this city;
It is like a granite rain
Falling from the immensity;
It is the chi-fa game,
Seven-Eleven, and yet others,
It is everything evil
In those hellish dens.

In the low quarters
Of those filthy dens.
Are found gamblers—
Those good-for-nothing wretches,
Who disobey the law,
Not performing their duty,
Robbing the children of bread
In Lucifer's game.

They are confirmed idlers,
Thus can they be called.
That is what common sense thinks
And there is no doubting;
If the law dealt proper punishment
With all its power and rigor,
Perhaps gambling would end
And things would be better.

Shame, infinite shame
Beyond the crisis that exists;
Fellow countrymen still play
Seven-Eleven and chi-fa;

It is a terrible misfortune;
They are unhuman vices
And these incorrigible people
Are the shame of the Portuguese.

Besides the great misfortune
Caused by games of chance,
There is another fraud
That leads to ruin;
They are the quack-practitioners,
Curandeiras and imposters,
Taking advantage of others,
Perverse, false doctors.

Some with books of dreams
Make prophecies from them,
Inventing thus fake knowledge
Leading to misfortune and perdition;
And pretending to be so pious
Actually hypocrites, false ones,
They have the devil's paws . . .
They wear Judas's trousers.

Mixing mockery on mockery,
The evil witches
Say they are casting spells
With divine words;
Should we not venerate them and
Caress those crowns of virtue?
We'd be better off to scourge
Them, making them rest in the coffin.

This matter of gambling and lotteries,
Of dreams and prophecies,
Causes wounds, sores, and cuts
Which damage the heart;
Accursed be the dark dens,
Caves of destruction,
May the idlers who gamble die
For the good of mankind.

TRANSLATED BY EDGAR KNOWLTON

Manuel Jesus Coito
"O FADO DE HONOLULU"

Belas ruas da cidade,
Só vestidos aparece,
Lá nas fitas não se falla
Que de tantas aborrece.

Ve-se luxos tão pesados
Ve-se fitas e mais fitas
Ve-se as rendas mais bonitas
Que os ricos ficam pasmados;
Ficam todos admirados
Por verem na mocidade
Tanto luxo, e vaidade
Em filhas de gentes pobres
Que figuram mais que as nobres
Belas ruas da cidade.

É tanta a galanteria
Que se vê no arredor,
E cada vez vae a maior

Esta enorme phantasia
É tal qual a maresia
Quando em marulhada cresce,
Aos censatos aborrece
Ver tamanhas presumpções,
Pois em certas occasiões
Só vestidos aparece.

É uma variedade . . .
De rendas, boquets e fitas,
Todas querem sêr bonitas
Que é mesmo rir sem vontade;
São p'ra fallar a verdade
Meninas de grande gala,
Embora a barriga estala
Anda para lá não me toques,
Com berliques e berloques
Lá nas fitas não se falla.

Mas isto deve acatar
Pois Deus nos castigou,
Já o cholera nos perturbou
Para os luxos se acalmar;
Agora a bobónica a grassar
Mal o cholera desaparece,
E coitados quern padece
Sem culpa de taes mesuras
São tantas as imposturas
Que de tantas aborrece.

"THE FADO OF HONOLULU"

Along the streets of the city
Only dresses appear,
One does not speak there be-ribboned
Since the multiplicity irritates.

One sees such annoying luxury,
One sees ribbons and more ribbons,
One sees the most lovely lace
Making the wealthy amazed;
Everybody is surprised
To see in young people
Such luxury and vanity
In daughters of the poor
Who appear oftener than the nobles
Along the streets of the city.

Much courteous behavior
Is seen about them;
This enormous fancy
Gets bigger and bigger;
It is like the smell of the sea
When it rises in billows;
It irritates sensible people
To see such hauteur,
For on certain occasions
Only dresses appear.
It is a refreshing change.

With lace, bouquets, and ribbons.
They all want to be pretty
Which is laughable, despite all,
If the truth be told.
Young women of splendid dress
Though their bellies burst
Go there; do not touch me
With hocus-pocus.
One does not speak there be-ribboned.

But this must impose respect
Since God has already punished us.
Now the cholera upset us,
For luxury to quiet down;
Now rages the bubonic plague,
No sooner has the cholera fled,
And unfortunate are those suffering
Blameless for such disasters.
There is so much calumny
Since the multiplicity irritates.

TRANSLATED BY EDGAR KNOWLTON

Manuel Jesus Coito
"A DESGRAÇA"

A cerca do Iwilei,
É o centro da corrupção
Onde vão as malfadadas
Vender alma e coração.

Vendem pelo Deus dinheiro,
A honra e a mocidade,
E no caminho da maldade
Zombam do Deus verdadeiro;
É este o ponto primeiro
Que n'estes versos direi:
Zombam da virtude e lei,

A Desgraça. ok 6/30/94

86

A cerca do Iwilei,
E' o centro da corrupção;
Onde vão as malfadadas
Vender alma e coração.

1

Vendem pelo Deus-dinheiro,
A honra e a mocidade,
E no caminho da maldade
Zombam do Deus verdadeiro;
E' este o ponto primeiro
Que n'estes versos direi:
Zombam da virtude e lei,
Desprezam sua existencia;
E' o antro da maledicencia
A cerca do Iwilei.

87 2

Até faz causar pavor
Ao povo que por lá passa
Ver as filhas da desgraça
D'um modo que causa horror;/
Oh /..victimas do impudor
Cahidas na perdição;
Tenham d'ellas compachão
Basta a malfadada lida,
D'essas miseras a guarida
E' o centro da corrupção./

3

Olhae, não escarneçaes
D'essas pobres desditosas
Que já foram lindas rosas
Mas,..venceu-as satanaz;/
Não zombem pois, se sois paes,
Se tendes filhas honradas,
Lembrai-vos que as desgraçadas
Tambem honradas nasceram;
Tenham dó das que cahiram
Onde vão as malfadadas.

4

Bem lhes basta a sorte escura
Que as arrastou para o mal,
E, por fim n'um hospital
Ter a morte negra e dura;/
Depoes de tanta amargura
Nas garras da prostituição,
Só restará a podredão···
A essas pobres maretrizes,
Castigo...por as infelizes
Vender alma e coração./

1900

Desprezam sua existencia;
É o antro da maledicencia
A cerca do Iwilei.

Até faz causar pavor
Ao povo que por lá passa
Ver as filhas da desgraça
D'um modo que causa horror;
Oh victimas do impudor
Cahidas na perdição;
Tenham d'ellas compachão.
Basta a malfadada lida,
D'essas miseras a guarida
É o centro da corrupção.

Olhae, não escarneçaes
D'essas pobres desditosas
Que já foram lindas rosas
Mas, venceu-as satanaz;
Não zombem pois, se sois paes,
Se tendes filhas honradas,
Lembrai-vos que as desgraçadas
Tambem honradas nasceram;
Tenham dó das que cahiram
Onde vão as malfadadas.

Bem lhes basta a sorte escura
Que as arrastou para o mal,
E, por fim n'um hospital
Ter a morte negra e dura;
Depoes de tanta amargura
Nas garras da prostituição.
Só restará a podredão . . .
A essas pobres maretrizes,
Castigo . . . por as infelizes
Vender alma e coração.

"THE CIRCUIT OF IWILEI"

The circuit of Iwilei
Is the center of corruption

Where the ill-fated women do
Go to sell soul and heart.

They sell for the god Money
Their honor and youth
And on the road of vice
Mock the true God.
This is the first point
To be made in these verses.
They mock virtue and law,
They despise their existence;
A cavern of ill fame is
The circuit of Iwilei.

It even causes terror
people passing by there
To see the daughters of misfortune
In a way that causes horror;
Oh, victims of immodesty
Fallen into perdition;
Let one take pity on them.
Enough of the ill-rewarded labor.
The lair of those wretches
Is the center of corruption.

Look, do not scorn
Those poor unfortunates
Who once were fair roses
But . . . Satan conquered them.
Do not mock, then, if you are parents,
If you have honorable daughters.
Remember that the wretched ones
Also were born chaste.
Have pity on those who have fallen
Where the ill-fated women do.

Indeed suffices for them the dire fate
That led them away to evil,
And, finally to have a dark, foul
Death in the hospital.
After so much bitterness
In the clutches of prostitution,

Only rottenness will remain . . .
Punishment for those poor
Prostitutes, since the wretches
Go to sell soul and heart.

TRANSLATED BY EDGAR KNOWLTON

MANUEL JESUS COITO (1876-1957) *came to Hawai'i from Madeira in 1886, a ten-year-old orphan in the care of an aunt and uncle, who worked on sugar plantations. Coito was employed in Honolulu for a number of years as a warehouseman, and he and his wife had a small store in the Punchbowl district of town, which was heavily Portuguese. He wrote poems in classical and popular Portuguese forms, a number of them about the local society of his times. He published in the Portuguese-language newspaper, and left a large collection of unpublished work.*

Evelyn Breckons

"COWBOY TONY"

The Oriental proprietor of the little "tin can" moving picture house was tacking up his posters near the entrance. Around him stood an admiring group of little boys of all colors and nationalities. "Look, Tony, look. One cow-boy picture. Look!" The little Hawaiian pointed excitedly to a multi-colored poster representing a band of impossible Indians fleeing from some equally impossible cowboys.

The boy addressed, a dirty Portuguese lad of about twelve, turned his attention to the poster designated, and his eyes grew round as he exclaimed, "Oh look, look! The Indian he got one gun. He been shot one cowboy. Hey," to the proprietor. "Cowboys catch him?"

"You come tonight, look see. You got too much money."

That night a crowd of ragged, dirty little boys assembled at the "tin can" theater. Each one had a hoarded nickel saved from selling papers, or some such occupation, and each one seated himself in a carefully selected seat in the front row and waited.

The first picture was received in silence, and so was the second and the third. What did they care whether the governor accepted the bribe or the penniless but handsome hero won the beautiful heiress? But at last the picture. When the title flashed "Cowboy Dick and Sioux Chief" there was a rustle and a murmur of expectancy.

And then came the picture! And such a picture! It showed how the Sioux chief stole Cowboy Dick's bride, and how he and his brave little band fought a host of Indians and killed them all, and how Dick bravely rescued the fair maiden. It was one of those cheap, melodramatic pictures so common to the "tin can" theaters. But to the little group of spell-bound boys it was better than grand opera. They sat tense and straight, with mouths open and eyes popping, and when it at last came to an end, there was a wild burst of applause, and a lusty shout.

The next day Tony greeted the other boys in a mysterious way. "You come," he said in a whisper, "You come." Without a word the boys followed him, for he was their acknowledged leader. There was no word spoken till they reached the now deserted moving-picture house. The pictures of Cowboy Dick were still up, but Tony passed them without a glance, and strode boldly into the theater. Breathlessly the boys followed him, and after looking around to see that they were alone, he slid his hand into his blouse and drew out a heavy blue-black object. It was a long-nosed Colt revolver!

The exclamations of mixed wonder, awe, and admiration that greeted the appearance of the weapon, would have delighted the heart of any boy.

"Oh Tony, where you been get?" questioned one little fellow.

"He belong to my father," was the proud reply.

At last one of the boys voiced the question which had arisen in the minds of all. "Oh, Tony, s'pose p'liceman come, what you do?"

With a look of absolute disgust at the question Tony replied: "I no scared p'liceman. S'pose he come, me shoot him."

This was the last step. Tony had reached an almost unattainable position in the minds of his comrades. Why, he was not even afraid of a policeman. Eagerly they listened to his plan. "I be Cowboy Dick. You, Moses, be Sioux chief. You, Manuel, be girl. All others be Indians and cowboys."

"I no like be girl," said Manuel faintly.

"S'pose you no like be girl you no need play. I no care."

"I be girl, I be girl," cried the little fellow.

At last they were ready. Moses seized the little Manuel and calmly sat on him. When Dick discovered her absence he was furious. According to the picture he ought to have waited for his band. But no, not so with Tony. Waving his revolver he dashed across the theater towards the chief and his fair (?) captive.

But, suddenly, a little brown foot struck out and—bang! Tony was lying flat on the floor—a smoking pistol in his hand!

Trembling with fear his comrades fled to a far-off corner. Too dazed to rise, Tony lay where he had fallen, still grasping the weapon. Then suddenly the door opened and in rushed—oh horror of horrors, Tony's father and a policeman. Across the rows of benches they rushed to where the scared boy lay.

Tony suddenly felt himself seized by a huge hand while another wrenched the revolver out of his hand. And then a gruff voice exclaimed, "What's the matter you steal my gun?"

And the gruff voice of the policeman broke the silence. "Come on down court."

Imploringly Tony threw his arms around his father while the latter turned angrily to the officer of the law. "Why you take my boy down court. He no steal you gun. I fix him." And with that he picked the trembling boy up in his arms and strode out.

There is little more to be told. Little Manuel is now the leader of the boys. As for Tony—well, Tony doesn't go to the moving pictures anymore.

EVELYN BRECKONS *wrote this story in 1915, when she was a student at Punahou School in Honolulu.*

Margaret N. Harada
from THE SUN SHINES ON THE IMMIGRANT

Yoshio was interested in growing things, and often brought home rare plants to set out in the yard and add beauty to his surroundings. He planted hibiscus plants with light yellow flowers and a few coconut palms. The landlady was not pleased, and said to him, "Take out the coconut palms you planted. I am afraid they will grow too big and the roots will turn over the house."

She was very annoying; she was forever interfering in Yoshio's business. The tenants didn't like her. She was a bully with a lordly manner. She often commanded her tenants to sweep the yards, and told the children not to bring any friends home to play. Once Jack took two boys home with him, but she chased them away with her broom. Her husband was a true gentleman, and the tenants tolerated her because of him.

Yoshio uprooted the coconut palms unwillingly. He told her, "Yes, Oka-san, I will take all of them out."

She was not pleased to be called "Oka-san," preferring the title "Honorable Mistress." Haru knew her eccentric ways and addressed her as she wanted, and soon she visited Haru bringing oranges, candies and cakes, and saying, "Please, for your Jack."

Yoshio made up his mind to buy his own lot, build his own house and become his own boss.

The landlady came to Haru one day and said, "I am going to raise the rent to twenty dollars, for the water tax has risen."

That night Haru told Yoshio the news.

"What! Twenty dollars for this small cottage! I would not mind if she would let me plant some trees and let me have my own way around my own home, hut she is always bossing me. I can't stand her bullying. We must look for a lot."

They began eating an early supper every evening and going to look for a lot where they could build. After some weeks they found a large yard, surrounded by beautiful scenery at Kaimuki on Seventh Avenue. In the yard grew mango trees, and the ground was covered with tall weeds. Diamond Head could be seen from the front of the lot, and the blue-green Manoa Valley from the back.

"This is an ideal place. I am going to buy this lot," said Yoshio.

A few days later, Yoshio received a letter from the coast from Mr. Davis, saying that he was recommending a Dr. and Mrs. Gillman to Yoshio for a tour of the Island of Oahu. He said that his friends were pausing in Hawaii for two days en route to the Orient.

"What luck! I am going to drive them around the Island," said Yoshio.

"How will you know who they are?" asked Haru. "The letter says that they will both be dressed all in white," said Yoshio happily.

On the day their ship was to dock, Yoshio woke up early. He drove to the wharf and bought two leis. The boat approached the dock slowly. The gangplank was lowered. A man and a woman dressed in white walked down it to the pier, and Yoshio went up to them. "Are you Dr. and Mrs. Gillman?" "Yes, are you Mori?" asked Dr. Gillman. "Yes. How do you do?" Yoshio greeted them, and put the leis around their necks. They walked to the street through the crowd of people who had come to meet friends from the coast.

"Please drive us to the Moana Hotel," said Dr. Gillman. "Yes, sir. Did you have a pleasant trip?" asked Yoshio politely.

"Yes, the sea was calm and we enjoyed our trip," answered Mrs. Gillman.

"We shall take a rest today. Would you come for us tomorrow?" asked Dr, Gillman. "I would like to go around the Island tomorrow."

They soon arrived at the Moana Hotel. The building was white, and the bellboys wore white uniforms.

The Moana Hotel was near the beach. The back of the building gave on the sea, where boys rode the waves on surfboards. When night fell Dr. and Mrs. Gillman could hear the breakers sweeping the shore. The waves of the sea sounded like a sweet serenade carrying them far out on the ocean.

The next morning, Yoshio asked Haru to prepare him a simple lunch of ham sandwiches and coffee, and with these he drove to the hotel. The Gillmans were ready, and climbed into the car.

"I am fascinated with the blue of the skies and the sea, and the greens of the trees," said Mrs. Gillman.

"We who live here are fortunate, for we are blessed with spring all through the year," said Yoshio.

He drove by the statue of Kamehameha I in his royal cloak and cap, a bronze and gold spear in his hand.

"Who is he?" asked the Dr. Gillman.

"He is Kamehameha the Great, who conquered the eight islands of Hawaii and founded the Hawaiian Kingdom," explained Yoshio. "He came with his men in canoes and landed somewhere near the Moana. Hotel, and pursued the king of Oahu to Nuuanu Pali, where the decisive battle was fought."

"What color was his cloak?" asked Mrs. Gillman.

"The royal colors were red and yellow," answered Yoshio.

"What was it made of?" asked Dr. Gillman.

"From bird feathers," answered Yoshio. "Today you no longer see red and yellow birds, for there are no more monarchs. The birds probably thought that they were no longer wanted and flew away to some other land."

"You spoke of the eight islands of Hawaii. What are they?" asked Mrs. Gillman.

"Oh! They are Hawaii, Kauai, Maui, Oahu, Molokai, Lanai, Niihau, and Kahoolawe," said Yoshio, counting the names off. "The largest island is Hawaii and the smallest Kahoolawe. Honolulu is on the island of Oahu."

"I wonder why Oahu was made the chief island of them all," said Mrs. Gillman.

"One reason is that Oahu has an irregular coastline and many good harbors, and ships from all over the world stop here for fuel."

"What does 'T.H.' mean?" asked Dr. Gillman. "It means 'Territory of Hawaii,'" explained Yoshio. "I see," said Dr. Gillman.

Yoshio drove them to the Nuuanu Pali, about 1,200 feet above sea level, where the mountains were yellow-green, passing the remarkable eucalyptus and ironwood forest on the way.

"What is that tree with the large crimson leaves?" asked Dr. Gillman.

"That is a kamani" answered Yoshio. "What are those with the twisting branches?" asked Mrs. Gillman. "There are some near the hotel."

"Those are called hau," answered Yoshio. "They are good for making a roof for a verandah, such as the one at your hotel."

They drove along the winding road through the trees, and at last reached the top of Pali. The sun was shining brightly and the breeze was gentle.

They got out to look at the other side of the island, and were captivated by the sight of the yellow-green kukui leaves, the dark brown koa beans and the red soil of the village. The red-brown roofs of the houses contrasted with the blue-green of the surrounding trees and the turquoise of the sea. Yellow-green grass and moss grew in the deep, sharp ridges of the mountains, and clouds floated across the sky.

"How beautiful!" said Mrs. Gillman.

"This was the place where the king of Oahu lost his battle with Kamehameha the Great," explained Yoshio. "The peak of Nuuanu Pali is unusually pointed."

Dr. and Mrs. Gillman looked toward the peak and said, "Yes, it is rather odd."

As Yoshio drove down Nuuanu Pali, his passengers often exclaimed excitedly, "How fascinating, how beautiful!"

The sun was high. To the right and left were green guava hedges with ripe yellow fruit hanging from the branches.

They passed a grove of banana trees with their long leaves and large green bunches of fruit. The papaya trees were heavy with orange fruit. The dark-brown, thin, curved trunks of the coconut palms swayed in the gentle breeze. The graceful hanging branches of the algaroba trees, laden with yellow-brown beans, and the rich brown koa trees added to the beauty of the tropical scene.

"There is something mild and calm about the atmosphere of the tropics," said Mrs. Gillman.

They drove to Kailua to see the awe-inspiring sight of the blue-green and yellow-green sea running in swift swells to the shore. The sand was fine and white, as though sugar or salt had been spread over the shore; beyond to the left was a mountain, its layers of sharp ridges casting deep, vertical shadows.

"From the mainland the sea is not so blue as here or the sky so clear and bright," said Mrs. Gillman.

"I heard you have a son, Mori," said Dr. Gillman. "Yes, he is now attending McKinley High School. Work to me is a great pleasure, because I have him and a daughter to think about."

"Parents are the same all over the world. They think of their children's future," said Dr. Gillman.

"Now, shall we have our lunch?" suggested Mrs. Gillman. They sat under the graceful branches of the ironwood trees and looked at the blue sea as they ate their lunches. "How very peaceful and beautiful," said Mrs. Gillman. After lunch they drove through acres of sugar-cane fields, and Yoshio commented on the importance of sugar to the economy of Hawaii. Dr. and Mrs. Gillman did not say anything; they were captivated by the variety of greens and the serenity of the surroundings. They passed rows of pineapple plants growing in the red soil and more cane fields. The road was frequently lined with alleys of algaroba trees.

"I know why Hawaii is called the paradise of the Pacific," said Mrs. Gillman. "The colors are marvelous, and the atmosphere seems so soft. Where a country has nothing but rocks and dirt, it shows that life is not very promising and interesting. But when a country is covered with greens as I see them here, I can tell that there will be plenty of work to satisfy the needs of its people."

They passed the Kalihi Valley and admired the dark blue range, and then drove back to the hotel.

"How much do we owe you?" asked Dr. Gillman. "We have enjoyed your tour very much."

"Twenty-five dollars," said Yoshio in a business-like manner,

Dr. Gillman handed him the twenty-five dollars, and added one dollar as a tip.

"Thank you," said Yoshio.

"Come for us again tomorrow," said Dr. Gillman.

Yoshio drove home bursting with pride to have so much money in a day. He took a bath and ate his supper, and at the table asked Jack to write a letter of thanks to Mr. Davis.

"I want to do well by Dr. and Mrs. Gillman, for they are Mr. and Mrs. Davis's friends," said Yoshio. "I am sure they were pleased with my service today, for he gave me a dollar tip."

"What about the lot?" asked Haru.

"I have already paid the real estate agent," said Yoshio. "I shall get contractors and carpenters to begin work on the house at once."

"When are we moving, Father?" asked Megumi.

"Probably next year," answered Yoshio. "The house is going to be a two-story cottage."

"We'll be able to do what we want, then! Hip! hip! hurrah!" shouted Jack.

The next morning Yoshio again picked up the Gillmans at the hotel. He drove them to Diamond Head. They brought their suitcases with them, since they would take the boat after the drive.

"The car rides comfortably on these smooth roads," said Mrs. Gillman.

"Yes, tourists are coming in great numbers, so the government is improving the roads by paving them with macadam," explained Yoshio.

They passed the lighthouse and stopped a little further on to look at the blue sea.

"I hate to leave Oahu. I wouldn't mind coming to live here," said Dr. Gillman.

There were some summer cottages near the shore. Yoshio drove through streets lined with coconut palms toward Koko Head, passing the forest of algaroba trees.

Koko Head was not so striking a sight as Nuuanu Pali or Diamond Head to them, for the mountain was a low red hill.

They then drove to Punchbowl where large cacti bore maroon fruits, and yellow blossoms grew wild from the rocky soil. When they reached the top they could see the whole city of Honolulu. Dr. and Mrs. Gillman were struck breathless by the sight. The harbor of Honolulu was calm. The eye took in the blue of the water, the green monkey-pod trees, the red, brown, white and orange roofs in a glance.

"Now, I shall take you to Tantlas," said Yoshio.

"After this, what can there be worth seeing?" asked Mrs. Gillman.

"Nothing, except for the green trees and the cool breeze," said Yoshio.

Ti palms, whose long, shiny leaves are used for wrapping fish and fruits, ginger, whose flowers are used in leis, koa trees, kukui trees, camphor trees, and evergreens grew in wild profusion along the road. The car passed guava and the bamboo hedges. The higher they climbed the cooler the breeze became. The air had a strange fragrance of some unknown perfume, and insects shrilled from the tall grass.

Yoshio took the Manoa Valley road along which many attractive houses had been built. Some looked like fairy homes; some were as splendid as castles, and others were like cozy doll houses.

The boat was to sail at five o'clock. Yoshio proposed that they leave enough time to visit his home to have some tea and listen to Haru play the koto.

"I would like you to meet my wife," said Yoshio.

"Yes, we would be delighted," answered Dr. and Mrs. Gillman.

Haru was at home practicing on the zither. Yoshio introduced her to them.

"How do you do," said Haru. "Please sit down and be comfortable."

She looked at her visitors. Mrs. Gillman had fair skin, bright blue eyes, and golden hair, and Dr. Gillman was tall and distinguished looking.

Tea was soon ready, and Haru began to play her favorite number, "Spring in Japan." The music echoed the twittering of birds, and evoked the image of clusters of cherry blossoms. Haru ended the piece with a bow.

"Wonderful!" exclaimed Dr. and Mrs. Gillman as they applauded vigorously.

"What is the koto made of?" asked Mrs. Gillman.

"It is made of paulownia wood and thirteen silk strings," answered Haru.

The Gillmans were interested in Japanese things for they were on their way to the Orient.

They bade a charming farewell to Haru and left for the dock. Well-balanced Hawaiian boys, their skin shiny and of olive-color, were diving for coins dropped into the water by the passengers.

Yoshio stood and waved good-by as the steamer pulled away from land.

MARGARET N. HARADA *attended the University of Hawaii; Doshisha Universty in Kyoto, Japan; LaVerne College in California, where she received her BA; the University of Washington in Seattle; and Columbia University, which awarded her a master's degree in 1942. She taught world history at Waipahu High School on O'ahu.*

Efren Baylon Sadorra
"HAWAII"

Disso a pagdidinnamagan
Pagbaknangan dagiti napanglaw
Maysamaysa a manggundaway nga umay
Iti uray ania a pamuspusan.

Tay balasang nga Ilokana ambisiosa
Uray addan nakaigalutanna
No adda Hawayano nga agpresenta
Likudanna karinkari a nalagda.

Napagasatan a dimteng "Impierno ken Gloria"
Dimtengda kano't Hawaii awan inanada
Parbangon no sumalogda, malemton no agawidda
Ay, gasat, kastoy gayam ti Hawaii yas-asugda.

No di maiwaksi tay kinasulit
Ditoy Hawaii, di panunoten ti agnaed
Rigatnan, Apo! sumken ta babawi
Awan inana, balud inggat inggana.

Hawaii, taeng da ragsak
No naanuska nga aggaud iti binigat
Naamo ti dollar a kumarab-as
Amin a kayat, ipaayna saan a mawas.

Disso nga ap-apalan, pangnamnamaan
Dagiti agar-arapaap di pay pulos dimteng

Dagiti makaigasat aglasatda't maika-maysa
Kastoy gayam! babawida dida mayebkas.

Hawaii, baknangan Ilokano a nagaget
Naanus nga agsukay, pagtatalonan naruay
Nadumaduma sapulen ta kaibatogan
Maumaka nga agpili no utekmo narnuoyan.

"HAWAII"

A place known reputedly
Where poor can become rich
So one by one come take a chance
By making remedies any way possible.

An ambitious young Ilokano woman
Even when she is tied to engagement
When a Hawaiiano presents himself
She'll turn her back to her vowed promise.

With fate she arrived in "Hell and Heaven"
Living in Hawaii, they have no rest
Before dawn they go out, evening they get home
Ay, what fate, so this is how Hawaii is, they moan.

If you can't throw off impatience
In Hawaii, you don't think of living here
Hard life, Oh, God! Is the recurring regret
No rest, a prisoner until the end.

Hawaii, work happy
When patient to row every morning
Money tamely jumps to you
All you like and buy never enough.

A place we envy with hope
The dreams have not arrived
The ones who lucked out, passed one by one
So it is like this! Regrets they can't let out.

Hawaii, makes rich the industrious Ilokano
Patient to till, the farms are many

Everyone seeks one's fate
Tired of choosing when your mind's bloated.

TRANSLATED BY VIRGILIO MENOR FELIPE

EFREN BAYLON SADORRA *was born in Salugan, Currimao, Ilocos Norte, Philippines in1952, of parents Monica Baylon and Gonzalo Sadorra. He came to Hawai'i in 1974, petitioned by his sister, Mrs. Venia Sidiaren. He has three children with Perlita, Jennifer Sadorra Padre, and Chester and Faith Sadorra. Efren is a good actor, loves to sing, and he raises fighting cocks for a hobby.*

———————————•◦•———————————

Naoto Nakashima
from HAWAII MONOGATARI

ワイアワ驛

I

ワイアワ驛——それは殆ど名のみで、たまに貨物列車が停つて肥料や家畜の兵糧袋を落して行く位のものであつた。だから、その床を持つた白砂塗りの四角な建物は、幅三間ばかりのワイアワ川の口の所で汽車を見送つてゐるだけだ。といふより・この驛は、もはや驛の任務を忘れてワイアワ部落の中央にあつて一つの記念碑となつて了つた。

試みに、この建物の中に入つてその四つの壁を仔細に見るならば、そこには雜然とでは

あるが、この部落の持つて来たあらゆる姿が鉛筆、インキ、小刀、白墨その他植物の汁な
どで銘記されてある。　悲喜哀樂！　その何れにせよ、私達はさういふやうな場合、何らか
の形に於てそこに表現しなくてはならなかつたらしい。

それは、また同時に子供の集會所ででもあつた。

2

で、私はよろこびに溢れてゐた。

私は、けふ、九月一日からホノルルのカイウラニ・スクールの七年生である。　ボールシ
チーの公學校を卒へると、七月から夏季休暇であつた。そして私達――姉、熊夫と私は、
魚賣りである父の馬車に乗つて、マウカ（山の方）へパイナツプルの仕事に出掛けたので
あつた。そして二タ月のキヤンプ生活の後、昨日、再び父の馬車で歸つて来たのだ。そし
て、昨日の今日、私は光榮なるホノルル、カイウラニ學校の生徒である。

私は、このよろこびを更めて母に告げると共に、この希望を何かに印銘しなくてはなら
ぬ。その時、私は、既にワイアワ驛へ向つて走つてゐた。

私は、そこに頑丈な驛の正面の半分開かれた戸口から這ひ上ると、川に面した側面の扉を半分ほど明けた。すると、二十呎と二十五呎の廣さの中は稍々明るくなつて壁の色もはつきりと解る程度になつた。貨物なに一つ積まれてゐない驛の天井は高かつた。私は側面の扉と向き合つた南の壁に向つた。四邊一面は少し油じみてワイザツな落書に鷄の足型のやうに汚されてゐた。

私は手近かに次のやうなものをざつと讀み取る事が出來た。

A、小口のヲバン（をばさんの意味）はバナナのア・サンとフアネ〳〵（怪しい〳〵）。

B、ミーはゆうべ、ここを通るとき、この眼でちゃんと見たんぢゃ。

B、ドイツのガイヤ號が金剛カンに降參して、日本勝つた！　勝つた!!

C、ミーは日本のエタジマ海軍兵學校へ、アア！　入りたくなつた。

D、ゆうべ、ミーがおそく小便しに出たら、てんじゃばに火が點いとつたが、なんぢゃろ。

E、醉ツ拂ひの兵隊が橋の上でひかれた。半分頭の毛がちぢれてゐる。

F、いまの夕方くらゐ、ペール・ハーバ（眞珠灣）がキレイと思つた事はなかつた。夕日

が、キビの丘で、ワイアワ一帯がかげると、長い陽足が夕映えをともなつて、丘のところから一せいに海の中へ流れ込んだ。すると、海は金波銀波もろもろの波をおこして、あつちへこつちへ轉つた。そしてワイピオの椰子の森の所へ行つて消えた。晝間夕立にあつた黒い椰子の森が食べてしまつたのかも知れん。やがて、日が暮れた。

G、ユキノの　の横に赤いイボがあると云ふとつた、ミーぢやない、健が。あのヤツ、ユキノのスキツト・ハートかも知れんて。ナッチヨラン。　　　，

H、その健が、ウヰリとキビを盗んでカフクのカラブース・ハウス（感化院）へ入れられた。あんなノーグル・ボーイ（不良少年）ここには入らん。

I、健はいらんが、姉さんのミサヨさんはいる。（熊夫の代筆生）

J、黒川順は高崎の家鴨の卵を、毎日五つづゝ盗んでゐる。青山先生に云つてやらう。だいたい後家の黒川のヲバンが悪いんぢや、男ばかりさがして歩いとるけ。ゴ―、ツ

I―、ヘルー（くたばれッ！）　　　　　　　，

K、アカンチューとボレー、アカンチューとボレー、ウェイ―（冷かしの文句）〔そしてこの戀人同志のやうな姉弟の事を一種の繪にしてあつた〕etc.

　　　，

私は私の書いたものを捜さうとしたが、短い感動的な文字は容易に捜せなくて、ただ鉛筆で覺束なげな英語で、書いては消し書いては消ししてある次の一文があった。

「ミーのパパーは癒るだらうか。パパーはもう一年近くねてばかりゐる。ワイバフのマツク・ガテガン（プランテーションの醫者）は、けふも來て口笛ばかり吹いてゐたが、一體どうなんだらうか。醫者の口笛なんか氣休めだから當てにならん。パパーはもうハシのやうに瘦せてしまった。ママーは相變らず病人につきつきりだ。ときどき夜中に眼をさますと、ママーは奥の佛ダンの下のパパーの寢床の傍に俯伏してシクシク泣いてゐる事がある。ある晩、パパーが突然呻くやうに「殘念！」と云った時などはママーは、一生ケンメイに何か祈りを上げるやうな譯の分らぬ聲を出してゐた。それにつけて可哀相なのはマリェ姉さんである。姉さんは姉さんで、炊事小屋（キチン）のカマドの下を焚きつけながら泣いてばかりゐる。學校も休み通しで、ハオレ（白人）學校は落第に決つてゐる。小さいよし子とミツメは、身の置きどころがなささうに、いつも二人で炊事小屋（キチン）の横の水溜りの周りの花壇の所へ、くつついてしやがんで他所へも遊びに行かない。ミーは、豚と馬の草を刈つて來ると、ニハトリに餌さをやる、ああ、夕暮のやうにいつも暗い家。ミーは悲しくなる。パパの

病氣、早くなほつてくれ！」

これは五年前の一家の事を書いたものらしい。その頃、父は過つて自分の馬車に轢かれて、餘病併發、一年餘り病床に臥したきりであつた。それは全く暗うつな絶望的な一年であつた。

その右手下に微かに次のやうな事が見出される。

「ミーにも兄さんがあつたのだ。茂といふ兄さん。名前がいい。十八、ミーと七つ違ひ・その兄さんと、ゆうべ始めて寢たが・體が大きいので、氣味が惡かつた。笑ふとき、右の眉毛を釣り上げて歯を子供のやうにみな見せて笑ふ。茂兄さんは繪かきらしい。日本のサムラヒの繪や女の繪をゑつと（澤山）持つてゐる。日本のむづかしい本も山ほど持つてる。餘り話好きでないやうだ。兄弟といつても、小さい時から一緒にゐなかつたためか、どうもよその人みたいで、餘り親しめぬ。ミーが重さうに草の入つたバイキを背負つて歸つて來ても、家の入口に腰掛けたまゝ譯の分らぬ笑ひ方をしてゐる丈だ。」

これは三年前、兄を日本から呼寄せた當時の事らしい。

ところが、その横に稍々新らしいインキで次のやうに記してあつた。

「やつぱり茂兄さんは家と合はなかつた。キャンプでも餘り働かないで繪ばかり描いてゐる兄と、さういふ兄を憎むパパー。ママーは間に入つて雨方から叱られてゐる。兄はいつか、パパに毆られてから寄りつかなくなつた。三年前、呼寄せた時の一家のよろこびの時には、いまのやうな事は思ひも寄らなかつたらうに。——」

しかし、その時、私はそこから眼を外らした。そして新らしい餘白を見出すと、新らしいシヤープ・ペンシルを輝かし乍ら力一杯に書き始めたのだ。

「九月一日！　なんと新鮮なよろこびの日であらう。けふ始めてホノルルの學校へ行つたのだ。ところで、父は朝の一番汽車でホノルルの魚市場へ魚の買出しに行く。私も一番汽車。父の青いシヤツと草履ばきの脊の高い格好。私の鳥打帽とニツカ・ボツカでハダシの格好。それが、ポールシチで一緒になり、同じ汽車に乘る。しかし、私達は同車する事が出來ない。父は二等車（三等なし）で、學生の私は否應なしに一等だ。私は父を氣の毒におもふ。しかし、パパは、却つてミーの事を自慢にしてゐるかも知れん。一番汽車は、ホノルル通ひの學生で一杯だ。みんな眼が希望に輝いてゐる。學校では、朝、揚旗式が了ると、ドラム（小太鼓）の莊重な合圖で二千の學生が默々と各々教室へ入る。その壯觀さ、

嚴肅さ、ちよつと想像がつくまい。ミーの先生はミス・ルヰズ。教室は三十八號。本館の裏二階である。ミス・ルヰズはカナカである。けふ、いろ〳〵注意を頂いたが、眼が大きくぎよろツとして。黒板を背にして「注意！(アテンション)」といつて一杯に睥睨する所は怖い。第二のミス・ホカノでなければいいが。ア・ツアウはミーの横。濱田はずつと前。アレスは直ぐ前。アレスのソバカス奴、入學早々教師の御機嫌を取り始めた。ロウズがカメハメハ學校へ行つたのは何かさびしい氣持。こんどホノルルへ越したのだから、もうあまり會ふ事もあるまい。ホノルルはいつも明るくて賑やかだ。九州屋旅館裏の富川秀夫を突然訪ねたら、吃驚しとつた。二人でアアラ公園へ行つたら、見世物小屋の猩々が逃げたと云つて、公園は大騒ぎ。猩々は公園の並木の上をあつちこつち逃げ廻つたが、とうとう環繩(ラツソー)で引つ捕へられた。その格好が悲壯で滑稽だつたので、みんなで大笑ひした。それで、ミーと秀夫も笑ひ止めないで、別れて了つた。」

3

　或日、私が「家鴨のダイアログ」について樂しく空想しながら線路を踏んで學校から歸

つて來ると、ユキノが驛の中で泣いてゐた。

「ユキノ、どうしたんか？」

私が家鴨の問答を止めて、訊くと、

「アカンチューとボレーが……」

と云つて、をえつが喉につまつた。見ると、脛のところに擦り傷を負うてゐる。

「打つたんか？」

私が云ふと、うなづいて

「なんにもせんのに、ミーを二人で追つ掛けて來て……」

と云つて、また喉につまつた。私は強いユキノが泣く位だから餘程ひどい目に遭つたに相違ないと思つた。

私は側面の入口から外を見た。すると、川に沿つた道をブブ！藪の間を見えつ隱れつして向ふの家の方へ一散に逃げて行く彼等の姿を見た。

「よし！」

私はアカンチューを憎んだ。

その晩、ユキノと熊夫の家へ行つた。三人してアカンチュー姉弟をこらしめようと云ふのである。熊夫の兩親は太平洋の方へ漁獵に出てゐて熊夫一人で網をすいてゐた。彼の家は川の向ふ岸に沿ひ、養魚池の上に半分臨んでゐた。

アカンチュー達は川を隔てて筋向ひである。三人は小石をポケツトや前垂れに忍ばせると、川に沿つて上つて行つた。さうして、石の屆く地點まで來ると、先づ聞耳を立てた。

彼等の鶏小舎に等しいブリキ張りの住居はユキノの家の田圃のマンゴの木の手前にカカイ（蘆の一種）とすれすれに低い。

「ワン、ツー、ツリ！」

私達は一齊に石を放うつた。すると、暗い空に「カン！」「カン！」「カン！」と三つの音がはつきりと答へた。と同時に、

「ゴツ、デム、サナガ、ベツチ」（畜生メ！）

と云つて、突然驚かされた雄鶏のやうに小屋から走り出て怒鳴る癎高い聲を聞いた。アカンチューのノツポの親爺らしい。

「チアウナミガシフアット！」

　私達はププーの蔭に隠れた。さうして、暫くしてぶつぶつ獨り言を云ひながら元通り家の中へ入つて行く親爺を見届けると、もう一度立ち上つてばらばら石を放つて熊夫の家の方へ駈け出した。

　すると、今度は親爺が兩手をかざして、興奮にふるへ乍ら譯の分らぬ支那語を浴せかけて來た。

　しかし、油斷は禁物である。私達は今夜のうちに逆襲のある事を知つて、協議した結果、今夜は徹底的に彼等姉弟を膺懲する必要があるといふ事になつた。ユキノが最も強便である。私達もユキノから夏休み中の事を聞かされて贊成したのである。彼等は私達のねない事を奇貨として方々のマンゴを食ひ荒し卵を盗み歩くのあらゆる暴狀を盡した。

　しかし、海の滿潮で、川は到底そのまま渡れなかつた。海月が泡のやうに浮いて來た。そこで、養魚池の中の小舟を川に滑らした。三人は、石、サーチライト、棍棒を用意して胸を躍らせてゐた。眠つてゐた川を渡る事にした。

　誓くして、果して熊夫の家と家鴨小舎の屋根の上にばらばら石の音がした。眠つてゐた

小舎の家鴨がおどろいて急に騒ぎ立てた。百羽餘り騒ぐので、吊り下つたランプが左右に搖れてゐる。

私達はかさかさ音を立てる藪に餘り欄れないやうに、少しづつ彼等に接近して行つた。

彼等は尙も放ちつてゐたが、反響をさぐるやうに一瞬投石を中止した。

その時、突然、私達は立ち上つて間近い彼等に一種の喊聲を放つと共に石を雨にした。

「テイスト、デイス、ユー、パケー！」（これでも喰らへ、このチャンコロ！）

「カム、オン、アカンチュー・アイ、フイクス、ユー、ナウ！」（さあ、さつきのぶたき打ちだ！）

ユキノが息を彈ませて、早口に怒鳴つた。

「ユー、ネバ、フォアゲツト、デイス！」（よく思ひ知つておくがいい！）

アカンチュー達は、この不意の伏兵に度膽を拔いて、一種悲鳴に似た癇高い聲とともに引返して行つた。私達は彼等の逃げる姿を強いサーチライトに寫し出して笑つた。

「チュヱ！ チュヱ！」

4

その翌日は土曜日。

私達は、驟雨の一時に通つた後の入江の小波のやうに、大膽に遊ぶ事を學ぶ。釣に飽き、マーブル遊びに飽きると、假装をして遊んだ。いつか、ワイアワ全體の子供二十數名が男女服装を取りまぜて、花冠りを頂き手に石油カンを持ち、ハーモニカを吹き、うたを歌つて練り歩いてゐたら、ポールシチの青山先生に見つかつて了つた。先生は、どこかの法事に來られたものらしい。ワイアワの生徒はどれもこれも操行點が丙になるであらう、と。カイに悄氣てしまつた。先生は、少し笑つて帽子を取つて行かれたが、私達は急にカイで家をいくつも拵へて寝る眞似をした。さういふ時には、誰れかア゛サンのバナナ畑へ行つて熟れたバナナを房ごと盗んで來る事であつた。それから自分の家の炊事小屋の膝手を知つた者はその中から一番いいもの──例へばオマカ（魚）のフライ──を持参せねばならない。もうタイナツプルの時季も過ぎたので、貨物列車は無愛想だが、それでも偶にはワヒアワからの貨車は私達目掛けて二つ三つ放うつてくれる。それを捜し出した。すると、どこかで必ず見てゐた小口さんかそのをばさんが「ヘイ、ユー！」と聲を勵まして、私達を反省させる。

夕方になって、ボールシチの方からお寺の鐘が鳴ると、私達はそろそろ歸る支度をする。歸りぎはにユキノが、みんなに蓄音機を聞きに來るやうに、と云つたが、さき程・ユキノの父親の小言さんに叱られたので、誰れも贊成しなかつた。

やがて、沖合の漁獵から歸つて來た矢部のおつさんの浪花節の聲が夜風となつて來た。

日曜日。勤勉の日である。

この日は私達日本學校上級生にとつて唯一日の授業日である。

ハオレ（白人）學校を卒業した者で上級の學校に行かぬ者も一週に一回の集會日である。

お互ひになんとなく年が入つたやうな氣がする。

女子はどことなく大人びてゐる。

それだけ互に多少遠慮が出來たやうだ。

この日、學校は忙しい。晝まで、私達上級生に授業があると、晝からは日曜學校。

學校が鐘を叩くと、裏のカトリツク教會でも塔の鐘がゆるやかに鳴り始める。

　、

學校の青山先生は土曜日の晩、大人達に說敎を、そして日曜の晝は私達にお經の讀方と
日本の怪談の話である。
それが濟むと、私達の自由な午後が始まる。私達はボールシチで遊んでワイアワワへ歸
る。なんと、長い一日！　私は急いで、豚二十四、馬二頭のために草を刈らねばならぬ。
驛附近には、釣の連中で、この村からも隣りの町の連中も一杯だ。日曜日働くべから
ず、なるが故に――。

5

ある朝、私は汽車に後れさうになつた。それだけではない。今日の辯當代五仙をまだ貰
つてゐないので、父に追ひついて、せびらうと思つて線路を走つてゐると、いつもボール
シチの橋を渡つてから出會ふ下り列車が來てしまつた。私は、しまつた、と思つて、その
列車をよけるつもりで、ワイアワ驛の waiawa といふ立札のところに立ち停つてその通
過を待つてゐると、どうした事か、段々スピードを弱めて來た汽車が驛の前で停つて了つ
た。いつか、さういふ事が一度以前あるにはあつたが、それにしても私は不思議におも

from HAWAII MONOGATARI

1.

Waiawa Station—a station largely in name only, a place where freight trains occasionally stopped to drop off bags of fertilizer and feed.

That is why, at the twenty-foot-wide mouth of the Waiawa Stream where it was located, the station's square white-mortared building with loading platform merely stood silently by as trains came and went.

Or, rather, perhaps we should say that this station had long forgotten its role, becoming instead a kind of monument in the center of Waiawa's small community. If one entered this building and looked closely at its four walls, he would find recorded there all of the village's faces over the years, scattered about in a jumble—jotted down in pencil and ink, or with knives, chalk or tree sap. Joy and sorrow, grief and pleasure! Whatever the community was feeling, it had to express itself in some manner on those walls. The building was also, at the same time, a gathering place for children.

2.

And so, today, I am overjoyed!

For on this day, September 1, I am a seventh-grader at Kaiulani School in Honolulu. I completed public school in Pearl City and summer vacation began in July. We—my older sister, along with Kumao and I—got into my father's horse cart (my father was a fishmonger) and headed mauka to work on the pineapple farm.

After two months of living at the camp, we returned home yesterday, once again aboard our father's cart. And today, I am a proud student at Kaiulani School in Honolulu.

Besides letting my mother know one more time how happy I felt, I had to record these hopes onto something. I found myself running toward Waiawa Station.

I scrambled into the station through its heavy front doors, which had been left half open. I opened another door on the stream-side of the building half way. This allowed light to shine dimly into the twenty by twenty-five foot interior, so that I could clearly make out the colors on the walls. The ceiling of the empty station, where not a single piece of cargo was stacked, seemed high. I walked toward the south wall, which stood opposite the side door. From top to bottom, the wall was slightly stained with oil and defaced with indecent graffiti, like the footprints of chickens.

Close up, in a sweeping glance, I could make out the following notations.

* Mrs. Koguchi is doing funny kinds of things with A-san, the banana man. I saw them here with my own eyes when I passed by last night.

* The German U-boat Gaea surrendered to the Japanese cruiser Kongo. Japan won! Japan won!

* Ah, it makes me want to go to the Edajima Naval Academy in Japan.

* When I went outside late last night to take a pee, the lights by the tracks were on. What was going on?

* A drunken soldier was run over on the bridge. Half of the hair on his head was curled with blood.

* I have never seen Pearl Harbor as beautiful as it was this evening. When the sun stood above the sugar cane hills and the whole of Waiawa began to darken, long streams of sunlight, glowing in the twilight, suddenly poured down the hills into the ocean. The sea produced waves of gold and silver which rolled this way and that way. The streams of light moved toward the coconut forest of Waipio and vanished. The black coconut forest, which was drenched by a sudden afternoon rain, may have eaten them. A little while later, the sun dipped below the horizon.

* He said that Yukino has a red wart by her. . . . I didn't say it, T did. I think that T is her sweetheart. What a lousy thing to say!

* T stole sugar cane with Willie and they were sent to the calaboose house in Kahuku. We don't want that kind of no-good boy here.

* We don't want T around but we do want Misayo, his older sister (she writes letters for Kumao).

* Jun Kurokawa steals five duck eggs every day from T's duck pen. I'm gonna report him to Aoyama sensei. It's all Mrs. Kurokawa's fault. She's a widow and spends all her time chasing after men. Go to hell!

* A. C. and Polly, A. C. and Polly: Wei! (Alongside, a picture has been drawn of this brother and sister, who act like a couple of lovers.)

I tried looking for something that I had written, but it wasn't easy to find words that were short and inspirational. Instead, I came across the following, which was written in pencil in faltering English and erased and rewritten several times.

"I wonder if Dad will ever get well. He has been confined to bed now for almost a year. The plantation doctor from Waipahu came to visit him again today but all he did was whistle. What in the world is going on? The doctor whistles to make us feel better but you can't count on that. Dad has gotten as skinny as chopsticks. Mama continues to spend all her time caring for him. Sometimes, when I get up in the middle of the night, she is lying face down on the floor weeping next to his bed below the Buddhist altar. One night, Dad suddenly moaned "It's so unfortunate." Mom then began earnestly praying, in a really weird voice. The person who should really be pitied is Mari-e, our older sister. She is always crying as she places firewood into the stove. She never has time to attend haole school and is sure to flunk out. The younger children, Yoshiko and Mitsume, are at a loss, and spend most of their time squatting next to the flower bed next to the drain outside the kitchen. They never go anywhere to play. Everyday, I cut grass and bring it home to feed the hogs and horses. Then, I feed the chickens. Ah, our house is always as dark as dusk. It makes me sad. I wish my father would get well soon!"

I had written this about our family about five years ago. My father had been accidentally run over by his own cart, suffered complications, and became bedridden for more than a year. It was a totally depressing year, when everything seemed so hopeless.

Just below this entry, on the right hand side, I could vaguely make out the following words.

"I found out that I have an older brother. His name is Shigeru. It is a good name. He is eighteen, seven years older than I am. Last night, I slept next to him for the first time. It was creepy sleeping with someone so big. When he laughs, he raises his right eyebrow and shows all of his teeth, just like kids do. I heard that he is an artist. He has a whole bunch of paintings of Japanese samurai and Japanese women. And he has a lot of difficult Japanese books. He doesn't seem very talkative. Although he is my brother, he feels like a stranger and I can't really get close to him because we didn't grow up together. When I come home, lugging a heavy bag of grass, he only sits near the front door of the house, smiling in a strange way."

This was written about three years ago when our family had arranged for my brother to come from Japan to join us here.

Right next to that comment, there was a newer remark written in ink.

"Just as I feared, Shigeru did not fit in with the family. He did not work much at the camp and was always painting pictures. Dad despised him for this. Momma was caught in the middle, blamed by both Shigeru and Dad for the situation. At one point, Dad hit Shigeru and Shigeru left home and did not return. Who could have imagined this situation at the time Shigeru joined us three years ago, when we were all so happy?"

But then I began looking elsewhere on the wall. When I found a new space to write on, I brandished my new retractable pencil and started writing vigorously.

"September 1! I've never felt this kind of joy before! Today, I went to school in Honolulu for the first time. Dad caught the first train to go Honolulu in the morning to buy fish at the fish market. I also got on the first train. Dad looked tall in his blue shirt and zori. I wore a hunting cap and a pair of knickerbockers, and was barefoot. The two of us met at Pearl City Station and rode on the same train. But we could not board the train together. Dad got on the second-class car (there were no third-class cars) and students rode first class, whether we wanted to or not. I felt sorry for him, but Dad was probably proud of me, riding in first class. The first train is always packed with students who attend schools in Honolulu. Their eyes are bright with hope. At school, after the flag-raising ceremony, two thousand students head silently to their classrooms to the solemn beat of snare drums. You cannot imagine how magnificent and solemn the atmosphere is! My teacher is Miss Lewis and our classroom is No. 38, on the second floor at the rear of the main building. Miss Lewis is Hawaiian. Today she told us what she would and would not allow in her class. Standing in front of the blackboard, she glares at us with her large, piercing eyes and says "attention!" It is quite scary. I hope she doesn't turn out to be another Miss Hookano. Atuau sits next to me, Hamada is way up in the front, and Alex has the seat directly in front of me. We have just begun classes and that freckle-faced Alex is already trying to polish the apple with the teacher. With Rose gone to Kamehameha, I feel kind of lonely. She has moved to Honolulu, so I don't think we'll see much of each other anymore. Honolulu is full of cheer and is bustling all of the time. When I made an unannounced visit to Hideo Tomikawa, who lives behind the Kyushuya Ryokan, he seemed very surprised to see me. We went to Aala Park, where things were in an uproar because a monkey had escaped from a show tent. The monkey was jumping from one tree alongside the road to another, trying to evade capture, but was finally lassoed down. The subdued monkey looked pathetic and comical at the same time, so everyone had a big laugh. When Hideo and I parted, we were still laughing about it."

3.
One day, as I was walking along the tracks on my way home from school, daydreaming happily about "A Dialogue of Ducks," I saw Yukino crying in the station.

"What happened?" I asked, leaving the ducks' dialogue aside. "A. C. and Polly . . . ," she said, heaving with sobs. I looked and saw that she had scratches on her legs.

"They hit you?"

She nodded and said, "I didn't do anything wrong, but they starting chasing me and . . . ."

She choked up again. I knew that if a strong-minded girl like Yukino was crying, something terrible must have happened.

I looked out the side door. Through openings in the puupu grove, I could see them running on the road along the stream toward home. They were running as fast as their legs would carry them.

"O.K., let's get 'em!" I began to really hate A. C.

That night, Yukino and I visited Kumao's house. We wanted to form a threesome to teach A. C. and his sister a lesson. Kumao's parents were out fishing in the ocean and Kumao was home alone fixing nets. His house was on the opposite bank of the stream and jutted out partly over the fish pond.

A. C. and his sister lived in a house located diagonally across the stream from Kumao's. The three of us, hiding stones in our pockets and aprons, walked upstream. When we arrived at a point within range of our stones, we pricked up our ears. Their tinplated house was like a chicken coop, standing as low as the kakai reeds fronting the mango tree in the middle of Yukino family's rice paddies.

"One, two, three!" We heaved our stones in unison and heard them bounce loudly off the house under the dark sky. Someone emerged from the hut like a suddenly frightened cock, yelling in a shrill voice, "Goddamn, son of a bitch!" It was A. C.'s father, who was very tall.

"Chow nami gash fat!"

We hid in the puupu bushes. After a while, he went back into the house mumbling to himself. When we were sure he was inside, we stood up again and began throwing our stones at our target. We then ran toward Kumao's house.

This time the old man came out with both arms in the air, trembling in anger, saying things in a mixture of Chinese and English.

We could not afford to let our guard down. We knew we'd face a counterattack that evening. We discussed the situation and concluded that we should thoroughly punish A. C. and Polly that night. Yukino was the most hawkish. When Yukino told us what had happened during summer vacation, we came around to her viewpoint. She mentioned how, taking advantage of our absence, A. C. and Polly ate mangoes off people's trees and stole eggs from all around the village.

We decided to cross the stream. However, because of high tide, wading to the other side was impossible. Jellyfish floated by like bubbles. So, we slipped the boat from the fish pond into the stream and paddled across. Armed with stones, flashlights and heavy sticks, the three of us were pumped up for the fight.

As expected, we soon heard the sound of stones hitting the roof of Kumao's house and duck pen. The startled ducks, roused from their sleep, suddenly began making a huge ruckus. With more than a hundred ducks inside, the pen shook and the hanging lamp swung from side to side.

We approached them very slowly, trying to avoid touching the bushes and making a rustling sound. After they had their thrown stones for a while, they stopped momentarily to gauge the situation.

It was then that we struck. We suddenly stood up and, at point blank range, raised a war cry of sorts and showered them with stones.

"Taste these, you pake."

"Come on A. C.! I fix you now," Yukino yelled fast, panting, "You never forget this!"

Caught completely off guard by our ambush, the A. C. gang retreated, yelling in high-pitched screams. We shined our strong flashlights on their retreating figures and had a good laugh.

"Chueh, chueh!"

4.

The next day was Saturday.

Like small waves on an inlet after the passage of a sudden rain, we learned to play boldly and imaginatively. When we became bored with fishing or marbles, we tried our hand at disguises. One day, all of the twenty-some-odd children in Waiawa exchanged clothing, with the boys wearing the girls' clothes and vice versa. We paraded through Waiawa, wearing hoku leis, beating empty oil cans, blowing harmonicas and singing songs—and were discovered by Aoyama sensei from Pearl City. He had come to the village to conduct a Buddhist memorial service at someone's home. With a slight smile, he took off his hat and went on his way. We suddenly lost our gaiety, thinking that now all the kids from Waiawa would get the lowest grade for deportment in the next Japanese school report. We built several shacks out of kakai and pretended to sleep in them. On these occasions, someone would sneak into A-san's banana patch and steal several bunches of ripe bananas. Those who knew what would be available in their own kitchens that day had to go home and bring back the best dish that they could find—for example, fried omaka. Because pineapple season was already over, the freight trains would just pass sullenly by. Even so, the crew on trains from Wahiawa would sometimes throw us two or three pineapples. This would prompt a stomp through the kakai bushes and a plunge into the rice paddies to find them. When we did this, Mr. Koguchi or his wife would always be there watching. They would shout "Hey you!" and make us reflect on the errors of our ways.

As evening approached and the temple bell in Pearl City began ringing, we slowly prepared to go home. Just as we were about to leave, Yukino invited us to her house to listen to their phonograph. But we had just been scolded by her father, Mr. Koguchi, so none of us agreed to go along.

Before long, the sound of a *naniwabushi* ballad wafted to our ears on the evening breeze. It was the voice of Mr. Yabe, who had just returned from fishing at sea.

Sunday: a day of diligence.

Sunday is the only day that we upper-grade students attend Japanese language school.

Sunday is also the one day of the week on which those who have graduated from haole school but have not gone on for further education assemble.

We all seem, in some vague way, to have grown older. The girls, especially, have an adult air about them. This has allowed us to be a little more reserved toward one another.

Japanese school is busy on Sundays. In the morning, upper-grade students have Japanese language classes and from noon there is Sunday school. When the school strikes its bell, the Catholic Church behind it also begins gently to ring its steeple bell.

Aoyama sensei delivers sermons to adults on Saturday evenings. On Sunday afternoons, he teaches us how to recite sutras and reads us ghost stories from Japan.

After class, our free afternoons begin. We play in Pearl City and then return to Waiawa. What a long day it is! I have to hurry to the pasture to cut grass for our twenty hogs and two horses.

The area around the station is packed with fishermen from Waiawa and from neighboring villages. They're here because nobody is supposed to work on Sundays.

TRANSLATED BY SHIGEYUKI YOSHITAKE

NAOTO NAKASHIMA (1904-1940) *was born in Waipahu, O'ahu, and grew up in Pearl City, on the same island. At the age of thirteen, he was taken to Japan, where he attended Kumamoto prefectural schools and Waseda University in Tokyo. Childhood memories, mediated by metropolitan literary influences, inspired the stories collected in* Hawai Monogatari *(Hawaii Tales) (1936), introduced by Yasunari Kawabata. Seeking material for a novel, he returned to Hawai'i, then moved on to California only to perish in an auto accident.*

―――――――――・・――

Carlo Mario Fraticelli
"LA ESCULA NO ES SUFICIENTE"

1
Padres que hijos tenemos,
fijemos nuestra atención
qué clase de educación
a esos seres les debemos.

1

Padres que hijos tenemos
Tejemos nuestra atencion
Que clase de educacion
A esos seres le debemos
Con meditacion pensemos
Que el niño nace inocente
Alli demos prontamente
A modelar su sentido
Segun estoy Convencido
La escuela no es suficiente

2

Se puede desarorel
La mente de un ignorante
Para que aprenda bastante
Leer escribir y hablar
Pero hay que Cultivar
De otro modo differente
Del niño su tierna mente
Por que debemos pensar
Que en la educacion moral
La escuela no es suficiente

3

Una madre tolerante
Que todo a su hijo perdona
Lo deja pisar la Zona
Del tramposo y el tunante
Para verlo en adelante
En la malvada Corriente
Que sigue el mundo presente
Segun yo vengo observando
Por eso es que estoy Cantando
La escuela no es suficiente

Con meditación pensemos
que el niño nace inocente;
allí demos prontamente
a modelar su sentido.
Según estoy convencido,
la escuela no es suficiente.

2
Se puede desarrollar
la mente de un ignorante
para que aprenda bastante
leer, escribir y hablar.
Pero hay que cultivar,
de otro modo diferente,
del niño su tierna mente.
Porque debemos pensar
que en la educación moral,
la escuela no es suficiente.

3
Una madre tolerante,
que todo a su hijo perdona,
lo deja pisar la zona
del tramposo y el tunante;
para verlo en adelante
en la malvada corriente
que sigue el mundo presente.
Según yo vengo observando,
por eso es que estoy cantando,
la escuela no es suficiente.

4
Los padres deben saber
reglas de buena crianza;
y si su saber no alcanza,
las debieran aprender.
Y si no saben leer,
buscar a uno inteligente
que les explique claramente
cómo es que el niño se guía.
Pues según se ve hoy en día,
la escuela no es suficiente.

5

Regad en el alma humana
las flores de la bondad
para que esa humanidad
nos las devuelva mañana.
Y en época muy temprana
inculquemos en la mente
del niño que va creciente
lo que aquí exponiendo estoy.
Porque en los días de hoy,
la escuela no es suficiente.

6

No concedas libertad
a una hija, mujer,
que a todo gusto y placer
pase por la vecindad;
pues detrás de la amistad
está el peligro imponente.
donde nace la corriente
de la odiosa corrupción.
Para esta educación,
la escuela no es suficiente.

7

La Europa civilizada
tiene escuelas especiales
que son puros manantiales
de educación esmerada.
La América está atrasada
en este punto eminente.
Y por eso es conveniente
la educación del hogar;
que en este particular,
la escuela no es suficiente.

8

Allá en la escuela europea
se enseña al niño a tratar;
y se enseña a respetar
aquel que superior sea.
Y esa virtuosa idea

cumple la madre fielmente;
allá delante la gente,
no se ve al niño gritar.
Pero para esto lograr,
la escuela no es suficiente.

9
Si un educacionista
de Europa nos visitara
y nuestra vida observara,
formaría una larga lista.
Y allá en una revista
de aquel otro continente,
probaría claramente.
Y en esto duda no hay
que en las islas de Hawaii,
la escuela no es suficiente.

10
Ni el ciudadano europeo,
ni los niños de la escuela,
estorban el paso en la acera,
como aquí en Hawaii yo veo.
Y el niño en su recreo
usa estilo diferente
y no forma esa imponente
algazara atronadora.
Yo digo con voz sonora,
la escuela no es suficiente.

11
Edificios escolares
en Hawaii se multiplican,
pero ellos no justifican
el gasto de esos caudales.
De las aulas escolares
no nace un sobresaliente,
no surge un hombre eminente,
ni un legislador de fama.
Por eso mi voz aclama,
La escuela no es suficiente.

12
Yo no veo aquí en Hawaii
un literato de fama,
ni una científica dama,
como en Europa las hay.
El pueblo se encuentra olrai
porque es un pueblo inocente
que rueda por la corriente,
sin saber a dónde va.
La culpa de quien será,
la escuela no es suficiente.

"SCHOOL IS NOT SUFFICIENT"

1
Parents who have children,
let's fix our attention on what
kind of education we owe those
persons. With meditation let's
think that the child is born
innocent; there (at that moment) let's quickly begin to
shape their judgment. As I am
convinced, school is not
sufficient.

2
One can develop the
mind of an ignoramus in order
for him to learn sufficiently to
read, write and speak. But one
must develop in another way
the tender mind of a child.
Because we should think that
in moral education, school is
not sufficient.

3
A tolerant mother who forgives
her child for every thing, allows

him to go to the world of the
swindler and the crook; only to
see him later on in the evil tendency which the world is now
following. According to what I
have been observing, for that
reason, I am speaking out (singing), school is not sufficient.

4
Parents should know the rules of
good upbringing; and if their
knowledge is insufficient, they
should learn them. And if they
do not know how to read, look
for someone intelligent who can
explain clearly to them how it is
a child should be guided. For,
according to what is seen these
days, school is not sufficient.

5
Water in the human soul
the flowers of goodness so that
humanity may send them back
to us tomorrow. And at a very
early age let's instill in the
growing mind of a child what I
am stating here. Because in
these present days, school is not
sufficient.

6
Don't grant freedom to a daughter, woman, who walks through
the neighborhood however she
pleases; for behind friendship
lurks imposing danger, where
the current of hateful corruption is born. For this education,
school is not sufficient.

7

Civilized Europe has special
schools which are pure sources
of a polished education. America
is behind on this prominent
point. And for this reason,
education at home is appropriate; that on this point, school
is not sufficient.

8

Over there in the European
school the child is taught to try;
and he is taught to respect one
who is superior. And the mother
carries out that virtuous idea
faithfully; over there in front of
people one does not see children
shout. But to accomplish this,
school is not sufficient.

9

If an educator from Europe were
to visit us and observed our life,
he would form a long list. And
over there in a journal from
that other continent, he would
demonstrate clearly. And on
this point there is no doubt that
in the islands of Hawaii, school
is not sufficient.

10

Neither the European citizen
nor school children
get in your way on the
sidewalk, like I see here in
Hawaii. And the child in his
play time uses a different style
and does not make that tremendous deafening uproar. And I

say with a loud voice, school is
not sufficient.

11
School buildings in Hawaii are
multiplying, but they do not
justify the expenditure of those
large sums. From school classrooms not one outstanding person is born, not one eminent
person has appeared, nor one
legislator of note. For this reason, my voice acclaims, school
is not sufficient.

12
I do not see here in Hawaii one
writer of note, nor a woman
scientist, as there are in Europe.
The people find themselves
"alright" because they are
an innocent people who roll
along with the current without
knowing where they are going.
Whose fault can it be, school is
not sufficient.

TRANSLATED BY AUSTIN DIAS

Wai Chee Chun
from FOR YOU A LEI

Characters:
MRS. LEE, *the mother*
MISS CARTER, *a school teacher*
AH MUI, *Mrs. Lee's daughter (about ten years old)*
AH QUON, *Mrs. Lee's son, (about fourteen years old)*
LEILANI, *a neighbor and Hawaiian friend of Ah Mui (about ten years old)*

Scene: A portion of a quadrangle inclosure surrounded by tenement buildings in the Aala Park District of Honolulu. The action takes place at the back of a tenement dwelling on a projection jutting out from the tall building and used as a porch and general playground for the children as well as a laundry room. A clothes line with a few pairs of faded sailor mokus and garments made of flour bags flapping in the wind is stretched across stage right from a tall pole to the back wall of the flat. An ironing board and a laundry tub are standing at stage right. A dilapidated railing surrounds the so-called porch.

Upstage left and center are seen in the near distance, the backs of rickety tenement buildings silhouetted against the pale blue sky. A few garbage cans hanging out crudely below the windows and flapping clothes lines relieve the sameness of the tall gray structures.

At the rise of the curtain AH MUI *and* LEILANI *are stringing purple bouganvillea blossoms into leis at downstage left. Both are seated on the floor.*

LEILANI: Shat ap, yerself.

AH MUI: C'mon. No make noise. By'm by da baby goin' wake up and my modda goin' make me carry 'im, you know.

LEILANI: Why? Your ole lady goin' come home today?

AH MUI: She wan come home already.

LEILANI: Oh, I thought she only come home Sunday.

AH MUI: Nah, da boss wan tal her come home, 'cause tomorrow lei day. Da boss goo-ood you know. Da boss let her come home spacial days, too.

LEILANI: Gee! da lucky, boy!

AH MUI: Yah, but she gotta go back and take care da boss baby tomorrow and stay dere.

LEILANI: Ah-h, waste time den, dat kind job.

AH MUI: Yah, dat's what we tal her, but she no like queet. She say if she no take da job she gotta work night time cannery anyway. So she rather have goo-ood boss and mo' dong-dong and no come home night time.

LEILANI: Gee, but my ole lady got one mo' batter job dan dat. She only gotta work day time, and every night she bring poi home. *(Sneeringly)* Your ole lady no bring not'ing home night time, huh?

AH MUI: Nah! I wan tal you she gotta take care da boss's baby and sleep dere. Now you t'ink she goin' bring anyt'ing home?

LEILANI: Yeah, dat's why my ole lady say da pake'wahine next door lolo for make money, boy. Da kind job she got, she mo' batter no work.

AH MUI: She wan tal dat about my ma?

LEILANI: Suah, and she say, waste time wan your ole lady come home. She only good for hit your seester, Ah Lan. Everytime we hear Ah Lan yell, boy. We no stink ear, you know.

AH MUI: Yeah, I know. *(Pause)*

LEILANI: Hey, for why she want to give Ah Lan goo-ood lickin' den?

AH MUI: For why you want to know, huh?

LEILANI: Naver mind for why.

AH MUI: Wal, mind yer own beeswax den. And anyway my ma always bring ono t'ings home Sunday, see?

LEILANI: Not so ono as da kind we get. Gee, da ono pipikaula, boy. And she wan tal me I can wear Kaiulani's white dress tomorrow for da lei program.

AH MUI: Gee! I wan get one peachy new dress for tomorrow, too.

LEILANI: Yah, show me, show me.

AH MUI: Nah, I not goin' show nobody, see?

LEILANI: Yah, you Jew, dat's why.

AH MUI: You t'ink me Jew only, but I no care. I not goin' to show nobody, see?

LEILANI: Yah, you scared, dat's why.

AH MUI: Who wan say I scared, huh?

LEILANI: I wan say, of course. I bet you no got da dress. *(Pause)* Yah, I t'ink you wan bull, hanh? Sure, you wan bull.

AH MUI: I naver.

LEILANI: Yah, I bet you wan bull.

AH MUI *(Louder)*: I naver. Cross my heart.

LEILANI: Go 'head, go 'head. Let me see. *(AH MUI makes the sign of the cross.)* You no crook now.

AH MUI: Nah, I no crook.

LEILANI: O.K. You gotta show me da drass by'm by, you know.

AH MUI: Maybe. Hey, look. Your lei wan feenish already. Gee, da swal bugga, boy.

LEILANI: Goo-ood, hanh? Gee, I naver know wan pau already. *(Displays the lei proudly.)*

AH MUI *(Rising from the ground excitedly)*: Try tie 'im, try tie 'im. *(Grabs lei from LEILANI.)* Gee, da swal, boy.

LEILANI *(Reaches for the lei, but AH MUI swings it away from her and hurriedly ties the two ends together.)*: C'mon, Ah Mui, give me back 'im. *(Starts chasing her)* Hurry up, boy, or I kick yer pants yet.

AH MUI: Yah? I like see. *(Starts off into a hula with the lei stretched before her and sings, "For You A Lei" slightly off key.)*

LEILANI: C'mon, I no kidding, you know. You like me slap your head down?

AH MUI: Suah. You try. *(Darts away.)*

(LEILANI finally catches her by her dress and raises her hand as if to slap her, but AH MUI, in giggles and laughter gives her the lei.)

LEILANI: I bet you wan spoil 'im already. *(Slaps AH MUI'S hands.)*

AH MUI *(Slapping her back)*: Aw, nuts. You look, same like before.

LEILANI: Yah? You lucky you naver wan spoil 'im, boy. *(She puts it around her neck.)*

AH MUI: O-oh, da swal, boy.

LEILANI: Goo-ood, yah? *(Starts off into a rhumba and sings "La Cucaracha" in a loud voice. AH MUI joins in with the singing and claps the time for her.)*
(A baby is heard crying offstage, although the children continue unheeding with their singing and dancing. MRS. LEE enters from stage right with a large basket of clothing in her hands and a baby straddled across her back. MRS. LEE is dressed in a two-piece Chinese costume of plain material. Her hair is disheveled, and, as she walks, she drags her ragged slippers along with her. Quite untidy, she is a middle-aged woman of slight build.)

MRS. LEE *(Amidst the baby's wailing)*: What's-a-matter you keeds, anyway? I wan tal you no make so much noise.

AH MUI: No, not me, not me.

(MRS. LEE sets basket on the floor.)

MRS. LEE: Yah, I wan hear you, too. Hurry up, carry da baby. I gotta iron clothes. *(She unties the strap around her shoulders with LEILANI'S help and sets the baby on AH MUI'S back. The baby stops crying.)*

LEILANI: Ah Mui, we go feenish da lei?

AH MUI: O.K. You make dis end, and I make da oder. *(They both take the same position as the opening of the scene.)*

MRS. LEE *(Picking up basket of clothes from the floor, walks towrad the ironing board. Turns on the heat and shakes out a wrinkled child's dress and dips her fingers into a bowl of water set on the board. She wets the clothing.)*: Ah Mui, where Ah Lan and Ah Hong?

AH MUI: Dey wan go peeck flowers by Aala Park . . .

LEILANI: Yah, near da river.

MRS. LEE: Why go tal 'em go peeck some mo' flowers? You feenish da lei already.

AH MUI: Yah, but no 'nough flowers for dis one. *(Shows the half-finished lei.)*

MRS. LEE: No make so long den, if no 'nough flowers.

AH MUI: Goofy kind if short.

MRS. LEE: Everyt'ing you say goofy kind. Mo' batter you no wear lei.

AH MUI: Yah? Da teacher say everybody gotta wear lei tomorrow.

LEILANI: Yah, and we goin' have program . . .

MRS. LEE: Ah Mui, you go tal da teacher only reech-kine peepul wear long lei all right . . . long kind, short kind, any-kind all right. Poor peepul go hana-hana, O.K. If no get flowers, no wear, see?

LEILANI: But we goin' have program, see? My ole lady goin' let me wear Kaiulani's white dress tomorrow.

MRS. LEE: Yah? Wal, Ah Mui goin' wear dis one, see? *(Lifts up an old, faded blue dress.)* Dis one all same white, huh?

LEILANI: Where her new dress for tomorrow?

MRS. LEE: No mo' new dress.

LEILANI: You naver wan get Ah Mui one peachy new dress?

MRS. LEE: Nah, no mo' dong-dong for buy clothes. You t'ink every day get new dress?

LEILANI *(To AH MUI)*: Hah! You wan cross your heart honest-to-goodness you get one peach new dress. Ah-h, you beeg crook!

MRS. LEE: Ah Mui, you wan tal lie, huh? You t'ink you funny? I slap your mouth yet.

AH MUI *(Carefully changing the subject)*: Ma, da baby wan sleep already. Take . . .

MRS. LEE: You wan tal lie or no, huh?

AH MUI *(in a frightened voice)*: Ma, da baby wan sleep already.

MRS. LEE: You damned liar. Just like da oder keeds . . . For why you go school anyway. For why, huh? Only good for learn how tal lie.

AH MUI *(Stamping her foot)*: Ma, I wan say da baby sleep already.

MRS. LEE: Wal, go put 'im in da bed. What's-a-matter wit' you? You dumbbell! *(Slams the iron down with a bang. AH MUI goes quickly offstage with the baby.)* All da keeds jest da same. Only know how kaukau planty, tal lies and dumbbell.

LEILANI *(Meekly)*: Ah Lan not so dumbbell. Wan you no stay home, she take care goo-ood da baby, Ah Mui, Ah Hong and Ah Quon.

MRS. LEE: Yah, take care! Nuts! She only good for go out and no stay home. Jest like now, wan I come home she no stay. Who wan tal her go, anyway?

LEILANI: Ah Mui wan tal her go, 'cause she no mo' not'ing to do.

MRS. LEE: Yah, no mo' not'ing to do. Get planty clothes iron, get planty clothes wash. She good for not'ing.

LEILANI: Yah, but now she get somet'ing to do. She go peeck flowers.

MRS. LEE: And maybe she goin' fall inside da reever wit' Ah Hong, huh?

LEILANI: Gee, maybe. *(Pause)* If she fall inside da reever by Aala Park you no mo' lei, Ah Hong no mo' lei, and Ah Quon no mo' lei.

AH MUI: Ma, somebody coming up da steps.

MRS. LEE: Yah? Who dat? Ah Lan? *(Puts down the iron.)*

AH MUI *(Turning toward stage left)*: Nah, one haole wahine.

MRS. LEE: Da one who before bring rent money?

AH MUI: Nah, not da one. *(LEILANI also looks toward stage left.)*

(MISS CARTER enters from stage left. She is a young school teacher of medium height and about 25 years of age. She is simply dressed in a sports outfit.)

MISS CARTER: Hello, girls, is your mother at home? *(AH MUI and LEILANI giggle.)* Isn't your mamma Mrs. Lee?

(AH MUI and LEILANI giggle again.)

AH MUI: Yah, she over dere. *(Points at her mother.)*

MISS C.: Oh, yes. *(Going over to* MRS. LEE*)* You're Mrs. Lee, Ah Lan's mother, aren't you?

MRS. LEE *(Stopping her ironing)*: Yah, I Mrs. Lee.

MISS C.: I'm Miss Carter, Ah Lan's teacher. Kalakaua Junior High School teacher. *(*AH MUI *and* LEILANI *step up to* MISS CARTER *and eye her curiously.)*

MRS. LEE: Yah, Ah Lan go Kalakaua Junior High. *(Resumes her ironing.* AH MUI *and* LEILANI *are in giggles again.)*

MISS C.: Are these little girls Ah Lan's sisters?

MRS. LEE: Yah, Ah Mui, Ah Lan seester. Leilani, Ah Mui friend. *(Pause)* Ah Mui, go breeng one chair out for da teacher.

AH MUI: O.K. *(To* LEILANI*)* You hol' 'im. *(Handing lei over to her.)*

MISS C.: Oh, I don't want to make you keep your friend waiting. *(*AH MUI *exits stage right.)*

MRS. LEE: Nah, dass all right. Leilani no care.

MISS C.: Mrs. Lee, is Ah Lan at home now?

MRS. LEE: Nah, no home. She go peeck flower by Aala Park, for make lei.

MISS C.: Oh, yes, tomorrow is lei day. Ah Lan has been picking flowers all day?

MRS. LEE: Me, I don't know. I go hana-hana every day . . . only today, after lunch time, boss tal me come home all right. *(*AH MUI *reenters with a chair.* MISS CARTER *sits down and thanks* AH MUI.*)* Maybe, Ah Mui know.

MISS C.: Ah Mui, has Ah Lan been picking flowers all day?

AH MUI: Nah, after school wan peeck only.

LEILANI: Yah, morning time she wan go movies wit' her boy fran.

*(*AH MUI *makes a dash for* LEILANI, *and both begin to slap each other.)*

AH MUI: You look out, boy.

LEILANI: Yah?

AH MUI: Suah, wait for wan she catch you, boy.

MRS. LEE *(Snapping a dress at them as they run before her)*: Shat ap, you keeds. *(A baby is heard crying offstage again.)* You wan wake up da baby already. *(Pause)* Ah Mui, go carry da baby go Aala Park play.

AH MUI *(With relief)*: OK, O.K., Yah, we go, Leilani, we go?

(They both exit stage right.)

MISS C.: Mrs. Lee, I came to see you about Ah Lan.

MRS. LEE: Yah?

MISS C.: You see, Ah Lan doesn't come to school every day, and we wanted you to know.

MRS. LEE: Ah Lan play hooky? No go school?

MISS C.: Yes, she play hooky. Sometimes she comes to school and says that you make her stay at home to do house work and to take care of the baby. Is that right?

(AH MUI and LEILANI reenter from stage right with the baby straddled on AH MUI'S back.)

MRS. LEE: Ah Mui, you go tal Ah Lan come home queek. And tal her take Ah Hong home, too.

AH MUI: O.K. *(She and LEILANI go offstage at stage left.)*

MRS. LEE *(To MISS CARTER)*: No, I no tal Ah Lan stay home take care baby. I tal her go school. Next door wahine take care until Ah Lan pau school. She only clean house and cook for da keeds.

MISS C.: Oh, I see. But, she says she has to take care of the house when you're not at home.

MRS. LEE: Yah, me no stop night time. Gotta hana-hana for kaukau. Take care boss baby night time.

MISS C.: But doesn't your husband go to work? *(Pause)* Hana-hana?

MRS. LEE: No, no got husband. Husband muckee.

MISS C.: Oh, I'm sorry. Then you come home only once a week from hana-hana?

MRS. LEE: Yah, me no can help.

MISS C.: I don't want to meddle into your business, but we like Ah Lan in school. She's good girl, and learns fast, but she doesn't come to school every day.

MRS. LEE: Yah, by'm by she come home, I lick her. Everytime she play hooky, I lick her.

MISS C.: Yes, she tells us you whip her many times. No, we don't want you to do that. *(Pause)* Mrs. Lee, do you think you can get job for only day time hana-hana?

MRS. LEE: Ho, no can get. No 'nough pay for five fellas. Big boy only sell newspaper get money. No mo' rent money pretty soon.

MISS CARTER: . . . because if you have day hana-hana, Ah Lan can have time for homework, to study. Then you can sleep every night at home.

MRS. LEE: Me, I try, but no can. Ah Lan bad girl, anyway. Dat's why she play hooky. I geeve her dong-dong for buy t'ings for baby and keeds kaukau, but she use dong-dong for go moving peecture. Dat's why I geeve her good lickin'. Yah, wan she goin' get one mo' good lickin' for play hooky today.

MISS C.: But, Mrs. Lee, Ah Lan is a young girl yet. She doesn't understand.

MRS. LEE: Yah? Me, I wan come Hawaii from China wan only fiteen year old. Me, I marry ole man, get keed, go hana-hana. Why Ah Lan no can?

MISS C.: But, Mrs. Lee, we want Ah Lan to come back to school every day and not only a few days. Principal says this time is the last time Ah Lan can play hooky. He's going to report to police. You don't want that do you?

MRS. LEE: Me, I no can help. Ah Lan I tal go school I lick her. She no go school I lick some more.

MISS C.: Well, we can put her in the reform school for girls, if you don't want to help Ah Lan. You want that?

MRS. LEE: Me, I don' know. Maybe yah, maybe no. You mean I geeve dong-dong for put in school?

MISS C.: No, you don't have to pay. This school is only for girls who steal and play hooky. Bad girls go there.

MRS. LEE: Yah, me likee. Too much good. Ah Lan bad girl.

MISS C.: You don't want to put Ah Lan in reform school, do you?

MRS. LEE: What dat? Refawm, huh?

MISS C.: School for bad girls.

MRS. LEE: Suah, good. Ah Lan put inside all right. Maybe pau one year she good girl, huh?

MISS C.: But, you don't have to put her in the reform school, if she goes back to regular school tomorrow.

MRS. LEE: Yah, but Ah Lan no like go school. P'oho dong-dong. Every time play hooky. *(A siren is heard offstage.)*

MISS C.: Don't you think you can help her by getting hana-hana during the day? Then she doesn't have to be staying at home with the children at night herself?

MRS. LEE: Nah, she no stay home. She go moving peecture. But me no can help. Put inside school all right.

MISS C.: Mrs. Lee, Ah Lan works hard, but she doesn't come to school every day. Please don't put her in the reform school.

MRS. LEE: Yah, but goo-ood put inside refawm. Mrs. Wong get her keed inside, too. No need lick 'em, no need kau-kau money. Not'ing. Yah, put Ah Lan inside all right.

MISS C.: Well, if you really want to, I suppose there's nothing I can do.

MRS. LEE: Pretty soon Ah Lan come home. I tal Ah Mui go tal her come home. You like her go refawm now? Now all right?

MISS C.: No, I'm not putting Ah Lan in reform school, but I want her to come back to regular school tomorrow, so that principal will not report to police. Ah Lan is not a bad girl. She's a good girl.

MRS. LEE: Nah, she bad girl. You tal principal I like Ah Lan for go refawm.

MISS C.: Are you sure you want to do that?

MRS. LEE: Yah, me suah.

MISS C.: Then I'll . . . *(AH QUON enters from stage left whistling. He is dressed in a work shirt that hangs loosely at the sides, and in a pair of faded sailor mokus. An old shoe box is strapped across his shoulders. He is barefooted)* Oh, is this your big boy? *(AH QUON stops his whistling suddenly.)*

MRS. LEE: Yah, dat Ah Quon. *(Tossing head toward MISS CARTER.)* Dat Miss Carter, Ah Lan teacher.

AH QUON: Oh, you Miss Carter?

MISS C.: Yes, I am.

AH QUON: Ah Lan told me about you. She said you help her all the time.

MISS C.: Oh, but we all are glad to help Ah Lan in school. She is a very fine girl. *(AH QUON shifts his weight from one foot to another and twists his neck in great embarrassment. He finally sets his shoe box in a corner.)* I was just telling your mother that we are anxious to have Ah Lan in school again. If you can get her to come back tomorrow, it would be wonderful, because we're having a lei program, and I'm sure that she would like that.

AH QUON: All right. I tell her by'm by.

MISS C.: Oh, would you? That will be fine. *(Getting up from her seat.)* Well, Mrs. Lee, you try to see what you can do for Ah Lan, We really would like to see her in school again.

MRS. LEE: O.K., O.K.

MISS C.: Good-by.

AH QUON & MRS. LEE: Good-by. *(MISS CARTER exits stage left.)*

AH QUON: Ma, what da teacher tell you?

MRS. LEE: She wan say Ah Lan play hooky again. Da principal like put her in refawm school if she mo go back tomorrow.

AH QUON: And what you say?

MRS. LEE: I say, O.K. Put Ah Lan inside.

AH QUON: Ma, you crazy wahine. Dat's calaboose, you know.

MRS. LEE: Calaboose?

AH QUON: Sure. Da teacher naver told you?

MRS. LEE: Suah, she wan say school for bad wahines. Wahine who play hooky and jabone.

AH QUON: Well, what you like put Ah Lan in dere for?

MRS. LEE: Wal, Ah Lan make me seeck, see? Everytime I gotta lick her. Evertime I come home, da house stink, and da baby no got not'ing for eat. Waste time dat kind wahine, so I goin' put her inside refawm school.

AH QUON: Yeah, in calaboose. Dat school make her worser. Where's Ah Lan now?

MRS. LEE: She wan go peeck flower Aala Park. I wan tal Ah Mui go tal her come home, but I t'ink she no listen to nobody.

AH QUON: Hey, ma, if I tell Ah Lan go back to school tomorrow, how much you goin' give me? *(As he is playing with knife on floor.)*

MRS. LEE: Not'in!

AH QUON: You know, I think she like go, only she scared you wild beast. Every time you give her good lickin', so she don't want to go when you tell her.

MRS. LEE: O.K. Tal her go back if you like. Tal her anyt'ing. I no care.

AH QUON: If I tell her, you give me two bits? Huh, ma?

MRS. LEE: Nah.

AH QUON: Ah-h, you Jew bugga.

MRS. LEE: Nah, no mo' two bits. *(She stops ironing and turns to gather clothes from line.)*

AH QUON: Wal, twenty sants den.

MRS. LEE: Nah, no mo'.

AH QUON: Sure you get. You only Jew.

MRS. LEE *(Throwing clothes gathered from line into basket and sitting down on chair.)*: Twanty sants for tal Ah Lan for go back school? Nuts!

AH QUON: Dime, den.

MRS. LEE: You pupule. Scram out. *(Pause)*

AH QUON *(Sighing)*: Den I gotta tall her for not'in. But I gotta geeve her somethin goo-ood, or else I t'ink she no go back, boy.

MRS. LEE: I geeve her good lickin' an' she still no go school. What you t'ink you goin' geeve her?

AH QUON: Dat's what I askin' you. I don' know. *(Pause. He gazes at the lei on the floor.)* Oh, ma, for who da lei?

MRS. LEE: Me, I don' know. For Leilani I t'ink.

AH QUON: Ah, ma! I t'ink I know what I goin' geeve Ah Lan for go back school tomorrow. One lei!

MRS. LEE: You look out, boy. Leilani goin' keel you if you jabone her lei, boy.

AH QUON: What you t'ink? I not goin' jabone her lei for geeve Ah Lan.

MRS. LEE: What you goin' do? Make one?

AH QUON: Nah! I goin' buy one peenk carnation lei for her. Yah! One peenk carnation lei. Sure t'ing she goin' back for da lei program, boy. Yah, den she no got to go reform school. Yah!

MRS. LEE: You one mo' pupule guy in da house, or what?

AH QUON: Sure, I pupule. I goin' buy one peenk carnation lei for Ah Lan go school tomorrow and tal her, "for you one lei." Yah! "For you one lei." Sur t'ing she go, boy. Yah! *(He rubs the palms of his hands together quickly and whistles the tune of "For You A Lei" and exits with his shoe box strapped around his shoulder.)*

WAI CHEE CHUN *wrote this play in 1937, when she was a student at the University of Hawaii.*

Michael McPherson

"AUNTIE KINA ON THE KING STREET TRAM"

Auntie Kina come from Molokai,
small kid time her family stay.
She come Honolulu for marry
the Irishman, come city lady.
When she go downtown, some dress
up she make. She put on her black
dress, her black hat; some kind
dignity this Hawaiian, you no can
believe. She come outside Alexander-
Young, the pastry shop, she go for
climb on top the trolley for go home.
The conductor, Mr. Kaahawai, he tell,
"Madam, kindly step to the rear of the car."
Whoo, auntie wild up with him. Some
kind stink eye she give, the kind no get
these days. Little more melt
the streetcar. But Mr. Kaahawai,
he old family, some kind stink eye
he give her back, the rails smoking.
She raise herself up, then she go
sit in back the empty tram. Bumbye
when come to her stop, Mr. Kaahawai tell,
"Madam, may I assist you to descend?"
Now auntie more piss off, but one more time
she summon up all her dignity, and she tell,
"No thank you, sir, I shall descend unattended."

MICHAEL MCPHERSON *has two poetry books,* Singing with the Owls; All Those Summers; *and a novel,* Rivers of the Sun. *His law review comments have been published in* Environmental Law *and* Ecology Law Quarterly. *He was inaugural fiction editor of* Hawai'i Review *in 1972 and editor of* HAPA, *1980-83. In 1988, the fourteenth Hawai'i House of Representatives honored his contributions to Hawai'i literature.*

Jeffrey Higa
"CHRISTMAS STORIES"

My father spoke of the Hakoloa Sugar Plantation like he spoke of death, something immutable that taunted him at every risky venture, greeted him at the end of every failure, and loomed like a buzzard over him, waiting for him to stumble so that it could pick his bones. Having grown up in the Japanese section of the plantation camps, I was used to this kind of traditional morbidity but my father's fatalism was different, He embellished his specters, animating them and seizing my imagination so securely that I continue to dream of death not as a rattling skeleton, but as a hidden cane worker, sweating flesh and dirt, his square hammertoed feet leaving bloody tracks on the porches and floors of my nightmares. We thought of the plantation as part of our family, a wicked stepfather, perhaps, someplace we could always go back to but without our self-respect. So, in January of 1923, when we left the plantation for the third time, we had no way of knowing for sure that it would be for good.

My parents moved into the Palama area of O'ahu, an area filled with Filipino and Japanese plantation expatriates, people like ourselves who possessed the immigrant's vision, like a blindered horse, of only looking forward. My father used to say that he didn't have time to look where we were, only where we were going. It would be many years before I realized that was because where we came from was too deeply inscribed upon his memory. But for me, away from the plantation, a whole world had opened up. Luxuries that I had only heard about and never believed, such as children's shoes, suddenly entered my life and all things seemed possible.

As his own boss, my father worked harder than ever, keeping the hours of his cane working days, sunrise till sunset, six days a week. He worked as what we called a "yardboy"—cut the grass, trimmed the hedges, tended the flowers. They're called gardeners now, but yardboy is what the haoles called it and to call it anything else would have been useless. He prided himself on being quiet and efficient, keeping immaculate flower beds and rarely chatting with the other domestic staff. I imagine the wealthy families in Mānoa that he worked for thought well of him, "a credit to his race," passing his name along to their friends, speaking of his reliability and industry. What they never discovered were his little acts of defiance: our eggplant vines growing amidst their hibiscus groves, the rose gardens he would let die and blame on the insects and later replace with tropical plants, the ponds he created upon request never warning them about the mosquito breeding.

As the oldest son, I helped him in November and December, so that he could charge a little bit more and try to pay off all our debts before the new year. I helped him for years, happily abandoning my schooling during those two months, eager in the promise of more "firsts"—our first radio, first icebox, first automobile, first house—which was the way we really measured our lives. My father's plans, however, were different, as he secretly squirreled away most of the money in the bank, waiting for that day when he could purchase us an entirely new life overnight, that first foothold in the American Dream.

So that December of '23, we were working the grounds of the VanHarding estate in upper Mānoa. It was the biggest place he worked for and he usually spent his Saturdays there, preparing the grounds for some kind of gala event: the welcoming of a new industrial pioneer to the islands or the hosting of a private charity. I liked working with him on Saturdays; it meant missing Japanese school, but mostly I enjoyed the bus ride from the fevered alleyways of our dusty community up into the cooler reaches of the Ko'olau Mountains and into the shaded valleys of oak and banyan trees. Once there, I was never very much help, just followed him around with the rake or rubbish bag, picked up fallen palm fronds, or watered the hibiscus. But I liked to go with him because sometimes I got near enough to the VanHarding house to catch a glimpse of the inside.

My mother used to call it the Ichiban white house, because although the other haole families had white houses, the VanHarding house was the biggest, the whitest, and the cleanest. My father, however, had another name for it, the obake house—ghost house. "Too white," he would say. "No more anybody there during the day. Just like one ghost house." Shaking his head he would go on, "Why anybody want a white house in the first place? So unnatural, like that. And hard for take care, every time chip and gotta repaint." He would conclude by spreading his arms and saying, "More better have one house like this. If little bit chip, little bit dirty, no matter. Brown paint anyway." Every time he said that I would look at our house and think how poor it looked next to the VanHarding's, like newsprint next to linen, and I would hunger even more for what I thought cleanliness and whiteness could buy: prosperity and satisfaction.

That Saturday, as my father piled bananas on top of me while I made a basket with my shirt, I planned my approach to the white house. I would have to run and stay out of sight until the last minute, because if I walked or crossed the open lawn too early, Otsu-san the maid would see me coming and meet me outside the kitchen door. But if I ran and knocked on the door, sometimes Mrs. VanHarding would answer and let me into the kitchen. This time I got lucky.

"Oh, it's the yardboy's son," Mrs. VanHarding said as she held the door open. "Come in."

"Okay," I said. My father would have wanted me to say "thank you" but at that age, I was only polite to people who scared me, like my father and his friends. It never occurred to me to be scared of Mrs. VanHarding. She was one of those haole ladies with a big bust, but the dresses she wore made her look soft, like an overstuffed futon pinched too tightly in the middle. Her dresses were fringed in layers of white lace, more lace, I imagined, than in all the dry goods shops on King Street. And she was always powdered and perfumed, even for just staying at home. As she took the bunches from me, I stood close to her and inhaled and was instantly reminded of the plumeria tree in our yard, wet with dew and still riffling in the morning breeze. It was an intoxicating but soothing fragrance, and once I was there, I didn't want to be anywhere else.

After she finished unloading me, she pulled two bananas from the bunch and offered one to me. "Banana?"

"Okay," I said and then remembered, "Thank you."

We both ate standing up. It was part of the ritual. When she was done, she stepped back and looked at me. "Good?" she asked, "The bananas, I mean?"

I shrugged. Big bananas were okay eating, but they couldn't compare to the sweeter and smaller apple bananas that I stole from our Filipino neighbors. "Anything else?" I asked. My father instructed me that anytime Mrs. VanHarding told me to do something, I was to ask if there was anything more I could do.

"How is your mother?"

I then gave her the answer my mother told me to say whenever the haole ladies asked about her, "My mother is good and thanks you for your generosity to our family."

Mrs. VanHarding smiled at me and looked like she wanted to say something else. In all previous encounters, nothing ever came out. Usually, a minute of silence would pass where she looked around the kitchen nervously, and I would inch closer to smell her better. "Well, goodbye," she would say and I would say bye, and walk out the door. The ritual complete.

This day, however, in the middle of my sniffing, she said, "Stand up straight."

"Hahh?"

"Stand up straight," she said, as she walked around me and looked. The smell of lavender had completely surrounded me. "You are eight?"

"Ten," I corrected, which I was, although I felt like I was lying. "Ten, missus."

"Yes, of course." She stood in front of me again, nodding her head. Her lips were a thin line as she looked me over, top to bottom. "Of course." She looked over her shoulder into the heart of the house, and then turned back to me. "Do not move. I will be right back." And she left the kitchen.

I didn't know what to do. My instincts told me to leave because good surprises rarely came from my father's employers. Extra hours, pay reductions, reprimands, and odious tasks were the kind of surprises I was used to. But I also knew that if I disobeyed Mrs. VanHarding and my father found out, I would be lucky to live the night. Even if I did manage to survive, I could foresee a long week of lectures on responsibility and the precariousness of our financial situation, punctuated by additional emphatic physical reminders. It seemed I had but one choice, so in the few minutes she was gone, I tried not to move. Soon I saw her coming towards me, but I still did not move until she handed me a brown paper bundle wrapped in string.

"Here," she said, "I think these will fit you."

The bundle was soft and I turned it over, but I couldn't see what was in it. I looked up at her and wanted to say something, but I didn't know the proper thing to say. No haole lady had ever given a gift to me before. I could only think of what my mother would have said. "Thank you for your generosity to our family."

"I have a son that is your age," she said. "He outgrew these a few years ago, and they were just taking up space in his wardrobe, so I thought—" she paused and looked around the kitchen and then at me again. "Well, your mother might have to alter them a bit."

"Thank you," I said and bowed like my father did when he got paid. "Thank you for your generosity to our family."

"Don't get them dirty when you get outside."

I nodded, bowed again, and ran out the kitchen door, across the lawn, and into the banana grove. "Look," I said to my father as I held up the bundle. "Look at what she gave me!"

"Who?" he asked.

"The haole lady," I said, "Mrs. VanHarding. She said she also had a son who was ten and that he didn't need these anymore because they too small for him now and. . . ."

"Gimme that!" he said as he dropped his sickle to the ground and threw off his gloves. He wiped his hands on his shirt and snatched the bundle from my arms. "Why you accept this? We taught you better than that!"

"But . . . but she said she didn't need these. And I thanked her for it. I did. I said, 'Thank you for. . . .'"

"No." He shook his head. "No charity. We no can accept this."

"But how do you know?" I knew my father would give the bundle back without even opening it. "She said they were too small for him. She said they were just sitting around. They're probably only boroboros anyway. . . ."

My father turned to me with a glare that stilled the rest of my thoughts. "Don't say stupid things, Ma-chan. Put away all our stuff. I going take this back." He turned around and walked towards the house.

I didn't try to stop him. I picked up the sickle and gloves. I knew there was no sense even hoping that he would change his mind. He couldn't accept the gift for some Japanese reason, and I knew from past experience that it was useless to try and convince my father out of his Japanese reasons. I just had to accept them.

Even now, I don't know if he could have explained his "Japanese reasons" to me anyway. In times of uncertainty, these traditions, rooted in his custom and history, were the springs he touched upon to propel all of us into our new future. It was a way I could never fully embrace and I would have to create a new way, balancing the forces of my past with those of my future.

After I finished putting the sickle, gloves, and ladder in the shed behind the white house, I started toward the kitchen door, knowing that my father would wait there, hat in hand, for Mrs. VanHarding to pay him. When I got to the door, my father was still trying to give the bundle back to Mrs. Van-Harding, who was shaking her head furiously.

"No," she said. "Please take it. These are just old clothes. I must insist you take it."

"No. Too generous. We no deserve such kindness." "No. This is not a gift. Christopher has outgrown these clothes." "Then please take the cost out from here," Dad held out the weekly salary Mrs. VanHarding had just given him. "To pay."

"No!" A horrified Mrs. VanHarding looked at me for help. I shrugged. She couldn't win. "Please take them," she repeated. "No charity," he said. "Not right."

"Yes," she said. "It is right." She took the bundle from my father and thrust it at me. "Anyway, I was giving them to your son. Doesn't he want them?" She turned to look at me. "Don't you want them?"

I couldn't believe that she was trying to get around my father. I knew if she had not been a woman and also haole, that he would have been very insulted and have left. Instead, he turned toward me and I could see the violence brewing in his eyes: I better not even raise my arms to accept the bundle—or else. But the look on Mrs. VanHarding's face was equally clear: She was not used to being disobeyed, and I was to take the bundle from her. It was up to me to do the right thing, and for the second time that day, I did not move.

"It would make my son very happy," she said to my father, "if your son would accept this gift from Christopher."

I almost laughed then, thinking, that's not going to work. You have to think of something better than that. But when I turned to look at my father, he had turned away from Mrs. VanHarding and was looking at the ground. He seemed suddenly bashful, something I had rarely seen, and after looking at his shoes for a few seconds, he lifted his head and asked, "How your son? Good, yes?"

She nodded her head but said, "No." And then added quietly, "The doctors say this might be his last Christmas."

My father looked back down at his shoes and then turned to look at me. "My son," he said as he nodded at me, "honored by gift from your son."

I stepped forward and then the bundle was in my arms.

The following Sunday and the entire rest of the week was frantic as my parents argued about what I should give Christopher. In the bundle was a white shirt and a pair of white shorts. Both of them were too big for me, and my mother refused to alter them because she said the material was too expensive and too nice to cut up. Instead, we draped the clothes over a chair set up in the living room, and all our neighbors came over to see and feel the silk shirt and linen shorts from Christopher VanHarding.

We knew that we could not afford to buy him anything that would be as fine as the clothes he had given me. We also knew that we could not make him the kind of food he was used to. So it was decided that I would give Christopher the koa carving that one of my father's friends had carved for me when I was born. The carving was of a carp twisting and fighting against the current, its tail flexed as it thrust its body out of the turbulence, determination and power barely restrained under its scales. It was a carving that had always frightened me as a child; its ferocity was more demon than fish. But my father thought it was an appropriate gift for a sick boy like Christopher.

The next Saturday on the bus, I asked my father why he had never mentioned that the VanHardings had a son my age. He said that he had seen Christopher only once, when Mrs. VanHarding had my father wash the windows. Christopher was lying in bed in a bedroom that faced the back lawn. He said he could see that Christopher was very sick but figured that the VanHardings could afford expensive haole doctors to take care of him.

"So is that why you decided to accept the gift? Because Christopher is sick and might not get well?"

"Yes," he said. "When number one son dying, it is a very sad time. Doesn't matter if they Japanese or not. Everyone sad."

I nodded my head and we remained silent the rest of the way to Mānoa.

My father waited until the afternoon before he sent me to the white house with the gift. The carving was heavy in my arms and was wrapped in the same brown paper and string that Mrs. VanHarding had given us. As I made my way across the back lawn to the kitchen door, I looked into the windows but did not see Christopher in any of the rooms. Mrs. VanHarding answered my knock and led me into the kitchen.

"How are you, Mrs. VanHarding," I said from the carefully prepared script that my parents had devised. "Fine, Masa."

"My parents thank you for the beautiful clothes you have given us." I offered the present to her, "And hope your son will accept this meager gift in return."

"Oh." Mrs. VanHarding looked over her shoulder and then back at me. "You did not have to do that."

"It is nothing so fine as the gift he has given me," I said. Then in proper Japanese fashion, "This gift is worthless and of poor quality." I bowed and held out the present in front of me. "Please accept this token of our gratitude."

According to the script, Mrs. VanHarding was supposed to take the gift, after which I would take a step back, bow again, and then leave. But as I waited, bowed over, she didn't take the gift. I was worried that maybe she wouldn't accept this token of our gratitude because of what I said about it being worthless. These proper Japanese things are always getting me in trouble, I thought. "Masa?"

I raised my head without straightening up. "You don't want this? It's actually very nice. My mother made me say that part about it being worthless. It's not really. . . . "

"This present is for Christopher?" I nodded.

"Then maybe you should give it to him yourself." I didn't know what to say. Meeting Christopher was not in the script. I was curious about seeing him, maybe through a window, but I wasn't sure I wanted to meet him. I wouldn't know what to say to a sick, rich, haole boy. I straightened up and tried to think of a tactful response, when Mrs. VanHarding said, "It would make him happy to meet you."

I knew then I had no choice, and said what my father would have wanted me to say, "You honor me."

Mrs. VanHarding motioned for me to follow, and for the first time, I walked out of the kitchen and into the VanHarding world. Even now, it is still hard to describe what I saw there. I can't really describe each room through which we passed. I remember thinking that it took a long time to cross the rooms, and there was something new to look at with every step. At the time, I had never seen so much material used to cover a window, with the excess allowed to spill out onto the walls. I had never seen a wooden floor shine. I had never seen chairs where cloth covered the entire thing, not just the seat. I had never seen doors made of glass. I had never seen plates and bowls and cups and pitchers that reflected like mirrors. I had never seen walls made of books. I had never seen an overhead light made up of diamonds, too numerous to count. But all of that did not prepare me for a sight I had never even seen in my dreams.

"There's a tree in your house," I said to Mrs. VanHarding but she had already moved to the other side of the room. It must be a mistake, I thought. Why would someone grow a tree in their house?

"Christopher, you have a visitor," she said to someone lying on the couch.

I knew that I was supposed to follow Mrs. VanHarding to the other side of the room and give Christopher his present. But I did not want to stop looking at the tree. It was, of course, a pine tree, but at that time all I knew was that it was a tree shaped like a green mountain, pointy on top and broader on the way down. I was going to touch it and make sure it was real, but I knew my father would not like me touching anything that belonged to the VanHardings.

"Masa," she said, "Masa, we are over here."

I carried the present to where Mrs. VanHarding was calling me, but kept my eyes on the tree.

"Christopher," she said as I got closer. "This is Masa. The yardboy's son. He is ten, also."

I turned my eyes away from the tree to the boy on the couch. I was surprised to see that Christopher, propped up by pillows, was not the tall, fat boy I had envisioned. Judging by the clothes he had given me, I had expected to see someone who was much taller and much heavier than I was. A boy version of Mrs. VanHarding. Instead, Christopher's skin looked like it didn't quite fit, like he had shriveled inside from staying too long in the ocean. Against his white clothes, his skin took on an ashy hue, like a shirt that had been worn and washed too often.

Even his hair looked weary of fighting the advancing white which had taken over his blond roots. When he looked at me, I felt I was looking into the worn-down eyes of an old plantation worker. Eyes that saw everything but kept it on the horizon.

"Hello, Masa."

"Hi . . . " I didn't know what to say next. I was trying to remember the beginning of the script so I could restart, but the tree and then Christopher made me forget. ". . . Christopher."

"Only my parents call me Christopher." He smiled at his mother. "Everyone else calls me Chris."

"Yes . . . Chris," I said and then frantically tried to think of something to say. I watched Mrs. VanHarding squeeze Christopher's hand, and walk past the tree, out of the room. "The tree," I said to myself, then I noticed Christopher looking at me. "You have one in your house. . . Chris."

"Yes, do you like our Christmas tree?"

"Oh yeah, Christmas." I had heard of Christmas. My parents had used the word once or twice, and one of my friends had said something about Christmas, something he had learned in school, but I always missed school during the last few months of the year. "A Christmas tree."

"This is the biggest tree we've had yet. How big is your Christmas tree?"

Our Christmas tree? I wondered if I should tell him the truth. "Not as big as this one."

"Yes, yes, but how big is it, anyway?"

I was about to reach up with my hands and say, about this big, when I realized I was still carrying the gift and had no way to gesture. "We don't have one."

"Your family doesn't have a Christmas tree?"

"No."

"Why not? What do you do for Christmas? How can you have Christmas without a Christmas tree?" Christopher pushed himself a little higher up on the pillows.

Although I didn't know what he was asking, I didn't like the way he was asking it, so I shoved the package at him and said, "Here, here's your gift." I knew it wasn't the proper thing to say, but I didn't care. It was my father's fault for getting me into this in the first place. Why did we always have to give something back? "Here, take it."

"Is this a Christmas present?"

Christmas present? What do I answer? Yes? No? Which answer did he want to hear? I chose, "Yes."

"Well, you have to put it under the tree, then." Christopher frowned at me. "Didn't you know that?"

"Yeah," I said and put the gift next to several other boxes that were beneath the tree. It didn't make sense to me, but if he wanted me to put it under the tree. . . .

"Don't you know anything about Christmas?" he asked.

I wanted to say yes because it sounded like I should know, but saying yes got me in trouble last time. "No."

Christopher continued frowning while I stood next to the tree. The tree had a pleasant scent, and it reminded me of my sister, Naomi, and the powder we put on her newborn skin.

"You don't know about Santa Claus or Bethlehem?" he asked. I wasn't sure if he was asking me or himself. "Don't you get presents either?"

"Well," I said as I considered his question. "I usually get presents on New Year's Day." Christopher swung his legs off the couch and sat up. "And then there's Boy's Day."

"But that's not like Christmas," he said.

"No." I thought about the tree behind me. "I guess not."

We then looked at each other. I could imagine my father kneeling among the orchids, wiping his brow, and wondering what was taking me so long. I was thinking I should probably leave now that my mission had been accomplished, and was just about to make that suggestion when Christopher said, "Come here. Sit down."

"Why?" I asked, even though my father had scolded me many times for asking "why" so much. No good ask too many questions, he would say.

"Because I'm going to tell you about Christmas." Christopher smiled at me. "I'm going to tell you a Christmas story."

I still don't know why Christopher decided to do what he did. I don't think he was trying to convert me to Christianity, because he barely mentioned the baby Jesus and Bethlehem. Or if he did, I didn't remember that part as much as the story about decorating trees and the flying animals and the fat haole man with the white beard and how he came through a hole in the ceiling instead of the door and gave you presents, everything you wanted if you were good and had listened to your parents that year. As Christopher told the story and I followed his voice and hands, I forgot that he was sick, that he was haole, and felt as if I were with any of my Palama friends just talking story. When he finished, he closed his eyes and leaned his head against the back of the couch. Suddenly, neither of us had anything to say as he breathed heavily and slowly as if asleep. We sat in silence until Mrs. VanHarding appeared in the doorway a few seconds later.

"Masa," she said. I stood up from the couch. "Your father is waiting for you outside."

I nodded at Mrs. VanHarding and turned to say something to Christopher. He had opened his eyes and was smiling weakly at me.

"I was just telling Masa a Christmas story," Christopher said to his mother as he slid his legs back on the couch. "But we ran out of time before he could tell me a story."

"Well, perhaps next week Masa can tell you a story." She turned to me, "You are coming back next week?"

"Yes," I answered although she didn't really seem to be asking me. "To tell Christopher a story."

"Good," she said and then to Christopher, "I will be right back with your medicine after I show Masa out."

Christopher nodded. "See you next Saturday, Masa."

"Yes, next Saturday." I nodded. "Chris."

My father did not say a word to me at the VanHarding's kitchen door or during the entire bus ride home. Even through dinner, he did not once look at me. So later that night after my mother had cleared the dinner dishes, I was relieved when my father finally said, "Why you cause trouble for the VanHardings?"

"I didn't. Mrs. VanHarding told me to give the gift to Christopher. She said that he wanted to meet me, so . . ."

"You see inside the house?" my mother asked.

"Yes," I said and proceeded to tell them all I could remember. My father did not say anything as I described the things I had seen, but my mother kept interrupting me for more details. What color were the walls, the rugs, the furniture? How big were the rooms, bigger than this house? Was Mrs. Van Harding wearing lots of gold and diamonds? When I got to the part about the tree, my father snorted.

"No make sense, I tell you," he said. "These haoles. Make me cut down live tree and put tree in house. After new year come, make me take tree out of house. Throw tree away."

I knew I had to wait until he was finished. But he didn't say anything else, so I continued. Then, in the middle of my description of Santa and the presents, my father blurted, "And how you throw tree away? Cannot. Got to burn." He lifted his empty teacup. My mother reached over with the teapot and refilled his cup. "Wasting tree, I tell you," he said.

"Go on, Ma-chan," said my mother, and so I did, ending with the part where Christopher had finished his story and Mrs. VanHarding was back in the room.

"Mrs. VanHarding," I took a deep breath, "wants me to come back next Saturday."

"Hahh?" Like most Japanese fathers, my father didn't like surprises from his children. "What you mean?"

"It's for Christopher. Mrs. VanHarding wants me to help Christopher."

"Help? Help with what?"

"She wants me to help him . . . " For the first time in my life, I lied to my father, ". . . learn Japanese."

My father started to stand up, "No shibai, you!"

"I'm not lying," I lied. "She wants him to learn Japanese."

"Why? Why he like learn Japanese?" He was standing now, looming over me.

"I don't know," I said, scared that this was starting to get away from me like an unraveling ball of yarn rolling downhill. "You told me never to ask why, especially to haoles."

"Don't say dumb things!" He raised his arm. My mother started tugging on his shirt but he ignored her. "Haoles no like learn Japanese, they like everyone learn English!"

"Let him go, let him go," my mother pleaded. "Maybe she pay extra for teaching."

I nodded at him, knowing that if I opened my mouth again, that hand would come down. He glared at me and I lowered my gaze to my feet. Neither of us spoke and I didn't raise my head until he exhaled loudly and said, "No embarrass us."

I nodded again and started to leave the room. I was almost out when I heard him say, "And no get me fired."

I didn't want to tell my father the truth because I didn't want him and my mother to tell me what story to tell Christopher. I knew they would pick a story about one of Japan's glorious samurais who did this or that brave deed and then died violently. Or some story about a child who did not listen to his parents and was tricked by demons and was now enduring eternal punishment. I wanted to tell Christopher a story like the one he told me: a story where animals had magical powers, and good things happened to children, and at the end of the story everyone was happy.

However, I did not know a story like that. All the stories I had learned from my parents or their friends were not happy enough, and Christopher probably knew all the stories I had learned in school. Every day until Saturday, while working with my father at one of the estates or afterward at home, I tried to make up a story. But every story turned out to be a thinly disguised version of the Christmas story, except with a fat Japanese man or flying mongooses. Saturday afternoon found me at the VanHarding's kitchen door, with no story to tell.

"Hello, Masa." Mrs. VanHarding opened the door. "Christopher has been waiting for you."

"Is he too tired to see me?" It was my last hope. "I don't have to see him today. Maybe next week?"

"Nonsense," she said. "Come, he's waiting for you in the sitting room." She turned and motioned for me to follow.

I slid my feet after her, barely looking at the things around me. This time, the VanHarding house did not seem so wonderful, just confusing and forbidding. I suddenly understood what my father meant by the obake house.

When we entered the sitting room, Christopher was on the couch near the Christmas tree. The tree had been decorated with ribbons of red and green, paper cutouts, white candles, garlands of silver, and glass balls that reflected the sunlight. The festivity of the tree only made me feel more empty-handed, like the hollowness I felt when I won a game by cheating. The carving I had given Christopher stood unwrapped on a table. Mrs. VanHarding whispered to Christopher, turned to smile at me, and left the room.

Christopher pointed to the end of the couch. "Hello Masa. Come sit here."

"Hello, Chris." I was hoping that he forgot I was supposed to tell him a story.

"So, what story are you going to tell me?"

I tried a change of topic. "Your tree looks very nice. Very Christmas."

"My father helped me decorate it," he said. "I did the bottom and he did the top."

Having exhausted all my knowledge on that topic, I switched to another. "Did you like the gift we gave you?"

"Yes, my mother was just telling me that I should remember to thank you for it." We both turned to look at the carving. "So thank you for this very nice . . . fish."

Both of us started laughing, but stopped almost immediately when Christopher started to cough. He coughed for a long time, and I waited until he was breathing normally.

"That's why we gave you this fish," I said as I stood up and took the carving off the table. "So you would get better." I handed the carving to Christopher. "It's a carp which is good luck for boys."

"Good luck for boys?"

"See this," I pointed to the base of the carving. "This is the water, the current." I pointed to the flank of the fish. "See this? The carp is bursting out of the water. It is a strong fish and can fight off the rough water."

I put Christopher's hand along the carved side of the fish. "Can you feel it? It is alive, full of power." He caressed the carving. "The carp is not afraid and does not give up."

And then it came to me. The story I needed to tell.

I drew up my legs onto the couch. "Once there was an old couple who lived in the countryside of Japan. Everything was good, and they lived simple and peaceful lives, farming rice year after year. But there was one thing that was missing. One thing that they really wanted but never had. Something that would make their lives much happier." Out the window, over Christopher's shoulder, I could see my father pruning the hedges. I watched him move from one bush to the next, each swing of the sickle fluid and assured, a movement he practiced hundreds of times a week. Then somewhere in a dim portion far back in my ten-year-old mind, I thought that if I were lucky, I would be able to move like he did in the world: deliberate and without shame.

"What!" Christopher shook my arm. "What was it?"

"A boy," I said. "They wanted a son." I told him the story of Momotaro, the boy born from a peach found by the old couple. I told Christopher of how Momotaro grew and brought much happiness to the couple, their lives made brighter by his presence. How Momotaro excelled in school and at games. How he was an expert wrestler and a good swordsman. "Then," I said, "when he was still a young boy, Momotaro decided to kill the demons stealing from his village." I told Christopher of Momotaro's journey and of the talking animals he befriended: the dog who could bite through anything, the monkey who was slier and trickier than any man, the bird who could see further and fly faster than any other animal. I explained how Momotaro was not afraid and sailed to the island where the demons lived and killed them all with the help of his animal friends. How Momotaro returned to the village and gave back everything the demons had stolen. And how, now that the demons were dead, the entire village celebrated but none more than Momotaro's parents who were just happy that their son was home with them.

When I had finally finished, Christopher looked up the from the carving he was still holding. "That was a good story."

I nodded, "When you get better, maybe we can play Momotaro sometime." I saw my father brush off his clothes, and walk across the lawn toward the house. "Like I do with my friends at home."

"That would be fun," he said. "As long as I get to be Momotaro."

"All right, it's more fun being the monkey anyway." And as soon as I'd said that, Mrs. VanHarding appeared in the doorway.

The next Saturday was the first week of the new year and I returned to Japanese school. I wish I could say that despite our differences, Christopher and I had become steady friends but in reality I never went back to the VanHarding estate and I never spoke with Christopher again. I didn't forget him, my days just became too busy. Regular school during the week, Japanese school afterward and on Saturdays, adventures with my Palama friends on Sunday—it seemed I always had something else to do, something too important to postpone. Then one Saturday halfway into the new year, I came home from Japanese school and found my father already back from work.

"Didn't you go to work, today?"

"Yes, but I had to come back."

"Why?" I asked but I already knew.

"VanHarding boy die two days ago." He shook his head. "Very sad. Funeral today, so no work."

Suddenly, I wanted to tell my father what had really happened between me and Christopher and of the story I told. But as the impulse to confess welled up in me, I knew that I wouldn't be able to tell him. I thought of the promise I had made Christopher and then abandoned. And as that wave of guilt sucked me out into an ocean of remorse, I turned away from my father, confused.

My father and I never talked about the VanHardings again; I suppose he felt there was no need. I did not understand what it meant that Christopher had died and my father could not afford the luxury of dwelling further upon it.

In a few years, my father saved enough money to open up his own restaurant in Palama, The Palama Inn. He gave his old clients to a friend of his, a recent immigrant to the islands. One day this man told my father that the VanHardings had decided to move back to the mainland. Massachusetts, the man said.

Now years later, after an old man's lifetime of knowing people and then letting them slip out of my life for no reason other than my own laziness, Christopher's is the friendship I think about the most. I wonder if I might have become a different person, if I had gotten to know Christopher better. So in my regret, I do the only thing I am able to. Every year, with my children and now with my grandchildren, I tell them the Christmas story. I tell them also of the boy, Momotaro, and his fearlessness while facing his enemy. And then, when they are ready, I show them the white shirt and shorts and tell them this story.

JEFFREY HIGA *was born in 1966 and graduated from Mililani High School on O'ahu before embarking on a twenty-three-year sojourn on the mainland, where he earned degrees from Rensselaer Polytechnic Institute and the University of Missouri–St. Louis. He has published humor and fiction in* HONOLULU *Magazine;* Bamboo Ridge; Zyzzyva; *and* Sonora Review, *and won the 2003 Kumu Kahua Playwriting Contest. He has returned to Honolulu with his wife and daughter and works as a director at Hawai'i's Plantation Village.*

Don Blanding
"BABY STREET (DOWN PALAMA WAY)"

I walk quite slowly down Baby Street
Babies are everywhere . . . under my feet,
Sprawled on the sidewalks, perched on the walls,
Babies in dydies, in blue overalls,
Babies in rompers of flowered cretonne,
Babies with not much of anything on,
Little brown babies in brown mamas' laps,

Philippine babies, Koreans and Japs,
Fresh, shiney babies right out of the tub,
Babies in scandalous need of a scrub,
Baby Hawaiians, the sons of a chief,
Rastus from Africa, black past belief,
Babies with yellow hair, babies with brown,
Babies with just a few patches of down,
Toddling babies on little bowed legs,
Very new babies much balder than eggs,
Portuguese babies, and Russians as well,
Babies whose ancestors no one can tell,
Toothless as turkeys . . . these tiny young tads,
But grinning as though they were dentifrice ads.

Walk very carefully . . . make your step hesitant.
One of these babies may some day be president.

DON BLANDING (1894-1957) *began his literary career in Honolulu in 1922, when he started writing advertising copy for the Aji-no-moto company. He penned a daily ad appearing in the* Honolulu Star-Bulletin *which consisted of rhyming verse extolling the virtues of the cooking additive. His simple, colorful verse and handsome pen-and-ink illustrations earned him the title "Unofficial Poet Laureate of Hawai'i." He is the author of many books of poetry, among them* Leaves from a Grass House; Vagabond's House; *and* Hula Moons.

Guy Cardwell
"ODALISQUE"

Chinese, Hawaiian, Portuguese,
Cloudy hair, lips cerise;
Romance eyes, slightly squinted,
Cathay cheeks, faintly tinted,
Ecstatic shoulders, carved in hell—
Angels never sculptured so well—
Keep cool, dearie, and you'll get
A decent haole husband, yet.

GUY CARDWELL *is the author of* The Man Who Was Mark Twain, *and the editor of* Discussions of Mark Twain *and* The Uncollected Poems of Henry Timrod, *among other works. He wrote this poem in 1928, when he was a student at the University of Hawaii.*

"On the Beach at Waikīkī

The sun shines on the tourist ... The sea is as blue as a peacock *lei* ... The wild waves lave them, one and all ... Somewhere an eukaleli thrills and cries ... Sweet brown maiden ... He saw the hula flower in her hair ... Camera angles ... Jack London on a surfboard ...

Rupert Brooke
"WAIKIKI"

Warm perfumes like a breath from vine and tree
    Drift down the darkness. Plangent, hidden from eyes,
    Somewhere an eukaleli thrills and cries
And stabs with pain the night's brown savagery.
And dark scents whisper; and dim waves creep to me,
    Gleam like a woman's hair, stretch out, and rise;
    And new stars burn into the ancient skies,
Over the murmurous soft Hawaiian sea.

And I recall, lose, grasp, forget again.
    And still remember, a tale I have heard, or known,
An empty tale, of idleness and pain,
    Of two that loved—or did not love—and one
Whose perplexed heart did evil, foolishly,
A long while since, and by some other sea.

RUPERT BROOKE (1887-1915) *was a charming and athletic English poet, "the most hand-*
some man in England," who befriended E. M. Forster, Maynard Keynes, and Virginia Woolf.
During World War I, he joined the Royal Naval Division, and died at twenty-seven, of blood
poisoning, on the island of Skiros.

———————————•◦•———————————

Henry Kailimai and G. H. Stover
"ON THE BEACH AT WAIKIKI"

Honi kaua wikiwiki
Sweet brown maiden said to me
As she gave me language lessons
on the beach at Waikiki

Honi kaua wikiwiki
She repeated playfully
Oh those lips were so inviting
On the beach at Waikiki

Courtesy of Bernice P. Bishop Museum.

Honi kaua wikiwiki
She was surely teasing me
So I caught that maid and kissed her
On the beach at Waikiki

Honi kaua wikiwiki
You have learned it perfectly
Don't forget what I have taught you
Said the maid at Waikiki

HENRY KAILIMAI (1882-1948) *was a well-known musician in Honolulu. At the Panama-Pacific International Exposition in San Francisco in 1915, Kailimai and the Royal Hawaiians were featured along with hula dancers. This started a countrywide craze for "Hawaiian" novelty music. Henry Ford hired the Royal Hawaiians. They played at the wedding of Thomas Edison's daughter, and made several records at the Edison Studio in New York. Kailimai was credited with "additional music" in Broadway musicals by Irving Berlin and Jerome Kern. "On the Beach at Waikiki" became a national sheet music bestseller. John Philip Sousa's band played it, and Shirley Temple danced a hula to it in* Curly Top.

Genevieve Taggard
"THE TOURIST"

He saw the hula flower in her hair
Drop to her bosom where it rose and fell:
Forgotten was her lover; slow her stare
Felt for his eyes; her warm body's smell—
The yellow-stamen perfume on her breath,
The poison heavy sleepiness of death
Made all her figure's slender golden grace
Seem like a censer in an altered place.

Swinging she danced the hula, and the moon
Hung on the mountain honeying the night:
Her dress of flowers whirled about her—strewn

Along the grass the fire-petals died.
Then like a bat against that disc of light
Leaped up her lover, and the lonely wide
Hollow and shadow echoed as he cried.

GENEVIEVE TAGGARD (1894-1948) *was the daughter of American church workers in Hawai'i. She graduated from the University of California at Berkeley, then moved to Greenwich Village, where she founded the journal* The Measure. *In the 1930s, she became active in left–wing causes. She is the author of a biography of Emily Dickinson, and thirteen books of poetry; some of her poems were set to music by Aaron Copland, Roy Harris, and others.*

Kathryn Jean MacFarlane
"FLAPPER'S ACRE"

There are too many girls
at Waikiki.
In the evening
they come out of the small houses,
out of the tree-top apartments,
and drift
down the moon washed streets,
across the moon drenched lawns,
like clouds
of moon pale butterflies.

KATHRYN JEAN MACFARLANE *wrote this poem in 1933, when she was a student at the University of Hawaii.*

Jerome Kern
from VERY GOOD EDDIE

ELSIE AND DICK AND ENSEMBLE:
On the beach at Li-Li-Wee
ENS: Shush shush shush
To the music of the sea

ENS: Shush shush shush
Sang a man whose heart beat fast
A love like mine will last.

Till the stars in the distant places
Far above the sea
Miss the sun-lit wave that races
Down the beach at Li-Li-Wee.

DICK:
On the beach at Li-Li-Wee
  ENS: shush shush shush
Stands a maiden fair to see
  ENS: shush shush shush
By her side a native son
So close they seemed like one
But the stars shining in their distant places
Far above the sea
Saw them kiss each other's faces
On the beach at Li-Li-Wee.

ELSIE:
On the beach at Li-Li-Wee
  ENS: shush shush shush
If you go there you will see
He's still waiting day by day
But she has flown away.
But the stars shining in their distant places
Far above the sea
Know a hundred just such cases
On the beach at Li-Li-Wee.

DICK AND ELSIE:
But the stars shining in their distant places
Far above the sea
Watch the old lies light new faces
On the beach at Li-Li-Wee
But the stars shining in their distant places
Far above the sea
Know a hundred just such cases
On the beach at Li-Li-Wee

ELSIE AND DICK:
On the beach at Li-Li-Wee
Lovers play their comedy
Some depart still others come
But only one tune hum
But the stars shining in their distant places
Far above the sea
Watch the old lies light new faces
On the beach at Li-Li-Wee.

JEROME KERN (1885-1945) *wrote songs and complete scores for more than a hundred movies and stage shows, including the Ziegfeld Follies. His most famous Broadway musical was* Show Boat, *with the classic "Ol' Man River." In the 1930s and 1940s, in Hollywood, he wrote songs for Fred Astaire and Ginger Rogers, Gene Kelly and Rita Hayworth, and won an Oscar for "Lady Be Good." Many of his songs became standards, including "All the Things You Are," "The Way You Look Tonight," "Can't Help Lovin' Dat Man," and "Smoke Gets in Your Eyes." The lyrics for "On the Beach at Li-Li-Wee," from* Very Good Eddie, *which ran for more than 100 performances on Broadway in 1915-1916, are in the New York Public Library for the Performing Arts at Lincoln Center.*

Jack London
from "THE KANAKA SURF"

T he tourist women, under the hau-tree arbor that lines the Moana Hotel beach, gasped when Lee Barton and his wife Ida emerged from the bathhouse. And as the pair walked past them and down to the sand, they continued to gasp. Not that there was anything about Lee Barton provocative of gasps. The tourist women were not of the sort to gasp at sight of a mere man's swimming-suited body, no matter with what swelling splendor of line and muscle such body was invested. Nevertheless, trainers and conditioners of men would have drawn deep breaths of satisfaction at contemplation of the physical spectacle of him. But they would not have gasped in the way the women did, whose gasps were indicative of moral shock.

Ida Barton was the cause of their perturbation and disapproval. They disapproved, seriously so, at the first instant's glimpse of her. They thought—such ardent self-deceivers were they—that they were shocked by her swimming suit. But Freud has pointed out how persons, where sex is involved,

-five, who had been born in the Hawaiian islands, & who had never heard of Ostend.

Hanley Black surveyed his wife's with a withering, contemplative eye. They had been married a sufficient number of years for him frankly to utter his judgment.

"That strange woman's suit makes your own look indecent. You appear as a creature shameful, under a grotesqueness of apparel striving to hide some secret awfulness."

"She carries her body like a Spanish dancer," Mrs. Patterson said to her

criminal shapelessness and voluminousness & antediluvian (spec) new-England swimming dress are prone sincerely to substitute one thing for another thing, and to agonize over the substituted thing as strenuously as if it were the real thing.

Ida Barton's swimming suit was a very nice one, as women's suits go. Of thinnest of firm-woven black wool, with white trimmings and a white belt line, it was high-throated, short-sleeved, and brief-skirted. Brief as was the skirt, the leg tights were no less brief. Yet on the beach in front of the adjacent Outrigger Club, and entering and leaving the water, a score of women, not provoking gasping notice, were more daringly garbed. Their men's suits, as brief of leg tights and skirts, fitted them as snugly, but were sleeveless after the way of men's suits, the armholes deeply low cut and in cut, and, by the exposed armpits, advertiseful that the wearers were accustomed to 1916 décolleté.

So it was not Ida Barton's suit, although the women deceived themselves into thinking it was. It was, first of all, say, her legs; or, first of all, say, the totality of her, the sweet and brilliant jewel of her femininity bursting upon them. Dowager, matron, and maid, conserving their soft-fat muscles or protecting their hothouse complexions in the shade of the hau-tree arbor, felt the immediate challenge of her. She was menace as well, an affront of superiority in their own chosen and variously successful game of life.

But they did not say it. They did not permit themselves to think it. They thought it was the suit, and said so to one another, ignoring the twenty women more daringly clad but less perilously beautiful. Could one have winnowed out of the souls of these disapproving ones what lay at bottom of their condemnation of her suit, it would have been found to be the sex-jealous thought: *that no woman, so beautiful as this one, should be permitted to show her beauty*. It was not fair to them. What chance had they in the conquering of males with so dangerous a rival in the foreground?

They were justified. As Stanley Patterson said to his wife, where the two of them lolled wet in the sand by the tiny fresh-water stream that the Bartons waded in order to gain the Outrigger Club beach:

"Lord god of models and marvels, behold them! My dear, did you ever see two such legs on one small woman? Look at the roundness and taperingness. They're boy's legs. I've seen featherweights go into the ring with legs like those. And they're all woman's legs, too. Never mistake them in the world. The arc of the front line of that upper leg! And the balanced adequate fullness at the back! And the way the opposing curves slender in to the knee that *is* a knee! Makes my fingers itch. Wish I had some clay right now."

"It's a true human knee," his wife concurred, no less breathlessly; for, like her husband, she was a sculptor. "Look at the joint of it working under the skin. It's got form, and blessedly is not covered by a bag of fat." She paused to sigh, thinking of her own knees. "It's correct and beautiful and dainty. Charm! If ever I beheld the charm of flesh it is now. I wonder who she is."

Stanley Patterson, gazing ardently, took up his half of the chorus.

"Notice that the round muscle pads on the inner sides which make most women appear knock-kneed are missing? They're boy's legs, firm and sure—"

"And sweet woman's legs, soft and round," his wife hastened to balance. "And look, Stanley! See how she walks on the balls of her feet. It makes her seem light as swan's-down. Each step seems just a little above the earth, and each other step seems just a little higher above until you get the impression she is flying, or just about to rise and begin flying . . ."

So Stanley and Mrs. Patterson. But they were artists, with eyes therefore unlike the next batteries of human eyes Ida Barton was compelled to run, and that laired on the Outrigger *lanais* (verandas) and in the hau-tree shade of the closely adjoining Seaside. The majority of the Outrigger audience was composed, not of tourist guests, but of club members and old-timers in Hawaii. And even the old-times woman gasped.

"It's positively indecent," said Mrs. Hanley Black to her husband, herself a too-stout-in-the-middle matron of forty-five, who had been born in the Hawaiian Islands and who had never heard of Ostend.

Hanley Black surveyed his wife's criminal shapelessness and voluminousness of ante-diluvian, New England swimming dress with a withering, contemplative eye. They had been married a sufficient number of years for him frankly to utter his judgment:

"That strange woman's suit makes your own look indecent. You appear as a creature shameful, under a grotesqueness of apparel striving to hide some secret awfulness."

"She carries her body like a Spanish dancer," Mrs. Patterson said to her husband, for the pair of them had waded the little stream in pursuit of the vision.

"By George, she does," Stanley Patterson concurred. "Reminds me of Estrellita. Torso just well enough forward, slender waist, not too lean in the stomach, and with muscles like some lad boxer's armoring that stomach to fearlessness. She has to have them to carry herself that way and to balance the back muscles. See that muscled curve of the back! It's Estrellita's."

"How tall would you say?" his wife queried.

"There she deceives," was the appraised answer. "She might be five feet one, or five feet three or four. It's that way she has of walking that you described as almost about to fly."

"Yes, that's it," Mrs. Patterson concurred. "It's her energy, her seemingness of being on tiptoe with rising vitality."

Stanley Patterson considered for a space.

"That's it," he enounced. "She is a little thing, I'll give her five two in her stockings. And I'll weigh her a mere one hundred and ten, or eight, or fifteen at the outside."

"She won't weigh a hundred and ten," his wife declared with conviction.

"And with her clothes on, plus her carriage (which is builded of her vitality and will), I'll wager she'd never impress any one with her smallness."

"I know her type," his wife nodded. "You meet her out and you have the sense that, while not exactly a fine, large woman, she's a whole lot larger than the average. And now, age?"

"I'll give you best, there," he parried.

"She might be twenty-five, she might be thirty-eight . . ."

But Stanley Patterson had impolitely forgotten to listen.

"It's not her legs alone," he cried on enthusiastically. "It's the all of her. Look at the delicacy of that forearm. And the swell of line to the shoulder. And that biceps! It's alive. Dollars to drowned kittens she can flex a respectable knot of it . . ."

No woman, much less an Ida Barton, could have been unconscious of the effect she was producing along Waikiki Beach. Instead of making her happy in the small vanity way, it irritated her.

"The cats," she laughed to her husband. "And to think I was born here an almost even third of a century ago! But they weren't nasty then. Maybe because there weren't any tourists. Why, Lee, I learned to swim right here on this beach in front of the Outrigger. We used to come out with daddy for vacations and for week-ends and sort of camp out in a grass house that stood right where the Outrigger ladies serve tea now. And centipedes fell out of the thatch on us while we slept, and we all ate poi and opihis and raw aku, and nobody wore much of anything for the swimming and squidding, and there was no real road to town. I remember times of big rain when it was so flooded we had to go in by canoe, out through the reef and in by Honolulu harbor."

"Remember," Lee Barton added, "it was just about that time that the youngster that became me arrived here for a few weeks' stay on our way around. I must have seen you on the beach at that very time—one of the kiddies that swam like fishes. Why, merciful me, the women here were all riding cross saddle, and that was long before the rest of the social female world outgrew its immodesty and came around to sitting simultaneously on both sides of a horse. I learned to swim on the beach here at that time myself. You and I may even have tried body surfing on the same waves, or I may have splashed a handful of water into your mouth and been rewarded by your sticking out your tongue at me—"

Interrupted by an audible gasp of shock from a spinster-appearing female sunning herself hard by and angularly in the sand in a swimming suit monstrously unbeautiful, Lee Barton was aware of an involuntary and almost perceptible stiffening on the part of his wife. . . .

But all, or nearly all on the beach, forgave Ida Barton her suit and form when she took the water. A touch of her hand on her husband's arm, indication and challenge in her laughing face, and the two ran as one for half a dozen paces and leaped as one from the hardwet sand of the beach, their bodies describing flat arches of flight ere the water was entered.

There are two surfs at Waikiki: the big, bearded-man surf that roars far out beyond the diving stage; the smaller, gentler, wahine, or woman, surf that breaks upon the shore itself. Here is a great shallowness, where one may wade a hundred or several hundred feet to get beyond depth. Yet, with a good surf on outside, the wahine surf can break three or four feet, so that, close in against the shore, the hard-sand bottom may be three feet or three inches under the welter of surface foam. To dive from the beach into this, to fly into the air off racing feet, turn in mid-flight so that heels are up and head is down, and so to enter the water head-first, requires wisdom of waves, timing of waves and a trained deftness in entering such unstable depths of water with pretty, unapprehensive, head-first cleavage while at the same time making the shallowest possible of dives.

It is a sweet and pretty and daring trick, not learned in a day nor learned at all without many a mild bump on the bottom or close shave of fractured skull or broken neck. Here, on the spot where the Bartons so beautifully dived, two days earlier a Stanford track athlete had broken his neck. His had been an error in timing the rise and subsidence of a wahine wave.

"A professional," Mrs. Hanley Black sneered to her husband at Ida Barton's feat.

"Some vaudeville tank girl," was one of the similar remarks with which the women in the shade complacently reassured one another; finding, by way of the weird mental processes of self-illusion, a great satisfaction in the money caste distinction between one who worked for what she ate and themselves who did not work for what they ate.

It was a day of heavy surf on Waikiki. In the wahine surf it was boisterous enough for good swimmers. But out beyond, in the *Kanaka*, or man, surf, no one ventured. Not that the score or more of young surf riders loafing on the beach could not venture there, or were afraid to venture there; but because their biggest outrigger canoes would have been swamped, and their surf boards would have been overwhelmed in the too-immense overtopple and downfall of the thundering monsters. They themselves, most of them, could have swum, for man can swim through breakers which canoes and surf boards cannot surmount; but to ride the backs of the waves, rise out of the foam to stand full length in the air above and with heels winged with the swiftness of horses to fly shoreward, was what made sport for them and brought them out from Honolulu to Waikiki.

The captain of Number Nine canoe, himself a charter member of the Outrigger and a many-times medalist in long-distance swimming, had missed seeing the Bartons take the water and first glimpsed them beyond the last festoon of bathers who clung to the life lines. From then on, from his vantage of the upstairs lanai, he kept his eyes on them. When they continued out past the steel diving stage where a few of the hardiest divers disported, he muttered vexedly under his breath, "damned *malahinis!*"

Now *malahini* means newcomer, tenderfoot; and, despite the prettiness of their stroke, he knew that none except malahinis would venture into the racing channel beyond the diving stage. Hence, the vexation of the captain of Number Nine. He descended to the beach, with a low word here and there picked a crew of the strongest surfers, and returned to the lanai with a pair of binoculars. Quite casually, the crew, six of them, carried Number Nine to the water's edge, saw paddles and everything in order for a quick launching, and lolled about carelessly on the sand. They were guilty of not advertising. that anything untoward was afoot, although they did steal glances up to their captain straining through the binoculars.

What made the channel was the fresh-water stream. Coral cannot abide fresh water. What made the channel race was the immense shoreward surf-fling of the sea. Unable to remain flung up on the beach, pounded ever back toward the beach by the perpetual shoreward rush of the Kanaka surf, the up-piled water escaped to the sea by way of the channel and in the form of undertow along the bottom under the breakers. Even in the channel the waves broke big, but not with the magnificent bigness of terror as to right and left. So it was that a canoe or a comparatively strong swimmer could dare the channel. But the swimmer must be a strong swimmer indeed who could successfully buck the current in. Wherefore the captain of Number Nine continued his vigil and his muttered damnation of malahinis, disgust-edly sure that these two malahinis would compel him to launch Number Nine and go after them when they found the current too strong to swim in against. As for himself, caught in their predicament, he would have veered to the left toward Diamond Head and come in on the shoreward fling of the Kanaka surf. But then, he was no one other than himself, a bronze Hercules of twenty-two, the whitest blood man ever burned to mahogany-brown by a subtropic sun, with body and lines and muscles very much resembling the wonderful ones of Duke Kahanamoku. In a hundred yards the world cham-pion could invariably beat him a second flat; but over a distance of miles he could swim circles around the champion.

No one of the many hundreds on the beach, with the exception of the captain and his crew, knew that the Bartons had passed beyond the diving stage. All who had watched them start to swim out had taken for granted that they had joined the others on the stage.

The captain suddenly sprang upon the railing of the lanai, held on to a pillar with one hand, and again picked up the two specks of heads through the glasses. His surmise was verified. The two fools had veered out of the channel toward Diamond Head and were directly seaward of the Kana-ka surf. Worse, as he looked, they were starting to come in through the Kanaka surf.

He glanced down quickly to the canoe, and even as he glanced, and as the apparently loafing members quietly arose and took their places by the canoe for the launching, he achieved judgment. Before the canoe could get abreast in the channel, all would be over with the man and woman. And, granted that it could get abreast of them, the moment it ventured into the Kanaka surf it would be swamped, and a sorry chance would the strongest swimmer of them have of rescuing a person pounding to pulp on the bottom under the smashes of the great bearded ones.

The captain saw the first Kanaka wave, large of itself but small among its fellows, lift seaward behind the two speck swimmers. Then he saw them strike a crawl stroke, side by side, faces downward, full lengths outstretched on surface, their feet sculling like propellers and their arms flailing in rap-id overhand strokes as they spurted speed to approximate the speed of the overtaking wave, so that, when overtaken, they would become part of the wave and travel with it instead of being left behind it. Thus, if they were coolly skilled enough to ride outstretched on the surface and the forward face of the crest instead of being flung and crumpled or driven head-first to bottom, they would dash shoreward, not propelled by their own energy but by the energy of the wave into which they had become incorporated.

And they did it! "*Some* swimmers," the captain of Number Nine made announcement to himself under his breath. He continued to gaze eagerly. The best of swimmers could hold such a wave for several hundred feet. But could they? If they did, they would be a third of the way through the perils they had challenged. But, not unexpected by him, the woman failed first, her body not presenting the larger surfaces that her husband's did. At the end of seventy feet she was overwhelmed, being driven downward and out of sight by the tons of water in the overtopple. Her husband followed, and both ap-peared swimming beyond the wave they had lost.

The captain saw the next wave first. "If they try to body-surf on that, *good* night," he muttered; for he knew the swimmer did not live who would tackle it. Beardless itself, it was father of all bearded ones, a mile long, rising up far out beyond where the others rose, towering its solid bulk higher and higher till it blotted out the horizon and was a giant among its fellows ere its beard began to grow as it thinned its crest to the overcurl.

But it was evident that the man and woman knew big water. No racing stroke did they make in advance of the wave. The captain inwardly applauded as he saw them turn and face the wave and wait for it. It was a picture that of all on the beach he alone saw, wonderfully distinct and vivid in the magnification of the binoculars. The wall of the wave was truly a wall, mounting, ever mounting, and thinning, far up, to a transparency of the colors of the setting sun shooting athwart all the green and blue of it. The green thinned to lighter green that merged blue even as he looked. But it was a blue gem brilliant with innumerable sparkle points of rose and gold flashed through it by the sun. On and up, to the sprouting beard of growing crest, the color orgy increased until it was a kaleidoscopic effervescence of transfusing rainbows.

Against the face of the wave showed the heads of the man and woman like two sheer specks. Specks they were, of the quick, adventuring among the blind elemental forces, daring the Titanic buffets of the sea. The weight of the downfall of that father of waves, even then imminent above their heads, could stun a man or break the fragile bones of a woman. The captain of Number Nine was unconscious that he was holding his breath. He was oblivious of the man. It was the woman. Did she lose her head or courage, or misplay her muscular part for a moment, she could be hurled a hundred feet by that giant buffet and left wrenched, helpless, and breathless to be pulped on the coral bottom and sucked out by the undertow to be battened on by the fish sharks too cowardly to take their human meat alive.

Why didn't they dive deep, and with plenty of time, the captain wanted to know, instead of waiting till the last tick of safety and the first tick of peril were one? He saw the woman turn her head and laugh to the man, and his head turn in response. Above them, overhanging them, as they mounted the body of the wave, the beard, creaming white, then frothing into rose and gold, tossed upward into a spray of jewels. The crisp offshore trade wind caught the beard's fringes and blew them backward and upward yards and yards into the air. It was then, side by side, and six feet apart, that they dived straight under the overcurl even then disintegrating to chaos and falling. Like insects disappearing into the convolutions of some gorgeous, gigantic orchid, so they disappeared, as beard and crest and spray and jewels, in many tons, crashed and thundered down just where they had disappeared the moment before but where they were no longer.

Beyond the wave they had gone through they finally showed, side by side, still six feet apart, swimming shoreward with a steady stroke until the next wave should make them body-surf it or face and pierce it. The captain of Number Nine waved his hand to his crew in dismissal and sat down on the lanai railing, feeling vaguely tired, and still watching the swimmers through his glasses.

"Whoever and whatever they are," he murmured, "they aren't malahinis. They simply can't be malahinis."

JACK LONDON (1876-1916) *grew up poor, was jailed for vagrancy, worked as a war correspondent, a gold-seeker, oyster pirate–and writer. At his height, he was one of the best-known authors in the world. Among his more than twenty novels are* The Call of the Wild; The Sea-Wolf; White Fang; Smoke Bellew; Martin Eden; *and* Burning Daylight. *He made three extended visits to Hawai'i, and wrote a good many short stories set in the islands, collected in* On the Makaloa Mat *and* The House of Pride.

Irving Berlin
from STOP!LOOK!LISTEN!

ACT 1

Version I:
Scene I: Honolulu, full stage
Scene II: Tropical drop: Hawaiian specialty
Scene III: Bathing houses, Song, VIOLETTE *and girls: "Take off a Little Bit."*
Scene IV: Landscape drop, garden, cottage @ right
   Duet: Teach Me to Love
   Sheriff specialty.

Version II:
Scene I: Bathing drop—"Take off a Little Bit"
Scene II: Farm House—Tempests and Sunshine Duet—Very Good Eddie Doyle and
   Dixon—Policeman specialty
Melody
Scene III: Moonlight drop—Hawaiian orchestra
Scene IV: Honolulu set—segue into Hula Hula
(Enter LALOR *with bicycle chair—Exit* LALOR *with* MRS. MORRISON *into hut;;Enter*
   SANTLEY *w/girls. Meets* MLLE GABY. *Song: "When I'm out with You."*
All exit. Enter DOYLE *and* DIXON. *Hula Hula business—they meet* FOX, *then*
   Lalor—Squish scene FOX *and* LALOR *exit leaving* DOYLE *and* DIXON *for Coon*

Specialty—after song, DOYLE *and* DIXON *exit—Entrance of* SANTLEY *with girls leading to USA number which finishes the act.*

Version III:
I: Honolulu chorus
II: "Teach Me How to Love"—Tempest and Sunshine
III: Sheriffs—Doyle and Dixon
IV: "When I'm out with You"—Santley and Gaby
V: Hawaiian sequence—Wheaton
VI: "Take a Little off"—Gaby
VII: Authors and Composers Foundry—Doyle and Dixon and Young
VIII: Melodrama (everyone) . . .

Act I

CONNOR: By George, this is funny. Quince Queen. A letter from a pal of mine in Honolulu. Listen: There is a girl out here you ought to see. Great looker. Nice voice. Peach of a dancer. Talent to burn. With a little booming she would be a great star in America.

COYNE: The town is going daffy over Hawaiian music. We'll go there and hear those wonderful native songs and you *(to* STEELE*)* shall compose them.

VIOLETTE: But please, where do I come in?

CONNOR: You will be the girl in Honolulu . . .

Act II

GIDEON: Do you understand Sandwich?

CONNOR: Do I? All the dialects—ham, tongue—all of em—
    (to STEELE *and* AYERS*)*—Hoochee-coochee-chinchilla?

STEELE: Back-sheesh Hashish Come-all-ye—Tush!

AYERS: Wulla-mulla Connemarra Squish.

CONNOR: I know these Russian towns but don't get the Squish

HORN: Squish means the police station is right down back of the post office.

GIDEON: Ask them if they know of this letter.

HORN: Tuscaloosa Ashtabula Ackyu acky ack.

AYERS: Mugaboola Squish.

GIDEON: Squish. Yes, so you said, we get to the police station back of the post office.

CONNOR: Not at all, in this case Squich means they don't like your looks and they will put a tarantula under your pillow.

GIDEON: Tell them nix on the Squish.

HORN: Sastree Simachee Singalacha Basy-ed/

STEELE: Lackawana Koko-Kola Ow. Ow. Ow . . .

GIDEON: Hey, Melican man lookee for Police Station. Muchee copper. You sabe?

CONNOR: Where do you think you are, a laundry? . . .

Hawaiian GIRL enters, comes in practicing a Hawaiian dance, pays no attention to GIDEON who admires her. He wants to flirt—but looks off to see if MOTHER is looking. As she in her practice lifts her skirts, GIDEON speaks:

GIDEON: Do you know you're a very pretty girl? You're what I would call a tropical exotic.

GIRL pantomimes: no understand.

GIDEON: Is there a quiet little cafe round here where you and I *(pantomimes a drink). GIRL shakes head.*

GIDEON: Well, you and I could get a taxi and take a little whirl around the nearest volcano.

GIRL shakes head.

MOTHER enters. GIDEON pretends not to have noticed.

GIDEON *to GIRL*: As I was saying, you poor benighted heathen, keep to the straight and narrow path and love your missionaries, rare or well done, it doesn't matter if you were my own daughter. *(pretends to see MOTHER for the first time).*

GIDEON: Ah, it's Mother.

MA: Who is this person?

GIDEON: Hannah Lulu. I was just going to give this little heathen a little fatherly advice.

Prelude to song. Hawaiian girl off.
Singer of song enters—
Hulu Hulu song.

Underneath the sad Hawaiian moon
  Chorus: Tell us about the sad moon
Where the sad Hawaiians love to spoon
  Chorus: Tell us the way they love to spoon
While the uka-lal-lies strum a tune
  Chorus: While the uka-lal-lies strum a tune
You can see them doing that hula hula.

Have you seen them do the hula
in Honolulu
the way they do
I know id you learned

how to do the hula hula
you'd be in Honolulu
doing the hula too.

I can teach you how to do the dance.
  Chorus: no one would ever think you knew it
Tell me you like to take a chance
  Chorus: show us the way and we will do it
Shake your head and quietly advance

Chorus: Show us some more and we'll go to it.
In another minute you'll be doing it . . .

> *Enter* STEELE *and* AYERS *as two coons—they come in to a dance step, or enter with an adlib quarrel as to who thought of the idea first (of disguising themselves).*

CONNOR *enters and watches them*: As I live, it's Frank Steele, the great composer *(shakes hands)* and Rob Ayers the book maker.

AYERS *(chagrined)*: Gee, this disguise must be a wash.

STEELE: You thought of it. I told you it was no good.

CONNOR: What's the idea?

AYERS: Our scheme to get Mary away from Gideon Gay.

STEELE: We must take her back to New York to play in our opera.

CONNOR: But why the Pittsburg complexion?

AYERS: We're disguised as a couple of natives.

CONNOR: You fellows remind me of the harmless coffee—everything extracted from the bean. The natives here don't get their clothes on 8th Avenue.

AYERS & STEELE: Don't they?

> *Segue into A Pair of Ordinary Coons*

We were born in New Orleans
Our mammies raised us there
We represent a race of a dusky face
and kinky inky hair.
We've traveled all around the map
We've been to every place
And we've found it's most convenient
To be traveling with a dark brown face.

In Honolulu, we pass as Hawaiians

Though we came from New Orleans
We go to South America
We're a couple of Argentines
They think we're natives—while passing through India
We sing their native tunes
and in Araby
We make them think we're Arabians
We pass through all these places on the faces
of a pair of ordinary coons . . .

IRVING BERLIN (1888-1989), *who lived to be 101, wrote words and music for vaudeville, Tin Pan Alley, Broadway shows, and Hollywood movies—more than three thousand songs, including classics such as "Alexander's Ragtime Band," "White Christmas," "There's No Business Like Show Business," "Puttin' on the Ritz," and "God Bless America."* Stop! Look! Listen! *which premiered in December, 1915, was his second Broadway musical. (He wrote 21 altogether, and 17 film scores.) The libretto excerpts here are from typescript production notes in the collection of the New York Public Library for the Performing Arts, at Lincoln Center.*

Don Blanding
"WAIKIKI SKIN-GAME"

The sea is as blue as a peacock *lei*
At Waikiki where the tourists play,
Those people who flock from far and near
In search of tropical atmosphere,
And what they seek they're bound to find
Either ready-made or the native kind.
    There are fat and thin and short and tall,
    The wild waves lave them, one and all,
    While the moon and the sun in the Island style
    Greet everyone with a friendly smile.
    There are people of every breed and class,
    Waikiki widows . . . both sod and grass,
    Gay, flirtatious and full of frills
    In search of husbands or maybe thrills.
There are streamlined maidens from Hollywood
With streamlined morals . . . though *some* are good.
There are rollicking sailors with tattooed arms

Who eye the sirens with curvey charms.
There are strutty fellows who snort and prance
And show more skin than a strip-tease dance,

There are Willowy Willies and Hairy Apes
With beefy Physical Culture shapes
Who flex their muscles and bulge their chests.
They are Waikiki's outstanding pests.
There are banker, bakers and bawds and prudes,
The chastely-clads and the demi-nudes,
    There are giddy swarms of red-hot mamas
    Who promenade in loud pajamas.
    There are young-old women with remade faces
    Whose figures bulge in the oddest places,
    They lie in the shade and preen and frisk
    And paint their toes like an *odalisque*.
There's the anxious Ma with the comely daughter;
Do you think they dunk in the lovely water?
Not much! They're out to get a man
Though it may take time . . . like a Five-Year Plan.

There are grandmamas and nice old aunties
And girls in batik "bras" and panties.
There are paunchy men with greasy eyes
And Busty Berthas with lardy thighs.
There are lonely women who sigh and swoon
When they feel the lure of the South Sea Moon.
    A day at the beach is a revelation
    In where folks put their vaccination.
    There are young and old and middle-aged,
    Embalmed stale cuties who can't be gauaged.
    There are plumpish ones who lie on their faces
    And look like the start of stratosphere races.
    There are nice plain folk who sit and bask
    And enjoy it all . . . that's all they ask
    As the surf-board riders poise and sway
    And race the waves through the drenching spray.
These tourists lie in the sun and broil
And smear themselves with cocoanut oil.
They turn like fowls on a roasting spit
In bathing suits of a skin-tight fit.

Despite all warning to take things slow
They loll in the sunshine, row on row,
They jump like fleas or lie like dead
'Till every last one of them turns bright red
Then fret and fume when the fun begins
And they blister and peel and shed their skins,
Their backs get raw and their tummies sore
 But they go right back to get some more.
 It may take time and it may be soon
 But they never stop 'til they're deep maroon.
 The new arrivals look forlorn
 As they do a shy September Morn
 In shame for their pallid oyster hue
 But it only takes a day or two
 To turn to the proper sun-tan shade,
 Then *they* belong to the Beach Brigade.
It's a funny place . . . this Waikiki.
Oh, the things you hear and the sights you see
As you lie like a stranded jellyfish
And join in the gossips' daily dish
Of Who Is Whose and Who Are They,
Of Where Are They From and Where Do They Stay.
And the sea is as blue as a peacock *lei*
And the clouds drift by in their aimless way
While the rainbows glimmer against the sky
And the winds in the palm-fronds moan and sigh.
 There's a golden sun and a silver moon
 And the steel guitars to sob and croon
 While the beach-boys loll in the *hau*-tree's shade
 And warble their South Sea serenade.
 There are things you'll like and things you won't.
 There are things you do and things you don't.
 It's a funny, fantastic *potpourri*
 But a grand old beach . . . this Waikiki.

Don Blanding

"CAMERA ANGLE, WAIKIKI BEACH"

Beneath the spreading banyan tree
The lady tourist stands,
A flower lei about her neck,
A kodak in her hands.
She stoops to focus on the view,
Her interest is intense.
How little does she realize
The view her rear presents.

The World Turning

Nothing had prepared me for Honolulu . . . I myself have seen it . . . The very new rubs shoulders with the immeasurably old . . . Electric cars rumble noisily along the streets . . . The valley is a woman lying on her back . . . Joe Garland is half kanaka . . . Every third house is a bank . . . My bare feet on hard earth . . . Carved idols with abalone-shell eyes . . . Hawaiian singing boys . . . The broad lanai of the Seaside . . . Out of the rising sun . . . Aw, it's just another air raid practice . . . You buggahs, you flying buggahs . . . Pearl Harbor is a sea of blood . . . Martial law and gas masks . . . All of Honolulu was black . . . Barbed wire barricades . . . They pressed my fingers into ink . . . The MPS were tough babies down there . . . Guards see you, they going shoot . . . A bayonet poked at my throat . . . Hot times on Hotel Street . . . My dad stands in a khaki uniform . . . Dance with me, soldier boy . . . Wave him goodbye . . . Back from the wars . . . Boy, Honolulu one dead town . . . . Ghosts of the past, dreams of the future . . . Which way is up? . . . This Japanese girl going around with a haole man . . . Barbara Hutton checks in at the Royal Hawaiian . . . Drive da tourists around da island . . . Stuck down there . . . If he fire me, he fire me . . . Dis place just like one prison . . . You like live in dis alley all your life? . . . Where are the Golden Men? . . .

Marc Blitzstein
from THE CRADLE WILL ROCK

The action takes place in Steeltown, U. S. A., on the night of a union drive.
Scene: Lawn of Mr. Mister's home

EDITOR DAILY:
Have you thought of Honolulu
Where your boredom would be banned?
Bid your family toodle-oo-loo,
Sail away to that fair land!
That's just the isle for you—
And you'll have your work, too.
(JUNIOR is startled.)
A little scribbling on our father's journal.
Oh, nothing ever happens over there!

MR. MISTER:
Son, they say the climate's fresh and vernal.

SISTER:
You could learn to play the ukelele.

MR. MISTER:
Now, Junior, listen to Editor Daily.

EDITOR DAILY:
Have you been to Honolulu?

JUNIOR:
(Up to this point perfectly sodden.)
Are the women nice down there?

EDITOR DAILY:
(Ever-ready.)
Demure, and so high born,
Just pure September Morn.

JUNIOR:
I don't care if they're high born
Just as long as they're highbreasted.

MR. MISTER:
Junior, please don't get arrested!

EDITOR DAILY:
Picture when the sun sets in Oahu;
(JUNIOR is blank.)
That's the island Honolulu's on;
Dusky maidens dancing in the starlight—

SISTER:
Wasn't some young debutante seduced there?

MR. MISTER:
You'd be our official correspondent.

SISTER:
(Almost tenderly.)
You're a fool if you don't go now.

JUNIOR:
(Fortissimo; the moonface bursts into radiance without warning.)
La la la-la-la la.
La la la-la-la la.

EDITOR DAILY, MR. MISTER, SISTER:
(In harmony; triumphantly.)
Junior's going to go to Honolulu!
Junior's going to be a journalist!

JUNIOR:
Can I drive over eighty miles an hour?

EDITOR DAILY:
(Undaunted.)
Ruby lips are waiting to be kissed!

SISTER:
(Not much on geography, but with the right idea.)
I'd be satisfied with one big Zulu.

EDITOR DAILY:
Chocolate arms are open like a flower.

JUNIOR:
(Dreamy.)
How the hell do you spell Honolulu?

EDITOR DAILY, MR. MISTER, SISTER:
(They whisper it, not disturbing the dream.)
Junior's going to be a journalist!

EDITOR DAILY:
There's a woman there who wants you . . .

JUNIOR:
(Fortissimo and sudden again; the baby is given the rattle.)
La la la-la-la la.
La la la-la-la la.

EDITOR DAILY:
Have you been to Honolulu?
Sail away to that fair land . . .
Dusky maidens in the starlight . . .

Fadeout

MARC BLITZSTEIN (1905-1964) *was a child prodigy classical pianist who grew up to be a composer. In the Great Depression years of the 1930s, he was associated with left-wing creative artists in New York, His socially conscious opera,* The Cradle Will Rock, *directed by Orson Welles, was sensationally closed down by the government hours before its opening night on Broadway in 1937. Blitztstein is best known for his English-language adaptation of* The Threepenny Opera *by Bertolt Brecht and Kurt Weill, which has had hundreds of productions all over the world and was the source of the hit song "Mack the Knife."*

W. Somerset Maugham
from "HONOLULU"

Nothing had prepared me for Honolulu. It is so far away from Europe, it is reached after so long a journey from San Francisco, so strange and so charming associations are attached to the name, that at first I could hardly believe my eyes. I do not know that I had formed in my mind any very exact picture of what I expected, but what I found caused me a great surprise. It is a typical western city. Shacks are cheek by jowl with stone mansions; dilapidated frame houses stand next door to smart stores with plate glass windows; electric cars rumble noisily along the streets; and motors, Fords, Buicks, Packards, line the pavement. The shops are filled with all the necessities of American civilisation. Every third house is a bank and every fifth the agency of a steamship company.

Along the streets crowd an unimaginable assortment of people. The Americans, ignoring the climate, wear black coats and high, starched collars, straw hats, soft hats, and bowlers. The Kanakas, pale brown, with crisp hair, have nothing on but a shirt and a pair of trousers; but the half-breeds are very smart with flaring ties and patent leather boots. The Japanese, with their obsequious smile, are neat and trim in white duck, while their women walk a step or two behind them, in native dress, with a baby on their backs. The Japanese children, in bright coloured frocks, their little heads shaven, look like quaint dolls. Then there are the Chinese. The men, fat and prosperous, wear their American clothes oddly, but the women are enchanting with their tightly-dressed black hair, so neat that you feel it can never be disarranged, and they are very clean in their tunics and trousers, white, or powder blue, or black. Lastly there are the Filipinos, the men in huge straw hats, the women in bright yellow muslin with great puffed sleeves.

It is the meeting place of East and West. The very new rubs shoulders with the immeasurably old. And if you have not found the romance you expected you have come upon something singularly intriguing. All these strange people live close to each other, with different languages and different thoughts; they believe in different gods and they have different values; two passions alone they share, love and hunger. And somehow as you watch them you have an impression of extraordinary vitality. Though the air is so soft and the sky so blue, you have, I know not why, a feeling of something hotly passionate that beats like a throbbing pulse through the crowd.

Though the native policeman at the corner, standing on a platform, with a white club to direct the traffic, gives the scene an air of respectability, you cannot but feel that it is a respectability only of the surface; a little below there is darkness and mystery. It gives you just that thrill, with a little catch at the heart, that you have when at night in the forest the silence trembles on a sudden with the low, insistent beating of a drum. You are all expectant of I know not what.

W. SOMERSET MAUGHAM (1874-1965) *was a greatly successful short story writer, novelist and playwright (and during World War I a spy for British Intelligence). His travels took him to Russia, East Asia, and the South Pacifc. Among his plays are* Lady Frederick; The Circle; Our Betters; *and* The Constant Wife. *His novels include* Of Human Bondage; The Moon and Sixpence; Cakes and Ale; *and* The Razor's Edge.

Jack London

"THE HOUSE OF PRIDE"

P ERCIVAL FORD wondered why he had come. He did not dance. He did not care much for army people. Yet he knew them all—gliding and revolving there on the broad *lanai* of the Seaside, the officers in their fresh-starched uniforms of white, the civilians in white and black, and the women bare of shoulders and arms. After two years in Honolulu the Twentieth was departing to its new station in Alaska, and Percival Ford, as one of the big men of the Islands, could not help knowing the officers and their women.

But between knowing and liking was a vast gulf. The army women frightened him just a little. They were in ways quite different from the women he liked best—the elderly women, the spinsters and the bespectacled maidens, and the very serious women of all ages whom he met on church and library and kindergarten committees, who came meekly to him for contributions and advice. He ruled those women by virtue of his superior mentality, his great wealth, and the high place he occupied in the commercial baronage of Hawaii. And he was not afraid of them in the least. Sex, with them, was not obtrusive. Yes, that was it. There was in them something else, or more, than the assertive grossness of life. He was fastidious; he acknowledged that to himself; and these army women, with their bare shoulders and naked arms, their straight-looking eyes, their vitality and challenging femaleness, jarred upon his sensibilities.

Nor did he get on better with the army men, who took life lightly, drinking and smoking and swearing their way through life and asserting the essential grossness of flesh no less shamelessly than their women. He was always uncomfortable in the company of the army men. They seemed uncomfortable, too. And he felt, always, that they were laughing at him up their sleeves, or pitying him, or tolerating him. Then, too, they seemed, by mere contiguity, to emphasize a lack in him, to call attention to that in them which he did not possess and which he thanked God he did not possess. Faugh! They were like their women!

In fact, Percival Ford was no more a woman's man than he was a man's man. A glance at him told the reason. He had a good constitution, never was on intimate terms with sickness, nor even mild disorders; but he lacked vitality. His was a negative organism. No blood with a ferment in it could have nourished and shaped that long and narrow face, those thin lips, lean cheeks, and the small, sharp eyes. The thatch of hair, dust-colored, straight and sparse, advertised the niggard soil, as did the nose, thin, delicately mod-eled, and just hinting the suggestion of a beak. His meagre blood had denied him much of life, and permitted him to be an extremist in one thing only, which thing was righteousness. Over right conduct he pondered and agonized, and that he should do right was as necessary to his nature as loving and being loved were necessary to commoner clay.

He was sitting under the algaroba trees between the *lanai* and the beach. His eyes wandered over the dancers and he turned his head away and gazed seaward across the mellow-sounding surf to the Southern Cross burning low on the horizon. He was irritated by the bare shoulders and arms of the women. If he had a daughter he would never permit it, never. But his hypothesis was the sheerest abstraction. The thought process had been accompanied by no inner vision of that daughter. He did not see a daughter with arms and shoulders. Instead, he smiled at the remote contingency of marriage. He was thirty-five, and, having had no personal experience of love, he looked upon it, not as mythical, but as bestial. Anybody could marry. The Japanese and Chinese coolies, toiling on the sugar plantations and in the rice-fields, married. They invariably married at the first opportunity. It was because they were so low in the scale of life. There was nothing else for them to do. They were like the army men and women. But for him there were other and higher things. He was different from them—from all of them. He was proud of how he happened to be. He had come of no petty love-match. He had come of lofty conception of duty and of devotion to a cause. His father had not married for love. Love was a madness that had never perturbed Isaac Ford. When he answered the call to go to the heathen with the message of life, he had had no thought and no desire for marriage. In this they were alike, his father and he. But the Board of Missions was economical. With New England thrift it weighed and measured and decided that married missionaries were less expensive per capita and more efficacious. So the Board commanded Isaac Ford to marry. Furthermore, it furnished him with a wife, another zealous soul with no thought of marriage, intent only on doing the Lord's work among the heathen. They saw each other for the first time in Boston. The Board brought them together, arranged everything, and by the end of the week they were married and started on the long voyage around the Horn.

Percival Ford was proud that he had come of such a union. He had been born high, and he thought of himself as a spiritual aristocrat. And he was proud of his father. It was a passion with him. The erect, austere figure of Isaac Ford had burned itself upon his pride. On his desk was a miniature of that soldier of the Lord. In his bedroom hung the portrait of Isaac Ford, painted at the time when he had served under the Monarchy as prime minister. Not that Isaac Ford had coveted place and worldly wealth, but that, as prime minister, and, later, as banker, he had been of greater service to the missionary cause. The German crowd, and the English crowd, and all the rest of the trading crowd, had sneered at Isaac Ford as a commercial soul-saver; but he, his son, knew different. When the natives, emerging abruptly from their feudal system, with no conception of the nature and significance of property in land, were letting their broad acres slip through their fingers, it was Isaac Ford who had stepped in between the trading crowd and its prey and taken possession of fat, vast holdings. Small wonder the trading crowd did not like his memory. But he had never looked upon his enormous wealth as his own. He had considered himself God's steward. Out of the revenues he had built schools, and hospitals, and churches. Nor was it his fault that sugar, after the slump, had paid forty per cent; that the bank he founded had prospered into a railroad; and that, among other things, fifty thousand acres of Oahu pasture land, which he had bought for a dollar an acre, grew eight tons of sugar to the acre every eighteen months. No, in all truth Isaac Ford was an heroic figure, fit, so Percival Ford thought privately, to stand beside the statue of Kamehameha I in front of the Judiciary Building. Isaac Ford was gone, but he, his son, carried on the good work at least as inflexibly if not as masterfully.

He turned his eyes back to the *lanai*. What was the difference, he asked himself, between the shameless, grass-girdled *hula* dances and the décolleté dances of the women of his own race? Was there an essential difference? or was it a matter of degree?

As he pondered the problem a hand rested on his shoulder.

"Hello, Ford, what are you doing here? Isn't this a bit festive?"

"I try to be lenient, Dr. Kennedy, even as I look on," Percival Ford answered gravely. "Won't you sit down?"

Dr. Kennedy sat down, clapping his palms sharply. A white-clad Japanese servant answered swiftly.

Scotch and soda was Kennedy's order; then, turning to the other, he said:—

"Of course, I don't ask you."

"But I will take something," Ford said firmly. The doctor's eyes showed surprise, and the servant waited. "Boy, a lemonade, please."

The doctor laughed at it heartily, as a joke on himself, and glanced at the musicians under the hau tree.

"Why, it's the Aloha Orchestra," he said. "I thought they were with the Hawaiian Hotel on Tuesday nights. Some rumpus, I guess."

His eyes paused for a moment and dwelt upon the one who was playing a guitar and singing a Hawaiian song to the accompaniment of all the instruments. His face became grave as he looked at the singer, and it was still grave as he turned it to his companion.

"Look here, Ford, isn't it time you let up on Joe Garland? I understand you are in opposition to the Promotion Committee's sending him to the States on this surf-board proposition, and I've been wanting to speak to you about it. I should have thought you'd be glad to get him out of the country. It would be a good way to end your persecution of him."

"Persecution?" Percival Ford's eyebrows lifted interrogatively.

"Call it by any name you please," Kennedy went on. "You've hounded that poor devil for years. It's not his fault. Even you will admit that."

"Not his fault?" Percival Ford's thin lips drew tightly together for the moment. "Joe Garland is dissolute and idle. He has always been a wastrel, a profligate."

"But that's no reason you should keep on after him the way you do. I've watched you from the beginning. The first thing you did when you returned from college and found him working on the plantation as outside *luna* was to fire him—you with your millions, and he with his sixty dollars a month."

"Not the first thing," Percival Ford said judicially, in the tone he was accustomed to use in committee meetings. "I gave him his warning. The superintendent said he was a capable *luna*. I had no objection to him on that ground. It was what he did outside working hours. He undid my work faster than I could build it up. Of what use were the Sunday schools, the night schools, and the sewing classes, when in the evenings there was Joe Garland with his infernal and eternal tum-tumming of guitar and *ukulele*, his strong drink, and his *hula* dancing? After I warned him, I came upon him—I shall never forget it—came upon him, down at the cabins. It was evening. I could hear the *hula* songs before I saw the scene. And when I did see it, there were the girls, shameless in the moonlight and dancing—the girls upon whom I had worked to teach clean living and right conduct. And there were three girls there, I remember, just graduated from the mission school. Of course I discharged Joe Garland. I know it was the same at Hilo. People said I went out of my way when I persuaded Mason and Fitch to discharge him. But it was the missionaries who requested me to do so. He was undoing their work by his reprehensible example."

"Afterwards, when he got on the railroad, your railroad, he was discharged without cause," Kennedy challenged.

"Not so," was the quick answer. "I had him into my private office and talked with him for half an hour."

"You discharged him for inefficiency?"

"For immoral living, if you please."

Dr. Kennedy laughed with a grating sound. "Who the devil gave it to you to be judge and jury? Does landlordism give you control of the immortal souls of those that toil for you? I have been your physician. Am I to expect tomorrow your ukase that I give up Scotch and soda or your patronage? Bah! Ford, you take life too seriously. Besides, when Joe got into that smuggling scrape (he wasn't in your employ, either), and he sent word to you, asked you to pay his fine, you left him to do his six months hard labor on the reef. Don't forget, you left Joe Garland in the lurch that time. You threw him down, hard; and yet I remember the first day you came to school—we boarded, you were only a day scholar—you had to be initiated. Three times under in the swimming tank—you remember, it was the regular dose every new boy got. And you held back. You denied that you could swim. You were frightened, hysterical—"

"Yes, I know," Percival Ford said slowly. "I was frightened. And it was a lie, for I could swim. . . . And I was frightened."

"And you remember who fought for you? who lied for you harder than you could lie and swore he knew you couldn't swim? Who jumped into the tank and pulled you out after the first under and was nearly drowned for it by the other boys, who had discovered by that time that you *could* swim?"

"Of course I know," the other rejoined coldly. "But a generous act as a boy does not excuse a lifetime of wrong living."

"He has never done wrong to you?—personally and directly, I mean?"

"No," was Percival Ford's answer. "That is what makes my position impregnable. I have no personal spite against him. He is bad, that is all. His life is bad—"

"Which is another way of saying that he does not agree with you in the way life should be lived," the doctor interrupted.

"Have it that way. It is immaterial. He is an idler—"

"With reason," was the interruption, "considering the jobs out of which you have knocked him."

"He is immoral—"

"Oh, hold on now, Ford. Don't go harping on that. You are pure New England stock. Joe Garland is half Kanaka. Your blood is thin. His is warm. Life is one thing to you, another thing to him. He laughs and sings and dances through life, genial, unselfish, childlike, everybody's friend. You go through life like a perambulating prayer-wheel, a friend of nobody but the righteous, and the righteous are those who agree with you as to what is right. And after all, who shall say? You live like an anchorite. Joe Garland lives like a good fellow. Who has extracted the most from life? We are paid to live, you know. When the wages are too meagre we throw up the job, which is the cause, believe me, of all rational suicide. Joe Garland would starve to death on the wages you get from life. You see, he is made differently. So would you starve on his wages, which are singing, and love—"

"Lust, if you will pardon me," was the interruption.

Dr. Kennedy smiled.

"Love, to you, is a word of four letters and a definition which you have extracted from the dictionary. But love, real love, dewy and palpitant and tender, you do not know. If God made you and me, and men and women, believe me he made love, too. But to come back. It's about time you quit hounding Joe Garland. It is not worthy of you, and it is cowardly. The thing for you to do is to reach out and lend him a hand."

"Why I, any more than you?" the other demanded. "Why don't you reach him a hand?"

"I have. I'm reaching him a hand now. I'm trying to get you not to down the Promotion Committee's proposition of sending him away. I got him the job at Hilo with Mason and Fitch. I've got him half a dozen jobs, out of every one of which you drove him. But never mind that. Don't forget one thing—and a little frankness won't hurt you—it is not fair play to saddle another's fault on Joe Garland; and you know that you, least of all, are the man to do it. Why, man, it's not good taste. It's positively indecent."

"Now I don't follow you," Percival Ford answered. "You're up in the air with some obscure scientific theory of heredity and personal irresponsibility. But how any theory can hold Joe Garland irresponsible for his wrongdoings and at the same time hold me personally responsible for them—more responsible than any one else, including Joe Garland—is beyond me."

"It's a matter of delicacy, I suppose, or of taste, that prevents you from following me," Dr. Kennedy snapped out. "It's all very well, for the sake of society, tacitly to ignore some things, but you do more than tacitly ignore."

"What is it, pray, that I tacitly ignore!"

Dr. Kennedy was angry. A deeper red than that of constitutional Scotch and soda suffused his face, as he answered:

"Your father's son."

"Now just what do you mean?"

"Damn it, man, you can't ask me to be plainer spoken than that. But if you will, all right—Isaac's Ford's son—Joe Garland—your brother."

Percival Ford sat quietly, an annoyed and shocked expression on his face. Kennedy looked at him curiously, then, as the slow minutes dragged by, became embarrassed and frightened.

"My God!" he cried finally, "you don't mean to tell me that you didn't know!"

As in answer, Percival Ford's cheeks turned slowly gray.

"It's a ghastly joke," he said; "a ghastly joke."

The doctor had got himself in hand. "Everybody knows it," he said. "I thought you knew it. And since you don't know it, it's time you did, and I'm glad of the chance of setting you straight. Joe Garland and you are brothers —half-brothers."

"It's a lie," Ford cried. "You don't mean it. Joe Garland's mother was Eliza Kunilio." (Dr. Kennedy nodded.) "I remember her well, with her duck pond and *taro* patch. His father was Joseph Garland, the beach-comber." (Dr. Kennedy shook his head.) "He died only two or three years ago. He used to get drunk. There's where Joe got his dissoluteness. There's the heredity for you."

"And nobody told you," Kennedy said wonderingly, after a pause.

"Dr. Kennedy, you have said something terrible, which I cannot allow to pass. You must either prove or, or . . . "

"Prove it yourself. Turn around and look at him. You've got him in profile. Look at his nose. That's Isaac Ford's. Yours is a thin edition of it. That's right. Look. The lines are fuller, but they are all there."

Percival Ford looked at the Kanaka half-breed who played under the *hau* tree, and it seemed, as by some illumination, that he was gazing on a wraith of himself. Feature after feature flashed up an unmistakable resemblance. Or, rather, it was he who was the wraith of that other full-muscled and generously moulded man. And his features, and that other man's features, were all reminiscent of Isaac Ford. And nobody had told him. Every line of Isaac Ford's face he knew. Miniatures, portraits, and photographs of his father were passing in review through his mind, and here and there, over and again, in the face before him, he caught resemblances and vague hints of likeness. It was devil's work that could reproduce the austere features of Isaac Ford in the loose and sensuous features before him. Once, the man turned, and for one flashing instant it seemed to Percival Ford that he saw his father, dead and gone, peering at him out of the face of Joe Garland.

"It's nothing at all," he could faintly hear Dr. Kennedy saying. "They were all mixed up in the old days. You know that. You've seen it all your life. Sailors married queens and begat princesses and all the rest of it. It was the usual thing in the Islands."

"But not with my father," Percival Ford interrupted.

"There you are." Kennedy shrugged his shoulders. "Cosmic sap and smoke of life. Old Isaac Ford was straightlaced and all the rest, and I know there's no explaining it, least of all to himself. He understood it no more than you do. Smoke of life, that's all. And don't forget one thing, Ford. There was a dab of unruly blood in old Isaac Ford, and Joe Garland inherited it—all of it, smoke of life and cosmic sap; while you inherited all of old Isaac's ascetic blood. And just because your blood is cold, well-ordered, and well-disciplined, is no reason that you should frown upon Joe Garland. When Joe Garland undoes the work you do, remember that it is only old Isaac Ford on both sides, undoing with one hand what he does with the other. You are Isaac Ford's right hand, let us say; Joe Garland is his left hand."

Percival Ford made no answer, and in the silence Dr. Kennedy finished his forgotten Scotch and soda. From across the grounds an automobile hooted imperatively.

"There's the machine," Dr. Kennedy said, rising. "I've got to run. I'm sorry I've shaken you up, and at the same time I'm glad. And know one thing, Isaac Ford's dab of unruly blood was remarkably small, and Joe Garland got it all. And one other thing. If your father's left hand offend you, don't smite it off. Besides, Joe is all right. Frankly, if I could choose between you and him to live with me on a desert isle, I'd choose Joe."

Little bare-legged children ran about him, playing, on the grass; but Percival Ford did not see them. He was gazing steadily at the singer under the *hau* tree. He even changed his position once, to get closer. The clerk of the Seaside went by, limping with age and dragging his reluctant feet. He had lived forty years on the Islands. Percival Ford beckoned to him, and the clerk came respectfully, and wondering that he should be noticed by Percival Ford.

"John," Ford said, "I want you to give me some information. Won't you sit down?"

The clerk sat down awkwardly, stunned by the unexpected honor. He blinked at the other and mumbled, "Yes, sir, thank you."

"John, who is Joe Garland?"

The clerk stared at him, blinked, cleared his throat, and said nothing.

"Go on," Percival Ford commanded. "Who is he?"

"You're joking me, sir," the other managed to articulate.

"I spoke to you seriously."

The clerk recoiled from him.

"You don't mean to say you don't know?" he questioned, his question in itself the answer.

"I want to know."

"Why, he's—" John broke off and looked about him helplessly. "Hadn't you better ask somebody else? Everybody thought you knew. We always thought . . . "

"Yes, go ahead."

"We always thought that that was why you had it in for him."

Photographs and miniatures of Isaac Ford were trooping through his son's brain, and ghosts of Isaac Ford seemed in the air about him. "I wish you good night, sir," he could hear the clerk saying, and he saw him beginning to limp away.

"John," he called abruptly.

John came back and stood near him, blinking and nervously moistening his lips.

"You haven't told me yet, you know."

"Oh, about Joe Garland?"

"Yes, about Joe Garland. Who is he?"

"He's your brother, sir, if I say it who shouldn't."

"Thank you, John. Good night."

"And you didn't know?" the old man queried, content to linger, now that the crucial point was past.

"Thank you, John. Good night," was the response.

"Yes, sir, thank you, sir. I think it's going to rain. Good night, sir."

Out of a clear sky, filled only with stars and moonlight, fell a rain so fine and attenuated as to resemble a vapor spray. Nobody minded it; the children played on, running bare-legged over the grass and leaping into the sand; and in a few minutes it was gone. In the southeast, Diamond Head, a black blot, sharply defined, silhouetted its crater-form against the stars. At sleepy intervals the surf flung its foam across the sand to the grass, and far out could be seen the black specks of swimmers under the moon. The voices of the singers, singing a waltz, died away; and in the silence, from somewhere under the trees, arose the laugh of a woman that was a love-cry. It startled Percival Ford, and it reminded him of Dr. Kennedy's phrase. Down by the outrigger canoes, where they lay hauled out on the sand, he saw men and women, Kanakas, reclining languorously, like lotus-eaters, the women in white *holokus*; and against one such *holoku* he saw the dark head of the steersman of the canoe resting upon the woman's shoulder. Farther down, where the strip of sand widened at the entrance to the lagoon, he saw a man and woman walking side by side. As they drew near the light *lanai*, he saw the woman's hand go down to her waist and disengage a girdling arm. And as they passed him, Percival Ford nodded to a captain he knew, and to a major's daughter. Smoke of life, that was it, an ample phrase. And again, from under the dark algaroba tree arose the laugh of a woman that was a love-cry; and past his chair, on the way to bed, a bare-legged youngster was led by a chiding Japanese nurse-maid. The voices of the singers broke softly and meltingly into an Hawaiian love song, and officers and women, with encircling arms, were gliding and whirling on the *lanai*; and once again the woman laughed under the algaroba trees.

And Percival Ford knew only disapproval of it all. He was irritated by the love-laugh of the woman, by the steersman with pillowed head on the white *holoku*, by the couples that walked on the beach, by the officers and women that danced, and by the voices of the singers singing of love, and his brother singing there with them under the *hau* tree. The woman that laughed especially irritated him. A curious train of thought was aroused. He was Isaac Ford's son, and what had happened with Isaac Ford might happen with him. He felt in his cheeks the faint heat of a blush at the thought, and experienced a poignant sense of shame. He was appalled by what was in his blood. It was like learning suddenly that his father had been a leper and that his own blood might bear the taint of that dread disease. Isaac Ford, the austere soldier of the Lord—the old hypocrite! What difference between him and any beach-comber? The house of pride that Percival Ford had builded was tumbling about his ears.

The hours passed, the army people laughed and danced, the native orchestra played on, and Percival Ford wrestled with the abrupt and overwhelming problem that had been thrust upon him. He prayed quietly, his elbow on the table, his head bowed upon his hand, with all the appearance of any tired onlooker. Between the dances the army men and women and the civilians fluttered up to him and buzzed conventionally, and when they went back to the *lanai* he took up his wrestling where he had left it off.

He began to patch together his shattered ideal of Isaac Ford, and for cement he used a cunning and subtle logic. It was of the sort that is compounded in the brain laboratories of egotists, and it worked. It was incontrovertible that his father had been made out of finer clay than those about him; but still, old Isaac had been only in the process of becoming, while he, Percival Ford, had become. As proof of it, he rehabilitated his father and at the same time exalted himself. His lean little ego waxed to colossal proportions. He was great enough to forgive. He glowed at the thought of it. Isaac Ford had been great, but he was greater, for he could forgive Isaac Ford and even restore him to the holy place in his memory, though the place was not quite so holy as it had been. Also, he applauded Isaac Ford for having ignored the outcome of his one step aside. Very well, he, too, would ignore it.

The dance was breaking up. The orchestra had finished "Aloha Oe" and was preparing to go home. Percival Ford clapped his hands for the Japanese servant.

"You will tell that man I want to see him." He said, pointing out Joe Garland. "Tell him come here, now."

Joe Garland approached and halted respectfully several paces away, nervously fingering the guitar which he still carried. The other did not ask him to sit down.

"You are my brother," he said.

"Why, everybody knows that," was the reply, in tones of wonderment.

"Yes, so I understand," Percival Ford said dryly. "But I did not know it till this evening."

The half-brother waited uncomfortably in the silence that followed, during which Percival Ford coolly considered his next utterance.

"You remember that first time I came to school and the boys ducked me?" he asked. "Why did you take my part."

The half-brother smiled bashfully.

"Because you knew?"

"Yes, that was why."

"But I didn't know," Percival Ford said in the same dry fashion.

"Yes," the other said.

Another silence fell. Servants were beginning to put out the lights on the *lanai*.

"You know . . . now," the half-brother said simply.

Percival Ford frowned. Then he looked the other over with a considering eye.

"How much will you take to leave the Islands and never come back?" he demanded.

"And never come back?" Joe Garland faltered. "It is the only land I know. Other lands are cold. I do not know other lands. I have many friends here. In other lands there would not be one voice to say, '*Aloha*, Joe, my boy.'"

"I said never to come back," Percival Ford reiterated. "The *Alameda* sails to-morrow for San Francisco."

Joe Garland was bewildered.

"But why?" he asked. "You know now that we are brothers."

"That is why," was the retort. "As you said yourself, everybody knows. I will make it worth your while."

All awkwardness and embarrassment disappeared from Joe Garland. Birth and station were bridged and reversed.

"You want me to go?" he demanded.

"I want you to go and never to come back," Percival Ford answered.

And in that moment, flashing and fleeting, it was given him to see his brother tower above him like a mountain, and to feel himself dwindle and dwarf to microscopic insignificance. But it is not well for one to see himself truly, nor can one so see himself for long and live; and only for that flashing moment did Percival Ford see himself and his brother in true perspective. The next moment he was mastered by his meagre and insatiable ego.

"As I said, I will make it worth your while. You will not suffer. I will pay you well."

"All right," Joe Garland said. "I'll go."

He started to turn away.

"Joe," the other called. "You see my lawyer tomorrow morning. Five hundred down and two hundred a month as long as you stay away."

"You are very kind," Joe Garland answered softly. "You are too kind. And anyway, I guess I don't want your money. I go tomorrow on the *Alameda*."

He walked away, but did not say good-by.

Percival Ford clapped his hands.

"Boy," he said to the Japanese, "a lemonade."

And over the lemonade he smiled long and contentedly to himself.

Genevieve Taggard
"THE LUAU"

Odor of algarroba, lure of release.
The smell of red lehua and the crisp scent of maile . . .
These words and images will help you after a little.
Hypnotic words emerge and bloom in the mind,
Anaesthetic names . . . Dry buzz of bees
Who make a honey eaten at early breakfast
From a comb like a broken coral . . .
Do dreams foretell the honey? Break the spell.

So I come home in the valley of Kalihi,
My bare feet on hard earth, hibiscus with stamen-tongue
Twirled in my fingers like a paper windmill,
A wheel of color, crimson, the petals large,
Kiss of the petal, tactile, light, intense . . .
Now I am back again. I can touch the children:
My human race, in whom was a human dwelling,
Whose names are all the races—of one skin.
For so our games ran tacit, without blur.
What brings me back with giant steps to them?
What was the feast that woke this fabulous thirst?
What was the summer fruit we found and ate
Boldly, with the children of Adam?

A game and a daily search
In the harvest of trees. We played a parable.
We possessed a valley, devoured the juicy, dense
Jewels of appetite hung in fresco sweeps,
In garlands and in fountains toward the sea.
Mangoes of golden flesh, with turpentine
Peel and odor. Cut plums of inky stain
And the pucker of persimmons. Dates to be got
By stepping up a tree trunk. Coconuts
With custard centers. Rose and custard apple,
Eugenia, pink, lemon and little orange,
Guava seedy and tart, and the hidden poha,
And the sacklike fig, to be ripped, to be seen, to be tasted.
How rasping sweet the suck of sugar cane—
Papaya and banana taken for granted.

With giant steps, in sleep and troubled pain
I return to the fabulous feast, the old communion,
With bodiless hunger and thirst. Why have I come
Away from the adult world where race is war?

Here we are dipping and passing the calabash
In the ceremony of friends; I also;
But in frenzy and pain distort
The simple need, knowing how blood is shed:
                                    To sit together
Drinking the blue ocean, eating the sun
Like a fruit . . .

Fanny Heaslip Lea
"MOON OF NANAKULI"

Nanakuli is a beach. It might, from the liquid, alluring, nonsensical name of it, be a song, or a perfume, or a woman, but it isn't. Although Lewis found all three there one hushed Hawaiian moonrise—after this fashion:

Lewis had been going around the island over the week-end alone, in his battered gray roadster, nursing a soul-scarring grouch. Undoubtedly he had his reasons, but two days of sun and wind and sudden fleeting rains and doubtful roads failed somehow to dislodge them, so that he came at the end, not of a perfect day, but of a sand-smitten, care-ridden Sunday, to the *kiawe* trees that hedge the way to Nanakuli and to the promise, glimmering vaguely through the *kiawes*, of the most perfect strip of ivory beach that he had ever seen.

It was just dusk—road and trees were powdered with shadow. There was an echo of surf in the air.

Lewis knew a sudden overwhelming desire for the sting of the spray on his eyelids, for the coolness of breaking waves on his sunburnt shoulders. He drew the car up at the side of a ditch, got out his bathing suit and a towel, selected in one sweeping glance the thickest clump of trees in sight as a likely dressing room, and plunged across the road.

Behind him loneliness settled, absolute and void. It was dark among the *kiawes*, and unpleasantly thorny. Lewis emerging after a little, straight and slim in his old gray bathing suit, cursed gently but with amazing attention to detail the discomfort of a pricked left heel. Then he came out upon the beach, and the loveliness of Nanakuli took him by the throat and silenced him.

Sunset had faded, only an eerie afterglow remained, smudging the clearness of the western sky with bloodstained gold, against whose dying ardors a line of black volcanic rocks thrust jaggedly, beginning midway of the beach and running down into the water to end in a smother of creaming surf.

Well up the beach, between the rocks and the dark of the *kiawe* trees, there was a shack, grass-roofed and shambling-walled, barely perceptible in the waning light, the one sign of human habitation in a place else free, delicious, wilderness.

Lewis turned away from the shack with a shrug of distaste.

"Squatters," he conjectured idly. "Smelling of stale fish and smoke and palm-tree gin. There every prospect pleases, of course—"

But the beach silenced him once more. To the east of the crescent of sand and over the high black shoulder of a treeless hill a glow was spreading—white fire, lambent, unearthly radiance, deepening with every breath.

Lewis had seen the moon rise before, but he stood there that night on the beach of Nanakuli and felt his heart stumble in his breast before the flawless, astounding magic of the thing. It came slowly, just at first; out of the watch-fire glow, tipping the blackness of the hill, a pairing of silver; then a sickle; then, before a man might catch his breath, a great gleaming beauty of a full moon, ripe with the mischief of all the centuries.

It washed the world in an exquisite pallor like the inside of a pearl—the sea gleamed like a great king's shield. It was then for the first time that Lewis saw the girl seated upon a grim black rock, her dark hair blowing out behind her. She was looking out to sea, and he thought he heard her singing.

"It's the moon, of course. I'm going mad," said Lewis succinctly and started off at once to dispel the illusion. His footsteps made no sound upon the sand. The world was still as death, or a dream.

The girl, however, was real. When Lewis came to the first black ledge of rock and stopped and looked up at her, she turned her head and looked down at him with an equal incredulity, but without a trace of fear.

"Hello!" said Lewis gently.

"Hello!" sad the girl, in the softest mellowest drawl he thought he had ever heard. She did not smile. She only sat there and looked at him and waited.

She wore a flimsy white shift of some sort that struck her between knee and ankle and that left her arms and legs and slender throat quite bare. Her flesh had a delicate darkness under the moon. The hair that streamed silkenly about her shoulders was darker even than her big questioning eyes. She had a wreath of white ginger flowers upon her head and the wide Apriline sweetness of them came strangely to Lewis's nostrils.

He stared until his own cheeks crimsoned. She was so unbelievably a creature made for the evanescent moment, for moonshine on southern seas, for untrodden beaches, and for dead-gold sunsets fading over black volcanic rock.

"Very nice moon!" he said with a feeling of deep chagrin at his own banality. He held his breath waiting for her answer.

"Yes," said the girl with a kind of naïve, soft gravity, "ver' nice moon. You too much like this place?"

"By gad! I should say I did!" said Lewis fervently.

"Where you come from?"

He gestured vaguely toward the road behind the *kiawes*.

"I go round island—automobile—too hot, too tired—I see beach—think I like swim—leave automobile beside road—(You cursed ass!" he finished fiercely to himself. "Talking pidgin to a dream like this.") But the dream only nodded its lovely head in unquestioning acceptance of his method of speech.

"This ver' good beach for swim—no coral—not many shark."

"You live here?" demanded Lewis irresistibly.

For an instant she looked away, smiling to herself as if she had not heard him. Then her eyes returned gravely to his.

"Long time I live here. I born Nanakuli."

"What?" Lewis had never heard so silken-soft a sound.

She repeated slowly: "I born—Na-na-ku-li—that's name this place. You think—pretty?"

"It's perfect," said Lewis softly. "I can hardly believe I'm awake." He put out one hand and swung himself up beside her. He smiled, and Lewis had in his softer moments a smile not easy to be denied. The Eternal Boy, at such times, looked out of his eyes. Women never failed to see it, and to waken before it.

"I like stay little while and talk to you—all right?"

"All right," repeated the girl serenely. She moved over to make room for him with just a touch of shyness, and the perfume of the wild ginger flowers in her hair floated to him as she turned. In that white, unearthly air her eyes were pools of shadow—her skin had a lucent warmth and smoothness.

"Sit tight, old boy," said Lewis to himself. "She's only a pretty little squatter after all."

But it took all his reserves of calm to keep that fact in mind. There was a fragrance about her and a delicacy. She might have been made of moonlight.

"You live in that house?" he asked at last to discipline his mounting excitement. She nodded sweetly.

"I got father, mother, one sister. My sister marry nice Portugee man. She live Honolulu—got plenty *holoku*, six small children. I never go Honolulu myself." There was a wistfulness in her lowered tones that tightened Lewis's throat. He thrust away from him the vision of the *holokued* sister (a *holoku* is a sort of native mother hubbard, very grateful to increasing curves)—thrust away the vision of the nice Portugee man and the six small children, fastened his eyes upon the slim flower-crowned thing beside him, and tried not to spill his heart at her feet before the moon should at least be overhead. Thus entangled, he made a desperate attempt at conversation.

"Your father Hawaiian man—where he stop now?"

She lifted a dreaming gaze. "My mother, Hawaiian. My father, Englishman—name—Edmonds-son. He stop inside house—sleep—drunk, I think." At Lewis's muttered exclamation she shrugged and gestured daintily with two small brown hands. "Oh—no *pilikia*! (trouble)—all time drunk. I think he like forget. Be-fore—he stop 'nother country. Not like this. All time—wear good clothes—all time wear shoes. He have money then—everybody like. Now"—she broke into a mellow note of laughter—"little fish; plenty drink, plenty sleep. He say like I tell you, he like forget. Tha's very' good way—eh?"

"Certainly it's one way, if you like," admitted Lewis curiously. "And you—you dream of old ivory and rose leaves!—I suppose you'll marry a nice Portugee man too and grow fat and clumsy and—"

"I not too old," she interrupted haughtily. "Eighteen—tha's not too old. But I no marry Portugee man"—her chin lifted proudly. "Some day I go England—marry Englishman." She pointed with a slender forefinger straight across the moon-swept empty splendor of the sea. "England over there?"

"Thereabouts," said Lewis gently.

"You think I b'long more better England?"

He smiled down into her eyes that dared him to deny her.

"If it comes down to that, I think you b'long in

magic casements opening on the foam
Of perilous seas, in faery lands forlorn.

You're just Romance—that's what you are! I'd begun to believe you didn't exist."

She frowned adorably. "I no understan' how you talk that way."

"No," said Lewis regretfully; "I suppose not. You see, it's like this. I'd heard all my life that these islands of yours were the Garden of Eden, and

I was disappointed after I got here because I simply couldn't see it—until tonight. By the way, you name is *Eve*, I suppose?"

"My name Kealoha," she told him softly. "You like that name?"

"It too perfect," said Lewis again. "I don't know what I ever did to deserve it."

She stopped him, impatient of obvious foolery. "You—you live Honolulu? I like you tell me where?"

Lewis saluted. "I live Schofield Barracks—know where that is? Oh well, it doesn't really matter."

"You soldier?" she cried triumphantly. "You come here from Cal-i-fornia?"

"From Georgia—if it's all the same to you"—a crooked little grimace of regret supplanted Lewis's careless smile. "I enlisted—some time ago—to go to France, you savvy? Beautiful child, did you know there was a war in France just now? Of course you didn't. Well—I—how the devil do you say it? I—too much like go France—I leave perfectly good job because I want like fight—for America. See? But kind Government sent me to Hawaii—to play around in the Pacific. Rotten luck, wasn't it? That, Kealoha, is what you call a cold deal. I'm a little sore over it still. Let's talk of other matters!"

"A little sore?" persisted Kealoha softly. "Grouchy—cross—unhappy, eh?"

She laid one cool little hand for the barest flutter of a second over his, and in that second Lewis's pulses raced. Then before he could stop her she sprang from the rocks and stood on the shining wet sand, a figure of sheer enchantment.

"If you not happy, I think more better we go swim—tha's good for forget—everything! No be sorry any more—eh?"

Laughing, she ran out into the sea, her white shift modeling her slender limbs in lines of an exquisitely tender youth: the wreath of flowers still upon her head, she flung herself into a breaking wave, and the moonlight glimmered upon one lifted arm as she struck out for the reef.

Lewis followed, not by any means so calmly as he might have wished. He was, in the majority of instances, a young man who knew his way about, and it startled him somewhat, annoyed him not a little, to find himself pursuing this creature of foam and faery with all the unconsidering ardor of the boy his earlier years had been. He fancied the scent of her wild ginger flowers came back to him on the wind. He thought he heard a luring sigh of laughter, and the sound tingled through all his veins.

Something sang in his mind like music while the water slipped away from his eager strokes:

A man had given all else for this—
To waste his whole life in one kiss
Upon those perfect lips!

"It's that damned moon!" groaned Lewis savagely, and quickened his way through the gray velvety shadow of sea that lay between them. The feel of that sea on his face and body was unadulterated ecstasy, cooler than April rain, sharper than breaking bubbles of pale gold wine. He caught up to her, a little way out, and they drifted side by side without a word.

After a long time she sighed to him sweetly, "You happy now, eh? You no need forget—any more?"

Like the inside of a great milky pearl the whole world set them round with silence. "I think maybe I no *can* forget any more," said Lewis slowly.

She turned her face to his, small and soft and mysteriously sweet like the fragile white flowers in her streaming hair. Her eyes held his for a moment—for a moment only.

"Listen!" she whispered.

From the shore a faint call came to them, twice repeated while they drifted waiting.

"My father," said Kealoha suddenly. "I think he not sleep any more." She put one hand to her mouth and cried back startlingly clear across the water. Then she swam very fast without parleying, straight for the beach, with Lewis close behind her.

"You go back by *kiawe* trees," she panted over one gleaming shoulder. "I no like he see you—please!"

"I'll do whatever you say," Lewis returned reluctantly, his idyll melting away before his eyes. "But I'm not afraid of your father, you know."

"Please—tha's more better for *me*," she begged.

So Lewis said simply that he would do as she told him. Only—when they came to the shallows where he could stand and Kealoha very nearly could, he stopped swimming and put his arms around her and caught her up against his shoulder, very gently. Her darkly dripping hair with its drowned white flowers, her dark questioning eyes and the childish sweetness of her mouth were very near his face—the slim little body was perilously still within his hold—and Lewis's heart was almost choking him with its unsteady heavy beating.

"I am going to kiss you good-by," he said a little huskily. "I shouldn't, of course, but I'll never see you again—I hope! and I know I shall be sorry—to the end of my life—if I don't kiss you—now. You're the kind of thing I've always dreamed about, you see, Kealoha—and you don't usually happen."

I don't know if Kealoha saw. I don't know if Kealoha could have stopped him. At any rate, she did not try. A little tremor ran through her—like the wind through the grass—when his lips touched hers and she hid her face against his shoulder for just an instant. But she was off and swimming desperately fast before he could even cry to her, and there was now a torchlight moving about near the stack behind the rocks. So Lewis let her go. She had said it would be better for her, and that, of course, was unanswerable. His last sight of the beach showed a scud of cloud coming over the moon.

Lewis got into Schofield about ten that night with a *kiawe* thorn in his left heel and a determined unbelief in his soul.

"Dreams," he said to himself, "don't happen." He added grimly, "I'll never see her again." But he did.

Just one week later he was sitting idly upon the railing of Molly Ledwell's *lanai* with the beach and the sea at his back and Molly's extremely engaging self languidly knitting in a low chair before his eyes—five of a murky afternoon it was, and Lewis's emotional barometer very low—when steps crossed the wide bare floor from the dining-room windows and Lewis, getting to his feet, looked suddenly and straight and unexpectedly into eyes which he had not in seven doggedly busy days been able for one moment to forget.

She did not at first seem possible, because Molly only said: "Oh, hello, Lissa Greenwood! I'm awfully glad to see you! May I present Lieutenant Lewis? Let him find you a chair; darling, isn't it a beast of a day? If it wasn't war time, I'd give you some tea."

And the girl only answered rather casually, without a sign of recognition: "Hello, Molly Ledwell! How do you do, Lieutenant Lewis? Still, one might have a drink of water, no? I'm just perishing—this dreadful Hawaiian weather of yours!"

Lewis watched her like a hawk while a soft-stepping Japanese servant brought water and while she drank it.

Those were Kealoha's eyes, but Lissa Greenwood smiled and spoke and moved with the evasive intrangible grace of a maid of honor of the court of Louis Seize. Her hair, dark and smooth under a wide flower-wreathed hat, her little feet exquisitely slim in white buckskin, her whole small self, cool in white organdy, fragrant of some dry, delicate flower scent, touched with a sheen and a bloom like the sheen and the bloom of old ivory, bespoke deliberation and finesse. She was consciously aloof, to her finger tips. Still it was there—the droop of the lip and the dark questioning glance, the little ripple in the low voice, the swift impatient gesturing of the childish-looking hands.

Lewis fetched a chair for her and drew himself up to his old seat on the railing facing the guest—and Molly.

"Do you live in the islands, Miss Greenwood?"

He had not meant to challenge her so abruptly, but wild surmises were lashing through his mind—bar sinisters on worthy English shields; all he had ever heard of the tangled relationships of the place came back to him charged with a new significance and all manner of breathless possibilities.

"No," said Miss Greenwood. "Oh, no!" She looked up at him coolly and shook her charming head.

"Have I lost my hall mark so soon? I've been here just four weeks. Isn't New York written on me somewhere? I live"—she drew an ambiguous little sigh—"I live on West Eighty-eighth Street, just off Riverside, if you happen to know where that is. Dear me, Molly! I'm feeling a little homesick at the mere mention of it."

"Nonsense!" said Molly briefly. She had been interrupted in her tête-à-tête with Lewis, who was both new and promising material, so felt at the moment no particular sympathy for Miss Greenwood's airy affectations.

"And you?" inquired Miss Greenwood indolently of Lewis.

"I come from Georgia."

They smiled at each other across an invisible barrier.

"My mother was a Southerner," she murmured. "That's the real Romance of the States, isn't it?"   ·

"Oh—Romance!" cried Molly suddenly. A glint of feminine malice came into her milkmaid eyes. She laid down her knitting.

"She's Romance-crazy! Make her tell you, Lieutenant Lewis, about the man she ran across last week. Where was it, Lissa darling? She was down at some beach place over the week-end."

"Really, Molly," said Lissa darling softly, "I hardly fancy Lieutenant Lewis would be interested. Besides—"

Molly swept on, the keener for the other's undeniable reluctance: "Nanakuli, that's the place! The Hattons have a shack there; just a grass-roofed hut, you know, native fashion—two rooms and a *lanai*. They took Lissa over there Sunday—It's a wonderful beach—to play at. Romance to her heart's content. And she *did*. Tell him, Lissa!"

"Tell it yourself," said Lissa with a gallant show of indifference. "You do it very nicely."

"Nothing near so well as you, my dear," protested Molly, and added for Lewis's benefit: "She kept a whole dinner party laughing over it a good half hour last night."

"What happened?" asked Lewis quietly, eyes on Lissa's face. Not even her eyelids fluttered. She was to all outward appearances as calm as a little carven Buddha.

"It isn't possible!" he told himself grimly, but something in him began at that moment to know it was.

Mrs. Ledwell broke out into a tinkle of laughter.

"I *shall* tell, anyhow! Why, Lissa was sitting down on the rocks, just at sunset, in a yellow silk bathing suit with a white *mu-mu* over it, and with a wild-ginger *lei* on her hair, when a man came along—weren't you, Lissa?"

"What's a *mu-mu*?" asked Lewis.

"Oh, a kind of Hawaiian thing they wear," said Mrs. Ledwell vaguely— "short, you know, this one was—picturesque and all that. Really, Lissa, you must have looked rather—"

Lissa smiled the chilliest little smile.

"The man," Mrs. Ledwell went on with sparkling determination, "was an enlisted man, a soldier, and of course he thought"—her voice broke delightfully—"that Lissa was just a little *hapa-haole*, half-white, you know. So he climbed up on the rocks and sat down beside her and they watched the moonrise together. Lissa said it would have made quite a wonderful scene for a play. He wasn't at all bad, you know: really educated and all that; quoted Keats to her when he wasn't talking pidgin—wasn't it Keats you said, Lissa? Don't look so annoyed, darling!"

"Keats or Kipling—I forgot which," said Lissa suddenly. She did not look at Lewis once.

"And Lissa, when she saw what he took her for, made him up a lovely long story about a beachcomber father, a Hawaiian mother, and a fat sister married to a Portugee man in Honolulu with six small children. Oh, Lissa, I should love to have heard your pidgin!"

"And then—" Lewis prompted steadily. His nice gray eyes had grown a little dark; his mouth was taking on a certain setness.

"Then they went swimming together. Lissa walked right down into the water, *mu-mu* and all, not wanting him to see her sophisticated yellow silk bathing suit, and when they had swum almost out to the reef, the Hattons missed her and began to call, so she told him her drunken father was awake and that he must go—and—he did as soon as they got back to the beach. He slipped off through the *kiawes* and Lissa went back to the Hattons. You said it was absolutely the most romantic thing that every happened to you, didn't you, Lissa? Full moon, and all that, and the poor man so obviously thrilled over the adventure he was having."

"Oh, he was—of course," said Lewis. He added, looking full into Miss Greenwood's impassive face: "Is that all?"

"Mercy, yes!" said Mrs. Ledwell.

"Wasn't there some sort of an affectionate parting? There usually is, I'm told."

"Was there, Lissa?" asked Mrs. Ledwell sweetly. "You didn't say."

"If there was," said Miss Greenwood, lifting soft, dark eyes to meet Lewis's squarely, "I have forgotten it."

Then she went home, hurt before she could make good her escape. Lewis, seeing her to her car, destroyed completely the foundations of her composure.

"I'm glad you didn't tell that I kissed you," he said very quietly. "It shows that part of it at least meant something to you. Am I to see you again?"

"I think not," began Miss Greenwood icily—finished in a rather breathless flame of fury. "I hope not—ever!" and was whirled off down Kalakaua Avenue crimson to her delicate eyebrows.

Nevertheless she did. This story seems to fall of itself into a triptych and approaches now the end.

She had no notion of seeing him. She said as much to Mrs. Ledwell, observing that she did not care for Lewis's kind of man and found life too short to admit such people into one's friendship. In spite of this, or perhaps because of it, he was unrelentingly in her mind, and since it is almost impossible in Honolulu to avoid even an uninteresting man forever, at the end of the three weeks more Lewis called Miss Greenwood up on the telephone one day and said, humbly as any woman's heart could wish: "First of all, won't you please forgive me?"

She said coldly—they had not seen nor spoken to each other since that unfortunate afternoon on Molly's veranda—"Nothing to forgive—"

"I'm ordered away, you know—by the next transport—"

"Why, I'm going next week myself." She thawed a little. "So you'll really get to France after all."

"Here's hoping!" said Lewis. "Now, listen, I'm having a beach party, for good-by, and I want you to come. Please! You might as well. Probably we'll never see each other again."

She said she couldn't of course. It was all of five minutes before, touched by the rather pathetic insistence in his voice, she relented and said she would.

"And you'll let me drive you out in my runabout?"

"Oh, impossible!" Eventually, however, she conceded that too—and swept by some inward weakening, some unadmitted longing, feeling rather like a queen bestowing a favor by reason of his outspoken and touching gratitude.

At the last he said carelessly: "Don't say anything to Molly—Mrs. Ledwell, that is—I'm not sure I'm asking her." That too rather pleased Miss Greenwood. Molly was apt to be very much in evidence of late.

So he came for her at half after four of a heavenly Sunday afternoon, and they drove off together through a green and gold and azure world.

"Who's going?" she asked as he seated himself in the car beside her and laid a hand on the wheel.

"Oh, just people," said Lewis vaguely. She felt his eyes on the curve of her cheek and blushed. It was a thing which, in spite of all her deliberation and finesse, she did readily.

About an hour and a half later they came to a strip of ivory beach glimmering vaguely through close-set *kiawes*.

"Why, this is Nanakuli, isn't it?" said Lissa Greenwood curiously.

"Yes," said Lewis, and added: "You don't mind?"

"No. Why should I?" But there was a certain uneasy stiffening in her tone. She thought that he was laughing at her.

He found the path through the shadowy trees and she went before him down upon the beach. Sea, sky, and sand were rosy witth sunset. Beside the big black rocks where she had sat and sung she faced him swiftly.

"Where are the others?"

"There are no others."

"You mean—?"

"What I say—there are no others."

"You wouldn't dare!"

Lewis smiled down into her widening eyes. "Why not?"

That and his smile left her silent.

"Then nobody knows"—she flung back her small dark head, and looked at him proudly. "What did you bring me here for, like this? It's unspeakable of you. Even if you're only—you *must* know better. Do you want me to be hideously talked about?"

"By whom? There isn't even a sea gull," said Lewis gently. He waited until she stormed at him again, her hands clenched tight against her sides.

"I never heard of anything so mad. It'll be dark in half an hour. You think I'm going to stay here alone, with you? *Why* did you do it?"

"Sit down and I'll tell you why," said Lewis very quietly.

When she obeyed him with an exaggerated aloofness he put his hand into the pocket of his service blouse and took out something small and yellowish, faintly discolored and a little dry.

"I brought you here to assist at a funeral."

"You must be mad."

Her eyes threatened him.

"The funeral of Romance," said Lewis, turning the thing over and over in his hand. He finished softly. "This is one of the flowers you had on your hair that night. I want you to dig a little grave for it and bury it, and say a little prayer over it. Then I'll take you home and never see you again."

"This is too utterly ridiculous," she told him coldly. "Bury it yourself, if you like."

Lewis leaned one elbow on the rocks beside her and shook his head unsmiling. "No. I bought you here to do it. Shall I tell you why?"

Her lifted shoulder betrayed a deep disinterest, in the face of which he continued evenly: "All my life I've had dreams—fool dreams, if you like—about the sort of thing that happened that first evening. Oh, I'm cured. But I'm going to keep the memory of that one—to see that it has a fitting end! My girl doesn't exist—the girl I found here on these rocks under the last full moon, the girl that went swimming with me in the moonlight with flowers in her hair and the loveliest smile in the world on her mouth. She's gone—she never really was—but she was mine when she lasted, and I'm going to—"

"She was *me*," said Lissa Greenwood abruptly. She took off her hat and laid it down upon the rocks, ruffled her sort dark hair, and flung him a look of defiance. "Kealoha was *me*—so that's all there is of *that!*"

The sunset deepened about them.

"You!" said Lewis and laughed insultingly. "You're just a nice little girl, no more, no less. Plenty like *you* in the world. You're pretty and clever and careful. They turn you out by the thousands from finishing schools in the East, but you're not Kealoha!"

"Who made her, then?" The big dark eyes were stormy; under the soft skin a flame of color was creeping.

"Nobody made her—I dreamed her. I dream of her every night!"

"Don't you suppose a girl has dreams as well?"

"Not your kind of girl."

His half smile mocked her. She caught her breath in a surge of helpless anger. "How dare you classify me like that! Didn't I play Kealoha in the beginning?"

"Yes, and didn't you boast about it to a tableful of sniggering idiots? No. Kealoha wasn't you. She was just an exquisite little wandering soul that slipped into your body for one moonrise. You'll never have her again!"

"Give me that flower!" said Lissa Greenwood between little white teeth. She took it from his acquiescent fingers and slipped down upon the sand with it. Just beyond the delicate ripple of the highest wave line she dug, kneeling small and slim in the roseate dusk, a little grave and laid the withered wild ginger flower therein. Lewis watched her without a word. When she had done she looked up at him, sitting back upon her heels, her face flushed, her eyes mysteriously luminous.

"Am I to say something over it?"

"Yes, and then I'll take you home—and never see you again," said Lewis.

She said very carefully in a slow, soft voice, her small hands folded in her lap, her look on the tiny grave:

I have buried sweet Romance
Beneath a tree
In a forest tall and black,
Where none can see.

I shall go no more to his grave
For the woods are cold;
I shall gather as much of joy
As my hands can hold.

I shall stay all day in the sun,
Where the wide winds blow—
But, oh I shall cry at night
When none will know.

There was a break in the even murmur. She sprang to her feet. "Now take me home. You promised!"

Lewis put a finger beneath her chin and tipped up the exquisite face.

"If you've got tears in your eyes," he said huskily, "it's Kealoha—and she's *mine*!" Seeing that she had, he finished with his lips on her cheek, her hands clenched tight against his heart. "You wonderful—beautiful—maddening—thing! Did you *care*, all the time?"

"Of course I cared," said Lissa Greenwood, choking back a sob. "Else why do you suppose I had to tell my soul to a silly dinner party?"

"You know," said Lewis softly after a little while, "things like this don't happen."

"Maybe we're different, you and I," said Lissa Greenwood wistfully. "Anyhow, Kealoha was *me*, wasn't she?"

He kissed her. She never forgot it; but it's no good telling you how. Either you know or you don't know, and if your pulses don't remember, printer's ink won't make them.

FANNY HEASLIP LEA (1883-1955), *born in New Orleans, came to Honolulu as the wife of a sugar executive. She performed, wrote, and directed for Footlights, an amateur theatrical company. Don Blanding wrote a poem for her, and drew her portrait. Lea wrote a number of novels, many short stories and romance serials for national magazines, some Hollywood screenplays, and a Broadway play.*

W. Somerset Maugham
from "RAIN"

S uddenly from below came a sound, and Davidson turned and looked questioningly at his wife. It was the sound of a gramophone, harsh and loud, wheezing out a syncopated tune.

"What's that?" he asked.

Mrs. Davidson fixed her pince-nez more firmly on her nose.

"One of the second-class passengers has a room in the house. I guess it comes from there."

They listened in silence, and presently they heard the sound of dancing. Then the music stopped, and they heard the popping of corks and voices raised in animated conversation.

"I daresay she's giving a farewell party to her friends on board," said Dr. Macphail. "The ship sails at twelve, doesn't it?"

Davidson made no remark, but he looked at his watch.

"Are you ready?" he asked his wife.

She got up and folded her work.

"Yes, I guess I am," she answered.

"It's early to go to bed yet, isn't it?" said the doctor.

"We have a good deal of reading to do," explained Mrs. Davidson. "Wherever we are, we read a chapter of the Bible before retiring for the night and we study it with the commentaries, you know, and discuss it thoroughly. It's a wonderful training for the mind."

The two couples bade one another good night. Dr and Mrs. Macphail were left alone. For two or three minutes they did not speak.

"I think I'll go and fetch the cards," the doctor said at last.

Mrs. Macphail looked at him doubtfully. Her conversation with the Davidsons had left her a little uneasy, but she did not like to say that she thought they had better not play cards when the Davidsons might come in at any moment. Dr Macphail brought them and she watched him, though with a vague sense of guilt, while he laid out his patience. Below the sound of revelry continued.

It was fine enough next day, and the Macphails, condemned to spend a fortnight of idleness at Pago-Pago, set about making the best of things. They went down to the quay and got out of their boxes a number of books. The doctor called on the chief surgeon of the naval hospital and went round the beds with him. They left cards on the governor. They passed Miss Thompson on the road. The doctor took off his hat, and she gave him a "Good morning doc," in a loud, cheerful voice. She was dressed as on the day before, in a white frock, and her shiny white boots with their high heels, her fat legs bulging over the tops of them, were strange things on that exotic scene.

"I don't think she's very suitably dressed, I must say," said Mrs. Macphail. "She looks extremely common to me."

When they got back to their house, she was on the veranda playing with one of the trader's dark children.

"Say a word to her," Dr Macphail whispered to his wife. "She's all alone here, and it seems rather unkind to ignore her."

Mrs. Macphail was shy, but she was in the habit of doing what her husband bade her.

"I think we're fellow lodgers here," she said, rather foolishly.

"Terrible, ain't it, bein' cooped up in a one-horse burg like this?" answered Miss Thompson. "And they tell me I'm lucky to have gotten a room. I don't see myself livin' in a native house, and that's what some have to do. I don't know why they don't have a hotel."

They exchanged a few more words. Miss Thompson, loud-voiced and garrulous, was evidently quite willing to gossip, but Mrs. Macphail had a poor stock of small talk and presently she said:

"Well, I think we must go upstairs."

In the evening when they sat down to their high tea, Davidson on coming in said:

"I see that woman downstairs has a couple of sailors sitting there. I wonder how she's gotten acquainted with them."

"She can't be very particular," said Mrs. Davidson.

They were all rather tired after the idle, aimless day.

"If there's going to be a fortnight of this I don't know what we shall feel like at the end of it," said Dr Macphail.

"The only thing to do is to portion out the day to different activities," answered the missionary. "I shall set aside a certain number of hours to study and a certain number to exercise, rain or fine—in the wet season you can't afford to pay any attention to the rain—and a certain number to recreation."

Dr Macphail looked at his companion with misgiving. Davidson's programme oppressed him. They were eating Hamburger steak again. It seemed the only dish the cook knew how to make. Then below the gramophone began. Davidson started nervously when he heard it, but said nothing. Men's voices floated up. Miss Thompson's guests were joining in a well-known song and presently they heard her voice too, hoarse and loud. There was a good deal of shouting and laughing. The four people upstairs, trying to make conversation, listened despite themselves to the clink of glasses and the scrape of chairs. More people had evidently come. Miss Thompson was giving a party.

"I wonder how she gets them all in," said Mrs. Macphail suddenly breaking into a medical conversation between the missionary and her husband.

It showed whither her thoughts were wandering. The twitch of Davidson's face proved that, though he spoke of scientific things, his mind was busy in the same direction. Suddenly, while the doctor was giving some experience of practice on the Flanders front, rather prosily, he sprang to his feet with a cry.

"What's the matter, Alfred?" asked Mrs. Davidson.

"Of course! It never occurred to me. She's out of Iwelei."

"She can't be."

"She came on board at Honolulu. It's obvious. And she's carrying on her trade here. Here."

He uttered the last word with a passion of indignation.

"What's Iwelei?" asked Mrs. Macphail.

He turned his gloomy eyes on her and his voice trembled with horror.

"The plague spot of Honolulu. The Red Light district. It was a blot on our civilization."

Iwelei was on the edge of the city. You went down side streets by the harbour, in the darkness, across a rickety bridge, till you came to a deserted road, all ruts and holes, and then suddenly you came out into the light. There was parking room for motors on each side of the road, and there were saloons, tawdry and bright, each one noisy with its mechanical piano, and there were barbers' shops and tobacconists. There was a stir in the air and a sense of expectant gaiety. You turned down a narrow alley, either to the right or to the left, for the road divided Iwelei into two parts, and you found yourself in the district. There were rows of little bungalows, trim and neatly painted in green, and the pathway between them was broad and straight. It was laid out like a garden-city. In its respectable regularity, its order and spruceness, it gave an impression of sardonic horror; for never can the search for love have been so systematized and ordered. The pathways were lit by a rare lamp, but they would have been dark except for the lights that came from the open windows of the bungalows. Men wandered about, looking at the women who sat at their windows, reading or sewing, for the most part taking no notice of the passers-by; and like the women they were of all nationalities. There were Americans, sailors from the ships in port, enlisted men off the gunboats, sombrely drunk, and soldiers from the regiments, white and black, quartered on the island; there were Japanese, walking in twos and threes; Hawaiians, Chinese in long robes, and Filipinos in preposterous hats. They were silent and as it were oppressed. Desire is sad.

"It was the most crying scandal of the Pacific," exclaimed Davidson vehemently. "The missionaries had been agitating against it for years, and at last the local press took it up. The police refused to stir. You know their argument. They say that vice is inevitable and consequently the best thing is to localize and control it. The truth is, they were paid. Paid. They were paid by the saloon-keepers, paid by the bullies, paid by the women themselves. At last they were forced to move."

"I read about it in the papers that came on board in Honolulu," said Dr Macphail.

"Iwelei, with its sin and shame, ceased to exist on the very day we arrived. The whole population was brought before the justices. I don't know why I didn't understand at once what that woman was."

"Now you come to speak of it," said Mrs. Macphail, "I remember seeing her come on board only a few minutes before the boat sailed. I remember thinking at the time she was cutting it rather fine."

"How dare she come here!" cried Davidson indignantly. "I'm not going to allow it."

He strode towards the door.

"What are you going to do?" asked Macphail.

"What do you expect me to? I'm going to stop it. I'm not going to have this house turned into—into . . ."

He sought for a word that should not offend the ladies' ears. His eyes were flashing and his pale face was paler still in his emotion.

"It sounds as though there were three or four men down there," said the doctor. "Don't you think it's rather rash to go in just now?"

The missionary gave him a contemptuous look and without a word flung out of the room.

Susanna Moore
from SLEEPING BEAUTIES

I n 1871, Clio's great-grandmother, a princess of full Hawaiian blood, married Redmond Clarke, a shipwrecked Irish sailor who won favor with the king. Included in her dowry was a coastal plain on the island of O'ahu that was one day to become the city of Honolulu. Wisteria House was Redmond Clarke's gift to his bride, and the princess used it as her town residence. Emma, who was the granddaughter of Princess Ruth, had inherited Wisteria House. The princess had been a shrewd, temperamental woman, rather large, and Emma's mother always liked to say, quite unfairly, that Emma had inherited the princess's character along with her house.

Clio used to imagine that nothing had come off the ships in Honolulu harbor that did not pass through the rooms of Wisteria House: the first grand piano ever seen in the islands, the first refrigerator, the first carriage and pair, the first Brazil nut. By the time Clio arrived at Wisteria House, faded red and yellow capes from the time of Kamehameha I, woven from the breast feathers of thousands of birds, lay stiffly over dusty *koa* tables. The capes looked like the crepe paper animals on abandoned carnival floats. Carved idols with abalone-shell eyes and mouths of sharks' teeth leaned disconsolately against the walls, their upraised arms bound in clotted webs, their shoulders powdered with the dried wings of bats and birds. The *koa* chests, full of folded layers of *kapa* cloth, were kept open so that the fragrance of dried *mokihana* flowers, like anise, could seep through the house, but even so, the rooms smelled to Clio as if damp towels had been kept in them for years.

The rooms where Emma lived, however, were clean and fresh. The wood floors were kept bare. The big koa calabashes and bowls were polished every day with bags of flannel dipped in *kukui* oil. The walls were covered with *lau hala* matting. There were pale, ghostly rectangles on the walls, lighter in color than the rest of the matting, where there once had been paintings, and Clio, years later, found a photograph in an old auction catalogue of a Gauguin that had once belonged to Emma.

Emma kept her heavy black hair in a chignon, held at the back of her neck with jade hairpins. She wore a white pique shirtwaist dress and brown-and-white, sometimes navy-and-white, spectator pumps. It was an old-fashioned way to dress, without variation and even without color, but Clio thought it daring in its simplicity and its deliberation. There was not much that Emma had not considered. There was little that surprised her, and although she had a ready understanding of how she wanted things done, the dereliction of others did not call forth her alarm or even her displeasure. She did not need much, not in the way of things, not even in the way of people.

Like her native ancestors, Emma believed in the power of dark forces. All of the ancient *kapus* had once had practical usages—the king's excrement had been borne away by his most trusted chief and destroyed in secret not because of modesty or shame, or even hygiene, but because an evildoer might use it for sorcery. If you were so reckless as to raise your head as the big calabash was borne past, you were taken to the *heiau* and strangled to death. During periods of mourning, no fires could be lit. Cats were muzzled and chickens were thrown into covered calabashes to keep them silent. At the death of the king, the people broke all the rules with exuberance. They burned, looted, and murdered, and the women joyously offered themselves as prostitutes—but only until the decomposition of the king's corpse was complete, when social order, with its system of *kapu*, was effortlessly restored.

A taboo existed in order to be transgressed. Violence, ritualized violence, had lain deep at the center of things. To be an ancient Hawaiian was to be terrified most of the time. It is a modern idea that to live in a subconscious state is poetic. It is also a sentimental idea, and Emma would have been the first to agree.

The thirteen-year-old child and the childless, solitary woman fell into an easy routine of study and domesticity. Clio liked very much that time of the evening, after their early supper (cooked by Emma, served precariously by Emma's servant, Lester, cleared and washed by Clio), when Emma would ceremoniously invite her to the library to talk-story. Emma drank a bottle of San Miguel beer and when she finished it, she banged loudly on the floor with a Maori war club for Lester to bring her another.

Emma talked to Clio of the things she had come to fear would be lost: the long songs without rhyme or metre called *meles*; the hulas and oral genealogies; the very history of her passing race: "Sandalwood was once plentiful in the mountains of the islands. It was of no commercial value to the Hawaiians—they used it only to impart fragrance to their *kapa*—but the Chinese needed sandalwood, and soon a commerce began between the foreigners and the agents of Kamehameha, one of whom was your great-grandfather Redmond Clarke. The Hawaiians readily, even heedlessly, gave away the trees in exchange for nails and rough cloth, and later for muskets and ammunition. As a consequence, by 1840 there was little sandalwood left in the Hawaiian Islands."

It was sometimes difficult for Clio to stay awake during the lessons. They worked steadily, surrounded by books and papers, until Clio would finally be sent to bed with a book that Emma had chosen for her, perhaps Isabella Bird's nineteenth-century travel letters. Clio would try to read the book that Emma had given her, but it would not be long before she succumbed and reached under her bed to pull out the books that she had been waiting all day to read, books that she found in her aunt's library, Rumer Godden and Somerset Maugham and Katherine Mansfield. She would read through the night. She kept the book that Emma had given her close by, so that she could open it if Emma came to her room, but Emma never disturbed her. It was not her way.

If Clio succumbed so easily, so willingly, to Emma, it was because Emma enabled her to wipe away her own small past. It was an extraordinary gift that Emma gave her. Clio was relieved to exchange the story of her own childhood for the vision that Emma conjured up for her. The myths that Emma told her, the legends that she whispered to Clio, became confused with Clio's dreams, and even her recollections, so that eventually Clio came to believe, willed herself to believe, that Emma's stories were her own memories. Because of Emma, Clio grew convinced that she'd come from the ocean, born of the marriage of earth and light. All cultures, all genealogies, begin with the marriage of earth and light, Emma said. "I myself have seen it."

Emma's servant, Lester, had come to Wisteria House in 1922 as Clio's grandfather's chauffeur. He was of Chinese and Hawaiian descent, and he had left the islands only once, the time he accompanied the Rolls-Royce sedan to Scotland for Mr. Junior's golf holiday.

As a young man, Lester had fallen in love with a Japanese girl whose father worked in the cane fields of Hale Moku. The girl had lived with her family in one of the small wooden houses in the workers' camp, a half mile from the plantation house. In the evenings, Lester would walk to the camp to watch her tend the vanda orchids in her mother's small garden. One night he found the courage to speak the few short sentences he had memorized as he walked down the beach. He stood in the road and persuaded her to take a walk with him.

Two days later, when he returned, the garden was empty. The girl's father came out of the house and shouted at him to go away. Lester walked through the camp every night for weeks until Emma told him what she had heard at the mill store. The morning after her walk through the camp with Lester, the girl had been sent to her grandparents in Japan. A romance with a man who was not Japanese was considered impossible, a shaming thing, and the girl had been sent away for the good of her family and even, some might have said, for the good of the community.

Lester had a collection of blues and jazz recordings that was unusual to find in Honolulu, a city where there were few places to hear or to buy such music, and few people who listened to it. Lester would invite Clio to join him in his room at Wisteria House, often on a weekend evening when she did not have schoolwork and Emma had gone to call on friends, where he played records for her, very loud. He smoked a Filipino cigar, his bad-tempered face dark against a frayed hand-me-down chair, and the cigar smoke filled the room as they listened to John Coltrane play "What's New?" Sometimes if Emma returned early, she would bring a bottle of beer from the kitchen and stand in the doorway and listen to the music. Emma liked the later Billie Holiday, those recordings in which the singing was a little dissolute, a little slurred.

It was during these evening sessions with Lester that Clio realized with both elation and fear that there was something in the world that might be there for the taking, something that she came to think of, perhaps unwisely, as romance. The world itself, she thought then, was romance.

Sometimes Lester would arrive soundlessly at her door or suddenly appear ahead of her on one of the garden paths and hiss morosely, "You want to see things, missy?"

Then he would take her into the attic, into the empty stables and carriage house, into rooms that had not been used for fifty years. He wore a heavy ring of keys attached to his stained waistcoat with a gold watch chain that had belonged to Redmond Clarke. He would unlock the doors of the rooms with deliberate, malicious ceremony, hunched over to catch the dust-filled light, taking his time. He never condescended to try the key in the lock, but insisted on finding each key by sight. Once inside, he opened the shutters with a clatter, flinging them back with impatience. He did not allow Clio to spend much time in the rooms. The dust made her sneeze, and this upset him. He thought it impolite, and even disruptive, as if the sudden noise might disturb one of her great-aunts, dead for years, bending over her embroidery. One afternoon, Clio noticed a small animal trotting down the center of the second-floor hall. She thought it might be one of the rats that sometimes slipped inside the house and she stepped back calmly to let it pass. To her surprise, the door behind her fell open.

A large *koa* bed sat heavily under a swag of faded striped damask. Festoons of dusty yellow feathers were tied to the top of each bedpost, an adornment, Clio knew, once allowed only the nobility. There was a slender chaise, its covering of gray sprigged silk faded and torn. There was a dressing table made of mother-of-pearl. She knew of the table; Lester had described it to her, a wedding gift to her great-grandmother from the ambassador of China. There were large mirrors in gilded frames, the glass blind with rust. There was a chamber pot under a tall *koa* chest.

She opened the chest. Hundreds of feathers floated to her feet. White doves, she thought in astonishment. And then she saw that they were not birds. They were shoes. Shoes sewn with feathers and lace and tiny rosettes of seed pearls, shoes with soles of thin white leather and the words Madame d'Espina, Rue Cambon embossed in gold in the faded satin linings. She sat on the floor and gathered the shoes into her lap.

A light fragrance of dusting powder rose from the shoes. Some of them had never been worn. She tried to pair them, delicately tucking her fingers into the toes so as not to soil them or injure the brittle velvet ribbons. She hesitated for only a moment, then slid her foot into a shoe that looked as if it had once been the color of lavender. She walked up and down the room, arms aloft, toes pointed like a ballerina.

Clio did not tell Lester that she had discovered the secret of the unlocked doors, nor did she fidget or otherwise give herself away while he
slowly searched for the key to the nursery. But she did avail herself night and
day of the rooms that her ancestors had left open for her.

SUSANNA MOORE'S *books include* Sleeping Beauties; The Whiteness of Bones; My Old
Sweetheart; One Last Look; The Big Girls; *and* I Myself Have Seen It. *She was raised in
Hawai'i and now lives in New York City.*

Lois-Ann Yamanaka
from BEHOLD THE MANY

T he valley is a woman lying on her back, legs spread wide, her geography wet by a constant rain. Waterfalls wash the days and nights of
winter storms into the river that empties into the froth of the sea.

In the valley, the rain is a gossamer cloth, a tempest of water and leaves.
The rain is southerly with strange foreboding. The rain is northerly with
cool rime.

The rain glistens on maiden fern, the wind rustling the laua'e, the palapalai touching her there where it is always wet and seamy.

The valley is a woman with the features of a face, a woman whose eyes
watch the procession of the celestial sphere; a woman with woodland arms
outstretched and vulnerable, a woman with shadowy breasts of 'a'ali'i and
hāpu'u, lobelias and lichens; a woman, a womb, impregnated earth.

O body.

When they find her, she is shiny, she is naked, she is bound, but for her
legs, spread open and wet with blood and semen. Tears in her eyes, or is it
rain? Breath in her mouth, or is it wind? Her thicket of hair drips into her
mouth, sliced open from from ear to ear. She is pale green, *the silvery underside of kukui leaves;* her eyes and lips are gray, *the ashen hinahina;* her fingers
and feet are white, *the winter rain in this valley.*

O body.

O beloved Hosana.

Anah knows her daughter is dead at the very moment of her passing. She is
sitting early dawn in the honey house, surrounded by the hum of the wild
swarms outside. Then the dead of a strange silence. Light enters the room
in a strand that illuminates the particles of dust, the luminescence of bees'

wings. Hosana enters the room in a flowing orange dress. She stops where the sunlight stills.

"Hosana?" Her daughter has been gone for weeks. Gone at fourteen with a man who called her beautiful. Gone to the other side of the island of O'ahu.

"Remember always, Mother," Hosana says without moving her lips, "love is sweet."

Honeybees move in the thick smell of the honey house.

She follows her daughter's slow gaze around the room as if placing the honey bins, the amber-filled bottles, the broken smoker, the dust of kiawe pollen, wooden frames, the scent of nectar, and finally her mother's face in her memory.

When the light fades, so does she. And then comes the wailing rain from a cloudless sky. Days of rain.

1916

The valley is a woman crying, a child's lonely wailing. Nothing but the river moaning down the mountain.

The valley is a woman's breath, a child's whisper. Nothing but the language of wind in trees.

In this valley, Anah's little sister died. On the night of her death, Anah walked down the steep staircases of the orphanage, Aki behind her holding on to the back of her nightdress. It was dark beyond midnight; the nuns were asleep in their small cells on the second floor. Anah stole a bottle of honey and a cube of honeycomb from the kitchen.

No one knew that Leah had died but Anah and Aki who sat beside her bed as she choked on sputum and blood. Her labored breaths grazed her throat, then crackled with hollow relief in her tiny chest.

"Okaasan coming tomorrow," Anah told her. *Don't die.* "And Charles, Charles too. He coming. *Don't die, don't die.* You have to be well so they can take us home for Easter dinner."

"Liar," Aki whispered. She looked away from Leah. "They never coming back for us."

Leah turned her face to the porcelain bowl with blue flowers on the bed stand beside her. She heaved thick strands of blood from the side of her mouth, missing the bowl. "He coming," she said.

"Yes, I promise," Anah told her, gently taking her hand.

"Who?" Aki asked. "Who coming?"

"No, Dai, no!" Leah rasped, her eyes fixed on the ceiling. "Dai, no!"

She died that night, that moment with her eyes open, horrified and stunned.

When little Leah died, Anah stole a bottle of honey from the kitchen, poured it on her face, a glaze over her sleeping eyes. *You're sleeping, that's all.* She poured it over her hair, brushed it to a glossy shine. *Never mind Sister Bernadine cut off your beautiful hair.* She rubbed the cube of honeycomb over her bloody lips, then placed it in her warm mouth. *In remembrance of me.*

Anah took her tiny right hand, Aki her left, and they bit off her fingernails. Anah cut off a thick strand of her hair with a kitchen knife. She placed these relics in the empty honey bottle filled with Leah's baby teeth and hid it in one of the dark closets on the third floor. Then hand in hand, they waited for morning.

1939

Ezroh finds his beloved Anah sitting in the honey house. He is holding their daughter's hand.

"Get out, quick, the bees swarming!"

Their child in a young woman's body, sings a child's song:

Sweet dreams for thee, sweet dreams for thee.

Anah sits in the midst of this odd, mad swarm, the certain pitch and hum at their untimely displacement.

"Why you naked?" he yells, waving his arms at the furious swarm.

There's not a comb of honeybee,
so full of sweets as babe to me.

He tries to pull her shirt over her head, then urges her to run. Their woman-child laughs at bees crawling on her hands, her father brushing them away from her face. He pulls her away from the honey house.

And it is o! sweet, sweet!

Anah sits in the blur of the old hive, stares at the green stinger barbs writhing in her hands, face, breasts, belly, thighs, and feet. And when she is fully pierced, she walks out of the honey house, the swarm emitting a high pitch behind her.

O BODY.

She places the corpse of her firstborn, her beloved Hosana, on a long table covered with her best lace tablecloth in the parlor. *Watch, O Lord.* She lights beeswax candles blessed by Father Maurice. *Those who weep tonight.* She folds her daughter's hands on her breast with the knotted sennit rosary. *Bless your dead ones.*

A snail slides across the threshold.

The woman-child sings:

Worm, nor snail, do no offense.

A rice sparrow hits the window.

The woman-child sings:
What nestlings do in the nightly dew?
An owl cries from the ironwood trees.
The woman-child sings:
Night is come. Owls are out.
She covers her daughter with foliage from the Koʻolau Mountains: woodland arms of kukui; breasts of ʻaʻaliʻi and hāpuʻu; hair of hinahina and lichens; body of palapalai and lauaʻe. She rains holy water on Hosana's body. And then she anoints her daughter with royal jelly, brushing honey into her beautiful long hair. She kneels before her daughter, then prays for her soul all night.

O beloved Hosana.

When Father Maurice and Sister Mary Deborah arrive in the morning, she is holding her daughter's cold hand. She kisses her face in this house one last time.

Glory be to the Father. The horse-drawn buggy pulls away.
To the Son. The church bells echo.
And to the Holy Spirit. She follows the body deeper into the valley.
As was in the beginning. The valley is a woman lying on her back.
Is now and ever shall be. The rain is a gossamer cloth.
World without end. Her many dead ones surround her.
Amen. A vincible God resides in this valley.

Someone is praying. The prayers do not end:

"Hail, holy Queen, Mother of mercy, my life and my hope, to you I do cry, poor banished child of Eve; to you do I send up my sighs, mourning, and weeping in this valley of tears.

"Hail, holy Queen, Mother of mercy, my life and my hope, to you I do cry to ask the Father on my behalf:

"Tell me how, O Lord," Anah cries, "how have I so offended thee?"

1913

Little Leah was the first to be taken to the orphanage deep in Kalihi Valley.

For months, Anah watched as Okaasan quietly burned the strips of old rice bag into which Leah had coughed up her contagious blood. Okaasan did not want Dai to discover their littlest one's illness. And she did not want Leah to infect the rest of the family.

Anah and Charles did as Okaasan had asked, collecting the soft tips of the ʻaʻaliʻi and white ginger blossoms as the crippled kahuna lapaʻau laʻau who lived among the Chinese in Pake Camp Two had instructed. His Hawaiian herbal remedies had helped many of the plantation's immigrant workers. So at the kahuna's behest, Okaasan instructed Anah to cut stalks of young sugarcane from the field behind their house in Portuguese Camp Four.

She held her sister Aki's hand as they watched their mother extract all of the sweet liquid from these plants in her hidden nook furnished with wooden crates and planks behind the makeshift furo house Dai had built far away from Japanese Camp Three.

The eldest, Thomas, skulked around the banana trees. "Go do your schoolwork right now, Thomas and Charles," Okaasan said in her native Japanese to her first and second sons. "I do not want the mean-spirited teacher to chastise you again." Okaasan twisted and squeezed the cheesecloth she had taken from the noisy tōfu-ya lady from Fukuoka-ken to strain the juices of the flowers and plants. "And you," Okaasan said to Aki, placing a kind hand on the little one's face, "go watch for your father. I heard the pau hana whistle. Give me a warning as soon as you see him coming." Aki's small body disappeared beyond the furo house.

"Okaasan, what about Anah?" Thomas yelled in anger. "She has schoolwork too. How come you never scold Anah?"

"Never mind about Anah. She is not your concern. She is helping me," Okaasan said to him. "Go, go, hurry. Get out of here," she said to Anah, pushing her back, "or Thomas might—"

"Okaasan!" Aki called in warning from the front of the house. "She is over there again in back of the house," Thomas reported to Dai in his native Portuguese, "making her useless plant medicine. She never listens to you, Father. She has not ironed your shirts. She has not made your dinner. And she is always talking in secret to the crippled kanaka man from Camp Two."

Anah moved to the opening of the nook to shield her mother from Dai's sight. Okaasan began pouring the juices together, haphazardly swiping the remnants of stem and leaf onto the ground.

Dai appeared as a huge, grotesque shadow in the shade of the nook. He pushed Anah out of his way, knocking over crates and planks. "Sumi," he called to his wife, "whassamatta you?" Homemade mead on his breath, he grabbed the tin can from her, sniffed it, then threw it over his shoulder.

"No, no! Baby sick-u, baby sick-u, Tomasu," Okaasan cried. She coughed into her hands to demonstrate the child's illness.

"How come you no cook my kaukau? Pau work, past pau hana time," Dai said, pulling Okaasan toward him by the sleeve of her cotton kimono. Okaasan would not respond. Dai was drunk. He spoke in Portuguese even though Okaasan did not understand. "My house is always filthy. And there is no food on my dinner table. My mother cooks better, anyway. Thomas and Charles," he called to his sons, "I am eating dinner with your grandmother. You can come with me or go hungry with your damned useless sisters."

Thomas followed Dai. They would eat a hearty Portuguese ham hock stew with sweet bread that Okaasan was forced to bake twice a week for Vovó Medeiros and various other Portuguese in-laws in the large community forno that the haole owner of the Oʻahu Sugar Company had built for his immigrant workers at the center of Portuguese Camp Four.

Anah helped her mother off the ground. She dusted herself off, then rushed to the kitchen to boil corn tea for their dinner of rice and pickled cabbage.

Anah motioned for Charles to follow her into the mountains above Kīpapa Stream to gather more sugarcane, ʻaʻaliʻi, and white ginger. In the dark of evening, in the nook behind the furo house, Anah extracted the juices of these plants.

Okaasan smiled at Anah when she presented her with the pulp-filled can. She sniffed it, dipped a finger, tasted it, and nodded. She quickly poured some of the liquid into little Leah's tea, then forced Anah, Aki, and Charles to drink the rest of the bitter tonic.

It rained the day they took Leah to the orphanage in Kalihi Valley cradled deep in the Koʻolau Mountains, one of two volcanoes that formed the island of Oʻahu. Freshwater streams and waterfalls ran from the wet upper peaks of Kalihi Uka to lower Kalihi Kai to Keʻehi Lagoon, just west of Honolulu Harbor but many miles away from the Oʻahu Sugar Plantation.

"Tuberculosis is highly contagious," the haole camp doctor had whispered to Dai in the quiet of the front room. "Many people world-wide, Tomas, living in unsanitary conditions I might add, have become infected by this epidemic. A terrible, terrible contagion." He tsked-tsked.

Dai nodded, utterly afraid for years of the leprosy that took a second cousin, then an older sister, then an aunt to the dreaded peninsula of no return, Kalaupapa, where a leper colony was established on Molokai's rugged north shore in 1886 by royal order of King Kamehameha V. Afraid of the bubonic plague that swept through an overcrowded and filthy Chinatown in 1900, the Board of Health forgoing quarantine and disinfection in favor of a purging by fire, leaving thirty-eight acres of slum in rubble and ash. Afraid of the epidemic of cholera, the worst outbreak since the maʻi ʻokuʻu that swept the Sandwich Islands in 1804, this time taking a paternal grandmother who shared living quarters with the Medeiros family soon after her arrival from the Azores in early 1889. Afraid of the influenza, typhus, whooping cough, the polio that crippled his younger brother, the smallpox that killed the newborn and the elderly. And now very ashamed of the stigma of the consumption that threatened his entire extended family living in Portuguese Camp Four. And all because of *his* infected youngest daughter.

"I realize that on your luna's pay, you cannot afford the sanatorium at Leahi Hospital, Tomas," the doctor said, snapping his bag shut with authority. "So it is my urgent recommendation that you make arrangements for your daughter to be taken immediately to St. Joseph's. Mr. Campbell has instructed me to make absolutely certain that the child infected with the consumption is gone by—"

"Haibiyo?" Okaasan stammered.

"Yes, Mama-san, tu-ber-cu-lo-sis," the camp doctor enunciated loudly as though she were deaf and stupid. "Con-sump-shun. Very ki-ta-nai. Very pi-lau. Very su-jo." He looked pleased to speak the word *dirty* in many plantation languages.

"Akachan no come home?" Okaasan asked the doctor.

"Your daughter is *not* a baby, Mama-san."

"*Akachan* no come home?" Okaasan repeated.

The doctor shook his head. "She will receive adequate care from the Sisters of the Sacred Heart," he said. "Many plantation workers in your si-tuation—no more mo-ney. Send sick child St. Joseph get better. When sickness all gone, maybe your child come home, Mama-san."

"No, me, I go," Okaasan insisted, patting her chest. "Me go with akachan. Me Mama. You talk to Nihon-jin doku-toru?"

The doctor, agitated and insulted now, knew of the Japanese doctors she referred to. "I am a better physician," he told her. The Japanese doctors were brought to eight sugar plantations in 1886 by edict of the Bureau of Immigration.

In his anger, he began making large, impatient gestures as he tried to explain to her. "Over there in mountain, Mama-san, there are German brothers and priests—very nice, very good men of God. They build very big foundling home." He paused, not wanting to frighten her with an explanation of *orphanage*. "Hos-pi-tal, three-story, Mama-san. Plenty nuns. Way inside the mountain. Clean air," he said, exaggerating a deep, robust breath. "Proper diet—tabe-mono. Consumption all gone. Girl must go now, Mama-san. You listen to me or else—"

"No, no," Okaasan told the doctor. "Way in mountain?" she asked. She did not wait for his answer. "No. Tomasu—" She turned to Dai. "You talk to the Japanese doctors the plantation brought to help us," she said to him in her native language, panicked and unable to find the words in pidgin.

"No, Mama-san, the girl must go now," the doctor insisted. "Very bad, very bad. You have four other keiki and family relations living close by. The girl is ki-ta-nai, Mama-san, *dirty*," he said with great impatience and import.

"Me take her back to Nihon," Okaasan said. "Maybe they can provide proper treatment in Japan," she consoled herself in Japanese.

"We have no money. The poor send their children to orphanages. It must be done or Mr. Campbell will take away my job," Dai said in an angry Portuguese. "It cannot be helped. It is God's will."

She did not understand his words.

"We no mo' money, Sumi-san. Listen doctor," Dai said, taking her face in his hands. "No mo' money for sanatoria. All kine family in plantation same-same. Children sick, go St. Joseph." He would have hit her had the doctor not been there. "Meu família," he said at last with great concern, looking out the window toward Vovó Medeiros's house. "I no like them sick from this *Japanee* illness—" He stopped, catching himself.

"*Your* family. You only think about your own kind. Your own kind is filthier than the pigs," Okaasan said in Japanese. "The Portuguese do not even bathe every night. Even the women are covered with hair. Your kind stinks worse than the Chinese. Our daughter was infected by the Portuguese."

"Speakee English," he said, glowering at her. "You listen me. And you listen doctor. All pau. No mo' talk." Dai looked at Leah lying on the futon by the window. "She go today," he said to the doctor. "You tell Mr. James Campbell, Medeiros like stay luna. Me listen Mr. James Campbell. Me not troublemaker." And then he muttered in Portuguese, "I will take her there myself if I have to."

Anah helped her mother, who collapsed into a chair. Dai left the house with the doctor, slamming the door behind him.

Anah rode with Charles and Leah in the back of the Andrade Dairy buggy full of empty milk cans and bottles. The smell of spoiled milk soaked deep into the wooden bed. Okaasan rode up front with Manuel Andrade. It would be a long day's trip from the O'ahu Sugar Plantation over the dry 'Ewa plains and into the city of Honolulu. The heat at sea level made the smell of sour milk unbearable.

They rode past groves of tall coconut trees, Chinese rice plantations, and taro farms near the huge ancient Hawaiian fishponds, twenty-seven in total, built by a chain of native men and boys from mountain to sea who moved rocks shoulder to shoulder to build the walls of the ponds. Hundreds of acres once the royal property of area kings and queens lined the coastal lands of the Pearl Harbor lochs.

They passed through the endless fields of rolling cane as they traveled along the train tracks of the O'ahu Railway built by a young, entrepreneurial Benjamin Franklin Dillingham. The train tracks, for years many called "Dillingham's Folly," would soon find the support of King David Kalakaua in 1889, the train tracks that brought king sugar to port, the train tracks that would lead Anah, her mother, brother, and little sister on this day to the city of Honolulu.

From the train station near the piers, Manuel Andrade clopped-clopped the horses along King Street, bustling with women under plumed hats and parasols, Chinamen mea 'ono pua'a vendors, stray cats, a Japanese funeral parlor, haole businessmen in formal suits, the candy man, fish peddlers, soldiers and whores, babies tied to the backs of mama-sans, noisy street merchants, and oxcarts filled with bags of rice or Japanese and Korean picture brides straight from the docks at Honolulu Harbor.

Anah listened to the slow squeak of the bed and the solemn creak of the wheels on the unpaved road. She had never seen the big, modern city of Honolulu, but fearing for the welfare of the little one, she turned her attention toward comforting her.

The buggy headed up into the mountains, past haole mission homes with vast lawns, Japanese flower growers, Okinawan piggeries, wet Chinese taro patches, and Portuguese and Hawaiian dairies, finally dropping them off on the deserted, narrow road leading to Kalihi Valley.

Charles hurried out of the back, Anah passing little Leah to him, as Okaasan bowed and bowed to Manuel Andrade, offering him bento, fresh produce from her garden, and a loaf of sweet bread that she had packed for the long journey. He smiled briefly with a tip of his straw hat. They did not exchange words. He accepted her obligatory gifts, then spit tobacco juice on the ground with a quick jingle of the harness. He pulled the buggy away.

It began to drizzle. They walked to the orphanage in the rain on a dirt road that followed Kalihi Stream, the muddy smell of the taro patches and duck ponds at the foot of the Kapālama Hills, the debris of fallen mangoes, pungent, the fuzzy gray seeds slippery underfoot.

Anah tended to little Leah, who began falling behind when the road became a meandering mountainous trail, the mud deepening with the whipping rain. She was so tiny, this winter of her fifth year. She stopped to fill the scoop of her dress with soft mangoes.

"They get 'ono kaukau ova there," Anah told her, taking the rotten mangoes and wiping the orange slime off her sister's dress. "You eat plenty good food, make you all pau sick."

"And they got real toilet paper so you don't scratch your little ass when you wipe your shit," Charles added. He spoke in the crude Japanese he had learned from the disgraced gannenmono samurai who lived in a lean-to beyond the whorehouse on the banks of Waikele Stream. "Steal some for me when I come to visit you. I can wrap some around my penis to keep it warm at night." He ruffled her wet hair when she laughed, punching at his stomach, then pushing him away from her. Large drops of rain fell from the trees. They took shelter from a heavy downpour.

Leah looked at Anah. "Where we going?" she asked tentatively.

Anah did not answer.

"You staying with me?"

No answer.

"When you all pau sick, I come back fast," Anah said at last, taking Leah's small hand in her own. "No worry, okay? Only chotto you stay ova there," she said with a small space between forefinger and thumb.

Anah hoped that Leah believed her.

Charles took out a long swath of rice bag that Okaasan had used to carry them when they were infants. He tied Leah onto his back like the strong big brother he was to his sisters even though Thomas was a full year older and Anah exactly nine months younger than him.

"My akachan," he said to Leah as she rested her cold face on his back. She always loved to pretend she was *his* baby.

"My paipa," she whispered into his ear, "my chichi." He always loved to pretend he was *her* father.

"Mine," Anah said, "my paipa!" She reached for Leah as Charles ran ahead. "My daddy, my chichi!"

Leah laughed at their game of keep-away.

Okaasan trudged on ahead of them, crying, wiping her face with both hands. She had no one, no family to turn to, disowned from Nihon to Hawai'i to Amerika to Kanada to Buraziru. She had disgraced the aggressive village matchmaker from Yanai City and her own desperate father by running away from her marriage contract, running from the docks of Honolulu Harbor with the filthy, hairy Porutogaru-go.

Anah stopped on the trail when she saw the foreboding three-story orphanage run by the Sisters of the Sacred Heart, built plank by plank at the turn of the century by two holy brothers, master carpenters from Germany, who were called on to serve the blessed church by Bishop Lanfranc Deusdedit, the third apostolic vicar of the Hawaiian Islands.

With a work crew of brothers and natives, the bishop himself had supervised the arrival, inventory, then hauling of each truss, joist, and main beam from Honolulu Harbor up the ominous valley by buggy. The holy brothers loaded their supplies onto mule wagons, then hand-carried them to the expansive site when the road narrowed from a horse trail to a mountainous path.

The cross on its rooftop made from chene wood imported from the bishop's native Fain-les-Moutiers stood white against a black sky.

Okaasan walked slowly over the spacious, soggy front lawn. Anah and Charles carried Leah and followed behind her. Then under a grove of mountain apple trees, near a patch of beautiful white ginger, on a bridge over a raging Kalihi Stream, they left her.

She clung to Okaasan as Anah untied her from the sling. And then she held on to Charles, who screamed her name as the nuns pulled her away from him. Leah wriggled loose and ran back to Anah's open arms, the huge white nun restraining her tiny arms and legs.

Anah felt Leah torn from her body, torn from that space in her belly left churning and empty.

Okaasan held Leah's coughing and gagging face in her hands as the nuns tried to separate them, Leah's arms outstretched, the wind pulsating with her cries, "Okaasan! Okaasan! No leave me!"

Her wailing, frantic voice echoed, and echoed, and echoed. A dog's long howling, an owl's plaintive cry, the high whinny of a whipped horse. Anah ran down the rocky dirt road for miles, the road that led them out of Kalihi Valley.

LOIS-ANN YAMANAKA *was named one of the "25 Most Influential Asians in America" by* A. Magazine, *and was listed among "Those Who Shaped the Isles in this Century: 100 Who Made a Difference," by the* Honolulu Star-Bulletin. *She is the recipient of the Hawai'i Award for Literature, the American Book Award, the Children's Choice for Literature, a National Endowment for the Arts Fellowship, and a Lannan Literary Award. She is the author of* Snow Angel, Sand Angel; Saturday Night at the Pahala Theatre; Wild Meat and the Bully Burgers; Blu's Hanging; Heads by Harry; Name Me Nobody; Father of the Four Passages; *and* Behold the Many. *She lives in Honolulu, where she is co-director of Na'au: A Place for Learning and Healing.*

James T. Hamada

from DON'T GIVE UP THE SHIP

I n another section of the city—in the highland of Kaimuki, a residential district perpetually swept by the trade wind, commanding a wonderful view of the sea—stood a magnificent two-story stone building, in the midst of four acres of well-kept lawn and fragrant multi-colored gardens.

This was the mansion of Stanley Ross, President of the Pacific-Hawaiian Steamship Company. To Mr. Ross there was much of sentimental interest in this mansion. He had built it, and he and his wife had moved into it on the day of their marriage. On that memorable day he had taken his bride into the new home and said to her proudly, "Jeanne, I'm not a college graduate, as you are. But I'm a self-made man, and this home and everything else I have, I have earned through my own efforts, with the assistance, of course, of a ship I got from my father. Now, all will be our joint property."

Years before, when struggling against overwhelming obstacles in building up his shipping business, Mr. Ross had been living in a humble cottage at Waikiki, which in those days wasn't the flourishing and popular resort that it now is. Along the beach were only a few scattered houses. It certainly was a lonesome beach in those days.

Memories of those early days persistently came back to Mr. Ross. Honolulu had made remarkable progress since then. The shipping magnate had long ago discarded the cottage at Waikiki, but every now and then he felt a poignant sting of nostalgia for those bygone days when he was working terrifically and dreaming of bright days to come. That was the happiest time of his life.

The Ross family was noted for its sea traditions. He was the descendant of a long line of seafarers, his grandfather having come to Hawaii as a whaler during the first half of the nineteenth century.

Mr. Ross was born in the old cottage at Waikiki. His father was skipper of a bark, the *Barbara Cook*, plying between Honolulu and the Pacific Coast, and until he was about seven years old he spent much of his time with his father on board that vessel. Thus, at an early age, the tradition of the sea was implanted into him.

Then he went to school—the old Royal School and Punahou. At fifteen he returned to the sea, as cabin boy on his father's bark. A decade later his father died.

Some years back—in 1876—a reciprocity treaty was concluded between the Kingdom of Hawaii and the United States. By its terms, Pearl Harbor, which has since grown into an impregnable naval outpost of Uncle Sam in the Pacific, was ceded to the United States, and Hawaii was granted the right of sending her sugar free of duty to America.

This gave a tremendous impetus to the Islands' sugar industry, which grew by leaps and bounds. This, and the shipment of the ever-increasing products to the United States, made it necessary to have more ships.

When Mr. Ross took over the command of his father's bark, the shipping business was on the threshold of an era of great expansion. He foresaw a brilliant future for it, and with his bark as a nucleus, started a shipping company.

It was hard work at first. There were plenty of obstacles and untold hardships, keen competition of foreign companies already well established. There were times when he came pretty near to giving up, but spurred by the glamorous sea tradition of his family, he kept on. The sailing ships eventually became out of date, and he replaced them with steamships.

Meanwhile the Hawaiian Kingdom was overthrown and superseded by a republic—later on annexed to the United States and became an American territory. And by the time the present century was ushered in, Mr. Ross's business had been well established. It was then that he built his present home at Kaimuki.

Then a new industry cropped up—pineapples—and became a considerable factor. Then came the tourist industry, which furnished still further impetus to the expansion of shipping, and Mr. Ross had to build a palatial ship to handle that branch.

The answer to this need was the S. S. *Honolulu*, a splendid vessel of 17,000 tons, built in an Eastern shipyard. Her arrival at Honolulu on her maiden voyage was a gala affair, serenaded off port by Hawaiian singing boys and girls in outrigger canoes and launches, and overhead welcomed by zooming army and navy planes. Practically the whole town was out on the waterfront to greet her. Every steamer whistle in the harbor and every factory whistle shrieked its welcome. The Royal Hawaiian Band blared forth its *Aloha Oe*, and that night there was a banquet and a pageant to celebrate the great event.

To Mr. Ross this was the greatest event of his life, next to the occasion years before when he took his bride into his new home.

James Michener
from HAWAII

Now, in 1927, Hoxworth Hale was these things, and in each he was an almost perfect exemplification of the archetype: he was a Hale, a Punahou graduate, a Yale man, the head of a great island firm, and a man married to his cousin. Therefore, when he spoke at his first meeting of the H & H board, his colleagues listened: "There is an unfortunate spirit of agitation in the world today, and I believe our first concern must be the protection of our position by exercising some kind of logical control over the legislature."

He outlined a sensible plan whereby his impressive cousin, big Hewie Janders, got himself elected president of the senate, while half a dozen assorted lawyers, treasurers and accountants who worked for the big firms ran for lesser seats. For speaker of the house Hoxworth shrewdly selected the jovial, relaxed Chinese politician Kangaroo Kee, to whom he offered several lucrative contracts; and so carefully did the new young leader plan that before long Hawaii passed into that secure and reasonable period when most of its legislation was decided upon first at quiet meetings held in the board room of H & H, whence it was sent to trusted representatives who could be depended upon to enact laws pretty much as proposed by Hoxworth Hale and his close associates.

The board room of H & H was on the second floor of a large, fort-like building that stood at the corner of Fort and Merchant, and from this combination of facts the powerful clique that ran Hawaii came to be known simply as The Fort. It included, of course, H & H and also J & W. The Hewletts were members, as were some of the lesser planters from the big island. Banks, railways, trust companies and large estate owners were represented, but exactly what The Fort consisted of no man could properly say; it was simply the group who by common consent were entitled to meet on the second floor of H & H, a close-knit, cohesive body of men who were determined to give Hawaii a responsible form of government.

The Fort rarely abused its power. If some crackpot legislator not subservient to it wanted to curry favor with his constituents by shouting, "I promised you I'd get a playground for Kakaako, and I'll get you a playground for Kakaako," they let him yell, and at one of their meetings Hoxworth Hale would ask, "Is there any reason why there shouldn't be a playground at Kakaako?" and if such a project did not imperil any fundamental interest of The Fort—and if its cost could be passed on to the general public without raising real estate taxes—the playground was allowed to go through. But if this same legislator subsequently shouted, "Last year plantation trains running without lights killed four people, so I insist upon lights where plantation trains cross public roads," then The Fort moved quietly but massively into action. "We've looked into costs of such lights," Hoxworth Hale would tell his directors, "and they would cut our sugar profits to the bone." Somehow such bills were iceboxed in committee, and no amount of yelling by infuriated legislators could get them unfrozen.

Any major bill affecting either sugar, pineapple or land had to be actually drafted by The Fort itself; such bills were too important to be left to the whims of a legislature. But it was to Hoxworth Hale's credit that he did not allow grossly abusive bills to be proposed: "My interpretation of democracy is that business must never intrude into ordinary legislative processes, except where matters of vital importance are at stake and then never for selfish motives." At some sessions of the legislature forty-nine out of fifty bills were not interfered with in any way; but this was partly because the legislators had learned to ask, before proposing a bill, "Will The Fort go for this?" It was common prudence not to propose something that The Fort would automatically have to fight.

It was under Hale's direction that The Fort insinuated its men onto the public boards that controlled things like the university and the parks, and once when an outside writer took pains to cross-reference the 181 most influential board members in Hawaii, he found that only thirty-one men in all were involved, and that of them twenty-eight were Hales, Whipples, Hoxworths, Hewletts and Janderses . . . or their sons-in-law. "A very public-spirited group of people," the writer concluded, "but it is often difficult to tell one board from the other or any from the board of H & H."

The Honolulu *Mail* was owned by The Fort, but its function in the community was never blatantly abused. It was a good paper, Republican of course, and it frequently supported positions which The Fort could not have approved but which the general public did; but when an issue involved land, sugar or labor, the *Mail* wrote forceful editorials explaining how the public good was involved and how government ought to respond. Once when a *Mail* reporter was sent to fifteen different sugar-growing areas to write a series of articles proving how much better off the people of Hawaii were than laborers in Jamaica, Fiji and Queensland, his returning letters were first studied in The Fort, "to be sure he maintains the proper historical perspective." The *Mail* was scrupulously fair in reporting activities of the underground Democratic Party, but the articles were written as if a benevolent old man was chuckling over the actions of imbecile and delinquent children.

The endless chain of appointed office holders sent out from Washington—too often incompetent and gregarious politicians—was quickly absorbed into The Fort's genial social life: hunting trips to the big island, boating parties, picnics by the sea. Sometimes a newcomer could sit on the bench for six months without ever meeting a Chinese other than a defendant in a court case or a Japanese who was not dressed in white and serving sandwiches. Such officials could be forgiven if they came to think of Hawaii as The Fort and vice versa and to hand down their decisions accordingly.

But Hoxworth Hale's greatest contribution lay in a general principle which he propounded early in his regime, and it is to his credit that he perceived this problem long before any of his contemporaries, and his adroit handling of it earned The Fort millions upon millions of dollars. He announced his policy flatly: "No military man stationed in Hawaii above the rank of captain in the army or lieutenant in the navy is to leave these islands without having been entertained by at least three families in this room." Then he added, "And if you can include the lower ranks, so much the better!" As a result of this rule, the constant flow of military people who passed through Hawaii came to think of big Hewlett Janders and gracious Hoxworth Hale as the two commanders of the islands, men who could be trusted, men who were sound; and in the years that were about to explode, making Hawaii a bastion of the Pacific, it was very difficult for Washington to send any senior admiral or general to Honolulu who did not already know The Fort intimately. Therefore, when a contract was to be let, bids weren't really necessary: "Hewlett Janders, the fellow I went hunting with ten years ago, he can build it for us." More important, when the procurement and engineering offices in Washington began to assume major importance in America's rush program of military expansion, the rising young men who crowded those offices almost had to be the ones that Hoxworth Hale and Hewie Janders had entertained so lavishly in the previous decade.

Nothing Hoxworth accomplished was more important than this establishment of a personal pipeline direct to the sources of power in Washington. Again, he never abused his prerogatives. He never called generals on the phone, shouting, as did some, "Goddam it, Shelly, they're talking about eminent domain on three thousand acres of my choicest sugar fields." Usually this made Washington determined to go ahead with condemnation proceedings. Hoxworth Hale acted differently: "This you, Shelly? How's Bernice? We're fine out here. Say, Shelly, what I called about was the proposed air strip out Waipahu way. That's a good site, Shelly, but have your men studied what the landing pattern would be with those tall mountains at the end . . . Yes, Shelly, the ones we went hunting on that weekend . . . Yes, I just want to be sure your men have thought about that, because there's another strip of land a little farther makai . . . Yes, that means toward the sea in Hawaiian, and I was wondering . . . Yes, it's our land, too, so there's no advantage to me one way or the other . . . Be sure to give Bernice our best."

Hawaii in these years of benevolent domination by The Fort was one of the finest areas of the world. The sun shone, the trade winds blew, and when tourists arrived on the luxury H & H liners the police band played hulas and girls in grass skirts danced. Labor relations were reasonably good, and any luna who dared strike a worker would have been instantly whisked out of the islands. The legislature was honest, the judges sent out from the mainland handed down strict but impartial decisions, except in certain unimportant cases involving land, and the economy flourished. It is true that mainland firms like Gregory's and California Fruit protested: "My God, the place is a feudal barony! We tried to buy land for a store and they said, 'You can't buy any land in Hawaii. We don't want your kind of store in the islands.'"

It was also true that Chinese or Japanese who wanted to leave the islands to travel on the mainland had to get written permission to do so, and if The Fort felt that a given Oriental was not the kind of man who should represent the islands in America, because he tended toward communist ideas, speaking of labor unions and such, the authorities would not let him leave, and there was nothing he could do about it. Hewlett Janders in particular objected to the large number of young Chinese and Japanese who wanted to go to the mainland to become doctors and lawyers, and he personally saw to it that a good many of them did not get away, for, as he pointed out: "We've got fine doctors right here that we can trust, and if we keep on allowing Orientals to become lawyers, we merely create problems for ourselves. Educating such people above their station has got to stop."

Once in 1934, after Hoxworth and his team had performed miracles in protecting Hawaii from the fury of the depression—it fell less heavily on the islands than anywhere else on earth—he was embittered when a group of Japanese workers connived to have a labor man from Washington visit the islands, and Hale refused to see the visitor.

"You'd think they'd have respect for what I've done keeping Hawaii safe from the depression. Every Japanese who got his regular pay check, got it thanks to me, and now they want me to talk with labor-union men!"

He refused three times to permit an interview, but one day the man from Washington caught him on the sidewalk and said hurriedly, "Mr. Hale, I respect your position, but I've got to tell you that under the new laws you are required to let labor-union organizers talk to your men on the plantations."

"What's that?" Hoxworth asked in astonishment. "Did you say . . ."

"I said," the visitor, an unpleasant foreign type, repeated slowly, "that under the law you are required to permit labor-union organizers access to your men on the plantations."

"I thought that's what you said," Hale replied. "Good heavens man!" Then, taking refuge in a phrase he had often heard Wild Whip declaim, he said, "If I saw a rattlesnake crawling onto one of my plantations and I shot him, I'd be a hero. Yet you want me voluntarily to open my lands to labor organizers. Truly, you must be out of your mind." He turned abruptly and left.

"Mr. Hale!" the labor man called, catching up with him and grabbing his coat.

"Don't you ever touch me!" Hale stormed.

"I apologize," the man said contritely. "I just wanted to warn you that Hawaii's no different from the rest of America."

"Apparently you don't know Hawaii," Hale said, and left.

In his cold, efficient governance of The Fort he manifested only two peculiarities which could be construed as weaknesses. Whenever he had a major decision to make he spent some time alone in his office, pushing back and forth across his polished desk a reddish rock about the size of a large fist, and in the contemplation of its mysterious form he found intellectual reassurance. "The rock came from his great-great-grandmother on Maui," his secretary explained. "It's sort of a good-luck omen," she said, but what the good luck derived from she did not know and Hale never told her. Also, whenever The Fort started a new building Hale insisted that local kahunas be brought in to orient it. Once a mainland architect asked, "What's a man with a Yale degree doing with kahunas?" and Hale replied, "You'd be surprised. In our courts it's illegal to force a Hawaiian to testify if a known kahuna is watching in the courtroom." The architect asked, "You certainly don't believe such nonsense, do you?" and Hale replied evasively, "Well, if I were the judge, I would certainly insist that any known kahunas be barred from my courtroom. Their power is peculiar."

One unspoken rule regarding The Fort was observed by all: The Fort did not exist; it was a phrase never mentioned in public; Hale himself never spoke it; and it was banned from both newspaper and radio. The building in which the men met remained as it was during Wild Whip's tenancy: a rugged red-stone commercial headquarters built like a fort and bearing a simple brass plate that read: Hoxworth & Hale, Shipmasters and Factors.

JAMES MICHENER (1907-1997) *wrote more than forty books, mostly novels. He published the best-selling* Hawaii *in 1959, the year Hawai'i became a state. His other books include* The Bridges at Toko-Ri; The Covenant; The Source; Texas; Alaska; *and the Pulitzer-Prize-winning short-story collection* Tales of the South Pacific, *which was made into the classic Rodgers and Hammerstein musical* South Pacific. *He donated his large and important collection of Japanese prints to the Honolulu Academy of Arts.*

Carlo Mario Fraticelli
"LA HORA SUPREMA"

Borincanos a la unión

Oh nobles puertorriqueños,
largo tiempo habéis sufrido;
en silencio sumergidos,
dormidos en los ensueños,
abatidos por los dueños,
tiranos de la opresión.
Hoy tenemos la ocasión
de mejorar nuestra vida;
por eso mi voz convida:
Borincanos a la unión.

La campaña electoral
puerta abierta nos presenta
para arreglarle la cuenta
al que nos trató tan mal.
En un estado fatal,
sin pena ni compassión,
vivimos la indignación
como seres muy fatales.
Para aliviar nuestros males:
Borincanos a la unión.

Necesitamos unir
todas nuestras voluntades,
y así evitar los males
de un ruinoso porvenir.
Necesario es destruir
el profundo malestar
si queremos disfrutar
de algunos días mejores.
A vencer los opresores
marchemos sin vacilar.

La política es un arte
en estos tiempos modernos;
luchemos para no vernos
con el mal de nuestra parte.
Vienen a desafiarte
y aumentar tu malestar;
si luchas podrás llegar
a conseguir la victoria.
A conquistar esa gloria
marchemos sin vacilar.

El bando republicano
representa la riqueza
y por eso le interesa
ver el gobierno en su mano.
El demócrata es más llano;
en su modo de pensar
él suele representar
de la pobreza el clamor.

Sigámoslo con amor
y veremos el altar.

Sería para nuestro bien
mayoría en el Senado;
según lo tengo estudiado,
en el congreso también.
No miremos con desdén
al alcalde y su sección;
votemos sin distinción
por toda la plana entera,
y veremos la bandera
de la santa redención.
La ley de ciudadanía
incluye en su reglamento
que el otro es un elemento
que sirve de garantía.
Con valor y energía
dejemos la postración;
levantemos la opinión
del Borincano algún día.
Veremos con alegría
nuestra santa redención.

La voz de este humilde hermano
todos debieran oír,
y el camino seguir
que marca su afable mano;
porque yo desde temprano
lo tuve por devoción,
en ir contra la prisión
del pobre y su malestar;
para verlo en el altar
de la santa redención.

"THE SUPREME HOUR"

Puerto Ricans, let's unite

Oh noble Puerto Ricans,
you have suffered for a long time;

submerged n silence,
asleep in dreams,
humiliated by the owners,
tyrants of oppression.
Today we have the opportunity
to improve our lives;
for this reason my voice invites you:
Puerto Ricans, let's unite.

The electoral campaign
presents us an open door
to settle the score
with those who have treated us so badly.
In a disastrous state,
without grief nor compassion,
we live through the indignation,
like ill-fated people.
To relieve our suffering:
Puerto Ricans, let's unite.

We need to unite
all our will power,
and in this way avoid the misfortunes
of a disastrous future.
It is necessary to destroy
the profound unrest
if we want to enjoy
some better days.
To defeat the oppressors
let us march without hesitation.

Politics is an art
in these modern times;
let us fight so that we do not end up
on the wrong side.
They are coming to challenge you
and to increase your unrest;
if you fight you will be able to
finally attain victory.
To win that glory,
let us march without hesitation.

The Republican party
represents wealth
and for that reason they are interested
in seeing government in their hands.
The Democrat is more straight-forward;
in his mode of thinking
he is accustomed to representing
the outcry of poverty.
Let us follow him with love
and we will see the altar.

The majority in the senate
will be for our benefit;
according to my study,
in the house also.
Let us not look with disdain
at the mayor and his department;
let us vote without distinction
for the entire slate,
and we will see the banner
of our holy redemption.

The law of citizenship
includes in its rules
that the other person is an element
that serves as a guarantee.
With valor and energy
let us forsake prostration;
let us raise the reputation
of the Puerto Rican someday.
We will joyfully see
our holyredemption.

Everyone should listen to
the voice of this humble brother,
and follow the way
that his genial hand indicates;
because from the earliest days
I have devoutly believed
in going against the pressure
on the poor and their unrest;

to see him on the altar
of holy redemption.

TRANSLATED BY AUSTIN DIAS

Jessica Kawasuna Saiki
"LEARNING"

I t did not matter that they hadn't seen it. The three girls had devoured enough data from glossy magazines about the movie that as far as they were concerned, the popcorn had already been digested and they had as good as seen it.

"I hear she runs nude through the woods."

"I thought she swam naked in a pool."

"Wasn't it a bathtub scene?"

"Everyone's talking about 'Ecstasy.'"

"Especially about Heddy Lamarr."

"It's really something."

During their senior year, the three girls had been the best of friends. Now each would go her separate way. Eileen and Myra looked forward to the university in September but Shizuko Hata said she wanted a permanent job. Distinguished in high school for her cuteness as head pom pom girl and attendant to the Senior Prom Queen, Shiz preened herself before a mirror. It was in preparation for a job interview. Carefully she outlined lips with carmine Tangee and re-arranged spit curls for the Flapper Fanny look. A final glance at the mirror, a tug at her skirt, and she was ready.

"Job hunting?" her mother asked, entering the room.

"Yeah, I have the ad somewhere here." She rummaged through her lauhala purse for a crumpled piece of newspaper. "Kinda strange sounding but interesting I think. Listen to this: 'Wanted, artistic type girl for design work,'" she read.

"Sounds like you."

"I thought so too."

"Well, see how it is."

"That's what I'm going to do. See you."

She repeated to herself the address then hurried to catch the bus. Located next to a car repair shop, in a semi-residential section of town, her goal was a warehouse fronted with a Palmer Enterprises sign. She entered the door marked Office.

A middle-aged man of average height, garbed casually in seersucker suit and polo shirt, rose to meet her. She noticed his slight paunch, dark curly hair and pleasant though ruddy face. Typical haole type, she thought to herself.

"I came to see about the job you advertised—artistic girl?"

"Sure, sit down." He eyed her thoroughly, up and down. He spoke in a relaxed way, leaning against the filing cabinet, fingering a cigarette in a hairy hand. "My name is Palmer, Ron Palmer. And yours is Miss—?"

The hand he offered was warm. "Shizuko Hata. People call me Shiz for short."

"Okay, Shiz, now let me tell you something about the job . . . ." He went on to elaborate details entailed in the position, the particulars of which she concluded she could handle easily enough. After the introduction, he took her through the plant where she saw five workers silk screening bolts of fabric with Hawaiian motifs such as breadfruit leaves, bird of paradise, surfers and so on. The usual stuff. Creating such designs would be her job.

While Mr. Palmer introduced the work crew, she felt an undercurrent of snide glances as though the likes of her were an all too familiar parade to the staff. Their stares gave her unease. It was certainly not Mr. Palmer's fault. On the contrary, he attempted to put them at ease with a limp joke about sleeping on and off the job, a joke greeted with snickers.

She was relieved to return to the privacy of Mr. Palmer's office. Consulting his watch, he asked "Did you bring your lunch?"

"No, I didn't expect to stay here all day."

"Okay, how about lunch with me?" It was his tone, as easy as turning on the tap. This was something he did every day. He was cool. She too would be cool. "Okay," she said.

Cupping her elbow, he guided her to his car, a Victoria Brougham, she remembered, baby blue enamel. Opening the door, he helped her into its beige leather seat. The fluid suavity of his conduct continued throughout lunch.

Fisherman's Lounge where they dined was a place she'd known only by sight. While riding the bus, she had passed its oversized neon sign. Its parking lot jammed with fancy cars. Popular with executives, at noon it bulged with businessmen, dark-suited professionals sipping martinis with clientele, secretary or an occasional wife. Seated at one of its spotlessly linened tables, beneath a hanging philodendron, she felt that she didn't belong here. She was not like one of those be-jeweled women, toying with their cocktail glasses and laughing easily.

Mr. Palmer, on the other hand, seemed to be swimming in his element. Background Hawaiian music, a blend of lethargic velveteen voices and steel guitars made him happy. His fingers kept drumming to its lazy beat. A waiter came to their table with menus. After a close study, reading even the fine print, Mr. Palmer asked "Now then, what'll you have? Any preferences?"

"I'll have whatever you suggest," she said, conscious of the waiter's eyes upon her. The air conditioning chilled her.

"Is there a house special?" Mr. Palmer asked the waiter.

"Sir, I would recommend the Parker Ranch beef today," said the waiter.

"Fine, we'll try it. I'll also have a bloody Mary just for kicks." He winked.

Leaning back in her chair, Shiz observed Mr. Palmer's cigarette choreography: thumping each against a shiny, gold monogrammed case, snapping a lighter, flicking ashes precisely into an ashtray so that a ruby eye of his gold ring flashed. "Now then, tell me about yourself, Shiz. Have you any hobbies?" he asked. He narrowed his eyes, which were a smoky gray.

"Well, I like to go to the movies a lot and I collect matchbook covers."

"You paint or draw in your spare time, I suppose?"

"Yes, I took a class at the Academy last summer that taught me how to draw things music inspires." She wondered if all this was kid stuff to him.

"Really?" He leaned back in his seat, squinting his eyes as if to snap a photograph of her. "That's very interesting. Abstract things?"

"Not always. Sometimes I see people or certain lines, flowers and things like that in the music. It depends." (Art interested him. She liked that.)

"Uh-huh." He hunched over, elbows propped on the table, hands clasped under his chin, re-garnering all his attention on her. Shiz nibbled at pebble-sized bits of steak and potatoes while talk rambled on about beach-wear and towels. Finally, the last course was served and consumed.

"Through with dessert?"

"Yes, the mango ice cream was delicious."

"Come on. Let's get out of here."

"Thanks for the lunch, Mr. Palmer."

"It was my pleasure," he said, assisting her out of the chair.

Leaving Fisherman's Lounge, Mr. Palmer drove down King Street to the banking district for an appointment he had with a shipping company. Shiz, meanwhile, waited for him in the car. When Mr. Palmer returned, he told her "Those people were real nice to me. Who says they have a stranglehold on the islands? They were real nice people."

His words meant nothing to her but she replied, "That's good," which seemed to satisfy him because he flashed another easy smile at her. It made him look handsome. He is a nice, generous man she thought as he asked her if the wind through the open windows bothered her. Considerate too.

"About your salary, Shiz, I think you'll find me a generous man. Giving bonuses for good work is how I keep my crew happy. You can ask them." Again he flashed that radiant smile. "I want you to be happy," he said patting her knee lightly.

They continued driving, not back to the office as she had expected but instead to the Waikiki district, onto a side street where sleek apartment buildings towered between palms bereft of coconuts. Parking the car in a private garage, he asked "Do you mind if I pick up some papers in my apartment?"

"No," she answered.

"Come with me then."

She followed him, entering a glass-fronted building where a doorman in red uniform said "Gooday, Mr. Palmer." With hand on her forearm, he led her through a foyer where they took a silent, carpeted elevator to the second floor and his apartment. Once inside its soundproof seclusion, he excused himself to change. He returned wearing a Hawaiian floral shirt and loose trousers. She was taken aback by the difference clothes made in this instance. He looked to her like one of the ubiquitous haole tourists she saw strolling the beachwalks any evening, prowling for quick pick-ups. She sat somewhat tensely on the edge of a chair close to the entranceway.

Again he left the room. She heard the slam of a refrigerator door. Ice cubes clinked.

Heaving a sigh, he flopped himself into a reclining, black leather chair, slipped off his shoes, and propped his stockinged feet onto a footstool. "Now then," he said, sipping a drink, "Let's talk about the movies. You said you see a lot of them?

"Yes, I do."

"Well then, are you up on the latest?"

"I think so."

"Have you seen 'Ecstasy'?"

"Yes," she blurted out before she could catch herself.

"What did you think about it?"

"Oh, it's a terrific movie all right," she continued to lie.

With a tiny stick he swirled ice cubes. "You think so, huh?"

"Everyone says so." She tried to sound casual.

"Come here, Shiz." he beckoned her with a crooked finger. "Come over here by me and I'll show you some real ecstasy."

Hearing this, the girl grabbed her purse and ran out the door they'd entered. She did it with such exigent speed that Mr. Palmer, groggy at the time, did not lift himself out of his chair. Her sudden dash had caught him by surprise.

She ran to the elevator. Drats, it was occupied. She tore open the exit door and scurried down stairs to the ground floor, past the doorman and into the harsh, sweet afternoon light of day. Luckily the Waihio bus pulled in just as she reached the corner. Quickly she boarded it and sat in back near the rear exist. She felt her heart continue to race. Steady, she told herself, you're safe now. You managed to escape. You're okay. She looked out the window seeing people carry on their humdrum lives as usual but she was not the same. She felt innocence race past her as swiftly as the day's traffic.

JESSICA KAWASUNA SAIKI *was born in Hilo, Hawai'i, to a fisherman father and a pic-ture-bride mother from Japan. She lived in the islands during the 1930s and 1940s, leaving after World War II to continue her education in Chicago. Her books,* Once, a Lotus Garden, *selected by* Publishers Weekly *as one the of Best Books of 1987;* Aloha: Goodbye and Hello; *and* From the Lanai, *chronicle the lives of ordinary people in Hawai'i before, during, and after World War II.*

Y York

from NOTHING IS THE SAME

Cast
GEORGE, *male, Filipino heritage.*
BOBI, *female, Korean heritage.*
MITS, *male, Japanese heritage.*
DANIEL, *male, Korean heritage.*
All are eleven years old.

Scene: A church yard. Early morning. GEORGE *draws a circle in the dirt with a stick.* BOBI *enters.*
BOBI: Hey, George, look dis, look dis.
GEORGE: Go home, Bobi.
BOBI: You gotta look dis.
GEORGE: I tink I hear your mahdah calling you.
BOBI: You nevah guess what I get.
GEORGE: You right, I nevah guess—I nevah like guess.
BOBI: I get one cat eye.
GEORGE: Whachu did to your cat?!
BOBI: Look at um. *(She shows him a marble.)*
GEORGE *(impressed)*: Ho!

BOBI: Good, yeah?

GEORGE: Nice dis. But not from your cat—

BOBI: No, but from one noddah cat.

GEORGE: Look like one *marble*, dis.

BOBI: *(Caught.)* Look little bit like dat. Dis cateye wen start out his life in da eye of one god—

GEORGE: I not going listen—

BOBI: One dark night in Africas . . . da ground shake wid fire . . . errybody stay shaking in dea beds, nobody come out fo see what shake da ground or make da fire. Den when da sun come out and errybody feel safe onacounta get light again, anybody go outside and find one tall black cat god. *(Triumphantly.)* Dis eye come from dat god was made outta stone.

GEORGE: . . . Sound more like da hist'ry lesson on Egypt Miz Hirogashi wen give.

BOBI *(caught)*: Sound little bit like dat.

GEORGE: Come on—we play marbles—

BOBI: No. You play fo keeps. I no can lose um.

GEORGE: You like play wid da guys, you gotta *take da risk*. Us guys take da risk. Lass cheer my Christmas keenie, was one good marble.

BOBI: *Was* one good marble.

GEORGE: I coulda kepp um in my pocket, nevah show, if I scared. If I too scared fo put um in play. Too scared *fo take da risk*.

BOBI *(mocking him)*: Yeah. You wen take da risk alright—you wen *lose* dat good marble. Mits get um now.

GEORGE: Yeah, but I *took da risk*.

(Enter MITS, he has overheard them.)

MITS: "Samurai nevah take his eye off da marble."

GEORGE: Hey, Mits.

MITS: "Samurai know da enemy marble going *make*." You ready fo play, George?

BOBI: I ready. I get one new kine marble.

MITS: Show me.

BOBI *(showing)*: No can touch um.

MITS: Nice cateye, dat.

GEORGE: You wen see dem before?

MITS: Castner's store got um.

GEORGE: "Eye of one god." Bobi, you such a liar.

BOBI: You nevah believe um, so no count as one lie.

MITS: Cost one quarter, dem.

BOBI *(impressed)*: Ho—Expensive da present.

GEORGE: Dis your birfday?

BOBI *(caught)*: . . . I don know.

GEORGE: Bobi . . . whachu wen do?

BOBI: Dis my Christmas present. I wen open um.

GEORGE: Hala! You going get lickens.

BOBI: Was going die from da wrapped-present disease. Could hear someting calling me from inside da box. "Come get me, come play wid me, I lonely." I going put um back before Christmas. Das why I no can take da risk. My fahdah see dat empty Christmas present box, I get lickens fo sure.

GEORGE: Fo'get her, Mits. We go play.

MITS: Who wen draw dis circle?

BOBI: George wen draw um.

MITS: All *hamajang*, dis. *(MITS picks up a stick to redraw the circle.)* Gotta concentrate when you draw da circle. Stand like dis wid chor stick touching da ground, den go all da way 'round like dis, nevah move your arm—move your whole body in one circle. I *stay* da stick.

BOBI: You no look like da stick—

MITS: I *stay* da stick. I stay da circle.

BOBI: Ho! Dat one round circle now.

MITS: *(Bows, a sort of prayer.)* "Today, I know I going lose my marbles. I know I going home wid no marbles."

BOBI *(derisive)*: Mebbe you wen lose your marbles already . . . *(MITS scowls at her.)* I no mean nutting by dat.

MITS: Wea da ress, George?

GEORGE: Das all I wen bring today.

BOBI: Why? You too scared fo *take da risk?*

GEORGE: *(A threat.)* Bobi, you like stay or you like go?

BOBI: I like stay. Quiet, me . . . Quiet like one stone. Quiet like one still night. One Silent Night, me!

GEORGE: Talk talk alla time talking, you. *(He misses.)* Shoots.

MITS: I go. Stand back. Samurai need plenny room fo shoot.

BOBI: Ho, you going lose George.

MITS: "Samurai take up one marble, da marble come one extension of his arm. Da Samurai stay da marble." *(MITS shoots and wins.)*

GEORGE: Oh, I no like lose dat one.

BOBI: You like I make some distraction, George?

MITS: "Da Samurai no can hear da distracting, talking talking from da noisy *wahine* on da sidelines." *(MITS shoots and wins.)*

BOBI: Who da noisy *wahine*? I not noisy.

GEORGE: Ho, I no like lose dat one, too.

BOBI: Should nevah play fo keeps wid one Samurai.

MITS: "Da lass lass, very lass marble. Da marble stay one long way away from da shoota, but da Samurai no fear nutting. Take in air, let out air, ready fo shoot". . . *(Shoots and wins.)*

GEORGE: I get no more.

BOBI *(disappointed)*: Mits da winna—errytime Mits da winnah—like one skipping record.

GEORGE: Mits, you going show me da Samurai kine?

MITS: No can. You Filipino—*(Proudly.)*—Samurai only Japanee.
   (Enter DANIEL.)

DANIEL: Hey! Why you here, Mits? Not your church.

GEORGE: Not my church, too.

DANIEL: More your church den his church—Buddahhead.

MITS: Howzit, Daniel?

DANIEL: No talk wid me. Who wen make dis circle in my church yard?

MITS: I wen make um.

DANIEL: Da minister going make you pray to Jesus, he see you here.

MITS: I going go before church time. Why you here so early, Daniel?

DANIEL: No ask me nutting, you. Go Japanese school, you, stay away from here. *(To BOBI)* Da minister wen come yet?

GEORGE: Yeah, I wen see him come in before.

DANIEL: I here fo da sugah donuts. He put um out fo da pigeons. Dey real good and fresh. I going get um before da pigeons.

BOBI: Dey not fo da pigeons doze donuts—

GEORGE: Shut your mout, Bobi!

DANIEL: Da minister wen say dey fo da pigeons. Whachu talking about, mosquito?

BOBI: I talking about—

GEORGE: She talking about talking. She don know what she stay talking about.

DANIEL: She like get um, das why. Stay here, you. Da sugah donuts, dey mines. *(Exits.)*

BOBI: Ho! Dat guy, he no like you, Mits.

MITS: His fahdah Korean, das why—He hate da Japanese.

BOBI: My fahdah Korean—we no hate nobody.

GEORGE: Mean Daniel, das why.

BOBI *(realizing)*: Hey—dey no more food, das why. He going eat da sugah donuts—

GEORGE: Yeah, you crazy or what? You was going tell how da minister put um out fo da poor kids. You call Daniel one poor kid, you going stay one dead kid.

MITS: I not scared him. Samurai not scared, das why.

GEORGE: Mits, I no care I not Japanee. I like you show me da power.

BOBI: I show, George. *(Tries to move like MITS.)* "Ho I one Samurai me—"

MITS: Hey—no can! . . . I show—little bit I show. *(Demonstrates.)* Look dis. Dis marble on da ground, all separate dis one. But when I pick um up— no more separate. Da marble wen come one parta da arm—connected tru da eye.

(There is the far off sound of rumbling. They look toward the sound.)

BOBI: Look dea.

GEORGE: Da army stay making maneuvers.

(They are initially surprised and quite indignant.)

BOBI: Hey, not allowed.

GEORGE *(to planes)*: . . . Hey . . . whachu doing?

BOBI *(shouts to planes)*: Go home. No can fly today. Dis Sunday.

GEORGE: How come dey's flying here? Dey supposed to go da oddah ways.

MITS: Close, dey coming. Low, too.

BOBI: Hey, look dea. Da army wen paint one red circle on da airplane. Too real dat kine. *(The sound of bombs.)* . . . Hey, what dey stay doing—? *(to planes.)* Whachu stay doing?!

GEORGE: Hey, no shoot ovah here. You stupid, you stupid—

BOBI: He coming, he coming—we going make we going make!

(More bombs and shooting. While the others duck, MITS raises his arms towards the approaching airplane. The plane veers and recedes in the distance. MITS is frozen, his arms raised.)

DANIEL: *(Centering.)* Dey going ovah da houses! I going check my house!

(DANIEL exits. BOBI throws her marble toward the planes.)

BOBI *(crying)*: You buggahs, you flying buggahs!

(BOBI exits. GEORGE gets up from the ground. The sound of bombs and planes in the distance continues. GEORGE discovers and pockets BOBI'S marble.)

GEORGE: Bobi wen trow da cateye. Hey, Mits, take down your arms. *(GEORGE pulls down MITS'S arms, then pulls MITS to the ground.)* We wait here 'til pau da bombs. Mits, you not breathing.

MITS *(gasps)*: George. Why dey wen do dat? Why da army bomb us?

GEORGE: You crazy? Dey not da army. Dey da Japanese.

Y YORK *has premiered nine new plays across the country since she moved to Hawai'i in 1999.* Nothing is the Same *was researched and written with support from TCG-Pew Charitable Trust. She has received support from TCG-Met Life, the NEA, the Rockefeller Foundation, and the King County and Seattle Arts commissions. She is a proud alumna of New Dramatists, member of the Dramatists' Guild, and still lives with Mark Lutwak, to whom many things are still dedicated. In 2006, she received the Hawai'i Award for Literature.*

Hong-gi Yi
"진주만 공격"

아침에 예배당에 가는 길에
왜놈의 비행기가 습격을 했다는 놀라운 소식을 전하자

시내와 시장들에 인파가 끊어지고
펄항에는 군인들의 시체가 가득 차 있다.

기도하는 정신은 전기와 같이 맹렬하고
너희들의 패망하는 소식은 우레 소리와 같으리라.

가족을 데리고 피난길에 오르면서
전화가 동결되어 심정이 몹시 혼란스럽다.

습격을 슬프게 맞으니 그만 나라의 원수가 되었구나.
일본을 숭배하던 것이 부끄러운 행동이 되어버렸구나.

도조는 수도에서 몰래 공격할 것을 꾀하고
구르스는 백악관에서 평화의 추파를 보낸다.

적의 폭탄이 떨어진 곳에서는 저승길로 가는 혼을 만들고
항만인 펄항은 피바다가 되었더라.

하룻강아지가 맹호의 지역을 침범하였으니
너희들이 패망할 것을 아느냐

"THE ATTACK ON PEARL HARBOR"

On my way to church in the morning,
I am surprised to hear that Japanese bastards' airplanes have
    attacked the harbor.

Usually filled with surging crowds of people the downtown
    marketplaces are empty;
soldiers' dead bodies fill Pearl Harbor.

Praying for peace is as intense as a spark of electricity.
And the news that will declare your defeat will be as sonorous as
    a clap of thunder!

Evacuating with family,
I feel disconnected because the phone line is down.

After the sad attack, we have become the country's enemies!
Showing respect to Japan now seems like a shameful action!

While Tojo secretly contrived the attack in Tokyo,
Kurusu was casting an amicable glance of peace at the White
House.

The place where the enemy's bomb falls becomes a site where
souls depart their bodies and head to the heaven.
Pearl Harbor is a sea of blood!

Consider a puppy that invades the lair of a tiger,
Don't you know of your doom?

TRANSLATED BY HYERAN SEO

Herman Wouk

from THE WINDS OF WAR

Janice Henry left her house and drove toward Pearl City in a cool morning echoing with distant church bells. Vic had wakened her at seven o'clock, coughing fearfully; he had a fever of almost 105. Yawning on the telephone, the doctor had prescribed an alcohol rub to bring the baby's temperature down, but there was no rubbing alcohol in the house. So she had given the fiery, sweat-soaked little boy his cough medicine, and set out for town, leaving him with the Chinese maid.

From the crest of the hill, under a white sun just climbing up from the ocean rim, the harbor wore a Sabbath look. The fleet was in, and ranged at its moorings in the morning mist: a scattering of cruisers, oilers, and tenders, clusters of gray destroyers and minesweepers, nests of black submarines. Off Ford Island the battleships stood in two majestic lines with white sun-awnings already rigged; and on the airfield nearby dozens of planes touched wings in still rows. Scarcely anybody was moving on the ships, the docks, or the airfield. Nor was any large vessel under way to ruffle the glassy harbor.

Only a few church party boats, with tiny sailors in whites, cut little foamy V's on the green still water.

Janice got out of the car to look for her husband's ship. To her disappointment, the *Enterprise* was not only absent from the harbor, it was nowhere in sight on the sea. She had been counting on a Sunday morning return. She took binoculars from the glove compartment and scanned the horizon. Nothing: just one old four-piper poking around, hull down. Tuesday would be two weeks that Warren had been gone, and now here she was with a sick baby on her hands, and a hangover. What a life! What a bore!

She had gone to the Officers' Club dance the night before out of loneliness and boredom, accepting the invitation of a lieutenant she had dated long ago, a Pensacola washout who now served on Cincpac's staff. Vic had had a cough for days, but his temperature had remained normal. Of course she would never have stayed out until after three, cavorting and boozing, had she known he would turn so sick. Still she felt guilty, irritated, and bored to the bone with this idiotic existence.

Since her return from Washington, she had been growing more and more bored, realizing that she had married not a dashing rake after all, but a professional Navy fanatic, who made marvelous love to her now and then and otherwise almost ignored her. Lovemaking at best took up very little time. What an end for Janice Lacouture—at twenty-three, a Navy baby-sitter! She had taken a half-day coding job at Cincpac to avoid being evacuated with the service wives, but that was dull drudgery too. Janice had spells of deep rebellion, but so far she had said nothing to Warren. She was afraid of him. But sooner or later, Janice meant to have it out, even if divorce ensued.

A small general store in a green wooden shack at a crossroads stood open, with two fat Japanese children playing on the rickety porch. That was lucky; it stocked a strange jumble of things, and she might not have to drive clear into town. As she went in, she heard gunfire pop over the harbor, as it had been popping for months off and on in target practice.

The storekeeper, a black-haired little Japanese in a flowered sport shirt, stood behind his counter drinking tea. On shelves within reach of his arms, goods were neatly stacked: canned food, drugs, pans, brooms, candy, toys, soda pop, and magazines. He bobbed his head, smiling, under hanging strips of dried fish. "Lubbing acoho? Ess, ma'am." he went through the green curtain behind him. The gunfire sounded heavier and louder, and planes thrummed overhead. A funny time for a drill, she thought, Sunday morning before colors; but maybe that was the idea.

Going to the doorway, Janice spotted the planes flying quite high, lots of them, in close order toward the harbor, amid a very heavy peppering of black puffs. She went to the car for her binoculars. At first, she saw only blue sky and clouds of black smoke, then three planes flew into the field of vision in a shining silvery triangle. On their wings were solid orange-red circles. Stupefied, she followed their flight with the glasses.

"Ess, ma'am? Many pranes! Big, big drir!" The storekeeper stood beside her, offering her the package with a toothy smile that almost shut his eyes. His children stood behind him on the porch, pointing at the sky and chattering in shrill Japanese.

Janice stated at him. Nearly everybody in the Navy disliked the Hawaiian Japanese and assumed they were spies. She had caught the feeling. Now here was this Jap grinning at her, and overhead Jap planes were actually flying! Flying over Hawaii! What could it mean? The nerve of these Japs! She took the package and abruptly, rudely offered him the binoculars. The man bobbed his head and peered upward at the planes, now beginning to peel off and dive, one by one, glinting silver amid the thickening black puffs. With a queer noise in his throat, he pulled himself erect and held out the binoculars to her, regarding her with a blank face, his slant eyes like black glass. More than the unreal, startling sight of the orange-marked planes, the look on his face told Janice Henry what was happening in Pearl Harbor.

HERMAN WOUK *was born in 1915. During World War II in the Pacific, he served as an officer on destroyer minesweepers, with time ashore in Hawai'i. Among his many best-selling novels are* The Winds of War; War and Remembrance; *and* The Caine Mutiny, *which won the Pulitzer Prize, became a Broadway play, and was made into a Hollywood film starring Humphrey Bogart.*

———————————•◦•———————————

Jon Shirota

from LUCKY COME HAWAII

When the first series of bombs fell, Kama Gusuda's number two son, Niro, was gazing out the kitchen window of the luxurious Whittingham house on Pacific Heights. He paid no attention to the rumbling sounds. Like most of the residents of Honolulu, he thought it was just another "simulated" attack the Army and Navy were going through. Lush-green Nuuanu Valley below was as quiet and lovely as ever. The crisp mountain breeze from the Pali was rustling the coconut palms bordering upper Nuuanu Avenue. Early-morning golfers in bright shirts and trousers were already out on the private course across the other side of the valley, their caddies following close behind.

Niro was the part-time, servant-chauffeur-houseboy for elderly Mr. and Mrs. Whittingham while attending the university. He had been with the Whittinghams the past year and a half, ever since Mr. Whittingham had a stroke and had retired as executive of one of the Big Five firms. They furnished Niro a room above the garage, plus board and ten dollars a week. He worked at the pineapple cannery during the summer for his tuition fees. The Whittinghams were cranky and demanding (especially Mrs. Whittingham, who was ill in bed a greater part of the time), but then, most of the haoles in the islands acted that way towards the Japanese anyway.

Niro had just finished the last of the morning dishes when the next round of muffled boom-booming echoes rattled the cups and saucers on the shelf, the floor recoiling under him.

Jesus! they're sure going through a tough maneuver, he thought, placing the wet dish towel on the rack above the shiny porcelain sink.

"Niro!" Mr. Whittingham called from the living room which adjoined the long dining room.

He hurried over to the dining room and opened the door. "Yes, Mr. Whittingham." He smiled graciously at the Old Man sitting on the couch reading the Sunday Morning Advertiser.

"Those sounds seem louder than usual, don't they?" Mr. Whittingham said, looking up momentarily over the paper, frowning, cluster of gray hair dangling over his deeply lined, pale forehead.

"I'm sure it's just another maneuver, Mr. Whittingham," he said politely. "—Is Mrs. Whittingham all right?"

"Yes, she's resting comfortably," Mr. Whittingham's eyes went back to the paper. His long wooden cane was placed beside him as it always was whenever he was sitting down. "I hope all that confounded noise doesn't disturb her."

"Shall I take her some warm milk?"

"That won't be necessary. I'll go in in a few minutes and see how she's feeling. —That damned noise is getting louder, isn't it?" he interjected when another round of reverberating boom-boom-boom vibrated the house. "You sure it's just another one of those maneuvers?"

"I'm sure it is, Mr. Whittingham," Niro said. He tried to hide the anxiety from his own face, holding his head sideways, small dark eyes narrowed with concern. The booming sounds were definitely louder and stronger than any other they had ever experienced.

"Go out in the front yard and see if anything unusual is going on," Mr. Whittingham ordered gruffly.

"Yes, sir." He quickly went past Mr. Whittingham through the spacious living room filled with old furniture.

Opening one of the double glass front doors and stepping out on the wide lanai, he quickly noted that it was a clear, warm morning with hardly any clouds in the blue sky, the breeze from the sea stirring the palms and hibiscus hedges along the driveway. The air smelled of fresh gardenias and roses. Aloha Tower, almost directly below at the waterfront, loomed majestically into the glittering sky.

Niro, short, stocky and comfortably dressed in white T-shirt tucked in his faded levis, stepped down the steps and walked over to the far edge of the big front lawn where Kato-san, the slight, wiry old Japanese gardener, was doing his Sunday morning chore, trimming the hibiscus hedges.

"Good morning," Kato-san greeted toothily, trimming away with his sickle. He was dressed in a patched denim shirt and baggy denim trousers wrapped at the legs with a roll of brown, threadbare Japanese leggings, an old pair of ta-bes meeting the leggings at the ankles. He stopped trimming now and gazed over his shoulder towards Pearl Harbor, then looked back at Niro, puzzled.

"Isn't that a big fire going on over there?" Niro asked, pointing beyond Kamehameha Heights. There was a column of black, ominous-looking smoke mushrooming up into the sky.

"I've been watching it the past five minutes," Kato-san answered in Japanese. "Those sounds seem real, don't they?"

"Aw, it's just another air raid practice," Niro said, trying to shrug it off, intense eyes concentrated on the black smoke, right hand over his forehead.

Kato-san dropped his sickle. He joined Niro watching the scores of tiny airplanes flashing silver in the blue skies over Pearl Harbor. "It sure looks like a real battle."

"Yeah, it looks like the real thing all right," Niro agreed, again feeling the ground trembling under him as another round of booming sounds rumbled through the city. "They're getting better all the time."

"Look!" Kato-san suddenly cried out, pointing excitedly over towards the ocean this side of Pearl Harbor. "That plane is on fire! It's falling into the sea! Look!"

Niro, squinting his eyes, quickly looked where Kato-san was pointing. "Jesus Christ!"

The tiny speck in the low sky crashed into the water, splashing up white foam before disappearing.

"There's another one! Over there!" Kato-san exclaimed, pointing slightly to the right this time.

"Whatdahell kind of manuever is that?"

"Niro!" Mr. Whittingham called out from the lanai. "What's going on out there!"

"They're sure putting on a funny kind of manuever, Mr. Whittingham," he answered. "They're shooting down the airplanes. And the bombs!—they're really setting fire to the ships!"

Mr. Whittingham came over, limping-hopping, breathing whizzingly.

"Good heavens!" he cried out, towering over them, stoop shoulders bent forward, right hand capped over his eyes.

Three of them stood there with mouths wide open, not saying another word, only staring, stupefied, towards Pearl Harbor.

Suddenly! an ear-splitting, weird whistling noise charged out of the sky. It was immediately followed by a deathly explosion near the base of the Heights.

"Good God!" Mr. Whittingham muttered, face turning chalk white. "That sounded like a bomb. What's happening! What's going on!—Niro, go into the house and call the police department."

Niro kept standing there.

"Niro!" Mr. Whittingham grabbed hold of his shoulder and gave it a hard shake. "Didn't you hear me? Call the police department."

Before Niro could turn to dash up to the house, a lone, single-engine aircraft, its motor sputtering falteringly, swooped over the Heights above their heads, made an abrupt turn, and headed back towards the ocean.

Kato-san, eyes squinting against the glaring sunlight, suddenly stiffened. He looked over at Niro, then back at the aircraft heading for Pearl Harbor. "Why, that was a Japanese airplane," he uttered, flabbergasted, eyes wide open. "Did you see that! It was a Japanese airplane," he repeated to Niro. "They're all Japanese airplanes!" he went on, awed.

Niro, stunned and shocked, exchanged quick, scowling glances with Mr. Whittingham, then looked over at joyful Kato-san.

Before Niro could stop him, Kato-san began yelling: "Japanese airplanes! Japanese airplanes!" waving a yellow, mucous-stained handkerchief at the planes miles away. "Did you see that!" he screamed into Niro's face. "Japanese airplanes bombing all the ships in Pearl Harbor. Banzai! Banzai! Banzai!"

"Why you goddamn little Jap!" Mr. Whittingham roared menacingly at the wiry old gardener. "You no-good Jap spy!" Mr. Whittingham screamed, raising his cane and swinging it down murderously on Kato-san's half-bald head. Kato-san reeled for a second, hands clutched over his head where the cane had landed, then collapsed helplessly on the grass.

"You sonofabitch! I'm going to kill you!" Mr. Whittingham threatened savagely, stepping over Kato-san's balled-up form, raising the cane high in the air with both hands, ready to strike the gardener again.

"Mr. Whittingham!" Niro cried. "Don't! He didn't know what he was doing."

"I'm gonna kill this little sneaking bastard!"

"Mr. Whittingham!" he cried out again, reaching up for the cane before it could land on Kato-san's head. He began struggling with Mr. Whittingham who suddenly lost his balance and, letting go of the cane, went sprawling backward onto the grass.

He meant to help Mr. Whittingham up, but the Old Man, pushing himself up with both hands, came charging for him.

"Why, you Jap bastard, you!" Mr. Whittingham cursed viciously, reaching up for the cane in Niro's hand.

"Mr. Whittingham! I was only trying to stop you from hurting Kato-san."

"You no-good Jap!"

Niro, realizing he could not appease the Old Man, heaved the cane way over towards the lanai. The Old Man grabbed his arm and began shaking him violently. He gave the Old Man a desperate shove and watched him stumbling hard on his back.

"I'm gonna get you two!" Mr. Whittingham screamed, pushing himself up. "I'm gonna get my shotgun and blast you two Jap bastards!" He went limping towards the house.

JON SHIROTA *was born on Maui in 1927. He is a graduate of Brigham Young University. He quit his job as a U.S. Treasury Agent, and moved to a writers' colony where he finished his first novel,* Lucky Come Hawaii. *The novel, adapted into a play, won the John F. Kennedy Center for the Performing Arts award. He also received awards from the Japan-U.S. Friendship Commission and the National Endowment for the Arts.*

Graham Salisbury
from UNDER THE BLOOD-RED SUN

T hinking about Papa being a prisoner drove me crazy. *Shikata ga nai*—It can't be helped. How could Mama and Grampa just accept it and go on like nothing had happened? Didn't they understand that he was a prisoner of *war*? But he was just a fisherman. He wasn't an enemy to anyone.

When I told Grampa I wanted to go looking for Papa, he got angry and told me to forget it. "You go there, they going shoot you," he said.

"But I'm only a kid."

"They shoot, I tell you," Grampa spit back.

Dawn. Sky dark and stormlike.

Grampa was already out with his chickens. Heavy gray clouds moved steadily toward the sea. Today I would tell Grampa I was going to see Rico.

But I would go to find Papa.

I put on a sweatshirt and a pair of shorts and made sure my ID card was in my pocket, then left the house as soon as it was light and the curfew had lifted. Leaves swirled around the yard. A shiver ran through me, as thunder rumbled far off in the mountains, muffled by the clouds.

In less than an hour I'd walked all the way to the harbor, down to where the freighters and passenger ships docked.

What I saw shocked me.

All around the water—everywhere—were barbed wire barricades wound in twisted and jumbled coils from post to post, the wire going all over like it was spun by a lunatic spider. It scared me just to look at it.

To get beyond it to the piers, you had to pass through gates guarded by soldiers.

I waited across the street, trying to figure out what to do next. Sand Island lay across the smooth gray harbor, less than a quarter mile away—a low, flat place covered with scrub brush and a few trees. I could see a white building with a red tile roof out there.

A convoy of army trucks rushed by. Stone-faced men peeked out from under the tarps in back. Behind the trucks, five tanks thundered by, shaking the street. I covered my ears. It was like I was in a nightmare.

The tanks rumbled on, and I crossed the street. How was I going to get over to Sand Island? I didn't even know if it was an island, or if there was a spit of land that connected it, or some kind of bridge.

Soon I came to where two army guards stood by an entry station. They had pistols on their belts, and steel helmets and dark arm bands that said MP on them. *They going shoot you. . . .*

I could see their eyes watching me even though they seemed to stare straight ahead. When I came up to them, they got out of that stiff position. I pointed past the barbed wire. "Is this how you get to Sand Island?"

"This area is restricted," one of the men said. He didn't smile or anything.

"I'm looking for my father. He was . . . arrested . . . by mistake."

The guard stared at me a moment, then said, "Better go home, son."

"But he's just a fisherman."

"Beat it," the other guard said.

I peeked past them. Nothing but ugly buildings and shipping boxes and a few trucks. A thick raindrop splattered down on my shoulder. The guards slipped army-green ponchos over their heads.

I headed back, and the rain let loose. Big drops bounced off the pavement. Rivers began to run in the gutters. I looked for someplace to get out of the rain and found an arched concrete bridge. I ducked under it and sat on a ledge, huddling next to the stream that ran out into the harbor.

What a stupid idea . . . I should have listened to Grampa.

The rain came down harder and the sound was deafening. The river started to swell and cloud with mud. I watched it rush by. Across the harbor Sand Island looked so desolate, a ghostly spit of land and the now barely visible red-roofed building.

It was pretty hard to see that far. The rain beat down onto the water so hard, it looked like it was boiling. But I could make out the shoreline across the harbor. No barbed wire over there. I figured they had it strung out on the other side, on the ocean side where the enemy could land.

Barbed wire!

I hadn't even noticed—there was no barbed wire. Not over there, and not here *under* the bridge. Nothing between me and Sand Island. I could swim out there. . . .

But what if someone saw me?

But it was raining, hard . . . Maybe no one would be out there looking . . . even if they were, the rain was making everything blurry.

I crawled along the ledge under the bridge to the harbor side. No people on the docks and no ships moving around, not even any small boats. It was a long swim, but I was sure I could make it.

Then I remembered the tugboats, like sharks with big magnetic teeth that pulled you under. I'd seen them moving ships up to the pier, huge, sucking propellers churning the ocean white behind them, making giant, ugly whirlpools. If one of those things came by while I was out there, it would chop me into shreds.

Another stupid idea.

But . . .

I took my ID card out and stuck it in a crack on the ledge, then covered it with my sweatshirt. If I lost that I'd be in more trouble than I wanted to think about.

The water was cool, but not cold. I dropped down into it and let the stream carry me out into the harbor, keeping low so I'd look like something floating, a coconut or some piece of junk in the water.

The rain thundered all around me. I turned and looked back. No one on the bridge. Still no boats, or anyone on the pier. When the force of the stream died out I started swimming . . . breast stroke, keeping low, making as little movement as possible. I accidentally swallowed a mouthful of oily, fuel-smelling water, and gagged. I tried to keep from coughing.

Pull. Easy, steady. Looking back. Watching for boats.

About halfway across the harbor I started to get tired, but at least I could stop worrying about being seen by anyone on shore.

Sand Island . . . were there guards there?

The rain started to let up. It would pass soon.

Move . . . stop thinking about being tired. . . . Keep going, keep pull-ing.

I didn't realize how tired I really was until I felt the soft touch of watery sand under my feet. I crawled out and stumbled up the small beach to sprawl in some weeds. The rain still fell, but not as hard as before. I curled up into a ball and thought about going back into the water where it was warm. But I stayed hidden in the weeds.

Soon the rain slowed to a drizzle, then stopped. A breeze brought the soft rumble of surf from out on the reef on the other side of Sand Island. It must have been about noon. I rested awhile, then crawled up to the flat land above the beach and into the waist-high weeds.

They going shoot anybody try go there . . .

Grampa was right. I should just be dutiful. I should be respectful and obey everything he says. *Papa should beat you. . . .*

But I was so close.

I crawled to a thicket of kiawe trees and studied what I could see of the white building. The whole island wasn't that big, maybe a half mile long and a quarter wide. I inched closer, hiding behind the trees.

The weeds broke onto a sandy field riddled with puddles. And beyond that, the prisoner camp.

My chin dug into the sand as I lay flat, straining to see. The camp wasn't much more than a barbed-wire enclosed yard of sand with a bunch of tents set up in neat rows. Beyond that was the white building, and a couple of smaller buildings.

But there was still the open field. How was I going to cross *that*? I could wait until dark and then crawl to the trees on the other side . . . but I had to be home before dark, before curfew. I should just get out of there.

Strange.

No guards. No prisoners. The place seemed deserted. Had I made a mistake? Had I come all this way just to find nothing?

The few trees that stood near the prison fence weren't that far away . . . about as far as from a pitcher's mound to center field. But it felt like three times that much. It was now or never . . . now or never.

I crouched and kept low to the ground. My feet thumped over the sand, making huge splashing sounds when I hit the puddles. I dove to the ground and rolled into some weeds around three trees. I lay there panting.

In the camp nothing moved. Where *was* everyone?

I counted more than thirty tents sitting in muddy dirt and sand, some shaped like pyramids and some like a sheet staked down over a clothesline. If Papa was there, was his tent near the fence?

The fence, I suddenly realized, was two fences, with about ten feet between them. You'll almost have to shout to talk to someone.

I waited, shivering. Wet shorts and no shirt.

After a while, a long line of men came filing out of one of the smaller buildings. When they got to the tents they broke up and went inside, or just gathered in groups in the yard. A few wandered toward where I was, talking to each other in low voices and looking at the dark sky. They were all Japanese. Still no guards in sight.

I recognized a fisherman I'd seen before . . . a friend of Papa's. He wandered into one of the pyramid tents that was near the fence. Too far away.

In a few minutes he came back out. My heart pounded with each step. Closer . . . closer.

"Pssst," I whispered.

The man stopped and looked around, out into the field, then back toward the tents.

"Over here." I stuck my head up out of the weeds, then quickly ducked back down.

When he saw me he looked around to see if anyone else had seen. "Lie flat!" he commanded, then walked casually over to stand right across from me.

I parted the weeds and peeked through. He stood with his hands in his pockets, looking up at the sky as if checking to see if it was going to rain some more. "Who you? What you doing here?" he said, without looking in my direction.

"Tomi Nakaji," I said in a shouting whisper. "I'm looking for my father, Taro."

He glanced in my direction, then quickly turned away. "No move, boy . . . the guards see you, they going shoot." He started to walk away, then stopped and looked at the sky again. "No even breathe."

He went into a tent and came back with Papa.

Papa looked . . . awful. Unshaven and grimy, far worse than after a month at sea without a bath. He walked slowly, limping. He used a stick for a cane. I wanted to call out to him, to jump up and run over to the fence. I could explain to the guards that they were all wrong, that they had an innocent man. But Grampa's words screamed through me: *shoot you, shoot you, shoot you. . . .*

"Tomi!" Papa whispered, not looking my way, a deep scowl on his face.

"Papa, I—"

"Shhh! No say nothing. . . You listen to me. . . . Stay in that trees until nighttime, then *go*. . . . You hear me? Go!" Papa looked scared. I felt sick.

He waited there with his friend, both of them scowling at the ground. Papa leaned on his stick, and once peeked over at me. The look on his face was as sad and lonely as I'd ever seen it. His friend said something to him and put his hand on Papa's shoulder.

Finally, Papa whispered, "Tomi . . . "

I lifted my head a little so he could see.

"You very brave . . . but also . . . Tomi, you tell Mama not to worry . . . Tomi . . . "

I wanted to call to him, to tell him I would get him out of there somehow . . . but I kept quiet, like he'd said.

A guard came out into the yard from the white building. Papa's friend urged Papa away from the fence. They separated, and Papa limped to his tent and sat between two mud puddles on a small stool. He sat straight, like Grampa, the stick lying across his lap. He stared out into the wet weeds, away from where I was, his weary eyes sagging.

It was almost unbearable to be so close and not be able to do anything but dig down into the dirt. I had to force myself to stop thinking about it before it made me crazy. I started thinking about food. But the thought of eating made me feel sick. And so did the salty smell of the wet, mushy sand I was lying in.

An hour passed . . . maybe two . . . or three. Papa never stopped guarding my hiding place.

I fell asleep, then woke with a twitch, suddenly remembering where I was. My neck was stiff and hurt when I moved. A blotch of sand clung to one side of my face. I wiped it away and ran my fingers over the grooves it left in my cheek.

I got up on my elbows and peeked over the weeds. Papa was gone. Everyone was gone. It was getting dark. They must have gone back into the building.

Night came down and hid the open field. I crawled back out of the trees and sprinted across the sand and puddles to the kiawe thicket, then slowed to a fast walk and picked my way through the weeds to the harbor. I must have been crazy to think I could help Papa. *Crazy!*

The water was warm and black.

The city across the harbor hid in a dark silhouette of buildings. An island with no lights. I swam slowly, evenly, trying to pace myself so I wouldn't get too tired. Except for the hum of a small-boat engine somewhere, the harbor was quiet. Off to my left a blue light moved steadily across the water. I waited until the boat passed, hanging in the water with only my hands moving back and forth.

I aimed toward where I thought the bridge was. It seemed like days since I'd hidden under it.

The cool, fresh water rushing out from the river pushed me away from the bridge. I had to swim harder. I turned and worked into it on my back, face to the sky. The clouds had cleared. There were stars by the millions. Seeing them like that, so peaceful, made me feel sad. And lonely.

A thrumming . . .

Churning.

Tugboat!

I swirled around, looking for it.

Blue lights bore down on me, growing larger. Sickening gray-white wake. Boiling wake.

I lunged toward the bridge, my arms so tired they dragged me under. I came up, gasping. The *thrum* grew louder. I could hear the swishing of water shooting out from under the hull, and a voice crackling over the tug's radio. A giant shadow loomed over me.

The sucking grabbed at my legs, dragged me backward.

Sucked me back toward the churning prop.

Nowhere to go but down. I went under, trying to dive to the bottom. Get out of the way.

Down.

The tug thundered above.

Down, down to where the water turned cold.

The tug passed and the sucking stopped.

I waited as long as I could, then clawed my way back up. My lungs felt like they would explode. I broke the surface, gasping for air. My legs and arms could barely hold me up. Swim. Swim to the bridge.

Swim . . .

The ledge was slippery with moss. For a few minutes I just hung on to it, then dragged myself up, the sharp concrete edge digging into my hands and scraping my legs. I lay panting in the dark, my mind dizzy with fear and exhaustion. I fell asleep without knowing it.

Sometime later I was awakened by a kick. A flashlight with a blue-painted lens burned into my eyes. A bayonet poked at my throat.

GRAHAM SALISBURY *grew up in Hawai'i and did not wear shoes until he was in the sixth grade. He is the PEN/Norma Klein Award-winning author of* Eyes of the Emperor; Blue Skin of the Sea; Under the Blood-Red Sun; Shark Bait; Jungle Dogs; Lord of the Deep; *and* Island Boyz. *He lives in Portland, Oregon, with his family.*

Kathleen Tyau
from MAKAI

T he islands were placed under martial law. That meant curfew, blackout, listen to the soldiers or you could be shot. My mind kept skipping back to school, to my friends. Annabel and Sammy, all of them. I prayed that Sammy made it all the way to Wahiawa. I wished that I had paid more attention in chapel, so that I had better prayers to say. Ones that would work overall, so I wouldn't sound too selfish in what I asked for.

My mother didn't want us to open the windows, even though it was so hot. I took a shower, but felt sweaty again as soon as I stepped out. The windows were wet. The whole house damp.

We slept together that first week, all of us, on the floor of my parents' bedroom. My father dragged the dresser across the window, and my brothers pushed the bed up against the door. We lay on the floor, my mother and me in the middle, with my father and brothers on both sides.

I was glad to be the baby, the girl, but I was so hot, lying in the middle, barricaded by my family. My mother cried, softly at first, then louder, as if it was such a relief. My father was quiet, like my brothers, only the sound of them breathing.

Finally, my father stood up and pulled the dresser away from the window. He went through the house, opening up the windows, banging the glass so it rattled each time, and every time my mother jumped a little and cried. Fresh night air poured in. It felt so good. I waited for my father to come back and scold her, but instead he pulled my mother close to him and rocked her back and forth. He hummed in a singsong voice until she quieted down.

My father, the bone doctor, all those bodies and feet he had massaged and healed, and I had never seen him embrace my mother, never seen them hug, not even touch, until that night.

It came to me then. Pearl Harbor was us. Not just the Navy or the U.S. government, but my father, my mother, my brothers, me. If we were attacked again, the bombs might hit our house. Even if we got away, where would we go? The island had never felt so small. It was stupid to hide, to think a shingle roof and thin, wooden walls could keep us safe.

I leaned against my mother, and my brothers leaned on me, and we fell asleep like that.

All of Honolulu was black. All of Oahu, all of the islands. No lights shining, everything shut down, everything quiet. I pressed my face against the screen and strained to see in the dark. The night sky punched with stars. The moon hiding too. A few cars creeping by with blue paint on their headlights or black paper, like big eyelids, with only a little bit of the white eyeballs showing. . . .

We lined up for everything. Gasoline. Rice. Sugar. Gas masks. We waited all day to get our identification cards. How tall are you? Five feet. But still growing. How much do you weigh? One hundred, but losing, losing. My stomach felt full all the time, but not from food. Not hungry anymore. Let the boys eat my rice.

They pressed my fingers into ink and then rolled them on the paper. My fingerprints like the rings of a tree. My fingerprints were all I had to show the world. Not my face, or my low forehead or baby cheeks. Not my hair that wouldn't curl or my short legs or my black silk stockings with too many holes.

How do you carry a gas mask? Around your neck. Over your back so it doesn't flop against your stomach. Tied to your waist so it bangs against your hip. Diagonal, across your shoulder, like a bag. It sits beside you at chapel, in class, on your lap on the bus ride home. It even has a little pocket for lipstick, so you don't need to carry a purse.

When Annabel Lee and I graduated from the Priory, along with the rest of the Class of 1942, all of us dressed in white, we marched down the aisle of the cathedral with gas masks slung across our breasts.

My brothers and I dug a hole in the back yard for a bomb shelter. We dug until the dirt turned to mud and clung to the shovel and water began seeping into the hole. We stood there looking down at the brown, wet hole—a puka in the ground, a puka not even deep enough to be black. . . .

After work we went dancing at the YWCA, at the USO. To the Richards Street Y, the Army and Navy Club on Hotel Street, Maluhia at Fort De-Russy, The Breakers in Waikiki. We went to every dance we could reach by bus, sometimes even as far away as Waimanalo or Haleiwa, wherever dance hostesses were needed. Most of the dances took place in the afternoon, because we had to be home before curfew. At least we didn't have to be inside by dark now. The curfew hours had changed, so we could stay out later, until seven or eight o'clock, and then catch the last bus home.

Lei makers took over my father's old shoe-repair shop. Aunty Vicki and her girls made camouflage nets now instead of leis, dyeing them green and brown. The walls of Annabel's father's restaurant were covered with camouflage colors too. If you looked closely, you could see a few coconut trees and chickens and dogs, not just blobs of color. The barbershop across the street had an Uncle Sam poster pasted on the door that made me stop to look every time. It said, Women Can Help Win the War.

That was us. Annabel Lee and me, Alice Lum. Working for the engineers, helping at the Red Cross, but what we cared about most was dancing. To us, that was as important as folding bandages and knitting, maybe even more. Like Annabel said, If you asked them which they'd rather have before they died, do you think they would choose socks?

I had to lie to my mother when we went dancing. Had to make up some excuse, and more often than not, that excuse involved going to the Red Cross or up to Annabel's house to sew. My mother worked now too, at Dole pineapple cannery and at Piggly Wiggly, so she was too tired to worry about me. At least she seemed happier now that she was bringing home some money and not just hounding my father.

I cashed my paycheck and gave all the money to my mother, except what I needed for bus fare. The bills felt good in my hands. Each one- and five- and ten-dollar bill with the HAWAII stamp. Money I worked so hard to earn. The whole U.S. of A. counting on us, counting on me.

In the ladies' room at work, Annabel and I changed into party dresses that we'd stuffed into our big handbags. We wore shorts under our skirts, black and tight and not too long. We rubbed our legs with thick liquid foundation and drew lines down the back of our calves to look like stockings. We shared lipstick, digging down into the tube with a lip brush, to make every bit of it last. Our favorite was Russian Sable by Revlon. So dark it was purple on our lips instead of red.

The buses were crowded, but we never had to stand. Sometimes the men fought to give up their seats. They said, Dance with me, sugar. Save me a dance.

Annabel ignored them. She sat straight in her seat with her knees together and stared out the bus window.

She said to me, Don't look at them, Alice. Don't answer.

But I couldn't keep from turning to see who they were talking to. Was it Annabel Lee they were calling sugar or was it me, Alice Lum? Were they blond or dark? Tall or short? Would they follow us off the bus? We fought for the window seat. I hated sitting in the aisle seat, with the men pressing against me as they moved down the aisle.

When we got off the bus, Annabel said, Don't look back, walk fast.

All those eyes on the bus and more on the street. The front of me grew bigger, the back of me too. My ankles felt weak and my knees shook, but I followed Annabel down the sidewalk. Quick quick quick quick. Gas mask spanking my hips, but I kept on walking and didn't look back.

We made up names for ourselves, borrowing from the movie stars. Irene Dung, Claudette Choy, Ginger Rodriguez, Marlene DeLima, but never Annabel Lee, never Alice Lum.

We danced with blond, brown, redheaded servicemen with big feet and rough hands and hair on their arms, most of them smooth talkers, some clumsy and shy. I worried about my slip showing, my heels breaking, slipping on the slick floor, my underarm odor. I thought of what Sister Martha Verity used to say about how a lady perspires, a lady never sweats.

Most of the boys couldn't dance fancy, just step together, step. Boring, and my side ached from moving the same way all the time. We retreated to the restroom from time to time to wipe the smudges off our dancing shoes.

I told Annabel Lee, My toes are so sore. If one more guy steps on me, I'm going home.

Tap the beat on their shoulders, Annabel said. When the music starts. Not too hard, just tap. One two three four, so they can feel the rhythm.

Dance with me, soldier boy.

Never mind who's watching. Just close my eyes and dance dance dance.

Before the band played the last song, we excused ourselves and went to the powder room, where we changed back into our work clothes and climbed out the window or sneaked out the back door. Sometimes we ran barefoot on the hot sidewalk because our feet were too tired for shoes. We ran quick up the steps of the bus, quick down the aisle, dropped into our seats, our hearts beating. Quick quick quick quick.

KATHLEEN TYAU *is the author of two novels set in Hawai'i,* A Little Too Much Is Enough *and* Makai. *She went to public schools in Waikīkī and Pearl City and then attended St. Andrew's Priory for three years before leaving the islands to attend Lewis and Clark College in Portland, Oregon. She now lives on a farm in Yamhill County, Oregon wine country, where she and her husband grow trees and play bluegrass music.*

Sandra Park

"MY DAD'S GIRLFRIEND"

W hen my parents divorced, the only bone of contention was the family photographs, two shelves of albums with wide cushioned covers embossed with golden curlicues. Black pages inscribed in white ink, in mother's

Palmer script, have grown thick and stiff with age. Snapshots are fixed onto the page with glued corner mounts, telling tales with smiles and linked arms. Only babies are caught unaware, mouths open, wailing.

My favorite pictures are of my parents when they were young, before my brothers and I were born. My mother and Kiki, high school girlfriends, are sitting back to back with a ginger lei draped around both of them. The soft rope of flowers snares their slender necks. Their shoulders rise high with pleasure. In another one, my dad stands in a khaki uniform with a crisp cloth hat shaped like a long envelope. His sister asked him to pose in front of the big mango tree at my grandmother's house. He is leaning against the old woven trunk, his hand on his thigh, looking out. My dad told me that he was gazing at their beloved dog, Lucky, who was eating good slop from a pan. On that day he was eighteen years old and leaving on an army carrier ship for war.

The most intriguing picture is of a woman. The caption reads, "Monty's girlfriend *From Here to Eternity*," a code for something. It is wallet-sized, slightly faint and blurred, an image caught in a cloud of bright light framed in night and vanishing walls. Mother found it in dad's cigar box of personal items, given to her by his family when he was officially pronounced dead— somewhere in the "Pacific theatre," a term used by General MacArthur on the radio.

Dad eventually showed up alive, curbing my mother's flow of tears and heroic stories. He had to explain the surprise in the cigar box. "An old girl-friend, before you, w-a-y before you." "Way before?" mother said. "When you were a boy drinking beer out of a baby bottle?"

As a child I studied this photo and tried to crack the old movie code. The woman is looking straight into the camera. Her leaning posture against a high counter, fine swirls of smoke teasing the air above her, makes me think it's a bar somewhere in Honolulu. She's wearing lipstick and a dress with a sweetheart neckline. Fine collarbone, fine hollow cheeks. Her soft hair is permed into waves barely touching her shoulders.

My dad told me she was "girlfriend material, not wife material." The word "material" sounded like "equipment," the way my dad talked about cars. She doesn't look like my dad's type. My mother is shorter and rounder with a habit of pressing children to her breast when she hugs them. The family acknowledges she is very smart and talks too much.

My dad first saw my mother at a church picnic. He asked her for her phone number and she wouldn't give it to him. So he asked Kiki, who gave him both her number and my mother's. Their first date was at my mother's house. Her thick black hair freshly washed, she wore pincurls snugly coiled and crisscrossed with bobby pins. She showed him a place to sit on the lanai, but he preferred to stand, nudging her to a shady spot, a low ledge protected by old split 'ape leaves as big as umbrellas. All seven of my mother's brothers stayed home that afternoon, feigning naps and chores. Her two sisters were also home, dipping white shirts in liquid blue Vano starch. Each finished shirt, ironed twice, could stand up without a man inside it. My mother wore no makeup because she hoped that my dad would see her inner beauty. He smoked cigarettes and talked her into meeting again the next day, a walk along Ala Moana beach. Her brothers thought my dad was a bad boy because he went to a tough high school. He was worried that my Uncle Danny was going to kill him if he kissed my mother. Uncle Danny had a hot temper and tattoos.

On a visit home to the islands, I again came across the coded photograph. By then, there were no family secrets and my parents were talking divorce. Settlement of property was swift and legal, but the photo albums were pawns in a family war. We ended up drinking too much and leafing through all the volumes. I looked for the telltale rise of my mother's belly under her wedding gown but didn't find any. (Conceived on a promise, not a vow, I still love the smooth, slippery feel of satin.) So, it was a shotgun wedding—seven brothers staring down my dad. Smiling, he said that true love is like surrender, it makes a strong man weak.

When I asked about the mystery lady, he pulled out a cigarette, rolling and tapping it slowly, then finally speaking. I crossed my legs and sucked on a coffee candy, resisting an impulse to fill the air with officious bits of California wisdom. If we had a day instead of an hour, I would advise my dad to stop smoking, eat whole fruits and vegetables, exercise regularly. But we had only a moment between a steaming lunch and a heavy dinner of meat and kim chee. My mother was out of the house and it was his turn to talk.

Her name was Mariko. My dad's family did not approve of him going out with a Japanese because of the historic slaughter and occupation of Korea by Japan. (Never mind World War II Axis and Allied loyalties. My dad said he went to war to prove he was American. He was young and not in a killing mood. He hated only his younger brother who borrowed his money and dress shoes without asking.)

My dad and his girlfriend rendezvous'd in bars around town and walked every street and side street of Honolulu. He did not have a chance to say goodbye to her before he went off to war. The days before he sailed—the first time he left the islands—were crowded with family and friends coming over to say goodbye. Uncles slipped money into his pockets, aunties covered his head with kisses. Children took turns sitting on his duffel bag. Uncle Danny was the only brother still at home on my mother's side because of his obesity and skipping heart. He came over and gave my dad a heavy jade ring, in case he ever had to bribe someone two-headed and foreign to save his life. Dad left the ring behind, in the cigar box.

After the war, my dad did not look for Mariko, but he heard things about her. Friends told him that after he left, she returned to the same bars on her own, asking about him and doing her best to piece together a chronicle of his time away. The war years were strange times in Honolulu with young uniformed men everywhere. Mariko's pretty face was not overlooked. She waved the men off and they kept coming back. She accepted cigarettes and drinks, and grew dependent on their attention.

She did not marry. She worked as a bank clerk. She rose in the ranks and became an expert at postwar home loans. Another of my dad's old girlfriends, Sylvia, told him that Mariko's ambition paid off, that she owned apartments in town. Sylvia said Mariko's beauty faded over the years from too much alcohol and hard work.

"Que sera, sera," Dad said. "Girls bring happiness and luck into life. When they're young, they're built for speed. When old, for comfort. Too bad your mother and I couldn't last. We made it through so much." Dad smiled as he told me this. I wondered what he would do apart from Mother. A handsome old man is not the same as a handsome young man. Who will pay attention? Old trees left standing, propped up, hollow with forgetfulness.

After a few years of push and pull over faded memories and storage boxes, my parents remarried. My mother said it was a short interruption in a long life. My youngest brother and his girlfriend witnessed the remarriage. Afterward, they went to a Chinese restaurant and drank a jigger of scotch with each of nine courses—all this before noon. My brother said he'd never been drunk so early in the day. I called from California and my kids sang Happy Anniversary to the tune of Happy Birthday.

Neither of my parents had been satisfied with division of memories and their attorney had openly wavered on the proceedings. A family friend, Henry refused to collect any fees. He said that over the years he ate and drank a fortune at our house. He wondered aloud if my parents would continue to host their New Year's Eve party after the divorce. My mother asked why. He shrugged, "I'm a bachelor. If you give up your parties, there'd be no excuse to use my connections for smoked duck." My mother nodded. Because of special favors owed him, Henry could get the best smoked duck in the islands, and he brought a big box to our house every New Year's. We ate the duck with warm steamed buns and curling tendrils of green onions, washed down with cold beer. Every year, we praised Henry's duck as if he sat on the eggs, raised them, and taught them how to quack.

My California wisdom is still evolving, it's past the basic food groups, beyond deep thoughts. Still, there's something nattering about it. My dad's school of thought feels richer, rooted in the loamy stuff of life and decay. The knack to assign provenance to ordinary things, to speak of the dead in daylight, to tell stories.

I watch *From Here to Eternity* whenever it shows on late night television. Frank Sinatra, young and skinny, slums around Honolulu with his dark-eyed twin, Montgomery Clift, looking for girls. Like the lost boys of Syracuse, they tempt fate along ancient highways, trading the familiar for the strange. In shadow, not yet first light, the dark twin is shot by military police on an oceanside golf course, dead before the war starts. I love his sad smile—he smiles when he insults an officer, he smiles when he gets the girl, he smiles while panting from a fatal wound.

The photograph of a pretty girl outside the family is a treasure claimed by both my parents. It resides in an early volume of history and cannot be removed or tampered with. My father's memory of it is an alcove, high and tucked away. Inside are gaudy bits of wartime romance—folded letters, hula girl swizzle sticks, the red target of Lucky Strikes. I look again at the artifact stolen from a cigar box, fixed on a page.

SANDRA PARK'S *recent work appears in* Iowa Review; New American Writing; Five Fingers Review; *and a PEN anthology,* Oakland Out Loud. *Literary honors include an Iowa Fiction Award (runner-up), AWP Prague summer fellowship, and an SLS Russia finalist scholarship. Born and raised in Hawai'i, she teaches at Ohlone College in northern California.*

James Jones
from FROM HERE TO ETERNITY

The street had that late-at-night deserted look fully developed now. Even the darkened silent houses and the street-lights had that look now.

There was no sign of Angelo, or of Tommy. To hell with Tommy. Angelo was the thing. There was no telling where the drunken little bastard went. He might have gone back up toward Kalakaua. On the other hand, he might just as easily have decided to go the other way, for a quick swim in the Ala Wai Canal. He put the paper sack with Angelo's clothes and shoes in it under his arm; the paper rustle was loud in the clear still night; and reached in his pocket for a coin. There was no coin, only Hal's four tens. He grinned again, and wandered over happily to the gutter to light matches until he found a flat pebble.

Chapter 27

The street had that late at night deserted look fully developed now. Even the darkened silent houses and the streetlights had that look now.

There was no sign of Angelo, or of Tommy. To hell with Tommy. Angelo was the thing. There was no telling where the drunken little bastard went. He might have gone back up toward Kalakaua. On the other hand, he might just as easily the other way, TO TAKE A have decided to go/for a quick swim in the Ala Wai Canal. He put the paper sack with Angelo's clothes and shoes in it under his arm; the paper rustle was loud in the clear still night; and reached in his pocket for a coin. There was no coin, only Hal's four tens. He grinned again, and wandered over happily to the gutter to light matches until he found a flat pebble.

There wasnt any hurry now, it was all luck now. No telling where he might have gone. A peaceful drunken fatalism filled him. Somewhere the MPs were hunting in pairs like hawks, but it might take a couple hours yet to find him.

He wiped the pebble off drunkenly carefully, taking his own sweet time in the stillness, feeling happily the stillness, and spit on one side of it and flipped it like you flip a coin. Just like you use to do when you was a kid, he thought.

Hell, the little bastard might even come back to Hal's. Hal would let him in, of course. Then Prewitt would be looking for him when he was back safe at Hal's.

Wet was Kalakaua. Dry was the Canal. He hunted for the pebble in the darkness with a lighted match. The wet side was up.

Courtesy of the University of Illinois at Springfield.

There wasnt any hurry now, it was all luck now. No telling where he might have gone. A peaceful drunken fatalism filled him. Somewhere the MPs were hunting in pairs like hawks, but it might take a couple hours yet to find him.

He wiped the pebble off drunkenly carefully, taking his own sweet time in the stillness, feeling happily the stillness, and spit on one side of it and flipped it like you flip a coin. Just like you use to do when you was a kid, he thought.

Hell, the bastard might even come back to Hal's. Hal would let him in, of course. Then Prewitt would be looking for him when he was back safe at Hal's.

Wet was Kalakaua. Dry was the Canal. He hunted for the pebble in the darkness with a lighted match. The wet side was up.

Okay.

He turned left on the main drag, back toward the Tavern, feeling like a hunter in the forest. Down the long blocks of the wide slightly curving street no thing moved. The street car tracks stretched away. Every other street light was turned off. Not a car, not a bus, no people, no life. His footfalls sounded very loud. He got off the sidewalk and walked on the grass.

He stopped to listen then, once, but he remembered Angelo was bare footed. And wearing trunks, no less!

The MPs were tough babies down here. These were from Shafter and Department Hq. All big boys, like the Schofield bunch, and always in pairs treading heavily in the GI shoes and tight whitewashed leggins. At Schofield the MP Company that covered the Post and Wahiawa and the road down under the two columns of tall trees alongside the reservoir, they had men just as big, and just as tough, but Prew knew several of them. So to him they were more human, somehow. He had come over on the boat with several, all good joes then, until they put on the whitewashed leggins. Up at Schofield, in a pinch, he had a forty-sixty chance of meeting one of the guys he knew, who could be talked into giving him a break. Down here he knew none of them. And Angelo out drunk bare footed in trunks! He began to laugh out loud tumultuously. The loud sound of his own voice stopped him.

He hunted carefully along Kalakaua, stopping to look in darkened yards and on the benches set on the sidewalk corners, and under them. Man, are you lucky you are not a big man. You might have been a goddam MP yourself. The Provost Marshal didnt take no for an answer when he looked them over as they came down the gangplank off the boat. When The Man picked the biggest for his very very own, they were his and thats all she wrote. He remembered one big guy of six foot four who had been signalled out just ahead of him. The only thing saved that guy was he was in the Air Corps, and was the Provost Marshal pissed off over that one!

He hunted for what seemed an eternity, expecting arms with brassards to grab him any minute from behind. And if they did, well it was dear john, thats all. Those boys knew how to work you over, and they did not have to hide the marks like the civilian cops. He passed Lewers Street, looking on both sides. Then, passing Royal Hawaiian Street he saw, or thought he saw, a shadow move across silent way up in front of him. He crossed Kalakaua and slipped into the edge of the Royal grounds and stalked it. When he got up to Seaside Street, where the Royal Hawaiian Hotel driveway went in off Kalakaua, he could see a figure wearing trunks sitting calmly on a sidewalk bench in front of the Royal grounds.

"Hey, Maggio," he called.

The figure did not move.

He crossed over to the curbing, keeping an eye on the bench as if it were a deer seen through the leaves that he was walking up on, walking down alongside the very tall smooth white royal palms and the vivid green, black now, of a thickness of plants and bushes growing almost to the sidewalk.

There was a streetlight a few feet past the bench. He could tell it was Angelo. He relaxed.

"Goddam you, Maggio," he said.

His own voice sounded eerie. The figure did not move the outstretched arms along the benchtop or the thick curly head that lolled back against it.

"Is that you, Angelo? Wake up, goddam you. Answer me, you bastard."

The figure did not move. He stopped in front of the bench and stood looking down at Maggio, grinning suddenly, feeling the still night around them, feeling suddenly the presence of richness and wealth and ease that seeped through the screen of bushes from the Royal Hawaiian Hotel.

This is where the movie stars stay when they come to Hawaii to rest and play. All the movie stars. Wouldnt it be nice, he thought. He had never been inside the screen but he had walked past the Royal on the beach and seen them on the patio. But wouldnt it be nice, he thought, if a movie star would come out right now and see me here and ask me back inside, up to her room. Maybe she's just been for a midnight swim and the water droplets still on her and just taking the bathing cap off the long falling hair, her arms up to her chin.

He looked up from Maggio suddenly, looking toward the darkened driveway where a faint light showed inside, thinking surely he would see this woman walking out, knowing it positively, her coming looking for a man and finding him available. They said these did it like that all the time. Suddenly there was a very large ache inside his belly, almost like a cramp and he thought about Lorene at the New Congress. He stood looking at the empty driveway. What a way to make a living.

"Hey, come on. Wake up, you dago bastard. Wake up and lets go down town and get a piece of ass."

"I'm sorry, Sir," Angelo said, not opening his eyes or moving. "I wont do it again. Just dont lock me up, Sir. Just dont make me re-enlist. Honest I wont."

Prew leaned down and shook him by the naked bony shoulder. "Come on, wake up."

"I'm awake. Its just that I dont feel like moving. I just dont feel like going back."

"We got to go back."

"I know it. But maybe if we was to sit here long enough some movie star will come out from there and pick us up and take us back to the States in her private plane and install us in her private swimming pool. You suppose? Maybe if we was to just sit here real still and dont move none except to breathe and dont open your eyes, when we open our eyes it wont be here. None of it, no street, no bench, no pass, no Reveille."

"Jesus Christ!" Prew snorted. "Movie stars, no less. My god you are drunk. Come on. Wake up. I got your clothes."

"I dont want clothes," Angelo said.

"I got em anyway."

"Well, give em back to the Indians. The Indians need clothes. All they wear is codpieces. Did I hear you say piece of ass?" Angelo opened his eyes and turned his head to look the question.

"Sure. I made your boyfriend for forty bucks. He was scared you'd get picked up and come back bringin the law with you. Sent me out to find you and take you home."

"Hell," Angelo said. He sat up and rubbed his hands hard against his face. "I aint drunk, friend." He paused. "Hell, man, you dont need no instruction from me, buddy. The very most I ever got out of him was twenty-two-fifty. And then I was suppose to pay it back. I aint though."

Prew laughed. "I couldna got it if he wasn't scared so bad he crapped his pants."

"Did he really?"

"No."

"See, Prew? I aint drunk. I sure had you guys fooled." He stood up and immediately fell back against the lamppost. He grabbed it with both arms to keep from falling. "See?" he said.

"No. You aint drunk."

"I aint. I just stumbled on that crack there." He pushed himself up straight and let go the lamppost cautiously.

"Whoops!" he yelled, throwing his head back and letting it out from the bottom of his lungs.

"Fuck it! I'M GUNNA RE-EN*LIST*!"

"Shut up, goddam it," Prew said. He stepped in quick and grabbed him by the waistband as he started to fall back flat, clear off balance from the throwing back of his head.

"You want the goddam MPs on us?" Prew said.

"MPs! MPs! *MPs!*" Angelo yelled. "COME AND GET US. HERE WE IS!"

"You jerk." Prew let go of the trunks suddenly and Angelo fell full length on the sidewalk, without moving a hand to catch himself.

"Look at me, Prew. I'm shot. I'm dead. A poor dead soljer, not a friend in the fuckinworld. Just send the medal home to mother, boys, maybe she can hock it."

"Get up," Prew grinned. "Come on. Lets get out of this."

"Okay." Angelo scrambled to his feet, using the bench to hoist himself up with. "How long you think before we get in the war, Prew?"

"Maybe we wont get in it."

"Oh, yes we will."

"I know it."

"You dont have to protect me," Angelo said, mimicking Tommy's deep bass feminine voice. He started laughing. "I wish I had a decent drink, this slop is filthy," he mimicked Hal's precise speech. "Hell with it. Come on," he said. "Lets go to town."

"We'll have to call a cab, but first we got to get you in your clothes."

"Okay, Prew. Whatever you say, Prew." Angelo grabbed the trunks and jerked them down to his knees and started to step out of them. His foot hung and he fell again.

"Who hit me?" he said. "Who done it? Let me at the bastard."

"God damn," Prew said. He grabbed the little guy by the armpits and hauled him off out of the light into the bushes.

"Hell," Angelo protested. "Take it easy, Prew. You're scrapin my ass on the sandy sidewalk."

"You'll have worse than that scraped, if you dont get into these clothes and get out of here. . . . Listen," he said.

They both held their breath and listened, and Angelo was suddenly very sober. From down the street they heard the heavy footfalls of the GI shoes. They were not running, but they were not walking. There were voices floating with them, and then they heard a single rattle of a billy against a post.

"Goddam it," one voice said. "For Chrisake, be quiet."

"All right, all right," the other voice said. "I want an arrest as bad as you. You and that corporal's rating."

"Shut up, then. Come on."

They came in pairs at night, dogtrotting heavyfooted, leggins scraping softly, clubs swinging silently, wherever soldiers ever lived. And the air of fear they carried with them went before them always, the Law, holding them inside it, and then they were mean to see the others turn away. They came in pairs, wherever soldiers ever drank to forget or yelled to forget or fought to forget or put their hands in their pockets to remember. Soldiers must not forget, they said, soldiers must not remember; all that is treason.

"Now you did it," Prew said. "Come on, back this way. Lets take off."

"I'm sorry, Prew."

Angelo followed docilely, sober now and ashamed for causing trouble, and they skirted the big wide drive to the movie stars' place of rest, working west through the Royal grounds and passing the Willard Inn that was for officers, and running through the bushes breathlessly till they came to Kalia Road, down near the beach and the rambling swank Halekulani Hotel that was so swank most tourists never heard of it and that was on the beach here where the surf was breathing gently against the sand.

"Now," Prew said. "Take them trunks off and get in these clothes."

"Okay. Gimme the sack. What'll I do with these, old buddy boy?"

"Hell, I dont know. Here, give em to me. Listen, Angelo, are you sure you're sober now? Those guys are going to be waiting back up on Kalakaua. One of them may try to go down Lewers and beat us to Kalia Road there. But our best bet is to walk Kalia down as far as Fort De Russy and walk out from there, without gettin inside the Post. Listen to me, goddam it."

Maggio looked at him, and then Prew could see the tears running down his cheeks.

"Oh, fuck," Angelo said. "Runnin like a goddam criminal. I'm sick of it. All the time scared to fart for fear an MP'll hear you. I'm sick of it. I aint going to take it, see? I aint, I say."

"All right," Prew said. "Take it easy, Angelo. You dont want to get picked up. You're still drunk."

"Sure, I'm drunk. Sure I am. So what? Cant a man get drunk? Cant a man do anything? Cant a man even put his goddam hands in his goddam pockets on the goddam street? Why not get picked up? You might as well be in Leavenworth, anyway, instead of always on the outside looking in and never getting past the glass front, like a kid outside a candy store. Why not get picked up? I aint no coward, to be running from *them*. I aint yellow. I aint no coward. I aint no bum. I aint no scum."

"Okay, okay, okay. Just take it easy. You'll be all right in a minute."

"All right? I'll never be all right again. Its all right for you, if you're thirty year man. I aint. I dont give a fuck for them, see? Not a single goddam solitary frazzle-assed fuck. I—just—got—my—belly—full."

"Breathe deep, Mack. Take ten, and breathe real deep. I'll be right back, soon as I ditch these trunks."

He stepped down to where the water was still lapping, very softly, an inrush and a froth and then a dripping back. He threw the trunks out into the water and stepped back to where he'd left the boy from Brooklyn. Maggio was gone.

"Hey," Prew said softly. "Hey, Angelo. Hey, buddy. Where are you?"

When there was no answer he turned and started running up the street, up Lewers Street, up towards the light, running hard, very lightly on his toes.

When he got to the edge of the pool of light from the streetlight he stopped and slid back off the sidewalk out of sight.

On the curbing at the corner, in the same pool from the streetlight, little Maggio was fighting the two big MPs from Shafter.

He had one of them on the ground and was hanging crablike on his back, punching with all his wind at the MP's head that was pulled down between his shoulders. While Prewitt watched, the other MP clubbed him on the head and dragged him off the first one's back. He clubbed him again, Maggio holding his hands up over his head, the club hitting skull and fingers, and Maggio went down. He crawled up on his hands and knees and was going for the MP's legs, but slowly now, and the MP clubbed him as he came.

"Go ahead," Maggio said. "Hit me again, you son of a whore." The first MP was up now and stepped over and began to club him too.

"Sure," Maggio said. "Come on, both of you. Is that the best two great big strong men like you can do? Go ahead and hit me. Come on, hit me. You can do better than that." He tried to get up and was knocked back down.

Prew moved then, back on the sidewalk and into the light and was running up the street at them, running lightly, figuring his footing and the steps before he jumped.

"Get back," Maggio yelled. "I'm handling this. This aint your affair. I dont need no help."

One of the MPs looked around and started down toward Prewitt. On the ground Maggio moved, crablike, and tackled him. As the MP fell, Maggio was on his back, bouncing his head against the street, punctuating his words there was not breath in him to say.

"Sure. You big jokers. And your clubs. Whats the matter. Cant you take it. You can dish it out though. Cant you."

"Go on, take off," he yelled at Prew. "You hear? You keep out of this."

The MP on the ground rose up slowly, Maggio riding his back punching at his head, and arched his back and bucked the demon off, like a horse will toss its rider.

"Go on," Maggio yelled. He lit on his hands and knees and came back up. "Get goin. This aint your affair."

The other MP, standing, was fishing for his pistol. He stepped toward Prewitt, tugging to get it from the holster. Prew turned and faded down the street out of the light and into the bushes. Over his shoulder he saw the first MP's pistol sighted on his back. When he hit the bushes he threw himself down and worked, like a rifleman under fire, crawling further in.

"Put that gun away," the second MP yelled. "Whats the matter with you? You fire in there and kill some moviestar and then we'll both be up shit creek."

"Sure," Maggio said, punching him. "You big ox. Without a paddle."

"Come here and help me with this madman," the MP sobbed.

"The other one'll get away."

"Let him. Come help me hold this one down, or he will too."

"Oh, no," Maggio sobbed. "Not this one. This one wont get away. Sure," he said. "Come on. You better call in another squad while you're at it, too. You think two's enough?"

Prewitt lay in the bushes, breathing hard, not able to see them but hearing all of it.

"Sure," he heard. "Come on. Hit me some more. Come on. Why, you cant even knock me out. Come on and knock me out. Or else let me up. You fucking sons of bitches. Come on. Is that the best you can do? Come on."

Prew lay listening and he could hear the fallings of the clubs, muffled and with a penetrating chunk. There were no sounds of fists now.

"You get on back to the Post," Maggio yelled. "I know what I'm doing. You get on back. You hear?" His voice was muffled.

"Sure. Come on. Why dont you let me up? Come on. I bet you eat Wheaties, dont you?"

The voice stopped after a little while, but the other, the chunking sound, did not. Prewitt lay and listened to it keep on after the voice had stopped. He noticed that his hands were aching and he looked down at them and then unclenched them. He waited till the chunking stopped.

"You want me to go back after the other one, Jack?" he heard one pant.

"Naw, he's gone by now. Lets get this one in."

"You ought to get your sergeancy for this one. I wonder what was wrong with this guy. He's a goddam madman."

"I dont know," the other said. "Come on, lets make the call in."

"This is a lousy job, you know it?"

"I dint ask for it," the other said. "Did you? Come on, lets get that call in for the wagon."

Prew started back down toward the beach and the road, Kalia Road, that led to De Russy, traveling low, keeping in the bushes. When he got to the beach he sat down in the sand a while, listening to the water. That was when he found he was crying.

Then he remembered the forty dollars in his pocket.

JAMES JONES (1921-1977) *was a soldier in Hawai'i when the Japanese attacked Pearl Harbor. His book about army life at Schofield Barracks,* From Here To Eternity, *won the National Book Award in 1952, and was made into an Academy Award-winning film starring Montgomery Clift. Jones' other books include* Some Came Running; The Thin Red Line; *and* The Pistol.

William Bradford Huie
from THE REVOLT OF MAMIE STOVER

As a matter of fact the Honolulu whores were the only group of American civilians who were asked by their government to do more work during the Second War at a reduced rate of pay.

In complying with their government's request for this Special GI Rate, the Honolulu whores proceeded to create the most famous *genuine* slogan of the Pacific war:

THREE DOLLARS FOR THREE MINUTES!

I say genuine because the other Pacific slogans—*Send Us More Japs, Praise the Lord and Pass the Ammunition*, etcetera—were phonies. Nobody said them. *Three Dollars for Three Minutes* was genuine. It was originated by a GI, and subsequently spoken by thousands of GI's. It was genuine, honest, original, authentic.

Prior to the Second War the brothels of the earth had operated on more or less the same slow and inefficient plan. The customer entered and found girls in the reception room. He chatted with them pleasantly, patted their bustles, perhaps bought a few drinks; and if further stimulation was needed the showroom provided it. He then chose his girl, went upstairs with her; and after an interval not so long as to be immodest nor so short as to be embarrassing, he came back down and made a dignified and leisurely departure. This was Standard Operating Procedure, and was varied only on such occasions as my first visit to Parchman's when one asked for a particular girl and was shown to her room by a servant.

There was some grace in this procedure. Through the years it had acquired a certain tradition . . . an honored place in our folklore. Like the two old Southern colonels arriving in New Orleans and one of them saying to the other, "Suh, shall we stop along the way and have a drink or shall we proceed directly to the who' house?" Everybody felt sorry for the neglected little tart who sat in the corner and sang plaintively, *They All Go Upstairs But Me.*

But when Bertha Parchman's girls were drafted into the Army, they knew that the old unhurried years were ended. Honolulu had to become the Detroit of harlotry. Whores had to embrace mass production; they had to build a better assembly line; they had to modernize or starve. So with their carpenters and plumbers they hovered over diagrams, took readings on sliderules, debated new plans for serving the largest number of customers in the shortest possible time. They had to arrange for a quick turnover. They had to become efficiency experts, speedup artists, if the fighting men of America were to be properly processed in the crusade for democracy.

One fact was recognized instantly: the day of the One-Bed Woman was past. In the graceful, leisurely old days if one woman kept one bed fairly warm she was doing a good night's work. But now, under the New Deal, even the oldest and laziest of them would have to operate two beds. And Mamie Stover, who was to become the Henry Ford of harlotry, produced the most ambitiously patriotic plan of all. She announced—and she presented carpentry blueprints to show how she would do it—that as her contribution to the war effort she would keep *four beds* running during the hours she was on the firing line.

As far as I have been able to learn, Mamie Stover was the first Four-Bed Woman in history. Her plan of procedure, therefore, deserves explanation and recognition.

Mamie began by asking Bertha Parchman for the big downstairs showroom for the duration. "We won't have time to put on any shows now, Bertha," she argued. "The only purpose of the shows was to help some of the old boys get in the mood. These GI's won't need shows to get in the mood; hell, they'll be ready when they come in the door. So let's close the shows and let me and Jackie and Maybelle use the showroom."

When Bertha agreed, Mamie had all the furniture moved out of the showroom. It was a large room, some thirty feet square. In the middle of the room the carpenters then built a plywood box eight feet high and fourteen feet square. They put a door at each corner, painted it a Chinese-red both inside and out; then they went inside the box and partitioned it into four rooms, each seven feet wide and seven feet long—about the size of a Pullman bedroom. On each of the doors was painted a yellow number—1, 2, 3 and 4—and in each room was placed a four-foot-wide couch. The only other furniture in each room was a tin wastepail, coat-hangers, and a wall light.

The finished "set" looked like a clever arrangement of dressing rooms on a beach. Or like fortune-telling booths at an indoor carnival. It was pretty—reminded one of Hollywood. There was space for traffic all the way around it, as the only other furnishings in the big room were two lavatories installed at the back and which were hidden by a curtain. Also, at the side of the room the carpenters cut a new outside entrance.

Thus, from noon until 9 P.M., each day for almost three years, there were two lines of uniforms at Bertha Parchman's. The longer line was at the main entrance. They were men who wanted to pay *Three Dollars for Three Minutes* with any of Bertha's girls. The shorter line was at the side entrance. They were men who wanted to pay *Five Dollars for Five Minutes* with Flaming Mamie. MP's kept the lines orderly.

At Mamie's doorway a soldier was met by a Japanese woman who took his five dollars and led him to the booth which had just been vacated. There he removed his cap, his pants, and his underpants—nothing else—and the Japanese woman affixed the contraceptive device and lubricated it. She went out and he waited. He could tell how long he had to wait because he could plainly hear Mamie working her way around the other booths. This was by design since nothing is so stimulating to a man as listening to an intercourse while he waits.

The moment Mamie finished in a booth she went immediately to the next one, wearing only her high-heeled mules. And as she walked out of a booth a Japanese woman darted in, handed the GI a towel, helped him to a lavatory, ushered him out, then rushed a new customer to the vacated booth.

The objective always was to keep the four-room set busy in this manner: from one room a satisfied customer was being ejected; in the next room there was action; in the third room a man was waiting "at the ready"; and in the fourth room a man, just ushered in, was being made ready. Mamie could not be held up and her time wasted by the mechanics of men dressing and undressing or being made ready. The three Japanese servants had to hustle to keep ahead of her.

Occasionally there was a minor tragedy in one of the booths. When Mamie entered she found the waiting soldier unprepared for immediate action. Mamie patted him on the shoulder and said to him under her breath so that no one could hear, "Don't let it worry you, Mac. Better luck next time." Then, as she passed quickly on to the next booth, she signaled to the Japanese woman to make a refund.

Mamie called this four-bed set the "Bull Ring," and she judged her efficiency by the length of time required to make a complete circuit. Ten minutes was par, though quite often she made it in eight. She was never longer than twenty minutes, for if any customer attempted to monopolize her services beyond five minutes he found himself jerked to attention by two alert MP's.

Mamie's record time—and, I assume, the world's record for this sort of thing—was one complete circuit of four operations in four minutes and forty-eight seconds. She admitted, however, that she was shooting fish on this run. She made the record against four seventeen-year-olds of the Fifth Marine Division; the sound effects alone set their teeth to chattering, and at least one of them never got any closer than Mamie's efficient right hand.

When a soldier emerged from Bertha Parchman's, MP's directed him across the street to the pro station where he lined up and got another processing by the medics.

Mamie's Bull Ring was in operation an average of nine hours a day almost every day for nearly three years. It handled from one hundred-fifty to two hundred men a day. Mamie, of course, didn't process all these customers personally. She was the Star Attraction—most of the men hoped to find her on the Ring—but she was assisted by Jackie and Maybelle, the other two deluxe values. Mamie usually came on stage about 2 P.M., took over from Maybelle without missing a beat, ran the Ring for an hour, until she was replaced by Jackie. Mamie then came back for a second shift at five and a third between eight and nine. At the end of a typical day when the Ring had handled one hundred-eighty customers, Mamie had handled seventy-two, Jackie sixty, and Maybelle forty-eight.

Jackie was a wiry little redhead from Houston; they called her "Texas Dynamite." She was as energetic as Mamie, and she commanded a considerable following of her own. But she wasn't tall and hot-looking like Mamie, and she lacked Mamie's big, luxurious breasts. She could never quite match Mamie on the Bull Ring, though she tried hard enough. Maybelle was a willowy brunette from Chicago with Latin blood. She was a beautiful woman—something like a brunette Rita Hayworth. She, too, had come to Hawaii as a sergeant's wife. But she didn't look as "mean" as either Jackie or Mamie, and she could never process a customer quite as fast as they could.

Usually there was bitching in the five-dollar line when the word was passed that Flaming Mamie was not on the Ring . . . like a theater audience bitches when they find the slip in the playbill announcing a substitution for the star. But any man who wanted to wait for Mamie, or for one of the others, could do so without losing his place in line.

When either Mamie, Jackie, or Maybelle took an offday . . . or on days when business was particularly heavy . . . some of the five-dollar customers got cheated because one of the three-dollar girls—usually Mamie's friend Kate—was shifted over to the five-dollar Ring. After a few complaints on this score had reached Major Sumac, Bertha was forced to adopt the policy of refunding two dollars to any GI who had paid five and then complained because he had to take Kate.

The Government of the United States couldn't tolerate any such chiseling on the fighting men.

Mamie's average of seventy-two operations a day on the Ring yielded her $252. She worked enough days each month to run this to $5000, and, in turn, she poured most of the $5000 into her speculative investments during 1942, '43, and '44.

My information about the Bull Ring came from Mamie herself. I wasn't in Hawaii when she set it up; I was away much of '42; but in November of that year, one night when I took Mamie back to Bertha's after curfew, I went in and looked it over. The Japanese maids were cleaning it, getting it ready for the next day's rush.

"You mean you finish an entire operation in three minutes?" I asked Mamie.

"Sure. Usually less. What the hell, you don't think these little Marines need as long as three minutes, do you?"

WILLIAM BRADFORD HUIE (1910-1986), *legendary investigative journalist, unearthed Pentagon secrets* (The Execution of Private Slovik), *risked his life exposing the Emmett Till murderers* (Wolf Whistle), *and was jailed in Florida for defending a black woman* (Ruby Mc-Collum). *Novelist Huie revealed the KKK* (The Klansman) *and presented admirable Emily* (The Americanization of Emily), *but he loved his Mamie* (The Revolt of Mamie Stover), *a symbol of success against huge, unfair odds in the Hawaiian paradise during WWII hell.*

Lisa Toishigawa Inouye

from REUNION

Cast

TAKASHI (TAKA), *young veteran of the 442nd Combat Team*
MIYO, *his older sister*
SHIGEYUKI (SHIGE)
MASAICHI (MASA)
All veterans of the 442; Takashi's buddies who fought with him in the same company
DUKE
JITSUO (JIT)
MRS. MIYAMOTO, *Takashi's mother*
TERUKO, *his younger sister*

Scene: The front of the Miyamoto home in Kaimuki, a modest white house built high above the ground. It has a neat porch with many steps leading up to it and a white picket fence surrounding both house and yard. There is a gate in the fence. It squeaks very loudly when opened.
Time: One Sunday.

MASA *(laughs)*: Well, what about pre-med? You know, why don't you switch to the medics, then both of us could go to the states to finish up. Remember the night before we left Repple Depple in Naples? We talked about going to the states. You said you wanted to go to Illinois and I couldn't see it. I still don't—Michigan's the school, man! Gee, we sure were ambitious . . . the plans we made.

TAKA: Yeah, I remember. Kinda funny . . . no fight now. When you're over there, you sure do some wishful thinking. You know one guy I admire is Yoshi. I hear he's right on up at the University. He's in everything, full of fight. Ha, I remember the time we went on pass to Paris. We went to eat in a black market restaurant and they soaked us sixty bucks for two guys! Wow, never again.

MASA: Yeah, that French black market was terrific. One Frenchman offered me several hundred francs for my combat boots. *(He lifts his boot to indicate.)*

TAKA: You should've sold them. But France, with all its Vosges mountains and wet and cold is some place! Paris nice . . . I'm going back someday for more of that Champagne campaign.

(SHIGEYUKI enters from stage right. He limps, the result of severe injuries received in combat. He has only recently returned from a hospital on the mainland and still walks with a cane)

SHIG: Hi! Whatchu guys doing like two old ladies?

MASA and TAKA *(together)*: Hi, Shig!

TAKA: Wea you going?

SHIG: When I come up Kaimuki, wea you tink I go? No dumb questions, you! Wat you guys doing, eh?

MASA: Nothing, just chewing the fat.

SHIG: Boy, Honolulu one dead town, boy. No more nutting to do. Mo betta when I stay in New York.

MASA: Yeah, you shouda got your discharge over there. I thought you going art school in N.Y.?

SHIG: Aw, da old lady tell me come home. Now no can go . . . too fool.

MASA: How about Chicago?

SHIG: No sir. Boy, das one pilau place and da cold wind! Tetsu guys shua can take it.

MASA: Oh, Tetsu guys went up? When?

SHIG: I dunno. Coming-home-time I wen see him ova dea. We wen go look around the art school, den go eat. Boy, Tetsu fat baga now.

TAKA: How he got in?

SHIG: Aw, he smart, da guy. He went regista befo he come home. Aw, anyway, I lazy go now. I going fool around li'l while.

MASA: Yeah, Shig, take it easy. Plenty of time. How's the leg?

(They all look at SHIG'S leg.)

SHIG: Okay. Only when cold time, eh, inside sore. Da doc said going be sore while. No can walk fast do' . . . Humbug. Mo betta cut 'em off.

TAKA: I dono Shig, I see Toku Motoyama walking around okay with his plastic leg, but he sure hates it.

MASA: Aw, well, he just got it, dat's why. Wait till he gets used to it.

SHIG: Boy, I had good fun in da hospital. De nurses, oh boy . . . some meats. Dey got a kick when I sing. One nurse especially ask me e-rytime, "go sing, go sing." Den she bring me candy and all kine stuff. Boy, her keed sista was some peach! Mama mia!

TAKA: You lucky bastard! Mo betta you stayed in the hospital.

SHIG: Yeah, come home no mo fun. Honolulu one small place, boy.

MASA: Sure, after New York, any place is small. I'd certainly like to be there now, huh?

LISA (BESSIE) TOISHIGAWA INOUYE (1925-1993) *graduated from the University of Hawaii in 1948 with a BA in English. She did graduate work at Columbia and the New School for Social Research in New York, where she worked for* Newsweek. *She also worked for the* Honolulu Star-Bulletin, Hawaii Hochi, KHET, KTRG, *the state legislature, and an oral history project for the Ethnic Studies Program at the University of Hawaii.*

Edward Sakai

from AND NEVER THE TWAIN SHALL MEET?

Cast

FATHER, *Japanese father of a family. Widower for the past few years and owner of a prosperous store. He firmly believes and values the ideas of family loyalty, Japanese pride, preservation of the family name, etc. For a "first generation" Japanese he understands and speaks English quite well.*

YOSHIO, *eldest of the children. He is married to Hanako and both are living with his father. He works with his father at the store. He has some of the racial prejudices of his father.*

KIMIKO, *only daughter of the family. She is twenty-two and is in love with Tom Bellows, a Caucasian. She is sweet and understanding because since their mother's death, she had to be a mother to the family.*

MITSUO, *twenty years old and the youngest of the children. He is a college student who can see things in their relative values. He is sympathetic with his sister. There is a spirit of comradeship between brother and sister.*

Scene: The living room of a well-to-do Japanese family.
Time: An evening in Honolulu. Any time today.

(As the curtain rises FATHER *is reading the evening paper in a chair up stage of the center table.* YOSHIO *is reading a magazine in the chair near the radio.* FATHER *rustles the paper, clears his throat.)*

FATHER: Another accident! Kids of today very careless. I hope car drivers will be more careful.

YOSHIO *(looks up from his paper)*: Another accident?

FATHER: Uh.. automobile accident. Lucky no one was hurt. Honolulu get too many cars.

YOSHIO: Too many automobiles and too narrow streets.

FATHER: When you drive downtown, you drive slow and watch out.. some people careless.

YOSHIO: Yeah.. I know. Only yesterday I almost had an accident.

FATHER: What happened?

YOSHIO: I was driving on Hotel Street.. then all of a sudden a fat wahine comes out from behind a car and starts crossing the street.. I jammed on the brakes.

FATHER: You never hit her?

YOSHIO: No.. but she almost see St. Peter. She's a damn fool anyway. She jaywalks without watching for the cars.

FATHER: Watch out when you drive a car.. you may be right; but maybe the other person careless. *(He looks down at the paper.)* But, look.. it says, "Miss Ruth Hasegawa was the other occupant of the car driven by Mr. Johnson".

YOSHIO: What about that?

FATHER: But this Japanese girl going around with a haole man.. What'sa matter with this kind Japanese girl?

YOSHIO: Japanese girls of today going to the dogs.

FATHER: They not like good Japanese girls. Before.. Japanese girls quiet and good.. now they run around like damn fools.

YOSHIO: All they want is good time now.. just like the other nationalities. And they think they big-shot when they go out with a haole guy.

FATHER: Haole no good. *(He returns to his newspaper.)*

(YOSHIO looks down at his magazine, looks up again at his father. He wants to say something more to his father.)

YOSHIO: Uh.. father..

FATHER *(without looking up from his newspaper)*: Uh?

YOSHIO *(hesitatingly)*: Uh.. maybe you better talk to Kimi about the guy she goes around.

FATHER *(looks up at YOSHIO)*: Why?

YOSHIO *(embarrassedly)*: I hear she goes out with a haole guy sometimes.

FATHER *(more surprised than angry)*: With what haole?

YOSHIO: I don't know but I think his name is Tom Bellows.

FATHER *(The newspaper is forgotten on his lap. He looks questioningly at YOSHIO.)*: Tom Bellows.. haole? *(YOSHIO nods assent.)* Kimi going out with haole?

YOSHIO: I think you better talk to her.

FATHER: What'sa matter with Kimi? Why she go with haole?

YOSHIO: I don't know.

FATHER: Maybe she only friend with this haole.

YOSHIO: My friends tell me Kimi go out with this haole plenty of time.

(Footsteps are heard on the front steps. Sounds of someone taking off his shoes. The door opens and MITSUO comes in. He opens the closet and puts his shoes inside; taking out a pair of Japanese slippers he steps into them. FATHER has watched MITSUO'S proceedings; but YOSHIO consciously goes back to his magazine and turns the pages.)

MITSUO: Everybody through eating?

FATHER: Yes.. where you been?

MITSUO: Oh, I was out with some of the guys. Anything left to eat?

YOSHIO *(looks up from his magazine)*: Kimi and Hana in the kitchen, I think.. cleaning up.

MITSUO: Well, I'll take a bite. *(He goes out the kitchen door.)*

FATHER: How long Kimi going with this haole?

YOSHIO: About five months, I think.

FATHER: Why you didn't tell me more early?

YOSHIO: I thought she'd quit him.

FATHER (*reflects a little*): Kimi is good girl.. she listen to me.

YOSHIO: She'd better.. but girls nowadays too fresh.

FATHER: Kimi, good girl. Maybe.. maybe I too easy with children?

YOSHIO: I was thinking about that. Since mother died you are not so strict. You do not ask where they go or who they go with.

FATHER: I try to be good father. I want my children to be good Americans.

YOSHIO: Kimi needs a good talking.

FATHER: I will talk to her now. (*He calls out toward the kitchens.*) Kimi.. Kimi..

KIMIKO (*from the kitchen*): Yes, dad?

FATHER: Come here.

> (*FATHER sits down again. KIMIKO enters from the kitchen. She wipes her wet hands on her apron as she comes out. She is smiling.*)

KIMIKO: You wanted something, dad?

FATHER: Sit down. I want to tell you something.

> (*The seriousness of her father's manner and voice causes her to stop smiling and she becomes puzzled. She sits in the chair left of the table.*)

KIMIKO (*quietly*): Yes, dad?

FATHER: Since mother died I tried to raise you children like good folks, eh, Kimi?

KIMIKO: Yes.. and we love you for everything you've done for us.

FATHER: Yoshi married; and Hana very good wife for him.

KIMIKO: We get along very well with her.. in fact, she's one of us now.

FATHER: Good. And how old you now, Kimi?

KIMIKO: Twenty-two.

FATHER: Pretty soon, you get married too, huh?

KIMIKO: Well—not immediately.

FATHER: You think of marrying someday?

KIMIKO (*embarrassedly*): Why, yes.. I think every girl does.

FATHER: Plenty of good Japanese boys.. and if you like meet some boys, I can fix that. My friends have big boys now. They all good boys.

> (*At the mention of Japanese boys, KIMIKO freezes and realizes what her father is leading up to.*)

KIMIKO: I know some Japanese boys.. good friends.

FATHER: One of them your boy-friend?

KIMIKO: No.. none of them.

FATHER: What'sa matter? You no like the boys, or the boys no like you?

KIMIKO: It's not that.

FATHER: You no have boy-friend?

KIMIKO: Oh, I have a good friend.

FATHER: You have boy-friend.. what his name?

KIMIKO: Tom.. Tom Bellows.

FATHER *(acting surprised)*: Tom Bellows.. haole?

KIMIKO: Yes.. he comes from Michigan.

FATHER: Haole no good. Japanese boy better.

(MITSUO comes in from the kitchen munching on a sandwich.)

MITSUO: Hey, Kimi.. Hana says to stop loafing and help her in the kitchen. She's almost through.

YOSHIO: Tell Hana, Kimi is busy.

(Until now YOSHIO has been paging through the magazine though not reading. He now closes the magazine, walks to the table and puts it down. He sits down in the chair at right of table.)

KIMIKO: Tell her I'll come soon.

(MITSUO stands by the kitchen door and yells out.)

MITSUO: Hana.. Kimi is busy. She'll come later. *(He walks to the desk and sits down on the chair there. He is still munching on his sandwich.)*

YOSHIO *(to KIMIKO)*: What's his job?

KIMIKO: He works for the army surplus.

FATHER: Soldier?

KIMIKO: No.. he was a soldier. He got his discharge over here, and he plans to make his home here.

YOSHIO: Soldiers no good.

KIMIKO: But you were one yourself.

FATHER: He had Japanese upbrining.

KIMIKO *(in desperation)*: What's wrong with a haole, even if he is an ex-soldier?

FATHER: Haole soldiers no good. You know what happened during the war. Plenty of haole soldiers came here. Now they all go back to America.

YOSHIO: Yes; and look around. You'll see a lot of bastard kids running about. Lots of Japanese girls were taken in by the smooth lines.. and now they're left holding the bag.. an empty bag.

KIMIKO: That was war hysteria.. everybody wanted a good time.. and anyway, the girls were wrong too.

YOSHIO: Sure.. the girls were damn fools.

FATHER: We do not like that to happen to you. We want the best for you.. We want you to be happy. You good girl, Kimi.

MITSUO: Everybody says that those kids are really good looking. Maybe I'll marry a haole girl and get some cute kids.

YOSHIO: Those kids cute? Maybe.. maybe.. but where's the daddy? On the mainland married to his kind of girl.

FATHER: Mitsuo.. if you marry haole girl, she not welcome in my house. To me, she not your wife. Haole no good.

KIMIKO: What's wrong with haoles?

FATHER: They.. they not honest.

YOSHIO: Yes.. we lost hundreds of dollars at the store because they lied about some goods.

FATHER: And they no pay the bills on time.

YOSHIO: They don't care about anything. They get drunk, they fight, they chase girls.. they worse than dogs.

MITSUO: Yeah.. but what you said is true of every nationality.. even the Japanese.

YOSHIO *(to MITSUO)*: Shut up.. nobody told you to butt in.

MITSUO: Shut up, yourself.

FATHER *(to MITSUO)*: Your brother is older.. you listen to him.

MITSUO: Yeah.. but he's dumb.. he says corny things.. he can't make sense.

YOSHIO: Dumb? I bust you up. *(He stands up threateningly and starts toward MITSUO. MITSUO stands up.)*

MITSUO: You try. I'm younger, but I'm stronger.

FATHER *(sternly)*: Yoshi.. sit down. You too, Mitsuo.
(The two boys stare fiercely at each other. They break apart and sit down.)

YOSHIO *(to MITSUO)*: You better not get fresh.

MITSUO: Dry up.

FATHER: Shut up, you two. What the neighbors going think? Two brothers fighting like.. like haoles? *(Angrily)* Kimi. why you go with this haole?

KIMIKO: He treats me nice.. better than the Japanese boys.

FATHER *(shouts)*: "Baka".. you fool. You think this haole treat you nice because he like you?

KIMIKO *(almost in tears)*: He loves me.

FATHER: Love? Love? What that? All foolishness.

YOSHIO *(caustically)*: Did he talk about marrying?

KIMIKO: Yes.. he wants to marry me.

FATHER: Love come from respect.. American love silly. Japanese love better.

KIMIKO: But we're in America, not in Japan.

FATHER: Make no difference. Look.. your mother and me.. we had good Japanese love, not American love; but we happy and get good family.

YOSHIO: Look at the divorces in America.

FATHER: No divorce in Japanese marriage.

KIMIKO *(to YOSHIO)*: Just because your marriage was a "go-between" doesn't mean that I must have one.

YOSHIO: What's wrong with a "go-between" marriage?

KIMIKO: Nothing; except that I'm going to choose my own husband when the time comes.

FATHER: You can choose own husband; but you choose Japanese boy.

FATHER (*more gently*): Kimi.. listen very carefully. If you go with this haole man and maybe marry him.. people talk. I going to lose good business.. lose my Japanese customers.. but that is all right. I'm old and I have money. What you do reflect on the family honor.. our ancestors and your brothers and their children, you must not spoil the family name for them. If you go against your brothers and me, then I will disown you. You may do like you want, but if I disown you I will not recognize you.. your brothers and relatives will forget you.. our family friends.. maybe talk to you but they will not treat you as one of my family. All family and friend connection will be "pau".. and you all alone. Think deeply, and long, before you do anything. (*He pauses, and* KIMIKO *stands sobbing*). I go bed now.

EDWARD SAKAI *wrote this play in 1937, when he was a student at the University of Hawaii.*

Milton Murayama
from PLANTATION BOY

I n March Barbara Hutton checks in at the Royal Hawaiian with her entourage. Chuck pays the hotel $15,000 to close the bar and lanai from 1:00 to 4:00 P.M. and invites his *mahu* and society friends to her party. She's thinking of building a house in Mexico for her new husband, the German tennis champion. He was refused a visa to the U.S. because he is a *mahu*. So they wintered in Cuernavaca, where she bought 30 acres from a Mexican contractor.

"She wants to build a Japanese-style mansion to house her collection of Oriental antiques. That's what millionaires do. They collect, then they build a house for their collections," Chuck explains.

Couple years back Doris Duke asked Chuck how much it would cost to gold-leaf a Moorish onion dome. She collected Persian antiques at Shangri-la, her Diamond Head estate. Chuck asked me to check out the cost of gold-leafing. I phoned Builders Gold. My pidgin accent must've turned him off. "No, you'd better forget it. It'll cost too much," the haole said, laughing. "Oh, okay . . ." I said, wondering who else I could call. "Who's your client?"

he asked just before hanging up. "Doris Duke." "I'll be right over!" In the end Doris Duke decided not to build.

Chuck practically lives at the Royal Hawaiian the next few days, sketching and developing designs for Barbara Hutton's *sumiya*, or "house at the corner." I do the elevations for the floor plans. What a program! Start with a detached guest house, a lanai and bar, a swimming pool, a tennis court, then an open entrance lanai to the sliding glass panels of the living room. A wooden bridge in an enclosed open court is to be the only access to the bedroom suite, which is to have tatami floors but a bed and dressing counter. The dining room is to be for floor-sitting with a well under the table for the diners' legs; the living room is all Western with wall-to-wall carpets. The spread-out plan includes a 40-seat Kabuki-style theatre.

A purely Japanese house doesn't need an architect. It builds itself up from the 3' x 6' tatami module. The number of tatamis used determines the spacing of the posts and height of the ceiling. The Japanese-style houses we did in Hawaii were *hapa*. The pitched roof and overhanging eaves suited our winter rains. We didn't have to contend with the Japanese winter so we used sliding glass panels between the posts, which brought in the outdoors. They were furnished with tables, chairs, and beds. Floor-based living and multi-purpose rooms are for making maximum use of limited space.

"You have to *spend* money to make money," Chuck says, all smiles. Barbara Hutton pays him a $10,000 retainer to build a $1,000,000 *sumiya*.

"She's leaving for San Francisco at the end of the month and then to Italy and France. We have to sign her before she changes her mind. It's a difference between ten thousand and one hundred thousand dollars."

"I cannot do it just with Ted. I need extra help."

He agrees to hire 2 temporary draftsmen.

"You can save thirty days if you pick a contractor now. I don't know how much materials and labor cost in Japan, but at three hundred sixty yen to a dollar, shouldn't be much. I bet you can get quality without asking for low bids," I say.

"I'm checking on references now."

The next day Chuck brings a set of photos and affidavits of her antique collection.

"It shouldn't be difficult," he says. "The collection isn't even one percent of Winterthur's. But the house has to be more than a mere envelope. It has to be authentic and conform to the periods of the pieces."

I examine the 6- and 8-panel screens, an antique door painted with peacock and chrysanthemum, ink-brush drawings, paintings, lacquer boxes, trays, etc.

"I cannot do it just by books. I have to go to Japan to look at the real stuff."

"I'll send you when I get the builder picked. Barbara has an exhibit of Chinese porcelain at the Academy of Arts. You should look at them too."

I have Ted break in Tom Chang and Sam Inoki, the temporary helps. Then I pile their "In" baskets with my prelims.

"You gotta convert everything to metric. Japan and Mexico are metric. No worry about the lettering and dimensioning. As long as they legible. Do the lettering and dimensioning lines freehand . . . like this. Nemmind if a little crooked or one-sixteenth inch off. This rush job. *Ukupau*."

Luckily we don't have the time-consuming details of windows and doors. Chuck flies to Cuernavaca to examine the site with a Mexican civil engineer. He checks the zoning laws and picks a project manager. I consult the engineers here. Electricians and plumbers will be Mexican.

I cram and cram. The *sumiya* came into being in the late 1600s with the rise of the merchant class. Without wars the samurai fell into poverty. Money, not rice, became the medium of exchange, and rich merchants built hideaway *sumiyas* for their mistresses. Barbara Hutton's "house at the corner" will be that in name only. It's too small. She'll need the bigger *shoin/sukiya*, which conforms to the period of her antiques. The *sukiya* is a later version of the formal *shoin*. It's less religious and more rustic and richly detailed, though the skeleton is the same—tightly joined Japanese cypress posts and beams, floor posts on small foundation stones, floor 2 feet off the ground.

Chuck stops by every day and stands over us. "We're talking ninety thousand dollars! Time is worth ninety thousand! She's leaving for Paris in a month and half!"

"How about helping us?"

"The first job of the architect is to bring in the job. I've done that. Your job is to do the drawings."

"Some offices, the bosses work on the board with the draftsmen," I say.

"Yes, I know. The ones that don't have enough to do."

He's good at schematics and design development, and he makes good presentation drawings and renderings, but he's sloppy in the details, knowing I'd fill them in.

I draw so hard and fast I see lines when I close my eyes. I stand at the board for hours, then come back after supper. I read in bed and wake up in the middle of the night, remembering one more detail. I work 16 hours, sleep 5 hours. I rush so hard food sits in a lump in my stomach.

"You have to slow down," Carol says. "Go get *shiatsu*."

I'm glad she leaves me alone at times like this. *A haole wife would demand her daily quota of attention.*

Then one night Carol says at supper, "You have to talk to Chrys."

"Cannot wait? I'm so busy."

"No," she says.

She won't bother me unless it's real important. She knows my work comes first. *I'm still struggling.*

Chrys vomited in Miss Kishi's first-grade class. It was parents' day, and when Carol and the other parents got to her class, Chrys burst into tears.

"Why you a crybaby, Chrys? You scared of Miss Kishi?" I hold her in my lap.

"You know what Miss Kishi told her afterward? 'You didn't have to do that in front of everybody,'" Carol says.

"How come you wen cry?" She hides her face in my shoulder.

"How come you wen vomit? You sick?" I say.

"You shouldn't speak pidgin. It's a bad example," Carol says.

"How come you vomited, Chrys? Why did you cry?"

"I hide the peas." She sniffs.

"Where?"

"Under the plate."

"So you don't like peas?"

She shakes her head.

"So why you vomit?"

"Miss Kishi wen make me eat the peas."

"Thass why you vomited?"

She nods and hides her face.

"But why did you cry today?" Carol asks.

She curls around me again. "I bet I know why," I say. "You want to show Miss Kishi up, yeah? You want to show she one mean witch, yeah?"

Quick nods.

"Phew! I thought maybe she was r-e-t-a-r-d-e-d," I tell Carol. It's the first thing the Kahana wahines bring up. Masaru Nakai worked for the Army in Japan and married a Japan girl. When he came back last year, the women said, "Oh, you know Masaru Nakai is back. His daughter is retarded . . ."

"She shouldn't be teaching first grade. She's such a disciplinarian. She treats them like they were fourth or fifth graders," Carol says.

"She's a Pepelau girl too."

"Yeah, she was two grades behind me," Carol says.

I take a night off. I drop by the Columbia Bar.

"Hey, I hear your society architect wen catch one beeg fish, eh?"

"Yeah, I busting my ass. He wants it finished before she change her mind. It's a difference between hundred Gs and ten Gs."

"So he giving you one bonus?"

"He better."

"Eh, you know what your *mahu* boss wen tell my boss?" Dike Masuo says. He works for a haole architect too.

"Yeah, what?"

"He says Orientals shouldn't get paid so much because they save half of what they make."

"Oh, yeah?"

"Yeah."

"Well, he going give me a big bonus. I saving him ninety Gs. Hey, you guys know what's a 'bidet'?"

"What that?" Dike says.

"Nobody know? Where's Lenny? He'd know. It's a washbasin sunk in the bathroom floor. The French wahines, they squat over it to wash their twats."

For the first time in 2 weeks I get a good night's sleep.

After couple of weeks, Chuck gets the name of a reputable contractor in Kyoto.

"He has his own crew of carpenters, plasterers, and roofers. No subcontractors. I have it from an unimpeachable source his craftsmanship is museum quality," he says.

"Great!" I say. We'll be saving 3-4 weeks, the time it takes for the contractors to send in their bids.

Now my specs can read "top-quality *hinoki* lumber; construction methods of the seventeenth century; all joinery, no nails except when unavoidable and they must be invisible; walls of earthen plaster . . ."

Chuck makes blueprints of each working drawing and specs and mails them to Mr. Harada, the contractor. The budget is the least of our worries. Time is worth 90 Gs.

We finish the drawings, but Barbara Hutton has left for Frisco and time is running out.

"I'll give you a twenty-five dollars per diem. You people can live on half of what it takes us," Chuck says.

"Bullshit! I got haole taste!"

"All right, bring back all your bills."

I ask Ted Noguchi, a Pepelau boy and travel agent, to reserve me rooms in cheap hotels in Tokyo and Kyoto. "I'll get you Japanese-style *ryokans*," he says. "They're half the price of swanky hotels."

"You going to Tokyo? Go see Mrs. Kanai," Masayuki Shiroma, my barber, says. "She one widow now." The Shiromas had a barbershop on Main Street in Pepelau before the war, and they were pillars of the Methodist Church. The Kanais left for Japan in 1939, and Rev. Kanai died during the war.

It must've been the 4 J&B's and the vibration of the plane—I sleep zonked out and wake up next morning in Tokyo. It's a sprawling shantytown, teeming with Japanese. I check in and take a cab. The driver is a white-gloved kamikaze, swerving into alleys at full speed, dodging oncoming cars at the last second. It's a maze of alleys and streets. Houses sprang up haphazardly after the firebombs demolished the city. He finally arrives at the address. "*Hai*," he says. It's a slum.

"Kanai-san! Kanai-san!" I call into the 2-story woodframe house.

An old woman in a faded print dress comes out and peers up at me through rimless glasses. Her hair, in a bun, is snow-white. The *okusan* I knew stood straight, a foot taller than her husband, the reverend. Unlike him, she spoke perfect English, and she dressed in the latest flapper hats and flowing silk gowns.

"*Okusan*, how are you? *Hisashi buri ne?* Do you remember me? I am Oyama Toshio. I was the bad boy Kanai sensei kicked out of Japanese language school." I crouch to show myself. *She must be only in her 50s!*

"Ah, Oyama Toshio. You weren't bad. You just had lots of energy," she says in English.

"I'm sorry to hear about Reverend Kanai," I say. I remember his hitting me in class when I told him I was quitting.

"It was merciful in a way," she says. "He suffered during the war. He kept telling people Japan can't win. They don't realize how vast America is, and its people are not spoiled and divided but individuals in a democracy, and they'd rise up in a body after an attack like Pearl Harbor and never settle for a negotiated truce. He refused to take part in the air-raid drills, and neighbors came to our house at night to throw stones."

"Why did you come back here?"

"Reverend Kanai and I were childless. We wanted to be among kin. 'It's *zannen* to die in a strange land,' I used to say. It seemed so important then. Also we thought we could do some good here with our knowledge of America and our command of English. All through the war we were forbidden to speak English. During the early years, they'd broadcast baseball games. The announcers were forbidden to say 'hitto' for 'hit.' The government had them say, *anda*, 'safe hit.'"

"Let's have lunch," I say.

"Do you realize you have a cousin living nearby?" she says when we sit down at a noodle shop. "She works at a toy factory across town. Did you know your late aunt, Chiyako? Yoshiko is her child from her first marriage. Chiyako divorced her first husband and remarried Takashi Kuni, the older brother of Mr. Kuni of Kahana. She had two children by him, then she died soon after the war ended. Mr. Kuni remarried and has two more children."

She's full of questions about Pepelau and the people in the congregation.

"The church is still there. I remember your tenth-grade class put on a Shakespeare play in Japanese for their graduation."

"Yes. *Hamlet*. Those were happy days."

I put ten 10,000 yen notes into her hand when I leave.

"No, no, no," she says, and pushes my hand away.

I fold the money and push it down her neckline.

"No, no!" she says, backing off, "people will talk."

It's only two hundred seventy-eight dollars American.

She's bowing and bowing when I look back. *It shakes me up. How can people change so much? She used to be so proud. Everybody called her "Okusan." She gave Mrs. Woods hell when Kiyo was hit by the car in front of the church. Now she's cowed by what people will say.*

I call on the Kunis after supper. He looks like his brother, Robert, who's now the principal of Kahana Grade School. The same round face and round *mempachi* eyes. Everybody looked up to Robert Kuni. He was the first success from Kahana.

I could've recognized Yoshiko anywhere. She walks like sister Ann— back straight, ass out. I make small talk with Mr. Kuni and his wife while I watch Yoshiko wash the dishes, bathe her 2 step-sisters and put them to bed. The older boy and girl are Chiyako's so they're Yoshiko's half-siblings. Finally Yoshiko is free and comes to sit with us on the tatami. I'm mad as hell! I came to see her, not them!

"How are you?"

"*Kekko*. How is your mother?" she asks.

"Fine."

We keep on making small talk, waiting for her step-parents to leave. But they sit there for the next 2 hours.

"Well, I better be going." I get up madder than hell. Damn Japs! They always take advantage!

"Thank you for all the gifts. Please give my regards to your mother and father," Yoshiko says, and follows me into the alley.

"You realize, they're making a *baka* of you!? Leave! You owe them nothing! You're not even the same blood! If you're not married the next time I come, I'm taking you to Hawaii! I'll find you a husband there!" *Even Kazuo Kawai would be an improvement.*

"*Hai*," she says, bowing. Then she says, "Please forgive my mother *ne*?"

"*Nani*?"

"All she talked about before she died was how badly she treated your mother."

"What are you talking about?"

"Mother was ten when your mother arrived in Hawaii. She treated your mother very badly. 'I should've apologized, I should've apologized,' she kept saying when she was dying. Please forgive her, *ne?*"

"That's ancient history. It's forgotten," I say. "But I'm warning you." I shake my finger. "They have no conscience. They'll treat you like a maid forever. *You* have to leave. If you're not married and out of here the next time I come—"

"Oh," Mr. Kuni says as he steps out, "I was worried when you didn't come back."

"*Sayonara.*" Yoshiko bows.

"Remember what I said," I say.

"What did he say?" I hear the parasite asking her as I leave, and I get even madder.

The next day I go to a swank hotel and "buy" a postdated receipt for the night, then get receipts from an expensive restaurant, and fly to Kyoto. Jiro Harada and his men meet me at the airport. One carries the prints, another a folder with the photos, a third with a fat valise. Harada is about my age, tall for a Japanese, 5'8".

"*Sensei.*" He bows and his men bow with him. *Nobody ever called me* "sensei"!

"Where dzu you wanz go firsto?" Harada asks.

"Take me to my *ryokan*, then I want to see some of the works you did."

We pile into his '56 Chevy coupe. It's the biggest car on the road. Kyoto was spared bombing during the war. American intelligence said there was nothing strategic there. It's serene compared to bustling Tokyo.

At the *ryokan* I dig out my prints and give Harada copies of the last quarter of the prints.

Then we drive to a *sukiya* he restored. Inside and out, the materials and craftsmanship are first-rate. A "floating" Japanese ceiling and *hinoki* framing. *Great!*

"Just like your *sukiya*," I compliment him.

"No, no, mine outside onry," Harada says.

"Did you study the photos?" I ask.

"*Hai, hai.*" He nods several times.

I say in slow English, "I need *ramma* and *fusuma* and other details that are of the periods of the antiques. For instance, the living room is all Western. Wall-to-wall carpets, Chinese rosewood coffee table and chairs, sofas and ottomans. *Wakaru?*"

He nods quickly. "Yes, yes."

"All the screens will be in both the dining and living rooms."

"One screen early Tokugawa, 1630 to 1730, other ones late Tokugawa, 1730 to 1880, Kano school," he says.

We drive all over Kyoto. He shows me more works he's done and the interior details for early and late Tokugawa. We sketch and photograph. It's not so much the periods and ideas I want to nail down, but the visual—how will they look beside the panel of ink-brush paintings. For instance, Hutton's little lacquer boxes are of Momoyama period, and would fit best somewhere in the bedroom suite. So I'll be dealing at most with 3 periods.

They offer to treat me to supper, but I say no, let's go to the compound and order take-outs and work on my latest prints and the interior details. It's past midnight when they drive me to my *ryokan*.

We spend another 15-hour day, now all at the compound. I push them like I pushed Ted and my 2 helpers. I keep selecting, discarding, selecting the right details to conform not only to the periods but also to the style of the pieces—the peacock and chrysanthemum door leading to the living room or to the screens in the vestibule. And I push them to work their abacuses to come up with estimates.

Finally, at dusk on the third day Harada comes up with an estimate—325,000,000 yen. "It can't go any higher," he says.

"Did you include ocean freight of the materials?"

"Yes."

"What about transportation of your men? And their room and board while there. The exchange will be in pesos. I don't know if you'll gain or lose with the yen. You're not including the wall and the main gate and stone lantern?"

"No, just insai house."

"You'll probably need the ten percent cushion. No telling how much the Mexican *yakunin* will ask. Sign it for three-sixty. There's bound to be hidden expenses. The steamship cost will be in yen? The yen is nothing if you have to pay in dollars."

"*Hai, hai, okage sama de,*" he says, bowing deeply, and all his men bow. I like the guy. He's like Bob Agena, a general contractor I use back home. I don't have to explain every omission and detail. He can follow my thoughts. He has a shock of black, greasy hair. He keeps his arms to his sides, feet together. They all have that stiffness, like they're ready to bow or click their heels. They could be niseis except for the stiffness and baggy pants. Hawaii is wide open compared to their packed-like-sardines space.

"We take you now to *sumiya* for geisha party," he says. "Onry *sumiya* in oru Jappan."

I ask them to drive me to the swankiest hotel and restaurant.

"*Chotto matte*," I say, and run in to "buy" receipts for my $50 per diem.

The *sumiya* is barely big enough for our party of 20. They must've reserved it months ago. I laugh. *Chuck would have a fit if we built a real* "sumiya." *It'd cost only 100 Gs at the most.*

We have *shabu-shabu*—a meat stew that don't exist in Hawaii. The geishas pour the sake. Harada and his men toast me one after the other and I toast them back, as is the custom.

I wag a finger at Harada. "You *sensei*. Me, *deshi*," I say, tapping my chest.

"No-no-no," he says, palm fluttering. You *sensei*. Me *deshi*."

"What you think Barbara Hutton house? Outside *sukiya*, inside all mix up?"

"Insai all mixu uppu orai," Harada says.

Pretty soon we're singing and clapping. I have a nice buzz and remember the Columbia back home. *Niseis too need booze to loosen up, but these guys get drunk faster and act real tipsy and silly.*

"*Sensei, kampai.*" They keep toasting.

The next morning Harada and his men drive me to the airport on a flight to Tokyo. I look forward to flying to Honolulu. It'll give me a chance to sleep.

When I get back, I show Chuck the receipts I "bought" in Tokyo and Kyoto and get my $50 per diem.

Chuck flies to San Francisco to see Barbara Hutton. He's gone for a week and comes back gliding into the office. All the *mahu* gestures come out, the prancing, the wrist action. He's collecting the 100 Gs in 3 installments to save on taxes and he's leaving on a 4-month cruise around the world.

"You're not giving us a bonus!?" I ask.

"I pay you more than any draftsman makes," he says.

"Yeah, but this was extra! I bust my ass! I push my boys!"

"Check the other offices. Nobody gets one thousand a month."

"Yeah, but this was overtime! I put in sixteen hours a day! We finish in three months what takes eight months!"

Just then a *hapa* shoe-shine boy pokes his head in the doorway. "Shine? Shine?"

"Yes, give these boys a shine," Ames says.

I laugh. "Yeah, we'd better take the shine. That's all the bonus we going get!"

But afterward I stew. I yell at Carol and the kids and go out and get stinking drunk.

The next day Ames phones the office and asks me to bring his valise from the office and drive him to the airport. He's flying to Los Angeles to catch his boat.

I have a throbbing headache as I drive up Tantalus in the blinding sun and look for the address. Metal numbers soldered on grillwork gate. A pastel '57 Lincoln with fat tail fins and another fat-fender car crowd the driveway. It's a large, open-style Spanish colonial, stucco walls, red tile roof. The view sweeps from Diamond Head to Ewa. The blue ocean rises to the horizon. It's breezy and fragrant with plumerias. Ames came slumming to Kaimuki a month ago to get one of the books on Japanese architecture. He stepped into our kitchen and said, "Where d'you get this!? It's mine! It's an antique!" "You mean this rug!? It was mixed up with the laundry at the office. I thought it was a rag," I said. "It's worth a fortune!" he said. Luckily the washing machine had not hurt it.

"Oh, Chuck, your boy is here!" a young, skinny haole shrieks. "Can I get you a drink?"

"No thanks."

Couple more young men come out. Mainland haoles not yet tanned.

"So he's the tiger of Malaya," one of them says.

"He doesn't look ferocious, he's more—"

"Like a trade number!" they shriek, kicking up knees.

I'm boiling.

Ames has leis up to his ears.

"You ready?" I snarl.

The boys follow with the suitcases.

I get madder and madder as I drive down the mountain. When I reach the bottom, I let go. "You and your goddamn *mahus*! You all the same! You think we nothing but houseboys! I going show you some day! I going get my license and I'll show you who needs who more! No draftsman in town working harder! Shit! I work around the clock for three months! I ignore my family! I push myself so hard I almost crack up and all I get is one shoe shine! Without me you nothing! You one parasite! Just like the plantation bosses! One more thing! You go around telling everybody Orientals overpaid, they save half of their pay!" I shake my finger. "You know, I can make you or break you! . . . " I yell and yell. He cringes against the door. I'm only 5'5" but I'm ready to hit this 6-foot slob!

I'm yelled out by the time we get to the airport. I help him with his suitcases.

"Have a good trip." I extend a hand, looking away.

It's a fingers-only limp handshake. *Why I offering this stupid handshake!?*

I drive back aimlessly. *What if he fire me? Shit, if he fire me, he fire me. Nobody indispensable. I sick of catching all the shit. I oughta blow up more often.*

MILTON MURAYAMA *was born in Lahaina, Maui, in 1923. He grew up there and on "Pig Pen Avenue" in the plantation camp of Pu'ukoli'i. The camp, once home to more than six hundred Japanese, no longer exists. During World War II, Murayama trained at the Military Intelligence Language School at Camp Savage, Minnesota, and served as an interpreter in India and China. He received a BA in English from the University of Hawaii and an MA in Chinese and Japanese from Columbia. He is the author of three novels:* All I Asking for Is My Body; Five Years On a Rock; *and* Plantation Boy. *The final novel in the tetralogy,* Dying in a Strange Land, *will be published in 2008.*

Edward Sakamoto
from A'ALA PARK

Cast:
JEANIE, *MANNY'S girlfriend*
MANNY, *about twenty, with dark, brooding eyes*
BEAR, *Manny's buddy, burly, mean-looking but good-natured*
UJI, *local Japanese man, late sixties*
JOJO, *MANNY'S brother, about fourteen*
CHAMP, *built like a boxer, age nineteen*
CABRAL, *a lanky Portuguese, age nineteen*

Place: A low-income section of Honolulu, in A'ala Park area.
Scene: The main playing area is an alley with a wall of gangrenous-green, peeling paint and termite-ridden wood. There is a beat-up trash can. At stage left is a back door which leads to an unseen pool hall. At stage right on an elevated platform are a table and two chairs, a section of MANNY'S tenement home.
Time: Late summer 1959, the year of statehood.

JEANIE: You serious about going to da Mainland?
MANNY: Yeah. I figga someday I going up.
JEANIE: Why you like leave Hawai'i for?
MANNY: Wat get here? Nuttin'. Dis place just like one prison, living on one rock, so damn small, no can breathe. Shit, take you just half a day drive around da island.

JEANIE: So wat? Who tell you drive so fast? If you go slow take one whole day.

MANNY: Sometimes I like just drive and drive, just me and nobody else, and I keep on driving till nobody around but me. And den I yell my head off till I go deaf and lose my voice da same time.

JEANIE: Wat good dat going do?

(OLDER MANNY joins the two.)

MANNY: Going make me feel happy, 's all.

JEANIE: Why dat going make you happy?

MANNY: Why you asking me all dese questions? You tink you my muddah or wat?

JEANIE: Why you no can be happy in Honolulu like everybody else? Maybe someting wrong wit' you. How come dey wen' fire you at da cannery?

MANNY: Aeh, I bust my ass dere and fo' wat? Only make da haole company rich. Dey get da money and I stay poor. You see wat I mean?

JEANIE: Not everybody can be rich. Some people gotta be poor.

MANNY: You gotta be poor, not me.

JEANIE: If you like be rich, why you neva study some more? Why you neva go University Hawaii? Nobody stopping you.

MANNY: Shit, Jeanie, now you sounding like my muddah.

(She kisses him full on the mouth.)

JEANIE: Your muddah kiss you li'dat?

MANNY: Aeh, no talk dirty, eh.

JEANIE: Well, no call me your muddah.

MANNY: I neva call you my muddah. I said you sound like her. "Why you no go school, you no shame o' wat?"

JEANIE: Your muddah no talk li'dat.

MANNY: 'S wat you tink, you dunno nuttin'.

JEANIE: I wish I was more smart. Den you no take me so cheap.

MANNY: Yeah, I betta look around fo' one girl wit' good head.

(She whacks him on the arm.)

MANNY: You see wat I mean. Wat da hell you hit me fo'? And clean up da way you talk, eh, you sound like one guy.

JEANIE: Yeah? I look like one guy too?

(She shows off a nice pair of legs.)

MANNY: Yeah.

JEANIE: Wat you mean, yeah? *(JEANIE jumps on him, and they wrestle playfully on the ground. Now she's on top of him.)* You give up?

MANNY: Yeah, you too strong fo' me.

JEANIE: Okay. Now you not going Mainland, right?

MANNY: Not wen you stay on top of me li'dis.

JEANIE: Good. Den I not moving . . .

(Lights change. It is late afternoon. BEAR enters, sits on the ground and examines his toes carefully, one at a time. MANNY enters, OLDER MANNY joins the two.)

MANNY: Aeh, Bear, you trying to count to twenty?

BEAR: No, I was tinking how come my toes so crooked. Look ugly, eh?

MANNY: You know wat dey say: crooked toes, crooked prick.

BEAR: Aeh, bull lie, who said dat? Sheila?

MANNY: Sheila? Wat, you fooling around wit' her?

BEAR: Maybe. Why? Wassamadda wit' Sheila?

MANNY: She too hairy. Why you no tell her shave her legs?

BEAR: Her faddah no let her.

MANNY: She get mo' hair on her legs dan you.

(BEAR pulls up a pants leg and admires his leg.)

BEAR: Yeah, I get nice legs, eh?

MANNY: Real bow-legged. Like one horseshoe.

BEAR: Jealous bugga.

(BEAR spots an ant on the ground.)

Aeh, look, see dat ant? All by himself. Where you tink he going?

MANNY: He going visit his girlfriend, tell her shave her legs.

BEAR: He coming dis way.

MANNY: Watch dis.

(MANNY puts a hand down to block the ant.)

BEAR: Now he going da odda way.

(MANNY puts his other hand down to thwart the ant again.)

MANNY: If ants can shit, he shitting right now. Look at him, back and fort', round and round. He dunno wat fo' do, everyting crowding in on him so fast.

BEAR: I like try someting.

(BEAR spits at the ant but hits MANNY'S hand.)

MANNY: Aeh, who tell you spit on my hand.

BEAR: Sorry, eh. I like circle him wit' spit so he no can escape.

(He spits again and again.)

MANNY: Now look wat you did. You spit right on him.

BEAR: No can help, he wen' run right unda my spit, da dumb ant.

MANNY: Now da bugga drowning in your spit.

BEAR: He lucky dog shit neva fall on him.

MANNY: He getting weak.

BEAR: Little bit mo' and ma-ke, die, dead.

(MANNY finds a rusty nail and uses it to lift the ant out of the spit.)

BEAR: He dead?

MANNY: No . . .

(Lights up slowly on alley. It is day. BEAR comes out of the pool hall's back door with UJI.)

BEAR: Dey make Hawai'i one state today? 'S wat da radio said?

UJI: Yeah. Too good, eh.

BEAR: Aeh, statehood no big deal. I no feel diff'rent today from yestaday.

UJI: We gotta celebrate.

BEAR: 'S why you wen' bring out da dry akule and lomi lomi salmon fo' everybody?

UJI: Sure, now we first-class American citizens.

(JOJO enters with a small American flag.)

JOJO: Look, dis flag get fifty stars.

BEAR: You sure?

JOJO: Yeah, try count 'um.

(BEAR starts counting but stops.)

BEAR: Too much trouble. I take your word. How you get 'um?

JOJO: One man passing 'um out. Free.

BEAR: Aeh, I going see if I can get some mo'. Wait, eh.

(He exits quickly.)

JOJO: You wen' see Manny today?

UJI: No. Why, someting wrong?

JOJO: No, no. He neva come home last night, so . . .

UJI: Maybe he feel bad because no mo' job. Too bad da cannery wen' fire him.

JOJO: Oh no, dey neva do dat. He wen' quit because, ah, he can get one betta job in Waikiki. In one of da hotels, Royal Hawaiian, I tink.

UJI: Yeah? Das good. Manny lucky den.

JOJO: Yeah, Manny no fool around. He know wat he doing.

(BEAR returns with one flag.)

BEAR: Da guy out dere manini bugga. He get plenny flags but he give me only one. If I get da flags he get, I can make money selling 'um half-buck one. Jojo, you and me go out again and try get some mo' flags. Da mo' you can get, da mo' we can sell.

JOJO: 'S not legal, eh?

BEAR: No worry about legal. I handle da kine. We go. Aeh, Uji-san, we see you, eh, me and Jojo going make some money. Jojo, now I split da profits wit' you, okay? You just give 'um your innocent face and keep asking fo' flags. Wat we doing is patriotic, so no need sweat . . .

UJI: Manny, Jojo was looking fo' you. He was worried.

MANNY: About wat?

UJI: He said you neva come home.

MANNY: Nah, dat was nuttin'.

UJI: He said you going work at Royal Hawaiian Hotel.

MANNY: Jojo said dat?

UJI: Good you going work dere.

MANNY: I dunno yet. I tink betta if I go Mainland.

UJI: Aaahhh, you no like go dere. Poho. Waste time.

MANNY: Get mo' chance on da Mainland.

UJI: No can beat Hawai'i. And now we get statehood.

MANNY: Wat statehood going do fo' me? Nuttin'.

UJI: Wat Mainland can do fo' you?

MANNY: Get forty-nine states to look fo' jobs.

UJI: Yeah but wat kine work you going do?

MANNY: Anyting betta dan da cannery.

UJI: I was like you wen I was young. I work on one freighta and sail to da Mainland. Was junk ova dere. Dose days was hard fo' guys like us. If you not haole, you hard luck.

MANNY: Ova here da same. Wat da diff'rence?

UJI: Maybe Mainland betta nowdays. But I still tink Hawai'i betta fo' people like us. We all stick togedda, no pilikia. Up dere, you going be all alone. I pity you.

(BEAR and JOJO reenter.)

JOJO: Dere Manny.

BEAR: No bodda him now. You no can see he busy? Okay, we get fourteen flags. We sell 'um fifty cents each, 's seven dollars. We split 'um even, four bucks fo' me, t'ree bucks fo' you.

JOJO: Aeh, 's not fair.

(MANNY and UJI enter the pool hall)

BEAR: Was my idea, right?

JOJO: Yeah.

BEAR: I olda dan you, right?

JOJO: Yeah.

BEAR: I betta-looking dan you, right?

JOJO: No.

BEAR: No? Aeh, I still win two outta t'ree. Chee, Jojo, no make me feel bad. Okay, I get t'ree seventy-five, you get t'ree twenty-five. And no ask fo' mo' dan dat, or I sell you to da gypsies on Hotel Street.

JOJO: I not scared. Da gypsies my friend.

BEAR: Yeah, yeah, everybody your friend. Aeh, Jojo, wen da tourists come in on da Lurline, you like be partnas wit' me?

UJI: Wat I gotta do?

BEAR: We go out in da ocean dive fo' da coins dey t'row from da boat.

JOJO: I no can swim dat good.

BEAR: Easy, brah. I put you on one rubba tire and you just wave at da tourists and tell 'um t'row some coins in fo' good luck Den I dive fo' da money. Haoles love da kine shit. Okay, partna, we go down Hall Street side make some money . . .

MANNY: Aeh, Bear, tell da guys wat wen happen at da beach.

CHAMP: Wat? You wen' naked and all da girls wen' faint?

BEAR: No get funny. Some service guys wen' get sassy wit' Gladys and Sheila.

CHAMP: Gladys and Sheila? Damn haoles go afta anyting.

BEAR: So dis one bugga wen' say, "Wanna hot dog, honey, you be da bun and I'll be da wienee."

CHAMP: 'S all? You act da same way wit' da haole wahines. In fact, you mo' dirty and sickening.

BEAR: I was going rap da haole in da face but two MPs wen' pass by. Jam everyting up. I was all set fo' one good fight and—

CHAMP: Yeah, yeah, I bet da haole could chop you down real easy.

BEAR: Look who talking.

CABRAL: See, da trouble is dese service guys come here, like make out wit' our wahines, eh. Den dey give da girls V.D. And whose hard luck? Us guys, man. 'Cause den we catch da disease from da girls,

JOJO: Get one good haole in my class. Real nice guy. We wen' elect him class president. Why you guys hate da haoles?

BEAR: Jojo, you no undastand. See, we no hate all da haoles. Sure, get good haoles too, but no ask me where dey stay 'cause I neva meet one yet.

CHAMP: Yeah, Manny, you no tell your bruddah nuttin' o' wat?

MANNY: Wat you like I tell 'um?

CABRAL: Tell 'um about da no-good haoles.

MANNY: Jojo, da haoles no good, no be friends wit' dem.

BEAR: Yeah, you listen to your bruddah.

JOJO: I tink haoles okay.

CABRAL: Manny, you get one hardhead bruddah.

CHAMP: Dey no good, Jojo, dey hit you below da belt.

BEAR: Dey like talk fancy, eh, use hybolic words, act like dey know everyting.

CABRAL: Dey like act bossy. Orda you around—do dis, do dat. And wat you tink dey doing? Sitting on deir fat asses watching you work your ass off. Dey let you do all da dirty work, jus' like my boss. Someday I going broke his mout'.

JOJO: But, Manny, if you going Mainland, you gotta mix wit' da haoles, eh? You gotta be friends wit' dem.

CHAMP: Aeh, wat dis about Mainland?

CABRAL: You neva say nuttin' about going to da Mainland.

MANNY: Nah, jus' talk, nuttin'.

BEAR: If you going Mainland, who I going hang around wit'? You no can go.

MANNY: Why? You like live in dis alley all your life?

BEAR: No. Someday I going get one place by da beach, maybe Waianae side.

CABRAL: Where you going get da money buy one place?

BEAR: 'S easy. Drive da tourists around da island, show 'um da sights, t'row 'um some bullshit. I know wat dey like see: Punchbowl, Crouching Lion, Chinaman Hat. I tell 'um stories about da menehunes. Dey going eat 'um up.

EDWARD SAKAMOTO'S *plays include* In the Alley, *which he wrote as a student at the University of Hawaii in 1961;* Yellow Is My Favorite Color; That's the Way the Fortune Cookie Crumbles; Voices in the Shadows; Manoa Valley; The Life of the Land; A'ala Park; *and* Pilgrimage. *He received grants from the National Endowment for the Arts and the Rockefeller Foundation, and was Rockefeller Foundation Playwright-in-Residence in 1981-82. He lives in Los Angeles.*

JAPANESE: THEY ARE SNEAKY
          THEY WILL SMILE IN YOUR FACE AND STAB YOU IN THE BACK
FILIPINOS: THEY ARE STUPID, ONLY GOOD FOR JANITORS
          AND GARDENERS
          THEY WEAR FLASHY CLOTHES - THEY ALWAYS WEAR
          PURPLE AND RED
KOREANS: HOT TEMPERED AND THEIR MOUTHS STINK
         FROM EATING TOO MUCH KIM CHEE
CHINESE: THEY ARE TIGHT WITH THEIR MONEY

Local

When I was young on an island . . . Coaxing the ocean out of our black hair . . . We gotta line up; no talk. Standupstraight . . . Small kid-time we cut school . . . Ah-h, shullup . . . Your Lucy was no angel. Ran away with haole sailor . . . I am from soft, fan-shaped Filipino brooms . . . Fot grade . . . Lots gots . . . Ho da plenny you get . . . Friggin' expensive go private school . . . Our chain link corner of Honolulu . . . The pineapples moved through the cannery on the conveyor belts . . . Walking distance to Kaimuki Dry Goods . . . She believes Japanese and Korean parents spoil their children . . . No need yell at me . . . Dim sum and my in-laws at the China House Restaurant . . . Broiled short ribs of beef . . . Tell you mama tanks eh . . . You no go mess with my sistah . . . Why can't I have double eyelids with long eyelashes and a small face? . . . I have just learned my Japanese eyes are dangerous . . . The smell of dog adobo floating lightly . . . Yeah, we cut open hees stoma' . . . I catch one shuga-ashflake on my tongue . . . The sun slipped in the water and darted through our hair like a yellow fish . . .

Hina Kahanu
"WHEN I WAS YOUNG ON AN ISLAND"

When I was young on an island
my brother caught gray baby sharks
on his bamboo fishing pole.
When he'd catch a shark,
he'd call the other kids and
we'd come running with clubs
of driftwood to beat the shark
to death.

When I was young on an island
my brother made moray eel traps
of silver pineapple juice cans
and a can opener, the kind that
makes triangle holes. When he'd
catch an eel, he'd give it to the
neighbor cat and we'd all watch
the tiger-striped cat
take the eel out of the can
and eat it.

When we were young on Paikō Drive
in Kuliʻouʻou and we played war,
my brother invented the battle charge.
He'd wait for a hard wind to pick
up the sand and just when the wind
was strongest, he'd yell, "Charge,"
and we'd run, head down, into a zillion
tiny bullets of stinging sand
hurled by the wind's hand.

When I was young on an island
my brother invented the jellyfish
test. He was an Apache Indian that day.
Tortured, he would cry out.
We caught see-through jellyfish
in our hands and held them
while they stung us. Whoever
cried out first or dropped their

jellyfish, lost. I remember sinking
to my knees with pain and finally
lying down in the cool, shallow water.
Only my burning jellyfish hand
held out.

HINA KAHANU *was born in 1945. A Hawaiian activist, she was raised by a Pirie mango tree. Her father sang to her in Pidgin English. Her mother drove her to Hauʻula and waited all day Sunday, reading the newspaper twice, so Hina could ride her horse, Calypso. Hina studied poetry with Harold McCarthy, Phyllis Hoge Thompson, and Nell Altizer. Today she writes with Ke-onaona, her* moʻopuna *(granddaughter). They are horse crazy, dog crazy, and they have a bird.*

Marie M. Hara

"FOURTH GRADE UKUS"

Until the right time came for me to meet my father, I would be patient. Mama made plans all the time. She had figured out what to do. Soon after we settled into a small rental house, we walked over to Lincoln School, a gracious stone building with many trees. None of the students there had to do any manual labor. They used the newest books. They were always featured in newspaper articles and photos that she pointed out to me. Mama had heard that the best Lincoln graduates were sometimes accepted into the private high schools, which was how they "got ahead." Once in the office I saw that all the teachers were haole, and it was a good thing I wore the socks and new shoes Mama had adjusted. I sat with each foot in her lap and great impatience to get accepted. Several teachers watched me watching the other kids playing on the immaculate playground equipment. This part was called The Observation. Once outdoors I took my time taking off my shoes and socks to keep them good for the next wearing. I kept munching softly on a strand of hair that hung comfortably near my mouth. Mama sat on a bench away from the other chatting mothers. She had one bare foot out of her slipper and rested it on top of the other foot still in its slipper. They, too, were new and hurt her. She looked tired. She was still waiting to hear about a better job than being a cook in a dormitory. I could see thoughts which made her cranky cross her face.

By the time we were back in the office for the part called The Interview, which was really a test to see if I could speak perfect Standard English, I knew something was funny. I could smell it.

The woman tester was young and Japanese and smiley. I relaxed, thought for sure I wouldn't have to act "put on" with her. But she kept after me to say the printed words on the picture cards that she, now unsmiling, held before my eyes.

"Da bolocano," I repeated politely at the cone-shaped mountain where a spiral of smoke signaled into the crayon-shaded air. She must have drawn it.

She shook her head. "Again."

"Da BO-LO-CA-NO," I repeated loudly. Maybe like O-Jiji with the stink ear on his left side, she couldn't hear: "We wen' go 'n see da bolocano," I explained confidentially to her. And what a big flat puka it was, I thought, ready to tell her the picture made a clear mistake.

"It's the vol-cano," she enunciated clearly, forcing me to watch her mouth move aggressively. She continued with downcast eyes. "'We went to see the vol-cano.' You can go and wait outside, okay?'"

Outside I wondered why—if she had seen it for real—she drew it all wrong.

Mama shrugged it off as we trudged home.

"Neva' mind. Get too many stuck shet ladies ova dea. People no need act, Lei. You wait. You gon' get one good education, not like me."

That was how I ended up at Ka'ahumanu School which was nonEnglish Standard. Its front yard sported massive flower beds of glowing red and yellow canna lilies arranged in neat rows, which were weeded and watered daily by the students. Teachers at Ka'ahumanu were large in size, often Hawaiian or Portuguese with only an occasional wiry Chinese or Japanese lady in sight. There was a surprise *haole* teacher who came in to teach art and hug kids. Many teachers wore bright hibiscus blooms stuck into their pugs of upswept hair. They didn't hold back on any emotions as they swept through the main yard like part of a tide of orderliness, lining up their wriggly children into classes. They cuffed the bad and patted the heads of the obedient as they counted us. They were magnetic forces with commanding voices, backbones at full attention and bright flowers perched like flags on the tops of their heads. When we stood in formation, the first ritual of the morning, rumors of all kinds went through our lines. I learned right away that on special holidays the cafeteria might even serve *laulau* and *poi* which we would help to prepare. Now that was worth waiting for.

I had resolved that in Honolulu I would have friends "fo' real." To this goal I studied the children at play and kept a silent watch before venturing in. When I forgot this logic and opened my mouth, it almost cost me my appetite to get educated. Because I occupied a fantasy world of vividly drawn characters from books and people I had made up for the lonely times in Kohala, I could go "off on a toot" and momentarily forget the real ones in front of me. I had gotten used to amusing myself in that way even while other kids swirled in activity around me.

I was in a dreamy mood when I first ran into Mrs. Vincente, who was to be my teacher. As a human being she was an impressive creation, since her bulk was unsettling and her head quite small. As she waddle-walked toward me, I made a fatal error. I mistook her for an illustration in a library book I had grown fond of in Kohala. She was a dead ringer for the character I thought I was seeing right before my nose. And why not? The first day of school was supposed to be the beginning of new and exciting things in my life. Everything so far had been surprising.

Therefore, I squealed out loud in pleasure, "Oh, Mrs. Piggy-Winkle!" at the sight of the pink-fleshed mountain topped by a salad plate-sized orange hibiscus. Did I truly think she would be equally delighted to see me? Mrs. Vincente, as I learned later, would never forget me. At the moment of our meeting, she grabbed me by the back of my neck and shook me fiercely until I blubbered.

Teachers came running; students formed a mob around our frantic struggling, and the school principal, Mrs. Kealoha-Henry, saved me.

As I stood sobbing in shivers from the wild shaking, Mrs. Vincente lectured me and the others on good manners. I shook my head in no-no-no when she asked in an emotional voice, "Do you understand now?" It took all of Mrs. Kealoha-Henry's counsel to keep Mrs. Vincente away from me.

Grabbing the opportunity, I ran all the way back home where long after she came home from work, Mama found me hiding out in the laundry shed. I didn't return to school for several days after that. But my mother's continual nagging, bribery and my own plain boredom finally wore me down. I vowed not to talk at school, in the name of personal safety. And I would forget imagination.

When I returned, I learned another lesson, although this one, also, started out in confusion. Back at Ka'ahumanu School the white-columned building seemed enormous. Without Mama for support, I needed to report my string of absences to the office. Retreating into passive silence, I stood in the. main hallway in front of the office with its impressive counter, convinced I was in trouble. The dark paneling and polished wood flooring came together into a tunnel of cool air where important things happened, and people spoke in official whispers.

Hanging high on the wall against the painted white wood, positioned to face the person entering up the broad steps through the columned entrance was a large portrait of Queen Ka'ahumanu, our school's namesake. Someone had placed an offering bouquet of many-colored flowers under the picture. I studied her fully fleshed face, the insignia of rank in the background and her guarded expression. In return her eyes reviewed me, a small girl who wasn't sure what to do next.

As I stalled and paced the corridor, the morning bell rang, and all the other children disappeared. Alone in my patch of indecision, with flashing eyes, I mapped out how and where I would run if I had to. I balanced on one bare foot and then the other, while I studied the ancient lady's clear-eyed regard.

When Mrs. Kealoha-Henry found me, she laughed in surprise.

"So you did come back. And now you have met the Queen. Do you know her story? No? Well, I didn't think so."

The principal, a plump woman who wore old-fashioned glasses which dangled from a neckpiece onto the front of her shirtwaist, told me then and there about Queen Ka'ahumanu, the *Kuhina Nui*. I learned that she was a favorite child and a favorite wife, that her hair was called *ehu*, meaning it was reddish unlike that of other Hawaiians of her time, and that she was *hapa*—of mixed blood, probably from Spanish ancestors. Mrs. Kealoha-Henry suspected the conquistadors, whose helmets the Hawaiian alii had copied in feathers, had been the first Europeans in Hawai'i. I heard the kindly stranger saying that I, too, must be *hapa*. To test me she tried out some Hawaiian, and when I answered correctly, "*Aloha kakahiaka*," she nodded favorably. She suggested a visit to the school library, where I would be welcome to read more about the Queen and what she did with the tremendous power she held at the end of her life.

Mrs. Kealoha-Henry put her hands on my shoulders and turned me in the direction of the polished *koa* wood steps that led to the second floor. She would take care of the absences.

Although I hoped that the principal had not confused me with someone else who was Hawaiian by blood, I was very pleased with the thrilling story. Her comments became the bond between the Queen and me. I felt lucky that I went to a school where a *hapa* was the boss—in fact, commanded tribute. After all, I did have the reddish hair, or some of it, and if I was *hapa* as she said, then that was the reason for my being different from the others. I felt lighter whenever I looked at Queen Ka'ahumanu's portrait from then on. Every day the Queen's round face gave me a signal that I was okay; a small thing, but necessary for someone so hungry for a sign.

Still, no matter how hard I squinted, the hair depicted in the painting showed no sign of being red. Never mind, I told myself, she was right there, up high, and she looked at me affectionately, if I kept up the squint. Whenever I needed to, I found my way back to the hallway to stand in the breeze and acknowledge the power of our kinship.

I had singled out Darleen Nishimura, a sixth grader, as my new model. I wanted to grow up to look just like her, even though she despised me.

Darleen looked so dainty and petite as she completed every action with grace. I tagged along behind her as she received smiles and praise, followed her as she delivered newspapers for her older brothers. But when she saw me, she looked annoyed and tried to shake me. She often escaped by cutting through a yard unknown to me. She made a clippety-clop sound with her merry flopping slippers, a sound which left you with a carefree rhythm. When she laughed, she covered her teeth delightfully with a hand in the way some of the older Japanese women did. I practiced and got nowhere. Never mind that Darleen wouldn't give me the time of day. Now I could forget it. Queen Kaʻahumanu was somber and regal; she never giggled.

One day I spotted another girl, this one chubby and my own age, standing in front of the painting. She quickly placed a white ginger blossom on the *koa* table and disappeared with a smile at me. Later, I heard her name was Monica. When we played in the school yard together, she revealed the secret of her full name; Monica Mahealani Michiko Macadangdang. Happily memorizing it on the spot, I learned that choosing friends wasn't the only way you got them; some chose you, if you were lucky.

Midway through the year I was happy enough to be going to school there, skipping down the streets extra early, eager to help water the taro patch and the red and gold lilies.

Three years later I was a bonafide Kaʻahumanu Kid, as accustomed as any one of my classmates to the school routine. Our neighbor Mrs. Lee, who lived on our block, must have seen my enthusiasm. She entrusted her only son, who had been living in Makawao, Maui, to my care since we were both in the fourth grade. Joseph and I walked to school together on his first day.

Just before the first morning bell rang, the whispers traveled around. We were aware that our teacher was moving down the line to study each one of us. Our voices were high, and our faces as busy as the noisy birds in the banyan outside. Always chattering, always in tune with our buddies, always watching, we knew how to move together on our quiet bare feet, without getting caught talking. We studied how to do it.

I felt a nudge from one side and a soft pinch from the other.

"Pssssssst . . . "

"Joseph. Make quick. We gotta line up; no talk. Standupstraight. Sing loud or she gon' make us guys sing one mo' time."

"She checking da guys' clothes first, if clean or what. Bumbye she gon' look our finganail and den check our hair behind da eah, l'dat."

The clanging bell brought us to silent attention.

Joseph looked completely blank. Unconcerned, he, being new, had no understanding of the importance of our morning classroom ritual. He didn't even pretend to mouth the words of Mrs. Vicente's favorite greeting, "Good Morning, Deah Tea-cha, Goooood Mor-ning to Youuu."

"W'at fo' she like check us in da eah?" Joseph's slow whisper tickled.

Before I could answer importantly, "'Cuz got ukus, some guys, you stupid doo-doo head," and think, "But not us guys," our teacher was standing right in front of us. Mrs. Vicente looked grim. Her gold-rimmed eyeglasses gave off glints in the pools of sunlight, evidence of real daylight outside, which invaded our dark, high-ceilinged and wood-paneled classroom.

She was the one who taught us to sing "Old Plantation *Nani Ole*" (Oooll . . . Plan-tay-shun . . . Na-ni . . . Ohlay) and "Ma-sa's (never her way, Massa's) in the Cold, Cold Ground," her favorite mournful melodies. She had turned to making us sing in order to drill us on our English skills, so lacking were we in motivation.

Frequently Mrs. Vicente spoke sharply to us about the inappropriate silences of our group. She complained that too often we spoke out of turn but "rarely contributed to the discussion." She must have believed that we didn't absorb anything that she lectured about repeatedly. She confided that she was "disappointed in" us or we had "disappointed Teacher" or she was "sorry to have to disappoint" us, "however," we had done something wrong again.

She was a puzzle.

The oriental kids—for that was our label—in the room knew better than to open their mouths just to lose face, and the part-Hawaiian and Portuguese kids knew they would get lickings one way or another if they talked, so we all firmly agreed that silence was golden.

Never would an adult female loom up as large to me as Mrs. Vicente did then. I could see her face only when I sat at a safe distance with a desk for protection. If she approached—in all her girth she was most graceful moving across her neatly waxed floor—her hands took my complete attention. When they were ready to direct us, I felt the way I did when Mama showed me what the red light at the crosswalk was for. When Teacher stood very near me, I couldn't see her tiny eyes, because the soft underpart of her delicate chin transfixed me so that I could not understand the words she mouthed. I got my mouth wrenched up to be ready for an alert answer, just in case she eyeballed me. Somehow whenever I had to respond to her I managed to get the subject and verb unmatched—"Yes, ma'am. We is ready fo' class"—even though she drilled us on the continual sin of the mixed singular and plural, because it was so fascinating to see her furious reaction to what she called Broken English, which none of us could fix.

Passing outside by Room 103, I overheard her passionate argument with another teacher who wanted to introduce the hula in our PE exercises. Mrs. V.'s reasoning escaped me, but I knew she was against it unconditionally. I stayed hidden in the *ti* leaves under her window just to hear the rush of her escaping emotions as she grew angrier and pronounced words more distinctly.

Mrs. Vicente's face was averted from the horrors she saw represented in the existence of our whole class. To her, we were not by any means brought up well, didn't know our p's and q's, often acted in an un-American fashion as evidenced by our smelly home lunches, dressed in an uncivilized manner, and refused moreover to speak properly or respectfully as soon as her back was turned. Her standards were in constant jeopardy.

Our concentrated looks centered on her totally. We followed her every move, a fact which unnerved her briefly each morning. To hide her discomfort, revealed by streams of perspiration, she swabbed her face delicately with a lace-trimmed hankie.

She shook her head at Francene Fuchigami, whose mother made her wear around her neck an amulet in a yellowed cotton pouch which also contained a foul incense and active herbs. The blessed *o-mamori* guaranteed the absence of both slippery vermin and casual friends.

Francene and I competed for Mrs. V.'s favor, no matter how much we accepted her obvious but peculiar interest in the boys only. She favored them shamelessly, but bullied them at every opportunity.

We brought Mrs. Vicente homegrown anthuriums, tangerines and sticky notes: "Dear Mrs. V, Your so nice. And your so pretty, too," with high hopes. *Maybe she will like me now*, ran the thread of wishful thinking. Winning her favor took all of my attention. I had to stay neat and clean and pretend to be a good girl, somebody who could "make nice-nice" and "talk high *makamak*." To win Mrs. Vicente over, I saw that I would have to be able to speak properly, a complicated undertaking demanding control of all my body parts, including my eyes and hands, which wandered away when my mouth opened up. Therefore, in a compromise with my desire to shine, I resolved to keep absolutely quiet, stand up with the stupid row and ignore the one I wanted to impress.

Mrs. Vicente was one of us, she claimed, because she herself had grown up in our "very neighborhood." Her school, too, she once let out, had been non-English Standard. We were surprised to hear her say that her family was related to the Kahanus who owned the corner grocery store. We knew them, the ones who used to have money. The brothers Eugene and Franklin Teves claimed they knew for sure she couldn't be kin to anyone they recognized, in answer to the other class who called her "The Portagee Teacha." She spoke, dressed and carried herself in a manner that was unlike any of the women I observed at home, but she fit right in with our other teachers who, like her, had gone to Normal School and shared her authoritative ways.

Difficult as she was, we could understand her preoccupation. Getting rid of *ukus* was a tedious job connected with beratings from your mother and lickings from your father. We always knew who carried *ukus* and were swift to leave that child alone. News traveled fast. All the same we could each remember what it felt like to be the "odd man out," which was the name of one of our favorite games.

To have *ukus*, to tell your close friends not to tell the others, and to have them keep the secret; that was the test of friendship. Like the garbage men who worked under the *uku pau* system, which meant that no gang or worker was finished until everybody on that truck helped the final guy unload his very last can, and everybody could quit, *uku* season wasn't over until every kid got rid of every last clinging egg.

At Christmastime, Mrs. Vincente wrapped up a useful comb for each and every one of us. At the end of the year we raced each other to be the first one lined up at her massive desk.

We would each shyly request her autograph with the suggested correct phrases, "Please, Mrs. Vincente," and, "Thank you, Teacha." So she must have been what we had grown to expect a teacher to be.

Because of Mrs. Vincente I wanted to become a teacher. I wanted to wield power and know how to get my way. I wanted to be the one who would point out a minute, luminous silver egg sack stuck on a coarse black hair, shake it vigorously with arm held out far away from body, and declare victoriously, "infestation . . . of . . . pediculosis!"

She would then turn to address the entire class. "This child must go directly to the nurse's office." She would speak firmly but in a softer tone to the kid. "Do not return to our room until you can bring me the white clearance certificate signed by both of your parents."

Completely silent during class, I practiced those words at home while I played school. I turned to the class. I gave the warning to the kid. Mrs. Vicente was not to be taken lightly.

The day Joseph learned about *ukus*, I figured out teachers.

Facing him, Mrs. Vicente demanded to know the new boy's name from his own mouth.

"Joseph Kaleialoha Lee."

"Say ma'am."

"Hah?"

"You must say 'Joseph Kaleialoha Lee, ma'am.'"

"Joseph-Kaleialoha-Lee-ma'am!"

"Hold out your hands, please."

Evidently he had not paid attention, the biggest error of our collective class, one which we heard about incessantly. He had not watched her routine, which included a search for our hidden fingernail dirt. He held his hands palms up. I shuddered.

Mrs. Vicente studied Joseph with what we called the "stink eye," but he still didn't catch on. She must have considered his behavior insubordinate, because he did not seem retarded or neglected as he was wearing his new long, khaki pants and a freshly starched aloha shirt.

She reached into the big pocket of her apron and took out a fat wooden ruler. Our silence was audible. She stepped up a little nearer to Joseph, almost blocking out all the air and light around us that her sharp features and steely voice cut through to reach our wobbly attention.

"What grade are you in now, young man?"

Joseph was silent as if in deep thought. Why wouldn't he say the answer? I nudged him quickly on his side with the hand nearest his body.

"Fot grade," he blurted in a small, panicky wheeze.

She turned on us all, enraged at our murmurs of anticipation. We knew for sure he would get it now.

Some girl giggled hysterically in a shrill whinny, "heengheengheeng . . ." Probably Japanese.

"Quiet."

Businesslike, she returned to Joseph with her full attention, peering into his ear. "Say th, th, th. Speak slowly." He heard the warning in her voice.

"Tha, tha, tha." Joseph rippled droplets of sweat.

"Th, th, th . . . everyone, say it all together: the tree!"

We practiced loudly with Joseph leading the chorus, relieved now to be part of the mass of voices.

"Say the tree, not da chree."

"The tree, not da chree."

"Fourth grade, not fot grade."

"Foth grade, not foth grade."

With a rapid searching movement which caught most of us off guard, Mrs. Vicente swung around to face Darcie Ah Sing, whose hand was still stuck in her curly brown hair when she was spotted scratching herself vigorously. Mrs. V. stared blackly into Darcie's tight curls with unshakeable attention. In a matter of seconds, with an upward swoop of her palm, Teacha found the louse at the nape of the exposed neck and pronounced her memorable conclusion, ending with "by both of your parents," indicting Darcie's whole family into the crime.

"March yourself into the office, young lady." Mrs. Vicente wrung a hankie between her pudgy hands with tight motions. Head hanging, Darcie moved out wordlessly to the school nurse's station for the next inspection.

We knew that she would be "shame" for a long time and stared at our dusty toes in hopeless sympathy.

When we were allowed to sit at our desks (after practicing the sks sound for desks: "sssk'sss, sssk'sss, dehss'kuss, dehss'kuss, dehss'kuss, not dessess, dessess, dessess"), we were hooked into finishing our tasks of busywork and wearing our masks of obedience, totally subdued.

Then she read to us, as she explained that she was "wont to do when the occasion arose," while we sat quietly at our desks with our hands folded as she had trained us. She enunciated each word clearly for our benefit, reminding us that by the time we graduated we would be speaking "proper English" and forgot the uku check for the day. Her words stuck like little pearly grains into the folds of my brain. I pondered how to talk *haole* while she continued to lecture.

"The child . . . the school . . . the tree . . . " I could not hear the meaning of her words and scratched my head idly but in secret, my head dodging her line of vision. I yearned to master her knowledge, but dared not make myself the target of her next assault. I was not getting any smarter, but itchier by the minute, more eager than anyone to break free into the oasis of recess.

When the loud buzzer finally shattered the purring motor of her voice, we knew better than to whoop and scatter. We gathered our things formally and waited silently to be dismissed. If we made noise we would have to sit inside in agony, paying attention to the whole endless, meaningless story which sounded like all the ones before and wasted our precious time. Even Joseph caught on.

He said, "Whew, 'as waste time."

Once we were outside, surveying the situation, we saw two teams of the bigger boys who pulled at a heavy knotted rope from opposite ends. Joseph's bare feet dug into the ground right in back of Junior Boy, the tug-of-war captain. Clearly he wouldn't need any more of my guidance if Junior Boy had let him in. Beads of wetness sparkled off their bodies as the tight chain of grunting boys held fast under the bright sun.

Noisy clumps of kids skipped rope and kicked up the grass, twisting bodies and shining faces, all together in motion. Racing around the giant banyan, for no good reason, I scream-giggled, "Wheeeeha-ha-hah!" Like a wildcat I roared up the trunk of the chree . . . just to see if I could.

Joseph spotted me. "Too good, you!" he yelled.

While the girls played jacks, and the boys walked their board stilts, Joseph and I moved around groups trading milk bottle covers and playing marbles. We wondered aloud to each other. We spread the word.

"Ho, w'atchoo tink?"

"Must be da teacha wen' catch *ukus* befo'."

"Not . . . "

"Not not!"

"Cannot be . . . "

"Cancan!"

"Yeah?"

"Ay, yeah. O' how else she can spock 'em dat fast?"

That made me laugh, the thought of Mrs. V. picking through her careful topknot. She would have to moosh away the hibiscus to get in a finger. I mimed her by scratching through the hair I let hang down in front of my face. When I swept it back professionally with the palm of my hand, I threw in a cross-eyed crazy look. Joseph pretended to "spock *uku*" in my hair as he took on Mrs. V's exaggerated ladylike manner to hold onto one of my ears like a handle and peer into the endless *puka*.

"Ho, man," he proclaimed, "get so planny inside."

The recess bell rang, ending our sweet freedom. We pranced back to the classroom in a noisy herd. Teacha gave us the Look. We grew cautious. We would spend the next hour silently tracking Mrs. Vicente's poised head, while Joseph and I smiled knowingly at each other.

Eyes gleaming, Mrs. Vicente never disappointed any of us, because she always stuck right on her lessons arid never let up at all. She stayed mean as ever, right on top of the class. As for us, fourth grade *ukus* could appreciate the effort . . . so much not letting go.

Philip K. Ige

"THE FORGOTTEN FLEA POWDER"

Two blocks past Johnson's Five and Ten in the town of Kaimuki, Satoshi Ikehara, standing in the rear of a jam-packed Honolulu bus, woke up from his stupor with a start, looked outside, and nudged his little brother who stood beside him. "Hey, Yuki, we pass da store again."

"Huh?"

"We forget to get off by Johnson Store an' buy flea powder—you know, for Blackie."

"Oh, yeah. How many times we goin' forget anyway? Four times already, no-o?"

"Yeah. We no can get off now—too late. We got to go home."

"'At's okay. We can buy 'em tomorrow—Saturday."

"I know; but Blackie cry, you know. He get so many fleas. He feel itchy an' he cry, you know."

"Yeah, I know. Yesterday I saw him scratchin' up. He no can scratch da back part 'dat's why he onny cry, so I been scratch his back for him. He *f-e-e-l* good. He no cry." An old Caucasian woman, sitting in a seat before them, looked up and smiled at them. The boys smiled shyly back and quickly turned their eyes away. They stopped talking.

The trolley slowed down to a halt at the end of the line in Waialae. They boarded a gasoline-engine bus, which crawled ponderously out of the terminal and roared down the tree-lined highway stretching toward Koko Head. Several minutes later in their front yard, which was also a part of the road going into the garage, a dog of mixed breed, not yet full grown, greeted them with yelps and leaps of exuberant affection.

"Hello, Blackie. Sit down, boy, sit down." Satoshi stooped down and patted the dog. "Atta boy, Blackie, good boy. Shake hand, Blackie. Come on, shake hand—" The dog began to offer its right paw, but withdrew it suddenly and began scratching its side vigorously. It scratched now under its belly, now behind its ears, now here, and there, scratching and biting and whining.

"Come on, Yuki, scratch his back for him. You no can see he sufferin'?" Yuki ran his little fingers through the animal's thick black coat as if with a comb. The dog complained no more.

"Come, we go in, Yuki." Satoshi opened the door and they entered. From inside, he saw, through the screen door, the dog scratching again. Then he saw it run toward the garage, stop abruptly, and resume scratching with painful, angry whines. An uncomfortable feeling of guilt swept over him and he said to himself that tomorrow, for sure, he was going to buy the box of flea powder at Johnson's Five and Ten.

The following morning, having been awake earlier than usual to finish their chores on the farm, they were on their way to buy the box of flea powder. The trolley stopped in front of Johnson's Five and Ten to take on more passengers. A clock within the store was visible from the trolley. "Hey, Yuki, onny about twelve o'clock," Satoshi said pointing to the clock. "What you say we go see movies first."

"Movies? Where? Downtown?"

"Yeah. We can buy da flea powder when we comin' back."

"Uh-h, boy, we go quick!"

They had seen the movies and at three thirty were out of the theater, seated on a trolley homeward bound. The sun was warm. The song of the speeding tires was like a lullaby. A lazy, drowsy sensation crept over them. Satoshi slouched down in the soft seat and closed his eyes. Yuki stared in front of him, his eyes half-closed. Twenty minutes passed. Satoshi remained nestled in his seat. Yuki stared drowsily at the bright red and yellow hibiscus stuck in a woman's smooth blonde hair in front of him. Presently the woman's hand reached out: and began scratching her head. A thought struck Yuki; he came to life.

"Fleas—," he said. The young woman's hand dropped down swiftly to her side. "Hey, Satoshi, wake up. We stay in Kaimuki already."

"Huh?"

"We got to buy flea powder—for Blackie."

"Oh, yeah!" Satoshi glanced outside. "Pull da buzzer quick." Yuki yanked the cord. The trolley stopped just across from Johnson's Five and Ten. They rushed off the trolley, hurried across the street and into the store.

When they reached home about four their father stood waiting for them at the front door. "Put that truck in the garage before it gets dark," he said to Satoshi.

"Okay." Satoshi turned to his little brother, "Now at las'," he said, "we goin' put da flea-powder on Blackie. Here, take dis flea-powder an' wait for me by da garage. I goin' put da truck in."

Satoshi walked to the old truck parked up the road which ran beside and in front of their house and into the garage. He jumped on and as he pressed the clutch pedal and put the gear in neutral, Blackie crawled out from under the truck to his accustomed place in the front of the truck, intending to escort it to the entrance of the garage. Down the small incline the truck began to roll, slowly at first, then gradually gaining momentum. The dog romped merrily in front of the truck, pausing now and then to bite into his flesh or scratch behind his ears:

"Doggone crazy dog," Satoshi muttered as he nearly struck the dog once.

Suddenly, with an angry, painful whine, Blackie dropped his hindquarters to the ground and fiercely began to scratch the side of his ribs. The truck rolled on. *"Look out, Satoshi, Blackie!"* An agonizing cry. A sudden screeching of brakes. Satoshi jumped out of the truck. Yuki dashed over. A moment of speechless watching and silent suffering followed!

"Why you never tell me stop more quick, you," Satoshi said bitterly.

"No can help. He been stop too quick in front da tire—was too late."

"See, look now. Blackie dead. 'At's your fault, you know."

"'At's not my fault. You been run over him."

"Why you never tell me stop more quick, den? 'At's your fault. If you been tell me stop more quick, I no was goin' hit 'em."

"I no care. 'At's your fault you no like buy da flea powder more quick 'at's why."

"Ah-h, shullup. You never buy 'em, too. 'At's your fault, too."

"'At's not my fault. I never drive da truck." "You like get lickin'. I said 'at's your fault." "I no care. I never—"

"*Shullup*, I said. You like get black eye. I said 'at's your fault—you never tell me stop more quick."

"I never drive da truck."

"Hey, you! You get sassy some more, I goin'—ah, look! Blackie movin'. He no dead. He shakin' his leg. Look!"

"'At's right! Look. He sittin' down now. He lookin' at us."

"Yeah, 'at's right, Ah, look, he *scratchin'* again! *Qweek*, Yuki, gimme da flea-powder—."

PHILIP K. IGE *was born in Kahaluʻu, Oʻahu, in 1925. He has worked as an English and social studies teacher, and later as an administrator in the Hawaiʻi State Department of Education and in the University of Hawaiʻi's Community College system. He also spent fourteen years in Toyko studying and teaching. He is married to the former Janet Okuma, and has three children and five grandchildren.*

Darrell Lum
"MARBLES"

What you get?
My marbles. Eh, no come so close!
Ho da plenny you get. Where you get 'em from?
I win 'em, of course.
How you get so many big kine?
As my bumboochas dat . . . and dese my pee-wees, da small kine . . . and I keep my keenee in one 'nudda bag with my puries . . . dis my best shooter, dis keenee. You like play?
Shoot!
How you like play? Regular or bumboocha style.
What bumboocha style?
Play only with bumboochas. Even your keenee gotta be bumboocha and den when pau, I take all the bumboochas I went win and if you like your bumboochas back, you gotta gimme five regulars for one bumboocha . . . and den pretty soon you no mo' nutting regular kine and I get all your bumboochas and you gotta steal marbles from your bruddah's aquarium and den he catch you and you get lickin's . . . hah, hah . . . .
Eh junk la' dat, play regular. How many inside?

Uku-billion!
No ack! How much?
Five, well!
'Kay, five. How many spams can?
One. No, two hand spams . . . two den. And no fun-nick and no mo'
Samoan style.
I no fun-nick anyway, so shaddup. I no cheat.
No only put junk kine, eh . . . gotta put two puries inside da pack and
den da junk kine, cats eye kine.
Jun-ken-a-po fo' go first.
Jun-ken-a-po, I-ken-a-show!
Slow hand, slow hand. Again! Two out of tree!
Jun-ken-a-po, I-ken-a-show.
What is dat!
Atomic bomb.
No such ting! You cheatah! Again, again!
Jun-ken-a-po, I-ken-a-show. Jun-ken-a-po!
Shet! You go den.
What kine marbles you wish you had?
I donno, jes' plenny puries . . . and plenny bumboochas . . .
Would be neat if had bumboocha puries, yeah?
No such ting! C'mon your turn . . . besides, ball bearing mo' bettah!
Nah, purie bumboochas . . . so sharp would be . . . so clear and
can see through . . . everything small and upside down. I wish
had purie bumboochas . . . Sometimes you know what neat, I
line up all my puries by da window and wait till da light shine
through and da stuff make colored light on da floor. Come
sharp, man. And if you look inside 'em, jes' like dey little crystal
balls. Can see everything inside each one. Can see everything, da
whole world, inside each one . . .

DARRELL LUM *is a fiction writer and playwright who has been one of the pioneering voices of*
Hawai'i's literature through his use of Hawai'i Creole English (pidgin). He has published two
collections of short fiction, Sun: Short Stories and Drama *and* Pass On, No Pass Back, *and his*
plays have been produced by Kumu Kahua Theatre and Honolulu Theatre for Youth. He and
Eric Chock co-founded Bamboo Ridge Press (www.bambooridge.com) in 1978 to foster the
creation and appreciation of local literature.

Ray Jerome Baker

"RUSTY'S EARLY LIFE AT TAKI'S"

Editor, The Advertiser:

On a recent sunny morning, Rusty, the neighbor's cat, sat down on our front walk and groomed himself meticulously as is his custom when absorbed in deep and contemplative thought. When I had shown an interest in his presence, he explained that he had been thinking about his early life and that he had recalled certain facts which he thought should be put down and made available for later publication in his Memoirs.

Rusty does not know a whole lot about his hereditary background, though his mother and grandmother have assured him that he comes from a long line of illustrious alley cat ancestors. Rusty's early recollections have to do with himself as a romping and frolicsome kitten in Taki's Store. Taki, it seems, adhered to the theory that the presence, even the odor, of cats about the store tended to inhibit the activities of mice. There were flour, rice, cereals, beans and many other foods in paper or cloth containers which were easy of access, via the gnawing route, to the mice. Rusty says that as a young and irresponsible youth he preferred to gambol about the rice bags, cases of canned goods, brooms and bamboo rakes rather than to take seriously his mission to drive the mice out of Taki's store.

At first Rusty and his playmate sister, Goldie, were too timid to venture out into the big front room where the patrons of the store came and where the cans, bottles and package goods were displayed. There was too much turmoil, tramping of feet, ringing of the cash register and curiosity of many shoppers for young cats to venture out. In the back room, if Goldie pulled a paper carton off the pile, or the two kittens in playing knocked the rakes or brooms over, the boys who worked in the store patiently set them up again and said nothing.

When the young kittens brew bolder and began to frisk about the big room, they ignored the presence of shoppers and often got in the way. It was here that Rusty's future mistress caught sight of him and asked Taki for him a number of times, but Taki invariably gave a negative reply. As the cats became more familiar and began to tear paper and damage packages, Taki's attitude became more uncertain.

The final act in this little play which was to determine the future course of Rusty's life, he admits, cannot be accurately described as an emotional and dramatic triumph. In fact there was considerable humility in it for Rusty. After the store was closed one evening the two kittens had a grand frolic in which Rusty chased Goldie about the big front room, up one aisle and down another and into the back storage room, with Goldie in the lead. To escape her playful pursuer, Goldie jumped on a pile of rice bags, then to a stack of empty cartons which swayed from the impact and caused Goldie to leap for a high shelf on which were stored bottles of washing ammonia. Goldie missed the shelf but caught hold of one of the bottles which came tumbling down, smashing itself as well as the demijohn of chlorine water below. Suffocated from the fumes of ammonia and with paws stinging from contact with the chlorine water, Goldie sought fresh air, and Rusty ceased the chase and followed.

The scene that met the astonished Taki the next morning can hardly be described. Rusty says the less said about it the better, but one thing was obvious—it was that Taki had made a decision. When Rusty's future mistress came in later, Taki waited on her. "Me too much hu-hu, suppose you like-a this cat, you hapai, aw-right," spoke the irate Taki as she seized Rusty by the nape of the neck and thrust him into a paper bag and into the hands of the new mistress. After a week of confinement, Rusty was allowed the liberty of his new home and has been loyal to it ever since. As for Goldie, she went to live in a remote community and though seldom seen, it is known that she has contributed generously to the population of alley cats.

RAY JEROME BAKER (1880-1972), *born near Rockford, Illinois, came to Hawai'i with his wife and son in 1910. He was Hawai'i's premier photographer during the first half of the twentieth century. His field photographs, studio portraits, lantern slides, and motion pictures document Hawai'i's changing population and landscape. He cooked a pot roast for himself once a week and took a cold-water bath twice a day.*

Lucretia Leong

"MANNA FROM HEAVEN"

The light shone through the slats as Leatrice formed mud pies from the wet, chocolate dirt that oozed luxuriously between her small fingers. Copying the motions she learned from watching her mother, she formed patties of various sizes: small ones for the picky eaters, medium-sized ones for the just right folks, and gigantic ones for her big, hungry girls. As she was about to put these delicious pies into the steaming oven, Leatrice felt a tugging at her right foot. Looking up, she saw her father's face appearing puffy, surreal, and stonewashed. She wondered how he had discovered her secret hiding place under the house.

"Wake up, Leatrice," her father said gruffly. Like her mother who sighed when he demanded something from her, Leatrice also rued the inconveniences that were put upon her. Her poor girls would have to wait for their dessert. By the time her father carried her out into the parlor and plopped her down on the sofa, she was fully awake. He sat himself across her on the *pune'e*, the one with the wild red and yellow plumeria flowers that now framed his silhouette.

Her father finally spoke. "Your mother," he said if he were swallowing rocks, "has gone to heaven where the angels will keep her well."

"What you talking about, Daddy?" she asked, rubbing her eyes vehemently, as she was often told not to do.

Her father paused and took a deep breath. "Leatrice, your mother was in a car accident. She was found with . . . " her father stopped talking for a while and then added, "Never mind, she has died and gone to heaven, just like Scotty."

Leatrice remembered crying her eyes out when her dog Scotty died. But her mother was different. She couldn't imagine not sitting on her mother's lap every day, twirling her fingers in her mother's black, silky hair which flowed down her shoulders like a dark, troubled river. Segment by segment, she had lovingly fashioned Shirley Temple "sausage curls."

She and her father sat wordlessly in the parlor for hours. Her daddy would not look at her. *What is happening*, she wanted to ask. But the only answer she received was from the bird in the cuckoo clock. Cranking out the time of day in its crazy falsetto voice, it said "coo-coo" nine times, then ten, eleven, twelve, all the way to five o'clock.

Throughout the night and day, Leatrice also heard the shrill sounds from an ambulance or a fire truck, which was inevitably followed by the cacophony of the neighborhood dogs howling in pain. She stared at the mock orange blossoms that her mother had picked in the morning, which lay forlornly scattered on the dinner table wilting and turning a deeper, deathly brown with each succeeding coo-coo from the yellow bird. Her mother's pink shrug hung lifelessly on the dinette chair as if it were waiting for its owner to give it shape and form. When the shadows from the trees flickered against the *tapa* hanging on the wall and the birdie announced it was six o'clock, her daddy galvanized himself into action. He lifted his only daughter up and carried her into the black Packard, and began driving like a demon toward the lights of Honolulu. As he approached the infamous hairpin turn on the Pali Road, he maneuvered it like a *kamikaze* pilot, and Leatrice hung on to the door handle for dear life. In her mind's eye, she saw the car being flung into the ravine far below.

The car skidded to a screeching halt in front of Halmuni's house on School Street. The lights were all turned on in vigilant watch like votive candles burning brightly. With tears streaming down her cheeks, Halmuni appeared at the doorway exclaiming, *"Ai goo chum."* Leatrice was comforted by her Halmuni's tears. She thought they were for her. But her daddy, who had no patience with the shenanigans of his coarse mother-in-law, only nudged Leatrice into the house and returned to the Packard. He gunned his engine and disappeared in a billow of gray smoke. Through the frame of the doorway, Leatrice felt she was watching a scene from a James Cagney movie where Al Capone engages the FBI in a wild escapade.

"Close the door," said Halmuni in a voice so sharp that Leatrice instinctively knew that in this house, a "we have no room at the inn" philosophy would prevail. She followed her Halmuni into a parlor filled with other ladies who were seated in a circle—some on chairs, others squatting Korean style on the floor with their feet on the ground and their knees spread apart in a wide V with the hems of their dresses covering their ankles for modesty. Halmuni and all the other *ajumones* were all wailing. *"Ai goo, ai goo chum,"* they shrieked. She recognized Mrs. Kim, Halmuni's bosom friend who was wringing her hands and crying *ai goo.* Mrs. Kim had been mixing *kim chee,* but when Halmuni called her, she dropped everything and came over immediately still wearing her white muslin apron with the *ko choo* stains forming a floral pattern that accentuated her round, middle-aged belly. Auntie Daisy, another friend of Halmuni's had been preparing *taegu* at the House of Lee's when she heard the news. She brought along with her the acrid smell of codfish. Halmuni, seated in the middle was wailing the loudest and beating her breast with her clenched fist. The other *ajumones* donned the role of the Greek chorus and slapped their knees and shook their heads and cried *"Ai goo chum."* Leatrice winced as if each *ai goo chum* was beating against her own chest. As Halmuni and the *ajumones* wailed louder, the din and clamor in the parlor heightened and intensified the smell of codfish, garlic, and *jang ju roam.*

Leatrice stood in a corner feeling invisible and alone. Her Halabugi walked up to her and looked into her eyes. For a brief moment, he rested his arm on her shoulders and tears began to fill his eyes. He started to speak, but no words came out of his mouth. He only motioned for her to follow him as he carried the Pan Am bag that contained her clothes and the wrinkled, brown grocery Foodland bag that held her dolls. She followed him into the bedroom of the house on School Street where she would now live.

At her mother's funeral at Borthwick's Mortuary, all the *ajumones* were there dressed in white with black bands around their upper arms. It was *ai goo chum* time all over again. Halmuni was crying *ai goo* the loudest as if its charm could redeem the sins of the dead. Amidst all the wailing, Leatrice, her father, and her Halabugi sat quietly on hard, wooden chairs with their grief encased in separate, steel armors of the heart.

Leatrice quickly learned that her Halmuni was the one who wore the pants in her new home. Her Halabugi, a gentle and soft-spoken man let his former picture bride have the last word on everything. He tried to keep out of his wife's way to avoid her scoldings and edicts. He spent most of his time smoking Lucky Strikes under the shade of the mango tree, sitting on the bench in the backyard with his nose buried in the *Korean Herald*, or sneaking off to see the latest Hopalong Cassidy "moam pictcha" show at the Liliha Theatre. Leatrice longed to run off with him. Her Halmuni's strident voice worked like a *gai sa gomg* pounder where the seeds of her brain felt like grist.

Late at night as Leatrice lay awake in her room listening to the creaks and groans of the house, she thought about her mother with her smiling black eyes and her father who never visited her. On the wall that separated her room from her grandparents was a two-foot by two-foot window that prevented any secrets between her grandparents and herself. Leatrice heard all her grandparents' bedtime conversations. It was her Halmuni's voice that droned on and on about converting new souls to the Catholic Church. When Tai Yun wasn't shredding *taegu* or lopping off the heads of chickens in her backyard, she spent her waking hours proselytizing for the Catholic Church. She firmly believed that doing good works was her guarantee into heaven. Many nights, she heard Halmuni say, "No, no, too tired, Kyoung Ho. Let's pray instead." Then Tai Yun would begin to say the *Hail Mary* in Korean.

One night Halabugi, giving voice to his thoughts said, "She cries every night. I tell you, Tai Yun, I no can stand it. *Pahmna ul rul.* Maybe we call Doh Won."

As if she were brushing off a fly, Halmuni answered curtly, "No need call. Go to sleep. Tomorrow morning, we go to Maluhia Hospital to convert Ok Soo and if her *kanaka* husband is there, him too."

"I wonder what goes on in our granddaughter's mind?" said Halabugi, who was not going to acquiesce easily this time. "She play with dolls all day, and no talk to us. She look sad and alone. She reminds me so much of my Lucy, with her black hair and eyes."

"You better not spoil her like you did her mother," said Tai Yun sharply. "And *your* Lucy was no angel. Run away with *haole* sailor. Maybe she was a *magui*," were Tai Yun's final words, and in the very next breath, she began to snore loudly. Whether awake or asleep, Halmuni always had the last word, thought Leatrice. She heard her Halabugi muttering under his breath, "How come so mean, God?"

Every day Leatrice went through the motions of life. She went to school, did her chores, and didn't bother much with anyone. She would sit for long stretches of time in the backyard waiting for the shadows to overtake the bright glare of day. Twilight was her favorite time of day—it was a peaceful no man's land. It bridged the sun's domain where all should be hunky-dory and the night where her mother's face appears laughingly in her dreams and her father follows, wrought and distressed. Only at twilight did Leatrice feel a surge of exuberance as she watched the wind glide through the tall grass and begin its spiraling ascent to shake the leaves of the mango tree. As it swept downwards, she felt the gentle trade winds coursing through her hair and face. For a brief moment, she was happy.

Leatrice also found comfort in her dolls of various sizes and ages that made the trek with her from over the Pali. Some were chubby baby dolls and others were grown-up with fancy party dresses. But before she could love any doll, she had one requirement: they must possess hair that could be styled. Leatrice showered with love the dolls with hair that could be combed and brushed. She took pains in braiding their hair and topping it off with ribbons and shiny barrettes. On special occasions, she swept their hair upward in a French twist and when she felt the need for casualness, she let their hair down so they too could enjoy the wind through their tresses. Those Korean dolls that were only for show were relegated to the bureau dresser where they sat forlornly as the ubiquitous dust fell on their untouched hair and synthetic eyelashes.

Her dolls lived a charmed existence. Mary, Linda, Juliette, and Laverne were all loved and cherished. At school, they were popular with everyone and were always picked first at all the games. Leatrice taught them to mind their manners and to say "Please" and "Thank you." She never said *ai goo* to them and never told them that children should be seen and not heard. Just as her mother had done with her, she kissed her dolls good night every night. She tiptoed ever so carefully around her four lovely daughters, for she knew life was fragile and that hearts were made of glass and could crack.

In spite of being their loving mother, Leatrice sometimes envied these dolls of hers. None of them looked *yobo* like her. They all had blue or brown eyes with oval, *haole* faces while her own face was so round and fat that it filled up the entire hand mirror. Most important, all her daughters had double eyelids. Even the Korean dolls on the bureau dresser had abandoned their own heritage with their *haole* eyes.

"Why can't I have double eyelids with long eyelashes and a small face?" Leatrice asked God. She began to copy Halmuni, and with her rosary twined around her finger, she knelt down by her bedside nightly and prayed for *haole* eyes and an oval face. Sister Martha Mary, her second-grade teacher said that God answered your prayers if He deemed it good for you. And Leatrice was convinced that having double eyelids would not be a bad thing. Upon awakening every morning, she headed straight to her bureau dresser to see if a minor miracle had occurred in her sleep. But instead of the granting of haole eyes and face, what rained down from heaven was manna of another kind.

One day when Leatrice came home from school, she discovered a doll's blue-dotted Swiss pinafore lying on her bed. Soon other gifts big and small followed. A package of *li hing mui* was left on her bureau dresser. On another occasion, a bright silver miniature kewpie doll that could be used as a *kini* for hopscotch was left on her black-and-white school composition book. Then came a crimson satin ribbon for her hair and hanging in her closet a pink taffeta dress decorated with white pansies and lavender roses. She was happy with these presents, but she valued them more as a symbol of her father's love for her. She wanted to ask Halmuni, "Did my daddy come today? What did he say when he left these for me?" But the words stuck in her throat. For to ask that question would be to open the floodgates of truth.

She daydreamed about her daddy carrying her high on his shoulders, so high that she could touch the sky and feel the wind blowing in her face. He would carry her to Chang Store where in a high glass case sat mouth-watering delights to satisfy every sweet and salty craving of all the kids. There was Tomoe candy, Cracker Jacks, cracked seed, olive footballs, lipstick candy, cuttlefish, waxed soda pops, Flick candy, and other *ono* morsels. As they left the store with her Flick candy and cracked seed in hand, all the kids would know that she too had a daddy who loved and cherished her. Leatrice knew her classmates at school and the kids that lived in the lane whispered about her parentless condition and about the way her mother died.

"Daddy must be coming by," she announced in a matter-of-fact voice to her dolls, who fell strangely silent and stared straight ahead at a spot on the horizon with full, thick eyelashes.

Each day when she returned home from school, she would check her room for new signs of her daddy's love. One day what she saw thrilled her to say, "Yes, he does love me." Sitting on her bed was a new doll with luxuriously long, blond hair. Leatrice named her Rapunzel because a prince could touch the sky as he climbed up the golden steps of her hair. In moments of play, Leatrice often extended the doll's movable arms so that she could receive the prince into her prison tower.

One day instead of manna from heaven, it was Halmuni who greeted Leatrice when she came home from school. She sat upright against the dinette chair in the parlor as if she were nailed to an invisible crucifix. Clenched tightly in her right fist and held upright like a shepherd's staff was a yardstick.

"Where you get dis *kine* new doll?" Halmuni screamed in a voice so shrill that the crystal vase on the shelf shook. Like a madman, Halmuni dashed to Leatrice's closet and yanked out the taffeta dress and flung it on the floor. Then out of her apron pocket came the kewpie doll *kini*.

"Where you steal dis *kine* from?" she asked menacingly.

"My daddy brought them, right?" Leatrice whispered, finally giving voice to the words she could never say. Now everyone would know that her daddy really and truly cherished her.

"Doh Won?" shrieked Halmuni derisively. "Are you *bakatari*? How can Doh Won give you these? Huh? Huh? Huh?" The shrillness and the volume in Halmuni's voice began to escalate into screams. "He no come here. You *kojinmal*, liar."

Halmuni picked up the doll's dress from the bureau saying, "And where the *ton* to buy this come from?"

Leatrice experienced both melancholy and terror at the same time. She wanted to indulge in the full weight of self-pity that her daddy hadn't come bearing these gifts, but fear of what her Halmuni was going to do to her was more imminent. Tai Yun approached her with the yardstick.

"You go church and *den* you steal. You bad girl," she said over and over and began hitting Leatrice with the yardstick. Leatrice felt the blows from the yardstick falling like sharp, prickly arrows upon her shoulders, arms, head, and legs. Crouched with her hands over her head, she tried to protect herself.

"*Kojinmal* and thief," Tai Yun was yelling at the top of her voice. "Sinner, you go church but you are *magui* like your *omoni*!"

The commotion brought Halabugi running into the house. "What you doing, why *teddyjo*?" he yelled as he yanked the yardstick out of his wife's hand.

"*Ai goo*, she steals!" Tai Yun shrieked as if she were exorcising a devil out of her grandchild. "Look at *dis*!" she said and pointed at Rapunzel, the dresses, and the satin ribbon.

"*Kaymani iso!*" Kyoung Ho shouted. "I *wen* buy all *dis* for her. She cry at night, she is so sad. *Pahmna ul rul*. Doh Won sends us plenty ton to take care of her. He like us buy things to make her happy."

"He give us *ton* to feed her and clothe her, *pau*, enough," retorted Halmuni. "What about *ton* for the church? Hay, hay? What about going to Choson to save the pagan souls? Hay? Hay?"

"To hell with the pagan," said Halabugi. "Why you going to Choson for? Only to make trouble for everybody. Leave alone! Maybe they no like be Catholics."

Yanking the yardstick from her husband's hand, Halmuni began flogging herself with it. Halabugi and Leatrice watched helplessly as welts began to form on Halmuni's legs and arms, and small pockets of blood like the stig-mata of St. Francis of Assisi that she coveted and prayed for finally appeared on her palms.

When Tai Yun felt that she had punished herself enough for her family's sins and those of mankind, she flung the yardstick at her husband, and grab-bing the white kerchief she wore to church, tore out of the house slamming the screen door behind her.

"You okay, Leatrice?" Halabugi asked after his wife's departure. He reached out his hand to stroke her hair but thought better of it and put it in his pocket.

"My daddy didn't buy those things?" Leatrice asked hoping against the truth.

"Nope, sorry," he said in a barely audible voice.

Leatrice was heartbroken and ran out of the parlor. Kyoung Ho heard the slamming of the back screen door this time.

"Koreans eat too much *kim chee*," he thought to himself. "The young ones blow up like volcanoes too."

Leatrice ran down the steps of the back porch and flung herself on the bench in the backyard. She sat there and cried for what seemed an eternity. Her daddy didn't love her. He mailed money, but he never came. Her mom-my left her for good and her daddy didn't care. She cried until her tears ran dry. She remained there until the sun's light diminished, taking with it the heat of the summer's day. She heard the deafening noise of the birds madly bidding each other good night. She watched as her friend the wind began its ritual of coursing through the yard and waited until she received its magical gift of love.

As night fell, Leatrice climbed the steps of the back porch. She found her Halabugi sitting at the kitchen table reading the day's *Korean Herald*. He had been waiting for her. As she entered the house, their eyes locked mo-mentarily and a smile passed between.

"*Annyonghi kaseyo*," he said to her as she passed him to go to her room. She acknowledged his good night by nodding her head and repeated his greeting silently.

As Leatrice lay in bed with Mary, Linda, and Juliette on her left and Laverne and Rapunzel on her right, for the first time since she came to her Halmuni's house she sang her favorite song.

How much is that doggy in the window,
The one with the waggily tail?
How much is that doggy in the window?
I do hope that he is for sale.

As Leatrice looked up at the ceiling, she saw Halmuni's ship sailing across the ocean blue to Korea, the land of the many *ai goos*. She stretched her arms out wide and smiled contently as she counted the gifts she received from her grandfather on the fingers of her right hand. "One, two, three, four . . . " she whispered to her children.

Maybe, just maybe she could go with him to the "moam pictcha" show and see Esther Williams cut through the water with graceful flourish. He could carry her on his shoulders all the way down School Street and turn the corner at Liliha for all the world to see.

LUCRETIA LEONG, *born in 1945, served as a language arts teacher, librarian, and library specialist for the Hawai'i Department of Education until 2006. Along with her newfound love of dogs and being able to sleep in, she finds time to step inward—through yoga, meditation, fiction writing, painting, and the creation of hilarious greeting cards for her beloved family and friends.*

Pat Matsueda

"INFLAMED"

for K., in adolescence

One summer when we were kids
we swam every day at Ala Moana Beach.
Dropped off in the morning by our father's parents,
we were picked up in the afternoon
wet, brown,
birds just out of the egg.
Later, we swam in pools, at other beaches,
eventually learned to do it right
in a college course, where you excelled.
but before that, in adolescence,
we again swam at Ala Moana.
In late afternoon, we went down
and swam till we were saturated with ocean,
our skins brown and our blood hot.
'Till the sun slipped in the water
and darted through our hair

like a yellow fish.
Then we left that caress
and showered.
I screamed and you laughed,
and for ten or fifteen minutes
we were under that cold, fresh water.
Rinsing, cleaning our skins.
Coaxing the ocean
out of our black hair.

PAT MATSUEDA *is the author of* Stray, *a collection of poetry; the managing editor of* Mānoa; *and an instructor of professional editing at the University of Hawai'i at Mānoa.*

Amalia B. Bueno

"WHEA YOU FROM"

I am from soft, fan-shaped Filipino brooms,
from Ajax, vinegar and salt.
I am from the daddy avocado tree
and the mommy mango tree
and their children the eggplant plants,
baby tomato plants and the jabong
branches with strong sharp thorns that got you
when you weren't careful.

I'm from bibingka and a curved tortoise shell comb,
from Eugenia and Alejo and Florentia and Placido.
I am from you have no shame and go fix your things
and go ask your lola and from aye, de goddamm
you are not using your coconut shell.

I'm from Ilocos provincia and crowded Quezon
and Palama Street in Kalihi where
even the fried fish has hard eyeballs
and the stinky bagoong releases its patis on top.

From Zamboanga Theatre to Hall Saimin
between dusty Book of Knowledge encyclopedias

old now among yellowed photo albums and and albums
of dreams distilled, of hopes captured
on our chain link corner of Honolulu.

AMALIA B. BUENO *was born in 1960 in Quezon City, Philippines, and emigrated to Hawai'i in 1967. She has a BA in English literature from the University of Hawai'i at Mānoa. Her poetry, fiction, and performance pieces have been published in* Bamboo Ridge; *the University of Hawai'i* Katipunan Journal: Voices of Hawaii; *the Meritage Press* Babaylan Series; Our Own Voice Literary Ezine: Filipinos in the Diaspora; *and are forthcoming in the Spinsters Ink Press anthology,* Bleeding on the Page.

Lee A. Tonouchi
"WOT VILLAGE YOU FROM?"

"WOT VILLAGE YOU FROM?"
My Grandma axes my friends
wit Okinawan last names.
I dunno why,
she always get
disappointed
when dey tell
Pālolo.

Lee A. Tonouchi
"DA WORD"

Back den I nevah know. I wuz only one six grader trying fo' make 'em into Punahou, 'Iolani, or Kamehameha. My faddah wanted me fo' get in. I dunno why. Friggin' expensive go private school. I nevah like go cuz pressure ah. Get dat debt dat I gotta repay my faddah now. Not only I gotta be grateful fo' him working hod, taking care me aftah my mom wen divorce us, but now I gotta be tankful dat he sending me to one "good" school so I can go "mainland" college and come one doctor. And not just anykine mainland school, but da kine "good" kine mainland school, preferably one of da

Ivory league kine schools. So to him I'm jus like one investment. He nevah axed me if I wanted fo' go private school. I guess wuz jus so he could brag to our family and all his friends, but wot about my friends?

Laurie wuz my friend, not by choice, more by default. She came our school from Oregon forth grade time. Since den da teachers always put us together in da smaht group. I mostly only talked to her in class, recess time I cruised wit my friends. We got along pretty good, except fo' da fack dat she wuz competetive, dat wuz one of her idiosyncrasies. Das my new word I wen learn. Da teacher wen make us learn one new word everyday and we gotta make one coconut-shape ornament and stick 'em on da Vocabulary Tree. Good fun wuz learning words. One time I called Laurie "demented" and she had to go look 'em up before she could give me her rebuttal, *"I'm not a person suffering from dementia or the irreversible deterioration of mental faculties. I'm not like stupid you know."* Yeah, right. Wotevahs. One noddah time I wen trick her li'dat wen I sed, "Ho Laurie, why you always gotta look so pulchritudinous, ah?" Ho, dat set her off. She nevah know wot dat meant, but she kept arguing, arguing wit me until finally she found out dat it meant beautiful and den wuz all like wop your jaws[1] ah. Some people, cannot take one compliment I tell you boy.

Of all da people I wuz going miss, Laurie wuzn't one of 'em. Chances wuz dat I wuz going be seeing a whole lot more of her though cuz she sed she wuz going private school too. None of her friends back in Portland wuz in private schools she sed. She wuz happy dat she wuz special. I guess I wanted fo' get in cuz I nevah like be lacking ah, but still I nevah like all my friends tink I wuz high nose li'dat. At least Laurie nevah have to worry about her rep cuz she had dat himakas[2] ting going down fo' long time already. Plenny people nevah like Laurie. Da girls nevah like her cuz she wuz pretty and she knew dat she wuz pretty. And she had dat "I'm one intellectual" kine attitude ah. She wuz da one always raising her hand in class, fully brown nosing, trying fo' be teacher's pet.

One day da teacher wuz going over everybody's essays on how wuz their summer vacation. He wuz really picking on Mits Funai and Barry Santos and he made dem go up in front da class and read their essays. Could tell he had problems wit Barry's body surfing at Point Panic papah. Teach sed he used to surf there too wen he wuz growing up so I nevah catch why he wuz geeving dem da business. At first I tot da problem wuz dat da essay wuz all "fiction" ah, cuz Barry, him, he talk da talk, but he no walk da walk ah, you know da kine. Him, he pressure out wen his head stay undah water li'dat.

---

[1] facial disgracial

[2] tantaran

Ninety feet and glassy. I no tink so. But wuzn't so much da content, but da manner in which Barry wen go write 'em.

"Barry, how many times must I tell you? You musn't write like how you speak."

"Hah?!" Barry's head jerked back.

"Who can tell the class what is wrong with Barry's writing?"

"Oh, Barry, he da kine. He stay abundantly writing in one freestyle kine manner using large quantities of informal neologisms, ah?" Mits attempted trying fo' incorporate as many of da new coconut-kine vocabulary words as he could remembah into dat one response.

"The problem is that both Barry AND Mits use too many colloquialisms," Laurie volunteered dis time witout raising her hand.

"Try like, das not wot I sed?" Mits whispered into my ear.

"I tink so, but maybe wuz too wordy or someting ah."

"That was an excellent response Laurie. You speak very well."

"Yeah Laurie, you talk sooo gooood," Fay added sacrastically.

"Laurie speaks WELL," da teacher correcked in his stern voice, silencing da snickering of da class as he banged da yardstick on da table. Talks good, speaks well. Same diffs. So long you get da idea. Laurie wuz fully irking today, couldn't wait till recess fo' play tetherball wit da gang.

Usually Laurie stayed in class during recess time. I tink so she sked da sun or someting, ass why she so white. I dunno wot she doing in da classroom. Probably kissing up to da teacher sa'more. Probably erasing da blackboard or straightening da desks or someting. Ass why all of us wen stare wen Laurie started walking toward da tetherball pole.

"No mo' caboose k," Barry sed, making like normal.

"Get swing?" Fay and Bernard wen ax.

"Ne'mine da rules, jus play already befo' we gotta go back class," I sed anxiously as I saw Laurie smiling at me.

"Hi, what are you guys doing?," Laurie axed as she stood on da outside of da concrete circle twirling her long black hair round and round wit her fingers.

"Wot YOU doing? You no belong hea, girlie. Jus go back wea you came from," Fay hollered.

Wuz so unexpecked wot Laurie's reaction wuz. I would've tot dat she would've jus make like one BANANA and split ah, make like one drum and beat it, jus make like one shovel and DIG li'dat, but instead she wen jus sit down and cry. Barry and da boyz wen go leave fo' go play on one noddah pole. I wanted fo' go have fun too, but I felt sorry ah fo' Laurie. Torn. Dat love-hate deals.

"Laurie, no cry," I sed hoping she would stop fass so I could go join my friends.

"Why . . . " she sed sniffling, her eyes coming all red.

"Come den, we go walk around befo' people tink wuz me who wen make you cry."

I helped her up and we moved from da grassy area to walking along da lanai. I got her paper towels from da bachroom so she could wipe her face. We walked togethers fo' awhile our shoulders brushing occasionally.

My body came all stiff li'dat wen witout looking at me she just locked her left pinky wit my right pinky as our arms swung together in unison. I made one strange face making quick kine side eyes, getting ready fo' make da break if in case had anybody looking ah. My eyes stopped scanning and focused in on her wen I noticed dat she wuz humming one song.

"Wot song is dat?"

"*It's from* Westside Story.*"

"Oh."

"*The musical.* Westside Story. *They made it into a movie. It's based on Shakespeare's* Romeo and Juliet. *You don't know it? How can you not know it? It's a classic.*"

"Oh. So. . . ." I sed not knowing wot else fo' say as I noticed dat we wuz all da way in da front of campus, by da office already. "So, uh, we go head back li'dat befo' da bell ring ah, you know da kine."

"*Why do you talk funny sometimes?*"

"Hah?! You saying I should be one comedian?"

"*Not funny, humorous, but funny, strange.*"

"Oh."

And den there wuz silence again as we continued walking back. We nevah talk until we wuz passing da libary wen Laurie wen ax, "*So when are you going to call to set up an appointment for your interview at Punahou?*"

"Ah, I do 'em bumbye," I sed casual kine, not really wanting to tink about it at da moment.

"*When?*" Laurie sed wrinkling her eyebrows together.

"Bumbye."

"*What's that, BUMBYE?*"

"Bumbye. Bum . . . bye," I repeated slowly.

"*Like ye-ah. That's not a word. You're making it up.*"

"It is too one word."

"*I'll bet you it's not!*"

Laurie wuz starting to piss me off. See, dat love-hate deals. Attractive, but get attitude. Since we wuz by da libary she sed we should go check da dictionary cuz das wea they had da big humangoso dictionary. Laurie wuz so confident dat she wuz right dat she even bet me dat whoever loss would have to carry da winner's books fo' a week while walking in between classes. I nevah like dat bet cuz to me ees like either way she win cuz I nevah like people tink dat she wuz my girfriend or noting. So I toll her if I won den she had fo' buy me one extra milk fo' lunch. Only ten cents, but ees not da money, but mo' pride ah. Cuz I knew I wuz right.

We walked into da libary and went to da stand wit da big American Heritage Dictionary, Unabridged Edition. Friggin' ukubillion[3] pages insai. My word garans going be insai there I tot, tinking of how sweet dat milk wuz going taste. I flipped through da pages wit Laurie friggin' tip-toeing and staring over my shoulders so she could be da first one NOT fo' see da word. Bumbye. As I flipped to da B's my mind wandered as I tot—das one word ah? Bumbye. Simple word too. Hakum Laurie dunno 'em? Nah, nah, no doubt. Laurie going be da one who lose out. Bumbye gotta be one word, I heard my Grandma use 'em sooo many times. "Grandma, wen you going take me Disneyland?" "Bumbye." So bumbye can mean later on, indefinite kine, possibly nevah. Or "Grandma, hakum you no always flush da toilet aftah you pau shi shi?" "Cuz bumbye pohō water." So bumbye is also like consequently or as one result of. See, so das two definitions already. So hakum dis friggin' dictionary no' mo da word?, I tot as I saw one smile begin to form on Laurie's lips. Maybe I stay spelling 'em wrong? B-U-M . . . B-Y-E. Das right ah? Maybe ees B-U-M-B-A-I? Or B-U-M-B-Y? I flipped frantically looking fo' da kine alternative spellings. I kept flipping back and forth, back and forth, making sure fo' double check each one. But nevah have none of da spellings. Bumbye wuzn't one word.

I quickly looked fo' da meejum size Webster's dictionary, cuz da big one had so many words dat ees possible fo' miss dat one word ah. But even da kine Webster's nevah get 'em. I wen check wot year da dictionaries wuz. If wuz old maybe I could get off on one technicality. Laurie wuz all jumping up and down, squealing small kine. Finally I ran to da librarian's desk and axed fo' borrow her little Random House pocket-size dictionary. Even though dat one wuz smaller, had all da important, high frequency, coconut-kine garans ball barans going be on da test kine words ah, so I figured gotta have 'em in dat one cuz ees pretty common ah, but still nevah get 'em. I held da small dictionary open not knowing wot fo' do. Da bell rang as Laurie turned and grabbed my arm fo' lead me back to class. I cradled da dictionary snug in my right hand as she pulled my oddah arm sa'more and slid her hand down to hold my hand. I let her fingertips slip through mine as she looked back once and den turned to leave toward da double doors. "Bumbye" wuzn't one coconut kine word. I stood, still looking at da dictionary in my palm, part

---

[3] choke

of me wanting to memorize every single friggin' word in there, part of me wanting to friggin' throw it at Laurie's head before she left, just to hear wot kinda noise it would make.

LEE A. TONOUCHI, *"Da Pidgin Guerrilla," wen author da Pidgin short story collection* Da Word *and da Pidgin essay collection* Living Pidgin. *He wen also compile* Da Kine Dictionary. *Literary publications Tonouchi wen edit/co-edit include* Hybolics *magazine;* Buss Laugh; Hip-Hop Hawai'i; *and* Bumbye Hawai'i. *Dis guy get one Elliot Cades Award for Literature, two* HONOLULU Magazine *Fiction Contest Grand Prizes, couple Kumu Kahua Playwriting Prizes, and two Kapalapala Po'okela Book Awards.*

Milly Lou Donnelly
"THE BARD IN PIDGIN"

A group of Oriental children were being taught the game, "Romeo and Juliet." Juliet, blindfolded in the center of the ring, must locate Romeo by the sound of his voice answering her: "Romeo, Romeo, wherefore art thou, Romeo?"
Little Ming Toy cut right through non-essentials, to
"Romeo, where you?"

Lloyd Stone
"KOBE"

I.
Kobe
(Our cook,
Not the city in Japan)
Seems constantly striving
To make the English language
More euphonious.

Only yesterday
When I asked him

If he had more soup in the kitchen
He replied
"Lots gots."

II.
One can always be certain
Of something startling
In the way of grammar
When Kobe answers the phone.
Today when someone called
Asking for Mr. White
(There are two of them on the place)
Kobe inquired
"Which kind, please?"

III.
Kobe is a stickler for politeness
Though his execution is unique.

"Yes, sir," he says to me
With an extra bow or two

And to the lady visitor
He smiles politely,
"Yes, her."

Mavis Hara

"AN OFFERING OF RICE"

T atsue wanted to stay downstairs and listen to the new Rudy Vallee song
on her mother's radio, but Okasan was sick with asthma again and it
was not easy for her to climb the stairs. Tatsue sighed as she uncovered the
pot of freshly cooked rice and pressed the sticky grains into tiny brass dishes.
The grains held together like a white moon. Okasan had taught her that
rice offered to the ancestors and the gods should be smoothed and round,
not triangular like the musubi humans ate because there were no corners in
heaven. In Japan, they said everything in heaven was a circle.

Tatsue carried the offering dishes upstairs and put one in front of the Shinto shrine and the other in front of the larger Buddhist shrine. She lit three thin sticks of black sandalwood incense and planted the sticks upright in a bowl of grey ashes. Then she sat back on the silk cushion and whispered the name of Buddha, "Namu Amida Butsu."

Tatsue did not sit long. She left the rice at the altar until the incense burned away and added itself to the ashes in the bowl. While she was upstairs, she collected the family's laundry—a rice bag full from the room that her four brothers shared, another from the room she shared with her sister Kei, and the last from Otosan and Okasan's room. She carried all the bags down the stairs and left them next to the galvanized tin washtub beside the copper furo.

"Tatsue, hayaku yasai wo arainasai," Okasan called, and Tatsue hurried upstairs to collect the dishes of cooled rice from the altars, then back downstairs to the kitchen to help wash the vegetables for dinner. When she got there, the two youngest children, Masao and Kei were waiting.

"I like eat the mamai-san rice," Masao was saying.

Tatsue wished that for once she could eat the cold rice in the brass dishes but she gave Masao one of the servings and six-year-old Kei the other. The two children smiled happily as they chewed on their prizes. Okasan was already at the sink slitting the belly of the fat mullet she had bought from the fish peddler that afternoon. Tatsue avoided looking at the red intestines and the gills that sent blood swirling into the sink.

After dinner, Tatsue finished washing the dishes, then went back to the laundry room where Otosan had already heated the water in the copper furo. Behind her in the back room, she could hear someone crying. Someone was always crying. This time it was the little one, Masao. He was tired of following Kei around the house and wanted to accompany his older brothers out into the neighborhood. And he didn't want to wear Kei's old dresses anymore.

"I like pants." he cried. He was three now and knew the difference.

"Yakamashii!" Otosan shouted, and Masao sat down on the floor reduced to soft whimpering. He had felt the belt before.

Tatsue scooped hot water from the furo into one of the tin laundry tubs, then set the wooden washboard inside. She wanted some new clothes too. How she envied Nii-san, her older brother who worked at Fair Department Store. He always got to buy new things then acted so high nosed when he wore them.

She filled the second tub with cold rinse water and opened the rice bags and began to sort the clothes. She pulled out a sweat-streaked shirt. It was Yoshio's now. She remembered washing it when it had belonged to Nii-san.

He and Otosan had not spoken to each other since the night Otosan had told him to leave school and go to work full time.

"Shikata ga nai. Can't help it. You have to work." Otosan had said.

"One more year until I finish!" Nii-san had argued. "One more year, I can work anyplace I like. I can make big money. Why you cannot wait one year and let me graduate?"

"Naze yuu koto kikan no?" Otosan yelled at him. "What kind of son are you? Men have to work." The old man had stood firm as iron. In the end, Nii-san did as he was told and handed over his paycheck every week. But he spent all the money Otosan gave back to him to buy all the latest styles.

"Hardhead. Big Face everytime," Tatsue whispered to herself. "Think he too good for us now."

Tatsue dunked and scrubbed. As she worked, she could hear her mother coughing in the back room. Okasan could never do all of this work by herself, and the boys would never set foot into the laundry to help. Woman's work, they called it. But beginning tomorrow, Tatsue would go to work too. This year she could work legally at the cannery without lying about her age.

The air outside was cool, the moon warm and silver through thin clouds. Tatsue finished hanging the wash and looked at the sky through her fingers. Her hands were thin and fragile-looking, and each oval nail contained the edge of a rising moon. Fred, the boy who walked her home every day from McKinley High School, said they were refined. She thought Fred was handsome. Otosan and Okasan didn't like him.

"His mouth is too big. His lips are too full. Your children will be ugly if you marry him." they said.

Tatsue looked down again at her hands and sighed. She didn't know if they were refined, but she knew they were strong.

Tatsue went back into the house and climbed the stairs to her bedroom. She opened her drawer and looked at her apron and gloves and white cannery hairnet. She pulled a glove over her fingers. Tomorrow she would earn fifteen cents an hour as a packer. The man in the window of the payroll office would hand her a numbered pay envelope heavy with silver dollars every week. It would be like Otosan's and Nii-san's. Tatsue lay in bed and drifted to sleep. She dreamed of buying cotton so sheer it would wear out in a year. She dreamed of wearing dresses that would never have to be handed down.

At five the next morning, the air was damp and smelled cool and sweet. Tatsue made her bento lunch then hurried out of the house and met her friend Edith at the corner.

"Hey, you going work my table this year?" Edith asked as they fell into step together. "If the forelady like us, she keep us on long time. We can make plenty money."

They walked out of Desha Lane down King Street, toward Iwilei and the cannery. Other girls joined them. Girls from thirteen to eighteen years old, dressed in home-made dresses, and carrying lunch pails, rubber gloves, aprons, and hairnets in their hands. They laughed as they greeted one another. The clouds above the mountains of Nuuanu swirled like incense high into the limitless blue sky.

The air at the California Packers Cooperative cannery smelled like baked pineapple. It was so thick it clung to Tatsue's skin. The girls walked past the guards, through the iron gates, and into the noise of the mechanical landscape. They walked past the trains that brought the pineapple in from the country. Twelve-hour shifts were usual at this time, the peak of the season. Everyone worked from six to six with one break for lunch.

Tatsue and Edith went to the locker room and put on their caps and gloves and hairnets. They pinned the bango numbers to each other's shoulders.

Edith said, "Last year, I went get sick and my sister took my number and came work for me. The man from the payroll office came with the clipboard and check the numbers. They went pay me anyway. They no care. So long as somebody wear this number. Same thing to them."

The girls walked out into the clatter of the thousands of metal teeth that moved the conveyor belts. The pineapples moved through the cannery on the conveyor belts that joined one machine to another like tongues that stretched across the room. The pine went from the railroad cars to the Ginnaka machine, which chewed them out of most of their skins. The almost-naked pines then rode to the trimmers who would pick up the fruit in one hand and trim out the spots of rind, called eyes, with the sharp knives they held in the other. Tatsue was glad she was not a trimmer. Their hands ached from holding the heavy pineapples and their arms were marked with round sores caused by the pineapple juice dripping down their rubber gloves.

"Eh, packers! I remember you two from last year, come over hea to my table," the forelady with the loud voice called to them. They followed the pine down the conveyor belt that led from the trimmers to the slicing machines, where a large, smiling Portuguese woman was standing behind girls packing pineapples into cans.

"You going be first packer this year," the forelady said as she pulled Tatsue into place behind the girl who worked closest to the slicing machine. When the whistle blew, the night crew stopped and Tatsue and Edith stepped up to take their places. The mechanical teeth kept clattering and the pineapple flowed endlessly by.

The year before, the two girls had lied about their ages and come to work scared and silent. They had been afraid of the loud voices of the fore-ladies. They had been afraid of the machines. But Tatsue had made it. She was first packer this year.

"No dream, no talk, no take too much time!" The forelady scolded the new girls, but Tatsue and Edith were old-timers now.

Tatsue picked out the sweetest slices emerging from the slicer and packed them in the small cans in front of her. These were the premium pieces and would be sold for the most money. The girls farther down the line picked out the slices that went into cans that were larger and less costly. Broken slices would be fed into machines again and packed into cans to be sold as tidbits, and badly broken pieces would be thrown into mashing machines and pressed for juice.

Tatsue liked her new position. The pineapple slices came out of the machine clinging neatly together. The vibration of the belt shook them out of their neat arrangement so Tatsue edged closer to the slicing machine to catch the pineapple just as it emerged from the metal mouth. As she settled her body into the chattering mechanical rhythm, she thought of Fred and the wonderful dresses she could make with the money she earned this summer. She would hand Otosan her pay envelope and he would give her back silver dollars to save in her drawer so that she could buy material to make new dresses for school. Tatsue could see herself walking home with Fred in her new clothes. "You look like Olivia DeHavilland in that dress," he might tell her.

Maybe this year Otosan would let her go to the movies with Fred. She would lean close to him and he might kiss her, his full lips on hers in a kiss she had seen in the movies at the Waikiki theater. She dreamed and smiled.

Tatsue reached higher into the mouth of the machine for her next slices. Suddenly, she felt a stinging numbness in her hand. She looked at her glove. The fingertip was open like a mouth trying to scream. She saw the pink flesh around a circle of white bone, all that was left of the tip of her finger.

She bit her lips and pulled her mouth smooth and hard across her teeth so that she would not cry out. The blood-spattered pineapple slices moved down the conveyor belt, and somewhere down the row, Edith began screaming. The girls farther down the line saw the bloody slices and screamed too. As the foreladies gathered around Tatsue and swept her off to the dispensary, she heard the screaming spread. It echoed down the line from slices, to chunks, to crushed. She did not open her mouth.

At home, she slept. After three days, she cried silently when her mother changed the bandage. Okasan thought she was in pain and tried to give her some pills.

"No, I no like drink anything."

Otosan made the face he always made when Okasan told him to call the mid-wife, and went downstairs to his chair. Tatsue sank into bed and gathered the thick, soft, cotton futon around herself. Her tears sank into the quilt made of dresses she had worn as a small child.

A week after the accident, she came downstairs to sit at the kitchen table where Okasan was sewing. Otosan had been laid off from his carpenter's job at the Libby cannery. He sat in his chair reading his books and smoking the hand-rolled cigarettes he made each morning. Tatsue looked down at her bandaged hand. Now Nii-san was the only one in the household working.

Tatsue left the table and went into the laundry room. She did not see Otosan put down his cigarette and watch her carefully. She got a bucket and filled the two washtubs with water from the furo. It was hard working with one hand, but it was dark in the laundry room, and no one would see her eyes. There would be no new dresses. The outline of her bandaged finger blurred.

Tatsue put the wooden washboard in one tub and dropped two balls of bluing in the other. She opened the old rice bag containing the boys' dirty laundry and pulled out Nii-san's crisp new shirt. She pushed it into the water in the first tub, then laid it on the washboard and rubbed the brown bar of soap over it. She moved the shirt up and down over the wooden teeth of the washboard. As she tried to squeeze out the soap she heard someone speak.

"Tatsue."

She looked up, startled. Otosan was standing in the laundry room. She didn't know how long he had been watching her. She had never seen him in the laundry room before.

"Sonna koto sen demo ii, you don't have to do that," Otosan said softly. Then he took the shirt that she had been washing and twisted it in his carpenter's hands to ring it out. Tatsue watched in amazement as he dipped Nii-san's shirt into the blue rinse water. He was clumsy and did not rinse like a woman. He was inventing the motions as he went along. Tatsue realized he had never learned this; a Japanese man never washed clothes. The bluing in the water clung to his nails. Each of his nails was grooved so that it looked like the ribbed cotton of his undershirt. Tiny ribs ran vertically the length of each nail.

"I like that one, you always get that one!" They heard Masao and Kei from beyond the laundry room door and the asthmatic coughing that constantly filled the house.

Tatsue watched the yellow carpenter's calluses in Otosan's palms become grey and soft as he washed his eldest son's shirt in the soapy water. He didn't say anything, he didn't smile at her, he just continued washing and rinsing. Tatsue took the clothes he had finished and fed each piece into the hand-cranked wringer. Otosan watched until he was satisfied that the work was light enough for her do. Then he went back to washing. Tatsue could feel her tears drying, her mouth softening again, her lips rounding into a smile.

Otosan helped her in the laundry room the whole summer. She loved working silently next to him. He smelled like sawdust, cigarette smoke and soft grey ashes. They worked through June and July, until it was August, the week before school.

Twelve hands turned the lazy susan in the center of the table quickly past the vegetables from Okasan's kitchen garden to the shoyu cooked fish. The ball bearings Otosan had built into the table clattered. He handed Tatsue three silver dollars.

"That is all that's left. Shikata ga nakatta. We had to eat your finger." Otosan spoke gruffly, avoiding her eyes. The table stopped turning. Everyone stopped eating and stared at him with open mouths. Tatsue did not understand.

"CPC kara . . . the cannery paid me money for twelve weeks after your accident. They said 'workman's compensation.' I didn't tell you. I had to use the money to buy food for the whole family."

Tatsue's eyes stung. Mean old man! The cannery had been paying her the entire summer! She pressed her lips hard over her teeth. He had not been able to work, and Nii-san's money had not been enough! Otosan had taken her money and used it. Tatsue looked down at her healing finger. Its tip was gone and it was shorter than the rest. The new nail was growing in wrinkled with tiny ridges.

Then she remembered Otosan squatting beside her in the laundry room. All her life, she had been taught that a Japanese man does not do women's work. She could not help thinking of that as she remembered Otosan pushing Nii-san's shirts across the wooden ribs of the washboard, the soapy water eating away the hard calluses on his palms and cutting into the deep grooves in his fingernails. He was a practical man. He did not say anything. He did what was necessary. She stared at his fingers as they held out the last three silver dollars he had saved for her.

She looked at Nii-san in his stylish clothes. He was looking at her finger; his eyes softened, then began to glisten. She looked at the younger boys and her sister Kei in their hand-me-down clothes, at Masao in his new pants made of Otosan's old workshirt, and at Okasan in her faded dress.

They were staring at her.

"Shi kata ga nai." It couldn't be helped. She began to mumble these words she had been taught. They were as familiar as the offerings she made every evening in a sweet cloud of incense to feed the hungry spirits gathering in the warmth around their family altar.

"Shi kata ga nai." She looked at them all sitting together in a circle around the kitchen table. And in her mouth, as she said those words, there was a satisfaction like the cold grains eaten from a small brass dish. It was a satisfaction which surprised her, and she felt nourished and warm as she swallowed. They were smiling at her in the last orange light, the bottoms of the windows filled with the curved edge of the sun. She looked at their faces, and the warmth she felt was like a circle, a round ball, an offering of rice.

MAVIS HARA *lives in Honolulu, where she was born at Kapi'olani hospital. Her book,* An Offering of Rice, *was published by Bamboo Ridge Press in 2007. She wishes to thank Mutual Publishing and editor Gavan Daws for selecting her work to be included in this anthology.*

Cathy Song
"THE GRAMMAR OF SILK"

On Saturdays in the morning
my mother sent me to Mrs. Umemoto's sewing school.
It was cool and airy in her basement,
pleasant—a word I choose
to use years later to describe
the long tables where we sat
and cut, pinned, and stitched,
the Singer's companionable whirr,
the crisp, clever bite of scissors
parting like silver fish a river of calico.

The school was in walking distance
to Kaimuki Dry Goods
where my mother purchased my supplies—
small cards of buttons,
zippers and rickrack packaged like licorice,
lifesaver rolls of thread
in fifty-yard lengths,

spun from spools, tough as tackle.
Seamstresses waited at the counters
like librarians to be consulted.
Pens and scissors dangled like awkward pendants
across flat chests,
a scarf of measuring tape flung across a shoulder,
time as a pincushion bristled at the wrist.
They deciphered a dress's blueprints
with an architect's keen eye.

This evidently was a sanctuary,
a place where women confined with children
conferred, consulted the oracle,
the stone tablets of the latest pattern books.
Here mothers and daughters paused in symmetry,
offered the proper reverence—
hushed murmurings for the shantung silk
which required a certain sigh,
as if it were a piece from the Ming Dynasty.

My mother knew there would be no shortcuts
and headed for the remnants,
the leftover bundles with yardage
enough for a heart-shaped pillow,
a child's dirndl, a blouse without darts.
Along the aisles
my fingertips touched the titles—
satin, tulle, velvet,
peach, lavender, pistachio,
sherbet-colored linings—
and settled for the plain brown-and-white composition
of polka dots on kettle cloth
my mother held up in triumph.

She was determined that I should sew
as if she knew what she herself was missing,
a moment when she could have come up for air—
the children asleep,
the dishes drying on the rack—
and turned on the lamp
and pulled back the curtain of sleep.

To inhabit the night,
the night as a black cloth, white paper,
a sheet of music in which she might find herself singing.

On Saturdays at Mrs. Umemoto's sewing school,
when I took my place beside the other girls,
bent my head and went to work,
my foot keeping time on the pedal,
it was to learn the charitable oblivion
of hand and mind as one—
a refuge such music affords the maker—
the pleasure of notes in perfectly measured time.

Cathy Song
"A CONSERVATIVE VIEW"

Money, my mother
never had much.
perhaps that explains her life's
philosophy, the conservation of money,
the idea of money as a natural resource,
the sleepless nights worrying
whether there is enough of it.
According to her current calculations,
there isn't.

I used to think it was because she is Chinese,
proud of the fact that her practical
nature is due to her Chinese blood.
"We do not spoil our children"
she is fond of saying as an explanation
for never having given in to our demands.
"Take care of the needs but not the wants" is another.

Place a well-behaved child
in front of her and my mother will say,
"Chinese, eh?"
She believes Japanese and Korean

parents spoil their children.
"Doormats to their kids."
And the bok gwai?—well,
they ship their offspring to camp or boarding school, right?
For the Chinese, discipline begins at home.
And it begins with teaching the value of money.

There are two things in life
my mother vows never to pay for:
gift wrapping and parking.
It hurts her to cough up the change for the meter.

Lucky is any day she can pull
into an empty space with time still running.
I was convinced my friends knew
that the birthday gifts I presented at parties
were wrapped in leftover sheets of our bathroom wallpaper.
—"Eh, how come dis paypa so tick?"

My mother's thrift frowns on the frivolous—
like singing in the shower
(it's a waste of water).
Her clear and practical sentences
are sprinkled with expressions
semantically rooted to the conservation of money.
They pepper her observations like expletives—
"Poho" if we bought something we couldn't use.
"Humbug" if we have to go out and buy
something we don't need.
"No need"—her favorite expression of all.

On shopping trips to the mall
she'll finger something soft and expensive,
letting her fingers linger on the exquisite
cut and fabric of a garment
when suddenly she'll exclaim,
like a kung fu battle cry,
"Pee-sa!"
(the one word she borrows liberally
from her Korean in-laws),
shuddering and releasing the price tag
as if she'd been bitten by a snake.

E X I L E "   489

My sister and I agree
she takes the price of things too personally.
Every morning there is her wake-up call—
"Diapers on sale at Longs."
"Price of lettuce up at Star."—
as though she were reporting the Dow Jones Industrial Average.
If I answer in the negative
to her interrogative
"Did you use coupons to buy that?"
—that being chicken thighs or toilet paper,
I feel guilty.

My father doesn't help matters.
He has heard enough from Mother
about Koreans being big spenders, show-offs—
"champagne taste on a beer budget"—
to have his revenge.
He thinks Mao Tse-tung is the best
thing that ever happened to China.
"How else are you going to get those damn pa-kes to share?"

Ty Pak

from "EXILE"

I wasn't too surprised when Deacon Shim asked me to a lunar New Year party at his house: somebody in the congregation was bound to make an occasion of it. This was the seventh party I'd had to attend in a month since the regular New Year's at the pastor's. Just bring yourself, they said. I didn't have to bring any food. At the door I presented my usual calling card, an envelope with a check enclosed, which the host accepted with a sigh of relief after the customary remonstrances and protests.

It all began last year, when Pastor Hwang came to the farm, smiling, speaking in a mellifluous Korean. I have no idea how he got my address. These pastors have a ferret's instinct for rooting out their targets. I didn't have a phone then, and I had assiduously avoided any association with my countrymen. Not only for the usual reason of self hatred, which is said to be very strong among Koreans. And you can't blame them, either. Korea, with its succession of incompetent, cruel, egotistic rulers, had not been much of a mother to her children. Shame, revulsion, bitter disillusionment were the primary emotions she had inspired and ingrained. And so long as Syngman Rhee and his henchmen enjoyed the support of America, the country where fortune had cast me adrift, I had more particular reasons to hide.

With the pastor's visit, the quarter century of exile from my country-men came to an end. My farm now crawled with Koreans, buying boxfuls of vegetables as if they had never seen them before. They came from Pearl Harbor, Hawaii Kai, even Waipahu, not considering the expenditure of gas and time that would more than offset the bargain. But then they are not known to be the most rational businessmen. I couldn't have cared less for their trade. Selling to wholesalers was much more efficient and ultimately more profitable. Sure I got more money per pound, and the cash income, a dollar here and another there, need not be reported, but I had to interrupt my work to accommodate them individually. Seldom did they come just for the produce; they took upon themselves the task of filling me with a lot of unsolicited information, the gossip of the Korean community.

I learned that there were about seven thousand Korean immigrants in Honolulu, most of whom had a female relative married to an American GI during the war, now divorced and operating a bar. Many lied about their in-come and lived in the disreputable government housing at Linapuni or Kalihi until after five years or so of saving they bought a house or a condominium, forever after to denounce the immorality of the American welfare system.

There were about fifteen churches of all denominations vying for aggran-dizement. The pastors sought out newcomers or stole members from each other with favors; in turn, people took advantage and hopped from church to church, not overstaying the hospitality of any one place. There were also the professionals, University of Hawaii professors, medical doctors, dentists, engineers, lawyers, accountants, who would have nothing to do with their inferior compatriots but whom the pastors sought after with obsequious flat-tery. Although it was a well known fact that these self made men were tight-fisted and believed in getting ten dollars back for every one they laid on the collection plate, their membership enhanced the church's stature. They came to dinners and picnics strictly as guests. The tithes and special offerings came from the lowly bar girls, hotel cleaners, restaurant operators.

Pastor Hwang's interest in me was therefore more substantial than pres-tigious. My three acre farm was probably as productive as twenty acres else-where; the subtropical weather allowed recropping throughout the year. I was in the fifty per cent or higher income tax bracket, despite all the business deductions my ingenious bookkeeper could devise. As the pastor was not slow to point out, my generous contributions to the church would be more than compensated by the tax credits they would earn. So I'd joined and in record time was made a ruling elder. With the honor came the dues. When they decided to purchase the pipe organ, all eyes turned to me. Whenever there was a wedding, a funeral, or a birthday and their occurrence was frequent and unending they invited me most cordially, expectantly. They felt no compunction about openly asking me for this subsidy or that, now that I wore the title. No royalty could have sold its dukedoms more dearly.

The main course was over, broiled short ribs of beef. Deacon Cho, the jeweler, observed that the motherland showed signs of unification. North Korea had agreed to meet with South Korea to work out the details of electing a pan Korea congress. Unification would never be realized, rose the skeptic's voice of Deacon Koo, the realtor. We shouldn't trust the rhetoric of politicians. On the contrary, retorted Deacon Lee, the upholsterer. The division of Korea was a purely external imposition; the power vacuum after Japan's withdrawal had to be filled by America in the south and Russia in the north. But during the Korean War Russia was edged out as Red China moved in to fight the Americans. China and America were now friends. A neutral peninsula was to the advantage of everybody concerned, he argued. Deacon Shim, our host, suggested that the moment Korea was unified, we should all pack up and return.

"Would they feed us?" asked Deacon Pyo, the auto body man.

"What kind of life is this that we have here?" snapped Deacon Chong, who worked as custodian at a Waikiki hotel but never lost an opportunity to remind others of the prosperous textile business he had had in Pusan. "My inwards twist several times a day to see these Japanese and Filipinos bossing over us. Caucasians are okay, but these second-generation Orientals are unbearable. Just because they came a few years ahead of us . . . "

"They sure kick us around," said Hishik Ho, part-owner of a bar. "Remember the dirt they threw at us in *The Advertiser* about Korean bars? Those lies about us fleecing customers? They can get away with anything because we cannot strike back."

"We need political power," said Byongho Lee, who had a Korean music and dance studio in town. "There isn't a single Korean in the state or city government."

"But there are other opportunities," interrupted Pyo. "One can be a scientist, doctor, businessman."

"They are all secondary," opined Professor Suh. "To be politically thwarted, even if fulfilled in every other respect, is like emasculation. We are living in a political limbo."

"I don't know about that," Pyo persisted. "I would be a millionaire anytime, even if I never got anywhere near a government office."

"Cite me a single millionaire who has made it without politics," pursued Suh. "Can you operate a body shop without going to the regulatory agencies, for example?"

This clinched the point. Everybody remembered going through irksome paperwork for business registration and inspection, filing financial statements, exhibits, balance sheets, all in confounded English.

"It boils down to having more children," said John Shin, who operated a gift and jewelry cart at Duke's Lane. "It is a patriotic duty. But you know how difficult it is to have a child. Between preschool and babysitters, our three year old is a four hundred dollar a month liability. I don't think I'll have another one even if he should be the next president of the United States."

"But what kind of life are we giving our children?" asked Deacon Lee. "Back home as children we thought of becoming president, congressman, general. I ask my son what he wants to be and he replies fireman. What kind of ambition is that?"

"They work short hours, retire early, make good money," said Pyo.

"What's a dollar more or less? When Korea gets united, I'll go," Lee declared vehemently.

"Me, too," said Ho. "Without the language I am an awkward clown here."

Everybody had a grievance or two against the new country of their adoption and seemed impatient for repatriation. For endorsement of the general sentiment they turned to the pastor who had sat aloof during the conversation. Somebody urged him to recount his Korean War experience. The pastor demurred at first but gave in. However, as he began from 1944, the year of his father's death as a forced laborer on Guam, even those who had steered him into this course were dismayed. He was a draftee in the North Korean People's Army, fought the South Korean forces and their allies, and was captured by the Americans in October 1950, shortly after MacArthur's Inchon landing and the collapse of the North Korean army. After three years of detention he was finally released as an anti-Communist POW. When the narration reached his conversion to Christianity and his eventual ordination, several hasty amens and hallelujahs went up, depriving him of the opportunity to draw some moral lessons, as was his wont. People got up, refilled glasses and plates, broke into twos and threes. This, however, must have portended to the orderly mind of our Deacon Cho the advent of anarchy to be averted at all costs.

"Does it mean you won't be going back to the united fatherland?" he shouted, edging up to the pastor by the buffet table, craning his head, dodging or shoving the people in the way. The concourse around the food was so thick and defensive that the pastor couldn't have been in a safer sanctuary. Finding himself unheard and next to me, the jeweller seized my arm.

"Grandfather," he said. He never called me anything else. "We should hear your story. Don't you have relatives back home? Quiet, everybody!"

Luckily, the hubbub drowned his shouts and clappings. In the meantime I had escaped to the lanai. The chilly night air had driven everybody inside. Waikiki blazed in the distance like a country girl's first night on the town. Her highrises, bedecked in multicolored, twinkling lights, defied the looming darkness of the Pacific behind. Suddenly, I felt lonely and old. The hollow feeling that grabbed my stomach spread and touched my heart. It could be any day now. Already I had outlived in age my parents and grandparents. I had the feeling that mine would be a sudden, no lingering, demeaning death. Instinctively I stroked my arm under the short sleeve. The goose flesh was bumpy to the touch. Who would mourn me? Would there be any trace of me after, say, ten years? My estate, intestate, would revert to the state, and my little tombstone, if there was one, would disfigure and crumble. I wondered where Yongmee might be. Was she divorced for the second or third time and operating a bar like the rest? Or was she a respectable matron with sons and daughters, maybe even grandchildren?

I saw her last as a passenger in the front seat of an American military jeep in Seoul thirty years ago. My bus lurched dangerously to a stop, making the curve by South Gate, its usual overload of passengers falling and piling like dominoes. While squelched under the weight of those on top of me, I saw the jeep drive up along the side right under the window. She was wearing dark sunglasses. The American soldier bent over and put his arm around her. The people in the bus straightened up. Oblivious to their own discomfiture, they smiled, feeling superior to this Jezebel, the fallen and untouchable. There was no trade lowlier than being a GI whore. They giggled, exchanging coarse jokes, loud enough for my sister's benefit. Some affected magnanimity and said her kind was good for the country's economy: the export dollars were 100 per cent net earnings as her ware didn't cost anything.

"Not entirely," a judicious wag pointed out. "Look at her get up. That must have cost her a pretty penny."

"Her honey gives that too," the trade expert said. "She must wear something, no matter what she is."

Yongmee sat erect and unflinching, staring fiercely into the space ahead. I sweated, squirmed, and wished I could disappear and erase the memory of it. It was painful. I saw only the shame and ugliness of prostitution, never the beauty or love. I blamed myself for everything, for not taking care of her and Mother properly. As the heir and namebearer of the family, it was my duty to shelter and feed the women. I had to do something fast, however desperate or irregular. Mother must have suspected all along what Yongmee was doing and got sicker every day. Yongmee moved out and soon stopped coming home altogether.

Then, a year or so later in the Pusan refugee swarms of July 1950, I ran into her friend Hesook. She told me that Yongmee was in America and had written her about my whereabouts. My papers had been ready and I should go at once to the American consulate. Hesook had been about to advertise in the papers. Relieved that she had not done so yet, I asked her whether anybody had come to her asking for me. She said no. After some hesitation I went to the U.S. Consulate, disguised as an old cripple. Surprisingly, things went fast and I was on the plane bound for America. Till the last minute, however, even after the Northwest Airlines DC 4 had taxied out and speeded up for takeoff, I momentarily expected it to be stopped and Kwak's men to board the plane to get me. Only when we left Haneda, did I savor the reality of my deliverance. Luxuriating in the velvet of the seat, I slept as I had never slept before.

It was a new world that I woke to in Honolulu, where the immigration procedure was completed. The ticket was for New York where Yongmee was waiting, but I decided to get off at Honolulu. Perhaps I was paranoid, but I felt I couldn't risk it. The long arm of vengeance or justice, I feared, knew no border. After trudging for days all over Oahu I chanced to be at Pupukea Plateau, on the North Shore. At an isolated papaya farm Mr. Kealoha, a big Hawaiian, six-foot three and nearly four hundred pounds, looked over my papers to verify that I was no stowaway and took me in, more willingly perhaps because I asked for no pay. I lived at the servant cottage and was on call twenty four hours a day.

When he went on a trip to the mainland later, I gave him a letter to mail from Chicago or anywhere in the middle of the North American continent. I told Yongmee not to look for me and promised to explain everything when the time was right. Although I kept her New York address, I have never written to her since. I should write her now. Perhaps they would forward the mail even if she has moved. Most of the Kwak gang have probably died during the war or forgotten about me in the intervening decades. Syngman Rhee died a long time ago, in Honolulu of all places, and his successors did not inherit his concerns. Nevertheless, nightmares and cold sweats were my frequent sleeping companions.

In fact I owed my saving of Mr. Kealoha's life to one of those nightmares. That night had been an especially bad one, and I couldn't go back to sleep. Getting out of bed, I noticed that Mr. Kealoha's pickup was not in the garage, nor were his fishing gear and boat trailer. He liked to go nightfishing and it was full tide. After looking around the property, I felt a strange desire to walk down the hill to the shore. The wind was high and sang shrilly. I fancied I heard something from the beach. The surf was throwing slammers into the cove, the salt spray fogging the air thick for miles around. The pickup was parked on the shoulder of the road at the edge of a haole koa grove. The boat had been un-hitched but the custom built eight foot surfboard was left on the pickup. I never had any interest in fishing, although I'd had to come down to the beach many times to help my boss. It seemed a singularly boring, unrewarding occupation, but he loved it. He said it made things right between him and his maker. I peered into the darkness, into the pale line dividing water and sky. Then as the wind whistled and the spray of salt dampened my skin, I heard a voice, a feeble desponding groan, that wafted uncertainly on the dashing wind.

"Hang on, Mr. Kealoha," I shouted at the top of my voice, although I was down wind and there was no chance of his hearing me. "Shout louder so I can see where you are."

There was silence for a few minutes. I was frantic. Perhaps a wave had swamped and drowned him. Then on the next shift of the wind I heard him again, out beyond the cove. Taking the surfboard, I splashed into the cold water. The wayward sea thrashed me and the jagged reef cut me up. Once the surfboard took off out of sight and I dismally contemplated swimming out unaided, but luckily I recovered it, jammed between reefs, and maneu-vered it over the inshore tumblers. He was clinging to a shelf of rock at the far edge of the cove. Every now and then a big incoming wave washed over his head and he hung on, unable to climb up or jump off into the water. It was uncanny how he had gotten washed up on the ledge after his boat had overturned some distance from the mouth of the cove.

Brought abreast of him by a wave, I pushed him off the rock. In vain I tried to steer him to the surfboard. This mountain of man, numbed with cold and fright, pinned me down and stood on top of me. I came up desperate for air, fighting off his strangling arms. In the next swell that washed over us, I kicked hard and dived with him in tow. Under water, his buoyancy made him lighter and more manageable. I propelled him toward the board, which twisted and bucked like a wild horse. Luckily, the big man's hands found the board and his arms went around it in an inexorable embrace. Using myself as a counterweight, I steadied its unruliness and nudged him to spread himself more evenly. From the rear I swam and pushed both man and craft until we were out of the swirling cove and headed for the open shore.

The huge but gentle and predictable undulations off the reef gave way to churning, boiling grinders that exploded into millions of fragments as we closed to the beach. We couldn't ride over them together. He was nearly done in from exposure and exhaustion. Though a fair swimmer, I couldn't have made my way in without the surfboard. Nobody could. But his condition didn't seem to allow any delay. I slid off and told him to move up the board and stretch himself, belly down, while I hung on behind and pushed it in. He told me to stop, divining my purpose. We should wait in the deep water until day came and people should come and look for us, he said, but even as he spoke, his big frame shook and convulsed with cold. I told him to hang on tight and shoved him off over the first rampart of the reef.

The board shot away like an arrow to disappear behind the ridges of surf, steel grey against the dark furrows. I barely managed to fight off a breaker bent on smashing and impaling me on the thousand subsurface teeth. The sea heaved up as high as Pupukea Plateau, then slid off to a great depth, to the very bowels of the earth, it seemed, blocking from view everything but the towering wave tops, roaring and breaking into showers, rivulets, and cascades. Something slimy caught at my feet; my whole body shrank with a scream, which was, however, quickly smothered by the clamor of waves that seemed like monsters poised on frothy rows of seething hills to pound and pulverize me. It was unfair to have to drown like this in the middle of the Pacific. Hadn't I paid my dues, those years of dodging and hiding in Korea, then the twenty years of servitude to an adipose Hawaiian? . . .

The sun had risen above the ironwoods of Pupukea, shining on my bed through the window. What a nightmare! I tried to get up, ashamed of my sloth. My arms and legs, in bandages, hurt. Mr. Kealoha came in with a deed of transfer making me owner of a hillside lot in Kahaluu.

"It isn't much now, nothing but rock and thistle, as you know," he said. "But you will make something of it. You are free to go to your own property as soon as you feel strong enough."

Nothing would dissuade this Hawaiian gentleman from making me this gift. He had a strain of royal blood in his veins and lived by a code of fairness unique to the native islanders. To refuse beyond what modesty required was to insult him, or worse, condemn him to the eternal vagabondage of the ingrate spirit in the nether world of Hawaiian theology. Eventually I learned to justfy the acquisition as a just payment for my years of free labor.

Roasting in the sun, I dug out rocks and boulders, some the size of a house, and battled the tough, exuberant weeds that would, if left alone, easily engulf a paved city. I sometimes doubted whether Mr. Kealoha had done me a favor at all, but five years of backbreaking, unremitting work, from dawn till long after sunset, began to pay off. Alas, I was a man of estate, a man of means, and these immigrant Koreans came to me for handouts.

A squall, sudden and gusty as usual, forced me to leave the lanai only to run into Deacon Cho, who smiled broadly, revealing all the gold of his molars. Somehow I didn't mind him at all. His officiousness, his vanity, his snakiness, all seemed more cute than diabolical, a perfect fit in the total design of nature. I smiled back to him cordially.

"Where have you been, Grandfather?" he said, grabbing my hand. "We are organizing a Committee for Re Immigration to the United Fatherland and we want you to be on it. You will, won't you?"

No Korean party was complete unless something grand was organized, to which everybody clapped and swore eternal allegiance. Of course nobody remembered a thing about it the next morning and it was bad manners even to bring it up. Deacon Cho was a well mannered Korean and so was everybody else at Shim's.

"Of course," I said cheerily, without the least reservation.

TY PAK *taught on the English faculty at the University of Hawaii from 1970 to 1987. His* *works include* Guilt Payment *and* Moonbay, *collections of short stories;* Cry Korea Cry, *a novel; and* A Korean Decameron, *a collection of Korean tales. In 2006 he moved to Honolulu, his true home, after living ten years in Los Angeles and ten years in New York City.*

Peter C. T. Li

"TAI CHI MASTERS OF DIM SUM CHECKS"

Like two Tai Chi masters practicing the art of the sticking hand
my father and my mother-in-law pushed each others' arms in
various circular motions while fighting for the prize of the *dim sum* check.
The check would be passed from hand to hand,
back and forth,
up and down,
round and round,
in sync with the Yin and the Yang motions of the universe.

Both dueled to save face in the name of family honor.
Armed with ancient secret techniques such as
"Crane Plucks Check from Tiger's Claw" and
"Buddha's Benevolent Palm Tipping the Waiter for Check."
It was no surprise that my father would defeat
my mother-in-law each outing and pay for the lunch.

The only time my father lost was when my mother-in-law
snuck away from the table while he was busy eating the last
siu mai of the meal.

I named her technique "Fox Stealing from Sleeping Monkey."

It was an unwritten Chinese tradition of the dining martial arts passed down through centuries from one generation to the next.

Dim sum and my in-laws at the China House Restaurant.

Charles Kong
"WELL, THEN"

I nevva had much for do and I was fooling around the corner of Ward and Queen when I sparked Donkey and his girl, Molly, crossing the street to catch the bus. "Hey," I yelled, "where you guys going?"

Molly waved at me, but that stink pot Donkey grabbed Molly by the arm and practically dragged her across the street without even telling me a "How'd do?" or a "Drop dead!" I tell you that burned me up. A punk like Donkey ignoring me as if I was nobody! Well, if you know my type, you know I no take no stuff like that from nobody, not from nobody. So I got my bumper up from the box I was sitting on and went up to them guys.

"What's the matta, Donkey?" I asked. "You steal your old lady's pants or something?"

Right away Donkey got his tail up in the clouds. "I nevva been do you nuttin', Flute. Why you stay everytime pick on me for?"

"Can you beat that, Molly," I says. "You no think Donkey's the super-stitches' guy you ever saw?" Then I faced Donkey and pulled in my mouth like them tough guys in the movies, and I let him have it from way down in my throat, like this guy Hogart or Bogart or whatever his name is. I says, "Donkey, I no like you insinyouwayshuns, see . . . "

Donkey thought I was mad and by the way his nose was twitching I knew he was plenty scared. "Flute, chee, you know how it is. No get mad. we was in a hurry . . . we . . . I mean . . . Molly . . . "

"You big fat-head! Why you blamin' me for? Why you no admit you stay scare of Flute?"

"What for I stay scare of Flute? Flute my friend. Nah right, Flute?"

What a worm! Trying to make good with me! "So you no scare of me, eh? Maybe you think you can lick me?" I gave him a jab in the shoulder. "You like pick me up?" I had the punk in the bag so scared he was. And the truth to tell I felt like rapping him right there and then. But I holded my temper, and I sasy to Molly, "what you ever see in this yellow insects?"

Donkey turned red in his big ears, and he opened and shut his fists as if he was squeezing . . . well, you know what. But I nevva give a care. I laughed. "You like make anything of it?"

He put his tongue in his backside and turned away. I took a swift step to him and grabbed his shirt, twisting him around. "What's the matta, Donkey? You no like my looks?"

"No . . . no, no, no, Flute. I tink you handsome."

"Leave him alone, stupid jackass!"

I swung around and almost pasted Molly. Lucky thing for her that me and her brudda, Kini, good friends. Not that I scared of him, but shucks, I no see no reason in going looking for troubles, especially with the boxing champ of the Navy. That's my style. I no pick on nobody. "Listen here, Molly, you shut you mouth or . . . " I sticked my jaw out like I saw Hopalong Cassidy in the show-house, and I let my body go relax. I bended my shoulders little bit and waited . . . that's how gunfighters supposed to look. Of course, Molly's no gunman, but I figga there was no harm in making her scare of me. I know I looked terrible, but with some womens you got to. You got to show them who's boss.

Molly barked like a dog with a belly ache. "Oh yeah! Oh yeah! You try! You try make me shut up." She swinged her purse overhead to konk me, but pitying her—I no hits womens—I ran behind Donkey.

"You jackass! You stupid jackass!" she screamed.

She slammed her purse down. I ducked, and Donkey was knocked flat on his okole. Poor Donkey. It was like the atomic bombs hitting him on the head. In fact, it was more worse. After all, considering the stuff womens carry around in their purse—from lipstick and candy and Exlax to cockroach powder—no wonder Donkey thought the angels had blowed their horns.

He had a silly look on his map. "What I been do you, Molly?"

"Oh, my baby Donkey . . . " She kneeled down on one knee and lifted Donkey's head onto her lap. "I'm so sorry, Donkey. I nevva mean hit you." She patted his head. "My poor, poor Donkey."

I tell you the sight of them disgusted me. I felt like spitting. "I no understand you womens," I says. "One minute you get teed off because Donkey blame you. Another minute you call him you baby jackass!"

Molly jumped up. She yanked at Donkey. "Get up Donkey and break his nose!"

"Hah!" I shifted on the balls of my feet like the main boy in "Gone with the Big Winds!" I put up my dukes and danced around Donkey the way I saw

Joe Louis do when he fought Sullivan in TRUE WONDER comics. But Donkey know me when I lost my head, and he standed there like a dummy begging me, "Take it easy, Flute. I no like fight. I no like fight."

"Yeah, Flute. Lay off Donkey. Someday you gonna get it. I feel like tell my brudda."

"Now, now, Molly, I not doing nothing. Chee, you guys no can take jokes?"

"Molly," Donkey said, "we gotta catch the bus. We no like be late."

"Where you guys going?"

"We going . . . "

Donkey groaned. "Molly, no . . . "

The damn Donkey. I was mad as hell. He get no right budding in. That's Molly's business if she like tell me where them guys going. I told Donkey. "What you say?" I was ready for kick his okole.

"Take it easy, Flute. Who you tink you? I tell you where we going. We going Punchbowl graveyard. 'At'swhere."

"You mean the graveyard where they bury the veterans?"

"Yeah. 'At's the one."

"What for? No more nothing up there for see except grass."

Molly laughed. "No be stupid, Flute. You know today King Kamehameha Day."

"Sure, so what? That no tell me nothing."

"You nevva read the papers?"

"Sure. You think I no can read?"

"Then you know they going bury King Kamehameha up Punchbowl graveyard. 'At's what the papers say."

"Oh, yeah! Yeah? I remember now. How could I forget! Now what that come out on . . . chee! Let me see . . . " I scratched my head. I nevva read no newspaper. I don't know even how to read. But I no like nobody know. Shame, eh, if they find out? I no like nobody think I'm dumb. So I says, "What the heck . . . chee, I sure get poor memory, Molly. I forget what page . . . "

"Came out in the o-bit-u-wary page. How come you fo'get? Boy, you sure get one lousy memory."

"Yeah, yeah, yeah, I rememba now."

"Plenty people going watch them bury King Kamehameha. He's the first veteran, you know."

"Sure, sure. I know all about that. You think I no can read for myself?"

Donkey was grinning. Molly grunted. "Okay, okay, Flute, you know everything. No bother us. We gotta go before too late. We no like miss see them bury Kamehameha."

"Okay, beat it. I going home dress. I meet you guys at the graveyard. I like see them bury Kamehameha too." I thought them guys was going to squawk, but they nevva open their traps one inch. I was surprised.

I took off home and shieked up. Then I went to the graveyard. But I nevva see nobody there. I nevva see Molly and Donkey, and I nevva see no peoples. I went look for the guy who take care of the graveyard, and I says to him, "Hey, Bull, they bury King Kamehameha already?" And he says, "You bet, Bub."

"Oh, no wonder."

"No wonder what."

"No wonder my pals nevva wait for me." I was turning for walk away when the guy says, "I don't get you, Bub?"

"What's the matta, Bull? You no read the papers?"

"Sure."

"Well then?" I walked away. Boy, I still no can see how stupid guys like him get all the slack jobs from the government.

CHARLES KONG, *part-Hawaiian, was born in 1931. His education ended in the eighth grade. When he was fourteen he was paralyzed in a diving accident. He was committed to a home for the indigent where for years a woman named Dorothy Blake carried packages of books up the steep hill for him to read. He began writing stories there. He left the facility at twenty-one and worked as a private instructor, real estate salesman, insurance salesman, stockbroker, hog farmer, and entrepreneur.*

Frank De Lima
"DA BLALLAH"

B ack in the late fifties there was a young local boy who emerged from the slums of Honolulu to become a rock and roll star. His first language was pidgin and he wrote his deeply personal and meaningful music in that dialect. In spite of the fact that no one could understand what he was saying, he had one smash hit.

But tragedy struck one day while he was driving his Volkswagen bug down Makapuu side on his way to a concert down Waimanalo Beach Park. His car flew over the cliff, got caught in one Japanese ulua fisherman's sugi line and sank to the bottom. He died.

But he left us with one island rock and roll classic that will live forever. His name: Itchy Valenz. The hit: "Da Blallah."

I'm a bla bla bla bla blallah
I'm a bla bla bla bla blallah
No boddah me
I stay Halekauwila
I work body and fendah
Stay live my car
My honey's place
My muddah's house
I stay eat Tasty Broilah
You no go mess with my sistah
I slap your head
I broke your nose
I bust your face
Blallah, Blallah
Blallah, Blallah
Blallah, Blallah
I'm a bla bla bla bla blallah
I'm a bla bla bla bla blallah
No boddah me
I make da kine big body
I like listen da radjo
Make any kine
Make any kine
Make any kine

There may be some of you unfamiliar with this local dialect. So, in fairness to you and to this sensitive song about the life of a local boy, we have translated it for you.

I'm a bla bla bla bla blallah
    (I am a large local fellow)
I'm a bla bla bla bla blallah
    (I am a large local fellow)
No boddah me
    (But it is of no consequence)
I stay Halekauwila
    (I frequent Honolulu's industrial district)
I work body and fendah
    (I am an automotive design specialist)
Stay live my car
My honey's place

My muddah's house
   (I have various places of residence)
I stay eat Tasty Broilah
   (Among my interests is gourmet dining)
You no go mess with my sistah
   (Please don't compromise my female siblings)
I slap your head
   (It does not sit well with me)
I broke your nose
   (And I can be very convincing)
I bust your face
   (Would you still like your ears in their present position?)
I'm a bla bla bla bla blallah
   (I'm a rather tall part-Polynesian male)
I'm a bla bla bla bla blallah
   (I'm a rather tall part-Polynesian male)
No boddah me
   (But it is of no consequence)
I like make da kine big body
   (I take self-improvement courses)
I like listen da radjo
   (I admire Beethoven and other classical composers)
Make any kine
   (I have a wide variety of interests)
Make any kine
   (I engage in a great range of activities)
Make any kine
   (I have a wide variety of interests and engage in a great range of activities)
Blallah, Blallah
Blallah, Blallah
Blallah, Blallah

Frank De Lima

"CAUCASIANS ARE STRANGE PEOPLE"

CHORUS:
Caucasians are strange people
Caucasians are strange, strange people
Caucasians are not like you and me

It's like they come from another planet
Their skin gets red when they try to tan it
They wear plaid socks, plaid shirts, plaid pants
They call their uncles "unks" and their aunties "aunts"
They talk too fast and they laugh too loud
They embarrass you when you're in a crowd
They got lots of friends and lots of money
They think Andy Bumatai is funny

Don't want no Caucasians, don't want no
Caucasians, don't want no Caucasians around here.

If you are at a party and everybody is hanging out,
drinking beer and grinding aku poke, and you jump
up and say, "Anybody want to play charades?" you are . . . HAOLE!
If your toes overlap from being in shoes too long, you are . . . HAOLE!
If you like pasta salad, but not macaroni salad, you are . . . HAOLE!

CHORUS:
Caucasians are strange people
Caucasians are strange, strange people
Caucasians are not like you and me
They're smarter than you and smarter than me
But they can't tell sushi from sashimi
Their men wear a size 14 shoe
They don't put tomato sauce in their stew
They'll eat kalua pig, but they won't touch poi
They always talk about life in Illinois

Don't want no Caucasians, don't want no
Caucasians, don't want no Caucasians around here.

If your name is Bruce, or Rick, or Betsy, or Laura, you are . . . HAOLE!
If you look older than you really are, you are . . . HAOLE!
If old Japanese men hate your guts, you are . . . HAOLE!

CHORUS:
Caucasians are strange people
Caucasians are strange, strange people
Caucasians are not like you and me

They buy aloha pants for their aloha shirt
They eat a Japanese dinner and they want dessert
They'll spend two weekends in Lahaina
And then call themselves a kamaaina
Their face, arms, legs, nose are all too long
They think "Tiny Bubbles" is a Hawaiian song
They put two pads of butter on their two scoops rice
They eat snow cones, but not shave ice
Don't want no Caucasians, don't want no
Caucasians, don't want no Caucasians around here.

FRANK DE LIMA, *born in Honolulu in 1949, is an award-winning comedian who has been entertaining audiences for more than thirty years. As the proclaimed Portuguese Prince of Hawaiian Comedy, he has headlined in nightclubs, and has performed at sold-out concerts and events throughout Hawai'i, along the West Coast, and in Las Vegas. He has produced numerous audio and visual works. He is also the founder of Frank De Lima's Student Enrichment Program, a non-profit organization devoted to Hawai'i's keiki (children).*

Kapono Beamer, Keola Beamer, and Bob Magoon
"MR. SUN CHO LEE"

Mr. Sun Cho Lee
Got plenty lychee
Got plenty lychee
But he no gives to me
And he's just a mean old pake man

Mr. Conrad Jones
Get plenty swimming pools
Plenty swimming pools
But he no gives to me
And he's just a mean old haole man

Mr. Maximo Concepcion
Got plenty fighting chicken
Got plenty fighting chicken
But he no gives to me
And he's just a mean old Pilipino man

Mr. Kazuo Tanaka
Got plenty camera supply
Got plenty camera supply
But he no gives to me
And he's just a mean old Kepanee man

Miss Momi Lomilomi
Got plenty experience
Got plenty experience
She no experience me
And she's just a mean old cocktail waitress

Mr. Kamakawiwoʻole
Got plenty not too much of nothing
Got plenty nothing
He takes it out on me
And he's just a mean old Hawaiian man

One ting I wen notice bout dis place
All us guys we tease the other race
It's amazing we can live in the same place.

KEOLA AND KAPONO BEAMER *are members of a multi-generational family of distinguished Hawaiian musicians and dancers. In the 1970s they performed highly successfully as the Beamer Brothers. Keola is a master of the Hawaiian slack key guitar style, kīhōʻalu. He was one of the first to blend traditional Hawaiian chants and instruments with contemporary influences. He composed "Honolulu City Lights," one of Hawaiʻi's top-selling songs of all time. Kapono is a guitarist, composer, singer, arranger, producer and recording engineer. He has won twelve Nā Hōkū Hanohano awards. His CD,* Slack Key Dreams of the Ponomoe, *was nominated for a 2006 Grammy Award for Hawaiian Album of the Year.*
EATON "BOB" MAGOON, JR., *a Honolulu real estate developer, wrote three Hawaiʻi-based musicals that had brief Broadway runs between 1961 and 1971:* 13 Daughters; Heathen! *and* Aloha. *He was also a founding partner of the famous Waikīkī club, Hula's Bar & Lei Stand.*

Charles K. Y. Khim and Wayne Takazono

from HE'S A NICE BOY, BUT ...

MONDAY AFTER THE GAME

SOME COMMON STEREOTYPES

HAOLES: LOUD-MOUTHED AND ALWAYS TRY TO PLAY UP
          TO THE TEACHER

JAPANESE: THEY ARE SNEAKY
          THEY WILL SMILE IN YOUR FACE AND STAB YOU IN THE BACK

FILIPINOS: THEY ARE STUPID, ONLY GOOD FOR JANITORS
           AND GARDENERS
           THEY WEAR FLASHY CLOTHES—THEY ALWAYS WEAR
           PURPLE AND RED

KOREANS: HOT TEMPERED AND THEIR MOUTHS STINK
         FROM EATING TOO MUCH KIM CHEE

CHINESE: THEY ARE TIGHT WITH THEIR MONEY

6.

Mavis Hara

"VISITING HICKAM AIR FORCE BASE, 1956"

He bursts through
the perfectly squared hedge
of a Hickam Air Force Base yard,
7 year old boy
in striped T-shirt and blue jeans.

"Get away from my dog" he yells.

I withdraw my 7 year old hand
from the soft fur of this puppy
that waddled under the hedge
a few moments before.
I sit back with a thump
but remember to squeeze
my thighs shut
and pull my skirt safely down
over my knees. My mother
told me there is something there
that is dangerous.

He straddles the dog
John Wayne style
blonde crewcut exploding
like glass from his scalp,
his eyes hard, blue
like veins.

"I know what you are!"
He yells, he advances.

"Don't you hurt my dog."
He hurls words at me
his fists clenched like grenades.

I run back to our car
and hide in the dark
on the floor of the back seat.
I cover my head with my hands.
I squeeze my eyes shut tight.
"You're a Jap," he screams.
I have just learned
my Japanese eyes
are dangerous.

Milly Lou Donnelly
"PART-SOJER"

A visitor in the Palama District noticed the blue, blue eyes of a dark-skinned lad and asked his nationality. In an accustomed manner, he replied, "Part Hawaiian, part sojer."

Edward Sakamoto
from A'ALA PARK

Cast:
JOJO, *MANNY'S brother, about fourteen*
JEANIE, *MANNY'S girlfriend*
SWEENEY, *a white sailor in his mid-twenties*
MANNY, *about twenty, with dark, brooding eyes*
BEAR, *MANNY'S buddy, burly, mean-looking but good-natured*
CHAMP, *built like a boxer, age nineteen*
CABRAL, *a lanky Portuguese, age nineteen*
Place: *A low-income section of Honolulu, in A'ala Park area.*
Time: *Late summer 1959, the year of statehood.*

JOJO: Aeh, wait, I tink I hear somebody coming.
　　　(The gang hides in the shadows. JEANIE and SWEENEY enter. He's dressed in a short-sleeved plaid shirt and khaki pants.)
JEANIE: Well, you betta go now. I gotta get home.
SWEENEY: I thought maybe I'd take you to your front door.
JEANIE: No, I'm okay.
SWEENEY: Meeting you at the bowling alley was lucky for me. I was getting bored at the Y. Can I see you again?
JEANIE: I work at the alley, so if you like bowling . . .
SWEENEY: Some of my buddies went looking for dames, but I had my eye out for somebody special. Someone like you.
JEANIE: Well, you know, I get one boyfriend.
SWEENEY: Yeah, I got a girl in Oregon. Her name's Margie. I kinda hope she's waiting for me, but . . . Been to Oregon?
JEANIE: No, neva left da Islands.
SWEENEY: Oregon's got some nice beaches too. Different from Hawai'i's but still beautiful. Maybe you'll visit me sometime.

JEANIE: Maybe. Well, gotta go.

SWEENEY: Wait. I was thinking maybe we could go have some coffee and talk.

JEANIE: I don't think so. Too late.

SWEENEY: I got no place to go. Haven't talked to a pretty girl in I don't know how long.

MANNY: Aeh, haole, wat you tink you doing here? *(The gang emerges and surrounds SWEENEY.)* You no going answer me? Who you tink you, eh?

JEANIE: Manny . . .

MANNY: Shaddup.

SWEENEY: I guess you two know each other. Sorry. I just met her tonight. I mean, hey, I wasn't trying anything.

BEAR: Lying bastard.

MANNY: You tink you was going get one easy time wit' her, eh?

JEANIE: Leave 'um alone. He neva do nuttin'. Let 'um go.

MANNY: Go 'way.

JEANIE: No.

MANNY: You like I kick your ass home?

SWEENEY: Boy, nobody told me the natives would be restless tonight.

CHAMP: Aeh, you making fun of us?

SWEENEY: No, don't take it the wrong way. I was just kidding.

CABRAL: We not laughing.

SWEENEY: Yeah, yeah. Hey, ah, wait. My friends call me Sweeney.

MANNY: We wen' ask you fo' your name? Wat da hell we care wat your name?

SWEENEY: Listen, I'm stationed at Pearl and—

CHAMP: One sailor boy, eh. I hear you guys get one girl in every port.

CABRAL: Yeah, you tink you one real lova, eh, one real Casanova.

SWEENEY: Bet I could learn a lot from you guys.

BEAR: Getting mo' and mo' cocky.

MANNY: You tink you so tarrific, eh, you really looking fo' trouble.

SWEENEY: No, no. Hey, why don't we shake and be friends, huh?

JOJO: I be your friend.

MANNY: Shaddup!

JOJO: We go be friends wit' him.

SWEENEY: Yeah, that's great, yeah.

> *(SWEENEY offers his hand to JOJO. MANNY shoves JOJO aside. OLDER MANNY stands next to MANNY.)*

MANNY: I said go home now!

JEANIE: Manny, he was only lonesome to talk to somebody.

MANNY: 'S wat you tink.

CABRAL: How 'bout we teach dis haole one lesson?

CHAMP: He tink he hot shit.

(*SWEENEY tries to get away, but* MANNY *blocks him.*)
MANNY: Where you tink you going, haole?
BEAR: You going get your medicine.
JOJO: Manny, no cause trouble.
MANNY: Go home befo' I slap your head. You hear me?
    (*MANNY shoves JOJO, who falls backward to the ground.*)
BEAR: Aeh, haole, we going make sure you neva come dis way again.
MANNY: I take my cut first.
    (*MANNY throws a couple of punches, then the rest of the gang piles into* SWEENEY,
    punching and kicking until he crumples to the ground. JEANIE *runs off.* OLDER
    MANNY *stands aside, watching solemnly.*)
BEAR: Weak bugga.
CABRAL: Wat you expect from one haole.
CHAMP: I got in one low blow fo' payback.
MANNY: Get your ass going. And if you like mo' trouble, you know where you
    can find us. (*SWEENEY struggles to get up, then stumbles weakly out of the alley.*)
BEAR: Now I can sleep good tonight.
CABRAL: Yeah, I had my fun.

Gary Chang

"THREE MAMMALS INDIGENOUS TO HAWAI'I BEFORE MAN'S ARRIVAL: THE HAWAIIAN MONK SEAL, THE HAWAIIAN BAT AND CAPTAIN ALOHA"

You got pissed off when the *haole*
wearing one Greenpeace T-shirt asked you if you wanted
for be their poster. Good thing plenty people
Lanikai Beach.

You stroked your Buddha-head, flicked off one stink-eye,
but your beard grinned. Sand funneled down your cut-off
jeans. Whenever you stood for shake 'em out, everybody
near us looked the other way.
            A blue-green Samoan
muscle ring tattooed your left arm just under the shoulder.
Construction scars—*Call me the Saw Man*—callused
your thick palms, Popeye forearms.
Least you kept all your fingers.
            "Can I go play water,

Daddy," asked Tiny.
You nodded.
How come when one four-year-old baby
weighs hundred twenty pounds, all his buds call
him *Tiny*?
"Go lie down some more, Captain Aloha,"
I said, "I watch him."

Good thing was Tiny woke you, your son
wearing the Greenpeace T-shirt.
Kolohe poured water from his plastic bucket
into your jeans.
"Their skin cannot dry out or they make,
like die," Tiny shouted, right
out of the Discovery Channel.
You jumped up,
Fucka
almost out your mouth. Now
everybody staring at us.
You think he cared? *Nah*, your son went shove his crotch
at you, grabbed his *ōkole*.
"Honk-honk."
Get out my face, you scolded him.
Tiny's thick legs pumping all the way
back to his cousins.
Braddah, you one sick puppy.

Must've been cold,
that water. But you never even wipe off.
Instead you reached
for your shades.
Gotta love 'em, Grey,
biker-beard grinning again.
"Yup, Captain,"
Tiny pointed at us, honking his butt.

"gotta love 'em."

GARY CHANG *was born and raised in Honolulu. His honors thesis won him the Hemingway Undergraduate Poet of the Year Award from the University of Hawai'i. At Colorado State University, Fort Collins, he received an MFA in poetry in 2001 while teaching classes in composition and ethnicity. He currently lives in Hawai'i.*

Jeremias A. Calixto

"MAYSA A MALEM ITI AALA PARK"

Adu ti napipintas a parke iti Hawaii: nalinongan kadagiti narukbos a kayo, naaplagan iti nalangto a ruot a kas berde nga alpombra, naarkosan kadagiti nadumadumat' marisna a sabsabong. Adda dita ti Ala Moana Park, ti Waikiki Beach Park, ti Manoalua Garden Park, ti Hanauma Beach Park, ti Sea Life Park, ti Waimanalo Park, ti Sand Island Park, inaganam laeng adda dita. Kinapudonona, kasla maysa a park ti sibubukel a Hawaii.

Ngem kadagiti Filipino old-timers iti Hawaii, awan kas iti Aala Park iti nagsasangalan dagiti kalsada nga Aala, Beretania ken King, Honolulu. Kadagiti lallakay a Filipino-dagiti immuna a sakada-ti Aala Park ti paglinglingayan ken pangpalabasan kadagiti darikmat a manglaglagip iti napalabas ken iti daga a nakayanakan. Napno ti Aala Park iti drama ti biag kadagiti lallakay a Filipino (kaaduanna ti Ilokano). Kadagiti Filipino nga awan pagtaenganna, ti Aala Park ti sangbayanda.

Maysa a malem, inrantak ti simmarungkar sadiay. Kas kadawyan, adu latta ti old-timers wenno senior citizens a nakatugaw kadagiti naipalawlaw iti sirok dagiti kayo. Nagtugawak a nakidenna kadakuada. Iluko ti pagsasaoda. Pagsasaritaanda ti maipapan kadagiti kabagianda a simmangpet manipud iti Filipinas ken dagiti pinanawanda nga ay-ayaten. Aggigidiat ti bengngatda. Adda bengngat taga-Ilocos Sur ken taga-Norte.

Adda lakay a Hapones nga agibumbunong kadagiti numero wenno tiket. Adda met gayam ay-ayamda a kasla hueteng a kas kadagiti small town lottery iti Filipinas. Adu met ti naggatang kadagiti numero kadagiti kailian.

Adda lakay nga agpakpakan iti pangen ti kalapati iti asidegmi. Adu ti kalapati. Ipuruak ti lakay ti ipakanna. Naamo dagiti kalapati. Iti Hawaii, saan a ranggasan dagiti tao dagiti tumatayyab. Saanda ida a paltogan wenno palsiitan. Pakanenda ida a kas taraken.

Adda sumagmamano a taripnong a nakapakleb iti karuotan. Agdengdengngegda iti tokar ti radio nga intogotda. Iti maysa a bangir iti parke, adda lalaki nga agsalsala iti moderno. Naparagsit. Lagto a lagto. Tiritir a tiritir. Pasaray agkinkingod.

Iti sabali a bangir ti parke, adda taripnong a nanglawlaw iti lamisaan iti sirok ti nasalumpayak a baliti. Immasidegak. Adda agay-ayam iti inipis, chess ken dama.

Adda dua a lakay nga agay-ayam iti dama. Adda pustada. Lima a doliar ti maysa a taya. Nagwingiwing ti maysa idi agkakanayon a naabak.

"Isunan," kinunana Inwalinna dagiti peon. "Maulawakon." Inruarna ti petakana. Nagbayad iti abakna. Aglimapulo a doliar.

Nakatakderak iti likudan ti naabak a lakay. Tinangadnak ti nangabak "Kayatmo met a padasen?"

"Padasek man no diak pay nalipatan," kinunak.

Implastarmi dagiti peon iti daina.

"Bassit laeng," kinuna ti lakay a kasangok. "Basta paglinglingayan. Lima a dollar?"

"Mapan," kinunak.

Sakbay ti ipapanko iti Hawaii, nagkamkampeonakon iti tournament ti dama. Saanak nga agsugal. Ngem maituredko ti makipusta iti dama.

Rinugianmi ti agay-ayam. Naabakak-wenno nagpaabakak-kadagiti immuna nga ay ayam. Padpadasek pay laeng ti gunayna.

"Nayonanta ti pusta," inkarit ti lakay. "Uray sagsapangulo laeng."

"Shoot," kinunak.

Tabla dagiti immuna nga ay ayammi. Ngem idi masanaykon ti gunayko. saanen a mangabak Napintas." ti lakay. Adda pay nagsasaruno a pito a kanayon a naabak. Idi agangay add an abakna nga agsangagasut a doliar.

"Nayonanta pay, manong?" inkaritko. "doblienta?"

"Saanen. Nasakiten ti ulok," kinunana. "Ken nadagsen ti gunayrno. Mano ti abakko?"

"Sangagasut ket sangapulo laeng" kinunak.

Inruarna ti petakana. Inyawatna kaniak ti limapulo a doliar.

"Dispensarem, adi. Daytoy laeng ti maitedko. Bassit ti kuartak," kinunana.

"Okay lang, manong," kinunak. Saan a ti inabakko ti nasken kaniak. Basta napadasak manen ti agay ayam iti daina ken makilangen kadagiti kailiak. Makayaman ti langana iti pannangawatko iti kurang a pagbayadna.

"Taga anotayo idiay Filipinas?" dinamagna.

"Vintar, idiay Norte. Ket taga Laoagka?"

"Apay nga ammom?"

"Iti heng atmo ammok latta."

"Agkaarrubata," kinunana.

Nagarn ammc kami. Crispin T . . . ti, naganna

"Immayyak pay la ditoy jdj 1928," kinunana. "Duapulo ti tawenko idi. Dakami ti iinmuna a sakada."

"Ket nagtrabahoka iti kaunasan?"

"Iti kaunasan,"

"Nabayag a panawen," kinunana.

"Dika pay nagbalikbayan?"

"Idi 1980. Napanak nangasawa."

"Nagimbagen," kinunak.

"Ubing. Duapulo ket lima laeng ti tawerina.

"Nagsayaaten."

"Ti kunam, adi. Ngem dakes a gasat. Innalak ditoy. Kunak la idi no kas iti pagpatinggaan ti santa ti banagmi a kanayonkami a naragsak. Ngem idi agbayag, nakasarak iti saan nga ubanan ken kuretret a kas kaniak. Napanna sinurot. Pinanawannak!" Natibnokan iti liday ti timekna.

"Kasta ti panagasawa. Kasla ay ayam 'ti dama. Mangabak.maabak," kinunak.

"Naimbag pay iti dama ta adda dagiti naimbag a mangabak a kas kenka. Mabalinka a saranayen ken pakawanen no maabakka."

Diak napuotan, limnek gayamen ti in it. Kaniton ti panagawidko idiay Salt Lake, paset ti Honolulu, a pagnaedak.

"Sadino met ti pagtaengam, Manong Crispin?" dinamagko.

"Saannak a sinungbatan daras. Kinitanak a kasla dma ammo ti isungbatna wenno sungbatannak wenno saan.

"Awan ti masnop," kinunana. "Kaslaak la balang nga agallaalla iti pagyanan. Kasla umang nga agakar akar. Ditoyak a maturog iti Aala Park."

(Adda dagiti awanan iti pagtaengan iti Honolulu. Agnaed, inaturogda iti Aala Park.)

Agsipngeten iti Aala Park.

Inruarko ti iriabakko a kuarta ti lakay. Im¬pisokko ti bolsanan. Ket napanakon limmugan iti asideg a bus stop.

"ONE AFTERNOON AT AALA PARK"

T here are many pretty parks in Hawaii: shaded with profuse trees, carpeted with fresh grass so green like alhombra, decorated with arches of flowers of different colors. There is Ala Moana Park, Waikiki Beach Park, Moanalua Garden Park, Hanauma Beach Park, Sea Life Park, Waimanalo Park, the Sand Island Park, name it they are there. The truth is Hawaii is like a whole park.

But for the Filipino old timers in Hawaii, there's nothing like Aala Park at the intersection of Aala, Beretania and King Streets in Honolulu. To many Filipino old men, the first sakadas, Aala Park is their place to rest and play and pass time to remember the past and the land where they were born. Aala Park is full with the drama of the lives of these older Filipino men, most of them Ilocano. Those without residence, Aala Park is their home.

One afternoon, I purposedly went to visit there. As usual, there are always many old timers or senior citizens sitting around the shaded tables that surrounded the trees. I sat down next to them. They are speaking Ilocano, talking about their newly arrived relatives in Hawaii and their love ones they left in the Philippines. Their accents varied, some sounds from Ilocos Sur, others from Norte.

There is also a Japanese old man distributing tickets and numbers papers. Ah, they have games here too, like hueteng, those daily lotteries in the Philippines. So many bought.

There is an old man throwing feed to a clan of pigeons near us. The pigeons are tame. In Hawaii, people don't harm the birds. They don't shoot or slingshot them. They feed them like pets.

There are some group of people laying on their stomachs on the grass listening to music from their radios. On one side of the park, there is a man dancing. He is very sprite jumping, twisting and sometimes heaving his hips.

On another side of the park, there is a gatherings around tables under the big shady banyan tree. I went nearby. Some were playing cards, chess and checkers.

There are two men playing checkers. They have bets. Five dollars for one bet. One shook his head when he kept losing.

"Enough," he said. He pushed the peons off the board. "I'm dizzy already." And he took out his wallet and paid his loss. Fifty dollars.

I was standing behind the old man who lost. The winner looked up at me and said, "You wanna try, too?"

"I will try . . . if I haven't forgotten," I said.

We placed the peons.

"Small bets only, okay?" the old man said. "Just to relax. Five dolyar?"

"Okay, we go."

Before I came to Hawaii, I was tournament champion in checkers sometimes. I am not a gambler, but I'm not afraid to bet in checkers.

We started to play. I lost or purposedly lose the first games. I was just trying so see his moves.

"Let's increase da bets," challenged the old man. "Ten dollars only?"

"Shoot," I said.

The first game was tie. Then I got my moves, and the old man never won again. After awhile he had lost a hundred dollars.

"We bet more, Manong?" I challenged. "Double?"

"Neh, enough. My head aches already. Your moves are heavy. How much is my loss?"

"One hundred ten only," I replied.

He took out his wallet. He handed me fifty dollars.

"Please forgive me, Adi, Younger Brother. This is all I can give. I only have little money." he said.

"That's okay, Manong," I said. It's not what I won that is important to me. As long as I tried playing checkers and mix closely with my townmates. His face was thankful when I received his reduced loss payment.

"Where are we from the Philippines?" he asked.

"Vintar in Norte. And you from Laoag?"

"How do you know?"

"Your accent I know."

"We are neighbors," he said.

We got to know each other. Crispin T . . . is his name.

"I came here in 1928," he said. "I was twenty years old. We were the first sakadas."

"You worked in the sugar cane fields?"

"In the canefields."

"Many long years," he said.

"Did you ever balikbayan, go home and come back?"

"In 1980. I went back and got married."

"That's good," I said.

"Young girl. Twenty five years old. Pretty."

"That's so good."

"Das what you say, Adi. But it was bad fate. I brought her here. I thought we would live happily together forever till the end of our times like we agreed. But not long afterwards, she found someone without grey hair and wrinkling skin, and she followed him. She left me!" His voice was doused with sadness.

"Das how marriage is. Just like the game of checkers. You win, you lose." I said.

"It's good with checkers, that someone wins like you. I can help you and forgive you when you lose."

I didn't realize that the sun had gone down. It's the time for me to go home to Salt Lake, a part of Honolulu where I live.

"Where do you live, Manong Crispin?" I asked.

He did not answer right away. He looked at me as if he didn't know what to say or even answer me.

"I don't have a home," he said. "I am like a loose animal, go wherever to stay. Like a loner go from place to displace. I sleep here at the park."

(There are homeless in Honolulu. They live and sleep in Aala Park.)

It's getting dark in Aala Park.

I took out the money I won from the old man. I put it in his pocket. And I boarded the bus at the bus stop near by us.

TRANSLATED BY VIRGILIO MENOR FELIPE

JEREMIAS A. CALIXTO, *born in 1917, is Dean of Student Affairs at the College of Education of Mariano Marcos State University in Laoag, Philippines. He is a World War II veteran. He was named Outstanding Ilokano Writer by the National Press Club in 1980; Outstanding Writer of the Year, by GUMIL in 1990; and received the UMPIL award Union Ng Mga Manunulat, in 1991. He worked with Pacita Saludes, the president of GUMIL Hawai'i, on Annak ti Kailokuan iti America. He has six children with Trinidad A. Camaquin.*

Elmer Omar "Hammurabi" Pizo
"BLACK DOG (PINOY STYLE)"

Beloved Frank de Limas, Willy Ks,
every time you meet me on the narrow
streets of waipahu or ewa or kalihi,
 in wedding celebrations or birthday parties,
in the mortuaries or pharmacies,
in the supermarkets or churches,
even in the schools or cinema houses,
you never fail to ask me about that
                                    black dog.

There's not a need to defend ourselves.
It's impractical, it's useless!
Yet, I, a typical pinoy dog eater,
considered the most shameful remnant
of this human race, still need to set
this black dog thing in a more relevant
perspective.

The smell of dog adobo floating lightly
through your aquiline noses is way,
way different from the real feeling,
from the real thing.
May it be tame or wild dog,
May it be trained or neglected dog,
May it be smart or idiot dog,
May it be rice-fed or chow-fed dog,
May it be pure-bred or native dog,
May it be yellow or brown dog,
When you roast them, their skin always
turns black anyway.

ELMER OMAR "HAMMURABI" PIZO, *born in 1960 in Asingan, Philippines, is now a seventeen-year resident of O'ahu. He was a Poetry Fellow at the Vermont Studio Center. His poems have been published by* Bamboo Ridge; Hawai'i Review; *and in the* Likhaan *of the Creative Writing Center, University of the Philippines-Diliman. He is an Inspector II at the Vector Control Branch of the Department of Health, State of Hawai'i.*

Henry Chun

from KINDNESS TO COBRAS

Cast

BENNY

JIMMY, *his younger brother*

KEELA, *his henchman*

COBRA, *his enemy*

YOUNG VOICE

Scene: The place is the outskirts of the Kalihi section of Honolulu. The scene is the interior of a small, unpainted, run-down shack of the type that boys like to use for clubhouses. Only two walls can be seen, the corner being at right center, from the audience's point of view.

Each wall has a window opening, with an awning-like shutter propped up by a stick. There is no glass, nor any window sashes. The left wall has a door at its left end. The door, too, is crudely made. In the beginning of the play, the door is ajar, and the windows open. Bright mid-afternoon sunshine comes in through them, flooding the bare dirt floor with light. Through the windows can be seen the dark-green koa haole trees in the background. A few of them grow right outside the windows.

When the curtain rises, a babble of young voices is heard coming from a distance. Some are high, shrill childish voices, others are low and grown-up, but all are tough and raucous. The wild discussion continues for some time. At last, after rising to a sudden crescendo, the bedlam stops. Several seconds pass, then COBRA, bound and gagged, is shoved violently from behind the room.

COBRA is a wild, ferocious-looking Filipino boy of sixteen. He is of medium height, and thin, but wiry. He wears very narrow-cuffed jeans and a red and blue striped tee shirt. KEELA, who had propelled him through the door, comes in next, followed closely by BENNY and JIMMY. BENNY is a tough-looking part-Hawaiian boy of eighteen. He is the biggest and huskiest of all the boys. He wears a dirty pair of khaki pants, but no shirt. JIMMY, his younger brother, is fifteen. He is a nice-looking boy, but has a truculent expression. He wears a dirty blue-yellow football jersey inside out. KEELA is almost as vicious looking as COBRA. He is about as tall as BENNY, but lean and stringy, not well-built like the Hawaiian boy. He is a Puerto Rican with brown, curly hair and long, curling eyelashes. He wears a filthy white tee shirt and black dungarees. None of the boys wear shoes, all except COBRA have knives stuck in their belts.

BENNY *(to someone outside the door)*: G'wan beat it, you yellow rat!

YOUNG VOICE: Okay, okay, no need act tough.

KEELA: You like one crack in da head? *(He starts towards the door.)*

BENNY: Led 'um go. *(KEELA stops in his tracks and turns around.)*

KEELA: Wy you let da kine small keed get smart weet' you? If he tell dat to me, I slap 'um in da head. *(turning to COBRA)* Now you going to get yours. *(He takes a spiked brass knuckle from his pocket, and puts it on. He is about to swing at COBRA when BENNY stops him.)*

BENNY: Hey, wait, no keel 'um yet, Keela.

KEELA *(grumbling)*: Wen you going be ready?

JIMMY: Lemme hit 'um once too, Benny, huh, Benny?

BENNY *(holding up his hand)*: Wait, wait, wait teel I tell you. We gotta decide what we going do wid 'um, first. *(COBRA glares balefully at him.)*

KEELA *(angrily)*: Wy da hell you no just lemme smash hees goddam face een, like he deed my brudda.

BENNY: Wassamadda, you like heem mahke o' hea? Den what we going to do wid 'um? Use you head, man. *(KEELA glowers at him.)*

JIMMY: Lemme hit 'um once, hah Benny?

BENNY: You wait.

JIMMY: Jus' once, okay?

BENNY: Bimeby, bimeby! Lemme teenk first!

KEELA: What da hell you like do, use 'um fo' decoration?

BENNY: Some day, Keela, I going feex you, you act smart.

KEELA *(exploding)*: You teenk I going wait all day fo' bus' up dees sonova-beetch? Heem an' hees gang wen go smash my brudda, an' I no going wait! *(anguished by the memory)* My brudda no mo' face, now, an' I going do da same to dees Goddamn bugga! *(Once again he draws his arm back.)*

BENNY: Keela, you dumb head! Bime by you keel 'um, yet! Den how you going make 'um suffa! *(KEELA reluctantly drops his arm. COBRA, who has been straining desperately at his ropes, lets out a horrible, animal snarl of helpless rage.)*

JIMMY: Look, hees leg rope coming loose.

BENNY: At's nottin. We makeum loose, so he can walk. Udawise, we have to carry heem all da way from Kalakaua School. *(to KEELA)* See, wen you use you head, you save trouble.

KEELA *(still grumbling)*: Okay, what we going do now? We bedda made queek. Bimeby hees gang come, den what? We all jam up.

BENNY: Wassamadda, you yellow? Da hell wid hees gang. In fact, how dey going find dees place? Nobody know owa hideout.

JIMMY: Yeah, nobody come o' hea. Too many bushes. Hey, we go make dees guy lie down, an' we sit on hees head, an' erry body else line up an' take turns keeck hees face in wit' combat boots.

BENNY: No can, nobody get shoes. Besides, no mo' 'nuff guys. Da uda guys all yellow.

JIMMY: Dey sked Cobra gang bus' 'um up, dass wy.

BENNY: Wat da hell you teenk dey been doing all yea? Playing hop scotch? Hell, almos' all us guys been lump up already, Dis damn son of a bitch *(indicating COBRA)* no geeve chance. Dey fight fo' keel, da damn buggas. Fo' of us guys lose eyeball awready, tree guys get broke ribs.

KEELA: Hell, he no going get chance from me! Een fact, nobody geeve chance in gang fight. Dey all fight to win, nobody care for fight fair. *(bitterly)* Ony us suckers!

BENNY *(threateningly)*: Wassamadda, you no like da way run da gang, or what?

KEELA: I tell you, we stupid fo' geeve chance! Nobody geeve us chance! Dey poke owa eyeball out, dey jump on owa ribs, dey do ennything!

BENNY: Okay, okay! Eef you like be like dat, wy you no join deir gang?

KEELA: Join what gang? Eef dey see me, boy, I dead duck.

JIMMY: Yeah, you mark' man, awready.

BENNY: All us guys mark' man eef dey ketch us by owa self.

KEELA: Come on, we wasting time! We gotta take care dees guy yet, *(spitting into his palms and rubbing them in anticipation)* Hey, I going to town on dis baby! Imagine, me busting up Cobra Cabotahe, da beeg shot of da Kalihi T'eata gang!

BENNY: I like take care heem, too! He da one wen go knife Mickey las' week.

JIMMY *(in surprise)*: Yeah? Heem da one wen knife Meeckey? *(COBRA strains at his bonds again, glaring hatefully at them.)*

KEELA: Heem da one smash my bruda face. I no going foget dat!

BENNY: He knife my bes' frien', too, wen he not looking!

JIMMY: Yay, we keel 'um

KEELA: We chop off hees toes! Make 'um walk from hea to home!

BENNY: Dass a good idea. Or we can deeg out hees eyeballs. *(He makes a clawing motion with his hands.)*

KEELA: How about pulling off all hees finga nails weet' one pliya, den stepping on hees feenga? Dass what hees gang done to Keala.

JIMMY: Cut off hees ea! Dass what, cut off hees ea!

KEELA: Naah! We cut off hees long john! Hey, dass da bes' one yet! *(COBRA, in a rage, shrieks a snarl of furious frustration at this suggestion.)*

JIMMY: I bet he hate us, no?

KEELA *(drawing a long, World War I bayonet from his belt)*: Mo' betta we keel 'um, so he no can do nottin' back to us! Jimmy! Close da weendos! *(JIMMY does so.)* Now I get my revenge!

JIMMY *(jumping up and down)*: Yeah, we cut open hees stoma' , an' pull out all hees guts, one by one! *(He makes a pulling motion.)*
(KEELA goes up to the helplessly struggling COBRA, and jabs his bayonet sharply into his abdomen. COBRA jerks back, and contorts his face in a horrible grimace

of agony, KEELA *keeps on jabbing harder and harder, and* COBRA *finds it increasingly difficult to keep from screaming in pain.)*

KEELA *(exultantly):* Haha! I keel you slowly, so you got planny time to remember all da tings you done to me an' my brudda!

BENNY: Keela! Enough! You like puka through? Den he mahke, we all jam up.

KEELA *(angrily):* Wuffo we bring heem up hea? Fo' make heem happy?

BENNY: Who running dis, you or me?

KEELA *(still furious):* Who done all da dirty work? Who wen go be decoy? Who get all bust up, jus' fo' trap heem? In fact, I teenk you sked smash heem! You sked hees gang!

BENNY: Oh, yeah? Who wen help you las' week wen you was bein' bust up by twenny guys? Who wen get keeck een da nuts jus' fo' help you?

KEELA: Den wy you no like I smash heem, den? Wy you so sked he mahke?

BENNY: Eef you keel 'um, you know what going happen? You no can make heem suffa no mo', an' you going be stuck wit' one dead body on your hans. What you going do den?

KEELA: Trow 'um een da ol' cesspool an' covayum up weet' dirt.

BENNY: Den where we going put owa guns an' knifes an' stuff?

KEELA: Eef you so smart, suppose you tell me what you going do weet' heem!

BENNY *(looking at his subordinate with a smile):* I like geeve 'um fair chance.

KEELA: What! You seeck? You mean we wait tree weeks fo' ketchum, we get all bust up, I get two lump on da head from black jacks, an' we drag 'um all day way from school ova hea jus' fo' geeve 'um fair chance? Like hell I geeve heem chance, I lookum first! Een fact, where you get da crazy idea of geeving guys chance? Every time we ketch somebody from 'nada gang all by heemself, we godda geeve 'um chance! Nobody last long een gamg war eef dey geeve chance! You know who was da last guy fo' geeve chance! Was Jojo! An' you know what dey done to heem!

BENNY *(in an anguished voice.):* No talk about Jojo!

KEELA: Dey wen keel heem, Benny! Dey keel heem! Dey ketchum all by heemself, twenny guys, an' dey wen stomp 'um! Mickey tell me! One 'nada guy tol' heem! Dey broke all hees reebs, an' dey smash hees head!

BENNY: Shut up! Shut up!

KEELA: I saw hees brains on da sidewalk, Benny, I saw hees bloody brains, right by da cafe! My beeg brudda! My beeg brudda an' your bes' pal! He neva had face, Benny, he neva had no face!

BENNY: Shut up, I said! Shut up! *(He draws his arm back to hit him.)*

KEELA: Go 'head. Go'head hit me! I no care! I no care fo' nuttin' now! *(almost in tears)* Jojo was da ony brudda I had. *(He lets the bayonet slip through his fingers. It sticks in the dirt by his feet.)* He teech me how to sweem, how to box, how to make feesh net. *(quietly)* He always like you, Benny. How many times he tell me he like you, you one good guy! Rememba da las' day he was alive? He was going show weet' you, Benny. He was going treat you go show.

BENNY *(in anguish)*: Oh, I weesh I wen go weet' heem to show dat day! Eef I know he was going to die dat day, I go weet' heem anywhere, no madda how fa'! I do anyting what he say! In fact, maybe eef I went wid 'um to Kalihi T'eada, maybe he still alive wit' us now! Wid' anada guy help 'um, maybe he could escape from dose bastards! Maybe he could be right hea, in dis room wid' us now, Keela! *(pointing)* Maybe he sidding down right dea, playing one ukulele, or cracking joke wid us now, or jus' smiling at us, like he used to.

JIMMY *(reflectively)*: He neva teenk he going die dat day, yuh, Benny?

BENNY: Nobody know wen dey going die, Jimmy. Maybe you going die to-day, you donno.

JIMMY: I no like know wen I goin' die. Bimeby I come sked. Yuh, Keela? Eef you know today you going die, you no sked? *(KEELA doesn't answer. He is busy tracing patterns in the dirt with his toe.)*

BENNY *(suddenly, recovering from his reverie)*: Hey, we wastin' time!

KEELA: Dass what I been telling you all aftarnoon. *(He picks up his bayonet from the ground, wipes it against his trousers, and confronts COBRA with it.)* We smash hees face, huh, Benny?

BENNY *(after some thinking)*: We leddum go, den I fight heem weet' knife. *(KEELA whirls around angrily.)*

KEELA: You nuts, or what? Afta what he deed to Jojo?

BENNY *(becoming angry too)*: An' you teenk eef we keel dees guy we can breeng back Jojo? Jojo gone awready, no can come back no mo'!

KEELA: I like know where da hell you get deese shetty ideas of play fair! From wheech nut head you learn 'um?

BENNY *(enraged)*: From Jojo, dass who! Dass da nut head who wen go teach me!

KEELA: An' look what happen to heem! You like da same ting happen to you? You read too mamy comics, boy!

BENNY: Eef you was een hees place, boy, you like chance fo' fight fair, ah?

KEELA: Shua, I like, but who going geeve me chance? Nobody! An' dass who I going geeve chance to! Nobody!

BENNY: No worry! I going fight heem, ah? I take care heem fo' you!

KEELA: An' what eef he ween? Dees damn manoong can fight weet' knife good, you know. I like slice 'um up now, make shua he get what coming to heem! I no like lose Jojo an' you, too!

BENNY: Queet talkin' about Jojo! Eef he was een my place, he do da same what I goin' do! He no play rat, he geeve fair chance! Dass why I like da guy! Now cut Cobra rope!

KEELA: Eef you like geeve chance to dat son of a beetch, you cut da rope yourself, Boy Scout!

BENNY: Okay, okay! No need squawk! Watch 'um good, now.

KEELA: No worry, no worry! I poke 'um eef he get smart. *(KEELA stands guard, while BENNY goes behind COBRA to cut his ropes. He starts to slash at COBRA'S wrist bonds, but finds the thick hemp too thick to cut through easily. Besides, there are too many ropes to cut. He sheathes his knife, and unties the ropes.)*

JIMMY: Benny.

BENNY: What? No bada me, I busy.

JIMMY: Somebody comn'. I hea dem comin' t'rou da bushes.

KEELA: Cobra gang! Dey comin' fo' us!

BENNY: You crazy! *(He stops to listen.)* Only da ween', Jimmy.

KEELA *(excitedly turning around)*: Dass Cobra gang, I tell you! Dey fine owa hide-out! Dey lookin' fo' heem! *(COBRA starts to reach stealthily for KEELA'S bayonet.)*

JIMMY: Yeah, I teenk dey comin'!

BENNY: Jimmy, go look outside da dowa. *(JIMMY does so. COBRA drops his attempt to snatch KEELA'S bayonet for the time being, as the latter slowly turns around. BENNY waits watchfully. Seconds pass, then JIMMY sneaks in again.)*

KEELA: Dey comin'?

JIMMY: I no see nobody.

KEELA: You shua? Go look again.

JIMMY: I sked. Maybe get ghost; I hea one guy tell me o' hea get one ol' Ha-waiian grave.

BENNY: A-ah! No mo' grave. I no see not even one small heel.

JIMMY: Get one behine dis shack, right by o' dea. *(He points to a spot behind the right wall.)* Planny guy tell me get blue light een dees place night time. *(KEELA looks nervously at the spot. BENNY goes back to untie COBRA'S remaining leg bonds.)*

KEELA *(after a short silence)*: Maybe dey sneakin' up on us.

BENNY: How can? Ony guys een owa gang knew about dees place.

KEELA: Maybe somebody wen go squeal. You know how dees keeds like brag, ah? I tol' you no let small keeds join owa gang! *(with increasing nervousness)* Hey! You no hea nuttin'?

BENNY: Shuddup, you make me nervous.

KEELA *(nearly hysterical)*: I tol' you fo' keel dees bugga queek! Now we trapped!

JIMMY *(after listening for awhile)*: Na-ah! No mo' nobody, Benny right, ony da ween'.

KEELA: Dea! You neva hea dat?

BENNY: Keela, you going nuts, or what? Nobody out dea! Besides, Jimmy wen go look.

KEELA: Maybe dey hidin' een da bushes, get plenny bushes out dea. Benny, no let Cobra go. Keel 'um now, den we run fo' get da hell outta hea!

JIMMY (*suddenly and sharply*): Benny! (*KEELA turns swiftly around to see. As he does so, COBRA sees his chance, and plunges his fist into KEELA'S midsection. He grabs the bayonet from the gasping KEELA'S hand, and, whirling around, stabs the crouching BENNY in the back. He slashes the few strands of rope on his feet, and breaks free. There is now nothing to stop him from dashing out the door to freedom except a stunned and helpless JIMMY. But he does not choose to run. He charges upon the still suffering KEELA, stabs him in the abdomen, and churns his long blade within the screaming boy's guts. Then he yanks out his blood-coated blade, and dashes after JIMMY, who runs toward the door. BENNY staggers to his feet, sees his brother's danger, hurls his long dagger, and misses. The blade quivers uselessly in the wall. COBRA catches up with JIMMY and stabs him once, twice, thrice. Then, with a horrible animal-like howl of triumph, he bounds out the door. His howl dies off in the distance, and so does the swish of his feet through the bushes of the forest. JIMMY staggers to the wall for support, then covers his mouth to hold back the gush of blood from his mouth. Bright red arterial blood streams between his fingers for awhile, then he retches, and a red waterfall of blood cascades to the floor. JIMMY grasps the wall for support, but his knees give way, and he sinks slowly downwards, his fingers leaving parallel trails of blood on the wall. BENNY stumbles across the still body of KEELA, nearly falls when he slips in KEELA'S spreading lake of blood, and reaches JIMMY'S side. JIMMY rolls over, an expression of agony and fear on his face, and looks up at his older brother. (The stage darkens slowly during the following speeches.)*

JIMMY (*fearfully, yet wearily*): Benny . . . Benny, I going mahke?

BENNY: No, Jimmy, you not going mahke. You soon be alright.

JIMMY (*plaintively*): I no like mahke. Gedding dark, Benny. Hol' my han', Benny, I sked . . . I sked ghost . . . I sked ghost . . . (*His speech trails off, and his head sinks back to the ground, lifeless. BENNY grips him, holds up his head, looks at his face for a moment, then drops him.*)

BENNY (*staring at the open doorway*): Jojo! (*He stares at the doorway for a few more seconds, then falls heavily across the body of his brother, revealing a bright red gaping gash on his back. The lights are very dim now, and nothing is heard but the swish of the wind through the koa haole trees and the bushes in the forest. Slowly the curtain falls.*)

HENRY CHUN *was born in 1914 in 'Ōla'a on the island of Hawai'i. He had six siblings. In 1917, the family moved to O'ahu and settled in Kalihi. He graduated from the University of Hawaii in 1937 with a teaching degree and taught on Maui for a short time before transferring to Farrington High School in Honolulu, where he taught science until he retired some forty years later.*

Christy Anne Passion

"WHAT ARE WE (FATHER TO DAUGHTER)"

You see dat stream, Waikalulu?
small kid time we cut school
go play in dat stream
we make raft, we play pirate, play
plum fight—our clothes get all purple stain
Huuuuuuu—grandma give me dirty lickens when
I come home, but good fun you know.
No can play in Waikalulu now
dirty da water see? Everything change
no mo da same trees
tamorine, kumquat, mountain apple all gone.
We used to fly kite up Punchbowl
by da Filipino camp
da wind so strong lift you off da ground
you no see kids fly kite today
everybody forget how to fly.
I taught you how find rosy apple in da mountain yeah?
Gotta look at da leaf real close
look like one star. And how fo trap opai
between da rocks. Lilikoi, guava—
you can tell when ripe
you remember yeah?

CHRISTY ANNE PASSION *was born in 1969 in Honolulu. Her works of poetry have been published locally by* Bamboo Ridge; Hawai'i Review; *and* Hawai'i Pacific Review. *Recent awards include the James Vaughn Award and the American Academy of Poets Award. The daughter of a multiethnic union, her work draws from the music of the pidgin dialect and blue-collar workers trying to make it in Hawai'i.*

Normie Salvador
"BIG SHUGA DADDY"

For KC

Is like I can see um dizzyflit ovah Gracie's,
Pas Arakawa's, Tsumoto's, an da Gym
Can smell um koge da air

I cradle Khrystall close, she only weeks old yet
We stay sittin on our lawn
My head tilted back
She jus watchin
Da black ash spiraldrift down
On one mango breeze

I neva know um den but
Big Shuga Daddy waz takin his las
Puff on his cigarette

I catch one shuga-ashflake
On my tongue
Charred caramel paypa wit
Da dark carbon tase

Small kid time
Sometimes I use fo run
Wit my stuck out tongue guiding me
Chryin jus fo catch one
Use for come tired
My tongue stay one dry pink

Gerald—he waz da bes
Twice our age an in da sixth grade
He waz cool
All he had fo do
Waz lean back an open his mouth

He stay li-dat fo one minute
Den one driftin flake
Would slowspiral down

Into his mouth
Sometimes, he flick his tongue

Den one yeah layta
I wen stop runnin
An jus wait
For one-half hour I stay in
One statue stance
Finally black ash wen lan
On my sanpaypa tongue

Bitta tatterflakes
Dissolved in saliva
Wen streak my tongue
Felt like waz charcoal
I wen spit long time afta
But waz worth it
I waz good now
Pretty soon, I waz jus leanin back
Fo yeahs, I wen tase ashes in my mouth
I had for show dat I waz da bes

I spit out ash grey
An chry make Khrystall open her mouth
For catch da flakes
My fingah tickle unda her chin
My mouth make like one fish
I chry again, my fingah press
Down her chin
Instead Khrystall giggle
And she suck my fingahs

I guess we jus gon wait
In da grey flakefall

NORMIE SALVADOR *was born in 1974. He is an editor at the University of Hawai'i at Mānoa's Outreach College. His work has appeared in* Bamboo Ridge; Hawai'i Herald; Hawai'i Review; Hybolics; KAIMANA; A Literary Lei; *and* Tinfish. *His goal is to be in every local literary publication. He is the author of a poetry chapbook,* Philter. *In 2007, he entered the NaNoWriMo competition—to write 50,000 words during the month of November. By midnight on November 30th, he had reached only 31,746 words. He plans on finishing the nascent novel and on entering the competition again.*

Michael McPherson
"KAIMUKI"

As soon as the cast came off his arm
his mother made him carry buckets of water
across the front yard to her pink plumerias.
After his chores, in the quiet before twilight
he climbed branches of the common mango tree.
From there he could see beyond the dark marshes
and low roofs of Waikiki, plumes of spindrift
tailing back over long blue first break rollers.
That first summer turned his limber body brown,
days on the beach held out their idle hours
and slowly surrendered to the persistent sea.
Sun poured down over dark men with flashing eyes
who sang in the shade of a broad banyan tree.
They rode that fertile ocean like effortless tides,
and handed away money easily as they breathed.
Those strains of ukulele notes beneath the banyan
stayed longest in his memory, after the university
and the war, and beyond sessions of bold strategy
among stuffed wild heads in the old Tropics bar.
The music played on when the king of beachboys
died wheezing alone in a borrowed room in Kalihi,
mind gone, tropic breezes waving invisible curtains
over faint tremors in frail and withered fingers.
In time the common mango tree came down,
and his memories of lugging the water bucket
faded like an old photograph too long exposed.
The plumerias and house on Maunaloa vanished,
marshes were filled and families moved away.
He never went back to see any of that happen.
Instead in his mind he held certain few moments
as though viewed through an inverted telescope,
or in a snapshot of long blue waves seen from a tree.

John Dominis Holt
"HAPA"

Dark waltzes
twirl and swirl
Inside my head tonite.
Three-four time reminders
of a pastel time
when gilded walls
and brilliant lights provided
backdrop to the dazzling
raiment of daring duos
lost in the banality
of place and sound
capturing me in my
softer parts so that
remembrance has no mercy—
I think of hula kahiko
and its vigourous beat
its mass gestures, its outdoor
splendor of fern and 'ohi'a
leaf

its abstract emotions
in the dappled shade
arms and bodies
swirling to the dictates
of another time—

I am not saddened, nor gladdened.

Dark waltzes like dark
lilacs, dark roses, or
frantic calls of violins—
excite and sadden both.

I could not stop to twirl
and swirl
left in the far universe
of lost hungers.

I reach out of the forest
fragrance of maile
the clean, clear perfume of ginger
the strong red flames
at the end of 'ohi'a branches

but I also hanker for rococo
ballrooms
ornate furniture and polished
floors.

Here I am between
the pala palai fragrance
of Laka's world
where drum beats
and the 'ohe flute notes
command the air
whilst part of my heart
clings to polished floors
and gilded chandeliers
where dark waltzes
are the music for the dance—
where dark lilacs, violets and roses
perfume the air.

Lloyd Stone

"CHINESE GRANDMOTHER"

Calmly she sits
In the darkened movie house
And politely watches phantom cowboys
Chase shadowy Indians
Across nebulous plains.
Modestly her hand is cupped
one within the other
Upon her silken lap.
Dignified,

Her lily-feet are placed
In careful order, side by side
Beneath her seat.
At her side
Her grandson sits
And chews and pops his gum
And loudly cheers
The hero on to greater deeds.

"It is not good that he
Should go alone,"
She tells the family quietly.

And he puts in,
"Aw gee!
The other fellows go alone!"

"It is not good,"
She says again.

And so it goes,
The matinee on Saturday.
Calmly she sits
In the darkened movie house
And politely
Watches.

Gary Pak

"THE GARDEN OF JIRO TANAKA"

After serving over thirty-eight years as a park keeper for the City and County of Honolulu, Jiro Tanaka graciously retired with the feeling that now he could enjoy life at his own leisure. At the small retirement party his co-workers held for him at the park pavilion, Jiro was given gifts and much praise from everyone. His friends asked him how he was planning to spend his retirement years. He smiled softly while scratching the back of his head. "Now I going do da things I feel like doing," he said.

"So what is it you going do?" they asked.

"Oh, I get plenty things to do. My yardwork. Make trouble fo' my wife. Do nothing." He laughed warmly.

Everyone laughed pleasantly with Jiro.

Jiro scratched his head again. "Now I can go play wit' my grandchildren any time."

"Jiro—you grandfather?! Eh, congratulations!"

Jiro smiled shyly. "No . . . I no have grandchildren. Not yet. Maybe soon, but."

The government gave him a comfortable retirement check every other week and free medical and dental benefits and a bus pass for the rest of his life. He often counted the blessings given to him as reward for diligently working the number of years he had for the City and County. The mortgage on his modest home was paid off; he had a wonderful, caring wife; and his only son was grown and enjoying a happy—though childless—marriage. Everything seemed to be taken care of, and sometimes as he lay in the darkness drifting off to sleep, Jiro would feel a mild sense of satisfaction and contentment with how favorably his life had seemingly turned out.

He woke up at four one morning—a habit he had followed like religion for most of his adult life—and went to the bathroom to wash and shave. In the water-spotted mirror he saw himself for the first time in all those years: a tired old man near the end of a comfortable yet uneventful and meaningless life. He stood there stunned, not knowing what to think, gazing at his shallow image: bleary-eyed, face swollen from sleep, short wet white hair standing on end.

Later, over a steaming cup of black coffee and with a lit but unsmoked cigarette between his fingers, he wondered how it was possible that over six decades of his life had passed by so fast. It was as if he had winked a couple times and life had become a liar and painted him an old man with thin white hair and deep wrinkles etched on his leathery face. He left the morning paper unfolded and unread on the kitchen table for the first time in all those years.

The next morning he woke and sat up at the edge of his bed, staring blankly in the darkness. He began to rise, but changed his mind and sat back down. His joints were cold and stiff and they ached. He lay back into his bed and covered himself with the blanket. Every morning his old bones were a discomfort to him. But this time the little aches and pains were a good excuse for him to stay in bed and not have the bathroom mirror brutally remind him of those lost years of his life.

With his eyes opened to the morning darkness, he listened to the sounds of the old house: the shifting of the old oak floor boards; the Venetian blinds softly tapping against the windows; the reliable purring of the old refrigerator down the short hall in the kitchen; the delicate humming of the electric clock. Then he tuned his ears to the warm silence that permeated the rest of the house. The sounds he heard were now like punctuation marks, devices that gave the silence time and depth and finiteness.

The sudden buzz of the alarm clock jarred him from his meditation. Hazel, his wife, stirred awake. She fumbled for the clock and switched the alarm off, then rose methodically off her squeaky bed. Jiro heard the track of her house slippers as they flip-flopped flatly on the wooden floor. He listened to the flushing of the toilet, the whining and gurgling of the ancient plumbing corning back to life. Finally, Hazel's footsteps shuffled out the bathroom to the hall where they stopped.

"Jiro? Jiro?" Hazel called out in an alarmed whisper. "You awake?"

He had not heard her come into the bedroom. He lay in silence for a few moments, resenting the fact that his privacy had been disturbed. "Yeah-yeah," he said finally. "I awake."

"Jiro—how come you still in bed? You sick? You not feeling good?"

"No, I all right. I feel like staying in bed fo' little while. Das all."

Hazel groped for the hallway light switch and turned the light on. The naked bulb radiated harshly into Jiro's eyes.

"Why you turn da light on fo'?" he complained. "Not'ing wrong wit' me."

"Den how come you not awake?"

"I stay awake. You jus' wake me up."

"But how come you not reading yo' pepah, drinking yo' coffee?"

"Cause I feel like staying in bed. Whas wrong wit' dat?" He paused, taking a deep breath to calm himself. "I retired, no? I can do what I feel like doing."

"I know but you always up so early. How come now? You sure you not coming down wit' one cold?"

"Yeah-yeah! I feel all right! I feel like staying in bed. Why you bugging me fo'?"

Hazel stood silent. "No need yell at me," she said painfully. "You no have to yell at me." She flicked off the light and shuffled toward the kitchen.

"I t'ink I going down da park today," he said to Hazel over a cup of coffee. For the most part, their breakfast together had been silent and tense. "I go see Kazuo and Fortunato . . . go talk story wit' dem guys."

Hazel nodded her head, turning the corners of her mouth.

"Maybe I ask dem if dey need help. Can help dem clean up da park. Not'ing to do ovah here since I retire."

"You can work on yo' own yard," Hazel said bluntly.

"I do. You nevah see how much da yard stay so clean since I stay home? Yesterday I wen cut da grass, da other day I wen weed da garden."

Hazel turned her dark eyes away from him, sipping her coffee sullenly.

"Be good to see dem guys," Jiro murmured.

Hazel went to the kitchen sink, taking her dishes with her. She rinsed off the dishes and washed her hands. "Bobby wen call yesterday," she said, while looking out the window and wiping her hands on a dishcloth. The sky was brightening with the morning sun. "He said Laurie went to da doctor." She paused for a moment. "He said da doctor tol' her she no can have babies. Something wrong inside."

Jiro was still for a long moment, then took a drag from his cigarette. "Whas wrong wit' her?" he asked, smoke streaming from his nostrils.

Hazel shook her head. "I dunno what da doctor wen tell her. But maybe . . . but maybe dey can adopt one baby."

Jiro shook his head slowly.

"Maybe," Hazel said. "But Bobby said dey going try one 'nother doctor. Fo' second opinion."

"Better if dey get dey own baby." He sighed, glancing at the wall clock. "I going down da park," he said.

Trash was piled high on every rubbish can, as if nobody had emptied them for weeks. The grass had grown high and wild, and as Jiro passed the public restrooms, he crinkled his nose because of the stench. He approached a young park keeper, a new face for Jiro, who was adjusting a sprinkler head. "You know where Kazuo or Fortunate stay?" he asked with a smile.

The young park keeper's eyes were red and vapid, he gave Jiro a look of indifference. Then, he nodded his head in the direction of the maintenance room where the park equipment was stored. Jiro found Fortunate there, kneeling and sharpening a sickle.

"Jiro!" Fortunato stood up, his face lighting up, his white-white teeth beaming in the dim room. "You looking good! Good to see you. So da retirement life good den, eh?"

Jiro nodded his head resolutely. They shook hands. "Is okay. Good change jus' stay home and no do not'ing." He chuckled. "Eh, no mind me asking," looking out the door, "but what happening over here? Ho . . . jus' like nobody taking care da grounds." He laughed uncomfortably.

Fortunato's smile faded. "I do my best," he said. "But da young guys . . . dey no geev one shit."

Jiro nodded his head. "I see dey wen hire one new guy."

"Three new guys. But dey always running away, hiding someplace."

Jiro shook his head.

"Young kids," Fortunato continued. "Dey no like listen to da old-timers. Dey t'ink dey know it all, dem buggahs. Dey like do ev'rything dey own way." He used the sickle to point out the door. "Look out dere. One big mess. Dem buggahs, dey go hide and smoke dey pakalolo allatime." He laughed uneasily. "I tell you, Jiro, nowdays, not like befo'. Ev'rything change. Not like befo'."

Jiro nodded his head. "So where Kazuo?" Jiro asked.

Fortunato's eyes widened with pain. "You nevah hear?"

"Hear what?"

"You nevah hear what happened to Kazuo?" Fortunato shook his head. "Last week he had one stroke. Right on da baseball diamond, by home plate. Lucky thing I was close by. I was da only one around. Da new boys was in da bushes smokin' dey grass."

"Kazuo? Stroke?" Jiro's voice cracked. "How him? He okay?"

"He in da hospital. Half his body paralyze."

"Oh no! And he was going retire in little while." Jiro shook his head. "Ho . . . I feel so bad fo' him. Fo' his wife."

They were silent for a long moment, the air in the room suddenly becoming heavy with gloom.

"And so how long he gotta stay in da hospital?" Jiro asked.

Fortunato shrugged his thin shoulders. "Dat, I dunno, Jiro."

"Where he stay? What hospital?"

"St. Francis. Intensive care."

"I go visit him today."

"I dunno yet if dey allow him visitors."

Jiro looked out the door. "I go ask. I call dem up." He turned to Fortunato. "And his wife? How she taking it?"

Again, Fortunato shrugged his shoulders. "I dunno, Jiro. Not too good, I t'ink."

They were silent again.

"Ah . . . but Kazuo he strong like one ox," Fortunato said finally. "He going recovah fast. No time he going be up and around."

"Yeah-yeah. But still . . . not going be da same."

Fortunato nodded his head. "Yeah. Not going be da same."

The two friends talked for a short while longer. Then Jiro bid his friend goodbye, promising to come back again.

Several nights later, in a dream, he planted a large brown seed in his garden. The seed sprouted before his eyes and grew fast into a thick, crawling vine. Yellow flowers bloomed everywhere. Then, from the flowers, oozed children. Dozens of children. And they were smiling and humming a strange melancholy melody. They jumped about and danced circles around Jiro, then ran off with their sing-song voices trailing behind, ringing in Jiro's ears. He ran after them with arms spread, in a desperate need to embrace them, but the vine roped his ankles and he fell face down. Helplessly, he watched the children run off and disappear.

When Jiro woke up the next morning, he forgot what he had dreamed. He went about his daily morning routine and, while reluctantly looking at himself in the mirror, was surprised to see his whiskers in a new way. Smiling and delighted at the discovery, he decided against shaving.

"You look terrible," his wife complained at the breakfast table, but all he did was grin and drink his coffee and smoke his cigarettes.

In a few days, Jiro raised a straggly, but healthy white growth on his face.

"You look like one old goat," Hazel said. But he just laughed with a boy-ish disregard, his dark eyebrows raising in jest. "Jiro, you embarrass me. I no like people see me wit' you in public."

Jiro laughed deliriously, frightening Hazel, chasing her out of the kitchen.

After breakfast, he went to work in his vegetable garden and discovered a small weed struggling between two maturing Manoa lettuce. It was a common weed. His garden had been infested with them a while ago and he had waged a bitter war against them. It was a war he thought successful until now. He bent down to pull it out when suddenly he became awed by the weed's simplistic beauty. Never before had he regarded a weed in this way. Gently he touched the shoot, examining closely the fine lines of the leaf. The weed moved him so that he decided to let it be. He yanked out the two Manoa lettuce, then watered the shoot.

Soon weeds sprouted all over the yard. Jiro was elated.

"Jiro! What happening to you?" Hazel asked with alarm. They were eating breakfast in the kitchen. She was aware of the yard going to pot, the wild growth on his face, but had not said anything for a long time until that morning when she just could not hold it in anymore. The weeds had practi-cally taken over the yard, the grass was knee-high.

"Da yard look terrible, Jiro, jus' like yo' beard. Da neighbors . . . dey talking 'bout you. I can hear dem talking behind our backs."

"So! Let dem talk 'bout me. Why should dat bother me? Is none of dey business anyway. All dey are is good-fo'-not'ing, lazy nosey buggahs!"

"But Jiro! What happening to you? What kind person you turning out? What kind grandfather you going be?"

Puzzled, he looked into Hazel's worried face. "What you mean? I not one grandfather."

Hazel dropped her hands into her lap. "Bobby called last night. He said dey adopting one baby, from Korea." She searched Jiro's face for a positive reaction; there was none. "Da pepahs went through already. Da baby coming anytime now."

Jiro brooded over the idea of being a grandfather. A smile slowly came to his face. "I going be one good grandfather," he said softly, his eyes twinkling. He stroked his beard. Then he clapped his hands loudly, rubbing them together. "Den I going be one good grandfather! I teach my new grandchild all I can how live one good life. Ho-ho!"

"But not wit' yo' beard. You going scratch da baby's face. And how yo' grandchild can play in one yard full of weeds?"

Jiro threw his head back, laughing heartily. He had not laughed like that for a long time. Suddenly he was back in his boyhood days, plantation days, swimming naked with school friends in an irrigation ditch. "Jimmy! We go swim down da ditch! Gome on! We go!"

Hazel looked at Jiro cautiously. "Jiro . . . what you said?"

"Come on—hurry up!" Jiro insisted. "Bumbye da big luna he come and catch us!"

The weeds thrived. They had taken over the vegetable garden and were spreading in Hazel's flower bed. Hazel worked furiously to get rid of them, and though she hinted that she would start digging up the rest of the yard, she dared not touch her husband's weeds.

Every night since the first night, without fail, Jiro dreamt of the children. They danced circles around him and sang their sad song, laughing and smiling, but they would never let him come near. The moment Jiro reached to touch them, the children would run off and disappear. And, also without fail, the moment he'd wake the dream would be forgotten.

Jiro's backyard became a miniature forest. In one comer was a grove of haole koa and in another tall buffalo grass. The squat house stood out starkly like a white mushroom on the fringes of a dark, quiet forest. Hazel had stopped talking to Jiro, and most of her time was now spent at Bobby's house with the new baby, she being afraid to bring the baby to their house. Jiro filled the silence by humming a song he had never heard before.

Must be my father's village, Jiro told himself in his dream. Long skeins of fishing nets hung in arches on wooden supports. The roofs of the cottages melded together. He saw the children, their moon-shaped faces with rouged cheeks peeking out of the doorways. He sang their song. Cautiously, they came out, smiling. They began to sing with Jiro. Jiro took a step forward. The children stopped. They ran back into their huts.

While tending to his garden of weeds one afternoon, Jiro heard melodic strains coming from behind the buffalo grass. He straightened up—accidentally dropping a can of chicken manure—and pointed his ears in the direction of the strange music. It was the song he hummed incessantly to himself throughout the day, the song that played in his mind at nights, lullabying him to sleep. Fear swept through him, making his heart tremble painfully; perspiration flowed from his face. As if possessed by a mysterious, hypnotic power, he ambled into the bush towards the music, his legs and arms moving stiffly, as if reluctant to go.

He came to a small clearing where the melody had taken a reedy quality and was the loudest. In the middle of the clearing was a tall, thick-trunked plant with large oval leaves. Small rotund fruits, smooth and shiny like tomatoes, hung from the tips of many branches, some fruits a creamy green color, some with a splash of yellow on green, one fruit ripened to a brilliant orange. The music was coming from the plant, its leaves vibrating with a warm gentle breeze.

He had never seen a beautiful plant like it before. Stunned, he sat on the ground, his eyes fixed on the plant. He noticed the ripened fruit dangling before him and touched it, and the fruit broke off cleanly and fell into the palm of his hand. It was soft and cool to the touch and had the smell of the ocean.

He fondled the fruit, then bit it. It was crunchy but bitter. Yet he was compelled to eat it all, not knowing why. When he finished, he was left with a large seed which he dropped at the base of the plant.

The fruit had an immediate soporific effect on him. His eyes lost their attentiveness and his body began to sway heavily, like a ship listing in port. He got up slowly and lumbered out through the bush, carefully covering the path. He entered the house and fell asleep before his head could touch the creases of his pillow.

The children peered from doorways. Jiro took a breath of air, calming himself, then began singing the song. The children came out slowly. Surprisingly, they came next to Jiro and let him touch their fine, smooth hair. Silently they hedged around him, their expressive eyes begging him to tell a story. So he did. And they smiled, then laughed cheerily. And when he finished telling the story, their eyes asked for more. Happily, he began another.

Everyday he secretly went to the plant, not understanding what this obsession was that was making him eat a bitter fruit daily. And every night he dreamed of the children. He played with them, sang songs with them, told stories. He let them run their thin cold fingers through his beard. He carried them on his back. And he buried his nose into their salty children-smell, closing his eyes and wishing never to lose that smell, though even in the dream he understood that he would never remember any of it when he woke.

Then, one night, he had no dream of the children. Instead, he had a nightmare of the fishing village being belted by a storm of waves as high as a mountain. And he woke up in the cold early morning with his body trembling, his mind swimming madly half absorbed in this only dream he remembered and half in the cold darkness surrounding him. And for an unknown reason, he became frightfully worried.

Quickly he got out of bed. Taking a flashlight from a kitchen drawer, he ran out into the garden, tripped on a hoe and fell face down, the flashlight spinning and rolling away into the bush. He got up, picked up the flashlight, and fought his way through the bush to the clearing. And there he saw, collapsed to a heap of wilted leaves and stems, the plant.

He ran out of the bush and returned with a bucket of water and a handful of manure, sprinkling the fertilizer over the plant and dousing it with water. But it was of no use. He fell to the ground and cried until his tears bled dry. He went back to the house, but returned teary-eyed to the clearing several times in the course of the day, hoping to find the dying plant miraculously recovered or to discover that it all had been just a bad dream.

He could not sleep that night, tossing and turning in bed endlessly. Whenever he closed his eyes he saw the horror of the village being lunged at by a stormy sea of monstrous waves.

Before dawn it began to rain. And through the fall of the rain, he heard laughter. A chorus of shrill laughter. And who was laughing and what was the laughter about?

Cautiously he got out of bed and put on a jacket, took the flashlight from the kitchen and went outside. He pushed slowly through the bush to the clearing and shined the flashlight left to right to left, down to the heap of dead wet leaves, then up at the bombardment of tiny raindrops which were caught in his trembling beam of light. He could not see who was laughing, though it was here that the laughter was coming out the loudest.

He stepped on something sharp and found the ground covered with broken shells of the seeds he had left.

And among the broken shells were the children.

They were the size of his thumb. They were wet and naked and rolling playfully all over the ground, their blushing skins picking up the dirt.

Jiro crossed his legs and carefully sat down. He watched them for a long time, as a smile slowly developed. Then, nodding his head in time with their song, he spread his arms generously to receive them into his warmth and protection.

GARY PAK *is the author of two collections of short stories,* The Watcher of Waipuna and Other Stories *and* Language of the Geckos and Other Stories; *and two novels,* A Ricepaper Airplane *and* Children of a Fireland. *He is at work on another novel and a collection of essays on contemporary Korea. He teaches creative writing at the University of Hawai'i at Mānoa in Honolulu.*

Patsy Saiki

"COMMUNION"

It was quiet, deathly quiet, and that was strange, for Morio Tamura's life had always been full of sounds. There had been the crickets and cicadas on the Tamura farm in Japan, and the rustle of cane fields and harsh commands of foremen on the sugar plantation on Hawaii. Here, in Honolulu, the sheathed thunder of cars, buses and trucks from below his locked and heavily draped bedroom window merged with his everyday life. Sound and noises were taken for granted, like the air around him, yet now there was this depthless, monotonous silence.

Was it time to get up? He had to be at the delicatessen by four if he wanted the coffee and doughnuts to be ready by five. A few faithful customers always came early for breakfast. What time was it anyway? He tried to open his eyes but couldn't. He then tried to reach for the clock by his pillow and again he couldn't. He didn't even hear the tick tock tick tock that put him to sleep every night. Am I dreaming? he wondered. Then he fell into motionless sleep once again.

The next time he awoke, he noticed not only the silence but the chill in the air. It was . . . it was . . . was there such a thing as antiseptic chilly? As if one were being preserved in a tub full of alcohol?

The tub reminded him of his iron vat with bubbling oil in which he made his doughnuts. How many more cases of oil did he have in his storeroom? And flour . . . should he order another forty bags? The newspapers talked about a shipping strike in a few weeks. But if the strike wasn't called, then he would be stuck with the flour and somehow the mice always got to the flour sacks. The health inspectors didn't like that.

Time . . . time to get up . . . what time was it? Surely it must be almost four. Why was it so quiet and cold? Where was Mama? Where was the alarm clock? I must be really exhausted, he thought, and fell asleep once more.

Two nurses entered the room in the morning, one with some towels and the other with a tray of thermometers. The first one said, "Mr. Tamura . . . Mr. Tamura . . . I'm going to wash your face, okay?" The second slipped a thermometer under Morio's tongue.

The first nurse asked, "How many days is it since he's been in a coma? Forty? Fifty?"

"More like ninety," the second nurse said, examining the chart at the foot of the bed. "Ninety seven today, to be exact."

"You think he'll ever come out of it?"

"Hard to tell. He's a tiny man . . . only five feet tall and weighed 110 pounds when he was brought in. He's 76 pounds now. But he looks like a scrapper, a fighter. The other day I was giving him an alcohol rub and it seemed like he tensed his right arm. First time I felt that. So he could be coming out of it."

"Sad . . . being pistol whipped for a few dollars. Honolulu was never like this. I can remember when we used to leave our windows and doors unlocked all the time . . . even at night."

"I know. Now I don't feel safe even in my own garage. And I lock myself in the car when I drive."

"Kind of a shame, isn't it, someone in a coma lying in this private air conditioned room. He can't even appreciate it, yet he has to pay for it."

"I think the police wanted him here. Anyone coming here has to pass through two stations."

"Must cost the family a fortune. I heard a rumor Admissions suggested the family take him to another hospital, when they found out he didn't have any health insurance."

"You can't blame the hospital. But we took him, didn't we?" She picked up her tray. "Hey there, Mr. Tamura, brave man, you in your secret world, have a nice day, huh?" She left, followed by the other nurse.

Morio Tamura, in his secret world, faintly heard Mama calling him. Or was it his mother in Japan? No, it was Mama. The paper cranes, he thought. The paper cranes Mama's making for my sixty first birthday party. What fool originally thought of making a thousand paper cranes for a sixty first birthday party, and what fools made this into a tradition? Fools with time, that's for sure.

I wish we had a daughter, he mused. A daughter in law is okay, but a daughter is different. Now I understand why Mama used to say that if we're going to have only one child, she would have preferred a girl to a boy.

He thought of Tom, his son, and Evelyn, his daughter in law. They were good kids, kind and considerate, but somehow not as close to them as a daughter would have been. His friend Shoda had a married daughter and always on Sunday afternoons this daughter brought some food over for her parents "So you don't have to cook tonight," she said. Then she cleaned the kitchen and bathroom and sometimes the inside of the refrigerator while her husband talked to her father. How lucky the Shodas were!

It must be time to get up and go to the shop. Must be close to four. What would the workmen say if the shop wasn't open by five? They depended on him for coffee, doughnuts and biscuits. Where would these truck drivers and construction workers have their large but cheap breakfasts? I must get up. But I can't open my eyes. Am I drugged? How could I be? Am I dreaming? Wake up, Mono Tamura. You don't have time to be sleeping. But he fell into another deep, unconscious sleep.

A few days later, Mrs. Tamura sat folding her paper cranes in the hospital room, as usual.

"Oto san" she whispered. "Oto san, Papa, can you hear me? Wake up! Try! You've got to come out of this coma. You can't die without saying goodbye to us. At least to me. Wake up! Look, I already have eight hundred cranes. Only two hundred more to go, and remember your birthday is only a few months away. You've got to be well by then. I sewed your red kimono for the party, and we have the guest list. So wake up, Oto san, for how can we have your party without you?"

Mrs. Tamura sighed. After three months she was exhausted with anger and worry. What would happen to them now? Should she sell the shop? Maybe the new owner would hire her. After all she was still strong at fifty seven, and she knew all the customers. Would she have to depend on charity in her old age when she had worked steadily for thirty five years, minus six months before and six months after Tom was born? Thirty four years of hard work in America, the land of the free and the home of the brave, Tom used to sing. The land of justice, of plenty, of love. And a land where someone wanted to kill her husband for a few dollars!

"What kind of country did you bring me to," she asked. "I gave up a country where I had relatives and I could understand the language. In that country I don't think anyone ever pistol-whipped another person from the back, even in the feudal days of long ago. The Japanese fought man to man, from the front, with warning. Why did we come here? What happiness have we had, working from four in the morning to nine at night, every day of the week?"

She pounded her husband's body in anger, heedless of different tubes attached to his body. "They say this country has justice, but there's no justice. The police didn't even bother looking for the boy. They said they had no clues. They just wrote something down on a piece of paper, that's all.

"They just accepted it . . . it wasn't anything unusual to them to have someone almost killed by another. When I try to talk to them they just move away. Oto san, how can you die now? You didn't have your party. You didn't see the thousand crane tree. What about that trip to Japan? You said we would go back on your sixty fifth birthday . . . when you retire. Lies . . . all lies! You aren't even trying to come out of your coma. It's easier lying in this air-conditioned room than working in a hot delicatessen and standing on your feet all day. You don't care about us . . . you're taking the easy way out."

"What? What?" her husband mumbled. "Four already? Time to get up, Mama?"

Mama . . . Mrs. Tamura . . . was so shocked she forgot to ring the bell to call the nurse. Instead she ran to the door and yelled, "Nurse! Nurse! Come quickly. My husband just talked to me!"

Two nurses came running. "Mr. Tamura, Mr. Tamura, do you hear us? Can you understand? You're in a hospital and we are taking good care of you. You have nothing to worry about. Your wife is sitting right here. Mr. Tamura . . . Mr. Tamura?" But Morio Tamura was back in his deep, deep sleep.

"Are you sure he spoke?" a nurse asked. "It wasn't a moan? Or a gurgle?"

"No," she answered. "He asked if it was four o'clock already."

"Four o'clock? Why four o'clock?"

"That's when he used to get up to go to work every morning."

"You're sure it wasn't wishful thinking? You didn't imagine it?"

"I'm sure. He spoke clearly." The nurses waited. But they had many other chores, Mrs. Tamura knew. So she said, "Thank you. Maybe I did dream it, after all." She picked up her bag from the floor, extracted some paper, and began folding a crane.

After the nurses left she leaned over Morio and whispered, "So! You make me look like a fool! Why did you stop talking? Listen, Papa, I know you can hear me. By the time I have my thousand cranes, I expect you to be out of your coma. You understand?" She scolded gently.

When, several days later Morio next awoke, he felt his mother pushing him. "Morio chan, Morio chan, wake up. Wake up and work in the fields for a few hours. Remember your brother is sending you to high school. You must work hard before and after school since he's making this sacrifice. Be grateful to him."

Be grateful to his older brother? But Morio knew why his brother was sending him to high school. Ever since Morio had contracted diphtheria when he was twelve he had stopped growing. Now he was fifteen and still so small he was of little use on the farm where strong labor was needed. His brother was hoping that with more education Morio would go to some city and not be dependent on his older brother.

"I would be grateful if I hadn't heard my brother discussing this with my sister in law late one night," Morio thought. "They were talking of ways to get me off the farm for good. They made me feel so unwanted. I wish I had never heard them talking about me."

So he continued sleeping although he could feel his mother pushing and pulling him . . . maybe even washing his face? Now why would his mother wash a fifteen year old's face? He wanted to protest, but instead he fell into his deep sleep again.

Five days later Mama said, "Well, that's the thousandth crane. Now I'll have to tie them to the tree branch Papa got from a friend. We have the invitations ready . . . "

"Mama, did you get white print on red paper or red print on white paper?" Morio asked, as if he had been in conversation with Mama all along.

Mrs. Tamura trembled and dropped the crane she had been holding. It took her a few moments to say quietly, "White print on red paper."

"Good. It'll be easy to read. Remember we had an invitation once with red print on black paper and we had to hold it a certain way to read the invitation? Poor Mama, a thousand cranes! But now you can relax a little."

"I enjoyed making them," Mama said, hoping one of the nurses would walk in on the conversation. "Somebody come . . . somebody come . . ." she prayed.

"Come to bed, Mama. We have to get up early tomorrow morning, as usual. I had a long day, standing on my feet, and they feel like lead bars attached to my body. I can't even move them. You sleep early, okay?"

"Sure . . . sure . . . as soon as I put my things away."

She pressed the bell. When two nurses came in she said, "My husband spoke again. Right now. He asked about the color of the print on the invitations we made for his sixty first birthday."

The nurses looked at each other. "That's wonderful, Mrs. Tamura. That's a good sign he might come out of his coma. Now listen, there's nothing more you can do for your husband now, so why don't you go home and rest? We'll take good care of him."

So they still didn't believe her. But it didn't matter. It was a matter of days or weeks before he'd come out of his coma completely. Papa was getting better and look what a clear mind he had. "Yes, I think I'll go home and rest," she reassured the nurses.

It was a week before Morio spoke again. "Where am I? I dreamed I was in Japan with my mother."

"You're in a hospital, Papa," she told him. "Remember someone hit you on the head with a pistol?"

A muscle twitched in his face. "Oh, I remember. A boy . . . a man . . . came in and bought doughnuts. One half dozen. He paid me and as I was going back into the kitchen I felt something hit me. That's all I can remember. How much money did he take?"

"All that I left in the cash register before I left. About six dollars in bills, nickels and dimes."

"Strange . . . he looked like such a nice boy. He talked so softly. I gave him two extra doughnuts because there were two left. He told me he wanted only six and I said the extra two were free. He said 'Thank you.' By the way, when can I leave here? I have to order some flour, in case we have a shipping strike later in the month."

"We already had a shipping strike, Papa, and it's been settled, so don't worry about the strike."

"We had a strike? But it was supposed to begin June 15!"

"It's September 9 today."

"September! How can that be? It was June 2 yesterday."

"You were in a long coma, unconscious, Papa. But thank heavens you're okay now. Listen, I'm going to call one of the nurses. They didn't believe me when I said you talked the last time. Talk to them . . . the nurses . . . so they'll know you can really talk."

When Mrs. Tamura returned with one of the nurses, Morio was again in his deep, motionless sleep. The nurse sighed in exasperation, but with sympathy. "Hang in there, Mrs. Tamura," she comforted her.

For another long ten days Morio Tamura slept, like an empty sack with tubes going into and out of him. Mama talked to him, pushed and pulled him, whispered, shouted, scolded, whimpered. Had he really talked to her? Even Tom wouldn't believe her, so she herself began having doubts.

"You know, Mama, when we wish and dream for something, it seems true," Tom told her. "You wanted Dad to come out of his coma and you wanted him to talk to you, so you heard him. It had to be in your mind, because how come he doesn't talk when anyone else is around?"

But the very next day he opened his eyes for the first time, although he couldn't move his head or hand. "Mama, forgive me," he said. "I lied to you. Well, I didn't exactly lie, but I didn't tell you how short I am, when I asked my brother to find me a wife in Japan."

Mrs. Tamura was surprised. He was now talking about what took place forty years ago. How his being short must have bothered him!

"I didn't want to tell you how short I am because I was afraid you wouldn't come to marry me. The white people on the plantation used to call me 'shrimp' and the plantation boss told me to work in the kitchen because I was so small . . . like a girl," he said.

"So what?" Mama answered. "I lied to you too. I told the go betweens not to tell you I'm 5'3" tall. At all my miai in Japan the mothers turned me down because they said I looked big and clumsy. They wanted a dainty daughter in law."

"Mama, remember when we were first married? When we took snapshots, I always took them on steps. I would stand one step behind you so I would look taller. How it bothered me, being shorter, yet I was happy because I had a tall wife and I wanted tall sons."

Mama waited for his next words but he closed his eyes, sighed, and went back to sleep.

The doctor and nurse came in, just a little too late to hear Papa talk. By now Mama refrained from telling the nurse about Papa holding a conversation with her.

"How's my husband?" she asked the doctor. "As well as can be expected," the doctor answered. "When will he be completely out of his coma?" "What do you mean . . . 'completely out of his coma'?" "Well, sometimes when he talks to me he's clear about things, but then other times he thinks I'm his mother, I think. When will he not go back to sleep again for days at a time?"

The doctor and nurse looked at each other. "We've had cases where patients have been in coma almost ten years," the doctor said. "Then we've had patients who came out of a coma perfectly normal and patients who couldn't remember anything or recognize anyone. We don't know about Mr. Tamura."

"Papa's mind is clear, and of course he recognizes my voice." "Remember, when your husband does regain consciousness, if he ever does, he may not remember much because of the brain damage and massive hemorrhage," the doctor warned.

"But he does remember," Mrs. Tamura insisted. "He even asked about the color of the print I used on his sixty first birthday invitations."

The doctor looked at his watch. "Fine . . . fine . . . let's keep working and waiting and hoping and praying. Miracles can happen. Now would you mind waiting outside for a few minutes?"

"What about this case, Doctor?" the nurse whispered after Mrs. Tamura left.

"Damage was extensive to the brain area . . . plus the hemorrhage . . . "

"It's a wonder he's still alive, isn't it?"

"He got hit two or three times in the back of his head, at the nerve center. I think the paralysis is permanent."

"Poor man. Better if he had died right away. Now maybe he'll be a burden on his wife for years and years, and they don't even have health insurance. Personally I'd rather die than be a vegetable fed by tubes."

"Sometimes you don't have a choice. Sometimes the next of kin don't have a choice too. Unless laws are changed." They left, and Mrs. Tamura entered to find her husband sleeping peacefully.

Seven days later Morio opened his eyes and said, as if he had not been unconscious for more than a week. "Listen, Mama, will you promise me one thing? Listen carefully, now. In case I turn out to be a bedridden invalid, if I'm completely paralyzed, promise me you'll help me to die."

"No, how can I do such a thing?"

"Mama, please. Won't you help me?"

"Even if I wanted to help you, what could I do?"

"I don't know. A healthy man can die in a car accident or drown in the ocean or fall from some tall building. But if one is bedridden and especially if he's like a vegetable, how can he die when he wants to? I don't know, Mama. That's where I have to depend on you."

"What are you talking like this for, just when you're getting well. Every day you're getting better, you know. I don't want to hear anymore. Besides, visiting hours are over."

"Please, Mama?"

"No."

"It's my only request. From my only life partner. For the sake of my life partner."

"I don't know what you're talking about." But she reached out to him. His thinness pained her. How could a man's arm really feel like a stick?

"Mama, is it daytime or nighttime?"

"Nighttime."

"Could you open the window and please turn my head so that I can see out?"

"There's nothing to see out . . . only a few stars."

"Stars? Oh, I want to see the stars . . . I never had time to see the stars while I was working. Remember when Tom was in kindergarten and he had to sing 'Twinkle twinkle little star' all by himself for a Christmas play and we practiced and practiced together with him?"

"And the teacher scolded him because he sang 'Twinkoru twinkoru litoru star . . . raiki a diamondo in za skai.'"

Did he chuckle? Mama thought so, and she too smiled. But then he seemed to have fallen asleep again so she left.

Morio opened his eyes and saw the stars. As he gazed at their shiny brilliance they seemed to break into little pieces and slide earthward, together with his tears that slid down his cheek to the pillow.

The next morning the nurses called cheerfully, "Good morning, Mr. Tamura. And how are we today?" But instead of wiping his face, the nurse called the doctor right away.

"Too bad Mr. Tamura passed away without regaining consciousness. One hundred and thirty-six days in a coma so he's really skin and bones," the nurse said.

"It's a wonder he lasted this long," the house doctor agreed.

"Kind of sad," the nurse said. "You know, there was such love between them, Mrs. Tamura is sure Mr. Tamura spoke to her several times. But that's physically impossible, isn't it? His throat muscles were paralyzed as much as the rest of his body, so he couldn't have talked, could he?"

"Most likely not," the doctor agreed. "But then there's a great deal we still don't know . . . "

The nurse pulled the pillow case from the pillow. Strange . . . it was wet, as if with tears.

PATSY SAIKI *is the author of* Sachie; Ganbare!; Early Japanese Immigrants in Hawai'i; Japanese Women in Hawai'i; The Return; *and* The Return of Sam Patch.

———————————•◦•———————————

Eric Chock
"MANOA CEMETERY"

for Moi Lum Chock

I.
I am late as usual
but no one makes an issue of my coming.
Candles are lit and incense burns
around the stone.
The rituals have begun.
We offer five bowls of food;
bamboo shoots and mushrooms
we've cooked for you today.

And there are five cups of tea
and five of whiskey
to nourish and comfort you
on your journey.
It's been a long year since you left,
and for me, the sense of regret
deepens into mystery.
It is not strange that we miss
your gracious presence,
your good cooking, or good smile;
but as we all take our turns
to bow and pray before your grave,
I begin to wonder who you are.

II.
I feel silly
to think I follow custom
pouring you a sip of whiskey
I never saw you drink.
But when I kneel before your stone,
touch my hands, and bow three times
I remember how you taught me prayer
before your parents' ashes
stored in earthen bowls
in a sacred room.
They've since been moved and now they're buried
with a proper stone
just one row up from you.
You know others on this hill.
We give them incense too.

III.
It was many years earlier
that an old Hawaiian king
offered a friendly Chinaman
all the land from Waikiki clear up Manoa
to this sacred hill
where we stand or kneel in worship
as our grandfathers taught us to do.
The old man refused,
saying, just give me enough

to bury my people.
I wonder if the Chinaman knew
what he was saying?
Even you, two generations before me,
were not born in China
but I think near Hanalei.
So what is it gains a place
among these laborers, merchants, tailors?
The repetition of names
sprawls across the hillside
and I remember once
I thought I saw a baby in my lover's eyes.
Now I keep an endless pain
regretting great-grandchildren
that were lost.
I forget what I tried to save
when I had to get on that plane
and fly away. Forgive me.
I cannot name the reasons.
And if you
who put your earthly life
in taro and in sugarcane
deserve a burial and worship on this hill,
surely I should have my ashes
scattered from an airplane!

IV.
But on this anniversary
we wash your stone,
we trim the grass around your plot,
and it is for you we sanctify
this world
with food, flowers, and firecrackers.
The sound and sulphur smoke
drive evil spirits away
but we stay, burning
gold paper folded into money.
V.
Whiskey, tea, and dust of incense
mix into the grass around your stone.
It's time for us to go,

but now, it's as if you were always dead
and we've come here every year
for a gathering of tears
and rituals
of fire.

ERIC CHOCK *is co-founding editor of Bamboo Ridge Press along with Darrell Lum. The press celebrated thirty years of local publishing on December 7, 2007. Chock worked for twenty years with the Department of Education and the Hawai'i State Foundation on Culture and the Arts as Poet in the Schools, was the Distinguished Visiting Writer at the University of Hawai'i Mānoa in 1995-96, received the Hawai'i Award for Literature, and now teaches writing and literature at University of Hawai'i West O'ahu.*

Maxine Hong Kingston
from CHINA MEN

There is a man who would be one hundred and seventeen years old now. He had a one-hundred-and-sixth birthday party in the Palolo Chinese Home in Hawai'i in 1969. He wore a wool cap. He told the guests he came to Hawai'i in 1885 on the S.S. *Coptic*. He brought with him pigs in cages, and chives and onions growing in cans. He had divided his ration of fresh water with the pigs, the chives, and the onions.

He worked in the sugarcane fields for four dollars a month, and his first job had been to clear the brush for planting. He lived in a grass house, but later moved into a dormitory, where he slept in a bunk covered with grass mats. He sent one half of his pay to his family in China. Here's how he spent the rest: He bought kerosene and wood; he paid off some of his debts, his passage to Hawai'i, and the twelve-dollar fee for processing his papers; he spent six dollars to join his Benevolent Association, which gave him room and board when he took his monthly trip to Honolulu on pay day. He rode to town in a horse cart for thirty cents; it carried five passengers. When he could not afford the thirty cents, he walked.

He rested by smoking opium, which the plantation foreman sold. A half-hour's worth of high was called a dragon seed and cost fifty cents. When Hawai'i outlawed opium, he switched to cigars.

He saw King Kalakaua and Prince Kuhio. In 1893 he did not go to town because of the American revolution against Queen Lili'uokalani, who was "big and friendly," he said. "I was for the Americans," he added.

Since 1885 he has left the island twice, once to go to Maui and once to Kaua'i.

On this one-hundred-and-sixth birthday, the United States was still fighting in Vietnam, and people asked him how to stop the war. "Let everybody out of the army," he said.

"In one hundred and six years, what has given you the most joy?" the reporters asked.

He thought it over. He said, "What I like best is to work in a cane field when the young green plants are just growing up."

"In the end," said Tu Fu, "I will carry a hoe."

Virgilio Menor Felipe
from HAWAI'I: A PILIPINO DREAM

We had to move out of that house, and the cheapest place I could afford to move to was here in Waimanalo. And I've been living here ever since. At that time, I figured that I was just over 65 and qualified for Social Security pension. If you figured that I was 22 when I came to Hawai'i in 1925, that made me 65 at the end of 1968, right? So, I moved here, and when the Japanese social worker came around, I told her I wanted to file for the pension. But there is no way I could prove it because I had no more birth certificate. I only had my blue contract card they gave me when I came to work for the plantations, but it wasn't good enough proof. I had no other identification papers, and she said she couldn't just take my word for it. It took almost a year after that to finally get approved.

I like living here. I prefer here to any place else. Sure, everything in the village is old and the roads are full of holes; the houses are termite-ridden and the toilets are outside, but there is life every place here. I am not a stranger here. There are fresh Filipino vegetables and fruits in the garden, and the cockfights, and best of all—friends to talk with in Ilokano.

No one really bothers me here even though I drink again. Except for a few, "Oy! Don't drink too much!" they accept me here for what I am. When I walk on the street, people don't just go on driving by without looking with some recognition. When I go to the store, I can talk stories there. And the cashier girl, a young Pilipina who is so nice, in the Japanee store, sometimes she pays for me my 99-cent bottle of Greystone wine when I don't have enough for the tax.

The only steady income for me now is the pension check I get from Social Security. I get $119, and that is more than what some of the others here receive. I get more for being sickly. The social worker tells me the President will give a 3% increase. That's for the election gift, eh? So that's kind of the government. But of course that's not enough for anyone in Hawai'i to live on. My rent is $25 a month with everything included. I pay it to Ciano's wife because their family has the lease, then he hands the lump sum rent to the Japanee.

But this retirement money is starvation pension. If I ate regularly and ate like the President or the governor and the mayor and all those politicians with the Security check I get, I would have to rob a store. But I can't do that so I drink more and eat less 'cuz then at least I get to feeling good and kill my hunger.

To help make it here, I plant for food. You can see the fence is crawling with beans and bittermelon. Of course we have our marungay tree. I don't waste land, and that is our Filipino custom. You cannot grow any by cementing over soil. You kill the land that way. But only money talks here, so maybe all this cementing will stop only when everything is dead. Anyway, the Security pension still is not enough. So I gamble for a few dollars here and there betting on the cockfights and playing cards. Sometimes, I go pick flowers for my Japanee friend there on his farm if there is no other way to get money, because every month, at least, I still like to ride one of those opihis when they come around.

Some people say that life is how you see it. Well, that's if you can afford. But in all my life in Hawai'i, and more so as I grew older, I can find no lasting joy in all that I have come to know. Even in the flower fields, when the Lord Sun is clear of the clouds, it gets hot, and even picking blossoms become plain work. So I tell myself, "Ay, 'Sus Apo! Look at what I've been fated for! I work away today, and I bet—I'll have to work away tomorrow! Yeah, but with my bare hands and calloused heart I helped build Hawai'i." Then I take out my bottle of Greystone wine, fits just right inside my pants pocket, and drink sweetly between the orchid rows until I see nothing but the Lord Sky.

On the Beach at Waikīkī One More Time

Well, here we are in Hawaii! . . . This is the famous Waikiki beach . . .
The water—it's clear, you can see yourself in it . . . The white sand is alive
with girls . . . The surfers beautiful as men can be . . . At play on a wind
rippled summer wave . . . Descending to the ocean only at dusk . . . Midnight in the Ilikai . . . Host culture . . . Package deals . . . Average day at the
hotel . . . It's getting drunk outside . . . Room service . . . Found I could not
eat the purple orchid in my drink . . . In Waikiki I'm something special . . .
A stray plover lost . . . The long swim . . .

Sam Isokane
"WAVES OF WAIKIKI"

The sound of the waves disturbs
The stillness of the seashore

Geof Hewitt
"LETTER"

for Kit Hathaway

Here in Honolulu a p.a. system squawks
directions to Waikiki and tourists bear news
on pink faces, tremble their money
on bad rum drinks. Dixie would love the beach
and the kid would go apeshit over all the sand
and the almost tame gulls,
but you'd sniff the mendacity from the soul
of Aloha Spirit, a motto someone wished
were true. The maidens don't swim to your boat,
but are still bare-titted in the nightclubs;
the beachboys walk silently past one another
and treasures, as advertised in the brochure,
wash up on the sand after big storms.

Tonight the clouds moved in on Oahu
and the palm trees nod like old men
waiting. Tonight I watch the lightning
and wonder where Linda is. She took everything
when she left, everything but the raincoat:
everyday she moves farther from my life,
I watch the storm move in, everyday
I forget a little more about her
good and bad habits. Forgetting is a death
invited, candles to follow the storm.
Moving changes people, I want back
the joy of storms climbing into Enosburg

over West Hill. My heart and stomach grunt
in Honolulu, my soul has married
to a coin, I thought that words
were important, I had forgotten speechlessness.

GEOF HEWITT *taught English at the University of Hawaii from 1969 to 1970. Since then, he has published three books of poetry and three books on teaching writing. Vermont's reigning poetry-slam champion, he works for the Vermont Department of Education and teaches at Vermont College. He and his wife Janet have two grown children and two young grandsons.*

Rap Reiplinger
"ROOM SERVICE"

(Phone rings.)
RECEPTIONIST: Front desk.
FOGARTY: Room service, please.
(Phone rings.)
WOMAN: Housekeeping. Oh, no no no, try wait, try wait. *(to someone else in the room)* YOU, PUNK, THROW ME OFF!
MAN: Oh, wop yo' jaws.
WOMAN: Room service, can I help you?
FOGARTY: This is Mr. Fogarty in room 1225. I'd like to order some dinner.
WOMAN: Hah?
FOGARTY: This is Mr. Fogarty. I'd like some dinner sent up to my room, 1225.
WOMAN: And what was your room numba?
FOGARTY: 1225.
WOMAN: One mo' time, please?
FOGARTY: Twelve-twenty-five.
WOMAN: 1225, that's a Mr. . . . Frogtree?
FOGARTY: Fogarty. Fogarty.
(Whistling.)
WOMAN: Can I help you, Mr. Frogtree? RUSSELL GUNFUNNIT I'M TRYING FO' TINK!
RUSSELL: Ahh.
WOMAN: *(sighs)* Now, where were we?
FOGARTY: I'd like to order some dinner and have it sent up to my room. Please.

WOMAN: OK, and . . . what room was dat?

FOGARTY: Room 1225. This is Mr. Fogarty and I'd like my dinner sent up to my room, 1225.

WOMAN: Okeydokey, and what would you like?

FOGARTY: I'd like a cheeseburger deluxe, French fries, and a chocolate malt.

WOMAN: Okay, that's a cheeseburger deluxe, French fries and a choc—try wait, yeah? EH, RUSSELL! YOU GET PEN?

RUSSELL: WHAT?

WOMAN: PEN! PEN! GUNFUNNIT, PEN!

RUSSELL: HEA, FO' CRYING OUT LOUD! HEA!

WOMAN: OK, now, uh, so that's . . . what?

FOGARTY: *(slowly)* a cheeseburger deluxe, French fries, and a thick chocolate malt.

WOMAN: Cheeseburger . . . oh, excuse me, yeah, but do you want the hamburger deluxe with cheese or, uh, wait, wait, wait, try wait? Now, you want now, the hamburger deluxe with cheese on the top or one cheeseburger deluxe?

FOGARTY: I'd like a cheeseburger deluxe.

WOMAN: Uh huh . . . and would you like that with or without cheese?

FOGARTY: With.

WOMAN: What?

FOGARTY: Cheese. CHEESE!!

WOMAN: Oh, why you neva say that in the first place? One side order cheese.

FOGARTY: NO!

WOMAN: Oh, wow. Eh, Russell, dis bugga giving me heat!

RUSSELL: Eh, go slap hees head!

WOMAN: No get uptight, sir, I was just trying fo' take your order.

FOGARTY: *(quickly)* Look, a cheeseburger deluxe, a French fries and a chocolate malt! All I want—

WOMAN: Eh, no go so fricken' fast! Cool yo' jets! What you tink dis is, au-to-ma-tion?

FOGARTY: I'd like a cheese—

WOMAN: I get 'em already, I get 'em already. And what else?

FOGARTY: And an order of French fries and a chocolate malt.

WOMAN: Ohhhh, try wait, try wait, try wait! We get special today, you know?

FOGARTY: *(flatly)* What is it.

WOMAN: No no no no no, we get two kinds, two kinds, we get.

FOGARTY: What are they.

WOMAN: Oh, numba one is pickle pigs' feet with Spanish rice on mashed potatoes, your choice of dressing on top' your fruit cup, and bread or toast. EH, MENTO! Oh, not you, sir. RUSSELL! EH, DEAF EAR!

RUSSELL: WHAT?

WOMAN: WHAT YOU GOING COOK FOR NUMBA 2 SPECIAL?

RUSSELL: NOTHING!

WOMAN: YOU GOING GET IT MAN, YOU WAIT TILL I TELL DA SUPERVISA! Oh, that's it, sir, only that one.

FOGARTY: I prefer my original order.

WOMAN: Oh, and what was that?

FOGARTY: CHESEBURGER, FRENCH FRIES, CHOCOLATE M—

WOMAN: Oh, yeah yeah yeah, right right right. You shua you no like the pickles pig feet? Hah?

FOGARTY: Yes.

WOMAN: Ono, you know.

FOGARTY: No, thank you.

WOMAN: You shua?

FOGARTY: Yes, I'm sure.

WOMAN: Really? Positive? Eh, you shua you shua? *(pause)* You still on the phone?

FOGARTY: Yes. Yes, I'm sure I'm sure.

WOMAN: Okay, just checking, yeah? So . . . let me repeat that order, yeah? Hello?

FOGARTY: I wish you would.

WOMAN: That was one cheeseburger deluxe, with a side order cheese, French fries, and one chocolate—AH HA HA HA! STOP IT RUSSELL! RUSSELL! RUSSELL, OH MY GOD! RUSSELL! YOU, OH, RUSSELL YOU DO THAT AGAIN I GOING KERANG YO' ALAS!

RUSSELL: Do it, do it, do it.

WOMAN: *(sighs)* Okay, now where were we? OK OK OK OK OK OK OK. Oh, OK try wait, OK? Ho da guy was Russell, what a pest! OK, so where were we?

(Dial tone.)

WOMAN: Hello? He-hello? *(sighs)* Tourists.

RAP REIPLINGER (1950-1984) *is acknowledged as the greatest local standup comedian ever. With the sharpest of eyes for social observation, perfect timing, and perfect pitch for the many different voices of Hawai'i, he raised live performance of pidgin to high comic art. He influenced a whole generation of local comedians. Twenty-five years after his early death, the mention of his name can still bring smiles to the faces of those who heard him live, and there are many who can quote whole stretches from his routines verbatim.*

Paul Theroux

from HOTEL HONOLULU

On another average day at the hotel, under the lovely sponged-looking skies of Honolulu, a young woman checking in asked for a discount because she was a travel writer. Guests could be ruthless, but ones claiming to be writers were the worst. I was summoned to the front desk to adjudicate.

"What's the most recent thing you published?"

She did not say, I did a think piece for *Forum* on penis size. But she might as well have.

At lunch I was told an elderly couple from Baltimore, the Bert Clambacks, had wet their king-size bed; another couple, the Wallace Caulkins from Missouri, a late check-out, had swiped the hotel's terry-cloth robes. Keola had put a bumper sticker on the staff bulletin board, *The Only Thing I'm Hooked On Is Jesus*, and Kawika countered with one of his own: *Hawaiian Sovereignty*. Rose said she wanted to change her name to Meredith. "Or Madison. Or Lacey. Or Brittany. But not Rose. And also I want a DVD player." Nigel Gupta, a guest from California, defying the rules (*No Glass Receptacles*), brought a jug of ice water, a bottle of whiskey, and a glass tumbler to the pool. He tipped over his table, resulting in so many scattered glass shards we had to close the pool. Among the guests who protested, Bill and Maureen Gregorian demanded a reduction in that day's rate and threatened a class-action lawsuit, since the pool was unusable. The elevator jammed; some guests were trapped for fifteen minutes; the thing itself was out of service for three hours. Guests had to be reminded not to hang wet bathing suits from the room lanais. A homeless man was reported wandering the corridors.

The homeless man was Buddy Hamstra. It was an example of how grim he had begun to look, how careless in his mode of dress, that the owner of the hotel, a multimillionaire in a dirty bathing suit and a Paradise Lost T-shirt, was mistaken for a tramp who had temporarily strayed from his shopping cart and his plastic bags.

Everyone found him funny; that became a theme. Without any effort on his part, he was rediscovered as a colorful character. This unasked-for comeback was so bewildering to him it made him furious, loudly so, resulting in more notoriety. "The old Buddy," people said, not realizing that his illness had made him seem clownish.

I waited for him to give me more material for his memoirs. "I'll tell you the rest later," he had promised. But there was no more. There was only pantomime, his blundering and shouting, and this unexpected excess energy made Buddy funnier than ever. He was angry at the world. Exasperated out-

77 The Last Laugh

Another average day at the hotel. A young woman checking in asks for a discount because she's a writer, she says to me.

"What, pray now, recent thing you published?"

"I don't think a piece for _Forum_ on penis size."

~~Why don't you ... publish ...~~

At lunch I was told a older couple from Baltimore had wet their bed, another from Joplin, Missouri, had stolen their bath/towels, Maria had put a bumper sticker on her car saying _The only boy I'm hooked on is Jesus_, my daughter and Rose said she wanted to change her name to Meredith.

"Or Brittany. Or Lacey. But not Rose." And also I want a CD player." A guest, ~~~~ defying the rules, (no glass receptacles) brought a jug of ice water or a whisky bottle in a tumbler to the pool, tipped over the table, resulting in so much broken glass we had to close the pool & consider draining it. Immediately there were protests from the guests. The elevator jammed; guests had to be reminded not to hang wet bathing suits from the lanai; a homeless man was reported to be wandering the corridors.

The "homeless man" was Buddy. It was an example of ~~Buddy~~ how given his bad beginning to look, how careless in his mode of dress, but the owner of the hotel was mistaken for a hippy who had temporarily strayed from his shopping cart & bulging plastic bags.

Everyone found him funny: had become a theme

rage is often the best comedy, for a protester's futile howls make him sound like a victim, the natural butt of a joke.

His cronies, constantly quoting him, attributed Buddy's new mood to the fact that he had found a method for getting rid of Pinky—to divorce her, give her some money, and send her away. The prospect of his new freedom, instead of concentrating his mind and making him lighthearted, confused him and made him explosive and forgetful. He had difficulty with names. He called Pinky, at various times, Stella and Momi. His friends found this hilarious.

Peewee said, "We're having dinner on the lanai. Someone asks Buddy to pass the salt. He just picks it up and drops it"—*dwops* it—"into the serving bowl of soup with a big splash."

"Is that funny?"

"We couldn't stop laughing."

To someone who asked for pepper, he made a big sprinkling gesture with the heart-shaped jar of Stella's ashes. "Just like the old days!" his friends said.

The mayor of Honolulu visited the hotel on a publicity tour of Waikiki, which was filmed for a promotion by the Hawaii Visitors Bureau. Buddy gave the mayor a lei, a raffia bag containing jar of Peewee's salsa, some macadamia nuts, and a Paradise Lost T-shirt.

Buddy poked my arm and told the mayor, "He wrote a book!"

A microphone was brought over. Buddy said, "It's getting drunk outside," and farted. The mike picked it up and amplified it, making it sound like a car backfiring, so percussive that people jumped.

The mike also picked up Buddy's explaining to the mayor, "I had an intestinal bypass, your honor. My table muscle."

Buddy turned his big serious doggy-jowled face to the camera as the bystanders laughed.

On another public occasion, the Waikiki Hotel Association's Annual Prize-Giving, at the Hilton Hawaiian Village Coral Ballroom, Buddy stepped up to receive an award for the Hotel Honolulu: honorable mention for dessert, Peewee's coconut cake. He stumbled, took a fall, knocked over a tub of anthuriums, and landed near the first row. Snatching at the flowers for balance, he ended up on his back with fistfuls of blossoms.

PAUL THEROUX, *born and educated in Massachusetts, joined the Peace Corps in 1963, in one of the first groups to be sent abroad—to Nyasaland, Central Africa. He taught in Africa for six years; lectured in 17th-Century Drama for three years at the University of Singapore; and later, abandoning the salaried world, spent seventeen years in Britain. He ultimately fled, and took up residence on O'ahu's North Shore, where after almost twenty years he still lives. He is the author of numerous novels, travel books, short stories, and a memoir,* Sir Vidia's Shadow. The Mosquito Coast; Saint Jack; Christmas Snow; The London Embassy; *and* Half Moon Street *have been filmed.*

Allegra Goodman

from PARADISE PARK

A ll this light was pouring in on me, and I started to open my eyes. I didn't know where in the world I was, and I reached over, but no one was there. The room was empty, and I didn't even know where the room was—it was all just floating in empty space, and I couldn't say what planet or star I'd landed on. All that was running through me in that one second was the loneliness of being this tiny insignificant particle in the universe, and how a life weighs nothing in all that light. And what is that light compared to God? Then I woke up and it came back to me. That the guy, supposedly my boyfriend, who came out with me to this joint, a flea-bag in Waikiki, was now gone, run off with a chick on her way to Fiji, and he—actually they—had left me with the hotel bill, which since I had no idea how to pay I was avoiding by just staying in the hotel and not checking out. But you know, the vision I had before, when I was just half awake, that was the important part. That was like the angels talking, when they speak to you and teach you right before you're born, and then they put their fingers on your lips—Sh! don't tell! You almost forget, but somewhere inside, you remember. At the time, that morning, I just lay there and had no idea what to do, not to mention I had never as far as I knew even believed in the existence of God. But in my subconscious, and my unconscious, and everywhere else, I had all these questions and ideas about this higher power and this divine spirit, and maybe I would have been dealing with them if I hadn't been so broke.

Finally I got up, sat on the edge of the queen-size hotel bed. The bedspread was halfway off, sliding onto the floor, and the spread was green, printed yellow and orange with bird-of-paradise flowers so enormous they looked like some kind of dinosaur parts. The headboard was white rattan. So was the dresser and the mirror frame and the desk. There was no chair. everything that could be nailed down was . . .

Here's what I took to Hawaii: my guitar, and my backpack with my name on it in black laundry marker. In the backpack: six panties, and a bra. Five T-shirts of different colors, a pair of shorts (I wore my jeans), two Indian gauze skirts wadded up in little balls, and a macramé bikini. A notebook and a ballpoint pen to write down my feelings. My wallet, my hairbrush, and toothbrush, and, from the free clinic, a good supply of the pill. I had a watch, a big silver man's watch that had been my grandfather's. Grandpa Irving's watch had a creamy face and bold black roman numerals. The crystal was scratched, and when you opened up the watch-case there were pawn marks inside, stamped in the silver. The watch was battered up, but lucky. Grandpa had kept it during the flu epidemic of 1918, when he holed up in his room for two weeks with a bottle of wicked germ-killing brandy, and he'd carried it though all his union organizing. It was his talisman—at least that's how it was told to me. He even brought it down to Mexico, when he'd tried to organize the tobacco workers in Yucatán. So of the things of value I had that watch and my guitar.

It was raining when we got to Oahu. Everything was gray and white and windy, like an old movie as we came down closer and closer, and out the airplane window I could see these little palm trees waving around hysterically by the tarmac. I couldn't take my eyes off them. My face was just pressed against that cold airplane glass. In the airport there was slack key guitar music and such a strong sweet scent of flowers I thought at first that everyone was smoking weed. There were servicemen, and tourists and honeymooners, who you could tell right away because they were all dressed up, everything about them new. And then there were scraggly folk like us, some with hiking gear. We all got free paper cups of pineapple juice.

The two of us piled into a station wagon taxi—which wasn't really necessary, considering how little luggage we had, but we laid our backpacks and my guitar in the back and we got in. All the car's windows were open in the rain, and I couldn't believe it, the air was so warm and soft and damp. We drove on the shortest freeway I'd ever seen. It was just like it was foreshortened, and there was Honolulu coming up so fast, just a few tall white buildings, a little clump right in front of Diamond Head. We'd got a two-week deal in Waikiki. Our hotel was not on the beach; it did not have views, its rooms were not equipped with many towels, but it was cheap. We figured it would be our launching pad.

The rain cleared up by the next morning, and we hopped a city bus, which was painted turquoise and had turquoise seats too. The windows were half open, and outside the colors were spectacular. I couldn't get over it. The greens were so green, the blue sky so blue. The leaves, the clouds, even the mock orange bushes. It was like everything on that island had just come out of the wash; it was like the trees were hanging out to dry. I just wanted to ride around all day. I just wanted to go out to a park bench with my guitar and write a song. But Gary had a look of disgust on his face. He hadn't come to ride buses and feel like he was still in the United States. He never said anything to me unless it was some kind of critical comment about tourist traps and raped ecosystems and the scummy bars in Waikiki.

We got off at the university, which was full of trees. There were trees that launched these seeds just like brown gold balls, dimples and all. And there were trees with big saggy phallic seed pods hanging down, just obscene looking. The buildings were all a mishmash, lots of dirty cement and glass. There was a tubular sculpture, bright orange, house high, with enameled pieces of metal bent into cones and big pointy curves. The top looked like lipstick scaled for a giantess. I loved all this. I was gawking at everything, but Gary just strode over to the zoology department. He was focused on digging up that ornithologist, the hero he had come all this way to meet and work with and learn from and basically get involved with his cause. There was real drama about it, the way Gary walked into Spaulding Hall. It was like it was going to be: Dr. Williamson, I presume? And Gary would be Stanley.

Well, as it turned out, Brian was a very down to earth feet-on-the-desk type guy. He was about Gary's age, mid-thirties, but shorter than Gary, and stockier. He had a lot of sandy blond hair and a beard, and basically looked like a mountain man. His eyes were dark and steady, his nose was peeling. His arms were thick and freckled, and his shoulders broad, as opposed to Gary, who was so tall and sinewy and fleeting. At the time I just thought Brian looked bluff and bland, and not as sharp as Gary. I thought Brian didn't have a lot of rhythm to him. Still, when it came to birds, he seemed to know his stuff. He thought it was cool Gary had read his articles. He said why don't we all have lunch. So we went to a lunch wagon on the street and bought big white dumplings with pork called *manapua*, and meat sticks, and that sweet cold *inari* sushi in a brown sugary-vinegary cone.

We sat out on the grass and Brian talked about his new project that he'd just got funded. It was a study of red-footed boobies, which were a very gentle lovely bird that traveled all through the Hawaiian islands to breed, even to certain tiny islands way northwest. They were one of those species that were indigenous to Hawaii and they weren't used to having any predators. They had no idea how to protect themselves against goats or pigs or mongooses. On Tern Island and various atolls they were being slaughtered by the jeeps and machinery the military was bringing in. They were flying into guy wires, and being sucked up the intakes of jet engines, which tended to crash the Air Force's precious fighter-bombers. Naturally, grunts had no sensitivity to this rare bird. In fact they liked driving around mowing boobies down when they stood in the middle of the road. Brian had been ridiculed by the Coast Guard when he'd gone out to defend the birds on island bases and installations. The government's official position was that the birds were dumb for getting in their way, while in fact it was the boobies' innocence and trust that was getting them killed. But now the Coast Guard was pulling back from a lot of places in the northwest, so Brian had a grant to sail out there and take a census of the boobies and other seabirds that were nesting happily on the islands the military had left. In particular, he was making plans to go out for three months to observe a bunch of red-footed boobies that he'd banded on Kauai when they were just chicks.

Gary listened closely all during lunch, but he didn't say much. I think maybe the Berkeleyites had made Brian out a little larger than life. Gary was becoming a little bit downcast.

After lunch when Brian went back to his office, Gary and I walked through campus.

"Where are you going?" I asked. "Isn't the bus the other way?"

Gary kept his eyes on the ground. He just kept walking. I looked over at him. He was making me nervous. What should I say to him? That I was having a great time? That those meat sticks and pork dumplings had made my day? It had been months since I'd had meat, and I wasn't exactly a vegetarian, even though in Berkeley I'd been living in a vegetarian co-op house. I just walked and walked along. It was hard to keep up, Gary's legs were so long, and he was so deep in thought. Finally I said, "Gary, could you just stop for a minute?"

He stopped.

"Don't you want to work on Brian's project?"

Gary looked at me like he'd never seen me before. I guess I should have realized the very suggestion was an insult. He'd come to Hawaii planning to work in the jungle looking for those endangered honey-creepers being driven out. He wasn't here to sit and watch a thriving seabird colony!

"How come you don't like it here?" I asked.

He didn't answer.

All of a sudden I lost it. "Well, what the hell *do* you like? What do you want? We've been traveling together all this time and nothing is good enough for you. Nothing is clean enough or wild enough; nobody is radical enough. Just what exactly are you looking for?"

He set his mouth, and still he didn't answer.

"You are the most selfish person I've ever known!" I raged. "I've come all this way with you and you are never satisfied. I'm not going to take it anymore. I'm not going anywhere else with you. I'm not walking with you; I'm not dancing with you, I'm not following you from—"

Then Gary floored me. He said, "Fine."

I couldn't believe it. I should have known. But it just hadn't occurred to me. I'd been too young and green to understand that Gary's goal in life wasn't just being with me! It hadn't occurred to me that we were different that way. I still had in my head some idea of symmetry, that since I loved him, he loved me the same way. And since I was all wrapped up in him, he was also all wrapped up in me. And that was the way it should be. I'd probably written too many songs.

He left me there right on campus with those ridiculous golf-ball trees, and I walked around and around, and my face twisted up like crumpled paper as I walked.

Finally, I went back to the hotel room and gathered everything that belonged to Gary. There were some papers, and his good hiking boots, and some extra clothes. He had his backpack with him, but I took everything he'd left in the room out onto the balcony. And if we'd had a room looking out on the ocean I'd have flung it all into the sea. As it was, we were on the tenth floor overlooking the street, and not far from an open-air shopping bazaar called the International Marketplace. I didn't want to kill anyone with the boots, so I left them on the balcony. Then I hurled Gary's shirts with all my might, so that they fell all the way down ten stories to the ground and flopped all over the sidewalk and draped on bushes far below. I wadded Gary's papers individually into little balls, and I tossed them too. All those balls of letters and notebook doodlings blew back against the building, and so did his socks, so they probably landed on the balconies below me, but Gary's jeans went straight down over the side, flapping in the breeze. And his underpants had a good wind behind them. Some hit the street, and some landed on the sidewalk, where the tourist couples in their matching aloha wear looked up to see what was going on.

ALLEGRA GOODMAN *was born in Brooklyn in 1967. At the age of two, she came to Hawai'i with her parents, both of whom were professors at the University of Hawaii at Manoa. Goodman attended Punahou School in Honolulu. Her first book,* Total Immersion, *a short story collection, was published the day she graduated from Harvard. She is the author of another book of short stories,* The Family Markowitz, *and three novels, National Book Award finalist* Kaaterskill Falls; Paradise Park; *and New York Times best seller* Intuition. *The landscape and people of Hawai'i figure prominently in her work, as does the city of Honolulu. Her forthcoming novel,* The Other Side of the Island, *takes place in an Orwellian future and features an island with some resemblance to O'ahu.*

David Lodge
from PARADISE NEWS

Dear Mother,
Well, we got here, but I'm not sure it was worth the journey. Waikiki is overrated—crowded and commercialized. All Macdonalds and Kentucky

Fried Chicken, just like Harlow Shopping Centre. We should have gone to one of the other islands, Maui or Kauai, but it's too late now.
Love,
Dee

Dear Denise,
Arrived safely. This is our hotel, I have marked our balcony with a cross. It overlooks the sea. Such a beautiful place, flowers everywhere. Nothing but the best for my Mum, Terry says! Unfortunately his girl friend couldn't come after all, so his friend Tony is keeping him company. V. hot here, doesn't really agree with your father.
Love,
Mother

Dearest Des,
Met that Bernard I told you about on the beach with a friend, another English chap called Roger who I thought would do for Dee. He is bald but you can't have everything. We went out on a Sunset Cruise with him (Bernard couldn't come), on this sailing boat, sails set by computer, ever so romantic, but Dee got seasick and I had to talk to Roger all the time, or rather listen to him, he's a university lecturer, likes the sound of his own voice. Better luck next time. Wish you were here,
Lots of love,
Sue

Dear Greg,
This is the famous Waikiki beach. Haven't seen much of it yet—been catching up on our sleep (nudge, nudge). How did you make out with the chief bridesmaid after the reception? Or were you too p----d?
Cheers,
Russ

Paradise Bakery
Paradise Dental
Paradise Jet Ski
Paradise Redicab
Paradise Yacht Sales
Paradise Erectors
Paradise Chapel
Paradise Ferrari and Lamborghini
Paradise Antique Arts

Paradise Video
Paradise Pets

Dear Sir,

I am currently enjoying, if that is the *mot juste*, which I venture to doubt, a holiday provided by your company at the Hawaiian Beachcomber Hotel, Waikiki.

Your brochure states quite unambiguously that the hotel is "five minutes" from Waikiki beach. I have explored every possible route between the hotel and the beach, and my son and I have independently timed these journeys on digital stopwatches. The fastest time either of us achieved was 7.6 minutes, and that was carried out at a brisk pace, early in the morning, when the pavements were comparatively uncrowded, and the traffic lights at pedestrian crossings favourable.

A normal family, carrying the usual accoutrements for a day on the beach, would take at least twelve minutes to get from the hotel lobby to the nearest point on the beach. The brochure is deeply misleading and seriously inaccurate, and I hereby give you notice of my intention to claim an appropriate rebate on the cost of the holiday. I will correspond with you again on my return to the UK.

Yours faithfully,
Harold Best . . .

Dear Sir,

May I suggest that, in future, when the *soi-disant* instructor in charge of snorkeling equipment hire under your auspices informs customers of the dangers of sunburn, he makes clear that it is possible to get burned *in* the water as well as out of it?

Yours faithfully,
Harold Best . . .

Paradise Finance Inc.
Paradise Sportswear
Paradise Supply Inc.
Paradise Beauty and Barber Supplies
Paradise Beverages
Paradise Puppets
Paradise Snorkel Adventures
Paradise Tinting
Paradise Cleaning and Maintenance Service
Paradise Parking

Dear Pete,

This is the best bit of Hawaii so far. First you get to see a film about the Jap bombing of Pearl Harbor (that's how they spell it here). Old newsreel, but quite interesting. Then you take a naval boat out to the wreck of the Arizona. You can look down through the water at the gun turrets. It's called a war grave, so you're not allowed to eat food there.

Best wishes,

Robert . . .

Dear Stuart,

Funny, I'd forgotten Pearl Harbor was in Hawaii. Very instructional tour. Did you ever see that film, *Tora! Tora!?* Apparently it cost the Americans more to make it than it cost the Japs to actually bomb the place. Thought you'd like to know the little yellow buggers were undercutting us even that long ago.

Best,

Brian

Dear Mum and Dad,

Having a lovely time here, apart from a few niggles about the hotel (Harold is writing to the company). Waikiki is more built-up than we expected, but quite nice. Cleaner than Marbella. Spotless toilets. The children love the water.

Love,

Florence . . .

Dear Greg,

I've discovered surfing! Fantastic! Better than sex! Met two great Australian guys who are teaching me how to do it.

Best,

Russ . . .

Dear Travelwise Customer,

On behalf of Travelwise Tours, I hope you are enjoying your vacation in Waikiki. As your stay on the beautiful island of Oahu draws to a close, we hope that we will have the pleasure of welcoming you to Hawaii again one day.

In the spirit of traditional Hawaiian hospitality, Travelwise Tours, in conjunction with Wyatt Hotels, invites you to cocktails and *pupu* at 6 p.m. on Wednesday 23rd, at the Wyatt Imperial Hotel on Kalakaua Avenue (in the Spindrift Bar on the Mezzanine Floor).

This invitation card entitles you to one complimentary cocktail and one plate of *pupu* per person. Cash bar also available. There will be a short video presentation of other Travelwise holidays available on the Neighbor Islands, including the fabulous new resort of Wyatt Haikoloa.

Aloha, Sincerely Yours,
Linda Hanama
Resort Controller

DAVID LODGE'S *novels include* Paradise News; Thinks ...; Home Truths; Therapy; Changing Places; *and* How Far Can You Go? Small World, *and* Nice Work *were both shortlisted for the Booker Prize. His works of literary criticism include* The Practice of Writing *and* The Art of Fiction.

William Stafford
"CUSTOMS DECLARATION: HONOLULU"

Clouds, when they come, belong, and the waves
to be rescued, these endless arrivals clasping
ever higher sand—yes, and the tourists
on corners begging for what they don't know,
trying for something that flowers have smuggled
into daylight all over these islands.

None of us invented summer, and the tourist
in the funny hat may bring what preserves
an island, being from afar. I won't
steal anything, and back home I'll prop
this place back of my prayers and celebrations,
making it real again and again by saying
in my mild way, "Yes. Yes, I was there."

WILLIAM STAFFORD (1914-1993) *was born in Hutchinson, Kansas. He was author of over fifty books, a recipient of the National Book Award for* Traveling through the Dark, *a professor at Lewis & Clark College in Portland, Oregon, and a traveling teacher throughout the world. As a conscientious objector during World War II, he began his unswerving practice of writing before dawn each day and his habitual generosity to other writers and readers.*

John Logan

"MIDDLE AGED MIDWESTERNER AT WAIKIKI AGAIN"

The surfers beautiful as men
                              can be
ride the warm
                   blue green
                              swells
and the white sand is alive with girls.
Outriggers (double boats) ride the waves back in
as the native warriors did.
I tried to swim and tried to look,
but ended up just going back:
a huge, perfect black
man at the beach
somehow drove me away a block
to St. Augustine's Church.
The bodies were giv-
                          ing me a fit
and I have come to see the momentary calm
we find sometimes in the must of Christ
(when he was awake
                       and sweat-
ing blood
              as other slept,
or like a furious bouncer
hustling out the money changers.)
The bodies of Mary and Christ
both still live, we're told. They're alive
and thus
must have dealt with the stress
of that long time
                       of turning on
to being young.
I speak of teens.
                       Fifteen and ten
years ago when I first confessed,
it was in this same church built then
as a gigantic shed
where the strange Hawaiian birds
(I forgot their names—no matter)

flew in and out of the high wood-
en rafters
like the whimsical winds of grace,
and grace gives back to sight
what beauty is—
                    as
that loveliness as the beach.
Now the church
                    has been rebuilt
in pointed stone across the street
from a much
                    higher new hotel
where at lunch
                    I almost spilled
and found I could not eat
the purple orchid in my drink.

JOHN LOGAN *was born in 1923 in Red Oak, Iowa. He is the recipient of the Helen Bullis Prize,
the Miles Modern Poetry Prize, a Rockefeller grant, and the Morton Dauwen Zabel Award of the
National Institute of Arts and Letters. He has nine children and fourteen books of poetry, among
them* Cycle for Mother Cabrini; Ghosts of the Heart; Spring of the Thief; The Zigzag Walk;
The Anonymous Lover; *and* Poem in Progress. *He has been a frequent visitor to Hawai'i.*

Terese Svoboda

"THE LITTLE GRASS SHACK"

Give, like blood, money—
let it flow or the Hollywood flat
that's Honolulu will fall
and the burrows behind tell.

You're here to buy the beaches
for the natives. See the fish
frenzying over your peas—
no parallels, please. Yet no one

sees you. No wonder you stare
at the water—it's clear, you can

see yourself in it. That's romance.
What about the asphalt that licks

the porches like lava? Say
it's the weather you love,
not the exotic. But do not invoke
with gin any god (you don't believe it,

do you?). Do not use star fruit
to mean subtle or ginger without
the man. Actual travel schools
refine this pact but you're not

the devil, you're "howl-ee"
as a full moon that rises apart
from the condos must be howled at.
What does the tourist earn?

The right to return,
As a wave covers wave covers
shark, the animals come,
or pollen.

TERESE SVOBODA *is the author of* Cannibal; Black Glasses Like Clark Kent; Treason; A
Drink Called Paradise; Mere Mortals; *and* Trailer Girls and Other Stories. *She spent a year
in the Sudan, making documentary films and translating the songs of the Nuer. A former Distinguished Visiting Professor at the University of Hawai'i, she lives in New York City.*

Lisa Linn Kanae

"ISLAND GIRL"

On the cover of the Royal Hawaiian
Shopping Center brochure,
a girl wears a crown of plumeria
tilted slightly forward—
grazes the top of her eyebrows.
Straight black hair
frames her airbrushed face.

During the photo shoot,
in the photographer's backyard,
Bach's Air in the Key of G
floats over tripods and wardrobe racks.
Silver umbrellas filter ten o'clock
sunlight.
She wears plaid boxer shorts
beneath a borrowed red pareau.
Between costume changes she studies
prerequisite world history 151, while
the stylist retouches her blush,
reapplies glue to an uncooperative
eyelash.

The girl's features are not Asian,
Caucasian, or Pacific Islander.
More like the "other" on a census form.
A face without allegiance to one
ethnicity,
ad agency exotic: one print hits
more than two market targets.

After the photo shoot,
she catches the number 47, Waikiki
gets off at the coffee shop
between Kalakaua Avenue and Lewers
Street.
She enters the women's restroom
before the dinner rush,
changes in to a kapa-print uniform to
greet three hundred guests, two to six
at a time.
She hands each person a dinner menu
printed in English and Japanese.

Tonight's special—
Try our authentic Hawaiian Pineapple
Boat
when you order a Porter House steak
with
French fries or rice.
Behind the cashier's counter she

slips coupons inside cocktail menus;
One free continental breakfast
with every twenty-five dollar purchase.

LISA LINN KANAE, *born and raised on the island of Oʻahu, is the author of* Sista Tongue, *a memoir/essay that weaves the social history of Hawaiʻi Creole English with personal experience. Some of Kanae's prose and poetry is published in* ʻŌiwi: a Native Hawaiian Journal; Bamboo Ridge Press publications; *Hybolics; and* Tinfish. *She teaches writing and literature at Kapiʻolani Community College in Honolulu.*

Hiroko Moriyama
UNTITLED

店内の人ごみ去りし片時雨

ワイキキのはぐれ千鳥の声ためて

Waikiki no
Hagure chidori no
Koe tamate

A stray plover
Lost in Waikiki
Unable to cry for help

TRANSLATED BY SHIGEYUKI YOSHITAKE

HIROKO MORIYAMA *was born in 1936 in Tokyo, Japan. She began writing haiku around 1989 and has been an active member of the Honolulu Haiku Dohkoh-kai (Honolulu Haiku Club) since its foundation.*

Frank Stewart
"HONOLULU: WAIKIKI NIGHTS"

Midnight in the Ilikai, high on acid
you remember Myra's face after the last senior game
when you were seventeen and she was willing
for the first time it seemed to be yours in a way
that was, why, it was just like being in love, like
in a song, and all the grimy nights since then
have made Myra some angel, if you were only Rilke—
oh yes, to sing the beloved is one thing—or Apollinaire
and possess a million Apollos, with his funny
bandaged head in the Italian Government Hospital,
Quai D'Orsay, or standing with Jacqueline,
"la jolie rousse" on the Boulevard Saint-Germain,
oh Myra. You could have been her Gui—onto
the elevator rising to the 43rd floor, blue and green
lights flash, copper lamps in a series. So far up
the harbor is rocking and the boats are still.
I am the fortress of the air and you my navigator,
Myra. Over Bremen I heard someone cough into the radio.
Was that you? We're so far off course, Myra. The gunner's
dead and we're so alone. I need your love, baby, I—
Come in. Come in. You said you were hitting the silk
but I still haven't seen you and we're going down fast. No
solution now no matter that you lean over the brink
and share a cigarette with a stranger who says
it's OK to go home now, you'll get a lot older and write
poems and not even remember this night. And Myra
will seem less real than Jacqueline or Rhonda Fleming.
But in one of those radio dreams you shake the stranger's
hand and when he turns you leap the railing like an athlete
and with a flurry of wind sail out like the last B-17
over the shiny waves, spin away until you've been
a tiny spot of white above the breakers and explode.

FRANK STEWART *was born in 1946. His publications include four books of poetry, most recently* By All Means, *and eight edited or co-edited anthologies, most recently* The Poem Behind the Poem *and* Wao Akua. *Since 1989, he has edited* Mānoa. *He has received a Whiting Writers Award, the Elliot Cades Award for Literature, and the Hawai'i Award for Literature.*

Byung Hwa Cho
"한풍경 – 하와이 와기기에서"

조병화

어두워서야 내려오는
한 쌍의 사랑이 있었습니다.

바닷물을 향하여 나란히 잠겨가는
한 쌍의 사랑.

짙어지는 암흑색 바다 멀리서
밀려오는 검은 물결

펼쳐지는 흰 파도
철석하곤 사라지는 먼 불빛.

어두워서야 바다로 내려오는
한 쌍의 하얀 사랑이 있었습니다.

"ONE SCENE AT WAIKIKI"

There once was a couple's love
descending only at dusk.

The love of a couple
sinking together into the ocean,
Where a distant light vanished
with the sound of a deep white wave,

There once was a couple's white love
descending to the ocean only at dusk.

TRANSLATED BY MICHAEL J. PETTID AND KIL CHA

BYUNG HWA CHO *graduated from Kyungsung School in Seoul in 1938, and from Tokyo University in 1945. In 1949, he became a school teacher in Seoul. He worked at Jungang University, Kyung Hee University, and Inha University, where he was vice-president of the university and president of the graduate school.*

Gary Snyder
"WAIKIKI"

A steep reef of concrete, steel, and glass
Owned by one man forty percent
Whose ex-lover watches the scene for him
While tending a classy bar,
And white people get a touch of symbolic brown
    at the shore,
Brown people get their symbolic touch of white,

Twenty-five thousand rooms, on a swamp.
In the heart of it all a Banyan:
Arching and spreading,
    surrounded by buildings,
Is the god of the place. Is a ghost of the past,
The life of the present,
    the hope of the future.
(A fortune-teller booth
    tucked away in a nook in the roots.)

GARY SNYDER *is a poet and essayist based in Northern California. He lives in a remote part of the mountains north of Nevada City. He has written eighteen books.*

Dan Taulapapa McMullin
UNTITLED

To J. K. Kauanui

In the middle of Waikiki, among the
crowds from Akron and Sendai,
are two wooden painted figures, a
hula dancer and a old 'ukulele player,
the only Hawaiians to be seen on the strand, as the
hotel workers come and go
twenty feet underground, through the
tunnels assigned to workers in
Honolulu.

A Native Hawaiian truck driver on the
edge of the hotel driveway is scolded
for taking his shirt off, while tourists
walk by in g-strings.
I come out of a mahu disco feeling like
the last Hawaiian when some locals
say to each other, What a pity,
as they watch me. And I say to
myself, Whatever, I'm from Hamoa.
My brother used to tell women he's
Hawaiian.
I met a Malaysian hula performance
artist
who made a career on being Hawaiian
in L.A.
I met a Pilipino hula dancer in
Minneapolis
who asked me for advice on being
Polynesian.
I dated a Native Hawaiian guy who
only admitted he was Puerto Rican.
I have been in valleys in Ko'olauloa
that remind me of valleys in
Lealataua,
where Native Hawaiians mow their
lawns and keep the gravesites clear.
I've been knee deep in the lo'i and I've
known many Kanaka.
I don't know where any of us is going.
But I know I'm not Hawaiian.

DAN TAULAPAPA MCMULLIN'S *paintings are available through Okaioceanikarts Gallery in Auckland, New Zealand and his work is part of the Mai Ka PIKO Mai exhibition at the Bishop Museum until April 2008. His poems won a 1997 Poets & Writers Award from The Loft and his film* Sinalela *received the 2002 Best Short Film Award from the Rainbow Film Festival, sponsored by the Honolulu Gay & Lesbian Cultural Foundation. His book of short stories* The Only Paradise Is Paradise Lost, *will be published soon in Hawai'i and Aotaeroa (New Zealand). Both his parents are from American Samoa. Some of his work can be seen at www.taulapapa.com.*

Howie Fukushima
"SURFSCAPE WITH CRUEL ACTION, 1966"

The secretary on the beach,
A fading thirty-five,
Watched the boy ride down a wave,
Furiously alive.

He laid his surfboard on the sand,
And eyed her, covert, stooping;
Her little breasts were lemon-sharp,
Her buttocks, mangoes drooping.

He fed her lots of local lore,
With surfing lessons daily.
She ate it up, she bought his time,
And strummed his ukulele.
For seven days he tolerated
Overwrought possession,
Then ditched her for a blonde co-ed
Hot from the summer session.

HOWIE FUKUSHIMA *(?-2005) was an elusive figure. He shunned society, and was reported at various times as living in a tree house on Kaua'i, in a van on the Kohala coast of the island of Hawai'i, and in his last years in a piano crate high up in the back of Mānoa Valley in Honolulu, in the feral pig zone. "Surfscape" was found among his sparse papers there.*

Frank Marshall Davis
"HORIZONTAL CAMEO: RITA"

27. Rita

One big difference
Between Hollywood and Honolulu
Is that in Hawaii
I know what I'm gettin'

In Hollywood
I put promises in my purse
And smiled as if content

Maybe this guy
Really had connections in films
(Who do you say "no" to?
How do you tell
Which shell
The pea is under?)
Gals like me
Are a dime a dozen
And for free

But in Waikiki
I'm something special
To the Midwest tourists
And the Oriental trade
I'm only a little busier
Use fewer Milltowns
And have more in cash
Than the average starlet
Anytime they ask
I'll be happy to contribute
Substantially
To the Hawaii Visitors Bureau!

FRANK MARSHALL DAVIS (1905-1987) *was a newspaperman, poet, expatriate from the mainland, and resident of Hawai'i for almost forty years. As a major national journalist and former editor of the Associated Negro Press, Davis analyzed the changing configurations of ethnic groups, class structures, foreign policy and strategies of control in Hawai'i. A collection of his poetry was published posthumously as* Black Moods.

Joe Balaz
"WAIKĪKĪ STREET WOMEN"

Waikīkī street women—
hundred dollars a crack.

JOE BALAZ *was born in 1952 in Wahiawā, O'ahu, and now lives in northeast Ohio. He is the author of* Domino Buzz, *a CD of music-poetry (www.joebalaz.com) and is also co-author of* JOMA—online, *an online gallery of concrete poetry and photography with Mary Ellen Derwis (www.jomaonline.com). He edited* Ho'omānoa: An Anthology of Contemporary Hawaiian Literature *in 1989 and was on the advisory board as an editor of* Hawai'i Review. Aloha 'Āina, *a similar collection was published later that same year.*

Mahealani Perez-Wendt
"HOST CULTURE (GUAVA JUICE ON A TRAY)"

"Host culture."
What euphemistic bullshit—
Pure, unadulterated H.V.B.*   Hawai'i Visitors Bureau
They act like
They was invited—
Like all these years,
We been partying
Or something;
It's like
Getting fucked in the ass
Is supposed to be
A turn on—
Get real!
Whoever thought up
That crap
Deserves to get whacked
Let's get one thing straight:
Nobody invited anybody—
They pulled a number on us,
Big time!
It's the same old, same old—
They move in
And before you know it
They take over:
The guys in the house
End up on the streets;
The guys with scratch
End up sucking wind;
The warriors,
They all in the joint;
The wahines
They all strung out;
The kids,
They getting hauled off
By C.P.S.*   Child Protective Services
The old folks
No can handle—
Nobody like listen to them anymore;

The "leftovers,"
They all "psycho out,"
Or in the churches
Thinking they fucked up.
How you gonna act
When you think about
The haole teacher
Giving your mother
A hard one across the face
For talking Hawaiian
Or the Queen
Tripping out in prison;
Or the old gods
On display
In New England parlors
Their balls cut off—
You know, they still trying
To castrate us
You hate to think like that
But seem like
They keep trying
To convince you that
Getting raped
Is very maika'i*   good
We supposed to
Catch our thrills
Because one stealth bomber
Named "Spirit of Aloha"—
Or because hula sell
Like Amway in Japan?
Every friggin' ripoff
Get one nice Hawaiian tag—
Like we all right with it
Like we gave permission or something
Too much, these guys—
We stay all bust,
All coma out,
And they act like everything 'way cool
That's probably why
N.W.A.*   Niggers With Attitude, rap group
Get nothing over the bruddahs

They doing crack
Smoking the crystal meth
They poking heroin
They pounding wahines
They kicking ass big time!
They 'way beyond
That red rag* bullshit   gang emblem
They carrying pieces
They taking guys out
They fucking nuts!
The way they feel
You can kick their ass.

MAHEALANI PEREZ-WENDT *has been published in over a dozen literary anthologies and was a recipient of the Elliot Cades Award for Literature in 1993. Her writing reflects her love for Hawai'i and its people. She is a long-time political activist and has been administrator and executive director of the Native Hawaiian Legal Corporation for nearly thirty years. A book of poetry,* Uluhaimalama, *was published in 2007.*

Haunani-Kay Trask
"WAIKĪKĪ"

all those 5 gallon
toilets   flushing
away tourist waste
into our waters
Waikīkī   home
of *ali'i*
sewer center
of Hawai'i

8 billion dollar
beach   secret
rendezvous for
pimps

Hong Kong hoodlums
Japanese capitalists

haole punkers
condo units
of disease
drug traffic
child porn

AIDS   herpes
old fashioned
syphilis
gangland murder

gifts of industrial
culture for primitive
island people
in need

of uplift   discipline
complexity   sense
of a larger world
beyond

their careful *taro*
gardens   chiefly
politics, lowly
gods

Waikīkī: exemplar
of Western ingenuity
standing guard against
the sex life
of savages

the onslaught of barbarians

HAUNANI-KAY TRASK *is a University of Hawaiʻi professor, activist, and poet. She received a PhD from the University of Wisconsin-Madison and has since lectured and taught at universities all over the world. She is the author of* From a Native Daughter; Eros and Power; Night Is a Sharkskin Drum; Light in the Crevice Never Seen; *and* Kuʻe. *She has been a Pacific-Basin Research Fellow at Harvard University, NEA Writer-in-Residence at the Institute of American Indian Arts, and a Rockefeller Residency Fellow at the University of Colorado at Boulder.*

Imaikalani Kalahele

"WAIKĪKĪ SAMATIME"

Good ting surf up
   in Waikīkī
   Samatime

   Bamby
   da wada
   com yello!

IMAIKALANI KALAHELE, *a.k.a. Dale Alton Meurlott Kalahele, was born in 1946. Artist, poet, musician, singer, philosopher, scholar, educator, activist . . . Hawaiian. Nuf said. You heard?!*

Richard Hamasaki

UNTITLED

   tourist
   drowns

in perfect
   waves

RICHARD HAMASAKI *has a BA in English from Boston University and an MA in Pacific Studies from the University of Hawai'i at Mānoa. He published and co-edited* Seaweeds and Constructions *with Wayne Westlake. He has taught for more than twenty years at Kamehameha Schools in Honolulu, where he helped to establish a Hawaiian, Pacific and World Literature program. He and his family live in Kāne'ohe, O'ahu.*

Michael McPherson

"MY UNCLES SURFING AT WAIKIKI, CIRCA 1935"

They're young in this picture.
Their lean hard bodies are erect
in the style of their place and time,
hair blown back as they race

My Uncles Surfing at Waikiki

They are young in this picture.
Their lean hard bodies are erect
in the style of their place and time,
hair blown back as they race toward
the camera on long redwood boards.
Behind them Diamond Head
is bare but for the ironwoods
along the wide white stripe
of beach, the outline of cliffs
and gullies offset by clouds
mingled with spray and rolling foam.
They are gone now, these hapa-haole boys
at play on a wind rippled summer wave.

Courtesy of Michael McPherson.

toward the camera on long redwood boards.
Behind them Diamond Head
is bare but for the ironwoods
along the wide white stripe
of beach, the outline of cliffs
and gullies offset by clouds
mingled with spray and rolling foam.
They're gone now, these hapa-haole boys
at play on a wind rippled summer wave.

Michael McPherson
"ZERO BREAK"

for Nina

Nobody surf today
all the boys on the beach
waves so big
little more
broke all down the pier
one wave
all one time
Elks Club to Gray's
no surf
no swim
no paddle canoe
only sit on the sand
in front the pink hotel
listen to Sammy play guitar
look how big
Tarball tell to Sarge

"Eh, kid
try move you nose
no can see Diamond Head!"

Michael McPherson

Dark waters of evening blue
as we clear Pier 14, industrial
dock, round Aloha Tower and motor
slowly from under these high glass
and stone spires of the waterfront.
The low drone of the city is left
in the wake, replaced by this single
diesel and lapping sea against our bow.
There to port is the spot we called Flies,
named for the incinerator, a secondary left.
Not great but rideable, best at high tide.
Now we pass the better of Waikiki's waves,
spindrift of a late spring swell.
Our course is toward the greatest of all,
Castle's, seldom seen to break these days.
Passing Public Baths and the Natatorium
a set rides under the hull, rises and
pitches over the reef known as the boneyard.
The long concrete seawall ashore marks
this spot we anchor. Petrels wheel in
the calm evening sky, drift down and light.
Brother shuts down the engine. I the elder
son take the calabash from my mother, unwrap
ti leaves and under the growing orange sky
pass my father's ashes through my fingers
out over these rolling waters. Papa, I say
to him watching him dissolve and become one
with the sea, guarantee tonight come big.
We leave for him garlands of ginger,
puakenikeni and pink plumeria, his mother's
favorite flower, watch as he drifts
with the current. Over the towers
of our city in the grey dancing light
next dawn, over the farthest reefs
first break Waikiki, the summer waves
are huge, long and tall and green.

Sadao Izumi
UNTITLED

うれふ身は物皆さみしワイキヽの渚に光る

小さき貝も

Ureu mi wa
Mono mina samishi
Waikiki no
Nagisa ni hikaru
Chiisaki kai mo

Those who lament
Are all sad
Like the shining shells
On Waikiki Beach

TRANSLATED BY SHIGEYUKI YOSHITAKE

Dislocated

Making the scene . . . Getting no satisfaction . . . I don't care for Chinese lion dancing . . . Arriving in Honolulu, I immediately started counting Asians . . . Silver lips . . . White owls past midnight . . . A young nouveau-hippie . . . Here, there, and everywhere . . . We drove right on in past the barricades . . . Sex'n'drugs'n'rock'n'roll . . . Naked at Hanauma . . . Graffiti wars . . . R&R with a hand grenade . . . We were so young, ignorant, and violent then . . . Wild chickens, abandoned cars and cats . . . Migrations of the mind . . . I like go bust something . . .

Eric Chock
"MAKING DA SCENE"

In '66, our hair
was hitting da tops of our collars
and doing da surfa flip,
we neva tuck in da tails
of our button-down paisley shirts,
and you could still wear Beatle boots
and make da scene.
All summer we cruised Ala Moana,
Conrad and me, new wrap-around
sunglasses making everything green,
rolling along with da Stones and
getting no satisfaction
in his brother Earl's '63 Dodge Dart,
lifted, quad carburetor, could do 90
on da new H-1 Freeway, but
we neva even think we was mean.
Everytime around,
we just leaned down in his
blue vinyl seats, hoping
somebody would notice us
as we rumbled through da park,
those wrap-arounds like protection
and a tease
for those cute chicks
who was out there every day,
doing da same thing.

Rodney Morales
"CLEAR ACRYLIC ENAMEL"

N*ow* it comes. Clear Acrylic Enamel. Funny how it hits you long after you've given up trying to remember. Boy, it had a good taste.
Wouldn't even bother to describe it. Like sex, acid, death, and adulthood,
you gotta try it to know what it's about. I let the feeling capture me. It

had long been reverberating in the inner recesses of my mind and now something—a smell, a taste, a sound—has summoned it to the forefront, ringing clear, to be absorbed NOW! before it is reduced to fragmented memories.

Silver lips. It is my memory now. Our insides must have primed, lacquered and enameled. I wonder if the paint eroded any in the past two years.

Lenny is trying to sneak in. Arthur's verbally seducing two chicks. Me? I'm watching. I've been watching since sixty-nine when my fingers were slammed by a yardstick and my terrified eyes watched her mouth moving "In my class you pay attention!" The mean, craggy, Oriental face. I had merely been leaning back on the two rear legs of my chair against the wall, with one ear pressed against it, trying to hear what went on on the other side. No. It must have been the paint. Sharpened me insenses or some-think. Made life a motion picture, an Edward Hopper painting come to life, with me, Lenny and Arthur the central characters, the subjects.

These nights were a movie. The same movie again and again, weekend after weekend, concert after concert—sneaking in. It's become a habit, me, Lenny and Arthur sneaking into concerts. HIC Arena, Waikiki Shell, Andrews Amphitheater. Wherever concerts were held, the film was being done on location. It was always challenging enough not to get boring, like the pinball machines at Rainbow Billiards, when we mastered them to the point that the games weren't fun anymore.

Sneaking in is hard. Well, not so much at Andrews, with its not-too-high chain-link fence, its relatively easy to climb walls. One could even go under the fence at one part, while the less risky (LRs) climbed one of the portable buildings around the amphitheater for the loftier view.

Getting into the Waikiki Shell is difficult. The fence is higher than that of Andrews. Once you get over the fence at most of the points around the place, you have to run across a field and hurdle still another fence (if you are able to avoid being tackled by a cop who is just itching (and I mean itching) to rough you up). The best chance is to leap the fence by the bathroom, run into it and calmly take a piss.

HIC Arena? Now that's a brand-new ballgame. Those of you with weak hearts better go and buy tickets right now, if any are left. It's a flying-saucer-(modern, I guess) shaped castle, complete with a moat around it. No alligators, though, just millions of tilapia, not to mention a sizable number of ducks. The best possible way of getting in without the ticket that lets you cross the drawbridge is to creep along the walls which have a fairly long footwide ledge, leap a waist-high railing, dart toward the stairs and either sit down conspicuously on the stairs if there are no empty seats or walk around all night like you're spaced out. The only problem is getting over that little railing without being grabbed by a cop or security officer who usually is waiting to knock you into the moat.

The cop—male, about thirty, local—is waiting for Lenny, who is standing along a ledge with his back against the wall. The cop senses he is there though he can't see Lenny because the ledge he is on projects like an *L*. The cop is at the top point of the letter and Lenny is balancing along at the bottom. It is only when Lenny turns the corner that the police officer can see who is crazy enough to make the attempt. I wipe my forehead, signaling Lenny that the cop is present. He retreats to the diagonally-opposite end of the top of the L-shaped wall and onto the safety of the grass.

It's important to me that Lenny gets in—I don't care if I can't do it and Arthur's more into scoring with chicks anyway—because Lenny's the best. Sneaky, clever, and gutsy as hell. What's more—dig it—he's on a streak. He's gotten in free eighteen times in a row, man. Not the last eighteen concerts (who wants to see the Carpenters?), but eighteen times in eighteen. He's *got* to get in. Our goal is twenty. That's why I'm standing here on the grass giving him signals. You follow me? Maybe there's paint in you. Remember, movies don't provide you with instant replays like T.V. does. And sometimes you have to read the book first.

The cop moves from his position and stands by the snack bar which is contained within the L-shaped wall. He is itching to bust Lenny's or any non-payer's (NP) head. There is and isn't a crowd outside. No cohesion. Not like that Hendrix concert when Lance was still around and before I began watching, when some weird sonofabitch pulls a fifth column by accidentally (hmmm) leaning on the wide bar that disengaged the lock on these side doors, doors flying open, with fifty bodies smashing through. Then, with the security officers (SO) chasing them all over the place and the notoriously-innocent guy yelling "Wha'd I do? Wha'd I do?" me, Lenny, Arthur, Lance and some other guys who later changed into Double Knit Assholes (DNA) are sucked in by the wide vaccum and settle on the steps inside just in time to hear Hendrix make the "Star-Spangled Banner" worth listening to, shortly before he was shot. Wait. Wait. It was King who was shot. Christ, I'm getting history distorted. I don't know who was murdered, who simply OD'd and who was watching as I am now.

Maybe that's what I'm doing: Seeing that history comes out straight and clear—truth in other words—because I know now that Lenny, who approaches me now, is making history.

"Pretty rough tonight," I say.

"Ah, fuck, we get 'em. Even if I gotta swim." His words make me look at the ducks for some reason. "Where Atta went?"

"Where else?" I turn my head toward Arthur and the two girls, and point with my index finger.

"The fuckah," he says. Lenny, with his hands in his pocket—as if to make his shoulders look bigger—approaches Arthur who is conversing with a couple of Oriental girls. Both Lenny and Arthur are the same height, about five-eight, but Lenny's features are obviously Filipino while Arthur's reveal some Hawaiian. I have never asked him what the rest is. Me? I'm watching. Not only watching, but following Lenny so I can also listen. I see that Lenny, perhaps instinctively, approaches the shorter of the two girls.

"Hey, you like fuck?" One thing about Lenny, he's honest. The girl turns color before my eyes, different shades of red. "Man, I know you like fuck." Color Arthur steaming purple, the other girl pale.

"We better go da odda side," the taller girl says. The two girls walk away. Arthur turns to Lenny. He is angry but doesn't want to speak too loud.

"You fuckah!" he says. "What you trying? I had the fuckah! Shit. Now I gotta start all ovah again."

Lenny glares back at him. "Shit. We no mo' all night! Man, if they like, they like! Why waste our fucking time? You like get in or not!"

"Fuck the concert!" Arthur yells. "I rather get laid!" For some strange reason, whenever they start to argue they glance toward me as if I should say something.

"Clear Acrylic Enamel." What else could I say?

"Hey, yeah!" Arthur says, "Thass the one!" Lenny does not look enthused, because he is. His facial expressions are incredibly downplayed, like the expressions of someone who knows there's a camera on him and wishes to deceive it.

"Thass the baby," Lenny says. "Taste so fucking sweet, man." Lenny's tone changes suddenly, addressing me. "Hey, you goin' try or what? This fuckah," he points to Arthur, "he retire already."

"I goin' try," I say. "But you gotta get in first."

"No make difference. I can get in by myself."

"Sure, Lenny," Arthur interjects. "Sure." Within a few minutes we agree that Lenny has to get in first. We try the same place with me and Arthur playing first and third base coach, respectively. It is too risky and we stop him before he gets thrown out. We decide to wait until intermission.

Minutes later the crowd starts pouring out of the inner sanctum. It is intermission.

You may leave now. Be back in about ten minutes.

What? You're still here? Intermissions can be important, too? Really?

The inside crowd is not a crowd. No cohesion. Faces are not faces. I see glazed eyes, eyelids painted blue, green, eyes drifting, eyebrows lifting, lids sagging, eyes passing eyes, ass grabbing eyes. But the clothes! Polyester, double-knit slacks, hip-hugging perma-press jeans, skimpy blouses, perma-wrinkled silks shirts, sandals, slippers, high-heeled shoes, all suggesting that the music is of secondary importance. One can always tell who's playing by the crowd. Most of the people wander around, captured in a web of paranoic tranquility. A few stand by the railing that keeps them from falling into the moat and stare, outward, at us. Actually, a lot of them are staring at the ducks.

The ducks! Why didn't I think of that?

"Lenny. Atta." I sound enthused. "We go give them one dee-coy." Arthur looks puzzled, while Lenny, though he may be puzzled, seems to have it figured out already. I tell Arthur to go along the *L* ledge and attract attention. Not too obviously, though. Lenny has already figured out his part. He heads toward another ledge about ninety feet to the left of the L-shaped one.

People on the outside see Arthur on the ledge and watch me play third-base coach, a job I relish. They seem to be united by this valiant effort. The cop, sensing something, acts like nothing is going on. He doesn't want to stop the attempt, but rather wipe out whoever reaches the railing. Those standing at the railing sense what's happening too. They're actually paying attention.

Arthur is all smiles. The cop *knows* I'm giving signals and pretends otherwise. Then, this lady security officer, twentyish, slightly overweight, who's been guarding the ledge ninety feet to the left senses that something's up and unobtrusively walks in the direction of the cop. Lenny steals across the ledge like no one else can, leaps the unguarded railing and is lost in the inside crowd. Number nineteen. One more to go. The outside crowd applauds. Arthur sticks his head around the corner of the L-shaped wall and smiles at the puzzled cop and equally puzzled security lady. Intermission is over.

After seeing the inside crowd and sensing that the cop is itching to get me, I don't try very hard to get in. I end up joining Arthur, who is now talking to the taller of the two chicks. I start talking to the other one, and me and Arthur end up heading toward the car with the two faceless girls.

The morning after, while me and Arthur are blessed with aching balls, Lenny is telling us how great a concert it wasn't. A wasted effort.

"Yeah, Lenny, yeah," me and Arthur harmonize.

"Fucking teasers," Arthur adds, "wasting my fucking dope."

"*Our* fucking dope," Lenny says.

"That's the trip," I say. "Painted eyelids are for teasing, Clear Acrylic does the pleasing." I do not know what the fuck I am talking about which is cool because none of us do most of the time. It is this absurdity that links us together. Words, by necessity, take on different shades of meaning in the continuously evolving process of language. We understand the absurdity, that's what matters. My words sent their minds back in time (Or did their minds summon a piece of their past? What goes where?) Anyway, we reminisce.

We live in a two-bedroom apartment in Makiki, the low-rise, apartment/condominium center of the Pacific that lies in the shadow of Punchbowl, the extinct crater now used as a national cemetery. The three of us sleep in the bedroom with wall-to-wall mattresses and floor to ceiling naked lady posters and assorted scrawls and drawings. In the other room we keep our guitars and assorted instruments—harmonicas, tambourines, maracas, parts of a drum set, and an old honky-tonk piano. We just play for fun now since Lance, our lead singer, is away. The combination living room/kitchen has only the essentials: a gas stove, a small refrigerator and a sink (of course) on one end; a foot high table in mid-center with *gozas* under and around it, which we now sit on; a telephone on the wall that bisects the apartment; and, against that same wall, a *Pioneer* stereo component system replete with the kind of speakers that make neighbors complain.

It had taken us about a year to fix the rust on our '64 Volkswagen. It belongs to me, Lenny, Arthur and Lance, should he return. That's how we got into the paint thing. Yesterday, Saturday, we sanded down all the rusty areas and patched up the holes with *Bondo*. Then we sprayed those areas with a primer. The scent sent us into our pre-car adolescent sniffing days, the pre-grass phase. Then, like right now, we reminisced on our spacing out, on our hearing the "Now I know I'm *stoned!*" buzz, and, unforgettably, we laughed over the time we didn't use the usual colorless acrylic paint and stood out at a dance-party because our silver lips glowed in the dark. Silver lips, the more we thought of it the more we laughed. It was the accidental yet obvious emblem of our defiance. Our own silly way of saying *fuck your world.*

But we couldn't figure out what paint gave us the best high until I flashed on it last night at the concert.

Sundays are dull, duller when it's cloudy. And they are dullest when it is early November and clouds are a sign of what's to come. Makes you almost wanna put on your Sunday best and go to church, just for the hell of it. I am on the verge of putting on something decent when Lenny suggests we go to Sandy Beach.

"If we goin' get wet, we might as well get drenched," he says. The day might be salvaged. The only problem is who is willing to drive. It's always a struggle.

"My leg sore," Arthur says, getting off to a good start, holding his left nut for emphasis.

"Fuck," Lenny says, "My eyes too fucking phased out, man."

"I'll drive," I mumble.

"Shit, my leg!" Arthur squeezes tighter.

"You only need one leg, pal," Lenny says.

"What about the fucking clutch?" Arthur counters.

"Shove it up your fucking nose," Lenny says, smiling.

"I'll drive," I say louder. They continue to argue for a full minute before they realize I have offered to drive, to everyone's surprise, including mine. "But everybody gotta chip in fo' gas."

It is a thirty-five minute drive to Sandy Beach from our apartment in Makiki, in the midst of the mess that is Honolulu, but if we're lucky we'll make it in an hour. First we stop for gas at the service station where we work. Then we head toward an on-ramp to the H-1 Freeway. All the car windows are open because the overhanging clouds and the tall buildings on each side of the narrow street box us in enough already. When we are on the freeway we breathe easier as this stretch of freeway on the way to Sandy Beach rises high above the city.

Honolulu is like a woman who doesn't know what she's got and does everything to look more like someone else every passing day, the someone else being LA.

They've shaven your pubic palm trees
and replaced them with a concrete slab . . .
Out of which grow sky high cement stubbles that
make you look so drab . . .
. . . Oh, no, Lulu, what have they done to you.

Nobody's singing. And the words aren't mine. Words from a song Lance wrote echo in my mind. I then flash on the last, unfinished lyric he showed me:

When you look at the world through high-priced cameras
there's an even higher price you have to pay
I'm sorry what you see is not more glamorous a snapshot
you want orange, you're only getting gray . . .
Take off the lens cap, take in the landscape
stay away from the mind traps that people call "escape"
Be sure it's not another trap that you're escaping to
and just as negatives develop, so will you . . .

"Hey," Lenny says from behind me. "You sleeping o' what?"

"No," I answer, snapping out of the daze induced by the highway, "just meditating my ass off."

"I just wanted to make sure you know wha's happenin' ahead."

"Yeah." We have come to the part where the freeway ceases to be a freeway and becomes a highway, with traffic lights and all.

As we cruise down the long stretch of road known as Kalanianaole Highway, most of the claustrophobia is gone. No tall buildings. Just good old suburban-type homes, wide streets and all. Everyone knows that the wider the streets are, the nicer the homes. Quite unlike the one-lane two-way streets in Palama . . . Whoops. Starting to daydream again. Better keep my eyes on the road. In other words watch.

Trees are abundant on both sides of the highway, swaying slightly in a gentle breeze that is not so gentle for us as we now fly down the road. Lenny tells me to stop at Koko Marina Shopping Center a little further up.

I turn in to the parking area of the shopping center and park alongside a curb, because parking's hard to find and me and Arthur will wait in the car anyway. Lenny dashes out. I turn up the car radio:

"*There must be some kinda way outa here,*"
    said the joker to the thief.
"*There's too much confusion,*
    I can't get no relief. . . ."

"Hendrix sings the shit outa that song," Arthur says. I nod. It starts to drizzle. Lenny returns in a couple of minutes with a package. Arthur asks him what he bought. Lenny says "Dig!" when I turn back onto the highway, I am in the right-most lane. Arthur tells me to shift into the next lane because the one we're in feeds into it up ahead.

With the drizzle, with my mind into Hendrix's frenzied guitar-work, and his rendering of Dylan's words: "There are many here among us who feel that life is but a joke," and with my eyes checking the side mirror for cars and my hands turning the wheel simultaneously, by the time my awareness is set on what's ahead by Arthur's "Hey!" I find myself running a red light. I blast my horn without knowing why. Perhaps it's an instinctive grasp for legitimacy. The other guys laugh and wave at the cars we pass. As we head uphill, I gaze into the rear-view mirror for a cop's flashing blue light but only see the two red traffic lights. As the lights get fainter, I am increasingly relieved, secure as the drizzle stops and splinters of sunlight penetrate the clouds.

We arrive at the beach. Somehow water lures us like nothing else, with the possible exception of music. Arthur passes by two chicks on beach towels—straining to maintain their tans, I guess—with scarcely a glance. He wants to bodysurf as much as me and Lenny do. I guess his balls still ache and he knows the therapeutic value of a whirlpool of salt water.

Lenny and Arthur are pros in the ocean. They carve through waves, weave under them, slice the fucking ocean to ribbons. Me, I get smashed. But don't get me wrong. I love every fucking shorebreak of wave that smashes me into the sand. I love when it sucks me in for more, and thrashes me again because I know I'll somehow manage to sneak in a couple of good rides.

It's funny how we take to the ocean after Lance's disappearance. The papers say he drowned. I don't believe what I read. They never found the body. I dive under a mother of a wave. Lance split. Me, Lenny and Arthur know that. It was the first and last time I dropped acid. The four of us were walking along the sea wall at Ala Moana when the acid hit. I am drifting now. At that instant we transformed into the Beatles walking down Abbey Road. I felt I was part of an album cover. Who could imagine how they felt, how me, Lenny and Arthur felt when it started to become a four-way street, when Lance broke toward the beach, dove into the water, and swam toward the crooked bowl of moon as water slowly filled it. All we saw afterwards, when we swam out there, was a blinking red light. We spent the whole night looking for him, long after the rescue unit gave up. I am drifting out more. He didn't know how to drown. Besides, he had plans. We don't talk about Lance much—his quiet, calculated movements that almost obscured his constant agitation—but we knew better than to go to a fucking memorial service. I tread water. He was weird but he was the sharpest of us. His conception of the world was getting people to sneak out of concerts. Damn it. He's just playing some super sly game, waiting for the right time. He's gone under— *yughh*, so have I. I've swallowed a mouthful. What a taste.

It sometimes takes hours to describe a moment. On the other hand . . . Hours later I fall down on the wet sand. I look up ahead and see Lenny ripping his towel apart.

There's a buzzing in my head. Someone is watching me. In fact there's a lot of them. I stare up from behind the sea wall. No choice. I make a run for it into the ethereal darkness. I stumble, scraping the tops of my toes. My mind runs back to a Santana concert at the Shell. There's at least a thousand of us outside. We have two things in common: we hate (or can't afford) to pay for music, and we want to get in. The vast majority of us are male. More than half are white guys, *haoles*. There are no fences between them and us shaded folks. There's a proliferation of attempts to get inside. Cops slam the ones they catch against the fence, then make them climb back out. Some return bleeding. Twenty police cars are parked at one end of Kapiolani Park, which partially surrounds the Shell. A couple of cops are giving tickets to cars parked along a dirt road in another part of the park. Cops on motorcycles drive through the crowd, dispersing us, as we get rowdier by the minute. The cops get even rowdier and force us to dive out of the way. Santana starts to play. The percussionistic spray of beat captures something in us, something wildly primitive. Some crazy fucker climbs the fence. Then another . . . and another . . . then a hundred. I start to climb as the screaming guitar pierces the wall of fear. Halfway on top I stop because I don't see Lance, Lenny, and Arthur. No! I stop because there's more going on outside! I leap back. Lance runs up to me with a bunch of parking tickets he pulled off the windshields of cars. The police department is gonna have one hell of a time convincing people that they got tickets tonight.

The buzzing gets louder. We drift from Abbey Road and float through a world of dark, only starlit space and metronomic, undulating rhythm. Secrets unfold as universes open like sleepy eyes. Seemingly impenetrable boundaries unbound, reveal themselves as clear walls of sound, soaking in an ocean of black, spacy void. Space. Rhythm. Space. Rhythm. The HIC Arena floats by. In the starlight of distance far beyond, I see Lance . . . filming it all. A silver circle is spinning, I am finding. Unwinding. Unwind.

I am staring at the door latch release button of the Volkswagen. I no longer hear the buzz. I see a piece of towel in my hand and realize it is dark. We are still at the beach, for Christ's sake! Hypnotized by a fucking release button?

I am freezing my ass as I get up to look for Lenny and Arthur. I am headed toward the bathroom when I see them walking along the beach with rags held to their mouths. I see a blinding flash right at Lenny's waist. It is the moon's reflection off a paint can, partially tucked in his shorts.

Monday. Arthur has managed to get the phone number of the girl he met at last Saturday's concert by calling up all the "Wongs" at random in the phone book. I laughed everytime he said "Wong numbah" and slammed the phone. He tries to make a date for Friday's concert at Andrews. She won't go unless her friend can come along. He tries to get me to take the other girl.

"Come on, you fuckah," he says, cupping the receiver. "I desperate, man."

"No way."

"Hey, come on. I really dig this chick, man. She all right."

"Find some other flower." He tells her he'll call her back later and hangs up the phone. He is quiet for awhile.

"Hey. How about if I pay for your ticket," he says, breaking the silence. He is desperate.

"I getting in free," I say, "along with Lenny's record-breaking shot."

"Fuck. He can get in by himself. He not one baby." He is silent for a moment. "Hey, come on. I know we can get us some fucking righteous lays."

"Later." I sense a wall forming. He's pretty pissed off at me, like he is several times a month. This time more so.

It's ten in the morning. Lenny started working at eight. Me and Arthur start working at eleven. We all work as service station attendants at the same place, Herb's Union (HU), in Makiki. I am getting ready to go to work. Arthur's on the phone again.

At work, we talk about the previous day and night and swear never to get nostalgic for a can of paint again, especially one that doesn't give us silver lips.

The week goes by fast. I anxiously await Friday's concert, which features local rather than mainland groups. Arthur is ecstatic to the point of actually being nice to us. The girl finally agreed to go with him to the concert alone. It bothers me and Lenny. We sense that he is one of the DNAs now. Me and Lenny have not discussed the matter but there is no need to. When you go through some profound changes with someone your wave lengths are generally on the same frequency. We know that only Lance's return could knock some sense into Arthur.

I spend my spare time (when I'm alone and it's quiet) drawing. I use the foot-high table for support. I try all kinds of styles, starting with straight forward, representational sketches, then moving toward the abstract utilizing my vague notions of cubism. Now I try to draw a map of Honolulu centering on three points, representing the HIC Arena (to the left of center), the Waikiki Shell (far to the right), and Andrews Amphitheater (above the center). I draw lines connecting them, then a pool-ball rack around them. Then I fill in other places, drawing more and more lines until the paper is a mess. I end up drawing conclusions:

This is fiction, not real. A sound is echoed. It reverberates, is endlessly distorted. Do you see yourself in these lines?

Andrews is quite a place; compact in size, as compared to the other arenas. Its situation in the center of the University of Hawaii guarantees a student audience. Portable buildings linger off two sides of the Amphitheater and their rooftops give far better views of concerts than a fairly large arena would. It isn't that difficult to climb the portable buildings either. Just balance yourself on the railing as I am doing now, reach for the roof, then pull yourself up, hugging the roof as if your life depended on it.

While I am struggling to get the greater portion of my body on the roof (being that most of me is dangling), one of the LRs pulls me up and I temporarily join their ranks. As I gaze inside while taking hits from the joints that keep coming to me, I recall the hardness of the concrete seats that circle around the crater-shaped amphitheater and the contrasting softness of the grass in the center, in front of the stage. The majority of the people inside huddle closely on the grass. The ones with meaty asses sit on the concrete, while some bony-assed freaks walk around. I see quadro-fiends, *stereoids*, lunatics, professors, but no Arthur. I guess he's just a part of the crowd. I decide to go down and join Lenny as, simultaneously, the red spotlight shines from its position on the grass, reflects on the polished steel of a guitar, stabbing my eyes, and the too-loudly-amplified instrument screams in agony. I almost fall off the roof.

I join Lenny outside a side gate, a position that allows for a partial view of the stage. "Lenny, pain is in my ears and in my eyes," I practically sing. I watch the stage act, remembering how a very nervous Lance once told me that each stage is a world.

Sneaking in seems so easy here. The fence-bordered hemisphere leads to a jungle of plants, an ideal place for balling if you don't mind bugs crawling up your ass. The other hemisphere is wall, with a railing on top so no one falls out. If you can race up the wall and into the crowd you're good—or nobody's watching. (Remember, Lenny's the best—and I'm watching.) The security here are not cops, usually, but guys hired by the promoter depending on the promoter's whims. Usually they're university dudes (DUDES) who've got the "ins" with the promoter or his brother. All in all, it looks like number twenty's gonna be no trouble for Lenny, who is biding his time right now.

It's hard to believe the same group is playing. The volume has been toned down and the sound is pleasing to the ear. The music permeates the atmosphere with a folk-rock haze. I stand soaking in the juxtaposition of a stirring bass and drum counterpoint and a high-pitched, intricately woven harmony. I recognize the song to be a Jackson Browne tune as I tune in to the words:

> . . . *I thought that I was free but I'm*
> *just one more prisoner of time,*
> *alone within the boundaries of my mind . . .*

There is a short instrumental break.

> . . . *I thought I was . . .*

Delicately piercing three-part harmony. Cut. One voice:

> . . . *A child.*

When the music's good who cares about anything else. I actually smile. The cool November air fills my lungs. Good fucking hit.

"I just wen' give it to one of yo' friends," a rowdy voice says, disrupting the acoustic blend. My first thought is to respond. Then I realize that the voice is addressing a haole guy a few feet to my right (Lenny's on my left). The haole guy looks at the source of the voice and says nothing. The source is a husky, Hawaiian-looking guy, carrying a gleaming silver object. It is a flashlight. There are a few other husky guys around him.

The promoter of tonight's concert has a mean streak.

"I talking to you, you fuckah." The husky guy's voice is not rowdy now. It is outright hostility. "I wen' give yo' friend one good whack with dis," he says, waving the flashlight. "I t'ink da bugga stay bleeding. Why you no look?" The haole guy says nothing, doesn't move. "He t'ink he can sneak ovah da fence, eh? I like see you try, you fucking haole."

The last words sting. The connection is clear now. What he is really saying is "I hit one of yours." Does this Hawaiian think of himself as "one of ours"?

My face is on fire. When I turn to look at Lenny's the glow in his eyes suggest the same. There are god knows how many of them. I stand immobile. Me and Lenny, the husky security men, and the two (an unsuspecting fool comes by) haoles form a curious triangle. Three sides rather than three angles. The inside of the triangle is solid, though invisible. We are the edges of clear acrylic walls. There is no straight route to any one of the other sides. Rather, one had to hit his outer edges and make a radical turn. There isn't time and space for that, especially when each side seems to rest on a different plane.

Who created these walls? Were they there all the time?

Moments fail to pass. I close my eyes to prevent their glow from being caught by the gleaming flashlight. I see it shining at me as I provoke assault with taunts: "What you doing in prison, brah? What you doing *inside?*"

The gate swings open and about ten of them charge me, Lenny and any haoles that are nearby. I swing wildly, seeing blood gush from cut eyelids, broken noses, seeing blood on oncoming fists. I see the flashlight coming towards my head. My hands are beaten numb. I can no longer defend myself. I see it all even though nothing has happened. I've just reopened my eyes. Everyone is still on their edge of their triangle side.

You see, I read the book. Does the movie, or should I say silver screen extravaganza, with a cast of god knows how many, end the same way? I turn to Lenny.

"You know what Lance would do in this situation," I say to him.

"Lance is dead!" Lenny screams. "The fuckah is dead!" He runs up to the gate and starts pulling on it. I am frozen.

"Hey, what you trying?" the husky Hawaiian says. "I no like hit you."

Still numb I too leap toward the gate, and pull. The haoles and other people on the outside, for some strange reason, run up to the fence and start pulling. I pull because I am burning inside because I didn't tear down the HIC walls to see Joplin before she died. No! I am pulling because when I leaned back against the wall in class I was listening to a message that Lance was pounding out from the other side. I am pulling because of the way walls are so strategically placed, so remarkably calculated. I pull and feel the fence come crashing down. I see the husky guy whack Lenny with the flashlight. I jump him. Lenny grabs the flashlight, runs into the inside crowd, throws the flashlight, and when I see and hear the red spotlight shatter I cease to watch.

RODNEY MORALES, *born in 1952, is the editor of* Hoʻi Hoʻi Hou: A Tribute to George Helm and Kimo Mitchell, *and the author of* The Speed of Darkness, *a short story collection, and* When the Shark Bites, *a novel. His stories have been published in numerous journals, and anthologized in* Rereading America *and* Growing Up Puerto Rican.

Kathy Dee Kaleokealoha Kaloloahilani Banggo
"NO MINDLESS DIGGING"

For Jeff

He used to call me pua, said he had been blessed with rain.

One time . . . many times . . . long before classic
Rolls Royce lipstick and stilletto heels,
when white owls past midnight meant my father's
ghost warned me home, my first love and I
claimed Hālawa valley. We picked flowers, ate
guavas, hiked barefoot,   let the mosquitoes bite,
examined insects, wrote poetry, ran our hands
over bark, got high, smelled leaves, b r e a t h e d,
listened to bird calls and answered back, planted
seeds, whistled, recited poetry, stripped and
kissed and made love, dozed, ate more guavas, hid
from the rifle-shouldering boys come to harvest
their pakalolo crops, dreamed of plump babies and
papaya trees, the rows of sleeping willows, the
kalo patch, the ocean just beyond the window,
the skateboard ramp out back . . .

Some days I want to turn around, turn my back on black stockings
and fax machines, the sticky adhesive of the city, lost love, new loves, cold
cream, offices, therapy.

We drove right on in past the barricades on
most nights. Other times, the boys bothered
to step out of the car to push those red-orange
striped barriers aside. No trespassing? Who
but a handful of misfit kids in worn out flannel
and torn denim would be interested in an
unfinished freeway?

We parked in the bushes, out of sight of HPD;
the boys drank beer and tossed their empty
Hinano bottles into the ditch running alongside
H-3. I scolded, being sober, and an environmen-
talist of sorts.

It could mean a return to a time before my own burial—digging, I mean,
Thoughtful digging. Ethical effort. Every measured meter of dirt uplifted
and cleared away could mean uncovering an old and forgotten simplicity.
My friend Kammie, a young nouveau-hippie with spacious eyes and a china
plate smooth forehead, told me about the job. She's working Hālawa
with an archaeology group contracted to excavate the valley. The pay is
good and I'm a penniless wanna-be poet burned out on poor, wanna-be
poetry. The real stuff is out there, means walking those trails again like we
did 8? 9? 10? years ago. Hell, I'll dig. If it means feeling the walls again
(2 feet high at the most), built beside the stream.

"Some old hippie dude built that wall," he says,
"Wanted to live like Thoreau."
"Crap." I'm kicking the shallow water with my
toes. "Little people did this."
"Littler than you?"
I snob slowly, the way a chameleon blinks but
without the drugged laziness, and say, "See
how low the walls are? And look at the way
the rocks are placed."
He grins.
"Carefully and with craftsmanship. One by one.
By hand." I nod. "Yup. Menehune."
"Yup," he mimics, "Menehune."
I am tired from speaking and lean against him.
My jaw hurts and I have cotton mouth from
all the effort it takes to pronounce my

English properly. He and his long-haired
buddies had teased the pidgin right from my
tongue so only traces of the melodic island
lilt remain.

I didn't know. I thought finding artifacts would save Hālawa. Isn't there a
law—? Like I said to my ma, it'll help to preserve the culture. She had been
up in arms against my wanting to dig. Not because of H-3—my mom, she
thinks in terms of white owls. So I told her, I told her, I said without really
saying that she was being superstitious. You see, I had forgotten. Somewhere between oceans I'd dropped the old blueprints, somewhere a long
time ago.

One time at high noon. Right on the hood of his
Duster, with a helicopter hovering and buzzing
overhead like some insane dragonfly.
I've never been so warm.

At night he drove mauka down H-3, flicking the
headlights off then on to the base of the
mountain where construction stopped. I didn't
know which was worse, driving with the lights
on or off. There's something ominous about
being the only hissing engine on a half-built
freeway. Slows the breath. All that bleached
concrete illuminated in the headlights thins
the air. It's paved desolation, a silence too
difficult to understand. We didn't try. Instead
we closed our eyes and kissed.
"Someday when we're old and this thing's built
we can tell our kids how and where and when—."
We stripped and kissed and made love because it
was easier. Because freeways cutting through
sacred valleys, like blue shadows darkening under
the eyes, was too burdensome a subject for the
churning, the arrogance of youth. *Why? Why?*

KATHY DEE KALEOKEALOHA KALOLOAHILANI BANGGO *grew up on Oʻahu and
graduated from the University of Hawaiʻi at Mānoa. She is widely published and has won a
number of writing awards, including an Intro Award for Poetry from the Associated Writing Programs.*

Hiroyuki Agawa
from "HANAUMA BAY"

T he heavy downpour that began at dawn let up. The sky was clear, and it turned out to be a warm day. Sakuma looked down on the street behind the hotel and saw an automobile encrusted with rust spots speeding through a puddle, raising sprays of light.

The others in his group had left on a tour bus, and it was quiet inside the economy-rate hotel.

Sakuma hadn't planned to see anyone, but he thought of Joji Taki, whom he remembered with fondness. He got out his small notebook, put on his bifocals, and reached for the telephone.

He heard the phone ring at the other end. He counted the number of rings, and after the seventh, decided he should try Taki's number at the university. He was ready to hang up when Taki answered.

"Where are you calling from?" Taki apparently thought it was an overseas call. Sakuma told him he had arrived the day before.

"By yourself? I'd like to see you," he said warmly. "I have to supervise a student experiment in the afternoon, but I'm free until then. Don't worry. Remember that beach we once went to? Why don't we go there for a swim?"

About fifteen miles east of where he was staying was a beautiful bay that was seldom frequented by visitors. Even beginners could use dive masks to watch many kinds and sizes of tropical fishes foraging for food amid the coral reef. Sakuma had first gone there five years earlier, when he was taken along by Taki, whom he had remet after a twenty-seven year separation.

Kaimuki, Kapahulu, Hukilau, Hunakai, Hanauma, Haleiwa—the Hawaiian language had so few consonants that all place names sounded the same, and Sakuma had trouble telling them apart. Hearing his complaint, Taki had said, "Think of it as 'Flower-Horse' Bay," and for Sakuma's benefit wrote out the Japanese graphs for *hana* ("flower") and *uma* ("horse").

"I come here often by myself after I've finished my classes, and have an early evening swim."

Sakuma, troubled by the uncertainty of his future at that time, had envied Taki, who would spend his days at the university, then enjoy a swim at this marvelous beach before dinner.

That feeling of envy had never left him. And now, having agreed to meet Taki at ten o'clock, he hung up. He was happily anticipating some time in the sea with tropical fishes, with no need to think about having to spend his time "usefully."

If one should wish to be free on this island without contacting people, without relying on their hospitality, one needed a car. Hardly the type to tolerate conversations with cab drivers, and feeling more misanthropic by the minute, Sakuma had walked into an establishment displaying a "U-Drive" sign on a nearby street corner and rented a car.

He was at the appointed spot above the bay early. He left his car in the parking area cradled amidst low-rising slopes and walked to the lookout bounded by a low wall made of volcanic rocks, beyond which a sheer precipice dropped dramatically to a vista of remarkably clear blue-green waters.

Although this was only his third time there, he felt as if he had "come home." Carrying a beach mat, snorkeling equipment, and a towel, he strode down the narrow winding path to the beach.

It had rained the night before, and the sand was wet. There were only a few sunbathers. Taki apparently had not yet come.

Sakuma had not at first known that Taki was a Japanese-American, born in Hawaii, or that his given name Joji was a Japanese phonetic adaptation of his real name, George. He found this out when they were both ninth-graders back home. Until then, he had thought of Taki, who tended to stay in the background, seldom speaking out, as an unassuming youngster typical of those who came from provincial farming families—and that his facility in English was due to some innate talent for acquiring foreign languages.

During the war Taki served in the Japanese military as a second lieutenant in the Transportation Corps, and soon after the end of the war he rejoined his brothers and sisters in Honolulu. Twenty years later, he was Professor George Taki at the University of Hawaii. Taki had not changed; he had never been talkative. Indeed, when the two remet five years ago, he talked very little about himself.

At last, Sakuma saw him lying quietly on a mat spread out over the sand, on his back, his arms and legs outstretched. He greeted him from above and lay down beside him.

All they heard were the onrushing waves and the wind and the occasional far-off hum of jetliners on steep climbs after leaving the airport runway. The slight sounds made by palm fronds reminded Sakuma of the rustling of a tattered paper fan.

When Sakuma closed his eyes, his eyelids became lined with a golden glow against which a row of green dots coiled lazily. The hot sun beating down on his aging body lent a delicious sensation. He lay quietly, his eyes closed.

Presently he heard Taki calling out to him.

"You came on short notice. Is it business or a New Year's vacation?"

"I ran away from home," said Sakuma, somewhat jokingly, sitting up on his mat. "The fact is, I quit K Corporation last year." His expression "ran away from home" was not a total jest. . . .

Sakuma had not intended to become a retired person. He wanted to experience a period—six months would be fine—when time flowed freely as a reward, so to speak, for those fleeting twenty-eight years of toil. He had job offers from a few firms, but had sent them extremely polite letters of refusal, which began "For the time being . . . "

He listened patiently to all his wife's sarcastic comments, then left the room to phone Ichihashi, who worked for an agency that took care of all overseas travels by members of K Corporation.

"The 3rd is impossible. If you can leave on the 5th or later, I have vacancies in the bargain five-night seven-day group tours to Hawaii."

On the night of January 5, Sakuma left from Haneda Airport, taking with him the dive mask, snorkeling tube, and swim fins he had brought back for Toshimichi on a previous trip to Honolulu. . . .

They decided to go in for a swim. Using his mask, tube, and pair of fins, Sakuma had a clear view of brilliantly colored fishes in water only waist deep. He had spent a little time the night before studying an illustrated book on fish classifications. He remembered the Japanese names for some of the fishes he saw: the tiny, blue *kobaruto-suzume*, and the *somewake-yakko*, whose body was covered with alternating stripes of black and yellow. The finely striped yellow fish whose dorsal fin resembled a row of needles was probably a variety of the butterfly fish, he thought. The black fish with red splotches around the eyes looked like a file fish.

The fishes near the shoreline seemed to have no fear of man. If Sakuma reached out to touch them, they would dodge his hand and glide away. If he floated inertly, they would ignore him and go about their business of foraging amid the coral reef.

Until a decade earlier Hanauma Bay was popular among fishermen. When the fish population was reduced almost to zero, the State made it a public park in an attempt to restore its pristine attractiveness. Stringent regulations forbade fishing as well as the removal of any shells, coral, or marine plants. Even rocks could not be taken from the premises. These regulations were posted at the snack stand on the beach. In time the fishes repopulated the coral reefs and evolved into tamed species. The bay had become a natural treasure trove of rare tropical fishes.

Sakuma worked his way along the reef toward deeper waters. From the lookout high above, the sea appeared bright and crystal clear. But as he swam out farther, the water became darker, and fishes larger. He noticed a huge fish with a protruding lower jaw lurking behind a boulder, studying him. He was reminded of the giant streamers in the shape of carps which are raised to pole-tops on Boys' Day.

Waves splashing about him, Sakuma surfaced and, like a whale, blew the seawater out of his snorkeling tube. He savored the taste of salt. Moving his arms and legs in leisurely strokes, he could move about freely in the water without exerting himself. In fact, by slowing down his movements he was better able to enjoy his sojourn among the tropical fishes.

Lying partly submerged on the sandy bottom was a creature, the same color as the sand, with long, trailing whiskers. In a small underwater cavern he saw a disagreeable, white, fluttering, noodle-like creature.

Soon he felt the pull of the tide. A large school of silvery fish flapped their tails, swimming against the tide. In magnificent formation the school of hundreds abruptly changed direction, swam forward, again changed direction, swam forward, continuing in this way to move gradually off into the distance.

Sakuma recalled having swum here three years before. He spotted a school of the same silvery fish and followed it, fascinated with the beauty of its formation and maneuvers. Suddenly he felt the tug of the tide drawing him toward deep waters.

The tug of even a slight tidal pull is formidable. Sakuma fought it but got no nearer to shore. As he struggled his breath became shorter. He realized he might be in danger. He held on tight to the coral, hoping to catch a wave sweeping across the reef, but his fingers were cut. They bled.

The sea churned as the receding water collided with an incoming wave, and Sakuma, forced to release his hold, felt himself being pulled out with the tide. His glance shot toward the shore. He saw Taki, in his snorkeling outfit, less than ten yards away. Apparently Taki, concerned with Sakuma's inexperience, had swum along to keep watch over him. As Sakuma breathed a sigh of relief, a friendly wave gave him a push toward safer waters.

Only experienced divers can safely negotiate the deep waters beyond the reefs. According to a guide sheet sold at the snack stand, a powerful current called the Molokai Express flows across the mouth of the bay.

Sakuma swam back through channel openings in the reef, observing the fishes but keeping aware of the tidal flow.

Taki, already back on shore, had bought coffee, and was waiting for him. "Were there any big ones?"

"Yes, there were. I feel lucky to be here at a place as pretty as the Dragon King's Realm . . . here only because I lost my job. I doubt that I'll be given many more opportunities like this one." The coffee he sipped from a paper cup was hot and good.

There were more bathers now. Sakuma looked up to the top of the precipice and noticed the many tiny figures clustered at the lookout point—tourists, no doubt. They probably came on the tour buses. Most just snapped pictures and left, but quite a few, carrying rolled up mats, came walking down the winding path.

"This place has become quite an attraction these days," Taki said.

The lifeguard was in his stand. A young black sat around, jazz pouring out of his radio. Girls in colorful bikinis lay stretched out on the sand.

There were a number of Japanese, and one could distinguish between the local Japanese and those from Japan by the shade of their skin. Taki and Sakuma, for example were quite different in complexion.

"It's still New Year's in Japan," Taki said. "Today is January 7th. Do families in Japan still have the traditional seven-herb rice gruel?"

"We did, because my grandmother grew up in Kyoto, a traditional city." Sakuma lay on his side, puffing on a cigarette. "We'd be in the kitchen before daybreak, singing a simple folk song that went like this:

Before the birds of China
Fly over to Japan,
Eat the seven herbs,
the nazuna *grass . . . "*

He set the words to the melody. "I remember singing that song as we chopped the seven herbs on the cutting board. Once the birds got to Japan from China the custom was gradually abandoned. At my house, at least, I haven't had seven-herb gruel since I got married."

Overcome by jet lag and fatigue from swimming, Sakuma felt drowsy. Just as he was comfortably dozing off, he sensed something of a turmoil erupting about him. He opened his eyes and noticed everyone on the beach sitting up and staring in one direction.

A young Caucasian woman was strolling along the water line wearing absolutely nothing. The tall, very slim woman had a nice face. A tree branch shaped somewhat like a crucifix in her hand, her eyelids lowered, she sauntered in leisurely steps in Sakuma's direction. She appeared to ignore the hum of whispers among the startled bathers. Her deliberate stride as she walked by Sakuma and Taki seemed to be an expression of a determined belief in a profound faith. The rich growth of her golden pubic hair assumed the hue of dried grass as it reflected sunlight.

Many of the bathers seemed to regard the incident as something ridiculous and resumed their napping. Sakuma kept watching. The woman turned right at the showers by the entrance to the beach, then stepped up onto the low wall made of lava rocks, standing tall like a prophet. Then, holding the branch in front of her breasts, she began walking up the sloping path.

Depending on the location, some observers looked up directly between her legs. The young black who had been playing his radio let out a shriek. A middle-aged American couple sat to Sakuma's side but a little closer to the water. The husband persisted in watching, his mouth agape. His wife gave him a sharp slap across the knee. Sakuma realized that his mouth, too, hung wide open.

"What was that?" he asked Taki.

"I've never seen her before. A hippie, most likely." Taki lay down and put a towel over his face. After the phantom appearance of the nude woman, the sunbathers became more congenial.

The chubby, graying American, whose wife had slapped him, winked at Sakuma and asked, "Where are you from?"

"Tokyo," Sakuma replied. "My friend teaches at the University here."

"We're from Minneapolis. Do you have a family?"

Sakuma's English sufficed for such simple exchanges. But when he was asked if he was a scholar too, he needed Taki's help to say that he formerly worked for a salary but was now between jobs.

The Minnesotan listened with interest as Taki interpreted, then returned a question for Sakuma, which Taki interpreted in Japanese:

"We, too, have a son in college and a daughter who's married. Are you in control of your son and daughter?"

"No," Sakuma said, with an anguished laugh, shaking his head. "What about you?"

The American shrugged his shoulder. "It's the same everywhere in the world," he said, and laughed.

The beach was again quiet. When Sakuma got back from his second swim, it was time for Taki to go to the university.

"What will you do about lunch?" Taki asked.

"I'll get a bowl of saimin at the snack stand and stay here until sundown."

"Why don't you come over for dinner tonight—that is, if you feel up to it?" Taki asked somewhat shyly.

"Perhaps next time," Sakuma answered. "I'm a runaway . . . remember? Give my best to your wife. I'm sorry I won't be able to see her."

Taki and his wife, a third-generation Japanese-American, were childless.

"Well, in that case . . . Call again while you're here."

"I'll do that. I ran away from home, but ultimately—actually four days from now—I'll end up back at home. I'll find a new job soon. That would be the right time for you to visit us in Japan."

On that note, they said goodbye.

TRANSLATED BY JAMES ARAKI

Gene Frumkin

"HAOLE IN HONOLULU"

Arriving in Honolulu, I immediately
started counting Asians and realized
they were more than I. People told me
I was a haole, Caucasian stranger
from another shore. I invented
a song for myself, not like Whitman's
I was not multitudes, but a grain of sand.

Here I am, writing about my ego
in the disconcerting waters of a cloud.
I want to go away and not pretend to be
a visiting professor. But the faculty
of the English Department knew me better.
My mind, via a small engine, traveled
west to the International Line. A day

this way or that didn't matter. I admired
a native of these Islands who had been
to Ohio, married there, and shy of men
ever since. She didn't mind calling me
"sweetheart" in a public place where she worked,
but meeting with me, the two of us,
was like a hatchet in the cupboard

of any domesticated flight. She was part
Asian, but I didn't know what part. Enough
though to imagine me in Ohio, and bad luck.
The department was kind and most
of the students, so I felt honorary, able
to construe myself as a member. She and I
were never alone, witnesses of a Hawaii,

from where, after all, I had to go home.

GENE FRUMKIN (1928-2007) *a poet and teacher, taught at the University of New Mexico for nearly thirty years. His books include* Freud by Other Means; Clouds and Red Earth; Saturn Is Mostly Weather; *and* The Man Who Swam Away and Left Only His Feet Wet.

Frank Chin

from GUNGA DIN HIGHWAY

It's a long long flight from Hollywood to China on Pan American Airways' China Clipper. I never made it, never went back to China to fight the Japanese before they bombed Pearl Harbor. My publicist's Hollywood myth about me says I was about to catch the Clipper back to China and make my way to the Chinese air force to fight for China against the invading Japanese. No such thing. But people enjoy thinking of me as a hero of my people. Everyone agrees, my people need a hero.

The flight from Hollywood to Honolulu via United Air Lines is long enough for me, though I have another flight to another island to catch yet to make exteriors for *Hawaii Five-O*. There's word of a new Charlie Chan movie in the air. NBC Vice-President David Tebet is on a much-publicized round-the-world search for a Chinese actor who speaks English well enough to be understood by American audiences to become the first Chinese to play Charlie Chan, the Chinese detective. The sons of Charlie Chan, Keye Luke, Benson Fong, Victor Sen Yung, and me, all feel the magic of the movies we made, setting us aglow. We strike casual poses by the phone, waiting for the thing to ring, just in case God happens to walk from one room to another with a camera.

I've come to meet my movie father, Anlauf Lorane, the Charlie Chan to my Number Four Son. We are old men when we are the money stars in the Bs of twenty years ago, though I always look and photograph younger, much younger than my actual age. And we are older old men now. He's too old to play the new Charlie Chan, and probably looks it, and doesn't want to. I don't understand.

I don't look too old, of all the sons of Chan I look the youngest still, and want to be the first Chinese to play Charlie Chan on the screen. Keye looks and acts too old, and the older he gets, the more foreign he seems. Not Chinese foreign. Some kind of European foreign with a pseudo-British accent. Benson is just too rickety. And Victor looks awful and has lost it. Of the four sons who've lived to take over the part of Pop in a Hollywood movie, I'm the only one. My time is near. Big screen or little screen: I want to be the first.

I land in Honolulu in one of those island rains with drops of falling water as big as eggs breaking on everything. The air is so thick with water it seems United Air Lines has landed me under the sea and I'm breathing watery goo and can't tell if the mud is falling on me or splashing up at me. All I hear is water and squawking muck. Through the water washing sweat and hair in my eyes I can see only blobs of grays and blues and vague greens and bluish reds. I can't see what is airplane and what is airport, what is slipping rainwater and what is glass and steel. Five blobs distinguish themselves from the mass by calling my name, and vague aloha shirts come into view.

A very wet toasty brown-skinned hula girl in a plastic hula skirt and toothpaste smile drops a wet orchid lei around my neck that immediately makes my nose run, and presses her wet gooey lips against my wet gooey cheek. The hula girl disappears and the five vague aloha shirts pat me on the back and laugh.

There is no difference between air and water, land and sea until I am in the dry quiet insides of the limousine the brothers from the tong hired to meet me. Old-time Honolulu brothers of the good-time Boom Boom tong are more good-time Charlie American than my Boom Boom brothers on the mainland. Not that they don't own and run honky-tonks, bottle clubs, and see girls run through their business and take their share during the war, but there is law in Seattle, and San Francisco and Los Angeles. In Hawaii the war is the law and boys of the Boom Boom tong are happy soldiers, judges, juries, and executioners of the law.

The brothers from the good-time Boom Boom tong tell me sometimes late at night when they get home from their business and turn on the TV and flip the channels through the old movies, looking for one to watch a while, not often, but sometimes, around four or five times a year, a movie I die in is broadcast from every station in Hawaii. The brothers think of me as a bigshot star of opera and movies still. Though I am here as a Guest Star on a two-part episode of *Hawaii Five-O* and expected McGarrett would send a limo for me, the brothers were only too pleased to meet me at the airport and escort me to my Waikiki hotel, and too happy to let *Hawaii Five-O* publicists take pictures and write stories about the old tongs of Honolulu looking on Chang Apana, the detective sergeant in the Honolulu police and the fat Charlie Chan the detective as the creators of the happiest memories of childhood and wartime businesses in their Honolulu Hotel Street China-town, on the piece of island real estate that suddenly is the bleeding end all be all of American honor. And in the movies of the time, I was, I am Charlie Chan's Number Four and most American-born and Americanized son. In real life, whatever that is, I was born in China. The South. Tang People. Cantonese. It all blends into a nice story about me that the newspapers and publicists blurbing me want to believe. I love it.

"The part I've come to Honolulu to play is nothing special," I tell the brothers. "But it is paying my way to party with my brothers in Hawaii and visit the last white man to play Charlie Chan still alive."

"You mean he's on the islands?" the brothers ask. "We had no idea!"

"I seem to be the only one he trusts with his address. He craves ano-nymity," I say. "He wants his privacy. I have several offers from advertising companies for him to put on the white duck and Panama straw hat of Char-lie Chan again and sell a few products for them. I'm going to try to talk him into coming out of hiding and making a little money."

They're impressed at my humility and loyalty and still want to know about my part in Hawaii Five-O. Do I live? Do I die? Am I Chinese? Am I Japanese? Am I southern artist? Am I northern bureaucrat? Does it make any difference? Am I squinty? Am I swishy? Am I bald? Do I have big eyebrows? We laugh a lot, stirring up old laughs, old short-sleeved Hawaiian shirts, old memories of old movies and happy days in the war. This ceremony over, the brothers grin at me, open-mouthed as catfish, their old bottomfeeder's eyes shine as if they'd swallowed strong drink. In the eye of their swirling wait, they're ready to know about my part on *Hawaii Five-O*.

I tell them, "I'm another cultured slimy warlord smuggling drugs into the United States through Hawaii who runs afoul of McGarrett, Chin-ho, Danno, Zulu, and the whole Five-O show, and, of course, I die in the shadow of Diamond Head."

They love it. *Hawaii Five-O* has really perfected the Charlie Chan for-mula, they say. They love the villains from World War II movies finding new life on the show. It's a breath of the old days.

"And it gives me work," I say, and we all laugh.

On the way to the hotel I see that *Tora! Tora! Tora!* is still playing in a big first-run Honolulu movie palace. "Ah, yes," I say, "A peace movie."

"A peace movie?" a brother asks.

"A war movie made in peacetime. I remember playing in war movies made during the war, with John Wayne, Van Johnson, Cary Grant."

Yes, the Hawaiian brothers remember the names and the stars who partied here after Pearl Harbor. The brothers ran restaurants or bars, or honky-tonks during the war and remember me flying over from Frisco or L.A. to play an ugly Japanese spy or sadistic Japanese officer who screams "Aiiieeeee!" when I die then head down to Chinatown for dinner and rice before painting Honolulu red, with the other sons of Chan and Willy and Kara chasing the tails of our fame and all the Chinese and Japanese women we can find from club to club from Chinatown to Waikiki. And the soldiers and sailors on the town and off-limits recognized us, grinned and laughed, put their arms around us, and we put our arms around them. They patted us on the head and we patted them on the head and watched them totter away to the whores or back to their bases.

Aiiieeeee! Aloha! Gung ho! Goong hay fot choy! The movies and Chinatown were exciting then. They had a future waiting for them after we won the war. There was an electric light night life. There was a Chinatown class and style. Padded shoulders. Wide lapels. Double-breasted suits. Straw hats. They were happy days for me too.

"There are people in Hawaii who object to the Charlie Chan movies and John Wayne war movies, and World War II movies on the late-night TV," the brothers tell me. "No sense of history."

"The younger generations don't remember when Americans thought all Chinese were sex perverts, opium smugglers, and torturers of women," I say.

"That's right, you and Keye, and Benson, and Victor were a more positive and real lifelike image of the Chinese," a brother says.

"As was our father, Charlie Chan," I say.

Yes, turn on your TV late at night to any old Charlie Chan the Detective or World War II in China movie and you are reading my life story. Every night from some tower over Honolulu or New York, or Chicago, one bit of my life or another unspools like smoke. I still like turning on the TV in another town to get away from it all, and being pleasantly surprised with the best days of my life.

For nearly fifty years, half a century, I am the most famous Chinese in America: an actor. I am Charlie Chan's Number Four Son; the Chinese nicknamed Die Say or Say Die. Yes, I am the rhythmic Christian of Charlie Chan's movie sons, the martyr, the one famous for saying nothing but "Gee, Pop!" and "Gosh, Pop!" I am The Chinaman Who Dies. . . .

The brothers of the tong give me a fine banquet and invite the stars, staff, and crew of *Hawaii Five-O*. All very straight for McGarrett. A good, straight-shooting Christian man. No drinking in sight. No smoking. No cussing. No dirty jokes. A round of speeches. The brothers are effusive. McGarrett in the same blue suit as he always wears on *Hawaii Five-O*, is serious, gracious, charming, and skeptical, and very low-key and cool. They call for me. They want Number Four Son. I give him to them.

"Gee, Pop! to you all, brothers, friends, *sum, moh, jiyeh, mooey,* and *Hawaii Five-O*. I say, Gosh, Pop! In the name of Charlie Chan, The Father, Keye Luke, the Son, and Earl Derr Biggers, The Holy Ghost. It's great to be an American and chew the fat with fellas who speak the same lingo."

A suckling pig for every table. A tea-smoked goose. Fish flesh of all colors and textures, and because we are Cantonese who must have our rice, a perfumed rice is one of the nine courses.

"I feel good tonight. My horoscope is just swell. Great biorhythm graphed in the paper. I feel good about today. I'm going to be okay. Say, this must be the Spirit of Aloha!" Even McGarrett smiles and applauds. The brothers laugh and nudge each other with their elbows.

"Let me say it right here and now. To us Charlie Chan is the Chinese Gospel of the New Testament. And Warner Oland, Sidney Toler, Roland Winters, and Anlauf Lorane are the prophets of Charlie Chan.

"I am the one lucky son of Chan who has had the privilege of meeting Earl Derr Biggers, our Holy Ghost, our creator, right here in Honolulu, in the bar of the Royal Hawaiian. He was working on his new Charlie Chan novel, *Charlie Chan in Winnemucca*, and I was over from the mainland with Benson about to die in a Gary Cooper missionary movie. Benson wasn't about to die. I was. I was having a laugh with Mr. Biggers about teaching the local Chinese children to sing 'My Old Kentucky Home' in Cantonese, to play Chinese mission school children greeting Gary Cooper to his mission in China.

"Mr. Biggers didn't laugh it up with me. Instead he became very serious. He said of all the sons of Chan I had a tragic dimension. For this certainly I was the most American of all the sons, he said, and at that moment he thought me the most likely to be the first Chinese to play Charlie Chan on the screen. I was surprised at how well he knew my acting. He said the roles that I played created a new character: the Chinese American as a casualty of the Fall, the Chinese American as victim, the Chinese American identity crisis as disease.

"The author Earl Derr Biggers saw all that in me. This was the Chinese American that sold, he told *me*. And he studies me for his next book *Charlie Chan in Winnemucca*. In the book and the movie, you will remember Charlie Chan has a chance meeting with a dishwasher named Chan from Pop's tong, in the kitchen of a Reno casino," I say, and people around the tables nod and smile in recognition.

"*Charlie Chan in Winnemucca* was Anlauf Lorane's first assay of the role of Charlie Chan. I was, once again, Honorable Son Number Four. Anlauf Lorane was a six-foot-four Belgian, five years my junior, and the fourth white man to play Charlie Chan. The role that almost brought him Hollywood stardom was General Yen, the seducer of Barbara Stanwyck, a young Barbara Stanwyck in Frank Capra's *The Bitter Tea of General Yen*.

"Anlauf told me Capra had him cut his eyelashes short, as he was convinced short eyelashes were the secret to making Caucasian eyes look Oriental. Until his eyelashes grew back he had to wear visored hats and dark glasses, he tells me.

"I tell him the word for the number four is *say* in Cantonese. And the word for dead is *say* in Cantonese. And *say yeah!* such a joyful exultant affirmative blast in English, is 'dead thing!" a curse, in Cantonese. And we have a good laugh together.

"In the book and the movie, but especially in the movie, Pop pities Chan the dishwasher for being as Chinese as the day he was born, a bigshot in the tong in San Francisco and Winnemucca's little Chinatown, but just a dishwasher in the real world, and in that real world, the dishwasher still looks on Charlie Chan, the detective sergeant of the Honolulu Police in immaculate white duck, with contempt, and Pop sighs and asks Why? Why is he contemptible in the eyes of the Chinese dishwasher? Because humble detective trod path away from the barbaric ways of old China, and toward the path of progress and became a Christian, became Americanized, Pop says."

The mood is down. The sounds of eating in the banquet aren't to be heard. They are moved. They're listening to me. . . .

The banquet is fit for the wedding of a prince and princess. McGarrett and Five-O give me face with my tong brothers, and vice versa. And they all give me face with the Honolulu papers.

Pictures in the morning paper with a story. "Charlie Chan and his Number Four Son gave me strength," Pandora Toy says in the *Honolulu Star-Bulletin*. "Neither his Hollywood brothers nor his own American sons see the great step Longman Kwan has made for Chinese America, for a new generation of actors, as Charlie Chan's Number Four Son and as The Chinaman Who Dies." She's a writing fellow at the Writers' Workshop at Iowa City. . . .

The shoot and my two weeks' work is done in ten days. Since I have four days to myself, I look up the Tiki Adult Bookshoppe and Arcade in the Yellow Pages.

Anlauf Lorane is the last prophet of Charlie Chan alive and I am the only son he trusts to keep his current identity, Henly Hornbrook, Honolulu pornographer, secret.

He's fat. He is very fat. Fatter than Charlie Chan. More bald than Charlie Chan. He turns and holds his bald head in one hand like a basketball. Fat, sleazy, notorious, convicted of obscenity. Oh, no, convicted of obscenity. Charlie Chan cannot be convicted of obscenity. I see dollars for Anlauf Lorane flying away into aloha—"Goodbye."

"If I did not care about being recognized as the last white man to play Charlie Chan alive, I might have made my little small business in rubber cunts and dicks, some made with human hair, a First Amendment case, gone to the Supreme Court," he says and laughs. I'm not prepared for the inside of this place, the smell of all this pink rubber in the dim, vulvalike interior of a Quonset hut. He lives in the Quonset hut next door.

His fantasy Tahitian bamboo and rattan porn parlor—adult books, adult toys, sex aids, adult films and 25-cent movies in private booths—has the look and unstated substance of Benson's tropical fantasy Chinese restaurants down cold. Plastic plants and inflatable rubber women. Yes, this is what's missing from Benson's. Rubber dicks and five-fingered French ticklers. And the tropical damp smell from the private movie booths, like the smell from dark stuff under the trees after a rain, I don't ask about and don't take for granted as natural.

His Charlie Chan moustache and goatee have grown wild and self-indulgent to Shakespearean pretensions. He looks like thousands of fat, goateed men with artificially inflated vocabularies I have seen in places like this, all on the edge of Chinatowns, all fat, watching a little TV set on a counter full of flesh-colored rubber genitals and faces with open mouths. His face is without worry and age lines, like an overinflated balloon. Pop is lost inside his own wilderness of fat globules, playing Henly Hornbrook, Honolulu pornographer, in his Tiki Adult Book Shoppe and Arcade, between the highway and Chinatown, looking out onto the street, not watching his little Japanese television set pouring the gray light of *The Hatchetman* all over his hairy right arm, that looks like a fat baby seal on a rock.

To the southwest is Chinatown and the prostitutes. Just around the corner is a street of men crouched over pinball machines and men in dark booths like the ones here, where they drop dimes and quarters into movie machines and stare into a slot to see a minute of sucky fucky with, hopefully, the woman with the face and body of their dreams. Every time he moves, bulbs and drooping bags of fat wobble all over and seem to ooze out from under his sleeves.

"Gee, Pop! You chose a hell of a place to hide!" I say, still hoping this is all a joke of some kind.

"I have to be where all those old movies are haunting the atmosphere for everybody to see. I wandered the Hawaiian islands for a year or so, so scared my asshole's afraid to open, sure the Chinese will assassinate me as soon as I try to take a shit and reveal my whereabouts, and there are Chinese everywhere, baby! Everywhere! Then Charlie Chan told me to *become* my hiding place. Hide Charlie Chan in a blob of shapeless fat."

"You're not hiding in the porn shop, you're hiding in your fat?" I ask.

But then another bald-on-top, fat white man with a moustache and goatee and a mouth full of vocabulary shows up, and Pop climbs down off his stool and ignores me as he makes pornographer's small talk with his look-alike. Then he walks me through sudden rain around a couple of tall skinny palm trees to the Quonset hut he calls home and introduces me to his fat blobular fifth wife.

To celebrate our reunion, our renascence, I hope, Pop announces he will make another five gallons of his world-famous chili con carne. While it simmers for five hours, he says, "We'll smoke, drink, and shoot the shit." Does he mean he's shooting drugs? I don't ask. No. He smokes Maui Wowie, the local super-duper *pakololo*. It's better than what we had in alleys behind the clubs with the bands during the war. One puff for the peace pipe effect and social cool, then that's it for me. He doesn't do cocaine. "Fat people shouldn't do cocaine," he says. "Otherwise I love being fat."

His wife helps him tie on a huge bibbed apron with "The World's Greatest Cook!" Day-Gloed from the right hip to left shoulder. He puts a large stainless steel pot on the stove and begins filling it. "I have good chili. I have good meat for the carne—sirloin. But the secret of good chili con carne is neither the chili nor the carne," he says, browning onions and garlic, a bay leaf and various kinds of fresh and dried chili peppers, "but the con, my son. The good con."

FRANK CHIN *is a Chinese-American writer of novels, plays, essays, and criticism. He was born in California in 1940 to a Chinese immigrant father and a fourth-generation Chinatown mother. He was the first Chinese-American to have a play produced on the New York stage, in print in* Two Plays By Frank Chin: The Chickencoop Chinaman, *and* The Year of the Dragon. *Among his fictions are* Chinaman Pacific & Frisco R.R. Co.; Donald Duk; Gunga Din Highway. *Non-fictions:* Bulletproof Buddhists *and* Born in the U.S.A.: A Story of Japanese America.

Jason Hui
"THE NEW CHINESE BOY IN SCHOOL"

No, I don't care
for Chinese lion dancing.
Fireworks aren't much fun.
I don't believe money from
those small red envelopes
will increase my luck.

No, I don't enjoy
shopping in Chinatown.
Parking is too hard to find.
I just go to Safeway instead.
It's closer to my house.

No, I don't think Jackie Chan is the greatest
and Bruce Lee isn't my idol.
I would rather watch *Baywatch* reruns.
Pam Anderson's a cutie.

No, sorry I can't translate.
Mandarin is just foreign to me.
I know a lot more Spanish.
I took it for two years.
Of course, I know English.
How else would I know
you're asking me a lotta
stupid questions?

Willyce Kim

"MIGRATIONS'"

I n 1903 the S.S. *Gaelic*, carrying the first boatload of Korean plantation workers from Inchon Harbor, arrived in the Hawaiian Islands.

Between 1910 and 1925 the second wave, largely comprised of Korean picture brides, continued the influx of migrant laborers.

In 1967, approximately sixty years after the immigration of her grandparents and four months before the infamous "Summer of Love," Penelope Frances Lee waved aloha to the island of Oahu and crossed the Pacific Ocean with a suitcase full of Thai sticks.

San Franciscans opened their golden gates.

She unlatched her suitcase.

The Yellow Pearl had struck gold, and the rest, as they say, was history.

In 1968 the Haight buried the hippie. Burned-out street urchins consumed cans of Alpo while fingering their love beads.

Penelope Frances Lee, disinherited daughter of the mayor of Honolulu, merchant emeritus of the Haight, honorary godmother to scores of aspiring tribal children, never looked back.

In 1969 she emerged from a phone booth as Ta Jan the Korean.

WILLYCE KIM *is the author of three books of poetry:* Curtains of Light; Eating Artichokes; *and* Under the Rolling Sky. *She is also the author of two novels,* Dancer Dawkins and the California Kid *and* Dead Heat. *In addition to these books, she has had numerous short stories published. She was born in Honolulu, in the year of the fire-dog. She currently resides in Oakland, California, but is an islander at heart.*

Joan Didion

from DEMOCRACY

"I magine my mother dancing," that novel began, in the first person. The first person was Inez, and was later abandoned in favor of the third:

"Inez imagined her mother dancing.

"Inez remembered her mother dancing.

"Brown-and-white spectator shoes, very smart. High-heeled sandals made of white silk twine, very beautiful. White gardenias in her hair on the beach at Lanikai. A white silk blouse with silver sequins shaped like stars. Shaped like new moons. Shaped like snowflakes. The sentimental things of life as time went by. Dancing under the camouflage net on the lawn at Kaneohe. Blue moon on the Nuannu ranch. Saw her standing alone. She smiled as she danced.

"Inez remembered no such thing.

"Inez remembered the shoes and the sequins like snowflakes but she only imagined her mother dancing, to make clear to herself that the story was one of romantic outline. You will notice that the daughters in romantic stories always remember their mothers dancing, or about to leave for the dance: these dancebound mothers materialize in the darkened nursery (never a bedroom in these stories, always a 'nursery,' on the English model) in a cloud of perfume, a burst of light off a diamond hair clip. They glance in the mirror. They smile. They do not linger, for this is one of those moments in which the interests of mothers are seen to diverge sharply from the wishes of daughters. These mothers get on with it. These mothers lean for a kiss and leave for the dance. Inez and Janet's mother left, but not for the dance. Inez and Janet's mother left for San Francisco, on the *Lurline*, reconditioned. I specify 'reconditioned' because that was how Carol Christian's departure was characterized for Inez and Janet, as a sudden but compelling opportunity to make the first postwar crossing on the reconditioned *Lurline*. 'Just slightly irresistible,' was the way Carol Christian put it exactly."

What I had there was a study in provincial manners, in the acute tyrannies of class and privilege by which people assert themselves against the tropics; Honolulu during World War Two, martial law, submariners and fliers and a certain investor from Hong Kong with whom Carol Christian was said to drink brandy and Coca-Cola, a local scandal. I was interested more in Carol Christian than in her daughters, interested in the stubborn loneliness she had perfected during her marriage to Paul Christian, interested in her position as an outsider in the islands and in her compensatory yearning to be "talented," not talented at anything in particular but just talented, a state of social grace denied her by the Christians. Carol Christian arrived in Honolulu as a bride in 1934. By 1946 she was sometimes moved so profoundly by the urge for company that she would keep Inez and Janet home from school on the pretext of teaching them how to do their nails. She read novels out loud to them on the beach at Lanikai, popular novels she checked out from the lending library at the drugstore in Kailua. "'The random years were at an end,'" she would read, her voice rising to signal a dramatic effect, and then she would invent a flourish of her own: "'Now, they could harvest them.' Look there, *random harvest*, that explains the title, very poetic, a happy ending, *n'est-ce pas?*"

She was attracted to French phrases but knew only the several she had memorized during the semester of junior college in Stockton, California, that constituted her higher education. She was also attracted to happy endings, and located them for Inez and Janet wherever she could: in the Coke float that followed the skinned knee, in the rainbow after the rain, in magazine stories about furlough weddings and fortuitously misdelivered Dear John letters and, not least, in her own romance, which she dated from the day she left Stockton and got a job modeling at I. Magnin in San Francisco. "Eighteen years old and dressed to kill in a Chanel suit, the real McCoy," she would say to Inez and Janet. Eighteen years old and dressed to kill in a Mainbocher evening pajama, the genuine article. Eighteen years old and dressed to kill in a Patou tea gown, white satin cut on the bias, talk about drop dead, bare to *here* in back. The bias-cut Patou tea gown figured large in Carol Christian's stories because this was the dress in which she had been sneaking a cigarette on the I. Magnin employees' floor when Paul Christian stepped off the elevator by mistake (another fortuitous misdelivery) and brushed the shadows away, brought her happiest day, one look at him and she had found a world completely new, the sole peculiarity being that the world was an island in the middle of the Pacific and Paul Christian was rarely there. "When a man stays away from a woman it means he wants to keep their love alive," Carol Christian advised Inez and Janet. She had an entire codex of these signals men and women supposedly sent to one another (when a woman blew smoke at a man it meant she was definitely interested, and when a man told a woman her dress was too revealing it meant he adored her), dreamy axioms she had heard or read or invented as a schoolgirl of romantic tendency and to which she clung in the face of considerable contrary evidence. That she had miscalculated when she married Paul Christian was a conclusion she seemed incapable of drawing. She made a love-knot of what she imagined to be her first gray hair and mailed it to him in Cuernavaca. "*Mon cher* Paul," she wrote on the card to which she pinned the love-knot. Inez watched her tie the hair but did not see the card for some years, loose in one of the boxes of shed belongings that Paul Christian would periodically ship express collect from wherever he was to Inez and Janet. "Who do you f— to get off this island? (Just kidding of course) XXXX, C."

She left dark red lipstick marks on her cigarettes, smoked barely at all and then crushed out in coffee cups and Coke bottles and in the sand. She sat for hours at her dressing table, which was covered with the little paper parasols that came in drinks, yellow, turquoise, shocking pink, tissue parasols like a swarm of brittle butterflies. She sat at this dressing table and shaved her legs. She sat at this dressing table and smoothed Vaseline into her eyebrows. She sat at this dressing table and instructed her daughters in what she construed to be the language of love, a course she had notably failed. For a year or two after Carol Christian left Honolulu Janet would sit on the beach at Lanikai and sift the sand looking for cigarettes stained with her mother's lipstick. She kept the few she found in a shoebox, along with the tissue parasols from Carol Christian's dressing table and the postcards from San Francisco and Carmel and Lake Tahoe.

Of the daughters I was at first more interested in Janet, who was the younger, than in Inez. I was interested in the mark the mother had left on Janet, in Janet's defensive veneer of provincial gentility, her startling and avid preoccupation with other people's sexual arrangements; in her mercantile approach to emotional transactions, and her condescension to anyone less marketable than she perceived herself to be. As an adolescent Janet had always condescended, for example, to Inez, and became bewildered and rather sulky when it worked out, in her view, so well for Inez and so disappointingly for herself. I was interested in how Janet's husband Dick Ziegler made a modest fortune in Hong Kong housing and lost it in the development of windward Oahu. I was interested in Inez and Janet's grandmother, the late Sybil "Cissy" Christian, a woman remembered in Honolulu for the vehement whims and irritations that passed in that part of the world as opinions, as well as for the dispatch with which she had divested herself of her daughter-in-law. *Aloha oe.* "I believe your mother wants to go to night clubs," Cissy Christian said to Inez and Janet by way of explaining Carol Christian's departure. "But she's coming back," Janet said. "Now and then," Cissy Christian said. This conversation took place at lunch at the Pacific Club, one hour after Inez and Janet and their uncle Dwight saw the reconditioned *Lurline* sail. Janet bolted from the table. "Happy now?" Dwight Christian asked his mother. "Somebody had to do it," Cissy Christian said. "Not necessarily before lunch," Dwight Christian said.

I saw it as a family in which the colonial impulse had marked every member. I was interested in Inez and Janet's father, Paul Christian, and in the way in which he had reinvented himself as a romantic outcast, a remittance man of the Pacific. "He's going to end up a goddamn cargo cult," Paul Christian's brother Dwight once said about him. I was interested not only in Paul but in Dwight Christian, in his construction contracts at Long Binh and Cam Ranh Bay, his claim to have played every Robert Trent Jones golf course in the world with the exception of the Royal in Rabat; the particular way in which he used Wendell Omura to squeeze Dick Ziegler out of windward Oahu and coincidentally out of the container business. "Let me give you a little piece of advice," Dwight Christian said when Paul Christian took up Dick Ziegler's side in this matter. "'Life can only be understood backwards, but it must be lived forwards.' Kierkegaard." Dwight Christian had an actual file of such quotations, most of them torn from the "Thoughts on the Business of Life" page in *Forbes* and given to a secretary to be typed out on three-by-five index cards. The cards were his hedge against a profound shyness. "Recently I ran across a thought from Racine," he would say on those occasions when he was called upon to chair a stockholders' meeting or to keynote the Kick-off Dinner for Punahou School Annual Giving or to have his picture taken, wearing a silk suit tailored in Hong Kong and an aluminum hard hat stencilled "D.C.," knee-deep in silica sand in the hold of a dry-bulk carrier.

That particular photograph appeared in *Business Week*, at the time Dwight Christian was trying (unsuccessfully, it turned out) to take over British Leyland.

I also had two photographs from *Fortune*, one showing Dwight Christian riding a crane over a cane field and the other showing him astride an eighteen-thousand-ton concrete dolos, with a Pan American Cargo Clipper overhead.

In fact I had a number of photographs of the Christians: in that prosperous and self-absorbed colony the Christians were sufficiently good-looking and sufficiently confident and, at least at the time Inez was growing up, sufficiently innocent not to mind getting their pictures in the paper. I had Cissy Christian smoking a cigarette in a white jade holder as she presented the Christian Prize in Sugar Chemistry at the University of Hawaii in 1938. I had Dwight and Ruthie Christian tea-dancing at the Alexander Young Hotel in 1940. I had Carol Christian second-from-the-left in a group of young Honolulu matrons who met every Tuesday in 1942 to drink daiquiris and eat chicken salad and roll bandages for the Red Cross. In this photograph Carol Christian is wearing a Red Cross uniform, but in fact she was invited to join this group only twice, both times by Ruthie Christian. "Spend time around that crowd and you see how the green comes out," she said when it became clear that she would not be included on a regular basis. "You see how the green comes out" was something Carol Christian said often. She said it whenever she divined a note of rejection or criticism or even suspended judgment in someone's response to her, or, by extension, to Inez or Janet. She seemed to believe herself the object of considerable "envy," a word Inez tried to avoid in later life, and perhaps she was.

"I detect just the slightest tinge of lime."

"Positively chartreuse."

"You find out fast enough who your friends are."

In fact it would have been hard to say who Carol Christian's friends were, since she had no friends at all who were not primarily Paul Christian's friends or Cissy Christian's friends or Dwight and Ruthie Christian's friends. "Seems like a nice enough gal," one of Paul Christian's cousins said about her when she had lived in Honolulu for ten years. "Of course I haven't known her that long."

I had, curiously, only two photographs of Paul Christian, and neither suggested the apparent confidence and innocence with which his mother and his brother and even his wife met the camera. The first showed Paul Christian playing backgammon with John Huston in Cuernavaca in 1948. Paul Christian was barefoot and dark from the sun in this snapshot, which would have been taken at roughly the time arrangements were being made for his wife to leave Honolulu on the reconditioned *Lurline*. The second photograph was taken as Paul Christian left the Honolulu YMCA in handcuffs on March 25, 1975, some hours after he fired the shots that resulted in the immediate death of Wendell Omura and the eventual death of Janet Christian Ziegler. In this photograph Paul Christian was again barefoot, and had his cuffed hands raised above his head in a posture of theatrical submission, even crucifixion; a posture so arresting, so peculiarly suggestive, that the photograph was carried in newspapers in parts of the world where there could have been no interest in the Christians or in Wendell Omura or even in Harry Victor. In most parts of the United States there was of course an interest in Harry Victor. VICTOR FAMILY TOUCHED BY ISLAND TRAGEDY, the caption read in the New York *Times*.

You see the shards of the novel I am no longer writing, the island, the family, the situation. I lost patience with it. I lost nerve. Still: there is a certain hour between afternoon and evening when the sun strikes horizontally between the trees and that island and that situation are all I see. Some days at this time one aspect of the situation will seem to me to yield the point, other days another. I see Inez Christian Victor in the spring of 1975 walking on the narrow beach behind Janet's house, the last sun ahead of her, refracted in the spray off Black Point. I see Jack Lovett watching her, a man in his sixties in a custom-made seersucker suit, his tie loosened but his bearing correct, military, suggestive of disciplines practiced for the sake of discipline; a man who is now, as he watches Inez Victor steady herself on the rocks down where the water meets the sea wall, smoking one of the five cigarettes he allows himself daily. I see Inez turn and walk back toward him, the sun behind her now, the water washing the rough coral sand over her bare feet.

I see Jack Lovett waiting for her.

I have not told you much about Jack Lovett.

Most often these days I find that my notes are about Jack Lovett, about those custom-made seersucker suits he wore, about the wide range of his interests and acquaintances and of the people to whom he routinely spoke (embassy drivers, oil riggers, airline stewardesses, assistant professors of English literature traveling on Fulbright fellowships, tropical agronomists traveling under the auspices of the Rockefeller Foundation, desk clerks and ticket agents and salesmen of rice converters and coco dryers and Dutch pesticides and German pharmaceuticals) in Manila and in Jakarta and around the Malacca Strait.

About his view of information as an end in itself.

About his access to airplanes.

About the way he could put together an observation here and a conversation there and gauge when the time had come to lay hands on a 727 or a C-46.

About the way he waited for Inez.

I have been keeping notes for some time now about the way Jack Lovett waited for Inez Victor.

JOAN DIDION *was born in Sacramento, California, in 1934. Among her books are* After Henry; Democracy; The White Album; A Book of Common Prayer; Play It As It Lays; Slouching Toward Bethlehem; *and* Run River. *The Year of Magical Thinking won the National Book Award in 2005 and was made into a Broadway play starring Vanessa Redgrave.*

William D. Steinhoff
"HONOLULU HAND GRENADE R & R"

We were so young, ignorant, and violent then. Now my anger has faded and I can see some bizarre justice in Clark giving Barbara Jean a hand grenade for a wedding present. We were in Honolulu on R and R from the Vietnam War, and more specifically, he gave her an anti-personnel concussion grenade. You see, Clark thought he was going to marry Barbara Jean in Honolulu, and I was going to be best man.

Originally, Clark was going to send the grenade back home with Barbara Jean, so she could give it to his brother. But Clark changed his mind about the hand grenade after Barbara Jean told him she was pregnant and was going to marry Harley Featherstone, who had an upholstery shop for cars in Flint, Michigan, called Harley's Cool Seats.

Getting back to the hand grenade, nobody knew Clark had it but me, and I thought he was going to send it to his brother Charleton. (Clark's mother named all of her eight kids after movie stars.) Clark said Charleton was going to throw it into a gravel pit and see if it would blow up some fish.

Clark still wanted to marry Barbara Jean even after Madame Magyar told him not to, the night before Barbara Jean arrived in Honolulu. But he never married Barbara Jean, then or later. And I forgot all about the hand grenade until after Clark sort of killed himself. Actually, he didn't kill himself, the Viet Cong did that. But he let them.

Anyway, the night before Barbara Jean arrived, we were walking around Waikīkī and we saw this little cubbyhole next to the restaurant where we had decided to eat outside. There was a sign with big red letters written in some kind of European-style writing. It said, "Madame Magyar, Vaticinator. Fortunes Told and Readings." Clark pointed at it, and I knew he would want to go there after we finished eating. He believed in all that mumbo jumbo stuff because his mother didn't operate on all eight cylinders. Like if a bat flew through the yard it meant someone was going to die, or garlic would keep girls from getting pregnant. I never did find out what girls were supposed to do with the garlic.

After dinner we went to Madame Magyar's and sat at a little table outside of her cubbyhole office and Clark paid her twenty bucks. Madame Magyar was real slick-looking. She had pitch black hair and she wore dark clothing that made her pale white skin look even paler. Before I said anything she looked at me and said, "You don't believe in my powers, but you will someday."

I just shrugged and smiled, because I had downed several beers and didn't feel like arguing with her. Besides, it was Clark's idea, and I went along because I always knew I could count on him to back me up, too.

So Madame Magyar started swishing these tea leaves around in a big cup and talking while she looked at the tea. She told Clark that she sensed a lot of confusion and doubt, that he should think long and hard before making some big decision or he would regret it. But most of all, he should not marry the person he planned on marrying. He should forget about her and not marry until the right combination of sevens came up. She didn't explain that, but said Clark would know when it happened. He would figure out the right combination because it would be obvious to him and not others.

Clark nodded in agreement, but I could see it really shook him because he was real quiet afterwards. I knew it would be useless for me to say anything against Madame Magyar. Clark believed her and he was between a rock and a hard place. I asked him if he wanted to get some more beer, but he said no and went back to the hotel room.

Clark really wanted to marry Barbara Jean because the months in Vietnam had turned her into some ideal woman in his mind. He never saw her the way she was. I realize now that what Clark hoped to gain from marrying Barbara Jean was a sense of security that he did not have within himself.

Our views of marriage were quite the opposite. After having listened to my parents fight over such stupid things as signing an income tax refund check, and having seen some of my fifteen brothers and sisters go crazy, I thought that anyone who got married was nuts, and having babies was totally insane. Clark's oldest brother was queer and Clark was ashamed of it, but in other things our backgrounds were very similar. Both of our mothers were very neurotic and our fathers very ignorant. My father worked as a core maker in the Buick foundry. Clark's father worked as a machinist at a Chevrolet plant. We both quit high school in the eleventh grade, and we joined the army together one year later. We'd been in Nam about six months when the Tet offensive came.

Sometimes now when I think about Clark, I feel the hand grenade was really my wedding present, too. I probably would have stopped Clark if I had known about it at the time. If I had stopped him, I probably would not be living in Honolulu now with Sandra Sachiko Mizukami, and working at the Pearl Harbor shipyard. I might have died, or gone back to Flint and spent my life heat-treating transmission shafts at Buick Motor Division, because that's what I did before I went to Vietnam. But it wasn't so clear then, and I only came to understand it fully when I went with my eight-year-old son Tommy to a replica of the Vietnam Memorial that some veterans' group brought to Honolulu.

Tommy asked if all of them were dead and I said yes, and he looked sad and said it must have hurt. And I said it only hurts when it happens, and when you think about it later. Beside Clark's name, Tommy taped a flower he had picked from our yard. Next to Tommy's flower was a page from a 1965 year book from Punahou School, which Tommy goes to now. Written on the page was, "We miss you. Love, Mom." On impulse, I snapped to attention and saluted with tears in my eyes, both for Clark and for the mother who left the yearbook page.

Tommy asked if he could salute and I said yes. When Tommy saw me crying silently, he cried silently too, and we walked away hand in hand. I told him someday we would see the real thing in Washington, D.C., and Tommy asked if we could take a live orchid from our yard and leave it in front of the wall by Clark's name. And I said that Clark would like that.

But getting back to where all this started, it was May, 1968, after the Tet offensive was over and we had helped kill over four thousand V.C. outside Bien Hoa, which is near Saigon. Clark and I and some others got a special ten-day R and R because the colonel said we had done a good job stopping the Viet Cong. We were the division recon, and all of us had walked point for units of the 101st Airborne during the clearing of the Bien Hoa area after the V.C. had shot their wad.

The colonel didn't know it, but we killed all the Vietnamese in our area. Maybe he did know and didn't care. Maybe he was playing a role, as Dr. Bahlman, my second psychiatrist, used to say about people when they were doing one thing but their emotions were telling them something else.

Dr. Bahlman said his name was very Freudian, but I didn't know what that meant at the time. He said he shot himself in the foot so he could get out of the Korean War, but I never believed him, though he did limp a little. Later when I was getting better, when he said it again I told him he didn't have the balls to shoot himself in the foot. He said I had made a pun on his name, and we all laughed in our therapy group. He said he had even considered turning queer and becoming a homosexual. He asked me if I would consider doing that if I had to face war again. I thought about it and laughed and said that I might, because it probably was less painful than being a hero. Everybody laughed at that, and Dr. Bahlman said I was growing emotionally.

But getting back to the colonel, he's now a big shit in the army because I see him on TV sometimes talking about the contras in Nicaragua. The only thing he did in Vietnam was stop the APC drivers from running over the piles of dead bodies when we heaped them along the roads that went through the rubber plantation. He didn't really stop them, because the APC drivers only stopped when he was around. When he wasn't, pieces of body were flying off the treads like gobs of brown, slushy snow from cars in Michigan. And there are lots of piles when you have over four thousand dead bodies.

The colonel didn't see it when one of the APC drivers ran over some live prisoners that had been taken to a collection point. I didn't see it either, but Clark did, and it bothered him. It was the only thing I can remember him saying about the war that bothered him. He said the Viet Cong had their hands tied and some airborne guys just threw them in front of an APC driver who wanted to run over them. When they tried to crawl away, they were picked up and thrown back in front of the APC as it turned around. Clark didn't throw anybody in front of the APC, but he said he didn't try to stop them. Nobody else did, either. Later he wished he had tried to stop them.

Anyway, Clark and I both got Bronze Stars and I came to Honolulu to be Clark's best man. Otherwise I would have gone to Bangkok with all the other guys, because the girls were easier to find and they were a lot cheaper.

When we left Saigon, both of us looked in the "no questions" box, which was a wooden box on a pole by the gate where you walked out to the R and R plane. You could drop in the box any illegal stuff that you had been thinking about taking on R and R with you, and there would be no questions asked. There was a kilo of marijuana in there, Thai sticks, all kinds of ammunition, lots of drug stuff, and a .45 caliber automatic pistol.

I picked up the kilo of grass and the pistol and thought about sticking them in my AWOL bag I was carrying on the plane. I would have kept the pistol and sold the marijuana in Honolulu. But I decided not to, because I didn't want to take a chance on messing up Clark's wedding, even if he was marrying Barbara Jean with her Cadillac body and her ten-cent mind. Clark looked in the box and glanced at me, but he had his grenade well hidden and didn't hesitate at all. The customs guy in Honolulu didn't even look in our bags. He jokingly asked us if we had any M-60 machine guns. We jokingly replied that we never went on R and R without them.

The day after Barbara Jean arrived, I was sitting in the bar of our hotel when Clark came in and motioned for me to come to an isolated booth. Clark was all pale-looking like he hadn't slept at all. He slumped down in the seat and in an almost pleading tone said, "She's pregnant. Harley Featherstone. She's going to marry Harley. She wanted to tell me in person, and she wanted me to have a good time on R and R."

I knew Barbara Jean. I even screwed her once, but I never told Clark that. I could just see Barbara Jean gossiping with her girlfriends about having to go to Hawai'i, and thinking how noble she would look to others for doing her duty. But I knew Barbara Jean really didn't want to miss out on a free trip to Hawai'i paid for by Clark, because all she would get from Harley was a weekend trip to Traverse City, or maybe a couple of nights at the Hawaiian Gardens Motel in Holly, down the road from Flint.

When Clark had recovered somewhat from the shock of Barbara Jean being pregnant, and he finally realized he couldn't change her mind to marry him, the thing that was really bothering him was having sex with a pregnant woman. Being very ignorant myself, I couldn't really give him any good advice. I tried to tell him just to let her sit in the hotel room and get home on her own. But I knew he wouldn't, because Barbara Jean was emotionally stronger than Clark and Harley put together. They were both smarter than she was, but no question about it, she was stronger. Barbara Jean would go after security and fight to control her nest with all the energy and the narrowness of her small mind.

I realize now that Barbara Jean was a good survivor, and that she used what little brains she had to the maximum, which is more than most of us can say. She knew what she wanted, and saw how to get there. Years later when I told my psychiatrist Dr. Bahlman about Barbara Jean, he said his first wife was like that. He said she wanted to marry a doctor, and she nailed him in his senior year of college with sex. He said she was much more experienced than he was.

Barbara Jean and Madame Magyar were a lot alike, too. They let others be emotional while they survived. I went down to the state courtroom recently and watched a trial where Madame Magyar was charged with swindling a Canadian woman tourist from British Columbia out of $25,000. It seems this woman believed she had an old Indian curse put on her by some medicine man, and came to Madame Magyar because she had heard about her helping another woman who was sexually inhibited and now had a good sex life, even though it cost her $10,000. After a week of private sessions the woman felt cured and went back to Canada, but the curse came back in Kamloops, British Columbia. So she wanted a refund. When the story hit the TV and newspapers, it turned out Madame Magyar had clipped several people for a total of $85,000 and was working on a few others when the shit hit the fan.

I can't be too hard on Madame Magyar because my father-in-law Takeshi, who is a descendant of a class of untouchables in Japan called Burakumin, is an exorcist in Honolulu. We have had a lot of friendly arguments about this. But he says since his ancestors had the untouchable jobs of dealing with dead bodies and slaughtering cattle, it was natural for him to deal with evil spirits, which, according to him, come in varying shades of evil. He says he lets the people tell him how evil the spirit is, and then God sets the price. Before I started living in Hawai'i I would not have believed all of this, and I still don't, but I have a more tolerant attitude toward evil spirits now.

When I first got out of the army I worked as an apprentice welder on the new football stadium. And when some of the supports started moving, most of the workers were convinced it was evil spirits. There were two schools of thought on this. One school thought there were really evil spirits, or the ghosts of old Hawaiians were getting pissed off at us for disturbing their graves. The second school was not so sure about the evil spirits and ghosts, but felt it would not be polite to show disrespect for old traditions. So all work stopped until a Hawaiian kahuna, or priest, was called in to bless and purify the grounds. The engineers said to themselves it was underground springs, but when they poured more concrete they made sure the kahuna splashed water on it.

You see, it's kind of hard to pin anyone down on evil spirits, ghosts, or religion in Honolulu because there are so many beliefs mixed together and existing side by side. Take this: a Filipino Catholic guy I know at the shipyard consults with a real live witch doctor, whom he refuses to name. But he never tells his priest at confession, because he would not want to hurt the priest's feelings. So he is quite willing to be tolerant even of me, an atheist.

Like he says, maybe I just haven't found the right spirits yet. He just tells me to be patient, because there are lots of them out there, and sometimes they are busy for years.

He told me he was arguing with his daughter, who wanted to marry a guy he didn't like. He knew the guy had bad spirits, because the witch doctor told him so. One day he very confidently handed me a newspaper story about how the guy was killed after he had downed a couple of six-packs and his car hit a big monkeypod tree. My friend went by and patted the tree afterwards and poured some fruit punch mixed with gin on the ground to say thanks. As he said to me, "Da kine monkeypod say geevum, brah. He can take it. Ford junk. Da buggah dead." I bought him a plate lunch that day to show him respect.

As the shipyard bookie, Philip Wong, says, "Hey, brah, you gotta go along because you nevah know what somebody got goin' for dem." I guess he should know, because he never seems to lose at the cockfights, even though he's lousy on picking football winners. As Wong says, if you were sure of winning all the time, there wouldn't be any fun in gambling.

One time we went to the cockfights and he won $5,000, but then the cops raided the place and we had to run. While we're running, he turns to me and says, "Hey, you take this. You can run faster and maybe you won't get caught. Besides, the cops won't believe a haole was at a cockfight." He never doubted for a minute that I would give the money back to him the next day. I had thoughts about keeping the money as I was running flat out through the kiawe brush, but the good spirits prevailed and proved Wong right.

So, even though I don't really believe in spirits myself, I do get the feeling sometimes that some unknown force in the spring of 1968 propelled Clark and Barbara Jean in one direction, and me in another. Like I said, I forgot all about the hand grenade, but Clark decided to give it to Barbara Jean for a wedding present. She didn't know it until she opened it after she married Harley Featherstone. I didn't know it until an agent from the Army Criminal Investigation Department came to see me at Tripler Army Hospital and asked me about the grenade and Barbara Jean.

By that time, Clark was already dead, and it was all mixed up in my mind who was responsible for killing him: Barbara Jean, the V.C., or Clark himself. I hated her for it just as much as I hated the V.C. But when you get right down to it, Clark just gave up on life and killed himself. If he hadn't wanted the V.C. to kill him, they probably never would have, because Clark was even better than I was at crawling around in the dark outside the perimeter and wasting V.C. That was what we did every night, and we were damn good at it.

To be more specific (specific is a word I learned from Dr. Deborah Bacon, my first psychiatrist at the VA clinic in Honolulu), Clark hit them with a ball-peen hammer that had a piece of guy wire attached to a hole in the handle. He would wrap the other end of the wire around his wrist so he would not drop the hammer and lose it in the dark. I usually stabbed them, but I sometimes used a hatchet rigged like Clark's ball-peen hammer. I kept experimenting with various things to find the perfect weapon for killing people in the dark, but I never did find it.

Sometimes we killed women and kids, too, but they were all V.C. because they all ran around in the dark after we told them to stay in the village. They would help the hard core V.C. plant mines and booby traps. Once I killed a grandfather. I knew what he was because I felt his beard afterwards. And once Clark killed a grandmother and a little girl. You could usually tell the ages of the V.C. by feeling their faces, but sometimes people there got old very quickly.

Clark had been real quiet ever since he said goodbye to Barbara Jean in Honolulu. On the plane back to Vietnam he didn't say anything, but then nobody felt much like talking. The first night back we were out all night crawling around, but I went back inside the perimeter by myself before dawn. Just after daylight, two guys from our squad came running into the mess hall and said they had seen Clark walking toward the V.C. village by himself, without any weapon in his hands. They said he just kept walking with his hands up until he disappeared into the jungle brush. They yelled at him, but no one was going after him until the area had been checked for booby traps.

With a sense of dread, I went out with the search party. I kept saying to myself, "Goddam that bitch Barbara Jean." We checked the village and threatened everyone, but since the captain was with us, we couldn't really get tough with them.

The next morning the V.C. left what had been Clark outside our perimeter. When I saw it, I burst into tears and felt my body going into convulsions. Before I fainted I heard the lieutenant say to make sure it wasn't booby trapped. Someone later told me that it wasn't.

The only thing I remember after that was getting on a plane with some wounded guys and flying back to Hawai'i. Some nurse asked me if I would help her change I.V. bottles. I remember that I held them up with my eyes closed. After I got to Tripler Army Hospital in Honolulu, I just remember sleeping and eating. I knew some people were asking me questions, but I don't know what I said.

The first thing I really remember was an older woman who came with a nurse, asking if she could have lunch with me. She had silver grey hair, she chain-smoked cigarettes, and she talked like a machine gun. Her name was Karen Sexton, and she was a volunteer. She just started asking me questions about where I came from, what I did before I joined the army, did I have a girlfriend. After a couple of questions and answers she said, "You can tell me to shut up if you want. I'm a compulsive hysterical type, but I don't bite."

When she said she didn't bite, I started to laugh and I didn't know why. I laughed and tears rolled down my face. Then she got up and said, "Wow, I'm on a roll. You know I tell jokes and I can dance, too. I once toured with the USO in World War II." She kept coming back every day, and the nurses kept giving me pills. Finally one day, she asked if I wanted to see her house. She lived near Diamond Head crater, right on the ocean. She even had a swimming pool and a bunch of guard dogs, but they only licked my hands.

She laughed and said, "For $2,000 I get hand kissers. Maybe I should have hired a bodyguard. No telling what he might kiss." Her husband traveled a lot for a pineapple company, and her daughters were away at college on the mainland. She said she was in charge of keeping the cockroaches and termites from taking over the place. We walked on the beach and I played with the dogs by throwing sticks into the ocean and they swam after them. She cooked all kinds of strange things I had never eaten before, like chicken paprikash and stuffed grape leaves. She went to cooking school to become a gourmet chef and wanted to open a restaurant, but her husband said he needed her to keep the roaches and termites in their place. So she cooked for herself and the dogs. She said the dogs refused to eat sauerbraten. She threw up her arms dramatically and said, "Can you imagine a dog refusing to eat sauerbraten? Next time I'll get German dogs." I thought that was very funny, even though I didn't even know what sauerbraten was.

We talked mostly about sex, or rather she talked and asked me questions about it. I didn't know much about any of this, but Karen went into great detail about everything. When I looked blank as she talked about diaphragms and spermicide, she even brought out a portable blackboard and drew pictures. She laughed and said that at heart she was a dirty old lady and really liked to perform for an audience.

The most important thing Karen did for me was to show me plants and flowers. She knew every damn plant and flower in Honolulu. Sometimes I helped her move big potted plants around, or trimmed the bougainvillea for her. She took me to meetings at Foster Gardens, and to the university arboretum. I even helped Karen make flower leis of plumeria blossoms and carnations for some of the guys at Tripler.

Before I met Karen I only ate things if they were sweet or not too sour, and in the tropical fruit area I only ate bananas and pineapple. Karen was always handing me a guava, passion fruit, lychees, and the thing that became my favorite, an avocado sandwich on homemade bread. I still see Karen sometimes. I think she drinks too much, and even she admits she is addicted to cigarettes. As she says, she is a compulsive personality type, and if she gave up cigarettes, she would become addicted to something worse. She is developing new types of orchids, and I see her at all the orchid shows. I always smile when I see her or think about her.

I wish I had been able to give her something in exchange for all that she did for me. Later, when I talked to Dr. Bahlman, he said she was very lonely and probably wanted to make love. At the time I couldn't imagine anyone with money being lonely. I was so overwhelmed with my own pain and confusion that I couldn't see other people's problems or give much to them.

Slowly I began to learn trust and let go of the anger. It may sound simple, but it wasn't. That was when I was still seeing my first psychiatrist, Dr. Deborah Bacon. I learned later that she didn't like men much, and Dr. Bahlman said she couldn't maintain objectivity with her patients. The VA sort of decided that she needed to find another job. She did two things for me, besides scaring the shit out of me most of the time.

There was this girl I met, and she was really putting the pressure on me to get married. Once she even claimed she was pregnant. When Dr. Bacon heard that, she said to take her to a gynecologist, and gave me the name of a woman doctor. But when the girl heard where I was going to take her, she said she wasn't pregnant after all. Also, Dr. Bacon told me to tell her that I was too immature and had too many problems even to think about getting married. Dr. Bacon said she would tell me when I was ready to get married, and then I could tell the girl. After that, the girl gave up and the next month she married someone else. So for a long time, I had this insurance policy against marriage. I would just tell girls that my psychiatrist said I was too immature to get married.

The other thing I learned from Dr. Bacon was that women were stronger than men. She said we are not living in a caveman society where we had to beat the shit out of animals, so muscles did not count for much. Dr. Bacon said it was mental and emotional strength that counted in our modern day society, and that women were superior to men in this. She recited all kinds of studies to prove her statements. The one that convinced me was her own statement that women live longer than men, therefore they are stronger. After I heard that, I started taking better care of myself and not working as hard. I also stopped feeling sorry for women.

Dr. Bahlman laughed when I told him all of this, but he did agree that women lived longer. He thought it was because men had more stress on them from their jobs. After hearing this, I decided not to marry any woman who did not want to work full time. If it came to one of us staying home, I was going to be that one and only. But that has never been a problem with Sandra.

The only problem with Sandra is her mother. She is a cold stone racist. As Dr. Bahlman said, she wants to deny my humanity because of my color.

She didn't want her daughter's pure Japanese blood corrupted by marrying a Caucasian, or haole, but Sandra's father Takeshi told me the Japanese were originally half Korean anyway. When I went to the house, Sandra's mother would go downstairs and not talk to me. Even after we got married, she wouldn't talk to me.

Sandra thought she would change after we had Tommy, but she didn't. So I refused to go to Sandra's parents' house on New Year's, or to let her take Tommy there. To Japanese, New Year's is the big holiday and everyone has lots of food and lots of relatives come over. There is plenty of sushi and beer. The men drink and watch football games. Sandra and I had a lot of arguments because I wouldn't let her take Tommy there, but I didn't back down. I said if she denies my humanity because of my color, then she must be denying half of Tommy's humanity, too. I said a half of a racist is still a racist, and I didn't want my kid associating with a racist.

I finally got even with Hazel Mizukami. She is a public school teacher and is always pushing education, both for money and status. She is what Dr. Bahlman calls hard core new middle class. She came from a poor family, and Sandra's father worked at the shipyard while Hazel went to the University of Hawai'i. Now she is a high school math teacher, and is embarrassed that Takeshi still exorcises bad spirits. But hell, he sometimes makes more in a week from that than Hazel does from teaching. Besides, Takeshi came from the Burakumin class and that bothers Hazel. She tries to cover it up, but everyone knows.

I finally fixed Hazel when Tommy turned five. Without telling anybody, early one morning I went down to Punahou School to turn in Tommy's application. Punahou is a very famous private school in Honolulu. There I was with all these pushy middle class mothers in line behind me. I had on my shipyard working clothes, because I had to go to work later. The women talked to each other, but not to me. Anyway, I handed in my application and it was number fourteen. Tommy could already read when he was three and a half, so Dr. Bahlman, whose two daughters went there, encouraged me to give it a shot. Dr. Bahlman said they might even give Tommy financial aid.

Well, Tommy aced the test and the interview. The woman who did the oral interview commented that Tommy was a very secure and mature child. I smiled and said his mother is very secure and his father is working at it. She sort of smiled, but also looked a little puzzled at that.

Anyway, when the letter came that Tommy had been admitted, they asked me to come down to the financial office and this very nice Chinese lady, Mrs. Lum, asked me questions about my finances. I said I was working at the shipyard and that Sandra was going to the University of Hawai'i studying to be a bacteriologist, but that she was an R.N. and worked at Queen's Hospital on the weekends. So Mrs. Lum did a little calculating on her calculator, smiled, and said they would offer us a half tuition scholarship, and I would have to pay the other half. She said when Sandra started working full time, then we would have to pay the full shot. I had no argument with that, and asked where I paid. She said all I would have to pay now was the deposit that would guarantee Tommy a place in the class of 1999.

I still hadn't told Sandra about any of this Punahou business until it was all double locked up. When I showed her the letter of acceptance and the paid deposit slip, she started crying, not because she was sad, but because she was happy. I asked her to make a reservation and invite all her family to come to the Pearl City Tavern, which is a pretty classy restaurant even if they do have live monkeys running around behind the bar in a glass cage. She started laughing and said, "You've done it! You've really done it! My mother can't say no to a Punahou grandchild. She will want to brag about that too much not to come to the Pearl City Tavern."

And sure enough, Hazel came. I waited at the bar with Tommy while Sandra sat at the table waiting for everyone to show up. Tommy was drinking a Shirley Temple, and I was drinking a double Singapore Sling. I looked at Tommy and told him he was a great kid and that I was proud of him and loved him very much. He wanted to play with the monkeys and feed them the fruit from his drink. When I saw that everybody had arrived, I picked up Tommy and carried him to the table. Everyone stood up and clapped, and Tommy asked if it was his birthday. I looked right at Hazel and said, "It's better than a birthday because you will have more of those, but today you're a member of the Punahou class of 1999, and you will be that forever."

Tommy didn't think it was a very big deal, and asked if he could have a cake. He was very happy when I told him we were going to have his favorite cake, chocolate, for dessert. I sat him down next to Hazel and said, "I don't know which half got him into Punahou, and it didn't say on the letter of acceptance. The lady in the admissions office told me he got a perfect score on the admissions tests."

Then I handed Hazel the acceptance letter and sat down at the far end of the table, next to Takeshi. He handed me an envelope under the table and when I started to raise it up, he motioned for me to put it in my pocket. Then he smiled and said softly, "You done a good thing. Sandra's done all right marrying you, and I just hope I live long enough to see Tommy playing football or baseball at Punahou."

He raised his drink and I picked up my Singapore Sling and he said, "Kampai!" When I got home, I found five one-hundred dollar bills in the envelope. I bought a thousand dollar U.S. savings bond for Tommy with it.

But it wasn't easy getting this far, and lots of times before I married Sandra I thought about going back in the army. In the army, you can avoid getting involved with people emotionally. All you have to do is do your job, and stay out of trouble. Nobody pokes into your personal life, and nobody asks where you go on the weekends. And after Clark got himself killed, I knew I never wanted to go back to Flint and the Buick Motor Division.

A couple of years after Sandra and I got married, we went to Flint to pick up a car that one of my brothers had gotten for us at a discount from GM. Sandra said at first she felt strange being around so many haoles, but later she learned that it was her problem. When she realized that no one was going to look at her funny, she relaxed and enjoyed herself. Sandra was always better than I was at adapting to new situations. She just took everything in like she was visiting a living museum. We went on a tour of the Buick assembly plant and when she saw how the people worked, she looked at me and said softly, "Now I know why you don't want to do this anymore." I told her it was even worse in the wintertime because you never saw the sun.

We went by ourselves to see Clark's grave. I poured a bottle of Clark's favorite Jim Beam whiskey on the grave after taking the first swallow. I gave Clark a casual salute and walked away.

I drove by Harley's Cool Seats and we saw Harley fixing somebody's upholstery. He was bent over, hard at work. I thought about stopping and giving him my Bronze Star for having set in motion all the things that changed my life. But we just drove by.

Clark's brother Charleton told me about Barbara Jean and the hand grenade. Clark had rigged it so it would not go off until the box was opened. Fortunately she was alone in the bedroom where she put the wedding presents. I was glad that she hadn't opened the present at the wedding reception. The explosion blew her through a sliding glass door, but it did not harm the cat that was sleeping on the bed. I didn't ask if it was a black cat.

Afterwards I thought that there isn't any justice in the world but what we make for ourselves. But this thought, like much of my life, is constantly being revised.

WILLIAM D. STEINHOFF *grew up in Flint, Michigan, and joined the Marine Corps in the 1950s. He has lived in various parts of Asia with the U.S. military, as a student, and as a freelance reporter. He graduated from the University of Michigan and earned an MFA from the Writers' Workshop at the University of Iowa. He lives in Honolulu with his wife Patricia, a professor of sociology at the University of Hawai'i at Mānoa, and their Bouvier, Teufel.*

Rita Ariyoshi

"JAMMING TRAFFIC"

The helicopter was filled with new guys, their burger-fed faces still warm from their mothers' good-byes. The hugs of sisters and sweethearts were almost tangible in the folds of their clothes. They had that typical American vacuity in their eyes, a blankness of soul that might be mistaken for innocence but was the result of having led, until this moment, a second-hand life. They had experienced lust and mayhem once removed, in their living rooms, on their screens, since first awareness.

The pilot and the door gunner, old Nam hands of seven and eight months respectively, exchanged conspiratorial glances. "Watch this," gunner Bobby Johnson said over the roar of the engine as the chopper slowed and circled. He looked at new guy Pete Pacheco as if he were about to feast on him. Six-foot-six, a brown giant, and every square inch was mush. A perfect case—medic—the guys whose testosterone tank ran on low. They were missing what Johnson called the K.I. chromosome, the killer instinct. They were hole pluggers, plumbers. With acute pleasure, Johnson sized up the tensile hulk of a man looking out on Vietnam with gee-whiz written all over his face.

Pacheco was from Hawaii, so he was accustomed to a world glowing in a hundred hues of green, but he had never seen, in all his twenty-two years, a green quite like the orderly squares of luminosity stretched out in the Mekong Delta below. He was seeing, for the first time, a rice crop in its full fecundity, an incredible sea of emerald, just before the tips start to go to gold for harvest.

A family—husband, wife, three small children—walked along the walls of the paddies, single file, accompanied by a platoon of ducks. From the air he couldn't see their faces, only the conical coolie hats. The wife had a baby in a sling on her back, a round lump curled in the shadow of her hat. It was a beautiful scene, could be the cover of a tour brochure. Visit sunny Vietnam. Pacheco had already heard about the surf at China Beach.

From the wide edge of its circle, the chopper suddenly aimed for the center, picking up speed, dipping as it neared target. Bobby Johnson shot the children first, one, two, three, "Pazooie," he yelled, then shot the wife in the very moment she raised her face to the swirling heavens and opened her mouth to scream. The chopper pulled up and Pete could see the face of the man, brown as his own, contorted in an anguish he didn't know until that moment was part of the range of human emotions. The man was looking up, shouting something at the chopper while his family lay like crumpled rags around him, staining the green. The chopper swept in again, so close the man's shirt blew in the wind. His hands were up, not in surrender, Pacheco knew instinctively, but in supplication—*take me, don't leave me.* Bobby Johnson obliged.

Radiant, blue eyes burning like a butane flame, the gunner turned to the men in the chopper, pulled his hat down snug on his head and said, "Gentlemen motherfuckers, welcome to fucking Hell." The hugs, the kisses, mothers, sweethearts, tenderness, naiveté, the whole nine yards were blown away in less than five minutes. Television and life merged. You had to do it. You couldn't take babies into battle, couldn't count on them not to break down and get someone killed. There were no thirty-second Pepsi breaks in Vietnam.

It wasn't Pacheco's worst moment in Vietnam, gore for gore, horror for horror, counting by bodies. The first time he killed a man, it was almost an accident. He didn't have time for the luxury of a moral decision. Danny Carew was down, both legs bloody pulps. Pacheco crawled toward him with his arsenal of Q-tips and tourniquets, which is how he sneeringly came to regard his army-issue medic's kit. As he knelt beside the black, twitching grunt, working quickly in the red slime just to dam the flows, he felt, rather than saw, a presence. He grabbed Carew's gun and whirled around shooting. The enemy fired aimlessly as he fell. The enemy couldn't have been more than fourteen, couldn't have weighed more than a skinny girl. He looked like one of the kids who hung around the Ching Lee store on Liliha Street, sucking on *li hing mui* and wet mango, trading milk caps.

Pacheco took some small moral satisfaction in the fact that he vomited after killing the kid. Carew, who would never walk again, tried to comfort him while they waited for the duster, "He would have killed us both. He might have been a kid, but he was the enemy. You did what you had to do, man."

Pacheco looked at the dead boy with his slim torso almost severed across the chest, and was ashamed. When the duster took Carew, they also took the boy's AK-47 and left the flesh behind to rot in the elephant grass.

In the evening Pacheco sat apart looking at the muted mountains bathed in moonlight, dangerously bright. He thought of the time he had crept quietly about his back yard, slingshot in hand, past the car port, stepping gingerly over the coiled hose, so close to the hibiscus bushes he got gold pollen dusted on his bare shoulders. There was a mynah bird owning the lychee tree, clear shot. Slowly he raised up the slingshot, sighted and sent the sharp rock flying. Got it in mid-squawk. The dark wings fluttered as it fell, the white undertips showing in the sunlight, like underwear. He rushed over. There was a hole in its head, something throbbing inside, pulsing. Life, mysterious force. Please die quickly. The bird was gasping air into its little orange beak. Suddenly another mynah came swooping out of the tree, diving at Pete, screaming, followed by a third bird. They pulled up and attacked again, taking turns diving at him, screaming. They drove him back to the hibiscus, then they went and stood beside the wounded bird, cooing softly until it died. Pete didn't go into the back yard for a week. He supposed a cat ate the body. When he was drafted into the army, he asked to be a medic, said he didn't want to kill.

Nobody screamed at you when you killed something in Vietnam. Most times nobody talked to you while you died and the last sounds you heard were not the cooing of kin, but the ear-splitting static of fire power. The delicate boy he shot was probably not missed yet by the mother who carried him. Pete wanted to remember the boy's details so a callus wouldn't form on his own conscience, as thick and protective as the ones his feet earned in a life spent barefoot. He knew it was entirely possible he would get used to killing, that he would take a land of pride in the outer limits of his actions, as he did in his ability to walk across fields of sharp, hardened lava, and to ride the monster storm waves that rolled into Waimea—the suicide surf. He also knew that Bobby Johnson was not unique, not an alien monster perverted from birth. Someday Johnson would go back to his real life and get married and have kids and maybe be a Little League coach and go to the mall with his wife.

That moonlit night when nothing moved, not even the bamboo, Pacheco thought that his first kill was some kind of a milestone in his life, the point from which nothing would ever be the same. But he was mistaken. There was no one turning point. Vietnam was cumulative. The overflow came the day his platoon burned some miserable thatched village and killed every man, woman, child and chicken. He did a post-carnage check—there were none to save. "Not a goddamn gook left," said one man, who then emptied a round into the dirt road, stirring up dust ghosts. The dead bodies looked like the Pachecos' neighbors. He took some Darvon from his medicine kit.

He didn't prescribe for himself often. There were men who might need the pills more than he did, men with visible, gaping wounds. He thought of his mother, her soft, too-sure voice saying, as she had hundreds of times in childhood when sibling quarrels erupted, "Little birds in their nest agree, why then, oh why can't we?" He swallowed his medicine and dozed in his Darvon nest.

Pacheco did two tours in Nam. They needed medics. The VC had a price on the heads of American medics. For every medic down, twenty soldiers would bleed to death in the field. It was an efficient, clever strategy. There were no Red Cross armbands in Fucking Hell. When the Americans went into battle, they had to have a code word for medic, because the VC would lie in the bushes and yell "Medic," and the poor guy crawling forward with his regulation Q-tips and cotton balls would buy the farm. The other, more compelling reason Pacheco had signed up for the extra tour was he had ceased to believe in a life outside Vietnam. He could not imagine reentering a two-sex world where you could be reasonably sure you would make it through the day, barring a traffic accident, and make it through the night without the sweet detachment of Darvon dreams. Then one day his sister Pua sent him a tape of Gabby Pahinui and his slack key guitar. The man sang "Hii lawe" as if he were weeping for joy and was so happy he almost couldn't stand it, and Pacheco remembered the beauty and peace of home, remembered those exact feelings. Hell had an exit that wasn't chemical. He was honorably discharged.

The whole family came to meet him at the airport, so eager, the tears, the hugs, up to his ears in leis. He had forgotten how sweet the air smelled, how soft upon the skin it was. How could this place exist in the same time, on the same planet? Pua, his mother, his older sister Kaui, his aunties, they had no idea. He had nothing to say to them. They remarked on how quiet he had become.

Whenever he checked the newspaper, Vietnam was page five, after the jellyfish sightings on the south shore, after the budget battle in the legislature, after the shipping news, after the Liberty House white sale. People are bleeding and dying. Young people. They are missing legs, arms, eyes. Mothers who nurtured little boys and packed lunches and poked thermometers and cleaned baseball uniforms got their sons back in anti-fungal body bags. A medic is the garbage man of war. Nobody wanted to hear that. They no longer cared about it. They said: *You are back. You are safe. I can relax. I can skip page five from now on. My boy is back. Praise the Lord.* If they could detect in his duffel bag the smell of burning hay from the roofs of small villages, as he could, they never said a word. He wanted to shake them. He swallowed his uppers.

Pete, because of his size, always slept Japanese-style on a futon on the floor. No bed was big enough, unless it was special order and too much money. He awoke the first morning at home and knew right where he was because birds were singing in the plumeria trees, in the lychee and mango trees dripping with fruit—greedy bulbuls with their beautiful song, doves incessantly cooing, little finches twittering, mynahs quarreling. Nam had no birds left.

Thanks to an uncle in the union, Pete got a job with Matson, unloading containers. He moved his futon to a place of his own so his mother wouldn't shame him into church on Sunday and so he wouldn't shame his mother with his sins. She had a way of pushing at the sides of her upswept hair before saying that Reverend Tamsing missed him and that his life would be wonderful if he would only come back to church.

He was grateful he was sleeping alone the night he dreamed he was in Nam. The dead boy had him by the throat, those slim wrists were hard as wing nuts. They rolled over, Pete was on top. He punched the grinning boy as hard as he could and woke himself with his own scream, his right hand shattered from impact with the concrete floor of his bedroom. He'd never work at Matson again. He couldn't even surf for awhile.

He met Cindy, a waitress who could swallow a tray of drinks like they were guava juice. They had a baby girl. The infant's dark hair peeked over the top of the flannel blanket, her shape round as—as the baby that first day in Nam. He wouldn't hold his child. He was terrified of the baby. Every time he looked at her he thought of that other baby sleeping so peacefully on its mother's back, in the shade of her hat. He saw small bodies all askew in a miserable village obscured by smoke. He knew that if he touched little Leilani he would break apart. Neither uppers nor downers helped. Not whiskey, either. Nam owned him forever.

Cindy pleaded with him, begged him to get help. They should go to AA together. They should go to his mother's church.

He'd walk out when she got like that, full of self-pity, giving him guilt. She had no idea what she might unleash, and the leash was fraying. Pete was relieved when she took her little round baby and went back to the Mainland. She had looked at him desperately, one last time before slamming the door.

At times, he missed her. But not the baby. He was afraid of the baby even in his dreams. He was afraid he might hurt her, and equally afraid something might happen to her, that she would die and he wouldn't be able to protect her.

His mother left letters from Cindy out on the kitchen counter. He'd walk out when he saw the familiar writing on the envelope.

When he was broke and couldn't buy dope, he'd go to the VA for medicine, for counseling, for job referral. He saw the slag of war, sitting in wheelchairs, missing limbs, parts of brain, and he wondered why he had tied those tourniquets.

Of the six medics who had gone through training with him and who were his friends, he was the only one to come home. He tried expressing his feeling in music. He wanted to communicate—what? He wanted to shake his head and clear it, but couldn't. Besides, he'd never sound like Gabby. It was too late for him to sing like that and play like that, the music piercing the heart with joy, when he had been to Nam and back.

Pete was arrested making his first heroin buy. He was brought into court in handcuffs and leg irons, like an animal, a pig from the mauka forest. His mother was there, along with Kaui and her husband. He had never seen his mother look so small, like a little girl. When she saw him, her honey-colored face aged eons in moments. Pete vowed he would never put her through this again.

First offense, vet. He got probation.

His mother revved up the church campaign. He wanted to please her, went once, liked the choir in their white nurse dresses singing "Rock of Ages," but he would have walked out if it wouldn't have embarrassed her. It wasn't that he didn't believe—quite the opposite. He believed every word of Scripture. When he tried to pray, he saw those little children in coolie hats, the Holy Innocents and their parents, up in heaven at God's right hand, whispering bad things about him in God's ear. He could never show his face in heaven.

He stopped in at his mother's when he needed a few bucks, and when he needed to be with someone who didn't really know him and so could continue to love him. Sometimes when he was kicked out of whatever shelter he had for not paying rent, he'd come and sleep on her floor.

Most times he slept under a tree in Aala Park. His sisters couldn't stand the sight of him, said he was taking advantage of their mother. They didn't know that he once in a while stopped in at the offices of their husbands and borrowed money. The husbands never told. Men are usually pretty decent about those things.

Pete's next arrest happened on the Lunalilo Freeway where he happened to be walking stark naked. He had been seized with a compulsion to be free, as if by shedding his clothes he could shed his memories. For a few glorious moments he was utterly free, walking in traffic in nothing but his pelt, the air touching every part of him gently. It made him giddy—or maybe it was the dope. He wanted to stop traffic, snarl up the whole highway, do something monumental for once in his life, but nobody stopped. They veered around him, looked back at the naked giant through rear-view mirrors, sneaky-like. When the police came, he raised his hands like the Vietnamese father, hoping to be shot. They spoke nicely. The ambulance came.

From that time on, he was in and out of Kaneohe State Hospital, the psychiatric ward. With the drugs he took on the outside and the drugs they gave him on the inside, he lost track of time.

Occasionally, over the years, he thought of his daughter. It amazed him that a parent could have a child and that the child would wander so casually in and out of his mind. There was some land of heresy going on here. He was little better than a stud dog who wouldn't recognize his own pup if it was eating out of the same bowl. He decided to call Leilani, to be a better father, even at a distance. The first time he called, he was surprised she could speak. He had been picturing her still round and curled. She was five. When she was eight he promised her a doll house. It was summer. There were no doll houses. Christmas shipments hadn't come in yet. By Christmas, he was back in Kaneohe. One more thing he didn't finish. He never finished his rehab programs because the truth was, he didn't want to be clean. It wasn't safe.

Years went by before he overcame his embarrassment and called Leilani again. She was thirteen. She didn't mention the doll house, but he heard it in her tone of voice, implying why call if you don't have the doll house like you promised. He asked for a photograph. Cindy wrote back, "You are not entitled to a photograph. You have never spent one thin dime to support your daughter. You just want to satisfy your sick-o curiosity as to what she might look like. You're not a father, you're just a sperm donor. Go screw yourself, Bastard, and leave us *A-lone*." Calling all uppers.

Pete begged money for dope on the Fort Street Mall. He hit up his brothers-in-law. When he was flat, he had his street friends and the surf rats—the haoles always had something. He'd like to say he didn't remember calling his mother in the middle of the night and taunting her, singsong, "Birds in their nest agree . . ." But he did remember and it didn't matter. The phone call to his mother just wasn't up there with his first day in Nam.

He was forty-three and he wanted to be free of Vietnam. The place was a lover who got into your blood, tantalizing, taunting, putting you through hell, leading you by the hand to the fires. He would strip himself of it once and for all.

He felt again those first glorious moments of utter naked freedom as he stepped into traffic. It felt so good he was sure he would succeed in stopping cars this time. He would explain to people about the little children in the coolie hats, the army-issue body bags. They had no right to their ignorance, to their nice day. He pictured the lines of cars obediently coming to a stop as he stretched his arms out and confessed. They would all look at him and admire him for his courage, waiting for his words. He would speak for all the fallen, the ones taken away in dusters, and the ones left to rot in the elephant grass.

He hardly heard the shouts, "Hey, Lolo," as the cars veered around him. One old Dodge pulled to the shoulder, another Hawaiian blalah. Peter staggered toward him, aware that he might topple over, that his head was an enormous mango without a pit. The man got out of the car, put his arms around him, "I know, brother. I know." Pete sobbed uncontrollably, and bent way over to rest his head on the man's shoulder. "'Not a gook left,'" the guy said.

Gently the stranger eased him into the passenger seat and said, "I'm going to get you some help, brother. Nobody knows who wasn't there." He drove him to Tripler, the big pink hospital on the hill, built for the invasion of Japan, before the atomic bomb made it unnecessary, promised to make all invasions unthinkable.

The man got him checked in. He came back to see him every day after work, made sure he got in the right programs.

The family was relieved. He was safe and clean, and they were very tired of dealing with him. They sent greeting cards.

Pete was released into yet another rehab program. No contact with anyone outside for thirty days. Inside, nobody presumed to have answers. They just listened. People like himself sat in a circle and took turns speaking their unspeakable private hells, the childhood rapes, the lovelessness, the self-inflicted humiliations, and the failures.

His road friend came to see him when he "graduated," helped him get a job in the produce department of Star Market. He had his own room in a boarding house, his own closet with hangers, an extra pair of pants, three clean shirts. He was happy for the first time since childhood when he'd surf all day off Diamond Head and come ashore with his board, and tourists would shoot him with their little cameras. Then the Veterans Administration said that if he put in those kinds of hours working at Star, he'd lose his benefits. He couldn't afford that. He quit, went surfing, had a few beers when the sun went down and the sharks cruised. His benefits and welfare always ran out before the end of the month. He worked the Fort Street Mall, developed a routine. He'd go up to a neatly dressed businessman and say, "Hi, am I glad to see you. How's it goin? Hey we gotta have lunch soon. Boy, I'm lucky I ran into you today. I forgot my wallet." While the man was trying to figure out how he knew him, Pete would talk him out of a five. "Thanks, Buddy, I'll call you next week." Pete hated himself for doing it. It had never bothered him before. Now he felt like a loser.

He kept going to rehab meetings, spilling his guts out. When he left the circle of pain and loss, he felt increasingly isolated, as if he had little in common with anyone outside rehab. They all lived in a plastic world, which by its very nature could not bleed. He escaped into his safe haven of uppers and downers, then confessed at the meetings.

You have to try, he was told. You have to make amends to break down walls. It's the ninth step to recovery. He called Leilani, apologized for being a bad dad. All she said was, "That's okay." Sobbing, he hung up the phone, his cries bouncing off some satellite in space, carried thousands of miles in darkness. Later he realized it had been three in the morning, her time.

He began to visit his mother more often, always being careful not to show up when he was stoned. She seemed so pleased with him, in her ignorance, but he could see her disappointment, her sorrow at the sight of him.

One night, a friend asked if he had ever tried free-basing crack. He said there was nothing on this earth like it. They sat down on the sidewalk on King Street in the arches of the old post office. A little flame flickered, rose then fell to a small spark as he sucked in. It was the most intensely pleasurable moment of his life, sexual, his entire being vibrated with pleasure, glowed like Bobby Johnson after a kill. He was walking on burning lava, hissing and crackling. No calluses. He became one with the pain, lost in its fiery magnificence, and entered the flame.

The police found him, alone and dead at five in the morning, when they made their sweep of the streets, before the secretaries in muumuus with paper cups of coffee came along, before the tourists off-loaded from their vans to gape at Iolani Palace.

His funeral was a curious mixture of family, his mother's friends from church dressed in white salvation nurse outfits, his own friends immediately recognizable in their ill-fitting hope as being from the rehab center, and some surfers dressed solemnly, thoughtfully in black tank tops. A young woman with long auburn hair sat beside his mother. It was Leilani, who didn't know what she should be feeling. When he had called her a month ago she had not been warm. She heard him eulogized as "a gentle giant."

He was to be buried with honors in the veterans' cemetery in Kaneohe. The extra-large casket, draped in an American flag, was eased into the hearse. The police escort revved their motorcycles, swung out into the street and stopped traffic on the Pali Highway for the funeral procession of Pete Pacheco. This was the only truth he could show them, and he was finally free.

His daughter was impressed by the escort. She didn't know that in Hawaii the police stop traffic for every funeral, not just for Peter Kaulana Pacheco, fallen hero, wounded 1968, died 1993.

RITA ARIYOSHI *is the author of* Maui on My Mind; National Geographic Traveler Hawaii; *and other books. Her writing has won many national and international journalism awards. Her fiction has been published in literary journals and magazines. She was awarded a grand prize in the National Steinbeck Center Short Story Competition, first place in the* Honolulu Advertiser *fiction contest, and first place in the Catholic Press Association fiction awards. "Jamming Traffic," originally published in* Witness, *received a Pushcart Prize for Literature. She lives in Hawai'i Kai, O'ahu.*

Denis Johnson
from TREE OF SMOKE

B ill Houston's Honolulu shore leave commenced with the forenoon watch, too early for a man with money to spend: on top of everything, the navy wished to deny him any nightlife. He took a shuttle bus from the naval station and across the open fields of the air force base and then through town to Waikiki Beach, wandered dejected among the big hotels, sat on the sand in his Levi's and wild Hawaiian shirt and his very clean shoes—white bucks with red rubber soles—ate grilled pork on a wooden skewer at a kiosk, took a city bus to Richards Street, booked a bed at the Armed Services YMCA, and started drinking in the waterfront bars at one in the afternoon.

He tried an air-conditioned place favored by young officers, where he sat at a table by himself smoking Lucky Strikes and drinking Lucky Lager. It made him feel lucky. When he'd collected enough change he called home on the mainland, chatted with his brother James.

That just made him more depressed. His brother James was stupid. His brother James was going to end up in the military like himself.

He strolled the waterfront with the beer thudding inside his head, a lonely feeling pulling at his heart. By 3:00 p.m. the pavement of Honolulu had baked so hot it sucked at his rubber shoe soles as he walked. He hid inside the Big Surf Club trading beers with two men slightly older than himself, one of them a man named Kinney who'd recently joined the crew on Houston's ship—the USNS *Bonners Ferry*, a T2 tanker manned mostly by civilians, of whom Kinney was one. But he hadn't just waltzed on board for a tropical cruise. He'd spent time in the navy, lived on ship after ship, and had no real home ashore. Kinney had attached himself to a barefoot beach bum who seemed hopped up on something. The bum bought the table two pitchers in a row and eventually revealed he'd served with the Third Marines in Vietnam before landing back home on an early discharge. "Yeah, baby," the bum said. "I got the medical."

"Why?"

"Why? Because I'm mentally disabled."

"You seem all right."

"You seem all right if you buy us a beer," Kinney said.

"No problem. I'm on disability. Two forty-two a month. I can drink a serious amount of Hamm's, man, if I sleep on the beach like a Moke and eat what the Mokes eat."

"What do the Mokes eat? Who are the Mokes?"

"Around here you got the Mokes and the Howlies. We are the Howlies. The Mokes are the native fuckers. What do they eat? They eat cheap. Then there's a whole lot of Japs and Chinks, you probably noticed. They're in the Gook category. You know why Gook food stinks so bad? Because they fry it up with rat turds and roaches and whatever else gets in with the rice. They don't care. You ask them what the fuck stinks around here and they don't even know what you're taking about. Yeah, I've seen some things," the bum went on. "Over there the Gooks wear these funny straw hats, you probably seen those—they're pointy? Girls riding on a bicycle, you grab their hat when you go by and you just about yank their head off, because they're tied with a string. Yank her right off the bike, man, and she goes down fucked-up in the mud. This one time I saw one where she was all bent like this, man. Her neck was snapped. She was dead."

Bill Houston was completely confused. "What? Where?"

"Where? In South Vietnam, man, in Bien Hoa. Right in the middle of town, practically."

"That's fucked up, man."

"Yeah? And it's fucked up when one of them honeys tosses a grenade in your lap because you let her get up beside you on the road, man. They know the rules. They know they should keep their distance. The ones who don't keep their distance, they probably have a grenade."

Houston and Kinney kept quiet. They had nothing comparable to talk about. The guy drank his beer. A moment almost like sleep came over them. Still nobody had spoken, but the bum said as if answering something, "That ain't nothing. I've seen some things."

"Let's see some beer," Kinney said. "Ain't it your round?"

The bum didn't seem to remember who'd bought what. He kept the pitchers coming . . .

Bill Houston thoroughly enjoyed beer, but there came a point where it started to stick in his throat. This tavern must face west, because the burning sun poured through the open door. No air-conditioning, but he was used to that in the places he drank in. It was a dive, all right.

He returned from the toilet, and Kinney was still interrogating the beach bum: "What did you do? Tell me exactly what you did."

"Nothing. Fuck it."

Bill Houston sat down and said, "I got nothing against you boys. Got a little brother want to go in the Marines."

The ex-marine was drunk. "That ain't nothing. I've seen some things."

"He's talking like he did something to some woman over there," Kinney said.

"Where?" Houston said.

"Vietnam, goddamn it," Kinney said. "Aren't you listening?"

"I've seen some things," the boy said. "What it was, they held this woman down and this one guy cut her pussy out. That stuff happens there all the time."

"Jesus God. No shit?"

"I did some of it too."

"You *did* it?"

"I was there."

Houston said, "You really"—He couldn't quite repeat it—"you really did that?"

Kinney said, "You cut up some bitch's cunt?"

"I was right there when it happened. Right nearby, right in the same— almost in the same village."

"It was your guys? Your outfit? Somebody in your platoon?"

"Not ours. It was some Korean guys, a Korean outfit. Those fuckers are senseless."

"Now shut the fuck up," Kinney said, "and tell us what the fuck you did."

"There's a lot of bad business that goes on," the man said.

"You're bullshit. The U.S. Marines would never put up with that. You're so bullshit."

The guy held up both hands like an arrestee. "Hey, wow, man—what's all the excitement about?"

"Just tell me you cut up a living woman, and I'll admit you're not bullshit."

The bartender shouted, "You! I told you before! You want beef? You want scrap?"—a big fat Hawaiian with no shirt on.

"This is a Moke right here," their companion said as the bartender threw down his rag and came over.

"I told you to get out of here."

"That was yesterday."

"I told you to get out of here with that talk. That means I don't want to see you yesterday, today, and tomorrow."

"Hey, I got a beer here."

"Take it with you, I don't care."

Kinney stood up. "Let's get the fuck out of this shit-hole Moke joint." He put his hand up under his shirt at the level of his belt.

"You pull a gun in here you gonna do time, if I don't kill you."

"I get mad easy on a hot day."

"Get out, you three."

"You making me mad?"

The young bum laughed insanely and hopped backward toward the door, dangling his arms like a monkey's.

Houston hurried for the exit too, saying, "come on, come on, come on!" He was pretty sure he'd actually seen a gun butt in the waist of Kinney's jeans.

"See—that's a Moke, right there," the bum said. "They act all rough and tough. You get an advantage on them, and right away they cry like little babies."

They each bought a jug of Mad Dog 20/20 from a grocer who demanded they buy three loaves of Wonder Bread along with the wine, but it was still a bargain. They ate a little of the bread and tossed the rest to a couple of dogs. Soon they walked, drunk, surrounded by a pack of hungry strays, toward a glaring white strip of beach and the black sea and blue froth crashing on the sand.

A man stopped his car, a white, official-looking Ford Galaxie, and rolled down his window. He was an admiral in uniform. "Are you fellas enjoying the hell out of yourselves?"

"Yes, sir!" Kinney said, saluting by putting his middle finger to his eyebrow.

"I hope like hell you are," the admiral said. "Because hard times are coming for assholes like you." He rolled up his window and drove away.

The rest of the afternoon they spent drinking on the beach. Kinney sat against the trunk of a palm tree. The bum lay flat on his back with his Mad Dog balanced on his chest.

Houston took off his shoes and socks to feel the sand mounding under his arches. He felt his heart expanding. At this moment he understood the phrase "tropical paradise."

He told his two comrades, "What I'm saying, I mean, about these Mokes. I think they're related to the Indians that live down around my home. And not just them Indians, but also Indians that are from India, and every other kind of person you can think of who's like that, who's got something Oriental going on, and that's why I think, really, there ain't that many different kinds of people on this earth. And that's why I'm against war . . . " He waved his Mad Dog around.

DENIS JOHNSON *was born in 1949 in Munich, raised in Tokyo, Manila, and Washington, and currently lives in northern Idaho. He is the recipient of a Lannan Fellowship in Fiction and a Whiting Writer's Award, among many awards. His books include* Angels; The Stars at Noon; Jesus' Son; *and* Tree of Smoke, *which won the National Book Award in 2007.*

Susan M. Schultz
"LOCAL POLITICIAN"

T he MC kept mispronouncing her name. She mouthed it back, corrected, but the MC looked the other way. She spoke in Japanese and sang a song by a former internee, old man who wavered beside her. Was it a song about the towers, the barbed wire, a woman's tubes tied without her knowing? *She looks good*, someone said. The crowd filed past a cut ribbon into the gallery. There were family photos: the Yamamotos in Arkansas; the

Hasegawas at Heart Mountain; the son in Italy; the son at Tule Lake*. Rows of barracks in the desert. And there was the proclamation, signed by a president, to say that words could not express. She'd served a year at Kailua Correctional for what she told the judge *all politicians do*. She didn't sing beyond the genius of barbed wire, but paused to say she had a job in recycling, did anyone know anyone with scrap.

Refers to internment camps for Japanese Americans during the Second World War; and to the 442nd Infantry Division, composed in part of the sons of internees.

SUSAN M. SCHULTZ *has taught English at the University of Hawai'i at Mānoa since 1990. She edits Tinfish Press out of her home in Kāne'ohe on O'ahu, and is the author of several volumes of poems, including most recently* And Then Something Happened, *and a book of essays,* A Poetics of Impasse in Modern and Contemporary American Poetry. *She cheers for the West Oahu Canefires.*

Kathryn Waddell Takara
"PLANTATION COMPOUND"

Off Kamehameha Highway
near Kahuku
the remains of the housing compound
for the sugar plantation bosses.

Next to the dirt road
which forks in three directions
after the slowdown tree bump.

Beyond the porches
several glens provide shade
for the wild chickens, abandoned cars and cats,
a dilapidated stable.
Occasional clusters of spider lily plants
and ti-leaves
suggest former lifestyles
hierarchies of landscapes
plantation lunas, workers,
and the elite.
One can ride in small circles

all day long
on these dirt roads
or choose
to go to the tip of the peninsula
on the Kahuku side of the large bay
feel free to while away the time
in nostalgia.

Or one can choose
to head out to "progress" and struggle
where workers, bosses,
tourists, police and ambulances
whiz by
armed with pagers and cell phones
and sometimes guns
toward modern destinations
on the circle island highway,
seeking to forget a failing economy
 ignore the growing homeless
escape the wedges of wealth
and crumbling aloha.

KATHRYN WADDELL TAKARA *has a PhD in political science and an MA in French. She is professor of Africana Studies with a focus on cultural politics, and a spoken word poet. Her poetry is inspired by place, nature, philosophical and cultural reflections, and her travels in Zimbabwe, China, Europe, and thirty-year residency in Hawai'i. She enjoys gardening, people, and studies in consciousness.*

Juliana Spahr
"GATHERING PALOLO STREAM"

•

A place allows certain things.

A place allows certain things
and certain of we of a specific
place have certain rights.

•

To go to the stream is a right for
certain people.

To go, to gather.

•

The stream is a right.

It is a place for gathering.

A place for gathering āholehole

or for gathering guava, mīkana,
maiʻa

or for gathering palapalai.

•

The stream is many things.

Is busted television and niu.

Is rat and kī.

Is mongoose and freshwater.

Is ʻawa and kukui.

•

Beside the stream is a parking lot.

Yet there is no road into the
parking lot.

•

The parking lot is surrounded by
buildings on two sides

by a fence on a third

by a stream on the fourth.

•

Where the road once was is now
a parking lot for a rental space
business.

The rental space business has
surrounded their parking lot with
a high fence.

The fence gets locked at night.

•

This is about how certain of we
have rights on paper yet not in
place.

Certain of we have a right to a
gathering of the stream.

•

While the parking lot is unused,

while the stream is rich and full,

the parking lot represents the
general feeling of the space.

There is the parking lot of
limited space

the parking lot of owned by
certain of we
the parking lot of no possibility of
use

the parking lot of being unable to
park

the parking lot of growing from
the stream of gathering's freshness
of water

the parking lot beneath the
highway beside the stream of
gathering.

•

It is because certain of we are
always driving that the parking lot
matters.

Certain of we are driving to
waking up.

Certain of we are driving back
to clear ideas about what certain
of we are.

Certain of we are driving to
finishing what got interrupted.

Certain of we are driving to
orange, sticky fruit.

Certain of we are driving to the
airplane's heat shimmering off its
wings.

Certain of we are driving to clear
water moving over rocks.

Certain of we are driving to
things are this way, this way.

Certain of we are driving from
what are things.

Certain of we are driving to
waiting.

Certain of we are driving to
thinking in rooms without walls.

Certain of we are driving to
the way of it all being clear.

Certain of we are driving to
bougainvillea.

Certain of we are driving from
little cubicles, overhead lights,
bright flickering screen.

Certain of we are driving from
the way of thinking of it as one to
the way of thinking of it as one
and one.

Certain of we are driving the
metaphor.

•

The metaphor here of how we
need

and how we reach

and certain of us have rights yet
the rights are kept from certain of
us
by certain of us who are owning
place.

Certain of we have rights and
these rights are written so that
there is a possible keeping, a
keeping away, that denies
gathering.

JULIANA SPAHR'S *books include* This Connection of Everyone with Lungs, *a collection of poems that she wrote from November 30, 2002, to March 30, 2003, that chronicled the buildup to the latest U.S. invasion of Iraq; and* The Transformation, *a book of prose which tells the story of three people who move between Hawai'i and New York in order to talk about cultural geography, ecology, anticolonialism, queer theory, language politics, the academy, and recent wars.*

Darrell Lum
"PAINT"

S ometimes I feel mean. I like go bust someting. Some guys like bust car antennas but I only like go spray paint. I donno, I feel mean and I feel good at da same time, you know. It bad, but still yet I like spray paint. I donno why. Make me feel mean when I stay painting but feel like I stay doing someting. Someting big you know, so dat I stay big, too. I no paint swear words la dat. I paint my name and make um fancy wit curlicues undahneat. Sometimes I paint my babe's name but I no like do dat too much, bumbye everybody know, you know. Sometimes I paint one surf pickcha. One real tubular wave wit one guy jes making it . . . cranking through, you know.

When you paint on one new wall, j'like you stay da first one in da world fo spray paint. Even if you know get someting undahneat dat you went paint before, when da wall stay new, I mean, when dey jes paint up da wall fo cover da old spray paint, j'like stay da first time you painting. You can feel da spray paint, cool on your hand. You can smell da spray, sting your nose but sweet, j'like. I no sniff, you stupid if you sniff, bumbye you come all stoned and you no can spray good. But j'like it make you feel big. Make you feel good dat your name stay ovah dere big. Like you stay *somebody*.

Coco. Ass my name. "Coco '84" is what I write. I no write um plain, I make um nice, you know. Fat lettahs. Outline um. Wit sparkles. Da kine dat you can make wit white or silvah paint, like one cross or one star. From far, j'like your name stay shiny. I stay undah da freeway aftah school fo watch my wall. I watch um from across da street by da school parking lot. Everybody who pass look at my wall everyday. I try put someting new everytime so get someting new fo everybody to see. Only little bit at a time, like some more lines on da wave or one diffrent color outline on my name, stuff la dat. Jes about everybody look at my wall, even if dey pass um everyday, dey look. Sometimes when get some other guys by me aftah school I no can paint new stuff but da people dat pass still yet try look fo figgah out what stay new.

Aftah school I gotta wait fo my mahdah pau work pick me up. Sometimes I stay by da guys when dey no mo baseball practice la dat but most times I stay by myself. Everyday gotta plan how you going paint. When you paint, you gotta plan um good. You gotta be fast. You gotta know what you going do. And you cannot get nabbed. How many times I almost got nabbed, man.

One time somebody went put "Rockerz Rule" on my wall. Was anykine way. Wasn't nice. Had some guys hanging around da wall and I went ask dem, "You went make dat?"

"So what if we did?" one of da guys went tell me. I told dem, "Eh, I know da guy Coco, and he going bust your head if he find out you went spray on his wall. He big you know, Coco."

Dey went look around first fo see if I had backers. Since nevah have nobody, dey went ack like dey was tough. But finally dey went go away. Dey nevah spray nutting else except fo dis one punk kid went spray and walk. Had one crooked black line all da way across my wall. I would've beefed um but I nevah like. I would've given um lickins. I could've taken um.

Nobody know I spray paint. Nobody even know I stay Coco. If they knew, they would say, "Naht, dass not you. I heard Coco stay one big guy. You too runt fo be Coco." Funny yeah, but dass me. Ass me, Coco. One time I going paint one big mural and everybody going know ass me. Would be good if you no need paint fast and hide when somebody come. Could make um nice and people would even buy da paint fo me. I would make da whole wall wit spray. I would paint faces, my face ovah and ovah and I would make um look mean and tough. And I would look *bad* and I would be feeling good. I would make sparkles and you could see dem shining in my eyes. I would use silvah and some black paint. People would tink, "Who did dat nice one?" Dey wouldn't paint um ovah. Dey would buy me paint. Dey would gimme money fo paint da walls all ovah da place. Wouldn't need to do work in school. Da teacha would gimme one spray can, not brush and pay pah, la dat. Junk, when you paint in school. Gotta do certain tings, certain way. No can be big. No mo feeling. Ass why spray paint mo bettah. Make you feel mean. And bad. And good.

One time had one lady came by da wall. She wasn't one teacha or nutting cause she had long hair and had jeans and tee-shirt la dat. I had to hide my spray can when I seen her coming. I nevah like her bust me. But you know what, she had her own spray can and went look right at me den she went spray on my wall:

REVOLUTION FOR THE 80'S
MAY DAY.

Den she went little mo down and went spray out my "Coco '84," and went put "WORLD WITHOUT IMPERIALISM, NO IMPERIALIST WARS" right ovah my surf pickcha.

When she was pau she went look at me and say, "You know what dat means?"

"No," I told her.

"Dat means we gotta tell people to fight da government. Gotta get da people together and tell da governments not to have wars. Gotta give da poor people money and food and power la dat."

"Oh," I said. "But lady, why you went spray um ovah da wall? You nevah have to spray um ovah Coco's stuff. You could've put um on da top or on da side or write smaller. Look how you went jam up my pickcha, I mean Coco's pickcha."

"Sorry," she went tell kinda sassy.

"Why you gotta paint da kine stuff?"

"Cause I like. So what, kid." She was coming little bit piss off. So aftah she went go away, I went try fix my wall up. But she went use red. Hard fo cover, red. She nevah have to put um right ovah my writing. I wanted dem fo come paint da whole wall awready, erase um so dat could start ovah. I jes went get my can spray and I went stand in front da lady's words. I was feeling mean. Not good kine, jes mean. I went write "LADY—HATE YOU" not nice wit fat lettahs or sparkles but jes anykine way. I nevah care. Was ugly, jes like her's one.

When my mahdah came pick me up, I seen her reading da wall. "Who went do dat?" she went ask me. I told her one lady wit long hair and tee-shirt. I went ask her who dat kine lady was and she went say, "Dat Communists dat. Not Americans. Hippies." She told me, "Dey good fo nuttings." I was looking out da window when we went drive away. Couldn't even see "Coco" anymore.

I couldn't tink about any ting except what I was going paint ovah da hippie lady's words. First I thought I could paint somemore surf pictures but I went check my colors and I figgahed would be too hard fo cover da words. Da lady, she went write big. I thought I could do "Coco '84" mo big but still couldn't cover da lady's words. Would use up all my paint.

Aftah school da next day, I went to my wall. Could see da lady's words from far away. I jes went look at her spray paint words. Ass all was, jes words. Ugly words dat nobody like read. Not like mines, not nice wit sparkles la dat or curlicues or one pickcha of one surf ah in da tube. Jes words . . . any kine words. Everybody going say, "Hoo da ugly. Who did dat?" What if dey tink was me? Betchu da painter guys going come paint da wall fast. J'like the time somebody else went write "Sakai Sucks" and everybody knew dey was talking about Mr. Sakai, da principal. Dey came right away fo paint da wall dat time.

Nevah feel good anymore fo look at my wall. Wasn't mine anymore. Wasn't Coco's. Wasn't even da hippie lady's cause she no care. Was nobody's.

And den da next day had posters pasted up on da wall. Was somemore stuff about May Day and had one pickcha of one guy holding up his fist. Dey nevah only put one, but dey went line um up. Had maybe six or seven or eight all line up. Cover every ting: my surf pickcha, my name, even my "hate you" words. And dey went paste um on good. Dey went use someting dat stick real good to da cement and den dey even put da paste on da top so dat da ting was stuck extra good. No can peel um off. Hardly can scrape um even. Only little bit. I seen da hippie lady aftah school looking at da posters.

"You went do dat?"

"What you tink?" she went tell me.

"I donno. You went do um, eh?"

"So."

"You shouldn't have done dat. Coco going come piss off, you know. Dis his wall. Maybe he might even call da cops or someting."

"Who's dat, Coco? Dat you? Betchu da guy no stay. If he so big, how come he no come talk to me himself? From now on dis is everybody's wall. Not only Coco can paint on dis wall. Anybody can paint. Me. You. Anybody."

She jes went keep on talking, "Eh, you no need be scared of Coco. He ain't so tough. What he going do to you?"

"Yeah but, not supposed to be writing on da walls. . . ."

"Who said? Da government? Coco? Coco went paint first. He went liberate dis wall first time. But now he no can hog um. Dis wall is fo everybody I tell you. Uddahwise he stay making up anykine rules. J'like one nudda government."

"Hah?"

"How come you gotta watch dis wall fo Coco? You jes being Coco's stooge, you know. You shouldn't have to be scared of Coco. Dat's jes like da people who scared of the government. I mean you no need be oppressed by somebody else. . . ."

Couldn't tell what she was saying cause one truck was going on da freeway and from far could hear one police siren. Da lady went stop talking and we went look up at da freeway listen to da siren coming closer. Went pass.

I jes told her, "No paint on top Coco's wall, eh. Or else you going be in trouble. Coco, he big, you know. He *somebody*, you know." She nevah say nutting. She jes went walk away but I was still yet telling her anykine stuff, "You no can jes cover up my wall la dat. Was *my* surfah. Was *my* wave. Was *my* name! I hate you hippie lady!"

I went get my can spray and I jes started fo paint one face right ovah her words. I donno whose face. Jes one face. Was black and red. Had plenny lines in da face. Was one mean and sad face. I jes went keep on adding lines to da face and came mo black and mo black until was almost like one popolo but wasn't. Jes was one face wit plenny lines on um. Da paint went run out when I was fixing up da cheek. Went drip. I couldn't finish um. I went cross da street and watch my face.

Had some guys in one truck, regular fix-da-road guys, went come and look at da posters. Dey took out anykine scrapers and some real strong kine paint thinner fo take da posters off.

"Awright," I went tell dem.

"Damn kids do anykine yeah," one guy went tell me.

"Naht, wasn't kids. Was da hippie lady," I went tell um.

"You know who was?"

"Yeah, da hippie lady who come around here sometimes."

"You not da one, eh?" da man went ask me.

"Nan, but da guy Coco spray."

"Coco spray dis kine words?" Da man was pointing to da word "hate" between da posters. Could only see "lady" and "hate" left.

"Nah, he make nice kine stuff. He no paint ugly stuff."

Dey went clean off all da posters and started to paint da wall.

"What fo you paint da wall awready? Da hippie lady only going paint um again. What fo?"

"At least going look nice fo little while," da boss guy told me.

"Eh, try look dis face," one of da guys went point to my pickcha wit his roller. "Not bad yeah? Look almost like somebody crying wit dis red drip ovah here. You know who went do dis one? Pretty good artist. Too bad gotta cover um up."

I jes went turn around. I started fo cry. I donno how come.

Frank Marshall Davis
"HORIZONTAL CAMEO: LANI"

1. Lani

Lani is at her best
Horizontal
No ponderous perpendicular prelude
Is essential
Unless one insists
Upon romance with love
But that is added expense
For as the slogan speaks
From the desk of the insurance executive
Time Is Money.
Lani, age 25,
Had distributed a fortune
Before she realized
There was gold in descent from the vertical
Lani, age 30,
Has 50 grand salted away
With no change in habits
And has had many husbands
Including two of her own;

But with success has come prejudice
Which never before existed—
Today she will not tolerate
Any man with less than $20
She is that rarity
Psychologists seldom find—
A woman working
At her best occupation
Without benefit of aptitude test.

Hunter S. Thompson

from THE CURSE OF LONO

October 25, 1980
Owl Farm

D*ear Ralph,*
I think we have a live one this time, old sport. Some dingbat named Perry up in Oregon wants to give us a month in Hawaii for Christmas and all we have to do is cover the Honolulu Marathon for his magazine, a thing called Running. . . .

Yeah, I know what you're thinking, Ralph. You're pacing around over there in the war room at the Old Loose Court and thinking, "Why me*? And why* now*? Just when I'm getting respectable?"*

Well . . . let's face it, Ralph; anybody can be respectable, especially in England. But not everybody can get paid to run like a bastard for 26 miles in some maniac hype race called the Honolulu Marathon.

We are both entered in this event, Ralph, and I feel pretty confident about winning. We will need a bit of training, but not much.

The main thing will be to run as an entry and set a killer pace for the first three miles. These body-nazis have been training all year for the supreme effort in this Super Bowl of marathons. The promoters expect 10,000 entrants, and the course is 26 miles; which means they will all start slow . . . because 26 miles is a hell of a long way to run, for any reason at all, and all the pros in this field will start slow and pace themselves very carefully for the first 20 miles.

But not us, Ralph. We will come out of the blocks like human torpedoes and alter the whole nature of the race by sprinting the first three miles shoulder-to-shoulder in under 10 minutes.

A pace like that will crack their nuts, Ralph. These people are into running, not racing—*so our strategy will be to race like whorehounds* for the first three miles. *I figure we can crank ourselves up to a level of frenzy that will clock about 9:55 at the three-mile checkpoint . . . which will put us so far ahead of the field that they won't even be able to see us. We will be over the hill and all alone when we hit the stretch along Ala Moana Boulevard still running shoulder-to-shoulder at a pace so fast and crazy that not even the judges will feel sane about it . . . and the rest of the field will be left so far behind that many will be overcome with blind rage and confusion.*

I've also entered you in the Pipeline Masters, a world class surfing contest on the north shore of Oahu on Dec. 26.

You will need some work on your high-speed balance for this one, Ralph. You'll be shot through the curl at speeds up to 50 or even 75 miles an hour, and you won't want to fall.

I won't be with you in the Pipeline gig, due to serious objections raised by my attorney with regard to the urine test and other legal ramifications.

But I will enter the infamous Liston Memorial Rooster Fight, at $1,000 per unit on the universal scale—e.g., one minute in the cage with one rooster wins $1,000 . . . or five minutes with one rooster is worth $5,000 . . . and two minutes with five roosters is $10,000 . . . etc.

This is serious business, Ralph. These Hawaiian slashing roosters can tear a man to shreds in a matter of seconds. I am training here at home with the peacocks—six 40-pound birds in a 6' x 6' cage, and I think I'm getting the hang of it.

The time has come to kick ass, Ralph, even if it means coming briefly out of retirement and dealing, once again, with the public. I am also in need of a rest—for legal reasons—so I want this gig to be easy, and I know in my heart that it will be.

Don't worry, Ralph. We will bend a few brains with this one. I have already secured the Compound: two homes with a 50-meter pool on the edge of the sea on Alii Drive in Kona, where the sun always shines.

OK
HST

HUNTER S. THOMPSON (1937-2005), *author of* Hell's Angels; Fear and Loathing in Las Vegas; Fear and Loathing on the Campaign Trail, 1972; *and* The Curse of Lono, *was one of the most distinctive American prose stylists of the second half of the twentieth century. Writing for* Rolling Stone, *he pioneered gonzo journalism (collected in* The Gonzo Papers). *In 1970, he shaved his head to run for sheriff of Pitkin County, Colorado, on a Freak Power platform that included tearing up the streets of Aspen, renaming the town "Fat City," and publicly punishing dishonest drug dealers with the stocks and the bastinado. He was a firearms fanatic who committed suicide with a .45 and had his ashes fired from a cannon into the sky above his home at Owl Farm outside Aspen.*

Chris McKinney

from HAWAIIAMERICA

I t begins in silence, about six AM, darkness giving way to coral-shadowed clouds that shock the sky. The engine starts up, shakes with a choking hacking early morning diesel cough, steadies itself, and a black shape rumbles off the trailer, out from under the blue tarp. Onto Laupele St., past new houses that do not look exactly alike but were built with the same parts. Left on Pahoehoe, two-story houses here, one skewered with a flagpole, Old Glory hanging limp. A woman out walking her dogs stands and stares; her three sand-colored Pom-Chis, mutt-mixture Pomeranian-Chihuahua, yap and skitter and tangle their leashes and show their little teeth. Right onto Meheula. Two joggers stop short at the curb, a man and woman in matching spandex shorts and green University of Hawaii plastic visors. The thing blows exhaust in their faces and rolls on, going the wrong way, into the early bird traffic heading for Honolulu. Cars brake and honk; a few flash high beams. The thing jumps the gutter and guns into pine trees on the nature strip. Three blocks down, at the Mililani Mauka Fire Station, a man coming out for his first smoke of the day hears the splintering whumps and an engine growling. He turns to look, his jaw drops, he loses his cigarette and runs back inside.

The thing slows, pauses, rotates. The driver looks through his periscope at the Castle & Cooke Real Estate Center. It has white flags all around it, saying START LIVING. He sights on the main office, built out of the same parts as the houses. He smiles and puts his foot down. The flagpoles snap like matchsticks. He has spent four months of nights and weekends welding sheets of half-inch steel over his Komatsu D375 bulldozer, two layers, sandwiched with concrete. He aims at the front wall with the big corporate logo, punches a hole in it, hardly trying. He reverses, comes on again, doubles the size of the hole, and rolls over the rubble into the sales area, treads crunching desks, computers, scale models of subdivisions. He punches an exit hole in the back wall, one-two, and swings onto XXXXAvenue, along the medial strip, taking out the Mililani, All-American Town, est. 1986 lava-rock plaque.

He hears sirens, checks his periscope, sees a blockade coming up—sawhorse barricades, cops in flak vests, straddle-legged, handguns gripped doublehanded. He puts his foot down. They scatter. A bullhorn yells at him, sounding strangled. He flips a police car, another, and flattens them both. Bullets ping off the steel plates, nothing to him, just fingernails tapping on an empty glass. A cop runs around behind, manages to scramble up and drop a dufflebag over the periscope. The dozer jerks and flails, like a bullride at quarter speed. The cop scrabbles and drops off, the duffle shakes loose.

The driver sights Mililani Town Center–Kentucky Fried Chicken, Star Market, McDonalds Express. The police cars are trailing him, but hanging back. He sees people lining the street, families, mommies holding babies, daddies hoisting kids on their shoulders. He thinks of his wife and his son, all the times he dragged them to Walmart, the Halloween candy and costumes, the Christmas decorations, the wire snowman wrapped in a string of red and green light bulbs, his boy's first bicycle, the chopper look, mock gas tank with flames and all. He can see the Komatsu reflected in the Walmart window, the steel plates, the periscope looking back at him. He is crying now. He cuts the engine, listens to the silence, reaches down to his boot top, and takes out a .22 caliber pistol. He puts it to his head and pulls the trigger.

CHRIS MCKINNEY *is the author of* The Tattoo; The Queen of Tears; *and* Bolohead Row. *Winner of the Ka Palapala Poʻokela Award for Excellence in Literature and the Elliot Cades Award for Literature, he grew up in Kahaluʻu and currently lives in Mililani, on Oʻahu, with his wife and three-year-old daughter. McKinney received his BA and MA in English at the University of Hawaiʻi at Mānoa, and is currently teaching at Honolulu Community College. This selection in from his novel-in-progress,* Hawaiiamerica.

The Streets of the City

He sits on a cold stone bench ... He squinted at the sky ... Old men convulsive ... She thinks she can fly ... His flute case hungrily opened ... If he only had ten cents more ... Don't cross me ... Put down the knives ... The silence of emptied guns ... The crimes of her man ... The cracks of sidewalks ... Bulldozers came and crushed metal and wood and us ... We passed two transvestite hookers standing by a traffic light ... The lady cackled and danced ... Yestaday we was shmoking one fat blunt ... The cops are patrolling the projects ... This place is worse than home, he says ... I stay in Halawa Valley maximum security ... My heart hurts so bad ... My mother lives in Las Vegas ...

Mahealani Perez-Wendt

"MY BUS IS TWO HOURS LATE"

Jack-in-the-Box smiles lurid
Through smoke-colored glass;
A midnight apparition in neon,
Formless and vaporized
At the Union Mall bus stop.
I'm a 99-Cent Special
Hanging with Jack,
A penitent for life
Consigned to steetcorner 'ukulele
And preacher's admonitions
Against Satan and his angels.
I'm a matron once a maid,
Lights gone out
With the one zillionth
Dream vacationer who,
Having luxuriated between
Hotel sheets
And a full measure
Of room service
Has gone,
Leaving me vacant,
Rank and unmade.
I sink quietly to knees
In the place prepared
By Jack's Faithful.
I kneel among their rancid offerings:
Paper cups, cigarettes,
Garbage strewn about
The silent streets.
I pray for lost sons
Struck senseless and star-crossed
By spirits;
For old men convulsive
In dirty felt hats;
For the hospital freed
Doing the thorazine shuffle;
I pray for preachers
Whose 'ukulele scriptures

Are Satan's bus stop nemesis;
For old ladies
Worrying behind
Grey spectacles
Fumbling at the pay phone
And giving up.
I pray for all
Seeking light
Missing important signposts
And going up in smoke.
Theirs are the voices
Of soft restraint
Whispering to the driver
Their wait has been long.
Jack-in-the-Box smiles lurid
Through smoke-colored glass;
A midnight apparition in neon,
Formless and vaporized
At the Union Mall bus stop.
I'm a graveyard shift conscript
Hanging with Jack,
Going with his angels
For one last ride.

Kate Ikehara

"THE IGNORED STORYTELLER"

Bypassed by marketers,
He sits on a cold stone bench,
Eyes shut with hair dreadlocked,
His flute case hungrily opened.
He willingly shares his life with
Strangers who may be deaf to the music.
A flute is his voice,
Polished and fluent, a contrast
To his tattered appearance.
A light dance tells of his childhood.

A final argument with his wife long ago
Expressed with high energy bursts.

He plays the solitary street life he lives now
As a sorrowful, slow funeral march.
He exposes his life, vulnerable to opinions.
But no one stops to hear the music.
Only a few stop and feed the flute case.

KATE IKEHARA *was born in 1990. She is currently a senior at 'Iolani School in Honolulu. During her free time, she loves to go to the beach, spend time with her family, and laugh with her friends. She plays the piano and is also a violinist in the school orchestra. The musical basis of her poem was inspired by a street musician in Hawai'i.*

Juliet S. Kono
"MISSING PERSON ALL POINTS BULLETIN"

C entral to all units: be on the lookout for an elderly Caucasian woman last seen in the area of Prospect and Magazine Streets. She was wearing a red, white and blue blouse, red pants, white walking shoes and a multicolored jacket. She is 85 years old. She wears glasses. She walks with a slight stoop. She thinks she can fly. About 5' tall, she has gray hair and answers to the name of Elizabeth, or Betts, or Mama. Shout "Hey!" or "Yo!" and she'll turn around. Party may be walking in circles. Party may be walking, looking at the sky. She may be talking to a leaf or tree, a bird or dog. Approach with kindness. Otherwise, she may scream and shatter; otherwise, she may think she's died and gone to heaven; otherwise, she may call you "Papa," take your face in her hands and kiss you. If seen, detain and notify her son, or Central, or God. KRO two four three, Missing Person APB, 2:45.

JULIET S. KONO, *born in 1943, has written two books of poetry,* Hilo Rains *and* Tsunami Years, *and a short story collection,* Ho'olulu Park and the Pepsodent Smile. *She also has a children's story,* The Bravest Opihi. *She received the Hawai'i Award for Literature in 2005.*

Kathlyn "Kiki" Furuya
"WHITE COTTON SOCKS"

High above the backed up traffic on Beretania
a kimono kit, just a grayish-blue stain
almost invisible against the naked January sky,
skirt open wide, suspended for a moment,
descending like an upside-down umbrella
with spokes bent at an obtuse angle,
and disappearing in an eye blink,
a mirage caught in the high-rise windows
becomes a discarded mannequin trapped
in the stiff green awning over a golf store,
exposing a pair of white cotton socks,
tiny feet stuck in mid-air punctuating the end
of a once vibrant life with two exclamation points.

KATHLYN "KIKI" FURUYA *was born and raised on the island of Hawai'i. After earning her bachelor's and master's degrees from the University of Hawaii, she went on to teach at numerous schools on O'ahu and the island of Hawai'i. She was diagnosed with ovarian cancer in May of 2006 and passed away July 29th, 2006. She was a mother to three and a proud grandmother.*

Christy Anne Passion
"SAND ISLAND"

I remember the totung roof and big blue fishing ball
hanging by the macrame net
open electrical wires, hibachi and ocean smell.
Try catch black a'ama crab
scream and drop them when we do.
Race to uncle's door when papio is running
I want to tie on the bait.
Everybody is auntie, so no need be hungry—
auntie always has food.
Mind your family, listen, and say grace before dinner

We got there too late that day, amazed
how quickly everything came down. Sand Island
after bulldozers came and crushed
metal and wood and us   scattered.
Say something to auntie and uncle
LOOK at their faces but
I can not.
I can only see the bags at their feet
and my cousins crying. Every auntie and uncle
with bags at their feet. Most cry
some scream, some quiet.
Dust and noise combined with HPD push   us   back
and I don't believe Papa anymore when he says it will be ok.

"SAND ISLAND REVISITED"

I drive past the rusted tower—
sewage salt water taints the air
rubbish weeds litter the view
was it here?
My uncle's fishing village, my weekend home? No
not here. Not this tent city this drug haven this
attemptable   manicured   park. I drive past

to where parking lot meets grassy field
bowed, I step here for the first time in twenty five years
Sand Island. I am not here
to fish or pick limu
those days are gone. I come
to make ipuheke with my brothers and sisters together
we go over the grassy slope to the sand divide, I see

waves still curl diamonds and sun still burns
my hapahaole skin. Sand still is large and coarse
not fine like imports at Waikiki
we need rough to smooth our ipu
we need rough to shape our way.

Our laughter carries over to Mokauea, resurrected
the shore break chants—*we remain we remain we remain*

Imaikalani Kalahele

"A POEM FOR CHINATOWN"

At the turn of the century
the plantation when buy the land.
So, Papa them when come Honolulu.
No more job. No more land.
Three generations no more place to go.
Ah, guess we going stay beach,
    That was then.
Guess again, Papa.
Now . . .
    you go jail!

Richard Hamasaki

"DA MENTO HOSPITO"

Eh, somebudi lik make one
big freeway tru my vallee
dey lik bill e'm reel beeg
and strong man
like one battl ship
so dey can send all dem kars
an trucs an busses
t'rew da mowntans
an make moa
condos an macdonals and purlridges
so da turists, an da grunts, an da locos
can bang each a'da moa

not only dat, but da air fors guys
like hāpai dere missos
tru da mowntans from heekem to mōkapu
an bak

one na'da hi'way aint gonna
keel dis iland brah

dis iland alredi dyin—
da hungry politishans
da govament
an da beesness mens
tink dey can ku'aku'ai da 'āina
lik one prostitoot

eh, so wat if get one moa hi'way
tru da mowntans
who gives a fricken "A"
about da farmas
da fishamen
da fresh wata
da wind
da rain
an da makas
ye, da eyes,
da makas dat luk da mowntans
an spak da new hi'way runnin
tru da vallee
da eyes dat see nottin'
but one beeg town

an pretty soon
we can drive dawreck—
from hālawa prison oneway
to da hawa'i state mento hospito
in kāne'ohe

Tracee Lee
"ROCKS"

Wednesdays I go
To Kane'ohe Boys Home
To see my brother
He got caught with his friends
for stealing a car
and beating up a retarded boy

in a chicken suit
in front of KFC.

This place is worse than home
he says,
and tells me about the ones
who cry at night
in their sleep.
He says the food's bad,
and that's when I give him
the *poke* and Twinkies I've brought.
They let him out for 30 minutes
and we go to the side of the mountain
and sit savoring
the fresh fish and seaweed.
He eats one Twinkie
and trades the other one
for a cigarette. I know it.

We just sit
and look up
at brilliant grey clouds.
He throws pebbles over the edge
and says he doesn't know
when he'll be out.

His time is up,
and he starts to head back.
But I do not move.
My life is here
throwing rocks off this cliff
With you.

TRACEE LEE *was born in 1973. She grew up in Kaimukī, in Honolulu, and now lives in Honoka'a on the island of Hawai'i. She received the Best Poetry Award in the* Bamboo Ridge *25th Anniversary Issue, and also received the Newman University Milton Center Award for Poetry in 2003.*

Lisa Linn Kanae
"OLA'S SON"

I told your receptionist
I did not want to talk to a haole.
I hope you understand.
I'm having a hard time trusting people.
It's my eldest son. He needs help.

> Palolo Valley Homes is a post-World War II
> "housing" project of 424 units and 1,500
> residents. Forty-eight percent are Laotian
> and Vietnamese immigrants; the rest
> Hawaiians, Samoans, some Tongans and
> Micronesians, and a few Filipinos.

He won't talk to me.
He is growing more withdrawn and depressed,
hardly comes home, hangs around
that basketball court.
He won't listen to me.
He'd rather throw metal folding chairs.
Last night at the dinner table,
he picked up his fork and threatened to stab me.

> *He started getting agitated when*
> *the guns were drawn,*
> *maybe because he was frightened.*

His brothers and sisters,
they mimic everything he does.
They slam doors. Punch walls.
My ten year old shoves his sister around
for the hell of it.
My three year old girl,
    Jesus, I'm afraid for her.
She won't talk at all anymore, period.

The Internal Affairs Lt. declined comment on the number of casings recovered at the scene except to say that "more than five shots were fired."

I want counseling for my kids,
but all the therapists are haole.
How are they suppose to instill
Samoan pride in my children?
These problems in my house
are about being Samoan.
These problems in my house
are about what happened to Uncle.

POLICE BARRAGE KILLS KNIFE-WIELDER

Today's UV index: 9: high
Use a sunscreen of at least SPF 15
when risk is moderate or above.
Trade winds are expected to
decrease throughout the weekend.
Skies will be partly to mostly
sunny today with a few brief
mauka and windward showers.

It was in all the papers.
Me and Uncle, we were cousins.
He used to watch my kids when
they were in diapers. My babies.
They can't understand why Uncle had to die.
When we heard our name on the six o'clock news,
we wept.

I know I could have gotten him to put down the knives, and others there could have, too, if they gave us a chance.

My son, he is big for a fourteen-year-old.
I mean physically large:
Five feet, ten inches tall, at least 175 lbs.
He took it the hardest.
You see, I'm a single parent.
My son really took to his Uncle.
No. My children's father is no longer in the picture.

PHOTO #1: the sky a receding gradient
two adult males with POLICE printed in
yellow across the backs of their dark
uniforms behind the officers five squad car
lights pop white to the right of the officers
is the front of an ambulance firecracker
paper litters the street screens peel from
windows and doors two civilians one adult
male and one adolescent male stare at the
ambulance one horizontal line police tape
curling divides the photo in two

Me? College grad. Just completed
my undergrad degree: Ethnic Studies.
I tell you, this whole thing is the result of
hegemony. colonization. misrepresentation.
If you're big and brown in this State, you're condemned.
If Uncle were an Asian man
the cops wouldn't have shot twenty rounds.

They just left him there, face down
on the road in the rain.
We had to go get a blanket to cover him.

My son looks half white. Hapa.
I hate to admit it but maybe that's a blessing.
He could pass for white if he needed to.

Have you heard the one about the
Ambulance and the Samoan? There was
an ambulance with its siren on rushing to
the hospital that passed by a tenement.
After they passed the tenement, they saw
a Samoan man running quickly to the
ambulance. The drivers were questioned
by his presence behind them so they
stopped the ambulance and asked the
Samoan what was his problem. The Sole
ran up to the ambulance and asked, "Eh,
U still get ice cream?"
http://www.e-hawaii.com

The cops are patrolling the projects,
I tell my son, if the cops stop you,
tell them you can't talk and run.
Trouble is he can't run away from his last name.
We can't hide from what everyone has
seen on television,
from what everyone has
read on the front page of the paper.
He is ashamed of being Samoan;
everything Fa'a Samoa.
He is already ashamed of the man
he has yet to become.

**POLICE: Catch flak for shooting man to
death in Palolo**
Police are trained that anyone armed with
a sharp-edged object within 21 feet of an
officer is in the "kill zone."

New Year's Eve night.
The cops get a call from the housing projects.
They had to have been wired on the way over here.
I know Uncle was drinking that night.

Might as well. I mean, another year goes by,
Same ole story.
So we party, pop firecrackers, eat, drink some more.
Somebody started an argument.
Things got out of hand.
My Auntie Ma'a yelled for the Matai,
but the cops showed up instead.
Next thing you know, squad cars
pull up to the center courtyard
in front of my screen door.
I run outside.
Yell for my boy to come home.

> . . . it is probably true that officers
> might be more likely to draw their
> weapons in a housing area instead of
> other areas . . . Officers have more
> of a chance of getting hurt here.
> It can be intimidating.

The police started to corral the men.
Arms up, faces and palms pressed against the wall.
The cops told Uncle to drop
his weapons—two fishing knives,
Uncle didn't respond. Fuck, he was drunk.
Next thing I know I hear,
"Don't shoot! Don't shoot!"

> PHOTO #2: adult Polynesian male six
> foot five almost three hundred pounds
> wide-set sleepy eyes rests his chin in
> the space between his left thumb and
> forefinger as if posing for an electric
> shaver commercial well-groomed
> goatee frames his smile big smile lots
> of teeth

Then there were gunshots.
White blue lights
punched through all the smoke.
My son saw everything.
Sometimes I think I see
the smoke in my son's eyes

> *He was already shot, face down in the*
> *pavement gasping for air,*
> *and the cops were just standing around*
> *not doing anything for him. The Fire*
> *Department, which responds fast to*
> *dumpster fires here, never came.*

I don't want just anybody to help my boy,
treat him like he is some stupid moke.
Did you know that they left Uncle in a
stretcher for two hours at Queens ER?
I don't care if I sound racist.

PHOTO #3: a hazy courtyard eyes look
out of the surrounding screen doors and
windows four boys eight to ten years old
walk alongside five police officers one boy
smiles and waves directly into the
photographer's lens second boy looks up
at the officers' faces third boy stares at
their holsters and guns last boy's head is
thrown back in laughter he aims his finger
and thumb like a gun directly at the
photographer

My son wet his bed last night.
Fourteen years old and he is pissing in his bed.
Can you imagine what it's like
to see

{
They shot twice, and he went down on his knees and dropped the knives. While he was on his knees, they shot three more times.

a fourteen-year-old boy weep
because he's ashamed that he wet his bed?

(Italicized text taken from Honolulu Star Bulletin, January 23, 1998.)

———————————•◦•———————————

Ryan Shinichi Saito

"THE MAN ON THE CORNER"

I see a homeless man and I wonder
What happened to him?
How did he get this way?
Does he have any family?
What is he feeling as he stares
straight ahead?

I think about talking to him.
But my mom says, "Ryan, don't stare."
When she turns away, I look again.
I feel so bad for him.

I can't just ignore him.
No shelter, no money, old clothes,
No food, no water.

I feel like I'm the only person
who notices,
Everyone else walks by, ignoring him.
I feel like I should welcome him
into my home

But my mom won't let me.

My heart hurts so bad.

RYAN SHINICHI SAITO *was born in 1995 on Oʻahu. A student at ʻIolani School in Honolulu, he resides with his parents and younger brother, Jordan. On his way to school one morning, Ryan was impacted by the sight of a homeless man sitting near the street corner. Bothered by the image, he was encouraged to express his feelings in a fourth grade homework assignment. The result was "The Man on the Corner."*

Darrell Lum
"THE MOILIILI BAG MAN"

O ne time by da Humane Society had one bummy guy at da drive in. He was eating from da rubbish can. Yeah. My fren tell, "Ass da Moiliili Bag Man dat. Try look, get anykine plastic bag hanging from his belt. I tink he got um from Star Market."

Da Bag Man was looking through da rubbish can, eating da leftovers. Yeah, da throw way awready kind. Mostly he was looking fo da plate lunches, fo da extra rice. He no care, da guy. We was looking at him from our table and da girl behind da counter stay shaking her head watching da Bag Man. Little while more, da cook guy wit one dirty apron and one broom and dustpan came outside from da kitchen part fo sweep rubbish. Da cook guy was so stink, man, cause he jes go empty da dustpan, all dirt and rubbish la dat, right in da can dat da Bag Man was looking. Da Bag Man no say nutting. . . but da cook guy was stink, yeah? He could tell da Bag Man was still yet using da can.

Da Bag Man nevah know what fo do. He jes went stand dere by da can. Den he went check his bags: cigarette bag wit plenny butts and bus up kine cigarettes, someting else in one nudda one, and look like one half orange, peeled awready in one nudda one.

Russo, das my fren, told me dat people sometimes go give da Bag Man money jes so dat he go away from dem. Even if he not boddering dem, dey give um money. I guess dey no like look at him or someting. Funny yeah?

Anyway, I no can tell if da Bag Man is happy or sad or piss off or anyting l'dat cause he get one moosetash and skinny kine beard wit only little bit strands, stay hide his mout. But his eyes, da Bag Man's eyes, stay always busy . . . looking, looking, looking.

I look back at him, and to me, he ack like he little bit shame. We stay da only small kids sitting down at da tables, me and Russo, but da Bag Man ack like he no like know us.

Had one nudda guy in one tee shirt was sitting at da table next to us was watching da Bag Man too. He was eating one plate lunch and afterwards, he went take his plate ovah to da Bag Man. Still had little bit everyting one top, even had bar-ba-que meat left.

"Brah," da guy tell, "you like help me finish? I stay full awready."

Da Bag Man no tell nutting, only nod his head and take da plate. I thought he would eat um real fast . . . gobble um up, you know. But was funny, he went put um down and go to da counter fo get one napkin and make um nice by his place da fork on top da napkin. Even he took da plate out of da box, made um j'like one real restaurant. I wanted fo give him someting too, but I only had my cup wit little bit ice left. I awready went drink up all da Coke and was chewing da ice. Da Bag Man was looking at me now, not at me but at my cup. I nevah know what fo do cause j'like I selfish if I keep my cup but, nevah have nutting inside awready, so shame eh, if you give somebody someting but stay empty. But I nevah know what fo do cause I had to go awready. I thought I could jes leave da cup on da table or be like da tee shirt guy and tell, "Brah, hea."

So I went get up and walk halfway and den turn back like I went foget throw away my cup. I went look at da Bag Man and say, "You like um?"

Da Bag Man nevah say nutting still yet, but I knew he wanted um so I jes went leave um on his table. I was curious fo see what he was going do wit um so I went make like I was fussing around wit someting on my bike. He went get out his hankachief from his front pants pocket and unwrap um. Had all his coins inside um and he went take out fifteen cents. Den he went take da cup to da window and point to da sign dat went say "Refills—15¢."

"Coke," he told da girl. Sly da guy! When I went pass him on my bike, I thought I saw him make one "shaka" sign to me. Wasn't up in da air, was down by his leg, j'like he was saying, "Tanks eh," to me.

Da next time I went see da Bag Man was by da shave ice place, Goodie Goodie Drive In. He was jes grinding one plate lunch, man. I donno if he went buy um. I doubt it, though. I thought I saw his busy eyes recanize me, but I donno. I jes went nod my head, jes in case he was telling "hi."

Aftah dat, j'like everyplace I go, he stay. Da Bag Man stay. One time me and my bruddah went Bellows Beach fo bodysurf and da Bag Man was dere. I heard my bruddah folks calling him Waimanalo Eddie but was him, da Moiliili Bag Man.

Was jes like I knew him by heart awready. I mean, j'like we was frens. I seen him by da Boy Scout camp checking tings out. One ting about Boy

Scouts, dey get plenny food, dey no run out, dem. But you know what, dey nevah know how fo cook rice. Dey went jam um up and had to dump um cause was too mooshy and wasn't right. Da Bag Man was right dere even befoa one scoop rice went inside da rubbish can. Could tell he was happy, boy. J'like he was dancing. His okole was wiggling and he was holding out his plastic bag for da throw way rice.

All da small kids, da Cub Scouts, started fo come around da Bag Man and ask him questions: "What you going do wit dat? How come you get so much tings in da bags?" One real small kid, wasn't even one Cub Scout went tell, "You one bum?"

Da Bag Man jes went smile and tell, "Dis fo my cat. He like dis kine rice." Den da Scout Mastah went try fo get all da kids fo go back by him. He went tell dem, "Come ovah hea. Da man jes going take da food fo his pigs or someting, *buta kaukau*. Come. I show you guys how fo make da fire so da ting no *pio*." But of course nobody was listening, dey still like hang around da Bag Man. Finally da Bag Man had to tell, "Eh, you fahdah stay calling you guys. Tanks, eh."

Aftah dat, I nevah see da Bag Man fo long time. I nevah see him, so I nevah even tink about him until one day, me and Russo went go Ala Moana beach and we went go fuss around by da end of da canal, by da pond part where sometimes get da guys wit da radio dat control da boats. Dose guys get piss off man, if you blast their boats wit rocks. Heh, heh, good fun though, sometimes.

But nevah have boats dis time so me and Russo was playing try come, try come. Ass when you try fo get da uddah guy come by you fo look at someting, but only stay bullshet like, "Try come, try come look dis doo doo stay look like one hairy hot dog." And you try jazz um up so dat da uddah guy like come by you instead of him trying fo make you go by him.

So Russo went tell, "Try come, try come. Get one *ma-ke* man stay in da bushes. He stay *ma-ke* on anykine *food*, la dat!"

Shet. I knew no can be. Dat Russo, he such a bull liar. So I was going tell him some interesting stuff about doo doo but Russo went tell real scared, "Da *ma-ke* man leg went move!" So I went by him.

"He only sleeping, stupit," I went tell Russo real soft, jes in case da guy was really sleeping.

"No, he *ma-ke* die dead," Russo went say.

"How you know?"

"I know. Maybe somebody went murder him!"

By now Russo was making up anykine stories and talking mo loud and I knew wasn't *ma-ke* man cause da legs was moving somemore and could hear somebody talking from inside da bushes.

"Sucka. Sucking kids, beat it befoa I smash your face."

Was da Bag Man. He was blinking his eyes real plenny and den he went look at us, stink eye. Russo was getting chicken and was backing up little by little, but I jes went stay.

We jes went look at each uddah, but dis time da Bag Man's eyes wasn't so busy. He jes started fo rip up one coconut leaf. Was sharp, man. He had one supah long fingernail on his thumb dat was jes right fo rip da coconut leaf into skinny strips yeah, and little while mo he went make one bird out of da coconut leaf. He nevah say nutting. He jes went stick um behind his ear. He went look at me, den at Russo, den at me again. I thought he was going scold us or someting, but he jes went start making one nudda bird. Only dis time he nevah go so fast. In fack, he went real slow, j'like he was teaching me how. When he was pau, he went give um to me and den he jes went split, even befoa I went tell um tanks.

When I went home, I went put da Bag Man's bird on top my bureau and even if I nevah see him long time aftah dat Ala Moana park time, I went tink of him everytime I saw da bird dere on top da bureau. Sometimes I try practice make birds, but I couldn't do um like da Bag Man. I could almost do um, but mines came out funny kine. I used to wonder if da Bag Man was in Waimanalo or if he was grinding food at da drive in or if he was making birds too at Ala Moana.

And den one day I was fussing around wit his bird, was all brown and coming had it. Nevah have nutting fo do, so I went try make da bird again. I kept looking at da Bag Man's bird and den back at mines one. Back and fort. Back and fort. I had to laugh cause must've been funny. Must've looked like da Bag Man's busy eyes . . . looking, looking, looking.

Den shet, was so easy. I went make um! Came out perfeck! I went make my bird look exact like his one. I went get somemore coconut leaf and try one mo time cause even I nevah believe. Da stuff came out again!

I wanted fo go Waimanalo or Ala Moana or drive in right away . . . but I nevah see him aftah dat time at Ala Moana park. And everyplace I go, I stay looking, looking, looking. But if I was to see him, I would make one bird fo him and den hold my hand down wit da shaka sign and make, "Tanks, eh."

Matthew Kaopio

from WRITTEN IN THE SKY

I stand on a sandy hill, and the salty air smells of geraniums and eucalyptus. I'm back at Grandma's house. I hear her banging around the kitchen and singing along to 1420 on the AM radio. I always loved being at Grandma's; it gave me such a strong sense of security. Safe. Sound. She calls my name. It's been some time since I've heard it. "'Īkau! 'Īkauikalani! Come eat, the food is ready. Hele mai, pā'ina!" I walk into the kitchen, where she's wiping the dishes at the sink. She still has her legs. I run up to her to give her a hug. She kisses me on the cheek and whispers in my ear, "Mariah Wong. Look for her, and remember."

The boy was jolted awake by a burning, stinging sensation on his left knee. With his eyes shut tightly, his blind fingers ran across a rapidly swelling mound of flesh with two small holes where the centipede had bit him. He jumped up and wildly searched through his things to see where it had gone. But with no sign of it, he settled back down and tried to resume his dream.

It had been weeks since his grandmother died, but sometimes he felt as if he was once again living with her on the farm in Kahalu'u. Along with his name, which he was ashamed of and never used, that time was gone and existed only in his memories. He was fourteen and had nowhere to go. His mother had left when he was seven, and his grandmother was his only family. Bills for dialysis and cancer treatments had run so high that the bank had foreclosed on their homestead. Without any income, they couldn't afford the rent in Honolulu. When she was hospitalized, most of their things were taken to the dump by the angry landlord. All that the boy owned in the world were a few clothes, his grandmother's quilt, and a braided lock of hair she gave him the night she died, which he kept tucked away in a pink Almond Roca tin can.

Eventually, he'd found a place to sleep under a bridge near the fishpond at Ala Moana Beach Park. It was dry, secluded, and safe. Although he had a centipede for a roommate, the soft grass formed a nest that cradled him as he lay under his grandmother's handmade quilt, and nobody bothered him.

He squinted at the sky. God was painting again. The boy admired the way the foamy, fizzy grape-soda clouds became streaked with strawberry sherbet. Lavender plumes turned into coral-rose flames, then juicy tangerine, and finally sweet lemonade. Every day, the sunrise was different, and each had its own story to tell. This morning, an orange dolphin cloud swam blissfully in a burgundy sea. From nowhere, a tangerine shark cloud billowed and began to attack. Just as the shark's teeth sank in, the dolphin swung around and jabbed its nose into the shark's side, shattering it into millions of canaries.

The dolphin then devoured the tiny birds one by one, the clouds merging. The boy knew this was a true sign that it would be a good day.

He loved dawn and dusk because those were the times that the sun was closest to the earth and that God listened to prayers and often responded. With reverence, the boy flung open his arms and embraced the morning, kissing the cheek of God. Then he got up.

He started his daily routine. Over his black T-shirt, he put on his denim jacket. Covered with original Hawaiian tattoo designs drawn with a permanent marker, it was his greatest work of art. Next, he dusted off his quilt, folded it diagonally, and tied the opposite corners into a knot, converting it into a pouch for his few possessions. He combed his tangled hair with his fingers and plucked out the leaves. Then he walked across the grass, noting that the beach park was not yet crowded with visitors. He marveled at the vividness of his dream. It was as if his grandmother was still alive, talking with him face-to-face. But it had been years since she could walk. Those days had been filled with trips to the beach to catch crabs, pick ʻopihi, and harvest hāʻukeʻuke or to the mountains to catch prawns and gather Hawaiian herbs. When her diabetes worsened, she became confined to a wheelchair, and he became her legs. He had helped her the best he could. What puzzled him about the dream was the name she uttered: Mariah Wong. And her telling him to remember. Remember what? he wondered. He was sure he'd never heard the name before. Was Grandma sending him a message from the other side?

The early-morning air tasted delicious on his tongue, and he drank the sweet tonic without wasting one drop. He was so hungry he could have eaten a rubber slipper. He entered the restroom to get cleaned up and found it deserted. Keeping his torn surf shorts on, he stepped into the shower and shocked his nerves with a cold-water blast. Hiʻuwai, he remembered. That's what Grandma called the first morning cleansing. Normally done either in the ocean or in a mountain pond, it gave one the chance to spiritually, as well as physically, wash away the debris of the previous day to begin the new day fresh.

The boy loved being clean. Despite what others thought, so did most of the other beach people. Spying a small hotel shampoo bottle on the shower floor, he opened it and lathered his body with the pearly liquid. Soon he was covered from head to toe in rich, perfumed lather.

He closed his eyes and let the water pummel his face. He imagined he was again standing under the mountain waterfall where his grandmother took him to catch prawns. They'd gather pepeiao, bamboo shoots, fern shoots, green papayas, and wild sweet-potato leaves, and she would cook up her famous jungle stew.

Grandma often let him swim before returning home, and once, while standing under the rushing waterfall, he'd felt as if he were undergoing a kind of baptism. Though the water was icy cold, a warm sensation had entered the top of his head and spread throughout his body, and he had imagined that his entire being had been touched by the finger of God. Now, for just a moment, it almost felt as if he was standing under that waterfall again. But then he heard voices echoing by the urinals, and the reverie ended.

He shut the shower off and dried his body with a towel he'd smuggled out of his grandmother's hospital room. He changed into his only pair of jeans, worn out around the knees, and put on his last clean T-shirt. He washed his dirty clothes in the sink with more of the shampoo and squeezed out the water. He slung his pouch over his shoulder and gathered up his wet laundry, then looked at himself in the mirror. Framing a slim, golden-skinned face were knotted, sun-bleached dreadlocks that fell to his shoulders. His thin nose and green eyes had been inherited from an unknown Caucasian father, probably some military transient his mother had brought home one night. Most boys his age suffered from acne, but his face was smooth. Bronze fuzz sprouted around his lips. He wasn't bad looking, and even though he was part Hawaiian, for years other children had called him "stupid haole."

He was used to harassment. In the park, people ogled his nappy hair or judged him by the images drawn on his jacket. He accepted their treatment as an ugly part of life.

He emerged from the bathroom so hungry that he felt his stomach was eating itself. He draped his wet laundry on a tree to dry, then stretched his body out in the shade below. Opening his pouch, he rattled the Almond Roca can and counted the few coins he had stashed inside.

If he only had ten cents more, he could buy a refillable cup of coffee. And for another thirty-five cents, he could buy a day-old poppy-seed bagel and have a decent meal. Instead, he had to settle for stale chips and a piece of garlic chicken from a plate lunch he found in the trash. He leaned against the tree and took a swig from his water bottle.

And then there were the homeless. Some were professionals: white-color or workers who were down on their luck and in desperate need of a temporary place to stay. Most were welfare recipients who'd been kicked out of low-income housing or 'A'ala Park. Others were teenage runaways, ex-cons, drug abusers, drunks, and people suffering from mental illness—all were scary looking, but most were harmless.

The old Chinese man was on the beach again, doing his morning exercises. The boy found the fluid movements mesmerizing. The man formed a small imaginary ball with his hands and pushed it away with a graceful sweep to his right; then he formed another imaginary ball and brushed it to his left. Next, he swept both arms outward as if swimming. On the park bench where she usually sat was the lady who fed the scavenger birds that dirtied the park with their droppings. The lady cackled and danced as if conducting an orchestra. Bobbing their heads before her were small turtledoves and larger, mostly white pigeons with bright, stop-sign-red beaks and feet. There were also fat lace-necked doves, brown mynahs with yellow beaks and eyes, red-breasted cardinals, and plenty of little brown and green birds that moved in waves like schools of fish, following the seeds that the lady sprinkled about.

Nearby, under a banyan tree, a red-eyed Asian woman was trying to wake her invisible friend and getting annoyed. The boy had seen her arguing with the air many times. Once when he'd politely said hello, she'd scolded her friend for not returning the greeting.

The boy often felt invisible himself: he would try to melt into his surroundings like a chameleon and observe the tourists who swarmed the park. Some of the Japanese had skin so pale and translucent that it almost appeared blue, and they shielded its delicacy from the sun by all means possible. Others applied liberal amounts of cocoa butter to their brown outer husks. Some of the young Japanese kids had bleached-blond hair, red spikes, or anime superhero-style wisps of pink and purple clumps. One young man with long, fake dreadlocks like a Rastafarian's would have passed for a light-skinned Jamaican if it weren't for his Japanese accent. "Bafaro soruja, borun in Amerika," he sang as he listened to a Bob Marley tune.

And then the boy noticed a man struggling to slip a dollar bill into one of the vending machines.

Sitting in a mechanized wheelchair, the man was small, in his midforties maybe, and had salt-and-pepper hair, a basketball-sized stomach, and two shriveled legs, which hung limply. His hands were so gnarled that he resembled a sea lion clapping his flippers together. The boy impulsively went over to him.

"You need help?" he asked.

"Thanks, brah!" the man said with a smile. The boy took the dollar.

"What's your name, cuz?" the man asked.

"Me?" The boy thought about the dream in which his grandmother said his name and how good it had felt. He swallowed hard. "'Īkau," he said softly. "I'm 'Īkau."

"Right on, Bruddah E! I'm Alex. Make a fist." The boy did, and the man tapped his hooked hand against it, saying loudly, "Bam!"

"Bam!" repeated the boy, grinning. He fed the dollar bill into the machine. "Which buttons should I press?"

"I like dah chips! Press A-4."

"Okay, it's fifty-five cents."

The boy pressed A and 4. The chips fell with a soft thud, and the change dropped into the coin-return slot with three loud chi-chings.

"You can grab 'em for me, cuz?" asked the man. The boy fetched the chips and scooped out the coins. "Here's your change," he said.

"Nah, brah, keep 'em."

Again, the man held out his hooked hand. The boy made a fist and they bammed each other before the man rode away, tearing his bag of chips open with his teeth. The boy gazed at the coins in his hand as if they were stars that had fallen from the sky.

He gathered the rest of his money, approached the fast-food counter, and bought the last day-old bagel and a cup of coffee. He ate ravenously. Because the coffee was refillable, he went back several times. Each cup was topped with loads of sugar and powdered cream. It was the best meal he had eaten in a long time.

MATTHEW KAOPIO *began his career as a mouth-brush artist and writer while going through rehabilitation after a 1994 diving accident that left him a quadriplegic. He is the author of* Hawaiian Family Legends *and* Written in the Sky. *He has a BA in Hawaiian/Pacific studies and an MA in Pacific Island Studies. In March 2004, he was accepted into the Association of Mouth and Foot Painting Artists, a for-profit company that supports hundreds of disabled artists around the world.*

Lois-Ann Yamanaka
"BOY WEN' FLUNK EIGHT GRADE ENGLISH AGAIN"

Like know what I doing hea?
I had one fuckin' old bag Japanee
teacha fo' English last yea'
and she neva like me
'cause I neva use to do
shit in her class.
I neva undastan' and her,
she no fuckin' help me.
So I said, "Fuck this shit,"
and I had fo' scrub walls afta school.

Fuckin' Maria ova dere,
she one prostitute.
How I know?
'Cause I know one tuna

when I smell one.
What?
What you lookin' at, fuckin' cunt.
No talk to me
until I talk to you.
What?
You like me slap yo' face,
hah, white shit.
Den shut up.
Why I gotta talk like dat?
'Cause dat's da way
I gotta talk.

I like write poetry
fo' extra credit.
Can make um rhyme?
Shit, whoeva heard poems
dat no rhyme.
Fuck, what kine teacha you?
Please.
Okay, I going write about Elbert.
He cool 'cause I was raggin' his ass
and he neva lick me.
Okay, Elbert—
Elbert you my friend . . . bend . . . send . . . mend.
Nah.
Elbert, Elbert you my man . . . fan . . . pan . . . can.
Nah, nah.
Ho, why no jes' give me
da fuckin' A.
Okay, I get um.
Elbert, Elbert you one lump.
You beeg and black j'like one stump.
Dere.

Alice, she sell drugs, you know.
Fo' real, you know.
I no shit you.
Why should I shit you?
Fuck, no believe den.
How I know?
'Cause, last summa when we was going,

she made one joint fo' me and her
from her stepfadda's stash.
We wen' get all stone
in da stairwell down KPT,
afta we five-finga discount at Sunny's.

Befo' when I was six grade,
my madda use to ask me,
"Son, you like try drugs?"
Den she go someplace
fo' buy me and her some ice.
Fuck, how come you *neva* believe me?
I tell you all dis shit and you,
you no believe.
What?
You calling me one fuckin' liar?
My-madda-use-to-buy-fo'-me-and-her-some-drugs,
okay? Den we smoke
and watch tv togeda.

My small sista and me from da same fadda.
My olda sista from one adda fadda.
My real fadda got kick out by my madda.
Now she get one military boyfriend.
Da grunt, he no like me.
Everytime he lick me.
So I wen' tell him,
"You wait, brah, til my real fadda come.
He goin' kick yo' ass."
My real fadda everytime tell me
he going come pick me up.
I wait outside my house 'til dark.
He no come.
Da grunt come ova.
He laugh.

Fuck, only haoles get da same fadda.

Chris McKinney

from BOLOHEAD ROW

A side from patronizing small, illegal casinos, I'd never really walked the streets of downtown late at night, and it got me to thinking that there were a lot of places on the island I'd never been to despite the fact that I'd lived here all my life. I'd never been hiking in the mountains, hadn't stepped foot on most beaches, and never walked into many dark pockets of downtown.

The people I saw that night were like roaches that had crawled out from the cracks of sidewalks in front of the old two-story buildings and the new bank high-rises.

I parked about a block from the police station and waited for B to peel himself from the truck. He was wearing a hospital gown over jeans, and he had brought a cane with him, a simple black one with a curved handle. We had to go slowly, so I saw more than I would have walking alone. We passed a woman sitting in front of the Honolulu magazine building in a portable nest of crumpled newspaper. We passed two transvestite hookers standing by a traffic light, one a dark Hawaiian with lines coming down from her mouth that made her look like a ventriloquist's doll. In Chinatown, a man was pushing a shopping cart filled with crushed cans and wearing these pants that weren't jeans, slacks, sweatpants, or khakis; they were just brown, straight-legged pants that looked homemade. Or maybe they were corduroys so worn down that the ridges had disappeared. Nearby, a woman in a soiled muumuu was mumbling something about God.

It seemed like every third person I passed asked me for a cigarette or five bucks. One guy stopped us and told us that his car had run out of gas. He was even holding a plastic red container to support his story. He asked to borrow money, then gave us a place of employment and a phone number. I was beginning to believe him and was about to pull out my phone to check out the number when B took off his shades, raised his cane and rested it on his shoulder, and said, "How about I knock you out, fill up your gas can, then come back and light your ass on fire?"

The guy started to say something, but he stopped himself and walked away. One of B's eyeballs was still completely red, the other was swollen shut, and there were patches of purple on his cheeks. The guy must have been tempted to take a shot at him, but B also had the look of the walking dead.

Gene Frumkin
"HOTEL STREET"

T—takes me to a nude bar in downtown
Honolulu on Hotel Street. One of the dancers
shows a scar on her stomach, from an accident
or some other cause. But there had been
an accident. She is lucky to be alive,
she tells me, after the first set, sitting
on the chair beside me at the bar.

Her boss soon takes her aside. I must order
drinks for us. She is telling the horror
of the crash, of her time in the hospital.
This is the first night back for her, dancing.
I'd noticed she was a bit out synch
with the music. I don't know if T—is hearing
any of our conversation. But I wonder

if she had ever performed in videos.
To ask this would infringe on her good nature,
but I ask anyway, ordering another round.
T—looks on, amused. Yes, she says, videos.
But they're out of print. But I'll give you
one out of my personal stock. We make
an arrangement for the following

night. T—drives me over again, approving
of my mission. She is not visible. I ask
her boss: she keeled over toward the end
of last night's show. Maybe she drank
too much, I ask. The girls' drinks are all
water. Can I visit her? If they'll
let you, at the hospital. But what's wrong

with her? Too much water or peritonitis.
She hadn't had a decent shit in two weeks.
Well, if you'll tell me where the hospital is
I'll give it a try. You must have fallen
for her big time. No, but she was very
pleasant to me, a nice woman who I guess
had a hard life. That's over anyway. She died.

Sean Sabal

from THE RETURN OF BRADDHA B

Cast

BRUCE, *recently unemployed, 21*
DION, *Bruce's close friend, 21*
KIMMIE, *Bruce's girlfriend, 20*
SONNY, *a good friend to everyone, 40*
NIKKO, *the neighborhood bully, 30*
BOY, *Bruce and Dion's friend, 16*
THE BOYS AT THE PARK, *just the neighborhood folks*
NIKKO'S GANG, *a gang of thugs*

Place: Honolulu, Hawaii.
Time: early 1990s

SCENE ONE

Lights up. BRUCE *and* DION *are sitting in* BRUCE'S *car.*
DION: Waaassup braddha B.
BRUCE: Wassaap. *(pause)* Eh, chro dat cigarette out befo you burn my ka.
DION: Oh yeah, I forgot cho rule, sorry yah. *(He flicks his cigarette.)* Nooo
    cigarettes.
BRUCE: Dats right you faka. *(smiles)* So what, we gon graaab or what?
DION: Yeah, bra, I waiting for Wayne call me back. He said he was gon call
    when he get da load.
BRUCE: Shit, fuck dat, I no like wait bra. What about da kine. Larry?
DION: Fuck Larry, he no mo shit, that fucken loosa.
BRUCE: Larry dat fat faka, everytime that faka nomo shit. *(pause)* What about
    fuckin da kine. What dat haole's name?
DION: Oh Davis. Dat crazy fucken haole. No bra, he stay fucken jail bra, that
    faka when beat his wife. Den his fucken kids when call 911 bra.
BRUCE: Fucken unreal. *(pause)* So what den.
DION: No worry bra. *(He takes out a gram of marijuana stuffed in a tiny zip-lock
    bag.)*
BRUCE: Oh you faka. Whea you got dat from.
DION: I wen pinch from Joe da day wen I wen hook him up.
BRUCE: Ho, right on bra.
DION: Yeah bra, smell this shit. *(holding a bud to* BRUCE'S *face)* Smell em bra.
    Try smell dis.
BRUCE: You know what, just roll da dubes bone head.
DION: Lick my balls bitch. *(pause)* Gimme something fo roll on.

BRUCE: Look in da glove ladat. (*DION opens the glove*) Right dea use dat. (*pointing at the car owners manual*)

DION: (*he starts breaking up the bud*) So what bra, what happen wit da kine, Kimmie?

BRUCE: I don't know bra. I no kea alrede. Fucken bitch ken do what eva she like bra.

DION: Oh yeah. (*pause*) Drama deals uh.

BRUCE: Nah, dis shit is ova.

DION: Why what happen.

BRUCE: Nah, jus da kine, too much stress you know, every time she open her mout I get fucken irritated.

DION: Oh yeah.

BRUCE: Yeah bra. She always say some fucken stupid shit bra. I wish I could put two wiyas on her head, and connect um to one ka batree, and everytime she way something stupit, I gon fucken zap her. I gon have one button I gon push everytime she say something stupid. Gon be jus "bzzt bzzzt bzzzt."

DION (*giggles*): You fucken crazy.

BRUCE: Yeah bra. So what, you almos pau O-what.

DION (*packing the ends of the dube*): Yeah bra. Wait! (*pause*) You get one crutch.

BRUCE: Right dea da match (*pointing to the passenger floor.*)

DION: OK. I see em. (*pause*) So what den, dat means you gon cruz wit da Boys again uh.

BRUCE: Shit. I cruz wit the Boys.

DION: Oh yeah.

BRUCE: Yeah.

DION: Whateva. (*pause*) Eh. Rememba Jimmy. (*long pause, then speaks with a bit of hesitation*) He go college now. (*pause*) He stay fucken mainland ladat.

BRUCE: Fo what? Play football?

DION (*pause, then speaks choppy*): Yeah bra, dat faka came huge. He one fucken monsta now.

BRUCE: Faak, dat fucken kid. (*pause*) Nah, I gon be cruzin mo often now.

DION: OK bra. (*lights the joint, takes a deep puff, holds it for five seconds, slowly lets it out, passes it to* BRUCE.)

BRUCE (*takes a hit*): Ho bra, dis shit is fuckin crip.

DION: Das what I was saying. Yestaday we was shmoking one fat blunt (*smiles*).

BRUCE: You can get somemoa dis?

DION (*receives the joint*): Yeah bra. (*pause*) So whea you put da ash ladat.

BRUCE: Outside.

DION (*rolls down the window, and attempts to flick the ashes*): Oh shit! Shtop da ka.

BRUCE *(notices that the joint no longer has the cherry on it)*: You fucken dumb ass. Why you no watch da fucken joint.

DION: Bra was da wind. See why you gotta drive like one fucken crazy faka everytime. Not oni my fault bra.

BRUCE: You fucken dummy.

DION: Bra, you know need amp bra. I tol you fucken sorry.

BRUCE: Eh fuck you bra, you when burn my seat.

DION: You no need amp.

BRUCE: Fuck you bra. Burn my seat and now you like talk shit.

DION *(long pause, he is contemplating about how he is going to change the subject)*: Eh, we go to da pak. That way save waste gas ah.

BRUCE: OK.

SCENE TWO

SONNY *(takes out a crystalmeth pipe, boils the drug that's inside and takes a hit and passes it to DION)*: Hea.

DION *(lights it some more and takes a hit and blows out a cloud of smoke)*: Ho, how's dat dragon ah.

BRUCE *(walks in on them smoking crystalmeth)*: Eh, you fakas smoke batu!

BOY *(receives the pipe from DION)*: Why you like take one hit.

BRUCE: Fuck no. When you guys started this? *(feels a thick film of smoke around him.)* Ho bra, get one fuckin cloud in hea. Fuck I gon cruz outside till you fakas done. *(takes a beer and the joint and goes outside stage right.)*

BRUCE *(talking to himself)*: Fuck I gotta get Kimmie back. *(glances inside the house and sees them still taking hits)* Fucking idiots. *(smoking the joint)* How can these fakas do drugs? Fuck, I no believe this.

SONNY: Eh Bruce. Come inside. We pau alrede.

BRUCE: Nah wait. Still get dat cloud.

SONNY: Nah. Nomo cloud.

BRUCE *(walks inside the house)*: Hey guys, time to call it a night. I getting tired and I gotta work tomorrow.

SONNY: Yeah. gimmi one ride.

BRUCE: Yeah yeah. *(shakes everyone's hand. Then him and SONNY leave.)*
Blackout . . .

SCENE SIX

Lights up. BRUCE is in his car driving. SONNY is in the passenger seat.

BRUCE: So what. How you guys stated smoking dat.

SONNY: Oh, I been smoke dat long time already. Off and on kine.

BRUCE: What about Dion and Boy?

SONNY: Oh those fakas. They started around the time you stop coming around.

BRUCE: Yeah.

SONNY: You know what. You should sell bra. *(pause)* You no smoke. You can make chook money.

BRUCE: For real. *(pause)* How much money.

SONNY: Bra. What eva you buy fo sell. We can turn it around and make double.

BRUCE: Oh yeah?! *(pause)* Where I gon get da stuff.

SONNY: I get da connec. You just gimmi da money fo pick up da load.

BRUCE: How much?

SONNY: I can get balls fo tree hundred. *(pause)* Dats one deal bra. Only I can get dat.

BRUCE: Why you can help me sell da stuff? *(pause)* Cause I don't know too much people who smoke dat. And plus too get all da undacovas ladat huh.

SONNY: Yeah. We all can help. And no worry about da pigs bra. We only sell to people we know.

BRUCE: Yeah maybe den. Just gimmi a few days fo come up wit da cash.

SONNY: Let's do it!

Blackout

SCENE SEVEN

Lights up. It's 2 weeks later. BRUCE *is at* KIMMIE'S *house.*

BRUCE: Kimmie, I sorry if I woke you up. I know it's early.

KIMMIE: It's cool.

BRUCE: Well I get my paycheck. I wen pick um up dis morning. *(hands* KIMMIE *the check)* I said I was gon help wit da baby.

KIMMIE: I no need yo money Bruce.

BRUCE: Nah just take em. Das my baby too right?

KIMMIE *(long pause)*: Bruce. I'm going to Vegas.

BRUCE: Oh yeah. Right on. I heard that place is the shit.

KIMMIE: No Bruce. I'm going there to live with my auntie and uncle. They have a big house and my cousins are away for college.

BRUCE: You gon move mainland?

KIMMIE: Yeah.

BRUCE: What fo?

KIMMIE: Hawaii no mo jobs. No opportunity for me. My auntie told me that Vegas is growing and they have way more opportunities.

BRUCE: That's good Kimmie. That's good. But what about me? I gon spend the rest of my life wondering about my child. Das just gon make things mo stress fo me. *(long pause)* Kimmie, I still had hopes fo us. You know wit our kid and all dat family shhh . . . shtuff.

KIMMIE *(long pause)*: You like come wit me?

BRUCE: Ho. *(long pause)* I can come wit you?

KIMMIE: Yeah.

BRUCE: Nah. What if things no work out? What if your family up dea no accept me? And what about all my friends and family ladat.

KIMMIE: Bruce, there is noting going on hea fo us. I bet you nothing gon change around hea. Da only change in Hawaii is just tings getting mo shitty.

BRUCE: I wish you would stay in Hawaii Kimmie.

KIMMIE: I know you try. But I already made up my mind. I'm going to Vegas to have this baby. Then after I'm going to find a job. I might even go to a 2-year college part time to study art.

BRUCE (*shows sad expression*): Das good Kimmie, I guess you gotta do what's best.

KIMMIE: I said you can come with me.

BRUCE: No no. Kimmie, das not gon work.

KIMMIE: It's the only way I see it working.

BRUCE: I no can live mainland. I no can handle dat. If you stay down hea, I gon support us.

KIMMIE (*long pause*): No. It's not that easy Bruce.

BRUCE (*gets up and begins to leave the house*): OK. Kimmie. Let me think about all dis. I was suppose to pick up Sonny.

KIMMIE: What, you gotta smoke your weed.

BRUCE: No Kimmie. I no even smoke dat much anymoa. I just gotta go pick up Sonny from where he sell his Sunday papers. (*pause*) And I gon think about all this. You know, put all das going on into perspective ladat. But I telling you, right now, bring the way things are, and how da situation is, I really no see myself moving to da mainland. I wish you would stay in Hawaii.

KIMMIE: Well you no need come if you don't want to.

BRUCE (*is at the door*): Yeah, well, I gotta go now. I give you one call.

Blackout

SEAN SABAL, *like anyone born and raised in Honolulu, was exposed to the melting pot of ethnic backgrounds, economic status, languages, cultures, and interests. He graduated from Kaimuki High School in Honolulu, then received his bachelor's degree in business administration from the University of Hawai'i at Mānoa.*

Normie Salvador
"NAMED BY NUMBERS"

HPD. Badge one-eleven.
I remember the badge number
from the investigation one month ago.

His name is
not one of our
own.   a shell I keep

Badge number 197 is the same as yesterday   across the Guerkbop   10/57/00
My grandfather sees saw   silence
himself reflected in the police officer's sunglasses,   numbers
watched the officer's mouth move in a question,   you   yellow + black
and did not understand.

I heard him, I did not speak about last night;   abandon "about"
about the black Civic that fishtailed to a stop   CRX   structure.
beneath the amber flight of our streetlamp; about
a license plate of personalized letters,   all highlights and chrome
no numbers allowed in the Speed Syndicate;   shine.
about four Filipinos, one related by marriage, two   , that shattered glass,
good as blood in our family, in this town;   shredded rubber, punched
about the fists that held guns,   four, the y   through the steel of.
named by numbers;   sleet   what had been the car
about the semi-automatic fire destroying the car
that had won the competition held the night before
about the sudden silence and blackout
as 94-prefixed addresses along the street went darkened   juggling finger
about the measured paces to our mailbox   like   searching a pocket
and the retrieval of still hot shells but for one, tossed to me
engraved with R P 7.62 × 39 mm, not my name
about the finger held to pursed lips,   scented with powder and
a smile that sealed my silence   night-blooming Jasmine
The officer repeated the question in Tagalog... in Ilokano... in Bisayan.
Silent shakes to each. No, we did not see.
No one will speak to him.
He does not live here.

                under a sky dark as his uniform blue

They did not know the meaning / of a bullet placed on the windshield.

His name was not one of our own.
My grandfather saw him first, saw himself
reflected in twin lenses, watched
the officer's mouth move in question,
and did not understand.
I understood the accented English.
Should I speak of what I saw?

Our neighbor did not understand the lone bullet
placed on his windshield two nights past,
a convention imported from the States.

Last night, under a uniform dark sky
a CRX, all highlights and chrome shine, fishtailed
into the amber pool of streetlight, flashing a license
plate of personalized letters.
There are no numbers in the Syndicate.

Two Filipinos, one related by marriage, the other
by friendship, good as blood to our family,
emerged from doors unfolding as wings. Their four fists
held four guns named only by numbers.
Four bucking barrels
let fly the semi-automatic sleet that shattered
glass, shredded rubber, and punched through steel
of what had won the car show
competition staged the night before.

Blackout
greeted the silence of empty guns
as number by number,
addresses along the street darkened,
no witnesses
save me.

My in-law measured six steps to my mailbox,
bent double and hissed in his juggling
retrieval of over a dozen still hot shells
but for one, tossed to me, a souvenir
engraved with numbers and not with my name.
It seared my skin. Its powder
scent mingled with fading rubber.

A finger held to pursed lips, his smile
sealed my silence as our eyes met
in agreement. No words were to be spoken.

The officer repeats the question haltingly
in Tagalog . . .
in Ilokano . . .
No one will speak to him.
He does not have to live here.

Because of the shell I keep
I will not speak
the two names and change them into numbers.
Not one neighbor has said
one word to break the silence of emptied guns.

Jean Toyama
"SPECIAL"

He broke my jaw more than once,
she said, as if giving her special
recipe for stew. But he was a good man,
always brought home his paycheck,
good to the kids. He broke my arm
only twice, she added, as if explaining the
making of a quilt. He was a good man.
Together 57 years, 57 years,
until he died five years ago,
two days before Thanksgiving.

Listen without interruption the words
of this old woman.
She bore the crimes of her man.

Respect, respect.

JEAN TOYAMA *is a poet, scholar, translator, and writer of fiction. She lives in Hawai'i, where she was born and raised.*

Ian MacMillan

"uhu"

H er eyes are so big when she says it, and Ikaika waits just outside the apartment door with no shirt on so she can see his muscles, "—an' can stay as long as you fee' like, 'kay?"

"'kay."

And Ikaika standing there waiting for you to go, jus' go awready, his eyes say. Take da speah an' go awready.

So slide on the zoris, next to the dusty thirteen size ones and Mommy's leather ones with the white and yellow daisies on them.

Traffic on Kapahulu, buses, cars, smoke that settles in the windless heat like a liquid on the hot pavement, and Kapahulu sweeps away toward the ocean, the glittering cars in the distance and the air all like boiling in the shimmering heat and all of it vanishing in haze into the zoo trees and the opening to the ocean. Spear point out front, the shaft jounces and bends, jounces and bends step by step while the fins squeak hanging from your fingers, the zoris flapping on the hot gum spotted concrete. Ikaika. On his tight jeans pocked the raised bumps of one circle over another circle over part of a third—Rayleen and Ikaika in the apartment. If Mommy ever find out. But she's at Liberty House, every morning make-up tubes and boxes all over the kitchen table and that little round mirror, and the little plastic badge on her chest that says Darla Leong moving while she paints.

Uh-oh. "Shoots. No mo' mask." Look back, past a lady in a red dress with a slit up her leg standing at the Rose Lounge door, past the corner, and Kapahulu boiling away into car exhaust haze under the black, cloud topped mountains. Gotta go back.

Stupid. Flap flap flap, jounce jounce the spear. Traffic. Jeep one way, BMW the other, Mazda with bondo spots. So Kenny, wheah yo' dad? Eh, he at Halawa—cah teff. Fo' real? How else to say it? Almost like it's cool that he's there.

The apartment sits at the back end of the two story building, Ikaika's black Scirocco pointing at the door. Stop. Now what? Walk past them while they're wrapped up and wrestling, Rayleen all squealing and giggling on the stupid couch?

So, gotta knock. Fist up—Uh-oh. Thumps, a squeal. Do it anyway.

"What!"

"Get no mask!"

Shadows on the frosted louvers—arm shoots out, a fuzzy brown, blob of body, oooo, brown too no clothes that's why. Then the door. The mask comes out dangling from Rayleen's finger. Take it. "'kayden, go awraddy." And Ikaika, "Chee, what a dummy—go ketch one sea slug."

"Hah—tink you so hot? What kine fish you get?" Nothing.

So say, "Babooze."

They laugh.

Sea slug. Flap flap flap, jounce and bend, the spear, the little hinged barb opening and closing.

Different way this time. Leahi Avenue, not past Japanee Tourist Beach or Gay Guys Beach or Family Values Beach or Outrigger Club. Flap past the school and the Nuns' Castle and Kapiolani Park Bow And Arrow Field. Go around the bend and left onto Diamond Head Road to Coconut Avenue and to the wall and left to the little beach where the haole girls go topless. Chi-chi Beach. But no chi-chis today. Why? Water junk today, that's why. Cloudy in close, whitecaps outside.

The sand on your feet hurts in the fins until you get in the water. Spit in the mask, pull the wooden handle up the spear and lock it, and flop face down. Cold at first. Then face down you motor off, little waves lapping over your back. Little fish, little fish. Chew on the mouthpiece and a gob of snot floats in the little bit of water in the bottom of the mask. Ahead, beercan like twice the normal size. Can't shoot that—last time just like practicing the spear got inside, took twenty minutes to get it off, people on the beach hiding laughs behind their hands.

What is that? A disposable diaper, moving lazily like a jellyfish, the plastic tabs low in the water. Bigger coralhead coming, so climb up on it into the cold wind, the parched rocky flanks of Diamond Head bright enough to hurt the eyes. Sitting, take off the mask and clean it, spit on the glass and—Ho, one haole girl on the sand. If you put your fingers on the outside edges of your eyes and pull Japanese style, you can see clearer. Lying on her back, chi-chis sitting on top of her chest, swaying when she moves. "'J' like jello."

Cold. So are Rayleen and Ikaika done yet? If Mommy ever find out. Big trouble, deep kim chee. Rayleen's a bad girl who put little x and o tattoos on her hands. Mommy talk talk talk—respect your body. Be responsible. Get good grades in school. I no like skoo, Rayleen says. So? You go anyway. Bumbye we'll be all right. Daddy will come home in five months. Until then it's franks and beans, soup base mixed with rice, burgers from across the street. Daddy—had fish all the time. Three times a week, on the hibachi wrapped up in bright foil sitting in the parking space.

And now Mommy looks at you, scowling—too skinny for someone twelve. You can go on one condition. Seventy-five feet out and no more. 'kay.

Flop in the water. What would you do with one little fish anyway? "Cgluk ubm ubp," you garble into the mouthpiece, and laugh, rattling the snorkel water. Cook um up. Farther out? No, Mommy says, only seventy-five feet, no more. But what is seventy-five feet? 'kay, motor out, the water a little more wild, bigger fish sweeping in the blue distance, bottom sweeping down, dancing pebbles in the bottoms of crevices. Scary. Keep going—what is seventy-five feet? Only means if you could see you wouldn't see chi-chis any more, too far that's why. And Ikaika and Rayleen at home, voices and squeals and thumps drowned out by traffic—bus, jeep, bondo-spotted Mazda.

Ho, how many manini? A hundred? The whole school sweeps away as one, black stripes on yellow like smoke in the wind swirling away. You pull the spear farther through the wooden handle, stretching the yellowish tubes. Aim—no, too far.

"Shblgit." Laugh into the mouthpiece. Can't even say shit into it. Can only hum, or groan, making the water rattle. Now so cold that the jaw vibrates, the body tenses into a long shiver. Gotta go in. Back to Chi-chi Beach. The waves push, sweep over and then drag so you scissor the fins and go backwards. Over a dark green rock to—

What is that? A tail in a hole. Big big tail. Something way over at the other side, in another hole, a rounded green something. The rounded green something moves back, more tail peeks out the other hole. A fish? "Nobgt." Not. Can't be that long. The tail moves back in a little and the rounded green front moves.

Then a wave sweeps you away. "Shblgit." But then the backwash floats you in reverse back to the hole, the tail still there. Daddy said, wind um up a little an' den hol' um steady steady steady, ahm shtraight, an' move close close close an' pulla trigga wit' ahm tensed so da spea get one good push.

Take one huge breath and dive down. Wait, scissoring to stay in one place. The head peeks out, close, close. The head goes back. Stay, wait, and the lungs start to hurt, and little hiccups jerk in your chest. Wait. Head moves out again—what is that? Like a white beak low on the curve of the head, then the eye. No air, the lungs like crushed flat. Hiccup. Pull.

The spear gone and as you explode for the shimmering silver surface sand balloons like smoke out of the hole, the spear jiggling and then being pulled in, ripped from your hand. Down again, grab the spear and push hard. The fish swims out—huge, the spear through the head, and it dances on the spear while you splutter and the mask slides down, strap around your neck, mouthpiece twisted out.

Shaking so much you can barely hold the spear. Cough water, up the nose. Another wave. Get the mask on. Calm. Its eye is on you, beak open. It shakes with a fine vibration, eye and beak open as if surprised or wondering. Calm. Red squiggle lines over the beak and under on the rounded head, the rest blue green, huge.

A dark man on the beach, watching. Work the fins, hold tight, the fish out front, twisting and then floating lazily on the spear, and your heart is high and ticklish. Keep going, hold on, no let go. Shallow. Stand up. Ho, bugga heavy, can hardly lift. So, do everything right. Fins off, mask off, splash hana butta off the face. The man looks.

"Ho da big," he says. "Way more den two feet."

"I—" Nothing comes out. "It—"

"'Uhu," he says. "'ass ono."

Now the chi-chi girl is up, and a guy wearing one of those okole thong things. She puts her yellow top on, and they come running. Hoist the fish up a little, green brown poop oozes out and plops on the water, then goes smoky and vanishes.

"You wanna get dat home," the man says. "Keep um fresh 'ass why. Wheah you live?"

"Up Kapahulu."

"I can give you one ride."

Look at him. Looks like Daddy, dark, beefy, big feet.

"Cannot. My mom tell me, no go wit' dakine. Strangers."

"What is that?" Chi-chis asks.

"Parrotfish," the man says. "Ne-vah see one dat big."

The guy looks. Ho, bet you wish you catch um.

Heavy. Don't want sand on him. The spear bends with the weight. "Yah, I get um home. I get my dad fo' do um up." Why did you say that? Liar liar pants on fire.

"Does it bite?" Chi-chis asks.

"It can," the man says. Then, "You get dat one home, 'kay?"

How to do this: maybe hook the fins and mask in the left hand and then carry the fish in the right, on the spear. Hike the spear on the shoulder. 'kay.

Sand in the zoris. Maybe clean them off in the little park? No, gotta get him home. Chi-chis and the boyfriend watch when you go past.

Every person in every car, every kite flying dad, every guy on a bike, every jogger—they all look, eyes wide, my god, where did you get that? Diamond Head Beach jus' backaways. Then Kapahulu. The shaft of the spear digs into the flesh by your shoulder, can't hold the arm up any more. Try carry it down by your hip. The slime on the fish has turned into a goo,—and smells like—Ho, like fish. Flap flap flap—he's so heavy, bangs sticky on the leg with each step, the slime making it slide. Past the water-works and the stores, more people, even tourists, my god, what a huge fish. One even takes a picture. And a girl, Eeeew, what is that? What does it look like?

At a light, have to stand there and wait, hike the fish up a little and it oozes poop onto the sidewalk. Can smell it. Cars go by with heads slowly swiveling to see it. Ahead Kapahulu rises a little as it vanishes into a point inside car exhaust under the black mountains and the clouds.

So are Rayleen and Ikaika done yet? Hope Ikaika's still there. Sea slug? One more block, past a bus that hisses and then groans to a stop, swaying, and heads turn in the tinted windows.

Uh-oh. Mommy's purple Tercel sits facing a brown dumpster. Ikaika's car gone. Uh-oh. And now just coming over the sound of buses and cars, screaming, first Mommy dada-dat! and then Rayleen wada wada what? Then whap whap whap. Keep walking, the fish so heavy now that the arms tremble trying to hold it up. The louvers are open, and in the gloom of the living room the yellow and white daisy comes up and then vanishes, whap, up and then vanishes, whap. "Why you do dat! Why you let him do dat! I send you bad girls home! What I do when you get hapai!"

And Rayleen, her voice almost a squeak, "I saw yo' marriage dakine!"

"So?" Whap, and Rayleen squeals.

"How come you was married when I was one hah?"

Silence. So, maybe you should knock. Step to the door, fist up.

The door sweeps open to Mommy, daisy slipper in her hand. Back behind the couch, Rayleen, eyes so big. "I got one big 'uhu." Rayleen slides out from behind the couch, toward the coffee table.

"No touch dat!" Mommy yells. Then looks down, and her mouth drops open.

Rayleen gasps. "Mommy, look!"

No touch what? Oh, can see it now, a crumpled up blue condom wrapper sitting like bad origami on the coffee table next to the Star-Bulletin.

"Can take one pitcha?" hiking it up higher.

"I'll get my camera!" Rayleen shouts, and runs into her room. Mommy turns. Rayleen comes out with her Polaroid, then slides around Mommy out the door. Mommy stares at the fish, something happening to her eyes, like there's something she looks at behind them back in her brain. Then she looks at Rayleen and her eyes go awful again.

"Turn around," Rayleen says. When you turn, she lifts the camera and shoots, and then the camera buzzes and grinds, and like a white tongue the picture comes out of the mouth below its single eye.

She's looking at Rayleen, still holding the slipper. Then, "Kenny, clean that and take a shower."

"I'll clean it!" Rayleen says. "Come. I do um."

She grabs you by the shoulders and slides behind, you a shield, "Watch da spea!" and drags you through the house to the back door where the deep sink sits on rusted legs. Turn the spear up, and in goes the fish with a wet thud.

"'kaywait," she says, looking through the window. "How we do dis?"

"A spoon."

"Yah, 'ass it, a spoon." She looks through the window. "You get it."

The spoon Daddy used is in the drawer along with a serrated steak knife. Mommy stands, slipper in her hand, staring down at the wrapper on the coffee table. Her eyes grow bad again, and she raises the slipper and throws it out the open front door. Then she half screams and half growls, coming into the kitchen. The spoon goes to Rayleen, who begins scraping it along the slimy green side of the uhu, and a scale pops up and glues itself to her forehead. Her hands are shaking. Mommy stands in the door and watches while Rayleen drags the spoon up the side, scales shooting off and sticking to the house wall, her forearms, your chest. "Ho da huge," Rayleen almost shouts. "Wait till we show Daddy da pitcha. Kenny, get one plastic bag fo' da guts."

Safeway bag, just inside the door. Mommy stands like a nasty statue, watching. Rayleen scrapes, sweat trickling out of the hair at her temple, the bright bead slowly making its way down her brown cheek. Scales fly. Then she grabs the knife and begins cutting the belly, and the gob of red and brown guts the size of a Softball plops out into the sink, grayish strands disappearing into the belly. "Yuk," she says.

Mommy, voice flat, "Where'd you get that?"

"Diamond Head?"

"How far out?"

Uh-oh. "Seventy-five feet?"

"'kay, we hibachi da back half 'kay?" Rayleen says.

Mommy goes into the kitchen and sits down before the little make-up tubes and pads. Then she takes a kleenex and begins dabbing at her eyes and nose.

"No take showah yet," Rayleen whispers. The bathing suit is dry and salty, the slime like half dry varathane. She gets up on her toes and looks in the window. Eyes so big. When she sees Mommy dabbing, she settles back on her heels, and whispers, "Oh chee." She scrapes more, but there is nothing to scrape. The scales are glued everywhere, one still on her forehead. "Wait," she whispers. "No go yet."

She washes her hands. Then, eyes big again, walks into the kitchen and sits down. Mommy doesn't look at her, so she thinks, then jumps up and runs into the living room and comes back with a pencil and paper. Sits down, waits, and then jumps her chair around a quarter circle of the table next to Mommy, and whispers, "Can you show me how to cook the fish?"

Mommy looks at her, thinking. Then she reaches up, Rayleen flinching, and picks the scale off her forehead, and puts it in her kleenex. Then Mommy stares at her until she looks down.

"Six steaks from the front," she says.

Rayleen writes.

"Fillet the back end."

Rayleen writes.

"No, that's f, i, two l's, e, t."

Ralyeen giggles and erases, writes again.

"Remember the fish cakes we made with green onions and potato?" Mommy asks.

"Oh yah!" Rayleen says. "'ass so ono."

"Let's see, then there's soup, and—" Mommy says, and then stops.

She looks at you, thinking, and then it seems that she is looking through, something working on the back of her mind. Is she huhu about the seventy-five feet? No, it's something else, like she's decided something. Then she jerks her head in the direction of the hallway.

Like paint, the slime feels. Rayleen stares at the side of Mommy's head, mouth open, so it's off to the shower, but on the way stop and check the picture. Body heaved way back to hold him up, spear bent. Uh-oh, eyes half closed, or open, but that's okay because it's mostly a picture of a fish. The sound of traffic comes from the street, the sound of whispering comes from the kitchen.

IAN MACMILLAN, *a resident of Hawai'i since 1966, has published seven novels and four short story collections, one of which won the AWP Award for Short Fiction. He has been reprinted in* O. Henry; Pushcart Prize; *and* Best American Short Stories *volumes. Recent books include* The Red Wind; The Braid; *and* Village of a Million Spirits, *which won the P.E.N.-USA-West Fiction Award in 2000. His new novel,* The Bone Hook, *will be published in 2008.*

Mark

UNTITLED

My mother lives in Las Vegas my father
lives in Hawaii. I am my father's son
and my sister is icky. Our family has
small noses and soft faces. If you

ask me one day I will soar like an
eagle to visit my mother.

MARK *wrote this poem in 1981, when he was a student at Makaha Elementary School in*
Wai'anae, O'ahu.

Kalani Akana
"DA 23RD PSALM"

The Lord my kahuhipa
I no need nobody else.
He go, "Lay down ovah deah in da grass, brah, rest;
Yeah, ovah deah by da stream." Cool;
Whoah I feel some good.
He lead me down da trails
Cuz he like dat, pono, cuz he no like me fall.
Even tho I stay in Halawa valley maximum security,
Brah
I no scared
Cuz he stay watch my back
His 'o'o and his ihe, brah, make me brave lai dat.

He wen make one lu'au for me, cuz
Right in front my enemies;
He go give me gel for my hair—make me look sharp,
Hook me up lai dat;
Wow, I stay all stoked.
So, I think only good stuff lai dat going happen now on;
When all dis pau.
I know dat fo sure.

KALANI AKANA *was born and raised on O'ahu. Hālawa Prison was in his backyard grow-*
ing up at Red Hill at a time when children still climbed trees, waded through streams, looked
for coke bottles, and hid the house key under the doormat. He is both an educator and student of
life, and spent some time in federal prison learning, teaching, and changing. "Da 23rd Psalm"
reflects the genesis of that change.

To be Hawaiian

I remember days when we were younger . . . Barefeet buying smokes . . . We were da bulls of Pakalana Street . . . Shanty houses, no-name roads . . . Damaged men . . . Girls gave birth in high-school johns . . . I thought I could kick ass, especially haole ass . . . I could kick your face, puncture both eyes . . . Greedy iss greedy . . . If da police come, too much pilikia . . . I cannot go back, I never left . . . Aren't we of this place? . . .

Leona Nāwahineokalaʻi Lanzilotti
"KEALIʻILOMA"

"When I die, I want my ashes scattered from that cliff."
I glanced up at the Pali, its lush, green face
overlooking our Hawaiian ancestral homeland, *Halekou*.
It was your favorite spot when you were younger, still is.
"Our ancestors were pushed off that cliff by King *Kamehameha*,"
    you told me.

I've heard the stories many times, that doesn't
bother me; they're our history.
When I was little, I scoffed, cringed at the mention of the name
    Kamehameha.
How dare he kill our ancestors, our blood,
our Hawaiian line.

You grew up running through the rain forest, mud sliding,
reading books in the tops of trees by your homes.
You always injured yourself in one way or another,
jumping from cliffs, riding horses, being a kid.
You drove Grandma crazy.

You learned how to speak pidgin from the daily bus rides to and
    from school
But you didn't get to learn Hawaiian.
You pleaded, of course, but Grandpa wouldn't teach you.

On the day Hawaiʻi became a state, you stood
on the porch of your aunt's house,
singing out Hawaiʻi Ponoʻi, tears falling
from your proud eyes.

I looked out the car window, staring at the peak
for a split second more,
breathing in the cool, strong Hawaiʻi wind.

Home.

LEONA NĀWAHINEOKALAʻI LANZILOTTI (NAWA) *comes from a richly mixed ethnic background. She loves the word, whether in Chinese, Hawaiian, English, or sign language. A 2007 graduate of Punahou School in Honolulu, she attends the University of Rochester.*

Kiana Davenport

from HOUSE OF MANY GODS

W AI'ANAE COAST, 1964
Morning, the air astonishingly clear. The sky so unblemished and wide, there is divinity in the light. Sun and heat already strong, the shapes of all things are revealed. Old roosters crowing, shopkeepers yawning, rolling back iron window grilles. The absolute poise of women with blood-leaping grace walking dusty roads to market.

In shanty houses, in rumpled beds, the piping cries of humans waking. A dozing father's muscular, copper-colored arm falls from a bed to the floor. An infant crawls across the floor, picks up the father's hand, and drools. The hand scoops up the child, cupping it like a well-loved toy. It lifts the child up to the day. Here is the still life. The sudden, static poem of being.

Down no-name roads, children stare from windows of abandoned, oxidizing buses, like little clusters of roe. Fresh from sleep, their faces are lovely to behold. Some windows have curtains, there is even a tilting mailbox near the road. A boy appears in a doorway, shaking out a sleeping mat. He rubs his eyes and stares as if in deep remembrance. An old man waters his taro patch, whispering to heart-shaped leaves that it is morning.

Life is not weary of these folks. They have held on to ancient rhythms in this world that was bequeathed to them . . .

This was the wild place, the untutored place, where the Grand Tūtū* of the coast, the rugged Wai'anae Mountains, watched over the generations. Here, thirty miles west of Honolulu, were the rough tribes of Wai'anae, native clans that spawned outcasts and felons. Yet their towns had names like lullabies—Ma'ili, Nanakuli, Lualualei—until up past Makaha and Makua the coastal road ran out, coming to a blunt point like a shark's snout.

And there was history here, many-layered legends. A reverence for the old ways, the good ways. Each town was set apart by a valley, by plains of weedy, rust-red dirt dotted with patches of taro fields and herds of sharp-ribbed cattle. The soil was coarse and punishing; it was unforgiving and bit back. Still, old *tūtū* men and women planted their taro at *Mahealani Hoku*, the full moon. And when they harvested the taro, underneath was good. And slogging in the *lo'i*, the taro mud, was good. Good for arteries and circulation. Good for hoof-thick fingernails.

And they ocean-fished by the dark moon when plankton came, bringing the big fish. And they gave back to the sea what was not needed. And they rested and worshipped according to moon phases. Living by the old Hawai-

---

*Tūtū—meaning grandmother or grandfather—is pronounced "too-too."

ian moon calendar, honoring their gods, they prayed that theirs would be a good death. That their bones would not lie bleaching in the sun.

Here too, among steep ridges in valley recesses were ancient ruins, sacred *heiau*, prayer-towers, and sacrificial altars. Here in caves hidden by volcanic rocks, in bags of rotting nets, eyeless skulls watched the land to see what *kapu* would be broken. And what the gods would do. In ancient days the coast had been a place of refuge for warriors weakened in battles. Here they had hid, tending their wounds, regathering their strength. Here, at night, across the valleys folks still heard those warriors marching back across the land to battle. Some mornings there were giant footsteps.

Seaward, the Wai'anae Coast was untouched and magnificent, its beaches great strands of soft, white powder. Yet only the boldest strangers ventured there. Last holdout of pure-blood Hawaiians, it was the skill of Wai'anae to keep outsiders out. Dark, husky local boys stalked foolhardy tourists at beach parks, vandalizing their rented cars. They ambushed soldiers venturing out from military bases. Sultry girls tossed back their hair, breathing self-esteem, hips swaying insolently as they strode by on crumbling rubber slippers.

Homestead youngsters raised on Welfare, their lives were circumscribed by landlessness, poor education, drugs. Outsiders saw in them the criminal intent, the wish to self-destruct, not looking deeper where hunger for beauty lay. Not hearing the suck and lisp of dreams, despair, then resignation. Yet here was tribal confidence, a sense of deeply rooted blood, of elders standing behind them for now, for good, for always. And the youngsters grew insolent and fearless. Even hardened surfers from Honolulu, out to catch the waves at Yokohama Bay, showed respect. They did not enter the sacred Kaneana Caves. They left the coast before moonrise.

In the town of Nanakuli, off the coastal highway, a house stood halfway up Keola Road, a sprawling Homestead house that vaguely resembled a shipwreck listing to the left. Generations earlier, it had been a house of pride, of people vivid with ambition. Then life, and neglect, had made the house seem very old. But scandals made it new again, embellishing its history.

The town itself was like that, constantly renewed, rewritten by its tragedies. There were shootings. Whirl-kick karate death gangs. Marijuana farmers were hauled off to Halawa Prison, while girls gave birth in high-school johns. But there was Nanakuli magic, too. Wild-pig hunting with uncles, their boar-hounds singing up jade mountains. And torch-fishing nights—elders chanting, bronzed muscles flashing, strained by dripping haunches of full nets. In tin-roofed Quonset huts, and ancient wooden shacks, women sang at rusty stoves, their shadows epic on the walls.

He leaned from his window, looking out at a bloodred valley, the color so beloved and worshipped by the ancients. A silent man, an empty room, only the white rectangle of a bed. He was Noah, and he had come home from combat in Korea without the will to speak. He did not, in fact, remember that war. When folks mentioned it, he shrugged, sure that they were making it up. This was his life now, leaning from his window, the windowsill grown shiny from the years of his forearms.

Having dismissed the past, he was acutely aware of the present, watching the comings and goings of his family, the neighbors, the progression of their small town, Nanakuli, slung like a hammock between mountain and sea. Knowing he watched them, folks behaved a little better. Sometimes while he dozed, children tiptoed close and left things on his windowsill. A mango, a green apple. He woke and leaned down, watching how the apple focused the glow of afternoon.

Since his niece had departed, he did not really sleep. He listened for the cries of little Ana, her abandoned child. He had watched the mother go, driving off with her arm waving out the window of Nanakuli's only taxi. A graceful arm, a careless arm, looking severed from the elbow. She never looked back. Her face was already looking toward the sea, already going *makai* and *makai* and *makai*, out into the world where life, real life, awaited her.

She was leaving behind intractable red dust, valleys that seized up and swallowed livestock, forests of mean kiawe trees whose barbed-wire thorns could skin a human clean. She was leaving, she said, a place of hopelessness, a coast of broken, thrown-away lives.

Noah heard a voice call softly in the dusk, like someone calling in a dream. "Mama . . . Mama . . . "

The child she left behind. Sometimes in the shock of early morning, he heard her chattering to herself. He rose, looked out the window where she was leashed by a harness to a wire clothesline. For hours she played alone in the gritty yard, building a little house with scraps of linoleum, then tidying each cranny.

In the heat of her chores, the child ran up and down the clothesline so it seemed to hum and sing as if she were a note running up and down a scale. After several hours, her hands grimy, her face bearded with dirt, she would grow lonely and would scream, which started the boar-hounds barking. She would scream until someone ran from the house and picked her up.

One day she screamed and no one came. Her screams grew so piercing, a young goat tethered to a tree fainted out of terror. Finally, Noah left his room, walked outside, removed the harness from the child, and pumped it with his shotgun, watching it leap and dance around the yard. Then he took Ana in his arms, humming while she slept. After that folks paid more attention, holding her more often. She grew up feeling loved, but quiet, a pensive child who sat alone like an old woman tired of talking.

There were so many elders in the house, for years she could not keep them straight. Fight-full uncles and great-uncles smelling of tobacco and gun bluing. Big-breasted aunties and great-aunties whose hands reeked of Fels Naphtha. At dusk they gathered on the *lānai* in competitive fugues of storytelling, and often they talked about her mother. Ana sat in the shadows and listened and, sensing her nearby, they fell silent, or sent her off to her cousins.

For years, she thought that sleeping alone was what people did when they were contagious, for she and her cousins grew up sharing beds; sleeping head to toe—husky boys with bronzed shoulders, and girls with names like Rosie, Ginger, Jade, one girl named Seaweed. Girls whose mothers were all headstrong beauties, famous up and down the Wai'anae coast—Emma, Nani, Ava, Mapuana, and for a while there had been Ana's mother, Anahola.

Along with its tempestuous women, the big house was famous for its damaged men. Ana's great-grandfather had come home from World War I with his nose shot off. Doctors had built him a metal nose which he removed each night before he slept. Folks said that's why his wife had gone insane, lying under his empty face. Great-uncle Ben, his son, came home from World War II without an arm. Ben's younger brother, Noah, returned from Korea silent as a grub.

Their cousin, Tito, a champion swimmer, had been a diver for the U.S. Navy. Deep saturation dives, day after day, year after year, until nitrogen bubbles trapped in his bone marrow turned his bones to rotting crochet. Now wheelchair-bound, he had become a poker master. There were other families, other vets. And sometimes they all came together, remembering war with fierce lyrics and metaphoric dazzle, as if peacetime were the nightmare.

Once a year on Veterans Day, folks came from up and down the coast, bringing baskets of food. They sat watching the veteran sons, and sons of sons, like people at a zoo. The damaged men would drink too much, strip off their clothes, and rave and dance with savage grace, while light hung in the space of a missing limb. Their mutilations glowed. Then they would wrestle their boar-hounds to the ground, play pitch and catch with great-grandpa's bronzed nose till everyone went home.

Of all her cousins in that house, Rosie, five years older, grew to be Ana's favorite. Smart and feisty with sightly darker skin, the girl gave Ana a feeling of security, a deep sense of okayness. Rosie's mother was Ava, and she was the one Ana kept her eye on. The woman had grown up wanting to be an Olympic swimmer, but then she turned beautiful and the dance halls found her. Folks said she looked like Lena Horne. Slow-hipped, honey-colored, each night Ava and her sisters dressed for the Filipino dance halls, rice-powdering their cheeks and arms to make them pale, puckering and rouging their perfect lips.

Sometimes an aunty mentioned Ana's mother, Anahola, how she had loved dressing up and going to the dance halls. How she had stood alone, measuring the men who never measured up. She hardly remembered the woman's face, but often in sleep Ana climbed behind her mother's eyes. She slipped into her skin. She glided with handsome mix-bloods at the dance halls, legs wrapped around thighs that ruddered her round the floor.

One night Ava turned to her, grinning in a twisted way. "Poor little bastard. Your mama didn't want you."

One-armed Ben took her aside. "You got one *loko'ino* mouth. Every time you open it, you swallow yo' damn brain. *Nevah* use dat word again."

Remembering what Ava had said, on her seventh birthday Ana walked into the kitchen full of elders. "Am I still a bastard?"

They cried out and scooped her in their arms. Great-aunty Pua took her on her lap while she mixed poi in a tub of pounded taro.

"Listen, child, anybody call you that again, you tell them *pa'a ke waha!* Keep the mouth shut. You our precious *punahele*. You going to be somebody, going make this family proud."

"If I'm so much, how come my mama left?"

Pua looked up at her sisters. "Your mama's on a voyage. One day when she's *pau*, then she come home."

Ana watched Pua add water to the tub, watched her squeeze the pounded taro, watched the poi ooze through her aunty's thick brown fingers. She listened as Pua instructed, telling her the secret to two-finger poi—not too thin, not too thick—knowing how much water, how much to squeeze.

"You squeeze too much, poi comes watery and runs away."

While she talked, the poi made sucking sounds, swallowing her hands and wrists. "Your mama's a little bit like poi, not always easy to hold on to. Have to let her go her way."

There were nights when all the aunties brought their men home, and the house bulged and rocked with human drama. In the mornings while they slept, Ana and her cousins slicked mulberry juice on their lips, turning them a ghoulish blue. They scraped green mold from the walls and smeared it on their eyelids, then pinned plumeria in their hair and slow-danced in couples like the grown-ups.

Rosie's father came, a handsome Filipino. He closed the door to Ava's room. Their singing bedsprings, call and response of human moans. Then, the sound of him slapping her, a series of screams, Ben aiming his pig-hunting rifle, the drummer running down the road. Ava stood in the doorway flicking ashes, throwing off perfumes.

One day for no reason, she hit Rosie so hard, the girl flipped sideways, landing on her head. Her eyes rolled back, showing white, a trick that took

Ana's breath. That night it was quiet, Ana was careful where she looked. Then Noah silently appeared, walked up to the chair Ava sat in, lifted her and the chair over his head, and threw them both across the room. Ava just lay there, her cheekbone's shadow on the floor.

Ben stood over her. "You going end up Kāne'ohe State Hospital, like Grandma."

Gradually, her face began to change. It grew bloated, blister-tight. She threw Rosie headfirst through a window. She slammed the girl's head with an iron skillet. One day she held Rosie's hand over open flames until Ben pinned her to a wall. Ana found Rosie hiding out behind the goat pen, and they slept wrapped together in a blanket. Through the years they grew so close, they could just look at each other and feel safe.

When Rosie was thirteen, Ava had another child. The father, a graceful Chinese famous for his tango, was only five years older than Rosie. Ben threw Ava out of the house; she never made it to the clinic. Her baby slid out on the backseat of Nanakuli's only taxi while the driver knelt in the bushes vomiting.

Much later she told the girls how she bit the umbilical cord, swung the baby upside down, and slapped it till it screamed. Then she wrapped it in her skirt, climbed up to the driver's seat, stuffed the man's jacket between her legs, and stole his taxi. For years, Ana pictured her speeding off in a rusty Ford, her newborn yelling itself purple while she shifted gears and struggled with her afterbirth.

Ava and the tango man hid out in Honolulu's Chinatown, living off the sale of the stripped-down cab. When they were finally arrested, Ben posted bail, Ava was put on probation and he brought her home. The baby, Taxi, was beautiful. But when Rosie bent to lift her little brother, Ava lunged at her.

"Touch him, I break your arm."

The girl stood straight so she and her mother were eye to eye.

"Guarantee. I never again come near your little bastard."

That word again. It was the first time Ana saw her cousin's edge. She saw something else that day. Rosie's walk was becoming obvious. For several years, she had listed slightly, as if her right foot were deprived of a natural heel. Each year the lopsided walk was more pronounced. Ben took her to a foot doctor who found nothing, but an ear specialist said her equilibrium was off. Tiny bones of her inner ear were permanently damaged.

Ana thought of Rosie flying headfirst through a window. She thought of Ava striking Rosie's head with an iron skillet swung like a baseball bat. Rosie's flame-scarred hand that took away her lifeline. Ana crawled into bed and held her.

Though folks in Honolulu called the Wai'anae Coast a "junk kine" life, somewhere in her early years, Ana began to see the forbidding beauty of her land. Slowly, the distant jade mountains and red valleys gained entry to her upcast eyes. The road past her house was paved, but dust lay so thick, it had always seemed a dirt road. Some days she stood on that road, hands on hips, as if barring entry to her valley, her attitude defiant even when neighbors drove by.

She would be a big girl, strong legs, wide, lū'au feet. She would never be a beauty. From her father, she had inherited wide cheekbones and slightly slanted eyes that went from green to brown, like hapu'u ferns. Her hair was black and curly and if not pulled back in a braid, made her look wild, electrified. She had the brown/gold skin and full, pouting lips of a local girl, so in that sense she did not stand out. But there was something in her eyes, always probing, asking why? that made her, even young, seem formidable. What folks remarked upon most were Ana's shoulders. Wide like a boy's, they gave the impression of double pride.

Some days when harsh, sobbing winds dried the membranes of throats, and left eyes gritty and raw, something would break loose inside her. Like a hunter of rain, she would run shouting up Keola Road, hair flying behind her like barbed moss. Boar-hounds—brawny warriors of the back roads— leapt alongside her like dark muscles exploding from the earth. And then the pounding of hooves, the gleaming, sweaty flanks of horses who shook their manes and galloped through meager grass beside her.

She would pass Inez Makiki's house where the Hawaiian flag stood waving in the wind, which meant a newborn baby. The Makikis were full-bloods and flew the original Hawaiian flag, showing a kahili in front of two crossed, pointed paddles, nine red, yellow, and green stripes for the major islands, and one to represent the entire Hawaiian archipelago. Twins ran in that family and folks were waiting for the day Inez would fly two flags.

Ana always slowed down as she passed Uncle Pili's house, an old bachelor who rented beds to field-workers and construction crews. "Dollah a day and suppah." There were eight rooms, two beds to a room, his kitchen so small, the table, chairs, and Frigidaire were chained outside to trees. No phone, no TV, no indoor toilet. For twenty years Pili's rates had stayed the same. Instead, each year he had lowered the wattage in the lightbulbs, leaving the house so dim, folks called his place The Lights-Out Inn.

"Beds fo' sleeping," Pili said. "Folks like read, go library."

Now guests brought their own lightbulbs, and neighbors watched them flickering on as folks screwed them in, and flickering off as folks moved out. With all the in-out traffic, sometimes at dusk the house resembled a mother ship signaling her pods for the final voyage home. As she passed, Ana would wave to Uncle Pili sitting on his porch in a broken-down obstetrics chair retrieved from Angel's Junkyard, his feet propped in the stirrups, his head thrown back, watching the day advance between his legs.

She would huff along, passing dozens of Quonset huts on either side of the road, left over from World War II, when the military occupied the land. Families lived in them now, and some were neat and hung with curtains, even miniature gardens. But some yards looked like dump sites—pyramids of rusted cars, skulls of hog heads, naked, running children, their bodies sequined with flies.

She would pass the chicken farm of the Chinese-Portuguese brothers, Panama and Florentine Chang, and then at the end of Keola Road, where it began to trickle out, Ana would slow down. Here were the turnoffs, de-graded dirt roads that people stayed away from. Down these roads were rusted-out Quonsets long ago condemned, hideouts for the death gangs. Men who dealt serious drugs and kept arsenals of guns. They were seldom seen in daylight, but at night they rumbled, their trucks skidding up and down the road. Gunshots were heard. A body found floating facedown in a feeding trough, nudged back and forth by the snouts of pigs. When police raided the huts, they always found them empty. The gangs had melted far-ther back into the valley.

Sometimes after a long run, Ana would hose herself down, then come in and sit under a big, translucent light globe, watching a gecko warm its belly against the genial glow. She would whisper to the small, transparent thing, observing its internal workings as it digested mosquitoes. She adopted a toad and three stray cats.

Ben shook his head. "This thing with animals, too much. She take that toad to bed with her, make conversation."

"She's lonely," Pua said.

"Why, lonely? She got a house of folks who love her."

"She doesn't have a *mother*. Not the same."

Each time Ana heard that word, a ship eased out of the corner of her eye and into the horizon. She would lie in the raw yellow light of a naked bulb, holding a textbook behind which she studied old snapshots of her mother.

"Maybe she never left the islands."

"What you mean?" Rosie asked.

"Maybe she's in Honolulu. Could be right now she's with some hand-some beachboy, sipping Mai Tais."

Rosie gathered her in her arms. "Ana, when she's ready, she'll come home. She only got one home."

"When she comes back, I'll make her beg."

Leialoha Apo Perkins

"KAMAKA OF MAMALA BAY"

W hen the white man came to the dark man's shores, what he saw was the virgin land that he had always hungered to own in his own old country but that he could never wrest from his masters who were of his own white kind. Among the American Indians, he conquered land by any means at his disposal—first by the gun, and then by his laws, and lastly by the delicacies of his language and arts, until there was nothing left for the American Indian but the isolation and the desert conditions of his reservation where he barely survived and when he survived, barely endured.

Then oil was discovered to rest under the reservation lands, deep below the burial pits of the Indians' dead ancestors. The white man came back, dragging behind him the paraphernalia of his laws and their orders allowing him to claim these reservation lands also as his own, in the name of public domain, the State, the nation, and even the survival of mankind.

Not all white men joined in the conspiracy to defraud and dehumanize the Indians, but enough did so—largely by their silence—to make the name of "pale face" synonymous with treachery. An Indian, captive on his own desert land, was left little but his hatred which, growing in the isolation of his bone dry surroundings, festered into rankling suspicion of all things connected with government, especially that of the people, for the people, and by the people, as the people were seldom, except as as a painful concession, non-white, and seldom, in any widely accepted sense, Indian—in color or in culture.

Some monetary restitutions were made to the American Indians by Congress. But by then the old Indian ways of life were virtually dead.

And the whole grim story of America's native populations awaits upon time to be repeated in the dehumanization and the defrauding of the Hawaiian people who lie the next in line for prey in the State's demand for their lands: But this time the "pale face" includes all intervening shades of color and of cultures.

For there is an avenging spirit that moves over the land like a swarm of locusts descending upon the panini of the arid Hawaiian plains where the Hawaiians have been pushed, with the ocean as the last roadway for escape. The locusts eat everything; green and dead; mature and promising; half maimed and partly recovered. In the Bible, men called such visitations the Lord's means of chastising man for his evil. Today men call such visitations "life" in the process of "the survival of the fittest."

The two fishermen, old friends, worked silently in the descending dark beaching their rowboat on the gleaming gold bar of sand that jutted into

Mamala Bay like a flick of the land's tongue. The sun hung, like a golden amulet, in the sky, and then sank slowly below the horizon. For a while it left behind it a flaming lake of an otherwise pacific ocean.

The two fishermen returned their nets and gear to a shanty where the colony's equipment was stored jointly. The door banged shut when Kamaka, the elder of the two men, finally came out. He dragged behind him the divided catch. He propped them beside the empty oil drums that were used among the shanties' colonists for chairs, tables, and sometimes shelves, as well as for bins for trash. Kamaka walked to the hut where his friends joined him.

"Okolehao." Kamaka said, pushing a tin cup toward his friend. He was proud to have such rare brew for such occasions as the past day's catch although he had also come to like Southern Comfort just as much. His friend sat down with a heavy sigh. He drank from the cup without a word. But when he drew the back of his hand across his mouth, he sighed in a deep throaty way that bore behind it the rattle of a thick cough,

"You go tomorrow?" the friend asked finally. "Or no?"

"Na-a-ah," replied Kamaka thoughtfully.

"If da police come, too much pilikia," Hiroshi, the friend, replied.

"Na-a-ah," was the reply.

"But da Pake judge wen' tell da State dat i's okay if da bull-dozer come. So tomorrow da gov'ment goin' come wit' da police. An-a' dese houses," Hiroshi waved his hand at the curved sweep of shanties that was huddled farther inshore of the sand bar, "goin' get broke down. No can stop 'em, Kamaka. Mo bettah you come live wit' me."

"Nah-a-ah."

"Den w'at you goin' do, den?"

"I goin' stay in diss place until 'i' fa' down . . . " Kamaka looked at the woven coconut leaf roof of the wall-less hut, where the fishermen of the colony sat every morning to study the ocean and sky for predictions of the day's promise of catch. All Kamaka could see were the white, curved driftwood of beams, all suspended together into joints of posts that had been discarded earlier as a legacy of the U.S. military.

Hiroshi said nothing for a while. Then he added, "Da state is Japanee state now, an' you don' know w'at Japanee like, inside, w'en dey no like somet'ing. Mo' bettah you come wit' me, stay wit' my daughter an' me."

In the deepening darkness, Hiroshi could sense a movement like the shaking of Kamaka's head. "You know dat young Hawaiian lawyer dat wen' come visit me last Sunday?" Kamaka asked. His friend nodded. "He tell me many t'ings, Hiroshi. One t'ing he wen' tell me iss dat da Mafia can help us, if we like, he t'ink. But we must go ask first."

"Da Kanaka Mafia!" Hiroshi exclaimed. "W'at you like dat fo'?"

"I no like, but maybe dey like, Hiroshi. Da folks heah say 'Okay, if da udda Hawaiians like help, good. We a' fight, toget'er, 'ohana style. Maybe."

"But, Kamaka, you da leader. You tell 'No!' An' da udda mens follow, fo shuah."

Kamaka shook his head, again, it seemed. Hiroshi could barely make out the gesture except in the quality of the silence. The night had descended too swiftly, too stealthily, like a hawk at prey. Across the waters of Mamala Bay, between the concrete fortresses of high rise buildings, marking the down-town waterfront face of Honolulu, the red traffic lights of Nimitz Highway blinked on and off, tinting the rippling waves a golden red.

"Da lawyer wen' tell me maybe i's okay fo' take Mafia help, because Mafia iss Hawaiian too. Da folks heah t'ink like dat. Hawaiian iss Hawaiian, dey say. We eit'er 'ohana o' we not. If we not, den bettah fo' all us give up," Kamaka paused. "Diss is too big Hiroshi, fo' one man say 'do diss,' o' 'do dat.' Diss decision iss fo' everybody, even kids, if dey fish like us old people. We need fo' somebody help us. Dat fo' shuah. But w'at I no shuah abou' iss who da Mafia really fo' e'en if dey fo' us an e'en if dey like be."

Hiroshi glanced at the rows of kerosene lamps, hung onto the nails of outside posts of the shanties. The lamps cast a pale circle of light on the un-dulating undersides of the corrugated iron ceilings. Shoreward, the harbour waters licked gently at the sandy spit of land on which the colony sat.

"W'en i's time fo' go, da Lord come get me, dass w'at," Kamaka said.

"You no scared?" asked Hiroshi, peering at his friend.

"Oh, shuah," Kamaka laughed. But he laughed as though he were also shrugging in the dark, as one might laugh even while twitching.

"W'at else da lawyer wen' tell you, so dat you no like move fo' not'ing now?" Hiroshi queried.

"Dat da best system fo' gov'ment iss one dat make Hawaiians partners wit' everybody else."

"An' you believe?" Hiroshi laughed wryly. "You don' know Japanee, dass why. I know. Kamaka, dey like haole now."

"Some like haole, not all. Some haole no' like haole. Some Hawaiians like haole, too. But w'at fo' I tell da folks dat? Dey must believe. If dey no believe, we all die fo' shuah. Some like haole, Hiroshi, but not a'."

"Too much, so no use."

"Greedy iss greedy," Kamaka answered. "One way fo' be greedy iss not udda way fo' be greedy, shuah; but greedy iss greedy, w'et'er haole, Japa-nee, Kanaka, o' w'at. W'at difference w'ich kind iss heah, Hiroshi?" Kamaka asked. "Mamala Bay iss Hawaiian kuleana. Keia ko'u one hanau: this sand is my place o' birth. I wen' been born heah. My family bury here: my fadda's white hair (one curl), my first wife fingernails, my t'ree sons' an' my second wife pictures. W'en da law say no can bury da bones heah, I bury da hair, fingernails n' stuff. Like mine goin' be too, maybe soon. I no like go anudda place fo' stay. Heah, diss sand iss my 'ohana land. An' yours too. if vou like go be my guest. because if diss land iss not my land fo' fish from—den w'ere my land fo' fish from? No more land, Hiroshi, if not heah. If I move, tomorrow gov'ment goin' like dat land, too, same as heah. Same t'ing goin' happen all ovah again. So I stay heah. An' da folks heah, now, dey like stay heah too."

"You pa'akiki, fo' shuah," Hiroshi said. "Now I t'ink i's no good you one fisherman."

"No make diff'ence—fisherman, o' taro plant man, o' w'at. If gov'ment like land, it take."

Hiroshi laughed, deeply, resonantly. "Nobody in particular wen' ask fo' dem take diss land fo' dem go build one pa'k heah, so w'at fo' dey like take diss land, ecep' fo' show you an' me dat we not'ing. Da State no got enuf money fo' pay fo' mowin' an' stuff. If dey no mo'e money fo' mow da grass den no mo'e money fo' mow da grass; den no mo'e money fo' weed da bush-es: it on'y get money fo' go broke down yo' house. Den dere's not'ing heah. An' i's all fo' dem. An' i' somet'ing like da 'same t'ing wit' da Kamehameha School: a' da Princess' land fo' da School iss now a'most not'ing, because da State say, 'Go sell 'em, o' we condemn, fo' shuah.' W'at State like iss fo' private kings' an' princess' land go get sold up, so Hawaiians no get not'ing, not even one free school fo' Hawaiian kids wit' a' kinds mixed blood in-side t'em too—no Hawaiians, no not'ing except poor mens, all o' us. Becos if da Biship Estate mus' sell da Kamehameha School land dat da Princess wen' go give in trust fo' one free school fo' Hawaiians, den no mo' ed'cate' Hawaiians left like go fight fo' dere lands. Da gov'ment like tax ev'rybody fo' go show who's boss, who's big shot, like da Lunas in da Plantation days w'en everybody must work fo' da Missionary sons' families an' nobody else, like you an' me remember real good, yeah? Da State iss da Big Time Land Owner. It get plenty land fo' sell da peoples dat like land, fo' build houses on; but it make da Biship Estate and people like you an' me go sell first. Wat it do iss take. Jes' take—take land, everywhere, from you an' me, an' dey say everybody, even w'en nobody go stay askin' fo' one pa'k heah. Da gov'ment iss not you an' me, t'ough dey tell you an' me dat story come vote time. Da gov'ment iss da mens in power, Japanee. Nevah befo' was Hawaiians pushed back in da sea. Da haoles nevah wen' do dat. Nevah. But da mens in power.

"Dey call me one squatter, on my own people's, my own king's land, even if I do not'ing wit' em but fish from. Dey no like one livin' pa'k wit' real Hawaiians.

"Yeah, squatter. Squatter iss one dog, no mo'e house, live on left ovahs.You fish, but dat no count. Who in da gov'ment fish? Nobody care. Dat judge who tell gov'ment okay da land iss fo' da State so dat da State come now fo' bull doze dis place—dat judge no come from fishing people; his kind on'y good fo' cooking. So w'at dey care if fish from you o' somebody else? So gov'ment like t'ink you squat. Maybe dey like you go buy Japan fish, altho' first, you need buy one freezer. Next, you must pay electricity fo' da freezer. So e'en je' t'inking you paying Japanee fisherman, den General Motors, den Hawaiian Electric . . . what da gov'ment like us fo' do iss pay' pay, pay. If no', dey get not'ing. If you go on welfare, den da Federal gov'ment pay some fo' you; dass good, because da State get somet'ing, yeah? If not, you get fish an' land, fo' free, like, an' dey get not'ing. If dey get not'ing, i's no mo'e money in da bank fo' a' dem, an' no mo'e power fo' make mo'e power, fo' make mo' money."

"Hiroshi," Kamaka replied, "I no care if I go on welfare o' not. W'at I no like iss no fish. If I fish, no need I go on welfare. Wat fo? I get fish fo' eat. I no sick. But w'at I goin' do if I no can fish? Like if I taro plant man. If no can plant taro, den do w'at? Fix telephone pole? Fo' w'at? I no need telephone. Fix stove electricity? I no need electricity."

"Dass w'at I say, too," Hiroshi added. Then he laughed ruefully. "Da State mens like da land so bad, dey get da bull dozer fo' go make one trench fo' push you in da ocean. One trench, fo' push you an' dese udda peoples heah in da ocean, maybe fo' you go drown. A' fo' dis small land right heah." Hiroshi peered around him. He could see very little of anything clearly in the night.

"Yeah, dey no let my uncle come take his sick wife go hospital dat morning. Nobody, dey say, can go makai, dis way—on'y peoples can go pas' da trench is us, go mauka, dat way, fo' go off diss land; o' else we go drown, fo' backwards; w'en we fa' in da water, go drown."

"Dass da Big Boss way fo' do, huh? Go bull doze da real people in da ocean like dey dead fish livin' on good land udda peoples need, dey say, fo' pa'k space. Jes like tourists like come Hawai'i fo' see mo'e pa'ks. Dat prove we no primitive mens, yeah? We a' civilize', good for business people come Hawai'i, invest dere moneys. O' maybe da State like fo' you go swim Japan, go fish dere." Hiroshi began to laugh. "So w'at you say, Kamaka: iss dat like one gov'ment dat iss fo' da peoples, by da peoples, of da peoples?" Hiroshi laughed so hard, he began to cough. Coughing fitfully, his laughter came to an end in a spasm of phlegm. He spat at some seemingly vile, invisible thing that lay in the sand at his feet.

Kamaka said nothing in reply. He seemed to be listening to the soft tatting sound of the waters at the far rock bound end of the sand bar. Hiroshi too listened.

"I no can live dat way," Kamaka continued, as though his train of thought had never once faltered or been stopped by intervening arguments. "I no can

work fo' get pay check fo' pay big companies a' my money, like I live fo' work
fo' dem, no' work fo' me live."

"Den w'at you goin' do?" Hiroshi asked. To his ears it was a plea to his
friend.

"I stay on dis land, an' fish."

"You goin' lose, I t'ink."

"Okay, but dass my way fo' lose, not somebody else way. Diss land was
my people's land fo' da king. Befo'e dat, diss was a' my people's land. Wen da
king die, his siste', Queen Lili'uokalani had diss land fo' her fish pond. Den
da Americans, da Planters, wen' lock her up, take her land. Dey said diss land
fo' ev'rybody, fo' a' da people, but w'at dey mean iss: it not fo' Hawaiians.
Jes' fo' udda peoples, Hawaiians wen' get not'ing. Now we like da Queen's
land back— i's our's, way back, we say. Befo'e da Queen, befo'e da King, too.
We leave w'at she wen' sell stay. We on'y want w'at left, fo' fish, fo' plant
taro, fo' live. I's good land fo' fish from, so I fish from. I stay. Da udda folks
stay. Dass my t'inking."

"Den I no goin' come tomorrow," Hiroshi said.

"Yeah, no good come," Kamaka said, simply.

"But I come next day, maybe."

"Yeah, you come next day."

"Maybe diss day was las' day we fish . . . "

"I Mamala Bay, yeah. Maybe las' day fo' us. But good day, yeah?"

"Too good," Hiroshi said. His throat was tight. He started to cough: a
deep, rumbling cough from way down inside his chest that seemed would
never leave him in peace.

The two men had been friends all their lives, since Hiroshi's grandparents, immigrants from Japan, had satisfied their contracts as Plantation laborers and then moved next to Kamaka's grandparents to fish with them.
The day that the two had first met lay now remote and untouchable in memory. When they arose to say goodbye, the moon was white and full.

"In da ol' kahiko loa days," Kamaka said, "One moon like dis mean dere
goin' be one human sacrifice."

Hiroshi was silent a moment. "You da sacrifice," he said, finally, and
walked away so quietly that Kamaka did not realize how he was in fact alone
on the edge of his shore, walled off from the rest of the island by a trench
and a dirt heap, his ocean lapping at his feet. Suddenly, he sensed the presence of his ancestors' spirits and the warmth of his family whose hair (one
curl) and nail pairings were buried, with photographs, in the sand. It was
then that he remembered what some Hawaiian folk had recalled of a prophecy, made by Ka'opulupulu of the death of O'ahu chiefs upon the coming

of foreigners, "Ke one 'ai ali'i o Ka-kuhihewa," the chief devouring sands of Ka-kuhihewa." But with the spirits of his ancestors upon him like a cloak, Kamaka began to sing.

E Hawai'i e, Ku'u one hanau e, ku'u home kulaiwi nei . . .
O Hawai'i, Sands of my birth, my own native home . . .

LEIALOHA APO PERKINS *was born in 1930, into a trilingual family (Hawaiian, Chinese, English), in Lahaina, Maui, Territory of Hawai'i. Her writing is inspired by her early years in Lahaina and Boston, from family life and changing Pacific multicultural ecologies. Perkins' books include* Natural Kingdoms of the Heart; Cyclone Country; The Firemakers; The Oxridge Woman; How the 'Iva Flies; Ancestral Crossing; The Balloon Hearted Whale; *and* The Missing Mo'olelo of 'Ohana Genealogies.

Imaikalani Kalahele

"ODE TO FORT STREET"

when pigs walked
from the harbor
to the ice house

Kalākaua played
at 'Alekoki
and Hawaiians
ruled their
homelands

now

where pigs walk
marble and MacDonald's
obscure the harbor

Kalākaua stands
frozen in bronze
and the missionary
sons are still
inventing history

pigs, pigs, pigs

once they walked
on cloven hooves
up dirt paths

now
they walk
on sidewalks and
wear Italian shoes

Mahealani Perez-Wendt
"KALUA"

I.

Sometimes I imagine
The grey corpses
Of early missionaries
Stirring lustily
In their vaults
Joining in
A rousing rendition
Of "Kalua"
The song from
Bird of Paradise
That Hollywood yarn
Starring bromide white
Deborah Paget
Who conjured up
A native woman
About to be sacrificed
To the great volcano god
By heathen Hawaiians
Somehow it seems fitting
Since missionaries
Brought that pilau
That they should fugue off—
Organist
Choir

Congregation
Included
(This is the night of love
This is the hour of
Kaa-luuuuuu-ah—)

II.

Whenever ma and Auntie Liz
Sang that song
Tutu would scold
A'ole maika'i kela himeni!
Meaning
That song is no good
Or more to the point
That song
Is not Hawaiian
She and the girls
Would kau lei
On the front porch
Of the old house
On Cummins Street
For boat days
Then they would sing
"Ku'u Pua i Paokalani";
"Kamalani o Keaukaha";
And "Kalamaula"—
But the sweet fragrance
Of those long ago gardens
Would soon disappear
Following Deborah Paget
To cinder and ash
Mother
What did you know
How could you know
Sneaking movies
At Kewalo theater
Except to lose
Hawaiian skin, lips, hair, heft—
Hollywood, after all
Wasn't about to save you
From volcano sacrifice.

III.

In the 1940s and '50's
All along Honolulu Harbor
The old Hawaiian stevedores
Would kanikapila
Late into the night
They would gather
At Mokauea
At Kewalo
At Kalia
Lifting sweet harmonies
To ocean, wind, stars
This was before
Walter Dillingham dredged
Caul and skull
Crushed and cured
For pavement
This was before
His asphyxiate tar
Blackened everything
This was before
Union bosses
Buried dissidents
In hotel footings
Then called in the kahu
To bless them
This was when Waikiki
Was ringed with loko i'a
And throw nets filled with
'Ahole hole, 'anae, a'ama
Were commonplace
Those days
Must have been sweet.

Haunani-Kay Trask
"RACIST WHITE WOMAN"

I could kick
your face, puncture
both eyes.

You deserve this kind
of violence.

No more vicious
tongues, obscene
lies.

Just a knife
slitting your tight
little heart

for all my people
under your feet

for all those years
lived smug and wealthy

off our land
parasite arrogant

A fist
in your painted
mouth, thick

with money
and piety

and a sworn
black promise

to shadow
your footsteps

until the hearse
of violence

comes home
to get you.

Haunani-Kay Trask
"PŪOWAINA: FLAG DAY"

for Kaʻiana, Lākea, Mililani, Hulali, and Kalaiʻolaʻa

Bring ginger, yellow
and white, broken stalks
with glossy leaves.

> Bring lei *hulu,*
> *palapalai, pīkake.* Bring
> *kapa,* beaten fine

> > as skin. Bring
> > the children
> > to chant

> > > for our dead,
> > > then stand
> > > with the *lāhui*

> > > > and burn
> > > > their American
> > > > flag.

Monica A. K. Kaiwi
"HEY, HAOLE LADY ... "

I
Hey, haole lady with your token Hawaiian in a head lock
    what do you mean,
      "being Hawaiian is the color of your heart?"
Do you feel the tug,
    push and pull of your kupuna through your naʻau?
Are you driven
    by a sense of obligation
    and responsibility to your people?

Do you rage
    and ache at the pain
    of the ʻāina and nā ʻōiwi?

    being Hawaiian is not skin or heart
    It is iwi and ʻuhane
        connecting me to my kupuna,
my moʻokū ʻauhau,
my heritage given by birth . . .
    not for sale to anyone.

II.
Hey, haole lady who wants to be Hawaiian
what do you mean I need
to "do" my incantations
to "pray" to the shark god
to protect us from all the man-eating sharks in the Kaiwi Channel
to put lākī in my bathing suit in order to win the race?

Keep your foolish superstitions to yourself
    and don't blame
    your ignorance
        on my ancestors.

MONICA A. K. KAIWI, *born in 1961, wrote her poem, "Hey, Haole Lady . . ." in 1998, while working on her MA in English at the University of Auckland, New Zealand. She currently resides in Kahaluʻu on Oʻahu.*

Naomi Clarke Losch
"BLOOD QUANTUM"

We thought we were Hawaiian
Our ancestors were Liloa, Kualiʻi and Alapaʻi.
We fought at Mokuohai, Kepaniwai and Nuʻuanu,
And we supported Liliʻulani in her time of need.
We opposed statehood.
We didn't want to be the 49th or the 50th,
And once we were, 5(f) would take care of us.
But what is a native Hawaiian?

Aren't we of this place?
'O ko mākou one hānau kēia.'
And yet, by definition we are not Hawaiian.
We can't live on Homestead land,
Nor can we receive OHA money.
We didn't choose to quantify ourselves,

1/4 to the left	1/2 to the right
3/8 to the left	5/8 to the right
7/16 to the left	9/16 to the right
15/32 to the left	17/32 to the right

They not only colonised us, they divided us.

NAOMI CLARKE LOSCH *was born in 1945 in Kahuku, a sugar plantation community in rural O'ahu, where she received her early education. She graduated from Kamehameha School for Girls in Honolulu, then completed a BA in anthropology and MA in Pacific Islands Studies at the University of Hawai'i at Mānoa, where she is an associate professor of Hawaiian. She has taught Hawaiian language and culture at the university level for over thirty years.*

Rodney Morales
from WHEN THE SHARK BITES

I t was almost vertical, the climb. I did what Manny did. I hung on tightly to rocks, hanging on to roots that stuck out like the roots of the orchid plants Grandma and Grandpa Wong used to grow. I would check first if they might be loose, all the time thinking *What the fuck am I doing? What the fuck am I doing here?*

After several minutes of scary climbing, I saw Manny standing on this ledge above me. He reached down and pulled me up like I weighed nothing. There was just enough room to sit, catch our breath. Manny then moved this boulder that appeared unmovable, unless you had a backhoe. Manny pushed it aside like it was papier-mâché. Turns out the boulder was hollowed out on one side, and not as heavy as it looked. But shit, it wasn't light either.

I was looking at a dark crevice, one that seemed to end right away. But that was part of the deception. I watched Manny as he moved another rock, revealing a low and very dark tunnel.

For the next few minutes we crawled. Ate dirt, I tell you. Wasn't scary, what I saw, was more of a revelation. I guess I shouldn't say more. There's been enough of this stuff on the news. And I tell you, man, by the time we crawled out, put the hollowed-out boulder back, and climbed our way down, when I looked up at the cliff and saw the precarious rock formation, I knew the earth was telling me something. And I knew I had to start paying attention.

We sat down on some boulders and drank water from a container that Manny had stashed up there. Then Manny started talking like he had never talked before.

"When I was a kid," he began, "I lived in Wai'anae for a while. Like you, I was into the ocean, I had no idea that all this stuff existed. And I don't jes' mean the caves and shit, but all the military facilities. Then my family moved to Wahiawa. Schofield Barracks, even though it was a few blocks away, it didn't exist for me. I was too preoccupied with getting out to Hale'iwa every day, hitchhiking with my board. Jes' had to get to where the surf was breaking.

"Then I got this job. I was in high school then, needed pocket cash 'cause my folks weren't giving it to me. The only jobs available were, da kine, busboy, dishwasher, or groundskeeper. Minimum-wage jobs. I figured if I'm gonna work for shit, it may as well be outdoors, so I applied for and got this groundskeeping job. It was at Schofield Barracks. So I became part of the grounds crew there. I used to mow the officers' lawns, water the endless trees. After a while I figured out that jes' about everybody in the crew had places where they could hide out and jes' cruise. I used to hang with this guy, Tommy LaBenz. He was a year younger than me. We used to hide out near the firing ranges. Nobody would ever think to look for us there. Sometimes we'd wander around. I liked the head of my crew, this guy Manuel Salcedo. Old Filipino man. Funny guy. He had a rascal smile, and always wore an L.A. Dodgers cap. He'd always make sure we did some work at least. But after a while he would go to *his* hideout and leave us to our wits.

"Sad thing is, two weeks before he was gonna retire and start collecting that pension he had worked all his life for, he sat at a bus stop on California Avenue. It was his day off; he was catching the bus to town, as he always did. Then all of a sudden this car came flying down the avenue—the brakes had failed—and it jes' crashed into the bus stop. I heard Manuel died instantly.

"If that wasn't bad enough, a few months after that Tommy and some of his cousins were goofing around at Nu'uanu Pali. They had found an abandoned grocery cart up there and were taking turns pushing each other around in it. I guess they lost control of it when it was Tommy's turn to ride, 'cause over he went. Over the fucking Pali. Shit. One more warrior gone.

"This was hard to take, I tell you. I was sixteen, going on seventeen—about the same age as you. I remember being bummed for the longest time, wondering what it all meant. Wondering if there was any justice in the world. I was still working at Schofield. I started going off-road, after doing my usual two-three hours of work, traveling among the trees. All that time I didn't even know that the main road in Schofield, Trimble Road, became Kolekole Road as it went through the Waiʻanae Range, then became Lualualei Naval Road, which took you all the way to Farrington Highway, Nanakuli side. That blew me away. Made me start readjusting the maps in my head. The lay of the land was so intriguing I began to wander all over the damn place. Got to know the area like nobody else. Found so many hiding places. Knew where I could pick fruit, berries, if I got hungry." Manny looked around. "Learned how to survive out here."

"Thass how you found this cave?"

"Well, not exactly. I would say the cave found me. One day I saw this old man. Another old man. And funny, he had the same kinda walk as Manuel, a slow, easy-going lope. I was curious, wondering what he could be doing on military land that was so out of the way. So I followed him. At first I was real careful. I watched him struggle to climb the same cliff we just climbed. One time he slipped, almost fell down. I thought, shit, what if he fall? He gon' die out here, all alone.

"So I walked to the bottom of the cliff and said, 'Papa, you need help?'

"He wen' look down, saw me, and said, 'It's about time.'

"It's about time," Manny repeated. "So he showed me the place I jes' showed you. And that was that. After that, I would always look for him, especially around the area of the cave, but—" Manny shrugged, holding his palms out. "So I jes' figured I would never see him again. I tell you, I wasn't about to enter that cave alone.

"Then one day, when I was near this very spot, I heard a scream. A woman's scream. I ran toward the road and saw this girl being pulled out of this car, being attacked by three guys. Crew-topped grunts. Without thinking I just charged. I was seventeen. I thought I could kick ass. Especially haole ass. I hit this one guy so hard he fell back into the bush. Then I charged this other guy, to tackle him, and we both went down. That was my mistake. While I was down wrestling him the third guy stabbed me on the side. I rolled over in pain. I was on my back when he came toward me. I kicked him in the nuts as hard as I could and he dropped the knife. I reached for the knife but the shithead I had knocked into the bushes stepped on my arm and *he* grabbed the knife. He went nuts, man. He started swinging the knife real wild, cutting my arms, my legs, my chest. . . . The girl—the third guy was holding her—she was screaming the whole time. Then the guy with the knife stabbed my arm and hit an artery. Shit, my blood started shooting up, like a fricken geyser. Then he kicked me in the throat and I started choking, gasping for air. At that point they panicked. They grabbed the girl—her clothes were all torn up—dragged her in the car and took off."

Holy fucking shit.

"I was losing blood fast. I tore off my t-shirt and tied my upper arm. I figured that was my only hope. At first it didn't seem to work. Blood kept shooting out, in spurts. So I made the tourniquet tighter. I was dizzy already. And then finally the blood stopped. Then I felt the agony of the other stab wound, the big slice along my hip."

"So it wasn't a shark," I said.

Manny looked me in the eye. "I showed you my shark wound. Now I'm telling you how I got the rest." He took a deep breath.

"Then I lost consciousness. Next thing I knew, the old man, that same old man, was treating my wounds. He was using what I thought was juice from the cactus, but was probably aloe. He nursed me, stayed with me for two days in the hills, using his shirt to keep me warm at night. The nights were fucking *cold*, I tell you. He gave me some stuff to drink. Some kind of tea he made. I tell you, it knocked me out. Then—I guess this was the third day—I woke up and he was gone. I thought he had left me there and thought I would never see him again. Thought I would die and join Manuel and Tommy. I was already thinking, gee, that wouldn't be too bad."

Manny cleared his throat, then drank some water. "Turns out he had gone back to wherever he lived and put some wheels on this paddleboard that he dragged all the way up here. It took a lot out of him. I mean, we're talking about a guy who's at least eighty years old. Man, he looked so wiped out.

"He lifted me up, asked me if I could walk. Every step was pain, but we got to the road. I almost shit when I saw the road again, thinking what if those guys came back, checking to make sure I was dead? Anyway, he strapped me to this paddleboard on wheels, tied himself to the board, and used his own body for drag. Imagine that, this old guy pulling against the downhill grade, easing me down the hill. For over four miles."

Manny stopped. Closed his eyes, pinching the bridge of his nose with his thumb and index finger.

"By the time we got to the bottom he was in worse shape then I was, and we still had a ways to go. We crashed for the night in the bushes. The next morning, we hiked the rest of the way, me limping, him dragging his legs. Finally we got to his house. It's that dilapidated shack near my bus. Thass where I recuperated.

"His house. Now that was something. Could tell right away he was a fisherman. He had throw nets all over the place. He told me that he had lived in that same spot for about thirty years, which was when the U.S. Army chased his family out of Mākua. You know, so they could practice their bombing. I tell you, this guy had ancestral ties to the whole Wai'anae Coast. I learned later that after his wife died, his children all split. They all went to live in Honolulu, or to one of the other islands. One of them moved to Vegas. None of them wanted to live the life of a fisherman-farmer.

"He kept giving me this tea he made, from I don't know what. He was an herb gatherer too, the way I figure. Anyway, whatever it was he was giving me knocked me out. Seems I slept for days. An' from time to time I would wake up—I couldn't shake off the drowsiness—an' I would hear this humming sound. Really weird. I would feel this tingly feeling on my skin. The lightest breeze would sting. Of course, it turns out he had been tattooing me. He was using India ink and this gun that was powered by a generator. Mind you, I learned later on that he was expert at carving designs into wood. Not bodies. I was his living, breathing guinea pig. When I recovered he told me that he wanted to create a network of tattoos to disguise my scars. He said I was too young to go around so disfigured. Now, of course, I'm a different kind of marked man.

"The old man also told me he wanted the tattoos to tell a story—one he wouldn't divulge, of course. He jes' said I'll figure it out in time. He said because of this scar—" Manny pointed to a diagonal scar on his chest opposite his heart—"he chose to invert and elongate the usual konane design that warriors wore on the left side of their chests. So instead of a checkerboard look it would be more diamond-shaped. The arm stuff is warrior bands, with a shark teeth motif. Supposed to protect me in the water." He smirked and snorted. "On my legs, birds in flight. Note there's one solo bird."

"What about the stuff on your back?" Those jagged lines, moving out from the center. They didn't seem to fit.

"What stuff?" Manny twisted his head, like he was trying to see what was on his back.

"You kidding me, right?"

He just stared at me for a moment. Then he had this look, like he was remembering something, speaking more softly. "While the old man did all this tattooing he got weaker and weaker, and funny, I was getting stronger and stronger. I began to wonder if this was his intention. And I wondered if he had willed himself to live only long enough to finish the task. But that kinda thinking, I don't know. Like I'm supposed to be special. I was a nobody.

"Anyway, by the time he was finished tattooing me he was too sick to eat. Then he started puking blood. He had an old car, a '59 Impala—yeah, the same one. I had the hardest time getting the engine to turn. When I finally got it going, I drove him to the hospital. The diagnosis was cancer. Terminal. The doctor said it had spread through his body."

Manny stood up. "Oh fuck, 'nuff a this shit."

I nodded. Manny offered me one more swallow from the plastic container. I drank. Then he drank.

We walked a bit and came to a road. It was bordered by the same kind of barbed-wire-topped, chain-link fences we had seen almost two hours earlier. I didn't make the connection at first, but slowly realized that this was the same road.

It was *the* road.

Manny slipped on his shoes. "We're gonna run this. You think you can handle? Four miles, downhill all the way." It sounded far, but I nodded. "I'll race you down," he said after he tied his laces, and took off.

Oh man, who woulda thought it would be so much fun. The road was so fucking steep. I couldn't stop my legs, man. Shit, we were flying. The wind blasted our faces. It wasn't even work. I bet we were doing four-minute miles, easy. Just flying downhill. We got to the bottom in no time. At that point Manny looked at me and cracked up. I must've had a shit-eating grin on my face.

Back in the bus, Manny pulled a 7-Up out of his icebox. Boy, after all that climbing and running and walking, it hit the spot. I finished the can so fast that Manny threw me another one.

Manny didn't seem tired at all, as he drank slowly from a bottle of Michelob.

"That's my training," he said, "the run back. My favorite run, though, is through Ka'ena Point."

"Man, that area's pretty treacherous. Not my idea of fun."

"You want fun? Try it with a flashlight at night. Plus, think of how much quicker you can get to the North Shore than if you drive around the Wai'anae Range."

"But that only takes you to Mokulē'ia. You still got a ways to go to get to Hale'iwa, let alone 'Ehukai."

"It's still a lot quicker to run to Mokulē'ia than it is to drive around the whole damn mountain range."

"I guess."

"So the old man died?"

Manny closed his eyes and nodded.

"His bones up there, too?" I got chicken skin, thinking about what I had seen earlier.

Manny shook his head. He was pretty quiet now, but it wasn't weird. Then he said, "His family had him cremated. I was a stranger. I had no say in the matter. . . . You know, funny, I jes' remembered. He had all these phonograph albums—78 rpm. You know what I'm talking about?"

"Yeah, the speed. Our player only get 45 and 33."

"What, in the age of CDs you guys play albums?"

"My dad's stuff. He no like get rid of 'om."

"He had all these old records. Old Hawaiian stuff, jazz, blues. He used to play these tunes while working on me with his tattoo gun. The needle on his player used to skip a lot, it was so old."

"Maybe he used it as a tattoo needle."

"Yeah, right. You really one clown. . . . Anyway, later on, after he died, I tried to find a needle to replace it, but no electronics place carried something that ancient. Then, in the army, I learned how to make one myself."

I was stunned. "You were in the army?"

"Surprised?"

"Yeah."

"Well, when you're eighteen, and you got no future, and somebody's telling you to be all that you can be. . . . The real reason is, I wanted to get those guys."

"Who? Oh, you mean the guys who—"

Manny nodded. "Nothing like a stint in army intelligence to get the information you need."

"Holy shit. You was one soldier."

"That wasn't the initial plan. I was really fricken naive in those days. After I recovered—thanks to the old man—I went to press charges. I talked to this lawyer, supposedly a family friend. All I learned was that I wasn't supposed to be on military property. *I* was the trespasser. So I got no help.

"But I remembered certain things about the car. I remembered the model, the California license plate. And, of course, I remembered the girl. . . . Through some family contacts with the police station, I learned that she had pressed charges. But what the military often does, I found out, is relocate soldiers who commit criminal acts on civilians. You fuck with your fellow soldiers, you're brought up for court-martial. You fuck with civilians, you get a vacation in some other part of the world. You fuck with dark-skinned civilians—" He paused. "I need more beer." He pulled another Michelob out of the icebox. It was his third bottle.

"So did you find them?"

Manny finished a long sip, then said, "Took me awhile, but I caught up with them, one by one. Second Lieutenant Nelson was the easiest to find. He was still on this island. Had married a local girl. He used to beat up on her. So she left him. I beat the shit out of him. Broke his jaw and a couple of his fingers. Fucking weak bastard when it comes to picking on someone his own size.

"Corporal Montero, same thing, though I had to go to fucking Oklahoma to track him down. I broke his fingers too . . .

"Now the guy I really wanted was Olvey. PFC Martin J. Olvey. The guy who cut me up. Fucking U.S. Army couldn't control that guy. They had kicked him out. Fuck, even those baby killers didn't wanna be associated with a scumbag like him.

"Him I woulda killed, I know I would've. You see, I had set out to kill all three, but found that I didn't have it in me—the killer instinct. But this guy Olvey, I could've. He had a record of felonies a page and a half long. Rapes, thefts, burglaries, assault and battery, you name it.

"Know where I found him?"

I shrugged.

Manny snickered. "In jail. Fucking guy was already in jail. Plus, he was in a fucking wheelchair. The story goes, he broke into the *wrong* house. The guy who lived in it was a card-carrying member of the NRA. He shot Olvey twice, once when he was turning to flee. Hit him right in the spine. Olvey's crippled for life. And serving life, for his catalogue of crimes.

"I went to see him, you know. Convinced the authorities that I was a relative passing through. I watched as they wheeled him in. He had no idea who I was. I told him I was the fucking ghost of Christmas past. I told him he was a lucky son-of-a-bitch. . . . And you know what he said?"

"What he said?"

"He said, 'I don't know who the fuck you are, but I wish you *would* do me in. Be a lot better than living like this in this shithole.'

"I opened my shirt, to show him the scars, but the fucker only paid attention to the tattoos. I told him, 'I hope you live a fucking *long* life, motherfucker,' and then I left."

"He didn't know who you was?"

"Fucker had no clue."

"Hard fo' imagine you being one soldier."

Manny was in his own world, staring ahead, muttering. "I was seventeen when it happened. The girl, I dunno, sixteen? You don't do shit like that to people and get away with it." Then he suddenly snapped out of it. "Hey, getting late, eh?"

I looked at my watch. "Holy shit! I gotta get home!"

Manny snickered. "Shit is right. Ay-ya, kid gon' be grounded again." He pulled out a cell phone from his backpack.

Wayne Kaumualii Westlake
"NATIVE HAWAIIAN"

how we spose
feel Hawaiian anymoa
barefeet buying smokes
in da seven
eleven stoa . . . ?

WAYNE KAUMUALII WESTLAKE (1947-1984) *produced a substantial body of poetry. He broke new ground as a concrete poet, translated Taoist classical literature and Japanese haiku, and interwove perspectives from his Hawaiian heritage into his writing and art. His work appeared locally, regionally and internationally in small press publications and anthologies.* WESTLAKE: Poems by Wayne Kaumualii Westlake *will be published in 2008.*

Imaikalani Kalahele
"HUI KAU"

Sitting on the beach
with the sunset reflecting
on his weathered face

A son of this land

Playing with the change
he hustled that day
from bottles and cans

(He thinks to himself.)

Saimin at 7-11 . . . maybe
musubi at the liquor store
Oh, the hell with it
Maybe one "40"

With his house on his back
and looking for a place for the night
he sits lost in thought

When the sound of
the shore break was
interrupted by a voice from
the shadows

WHAT YOU DOING HEA!
What?
BRA, WHAT YOU DONG HEA?
Nothing!
THEN WEA YOU FROM?
Me?
YEAH, BRA, YOU! WEA YOU FROM?

Me, I from hea!
FROM HEA? OH, THEN WEA YOUR HOUSE?
House? Bra, I no more house!
    YOU NO MORE HOUSE!
No! This my house. He point to his tent on his backpack
    THEN YOU NEVER SEE THE SIGN, HUH?
No! What sign?
    THE SIGN SAY "NO SQUATTERS"
    YOU KNOW WHAT THAT MEAN?
    THAT MEAN NO HOMELESS GUYS
    LIKE YOU, BRA

Whoa Bra, I no more HOUSE, Bra! That's all!
You know what?
From the time when Kane and Kanaloa
first made Awa ova hea
this was my HOME!

When Kamohoalii brought Pele
I was hea already

Us guys was home
wen we saw Captain Cook
get off the boat

And wen Kamehameha
started his rampage
from Kohala to Oʻahu
we were hiding in the mountains

We saw Ka'ahumanu
burn the ki'i
and disrupt the temples
and cried when Liholiho
broke the Kapu
and lost out at the Great Māhele

And when the whalers
wen come, it was
our sisters that ended up
on the streets and in the bars

Then, wen the sugar guys come
mega farming plantations
thirsty plantations
relocating lands, water and people
we the ones with no jobs
mo easy bring in cheap labor

But had problems! New guys
New kine ma'i
And again was us guys
that carried most of that kaumaha
It was our children, our mothers, our grandmothers,
Our ancestors were the ones when make

No jobs, no land, new kine economy
We when come ova hea, Honolulu
from Hōnaunau to Kapa`a
to Maunakea and Smith streets
From lo'i to the slums
looking for a job

Heart diseases, TB, asthma
high blood pressure and cancer
leprosy, alcohol, obesity and drugs
A people lost in their own home
    Huikau!
Lost in the shuffle

High rent. Low wages, no place to go
    Huikau, yeah!

Lost in the shuffle
No can live in the mountain
No can live on the beach
    Huikau, yeah!
Lost in the shuffle
    Huikau, yeah!

Now look,
hea we are
two Hawaiians
You! Questioning me
about wea I from
and Me! Looking
fo a place to put down
fo the night
Huikau, yeah!

Because, you see, bra, I not Homeless!
I Houseless, bra!
Huikau, yeah!
And, what about you, bra?
Wea you from?
Wat you doing here, bra?

Huikau!
Huikau!
Huikau!

Auwe!
Auwe ka Maoli!
Auwe ka Maoli o ka pae āina!

Joe Balaz
"MOE'UHANE"

I dream of
the ways of the past—

I cannot go back.

I hike the hills
and valleys of Wahiawā,
walking through crystal
        streams
and scaling green cliffs.

I play in the waves
        of Waimea
and spear fish
from the reefs of Kawailoa.

I grow bananas, 'ulu
        and papayas,
in the way of the 'āina.

I cannot go back—

I never left.

Jerry Santos
"KU'U HOME O KAHALU'U"

I remember days when we were younger
We used to catch 'o'opu in the mountain stream
'round the Ko'olau hills we'd ride on horseback
So long ago, it seems it was a dream
Last night I dreamt I was returning
And my heart called out to you
But I fear you won't be like I left you
Me ke aloha ku'u home o Kahalu'u

I remember days when we were wiser
When our world was small enough for dreams
You have lingered there my sister
And I no longer can it seems

Last night I dreamt I was returning
And my heart called out to you
But I fear I am not as I left you
Me ke aloha ku'u home o Kahalu'u

Change is a strange thing, it cannot be denied
It can help you find yourself, or make you lose your pride
Move with it slowly as on the road we go
Please do not hold on to me, we all must go alone

I remember days when we were smiling
When we laughed and sang the whole night long
And I will greet you as I find you
With the sharing of a brand new song
Last night I dreamt I was returning
And my heart called out to you
To please accept me as you'll find me
Me ke aloha ku'u home o Kahalu'u

JERRY SANTOS *was born Gerald K. Santos on June 23, 1951 in Honolulu and raised on the Windward side of O'ahu. The youngest of nine children, he attended Waiahole Elementary School, Kamehameha Schools, the University of Hawai'i, and Kapi'olani Community College. Best known for his work in the musical group Olomana, he is an award-winning singer and songwriter whose career in island entertainment has spanned almost four decades.*

Plop! Rain dropping on my roof,

creating a waterfall down my window.

Around
the Island

Every place has its own wisdom . . . Honolulu late night . . . Chinatown herbs . . . Lion dancing . . . Mōʻiliʻili cats . . . Mānoa bus ride . . . Kalihi hypocrite . . . Bird of paradise . . . Wild yellow ginger . . . Rainbows on the old battleground . . . Windward weather . . . Mango trees in Waipiʻo . . . Hushed bamboo . . . Honeycreepers . . . A Haleʻiwa fisherman . . . Shorebreak . . . The goddess Hiʻiaka at Hāʻena . . . Mākua, still Iz . . .

Michael Ondaatje
UNTITLED

Every place has its own wisdom. Come.
Time we walked about the sea,
the long waves
          'trapped around islands'

MICHAEL ONDAATJE *is the author of the novels* In the Skin of a Lion; The English Patient; *and* Anil's Ghost. *His other books include* Running in the Family; Coming Through Slaughter; The Cinnamon Peeler; *and* Handwriting. *His new book is* Divisadero. *Ondaatje was born in Sri Lanka and came to live in Canada in 1962. He lives in Toronto.*

Author Unknown
"HENEHENE KOU 'AKA"

Henehene kou 'aka
Kou le'ale'a paha
He mea ma'a mau ia
For you and I

Ka'a uila mākēneki
Hō'oni'oni kou kino
He mea ma'a mau ia
For you and I

I Kaka'ako mākou
'Ai ana i ka pipi stew
He mea ma'a mau ia
For you and I

I Waikīkī mākou
'Au ana i ke kai
He mea ma'a mau ia
For you and I

I Kapahulu mākou
'Ai ana i ka līpoa
He mea ma'a mau ia
For you and I

Our eyes have met
Our lips not yet
But oh, you sweet thing
I'm gonna get you yet

Ha'ina mai ka puana
Kou le'ale'a paha
He mea ma'a mau ia
For you and I

"YOUR LAUGHTER IS SO TEASING"

Your laughter is so teasing
That seems to be your delight
It's the usual thing
For you and I

The streetcar jiggles
and jolts your body
It's the usual thing
For you and I

We were at Kaka'ako
Eating beef stew
It's the usual thing
For you and I

We were at Waikīkī
Swimming in the sea
It's the usual thing
For you and I

We were at Kapahulu
Eating līpoa seaweed
It's the usual thing
For you and I

Our eyes have met
Our lips not yet
But oh, you sweet thing
I'm gonna get you yet

The story is told
It's your delight, it seems
It's the usual thing
For you and I

TRANSLATED BY PUAKEA NOGELMEIER

J. Kokolia and Solomon Hiram
"SASSY"

Kaikamahine no Iwilei lā
Sassy hoʻi kāu lewa ʻana
Ua maʻa wale i ka ʻai ʻalamihi lā
Sassy hoʻi kāu lewa ʻana

Kaikamahine no Kalihi lā
Sassy hoʻi kāu lewa ʻana
Ua maʻa wale i ka inu pia lā
Sassy hoʻi kāu lewa ʻana

Kaikamahine no Kapālama lā
Sassy hoʻi kāu lewa ʻana
Ua maʻa wale i ka ʻai laiki lā
Sassy hoʻi kāu lewa ʻana

Kaikamahine no Kakaʻako lā
Sassy hoʻi kāu lewa ʻana
Aia i ka papa ABC lā
Sassy hoʻi kāu lewa ʻana

Wahine haole no ka Moana Hōkele lā
Sassy hoʻi kāu lewa ʻana

'Elua kālā me ka hapalua lā
Sassy hoʻi kāu lewa ʻana

Kaikamahine no Waikīkī lā
Sassy hoʻi kāu lewa ʻana
Ua maʻa wale i ke ʻai līpoa lā
Sassy hoʻi kāu lewa ʻana

Kaikamahine no Waiʻalae lā
Sassy hoʻi kāu lewa ʻana
Ua maʻa wale i ke kau ʻēkake lā
Sassy hoʻi kāu lewa ʻana

Haʻina ʻia mai ana ka puana lā
Sassy hoʻi kāu lewa ʻana
Ua maʻa wale i ke kau ʻēkake lā
Sassy hoʻi kāu lewa ʻana

"SASSY"

Girl of Iwilei
Sassy straying
Always eating black crabs
Sassy straying

Girl of Kalihi
Sassy straying
Always drinking beer
Sassy straying

Girl of Kapālama
Sassy straying
Always eating rice
Sassy straying

Girl of Kakaʻako
Sassy straying
There in the ABC class
Sassy straying

White woman of the Moana Hotel
Sassy straying

Two dollars and a half
Sassy straying

Girl of Waikīkī
Sassy straying
Always eating seaweed
Sassy straying

Girl of Wai'alae
Sassy straying
Always riding a donkey
Sassy straying

Tell the refrain
Sassy straying
Always riding a donkey
Sassy straying

TRANSLATED BY PUAKEA NOGELMEIER

Joseph Stanton
"DRIVING THROUGH LATE-NIGHT DOWNTOWN HONOLULU"

suggested by the cityscapes of Ka-Ning Fong

1. Agree with the Night

It is best
it agree with the night
because the night is teeming
with light
and there is no other way
to see it.

2. Steal Away

Sometimes we stumble upon
bus-stop compulsions

at intersections
on the edge
or beyond,
where Faustian scenarios
make light
of all
their arrangements.

3. Promises in the Dark

There are alleys
through darknessess
between urban cliffs
that seem to lead
by sleight of light
to dream visions
of long-gone childhoods
that will,
when we get there,
be backdoors to bars
or worse.

4. Orpheus's Glance

Orpheus's glance—
though it has,
now,
a thousand eyes—
leaves
the woman without a shadow
to fall back
into the urlight of dawn.

5. Bluer than Midnight

At this hour
the palette inclines to saxophone.
Dreaming it is green
that makes people confess
and playing a floating
dark-note trill—

an idea leans,
lost or lonely or both,
against walls
down narrow passages
between tall buildings,
bluer than midnight.

JOSEPH STANTON'S *books of poems include* A Field Guide to the Wildlife of Suburban
O'ahu; Cardinal Points; *and* Imaginary Museum. *His poems have appeared in such journals
as* Poetry; Harvard Review; *and* Bamboo Ridge. *Among his other books are* Stan Musial; The
Important Books; *and* A Hawai'i Anthology. *A winner of the Elliot Cades Award for Literature, he has lived in Hawai'i since 1972.*

Susan Lee St. John
"GETTING GROCERIES"

On Saturdays we drive
our red Chevy
to Maunakea St.
Chinatown.
First the herbalist
in his dark room
Rows of drawers
filled with crumbling plants
lizard bile
desiccated bat eyes
wanting water for rebirth.
His brass balance
tarnished and still
in the stagnant air.

Three dirty old men
sit on a sidewalk bench
One pretends to read
a Chinese newspaper.
Don't look at them
my sister whispers.

They'll spit on you.
Hurry up, mama says.
We walk on the far edge
looking straight ahead.

Fermented duck eggs
fuzzy winter melon, gingko nuts
salted black beans
Let's have hamburger,
I say.
Shut up, mama says.

At Young's Noodle Factory
young women, gleaming with sweat,
swirl a white batter
over metal sheets,
shove them in a huge steamer.
We buy jee cheong fun:
glistening layers, folded
and wrapped
in butcher paper.
Across the street
a flashing marquee.
BOYS WILL BE GIRLS REVUE.
Mahus, mama says
under her breath.
One waves an emerald silk
handkerchief at us
Another in gold brocade
pouts full red lips.
I watch mama's face.
Be quiet and keep walking
she says.

SUSAN LEE ST. JOHN, *born in 1956, lives in Kailua, O'ahu, with her husband, Robert, and their three children, Eliot, Madeline, and Sam. Her poems and short stories have appeared in* Bamboo Ridge *and* Calyx. *She has had short plays and monologues produced by the Honolulu Theatre for Youth. She currently teaches at Le Jardin Academy.*

Zoe Wang
"DANCE TO THE RHYTHM OF CHINATOWN"

Lions prancing, jumping, climbing
fun to watch

Firecrackers
leaping, spinning for good luck

People
old ones shuffling slow and slower
young ones stomping, bumping in a rush

Cats
creeping, sneaking, slipping into shadows

Zoe
arms swinging
legs dancing
shoes clicking, tapping
as I dance to the rhythm of Chinatown

ZOE WANG, *born in 1996, wrote this poem because whenever it is Chinese New Year in Honolulu, she and her family go to Chinatown and watch the lion dancers, hear the drums and the firecrackers, and watch the fireworks. She would like to thank her third grade teacher, Mrs. Ueda.*

———————— •◦• ————————

Sue Cowing
"LION DANCER"

Ever since Kevin was almost three
he's known for sure what he wanted to be:
a dancing lion in Chinatown
who rears up and swallows the red money down
and flutters his lashes and shakes his fur
to the clang of gongs in the smoky blur
from fireworks popping around his feet
as he prowls down Maunakea Street.

He always pictured himself as the head,
but he wound up being the tail instead
of the smallest lion owned by his group.
The whole time he's dancing, he has to stoop
and follow Keoki wherever he goes
(and jump to the side to protect his toes).
Though he hears people shouting, *Kung Hee Fat Choy!*,
Kevin's missing the fun. He's the back-up boy.

He sees mostly his feet. When they go round a bend,
he has to watch out for Keoki's rear end.
Kevin knows he is lucky and shouldn't grumble.
They say it's a good thing in life to be humble.
But shouldn't Keoki be learning that too,
instead of hogging the lion's-head view?

SUE COWING *has lived in Honolulu since 1961. Her poems have appeared in* Bamboo Ridge; Sister Stew; Chaminade Literary Review; *and several mainland journals, including* Virginia Quarterly Review *and* Cricket. *She has published two Po'okela Award–winning books:* Fire in the Sea: an Anthology of Poetry and Art; *and* My Dog Has Flies: Poetry for Hawai'i's Kids.

Frank Stewart

"CHINATOWN"

At every stroke of rain
The half-eaten, pre-war walls sag
Into becoming a pond of sticks and slag.
The roaches with their backs like battered
Thumbnails are everywhere; and they, like us,
Are concerned but systematic. They are used to rain
Falling through nights that are not black for them
But only wet. The sludge, after all, can be forded.
And if the retreat is made without panic, if there is
Some grace to be salvaged, they will find it
Shining deep in the lengthening cracks
Down which a woman might lose
Everything. Or a man press his tongue or eye
To the wood, and see skin like flecks of reddish

Mica in the dark, her disordered fingers
Grasp at the peeling walls. And all around
Their insect feet like lashes blink softly back.

Carol Reynolds
UNTITLED

Kamehameha,
On your feather helmet sits
A brazen mynah.

CAROL REYNOLDS *first visited Hawai'i in 1965. She and her husband, the Reverend Craig Reynolds, returned in 1972 to live and work on Maui, O'ahu, and the island of Hawai'i. She edited the "Hawaii Haiku" column in the* Honolulu Advertiser, *and published* Pebbles and Pearls *and* Haiku of Hawaii Nei.

John Dominis Holt
"REMEMBERING KAKA'AKO"

Kaka'ako used to
be a different place.
One of boot leggers,
pipi stew . . .
sweet-meated 'alamihi eaten raw
and sweet late night strummings
of Mary Lukini
Ukranian born artiste
of the slack key style—
Iolani lived at Kaka'ako
for a time
and years before that
my great grandparents
and before them
Keopuolani and her
infant daughter Nahienaena.

William Stafford
"THE R. L. STEVENSON TREE ON OAHU"

Here under the Trade Wind that breaks off
boughs for the doves, he lost his breath
and began to know that scenes don't care.
He hid in the hotel room and wrote
whatever story trees and clouds had prepared
for this head. Mornings, outside the window,
pressure of doves built up in the banyan;
he heard Old Pew sweep the courtyard, tapping
the ash trays out, and waiters whisper
a plan to take over the place, once
their bosses were gone.

     Friend, you and I,
twin ghosts of that writer, now meet
on a world become an aircraft carrier:
may the plans he made, the stories
the smuggled poems, master this craft,
bring all islands under the sound they belong to—
Trade winds, friend, banyan, dove.

Richard Hamasaki
"MŌʻILIʻILI"

cats walk across the field

at noon

I get up sneezing
mountain peaks behind clouds

prowling in cut grass—like wheat chaff

cautious   hunter

Courtesy of Richard Hamasaki.

your world includes time for lust

you kill as well

beneath apartment walls
or ruins
beside damp garbage   black cats
walk between cracks and make love in private

Cat in yellow field   slung low   I see your rhythm

hear your smooth talk in the evening near my screen door
and ignore you—couldn't bear to be like Hemingway
on his island in the stream

eyes that tell time
so they say

you watch me tonight

riding home drunk
bicycle wobbling

awake   crouched on a car's warm, metal skin
         your friends are crossing the field.

Darryl Keola Cabacungan
"KA LOKE HĀKEA A KA MAHINA"

Hakū mai lā ka mahina
Ma luna o Waʻahila

Hoʻopiha ʻia lā ʻo Mānoa
Me ke kōnane lā

Nui ka ʻiliʻili ma ke kahawai
He kahawai me ka ulu paina

Inā iho lā ʻo ka pua
Ka pua loke hākea

Ke ʻālohilohi o ka pua
Ka loke lani o ka mahina

Ke kali nei au me ka ʻiʻini
No kou waianuhea

Mōhalahala mai ʻo loke hākea
Hoʻike mai i kou manaʻo

Haʻina ʻia mai ana ka puana
He mele nō ka pua loke lani

"PALE ROSE OF THE MOON"

The moon rises over Waʻahila Ridge.
Filling with soft light the lap of Mānoa.
Weathered stones that glow as white eggs
Line the path of a stream through an ironwood grove
Where a pale rose blooms.

This is the fourth day
Of the fourth month.
My waiting is ended.

Unfold your petals
Daughter of the moon.
Reveal your dream sin—
Your heart, a coil of white flesh.

DARRYL KEOLA CABACUNGAN'S *work has appeared in* Chaminade Literary Review; Hawaiʻi Review; Oceanic Linguistics; Chain; Hyundae; Hybolics; Historic Hawaiʻi; *and the* Honolulu Advertiser. *He has read his work at the University of Hawaiʻi at Mānoa, the Honolulu Academy of Arts, the Louis Pohl Gallery, Honolulu Hale, Washington Place, ʻIolani Palace, and the Gay & Lesbian Film Festival. He was commissioned to compose* oli *for the Polynesian oceangoing canoe* Hōkūleʻa's *return from its Voyage of Discovery, and for the Honolulu Men's Chorus.*

10/1/05

The Mānoa Rain
By Kaci

Plop! Rain dropping on my roof,

creating a waterfall down my window.

Dark clouds sweep the blue sky away.

The heavy mist erasing the top of

the mountains from view.

Watching from the safty of my room.

Beautiful poem, Kaci
I sens can almost smell
the rain!

Kaci X. Tavares
"THE MĀNOA RAIN"

Plop! Rain dropping on my roof,
Creating a waterfall down my window.
Dark clouds sweep the blue sky away,
The heavy mist erasing the top of the mountains from view,
Watching from the safety of my room.

KACI X. TAVARES, *born in 1997 in Fuzhou, China, is a fourth grader at Punahou School in Honolulu. She is an avid dancer of ballet, hula, and musical theater. She enjoys drawing fashion models. Any free time she has is spent reading novels of various genres.*

Walter K. Lew
"MĀNOA RUN"

If I stretch it out, turn and go

Up the hill, the circling road
Behind the widow's house

I will see an ocean sunset, flotillas

Of cirrus blazing in their chassis.
I will follow the curve, the lush bend up into the better

Neighborhood: silk dogs, children tumbling like deaf-mutes,

The crying iridescent flora
Shrubbed and rinsed and shaken clean.

A cold flame of wind will grab

Fallen, lung-sized kamani leaves
And gust them into a walking companion

Rushing and treading beside me, at shoulder-height:
Its head's milled peat, belly, shins
Unceasingly thrashed and shat into each other

As if this were no mere exercise

But a face of the hidden urge, whispered
Mind of things to pace and speak with us.

By this I will be made helpless, and jog on

Knowing like a scar, that I cannot remember, cannot
Say the spell exactly, or dare to embrace

The falling figure, weep and pray

For the burning prisoner kneeling into his
Dissolving shins. *Grandfather!* I may whisper, *Father!*

My father says all his life here. The flame withdraws,

The head keels, flops open like a gourd
Into a hopping gyre of mute leaves

On the black road, if I stop and turn around.

WALTER K. LEW, *born in 1955, teaches at the University of Miami. His books include the award-winning* Treadwinds: Poems and Intermedia Works *and* Excerpts from: ΔIKTH DIKTE, for DICTEE. *He has edited* Kôri: The Beacon Anthology of Korean American Fiction *(co-editor Heinz Insu Fenkl);* Crazy Melon and Chinese Apple: The Poems of Frances Chung; *and the groundbreaking poetry anthology* Premonitions. *Formerly a documentary producer, Lew has performed his multimedia "movietelling" pieces at many film festivals.*

W. J. Illerbrun
UNTITLED

Bus from Manoa
Always the same hair and dress
Japanese tutus

W. J. ILLERBRUN *was born in Edmonton, Alberta, in 1944. It took him twenty-three years to get to Honolulu, and learn that his birthday was a holiday. Nice place, he thought; friendly people. He still thinks so, though he hasn't lived there for decades. But who ever really leaves Hawai'i? He has a son whose middle name is Kalani.*

Courtney Sato
"MARINER'S RIDGE"

Driving up the hill today,
past the bougainvillea bushes,
past the shower trees,
even past the first few houses,
I kept glancing down at the valley.
Where is the dirt pathway we carved
with our bikes every June?
June was always perfect: the grass,
dried in long gold wisps reaching
knee-length as we rode our bikes,
calling out names. As we rode,
we would look up at the mountain
casting shadows on the path, sometimes
dark patches, like bruises in the dry dirt.
For several years, I thought the mountains
shifted, but it was only the sun
carving its own path,
past the steaming clouds,
stopping for no one. Now, mid-June,
where is the gold grass?
Why is the only sound I hear the murmur
of wind in the rolled-down windows?
Soon there will be whispering, a thousand
flowers placed against the bottom of the hill
bundled in ribbons that crinkle in the wind.
Why a cemetery? There is nowhere else.
Their voices will be unrecognizable,
a string of rising sorrow that will settle
in the valley, no longer voices of children.

COURTNEY SATO *was born in Honolulu in 1987. She is a junior at Wellesley College, majoring in English. Her poetry has recently appeared in* Bamboo Ridge; Aeolus; *and the* Wellesley Review. *Past poetry honors include the National Scholastic Art & Writing Awards and the Hawai'i Council Teachers of English Language awards. She is currently taking a seminar with poet Frank Bidart. In her free time she enjoys dancing and playing with her dog Ollie.*

Manuel Jesus Coito
"TASCA DO MONTE, KALIHI"

A bella tasca do monte,
De verduras rodeada,
Cauzando infinda alegria
A bella rapaziada.

1

O "Pão e Peixe" Companhia,
Ao balcão junto à barra
Fazia gemer a guitarra
Que era uma bizarría;
O "José Canhoto" vendia
Da alcoolica fonte,
Estava bello o horisonte,
A luz da lua brilhava
No sabbado quando eu chegava
À bella tasca do monte.

2

Estava tudo para agradar
A cebola de excabeixe
E o fadista "Pão e Peixe"
O bello fado a cantar;
O "José Canhoto" a jugar
A sua bisca fallada,
Estava a tasca illuminada
Com duas bellas lanternas,
Era uma tasca das modernas
De verduras rodeada.

3

A agua gasoza ardente . . .
Tremoço e fava corrida,
Oh que cousa apetecida
Para um estomago fervente,
Estava tudo em fim contente
A fresca aragem corria;
No Domingo, já alto dia
A musica harmoniava;

Ao charamba alguem cantava
Causando infinda alegria.

4
De tudo, o melhor a tasca,
A cerveja evaporou-se,
A agua gasoza acabou-se,
Do presunto já nem lasca;
Do tremoco, só a casca
Pelo chão estava espalhada;
A fava estava papada,
E, já o sol no horisonte:
Deixava saudades do monte
A bella rapaziada.

"TAVERN OF THE MOUNT, KALIHI"

The beautiful tavern of the mount,
Surrounded by verdure,
Causing infinite joy
For the fine gang of lads.
"Bread and Fish" and Company
In the balcony next to the bar
Made the guitar sing
Most marvelously;
"Jose Canhoto" was selling
From the fountain of alcohol.
The horizon was beautiful,
The light of the moon shone
On Saturday when I arrived
At the beautiful tavern of the mount.

Everything was to give pleasure
The onion was in the escabeche
And the "Bread and Fish" fado singer
Singing the tuneful fado;
"Jose Canhoto" playing
His well known card game, bisca.
The tavern was illuminated
By two splendid lanterns.

It was a very new tavern
Surrounded by verdure.

The fiery gaseous water,
Lupine and soaked beans,
Oh, what a savory dish
For a stomach on fire.
Everything, in short, was happy.
The cool breeze was blowing,
On Sunday, already high noon,
The music was harmonious;
Someone was singing with the band
Causing infinite joy.

Of everything, the tavern's best,
The beer evaporated,
The gaseous water was depleted,
There was left not a slice of ham.
Of the lupine beans, only the shells
Were scattered on the floor;
The bean was eaten up,
And already the sun on the horizon:
It left yearnings for the mount
For the fine group of lads.

TRANSLATED BY EDGAR KNOWLTON

Emily Callejo
"AN ETCHING"

Poetry is Kalihi,
Irene and Soriano Palongao who immigrated
from Langiden, Phillipines.
Poetry is the tangerine ripening on the tree
in the backyard,
the marungay trees rising towards the sky,
Bantay, the dog, and Concordia who died.
Poetry is ruby, the color of the fiery eyes,

and azure, the color of the jeweled sky.
Poetry is long rice chicken that giggles in the pot,
halohalo that dissolves in a sweet swallow
down my throat.
Poetry is the golden bracelet
my grandma will hand down to me in the future.
Poetry is racism and hatred, goodness and love,
Poetry is my goals and ambitions,
washing dishes for dinner, romance books and Usher.
Poetry is my bursting anger devouring myself,
my kind heart painting the heavens.
Poetry is the sky, the clouds etching the air,
the mejiro singing across the lychee trees,
the sun ascending above Kalihi,
I am flying through the silky air with my words.

EMILY CALLEJO, *born in 1990, grew up to be a compassionate, determined Filipino girl from Kalihi in Honolulu. Emily's sixth grade poetry teacher, Lois-Ann Yamanaka, inspired her passion to write poetry. Dancing Tahitian is another passion of hers. She is a part of Na'Opio O Ko'olau Hula Halau. Emily is a hardworking, busy Farrington High School student involved with many extra-curricular activities. She aspires to become a doctor, join the Peace Corps, and save many lives.*

Salt

"KALIHI HYPOCRITE"

It's like, my dog's a killer.
I hafta keep her on a leash
far enough
Till I don't care if she kills something.
In the yard if
Some stupid hen somehow comes walking in,
Wham, first thing you know,
Squawk, squawk, feathers and yellow guts.
The one time it was okay was
Way up by Ice Pond
She roared off through the brush
And then this long squeal,

the bush shaking and leaves shuddering
   like mad.
Up she trots with this really large mongoose still twisting,
Still trying to slice at her neck.
She glances at me and—very
Doggy deliberate—
She takes that mongoose down to the
   rocks at the edge of the pond and
Holds it under water till the thrashing stops.
She does it for pleasure.
But what! This giant tan mongrel
Comes at us just before the bridge,
Gets her rear in its teeth. Panicked
I jump at the dog, barking my head off
Before I think. The surprised mongrel
Steps back unhinged. My killer dog
Quick as a wink slips behind me,
Leaving me looking at teeth.

SALT *is the author name Nancy S. Young chose for her creative work. She was born in 1941. She married at age twenty. She and her husband have a large family, with two teenagers still at home. She has written poems, short stories, and her journal; and has sculpted since kindergarten. She taught school for a living. She thinks when she walks the dog up Kalihi-uka in Honolulu, and when she wakes up during the night.*

Emily Day
"MIDNIGHT"

Let there be poetic nights
on the streets of Kalihi.

Let the night heal the crying baby,
the lady with the injured leg,
the wild shrieks from the next house,
the trees wrapping their branches around
the sadness of our Kalihi neighborhood.

Let the sadness fly up to the sky
to the enormous clouds who heal

the pain from the heart of the streets,
the faceless rain comforting us all
each and every poetic night.

EMILY DAY *wrote this poem in 2003, when she was in the fifth grade at Fern Elementary School in Honolulu.*

Puanani Burgess
"'AWAPUHI"

Mama loved the scent
of the wild yellow ginger,
growing thick on the slopes of Tantalus.

In its blooming season,
she would walk up that steep, curvey road
to pick two or three.

These she would weave into a brooch,
to be pinned to the inside
of her blouse—hidden,
but for that warm perfume.
On the day she was buried
she wore a lei of wild yellow ginger,
freshly picked from the slopes of Tantalus,

And left for me,
in a blue shoe box,
a thousand, neatly-woven, dry
fragrant brooches.

PUANANI BURGESS *was born in Honolulu, Territory of Hawai'i, in 1947. Her full birth names, Christabelle Yoshie Puanani Sonoda, represent the political and cultural times in which she was born. She lives with her family in Wai'anae, O'ahu, and is a community developer, popular educator, facilitator, mediator, and cultural translator. She helped develop the 'Opelu Project; Ka'ala Cultural Learning Center; the Backyard Aquaculture Project; the Wai'anae Coast Community Mental Health Center; and Pu'a Foundation.*

Michael Darnay Among
"NEAR MY HOME IN THE VALLEY"

for Mikahala

near my home in the valley
i stand still among white ginger

my waiting has been a pleasure
and the clouds wait for rain

the wind blows swiftly through the bamboo gate
i haven't any time to ask your name

i listen to the ribbon tails in a flurry
spreading their feathers in the mist

in the stillness i move
with certain steps in the Tantalus mountains

dark faces escape my hands
as i fall between boulders

washing away the black stone
you remain there upon cold grass

now i see you leap from path to path
wet feet zigzagging on jade stones

dawn breezes take you
leaving your slippers in the final pool

MICHAEL DARNAY AMONG *has recently created T-shirts with the logo "NevaSaNeva," with quotes that flow around boulders. He started the business in March of 2003. As an educational entrepreneur, he counseled students in preparation for college and careers; he also tutored students in English and writing poetry. "Taking a chance is the only safe thing to do" is a quote on one of his T-shirts. His website is nevasaneva.com.*

Ruth B. Canham
"'LITTLE 'AMAKIHI"

Once upon a time in the forests of Tantalus, high in the mountains of Oahu, lived a small 'Amakihi. Because he had been the last of the eggs to hatch in a large group of five, he received his mother's last and least attentions. When she fed the chicks, some would eat many insects before Little 'Amakihi had his first, so Kihi remained the smallest and thinnest of the lot. Nonetheless, Kihi was happy and satisfied. He enjoyed watching his stronger brothers and sister as they grew into fledglings, tested their wings and voices, and began to fly, for in only seventeen days they started to leave home. One by one they all deserted the nest until Kihi was alone with his mother. His mother took great pride in singing about the success of her large family: one son had nested in the best koa tree in the forest, her daughter would surely draw attention next mating season for she was stunningly beautiful, another son had a mind which was so sharp that he could solve any problem in the forest, while the last son had the greatest gift—his song was the loveliest of all the 'Amakihi. No mention was made of Kihi. He was just an ordinary bird, rather scrawny and pale, in fact, with no special talents.

Finally the day arrived when Kihi gained the strength to fly away. His departure was difficult, for all the trees nearest the nest were taken and he had to fly all the way to Makiki to find a new home. But, at the very edge of the forest, he discovered an Ohia tree and decided that it was just suited for him. Here he made his nest. He collected the finest grasses, some lovely lichen, and built high in the leafiest branches of his tree, where he would be safe from the mongoose and other predators. Each week Kihi flew all the way back up to the top of the mountain to visit his family. This was often difficult since he had to struggle against the powerful Tantalus rain and the strong mountain winds. But, so important was his family that he did not think of missing a visit.

The shower trees had long ago dropped their blossoms and now the bright red flowers of the winter poinsettia had begun to bloom. Little Kihi realized how true his mother's song had been: his sister drew everyone's admiration for her beauty, his brother continued to sing the most beautiful song on the mountain, and his other brothers were leaders of the forest, with the grandest nests in Tantalus. Kihi was proud of them all. "What a wonderful family I have," he thought.

Kihi had grown in the past months. His body, now plump from the sweet juice of guavas, had changed into lovely colors—his tail was a deep dark green, the bright green of his wings was accented with delicate black markings, and, as he fluttered, the yellow of his breast showed vividly against the blue sky. He was ready to find a mate.

But just as Kihi thought of his weekly flight up the mountain, the mild Oahu weather turned into a December storm. Fierce gusts of wind and pounding rains blew through the branches of his Ohia tree. Before he could even begin his flight, he was suddenly knocked to the ground by a falling branch and when he hit, he broke his left wing. It hurt badly, too badly for him to move, even when he saw a man come out of a nearby house. Noticing Kihi on the ground, the man picked him up and gently carried him into the house. The man called for his wife as Kihi, shuddering with pain, looked up to see a small tree, decorated with beautiful lights and glittering as brightly as the Hawaiian sun.

"Oh no, not our favorite friend," Kihi heard the wife exclaim.

"I'm afraid so," replied her husband sadly, "the very one we've watched grow from a fledgling. The bird whose beautiful flight gave us so much pleasure, whose wings have turned to the green of Christmas. Let's call a vet and see what we can do for him."

"Beautiful flight . . . our favorite friend . . . given us so much pleasure," mused Kihi—were they talking about him? Surely they were. He couldn't believe it—he had never thought about himself like that. He stirred only slightly in the man's hands, for his wing gave him great pain, but a feeling of warmth filled his small body. This Christmas season had given him the greatest gift of all, for now he knew that he was important—he had been noticed and he, too, was special.

RUTH B. CANHAM *was born in West Virginia in 1946, grew up in Maryland and California, and has lived in Hawai'i for nearly thirty years. She wrote this story for her elementary school students while teaching at the Kamehameha Schools in Honolulu.*

William Charles Lunalilo
"KA 'ŌLELO A KE ALI'I KĀNE I KE ALI'I WAHINE"

'A'ole i mana'o 'ia
Kāhi wai a'o 'Alekoki.
Ho'okohu ka ua i uka,
Noho mai la i Nu'u-anu.

Anuanu makehewa au
Ke kali ana i laila.
Kainō paha ua pa'a
Kou mana'o i 'ane'i.

Āu i hoʻomalu ai
Hoʻomalu ʻoe a malu,
Ua malu neia kino
Mamuli o kō Leo.

Kau nui aku ka manaʻo,
Kāhi wai aʻo Kapena.
Pani ā paʻa ʻia mai
Nā māno wai aʻo uka.

Ahu wale nā kiʻo wai
Nā papahele o luna.
Maluna aʻe nō wau
Ma ke kūʻono liʻiliʻi.

Ma waho aʻo Māmala,
Hao mai ana ehuehu,
Pulu au i ka huna-kai
Kai heʻeheʻe i ka ʻili.

Hoʻokahi nō koa nui,
Nāna e ʻalo ia ʻino.
ʻInoʻino mai nei luna
I ka hao a ka makani.

He makani ʻāhaʻi lono,
Lohe ka luna i Pelekane.
A ʻoia pouli nui,
Mea ʻole i kuʻu manaʻo.

I ʻō i ʻaneʻi au,
Ka piʻina la aʻo Maʻemaʻe,
E kilohi au i ka nani
Nā pua i Mauna-ʻala.

He ʻala onaona kou,
Ke pili mai i ʻaneʻi,
O aʻu lehua ʻula i luna,
ʻAi ʻoho a nā manu.

"THE PRINCE'S WORDS TO THE PRINCESS"

I've no interest in the Pool of 'Ale-koki.
I scorn people who live in flatlands.
Here where cold rains haunt Nu'u-anu's slopes
I weep and wait and freeze—waiting for nothing.

I loved you once, I believed you.
Even I thought you were true.
You made me swear to be loyal and remember.
Remember your own oath and keep it true.

For this body, beloved, brims with my love.
At the thought of your mouth my heart leaps
With love remembered in a magic pool.
At brink of Ka-pena Pool no magic now
In this cool watershed of upland Nu'u-anu.

You tell me it is fenced, cut off, kapu.
Oh yes, the water-heads are tightly sealed.
Why hide your fountains, dear?
Let descending skies pour down their lesson.

Perhaps you keep me lodged here hung up in the cleft
Of a dainty rock because teasing amuses you.
Perhaps more than you know, or even I fear perhaps,
I am a man already lost and sinking, in a gulf of sorrow.

As a wild wind hurls itself against an unyielding surf
I too am hurled naked against Māmala's spume.
But when did sailor-warrior of old question his insistent heart
If committed by it to outface the furious brine?

Dark clouds scale a tempestuous sky.
Driven by gossiping winds this tale of ours
Reaches lofty ears at Beretania.
Though tale-bearing winds gossip afar
Nought care I for darkest storm.
Much less for royal listener!

Now as we climb a winding way at Ma'ema'e,
Here where buds of Mauna-'ala shed the fragrance

We knew from childhood only too well,
What flower will burn from your body
If I, beloved, lie in your arms?

When will mine, Pele's scarlet *lehua,*
Breathe again for you such sweetness as forest birds
Seek in fire of sunlight, fire of darkness,
Before tiring into sleep?

TRANSLATED BY MARY KAWENA PUKUI

WILLIAM CHARLES LUNALILO (1835-1874) *was the sixth monarch of the nineteenth-century Hawaiian kingdom. He is the likely composer of this chant. The setting is 'Alekoki, in Nu'uanu valley, Honolulu.*

Eric Chock
"WAOLANI STREAM, 1955/1975"

W hen I was a small boy I looked into a pool and saw the sky passing through. When the glare passed, I saw snails and mud. Leaning forward, my face appeared at the edge, straight dry bangs fringing my forehead. But snails seemed to be crawling out of my eyes, so I collected the biggest black shells and corralled them with rocks, blanketed them with moss, threatened them with crayfish. The snails strayed in their cones, waiting. I pretended to be part of the sky, blue air, hovering above the surface.

The snails and crayfish must have been afraid of the breaking of their sky, for everytime my hands shattered that glass, they'd look for darkness to hide in. But my hands moved quickly in their world. Tired of waiting, I tried to bait them out with flesh from other shells I crushed, and they would risk the breaking of the sky to taste it. With the odds so high against them! What game is it they played, what love of risk they lived, what hunger under a breaking sky!

I've not grown older than snails or crayfish, but there is some flesh out there I seek. These hands grasp air, grasp mud, pass through like water moving through water, like blue air through sky, these hands reaching through my body out of my flesh.

Susan Heroy

"JAPANESE CEMETERY, NUUANU, HAWAII"

There is neither light
nor fuel for light in the paper
lanterns swinging on slanted poles.
I stand before the stones, touching
names that coil and swing out,
a braille that even with more light
I could not read. From the silence
birds fly up at my step,
their blue wings opening like fans
women might carry on a river
thick with fog.

Fruit sits ripe on the graves
as on altars—oranges, mangoes—
and birds of paradise,
their petals spiked, ablaze,
as if colors that could lure
Gauguin across the world
might lure someone from
much further away.

So we give them
what they loved in life,
just as we gave or held back love.
In other times flowers,
even food, were not enough,
but we would load the boats
with weapons and jewels
before we cast them off into the mist,
or we would lay on the fire
fine cloth, gold, even a woman
still warm with her own breath.

We know better now.
And these are not my dead.
But when I find a glass of wine
mixed with rainwater on a marble ledge,
and the mountains before me

rising to cloud, I bend down,
I pour out the wine,
I whisper into the ears of the air,
drink! drink!

SUSAN HEROY, *a native of Rochester, New York, lives in Richmond, Virginia, with her hus-band John, a photographer. The have one daughter, Sasha. Susan has taught English at the University of Richmond and Virginia Commonwealth University, and currently teaches creative writing at Randolph-Macon College in Ashland, Virginia. In addition to* Bamboo Ridge, *she has published in* Prairie Schooner; Southern Poetry Review; *and* Three Rivers Poetry Journal, *among others, and has won a Virginia Prize for Poetry.*

Hiroko Moriyama
UNTITLED

古戦場跨ぐヌアヌの虹の橋

Kosenjo
Mataga Nuuanu no
Niji no hashi

Straddling the old battleground
A bridge of rainbow
At Nuuanu

TRANSLATED BY SHIGEYUKI YOSHITAKE

Haunani-Kay Trask
"RETURNING TO WAIMĀNALO"

between two worlds
shorelines of meaning form
edging closer, farther
marking the one space

where all my selves
cease transforming

war continues on one side
from the other beckons
a different front:
all battle, scarred
and scarring
two worlds, two
world wars

but here, there is a moment
a fall of light along
the shore, gleaming
a changing shoreline
this is not peace, or
solitude. i am too
unseasoned for that

it is something strange:
intelligible space
in a bitter universe
rhythm amidst terrifying noise
human need that does not
suffer

it is my experience
when struggle wanes

myself, and my people
absorbing sounds
near a silent sea
forming ancient
contours of meaning

Kapulani Landgraf

"HE AU KO'OLAU LĀ"

'Iu'iu Ko'olau i nā pali lupalupa
i ka uhi 'ia e ka 'ohu
Kumukumu ola 'o Hi'ilaniwai
Kalo kupu o ka 'āina 'o Luluku
i pōhai 'ia e nā pua kukui 'olili,
ke ahe a Kāne
'I'ike i ka nani o Kāne'ohe,
'a'ohe mea 'imi a ka maka.

Kaukolo nā maka o ka makani
i ka mālie
Ka'alina e ka ua lehu i Ha'ikū
Ha'imalule nā pali 'o Keahiakahoe
i nā wili Ko'olau
Nākolo nā pōhaku kapu o Kahekili,
ko'ele ke ahi o na lani
He au Ko'olau lā.

Nahā i ke kōlea ka huewai ola
a Kāne
Pauka'a i nā i'a hao o ka 'āina
ka papa o ke kuahiwi
Īhe'ehe'e ka wai 'ula,
pu'ua ka 'āko'ako'a kohe
'Iliki maumau ka ua Kani Ko'o
o He'eia Uli.

Ho'opouli i ka umauma o ke kōlea,
ho'i i Kahiki
Hanupa'a Kāne'ohe i ka pāulihiwa
haha'i ka iwikuamo'o
Kāluli kāmau ka 'ohe kupa
i ka Moa'e kū
Meha ke kula, 'a'ohe lele pueo.

"THAT IS KO'OLAU WEATHER"

The glory of Ko'olau are its verdant cliffs
concealed by mist
The source of life is Hi'ilaniwai
Taro grows on the land of Luluku
surrounded by the shimmering kukui
blossoms, the breath of Kāne.
Behold the beauty of Kāne'ohe,
nothing more for the eyes to search.

The eyes of the wind follow one another
in the calm
The ash rain pelts Ha'ikū
The cliffs of Keahiakahoe are weakened
by the Ko'olau whirlwind
The sacred stones of Kahekili rumble,
fire cracks in the heavens.
That is Ko'olau weather.

The plover bursts the water gourd
of Kāne
The iron fish of the land consumes
the spine of the mountain
The red waters run,
the coral suffocates
Relentlessly pours the cane tapping rain
of He'eia Uli.

The breast of the plover darkened,
it returns home
Kāne'ohe is breathless in the dark clouds
The mountain crumbles,
the backbone breaks
The native bamboo bends continuously
by the persistent tradewinds
not a sound is made.

KAPULANI LANDGRAF *was born and raised in Pū'ahu'ula, Kāne'ohe, O'ahu. Her books,* Nā Wahi Pana O Ko'olau Poko *and* Nā Wahi Kapu o Maui, *received Ka Palapala Po'okela Awards for Excellence in Illustrative Books. She currently teaches photography at Kapi'olani Community College in Honolulu.*

Jeremy Walter

"IF I WERE THE KOʻOLAU MOUNTAINS"

I would inspire the people
who walk on me to listen
to the echoes of children
running and playing.

I would sleep in the dark night
under the moon who whispers
a humming secret to the stars.

Endless craggy rocks resting high above
the clouds, dragonfly over the ponds
as I shimmer in the cold wind.

The mountain apple trees touch
the moon when the splendid night
enchants the beauty of the city

below. If I were a mountain,
solitary and calm, I'd remember
the happiness of my tree friends forever.

JEREMY WALTER *was born in 1996. He is Micronesian. His mother is from Chuuk. He is a student at Fern Elementary School in Honolulu and Naʻau, a Place for Learning. His favorite subjects are reading and social studies. He enjoys paddling, playing basketball, and spending time with his mother. He would like to be a lawyer so he can help his clients win their trials.*

Kaʻimi Medrano

"MAIKAʻI NŌ! VERY GOOD INDEED!"

The twittering of a manu (bird)
The gray kai (sea)
The comfort of this puneʻe

Beyond lies Chinaman's Hat
below
the pili (grass)
A'e the heavens
Iho the kai
Beyond
Chinaman's Hat.

'Olu'olu 'oe
Pleasant to the maka
Ka manu
Ka pili
Ka lani
Maika'i nō!

KA'IMI MEDRANO *was raised by her* kūpuna *(grandparents) in Laupāhoehoe on the island of Hawai'i. Inspiration from Windward Community College* kumu *(teachers) Lillian Cunningham and Kawaikapuokalani Hewett, and the view from her oceanfront Kāne'ohe Bay home, culminated in the writing of "Maika'i Nō! Very Good Indeed" as she lay on her* pune'e *(daybed). She received a master of science degree in nursing and is active in her professional career as a registered nurse in Windward O'ahu.*

----◆----

Emalia Keohokālole, Fred Kalani Meinecke, Earl Pāmai Tenn
"WINDWARD COMMUNITY COLLEGE HULA"

He mele kēia nou e ka hale
Nā hale kū hanohano
Nā hale kūpono o Hawai'i
Kulanui no ka lehulehu.

Kū kilakila nā Ko'olau
Ka'u mahalo a'e ana
Me Ke-ahi-a-Kahoe
Me Ke-ahi-a-Kahoe
Kuahiwi kau i ka 'iu

'O ke ānuenue, ke ānuenue
E pi'o mai la iluna,
Pā mai ka noenoe, pā mai ke aheahe,
Luana wale ka mana 'o.

He kahua 'olu ia, he kahua 'olu ia,
No ku'u hoa, ke kōlea
Āhui mai nā hulu, Āhui mai nā hulu,
I ka malu ulu o ia ne'i.
'O ka'u nō ia, 'o ka'u nō ia
E li'a mau a'e ana,
Nā mea kū kahiko,
Kūpono iā Hawai'i
Ku'u home piha aloha.

Puana ku'u mele, puana ku'u mele
Nā hale kū hanohano
Kulanui kaiāulu, E ō i kou inoa
Kaulana o nā Ko'olau.

"WINDWARD COMMUNITY COLLEGE HULA"

This is a song for you
Halls standing proudly
Halls befitting Hawai'i
A college for the multitudes.

The Ko'olau stand majestically
Evoking my admiration
With Ke-ahi-a-Kahoe
With Ke-ahi-a-Kahoe
Lofty mountain placed on high.

The rainbow, the rainbow
Arcing up above
The mist caresses, the gentle breeze soothes,
The mind reposes.

It is a pleasant campus,
For my friend, the plover,
The precious ones gather,

Under the verdant shade here.
It is indeed
My desire
To continue the traditions
Befitting Hawai'i
My beloved home.

Let the refrain be sung,
Hall standing proudly
Community college, reply to your name song
Renown of the Ko'olau.

EMALIA KEOHOKĀLOLE *is a lifelong resident of Kāne'ohe, O'ahu. She is a native Hawaiian researcher, musician, and cultural practitioner of the Hawaiian heritage.*
FRED KALANI MEINECKE *is a professor of Hawaiian language and culture at Windward Community College in Kāne'ohe.*
EARL PĀMAI TENN, *born in 1940, instructs hula at Windward Community College. He has studied with Henry Pa, Maddy Lam, Rose Joshua, Morrnah Simeona and Kawena Johnson. He is advisor to Ka Leo O Na Hula, a hula teachers association in Mexico City; founder of Ka Pa Hula Manu; and liaison for Nadine Kahanamoku (Mrs. Duke Kahanamoku) estate.*

Abbie Kong and Johnny Noble
"KĀNE'OHE"

'Ōlapa ka uila i Kāne'ohe
Ka hui laulima o 'Ēlaniwai

Me ka ua 'Āpuakea
Ka la'i a'o Malulani
Me ke anu o ke Ko'olau

Kaulana mai nei Ko'olaupoko
Ua 'ā ka uila a i Kāne'ohe

Walea ana 'oe me ke onaona
Ku'u lei hulu mamo pili i ke anu

Hanohano Mōkapu i ka 'ehu kai
Te tua motumotu a'o He'eia

Ho'okahi mea hou ma He'eia
Ka uea kelekalepa leo nahenahe

Aia 'ike lihi o ka 'āina
Kahi a ke aloha i walea ai

Ua ana ho'i au a i ko leo
Ko pane 'ana mai pehea au

Ha'ina 'ia mai ana ka puana
Ua 'ā ka uila a i Kāne'ohe

"KĀNE'OHE"

The lightning flashes at Kāne'ohe
The working team of 'Ēlaniwai

With the 'Āpuakea rain
The calm of Malulani
And the coolness of the Ko'olau

Ko'olaupoko is famous
And lights go on at Kāne'ohe

You delight with the sweetness
My mamo feather lei with me in the cold

The glory of Mōkapu is the sea spray
And the jagged ridge of He'eia

A new thing at He'eia
Is the sweet-voiced telegraph wire

Glimpses of the land
Where love finds delight

I am fulfilled by your voice
You asking how I am

Tell the refrain
Lights go on at Kāneʻohe

TRANSLATED BY PUAKEA NOGELMEIER

JOHN AVERY NOBLE (1892-1944), *a part-Hawaiian, took early twentieth-century Hawaiian songwriting in the direction of jazz rhythms and pop song stylings, with lyrics mostly in English and a sprinkling of Hawaiian words—what became known as* hapa-haole *music. He spent ten years on the mainland, organizing Hawaiian shows for radio and vaudeville, and he worked on Hollywood film scores. Several of his songs were national hits in the 1930s, including "My Little Grass Shack" and "Hawaiian War Chant," which has been recorded since then in scores of versions.*

Faye Kicknosway
"SHORT TAKE 16"

There is an island, but it is a hat
and a photograph of
a hat, and breath—so tenuous—

overhangs it

as does an inkwell; no;

an octopus
in a black suit
            sewing an umbrella

because it's a comical shape; no;
            because it's a conical shape

and so pious

and so envious
of Aristotle's salamander:
                        four elbows

instead of eight—and a heart

that is its eyes' engine
              all drawers of it
              all handstands
              and cartwheels of it

FAYE KICKNOSWAY *has published twelve books of poetry; the two most recent are* Mixed
Plate *and* Still Windows Run Deep. *Her work has appeared in numerous anthologies and
literary journals, including* The Paris Review; The Little Magazine; New Letters; Hanging
Loose; *and* Hawai'i Review. *She has received two artist's grants, an Arts Achievement Award,
an NEA, and a PEN Syndicated Fiction Award.*

Michael Ondaatje
UNTITLED

The cabin
              its tin roof
a wind-run radio
catches the noise of the world.
He focuses on the gecko
almost transparent body
how he feels now
everything passing through him like light.
In certain mirrors
he cannot see himself at all.
He is joyous and breaking down.
The tug over the cliff.
What protects him
is the warmth in the sleeve

that is all, really

Sojin Maruyama

UNTITLED

ずうと草が空へゆけば家があるといふ

Zuutto kusa ga sora e
Ikeba ie ga aru to iu

Grasses grow all the way up to the sky
People say houses are there at the end

TRANSLATED BY SHIGEYUKI YOSHITAKE

SOJIN MARUYAMA *migrated to Hawai'i from Japan in 1906. With three other people, he cleared forty acres of land in Wahiawā and planted pineapples. He studied with Ogiwara Seisensui, a famous freestyle haiku poet in Japan, and published his own collection,* Sora to Kusa (The Sky and the Grasses) *in 1941.*

Tatsuo Teraoka

UNTITLED

Kuraki hi ni
Umareshi tokoro
Ie mo naku
Waipio-tani ni
Shigeru Mangoju

No house remains
Where I was born
On those dark and dim days
Only the mango trees
Remain in Waipio Valley

TRANSLATED BY SHIGEYUKI YOSHITAKE

Noelle Elizabeth Spring

"THE WHITE MAILBOX"

We both lived on Kam Highway,
the fastest lane in Laie
We prayed for a car so we could ride that
Highway out of here
But we were short on resources
So we ate extra cheesy goldfish
and watched
Our favorite '80s movies and
gazed out her beachside window
To see old ladies in hot floral
pink bikinis
Greasing up their tan spotted wrinkles,
Or I'd look through her magazines
at hot guys
(I'm shallow like that sometimes.)
We blasted the Beatles and ruminated
on our latest infatuations

We never needed to entertain each other
We had the best conversations
without saying anything
A rusty mailbox, old, corroded,
And disintegrating in between
our houses
Was our meeting point.
The last day she was here,
she came to say goodbye
I walked her to the mailbox.
the year she left me for Oregon
It rained more than ever before.

NOELLE ELIZABETH SPRING, *born in 1988, was raised in Lāʻie, on Oʻahu. She has always enjoyed school and found her voice as a writer early. Throughout high school she participated in activities such as speech and debate and show choir. In seventh grade, she was chosen to present a historical performance that she had written on the life of Hawaiʻi Congresswoman Patsy Mink at the National Archives in Washington, D.C. She is currently a sophomore at Stanford University.*

Kimo Armitage
"AWAWA O WAIMEA, OAHU"

Barren is Kailiilii
her monkeypod is gone, fallen.
Kaneaukai, this strong rock shrine,
attracts *uhu* and *kumu*.

The fertile *ha* of Kane
blows her moss womb wide open.
Rain slicks her thick *hapuu*,
red mud beads over her banks.

Touch this gulch Kamanaiki,
from that gulch Kamananui.
Ending in Waikakalaua
thirsty for the next rain, blowing.

Her smell is *pakalana*
blooming tiny random pearls.
Sheathed *maia*, peppered black,
engorged, bursts pockets of ripeness.

For the expert is Puulu,
thick, covered by *palapalai*.
Punakai the freshwater spring,
gushes into Kukuiee.

In June, *kuawa* and mango
satisfy honeycreepers.
While *lau* chop slanted sunlight
into blocks of purple shade.

KIMO ARMITAGE *was raised in Hale'iwa, O'ahu, by his maternal grandparents, Beatrice Lau Akina and George Poepoe K. Akina. He has authored and edited more than twenty books, and has published his poetry locally, nationally, and internationally. He may be reached at kimoa@hawaii.edu.*

Paul Nelson
"WEST OF WAIMEA"

Heeling like frigate-birds,
mum as the sublime,
gliders steer the thermals, and chutes
pop open like Disney blossoms,
chartreus, neon pink, blue-blue, swaying
down the long trail of the Trades, down,
spiraling to a walk on the drop-zone
near Kaena.

Grounded, we remember
something without tether.
The children haul along,
miserable as need.

So who are these crazies
inspiring children with yearning,
finding it lovely as damp orchids,
dangling on tender stems?
Glider pilots, sky-divers say the ride
is ecstasy, but that they do it
for the rush, seconds of free-fall
when the tow-hook releases
or yours is the next vacancy
in the small bright door.

Walking around under them, all day long,
groceries get heavy, the door
sticks in its frame, A/C fails, friends stick
and the children plan to leave you,
travel where peoples get slaughtered in sand.

Impatient for night's reward
you forget stars, whole constellations
that float over the Pacific, hanging like hardened
souls above your gratitude.

PAUL NELSON, *born in 1934, taught for Punahou School in Honolulu in the early to mid-1960s, and returned to retire on the North Shore of Oʻahu after years as professor of English and director or the creative writing program at Ohio University. He has published five books of poetry, received an NEA fellowship, the AWP Award for Poetry, and the University of Alabama Poetry Series award. He is a board member for the Hawaiʻi Literary Arts Council.*

Tino Ramirez

"SHOREBREAK"

I wonder, too, about how it's going to turn out.
Of course, I want it simple, like those first words
We exchanged at Wahiawa Theater last year
Before they tore it all down. Something of you
Is stuck with me, and as the rumble of surf drifts
Across the empty lot tonight, I find myself humming

Arcane tunes of regret: how we both knew enough
To know the Koolaus can offer a view of both sides,
And how one evening we hiked up anyway
To a resting place above the windward coast
Where ridge lines arc down to sea

for what seemed
A pleasant walk of just a few more hours. But before
Our first steps fell and we could choose which strip
Of beach to aim for, the wind shifted due west,
Booming like groundswells in the trees behind us.

I remember looking up next day
At midafternoon and the salt haze floating
Above an ocean so agitated in that rip of events,
My eyes burned looking at it. Premonitions rose
In the tears, and when the beaches were washed out
Back to the treeline, I knew it had already
Been too late. And though neither one of us
Will ever say what happened, the waves have a knack
For sorting themselves out. Go ahead and pick one.
The sand rising in its face will testify
That tomorrow is not hidden, but suspended,
Floating in view for a long moment
Before it falls on shore.

TINO RAMIREZ *was born in 1955 in Fukuoka, Japan. He lives in Waialua, Oʻahu, and is administrative assistant at Kamakakūokalani Center for Hawaiian Studies, University of Hawaiʻi at Mānoa.*

Nell Altizer
"HALEIWA CHURCHYARD"

The common hands of a girl and
woman I love as well as
grass on this good field

lay their inquisitions
like flowers over the years
of the narrow dead.

Under us are oceans
of birds and spring roots
and the long sound of rain.

One after one tonight,
while we lie
miles from these travelers,

the stars will wash the stone
calendars with silver water.

So that our sleep is no
more difficult than this,

the old earth sails again
toward its appearances.

NELL ALTIZER, *born in 1936, has taught at Emory University, the University of California at Berkeley, and the University of Hawaiʻi at Mānoa. She is co-author of* Handbook of English Composition. *Her poetry has appeared in* San Marcos Review, Hanai, *and* The Little Magazine.

Alison Tomisato
"HALEʻIWA FISHERMAN"

A woven lauhala hat, frayed at the brim
shades his face from the rising morning sun.
The hat sits low on his forehead,
casting shadows over his age-trenched skin
as his eyes squint into the horizon.

He sits on the pier that juts into the sea,
just past the breaker wall;

the concrete, still cold, seeping through
faded khaki shorts.
Dipping a notched bamboo pole into the calm harbor water,
he patiently waits for that first, hesitant tug:
A silent, watchful statue
with eyes that have seen too much.

As I walk along the edge of the pier,
staring at the water lapping against wooden pilings,
his gaze trains on me.

Vulnerable, I look up.

His eyes are ancient and probing.
I walk toward him, and when I stand
no more than two feet away,
he reaches out and places an identical, notched bamboo pole
    next to him.

Taking this silent invitation, I sit
and dip my fishing line into the placid water.

ALISON TOMISATO *is a 2003 graduate of 'Iolani School in Honolulu and a 2006 alumna of Boston University, where she graduated summa cum laude in communications. She wrote "Hale'iwa Fisherman" after spending a fruitless late afternoon holding her bamboo pole off the stone wall bordering Hale'iwa Harbor on O'ahu. She currently works in special events in Boston, Massachusetts.*

Cameron Sasaki

"THE SONG OF CAMERON SASAKI"

I sing of Kupiapia Place in 'Ewa,
my grandparents Matsu and Sei Shimizu
who always plant flowers like anthuriums and orchids;

I sing of soybeans, lettuce, and cherry tomatoes,
Yuki, the furry white dog who died of diabetes;

I sing of indigo the color of the sky
and of teal the color of marlins;

I sing of miso soup with egg that we eat at Catch of the Day
and samurai ice shave with two flavors,
vanilla and strawberry;
I sing of the Yu-gi-oh cards that I keep in my drawer;

I sing of my fright of being grounded,
my love of drawing,
and being with my cousin Tyler;

I sing of being a couch potato,
but rising early in the morning on Saturday and Sunday;

I sing of the ocean:
the distant, clear sea hushing to me,
the fish gently breathing and looking at me,
the soft waves tickling my feet;
I am diving through the calm sea
whooshing through my veins.

CAMERON SASAKI *wrote this poem in 2004, when he was in the third grade and studying writing at Naʻau in Honolulu.*

Ali S. Y. Nakashima

"KUHIO VINES ARE PEACEFUL"

Hala are peaceful.
Manu-oku are peaceful.
Aloʻiloʻilo is peaceful.
Kualoa Regional park is peaceful.
Makena Beach is peaceful.
Kaneohe district is peaceful.
The South Shore is peaceful.
My sister is peaceful.
My heart is peaceful.

My Hawaiian Christian church is peaceful.
My mom is peaceful.
My dad is peaceful.

ALI S. Y. NAKASHIMA, *born in 1999, is a second grader at Waiau Elementary School in Pearl City on Oʻahu. Besides writing, she enjoys art. Her artwork has been featured at the State Capitol, City Hall, and the Board of Water Supply's annual water conservation calendar. Among her other interests are karate, piano, and gymnastics.*

Haunani-Kay Trask
"INTO OUR LIGHT I WILL GO FOREVER"

Into our light
    I will go forever.

    Into our seaweed
        clouds and saltwarm
            seabirds.

Into our windswept
ʻehu kai, burnt
    sands gleaming.

        Into our sanctuaries
            of hushed bamboo,
                awash in amber.

Into the passion
    of our parted Koʻolau
        luminous vulva.

    Into Kāne's pendulous
        breadfruit, resinous
            with semen.

Into our wetlands
    of Heʻeia
        bubbling black mud.

Into our spangled,
blue-leafed *taro*,
flooded with *wai*.

Into Waiāhole,
chattering with rains
and silvered fish.

Into our shallows
of Kualoa,
translucent Akua.

Into the hum of
reef-ringed Ka'a'awa,
pungent with *limu*.

Into our corals of
far Kahana, sea-cave
of Hina.

Into our chambered
springs of Punalu'u,
ginger misting.

Into the songs of
lost Lā'ie, cool
light haunting.

Into murmuring
Mālaekahana,
plumed sands chanting.

Into the sheen
of flickering Hale'iwa,
pearled with salt.

Into the *wa'a* of
Kanaloa, voyaging
moana nui.

Into our sovereign suns,
drunk on the *mana*
of Hawai'i.

Author Unknown

"KAU A HI'I-AKA I KA-'ENA"

Lele ana Ka-'ena me he manu ala,
I ka mālie me he kaha 'ana nā ke ka'upu
Ke one o Nēnē-le'a,
Me he upa'i ala nā ke koa'e
I waho la o ka 'ale o Ka'ie'ie.

Me he kanaka ho'onu'u ala i ka mālie,
Ka papa kea i kea lo o ka 'alā.
Ua ku'i 'ia e ke kai a uli, a nono, a 'ula,
Ka maka o ka 'alā,
E noho ana i ke kai o Kāpeku,
Ka leo o ke kai o ho'oilo ka malama.

Ke kū mai la ka pā'ulu'ā hiwa
Makai ka hō'ailona o ka 'āina.
Ahuwale ka pae ki'i, ka pae newanewa,
Ka pae manu a Kanaloa,
E ho'opaepae ana i ka lae o Ka-lā'au,
Kīhe 'ahe'a ana i ke kai o Ewelua.

Nā'owae pali o Unulau,
Inu aku i ka wai o Ka-'apu.
Hō'ole ke kupa hūnā i ka wai.
'Ehā ka muliwai wai a Ka-'ena
'E'ena iho la i ka lā o Makali'i.
'O'io mai ana i ku'u maka,
Me he kālana pali ala o Lei-honua.

Honua iho nei loko i ka hikina 'ana mai a nei makani.
Heaha la ka'u makana i ku'u hilahila?

O ka'u wale nō ia o ka leo a.

"HI'I-AKA'S SONG AT KA-'ENA"

Ka-'ena reaches out like a bird flying overhead,
a sea-gannet soaring in a still sky
above sandy Nēnē-le'a,
a bo'sunbird high over the channel of Ka-'ie'ie—
a flapping of wings.

Like a thirsty man drinking from a pool
so do rocks near Ka-'ena drink of foamy waves.
Silent pounding has darkened those quiet faces of stone.
Bruised black and red, waterworn,
they have grown ghostly from long attending the sea of Kāpeku,
a wintry season's song.

Blackened and red from perpetual pounding
stand these sea-wardens of the land:
naked god-forms, unstable god-forms
assumed by Kanaloa who shaped them,
sea-washed bird-forms of the high god
guarding the shore at Cape Ka-lā'au,
sprayed by the sea of Ewelua.

In cliff-steep gullies at Unulau
I too drink of Kā-'apu's water.
(The countryman, with surly denial, would hide it from strangers.)
Yet at Ka-'ena four shy streamlets wind seaward
in heat of summer sun.
Their living waters file before me in parade.
Lei-honua's great wall beholds the procession.

With the rising of the wind I am caught by a sudden thought.
What shall I, in my shame, give to the four bathers?

My sole gift is a song.

TRANSLATED BY MARY KAWENA PUKUI

W. J. Illerbrun

"STILL IZ"

Everytime,
driveen pas Makua
I teenk of you
on da beach deah
wit da surf comeen in

Sometimes,
when it's only me in da cah,
I turn off da radio
geev leesen

First comes da weend,
den da waves
Den . . . .den comes yoah voice again
jus like befoah you wen go

Funny ting dough
If I stay by da side da road
dere is only da weend
and da waves

And now and den
one rainbow rideen in

Private Passion

Heart clapping like green bamboo . . . I drink oceans . . . Crazy for beauty . . . The pure murmur . . . Waiting for the pounce . . . Not bending to call or caress . . . Passion flower my scent . . . Floating through the green water . . . Please send me a letter . . .

Michael Ondaatje
UNTITLED

All this noise at your neck!

heart clapping
like green bamboo

        this earring
    which
has flipped over
   and falls
        into the pool of your ear

The waves against black stone
that was a thousand year old
burning red river
could not reach us

Tracee Lee
"MĀNOA PARANOIA"

I am out of my mind
and deep in the rainy valley, waiting for you
under the wet ʻiliahi tree.

I linger in the lush damp
until my limbs take root
and my hair curls around the lace fern.

One day you'll come back to me,
not on the crest of tsunami, or spray of lava,
but gently on trades.
Is that your voice riding the offshore wind?
I chase it down to the foot of Kahana
and open my eyes for you in the brackish water.

Smoke rises up from the leeward side:
a brush fire, burning rubbish, huli chicken?
You're trying to signal me, I know it.

Up on the ridge, I vanish by the waterfall.
Come search for me with sniffing dogs—
I'll leave a trail of white ginger, just in case.

I remember us up to the knees
in the taro patch, pulling thick stalks;
the silty earth, and our legs mingling under water.

You remember my foolishness—
reticent as a clam, hard as a coconut husk.
I turn my back to the waves.

I'm missing you so I report you
missing. Your mug on the milk carton
is not smiling.

They dredge the Ala Wai—but no sign of you:
a gun, a key, a wedding ring.
Nothing I can claim.

This is no mystic love affair
waiting to happen. This is
an ordinary woman loving her pig.

I'll wait for you at Hunakai, low tide lapping up shore,
our spot by the fallen tree. If you don't come
this time, I'll try to learn a lesson.

Forest green. Ever green. Ocean green.
One day I'll want more than rain
and lime-colored vistas.

I am earth bound for now.
Down here I wallow in the wet dark,
moss-covered and hidden beneath the valley's overgrowth.
My landscapes are always raining.
Each drop on the tongue is a promise of you
and so I drink oceans.

Paul Oliveira

"HOʻOMALIMALI"

crazy for beauty in the Academy of Arts
        a yellow field by one ear,
and crooked nose who loved shy brown wahines
        sing to me

a local wahine
much attracted to the field
        and I know
he would cut off his other one for her

the thought of what life
        would be like
    if local women mingled more
           corrupts my mind

the thought of what life
        would be like
    if local women wore no mask
           surreals my vision

the thought of what life
        would be like
    if local women sang to me
           troubles my sleep

PAUL OLIVEIRA *wrote this poem in 1976.*

Jane Anderson

UNTITLED

you approach in a safari hat
And speak of thick furred animals
I begin to cover the erotic parts of myself

Frank Stewart
"HONOLULU, WINTER MORNING"

The dawn's wine tilts
up the mountains, the green ranges'
light washing up, edges to orange
below the day moon, red air, red clouds.
The glassy yellow haze begins to clear.
I turn from the window to your bed's white.
I've been so far into the walls
during the night my heart's become white cinder, a spell
or disease of the glass, the white curtains'
wavering towards that amber and silver city below.

Now daylight goes blue.
The flood of your hair against the sheets
is all that's left of the night.
Silver ghosts fly from it, turn to white
all our tears, the children's voices, grief
for lost parents, every unhappiness
and homelessness, gone or turning away.

The Episcopal bells across the city ring.
What can I give you that's not another cruelty?
I'm worn out with desire, want to return, if I could,
the healing that's the kingdom of your body, where
though it's barely light, I've broken too many things.

Marjorie Edel
"KIMI"

1 Now that I've decided to go back, I remember everything I wanted to
forget. If I hadn't seen that beautiful collection of her pottery in Gump's
window in San Francisco . . . The old pain returned, but it was quieter; and
the longing to recover—what can I call it? A harmony—which I have never
fully understood. It was more than twenty years ago. In between I've had my
life with Annabell and the kids, my work . . .

In my room at the Royal Hawaiian Hotel. I listen to the sea. The surf shuts things out, dims anxiety, old jealousies, angers. I know her studio is not far from here. I could walk there, I could surprise her. I might even look in the window, and then walk away, not even see her.

When the end came between us—though I've learned that nothing really ends—I thought I would never recover. I would die. I wanted to die. I drove wildly to the cliff's edge. I looked down onto the black rocks and the sea foam. I could see my broken body. I pitied myself; I thought of how she would feel.

Why didn't I throw myself down on the black rocks?—I couldn't. I did what I could do. I went to his house and took a machete. There I saw George's car. I hacked until the tires were shreds. He never said a word about it. Kimi never said a word. I hated their silence. It was as if they had a conspiracy, George and Kimi, and I didn't know how long it had gone on.

One thing is clear. I can never again live with the intensity, with the wide dimension of dream I had during my three years with Kimi. For two of those years I was working on the novel I never finished—an effort left over from a university course. She was doing her first work in pottery, learning the art which ten years later made her famous. I was a macho snob. I assumed I would become the great one, and Kimi was just playing, womanlike, with clay. The intensities, I know now, were in her, not in me. The passion for art was in her—it struck fire in me while we were together. I have not felt it since. Oh, a little, perhaps, after I started my collection of paintings.

I remember the baths we took together in the furo. It was at the small shack on Kauai which belonged to her grandparents. Every afternoon Kimi lit the wood fire under the tub of the bathhouse. The smoke slid out between the boards, drifted among the trees until the wind caught and dissolved it. It made the whole wooded slope fragrant. We undressed in the bathhouse and hung our clothes on a peg. The wooden floor under our feet was soft with years of soaping and scrubbing. From a large galvanized iron tub we dipped cold water and poured it over ourselves. We soaped our bodies and then embraced to feel the smooth sliding of body on body. Her breasts were small with brown nipples. Her hips and thighs glistened along their whole delicate length. We rinsed ourselves clean of soap. We stepped into the steaming water of the wooden tub, slowly sinking until the water was up to our chins. Her long hair trailed on the water's surface like a drift of seaweed. My white skin turned red. Hers remained its own pale gold. We put arms around each other—our skin was charged as if with electricity. We made love endlessly in that old bathhouse where several generations of a family had bathed and put on their cotton evening kimonos. We spoke of this and felt a curious continuity of life. For me in the painful throes of my unfinished novel, it was as if I shared in ancient generative forces that were compensation for my limited imagination. The bath was ritual: purification, rebirth.

Another ritual we observed each year was the gathering of plums. Kimi's family showed us an old grove of plum trees on the slope of the hills. Sometimes the whole family would go with buckets; afterwards Kimi's mother made a delicious jelly from the harvest. Other times Kimi and I stole up alone. We lay in the fern bed at the edge of the grove and watched the flowing movement of clouds, foliage, light. We listened to small thuds when plums fell. We ate the fruit, sour-sweet and sun-warmed. Lying there in the dappled light I came to know in detail the beauty of her body—the roundness of her arms, the delicate narrowing from the elbow to wrist, and the strong flowing articulation of wrist to hand. Her small belly was like a shallow saucer of the faintest gold, her thighs rounded, firm; they had amazing strength. It always amazed me, her strength—hand and wrist, foot and ankle, thigh. She could lift things I could barely budge. This controlled power slowly poured itself into her work, the bowls and plates and teapots, the free forms she occasionally indulged in and of which she was always slightly ashamed.

Sometimes in that warm fern bed, after making love, we would sleep. She always wakened first. I would come through the shadowy tide between sleep and awareness—the flow of cool wind over my body, a faint darkening of the sunlight, and finally her eyes looking at me. Shining, watching, smiling lightly. Occasionally I sensed that she had gone off, leaving me sleeping in the fern. For how long? Why? I never knew, I never asked. I was always vaguely jealous.

After she told me about George and I suffered that final brutal hacking jealousy, I fled from her and from Hawaii. For a year or two I continued to see dark eyes like night on the water, the eyes that watched me sleeping in the fern bed. Often I smelled the plums. Even on Madison Avenue when dust and exhaust hung in the air and brakes screamed, I smelled the plums. I was lucky to meet Annabell so quickly after my flight. But she was only a substitute, a shadow. I had to make her real by constantly reassuring myself of her beauty and her gracefulness of manner. I said to my friends, "Annabell's lovely, isn't she? So beautiful, so serene." I said these things until I believed them.

There were times, however, when the old spell returned, when Kimi haunted me. I would see her on streets, in shops, in cafes and art galleries. Once in the Metropolitan Museum I saw her walk from one gallery to another, just slipping through the archway of the door. Her long hair flowed behind her, and I was sure I saw her beautifully formed strong wrists. I hurried after her. She turned. A stranger. In Paris once I saw her sitting at a sidewalk cafe reading a newspaper. Her head was bent and the dark hair fell about her face. I remembered how I had pushed my fingers and arms through that hair—the experience of Kimi remained in my body. I sat near her, a little frightened, to wait. In time she did what Kimi often did—she thrust her thumbs through the fall of hair next to her cheeks, pulled it back, fastened it behind her head with a small loop. The face was not Kimi's.

For more than twenty years I have followed girls with long dark hair. And faced the inevitable disappointment. I wonder what it was that held me, that was so haunting and stirred me with old recognitions which somehow were a part of earth and sea, a part of the ongoing generations. Baths in an old bathhouse . . . Annabell has never known about Kimi, nor of course have the children. As my wife she pursued her own way—golf, bridge, parties. The children are now at the university. I fashioned a conventional businessman's life. A good life, in ways, and satisfying. I guess I can be smug. There continue to be, however, small moments of doubt and regret. Then comes Annabell's sensible voice, or one of the children asking help in making or buying. They believe in the value and immutability of things.

Here at the Royal Hawaiian, the sea beyond my lanai crashes restlessly. It bites the sand. Just a few blocks away she works or sleeps or talks.

2

It has taken a few days to manage those few blocks, not so few as it turned out. The studio is off Beretania Street on a little lane buried deep in large mango and breadfruit trees and a monkey pod. I walk down the cracked walk spiked with grass. The studio is an old house. The window to the display room is dusty. There is a semblance of dilapidation. The studio doesn't suggest the elegant shops in Japan. New York. London, Paris that display her work. Perhaps she is in one of those far-off places now. I almost hope so. Then I could turn around and go home. Annabell is uneasy about my absence, she calls me from New York every day. She would be glad.

I see myself suddenly in the window. My hair thinning and graying, my stomach rounded so that I have no waist. I look sloppy in these vacation clothes, pale-blue slacks, a white sport shirt with some sort of animal symbol on the pocket. Do I want to see her, to let her see me? Like this? Does she remember the lanky brown-haired boy?

For years I have not felt this uncomfortable, this reluctant about meeting an old friend. Is this what I want? To resurrect a ghost which belongs more in that grove of plum trees or that decaying cottage in the countryside of Kauai?

But I have come. I step across the threshold. A bell tinkles. There are some new pots, thin and delicate as leaves dried in Hawaiian sun. She continues her explorations in clay. A middle-aged Japanese woman comes from an inner room. She is carefully dressed in a dark color, and her hair is molded as if she had just come from the hairdresser. She wears high heels and has beautiful slender legs. "May I help you?"

It is Kimi's sister Janice. I know her voice. That scrawny child who had been the despair of her parents because she ran wild in the hills and loved animals. She has become this primly fashionable woman.

"Do you remember?" I ask.

She studies me a moment. Then she smiles, bows slightly. "Dennis. It's you."

We exchange a few memories before she asks. "You come to see Kimi?"

I nod. "She's been ill," Janice says. "She's better, but . . . " Janice shakes her head. "She's still too young." After a moment, she giggles in the nervous Japanese fashion, "We're still quite young, aren't we?"

I pick up one of Kimi's pots. "Yes, we're always young." We both recognize how silly our remarks about youth are. Things to be said when a person doesn't know what else to say.

"I'll get her. Sit down and I'll bring some tea."

The tea comes quickly in a beautiful cup of Kimi's design. Janice says, "She'll be out in a minute. She really has been very sick." She returns to the inner part of the house.

I sip green tea. My heart almost deafens my ears. I stare at the pattern of leaf shadows on the lawn outside. Two mynah birds are chasing each other. I want terribly to stay with external things, to fasten my mind upon them.

Kimi comes in before I realize it. Standing at my side. "Dennis!" Her voice still has all the soft huskiness I remember.

I put the teacup on a shelf and embrace her. I can feel the frailness of her bones. There is nothing of the firm flesh of the past. "Kimi!" I whisper.

She is shrunken like an autumn leaf and as delicate. She talks in that husky voice and sips tea. I scarcely listen to what she says. Her presence overwhelms me. Her long hair done loosely in a bun with a silver chopstick through it. Her eyes rounder than I remembered, and larger. Her skin wrinkled but transparent. She is all around me, voice and cadence, demeanor and gesture, her whole persuasive self.

As she rises to go for more hot tea, I recognize myself—my sweating flabbiness, the head going bald and hair graying, the eyes fading and sinking, my nose grown larger somehow. How can she bear to look at what I am? Has she ever thought of me during the years? I was wrong to come. But I have been wrong about so much. She makes me feel the waste, a tedious channeling of the days.

"Your children?" She pours more tea.

"Like others these days. Puzzled, uncertain, materialistic."

"You're lucky. You've a family." She sighs. "You belong to the great stream of life, of human energy and spirit." She pauses. "I have only pots." Her tone is sad. "Now, as I am now"—he holds out her thin arm, touches it, then strokes the lines of her cheekbone. "I feel a loss. The loss of time." She waves a hand at the pots. "These are inanimate. Their voice is silence."

"Kimi," my tone is much too somber. "You are a great woman."

She laughs. "Come, Dennis—remember the plums we used to eat?"

3

I wait awhile before returning to the studio. The days are crowded with remembrances. The old house, how she put buckets down when the roof leaked in drenching rains, her fingers stained purple with plum juice, soap bubbles running down her arms and thighs. When I walk from the Royal Hawaiian out on Kalakaua Avenue, I see her ahead of me, her long hair flipping in the tradewinds. It is always the young Kimi. Not the fragile Kimi of today. The Kimi who in strange fashion does not exist, who is translated into the stream of pots and jars and plates which have come from her fingers and were fired in her kiln.

I want to see her once again before I leave. I want to free myself by looking at that pale transparent skin, the hair still dark but thin, the face in which the bones stretch the skin. Such looking will free me. I am sure of it. I am desperate—this is not the Kimi I knew. This is not the self I want to be—plump and middle aged after a life of successful conformity. (The novel lost long ago, but then I could never have finished it.) I am not the Dennis of the plum grove.

The day is overcast. Showers in the mountain areas drifting down to the sea. I walk from the Royal Hawaiian to the studio. I will only glance at her. I will see very little. This is to be the moment of renunciation. Such a silly word to use. What is there to renounce? But I need this moment.

The door of the studio is open. No one is there. I step in. No bell. I can hear only wind in the foliage and a passing gust of rain. The dried leaf of a breadfruit tree lies on the floor like a shrivelled hand. Yellow spindly leaves from a croton are twisted into a corner. Among the pots is a bouquet of flowers—their stems have turned black, and they droop. A faint odor of rotting green comes from the vase.

Kimi is there suddenly. She seems not to notice me. She walks to the display of her work, picks up a pot, examines it, puts it down. She moves uncertainly to another pot and touches it. Her fingers run lightly over the surface. I feel her fingers on my skin in the furo. The texture—she wants to feel the texture. There is something about her demeanor that keeps me from speaking. She turns toward me but gives no evidence of seeing me. I stand perfectly still. I feel like an intruder. I want to leave quietly without her discovering me. I shrink toward a shadowy corner. She moves suddenly to the inner door and disappears. I do not hear her footsteps. I am alone as I have never been alone. I shiver slightly. The dried breadfruit leaf scrapes along the floor.

MARJORIE EDEL (1913-2005) *is the author of* Kona; The Wild Wind; *and* Nahiʻenaʻena; *and the editor of* The Path of the Ocean. *She taught English at the University of Hawaiʻi at Mānoa, and worked for over twenty-five years with the Hawaiʻi Literary Arts Council. She received the Hawaii Award for Literature in 1981.*

Courtney Sato
from "WISHES"

3 I Just Don't Want to Die

Years ago, we walked on the wall
leading out into the murky Kahala water.
It was so quiet as we balanced on the thin
cement blocks, just your sighs when you
looked back. The salt water pooled
at my ankles as I watched you
dive off the pier. I heard your voice,
strained by salt and laughter.

Once night arrived
and the moon crawled above us
you returned, your arms slowly slicing
dark water, reaching for my tiny body.

Joy Hiromi Uyeno

"TREETOPS FLYING"

Deep in the rich green of Wahiawa, past the scent of pineapple and chicken manure, summer rises in the damp, tangled forest, thick and moist like the breath of someone near. Mock orange blooms with the red, featherlike blossoms of the low-hanging trees as the five of us walk quickly, barefoot on the watermarked trail. We reach the first river, crossing the rocks without speaking. At the last one, I reach for a branch on a nearby tree to steady my balance as I step to the land, and a sharp one cuts across my wrist lightly, opening the nearly healed scars that lie lumpy on my wrists. I can already feel the blood trickling, mingling with the mud that speckles my arms.

Jonah notices, and steps up to take my other hand, helping me to the muddy bank. Blue tinged shadows from the trees dance on his light skin, and I wonder if we'll make it back before sunset. I make a silent wish that we won't.

His familiar scent hangs in the netting of late June's breeze as we make our way to another trail. I lift my free hand as Jonah's smell wafts over me, hoping to catch it in the cross hatched patterns of my palm.

At the vined entrance to the creek, Kamaile and Aaron run ahead, already laid out and glinting like washed up seashells, on the largest rocks by the time the rest of us reach the water. Anne sidesteps her way to a shaded platform carved in the cliff. Jonah and I snake through the banyan tress, over the carpeting of fallen leaves, to a hollowed log overlooking the rest of the scene.

"Will you jump?" Jonah asks. He always does, just in case.

"Maybe. You go first," I answer, sitting on the log to examine my arm.

"Let me see," he says as he kneels down and touches three fingers to my wrist, wiping away the brown to reveal the red. I wince.

"Sorry." With his teeth, he pops open the top of his water bottle and cleans off the area around the cut. I look in fascination at the contrast of my gold against his white skin.

"Jonah?"

"Yeah?"

" . . . Nothing," I say, taking my arm back. "Thanks."

I watch as he steps to the edge to jump into the creek, holding my breath even though I know he's not. "Last chance, Kai," he singsongs. Before jumping, his sharp shoulder blades move as he brings his hands to the center of his chest, until he is folded, head down, arms bent, eyes closed, like an origami crane. Then he's flying, suspended in the air for a split second, as though he knows my hand is already reaching into the depths of my backpack, tangled in the straps of my camera.

Once, Jonah told me that he wished to fly. We had first known each other that year, and by then I was used to his endless one-sided philosophical debates, and he had come to understand my cynicism. The night he'd confessed his wish to me, I was sorting through numerous slides I'd taken in Waikiki—tourist shots, of the crimson clouds moving over the beach, of the cherry blossoms, and red hibiscus.

"That's a trite wish," I said, holding a slide up to the light. "Everyone wishes to fly."

"Well, what do you wish for?"

I shrugged, "I could use a new lens."

Through my bangs, I looked up at him, waiting for his smile to meet mine.

Instead, his eyes were focused just to the left, halfway to the lamp, on my arm. Quickly, I brought the slides to the ground, covering my wrists with my hands. Panic rose in a white sound that echoed though my ears. I pressed my spine down into the white carpeting, wishing to melt into the kaleidoscope of scattered slides before me. Shallow breaths passed through my dry lisps as Jonah reached over to push back the sleeve of my right arm.

The underside of my wrist was white, like the belly of a fish with veins, crimson from the point of my razor. Jonah traced his finger lightly along the trees I'd carved into my skin—a hundred nights of yet unfinished poetry. I didn't pull away; he didn't speak. if he were to ask why, my only answer would be one he already knew: that I was, somehow, already gone.

Bringing both his hands around mine, he pulled them toward him, to the smoothness of his T-shirt. My pointer finger touched his Adam's apple, and I felt it move up and down as he closed his eyes and swallowed.

I watched him pray for me, studying the way his sandy lashes rested on his cheeks, wishing that I could capture him like that in a black and white photograph.

Instead, I whispered, "I shouldn't be prayed for."

I thought he hadn't heard me; he kept his eyes shut for a few seconds longer. When he opened them, he said, "Of course you should be."

A breeze whispered through the leaves of the ginger stalks outside, and the weight of the glass louvers, and the darkened mesh screen. Jonah picked up a slide and held it close for me to see. I'd taken it while sitting on a branch that hung over the edge of a cliff at Kolekole Pass. Dozens of treetops flushed in noontime sun filled the view. A white good luck bird was poised just below, wings bent like white tents.

"I think you wish to fly too," Jonah said, placing the slide back beneath the blue safety of my ocean shots, all wide angled, flat, and empty.

I snap a shot of Jonah just before he hits the water, his spiky hair looking even more shocked, one hand balled up, pinching his nose shut. My throat tightens for the few seconds he's underwater, until he surfaces, sputtering, smiling, paddling back to the trail. When he's back, putting a dripping arm around my shoulders, my toes are already an inch from the edge. I pass him my tank top and camera. He steps backward, the rhythms of his quickened breath beating with the blood pulsing through my head.

A gust of wind carries through the trees, rippling the water, smelling heavily of mock orange swirled with dampened earth. I contemplate saying something to Jonah, but fear losing this moment. Instead, I touch my wrists, then jump while the wind is still blowing, until it is through my hair, in my nostrils, filling my ears, its fingers rolling down my spine. I fall until I am floating through the green water like leaves of *mamaki* tea, drifting to the bottom until they can be read.

JOY HIROMI UYENO *grew up in Mililani, on Oʻahu and graduated with her BA from the University of Hawaiʻi at Mānoa. Her work has appeared in* HONOLULU *Magazine;* Talk Story; *and* Leader *magazines, and she writes a column for the* Honolulu Star-Bulletin *called "Hit the Road." She writes about travel, fashion, and food from her home in Boston, Massachusetts.*

Debbi Pughe
"SITTING VIGIL WITH PABLO CARLOS"

A big old calico
    black cat
licking lines like
    'just for tonite
    let's be romantic'
around your too soft lips
and that tail that
slips
between my legs
and starts to wind its way up.

You rasty old black
    tongue-creature
who assentingly
listens to reason
and truth
waiting for the pounce.
And could I ever trust you
    enough
to show you
    in person not letters
the vulnerable and purely
    mousekin in my soul
that holds you,
cares
and is a warm furry paw.

You'd still,
    calicoed salamander lips
        wet and soft,
    stand on my tail
    and try to take
        me down.

Your needs are
    still your own.

I'm curled alone
    in a warm bed
and quite happy.

Debbi Pughe
"MIYAZAWA NO YOMU TOKI"

Bending neither to
the push of Manoa wind
or to you
and the desires erupting at the tip
of my breast

Bending neither to idle talk
or huge stories
or black blood
frozen and tired
or blatant gambles
lost and won and
bought away with fresh fruit
Alone later
Bending neither to
darkness falling
disquiet
disfiguring the hour

Not bending to call or caress

Nor filling my mouths
with
you or
anything but
poetry
and the stick to grind sesame.

DEBBI PUGHE *wrote this poem in 1977.*

Debra Thomas

"RAINBOW FALLS A STAIR"

Rainbow falls a stair.
You, my Prince, smile in mist.
My, how your skin gleams, dark as the bark
of the koa tree
and your eyes gleam in the moth shadow of your cape.
Come, in the dusty rafters of the banyan tree
I'm in vines entangled, morning glories I
bloom for orange moon Manoa Valley Prince.
My house is fine, full

my lips smooth, pomegranate red
my heart, passion flower
my scent, sweet awepahuna breath.

DEBRA THOMAS *was born in 1955 and grew up in Pālolo and Mānoa on Oʻahu. She has
studied at the University of Guadalajara, the University of Hawaiʻi, and the University
of California at Irvine, where she received an MFA in poetry. She teaches transcendental
meditation.*

This is Paradise

Peaceful postcard paradise . . . Bright prismatic people . . . Missionaries beat holy drums . . . The aristocracy of the dollar . . . People, pineapple, sugar cane and Pearl Harbor grown dependently together . . . Race prejudice? There's none in Hawai'i . . . The pot melts and boils . . .

Frank Marshall Davis

"THIS IS PARADISE"

I

Here is the peaceful postcard paradise
A considerate sun slaves overtime
The moon dances to a soft guitar
The champagne rain bubbles and warms
And June lasts a full twelve months;
Here live the bright prismatic people
Sun-washed, moon-dried,
Diamond set in the lava ring
Of brown green mountain and rainbow valley
In the blue jewel case
Of the Pacific.

The seven main islands of Hawaii
Born two thousand miles from California
Are inhabited by people, pineapple
Sugar cane and Pearl Harbor
Grown dependently together—
This much is in the travel folders.

The rich cruise here in winter
Planes bring the middle class in summer
(The poor see the sights any time
At their neighborhood movie or on T-V:
Who says there's no equality in America?)
With air above and water below
Subject to municipal regulations
And official boundaries
Afloat on the ocean,
You enter the City & County of Honolulu
A thousand miles
Before you reach
The City & County of Honolulu
(Discount any comments
From birds and fishes—
They have neither voting rights
Nor civic consciousness)

Bring along a blank paper mind
Until the Island of Oahu
Inflates from dime to dollar
And then a sack of bulging bullion
Split by the worried brow of Diamond Head;
See the languid palms
Dressing the shining coral shores;
Bright houses and slick buildings
Like quarters and dimes
In a pocket of greenbacks;
Come by luxury liner
And see the little welcoming boats
Like chicks around a mother hen;
Brown boys in bright trunks
Diving to spray tourists
With splashes of Local Color;
Hula dancers waving their hips
To conduct the Royal Hawaiian Band;
Come by air
And see the fly-speck mountains
Spring into gaunt giants
As the land reaches up
Like a friendly hand;
Come either way
And wear a lavalier of flowers
On that greeting drive through strange streets
Glowing with the bright prismatic people;
Now enter into the baited door
Of your tourist trap in Waikiki,
Pour your eager flesh and bone
Into a bathing suit,
Dash to the nearby beach
And sit;
Sit while barefoot boys bob by
Twanging ukes;
Sit while waves regularly report
Their quotas of spray and surfboard riders;
Sit for dinner under soft stars
Sit until the night grows confidential
And solicits for his scented woman, Sleep
Now take a postcard to your room

Write "Having wonderful time—"
And go to bed, murmuring
"It's really true!
This really is Hawaii!"

Tomorrow, long after the sun
Has wandered into your room
Sat awhile, and left his calling card
You will leisurely arise
Breakfast on papaya,
Guava jelly and Kona coffee
Then buy a gaudy Aloha shirt;
Now start your conducted tour
Of the island,
See for yourself the fabled sights
Leap to life from the guidebook;
Go to a luau and eat like the natives—
The quaint, friendly, childish natives;
Pinch the buxom bottoms of the island girls
While your wife makes eyes
At the sleek brown boys;
Loaf and live
By all means live;
Go to the Outer Islands
Visit the bubbling volcanoes on Hawaii
Huge Haleakala crater on Maui
Wonderful Waimea canyon on Kauai
Or stay in Waikiki;
This is Paradise
Anyway you take it—
And so two weeks, a month slip by.

Now it is time to leave
Return as president of that Iowa bank
(Good old Iowa, the REAL U. S. A.)
Back as buyer for the Boston store
(Good old Boston, pride of New England);
You've had as good a time
As money could buy
At prevailing prices;
(That explanation

By the Hawaii Visitors Bureau
Was logical:
"Everything's shipped in, you know")
You'd like to come again
Not next year but sometime
But no matter
You've plenty to tell the folks back home,
You've seen the peaceful postcard paradise,
You've seen the bright prismatic people
And now you know Hawaii!

II
Pardon me, Paradise
But under your cool stylish frock
Designed by the Chamber of Commerce
Tailored by the Visitors Bureau
Your soiled slip shows . . .

Hawaii is more than pineapple and sugar cane
Tall mountains and green valleys
Grass shacks under pandering palms
Gleaming sands and green-blue ocean
Smoking volcanoes and cascading waterfalls
Gliding guitars and ripe red laughter—
For these
These are but props and a stage setting,
Painted scenery for continuous drama.

Pick it up at Scene I, Act the Second
Pick it up when old Captain Cook
Blasted the dam of silence
And the raging waters of missionaries
Roared through the widening breach

Sweeping over the old ways
Inundating the ancient gods
Flooding the sacred soil of custom and tradition
Leaving seeds of civilization in the thin silt;
Fruitful civilization bound to bless
The heathen sinners.

And the missionaries were magicians, too;
These magicians of missionaries
The conjure men of Christianity
Placed the vanishing cloth
Of Mother Hubbards on the women
Then Whoosh and Presto
Nudity into nakedness,
A factory-fresh set of morals
And a rise in illegitimate births.

Now that it was uncivilized
To kill by spear or club
Guns became a symbol of progress;
Guns with a silent sting
More poisonous than the bite of the scorpion
Sharper than the sudden kiss of the centipede—
Thus the natives advanced.

The missionaries beat holy drums for the good life;
People who had never heard of Satan
Were sold on the idea
That they had been bound for hell
That material things
Were bait in the devil's trap;
"Put ye the world behind you,"
Spake the come-on men for the church
"Now take the Word of God
As it is written in the Bible,
Believe,
And you shall find mansions in heaven."
The people heard and found salvation
Kings, chiefs, common people found salvation
And they turned their backs on the verdant islands
Lifted their eyes from the land that bore them
And began making reservations
For life eternal beyond the skies;
The missionaries came with Bibles
The heathen natives had the land
Now the natives are no longer heathen,
They have the Bible and Jesus
And in this equitable trade—

This oh so reasonable swap
The missionaries got the land:
End of the last scene of the Second Act.

(Maybe you've viewed this show before
Maybe you recognize this whitehaired plot
If that is the case I'm sorry
Nevertheless . . . anyhow . . . regardless
The drama still goes on)

III
Under the manure of the missionaries
Sprouted the Big Five
Monster all arms and mouth
Grabbing and gorging
Taking the best and the most
Packaging the crumbs
To sell at a price
Thus proving,
Say the public relations men,
The virtue of Free Enterprise
Which allows any man
To make a million.

God and the Big Five
(God ruled
Like the King of England
Tolerated
By the Aristocracy of the Dollar
If God got rambunctious
Out He went)
Time was
When the Big Five had God on their payroll
To care for the Sunday trade;
Weekdays they handled the people direct:
Sneeze, and they sold you handkerchiefs
Eat, and the food came by Big Five boat
Dress, and their stores peddled you cloth and clothes
Read, and the words had passed their censors
Die, and ride to glory in a Big Five box on a Big Five hearse
(One day the president of the largest bank

Delivered the commencement address
At the University of Hawaii:
"The best things
Yes, I say the best things in life
Are free.")

But that was before the Union
(Given free choice
Satan is preferable
The devil doesn't ask shorter hours, higher pay
Like Harry Bridges and his ILWU)
Men on the wide plantations
Those handling cargo on the waterfront
Hung hand me down hates in the closet
And organized
In one big union
Japanese, Chinese, Filipino, Portuguese, Puerto Rican,
    Hawaiian, Korean
And together
Raised their voices for a living share of the take
And treatment as men and women;
The Big Five sneered
Flexed its muscles
And hit—
But the Union stood and fought
Growing strong in struggle;
Then the onlookers
Seeing the Big Five no longer king
Themselves grew bold
Forming their own corporations
Biting the sweet apple of independence—
Nevertheless Directors of Big Five firms
(Interlocking, naturally)
Take two full days each year
To count their annual profits.

In the old days
Those oh so good dead days
(Shed a tear for the pungent past)
When the Big Five decreed
Finis for the militantly articulate

They bought one way passage
On the next outgoing ship;
But Time whistles a new tune
The plain people
Are no longer concubines of Fear.

No longer the hungry whip of the overseer
Eats soft flesh of the plantation hand,
No longer the boot of the waterfront boss
Underlines orders to the stevedore,
Still
The road to Heaven
In this island paradise
Is rough and long.

Behind the rows of rotting shacks
Herded together to leave more room
For growing pineapple and sugar cane
Rats and babies
Race for the privvies;
Seated in his office
Looking out into the lavender water
Of his private swimming pool
The plantation manager spoke
To the grievance committee
Of the union:
"It is your duty
As good citizens
To help preserve
Our American way of life."

During the big shipping strike
Somebody wrote to the stevedoring firms:
    For those who know
    The day they'll die
    Moons whiz by
    But minutes ride snail-back
    For the anxiously waiting.

IV
America is more than white
America is more than extension of Europe
In Hawaii the pot melts and boils
Orient and Polynesia
Caribbeans and Philippines
Pour in their pounds
To blend with Europe and a dash of Africa
And we have the people of Hawaii—
The bright prismatic people—
Blonde to black
With the tan pastels
Of Japan and China dominant.

A haole* tourist from Birmingham
Went home after two days of his intended month:
"You can take these Goddamned islands,"
He told friends in Dixie
"And shove them up your ass
I don't like Hawaii—
Too many niggers there."

A Hawaiian dark as ginger root
Said to his new neighbor from Nebraska
(A Negro light as a lemon)
"We ought to get along real well—
During World War II
My best friend
Was a colored boy from Pittsburgh."

Koji Takemoto sells soap powder on television
Ching On Mau buys Mickey Mouse boots for his son
The corner grocery is owned by Calixto Balbag
Antonio Rezentes and Kaleo Fanane drink Milwaukee
    beer and argue about the Giants and Dodgers;
Yesterday Mun Ng the printer
Setting type for Epstein and Ellison, Ltd.
Laughed and said
"What funny kind names, these."

---

*originally foreign, now means a white person.

Mrs. Yoshiko Saito Hanks has returned from Texas;
She plans a trip to Tokyo
After she becomes plain Yoshiko Saito again;
Texas was all right
It was big and broad and hot in summer
But it grew lonely
At the cottage in Dallas,
Her haole in laws could not climb the mountain
Of a Japanese in their family
And soon gave up trying;
Neighbors said to her husband,
It's all right to sleep with 'em
But for Christ sake
Why do you have to marry 'em
So after a year in Texas
With her soldier husband
Mrs. Yoshiko Saito Hanks
Has come home.

Each Friday night brown John Keakana crams his wife and four
    kids into their sputtering jalopy and drives from Honolulu to
    the country to weekend camp and fish on a sandy beach
And the tourists from Topeka and Joliet riding around the island
    in the prancing buses smile pinkly and murmur: "How
    quaint, how carefree the Hawaiians are, not a worry in the
    world, nothing to do but loaf and fish just like their ancestors"
Sunday afternoon John herds his Keakanas home and weighs his
    fish. Some he sells and some he keeps to help stretch monthly
    pay within $40 of what the social scientists call necessary for
    minimum health standards

Four stood by the gaping grave:
Book reading priest in black
Woman poking wet eyes with bright apron
Husband silent and circumspect
Young boy aiming his curious gaze at the quiet home of the
    buried dead around him—
This was all
The old man's world was small;

Neighbors noted "Kawasaki has another mouth to feed"
    seventy years before in Kyoto
Two days ago somebody mentioned "Old Man Kawasaki
    kicked off last night" in the little lane in Honolulu;
Both main events in this history
Flattened to the casual;
Now four stood by the gaping grave—
This was all
The old man's world was small.

Outside a country church
I heard a young woman say:
"If it's true the good die young
My boy! lost at the age of eight
Must have been near perfect.
But think what a no-good bum
Methuselah must have been."

One delegate to Congress
In the first half of the century
Given the run-around on statehood for Hawaii
Left this final request:
    When I die
    Burn these brittle bones
    Then take the thin ashes
    Some blowy snowy day
    And scatter them on the Senate steps
    So those who stomped upon my living soul
    May complete their act.

V
"Race prejudice? There's none in Hawaii"
Said blonde Bob Bowser
Driving from his beachside home in Kahala
(You'll love this exclusive section, said
the realtor. No Oriental neighbors)
To an evening at the Outrigger Club
(Membership restricted to Caucasians)
"Never could understand why
The damn Japs always stick together
Unless maybe they're just clannish."

"We don't say nothin'
When those haole boys from the Mainland
Get in our high school
And act like they're better'n us,"
Grinned the clove brown Samoan,
"We jus' sit tight 'n' wait
'Til they come out fo' football practice."

Moses, mud black Hawaiian
Was fired as tour car driver
After socking that visitor from Denver
Who innocently asked
If Moses was Negro.

Three Oriental lads
Studying at the University
Stood at the bus stop
Drenched in grave sarcasm;
Bowing, low
They spoke to the lone Japanese co-ed:
Who had twice dated a Canadian classmate:
"We salute you—
From now on
You're white man's meat
You haole-lover you."

"You gotta understan',"
Said the red-headed sailor from Savannah
To Anna Kahakapai
Nutmeg toned bedmate
"You're better'n any damn nigger
So don't never
Even talk to 'em
If you can help it
Or none of us
Ain't gonna pay you no min'."
And the graduate from Ole Miss
Supervising at Pearl Harbor
Looked around his first day
At strange yellow faces
Ancestor-flung from Korea, Okinawa, Japan, China

And one lone mulatto
With the map of familiarity
Then he smiled
And he walked over and spoke
Confidentially: "You and me
We have to stick together—
We understand each other."

One week in the country
And the navy wife phoned her landlord:
"Across the street
Lives a bunch of dirty Hawaiians;
Next door on our right
A family of lousy Japs;
On the other side
A house full of slant eyed Chinks;
And in front of us
On our very same lot
A white bitch married to a nigger—
I want our rent money back."

After a lifetime
Of crusading for black causes
Outwitting three lynch mobs
And six shotgun sheriffs
Africanus White
At the age of sixty
Came to Hawaii
Only to die one year later
In the unfamiliar jungle of superficial equality
From mental malnutrition.

VI
The night
Slippery as a black eel in Kaneohe Bay
Slices softly down zig-zag mountains;
Hotels in Waikiki
Mark feeble protests
In neon and mazda;
White buttons of light
Fasten homes to high dark hills;

A gay full moon
Spills champagne bubbles
Bursting in dancing splashes
On the rambling waves
Of the ocean;
Stars wait
Like patient white lizards
On the dark rock
Of the sky;
Slowly the night sinks
Into the confusion of history
As the peaceful postcard paradise
Sleeps.

The Way We Live Now

My girlfriend loves to shop at da Generations depahtment at Liberty House . . .
Hawaii makes rich the industrious Ilokano . . . No high heels but walk barefeet . . .
Rubbah slippahs . . . Beware of the Ala Wai . . . Sittin down wit mah Papa insai his
boat . . . Hooking up on the Web . . . GurlStar signed off at 8 o'clock . . . Rueful-
ness in the coffee shop . . . Move two one-night stands to the left a handful of
"I'll call you's" to the right . . . Heard you went to a party in Waipahu . . . Drinks
and pupus at eight . . . WHERE IS DICKEY BOY JR? . . . Chicharon widows . . .
Sensible women nearing forty do not marry fishermen . . . Quiet sansei guys
great at electronics . . . Local guys are Not like cops on the main-land . . .
Rough times in the classroom . . . Great big girls with great big curly hairdos . . .
Road rage . . . Miles from Normal . . . They think life is a video game . . .
Gangsta surf . . . You bettah watch out . . . Boy! Come hea! . . . Kimother-
apy . . . I no shet you . . . SEE YOU LATER IN COURT . . . We Young
Asian Professionals gave him space . . . Stalking Haunani . . . Island enter-
tainment . . . Herbert K. Wang, Doctor of Herbal Medicine, Ret., No So-
liciting . . . There's a gecko in my kitchen . . . 47 million termites . . . Da
Lemon Tree Billiards House . . . Tink positive. You one negative buggah . . .
Museum views . . . Topless time . . . Round and round at the Lollipop . . . There
is no short season on the island . . . Tell me all you know about bamboo . . .
Temple bells . . .

Faye Kicknosway
"THE OTHER SHOE"

did you know Melville worked
in a bowling alley in Honolulu?
Bela Lugosi tried to outwit
Charlie Chan in Kailua?

he paused, whoever it is
writing this.
it was 1843 and civilized enough
for beaver hats.
There was a lens of fresh water

above the ocean not to mention claw
hammers, salt pork, ordnance,
the understanding

kerosene would be the death
of whaling.

Answer the following: What's
a pineapple? A sheep? A night blooming
cereus

What's a South Sea Islander?
Measles? Immigrant labor? Cholera?

What's a rat? A horse?
Plague? What's history? And why

is it time sugar moved to Thailand?

I'll tell you: Because Max Von Sydow
and Julie Andrews
put long grey shirts on it.

Roxanne Mapuana Cottell
"TREASURES"

i. Take a short ride on *The Bus*,
    end up at the end of the earth.
    Wonder where it begins,
    again

> at Ala Moana, Longs Drugs,
> slippers on sale—two for a dollar.
> Always wear slippers,
> Never wear a jacket,
> > even in winter.

ii. McDonald's saimin!

iii. Leftover stew and rice.
     Portuguese sausage, eggs with rice.
     Spam fried slightly—never burnt or dry.
     Fight with Auntie Napua for the
     last manapua, then
     run.

iv. Summer fun in Booth Park.
     "Kawaipunahele" loud like Metallica.

     Saturday:
     > Seven kids and Nana packed in
     > Tutu's brown Ford Pinto station
     > > wagon.
     > Kahaku jumps down the stairs.
     > Hula at Chris & Lori's.
     > Roland and Sam play slack key
     > > guitar.
     > Maile and Kawika water the yard.
     > String lei at Nana's house.
     > String lei at anybody's house.
     > Uncle Ronnie calls about the toilet
     > > again.

v. A feather lei on a straw hat.

ROXANNE MAPUANA COTTELL *lives in Helendale, California, with her husband, three kids, and two stupid dogs. Her writing can be viewed online. She teaches hula, and is a life coach, student, and entrepreneur. She spends her days writing in the heat of the Southern California desert.*

Lee A. Tonouchi

"DA HOUSE OF LIBERTY"

My girlfriend loves to shop at da Generations depahtment at Liberty House—Pearlridge, Ala Moana, Kāhala Mall, Windward Mall. She even goes to da Liberty House in town during her lunch break at work. If you's a frequent shopper, you bound to take notice a her. She's da one . . .

who gets all da sales announcements in da mail before da ad comes out in da papah. Seems as if she's always looking fohward to da Zooper sale, Safari sale, Rainbow sale, White sale . . . Blue Tag sale . . . One Day sale . . . 12-hour sale . . . 13 minute 33 and a half second sale—starting, not now, but NOW.

who longs to buy expensive, high-quality, name-brand shoes from da LH shoe depahtment wea my friend Matt Takamine works, so he could probably geev us off, but we end up going to Payless and getting 5 pairs of shoes for $6.99, which of coss geevs her feet blisters da next day at school, jus walking from da pahking structure to Kuykendall. Three weeks later dey break and we repeat da whole process—again.

who buys her make-up from the Clinique conter, but only wen dey have their free gift offer—usually a container filled wit trial sizes of lipstick, mascara, eye shadow, lotion, and soap, which she brings home and jus keeps in her drawers, cuz she usually doesn't use dat much make-up, but still she likes to go during these special limited times, cuz she wants da free gift, jus because ees free.

who dreams of purchasing a Dooney & Bourke handbag behind da glass case in da handbag depahtment, a real Dooney & Bourke, not da faaaake $15 kine from da swap meet, cuz women can tell dat sorta ting. Eh-verytime we go to da store, we gotta set aside special visiting hours jus so she can point out to me da exack shade and style she prefers. Finally I get tie-ed of going all da time, so I get her one for our one-year anniversary. However, I failed to forsee dat now we would haff to get da matching checkbook, pocketbook, wallet, coin purse, and key chain. Wot did I start?

who tries on at least one garment from every dehpahtment—swimsuits, shirts, blouses, shorts, slacks, even socks muss be carefully selected and fitted insai da dressing rooms while I wait patiently outsai, looking desperately for a wall or pillar, SOMEting to lean against, so I can ress my weary shopping fatigue body in one attempt to look cool, like I wanna be shopping, like I'm enjoying myself, like I belong by all da bra and panties.

who pays for eh-vryting on top her LH charge card, and wen assed if she wants it deferred, she sez "YESSS," as if she's a member of da secret sisterhood for da shopping elite. Aftah she signs, me, being da big strong guy dat

I am, get to carry all da bags from all da separate depahtments, Luckily, she always asks for a shopping bag for her final purchase so I can put all her od-dah bags in da bigger bag, which I suppose does make my life a little easier.

who lets me look at da aloha shirts for approximatelee, two minutes before she goes "sigh . . . " and looks at her watch like she's anxious to go back and buy something she had previously decided she didn't want, but apparently during those extra two minutes of tink-time had decided it wuz some item she couldn't possible live witout, or at least some item she can always, ALWAYS return later for a full refund, no questions assed, wit ony da occasional stink-eye from da sales girl who recognizes it as being in style two or three seasons ago.

Now dis might seem like a lot to endure for a guy my age, spending his most vital years being bag-boy to da almightly shopping queen. But seeing her happy, is wot makes me happy. At least, so she sez.

Kalei Talwar

"WALMART IS THE SUPERSTORE OF THE UNIVERSE"

S o i am standing outside of **walmart** the superstore of the universe, where there are *always low prices, . . . always!* and i am waiting, waiting for the end of the world, for the sun to explode and below its toxic and burning **gasses** to engulf earth and for us all to find out what exactly happens when we slip into darkness, that and for my dad to finish his haircut and pick me up. whatever comes first, i love going to **walmart**, i think it's the best place in the world, actually, that's a lie. but it's definitely in my top ten. there is just so much stuff. toilet paper, country music, fabric by the yard, paint, plastic boxes, industrial sized **maui** macs, industrial sized living, whenever i go to the mall, i just end up roaming the aisles of the walmart across the street, then i see my dad drive up in our 2005 **mercedes benz** SLK 500 with eggshell blue paint.

nice.

so i open the backseat of the 46k horseless carriage and throw my purchase of 6 canisters of bubbles and one gallon of bubble canister refill onto the leather cushions, i make loud noises slamming car doors, my dad looks good, if not plumper than usual, with his new hair, cut at **bottega antoine's** half an hour ago, white shorts, and freshly pressed tommy **hilinger** blue and white shirt, i quite literally hop in and change the music to my mix cd containing the best of **edith piaf** and the clash, "how's about not," my dad says whilst pressing the button reading radio and then another button with a number 6 on it, which is preset to a tacky Hawaiian station, I detest it.

then we start driving.

the windows are down and the sunroof has retracted into its slit and i put on **myYSL** vintage **sunglass** that i found at this preschool/ church consignment store and my dad turns up the music and we exit the parking garage and turn left onto the street and we soar down the empty street and we slam back to reality as the **stoplight** blazes neon red.

"i hate walmart," my dad says as we wait. "it represents everything bad in all **ofamerica**." he enumerates numerous reasons why **$1** for a pack of 50 multi-colored, **bendable** straws is unmoral and this leads him to his "the world is going to hell" talk.

come on.
he doesn't even go to church.

then as we start driving again he shares his feelings about how terrible all these new condominiums are for the environment and how if you look out the window in some places all you can see are hotels and office buildings and that there should be a law to how high a building can go and **blacha dkj** blah **asdkcblah** this is coming from the vice president of **hawaii** visitor's bureau, it's his freaking job to get people to come to hawaii and fill up these so-called "blemishes to the environment."

so, true to his vow of eating healthier, we pick up Indian **takeout** for the second time this school week. how organic.

and so we drive home over the **pali** highway to our domestic looking neighborhood that has (at last count) 7 white picket fences within three streets of my house, "let's take the scenic route!" My dad thinks he's somehow young and edgy by doing this. the same way my mom tries to dance to my music, please accept your age. now. the scenic route takes all of 45 seconds longer then the normal one, and all we really see are more picket fences, i hate ourselves, our **hypocrisy,** our ignorance, our lame attempts at normal life. we've become the kind of people who call the other of our two phone lines and wait for someone to pick up so the caller can tell the family member who picked up the phone upstairs that dinner is ready, that's gross.

somehow i still don't really care.

KALEI TALWAR, *was born in 1990 to "Tutu" Chang and Madan Talwar. She wrote her piece during her sophomore year at Punahou School in Honolulu, and spends most of her time either merry-making or creating art in the theatre. She enjoys krumping, learning about Bacon's Re-bellion, and independent projects. She currently resides in the Nuʻuanu house her grandparents built, sleeping in her mother's old room across the hall from her favorite Korean—her brother.*

Dawn Sueoka
"CAPTIONS FOR AN IMAGINARY BOOK ABOUT HONOLULU"

INTRODUCTION

1. Swimming pool by sleeps teenager, hand on crotch, awaiting tradewinds.

2. Imported gallery strangers, windows flung wide spahking blasé sunset.

3. Good-time girls (classy shoes, classy panties, classy gasoline) on lanai scarf cakes.

CHAPTER 1

1. Vernacular contemporizes native idiom.

2. Double-hipped indigenous vernacular.

3. Contemporary idiot hips.

4. Getting forgetty.

CHAPTER 2

1. Intermittent streams, dazzled.

2. Don't remember which one was what one.

3. Or who was here here.

4. Or what was thug.

CHAPTER 3

1. Dakine, circa late-1800s.

2. Dakine, circa late-1950s.

3. Dakine, circa dakine.

CHAPTER 4

1. Each of one thousand.

2. Empty.

3. Pawned-ring apartments.

4. Claims only glass shakes off.

5. Since nothing.

6. Ain't here.

7. No more.

CHAPTER 5

1. International Group 69.

2. Bench-press baby.

3. A warm teriyaki.

4. Vast clarity of fridge.

CHAPTER 6

1. Li-hing summer.

2. Sorry, always.

3. Getting on jets.

CHAPTER 7

1. Traffic.

2. More traffic.

3. Traffic gussied-up.

4. Traffic with mangoes.

5. Sad traffic.

6. Infinite traffic.

EPILOGUE

1. Scrap hectic blueprint, wing-lit corridor.

2. Two months then, finally rain

DAWN SUEOKA, *born in 1980, has an MLiSc from the University of Hawaiʻi at Mānoa and is earning an MFA in creative writing from the Jack Kerouac School of Disembodied Poetics at Naropa University, in Boulder, Colorado.*

Carol Ayento
"KING KONG ANTS"

We are fields of ants,
running through the tight streets
of Kalihi.

We are the ants,
who are down below
with our private lives,
soap operas and TV shows.

We are wealthy ants,
zigzagging in the crowded downtown streets,
through the wide Kahala sidewalks.

At night we are the young ants,
asleep in cloudy rooms.

In the morning,
we are the dead ants,
struggling to get up.

Throughout the day,
we work hard to find our money.
We are ants coming home,
all exhausted.

We are ants fighting
through the tight dirt.

CAROL AYENTO *wrote this poem in 1990, when she was a student at Kalakaua Intermediate School in Honolulu.*

Chan E. Park

IN 1903, PAK HŬNGBO WENT TO HAWAI'I

(Slide: Plantation cottage)
One *Makahiki* season,
Everyone was busy celebrating the harvest,
Hungbo and his family didn't have much,
So they harvest the gourds for donation.

Sung: *Sirirong silgun*, let's saw it.
       Eyoru, pull it.

"Look, Wife, sing with me."

"I would, but I'm too hungry to sing."

"Well then, tighten your belt, let's roll."

Spoken: *Keikis!* Come out and help us saw the gourds!
       Invite Mr. Ka'uhane to come and bless the gourds.

He has a great voice!
(Escorted by the children carrying ipus, a Hawaiian chanter enters.)

"Mr. Ka'uhane, good to see you! Can you bless these gourds?"

"At the already prepared planting spot, the farmer drops the seed with a sudden outward motion of his hands with his palm up. If the palms are down, the gourds will grow crooked and shriveled. While dropping the seeds, the farmer says a prayer-suggestion."

"Then let's do a Korean-Hawaiian gourd-sawing chant!"

Sung: *Sirirong silgun*, let's saw it!
Eyoru, pull it!

He ipu nui! (A huge gourd!)
O biki ku mauna (Growing like a mountain)

When this gourd opens,
I want nothing but a pot of rice.
A big pot of rice is my lifelong wish.

He ipu nui! (A huge gourd!)
O biki kua (To be carried on the back)

Eh—*yoru*, pull it!

He ipu nui! (A huge gourd!)
Nui maoli keia ipu! (Really huge is this gourd!)

Sirirong sirirong sirirong sirirong, ttukttak!

Spoken: The first gourd opened, it was empty.
Good heavens! If you're unlucky,
You crack an egg to find bones in it.
"Who ate the fruit?"

(Lights change for mysterious atmosphere)

"Look! There's a chest inside, two!"

When Hungbo peeped into one, it was full of money.
He peeped into the other, it was full of rice.

Ecstatic with joy, they unload the chests with amazing speed.
Money and rice pile up like mountains.

Sung: Hungbo's ecstatic, Hungbo's ecstatic,
Empty the chests, they fill up.
Empty the chests, they fill up.

"Wonderful! May money and rice come out like this every day!"

Spoken: Money, rice, treasures, computers, DVDs, muumuus, aloha shirts,
surf boards . . .
Do you know what came out of the rest of the gourds? Fresh batches
of kimchee? Of course!
The best-rated real estate agents from ERA, King Thompson,
Savio . . .
But there's nothing like building your own home,
So this time, master architects, building inspectors,
And the entire construction crew!
Then a team of escrow, legal, tax experts, and financial advisors,
Butlers, maids, landscape artists,
Pets groomed, shampooed, and manicured!
In no time assembled a most exquisite mansion up on Wai'alae Iki,
With a postcard view of Diamond head and the blue Pacific.
*(Slide: Several photos of the interior and exterior of a mansion with ocean and
Diamond Head views)*

Hungbo became one of the wealthiest people in Hawai'i.
He spent his wealth wisely,
For the welfare of the elderly and immigrants,
Education for youths, and the Korean Independence movement.
His children and grandchildren inherited his legacies,
And have served the community well.
So ends the story, with da Hawaiian-style celebration!

Corey Egami
"CASCARON"

"Kumusta ka sweetheart"
Hi manang

Seven o'clock Downtown
The sun late for work again this morning
It is cold in Oahu
Dispelling the sleep from my eyes
Flicking the sharp mukat to the floor
Nanas bustle about setting out
The saluyote and the Pakote
Squeezing past the frozen trays
Of milkfish and catfish
Shuddering at the sight of the pink aramang
With its black eyes staring at me

Manang, I like two cascaron
"Last two sweetheart"
My journey through the market has ended
The reward in my hand
Mochi, fried to perfection
Melted sugar dances in the filtered sunlight
"Bamboo shoots come in Tuesday"
Salamat po manang, I come back later

COREY EGAMI, *while attending the University of Hawai'i at Mānoa, was introduced to Filipino culture and food by his future wife Jennifer. They live on the island of Maui with their daughter Cara.*

Perlita Tapec Sadorra
"BIAG DITOY HAWAII"

Kadagiti nariwet a parbangon
Kadagiti nawawasnay ken nalalawa a kalsada
Adun dagiti agin-ini-in a luglugan
Awitda dagiti nataengan ken nakabalkot a maladaga.

Ay-ay pay dagiti maladaga
Awan unmanay a turogda
Pigerger gapu't lam-ek sagrapenda
Iti parbangon a pannakaiyulogda.

Gapu't kinapateg ti trabaho
Annak saan unay a maasikaso
Para aywan dika pay unay am-ammo
Iti kabibiagada ken kinatao.

Naanus nga Inna ken Amma
Agmalmalem nga agtrabaho
Tapnon makaurnong iti pirak
Agserbi ken pagadal dagiti annak.

Ar-arigen dika pay nakamulagat
Umulogka't pagtaengan iti bigat
Uray ta magatangmo amin a kayat
Biag ditoy Hawaii, narigat a naragsak.

"LIFE IN HAWAI'I IS DIFFICULT"

In the many dark early dawns
On the many long and wide roads
There are many slow moving vehicles
Carrying grown women with children wrapped.

Pity all the women
With never enough sleep
Shaking 'cuz of the cold chill
Of early morning as they go out.

Because work is precious
With children, little time to care
The baby sitters we hardly know
Their lives and what kind people.

Kind mothers and fathers
Working all day to the evening
So they can accumulate money
For their children's education.

Seems you can't even open your eyes
Leaving your home in the morning
Although you can buy all you like
Life in Hawaii, happiness is difficult.

TRANSLATED BY VIRGILIO MENOR FELIPE

PERLITA TAPEC SADORRA *was born in 1953 in Brgy. 15, Suba, Paoay, Ilokos Norte, Philippines. She graduated from the Northern Luzon Teachers College in Laoag and Cannon's Business College. She arrived in Hawai'i in 1974 and worked at Woolworth's, the Bishop Trust, and with HMSA since 1975. She has three children with her husband Efren, all of whom are college graduates. A member of the Legion of Mary of St. Joseph's Church in Waipahu, the Paoay Currimao Organization of Hawaii, and GUMIL Hawai'i, Perlita loves dramas and comedies.*

Janet Ulep Tolentino
"GRANDPA JUAN"

Juan Tolentino, my grandfather
he works as a bus boy
at Kenny's Restaurant.
He collects dishes
in a noisy bright room
after the people
finish eating.

After he's done
at Kenny's
he rides the bus
to Makiki to care
for the plants at a house
that a lady named Laura owns.

From five
to seven thirty at night
he plants, waters and cleans.
Even when the heavy winds blow
he still works.

He goes into a small shack
down the road
changes his clothes
so he won't look dirty
while riding the bus.

All out of breath
from walking up the hill, Grandpa strolls
to the room,
lays on his bed,
and caresses his pillow.

JANET ULEP TOLENTINO *of Honolulu was born in 1976. Being proud of her Filipino culture, she was inspired to write a poem expressing her grandfather's dedication and hard work. During her free time, she continues to write poetry based on her life experiences. With her passion for creativity and love of working with people, she hopes to start a business in event planning.*

Helen Rogerson

UNTITLED

Jogger with his dog
Puffing along Ala Wai—
Two tongues hanging out.

Sarah Omura

"BEWARE OF THE ALA WAI"

O bid me walk
Rather than fall into the Ala Wai,
Barefoot on a mile of razor-sharp holly leaves.

Or have me chew the petrified gum stuck to the bottoms of all
movie seats,
Or force me to watch "The Sound of Music" continuously for
forty-eight hours.

I would rather sniff a line of wasabi as if it were cocaine,
Or eat a steamy plate of Rocky Mountain oysters,
Whose origins and whereabouts I'd rather not know,
While sitting Japanese-style for a week.

And I will do it without hesitation or fright,
So that I may stay dry and never fall into the Ala Wai ever.

SARAH OMURA *is currently a senior at 'Iolani School in Honolulu. She lives in Niu Valley, O'ahu, with her mother, father and grandmother; her older sister is at college on the mainland. When she is not hanging out with her friends and being a typical seventeen-year-old, she is sailing on the ocean or practicing yoga. She enjoys photography, filmmaking, and traveling to foreign places. She would like to thank her English teachers for their encouragement over the years.*

Walt Novak

from THE HAOLE SUBSTITUTE

My first day of substitute teaching is at radical Ranford High School. My number one son is a tiny infant, my wife has not yet turned twenty, and I am impoverished. I wonder if all subs enter the field under similar circumstances. Personally, I'd rather be surfing.

Having ready my "Sub Teacher Handbook," I show up promptly at 7:45 a.m. The office secretary hands me a classroom key and a sub teacher report form. I sign my name on the appropriate line and am asked to show proof of being a real live substitute person. I proudly whip out my Xeroxed form. Then, acting unimpressed, she adds, " . . . and a driver's license, please." Convinced that I am Paul Kodak, Substitute Teacher, in person, she almost smiles and says, "Check the box." Thinking that I need to scribe a ☒ or a ☑ in a designated cubicle, I ask, "Which one?" She replies, "Matsumoto's." Being of at least average intelligence, I recognize this as being the name of the teacher I am replacing. My eyes notice a list of names on the counter. Apparently teachers are taking turns checking off their names and walking away. I look up Matsumoto and put an "x" in the properly dated cubicle. "What are you doing?" demands the disapproving secretary.

"I checked the box."

"No, the box!" screeches this pleasant lady, apparently believing an increase in decibels increases communication. She reaches for her Boo Boo

Glue (also known as White-Out). She blots out my first official act as a substitute teacher. Then, she does something really useful. She silently, but with an exaggerated air, points her manicured finger at two walls full of wooden drawers.

"Ah hah. Boxes!"

The first bell rings and I find myself seated in a "portable" on the far side of the campus. Kids wander in. Some of them are friendly. Two or three warn me that I'll have trouble with Period Five . . . but I don't have to wait that long.

"Tittas" are great big girls with great big curly hairdos. Their nationality is "local," their language "pidgin." They dress for school as if it were the disco. Fine silk and expensive satin cover their fine, often voluptuous, bodies. They are sexually active and academically inactive. Most sensible minded people stay out of their way; they are known to beat up boys.

Faye Ornelles walks into my room with two others. She takes one look at me and laughs. Then she sits down. The half-dozen already seated kids stiffen their backs and stifle the chatter. Her fingernails appear freshly sharpened. They're nearly two inches long and polished shiny black.

"Honey Girl" Keale enters with her group. They sit across the room. Like Faye, Honey Girl is dressed to the hilt and laced with necklaces. Her wrists have three gold bracelets each, compared to Faye's mere two. Her face is also caked with makeup and her nails are newly honed. Her fingernail polish? Dark green with shiny glitter.

Two things are required of a sub teacher during home-room: 1) take attendance, and 2) read the daily bulletin. I make it through the attendance without mispronouncing too many names, but halfway through the bulletin, things go wild. Apparently, Honey Girl has flirted with Faye's boyfriend before school (or some such major crime). As I'm announcing the pep rally schedule, Faye stands up and hurls a foul string of expletives at her rival. Honey-Girl, the blood rising to her Maybelline, gets up deliberately and hurls an equally profane phrase right back. Then they charge like two large cougars. They clash at the classroom's center in a whirlwind of fury. Stunned, I lamely bark, "Stop it!"

Faye's fingernails immediately lacerate her enemy's face. Honey-Girl, a notorious street fighter as it turns out, responds with an uppercut to the groin area and uses her head to butt Faye solidly in the teeth. I snap out of my momentary stupor and race for the juggernauts. By this time, they are rolling on the floor like two wicked witches gone berserk. One thick earring falls off to the side—attached to it is a small piece of ear.

Three blond boys scram out of the classroom. I suspect they're cowards. Actually, they've wisely gone off to fetch the CPOs (Campus Patrol Officers). One of the companion girls screams, "Leave 'em alone, you haole fucka!" as I grab Faye's ankle and attempt to drag them apart.

The problem with girl fights is—even when they're over—they're still not over. I'm reminded of stags who angrily bang antlers in the forest. Even the winner dies of starvation. They realize their gross error in judgment when the harsh winter freezes them stiff. In April, a squirrel hunter finds both deer bodies well-preserved, still locked together.

The GPO sees the bloody, screaming, kicking mess on the floor and radios for backup on his red-buttoned Walky-Talky. Then he grabs the other set of ankles and we pull like crazy.

They are unresolvably tangled. Well-braceleted wrists and multi-ringed fingers are hopelessly knotted in the formerly-elaborate hairdos. Faye's earlobe has a vent. Stretched straight out on the floor, both still hiss and struggle, but have calmed considerably. The second CPO shows up and realizes that the only solution is a pair of scissors and an ambulance.

WALT NOVAK *has taught English in Hawai'i's public schools since 1981. He spent most of the 1980s surfing Pipeline, substitute teaching, raising infants, and writing for surf magazines. That decade became the basis for his first novel,* The Haole Substitute. *He now has three grown children, one daughter-in-law, one grandson, one convertible, and one midlife crisis. He lives in a coastal penthouse on O'ahu, thanks to* The Haole Substitute *and its sequel* Half of September, *which earned Hollywood contracts with director-producer David Mickey Evans.*

Lee A. Tonouchi and Da Fall 2001 PCC Classes at KCC
"DEY SAY IF YOU TALK PIDGIN YOU NO CAN . . ."

Dis group of poem wuz edited for flow li'dat, but da stuffs is all from their lists. Mahalos to da students for geeving me their two-minute brainstorm lists of wot people toll dem dey cannot do wit Pidgin. Shout out to Jhoanna Calma for letting me use her PCC class too. To da students who came dat day—look get your name stay insai hea—Hanna Chang, Wendy Chang, Artemio Jubilado, Jessica Kim, Kathy Lam, Alvin Lo, Mandy Lo, Mark Lunasco, Leilani Montenegro, Melanie Montenegro, Janice Munar, Tiore Malia Nakaahiki, Jonathan Nitullama, Adore Ngo, Tarseny Otis, Kelly Pong, Gaily Siddayao, Jarnell Spencer, Uoleni Tupuola, Juliet Vallesteros, Tiffany Wong, and Kelsey Yamane. For da students who wuz absent—too bad, so sad. Next time no play hookey.

DEY SAY IF YOU TALK PIDGIN YOU NO CAN . . .

BE SMART
BE IMPORTANT
BE SUCCESSFUL
BE PROFESSIONAL
BE TAKEN SERIOUSLY
BE ONE TEACHER
BE ONE DOCTOR
BE ONE LAWYER
BE A GOVERNMENT WORKER
BE BIG BUSINESSMAN
BE DA POPE
BE THE PRESIDENT
BE THE WIFE OF THE PRESIDENT

DEY SAY IF YOU TALK PIDGIN YOU NO CAN . . .

COMMUNICATE
EAT AT FINE DINING RESTAURANTS
ENTER A BEAUTY PAGEANT (AND WIN)
FLIRT
FUNCTION
GO OUT TONIGHT
GO TO JOB INTERVIEWS
GO MAINLAND
GO MAINLAND SCHOOL
GO OPERA OR SOMEPLACE ELEGANT
GO FORWARD

DEY SAY IF YOU TALK PIDGIN YOU NO CAN . . .

GET GOOD GRADES
GET ONE GOOD EDUCATION
GET GOOD JOB
GET A SMART GUY
GET A SOPHISTICATED GUY
GET CHICKS

DEY SAY IF YOU TALK PIDGIN YOU NO CAN . . .

GIVE PUBLIC SPEECHES
JOIN THE MILITARY
LOOK HIGH CLASS

MAKE IT IN HOLLYWOOD
PRAY TO GOD
READ
RUN FOR GOVERNOR

DEY SAY IF YOU TALK PIDGIN YOU NO CAN . . .

SCORE
SOUND INTELLECTUAL
SURVIVE
TALK PROPER
TALK TO DA PHONE OPERATOR
TALK TO DA JUDGE
TALK AT FUNERALS
TALK TO DA HAOLES
TALK TO TOURISTS
TALK IN EUROPEAN COUNTRIES
TALK IN THE CLASSROOM
TAKE TESTS
TEACH
UNDERSTAND

DEY SAY IF YOU TALK PIDGIN YOU NO CAN . . .

WORK CUSTOMER SERVICE
WORK AT NEIMAN MARCUS
WRITE A "PROPER" SENTENCE
WRITE LETTERS
WRITE FORMAL ESSAYS
WRITE PAPERS FOR CLASS

DEY SAY IF YOU TALK PIDGIN . . .

YOU NO CAN.

John S. Pritchett

"KIDS AT THE BUS STOP"

JOHN S. PRITCHETT *was born in 1950. Originally from Florida, he moved to Honolulu in 1974. He worked in advertising until 1987, then pursued a cartooning career. In 1988, he worked with world-famous cartoonist Ranan Lurie in New York. He has published a weekly cartoon in the* Honolulu Weekly *since 1993, and has received awards from The Hawai'i Publishers Association, The Society of Professional Journalists, Common Cause Hawai'i, Small Business Hawai'i, the City Council of Honolulu, and the United Nations Correspondents Association.*

Puahaulani Takushi

"CONVERSATIONS ON ROUTE 51"

Characters:
GIRL ON THE RIGHT
GIRL ON THE LEFT
HAOLE GUY WITH ALOHA SHIRT *(audience hears his thoughts)*

OLD FILIPINO LADY
JAPANESE LIBRARIAN
MAHU

Onstage is the JAPANESE LIBRARIAN and other bus riders.
Enter two girls. They deposit bus fare and find appropriate seats.

GIRL ON THE LEFT: No worry, my aunty so cool she not going mine us coming ovah.

GIRL ON THE RIGHT: You shuah? I going be so shame we get ovah deah and den she tell us fo' go back school.

GIRL ON THE LEFT: I telling you, no worry. She not li' dat. She real, real, real nice.

GIRL ON THE RIGHT: Okay, whatevahz.

GIRL ON THE LEFT: So wassup wit you and Matt? You tol' him dat you love him yet o'what?

GIRL ON THE RIGHT: Nah. He tol' me dat he love me, so I tol' him dat I love him too. But den I really, really like him.

GIRL ON THE LEFT: Dass good 'cause you shouldn't say dat jus' fo' please him.

GIRL ON THE RIGHT: Yeah, plus I tol' him dat Waianae guys only like one ting and aftah dat dey donno you any moa.

GIRL ON THE LEFT: Ae, you! You tol' him dat?

GIRL ON THE RIGHT: Yeah, and he tol' me, "Dass what you tink of me?" So I tol' him, "No, I hope you not li' dat 'cause I like one solid relationship." Den he tol' me dat I jus' too good fo' him dass why I cannot say dat I love him. But I no tink dat I bettah. I jus' like take tings slow, dass all.

Enter OLD FILIPINO LADY. Shows bus pass and walks down the aisle, hitting passengers on the head and shoulders with her large handbag. JAPANESE LIBRARIAN allows FILIPINO LADY to sit by the window.

OLD FILIPINO LADY: You know deez students now days? Dey don't go school and den dey come on dee bus and take up all dee front seats. Don't have room for me to sit over dare, all dee time.

JAPANESE LIBRARIAN: *(turns toward OLD FILIPINO LADY, smiles and nods.)* Yes, that's too bad.

OLD FILIPINO LADY: Where dey going? Dey don't want to go school, but where dey going on dee bus? How come dee police officer don't arrest dem and put dem in jail? Den dey go to school. More better dey go to school den go jail, yeah?

JAPANESE LIBRARIAN: I would think so.

OLD FILIPINO LADY: And look dat girl over dare. *(Points to front of bus.)* Look like dee same age as my granddaughter who only fourteen. But dat girl get baby already and going to have one more. So young, how she going to take care? Look, her chee-chee so small. Dat mean she don't breast feed. How she get de money for feed her baby? And look, her stoller take up dee whole chair over dare. I could have sit dare, but I thought dat was a person.

JAPANESE LIBRARIAN: *(Smiles at OLD FILIPINO LADY and turns away).*

Enter HAOLE GUY WITH ALOHA SHIRT. No seats available. Stands next to girls.

HAOLE GUY: *(Looks down at GIRLS.)* Whoa, baby! Nice tits! Real nice!

GIRL ON THE RIGHT: *(Points to pregnant girl.)* See dass why I no like fall in love wit Matt. I no like end up hapai like her. Look her, muss be so hard catching bus wit one bebe, one strollah, and two bags. I raddah carry books.

GIRL ON THE LEFT: Lolo, jus' 'cause you fall in love wit somebody no mean you going get pregnant.

GIRL ON THE RIGHT: I know dat, but I scared dat when I really, really fall for Matt, I going like da kine with him. And when dat happens, I not going like stop.

HAOLE GUY: *(Stares at GIRL ON THE RIGHT'S cleavage.)* Damn, I really got to get me some of that fine Hawaiian titties!

GIRL ON THE RIGHT: I already get buttahflies when he kiss me. And when he stay kissing me full on and rubbing my shouldaz, I jus' like faint. Ho, feel so good I jus' like take off all my clothes. But I promise to God dat we nevah da kine yet, but I like so bad. Sometimes I gotta cross my legs when we kissing so dat notin' happens.

HAOLE GUY: *(Looks at GIRL ON THE RIGHT.)* I'd do her, hell yeah! *(Looks down at his crotch.)* Whoa! Sit, boy, sit!

GIRL ON THE LEFT: Den do it already, jus' use rubbaz.

GIRL ON THE RIGHT: But I did dat wit all da'adda loozaz I was wit. I no like use rubbaz wit Matt 'cause he so different. I telling you, I really like be wit him. I cannot explain. I no like just have sex, I like . . .

GIRL ON THE LEFT: Yeah, right. Dass what you said about da'adda guys befoah Matt.

GIRL ON THE RIGHT: Not!

GIRL ON THE LEFT: Yes!

GIRL ON THE RIGHT: Not! I promise fo' real kine, I really like be wit Matt. But I like 'em be special.

GIRL ON THE LEFT: Fo' somebody who wanted fo' take tings slow . . .

GIRL ON THE RIGHT: I know, but I nevah tell him all dis so he donno.

GIRL ON THE LEFT: Jus' rememba' dat girl up deah. Rememba' dat you no like end up li' dat.

HAOLE GUY: *(Looks down at girls.)* Shit, I sure wouldn't mind having the two of them at once! That would be fuckin' heaven, man!

Enter MAHU. Pays bus fare and speaks to bus driver.

MAHU: *(Loud deep voice.)* Can I have a transfer, please.

All passengers look forward and stare. MAHU ignores them and sits next to the pregnant girl in the front.

OLD FILIPINO LADY: Ae, dat one get dee man's voice but dat one look like on female. If dat was my grandson, I tell him, "You like be one female? I cut dat ding-ding off with my bolo knife, den you can be one female. You don't want dee bolo knife, den you bedder act like one man!"

JAPANESE LIBRARIAN: Then she's . . . I mean he's lucky you're not his grand-mother.

OLD FILIPINO LADY: If I was his grandmoder, he would be lucky because today he be one boyee.

HAOLE GUY: Damn, I can't believe that fine piece of flesh has a dick!

GIRL ON THE RIGHT: *(Looks at MAHU.)* Ho, how's that shim ovah deah.

GIRL ON THE LEFT: Why, jealous 'cause he moa pretty den you?

GIRL ON THE RIGHT: Yeah, he pretty ugly!

GIRL ON THE LEFT: You know he pretty! Look him, he stay wearing one short, tight skirt and he no even look like one tuna. His body look way bettah den most of da girls' ones at school. In fac', his face look way moa bettah den da girls.

GIRL ON THE RIGHT: He all right, but he not pretty-pretty.

HAOLE GUY: *(Scopes MAHU.)* Oh, yes, she it!

GIRL ON THE LEFT: What evah you say.

GIRL ON THE RIGHT: What da sense of looking li' dat when he still sound man-nish?

HAOLE GUY: Shit, just give her one night with me and I'll make her a natural soprano!

GIRL ON THE LEFT: Going take time, but his voice going change so he sound moa like one female.

GIRL ON THE RIGHT: Yeah, but he still going have his da kine.

GIRL ON THE LEFT: So, nobody going know as long as he have on clothes. Eh, what you tink, he sit down when he make shee-shee or what?

GIRL ON THE RIGHT: I don't know, I look like one mahu?

GIRL ON THE LEFT: Yeah, small kine.

GIRL ON THE RIGHT: Not even!

GIRL ON THE LEFT: Nah, I only kidding. I no tink mahus can have big tits like you.

GIRL ON THE RIGHT: Dass right. *(Sticks out chest.)*

GIRL ON THE LEFT: I no tink dey can even make implants dat big.

GIRL ON THE RIGHT: Shuddup!

GIRL ON THE LEFT: Serious kine, I not teasing you. Why, what size you take?

GIRL ON THE RIGHT: 30 D.

HAOLE GUY: Holy, tit heaven!

GIRL ON THE LEFT: Fo' real?

GIRL ON THE RIGHT: Yeah, you like see my tag?

GIRL ON THE LEFT: Ho, dass what you call Mauna Kea and Mauna Loa!

HAOLE GUY: Call it whatever you like, but what it all boils down to is really big tits!

GIRL ON THE LEFT: Eh, you know what? Dat mahu look so familia'. I know him from some place.

GIRL ON THE RIGHT: Not, if you know him, den I would know him too and he no look like anybody I know.

GIRL ON THE LEFT: Yes, I telling you I know him. Dass . . . Dass um . . . Eh, dass Jimmy Coon.

GIRL ON THE RIGHT: Who?

GIRL ON THE LEFT: Jimmy Coon, remembah? When we was in da third grade he was sixth grade.

GIRL ON THE RIGHT: Oh, yeah! He was da bull of da school, eh? No way, dass not him.

GIRL ON THE LEFT: Believe me, I remembah dat face 'cause I was all in love wit him when I was one small kid.

GIRL ON THE RIGHT: How can dat be him? He was da bull of da school, he wasn't sof'.

GIRL ON THE LEFT: I telling you, dass him.

GIRL ON THE RIGHT: Maybe dass da sista . . . I mean da brada dat like be one sista.

GIRL ON THE LEFT: Dass Jimmy!

GIRL ON THE RIGHT: But all da girls wanted fo' go wit him. And he could scrap so good. He cannot be one mahu now.

GIRL ON THE LEFT: You donno 'cause we nevah see him aftah elementary. Remembah? He nevah wen come back aftah his fadah went lick him in front of da whole school.

GIRL ON THE RIGHT: Ae, yeah. Why his fadah went do dat fo' anyway?

GIRL ON THE LEFT: I donno. But all I know is dat da stupid principal was so scared fo' stop da fadah, he wen wait until da cops came. By den, Jimmy was all buss up.

GIRL ON THE RIGHT: He nevah even cry, yeah? He jus' went let da fadah lick him. No way, dat cannot be him

GIRL ON THE LEFT: It is . . . trippy yeah? He was so handsome, but now he pretty. Eh, we gotta get off da next stop.

GIRL ON THE RIGHT: Eh, you shua your aunty not going scold us?

GIRL ON THE LEFT: She not going, so stop worrying alredeh.

GIRLS stand, then slowly make their way down the aisle.

HAOLE GUY: Damn, they didn't give me a chance to make my move!

OLD FILIPINO LADY taps the JAPANESE LIBRARIAN on the shoulder while girls pass.

OLD FILIPINO LADY: If dose were my granddaughters, I would pull dare ears for not going to school.

As GIRLS exit, they make eye contact with MAHU. The GIRLS smile. MAHU smiles back briefly and looks down quickly.

GIRL TO THE LEFT: *(Hits friend on shoulder.)* See, I tol' you dat was him!

PUAHAULANI TAKUSHI *works as an educational assistant at a public charter school on Oʻahu. She is married with two children. She enjoys reading and watching her children play sports.*

Alecia M. Tumpap

"THE BUS DRIVER"

I'm on a bright, post-it yellow bus of life
That won't stop until darkness
We're leaving childhood
But I don't want to trade

Roller blades for polished shoes
Scooters for an overpriced used car
My chores for a job I don't even like

This trip frightens me
I have to turn this BEAST around
"Let's go back!" I shriek at the driver
Who turns without stopping
I look
It's ME.

ALECIA M. TUMPAP *was born in 1991 on Maui to parents Francisco and Pamela Tumpap. She first attended Seabury Hall in Makawao in 2002 to begin middle school and wrote "The Bus Driver" while in the eighth grade. She was mentored by English teachers Carter Latendresse and Gayle Martelles. She is presently a junior at Seabury Hall. She spends her free time at the beach, with friends, and enjoying her new license.*

Dorothea N. Buckingham

from STARING DOWN THE DRAGON

T he doorbell rang. I sprayed myself with vanilla perfume.
"Is anyone going to get the door?" Dad called out from his den.
"I've got it, Dad."
When I answered the door a dark figure with spiked black hair, wide cheekbones and duct tape over his mouth appeared. It was Nate. His eyes were shouting at me, "Go ahead, ask me what the duct tape is doing across my mouth?'
I acted like there was nothing unusual. "I'm going to say good night to my folks," I said. "I'll tell them you said 'hello.'"
"When I got back I asked Nate, "Is this a new version of man talk?"
He shook his head "no."
"Is this a game?"
He nodded, "yes."
"What kind of game?"
As we walked to his truck he handed me an index card marked "Number One." Then he made a flipping motion with his hands. The back of the card read, "You can find your dreams if you follow the clues."
"Dreams? What dreams?" I asked.
He pointed again, stabbing the card.
"Okay, I'll play," I said. "Dreams? Dreams at the end of a rainbow? Are we going to Rainbow's for chicken katsu dinner?"
He shook his head "no."

"Dreams? Dreams like fortunes? We're going to Chinatown to get our fortunes told."

This time a vigorous "no."

I climbed in the truck and he closed the door behind me. As he drove away I wondered if it was legal for him to drive with duct tape across his mouth.

He pointed to card number two on the dashboard. I read it out loud. "To follow your dream you must take one step after another."

"Okay, Nate, what is this?"

He turned toward me. I thought he was smiling. His cheeks were puffed out, his eyes narrowed, and under the duct tape I detected an upward curve of his mouth.

"One step after another," I repeated. "It's not the marathon, that's for sure." I fidgeted with the card. "Night hiking?"

He kept his eyes on the road.

"Are we going hiking?"

Another "no."

"Maybe a walk. Honolulu Time Walk? The Ghost Tour."

I was wrong again.

I thought out loud. "One step after another, but not a hike and not a walk. A street? A road? The road less traveled? The yellow brick road? The road to where? Where in the world is Carmen San Diego?" I turned to Nate. "Got it! We're flying to San Diego."

He laughed a muffled laugh and pointed to the glove box where, buried among half eaten Lifesavers and parking stubs for Honolulu General Hospital was card number three, stuck to a crumpled up Power Bar wrapper.

I peeled the card off and read, "Tonight you will receive a gift that was inspired by dreams."

I looked around in his truck. There was an old milk crate jammed in the cubby behind my seat, overflowing with basketball shoes, stained towels, sunscreen, dirty T-shirts and probably last week's gym clothes. "Dreams? This truck could inspire nightmares."

Nate shrugged.

We were headed into the first Pali tunnel. Between the first and second tunnel was a view of the windward side from Lanikai to the North Shore. It was my favorite view on the island.

Nate jabbed the card with his finger.

"Yes, sir." I snapped an exaggerated salute. "This is my dream that's going to come true, not yours," I said. "Fat chance of any of your dreams coming true, buster." He took his hands off the wheel, clasped them in prayer and leaned toward me in a fake plea.

"Hey! Pay attention to the road." I pointed to the car in front of us. "Fooling around on the Pali makes me very nervous."

Right outside the second tunnel was an emergency parking lot with a phone, a first aid kit and a bench. Nate pulled over. He reached into his pocket and delivered another card: "From now on I will only go where you tell me to go. You can either continue to play or give up and never find your dream."

"I'll play," I said.

Card number five read: "The memory of its city lights brings the islander home again."

"Honolulu," I said.

By the eighth card I was standing next to the hula girl statue at the Aloha Tower Marketplace. Nate still had the duct tape over his mouth, unbothered by the stares of tourists.

One old guy in a porkpie hat and brown plaid shorts that were pulled high over his belly called over to Nate. "You look like you're in training for being married."

"Stop it, Harry." The man's wife jabbed his belly, setting off a tidal wave of fat rippling across his shirt—a rayon Aloha shirt that matched her hibiscus mu'u mu'u.

Nate gave Harry a thumbs up.

By time I read the last card I was in front of the cash register at the Blue Hawai'i Bookstore.

The last card said, "Hand this to the clerk and claim a gift for Estrella DeMello."

The clerk exchanged the card for what appeared to be a wrapped hardcover book.

The gift tag had Nate's handwriting. "To my Beautiful Star, From Nate."

"You know what my name means." I beamed.

Nate took a sweeping bow.

I gently pulled off the wrapping paper to uncover *The Dream of Light, A Path through the Grand Canyon*, by Makana Johns.

"I've wanted this book for so long." I threw my arms around him and kissed the duct tape across his lips. As I leafed through the book, he peeled the tape off his mouth. Silver strands of adhesive stuck to what looked like an instant rash across his face.

"You okay?" I asked.

"I think so." He patted his mouth with the back of his hand.

I stood on my tiptoes and gave him a kiss.

"Ouch."

"Ruin the moment," I said pretending to be annoyed. "Pure romance ruined by a mouth pansy."

"I'll show you 'mouth pansy.'" Nate put his arm around me, dipped me back and kissed me. "Jeez, that stings." He squeezed his eyes and pursed his lips.

"You know, for a smart guy, you get zero in common sense."

"Is that zero a mean, a median or an average?"

I wanted to give Nate a big Santa Claus hug and cover him with hundreds of kisses. I hugged him again and told him, "This is the best gift I ever got."

He beamed with "man pride."

"Are you ready for what's next?" he said.

"There's more?"

"You bet."

The more was more fries, more ketchup and more beef in your burger. We ate at Bruddah's Grill at the end of the Aloha Tower pier at a table over-looking the harbor. The SS *Independence* cruise ship was berthed next to us. It was all lit up like a birthday cake with strung white lights for candles and red and blue streamers for frosting. Halfway through our meal I felt a low pitched rumble—the pier vibrated and the ship got underway. Her horn blasted, little girls in ti leaf skirts danced hula on the dock, and right on cue, a helicopter showered the ship with plumeria blossoms. It was just like the movies. I reached over for Nate's hand and braided my fingers into his.

He handed me a napkin with his other hand. "You want to wipe the ketchup off your hands first?"

I crumpled the napkin and threw it at him. "Right after you quit the red lipped reindeer routine."

"Wound me," he said, grasping his heart.

"I already did."

Our waitress refilled our drinks then rested the pitcher of water on her hip. "Are you on vacation?" she asked.

"Yes. We're from San Francisco," Nate answered.

"You may want to stick around." She lifted her pitcher in the direction of Diamond Head. "The Hilton puts on a fireworks show in fifteen minutes."

"Thanks, we will," I said.

The night was perfect.

DOROTHEA N. BUCKINGHAM *was born in 1949. Her novel,* Staring Down the Dragon, *was awarded a Best Books for Young Adults Award in 2004 by the American Library Associa-tion. Her other works include* The Essential Guide to Sumo; *the historical novels* My Name Is Loa *and* Poisoned Palms, *both set in Hawai'i; and a historical cookbook of Sackets Harbor, New York,* Delicious Tidbits. *After living in Hawai'i for nearly twenty-three years, she now resides in Wilmington, North Carolina, with her husband Jack, and their dog Ajax.*

Karri Leilani Villanueva
"RUBBAH SLIPPAHS"

Left, right,
       left, right,
              left, right,
then   Stumble!
I stay lookin down and eh,
       deez slippahs not mine . . .
You took my slippahs?
How I wen end up wit dis pair?
Deez *Locals* not mine
I no remembah dis hole at da sole,
or dis tear on da strap,
or dis gum dat stay stuck on my left!
Wea *my* slippahs stay?
Dey my *protecktahs*, you know!
From da gravel,
da dirt,
da pokey-kine grass,
and da rubbish from da dogs!
You took my slippahs?

Or I wen take yours?

KARRI LEILANI VILLANUEVA *was born in 1988, and grew up on the islands of Kaua'i and O'ahu. She is currently attending the University of Hawai'i at Mānoa and pursuing a bachelor of science degree in nursing. Her original screenplay was selected by the State Teleschool Department for the Department of Education's Teen Stories series. Her poems from the 2005 and 2006 Star Poets Contest were published in the* Star Poets Journal.

MOTHER DEAREST

70 "Boy! come heah!" echoed thru da Plantation Village.
Mom would wait in da house,
1 wit one guava switch in her grasp
2 and her lips pursed tight.
new stanza → 3 Da stick cut thru the aiah
4 wit dis WHOOSHIN sound,
5 and came SMACK
on my okole.
new stanza → Any time I make trouble:
not doin chores,
makin stink to my sista,
comin home late;
6 I hear da leaves rustle outside
as my mom wen cut down
one new guava switch.
"Boy! come heah!"

Courtesy of Kyleena Lamadrid.

Kyleena Lamadrid
"MOTHER DEAREST"

"Boy! Come hea!"
echoed tru da nebahood

Ma waited in da house
as she gripped one guava switch,
pursed her lips tight,
and shot me stink eye
that could make one rock squirm.

Da stick cut tru da aiah,
easy as fish swim tru wata,
wit dis whooshin' sound.
It came, smacked my okole,
leaving behin' one stingin' mark
'cross bot cheeks.

Any time I make trouble—
forget to do chores,
makin stink to mai sistas,
comin' home late—
I hear da leaves rustle in da backyard
as mai mada wen cut down
one new guava switch.

"Boy! Come hea!"

KYLEENA LAMADRID *created this poem her sophomore year at the University Laboratory School in Honolulu. She became interested in the pidgin style of writing after reading* Growing Up Local *in English class. Inspired by the words of local authors, she tries to use pidgin to illustrate her own views of Hawai'i. Besides writing, she also enjoys drawing, studying sciences, and playing basketball on the University Laboratory School's Girls Varsity team.*

Richard Hamasaki
"KAPAHULU GIRL"

chorus:
Kapahulu girl,
Jus make 16
Kapahulu girl
wattsa matta' you?

Kapahulu girl
poppa's only one
Kapahulu girl
she rappin'

> *my daddi wen name me Bobbi*
> *he need me fo' be one caddy*
> *my fadda like me be a Rainbow*
> *he even t'ink I can be one golf pro*
>
> *monky monku*
> *yeah yeah*
> *monky monku*
> *yeah yeah*

repeat chorus:
Kapahulu girl,
Jus make 16
Kapahulu girl
wattsa matta' you?

Kapahulu girl
poppa's only one
Kapahulu girl
she rappin'

> *my fadda don't mine my boifrein*
> *my boifrein get one job downtown*
> *my mudda, she teach me fo cook an' sew*
> *ah, but she bodda me about what fo' do*
>
> *monky monku*
> *yeah yeah*

monky monku
yeah yeah

chorus:
Kapahulu girl
poppa's only one
Kapahulu girl
she rappin'

Kapahulu girl,
yr his samurai
Kapahulu girl
like one numba one son

> *my mudda, she luv my boifrein*
> *my fadda, he favor my boifrein*
> *but my fadda he no say nuttin*
> *even doe da boi one good Japanee*

> *monky monku*
> *yeah yeah*
> *monky monku*
> *yeah yeah*

Kaui Hart Hemmings

from "HOUSE OF THIEVES"

We are floating on our surfboards in a loose circle beyond the break so we can talk about the emergency: Wendy's brother is back. "What does he want?" Nicole asks. She's holding the nose of Wendy's board to keep from drifting away.

"I don't know," Wendy says. "Maybe he wants to come home."

Belle is tucking her breasts back into her bathing suit top. They are getting really sloppy. I look down at my chest. I have nothing to fix and arrange. I'm twelve.

"Did he look good?" Belle says.

"I guess," Wendy says. "I didn't see him up close."

Wendy is sad, though I could be wrong. I'm a writer and a diarist and also an actress at the Diamond Head Theatre so sometimes I see things that aren't really there. We are moving farther away from shore, past the rocky fingers of reef. The water here is a blackish blue. I'm thinking about Wendy's brother, but also about sharks. Echo Point is known for having them. We're all gripping our surfboards between our thighs. The sun stings our backs; eight legs dangle in the water. To any sharks below us, we must look like sea turtles. When I tell this to the others, they lie on their stomachs. Sometimes my prose is very effective.

"He was swimming at our beach," Wendy says. "He must have used the access by the lighthouse."

"Whack job," Nicole says.

Wendy shrugs her burning shoulders. "It's his beach, too, I guess."

"Why don't we like him?" Belle asks.

"I like him," Wendy says. "He just makes me angry sometimes."

"I like him," I say, even though I feel guilty about it. I know that her brother has done more than steal a car. Belle and Nicole think Perry's just a runaway thief who has abandoned Wendy and scarred her emotionally. My dad scarred my mother emotionally. He has a license plate that says SUE EM. My mom divorced him then sued him, but now they're back together again. They dance on our balcony to "Shake Your Groove Thing," their second wedding song.

"He's a thief, that's why we don't like him," Nicole says. "He's come to take our money, I bet, but we'll kick his ass. We'll egg him."

I imagine how we'll do it, like the Sharks and the Jets. I choreograph fight sequences: Pas de bourrée, kick kick, neck hold. Pirouette, layout, punch punch, jazz hands. If we get caught for fighting or vandalism I will simply say that we're just kids growing up on an island, doing bad things in pretty places. I test this line on my friends because it sounds stylish and dramatic and just right.

"Niner," Nicole says, which is this week's term for loser.

Sometimes my verse doesn't work so well, but Nicole's a skank and I take this into consideration. She's always reaching behind her legs to pull the flesh of her inner thighs apart and saying, "If I looked like this I'd be perfect." Tomorrow, at Secrets, or Old Man's, or No Place, I will drop in on all her waves. I'll do a cutback. I'll pump my board and ride out a wave to shore like a boy. This is how I win arguments with Nicole, my third-best friend.

We paddle in closer to shore. There are no waves. We're lifted and dropped by swells that don't break or take us anywhere. "Let's go," Belle says. "This sucks."

"You go," Nicole says. "You suck."

Belle and Nicole are sisters. They don't like each other much, in a sisterly way. On dry land they wear their dad's scrubs—just the pants part. They pair them with bandeau bikini tops and claim that the other has copied.

"Race you," Nicole says. She splashes water on all of us and it's freezing since we've been cooking in the sun. Then she paddles in so fast her arms blur like insect wings. Nicole gets babysat by this white pill her parents force her to take, and it makes her either freak out, or focus intensely on inanimate objects, or get angry and cranky and two-year-old-like. I've caught her sucking her thumb.

Wendy doesn't want to go in, I can tell. Seeing her brother again has upset her. It's truly a disaster. He's really sweet and really real and handsome, but he moved out of the house when he was sixteen because he accidentally touched her inappropriately or something. I know this because I accidentally caught a glimpse of her Dec. 12 entry in her old diary. The glimpse said something about them playing Escape from Sing Sing. She was eight years old. He'd give her five seconds to escape from his room before he tackled and pummeled her. One time he tackled her and they starting kissing and their mom found them kissing and touching inappropriately. She called a professional who was like a referee but with a pen and weird glasses. The family hugged and cried. Wendy is a good writer. Due to the suspense she created I couldn't help but read more. The entries stopped on Feb. 18 with this very emotional paragraph: When he said he was sorry I thought he meant for the charley horse, but maybe it's cause of the before part. Now he's going to the North Shore. He stole Dad's car, but Dad's not telling. I'm worried for Perry.

Because he banished himself, I find myself truly believing that Perry's a good person, noble even, like the Christ figures in the plays I've been in. I got to play a Christ figure once. I played Annie in Annie. In addition to being noble, Perry is a very good long term connection for us because we're planning to live in Haleiwa one day on the North Shore. It's where all the real surfers live—Mark Occhilupo, a.k.a. Occy, a.k.a. the best surfer ever, Shaun Tomson, Curren, Hans, the Ho brothers, and the lost at sea legend, Eddie Aikau. I know their stats and bios, their likes and dislikes, their favorite bands, their sponsors, if they have a cat or a dog or a wife. Perry is just like these guys. He used to be the best of the amateurs. We watch his old contest videos, which proves Wendy has forgiven him for whatever happened. When he surfs he looks like he's doing something illegal. I bet one day he'll have his own line of shoes.

Wendy stays by my side as we paddle in though she can go much faster. She's the strongest girl I know. I feel so lucky that we like to surf even when no one's looking. I feel lucky that we aren't girls who sunbathe, although I know that Belle and Wendy have given blow jobs. Nicole told me what a blow job was and I can't see why a guy gets pleasure from someone blowing on his dick. My friends are in seventh and eighth grade and they have knowledge I don't have yet. I can't wait 'till November when I'll be a teenager. I can date guys like Perry and it won't be considered harmful to my childhood. Except now he's twenty one—I think that's still in the danger zone. I want to be older. I hate my grade. Kids my age listen to Tiffany and Debbie Gibson and know nothing about Oingo Boingo or life.

Kaui Hart Hemmings
from "SECRET CLUTCH"

T onight is the Fourth of July and they are now at his mother's wedding reception, which is at her and her new husband's home on Wailai'iki Ridge. The yard is shaped like a broom, a triangular expanse of grass with a long handle of ledge that hovers over a valley. Kent and Noe stand on the handle in the wind. They float above the valley and the black and wrinkled sea.

Kent surveys the yard, the people by the bar and under the tent, which is made of sails and is staked to the ground with bamboo poles. "I need to get back to work," he says.

Kent has given himself a mission and calls it Mission Imbecile because that was what he once was: an imbecile, and he doesn't want to be one any longer. He has finally seen the light. He thought his stunts were so clever and shocking but, as his grandfather said, he was just another dim-witted participant in the great island tournament of pleasure. Now, in honor of his recently deceased Gramps, he is looking to add something new to his life. He wants to add some dignity. He wants to engage in mental combat always and forever. Most of all, he wants to show Noe that he has the potential to become a responsible man.

"Let's get this over with," Noe says. "There's Mr. Wong."

Her hair is black like charcoal. Her hair is his fuel. Kent walks toward his victim. Mr. Wong owns a chain of crack seed stores that Kent has stolen from. He loved the wasabi peas and the dried, crinkly plums soaking in li hing sauce. He'd reach his hand into those glass jars, in the thick juice, and then he'd run out of the store with a handful and jump on the Express 27 that always came to the corner of Koko Head and Wilhelmina at 3:22.

Mr. Wong sees Kent and raises both of his hands as if it's a stickup, then makes a tiny bow and laughs.

"How are you doing this evening?" Kent asks.

"You like my treats," Mr. Wong says. "You take." He presents a package of dried shredded mango from his pocket and pushes it into Kent's hand.

"No," Kent says. "I would like to apologize for my old ways," but Mr. Wong is backing away before he can continue with the spiel. He is smiling, amused, as the others were. Kent is becoming more disappointed with each response. It's as if he's going from door to door and nobody's home. To others, his desire to lead a noble life isn't admirable; it's adorable, irrelevant. Earlier this evening he apologized for ages thirteen and fourteen to the Sigfrieds, the Richardsons, and the Johnstons, people from his dad's neighborhood. He rode the Sigfrieds' mini horse to the Circle K. While the Johnstons were away in Sun Valley he had their pool drained and used it for skateboarding, and he taught the Richardsons' parrot how to say, "My nads are on fire." All three families accepted his apology immediately. Mrs. Sigfried told him that divorce could be hard on children. Mr. Richardson said that Joshua snorts pain killers and that Kent looked like Father Damien next to his sorry sack of skin of a son.

Gramps gave Kent this apology mission about a year ago when he and Noe first moved into Gramps's house on Diamond Head. They moved in after Kent received straight C's on his report card, even a C in Glass Blowing, but Kent was a different person back then and he ignored his grandfather's various tasks, ignored all of his prescriptions that would help kill the wise ass within.

His grandfather was a flyer in the Korean War. Kent wants to be like him, though not look like him. His teeth were different shades of khaki, though he only smiled when he saw Mrs. Sees on a chocolate box. He'd see her picture, smile, and say, "I bet she was a real good girl." In his grandfather's later years, he grew puffy and neckless. He had scattered discs of liver spots on his bald head and his left arm from sticking it out the window as he drove, and the spots were always bathing in a petroleum jelly-like substance. Gramps looked like Jabba the Hutt if Jabba were to undergo gastric bypass surgery, yet Kent would rather resemble him than his other male role model, his handsome father, because his father is a reckless pervert. Kent has seen videotapes of him having sex with women, and the women in the videos don't look conscious. They look as if they're sailing the high seas listing back and forth, their faces pale and vacant with motion sickness. Kent has also seen his father having sex live. Twice, he caught him in the living room. He never got to see the woman's face—just her tan leg draped over his father's shoulder and his father heaving into the body as if attempting to break down a locked door. He overheard the woman saying to his father that he makes her feel like a cavewoman, and then she made a roaring sound.

Girls are fond of Kent, too. He has been kissed, groped, and dry humped on numerous occasions, but during these moments he always thinks of his father, and of his inner caveman, and his dick droops like a Dali watch.

What kind of man do I want to be? Kent thinks about this a lot ever since his grandfather died. What kind of man am I now? He looks at Noe's face, her body, and then his shoes. He allows himself to imagine her nipples before putting on his metaphorical coat of armor. He wonders if he has the same thoughts as his father, the same fantasies of swiveling hips and nipples with craters and hills like the surface of the moon . . .

Who's next?" Noe asks. "Who else have you robbed or insulted?" She takes a pull from a longneck beer bottle. "I feel like insulting someone."

Kent puts his arm around her. "Cheer up," he says. Poor Noe. Her engagement to Racer McNaughton has been broken. Racer is a beach volleyball player, a grunting jock, a pro asshole. He's also a sugarcane heir, a literal sugar daddy. Like her predecessor, Noe didn't get to upgrade. Noe is a descendant of the Scottish Hawaiian Princess Victoria Kaiulani, the princess who never got to be queen because the monarchy was overthrown and she died of disease and heartache. Kent knows everything about Princess K. because of Noe—she clings to her heritage because she thinks that it somehow makes her royal, but Kent has trouble reconciling her bloodlines with her profession. She's a nanny and a Tahitian dancer—she wears bras made out of coconuts and she shakes her ass while the male dancers around her waggle their tongues and swallow fire. There's nothing regal about it. Poor Noe.

Tonight, he'll have to apologize to her as well for what he has done and for what's about to happen.

"You should get drunk," Kent says. "I'll drive home."

"Yeah right," she says.

His grandfather banned Kent from any kind of vehicle including golf carts. Kent is reminded of Russell Clove and scans the area for him. Kent spots him and tugs on Noe's wrist. They walk toward Russell, who unfortunately is with his daughter, Brandy, a senior at Kent's high school and a constant presence at family functions. Kent hesitates. Brandy is sulky and skinny—a walking rib. She's also very cool. When she talks it sounds as if she's simultaneously yawning. Kent doesn't bother with formalities. He recites his memorized speech so that it will be a proper apology:

"Sorry, Mr. Clove, for ruining your golf game with my foolish antics. Like a moth to a flame I was drawn to destruction and tomfoolery." Kent looks over at Noe and she's mouthing parts of the speech along with him in a mocking way. "By chasing you and your party into the pond with my cart I was fulfilling my need for attention since my parents didn't give me any." Kent pauses. Russell is looking at him with a smile on his face as if Kent's telling a joke that's about to reach the punch line. He doesn't look at Brandy, knowing that she'll kill his flow. He's embarrassed, but reminds himself that the new Kent need not be embarrassed. The new Kent does not care for peer approval, nor does he dig through cow manure for magic mushrooms or make mustaches out of pubic hair and offer them to the drama dorks to use in their musicals. He is not like his father, he is like Gramps, and the only thing that can be depended on is his own brute strength. He will not be a pervert. He will not mistreat people because he knows what it's like to be discarded. He will recite his speech. Still, with the hope that Brandy won't be able to hear him, he mumbles the next line: "I'm now in a better environment and am on my way to becoming an upstanding citizen."

"Christ!" Russell yells. He elbows his daughter. "Did you get all that, honey?"

"Whoa," she says. "Scary."

Kent knows he's dead at school on Monday. Brandy will tell her crowd all about his apology, a crowd he once aspired to. She hangs with the mushers—skaters and stoners whose girlfriends manage to look hot in baggy clothes and DC shoes. However, Brandy is a poser and wouldn't want her sticky friends to know about the glam parties she attends. Tonight she wears a turquoise dress slit up the side of her leg and she carries the exact purse Noe coveted when she dragged him to Neiman Marcus last Saturday: the Murakami Louis Vuitton. There was no way Noe could ever afford it. How he loathes this purse. Everywhere he looks he sees it, its fluorescent logos, the white leather, women cradling it as if it's a newborn. He sees Noe nod at the purse. Brandy looks at Noe's purse, vintage Chanel, given to her by Kent's father, and nods. Hello, Louis. Why, hello, Chanel.

"Didn't you get suspended from the club?" Brandy asks, laugh/yawning into her dad's shoulder.

Kent knows that she knows very well that he got suspended for his antics on lobster and a movie night when he went from table to table imitating the scream a lobster makes as it burns and drowns. Everyone laughed as they dunked their slabs into their tins of drawn butter, but that was months ago when he was still on the thorny path. Does Brandy want to partake in a little game of "Didn't You?" Oh, he'll play. Rumors have her putting chicken salad on her pussy and Chad Nikolai licking it off.

"Are you sniffing glue or something?" she asks.

"Oh, real clever," Kent says, then flicks his tongue and tells her there's chicken yakitori by the bar if she gets a hankering for some bird. After this, he immediately says: "Sorry."

"Whatever," Brandy says. "I don't even know what you're talking about."

"Kent," Russell says. "You did that when you were ten years old. I've gotten over it. It's dinner party material now. It's great."

"Please, Russell," Noe says. "Just say you accept his apology. The boy has gotten into a lot of trouble and he's trying to amend his wrongs in honor of Gramps—one of the steps is apologizing."

"Oh, sure," Russell says. "I had to do that once. Twelve steps."

"I only have nine," Kent says. "I don't have to carry my message to others and I don't have to seek through prayer."

"Decided to pass over the God parts," Russell says. "Not bad. But what about steps two, and five, six, seven?"

"You sure know your steps," Noe says.

Russell looks down at his cocktail and shrugs.

"I still have those steps," Kent says, "except instead of 'God can restore,' 'Admit to God and others,' it's 'Gramps can restore,' 'Admit to Gramps and others.' That was my grandfather's idea, but now that he's gone I guess I don't really have those steps either. Stop staring at me, Brandy."

"Well, Mr. Halford ran a tight ship," Russell says.

"I've run amok for almost sixteen years," Kent says.

"Well, amen, soldier. Over and out!" Russell salutes and shakes his glass then moves along with his slouching daughter, the collapsed rib. Brandy looks back at him and smiles. It seems genuine.

KAUI HART HEMMINGS *grew up in Hawai'i and has degrees from Colorado College and Sarah Lawrence College. She is also a former Wallace Stegner fellow. Her work has appeared in* The Sun; StoryQuarterly; Zoetrope; Best American Nonrequired Reading; Best American New Voices; *the* LA Times; *and* Bad Girls. *She is the author of* House of Thieves *and* The Descendants. *Her debut novel was a New York Times Editors' Choice and has been optioned by Fox Searchlight and translated into five languages. Visit her website: www.kauiharthemmings.com.*

Matthew Rikio Nihei Sakumoto
"GURLSTAR'S REPLY"

O sk8erboi6948
Whose love for me will not abate
No, all your charm cannot persuade
Me to become your online maid.

Your profile pic looks pretty cute
Tall, muscular, and tan to boot
But what's to say your info's true
My age says twelve; I'm fifty-two.

Our conversation lasts an hour
'Cause after that my mood grows sour
For everything looks slightly green
From staring at my laptop screen

I never did make much ado
'Bout silly text like "I ❤ you'"
I need a real man face to face
A thing your webcam can't replace.

I'm sorry but I must decline
The one who wastes his time online;
Your name is one that I will block
GurlStar signed off at 8 o'clock.

MATTHEW RIKIO NIHEI SAKUMOTO *was born in 1988 in Honolulu and grew up in Kāne'ohe on the Windward side of O'ahu. A 2006 graduate of 'Iolani School, he is currently studying biomedical engineering at Washington University in St. Louis, Missouri. In his free time, Matthew enjoys going to the beach, playing basketball, and playing guitar and jazz trumpet. He would like to thank Dr. Peter Webb for encouraging him to submit his poem to the Starbucks Star Poets competition and to this anthology.*

Carolyn Lei-Lanilau

"CAROLYN AND THE COP"

It started with my waiting and waiting and waiting for the bus starting at 6:30 am to catch the Ala Moana bus to transfer to the other bus to Pearl City, While waiting and waiting and expecting Mildred to walk out to see if I caught the bus (because she wanted to drive me to Ala Moana) what should re-invent itself in front of my brown black eyes but a blue and white cop car ccrrruis-singing by and at that very moment I flashed on HIM.
No mere mortal.
HIM: not just a thickly padded jewel.

Not just a cop but a **legend**,
a nightmare:
the something you want to forget in your early early profoundly bad
adult life.
The cop car and the cop inside were not the archetype, but the Symbol of
the man in blue reminded me of HIm.

HOw did he—him even have access to ME?
well, heh heh, He was teaching *karate* at Summer Session
and I
was taking the very first *tai qi* class offered at the UH.
We had to share the same gym. Our side, the *tai qi* class was delicate and
tranquile and
their side was rough and brutish—noiseyand sexual.
Our side was advanced and intelligent
and *something* about uniforms—However, while I hate to admit it, from the
distance, I noticed this Guy, good looking from far away, and purveyor as I
was, I
scoped him out.
I cannot remember anything precisely as what led to what,
but one day he noticed me in my extraordinary aura.
He asked me if I wanted a ride home and of course, now I would refuse, but
then. Then, I had never been with a cop before and only knew them col-
lectively as PIGS.
Locals guys are Not like cops on the mainland.
At home, we can come face to face with a cop and
not take them at all seriously They just all look like our cousins or brothers
and we just know they are juvenile delinquents.
So he gave me a ride home in his own cop car because in Hawaii, the cops
can drive their own cars on the job—or at least they used to. It was blue.
It was a sedan. We were both sweating from the humidity. We were both
young and both cocky. I'd like to remember if we went for a ride before he
brought me home or what. I remember we went to Nuʻuanu and I let him
know I was the sexually advanced type. He was cute.
He was as cute as all the Hawaiian boys I ever saw.
Hawaiian guys are so incredibly good-looking.
Young Hawaiian guys, old Hawaiian guys are so wild, so naughty, so
so good-looking. And they are horrible—worst than Chinese because
they are so good–looking and because they are so phy-phy-physical, it is
such a goddamn downer when you discover they are so royally stupid—
not no brains—that they impulsively do something stupid Because:

It Was Good Fun at the Moment.
That was Bumpy who smelled good and felt thick and young in my hands.
That
was
Bumpy who was so strong and is probably dead by now.

When it came to fucking me, it was no french movie. He just pulled and
down came my panties at Kuli'ou'ou. Crushed and pounded, the taro roots
became the milk and *poi* quiche—served which managed to come together
somehow.
There was no conversation.
The ocean's voice stirred in and out.
The palm fronds wondered.
He was a cop and I was a writer but we were both Hawaiian and he was *one*
guy—besides Big Kenny that my father watched. My father addressed in
orders. My father wasn't nice to any of the guys that I dated with the exception of Godwin—what a name! And one thing led to another. I had a real
boyfriend for a change, not some stupid student in Creative Writing. Or
some membrane in Philosophy.
Bumpy was just an ordinary Hawaiian guy who was divorced and had a kid.
He fucked me quite a bit at my parent's house when they went out. I can't
believe I'm even writing about this: I really should be ashamed, but this is
dime for three or four dozen stuff so people at home wouldn't even consider
Telling anyone about this but there Is a connection and that is up until I
remembered the legend of My Very First Hawaiian Boyfriend

I didn't even know I had one and was in the meantime dreaming about—
formatting da
buggah like he was sen-sitif
and of course good-looking and first ting, had to be smart;
and with a good sense of humor and strong and healthy so he surfed and
could
build house and do yard work
and was nice to all the aunties
and went fishing with the boy cousins.
Had to be able to sing and play music
and know how to get good deals
and was so nice to me and wrote music for me
and was original and of coss, I, the Bestest, deserved him.

I forgot Bumpy because I thought I as goin to turn him on with my grass
one day while my parents went holoholo and right away Bumpy goes to the

phone and pretends to be calling the vice squad. Of coss, I don know dat and I'm already stoned.

All I saw were the headlines in the Honolulu Advertiser *"O NO ONo GIRL Arrested fo Possession of Pakalolo at Uncle Jackie and Aunty Mildred's, 1893 Iolani Palace."* I was sure that I had pressed my luck that time. I really expected the police truck to haul me off but no, Bumpy gives me a lecture and takes the stash. And I am left to recover from my worst challenge in life.

But a few days later, that fucker drives up like nothing happened. Like I had no memory HE had forgotten, *mais non, pas moi merci.* He wants to visit with me and I'm like

requiring Gestalt Therapy. I don't want to see him.

My mother said I wasn't home and of course, she asked why? I made up some excuse.

And then, he drove by several times and each time when I happened to be by a window, I sunk a little lower.

Then he continued to come by and the summer was over and I ws on the plane back to the Haight.

No wonder I fell for Steve: he and Bumpy have that raw instinct that I love and that dull memory which I hate.

Their fucking style is similar too: simple, coarse, hard, and good.

(usually B+ for style, A for orgasm, A++ for engaging my idiocy)

CAROLYN LEI-LANILAU *is a poet, artist, and scholar who lives in Oakland, California, and in Honolulu. Her book* Wode Shuofa (My Way of Speaking) *received a 1989 American Book Award. Her poems have been anthologized in five books, including* The Best American Poetry of 1996, *and have appeared in such journals as* The Bloomsbury Review; The American Poetry Review; Mānoa; Yellow Silk; Zyzzyva; *and* Calyx.

Davin Kubota

"BOYFURENDO/GARUFURENDO"

In Kaimukī,
"Auntie," 'round 65
wit one pen in one ear, some bobby pins
ovah da oddah,
and one massive black hairnet,
brings da tray—
black lacquer bowls and

wooden hashi stay on top.
Unlike da waitress who no take off da lid,
Auntie hemo da lid off da miso soup,
So can see steam come up
And smell green onions
Mixing pungently wit' da tofu.
"Chee Auntie, t'anks, ah," I say, as I take out
da hashi and rub 'umm fasttogeddah, jes like
I one excited Boy Scout at
Camp Erdman making fire fo' da
firs' time.
"Doan mind, doan mind," says Auntie, as she
pours me
one noddah cup green tea.

Da waitress who no can hemo da lid
Reminds me of da hotties at Ocean's
Or Dave and Busters—dey nice, but dey nice
Cuz dey know dey going
karang you on da tip.

But not Auntie. Auntie give me
One okawari of rice—one extra
Serving—wit'out me even asking.
she just eye da specks in da bowl and
she know—BAM—da rice is dere.

On top of dat,
Auntie hooks me up with extra wakame,
or sometimes bean sprouts,
and okra dat she made herse'f.
Dese seaweed, bean, tofu-kine
dishes not even on da reg'lah menu,
but Auntie is cool li'dat.

Da grumpy-face Nakatani-man,
da one who grunt at Auntie when she
give him da wakime-bean-okra,
as if wuz expected ten minutes ago,
give her fifty cents tip
and she still
treat him good, pouring him
coffee again and again.

Cuz wen Mrs. Nakatani wuz alive,
she gave Auntie all kine daikon
and Mānoa lettuce from her yard.
Ass why Auntie feel obligated.
So I like figgah why Auntie treat me
so good—jes like she
my real Auntie—but not
obligated to be nice to me.

I tink she like me cuz I can talk Japanee.
In her mind, mebbe
preserving da language stay essential kine.
She tell, "I wish my daughta, Patrice,
wa Nihongo o tsukaeru like you.
She almos' 30 you know, and
only speak Engrishu.
You can teach her?
You like me shinpai you
togeddah?"

So I guess I kinda flattered
dat Auntie making me out
fo' be one good catch, or her
future son-in-law, but
I not interested.

Cuz Auntie not too good
at making her daughta out fo' be
one appealing bride:

"She no eat Japanese foodo!
I make dis kine fo' her and she
only like eat Macudonarudo and
expensive Itarian spaghetti!"

"She no can cook!
I tell, 'How you can
get good husbando
if you no can make
food?!'
She say, 'Ma!
Ass why I get
rich lawyer husband

fo' take me eat
Assagio's!'"

Ass why, if it wasn't for
da massive hairnet, da blue smock, and
da forty year age difference
between da two
of us,
garanz me and Auntie would be
boyfurendo and garufurendo;
I no shet you.

DAVIN KUBOTA *was born in 1976 and is an instructor of English at Kapi'olani Community College in Honolulu. He enjoys eating the Japanese breakfast at Victoria Inn in Kaimuki because it reminds him of an old Hawai'i that now seems to be increasingly hard to discern.*

Andrea Castillo Simeon Baptista

"LOVE, FIL-AMER STYLE"

Makalawasen a di simmangpet ni Carol. Diak ammot' napananna. Nagpasugnod. Namin-adun a timmalaw manipud nagasawakami. Agsubli met latta uray diak biroken. Daytoy ti kabayagan a panagtalawna. Innak koma sapulen ngem amangan no dumakkel ti sarana. Uray ipatpategko, diak kayat ti ma-under.

Kadawyan iti agassawa, adda pagsubanganda. Manmano met ketdi no agasingkami ngem awan paabak. Diak pinagtalaw ni Carol. Kinapudnona, pinagiddanak iti sopa iti karabiyan ti talawna. Diakon nabangonan iti agsapa! Pudno a diak maawatan dagiti babbai.

Padasek ti agmaymaysa. Kas gagangay nga aramidko iti Sabado, agdalusak iti arubayan. Sinukitko dagiti barsanga iti lawn grass. Inabunuak dagiti agkurkuriripit nga anthurium ken orkidia. Sinibugak dagiti nanglaylay nga snowballs. Sinigpatko dagiti duyaw ken nagango a palatang ti palmera. Kalpasanna, pinasilengko ti karrok, sako inis-is ti garahe. Kasla mangus-usig ti tungga kaarruba a makakita kaniak. Gapu ngata ta nabayagen a dida nakita ti karro ni Carol. Pakasikoranda? Diak met bibiangan dagiti aramidda! Diak ugan ti makikakarruba.

Nagay-ayamak a dinalusan ti swimming pool. Duan a lawas a di nausar. Kasta unayen dagiti limned ken agtatapaw a bulong. Linumoten ti leblebna.

Gimsaaden _____. Binalayan payen ti kuyamkuyam. Smuktak ti danumna. Makaay-ayo manen a pagpapaan. Mangawis pay iti panaglangoy ti dumardarang nga init. Inyusokko ti swimming trunk. Nagpiapiak iti ngarab ti swimming pool.

Kalpasanna pinukisak dagiti aglulumbat' rangawna a mock-orange a nayalad iti solar. Pinormak ti ulo dagiti pine tree iti lauden ti balay. Mariknakon ti bisinko idi lumabaga ti init iti nagsabatan iti langit ken taaw.

Nagbuyaak iti telebision. Awan regular a programak ngem naanusak ti nagbuya inggana't nagserra dagiti estasion. Ipatok no yepyepenak iti sangkalidokko a Scotch ngem saan. Ad-adda a naggitebgiteb ti barukongko. Kasla di agdisso ti bukotko iti iddak. Saanak met a nabartek. Kasko la im-impen a dumteng ni Carol iti tunggal daranudor dagiti karro. Isagsaganak pay met iti parbo nga urok.

Kabigatanna, awan ammok nga aramiden. Makimisa? Diak ammot' mapan iti simbaan no awan ni Carol. Duan sa nga orasko a nangig-igup iti kape. Dimmegdeg ti lidayko. Nalagipko a kinita ti kloset ni Carol. Naksayan, dagitay la kunana a junkies ti nabati. Linuktak ti jewel box iti dresser. Awan dagiti alahasna, malaksid ti wedding ringmi. Naiparabaw iti bassit a papel. Kastoy ti naisurat: ENOUGH IS ENOUGH! I'M SICK OF EVERYTHING. SEE YOU LATER IN COURT! CAROL.

Nagdanagak. Ita la nga imbati ni Carol ti singsingna. Paypaysuennan? Tineleponuak ni Nanang iti Kalihi. Sinaludsodko ni Carol. "Diak pay nakitat' alliwitna. Dagiti la yaayna idi kanaganan iti Tatam. Apay, aya?" kinunana.

"Nagpauyon sa ta di simmangpet idi rabii," inyulbodko. Nagkullayawak.

Nagapakami idi naminsan a Sabado. Nangrugi iti innimon. Dimmar-aykami ngamin iti kallaysa ti gayyemmi. Namin-aduka mi a nagsala ken Pilar. Kasta unay met ti dekket nga agsala da Carol ken Mr. Wilson a bossna. Nasudak ngata ti riknana, kasta met kaniak. Iti panagrinnasukmi, naisidirko daydi nasukalak a suratna ken ni inana. Mangibagbaga iti kuarta. An-anuenna? Kunanto pay da katugangak a bisinek ti anakda. Filipino, apay, kapuy?

Daydi ti namagsibo iti riknak. Nagramaram idi kunana nga innak sumapul iti kadutdotko. Ita, nabaawen ti ulok. Masapul a birokek. Asawa la ti asawa. Mailaak met gayam!

Iti Lunes, diak simrek iti opisina. Pinallikosak ti opisina da Carol ta amangan no adda met la ketdi nga agtrabaho a kas kadagiti napalabas a panagtalawna. Awan ti karrona iti parking lot. Simrekak iti opisinada. Nagsaludsodak iti baro a receptionist. Imbagana la a nagbakasion ni Carol. Nakitak met ni Mr. Wilson a bossna. Sipapasnek nga agkuditkudit iti boothna. Damagek koma kadagiti katrabahuanna ngem "Is that Filipino Style?" kunanto man dagiti sutilen.

Nagsaludsodak kadagiti am-ammomi. Nagteleponoak pay ken ni Velma, ti kabsatko a kagayyemanna. Awan. Nasdaawa pay ketdi: kabainko payen dagiti unton.

Nagteleponoak idiay Florida, ti baro a destino da katugangak. Awan latta. Idi agangay, isudan ti agkaraawag. Nagulbodak. Imbagak a simmangpeten ket addan iti trabahona.

Insardengko ti agbirok. Namak pay no agwaras a nagapakami. Maipaduyakyaken ti ap-apalanda a relasionmi. Naragsak kano ti panagdennami, kadagiti dadduma, mabalin a kasta. Ngem no ipaypayso ita ni Carol . . .

Amangan no ur-urayenna nga innak ay-aywen? Ngem sadino ti pagbirokak? Missing Persons iti Police Deprtment? Saan! Diak kayat ti maim-imbestigar. Hospital? Naawaganak koman. Urayek laengen ti ayab ti korte no impaysona.

Piman dagiti nagbannoganmi iti pito a tawen. Daytoy ap-apalanda a balayni ditoy Oceanfront ken ti 16-unit apartment a naigasatanmi iti trust auction sale. Tuok, rigat, nagbagaykami a nangibaklay. Awan reklamona idi karigatmi. Ita, addan bassit pagnam-ayan. Awan anakmi a mangsiglot koma iti kasamientomi. Dagitoy kukuami ti amok a pakirinnisirisanna iti Korte. American style dayta. Apay ngamin a nakatumpongak iti sabali a puli?

Haole ni Carol. Adda bassit darana nga Aleman. Nayanak idiay California. Sangapulo ket walona idi damomiti ti agkita iti Hawaii State Employment Office. Agbirbirokak iti trabahok idi uray isu ta kayatna ti agnaed ditoy Hawaii. Tinulongak iti aplikasionna. Naperdina ngamin ti porma nga inted ti clerk. Dakesdakes ti espelingna. Kasla kinaraykay ti manok ti suratna. Kunam lan' di graduado iti haiskul. Anak ti kapitan a naidestino iti Clark Air Base idiay Angeles, Pampanga.

"Why aren't you with your family down there?" sinaludsodko.

"I've been there for years. I came back recently. I'm grown up now. I wanna live my own. Anyway, my parents will soon be back to the States," insungbatna.

Natured a pakinakem, nakunak.

Duapulo ket walok idi. Masters degree in economics iti UP ti panangsakadak iti bisak. Ayatko la a sumurot koma ken ni Pila, ti nobiak idiay Manila iti tallo a tawen. Inkarina nga agsublinto ta agkasarkami ngem di kano makaurnong iti pagpletena. Intuloyna ngamin ti adalna ditoy. Siakon ti dimmanon. Reprep idi ti umay a propesional. Panawen daydi agdindinamag a brain drain. Idi sumangpetak, agkasardan ken Elgin a kapiduana. Diak ammo no nagkinnaawatanda ken Elgin wenno remedioda laeng tapno makapagnaed ni Elgin ditoy Hawaii. Nadamagko a mausigen ti kaso ti panagwinnaswasda. Iti panagkunak, immay ni Elgin a bogus a negosiante.

Nadekket a dagus ni Carol kaniak. Inyumanna no ania ti maibagay a job training a serkenna. Parking lot attendant ti immuna a trabahomi. Kabayatanna, nagsanaykami iti travel service.

Karissabong ni Carol no idilig iti tawenko. Ngem tawen kadi ti pagrukodan? Napintas ni Carol. Nagaget. Debosionada. Saan a bastabasta maidate. Simbolo ti kinadalusna ti puraw a trahe de bodana.

Kaay-ayona ti agbaniaga, agkakangina nga aruaten ken alahas. Dua a tawennan iti travel agency idi agkasarkami. Dua nga annual vacation. Sinursorna dagiti siudad iti Europa ken Sud America. Iti koma maikatlo a bakasionna, lawlawenna ti Asia.

"Save your dollar, Honey. We'd rather settle down," inlap pedko.

"I'm entitled to my own earnings . . . to my life ambitions!" Natangig a simmungbat.

Daydi la ti panagginnurami bayat ti panagnobiomi. Maysa a rabii, immay iti apartmentko. Nagsangsangit a nagpakawan. Ket nagkasarkami.

Naghoneymoonkami idiay Tokyo, Seoul, Taipei, Hong Kong ken Manila. Butbot ti bolsami a nagawid. Nagasat ta naital-oak idi iti akemko iti airline a pagserserbiak. Pinagsiddaawnak ni Carol idi impabus-oyna kaniak ti kaha. Akuenna nga ukrad ti dakulapna iti kuarta.

Immadu ti urnongmi. Adda naitinnagmi iti balay. Pili ni Carol daytoy a lugar a mataptapliakan ti danum-baybay. Saan a mabayag, nakagatangkami iti vacation house idiay Hauula. Idi malakomi ti vacation house, nadoble ti equitymi. Daydi ti ninayonanmi nga intinnag iti 16-unit apartment.

Itay napan a tawen, nariknami ti pagkuranganmi. Mailiwkami iti garakgak wenno sangit ti ubing. Pito a tawen! Nagpakitakami iti doktor. Adda cyst ti maysa nga cbario ni Carol. Naopera. Adda kano met depektok ket masapulna ti medical attention.

Idi maital-oak manen, pinagsardengko ni Carol iti trabahona. Naunget gayam ti babai a saan a naruam nga agyan iti balay. Orasanna payen ti sangpetko. Intedko ti kaha tapno adda pagliwliwaanna, ngem dina nasurotan ti badyet nga insaganak. Nagpilit nga agsubli iti trabaho. Natungpal ti kayatna. Nasaysayaat ti nastrekanna. Idi ngumato ti sueldona, dimmakkel metten ti ulona!

Nagtelepono ni Nanang. Kablaawanna kano ni Carol. Nalipatak a kasangayna gayam. Imbagak a bimmaban ta inkami ag night club. Magustuan ni Nanang ni Carol. Gapu kenkuana, nakaayda ditoy Hawaii. Idi makapagcitizenak, dinurogannak ni Carol a mangpetision kadakuada. Isu ti nakaammo iti amin. Diak kayat idi nga umayda ta kagurak ti agsiuman kaniak, ni Tata Simo. Immay ti amak ditoy Hawaii idi 1946 ngem nakalipat apaman a nakatiliw iti Kanaka. Nagrigatkami nga agina. Nakikabbalay ni Nanang ken ni Tata Simo.

Dimteng ti Domingo, ngem awan pay ni Carol. Awan ti damagko maipapan kenkuana. Napanak nag-bowling tapno malisiak da Nanang. Malemen idi sumangpetak ngem isu met ti yaayda. Inur-uraydak iti garahe. Kaduada ni Donato a kabsatko iti bu niag.

"Komusta, kabagis. 'Niat' naknakanmon?" inkablaawko.

"Ay, kabsat, kitaem lat' gasat, a," insungbatna.

"Dumagas ditoy iti makalawas. Mapan idiay Marlboro, Massachusetts," kinuna ni Nanang.

"Kuem idiay? Adda puraw a kueliom! Agpadikan?"

"Wen, kabsat. Simrekak iti seminario iti La Salette Congregation. Maysaakon a Brother ngem innak pay ituloy ti agadal. Daytoy ngata ti pangawagan ti Dios kaniak."

"Ayan ni Carol?" sinaludsod ni Nanang.

"Adda kinuyogna a tour a nagpa-Mexico. Sumangpetto no umay a lawas," inlibakko.

Pinerrengna ni Brother Donato. Nagkinita da Nanang ken Tatang. Diak naitured ti agpudno.

Nagbirok ni Nanang iti lutuenna a pangmalem. Awan. Nabayagen a diak naggroseria. Inawisko ida mangan iti ruar. Kalpasan ti pangmalem, imbatida ni Brother Donato. Diakon nailemmeng ti problemak.

"Nagtalaw ti baketko, Brother. Dua a lawasen."

"Apay?"

"Diak ammo. Ania ti aramidek?"

"Umanamongka kadi nga agsinakayo?"

"Saan. Patpatgek. Ur-urayek nga agsubli. No koma ammok ti yanna, siakon ti agpakumbaba."

"Napudno met la nga asawa?"

"Dayat' diak masungbatan, Brother."

"Wenno agimon ketdi?"

"Ken ni Pilar ngata!" Inestoriak ti ipapanmi iti pakasar. "Ngem uray met isu. Kasta unay met ti dekketda nga agsala ken ni . . . "

Nadlawna ti irarasukko. "Cool off, Brother. Isut' agimon wenno silka. Adda pay sabali a nagsubanganyo?"

"Tinubngarko ti panagdawatna iti kuarta ken ni katugangak. An-annuenna koma? Adda met itedko nga allowancena. Apaman a makayentrega iti sueldona, e . . . e . . . " Naalak ti agbain. Saanna nga ammo ti financial arrangement ken ni Carol. "Naim-imbag pay ti nastrekmo, Brother. Awantot' parikutmo iti nagulo nga estado. No agpilit ni Carol nga agsinakami, surotenka iti seminario tapno agtalna metten ti lubongko."

"Saanka a naikari iti seminario, Kabagis. Urnosenyo ti kasasaadyo nga agassawa ta isut' naituding nga aramidyo."

"Awan maaramidko no dinak kayaten ni Carol."

"Saanka a nagpudno kaniak. Adda pay sabali a nagsubanganyo. Naun-
uneg ngem dagiti imbagam."

Napadumogak. Naabakak iti perrengna. "Awan," kinunak "Kayatna
ngata a maneharen ti panaggastosmi ngem gastadora met. Kuestionenna
amin a numero iti badyet."

"Umanay met la ti itedmo nga allowancena?"

"Sobra pay, Brother!"

"Iti isu amin a kasapulanna?"

"O, yeah! Uray mano, mangtedak no mangibaga!"

"Excuse me for a while. May I use your phone?" kinunana. Nag-
turongak iti banio. Ammok a ni Nanang ti kinasaritana, ngem diak
maawatan ti panagungap ti ngiwatna. "Ninto Velma ti kasaritam, Nana,"
kinunana.

"Imbagam ti problemak ken ni Nanang, Brother?"

"Dayta ti narigat kenka, Kabagis. Nalimedka la unay. Kasanot' panag-
warwarmo iti problemam no dika makruman kadagiti adda padasna? Reb-
beng a maammuanda. Maturogtan. Agdawatka iti dakkel a kaasi ni Apo Dios
ta mayadayo ti asawam iti dakes."

Intulnogko iti guest room. Diak nakaturog a nagpatnag. Nasapaak
a timmawag ken ni Nanang. Immayda a dagus ken Tatang. Di mabayag,
adda metten ni Velma. Lumlumnekak iti kasla mangus-usig nga ikikitada.
Inurayko ti sermonda.

"Velma, dimo la nakitkita ni Manangmo?" kinunak.

"Aha, birokem met la, aya? Ipatok no saanen!"

"Ania a saan ket asawak?"

"Di ngamin agtalaw ket adda naalas a rasonmo! Isardengmo dayta. Man-
gibabainka!"

"Ania a rason?"

"Kuripotka! Naagumka! 'Tan sa la tsekena ti intresem kenkuana. An-an-
uemto ti kinabaknangmo? Dumawat la iti para dockor, adu la unay a saom.
Asino ti di mabainan?" Kasla agbusi ti ngiwat ti kabsatko.

"Ania a para doktor ket ammok met a nasalun-at? Agurayka, apay nga
ammom maipanggep iti doktor? Ammom ti yanna, ibagam!" Winagwagko ti
abagana.

"Nadagsen ti bagim ti asawam. Impanko iti doktor idi kalman. Nagtarus
idiay apartmentko. Adda dita karrok, ita, naimas ti turogna. Inka kitaen!"

Nagpayak dagiti sakak a rimmuar. Agdudumog ni Carol iti lugan. Sar-
sarapaenna ti rusokna. Binagkatko nga inyuli iti balay. Nabessag. Nalnek
dagiti matana. Naguk-ok iti nairut. Agsalsalungayngay ngem napigsa met ti
pusona. Intarusko iti kama. Naguk-ok manen. Pinunasan ni Brother Donat

ti napalet a katayna a nagayus iti t-shirtko. Adda impatomar ni Velma a kap-sula. Kinitak ti label ti botelia. Reseta ni Dr. Lim.

Inarakupko ni Carol. Umis-isem dagiti uppat idi matmatak ida.

"Thank you kadakayo amin!" kinunak idi pumanawda koman. "Ay, agu-raykayo man pay bassit. Pakitaliawyo ni Carol ta tumawagak dita opisina. Masapulko ti paternity leave, with or without pay, I don't care!"

"LOVE, FIL-AMER STYLE"

I t's already a week that Carol did not come home. I don't know where she went. Many times she has left since we got married. She always comes back, even if I don't look for her. But this is the longest she's been gone. I think of going to find her, but that may grow her horns bigger. No matter how much I care, I don't want to be under the skirt.

In the ways of a husband and wife, there are disagreements. We have few arguments, but no one wants to lose. I didn't make Carol leave. The truth is that she made me sleep on the couch the night she left. When I woke up early, she was gone. Honestly, I do not understand women.

So I try to live alone. I do my routines on Saturday, clean the yard. I weeded the lawn, and fertilized the wrinkling anthuriums and orchids. I watered the drooping snowballs. I chopped off the yellowing and dried palms. After that, I polished my car, then cleaned the garage. Neighbors passing by giving me an investigative look; maybe 'cuz they haven't seen Carol. What's their business; I don't mind what they do! It's not my habit to be neighborly.

I played cleaning the swimming pool. It's been two weeks unused. So many leaves have soaked down and more leaves still floating. Algae are growing on the edges. The chlorine's solidifying on the bottom. Paramecium are swimming. So, I changed the water. Now it's inviting to go soak in. The hot sun is enticing me to swim. I put on my swim shorts. But I only sat on the edge splashing my legs.

After that I trimmed the mock orange hedge that surrounded the yard. I shaped the heads of the pines west of the house. When I felt hungry, the sky was turning red where the sun meets the ocean.

I watched TV. I don't have any regular programs I watch, but I endured watching 'til the station closed. I thought a shot of scotch would make me sleepy, but no. My chest heaved more. It seems like my back doesn't touch my bed. I'm not drunk. I keep thinking it's Carol arriving home every time I hear a car running. I even readied myself to pretend snoring.

In the morning, I don't know what to do. Go to mass? I don't know how to go to church when Carol is not here. I think I drank coffee for two hours. My sadness became more severe. I remembered to go look inside Carol's closet. She took out good clothes and left what she calls junkies. I opened her jewelry box in her dresser. All her jewelries are gone; except her wedding ring put on top a small paper. This is what is written: ENOUGH IS ENOUGH! I'M SICK OF EVERYTHING. SEE YOU LATER IN COURT! CAROL.

I became fearfully worried. It's only now that Carol leaves her ring. Is she leaving for real? I phone Mother in Kalihi. I asked for Carol. "I haven't seen her shadow. Only on your father's birthday. Why . . . ?" she said.

"I think she is sulking, 'cuz she didn't come home last night," I lied. I felt my stomach go up my chest.

We had a fight last week Saturday. It started with our jealousies. We went to our friends get together. I dance many times with Pilar. And Carol was so close when she danced with Mr. Wilson, her boss at work. Her feelings must have been pierced, and me too. When our fight was at peak, I brought out her letter to her mother that I found. She asking for money. What for? My in laws will think I'm starving their daughter. Why, you think Filipino is weak?

That's what boiled my feelings. It got worse when she said for me to go find someone else like me. But now my head is cool. I must find her. A wife is always a wife. I feel so alone!

On Monday, I didn't go to the office. I drove around the office where Carol works, 'cuz she always went to work whenever she left. But her cart is not there. I went inside their office. I asked the new receptionist. She said that Carol is on vacation. I saw Mr. Wilson her boss busy in his booth. I was going to ask her co-workers but "Is that Filipino style?" the teasers will say.

I asked those who know us. I even phoned my sister Velma, who she is close friends with. Not there. She's very surprised. I was very ashamed by her many questions.

I phoned my in laws in Florida where they just moved. Not there. After that they kept calling. I lied. I told them she came back and that she's at work.

I stopped looking for her. That might spread that we fought. It will open our relationship that they are envious about. They say that we are so happy together and with others. But if Carol do this for real—

I wonder if she is waiting for me to go be lovely? But where do I go to find her? Missing persons at the Police Department? No! I don't want to be investigated. Hospital! She would've called me. I may as well wait the court to call, if she's for real.

Too bad what life we've built together in seven years. This ocean front home people are envious of; and the 16 unit apartment complex we luck out on in a trust auction sale. Pain, hardship we both endured. She did not regret our hardship. Now we have pleasure time. We don't have a child that would tie our matrimony. I know it's our properties that she wants to contest in court. That's American style. Why did I fall for some one of a different feather?

Carol is haole. She has little German blood. She was born in California. She was eighteen when we first met at the Hawai'i State Employment Office. I was looking for a job and so was she 'cuz she wanted to live in Hawai'i. I helped her with her application, 'cuz she spoiled the form that the clerk gave. Her spelling was very bad and her writing was like chicken scratch as if she didn't graduate from high school. She's the daughter of a captain stationed at Clark Air Force Base in Angeles, Pampanga.

"Why aren't you with your family down there?" I asked.

"I've been there for years. I came back recently. I'm grown up now. I wanna live on my own. Anyways, my parents will soon be back to the States," she answered.

Brave values, I told myself.

I was twenty eight. Masters degree in economics from UP (University of the Philippines) is how I got my visa. I just wanted to follow Pilar who was my girlfriend in Manila for three years. She promised to come back and marry me when she's accumulated enough money for fare. But she continued her education, so it's me that went to her. So many professionals were coming. Those years were known as brain drain. When I arrived, she was already marrying Elgin, her second cousin. I don't know their understanding, or maybe just to remedy Elgin staying in Hawai'i. I heard that the case of the marriage is investigated. To me, Elgin came as a fake businessman.

Carol came close to me immediately. She asked me what job training would be good for her. Our first jobs were parking lot attendants. Next we went to travel service.

Carol is a young flower bud when you compare her to my age. But is age the measure? She is pretty. She is industrious; very devoted. She doesn't go dating around. She's very clean and white as her embroidered dress.

She likes to have fun and her jeweiries and clothes are expensive. She had been with the travel agency two years when we wedded. Two annual vacations, she visited cities in Europe and South America. On her third vacation, she was going to go around in Asia.

"Save your dollar, honey. We'd rather settle down," I hinted.

"I'm entitled to my own earnings . . . to my life ambitions!" she answered firmly.

That's the only time we got angry while we were courting. One night, she came to my apartment. She was crying and apologized. So, we got married.

We honeymooned in Tokyo, Seoul, Taipei, Hong Kong and Manila. Our pockets were holes going home. I was fortunate bring promoted by the airline I worked. I was surprised that Carol let me hold our monies together.

Our savings accumulated. We had down payment for a house. Carol chose a house that is sprayed by ocean water. Soon after that we bought a vacation house in Hauula. When we sold the vacation house, our equity had doubled. That's what we added to buy the 16 unit apartment.

Last year, we felt something was missing. We were yearning so much for the laughter or cry of a child. Seven years! We went to see a doctor. Carol has a cyst in one of her ovaries. She was operated. I was also told that I have a defect that needs medical attention.

When I was promoted again, I told Carol to stop working. I realized when a woman used to working stops working, she angers a lot staying home. She even time the hour that I get home. So, I handed her our monies to hold, but she cannot follow the budget I prepared. She forced to go to work. She did what she likes. She found a better job. When her salary went high, then her head got bigger!

Mother phoned. Said she wants to greet Carol. I had forgotten she flows with her. I told her she's gone downstairs and that we're going nightclubbing. Mother really likes Carol. Because of her, my parents came to Hawai'i. When I became a U.S. citizen, Carol kept pressing me to petition them. She did everything. I didn't want them to come because I hate my stepfather, Tata Simo. My father came to Hawai'i in 1946, but he forgot us when he got a kanaka, Hawaiian. Mother and I were in hardship. So Nana housemated with Tata Simo.

Sunday came but Carol still not here. I have no news about her. I went bowling so I can avoid Mother. It was afternoon when I got home, but that's when they came. They were waiting for me in the garage. They were with Donato, my brother in baptism.

"Komusta brother. What have you been eating?" I greeted.

"Ay, brother, look at my fate, a," he answered.

"He is here just a week, going to Marlboro, Massachusetts," Mother said.

"What are you gonna do there? You have a white collar. You become a priest?"

"Yes, brother. I entered the seminary of La Salette Congregation. I am now a brother, but I'm going continue studying. This must be my calling from God."

"Where is Carol?" Mother asked.

"She took a tour group to Mexico. She'll come back next week," I lied.

She looked into Brother Donato's eyes. Mother and Father looked at each other. I didn't have the braveness to tell the truth.

Mother looked for what to cook for dinner. Nothing. Been awhile since I groceried. I invited them to eat out. After dinner, they left Brother Donato with me. I couldn't hide my problem anymore.

"My old lady left. Two weeks already."

"Why?"

"I don't know. What should I do?"

"Do you agree that you two part?"

"No. I really care for her. I've been waiting for her to come back. If only I know where she is, I'll be the humble and lower myself."

"An honest true husband?"

"That's what I cannot answer, Brother."

"Maybe she is jealous?"

"Maybe of Pilar!" I told him about the wedding party we attended. "But she is the same. She dances so closely to . . . "

He felt how I was getting hot. "Cool off, brother. She is jealous or you are jealous. Is there something else you fought about?"

"I stopped her from getting money from my in laws. What's she gonna use that for? I give her allowance money. After her paycheck is deposited, e . . . e . . . ." I got ashamed. He doesn't know my financial arrangement with Carol. "What you are getting into is much better, Brother. You will have no problems of scrambling conflicts. If Carol forces to split, I am following you to the seminary so my world settles into calmness."

"You were not promised for the seminary, Kabagis, Brother. You two put into order your ways as husband and wife; that's what you were meant to do."

"There's nothing I can do when Carol doesn't like me anymore."

"You are not being honest to me. There is something else you argued about. It's deeper that what you've told me."

My head hung down. I lost to his stare. "Nothing," I said. "Maybe she wants to dictate our spending, but she is a spender. She questions all the numbers in the budget."

"Is it enough what you give her for allowance?"

"More than enough extra, Brother!"

"For everything that she needs?"

"O, yeah! No matter how much, I give when she asks!"

"Excuse for awhile. May I use your phone?" he said. I went to the bathroom. I know that he talked to Mother but I didn't understand what was said. "You talk to Velma Mother," he said.

"Did you tell my problem to Mother, Brother?"

"That's what is hard with you Brother. You are too secretive. How can you untie your problems when you don't consult those with experience?

They should know. Let's get to sleep. You ask for a big kindness of Lord God that your wife is taken farther from bad."

I took him to guest room. I did not sleep all night. I called Mother early. She and Father came right away. Shortly after, Velma arrived. I was shrinking from their investigative looks at me. I waited for their sermon.

"Velma, you didn't see you Manang (Carol)?" I said.

"Aha, you are looking for her, aya? I thought you were not already!"

"Why not? She is my wife."

"She leaves because of your ugly ways! You stop that. You are shaming us!"

"What ways?"

"You are a selfish tightwad. You are envious! You are only interested in her paycheck. What are you going to do with your richness? She is only asking money for the doctor and you say so much. Who will not be ashamed?" My sister's mouth is exploding like popcorn.

"What for the doctor, she is healthy. Wait, why do you know about the doctor? You know where she is, tell me!" I shook her shoulders.

"Your wife's body is heavy. I took her to the doctor yesterday. She came to my apartment. She is in my car now. Her sleep is delicious. You go look at her!"

I had wings on my feet going outside. Carol's head was down in the car. She is holding on to her solar flex. I carried her up inside the house. She is pale. Her eyes were sunk. She heaved tightly. She's hung loose dangling but her heart is strong. I took her directly to the bed. She heaved again. Brother wiped her thick drool that streamed on my t shirt. Velma gave her a capsule medicine. I looked at label of the bottle. It's a prescription of Dr. Lim.

I embraced Carol. Smiling were the four when I looked at them.

"Thank you, all of you!" I said when they were leaving. "Wait just a little bit. Will you look after Carol while I call the office? I need a paternity leave, with or without pay, I don't care!"

TRANSLATED BY VIRGILIO MENOR FELIPE

ANDREA CASTILLO SIMEON BAPTISTA *was born in 1939 in San Mateo, Isabela, Philippines. She has a BS in education from the University of Santo Tomas, Manila, and another from the Philippine Normal University. She is a teacher and human services worker. In addition to publishing in* Bannawag *magazine she has written more than a hundred songs, including the classic "Sakada" song.*

Virgilio Menor Felipe

"LOVE LETTER FROM LAOAG TO WAIPAHU"

Napan ka kano naki-party diay Waipahu
Heard you went to a party in Waipahu

Baptismal da Magdalena ken Jhun-Jun
Baptismal party of Jhun-Jun and Magdalena

A kabagyam, ken karoba ditoy Laoag.
Your relatives, our neighbors here in Laoag

Adda kan, metten sabali a date mo?
They said, now you have another date?

Naka-rag-ragsak, kay kano
Verrry happy, you two, they said

You kar-karaoke, Macarena ken lag-lagto
Singing, dancing Macarena and jumping

Apay kastan aya ti aramidmo?
Why do you do this?

Apay? Awanen ti ba-ba-in mo?
Why? You have no shame?

Awan cuentan ti kina-edamon?
Your laying down with me is nothing?

Napukaw amin a lagip mon?
Are all your memories gone?

Dagidi gan-ganas ken kat-katawa
Our thrills and laughters?

Ken ti panag-romans ta?
How we romanced . . . all gone?

Gapu't kastan aramidmo
Because you are like that now

Diyak pay maka-pangpanganen
I cannot even eat anymore

Agkutongak kano metten
They say I'm getting very skinny

Kuna ti ta-tao am-ammo
People that know us, say so

Lumneken ti ping-ping ko
Sinking-in are my cheeks

A di-nil-dilam ken bisito
That you kiss and licked

Agpaparangen ti tul-tulang ko
All my bones are showing

Ti pispis ken tenged ko
My temples and neckbones

Awanen polos na-imas a kayat ko
Nothing is delicious anymore

Dagidi kut-kutsara inted mo
The spoon sets you gave

Nang-nanganan ta, awanen ramanda
That we ate from, has no more taste

Dagidi ping-pingan inted mo
The dinner set you gave

Nat-nag idi ag-in-inawak ta na-ibatak
I dropped when washing dishes

Isu in-burak ko la aminen
So I cracked them all

Ti sakit ti gulib mo a na-palalo
Because of the pain of your cruelness

Dagidi bang-banga inted mo
The pots that you gave

Nalipatak pinatay ti stob
I forgot to turn off the stove

Ket nagdiwig ta na-uramen
Burned bad and misshapen

Isu ti usarekon a banga
Now I use them

Panganan ti aso ken pusa
To feed the cats and dogs

Pag-inuman ti manok ken pato
Water for ducks and chickens

Bom-bom-sog kanon ti matak
My eyes are swelling, they say

Ngata haan umanay inana
Maybe not enough rest

Ti kidem ken turog ko
Not enough sleep and shuteye

Ibagak kenca ita
So now I tell you

Lag-lagipem ti sa-ok:
Remember what I'm saying:

Na-ibusen ti luak kenca
All my tears are gone for you

Apo Diyos, ka-asianak kadi
Oh God, please be kind to me

Ta awan metten kaasi ni lakay ko
My man has no more kindness

Nag-American istyle'n, adda girlfriend nan
Now he is American style, has girlfriend

Ay, biagko, garupko no napudno ka
Oh my life, I tho't you are true

Garupko'n haan ka nga plastik
I tho't you are not a plastic

Kinorosam ti pusom ken nag-sapata ka
You swore and crossed your heart

Im-bagam, "Ay-ayaten ca
You told me, "I love you

Tungpal ti biag ko,"
Forever with all my life"

In-yarasaas mo ket dinilpatam lapayag ko
You whispered and tongue my ear

Ket anya ngarud?… amin dayta'n?
So what now? . . . what is all that?

Awanen ti kuentak kenca?
I mean nothing to you?

Anya! Pag- patang-ken mo lang?
What! I'm only your . . . hard-on?

Apay nag-kasta ka?
Why do you do that?

Nga ag-si-silpo ti olbod mo?
Make all these chain of lies?

Apay usarem laeng ti padam a tao?
Why only use another person?

Dagiti bedrom sets nga inted mo
The bedroom sets you gave

Amin mattress caber, balentyn blankets,
The mattress covers and valentine blankets,

Bedsits, ti familyam in-yawat ko
Bedsheets, I gave all to your family

Dagidi regalo'm alahas, aritos
Your gifts of jewelries, earrings

Kuentas, sing-sing ken porcelas
Necklaces, rings and bracelets

Inted ko amin ken Nanang mo
I gave all to your Mother

Dagidi ar-arwaten nga inted mo
The clothes you gave me

Da latest pasions nga Americano
The latest American fashions

Bestidas ken sapatos…istyle ni Imelda
Dresses and shoes . . . the styles of Imelda

Dagiti satin gowns, parang-pakita bras ken kalsones
Satin gowns, see-thru silk bras and panties

Agapu't Secreta ni Victorya
From Victoria's Secret

Ti kakabsat mo, amin inted ko
To your sisters, I gave them all

Sumunu nga ag-balik-bayan ka
The next time you come home

Ditoy Pilipinas, agbakasyon ka
To the Philippines, and vacation

Yawat konto amin arwatem
All your clothes, I will hand to you

Ta awanen ti riknak kenka
I have no more feelings for you

Ngem no siak, saan ka a ka-gura
But me? I don't hate you

Saanak a tao nga na-gura
I am not a hateful person

Haan ka kaguraen
I don't hate you

Ti pag-say-atam ti ibagak
For your goodness I tell you

Buenas suerte latta ti bilin ko
Good luck, is my advice

Makitam wenno apay?
Can you see or why?

Gapu'ta amok, ket siyerto-ak
Because I know, I am sure

Malasat ko dagitoy nga to-ok
I will live thru all this misery

Uray pirsayen pusok toy a pa-naas
Even with my heart piercing with pain

Ag-biagak... ta napudno-ak
I will live . . . becuz I'm honest

Ammok ta . . . ti pusok ket ag-kaykaysa
I know . . . 'cuz my heart is faithful

Dayta ba-ba-im, ket baknang kano
Your woman, they say is rich

Ubing, a na-balo, ak-sidente ti karro
Young, widowed from car accident

Kuarta't insurance, addu kano na-awat na
So much insurance money she got

Ngem no siak? Haan umanay dayta
But for me? That's not enough

No kwarta? masapulanto latta
If money, can always earn

Narag-ragsakak to ngem sika
I will be more happy than you

Ta ti asawaek, nagaget ken anos
'Cuz a patient man, I will marry

Uray haan a guapo, no napudno
Even not handsome, but true

Ken nautog laeng kanyak.
And horny only for me.

Umanayen kanyak
(Now goes into refrain.)
Das enuff por me

Husto na!
Das enuff!

Bastante na!
Das enuff!

So . . . enuff! . . . oredi! Enuff! . . . oredi!
(Ends with a sudden door slam!)

Wendy Miyake

"GETMYMOI.COM"

Hamachi Oe scrolls down the list of new messages on her computer. There are as many as fifteen since yesterday but only the one entitled VD woos her attention. She clicks open the file. Only seven words appear on the screen, but in the ocean or white space, there are a hundred nets of hidden meaning. The style does not surprise her. This message is from the same man who has to hand-deliver all his mail to the post office, who takes down the employee's name, Social Security number and date of birth should any promise be broken. He crafts his messages with fewer than ten words, still paranoid that electronic mail is really a letter without an envelope, an invitation to the world to come see about you.

She stares at the screen, drags her eyes over the words:

Be here by five. Fish delivered. Dad.

She reaches her parents' corner house before five o'clock, and steps onto the asphalt driveway covered with the moss that mocks her father's attempts to kill it.

And there he is. The man with the red truck who smiles at her is Fisherman. She doesn't give him a name. That would make their relationship personal. It's not. He is just Fisherman to her—the man who, when he was four, convinced her father that to name her after an expensive fish would be an honor; the man who has delivered to her father an ulua every Valentine's

Day, gutted, cleaned and sealed in a recycled Ziplock bag; the man who attaches that ringy-dingy of a boat to his truck at 4:30 in the morning with a smile, an almost giddiness that makes you wonder if he's obsessed.

She crosses the threshold into the house and finds her father stationed at the master bedroom window, looking out across the street. He can do this without being seen after having planted the trees just so—so that he can see out, but passersby cannot see in. Fisherman makes no attempt to come over with the fish. It gets later. She watches her father's eyes forbid the sun to fall behind the Wai'anae mountain range. The sun ignores his pleas and the light outside turns the clouds a deep amber, the house across the street suddenly enveloped in a dusk glow. Fisherman leaves his truck outside and disappears into his house.

The sky relinquishes its colors and with the first patches of darkness spilling above the mountains, her father begins to go through withdrawal. He turns his tongue in his mouth like a wave, salivating as if the wasabi shoyu were washing across his tongue. His eyes are closed as if trapped in a seafood seduction, a culinary hallucination, imagining the flesh of the ulua breaking up in his mouth.

For her father, withdrawal was an immediate reaction to a promise that had not been fulfilled. The longer he waited, the deeper he descended into varying degrees of delirium. Hamachi was used to waiting. Ten years ago on a Kona weather afternoon, she stood at the edge of her parents' street, behind Fisherman's red truck as he washed it down and asked in her prettiest voice, as if that made a difference, "My birthday is coming up soon. Could you catch me a moi?"

He smiled, not one of those smiles he had at 4:30 in the morning, but one that was gentle and let her know that he had heard her.

Moi is a good fish. It has a season. Only rare fish have seasons. And moi is rare. In the old Hawaiian days, the only people who could eat it were royalty. Hamachi felt pretty privileged in this life as a young Japanese woman to be able to even ask for it.

Moi is hard to catch, her uncle told her five years ago when she wanted to give up on the promise. *You must watch the sand. In the winter, the ocean takes the sand away, moves it from the shoreline. You must wait for it to return. You must watch the tide. You must have a moon.*

Hamachi hears the gunning of the Volvo vibrate throughout the house. She knows where her mother is going. Star Market has $25-a-pound 'ahi poke and she knows her mother hopes two pounds of it will bring her father back to reality. Her father does not hear her mother leave; instead, he continues to talk, his brain floating somewhere off the North Shore.

He tells Hamachi that Fisherman wants to marry. He's getting older. He sees the same fish getting larger every year. They mock him. Fisherman has even seen an ulua crack a smile, as if Nature were keeping track.

Her father tells her he wants her to marry. He cannot imagine his only daughter alone. What will our family think? Alone is good, Hamachi thought. *You can evolve quickly like being caught in a fast-forward of time-lapse photography. Be one of those senior citizen women who believes in her heart of hearts that purple and pink really do match, who dyes her hair so regularly that her scalp turns black and who doesn't care about passing gas in the middle of the frozen foods section at Star Market where the odor will just linger.*

Hamachi's father wants her to marry. The truth is, he wants to fish. Fisherman has a boat. These are the kinds of connections he makes in his retirement—ones that ultimately benefit him.

Sensible women nearing forty do not marry fishermen. If they're smart, they marry people who work for the state of Hawai'i so they can be fully covered by medical insurance, go for chiropractic treatments twice a week, snag a four-bedroom house with a rock wall in Mililani, a Honda Accord that will be stolen anyway.

The problem with Hamachi is that she's unique. She's not the Hawaiian-bracelet-girl type. That's what her father calls them. He's not talking about all the actual Hawaiian families that pass down the bracelets as a symbol of love or whatever. He's talking about all the girls who beg for gold jewelry or this dress or that car for the Buddha's birthday, Girl's Day or any other holiday or three-hour anniversary. The problem is that Hamachi doesn't like stuff and if she did, she could buy her own stuff. She never thinks to ask others for stuff.

When she told her father she was going to be a yoga teacher, he thought that was too unique for his only daughter. She told him, "Hey, they look happy. I don't know what they're on, but they're always smiling."

And like a suburban oracle, her father said to her, "Twisting your body into a pretzel will not bring you a man. All you will get is tangled."

Now Hamachi is a thirty-eight-year-old yoga teacher moving into no-man land, and her father has regressed to ancestor worship. On any given Sunday, you will find him at the graveyard cleaning other people's graves. He talks to the dead, tells them his story, "Tell her grandfather what I just said. Just in case he didn't hear me the first time."

The dead will rise only when her father is not there. They are probably sick of his requests. He tells Hamachi that he is positive that someone among the many prostitutes in their family tree was, in fact, a samurai.

"That's the way they did things back then. Arrange marriage," he tells her, bringing his two hands together in prayer. She looks at him with eyes of disbelief. She cannot believe that her father is actually considering this. "Those people look happy," he says, patting her shoulder. "You learn to love them."

"Really?"

When her father has deep thoughts like this, it scares Hamachi. She doesn't know what to expect. The last time he had deep thoughts about being prepared for hurricane season, he actually constructed a cement igloo in the backyard that housed at least forty packs of MD toilet paper, several gallons of bottled water, a Japanese futon, and a hundred cans of sardines in tomato sauce. He even started making wine with his tangerine juice, finding the temperature of the igloo perfect.

And now, her father is having thoughts of arranged marriages. She tries to convince herself that it is fish withdrawal and her father is not thinking straight.

Two days later, he e-mails her another cryptic message.

Five thousand hits. Two days. My own Web site. Dad.

Five thousand hits? Two days? This is a little obsessive, even for fishermen who want to share. Hamachi wonders what kind of side business her father is running. One never knows.

It's been only two years since her father bought himself a computer to keep his mind active. But over those two years, the computer has made his mind too active. He wakes at two in the morning, when his insomnia kicks in, and *accidentally* buys things like a $4,000 tricycle on eBay. Then he calls Hamachi on his cellular phone asking how to unbuy it because his Social Security checks will not cover the cost. But lately, he's become so adept with the computer that he created his own Web site, scanned in pictures of himself with the fish he's caught, wrote fictitious stories that he paraded as the truth but were really rip-offs from Hemingway's *The Old Man and the Sea*.

That evening, Hamachi's mother calls. She tells her that her friends from the Europe trip, yes, Kristee-Ann and Dwayne, have a friend.

"You'd love him. He's haole, six feet tall and an engineer. He can provide for you, dear."

Hamachi doesn't respond. That doesn't stop her mother.

"You know, Kristee and Dwayne are just recently married and, oh, they are so cute."

"Big boobs?"

"Yes."

"Beautiful face?"

"Yes. In fact, she has an uncanny resemblance to Kristi Yamaguchi."

Hamachi doesn't say anything.

"Your brother has a friend who was an engineer and now is a kindergarten teacher. He likes making crafts. You're pretty crafty yourself, aren't you, dear?"

"I guess."

"Oh, by the way . . . " Hamachi almost doesn't hear her mother's words.

Did she know that her picture was on her father's Web site? Did she know that's why there were so many hits? "Your father said you *love* fish."

He wasn't lying. Hamachi craved moi, but not this way.

She ignores her father for the next five days, but he eventually convinces her to come over, see the Web site for herself.

"We can narrow down the field," her father says, trying to console her. "Only those who catch the biggest moi need apply. How's that?"

Hamachi squints into her father's one good eye. He smiles, but probably doesn't even see her. She's skeptical. Although her father was a rather epidermal man—you had to pass through him to get to her—he had a history of attracting freaks. Once, at Ala Moana, he waited for her by the benches outside of Sears. A relatively normal-looking lady with an icee was pacing back and forth to the side of him. "I wonder if I should cut my leg off," the woman pondered out loud to herself. Her father thought she was talking to him, but, before he could answer, she asked, "Should it be the right leg or the left leg?" When he realized that she was talking to herself, he moved away. Hamachi thought this marked a new phase in his life. Before, he used to attract women who wanted someone to tell their problems to. He had that face. They could read sucker in his eyes.

"Dad, I don't want love to be about fish."

"No, of course you don't. Don't worry. You'll love this. Look." He scrolls up to the home page of his Web site. In big red letters it says, "Get-MyMoi.Com."

"Okay," she agrees. "But the moi has to be over five pounds."

"Fair enough."

Two weeks later.

Hamachi is surprised they're even here. Leaving the house was a chore. Her mother kept pestering her to change her clothes.

"I'm going to be in the car, Mom. They can't even see me," Hamachi told her. Her answer seemed to subdue her mother, but then, just when she was ready to leave the house, she heard her mother, in her small mosquito-like voice, "Aren't you going to *access*-orize?" She hit the accent on access like that Asian double meaning—let someone access her heart. *I know that's what she means.* Hamachi closed the door in her face.

Hamachi watches from the car. She can see her father through the opening in the headrest. He looks like he's in a Norman Rockwell painting, something titled, *Schoolboy Waiting for Dessert*. Only her father is in Starbucks Mililani, drinking a cup of Brazilian coffee, holding a cellular phone and giving her a thumbs up sign through the window. His painting should be called *Senior Citizen Waiting for the Moi Catcher*. She smiles weakly and turns to the big buns on the Stairmasters blooming in the window at 24 Hour Fitness.

The first man to walk through the door has that fermented look of eighty. He sits across from her father, who looks rather surprised. The man doesn't look anything like his picture. He reaches into his pocket and pulls out a bottle full of Viagra that can be refilled at least three times. Her father shows him to the door. The old man refuses to leave without a free coffee for his time. Hamachi suspects that's the real reason he showed up.

Her father gets on the cellular phone. "Don't worry. There are at least twenty more guys!"

They go through them all. Fat ones with money, short ones with moles on their eyes, old ones with hair sliding off their heads to repopulate their ears.

The twentieth man is fifteen, the type who scores 1600 on his SATs and dresses like a senior citizen. He wants to know if Hamachi will go with him to his prom dressed like a mermaid—topless and all. And can she grow her hair out just a little more and dye it red? Her father prods him out the door like cattle ready to be slaughtered, threatening to inject him with large amounts of coffee to make him impotent.

Then all of a sudden, Hamachi sees a red flash just to the side of her eye. Tell me he is going to Foodland. Tell me some cool Spanish guy owns that red truck. He isn't and it's not. Instead, he parks his truck, takes out a large Liberty House package and walks into the cafe. After the usual pleasantries, he offers the package to her father ceremoniously, like dowry. She watches her father take out a large gold platter with a beautiful seven-pound moi, steamed in a Chinese red bean sauce. Where did he get that? You can't find that size moi anymore. Hamachi picks up the cellular phone.

"Bingo, darling! We hit the jackpot!"

Before Hamachi can ask for the details, Fisherman pulls out a card. Her father turns it in his hands again and again until he begins weeping.

"Dad, what's wrong?"

"Buddha has blessed us, Hamachi. He has taken us in his palms and exhaled his holy breath on us." Her father begins reciting an entire Buddhist sutra.

"What are you talking about?"

Her father sips his coffee and clears his throat several times.

"He has his own insurance!" her father shrieks into the phone, hardly able to contain his joy. "Medical, dental, vision, drug! With one phone call, darling, I can verify the claim number now. And, get this—he has his own

Web site, Ulua.com. Isn't that clever?" He lifts the platter to the window, running his palm across it like some spokesmodel.

"My daughter," he cries, bowing his head in a dramatic pause like James Brown, "is getting married!" He lifts an 8-by-11 picture of Hamachi above his head to thunderous applause.

She watches as her father turns a quiet Starbucks into go-between central. He weaves through the growing crowd passing out moi and Frappuccinos and little red-and-white business cards that read Arranged Marriages at Get-MyMoi.Com. Fisherman ignores the spectacle and gazes through the glass at Hamachi, the girl he named when he was four years old. She sighs, her body sinking into the vinyl of the seat. So it is true. Fisherman has watched the sand. He has waited for the tide to rise. He has looked for a moon.

WENDY MIYAKE *was born and raised in Mililani on Oʻahu when it was known for red dirt rather than Wal-Mart. Her short story "GetMyMoi.Com" won the* HONOLULU *Magazine fiction contest in 2001 and is included in her first book,* Beads, Boys and the Buddha. *Her second book,* The Bodhisattva Club: Adventures in France with the Great Mother, *was published in 2007.*

Carrie Y. Takahata

"WHAT I CARRY"

The coffee shop could have been any
anywhere across the country but
we happened to sit there
in the middle of Honolulu
each of us cupped
by the vinyl seats
and cold, dry air. Unaware
of our on-going conversation
I mentally unpack each
of the seven suitcases I always
carry with me into such
relationships. I pause
proud of my
contents; reach into each opened case
caress my pasts: bag one is always
Josh, I remember

he's the one I should have loved
but left for the contents of bag number two
who liked me more
attached to Josh;
Steve, he's three
because I left on Tuesday for a business trip
and returned on Wednesday to surprise him
in the middle of
two other women; number four and five
I reserve for Ed
who asked me to postpone
my move in with him
until after
his girl
from Japan
left; number six
I show with pride,
the seven-year relationship
which carried me through my twenties
only for Dave to finally admit
that he could never love me
or any woman
for that matter. This
I open up for my newest companion to see
challenge him to choose a favorite
and when he refuses
when he fails,
I open up bag number seven
move two one-night stands to the left
a handful of "I'll call you's" to the right
and place this memory right there in the middle,
secure.

CARRIE Y. TAKAHATA *obtained a BSW in social work and an MA in English from the University of Hawai'i at Mānoa. She has written for* Honolulu Weekly *and has seen her poetry published in* Asian Pacific American Journal; Bamboo Ridge; Tinfish; Hawai'i Review; Social Process in Hawai'i; *and* 27 Hours. *Currently, she resides in Oakland, California, sits on the Board of Intersection for the Arts, and co-edits* Hybolics.

Keola Beamer

"STALKING HAUNANI"

Haunani Freitas is one angel dat came from heaven. She live at 457 Wai Nani Way in apartment numba twelv. I know dis because I was stalking her so hard, I almost drove myself nuts.

Me, I was tryin foa learn from my past mistakes. I was married twice befoa, but I neva kno how foa act. Worse yet, my second ex was part Korean eh? Ho dey get mean tempa, I tell you. Living wid dat *wahine* was like trying foa sleep next to one cherry-bomb on New Yea's Eve. In fact, dat whole second marriage ting wen blow up in my face like one big can Spam filled with dynamite. I still trying foa heal from da blast. At da final court ting, da judge wen say, "Honey Boy Rodrigues, you gotta do dis, you gotta do dat, you gotta pay dis, you gotta pay dat." I wen home, try look myself in da mirror, ho, my face stay all covered wid black soot and my hair was pokin out da sides, all funnie kine, like Neil Abrahcromby afta he run tru one wicked brush fire.

My hair was alredy spooky lookin anyway, from wen I was baby. My modda, she look at me, an say,

"Look Daddy, he get *ehu* hair!"

But my Daddy no moa *ehu* hair . . .

"We go call him Honey Boy," my moddah said, "cause his hair jus like honey!"

Den Daddy said, "Nah, we goin call um Bozo, cause his hair just like dat clown, Henry Santos who live next doah!" Ho, my moddah was ready foa beef my foddah afta dat.

I figga, from now on, I no go make da same kine stoopid mistake in marriage again. I goin take my time and no make no moves, until I get um all scoped out, li' dat. I was tired loose eryting. In fact, I was tinking, maybe next time, I save erybody planny humbug. I jus goin pick out some pretty *wahine* dat I no even like and give her one house.

Dis my story, my *kapakahi* love story, of how I wen stalk Haunani Freitas.

I was workin at da A1 Transmission Service on King Street. Was one good job, 'cept even in Decemba, was hot and da shop smell like transmission fluid. Not da new tranny fluid, but da stink, old kine. Da exhaust fan wen broke insai da shop, and da boss so dam cheap, he no goin fix um. Da smell, no leave. He jus stay around yo head all day. Like one frickin hat. But I wen work planny worse places befoa and us brokanics made some pretty good dough. I still remembah da time, one Filipino kid from Mayor Wright Housing wen pay us $300 for change da fluid in da tranny of his Sentra. Tree-hunred bucks! So us guys wen trow in one lube foa free! Ha Ha. We wen bus out laughing afta da kid pay da bill. Ho, shet foa brains, you got lubed alright. And because you so stupid we all wen grind at Benihana and drank sake till dey wen trow us out. We got all bus' up and no can drive home. Me and Harlan Miyasaki had to ride taxi part of da way home, cuz Harlan had one small kine accident and da Vietnamese driva tole us in a voice like squealing brakes, "Get Da F&^* out of cab!"

Afta my second ex Su Yen wen divorce me, I was feeling jam-up. My small seesta Bernice-da-butinsky, told me "Eh, go buy one cat. Dey keep you company, you know." So I wen down da humane society and get one small black one. Foa real kine cat. Had tail and fleas and whiskas an eryting. And cheap! I wen name him "Rocky" foa Rocky Galunta, who wen grad wid me, Farrington class of 79'. Rocky was da bull of automotive shop class, except he was kinda on da short, cranky, piss-ant side. He carried one big frickin chip on his shoulda and one huge tractor wrench in da back of his truck cab. One time he got stopped and da cops dey acks him if da big wrench was one weapon. "Not even" he said, cracking his gum. He use um for "fix da radio."

Rocky was always beefing and afta high school, his faddah told him, "Eh, shet for brains. Go get one job, prefably in one nodda country." Rocky wen move to Oregon foa cut down trees and beef. I tink he still up dea, kickin da shet out of da trees and waitin for kill *haole* day, which I pretty sure, dey no get in Oregon.

I wen name da cat afta him, cause he all futless and mean too. Sometimes I walk down da hallway and dat cat, he look at me like, "What? I owe you money?" Den he like try foa duke um out wid da cuff on my work jeans.

Was coming up on Cristmas time. As da worse time foa be single, I tell you. What? I going wrap one present foa myself and pretend I no know what get insai? Shet. Worse, yet, I still neva had one Cristmas tree so Rocky could spray um wid his Merry Xmas cheer. My oldah seesta, Nadine-da-Queen, kept calling every oddah night, acting all nosey, and whining in her high pitch voice, like one burnt bearin in one 82' Pinto, "What . . . you neva get yo tree yet? You no get um yet?"

"Uhh . . . I neva get um. Becuz, no moa. Star was . . . all . . . sol out."

"NOT!—I was jus dea! No Lie, Honey Boy! You jus too dam lazy for put um up! I not goin bring da kids by, den. What kine Chrstmas dat? Dea own Uncle, too lazy foa get one tree. Foget it. And Merry *#@#*^* Christmas to you." Nadine was da drama Queen and since small kid time, I had it wid her alredy.

Trutfully, she wen nag me so bad last yea', I wen make da dam tree. But Rocky was only baby kine yet, eh? So he wen climb on top'yom and hang on da branch till da tree wen *huli* ova. TimBAAAAH! Jus so happen Nadine was visitin and ackin all high makamuk and feeding her rugrat candy, when da tree had crash and da ackspensive glass ornament she wen jus give me had bus' on da cement. Ho, Nadine was so piss off. Den she got even more piss off when Rocky eye her rugrat and dive bomb da liddle sock hangin from his foot like some kine demented kamakazi. Why she like come ova foa anyway? Geez!

Anyway, Cristmas time was OK, but da nights was long and only had "Its A Wondaful Life" on TV, ho I seen um so many frickin times, I like bus' da TV alredy. Eh KITV, why no show um 50 times a night? We want moa!

Den one Decemba night, around dat same Christmas time, one Kona wind stay come slinking up da Ala Wai from behind da Zoo. Ho, dat wind was all sticky and *hapai* wid dakine elephant shet scent. I had one funnie feelin in my guts dat night. Like small kid time, wen I swallow gasoline, tinking it was gramps pineapple swipe.

I wen crack open da window and inhale da night air. Ho . . . neva smell too good. Rocky wen inhale too, den his eyes wen come beeeg. He krinkle his black nose. He wen smell da zoo smell, an tought, "Africka!" He wanted to beef right dea! He wen run all around da place, but no can find no wild Afrikan tigas foa beef wid. He look at me like, "You! Rodrigues! Wea stay? Whose lion okole I goin kick?"

"Rock," I tol him. "Get one grip." He went sulk unda da bed, wea I wish he would spend moa of his time, da bastid. Dat night also had dakine high, tick, humi-ditty. You know what I mean, eh? You go put on one t-shirt and walk tree feet foa turn on da TV. Wen you get back to da sofa, you stay soaking wet, and you get one terminal case BO.

I was kine of antsy too, eh? So I wen pop open up da binoculas dat I wen buy for one Moloka'i hunting trip. I was trying foa spock some decorations across da Ala Wai and I was lookin at one string of lights on one balcony in da distance, when dat dam liddle Rocky wen punctcha my big toe wid his claw. As I wen lurch foward, cuz of da xcrutiatin pain, I wen drop da binoculas down and saw right insai da apartment across da street! Holy Frickin Moley and Deah Moddah of God. Deah she stay, my dream come true. My Christmas Angel. God help me. I wen stalk my first Haunani stalk.

Soon da eye pukas around da binoculas was getting all sweaty, cuz she was mosly naked except foa one short, pink neglahjay dat showed off her bootiful *malasadas* and one excellent pink lace pantie. She was watching some kine ESPN sports ting, brushing her hair and drinking from one small kine tea cup. Even tho Rocky was engage in some kine surgery of my big toe, I wen make da focus moa sharp. Haunani stay undaneat one really nice, tick, Xmas tree. She tie one red ribbon on her hair. She was so bootiful, like one goddess, floating in one sof, pink cloud. Ho, I tell you, da whole pikcha look like one Longs Drugs Stoa Christmas card, except foa da panties. Uhh. Longs no make li' dat.

Da Xmas lights was all shining and making disco on her skin as I wen look around her place wid da sweaty binoculas. I could almos hea da music from her stereo speakas. Wen I stay look at her face, she seemed so innocent, I felt shetty for ereyting bad I eva did in my whole life. Moa worse, I felt bad foa stuff I neva even do yet! Dat is da powa of one angel, I tell you! I almost bus'out crying, because of da murda of my boss. Ho, I felt terribal! Den I wen pull da binoculas away and get all piss off. Why? Cuz I remembah. I neva kill him yet.

Afta couple minutes, my bootiful angel wen notice da drapes stay open and she wen pull da cord ting. Aw shet. I was alone again in my cruel world. I trew down da binoculas and wen into da living room. I turn on da TV cuz, I like foa watch da same ting as her. Romantic ha? Da TV was kine of interesting, but I neva unastan 'um. I wen make one mental note, foa go down to da library and try figa out dat Hockey ting.

Afta a while, I wen get hungry and dat stooped Rocky, sensing movement and possible beef conditions, wen flyin out from unda da sofa foa try kick my ass. I was so depress, I neva even notice. I jus kept walking down da hall in some kine angel-love-fog. Rocky wen hitch one ride on my right foot to da fridgerator and back, his tail all puffy and his front paws wrapped around da back of my leg, holding on foa deah life. When I finally looked down at my foot tru two cans of cold beer, his eyes was all wide and his liddle black ears stay pressed flat against his head like da small horns of one mentally challenge billy goat.

Of course back den, I neva even know her name was Haunani. I had to find out da hard way, by bus'ing into her car and stealing her registration. I felt bad about dat too. But I neva mess up da car, I jus when use da slim-jim from da tow truck dat Binky Ka'ahane from "Unreal Toeing" wen loan me.

Binky's shop was right next to us guys. And dat day, foa some stoopid reason, I wen acks him why he name his company, "Unreal Toeing" anyway. Binky was huge. He looked at me, like one bullfrog sizing up one pipsqueak fruit-fly. I tink he was calculating if da effort foa open his mout' was wurt our many yeahs of friendship. Den da whole worl got really frickin quiet and I could hea one mosquito fut in shop #108. Da silence came even moa loud. An ant hiccupped way the f%^& down by Schofield Barracks. Unreal. Finally, Binky wipe da swet from his head and acks in one really low voice, "What you tink dey say, wen dey find dat da car no stay?" He squint at me, and whack one beeg wrench slowly against his hand. Den he tilt his truly humongous head towards me and lock me in his swety gaze.

Shet . . . I almost black out. No can tink. No can tink!

"F*@#*#* Unreal!" he wen roar, his big voice shaking da dirt from da rooftop of da ol' warehouse. Dat dust, she fall down in slo motion, like midget snow insai one Xmas papahweight. Off in da distance, da shop radio was playin, "White Christmas" as my life was spared and da tiny warehouse snow wen drif down tru one sunbeam high above bruddah Binky's big ballahead.

Afta I busted into Haunani's car, I wen copy her registration at Kinkos and slide um back insai da glove compartment of her Mazda. Den I saw da security camera in da garage. Shet. My mind wen trip out. How foa make so no can identify? I wen dig out fast-kine while making one academy award acking job like I had one gimp leg. Ho, smart eh?

Speaking of smart, I pretty shua Haunani wen Kam school. Cuz ontop on her Mazda had one "The Kamehameha Schools Est. 1887" bumpa sticka. Erybody know dat if da cops see dat, you can make anykine and still no go jail. Dat bumpa sticka not jus one piece papa, das one Hawaiian cloaking device. You can be goin freakin nuts on H1, and dose *kanakas* dey no stop you. Why? Cuz dey all wen grad Kam school, das why. Da machinist down at work, Milton Kamanu wen grad from Kam School in '82. Milton can go 500 mph in one 15 mph School Zone, wid his stereo blassin "Shoot da mother*#@#*@* Cops," and as long as his "The Kamehameha Schools Est. 1887" bumpa sticka stay on his vehicle, da cops jus smile! "Ahh . . . Kam School," dey sigh, flashing da warrior ring and making shaka sign. Den dey sing da school song, make one small *ami* and salute smartly, as Milton, dat rat bastid, goes and brok tru da sound barrier in his red Tundabird.

On day, feeling hemo-jang and small kine lonely, I went down to Haunani's building. I took one quick look at her laundry in da machine. Ho! Nice! Den I wen spock da dumpsta by da alley way and insai my brain, one light wen on. Heh heh heh. You can learn a lot about one angel from her trash! Afta all, even angels from heaven gotta trow away dat *manapua* cardboard ting. And ho . . . planny kine Jasmine tea bags . . . dis girl like her tea. And she no drink alcohol and no smoke. Lucky ting was one small building, so not dat much trash foa go thru. Worse part was da lef ova hum-ha from da *Pake* family in 17. Strong I tell you, and da smell last foa days. I almost no can dive on da hum-ha days, even wid da spray paint goggles and resparetah from Duke's Auto Painting. Afta awhile, dat hum-ha smell give one mean headache. Pretty soon I going file workmen's comp against my boss, Freddy Pacheco, foa no reason, except dat he wen hire me for fix transmission and he still alive.

By nosing around li dat, I found out so many stufts about Haunani. She was working foa one Polynesian review in Waikiki and she was dating one rich punk named Bobby Renton. Ho, I wen lay net foa dat bastid!

Stoopidhead Bobby neva knew what he was in foa, and to dis day, he still missing. He wen drive up in his 40 tousand dolla Lexus and park 'um on da side street of Haunani's place. Da leatha seat was still warm from his skinny okole when Binky had da Lexus up on da tow truck, and on da way to da shop. Us guys made some quick "adjustaments" and Binky put da Lexus back in da exact same place. Next mornin' dat stoopidshet Bobby wen go outside and da Lexus no start, why? Cause no moa transmission das why. Also, no moa engine. Binky needed um foa one trade deal or someting. I remembah him acksin' me, "What, Rodrigues, you need da muffla?"

"Nah, you get um," I said smiling. Was easy to give away Bobby's stuff.

Dat jackass Bobby wen finally give up turning da key (Duhhhh!) and notice da small note I lef on da passenga seat:

> Eh Bobby,
> Dis time, its just da car. Next time we goin take out your guts and feed um to da SHARKS. No eva come back dis way again. Stay away from My Christmas Angel. We know wea you live, and we see you again, we goin bring one gas can wen you sleepin and make Bobbyque.
> Signed,
> Bozo and da sout street boys

Bobby wen jump outsai da car, acking all futless. He go pop da hood. He look at da big black *puka* of what use to be da engine. His legs shaking.

Now me, I was idaling in da black Camaro across da way spocking Bobby's face insai da binoculas. Ontop da radio had Nat King Coal singin "Chessnuts Roasting On One Open Fi-ah." Ho, I tought to myself, dat Jack-Fross-nipping-at-yoa-nose must be one mean Chihuahua. Much, much, worse den my Rocky.

Anyway, I see Bobby face as he go slam down da hood and I try foa read his lips. I tink I hea his high girlie voice spitting out:

"F*&#*****^@ Unreal!"

Den he stumble away, real spooky like, looking behind him every coupla feet. Was time to swing into action. I grab da chrome ball on dat short trow gear shif and bang um into second. Den I pop da clutch and floor 'um. I come up behind his ass and flick on da nitro switch. Da Camaro, she scream sideways down da sidewalk, da rubba burnin' an smoke pouring out from da jacked up reah end. Da ting mus have look like one Sherman tank bearin down on pooah Bobby. He take one look behind him, run like one *mumu* orangutan and go make one ugly ass swan dive right into da Ala Wai Canal! Excallent! I screech to one stop an lean ova da window foa give him da bird. But he no look, he only swirl around in da oily wata and dissapeah from view. Hey. Maybe no can swim! Way to go Rodrigues!

Coupla nights lata, Haunani was watching da Wings–Hurrahcaines hockey game on TV. Jesus, dat wahine was scrumptious. I spent some moa time admiring her in one blue neglahjay. I let da binoculas drif around her place, you know, jus checking 'um out. On top her stereo had one Willie K. CD. Ho, you gotta love dis girl! I wen to sleep reading "Rolla Hockey, Skills and Stratagey Foa Winnin On Wheels." I had borrow 'um from da Waikiki-Kapahulu Public Library.

I wanted foa watch her dance, too, but I no like come on too strong, eh? I was tinking dat that she might wea fancy-kine shells foa one brassiere. Ho, toughts of dose sweet malasadas snuggling in moddah-of-pearl shells was enough foa make me all hot. While I was tinking dos UnChristmas-like toughts, Rocky came prancing down da hallway, wid one dead geccko hanging from his mout. I said to him, "Rock, I goin out tonight." He look at me, like . . . "You Shet. You still owe me money. No gecko foa you!!" Den he stick up his skinny tail and disturb me with one startlingly clear piksha of his tiny butt hole. Now, guarantee bad dreams. Tank you, stoopidbastid.

I thought about Haunani and dose sweet *pan duce* all day at da transmssion shop and I no can even work. May as well sleep, but no can, cuz Futless Freddie stay wid his feet up in his cheap ass office.

At lunch break, Harlan told me Nadine lef one message on da shop machine, dat her oldest boy Derek wanted one Pokemon for Christmas "from his favorite uncle, Honey Boy." Favorite my ass. Da kid no even like me! Maybe Harlan know what to do. Harlan was moa smart den me. He wen graduate M.I.T. wid one doctarite, but now he gotta work transmission, cuz, his moddah no can fine his diploma. Pooah Harlan, afta all his edumacation, still no can catch one break. We was eating lunch at da saimin place wen I acksed seriously,

"Eh, Harlan. What's a Pokemon?"

"One Jamaican Proctologist," he said giggling. "Ha Ha Ha! I wen see dat joke on da intanet . . . " he wheeze speaktacularly, one noodle spanking his greasy Japanee chin.

"Damit, Harlan, take it easy." I say. "You know what happens when . . . "

But Harlan keep on laughing really loud and almost brok one gut. His face got so dakine red, look like his nose was changing color. Da Chipmunks record insai da coffee shop was playin' "Rudolph Da Red Nose Raindeah" as Harlan's honka was turnin all red and and lightin up da frickin booth. Harlan was still laughing, dat Kaneohe-bound nuthouse laugh, and wheezing like one bastid wen I lef. I no like stick around, eh? Cuz wen Harlan laugh li' dat he catch azmah, den he go pass out and make ass. Da Saimin place call da ambulance tree times already and pretty soon dey goin' 69 us.

Back at da shop, still no can concentrate, no can tink. Only dreams of bootiful, pink malasadas and naughty kine toughts. Jesus H. Christ In A

Mustang. I trow down da wrench, wid one big clang dat almost wake up Freddie. I like marry her right now! I nergeously drop one bearin and he roll down da street. A . . . lo . . . HAA. Ah shet, what's a bearin or two, I tought, and put back da tranny of one Oldsmobile Cutlass, missin bearin an all. Den I put dakine special ingreedament insai for keep da noise down. At 4 PM sharp, I wen dig out, jus wen Futtless Freddy had wake up an was goin acks me about da hubcap filled wid sawdust by my work bench.

I drove home and took one long, cold shower. I wen shave. I put da maximum amount of Brut Cologne dat one man can put on, befoa crossing into da treshold of *mahu* status. I wen comb my hair and put planny Pomade. Ho, sticky da hair came. I wen bus' out my best shirt from da closet. I wen shine my shoes an shoot one tremendous blast hairspray insai my left ear. Oops. "U da man!" I said to myself, den I look moa close and tought, "Shet. Too much Pomade!" What da hell. I figgah if dey was goin make one "Transmission Repair Specialists that Stalk Haunani Freitas Calandar" I goin be in da runnin for Mr. Decemba.

I jumped insai da Camaro and dig outta da garage. Half way down Kalakaua, I hit da nitro button and da tires on da back wen smoke one good, long patch. Ho, da Japanee tourists by da curb wen get all futless and run back insai da Royal Hawaiian Shopping Centa. "Godzilla approaching Tokyo! Godzilla approaching Tokyo!" I yell in my best Japanee movie accent. Ho, felt good! Den I saw da motocycle cop in da rear view mirror. He look at da bumpa of da Camaro. Get dakine Kamehameha School bumpa sticka dat Milton wen give me but, somehow da buggah no work! What da F*^#? Da blue light go on. Shet . . . Busted.

"I like give you some advice dat I wen learn at Kam School," Offissa Joseph Kamuali'i said, all police like, afta he wen write da ticket.

"Uhh . . . OK." I say.

"No use so much Pomade, Meesta Rodrigues. Wid yoa *ehu* hair, look like you get one dye job. Da chicks, dey no dig it. Seriously."

"Tanks Offissa," I said unda my breath all, piss off. He wen hand me da citation. I look at 'um. Den I look at 'um again, not really undastanding . . . what da hell?. Offisa Kamuali'i had scrawl on top da ticket in big block kindagarten moron-lettas,

TOO MUCH POMADE

Den he see my red face and bus' out laugh.

"Only kidding, Meesta Rodrigues. "Us Kam School boys gotta stick tooggedah, no? No worry, you no goin get ticket. Only warning! Take it easy on da pomade! Ha Ha . . . What yea' you wen grad?"

"Uhh . . . 1982?" I said lying like one cheap-ass rug.

Offisa whats his name stood at attention, salute me and give da supa-secret shaka sign. "Milton, my bruddah," I tought to myself. "Wen I die, you goin get my complete Batman comic collection."

"Tanks foa da break, Offisa." I said humbly, "and . . . uhh . . . Imua to da lua."

Den I drive away real easy-kine. In da rear view mirror, look like da bastid was dancing hula in Adolf Hitler boots. Ho . . . kina trippy.

Because of da fake ticket, I arrived late to da *Luau* show. Was late too, because I no goin pay da $32.50. I snuk in from da beach and came in back by da hau tree. Da band began to play one lame-ass version of "Jingle Bells" wid da hula girls shacking da gourd ting. Ho, maybe going get catfight? Exciting! Could be some kine chorenography or someting, but still look sexy to me.

I neva have dakine female companionship for long time, I tought, nailing two double Mai Tai. But unlike dat piss off and mean Rocky, me an my *lahos* was still installed in da same vehicle, if you catch my driff. Hey, no wonda Rocky so piss off at me! Mines was lonely and unused, but dey was still dea for Christsake! "*Hui* Haunani!" dey wen sing insai my nice grey slacks, "Ova hea! Come see da buggah dat goin sweep you off yoa feet!" I drank two moa Mai Tai.

In da flickaring torchlight, drums was beatin sofly and da demon rum was bending my toughts. I was feelin mental. Could also be I was nergeous cuz da angel of my dreams, was right deah. She came on stage, perspiring slightly in da warm tropical night. Da music came really sweet. She wen dance on one small kine platform, da brown skin of her naked back glistening in da sof moonlight. "*Godfannit! Go get dat frickin ting and bring um ova hea.*" I wen say liddle bit too loud, sounding a lot like my deah departed foddah. In fact, I was beginin to tink I was a lot like my pooah foddah, an so far wasn't workin out too good.

Maybe I was getting too hot. Da Pomade was starting to melt down my sideburns, I could taste um if I stuck my tongue out da side of my lip. I put da Mai Tai glass against my sizzling forehead. "Lawd take me now," I wen mumble stoopidly. Next to me, had one nice old white-haired lady from Nebraska. She wen drop her napkin and in da process of pickin da ting up, she look under da and table see da impressive garage I had construck on my own premises. Wen she come up from da table—all buggy eye, I smiled at her and wiggle my meltingly-hot hair. "A licensed transmission specialist, if lubed to the max, may sometimes service antique vehicles," I tole her sweetly. Her eyes came really beeg!

The stage manager of da Polynesian show was one Samoan kid. To tell you da trut, I tink dat buggah wen bus' trough da Brut Cologne barrier back in kindagarten. Still, dat bastid held da key to my fucha. At first, he seemed upset by my approach to da backstage area. Could be he was tinking foa call da cops or someting. But in my pocket had one $20 bill, and da chicken-scratch love note I made foa Haunani on one napkin from my pineapple spear. "Exquiseme," I said all polite like, and *haole*-fied, handing him da note and da $20, "You tink you can help me out?" He looked at da $20 in his hand and da note. He try foa figure out exactly which shiney socket in da tool kit da brokanic was reaching foa.

"Hmmph," he snorted, "an foa whom do you wish me foa give dis?" he said all sassy. Sounded like he was talking to me tru his stuck up nose.

I was confuse. "Uhh . . . da 20 bucks is foa you."

"Duuuhhh . . . " da Samoan kid said even moa sassy, "I kno dat! I MEAN DA NAPKIN!"

Da ring and pinion gears was stripping in my portagee head. My personal pressha gauge was moving rapidly towards da red. Soon, smoke was goin come out my okole and *Mahu* or not, I would disconnect dis bastids driveline right now if he keep acking all sassy to me.

"Hau . . . na . . . UHH . . . Da girl on da pedestal!" I slobbered loudly. There was silence.

"As what I wen figgah," da Samoan Kid said finally, shaking his head disgustedly, "she always get da weird ones." He fluttered his made up eyeballs, threw his hair ova his shoulda and said, "MEN!" Then he run all mahu-like over to da girls' dressing room.

"Wait!" I said, kine of pleading. And den I tought to myself . . . can I be so desperate I goin kiss this *mahu* kid's okole?

Uhh. Yup . . .

"Dat girl, uhh . . . what kine flowa she like?" I blurted.

He look at me with pity on his face, and sigh. I wen smile at him and look homeless.

"Please . . . uhh . . . what kine flowa she like?" I asked again, moa softly this time. Like the doofus-dork-dumbass-moron I seemed to be acktually turning into.

"Carnation—pink, da long stem kind and no get da cheap one." He said, still sassy. Den he made a "humph" sound wiggle insai da dressing room door.

I goin let him live.

My Christmas angel was removing her makeup in front one zillion watt mirror. In my umbrebriated toughts, I wen imagine her sweet lips glistening, as she opened my sticky, pineapple-scented napkin to read:

Howzit honey,
you dance so nice, an you so talented.

I hope I get to meet you sometime.
From,
Honey Boy Rodrigues—Hockey Playa

Beneat her dressing room window, da pistons of my heart was all funnie-kine. I tink I in love. Hah la! I stay spinning in one weird kine auxiliary overdrive. Spooky you know, das da kine repair you no can touch um. Only da factory can fix.

I stumble back for one seat at da bar, wiping one teah from my eye. I tink one dirt wen blow insai 'um. "Cohffee!" I wen bumble out drunkenly, hiding my stoopid face in da napkin. Da ol lady from Nebraska wen slide in on da stool next to me. She make eyes at me. Aww . . . shet!

As my ancestor, da great Portagee-*Kanaka* chief Manuel "Flopping *Uhu*" Braga once said, his *malo* unraveling as he dug out from one fierce-kine battle, "I will retreat to fight one noddah day. Preferably not right away, but in da distant futcha with some moa guys and one really big machine gun. Alooooha and **PAACOCK!**"

I split. I neva like meet Haunani Freitas all shet-faced, plus da ol lady from Nebraska was freaking me out. Foa da firs time in my life I felt shame, you know.

I wen drive home reallyreallysloe. Den I eat one can Vienna Sausage, followed by some moa foa Rocky. I tought about it a lot dat night, about how I neva like foa her see me all *pilute*. Maybe I can be one betta person and afta dat sawdust ting, maybe I can try foa be one betta brokanic, too. I could be moa betta at a lotta stuff, now dat I was tinking about it! Shame Rodrigues. Shame.

My mind was all confuse and still pilute. I crack open da window. I put on one old tape of Ed Kenney singing "Da twelve Days of Christmas" and sing along wid my favorite part, da 40 Stinking Peeegs. Afta about 10 times tru, and trying foa remembah all da words (Ed nail um every time), I wen crash. Rocky drag one moa stray Vienna Sausage unda da bed and grind 'um. Den he roll ova on his back and snoa like one dam doofus. Me, I had neva eva snoa, even once. Despite da huffy testamony to da contrary insai da courtroom on dat black, black day.

I close my eyes and remembahd dat last day in court. Was like one nightmare. I gotta change my life. I really gotta change my stoopidlife.

"Was he hostile?" Da judge wen acks, all serious and formal like.

"Ho judge!" Su Yen wen hiss tru her pouty lips. Steam was comin out of her eeah, like da funnel from da smoke stack of one model train. Da pooah ting was strugglin wid her mean tempa. She wen rake da hair from her forehead, an stan up quickly from da chair.

"Hostile, dogstyle, anykine style!" she yell out. She point at me, "And den, right afta dat, all da time **ZZZZZZZ, ZZZZZZZZZ,** like one chain saw, yoa honah. I res my case!"

Da sherif by my side was ready foa bus out laughing. His face was all red, an his eyes was buggin out, like he was holding his breat unda da wata. Da judge, he get up and run insai his chamba. I tink dat bastid was laughing too, cuz could hea tru da doah. Ho, right dea I wanted foa turn into one small inseck and axcape into da alley.

Maybe das what was goin happen to me if I neva change my evil ways. I goin stand up on judgement day, say "howzit" to St. Peeda and feel someting funnie kine coming out from da top of my head. Maybe I was goin make one big carmic-cannonball into da giant pool of heaven and come back in one noddah life as one crooked politician, one defrocked trustee or one noddah kine awful ting wid "feelers." Holy Shet! At da rate I was going, St. Peeda not even goin give me one "The Kamehameha Schools Est. 1887" bumpa sticka foa paste on my pooah cockaroach *okole*.

So, early da next morning, I made one cup coffee and strugglin' tru one epic hangova, wrote Haunani one letta. I told her I seen her dance, and was wondering if she would like to see da Willy Kay concert at da Shell next week. I wrote um all nice, too. Took me tree tries.

I showed up in da hockey unifoam I had jus get from da UPS guy, cuz da mainland Sports Authority lady on da telephone had come thru. In my hand I had one dozen pink carnation, long stem flowers, da really ackspensive kine.

"I didn't know there was hockey in Hawai'i" she said sweetly looking at my unifoam.

"We just getting started. Me and Binky and da boys. Binky da goalie, cause he build like one brick sh . . . er . . . house. And no moa ice, so us guys use da in-line skates. Except for Binky, dat is . . . his feet too big. He just wea slippas."

"How Fun! Can I watch you play sometime?"

"Shoots. Next week we goin play Stan's Auto Body Shop in Kalihi."

We had fun at da Willy Kay Concert. Ho Braddah could sing! He take da guita and he shred um. Nice you know! Willy sang "Oh Holy Night" and my Christmas Angel almost wen cry. Me too. Jus sittin dea wid her unda a bazillion stars, I was so happy, like one dream come tru. Afta da show, I drop her off all gentleman like, and I even open da doah of da Camaro and walk her to da elavatah. Funny ting how I know which button to press. Den I step out befoa da ting goes up and say "aloha." Foa shua, I no move too fas dis time.

Da week went by quick. Me an da boys wen practice couple times afta work in da parking lot. Ho, da hard foa teach mokes to skate wid dakine, inline skates. Wid any kine skates, acktually. Wen came time foa da game, we neva play too good, but we had fun. Stan dem was pretty lousey. Shet, dey was just doing me one fava for fixing Stan's wife's tranny last yea.

I zipped around and bodychecked Martinez wid one shoulda in da chest. He went fly off into da hibiscus bushes. I guess Mexicans no can skate too good eeddah. "Way to go! Honey Boy!" Haunani shout excitedly from da sidelines. Den I skated on da outside around Stan's fenda guy Leo, and crank da puck wid one sly backhand shot. Da buggah slip past dat big ape Eric Nakasone and went into da empty dumpster dat was da goal. Ho, I SCOA!

Haunani got togeda wid some of da odda girls and wifes and dey started making cheers li' dat. Dey wen yell:

*"Float like one dragonfly, bang um in da yoys
Geef um, geef um, Honey Boy!"*

Ho, I was so proud, I was skating like one lunatick. Binky was running around all happy. Instead of taking something, dat big bastid was acktually protecting something, even if it was jus one empty dumpsta, nocked ova on da side. Bein one goaly seemed to agree wid him. His boys an his ol lady was cheering foa him too. Haunani had teach dem some cheerleading stufts. Dey wen make dakine chearleada dance kine moves. Dey was yellin:

*"Standing by da dumpsta, man of steel
Binky, Binky, he's unreal!"*

We was all having so much fun, like we was all *ohana*, instead of jus a bunch of guys who no give one rat's ass. I wen skate pas Eric for one moa goal. "Gee Portagee," he said grudgingly, "you not too bad."

"Hurray for Honey Boy!" Haunani screamed. "Way to go, Rodrigues!" Ho, I was burnin da bearins in my in-line skates and looking at her sweet face, all happy and perspiring. I guess my liddle angel jus needed somebody foa cheer in her life.

I tink I can be dat guy. I goin work real hard foa show her dat I love her and I no goin let her down. Me: Honey Boy Rodrigues, Licensed Transmission Repair Specialist and, oh yeah, "Hockey Wing."

Afta da game, da boys wanted to make one game foa next week and drink beer foa celebrate, but I leaned ova and told Haunani,

"I no drink alcohol. You like Jasmine tea?"

"Do I!" She smile and touch my swety arm.

On Christmas day, she came ova to my place and watch Rocky beat da crap out of a ping-pong ball she wen give him for Xmas. Da Rock was so happy, he neva like beef, even once. I had a feelin tings was goin change in my life. In our lives. Maybe I had finally begin to learn stuff dat I should have learnt long time ago.

"Wow," she said, looking down across da street, "you can see my place from here!"

Whoops. No moa stalking Haunani foa me. From now on, I goin try learn stuff about her da regula way. By paying attention and caring. Oh, yeah and something else I was neva any good at. One ting called "listening."

I stood up ackin all surprise and look out da window across da street.

"Not. You mus be kidding. Whea stay?" I said laughing. Rocky look at me and shake his little doofus head.

She opened her Christmas present, one light yellow neglahjay from Macy's dat was goin fit her dead solid perfect. She excuse herself and was gone for liddle while, den came back insai da living room.

"Merry Christmas, Honey Boy," she said giggling.

pau

Author's Note;
Once, I played a series of concerts for the University of Hawai'i. On the same bill was an excellent jazz guitarist by the name of Frank Vignola. Frank hailed from New York City and after playing a couple of shows together, we became friends. We were staying at the same high-rise hotel in Waikīkī and had a few hours free one afternoon, so I decided to play tour guide. Frank and I walked over to the Honolulu Zoo. When we got to the monkeys—the ones with the bald 'elemu; don't know the species—Frank's eyes lit up. He was so happy standing there watching their naked buns. In front of my own eyes, a studied and talented musician had apparently turned into a little kid. That's what I love about my musician friends. Sooner or later a "quirk" appears and it is usually a pretty damn good one. Later, having a drink on the balcony, I accidentally noticed a lovely maiden, partially clothed in the window of an adjacent building. This was way better than the monkeys, I thought. The sweet scent of the zoo drifted in the air and "Stalking Haunani" was born. The Hawaiian words in this story are from the character's point of view and as such, are intentionally misspelled.

Peter Van Dyke

"WORDSWORTH AND DR. WANG"

T he apartment block was one of those old two story places you still see
here and there in Waikīkī, with just 22 units altogether. The land it was
built on must have been worth a fortune. All around were big, gleaming towers, and the Japanese were cruising the streets looking for real estate.

Dr. Wang owned the whole complex. He lived in No. 4, where he could
watch out over the parking lot, the mailboxes, and the laundromat. The sign
on the apartment door announced:

> Herbert K. Wang
> Doctor of Herbal Medicine, Ret.
> No Soliciting

You could see him every day at the mailboxes just as the carrier finished
delivering the mail. The mail carrier was a woman named Karen. Dr. Wang
was more outgoing around her than around any of his tenants, even those of
us who had been there for years.

"What did you bring me today?" he'd say, "not more bills, I hope."

"Looks like a lot of love letters," she'd reply. Karen got her job done, but
she was willing to exchange pleasantries too.

Dr. Wang was a short old man, almost completely bald, with large liver
spots on his head and a dark, fleshy mole just over his left eyebrow. He
avoided eye contact. Even if he was right in the laundromat with somebody he'd known for years, he wouldn't say anything. He just pretended
he was alone. He'd nod back if you forced him to, and he'd say a few things
like "No change" or "Machine broken," but he kept the conversation to a
minimum.

He was a man of letters. He communicated through the written word.

There were signs plastered all over the apartment building, all the usual
ones: "Parking for Tenants Only," "No Soliciting," "Visitors Park Outside";
and a few weird ones too: "No Loitering," "No Firearms," "Post No Bills,"
and "Beware of Dog."

This last one was unusual because dogs were forbidden by the lease
agreement signed by all the tenants. Dr. Wang wasn't the kind to use a standard lease form, either. He wrote his own, and the rule against animals was
especially stringent:

> Tenants shall neither keep nor allow on the premises any pet,
> animal, bird, reptile, amphibian, or insect. Nor shall tenants en-

courage wild birds or other wild or feral animals on the premises, including pigeons, cats, mongooses, or stray dogs. Violation shall be cause for immediate eviction, with tenant held responsible for treatment for fleas, mites, or other pests resultant thereof. Said animals shall immediately be surrendered to humane authorities and destroyed.

The lease was full of all sorts of unreasonable rules and regulations: No radios after 10 p.m., no overnight guests, no slippers left outside doors, no nails in the walls. We all broke those rules all the time, of course.

He wouldn't tell you to your face when he thought you were breaking the rules. He'd write notices and put them on the bulletin board in the laundry room:

> Residents were extremely disturbed last night by the raucous gathering at a second floor apartment between the hours of 9 p.m. and midnight.
>
> Remember that our sleep restores us, and makes us bright, active, and productive. You may be able to sleep during the morning hours, but duty calls the rest of us to be up and about with the sun.
>
> Rule No. 8 in the Rental Agreement clearly states that all noise-making is to cease at 10 p.m.
>
> Repeated violations are grounds for eviction.
>
> Respectfully,
>
> Dr. Herbert K. Wang

Under the signature, someone wrote: "Wang Wanks His Weenie."

The parties went on for about five months before Dr. Wang had the tenants evicted. They were university students and they loved their reggae. Just before the eviction, Dr. Wang had one of his frequent letters to the editor printed in the local paper. Those of us who made a hobby of poring over his works—we called ourselves "Wangologists"—could tell that he was planning a move. This was the letter:

LOUD MUSIC MAKES POOR STUDENTS

What passes for study among modern youths looks more like moral dissipation to a member of the older generation. The brain is nurtured in quiet and harmonious peace. No Einstein can develop under the influence of the screeching, nerve-wracking "music" of the day, yet our modern students seem to spend most of the time with the stereo turned too loud.

We must take care of our bodies in every respect, in order to succeed in our studies. The ears must be protected from loudness. Regular hours of sleep must be maintained. When the body is healthy, the spirit is strong, and education can proceed.

Today's students seem to be insensitive to their community. The student's job is to study. It falls on the rest of us to work.

The university should take responsibility for its unruly members. Is discipline no longer practiced? Sometimes a harsh action is the best lesson.

Dr. Herbert K. Wang

There was little doubt among the Wangologists as to what the letter meant, and sure enough, just two weeks later, the reggae beat was stilled.

Those students were not the only ones to rate a mention in one of Dr. Wang's letters to the editor. Many of us had our turn. Marsha Yost inspired a letter. Newly divorced from a military man, she had moved from base housing to the Waikiki Sea Villa apartments, as our place was called.

YOUNG LOVE NEED THOUGHT

We are all swept away by young love at some juncture in our lives. Who has not looked at a starry-eyed lover and wanted to say, "Yes! I will!"

But when it comes to love, we would do better to look before we leap. Too many young marriages break asunder these days. Too many happy couples flounder on the rocks of dismay.

The real tragedy visits the little ones, the fruits of the ill-begotten love. I have seen many examples in my life of children of a broken home. There is no strong man about the house to call "Daddy." There is nothing to counterbalance the kindly, forgiving love of the mother. The child may take advantage of this situation and grow up without a proper sense of respect for his elders.

Young people of Hawaii, think before you say "I do." Our children are our most precious heritage, and let's give them a good start in life!

Dr. Herbert K. Wang

Marsha told us that the boy had started calling Dr. Wang "Dr. Doo-Doo-Head" in the last few weeks, in spite of the "good licking" she administered every time he said it.

Marsha got into more trouble with Dr. Wang over her boyfriend, Roy. Like everyone, Roy had trouble finding a parking place, and when he stopped in for a quick visit, sometimes he took a chance and parked in an empty space in the parking lot. After all, Marsha's place was on the ground floor, so they could just jump up and move the car if the person who had the stall came back. He was parking in Chong Be's place anyway, and Chong Be worked all day for Duty Free at the airport.

One day we heard Roy shouting and cursing in the parking lot, and we knew Dr. Wang had done it again. There was a notice pasted on the tinted window on the driver's side of Roy's El Camino. It read:

> WARNING: This car is parked illegally. The parking lot reserved for tenants only. Visitors must park on the street. If you park here again, you will be towed immediately.
>
> The Management

Roy was angry and he let everybody know it, but that was the last time he parked in the parking lot. You needed a razor blade to get those notices of Dr. Wang's off your car window.

Dr. Wang always seemed to get his way, in spite of his curious methods of enforcing the regulations. After all, he was the landlord.

Then one day in January, a crumpled notice in an unknown hand appeared tacked to the laundromat bulletin board. It certainly wasn't the work of any of the tenants, and Roy would never resort to the written word. The whole note was in capital letters, and there were stray ink marks here and there. The paper had been wadded and unfolded and pressed by hand before it was tacked to the board. It read:

> GODDAM YOU AGENTS OF THE RED CHINESE GOVERNMENT ARE TAKING OVER THIS CITY THEY ARE CAPTURING THE MINDS OF THE PEOPLE BY THEIR INSIDIOUS PROPAGANDA. YOU CAN HEAR IT IS BROADCAST LATE AT NIGHT WHEN YOU ARE ASLEEP. THEY ARE AGENTS OF SATAN AND ENEMIES OF DEMOCRACY. IT IS TOO WARM HERE SO YOU CAN'T WAKE UP AND CATCH THEM ONLY THE PEOPLE WHO SLEEP OUTSIDE ARE FREE.

It didn't take an expert to figure out that whoever wrote this probably did sleep outside. Waikiki has its share of street people.

The note stayed on the board for three days amidst the lists of rules related to the laundromat, homilies, clippings of Dr. Wang's letters to the editor, and a few desultory want ads put up by the tenants.

When Dr. Wang saw the note, he read it carefully, and then removed it and carried it between his thumb and forefinger to the trash can by the Coke machine. He washed his hands in the laundry sink before he left.

That afternoon, the author of the note showed up. He came through the parking lot pushing an empty shopping cart. He parked the cart by the laundromat door, went in, and used the sink. He washed his hands and ran the water all over his head. When he was finished, he pushed his tangled gray hair back and ran his fingers through it a few times, and then shook his head so violently that drops of water flew over the folding table halfway across the room.

He walked to the bulletin board and stared. He muttered, closed his eyes, and wagged his head back and forth, and then looked again. He cursed. For the next few minutes he stared intently at Dr. Wang's notices and letters.

As he read them, he erupted in scornful laughter from time to time. When he was finished, he walked away, and as he left, he stopped at the trash for a routine inspection. After digging down a bit, he uncovered his note, and he immediately lost interest in the remaining contents of the trash can. He walked out of the room reading his note. He folded it carefully and put it in his pocket before he pushed off with the shopping cart.

We called him Wordsworth, after the poet. It was just a name somebody came up with, but it stuck. He was a big Caucasian man. One eye looked off to the left and half his teeth were missing. He never wore shoes and his bare feet were encrusted with grime.

The next day, he was back. He posted another note. This note was a little fresher looking.

I HAVE TALKED TO GOD DIRECTLY ON THE RADIO AT KAPIOLANI PARK HE IS VERY ANGRY, HE SAID HE WAS GOING TO SEND THE PEOPLE TO HELL, TO BURN THERE BECAUSE THEY REFUSED HIM AND THEY WOULD NOT ACCEPT HIS WARNING. HE IS GOING TO LET THE DEVIL HAVE HIS WAY WITH THEM. THERE IS A MAN IN PUYALLUP WASHINGTON WHO WILL TELL YOU ABOUT THE RADIO WAVES THAT ARE FILLING THE AIR RIGHT NOW WITH COMMUNIST MESSAGES. THEY ARE GOING TO UNDO EVERYTHING AMERICA STANDS FOR. I KNOW BECAUSE WE TRAVELED TOGETHER FOR 6 MOS.

This letter was posted for no more than an hour when Dr. Wang appeared to empty the change machine. He treated this note with the same contempt he had shown the earlier one. This time, however, immediately after disposing the message, he went to his apartment and hammered out a reply, which he stapled neatly on the board in the laundromat.

TO WHOM IT MAY CONCERN:
This board is to be used for approved notices only. A person or persons wanting to post notices must obtain permission of the apartment manager before posting them. This is not a public forum. Go to the "Free Speech" areas of the university if that's what you want. These facilities are for the use of persons doing their laundry only. Other individuals are asked to leave the premises immediately.

Dr. Herbert K. Wang

Wordsworth was back the next afternoon for a wash-up. He went to the board and studied Dr. Wang's latest pronouncement. After a few derisory snorting noises, he addressed the notice board with an emphatic, shaking, raised middle finger. He held his posture for several minutes; at the same time, he clenched his teeth and uttered a strained growl. He seemed ready to explode into violence, but before he did, small Jack Wray, the only witness to this display, slipped out the side door and retreated to his apartment.

The next morning was remembered in the annals of the conflict as "The Morning of the 'Fuck You' Notes." To compare the litter of notes in the parking lot with snow would be an exaggeration, but nevertheless, the comparison was made more than once. What seemed to be flakes were torn up deposit envelopes from the automatic tellers of several banks in Waikiki. On every bit of paper, in angry capitals:

FUCK YOU!

It was a work of prodigious madness. Dr. Wang was out sweeping up for hours, and for days afterward we found the odd notes here and there in the corners: FUCK YOU!

Dr. Wang responded carefully. He strengthened his basic sign collection with the strategic addition of a dozen or so "No Trespassing" and "Tenants Only" signs. We waited for the next move.

Wordsworth was around the parking lot more and more. He found a shady spot to slump against the laundromat wall for an afternoon nap. When he wanted sun, he took to sitting on the chain that separated one side of the lot from the street, humming an odd, mad tune so that the pedestrians on the sidewalk skirted wide around his spot.

The police showed up frequently. Usually when they pulled in and conferred with Dr. Wang, Wordsworth was nowhere to be seen. Once or twice they talked to him, but he paid no attention to their threats.

Four days after The Morning of the "Fuck You" Notes, Dr. Wang posted a new letter in the laundromat:

TO WHOM IT MAY CONCERN:
A certain unpleasant man has taken up residence in our common area. At first, I did not force him to leave, for I believe that charity and kindness of one human being to another is dear to the human spirit. I tried to walk in the footsteps of Lao-Tse and Jesus, who advise us to love one another.

But this man does not deserve our love and charity, for he has shown his true character through acts of vandalism and violence. He has shown that he has no respect for the principles of private property which are guaranteed in our Constitution. His "letters" talk of God and American values, but his actions speak otherwise. Love is not returned upon the man who would take your charity and spit in your face.

So, a word to the wise is sufficient. If you see this man, tell him to leave immediately. If he will not obey, please call the police (911).
Dr. Herbert K. Wang

For several days, an uneasy peace prevailed. Wordsworth was somewhat less in evidence, and Dr. Wang's letter remained unmolested on the notice board until some third party added, just below the signature:

Wang's brain needs liposuction.

A little later, in another hand, this was added:

What about Wang's butt?

It was difficult to see the justice in this last remark as Dr. Wang was a skinny old gentleman who had no backside at all apparent within his trousers.

Then one early morning we awoke to the sound of hammering. Wordsworth was tacking his rebuttal to the laundromat door.

The rebuttal was in the form of a list. There were gouge marks in the door from the chunk of concrete Wordsworth had used as a hammer.

1. WHAT IS THE MATTER WITH YOU? AREN'T YOU
   AWAKE? THIS MAN IS THE ENEMY!
2. GOD HAS SAID THAT HE WILL STRIKE DOWN THE RICH
   SINNERS. WHEN ARE YOU GOING TO WISE UP?
3. I PAID MY TAXES EVERY YEAR THROUGH 1971.
4. THE RADIO WAVES HURT MY HEAD.
5. I HATE IT HERE.
6. HOW CAN HE TALK ABOUT CHARITY? WHAT DOES
   THAT COMMUNIST KNOW ABOUT CHARITY?
7. I THOUGHT THE PEOPLE IN HAWAII WERE SUPPOSED
   TO HAVE SOME ALOHA.
8. WATER IS FREE. AIR IS FREE. HOW CAN I STAY CLEAN IF
   HE WON'T LET ME USE THE WATER?
9. THERE ARE A LOT OF EVIL PEOPLE IN THIS WORLD.
10. WHY DO THEY LET THOSE PIGEONS FLY AROUND AND
    SHIT ON EVERYTHING? WE COULD EAT PIGEONS.
11. I AM A PERSONAL FRIEND OF THE GOVERNOR OF THIS
    STATE. HE IS GOING TO DECLARE THIS APARTMENT
    BUILDING CONDEMNED AND MAKE IT INTO A SHEL-
    TER FOR THE HOMELESS.

The police came a couple of hours later and Dr. Wang showed them the list and the marks on the door. In the evening, he posted a triumphant notice:

VANDAL ARRESTED
The police arrested the vandal who harmed our laundromat door. He is the same man who has been disturbing the peace here for the last few days. We owe a sincere debt of gratitude to the officers of the law.

Dr. Herbert K. Wang

However, Dr. Wang's triumph was short-lived. Two days later, Wordsworth was back in the parking lot.

There began a running battle. Every day one side or the other posted some new diatribe. Dr. Wang's, of course, were neatly typed and tacked up in the corner of the bulletin board that he reserved for his regular pronouncements. Wordsworth's, on the other hand, were scrawled everywhere: on the walls, over Dr. Wang's notices, on scraps of paper strewn here and there, stuck under windshield wipers, and stuffed into mailboxes.

It was like a battle between two well-matched boxers. Each delivered damaging blows, but neither flagged. Dr. Wang fought with precision and artistry,

Wordsworth with zeal and energy. Their respective themes never changed: Dr. Wang insisted on the rule of law and the rights of property; Wordsworth reiterated his mystical revelations of God and the Communists.

Then after two weeks, Dr. Wang had another letter published in the newspaper:

HOMELESS PROBLEM AND THE LAW

There is a scourge upon the land. It is called the "homeless problem." Perhaps you have seen them on your street.

The police are powerless to act. Government cannot put its foot down. Property owners must stand by and see their constitutional rights trampled by this vocal minority.

Why are we supporting these freeloaders when there are "Help Wanted" signs in every store window? Perhaps in our compassion we have gone too far, for is it not more compassionate to teach a man to fish than to give him a fish dinner?

Are certain people above the law? There is a law on the books in every community that states very clearly that you cannot sleep outdoors. If I were to rob a bank, I would be arrested. Why aren't these people recognized for what they are, common criminals?

I hope that our leaders will come to their senses before it is too late. We must act swiftly and sternly, with gentle wisdom, to end this "scourge upon the land."

Dr. Herbert K. Wang

With the publication of this letter, the conflict entered its final phase. Two days after the letter was published, Dr. Wang posted it in the laundromat. Wordsworth spent that afternoon sulking under the corner folding table.

By 4:30, Marsha's wash was done, and she went to the corner table to sort and fold. She set to work methodically, without ever having noticed Wordsworth right at her feet.

Wordsworth moaned, but Marsha took it for the sound of an out-of-balance washer in the row right behind her. Then Wordsworth flailed his arms about mindlessly. He was probably as unaware of Marsha as she was of him.

One of his hands came to rest against Marsha's ankle. A rough, wrinkled, battered hand against an ankle smooth and slightly plump. Marsha screamed.

She backed up in horror and shouted, "What the fuck are you doing down there?"

Wordsworth stared at her, but did not reply.

"I'm getting Wang, you creepy old bum." Marsha rushed out of the laundromat.

Minutes later, she came back. Dr. Wang followed her to the corner table. He was shaking. "Get out. Out, Goddamn you. This is for tenants only," he said.

Wordsworth struggled to get out from under the table, knocking it hard with his head and elbows several times in the process. As he emerged, Dr. Wang backed away. "I'm warning you. I'll call the police."

Marsha retreated behind the Coke machine. Wordsworth moved toward Dr. Wang with his fists clenched. Jack Wray's afternoon paper was on a chair between them, and when Wordsworth saw it, he picked it up and threatened to beat Dr. Wang with it like a dog.

Dr. Wang stood his ground for a few seconds, and then broke and ran, with Wordsworth close behind. "I'll get you," Wordsworth shouted as they ran across the parking lot. "I'll get you, old man."

Dr. Wang barely made his apartment in time, but when the door was shut, Wordsworth gave up the chase, tossed down the paper, and walked away laughing.

An hour later, Dr. Wang left the apartment complex in his car. When he returned, he was not alone. In the car with him was a German shepherd.

It was hard to sleep that night. Just after midnight, somebody's car alarm went off on the Ala Wai across from the apartments, and wouldn't shut down for an hour. Then Roy and Marsha had an argument that didn't quiet down until Roy finally slammed the front door and stomped off into the night.

The next morning there were no clouds anywhere, not even over the mountains, and there wasn't enough breeze to move the coconut leaves. Sensible people were getting ready to go to the beach. The Wangologists, however, were gathering in the laundromat, one by one, each drawn independently by a sense of impending crisis.

The morning hours ticked by and there was no sign of either Dr. Wang or Wordsworth. By 11:30 we were tired of waiting. Jack Wray said he was going to give up and go to the bank. His laundry was long since dried and folded.

We heard a rattling noise, like the sound of Wordsworth's shopping cart. Marsha looked out. "It's just Karen with the mail," she said.

There was more rattling, and Marsha looked again. "It's him," she said. Wordsworth was cutting across the lot, right in front of Dr. Wang's apartment. He leaned heavily on his cart and stared at his feet as he walked.

Dr. Wang's door cracked open and the brown shape of the dog emerged. He stopped and stared at Wordsworth and his cart, then flew out after him, barking furiously.

Wordsworth was slow to react. At first he tried to push his cart before him as he ran; then he abandoned the cart and started for the laundromat. The dog was all over him, barking and snarling, jumping as high as his shoulders. Wordsworth seemed to see us staring at him from the laundromat, and he swerved away. He went back to the hall where the mailboxes were, disappearing from our view behind the mock orange bushes between the parking lot and the walkway.

We were all afraid of the dog except for Jack. He was the one who went out and saw what happened.

When Jack got around the hedges to the mailboxes, he saw Dr. Wang struggling to get a leash clipped onto the dog's collar. The dog meanwhile had his jaws locked around one of Karen's muscular calves. Wordsworth had escaped.

Karen needed thirty stitches in her leg. Mail service to the apartments was suspended for a week until Dr. Wang finally took the dog back to the pound. We all had to go to the branch office to pick up our mail.

Wordsworth never showed up at the apartments again, although from time to time, people saw him around Waikīkī.

Karen was taken off our route, and the new mailman was old and taciturn, and predisposed to dislike Dr. Wang. It must have taken some of the pleasure out of Dr. Wang's life; he stopped posting notices in the laundromat all the time, and it was a full five months before he had another letter to the editor published:

MAIL CARRIERS DESERVE OUR PRAISE

The mail must get through. We owe a real debt of gratitude to the people who carry out this solemn oath, for our whole democratic system relies on the U.S. Mails. These men and women serve us without thanks or recognition for a job well done. They face real dangers, even in Hawaii, where our gentle climate spares us of the sleet and snow that plague the Mainland states.

The dangers here are of a human variety, in the person of the common street criminal. Their motive may be robbery, or merely vicious assault, or the mail carrier may be innocently caught in a crime in progress. The result is just as deadly.

These troubling times call for tough measures. Maybe our postal workers should be armed. Wouldn't we all sleep a little better knowing our friends were well protected on their daily rounds? I know I would.

Dr. Herbert K. Wang

PETER VAN DYKE *was born in 1947 and grew up in Santa Barbara, California. He has lived in Hawai'i since 1973. His stories follow seams of amusing detail in ordinary lives. Most are set in Honolulu, where the human inhabitants regularly ignore the outrageous natural beauty of the place to pursue their foibles. He pursues his personal foibles in Kona, on the island of Hawai'i, among his family and a legion of restless pets.*

Mary Troy

B y the time I was twenty-eight, I'd had the usual disappointments and surprises, like in the eighth grade getting points taken off a math test for writing it in lipstick when my pen ran out of ink; like in the tenth grade, sitting on the bench all during volleyball season because most of our games were close; like when I was seventeen, the guy I had gone out with once or twice and who I thought was a sure thing, asking some other girl to the Winter Wonderland dance; and like being forced to take college algebra at the University of Illinois, even though I told all the advisors I was a history major and would not remember a bit of algebra anyway. So I knew life was unfair, perverse, and illogical. And having been in and then quickly out of what passed for love four times in my twenty-third year alone, followed by three unrequited crushes the following year (one on my mail carrier, who flirted with all the women on his route), I believed true and lasting love was a myth. I also knew we lived tentatively between natural and man-made disasters, and, given the built-in belligerence and hardheadedness of mankind, any version of a sustainable worldwide peace was a bigger myth than love. I worried about all of these things a little, as well as about tsunamis (Frank and I lived in a converted pigeon coop in someone's backyard not fifty feet from Kailua Beach, and I knew we'd be gone before the sirens sounded), about getting my papers graded (I taught seventh and eighth grade social studies at St. Barbara's in Kaimuki), and about whether cockroaches would eat holes in my diaphragm when I left it out on the bathroom sink to air dry. Mainly, though, I enjoyed myself: boogie boarding every Saturday; watching my skin turn an ever-deeper shade of brown; giggling at parties after too much scotch; and sleeping soundly and dreaming in technicolor, with or without Frank. Then I moved next door to Robert Randall, a day care center operator, a former member of the Rainbow Boys dance troupe, and a soon-to-be-famous pervert, alleged sicko, bully, and creep.

For a few months, I had been living with Frank, the math teacher at St. Barbara's, but I had been on my own too long for it to work out. For the eight years before Frank, ever since I had come from the perpetual dusk of Peoria for summer school at the University of Hawaii and decided to stay, I had answered to no one, had taken care of myself, and had done a damn fine job of it, too. I found my new place by myself and didn't even let Frank see it, knowing his comments would irritate me, make me contrary. When I told him I was moving out, he said, "I guess I should just go eat worms and die." He said I made him feel worthless, unloved, cast aside. "I'm in *loke* with you," I said and tried to explain that *loke* was more than like but less than love. He looked at me as if I had just told him there was no such person as Officer Friendly or that God was dead. I could tell he felt sorry for me.

He insisted on helping me move, though, and since we did it on a Saturday, I agreed to let him stay over. Christen the place. But after we made love, enjoying the familiar actions and reactions—his cries, my shudders, the viselike hugs, the final gentle kisses—I moved away and lay there not touching him, pretending to be asleep, savoring my new home by myself.

That was Saturday, and it was on Monday, my first Monday morning, when a blue and white plastic ball came through my screenless bedroom window—the landlord had promised screens soon—flew across the room, and landed on my right knee. There were no primary colored signs in the front yard, no wooden cut-out clowns and ducks as clues, but from about six thirty, I had been listening to doors slamming, grown-ups saying "Bye-bye" and children whining, all coming from next door. I raised myself on an elbow, grabbed the ball, and with perfect aim, sent it back the way it had come. I knew I should have looked at the place on a weekday.

About an hour later, Robert stopped me and apologized as I was getting into my car. I suppose I stared, but I expected the day care center operator to be a middle-aged, large-bosomed woman in a baggy T-shirt and gym shorts, not a pale, fragile-looking, sixtyish-year-old man in pleated khaki slacks and an aloha shirt that looked pressed. "I surprise you?" he said, using the back of his hand, fingers curved delicately, to brush his thick white hair from his forehead.

"Not a bit." I hated to be caught doing what I knew I was too sophisticated to do, typing people according to age and sex. "I'm just amazed at anyone who wears good clothes around little kids."

"You should see my good clothes sometime," he said. He rolled his eyes elaborately as if he were on stage, and as he stood there, palms flattened against his hips, elbows jutting out, I was not certain if he meant to be funny or not but took a chance and laughed anyway. He did, too. Then he said Patrice-Leilani wanted to meet me, and so I was invited to dinner that evening. "Drinks and *pupus* at eight," he said. I accepted partly for the chance to see the inside of his house.

We lived in the cheap, boxy, single-wall construction houses common in Hawaii and other places with benign climates, but because he was dressed like the *haoles*, who carry canvas bags on their arms as they shop the open air markets, sniff delicately at the mangoes, know the names and regions of wines, I expected the inside of his to be decorated just so with brass floor lamps, blond hardwood floors, natural straw mats, and dried flower arrangements on hall tables. Instead, it was all velvets, brocades, lace, cut glass, fringe, and tassels. The word whorehouse kept coming to mind, though I had seen those only in plays and movies, old west kinds of *whorehouses*. Patrice-Leilani was a further surprise. I had expected a relative of some sort, a wife, perhaps a grown daughter, but not a ten-year-old, not as black as the ripe olives that garnished her casserole, and not wearing gold lamé.

Patrice-Leilani had taken her recipe right out of *Seventeen* magazine—baked chicken and noodles drowned in cheddar cheese soup. "Robert doesn't like to cook," she said. "I made this with Campbell's."

"M'm, M'm good," I said, another expectation of Robert vanishing. "Patrice, the Campbell's kid."

"Patrice-Leilani," Robert said. "It's hyphenated."

"Robert says when people shorten your name, it's like they're just too busy to say it all. It's an insult."

I apologized, and during dinner, Patrice-Leilani shared some of her cooking secrets with me: canned chow-mein noodles were good in tuna casserole, and dry cake mix covered with maple syrup made a yummy last-minute dessert. "Course, I can't fix all that for Robert's kids," she said.

"Dietary restrictions," he said to me. "Some can't have sweets, not even pop. Others, no meat. One breaks out from tomatoes."

"One eats anything," she said. "Even his own boogers."

Her dress was a short tunic with full raglan sleeves, the right one of which she dragged through her plate each time she reached for her milk. I was sure Robert noticed it, too, but though lamé is not washable, he did not so much as wince.

"Robert made it," Patrice-Leilani said of her dress, probably because I was staring at the soiled sleeve. "He makes all my good clothes."

After dinner, when Patrice-Leilani went to her room to trace a map of the United States and mark the capital cities, Robert and I pushed away from the crocheted lace tablecloth and moved to the white brocade love seat in the living room. There were furry magenta-colored pillows at the two corners, and we leaned against them, facing each other at an angle, knees almost touching, our wine goblets within reach on the pink-marble-topped coffee table. Then, as people who are new to each other do, we summarized selected chunks of our lives. He talked first about Patrice-Leilani. She had been left in his yard when she was nine months old. He found her sleeping in the grass, a paper bag with a few changes of clothes beside her. He turned her in, of course, but kept track. He was, he said, already enchanted. It turned out he knew the foster family who got her first, and so he visited often. "Take me back," she said each time, and he finally did, though he had to work around many refusals—a single man, an old "flaming queen," was not a fit parent for a young girl. But Robert was from an old *kamaaina* family, one that went back as far as Queen Liliuokalani's imprisonment by her advisors, and his Auntie Elena was not only a Randall and a Cabot, but was also Mrs. Joachim Waters and heir to the shipping company fortune. Auntie Elena's nod helped overcome the refusals, and Patrice-Leilaini was finally Robert's. She was nearly four by then.

Though his auntie had helped him with Patrice-Leilani, she had also disowned him, had had his name specifically removed from her will when she realized his homosexuality was not a phase. "No *hu hu*. I won't worry," he had said at the time: he had a substantial trust fund from the Cabot side. Once he got Patrice-Leilani, though, he realized he was a natural with kids and opened his day care center a year later. "I miss my kids on weekends," he said.

When it was my turn, I talked about St. Barbara's, saying it was an OK place, not admitting that teaching those snot-nosed brats was all that made me feel I had worth, did anything valuable. I said I had been in Hawaii eight years and tried to explain why I never wanted to go back to the Midwest. "It's more than the thick, clean sand and the salt air," I said. "It's because Chinese here are stingy *pakés*, Filipinos are *bok-boks*, Arabs have halitosis, Koreans are manic paranoids, *portagee* are dumb, Hawaiians are lazy, but as *haoles* we're loud, rude cheats." I hoped I had not offended him, but I did not know how else to explain it. "It all evens out here," I said.

Suddenly, he moved closer, so close we shared the same love seat cushion, and I leaned as far back as possible into my pillow. "What about Samoans?" he said. "See this?" He held his wrist, his gold ID bracelet with nothing inscribed on it, at my chin level. "I almost lost this to a Samoan I had with me for a while. He tried to pawn it. He took always, never giving in return. They're like that. They have no class."

I reached in front of him for my wine so he would have to move back. I wasn't concerned about his sitting so close, but I needed more room. He did move back, then looked at me with his pale, soft blue eyes. "Of course, it wasn't the worst thing that ever happened to me. I got over it."

"Swell," I said, raising my glass in a toast, only slightly disappointed that he had missed my point. "Here's to getting over it." I stood then, explaining that I was starting World War I in the morning and had to be well rested.

Before I left, Robert gave me a standing invitation to the open houses he held every first Sunday. They were primarily for his charges and their parents, he said, but other friends dropped in every now and then. He said I could bring a guest.

About thirty people were at the first one Frank and I went to, and Patrice-Leilani wore an aqua chiffon dress with spaghetti straps that kept sliding down her shoulders and a full skirt she swirled as she walked by violently swinging her hips. "Sammy threw up," she said as soon as she saw me, as if it were the big news I had been waiting for. "In the kitchen. PeeYuu. Robert's cleaning it up now."

"Oh yuck," I said. "Thanks for telling me."

Most of Robert's clients were university people—teachers, researchers, grad students. They all had calloused feet, and the women's muumuus, typically, had too many ruffles or buttons or just hung funny, like sheets. They studied and wrote reports on what goldfish did when startled and on whether breast feeding affected sense of humor. "The kid's or the mother's?" I asked. The other guests, the friends who dropped in every now and then, were entertainers, not well-known types either, but the kind who supported themselves by playing piano in lounges or in expensive Mexican restaurants with Naugahyde booths and recessed lighting. They were mostly men, carefully styled, jeweled, and wearing nylon aloha shirts. They got on Frank's nerves. "They're the kind of people who would never be surprised by their reflections," he said, and rather than talk to them, he went to help Patrice-Leilani pass around her chips and dips, invariably made with onion soup mix.

We went to five open houses, and at each one, someone, a parent or an entertainer, asked us if nuns really said that stuff about patent leather shoes. We were considered oddities for being Catholic, were considered superstitious Rome and virgin worshippers. We kept the old gags going, too, a perverseness in us, I guess. We confirmed the patent leather story and added the ones about mud puddles and oranges and white tablecloths.

I liked Robert's parties for the ease with which people moved in and out of conversations, and once when I had run out of chit-chat and was sitting alone on one of the wooden front porch steps, I saw Robert and a little girl at the edge of his driveway. Their backs were to me, and the way he held her had caused her yellow dress to stick up over his arm in back. Her blond hair, thin wispy baby-fine strands dangling to her shoulders, seemed fragile. And as I watched him point out the bird-of-paradise across the street, I thought of how her hair would become fuller and stronger. I was struck by that thought, realized it was the origin of hope. I thought I heard the girl giggle, but there were other kids closer, and I couldn't be sure.

At dusk, when the open houses were almost over, one of the old friends, a little kewpie-doll of a man named Mitch, would beat out a rhythm on a set of bongos and chant while Robert danced the hula. "Gag," Frank would say in my ear. I would tell him what he already knew, the hula was originally a male dance, and he would make some smart-alecky remark about the maleness of the male dancer before sneaking off to my house to wait for me. But Frank really had no need to sneak; all attention would be on Robert, his knees slightly bent, his upper torso held rigid, and his pelvis rotating, swiveling widely as his knees jutted in and out. It was, of course, a dance of sex, a dance largely responsible for Frank being allowed to stay over on first Sundays.

Though we were neighbors, Robert and I were too busy with our separate lives to see each other often, but every now and then, every two weeks perhaps, we would drink a scotch on the rocks together at the end of the day. He talked then about his computerized sewing machine and about hiring a math tutor for Patrice-Leilani. I usually told him how the candy-for-band-uniform sales were going or the latest joke from Jo—Sister Joseph Ann, the stand-up comic of the faculty lunchroom. "There was an engineer and a priest," I'd say, or "A *portagee* and a *haole* walked into a bar." I've never been good at jokes, but Robert would smile anyway, chuckle politely, sometimes recite a few of the limericks he liked about farts or genitals.

We knew each other in this way, superficial maybe, but real, too. No matter what the blond girl had said, I knew he was not a child molester. I knew it just as certainly as I knew his gold ID bracelet had been given to him by a lover, one he missed. Some things you can just tell.

After the blonde came forward, though, another little girl told a similar story, and it looked bad. I learned about the accusations from a psychology department secretary I ran into at Safeway. She had been to one of the open houses, and when she recognized me, she got right to the point. She was dying to tell what she had heard that very day, and maybe I called Mitch later for the same reason. "Isn't it awful?" I said to him as if I were a backyard gossip, but I did not know what else to say, how else to say it.

"Awful," he said. "Sure. But not surprising."

The day care center was closed pending investigation, and on that first morning, I overheard a plea, heard one of Robert's customers saying, "I don't care about all that nonsense. You have to take Sam today." Robert refused her over and over before she gave up, but they both laughed at something and I was relieved. This would blow over. It could be laughed at.

Robert came over for a scotch that evening, but he did not want to talk about the charges. Rather, he reminisced about island entertainment of the '70s, the attempt at reviving the old *Hawaii Calls* radio show, parties at the Moana Hotel, Andy Cummings and other celebrities. He hung around for the parties, he said, and sometimes they would take turns making up dances. He and Mitch were still in high school then, star-struck and eager to please. They did a dance called the Tourist—everyone had a version—craning their necks, pretending to be jumping around on hot sand, carrying heavy shopping bags. "We were groupies," he said. "We would do whatever the big stars told us. No pride. Someone would say 'Hey kid, do the Pipeline,' and I would pretend to surf and tumble. I was good at tumbling." He sat in silence, and I was quiet, too, not knowing if he was in the past or the present. "It was something just to be there," he said. "To think that against all odds, you might make it, too. Someday.

"I did finally perform for a while. I was in a group. The Rainbow Boys." He asked for another drink, neat this time, forget the rocks, so I just brought out the bottle and let him pour. "There were four of us. We stripped. It was at the old Boys Will Be Girls club in Chinatown. This was in the mid-eighties. We'd dress up as women, see?" He leaned forward, perching on the edge of my white wicker chair. "Sort of vampish. Over-made-up, slinky. Then we'd strip, so the joke, the one the audience was in on all the time, that we were men, was obvious." He leaned back, sipped his drink, and said, "Shit. I was better than that. Shouldn't have lowered myself, but I was mad that I hadn't made it. I wanted some sort of publicity."

Before he left that evening, he told me his lawyer might be calling for a character reference. Lots of his friends and customers were being asked. It probably would not be used, he said. There was already enough evidence he had no character. I disagreed right away, and, taking my cue from the woman I had overheard who called it all nonsense, I offered to get letters from all the teachers at St. Barbara's, including the three nuns—one deaf and nearly blind who no longer taught but merely cruised the halls and smiled at the children. So what if no one but Frank and me knew him? What I said was a joke, at least mainly a joke, but he didn't crack a smile.

"Everyone wants to be funny about it," he said. "Even Mitch. He says I'll finally get my name in the paper."

"Sorry," I said. "But really, Robert. Jokes don't hurt."

The accusations turned into formal charges, then to an arrest, then to a trial. On the Friday before the trial was scheduled, Frank and I started on wine, but somewhere along the line switched to brandy. I had been telling myself for weeks that I did not know Robert at all well, did not *know* he was innocent. Nevertheless, I *believed* it. I reminded myself that all any of us have is our belief, but when I said as much to Frank, he launched into a long-winded explanation of why that was wrong, then listed all the things he truly knew, beginning with the laws of physics. When he finally wound down, I got back to Robert. "They won't convict him," I said. "He's innocent." I didn't know that. I could think of no reason for the little girls to lie, and I reminded myself that even tyrants, dictators, mass murderers had friends, family members, former classmates, someone who liked them, believed them, laughed at their jokes, and prayed for them. "Please don't let Robert be convicted," I prayed then, not brave enough to say, "Don't let him be guilty," because God never did change the past. "If he is guilty," I told God, "don't let me ever find out."

"Crappola," Frank said, though I had forgotten what I'd said to earn such a response. "Innocence has nothing to do with it. Parents are afraid. They say, 'Where else did he touch you? And where else?' Besides, look at him, a former stripper in a transvestite bar, disowned by both the Waters and Randall families."

"That's all in the past," I said, trying not to slur my words.

"Hell, look at his living room," Frank said. "It looks like a bordello."

I agreed, and when I nodded, Frank got blurry as if he were inexpertly superimposed upon himself. "He should get rid of those velvet curtains," I said, then I looked at Frank again to see if he had come back together, and we both laughed, spraying our brandy at each other. I didn't know why I was laughing, but *bordello* was a funny word, and just as we would start to calm down, one of us would say *tassels* or *fringe* or *bordello*, and we would start up again. My face was hot. It hurt. "Hung for tackiness," Frank said over and over, as if it was the truest thing either of us could say.

When we finally got to bed, I had to press my temples, hold my head together with my thumb and forefinger. I dreamed of Patrice-Leilani jumping nude over the brocade love seat and the magenta-colored pillows.

The trial was fast, and Mitch was right: Robert got his picture in the *Honolulu Star-Bulletin* more than once. The little girls testified behind closed doors, but their mothers took the stand. They said their daughters said, "Robert touched me here," and then pointed right between the legs of the plastic doll used for questioning. "Children don't lie," the expert witness psychologist said. "Not about that." Robert was the only witness for the defense. He said he did not do it, but he looked down, fiddled with his ID bracelet as he talked, not once raising his eyes to the jury or the prosecutor. The headline read "Scion of Missionary Family Offers Little Defense."

He got ten years, and Patrice-Leilani once again became a ward of the state.

When they led him from the courtroom after the sentencing, a reporter asked how he felt, and Robert screamed, called him a bastard, and spit at the camera. I was proud of him, and the next morning when I saw his picture, lips rounded in mid-spit, eyes bright and frightening, I cut it out to save.

Robert's lawyer was all silk and grease when he explained to me that it was Robert who refused to let Patrice-Leilani testify, even though it would have helped him. And the lawyer also said the prosecution showed restraint by not bringing up the Rainbow Boys. "Not that they had to," he said. "You just can't beat the testimony of kids."

Robert's auntie apparently would not help Robert this time, not Patrice-Leilani either. I wrote to her, Mrs. Joachim Waters, and told her why I believed Robert was not guilty. Forget the logical, like why would a pervert who wanted to snatch at private parts of kids go to all the trouble of fixing food for them, teaching them, cleaning up after them? Why not just hide in the beach restrooms, cruise Makiki Park? Forget all that I said in my first two letters, and remember he's a good man. That's all. In the third letter, I just said please. I don't know if my letters were ever read. They weren't answered or returned. After five letters, I stopped trying to help Robert and concentrated on Patrice-Leilani. "She's your great-niece," I said. "Don't abandon her." As I expected, nothing.

I was afraid to visit Robert. I did write to Patrice-Leilani, who was living in a group home on the Big Island. I told her I hoped she knew Robert was innocent. She answered my letter, saying she was happy they let her help fix dinner at her new home, but I shouldn't bother to visit her or anything, because she had cancer. She wanted to be buried in her green taffeta with the ruffle on the hip. Her court-appointed social worker, whom I called and wrote to, said not to worry. It was just a phase, and there was nothing I could do.

Now when Jo tries to tell me her jokes about a gay *paké* and a Congregational minister, I interrupt her. "Life sucks," I say. "Like a Hoover Deluxe." She purses her lips, squints at me. "Grow up," she says.

Anyway, I'm back with Frank—I used the still screenless window as an excuse to break my lease—and we are planning to be married sometime in the next few years. I often play a game of comfort and imagine we adopt Patrice-Leilani as soon as we're married, but I know we won't. When I've had a touch more scotch than I should, Frank undresses me, leads me to the bedroom, and tucks me in. He holds me tight all night, and I hold on to him, too, believing in the crack in the ocean floor thousands of miles away that is my doom. I listen until I can hear the smack and thud of the wind throwing the giant tsunami waves down hard on the thick and wet expanse of sand, and I prepare myself to be spun around and around until my breath is gone and my lungs burst from emptiness.

MARY TROY, *born in 1948, is the author of three collections of short stories:* Cookie Lily; The Alibi Café and Other Stories; *and* Joe Baker Is Dead. *Her stories and essays have been published widely in newspapers, literary journals, and anthologies. From 1977 to 1983 she was a researcher/writer for the University of Hawai'i's College of Engineering. She teaches creative writing and literature and directs the MFA program at the University of Missouri–St. Louis.*

Linda Spalding

from DAUGHTERS OF CAPTAIN COOK

S ometimes after sailing at Waikiki, we drove home to the windward side the long way around the edge of the island, taking the beach road past Black Point and Koko Head and Hanauma Bay, enjoying the purpling light of the shore, past Fort Ruger, where the military let its officers relax next to a perfect beach that had once been, Paul said, choice Hawaiian land. Now the Hawaiians had been given housing lots close to the highway, far from the beach, one of those places called "Hawaiian Home Lands." We stopped, when we went that way, at Sandy Beach, where a truck at the side of the road sold manapua, steamy and hot to hold, a puff of dough with meat buried inside. If it was late enough, we ordered a whole plate of food—chili and rice or stew and rice with two scoops of macaroni salad for a dollar eighty-five. After a year here, we had a taste for local things, for manapua and plate-lunch.

But this time the late sunlight followed us up the Pali highway instead. Into the mountains, across the middle of the island and down, passing through the long tunnel without a word because it's bad luck to talk in them. Ahead of us was the windward plain and Kailua, our own town. Kailua is a small place—orderly and middle class, built up along the beach, and not very old—although there was a settlement here once long ago. It's called the bedroom of Honolulu now, a bedroom full of families and Marines. Once there were pastures and taro groves, an ancient *heiau* or temple called Ulupo, and, at the end of the beach, a jungle under a cliff. Now there are houses and churches and stores. On one side Kailua stretches out into a thin finger of land between the beach cliffs and Waimanalo. That's where Revere is. In Lanikai. Our house is about two miles away, toward the Marine base, in a section of town that was reclaimed from the bay. The land there is flat and covered with coconut trees.

Now, as we drove, Kit leaned against Paul's arm and fell asleep, breathing soundlessly against her father's pulse. All the way home, once you hit the Pali, is downward, a long sweep against softening hills, and at the bottom Paul stopped for ice cream, nudging Kit awake at the Chinese store.

"Shouldn't I just take you home first and then go unload the boat? Wouldn't it be a lot easier? I can take you home and double back."

For the second time during that ride I was disappointed. It was always strangely thrilling to visit Revere, to stand on the threshold of what might have been our house.

To avoid the traffic on Oneawa Street, or to satisfy that wish for something more exotic than the streets of our settled and respectable town spent another hour watching dark leaves ~~overhung up~~ under bright ones drying out after a little ten minute rain and swaying over the narrow overhang of my roof. I see the tree from underneath, looking up to its branches which are several inches thick and spread open like a hand ~~awaiting~~ waiting for a gift to be dropped into it. The whole shape & size of the tree comforts me ~~(in fact it may be the have been a reason for choosing this house)~~ because it seems so like a tree anywhere else. It doesn't look tropical from this angle - except that when the leaves fall they are still green. Beyond my tree are others: ~~is~~ the fan-shaped coconut palm at the corner of the house, ~~partly visible seen at the other side of the window,~~ 3 or 4 huge waving tendrils at the ~~far~~ left corner of the window ~~frame~~ &, beyond that, between the two trees, is a tall, handsome kukui nut tree - almost regal in its messy indifference, it seeds my sandy side yard with its daily droppings as if I should be delighted to ~~sweep~~ attend to the business of its toilet. But, to spite it, I refuse and leave a mess there so surround my side of it - it's not my tree, but hangs over from the neighbor

Courtesy of Linda Spalding.

offered, Paul took the swamp road over the last stretch of afternoon—a narrow, winding road through *halekoa* and *kiawe* trees. It is a place of birds and knee high grasses—this ancient swamp—and on its high side, a huge landfill where bulldozers plow through the daylight hours, terracing the hillside with the rejected stuff—old beds and bureau drawers—of everybody's lives. Like ornamental carapaces, like the fossilized armor of prehistoric beasts, old metal skeletons of cars festoon the winding road below this burial ground.

Along the way, just visible behind a high wire fence, hangs what we called the Lady of the Swamp. Kit was the first to notice her one day soon after we arrived, aloft on her tree trunk. She stared past us unsmiling but not quite expressionless. Ship's maiden? Mannequin? Her wooden nakedness was so benevolent among the metal shards, her gesture was so eloquent, that we looked to her each time we drove by with expectation and anticipation.

Somewhere behind her the old *heiau* called Ulupo crumbles and dissolves. Its sacred stones lie scattered under silty water and marsh grass although part of its huge stone platform is still visible on a slight rise. A sign claims it was built by the *menehunes*, the earliest inhabitants, which means it has stood on that rise between the mountains and the sea for more than a thousand years At that time we knew Mihana used to visit it every few days, walking around it, squinting up at it, trying to get a feel for its size and shape, tucking back into place—little by little—the fallen stones. She was a healer of some kind—the locals believed in her. But she was Christianized. All she had left of her heritage were stories and recipes for cures. People who had a need for cured stomachs or cured hearts still appeared sometimes at her door. Our door, Paul said.

Paul said Mihana shouldn't have inherited Revere. I think it seemed to him that she had locked him out of paradise and that because of it, no matter how polite she was, we were confined to a small rented house—in a Kailua tract built on old landfill.

The house, as we approached, looked small, but it was ours, where we lived with our mango tree, the flowering plumeria, the fig tree in the deep front yard, the growing be–still and the birds and small sounds of the place quietly humming. Paul turned the corner at a wide angle, driving slowly, being careful that the boat did not disturb the balance of our narrow and untraveled street; then let us out, telling me to take the bags and cooler, telling Kit to help me take the gear inside.

The cat wound himself around our feet, hungry and pleased to have us home. "Lukie . . ." Kit crooned. I ran a bath for Kit and urged her into it, then went outside the way I always did and walked around the mango tree. The shape and size of the old tree were comforting—almost what I remembered trees to be. Tall and tough and even limbed, it looked almost deciduous, except that when they fell, the leaves were green. Beyond it, on the other side of the slat fence, a tall *kukui* tree seeded our yard daily with the hard black nuts the old Hawaiians used as lamps. They used to string them up on the spine of a banana leaf, then light the oil inside and count the hours as each *kukui* nut went out. Now they're made into necklaces and sold to tourists—there must be a million strings of them in Waikiki. I didn't mind about the seeds that lay in my yard. I took each tree at its face value. They didn't have to earn their keep or be domestic. I kept the garden trim but I let the trees be.

The one tree I took care of was the yellow be-still I had planted when we took the house. A seedling from Revere, I'd put it over the old cesspool right outside the living room, where, on its rich diet, it grew at an unnatural rate and bloomed continuously, its yellow flowers small bright torches that were always there. It was surrounded by the greens and reds and floral shapes and hues that grow so easily in gardens there. Without much effort things will bloom and multiply. And because the wall between the living room and the yellow tree was sliding glass and screen, the garden became part of the still, dark rooms where we lived. We became part of the garden.

From the garden, I looked inside and eyed the dented sofa and the mail. There was gear to unpack and a meal to get ready, but the old rattan sofa covered with pillows looked inviting. I could lie there and wait for Kit to finish her bath. I could stretch out and throw a magazine across my face or leaf through the envelopes of empty news, of bills and coupons that had piled up. I could lie there and think about Revere and what it was about it that had got into our skin, under our skin, buried head first like a chigger from my old Kansas backyard so that its tiny venom moved around in us, coursing as close as it could to our hearts.

I opened my back door, sliding it wide. After the winter rains, I knew the exact rumble of the wood and glass, the light resistance of the screen, so that I opened the door each time with a flourish as if, in that way, I could join the two worlds—outside and in. As if having found a place to put down roots, I wanted to put them down in this ground on this island again and again.

There is no short season on the island. No brief summer moving into fall. The flowers bloom endlessly. Soon, I thought, we would belong here. The banana trees would feed us, and the mango trees and coconut palms.

I left the doors pushed back when I went in and peeled off shorts and shirt and underwear and went to the old sofa sleepily, reaching into the mail. The neighborhood was quiet at this hour. It was a Monday afternoon. The men were busy coming home. Soldiers and civil servants most of them. Women and children, back from jobs and school, waited for them. Except for us, this was a neighborhood of homeowners, of the middle class. Many were from the mainland—servicemen and businessmen and their wives. They shopped at Safeway for the most part although all the children went to the Chinese store close to the beach for shave ice and crack seed. Children acclimatize. This was a neighborhood of childish dreams.

Paul would be pulling up the long, sandy driveway at Revere, trying to think of the best way to unload the heavy boat. He would have to cut across the grass at the only spot left unprotected by Mihana's hedge, then turn the whole thing around and back the car down to the beach. Or he would not drive as far as the house at all but use the boat ramp at the entrance to Lanikai, that thin strip of land hugging the cliffs. Revere covers ten acres of jungle and lawn at the far tip, inside the crotch of land where the ocean presses almost into it. The one-way road begins at the boat ramp, then circles Lanikai. The road, in its circle, passes through a different kind of neighborhood than ours. The houses on the beach had been built for the rich. Flower children lived in them now, and drug dealers and surfers, living communally. In the rest—in the smaller houses on the hill—there were families. At the end of the road Mihana lived. Having no place more to go, the road turned around at Revere, and looped back out again.

Paul would use the boat ramp, I decided, and sail down to the old house, preferring the long walk back to the car when he was done. He would sail close to the shore because he had no light yet on the boat and he would think of the great, empty house ahead of him and of the times behind him when he had lived there, when he was a little boy. His disheveled childhood. Sent away to school at the age of nine, he had been an academic failure. He'd been looking toward Revere for years, wasting precious time. Now it was before him. He would see Maya running toward him in the darkness like a sandpiper, wild and thin and childishly excited, trying to stand still, trying to look poised, but forgetting and skipping around in that way she had because she was still a child. Inexperienced and untouched, Maya seemed closer to love and sex, and death than any of us. She was on the edge of it all, peering in. She had the hesitation of virginity. She would stare past us, into the windows, into the banyan tree, as if waiting for something, as if someone might arrive with an unimaginable message that would change everything. Or maybe it was something waiting for her behind the tree, ready to step out, and she was afraid but watching anyway so that she would recognize him when he came, dressed in colors of clay like the first man who had been created by the gods Lono and Kane on Makapuu Point, where the Marines lived.

Maya was wide-eyed, curious about everything, wandering in the jungle around Revere as if whatever was going to happen would happen there, as if knowing it would carry with it the strong smell of salt and blood.

Mihana kept her thoughts to herself. Perhaps everything was a danger, perhaps nothing. There were men everywhere. There were the Marines. There were the flower children with their drugs. They had come from California. They had come from far away. But Maya was too young to care, and Kailua had attractions for her; it sold the hibachis we took to the beach for week-end picnics, and throwaway diapers and rubber slippers and plastic jewelry and cigarettes. There were pizza places and a Korean restaurant and a small department store and a large drugstore. There were three streets which met the Pali highway. There was a gas station on every corner, and there was our house. Kailua was a town that might have been chipped out of the Midwest, except that in the center of it there was a patch of grass surmounted by a huge, clattering evening-full-of-birds banyan tree. Like the tree in Revere, only noisier, it functioned as the town clock, the scattering and regrouping of the mynah birds signaling morning and night. Kailua town—sleepy and self-satisfied, but vigilant, ready for some amusement, some entertainment, like Maya watching us.

I lay on our sofa, naked, knowing that by now the lights were on inside the small part of Revere that was inhabited, that Paul was relishing the thought of the cold beer he would drink there in the old house that looked, to him alone, in spite of termites and dry rot and a generation's softening decay, exactly as it had a quarter of a century before; that he was watching Maya running toward him, and Mihana standing on the slope above him, immense in front of the tall stand of ironwood that hid the house. And he would be glad he had come by water so as not to disturb the lawn, such as it was, or Mihana, such as she was. I lay on the sofa, our bills in hand, and thought about all that. I knew these things. I could follow Paul's course, I could look up the shore and through the dense jungle of ironwood trees that held the great and wasted lawn back from the collapsing beach. I could see where he passed and where he went—in which direction. Or so I thought. Just as I could listen to the song of Kit who would soon fall asleep in her bath and who would later blame me for it, although she lay in it like a snow angel, hair spread out around her head. She was making noises there now while the birds outside caroled and squawked their final evening messages, settling into trees, and while the neighbors in their matching small tract houses—mainlanders like us—settled around their dinners and TVs, and while the flowers opened their hearts and bodies suddenly and threw their fragrances into the air like offerings.

The cat, who sat outside on the well clipped grass, listened along with me, and I held the unopened mail, believing there was no news that could matter very much to us anyway. Probably I should have felt just then a pull—a warning—that sense of small alarm that makes the hair rise on the neck's thin skin.

It was twilight, the hour when a mother calls her children home, and mine was here; my house was safe; my future still connected to my past. The press of Paul's hand, the color of Kit's hair, the things that I knew were all around. When the phone rang I got up to answer it as unprepared as I was unarmed.

LINDA SPALDING *was born in Kansas and lived in Hawai'i before immigrating to Toronto in 1982. She is the author of* Daughters of Captain Cook; The Paper Wife; *and* Mere, *written with her daughter Esta. Her nonfiction work,* The Follow, *was short-listed for the Trillium Book Award and the Pearson Writers' Trust Prize.* Who Named the Knife *is short-listed for the Arthur Ellis Award. She received the Harbourfront Festival Prize for her contribution to the Canadian literary community.*

Helen E. Dalton
UNTITLED

On highrise lanai
Japanese linnets build nest
With a bird's eye view.

Lynelle Thon
"MY ROOMMATES"

There's a gecko in my kitchen
Getting fat on ants
There's spider mites and mealy bugs
Living on my plants.

A mouse who rents the room
Beneath the kitchen sink
Tells me to take the trash out
When it begins to stink.

There are spiders in the attic
And termites in the walls
There's moths in all my closets
Despite the many moth balls.

The roaches clean up all my crumbs
I never have to sweep
Bedbugs keep me up all night
Preventing any sleep.

It's getting pretty crowded here
And if my landlord ever found out
He'd either raise the rent up
Or else he'd kick us out!

LYNELLE THON *wrote this poem in 1992, when she was a student at Kapi'olani Community College in Honolulu.*

Tony Quagliano

"MAN ALONE THE BEAST"

47 million termites
  swarm
   my 60 watt bulb in Kapahulu

I try to love nature
   and nature
  poets tell me wolves
    say, kill
  necessarily, predators
    are non-intentional

   scorpions
  have no Hiroshima
    rats
  no Dresdens
    vultures, Belsens
    barracudas, crucifixions

nature poets tell me
man alone
has killer mind

I try to love
the food chain
animal murder
as transfer of protein

nature
poets tell me
calling cops pigs
insults pigs
whales
are tuneful
crickets wise
gulls
screech overviews
monkeys sign direct
and uncorrupted

nature
poets say subhuman
assassination god's
plan
man alone the beast

so as I spray and spray
my 60 watt bulb
typewriter, desk
and window on Kapahulu tonight
I feel
quite natural.

TONY QUAGLIANO (1941-2007) *has various works including poems in* New York Quarterly; Harvard Review; Rolling Stone; New Directions; Yankee; Spring: The Journal of the E.E. Cummings Society; *and* The Pushcart Prize, *as well as in numerous Hawai'i literary journals. His books of poetry include* Language Drawn and Quartered; Fierce Meadows; *and* Snail Mail Poems. *He edited the special Bukowski issue of* Small Press Review, *which appeared in 1973. He edited* KAIMANA—The Journal of the Hawai'i Literary Arts Council *from 1990 to 2007.*

Wing Tek Lum

"TO LIVE AND LET LIVE"

" . . . the tree of life also in the midst of the garden,
and the tree of the knowledge of good and evil."
—Genesis 2:9

We live on the side of a mountain, an old volcano in fact,
and all manner of insects pass through our condo
as we're on a low floor
and have never bothered to install screens to our windows.
Usually it's a moth or mosquito or a honeybee lost in the night.
In the summer there are also termites that rise as we dine.
Some of these bugs I have never seen before
like those lanky brown beetles
and that bright green one with a hard shell
I would have thought to find only in a museum.
The larger ones with stings I shoo away with my broom.
I will not hesitate to swat a fat roach.
But these are the exceptions.
Most others we have simply taken note of and ignored.
It's only been after the birth of our daughter
that we've had to reconsider our pact of indifference—
not in fear of their biting our new girl:
she just hasn't learned yet
to discern all the objects of her world, to live and let live,
and not devour each smaller thing within her grasp.

Kathryn Waddell Takara

"ISIS THE CAT: ELEGY"

Isis
a cat of strange origin
was not responsible
for the geckos she ate
that were carriers
of the hepatitis
which killed her.

Richard Hamasaki

"DOES THE TEMPLE BELL STILL TOLL AT THE MŌʻILIʻILI HONGWANJI?"

on Kapaʻakea Lane
memorizing
shades of green

walking home
with another letter
evicting me

he turns the corner
precious face
like his plantation house

with gravity he
shakes my hand
grins widely

"Get plenty t'ings fo' do"
he declares
then disappears

pumping down
the narrow road
in his wheelchair

Cedric Yamanaka

"THE LEMON TREE BILLIARDS HOUSE"

The Lemon tree Billiards House is on the first floor of an old concrete building on King Street, between Aloha Electronics and Uncle Phil's Flowers. The building is old and the pool hall isn't very large—just nine tables, a ceiling fan, and a soda machine. No one seems to know how the place got its name. Some say it used to be a Korean bar. Others say it was a funeral home. But all seem to agree that it has a lousy name for a pool hall. At one point someone circulated a petition requesting the name be changed. But Mr. Kong, the proud owner, wouldn't budge. He said his pool hall would always be called the Lemon Tree Billiards House.

Mr. Kong keeps his rates very reasonable. For two dollars an hour, you can hit all of the balls you want. One day I was in there playing eight ball with a sixty-eight-year-old parking attendant. The guy played pretty well—I was squeezing for a while—but he missed a tough slice and left me enough openings to clear the table and sink the eight ball. I won twenty bucks.

Another guy walked up to me. He had a mustache, a baseball cap, and a flannel shirt.

"My name Hamilton," he said. "I ain't too good—but what—you like play?"

I ain't too good. *Sure.*

"My name's Mitch," I said. "Let's play."

We agreed on fifty bucks. Hamilton racked the balls. I broke. It was a good one. The sound of the balls cracking against each other was like a hundred glass jars exploding.

As three striped balls—the nine, twelve, and fifteen—shot into three different pockets, I noticed a good-looking girl in a black dress sitting on a stool in the corner. I don't know if I was imagining it or not but I thought I caught her looking my way. I missed an easy shot on the side pocket. I'd burned my finger cooking saimin and couldn't get a good grip on the cue stick.

"Oh, too bad," said Hamilton. "Hard luck! I thought you had me there." He was what I call a talker. The kind of guy who can't keep his mouth shut. The kind of guy who treats a game of pool like a radio call-in show.

Anyway, Hamilton hit four balls in but stalled on the fifth. I eventually won the game.

Afterward, the girl in the black dress walked up to me.

"Hi," she said, smiling.

"Hello," I said.

"You're pretty good," she said.

"Thanks."

"You wanna play my dad?"

"Who's your dad?"

"You wanna play or not?"

"Who is he?"

"He'll give you five hundred bucks if you beat him."

"Let's go."

I'm a pool hustler and the Lemon Tree Billiards House is my turf. You see, I've been playing pool all my life. It's the only thing I know how to do. My dad taught me the game before they threw him in jail. I dropped out of school, left home, and traveled around the country challenging other pool players. I've played the best. Now I'm home.

All right, all right. I'm not a pool hustler. I'm a freshman at the University of Hawaii. And my dad's not in jail. He's an accountant. And I never challenged players around the country. I did play a game in Waipahu once.

I have been playing pool for a while, though. Sometimes I do real well. Sometimes I don't. That's how the game is for me. Four things can happen when I pick up a cue stick. One, sometimes I feel like I'll win and I win. Two, sometimes I feel like I'll win and I lose. Three, sometimes I feel like I'll lose and I lose. Four, sometimes I feel like I'll lose and I win.

I'll tell you one thing, though. I could've been a better pool player if I hadn't been cursed. Yes, cursed.

It all happened back when I was seven years old. My dad had taken me to a beach house. I'm not sure where it was. Somewhere near Malaekahana, maybe. I remember walking along the beach and seeing some large boulders, I began climbing on the rocks, trying to get a good look at the ocean and the crashing waves. The view was stunning. The water was so blue. And I thought I spotted some whales playing in the surf offshore.

All of a sudden, my father came running down the beach. "Mitch!" he said. "Get off da rocks! Da rocks sacred! No climb up there! No good!"

Ever since that day, I've lived with a curse. One day in the eighth grade, I dropped a touchdown pass and we lost a big intramural football game. I smashed my first car three minutes after I drove it off the lot. My first girlfriend left me for a guy in prison she read about in the papers. I'm the kind of guy who will throw down four queens in a poker game, only to watch helplessly as some clown tosses down four kings. If I buy something at the market, it'll go on sale the next day.

It hasn't been easy. The only thing I do okay is play eight ball. But I could've been better. If it just weren't for this curse.

I don't know why I agreed to play pool with this strange girl's father. Maybe it was because she was so beautiful. The best-looking woman I've ever seen. Six feet, two hundred pounds, hairy legs, mustache. Okay, okay. So she wasn't *that* beautiful. Let's just say she was kind of average.

Anyway, we got into her car and she drove toward the Wai'anae coast. She had one of those big black sedans you saw in the seventies. The kind Jack Lord used to drive to Iolani Palace in *Hawaii Five-0*. In about a half hour or so, we wound up at a large beach house with water mills and bronze Buddhas in the yard. Everywhere you looked, you saw trees. Mango, avocado, papaya, banana.

"My dad likes to plant things," the girl explained.

We walked past a rock garden and a koi pond, and she led me into a room with a pool table. There were dozens of cues lined up neatly on the wall, just like at the Lemon Tree Billiards House.

"You can grab a stick," the girl said. "I'll go get my dad."

In a few minutes I realized why she didn't want to tell me who her father was. I was standing face-to-face with Locust Cordero. *The* Locust Cordero. All six-five, 265 pounds of him. Wearing, of all things, a purple tuxedo with a red carnation in the lapel. Locust Cordero, who stood trial for the murder-for-hire deaths of three Salt Lake gamblers several years back. I was about to play eight ball with a hit man.

"Howzit," he said. "*Mahalos* for coming. My name Locust."

What should I say? I know who you are? I've heard of you? I've seen your mug shots on TV? Congratulations on your recent acquittal? Nice tuxedo?

"Nice to meet you, sir," I said, settling on the conservative. "I'm Mitch."

We shook hands. He wore a huge jade ring on his finger.

"My daughter says you pretty good."

"I try, sir."

"How you like my tuxedo?" he said.

"Nice," I said.

"Shaka, ah?" he said, running his hands over the material. "Silk, brah. Just bought 'em. What size you?"

"What?"

"What size you?" he repeated, opening up a closet. I was stunned. There must have been two dozen tuxedos in there. All sizes. All colors. Black, white, maroon, pink, blue, red. "Here," said Locust, handing me a gold one. "Try put dis beauty on."

"Uh," I said. "How about the black one?"

Again, I was leaning toward the conservative.

"Whatevahs," said Locust, shrugging.

I changed in the bathroom. It took me awhile because I'd never worn a tuxedo before. When I walked out, Locust smiled.

"Sharp," he said. "Look at us. Now we *really* look like pool players."

Locust chalked his cue stick. He was so big, the stick looked like a tooth-pick in his hands.

"Break 'em, Mitch."

"Yes, sir."

I walked to the table and broke. I did it real fast. I don't like to think about my shots too long. That always messes me up. *Crack!* Not bad. Two solid balls shot into the right corner pocket.

"Das too bad," said Locust, shaking his head.

"Why's that, sir?" I asked.

"Cause," said Locust, "I hate to lose."

One day not too long before, I'd visited an exorcist. To get rid of my curse. He was an old Hawaiian man in his late forties or early fifties, recommended to me by a friend. When I called for an appointment, he said he couldn't fit me in. There were a lot of folks out there with problems, I guessed. I told him it was an emergency.

"Okay, come ovah," he said. "But hurry up."

I drove to his house. He lived in Palolo Valley. I was very scared. What would happen? I could see it now. As soon as I walked into the room, the man would scream and run away from me. He'd tell me he saw death and destruction written all over my face. The wind would blow papers all over his room, and I'd be speaking weird languages I had never heard before and blood and mucus would pour out my mouth.

But nothing like that happened. I walked into his house, expecting to see him chanting or praying. Instead he was sitting behind a koa desk in a Munsingwear shirt and green polyester pants.

"Dis bettah be good," he said. "I went cancel my tee time at Ala Wai for you."

I smiled. I told him my plight. I started from the beginning—telling him about the day I climbed on the rocks and the bad luck I've had ever since.

"You ain't cursed," the man said. He bent down to pick something up from the floor. What was it? An ancient amulet? A charm? None of the above. It was a golf club. An eight iron. "Da mind is one very powerful ting," he said, waving the eight iron around like a magician waving a wand. "It can make simple tings difficult and difficult tings simple."

"What about the rocks?" I said.

"Tink positive," the man said. "You one negative buggah. Da only curse is in your mind."

That's it? No reading scripture? No chanting?

"I tell you one ting, brah," the Hawaiian man said. "One day, you going en-countah one challenge. If you beat 'em, da curse going be *pau*. But if you lose, da rest of your life going shrivel up like one slug aftah you pour salt on top."

"Anything else?" I said.

"Yeah," said the Hawaiian man. "You owe me twenty bucks."

Locust and I had played ten games. We'd agreed on eleven. I'd won five, he'd won five. In between, his daughter brought us fruit punch and smoked marlin. It was already dark, and I had an oceanography test the next day.

In the final game, I hit an incredible shot—the cue ball jumping over Locust's ball, like a fullback leaping over a tackler, and hitting the seven into the side pocket. This seemed to piss Locust off. He came right back with a beauty of his own—a massé I couldn't believe. In a massé, the cue ball does bizarre things on the table after being hit—like weaving between balls as if it has a mind of its own. Those are the trick shots you see on TV. Anyway, Locust hit a massé, where the cue ball hit not one, not two, not three, but four of his balls into four different holes. *Come on!* I was convinced Locust could make the cue ball spell his name across the green velvet sky of the pool table.

Pretty soon it was just me, Locust, and the eight ball. I looked at Locust real fast, and he stared at me like a starving man sizing up a Diner's chicken *katsu* plate lunch. I took a shot, but my arm felt like a lead pipe and I missed everything. Locust took a deep breath, blew his shot, and swore in three different languages. It was my turn.

And then I realized it. This was the moment that would make or break me. The challenge the exorcist guy was talking about. I had to win.

I measured the table, paused, and said the words that would change my life and save me from shriveling up like a slug with salt poured on it.

"Eight ball. Corner pocket."

I would have to be careful. Gentle. It was a tough slice to the right corner pocket. If I hit the cue ball too hard, it could fall into the wrong pocket. That would be a scratch. I would lose.

I took a deep breath, cocked my stick, and aimed. I hit the cue ball softly. From here, everything seemed to move in slow motion. The cue ball tapped the eight ball and the eight ball seemed to take hours to roll toward the hole. Out of the corner of my eye, I saw Locust's daughter standing up from her seat, her hands covering her mouth.

Clack. *Plop.*

The ball fell into the hole. The curse was lifted. I had won. I would have been a happy man if I hadn't been so damned scared.

Locust walked up to me, shaking his head. He reached into his pocket. Oh, no. Here it comes. He was gonna take out his gun, shoot me, and bury my body at some deserted beach. Good-bye, cruel world. Thanks for the memories . . .

"I no can remembah da last time I lost," he said, pulling out his wallet and handing me five crispy one-hundred-dollar bills. "*Mahalos* for da game."

Locust asked me to stay and talk for a while. We sat on straw chairs next to the pool table. The place was dark except for several gaslit torches hissing like leaky tires. Hanging on the walls were fishing nets and dried, preserved fish, lobsters, and turtles.

"You must be wondering why we wearing dese tuxedos," said Locust.

"Yeah," I said.

"Well, dis whole night, its kinda one big deal for me." Locust leaned toward me. "You see, brah, I nevah leave my house in five years."

"Why?" I said. I couldn't believe it.

"All my life, everybody been scared of me," said Locust, sighing. "Everywheah I go, people look at me funny. Dey whispah behind my back."

"But—"

"Lemme tell you someting," he continued. "Dey went try me for murder coupla times. Both times, da jury said I was innocent. Still, people no like Locust around. Dey no like see me. And das why I nevah step foot outta dis place."

"Forgive me for saying so, sir," I said. "But that's kinda sad. That's no way to live."

"Oh, it ain't dat bad," said Locust. "I play pool. I go in da ocean, spear uhu. I throw net for mullet. Once in a while, I go in da mountains behind da house and shoot me one pig . . . "

"But don't you ever miss getting out and walking around the city? Experiencing life?"

I was getting nervous again. I mean, here I was, giving advice on how to live to Locust Cordero. After I had just beaten the guy at eight ball.

"Whasso great about walking around da streets of da city?" said Locust after a while. "People shooting and stabbing each othah. Talking stink about each othah. Stealing each othah's husbands and wives. Breaking each othah's hearts."

"You scared?" I said, pressing my luck.

"Yeah," said Locust, looking me straight in the eye, "I guess I am."

We didn't say anything for a while. I could hear the waves of the ocean breaking on the beach.

"So," said Locust, shifting in his seat, "where you went learn to shoot pool?"

"The Lemon Tree Billiards House," I said.

"Da Lemon Tree Billiards House?" Locust said, shaking his head. "What kine name dat? Sound like one funeral home."

"Sir," I said, "I'm sorry. Can I say something?"

"Sure."

"You're living your life like a prisoner. You might as well have been convicted of murder and locked in jail."

Yeah, sometimes it seems I just don't know when to shut up.

"Evah since I was one kid, I had hard luck," said Locust, moving closer to me and whispering. "You see, I'm cursed."

"You're what?" I said, surprised.

"I'm cursed," Locust repeated, raising his voice. "Jeez, for one young kid, you get lousy hearing, ah? Must be all dat loud music you buggahs listen to nowadays."

"How'd you get cursed?" I said.

"One day, when I was one kid, I was climbing some rocks looking out at da ocean. Down Mālaekahana side. All of a sudden, my bruddah start screaming, 'Get down from there. No good. Da rocks sacred.'"

I couldn't believe it. Locust and I were cursed by the same rocks. We were curse brothers.

"Da ting's beat me," said Locust, shaking his head.

"You're talking like a loser."

"A what?" said Locust, getting out of his chair.

"Locust," I said, my voice cracking, "I lived with the same curse and I beat it."

"How?" said Locust, sitting back down. "I tried everyting. Hawaiian salt. Ti leaves. Da works."

"You gotta believe in yourself."

"How you do dat?"

"With your mind," I said. "See, the first thing you gotta do is meet a challenge and beat it," I said. "Go outside. Walk the streets. Meet people."

"You evah stop for tink how dangerous da world is?" said Locust. "Tink about it. How many tings out there are ready, waiting, for screw you up. Death, sickness, corruption, greed, old age . . . "

It was scary. Locust was starting to make sense.

"I don't know," I finally said.

"Tink about it," said Locust. "Tink about it."

One day several weeks later, I was playing eight ball at the Lemon Tree Billiards House. Several people were arguing about the source of an unusual smell. Some said it came from a cardboard box filled with rotten *choy sum* outside on the sidewalk in front of the pool hall. Others said it was Kona winds blowing in the pungent smell of *taegu* from Yuni's Bar-B-Q. Still others said the peculiar smell came from Old Man Rivera, who sat in a corner eating a lunch he had made at home. Too much *patis*—fish sauce—in his *sari sari*.

"If you like good smell," said Mr. Kong, the owner of the Lemon Tree Billiards House, "go orchid farm. If you like play pool, come da Lemon Tree Billiards House."

I was on table number three with a young Japanese guy with short hair. He had dark glasses and wore a black suit. He looked like he was in the *yakuza*.

I had already beaten three guys. I was on a roll. It gets like that every now and then. When you know you can't miss.

The *yakuza* guy never smiled. And every time he missed a shot, he swore at himself. Pretty soon he started to hit the balls very hard—thrusting his cue stick like a samurai spearing an opponent. He was off, though, and I eventually won the game.

"You saw how I beat the *yakuza* guy?" I said to Mr. Kong, who was now on a stepladder unscrewing a burned-out light bulb.

"*Yakuza* guy?" said Mr. Kong. "What *yakuza* guy?"

"The Japanese guy in the suit," I said.

"Oh," said Mr. Kong, laughing like crazy. "You talking about Yatsu! Das my neighbor. He ain't no *yakuza*. He one preschool teachah!"

Just then, Locust Cordero walked into the Lemon Tree Billiards House. Mr. Kong stopped laughing. Everyone stopped their games. No one said a word. The only sound I heard was the ticking of a clock on the wall.

"Mitch," said Locust, "I went take your advice. I no like live like one prisonah no more."

I was speechless.

"You know what dey say," said Locust. "Feel like one five hundred-pound bait has been lifted from my shoulders."

"Weight," I said.

"For what?" said Locust, obviously confused.

"No, no," I said. "Five hundred pound *weight*. Not bait."

"Whatevahs," said Locust. "Da curse is gone."

He walked over to one of Mr. Kong's finest tables, ran his thick fingers over the smooth wood, and looked into the deep pockets like a child staring down a mysterious well.

"Eight ball?" he asked, turning to me.

"Yeah," I said, smiling. "Yeah, sure."

CEDRIC YAMANAKA, *born in 1963, is the author of* In Good Company, *a collection of short stories. He is the recipient of the Elliot Cades Award for Literature and the Helen Deutsch Fellowship from Boston University. He is also a two-time winner at the Hawai'i International Film Festival.*

Jean Toyama

"SARUMATA"

"You're wrong, dear, it was a new pair, flesh-colored. My mother wouldn't give you an old pair of panties," he repeated. Tom Nakamura turned to me. His brow furrowed, while the creases around his mouth deepened then sagged. His wife, Betsy, looked toward me, too. Her lips tightened as she shook her head in silence. He slouched in his chair.

"You don't remember. You never remember. I told you before, I opened the box. I know what I saw. It was that rough material they used to use for rice bags. You know the kind, don't you, Dr. Belli?" She pointed at me, then rubbed her hands together as if fingering some material. Her voice grated like sandpaper. Turning back toward her husband, she continued, "She made underpants out of all those hundred pound rice bags. Remember, Tom?"

"One hundred pounds of rice?" I asked keeping my voice monotone. After weeks of marriage counseling this new detail intrigued me. I looked at Tom but he did not respond, though his wife became more animated.

"It used to last a month. There were ten of us. I was the only *yome*. You know what that means, don't you?" Again the finger.

I shook my head indecisively and said, "Something about daughter-in-law, isn't it?"

"Not bad for third generation with a *haole* last name, Italian, isn't it?" She stared at me, as if saying, You did not marry 'a good Japanese boy.' "You're *sansei*, right? Third generation. I bet you never went to Japanese school." Without waiting for a response she continued, "I married the eldest son; I was the daughter-in-law. None of the other boys were married yet. 'California rice,' it said with a big red rose." Her hands came up in a blossom. "Right, Tom? That's what it said. I had to cook the rice for every meal. She said she had to teach me how to cook the rice. Imagine! I'd been cooking for my family since I was eight, and she had to teach me how to cook rice." Her gaze switched back and forth, between me and her husband, who remained still, staring ahead. "Your husband Italian?"

Her voice rose and fell like rough waters against a stone wall. I surmised that she was feeling more comfortable with me; she had never asked me personal questions and her tone had changed.

Without answering her, I turned to Tom. He was in his 70's, retired for about five years. He'd been the manager of a hardware store on Beretania Street and could tell you which stud, split pin, or locknut you needed. In our individual sessions he would go on and on about the contents of his store and his customers, but with her he was mostly silent.

Throughout their fifty-year marriage she had worked alongside him while raising their three children but for the last ten to fifteen years she also cared for his parents until their deaths. Tom's father was the first to go; then about five years ago his mother passed away.

At a time when things should have been easier, they were talking separation. The children were baffled. After strenuous intervention by family and friends, the pair started therapy, first individually then as a couple. This was an unusual case; normally second-generation Japanese couples don't seek counsel. They're too reserved and closed mouthed, preferring to grin and bear it rather than seek a solution. Ten years of caregiving is no easy life. They should have felt liberated.

"So when she taught you how to cook rice, how did you feel, Betsy?" I asked.

"You know how I felt, I told you already! I was angry, I felt insulted."

We had discussed the rice-cooking issue before, it was one we kept going around and around on. What I gather is that her mother-in-law was never openly hostile to their marriage at least not in front of Betsy. Relations may have been strained but nothing more than the everyday, normal tensions of adding someone new to an established household. This is what Tom thought anyway. Mrs. Nakamura, the mother, had expressed some reservations (his word) about the marriage when he first announced it to the family. However, he was adamant about marrying Betsy and would brook no objection, which is unusual, given that he is second generation, *nisei*. Studies of this immigrant group indicate that the children of *issei*, first generation, were especially pious in their filial devotion. Tom must have been the exception that proved the rule or else his mother really did express only minor objections. When I asked him what these reservations were, he only replied that Betsy and her family lived on a different island. I wondered whether this really could have been the only reason.

"Was the rice any better, when you followed her instructions?" I asked for the first time.

"I'd say!" her husband interjected.

Not saying a word Betsy turned to look at him. He lowered his eyes to pick some lint off his trousers.

While this issue of rice washing had turned up before, we had not moved beyond it. With my question I could see that I had provoked an unexpected affirmative from Tom and a surprising silence from Betsy.

"Would you say that your mother-in-law treated you unkindly."

"No," Betsy replied still mulling over Tom's previous response.

"Then why do you suppose we spend so much time talking about her?" I asked. It was usually this question that silenced both of them, so I was surprised that Betsy changed from her previously curt answer and continued talking.

"I've been thinking about this question, you know, for the past week. It's not exactly what she said or what she did, but I always had this feeling that she wished I wasn't there, that she would have preferred another daughter-in-law. But I could never complain, because she never did anything to make me complain, except for that pair of old . . ."

"New . . . Are we going to do this again? They were new."

"Why do you say they were new, Tom?" I asked.

"I distinctly remember the pink color, and how it looked too large for my wife. You see for yourself how thin she is." He pointed to his wife who didn't turn away but looked full face into her husband's eyes.

For the first time Tom pushed his version of the event. Till now he had deferred to his wife.

"She's always been that way. Thin. Betsy, why do you bring this up anyway. It was so long ago. My mother's dead. Why are we talking about her, anyway? It's not important."

"For you, maybe. It wasn't your gift. Imagine receiving a Christmas gift like that! I still remember my face getting hot and my hands trembling . . . "

"Let's not go through that . . ."

"There you go, cutting me off again. Why don't you ever let me finish?" Her head bounced up and down, punctuating every word like a pigeon picking at an earthworm. "The faded rose was double printed. I saw it hanging on the clothesline many times, so when I saw it in the box I knew it was the same one. Hers. Her old pair of *sarumata*."

"*Sarumata*? Is that what you called it, *sarumata*?" I asked.

"Sure, underpants. That's what they were called in Japanese. Everyone wore them in those days. I bet your mother wore them. We couldn't afford to buy underwear, so we sewed up old rice bag material. Waste not."

"I tell you, they were new pink panties."

"Oh, Tom, that was another Christmas, and those were the panties Irene gave me when she was ten years old. You remember that Christmas we all laughed because they were so big."

I could see by then, that Tom had decided to retreat. He closed his eyes and leaned back in his chair once more.

For some reason Betsy had invested this incident with extra meaning or it was actually full of meaning. The insult of giving a gift of a used article of clothing, especially of such a personal nature, is clear. But was there more to the gift? Tom's denial is easily understood.

"She was insulting me, don't you think? As a psychologist don't you think that was a hostile act? You know, maybe when it happened I didn't really understand, but I've been watching Oprah for years. I think there was more to the message than just the insult. At that time I thought, she thinks you're only worth an old pair of *sarumata*."

"Do you know why they were called *sarumata*, Betsy?" I asked.

"I don't know, that's just what they were called."

"Do you think it would help to know the meaning of the word?" I asked.

"What does it matter? You call something "underpants" or "panties" or "sarumata." Does it matter what word you use? Aren't we trying to find out why Tom and I can't get along? Why I'm so angry all the time?" she burst out as she glared at me.

A breakthrough. Never had she admitted that she was angry, "so angry all the time." Now we're getting somewhere, I thought. Press the advantage.

"Well, I never really studied Japanese, but I do know that the characters used to create words have meaning in themselves. I thought that perhaps your mother-in-law was conveying a meaning with *sarumata*. What do you know about the word?" I asked.

"I don't want to talk about the word," Betsy shouted. "We're not here to give you a Japanese lesson."

Betsy's explosive response took me aback, but Tom quickly intervened.

"Well, the Chinese characters are *saru* which means monkey and *mata* which means the crotch," Tom explained. "Does that help?"

I watched Betsy who, becoming more agitated, said, "That's what your mother wanted to tell me."

"What do you mean by that?" Tom asked bewildered.

"Monkey, monkey, monkey."

"That's not fair. My mother never called you a monkey," Tom said, his voice raised.

"She didn't have to. You understood. You always understood, though you never said anything. You knew I didn't like to be teased about that. You knew, and you never said anything."

Disheartened, Tom said, "I don't understand, Betsy."

"She'd always talk about how much hair I had on my arms and my legs. Of course, she seemed nice about it. But she really wanted to say, 'Go shave!' Like I should be ashamed," Betsy said, making a dull sound as her hand hit her chest. "You never told her to stop teasing me. She never had to say monkey; she just gave me a pair of *sarumata*. 'Monkey crotch.' It's even worse than I thought."

"Did you know about the meaning of the kanji?" Tom asked. They were silent for a time. "I never made the connection. Did you? *Sarumata* is *sa-rumata*. I just looked it up, after we started talking about it with Dr. Belli. If you didn't know the kanji characters, how could you have been insulted? How could you have known you were being called a monkey?"

"I got that old pair of *sarumata* for Christmas, remember?"

Tom threw his hands up in despair.

William Pascua
"MILES FROM NORMAL"

The rusty red car
Crunches up the driveway.
He's late since eight
When he said he'd be here.
We get in his car for a half-hour drive
All the way from Pearl City to Kalihi.
The garage stinks of a mix
Of Grandpa's Skoal and dead cats.
The floor in front of the door
Stained with tobacco spit.
The grout brown with dirt and Grandma's dogs
We sleep in my dad's room
The cleanest in the house
That he built with his own hands
Familiar old furniture from Ewa
Has found their way into his room.
Reminds me of when they were together.
Quality time and the weekend's too short.
The streetlight ride home
Takes us miles from Normal.

WILLIAM PASCUA *has been a student at the University Laboratory School in Honolulu since the eighth grade in 2003. He grew up in 'Ewa on O'ahu for most of his early years, but spent most of his time in Pearl City, attending Momilani Elementary School and Highlands Intermediate School. He enjoys listening to and playing music, watching R-rated movies, playing video games, and bowling with friends. He is always trying to find new ways to solve problems.*

Ida Yoshinaga
"UYESUGI GUMI: SONNETS FROM THE NON-SAMURAI SANSEI BOYS' CLUB"

Part I. Contingent Worker *Enka*

He was a quiet neighbor, a hard worker,
fixing his father's old 'Stang and
designing furniture on weekends.

We don't want to bother the family.
Besides, he seemed like such a nice
Japanese boy, collecting prize carp and
making his own fish tanks. But seven bodies,
expecting machine fixings, opened suddenly
to heaven in a boom-boom of reddened
office blossoms. *On Easy Street,* he'd said,
the shadows poked at my head all night.
Three men in one suburban house,
rifle collections, unspoken pain about work;
technical pride hides shame and fear.

Part II. Off the Yappie Track

Why wasn't I surprised? I had known
Byran Uyesugis all my life—that hapa-haole
Tanaka boy, who'd absorbed
too much counter-culture to be a dull
doctor, lawyer, or CPA. In college,
he'd DJ'd and cartooned, coked and toked,
phoned surprised friends to "share"
light bondage fantasies (including me).
We Young Asian Professionoids
gave him space, blank faces, pity.
His best friend's now an engineer,
but the wife—who oversees hotel PR
so wealthy tourists can golf glamorously—
says *Stay away, things have changed.*

Part III. The MUD Pack

Then there were my ex-boyfriend's friends—
quiet *sansei* guys great at electronics
and programming. Spoke more pidgin
than Standard, drank beer in parking lots
aftah work, 'cuz, shoots, you see da stahs.
They MUDded, gamed, played Magic cards.
The ones who knew real girls (not *animé* queens)
were petrified of being dumped . . . so they were.
Others seemed so shy, they could barely say
anything but *Yeah, but.* Then life'd shit on them,

they'd swarm a karaoke bar—this gang of
unshaven, greasy-haired, junk-food-ed, slightly
plump keyboard jocks–wearing their sharpest
collectible knives on the belt. *Betta watch out.*

Part IV. Why He Lives Mainland

He used to live Lehua tower, Hale Aloha,
amidst legions of *sansei* and *yonsei* boys
from Wailuku, Lihu'e, and Hilo, mid-'eighties.
He was a good dorm-mate, who sampled Coronas and weed
late-night with the guys, who counseled both sides
during breakups, who walked girls back from Sinclair after studies.
On breaks, he stayed O'ahu to save his folks airfare,
toured new Mililani, met roomies' classmates and family,
learned Honolulu townie. But it got to him—
who didn't like football so much as poetry,
who didn't call girls *chicks* and *bitches*, who read Doonesbury,
who painted like Pollock instead of frightening the "faggots"
by dumping trashcans of water in their rooms. After he grad,
he moved up to a city of museums. And never looked back.

Gary Pak

from CHILDREN OF A FIRELAND

T he last showing at old Kānewai Theater was to a crowd of two. The
movie playing was George Lucas's *The Empire Strikes Back*. Earlier in
the week, the first showing of the movie drew a crowd of twenty-three, and
each night thereafter the crowd diminished by half. It didn't help that the
movie was showing after premiering seven years earlier in a more posh theater one town over. And it didn't help the theater's turnstile that most of
the young folks of the community would rather hang out at the new bowling alley or the family billiards parlor than at the theater to see the latest
third-run movie. And, anyway, when there was a new movie to see, most
of the residents would make the trip to Honolulu and pay five dollars for
admission, more than three times what they would pay for a ticket at the
Kānewai Theater. The downtown theaters were always air-conditioned and

reasonably clean, though one thing that the Kānewai Theater had over its ultramodern rivals was its fresh popcorn. The old-timers always made the point that you couldn't get better-tasting popcorn than at the theater's concession, which made its own popcorn from scratch using a popper purchased secondhand from a renovated Savoy in Brooklyn. The uniquely good taste of the popcorn came from the touch of sesame oil and pulverized Hawaiian salt that were used to flavor the butter. And at fifty cents a bag, it was a bargain that was hard to pass up.

The old theater, the first on the windward side of the island, had seen better days. The doors had initially opened to the public in 1946. Those days the showings started on Thursday and ran to Tuesday, with matinees on the weekends at noon and 4:00 p.m. People from miles around came to the theater on horses and in buggies; and, later, with the popularization of the automobile, in cars. The walls of the building were constructed with crushed-coral hollow tile and its roof was covered with corrugated iron sheeting that was painted a metallic avocado green; when it rained, the projectionist had to turn up the volume so that people could hear over the drumming from above.

The original owner of the theater was Casey Akana, the only son of a prominent Chinese-Hawaiian family in Kānewai who had owned several sizable properties in Kānewai before the big earthquake. He had left the islands in the late thirties and went to a small liberal arts college in upper state New York. Dropping out during his third year following an unfortunate relationship with the son of the college president, he bought a one-way train ticket to New York City and joined a small off-Broadway company, getting bit parts in a few productions but being mainly the company's all-purpose techie. After seven years of living hand-to-hand and being frustrated professionally—at best, the only acting parts he could get were that of Oriental servants and the like—he began yearning for the country living in Kānewai and the life of leisure and dignity that he had taken for granted, being the son of rich parents. He returned home for good right before the war ended. Back in Kānewai and immediately missing the social life of New York, he cajoled and finally won over his mother to manipulate his father into liquidating a large portion of the family's land holdings. With this small fortune, he built a theater on a small leftover parcel in the middle of the town. In three years he was forced to sell out because poor management had turned the theater into a disastrously losing business.

The theater was bought by Wah Lau Ching, the autocratic family head who owned one of the two grocery stores in Kānewai. One son, Hennesey, was the town drunk and dunce, denounced by the senior Ching as "unworthy to be part of my family" (translation from the Cantonese). Early one

Sunday morning, while driving to Mass, Claudio Yoon saw him wading out on the mudflats, and that was the last time anyone in Kānewai ever saw him again. With the help of his other son Hiram, Mr. Ching began the renovation of the front of the theater, which Hiram finished after his father's death only three weeks into the project. Two small commercial store fronts were added; a carpet of deep carmine was laid in the lobby and aisles; and the exterior of the theater was repainted in a Kaiser pink, according to the wishes of Mr. Ching. One year and one day after his father's death, Hiram hired Paul Navarro to repaint the theater a light sienna. One of the store fronts became storage for the theater, and the other was rented to Mr. Pedro Rizon, a barber, who stayed in that location for forty-three years. Rizon gave the best scissors-cut this side of the Koʻolaus, and for twenty-seven years no one could find a better bargain than his fifty-cent haircut.

The last showing was announced in a one-by-two-inch ad in the local daily. Nobody in the community seemed to care, for the theater had lost its purpose, which was to provide the source of Hollywood entertainment in town, years before. For every household now had at least one television with a VCR and almost all subscribed to some form of cable TV service. And, if anyone wanted to see the latest movie, all that it took was a trip to Honolulu, an excellent excuse for a family to go holoholo.

Three months before the announcement, negotiations were fast being finalized by the Ching family with a fast-food corporation based in Carson City, Nevada—Mama Mason's Country Fried Chicken & Tacos. There were already three franchises in Honolulu and another on a neighbor island, and this would be the first one on the windward side. The Chings had given Mama Mason a twenty-five-year lease, which would give them a gross income of $3.6 million. The plans called for the tearing down of the ancient structure one month after the last showing and the start of construction shortly after. Everything seemed to be on schedule until the signs started coming up on the side of the theater, one week after the theater officially closed its doors.

No one knew who was spraypainting the graffiti, and everyone wanted to know. The signs started innocently enough. The first graffiti was a large red heart with the words "Richard 'n Cindy" inside. People smiled or laughed at the sign, for they knew that the names were for Richard Cordeiro and Cynthia Naelehu, who later became Cynthia Cordeiro. There followed others—"Katie 'n Norton," "Lance 'n Lily," "Harry 'n Amy"—who were all legitimately paired off. Everyone thought it was a big joke, someone playing a nostalgic prank using the side of the condemned theater, which had once been the social gathering spot for the entire community. But it became disturbing when other messages started showing up on the wall, like "Charley

McKinley's father is not his real father," and "Bobby Kim 'n Sandy Wakashi-da" (who were both happily married, but not to each other), and "Matilda Nunes got pregnant in Row 37" (whose only child, Jason, was told that his father had died in Vietnam), and so on.

"I t'ink is da humbug boy doing all dis," said George Hayashida, referring to Kalani Humphrey, the community bad boy.

"How can?" his wife, Joyce, remarked. She cracked two eggs in the hot cast-iron frying pan. George liked his eggs with the yolks intact and the whites just turning solid around them. "He in jail."

"But den mus' be one of his friends coming 'round and putting up dose signs, making trouble. Maybe he wen go visit da bastard in jail and da bastard wen tell him put up dose kine stupid signs, fo' make trouble fo' everybody, like he always doing."

Joyce Hayashida shrugged her shoulders, though nodding her head in tentative agreement. No one could pass any fair judgment on Kalani Humphrey. He had earned his notoriety by ripping off almost every other household in the community. He had knocked up at least a half dozen maidens of the town. He even stole twenty dollars from his great-grandfather's coin purse when he was eight years old, though he didn't know that the old blind man was a relation. Nobody liked Kalani Humphrey, and whenever something went wrong in Kānewai, it seemed that somehow Kalani Humphrey was connected to it.

"But you know," Joyce Hayashida reflected, "he been in prison fo' t'ree years already. I dunno if he wen do 'em."

"If I say he did it, then he did it," George growled. He gave an extra stir to his coffee. "I know he did it. If he nevah do it, den wouldn't have no mo' stupid signs like on da side like dat."

Joyce shook her head, her lips pursed. It wasn't worth arguing with her husband. Let him think he always right, she thought. Then she broke the egg yolks and turned off the stove.

When Hiram Ching and a representative of Trinity Corporation, the mother company of Mama Mason's Country Fried Chicken & Tacos, went to inspect the premises early one morning, they could not get in. A six-foot-high pile of garbage was pressed against the front glass doors from the inside. Hiram Ching went to the back to unlock the door, but this door, too, would not budge.

"Damn vandals," he quipped to Mr. Henderson, the representative of Trinity.

"Do you have problems like this all the time?" Henderson looked a bit worried.

"No–no–no–no," Hiram rattled off. "This the first time. Kānewai is one peaceful town. We cleaned up our act long time ago. All the bad elements either left town or in jail right now." For a moment he thought of Kalani Humphrey. He shook his head, thinking how stupid he had been to hire the Humphrey boy as an usher a few years back; the boy had scammed him by taking in kids for half the price and pocketing the rest of the money.

"Is there any other way into the building?" an irritated Henderson asked.

"Yeah-yeah. Let me think." Hiram tried the back door again, then sighed and led Henderson to the side of the building, where there were two windows, one for the women's restroom and the other for the men's.

"What's all this?" Henderson asked, referring to the graffiti-covered walls.

"Ahh . . . just some of the young punks around here. They don't have anything else to do."

"Do you have problems with graffiti? I thought you said you didn't have problems with vandals?"

"No, not really."

"Then what's all this?"

"Must be the work of outsiders coming in. This the only time we been getting this. Like I told you, this community is real quiet and peaceful."

The window to the women's restroom was ajar. Hiram placed an empty wooden box under the window of the men's restroom, which was locked shut, and stepped up on the box. He slipped one of his keys under the lower edge of the window and ran it to the middle to find the lock.

"What are you doing?" Henderson asked, looking at the other, open window.

"I'm going inside," Hiram answered, thinking to himself how stupid the haole was, though he didn't think it necessary to explain that it was improper to enter the building through the women's side.

"But . . . "

Before Henderson could verbalize his thought, the lock popped free. Hiram pried the window open with his fingertips, then wiggled his pear-shaped body through the opening and climbed in, balancing on a narrow ledge inside the window. Catching his breath for a few seconds, he stepped down from the ledge, misnegotiated a shadow as a foothold, and fell to the concrete floor. But it was a small fall, and no physical damage was done.

"Come inside," Hiram puffed, picking himself up from the floor and dusting off his jacket.

"Why don't you open the back door for me?"

Hiram muttered an "Okay," but not without feeling like a guinea pig. He shook off the remaining dust and dirt from his pants, picked up the pen and bits of paper notes that had fallen out of his shirt pocket, then proceeded to the auditorium. He passed the entrance to the women's restroom with a touch of apprehension, for though he never personally saw or experienced it, he was very aware of the many stories about a milk-white, faceless apparition that appeared behind the backs of women touching up their makeup in the mirror. It became a common practice for them to use the restroom in pairs. Hiram's hands became sweaty and his heart skipped a beat. No, there's no ghost here, he reasoned to himself, but that couldn't settle the skin crawling on the back of his neck.

In the semi-darkness, he felt his way along the hallway to the switch box and turned on the interior lights, then entered the auditorium, where his nostrils were smacked with the awful odor of cheap perfume. It was as if someone had dumped an entire bottle right in the middle of the room. He swore loudly at the vandals whom he was sure had broken into the theater and committed this foul-smelling play. Later in the afternoon, he told himself, he'd see Val Rodriguez, slip him a twenty, and ask him to visit the pool hall and find out who among the punks did it. Then he'd slip Val another twenty, and Val would know what to do with those bums. Hiram nodded and smiled in selfish glee as he visualized Val busting their heads.

But he stopped in the middle of an upbeat of an assuring nod. Slashed in bright red paint on the baseboard of the movie screen was a message in large, bold letters: "KALANI HUMPHREY WENT SLEEP WITH CLARISSA IN THE LADY'S BATHROOM."

For a moment, he actually had some doubts about his wife, but he shook off his uncertainty and cursed at the ridiculous fiction of the punks.

Henderson was pounding at the back door.

Hiram rushed to the janitor's closet and took out a bottle of cleaning fluid and raced back to the sign. But no matter how hard he scoured, the paint wouldn't rub off. Henderson was now pounding and shouting for Hiram to open up. Hiram hoofed it to the front office and brought back a fresh gallon of paint. Using an old mop, he sloshed the paint over the graffiti, then hid the paint and mop in the janitor's closet. He hurried to the back door, which had been latched from the inside, and let Henderson in.

"How come it took you so long?" Henderson asked, scanning the dim interior for clues.

"Oh, I had to do something."

"I hope you didn't start painting the interior," the representative of Trinity Corporation commented, noticing a splash of paint on Ching's right hand. "Smells like fresh paint in here."

Ching thought quickly, rubbing off some of the paint on his hand on a wall. "Ah—the stupid janitor—he was painting the wall and he never tell me about the wet paint." He laughed and before Henderson could pry more said, "Tell me, why you want to look inside the building for anyway?" He wished he had thought of the question earlier.

"Well," an observing Henderson began as they entered the auditorium, "my company thought that we might keep the existing structure if it was unique in design, but . . . " He turned to the stage and regarded the ratty drapery for a moment. "But from the looks of what I've seen so far, this building is just four tile walls and an old rusty roof. I think our best bet is to tear it down, rather than renovate an old junk building."

Ching nodded his head, then led the representative of Trinity on a short tour of the projection room.

The graffiti on the outside walls continued, becoming progressively more scandalous.

"HARRY AND ELLA HAVE NOT DONE IT IN EIGHT AND A HALF YEARS."

"PAUL NAVARRO AND CASSIE CHUN USED TO MEET EVERY THURSDAY IN ROW FOR-TY-FOUR." (Thursday nights were Pat Navarro's night for blackjack with her friends; her husband was a member of the Thursday Night Jackpot Bowling League.)

"WHERE IS DICKEY BOY JR.?"

"I think I going down there and burn da friggin' building down," Richard Pimente said to his wife Jackie, setting down the Saturday morning paper on the breakfast table. He had browsed over the baseball box scores without paying attention to whether his favorite teams had won or not. "Is one real eye sore. All dat graffiti on da side wall."

"Why you so concerned about all that?" Jackie said. She stirred the cream into her third cup of coffee. "You never was before. Did you tell Darren and Micah that breakfast is ready?"

"Yeah, but is different now."

"What is different?"

"Because—because—" He reopened the newspaper, searching for a good excuse. "Because how da hell Ching going sell da property to da Mama Mason outfit if get all dis kine vandalism all over da building?"

"Ching already signed it over to the restaurant. And anyway, since when you started getting cozy with Ching? I thought you hated his guts. Eh, where are those kids? Playing Nintendo so early in the morning? Did you call them for breakfast?"

"No. But I jus' no can stand dat sneaky old pake," said the former high-school star lineman. He shook his head, set the newspaper to the side, and sipped his coffee.

Years before marrying Ching, Clarissa Lee had been Richard Pimente's sweetheart, though Clarissa's parents disproved of him. And when Clarissa, the head song leader of the Wilson High School Warriors, had to leave school three months before graduating, Hiram Ching, twelve years her senior, agreed to marry her, but with the ironclad stipulation that the baby had to be put up for adoption.

The couple was silent for a minute, Richard going back to his newspaper and Jackie staring into space.

"Honey, who you think is putting up all those signs?" Jackie asked.

Richard put down his newspaper. "You asking me? I dunno. But I sure as hell would like to know. I string da buggah up so fast if I find out, faster den he can say 'I nevah do it.'"

It pained Clarissa Ching to hear rumors about how bad her son was. She knew he wasn't born a bad egg. It just wasn't fair that everyone in the community had written him off even when he was just a little boy. And it pained her more that it had been impossible for her to take care of him when he needed it the most. She had seen how the Humphreys, that childless, elderly haole couple, schoolteachers for many years at Wilson High, were not suited to the raising of children. They were too strict; they refused to feed him when he was bad; and they punished him severely when he peed in his bed. Their abusive tendencies were so widely known that Father Rosehill from the Catholic parish had visited them at least twice, even though the Humphreys were Congregationalists, and pleaded them to be more tolerant of their son's hyperactivity. And through this all, Clarissa was unable to come to her son's rescue, for the agreement that had been made was the Humphreys would adopt the baby only if Clarissa never exposed herself as the boy's true mother. Though she hated the Humphreys and herself for making that promise, Clarissa was a woman of her word, and this hurt her terribly.

"You know, all dis is very, very strange," Matt Goo was saying to Freddie Tanaka at Freddie's service station, which was just a traffic light down from the theater. The two men were sitting on the removed back seat of a '69 Dodge Dart set in the front of the station. Freddie was listening with his short, hairy arms folded, the fingers of his right hand rubbing the left elbow. "You know, all dis business dey putting da blame on Kalani Humphrey. I tell you fo' one plain fact, da Humphrey boy is in jail. And one nada fact—"

"Try wait," Freddie Tanaka interrupted, unfolding his arms. "I get one customer." Freddie went out to the pumps and filled up the gas tank of a tourist car. Upon returning, he said, "What you was saying again?"

"I dunno. What I was saying?"

"About da Humphrey boy. You think he not da one who doing all dis."

"Yeah. I no think he doing all dis. How can? Fo' one, he in jail. And fo' one nada fact, how he know all dis stuff he putting up on da wall?"

Freddie nodded his head in agreement. He chased a fly off his arm. "Then who you think da buggah doing all dis, then?" Freddie asked.

Matt sipped a can of soda. "I dunno. Maybe is da ghost haunting da moviehouse."

Freddie switched his rubbing to the other elbow. "Could be," he said.

It was a well known fact that a ghost—or something—was or had been living in the theater. The old-timers pointed to the fact that the theater had been foolishly constructed next to an ancient Hawaiian pathway to a heiau. Some said that the ghost was the spirit of Casey Akana, coming back to haunt Hiram Ching, whose father had bankrupted him and thus forced him to sell the theater at a loss.

"If I was Ching," Matt said, "I wouldn't knock down da building."

"Why?"

"'Cause if I was him, I no like die."

"Whachu mean?"

Matt Goo shook his head slowly. "If he break down the building, maybe da ghost might . . . " Matt didn't have to finish the sentence; Freddie was nodding his head in agreement. Then he got up with the arrival of another tourist car.

It was becoming a community habit—or rather, passion—to visit the theater's wall on a daily basis. It was becoming, for many of the residents, a kind of daily bulletin board of gossip. For every day—no miss—a new quip of scandal would be painted on the wall. It was becoming customary to drive by there, even if it was out of the way, to see the latest news of the unexpected. And it was becoming acerbically amusing for the others to witness what the backstabbing messages were doing to the marital stability of those individuals selected as targets, though deep down inside each and every resident who had not as yet been elected for representation was the fear that perhaps the next time around his or her name might grace the wall.

A small group from the bowling league became so concerned with the lambasting that they decided to organize a twenty-four-hour vigil at the theater. Their stated intention was to catch the vandals, because "all they want to do is make trouble fo' our town." Of course, the real reason behind the forming of the group was to contain any further disruption that would threaten the stability of their organization. One of their own, Paul Navarro, had been exposed. It would be only a matter of time, if this was allowed to continue, that the unstated purpose of the group for a significant minority of its members—that of providing an alibi for their extramarital activities—would be exposed.

So they organized an around-the-clock watch one weekend, divided into four-hour shifts, with the robust determination to nab the troublemaking sign-maker. Tiny Vierra, all 267 pounds of him, pulled the first evening shift on the Friday, from 6:00 to 10:00, sitting in the darkness of his parked pickup across the street from the wall. And everything went well during Claudio Yoon's 10:00 p.m. to 2:00 a.m. slot; the watch was as quiet as the man himself. (As a fine example of the group, Claudio was not the cheating type. To be exact, he had no one to cheat on.) And things were going routine for Henry Kila—up to the time he dozed off for a few minutes, an hour before the end of his shift. Quintin Lee arrived for his shift forty-five minutes early to talk story with his good friend, bringing along fast-food breakfast and coffee, and noticed Henry snoring and a freshly painted sign gleaming and dripping from the wall. Silently he read the sign, then began laughing loudly, then cursing after dropping one extra large coffee (he had bought four) on his foot. Henry was wakened by Quintin's painful, unholy deprecations to the gods of defecation and jumped to attention. The off-duty firefighter habitually grabbed for his pants and boots before realizing where he was.

"Whas so funny," a dopey Henry asked, scratching his head, "and whas wit' da racket? Gimme one coffee."

"I thought you was supposed to be watching da place?"

"So I wen nod out fo' couple minutes. So what?"

"Couple minutes?! Couple minutes is couple minutes, brah. Couple minutes was enough fo' dis. Look." Quintin pointed to the new sign and began laughing.

Henry read the sign out loud. "HIRAM CHING JAGS OFF IN HIS OFFICE WITH HIS DIRTY BOOKS." A smile came to Henry's chunky face and he laughed guardedly with Quintin. Then he was quiet. A concerned look came to his face, and he aspirated a sour "Shit."

"Whas dah mattah?" Quintin asked.

"Eh, brah. Dis sign gotta come down. Right now. Dis sign no mo'. . . taste."

"Hah? Whas wrong wit' dis?"

Henry shuffled his feet. He looked up at the sign, the whites of his eyes reddened and wide and begging with a simple innocence. "Stuff like dis . . . is private. No man in his right mind wants da world to know he whacking off on da side."

"But everybody jag off. Whas so secret 'bout dis?"

"Dis not moral, not in good taste."

Quintin looked hard at Henry, who was now regarding the sign with a strained expression, as if he was becoming more and more emotionally attached to it. Quintin was about to say something about the morality of Henry's extramarital activities since the birth of his third daughter, but decided against it. It wasn't the time and place to argue with a disturbed Henry Kila, who was known for his slow-burning fuse and a fist that could break burning bricks in half. "Yeah, maybe you right," Quintin conceded. "But what we going do?"

Henry silently went to the wall and touched the fresh paint with a fingertip, then sniffed the tainted finger. "Oil paint," he said to no one. "Who use oil-base in dis day and age?"

Quintin touched and smelled, too. "Smell like old paint."

"And da buggah use da same kine all over." Henry scanned the wall of graffiti.

"At least da buggah wen spell da names right." Quintin broke into a laughter that was quickly suppressed when Henry suggested what they must do. "What?" Quintin protested. "How da hell we going do dat? Da sun coming up already."

"Den we gotta work fast. Go call Dennis come down with da stepladder. And Val. Tell him bring some oil paint and brush. You go home and get what you get. Me . . . I stay down here and try cover up." Henry was already trying to smear the tacky paint with his hands, though the paint was already being absorbed into the pores of the wall.

Within a half hour, the gang was repainting the wall, covering all the graffiti. It took them an hour to paint over every bit. But somehow, the most recent message had already leaked out of their circle and had spread through the community grapevine, and a good laugh, as well as a singular degree of pathos, was had by most of the community.

Henry's spontaneous plan to vanquish all the graffiti didn't last too long. Approximately twenty-four hours later, during Dennis Umeda's shift, the signmaker broke through Dennis's watchdog defense. So jolting to Dennis was the content of the message (now painted in black on white) that he thought he was going to have a heart attack. When he recovered from the shock and the heartburn, he limped off to the pay telephone across the street and called Watson Kamei, who was to relieve him. "Come down now," Dennis said tersely.

"But it only five o'clock," Watson whined, yawning in the phone. "I still get one hour mo'."

"Come down now," Dennis demanded, then hung up.

He waited at the phone booth until he saw Watson's monstrous black four-wheeler trundle to a stop next to his Toyota. Watson had his engine on for nearly a full minute, the headlights of the truck switched to high, lighting up the wall. Finally, he killed the engine and got out. Dennis called from the booth, and Watson crossed the street.

"Whas da meaning of dat?" Watson whispered. "Who did dat?"

"You . . . asking me?"

"You wen fall asleep, too?"

Dennis shook his head. Watson noticed the slight trembling of Dennis's hand, which was still clutching the hung receiver.

"Nah, all dis gotta be part of one big fucking joke," Watson said, smiling as wide as his sleep-stiffened cheeks could give.

Dennis nodded his head. "But what should we do?" Watson stuffed his hands all the way in the pockets of his blue jeans, rubbing the sides of his testicles. "We gotta go paint 'em over. Das what we gotta do."

Dennis agreed. But before they could cross the street, a sleek white car whizzed by, slowing to check the bulletin board. Though it was moonless and the incandescent light from the streetlamp feeble, the message was brazened by the bleak whiteness of the freshly painted wall: "HIRAM CHING IS TO DIE." The car stopped, its radiating brake lights gripping the mute, watching men, then sped away.

"Who—dat?" Watson gasped after realizing that he had momentarily stopped breathing. They crossed the street. "You saw who . . . was dat?"

"Was Clarissa Ching," Dennis said. Then he jumped in his car and drove off.

Sue Cowing

"AT THE HONOLULU AQUARIUM, WITH CAMERA"

I frame the outdoor tide-pool exhibit
in my finder. Who would know
this rush and backwater over reef rock
is simulated? Instead, I shoot the sign
over the Hawaiian monk seal's pool, warning me
to keep my body parts behind the rail.

Zoos and aquaria yank species from the brink
to mate in tanks and cages.
                              Ships aren't arks anymore,
Their invisible nets trail wakes of silence.
Last Saturday, customs men boarded the *Bum Dong*
looking for drugs, found ordinary cooking oil
in the hold. But in the living areas,

eight sea turtles, stuffed, and eleven hundred blooms
of Philippine coral. Almost five tons.

Down the hall, the Reef Machine, complete
with charcoal filters, plastic pipes, fresh-water pumps,
shows us how reefs really work. Reminds me
of health class, when we were to think of our body
as a car whose engine needed regular maintenance
to stay tuned. Fathers respond to this. I snapped one
telling his son, "The reef purifies the water
for the animals, sort of like a kidney."
We do try to get closer to this other world,
naming its animals for our familiars.
Sea-horse we say, or Lemon Peel Butterfly,
Hogfish, Frogfish, Five-horned Cowfish,
Fiji Fox Face, Convict King.

The Day Octopus is always flattening himself,
falling again for the illusion of glass,
propelling backwards with all eight arms behind
like a long banner, smack into one wall
of this four-by-one-by-two-foot tank.
His sac-like body looks instead
like a scrotum or a large, soft, comic nose.
At the end of each arm, a permanent tendril curl.
These arms are never still. He pulls his silk sleeves in
and out of themselves, shakes out his scarves
as though in a light wind.

Today, instead of taking refuge at the back,
the octopus dances in the window of his tank.
His audience, a shirtless surfer with wind-burnt hair,
has kicked his slippers off and kneels
at soft attention close to the glass.
Each time the octopus unfurls an arm and flourishes it,
the surfer chuckles, whispering *tako, tako,*
traces the movement gently along the glass.

If you could say what goes on in any one
of his three hearts, the octopus delights in this.
The movements of the two
grow slower and more intricate.

No lovers' stroking could be more tender.
I hesitate, then slip on a close-up lens
and steal this shot.
                    What won't come out on film
is the second after the click, when first the surfer,
then the octopus, turns stone red.

Tony Quagliano
"POETRY ON THE BUS"

on Diamond Head, the morning rain
has started
swept leeward by the daily trades
which certainly will later sweep
across this rock
some blue and white amazing sky

Michael Ondaatje
UNTITLED

Tell me
all you know
about bamboo

growing wild, green
growing up into soft arches
in the temple ground
the traditions
driven through hands
through the heart
during torture

and most of all

this

Diamond ~~Dimond~~ Head Hike

Diamond
~~Dimond~~ Head, I went on the

~~hike~~, I see ~~saw~~ the ocean crashing
against ~~rus~~ rough
~~gins~~ rocks. The green plants on the

hillside grow high. I hear
chirping
birds ~~criping~~ loudly. I feel the

wind whipping my hair behind

me as I hike up the ~~Dimond Hea~~
excitement
stairs. I shiver as my ~~excitment~~
through   have reached
goes ~~though~~ my spine. as I ~~ta~~
of
~~hike the~~ Dimond Head!~~stairs~~

Courtesy of Emily Pasch

small bamboo pipe
not quite horizontal
that drips
every ten seconds
to a shallow bowl

I love this
being here
not a word
just the faint
fall of liquid
the boom of an iron buddhist bell
in the heart rapid
as ceremonial bamboo

Emily Pasch

"THE DIAMOND HEAD HIKE"

Diamond Head!
I see the ocean
crashing against rough rocks.
The green plants on
the hillside grow high.
I hear birds chirping loudly.
I feel the wind whipping
my hair behind me
as I hike up the stairs.
I shiver as my excitement goes
through my spine.
I have reached the top of
Diamond Head!

EMILY ANN PASCH *was born on August 9, 1999 in Irvine, California. At age four, she and her parents moved to Hawaii, where her father is stationed with the Marine Corps. Emily attends Kāne'ohe Elementary School, on O'ahu. She enjoys playing soccer, collecting Webkinz, and reading. Her favorite series is the Animal Ark books, especially the stories about horses. Someday she would like to have her own horse.*

Lee Hartman

"MUSEUM TOUR: HONOLULU ACADEMY OF ARTS"

I

(Bridge at Uji, 17th Century)

In the Japanese room
we crossed the bridge
from one painted screen
to the next: a kind of
an extension of hands.

II

(The Gion Festival in Kyoto
with Scenes of Temples and
Shops in and around the City,
ca. 1600)

In the Chinese room
we entered crowded cities
and finding any city too crowded
for our desires, we tasted
the brightness of yellow cups.

III

(European Room: Two Nudes
on a Tahitian Beach, 1892)

Gauguin's two nudes:
like looking in a mirror
of dark blues and white crests
the two nudes are us.

IV

(Wai Aniani—Transparent
Colors, 1975)
In the prism of the Modern Gallery

of European and American Art
in a maze of
cool lucite beams
our eyes refracted
orange, purple, red and green;
while you enjoyed the vertigo
I strummed the nearest tall
steel bass which seemed to sing:
"gently you may touch" (alas).

V

(Outer Garden: Red Untitled,
1965-1966)

By Noguchi's carved out oval wall
pink and sanded to a smooth
I found you through the oval
surprised and happy in this first intercourse.

LEE HARTMAN *lives in Upperco, Maryland, and teaches creative writing and literature at Howard Community College. He dedicates his poem to the memory of John Unterecker, writer, scholar, and former professor at the University of Hawai'i at Mānoa, and the director of the National Endowment for the Humanities fellowship course of study that provided the author the occasion for this poem.*

Susan Heroy

"LE CHINOIS, HONOLULU"

Inside the gallery, cool and quiet
and redolent of musk, the head

of a Chinese man glows in the shadows
as if taking light into itself.

This black metal, lambent as silk,
pulls me inside even on mornings

the whole island seems to float
in mist. I touch the temples,

amazed each time that the metal can be so soft,
soft as fingers that rubbed it

a hundred years ago with wax.
Think of a head on a stake, fetid and blown,

while the compacted atoms of this face
balance forever on a bone-white pillar.

When I leave, someone will take my place.
Perhaps a woman with a cord

of kukui nuts, warm and brown
as snake eggs, around her neck.

Sherman Souther

"BUFFO NIGHTS"

The mannequin with alabaster breasts and a
plumeria lei stands over the aromas of dark
coffees and words as a boy who would be a
surgeon translates a gilt-edged text undisturbed by warped covers; " . . . here in certain
seasons, toxic toads ohm from lotus-lined
ponds, their parotid secretions place dogs at
risk and . . . " Across the table the student of law
covers the holes in her stockings with layers of
undergarments, the skin of her back soft from
the scents and sounds.

SHERMAN SOUTHER, *born in 1941, is a physician and writer who has made Honolulu his home several times during the past thirty-five years.*

Michael LaGory

"DOUBLE RONDEAU"

Round and round at the Lollipop,
Put it on to let it drop;
  Doff and don; clasp, unhitch;
  A penny a tingle, a nickel an itch;
Lace by nylon, peel, unprop.

The record turns without a stop;
About the brims the bubbles pop;
  Pinballs spin as slots grow rich
    Round and round.

Sweets in a dancing candy shop
Bob and dangle, hip by hop;
  From stage to stage the dancers switch,
  The men forgetting which is which,
The whole room spinning like a top
    Round and round.
Round and round to appetize
The thirsty throat, the circling eyes,
  The glance steel-cupped as an ice cream scoop
  That follows a loll and ponders a droop,
The palm that moistens, the calm that lies

In silvered bankers, shorn GIs;
Table after table buys,
  At two bits a holler, a dollar a whoop,
    Round and round,

The cocktail wets, the dancer dries;
Off and on, the same disguise;
  In and out the door men troop;
  From stage to stage the ladies loop:
A room of clocks that synchronize
    Round and round.

MICHAEL LAGORY *was born in 1954, in Maryland. He has lived in Hawai'i since 1957. He teaches English at 'Iolani School in Honolulu.*

Nora Okja Keller

from FOX GIRL

"C oca-Cola," she said to the stewardess, peering at the drinks in the cart. "7 UP. Orange juice. And that—" she added, pointing to a slender red-and-white can.

"Bloody Mary Mix." The stewardess filled a plastic cup with ice and soda and another with thick red juice that Sookie refused to touch. Leaning over me and Myu Myu, she lined them up on Sookie's tray. When she noticed Sookie eyeing her cart again, she turned away and pushed it farther up the aisle.

I opened the bag of nuts and chewed one up. Spitting it out, I placed it on Myu's tongue. She wrinkled her face and gagged. Crushed peanuts came out in a long stream of drool, which I tried to catch in the small square of napkin the stewardess had handed out.

"Disgusting." Sookie shuddered, adjusted the earphones, and turned her face to the window.

The smell of peanuts made my stomach lurch. After fumbling with the seat belt, I managed to unbuckle myself and stumble into the aisle. With Myu Myu on my shoulder, I made my way to the back of the plane. Behind the line of people waiting for the toilet, I paused, noticing the rear exit door. I stepped up to the small window, skimming the emergency release handle with my fingers. For a moment, my hand tightened with the urge to pull down, to open up, to float into that endless dream of blue and white, suspended between heaven and earth. I exhaled, fogging the glass with a cloud of breath, and forced myself to step away.

We filed off the plane like cattle, jostled into lines for processing. Our passports stamped, we shuffled through a corridor toward a glass door. A pack of people pressed close to a doorway that opened and closed as passengers neared it. Peering in, their faces eager, anxious, they waited. A woman behind me cried out and pushed past me, through the doors that parted like water, and into the arms of someone who could have been her sister, or mother, someone who loved her. Travelers were claimed, enveloped in garlands of flowers, their bags taken by other hands. Yoon was there to claim Sookie and me. Her eyes widened, then narrowed on the baby I carried. "What the fuck?" she squawked, pinching me in the ribs when she pretended to embrace me. But she pasted a smile on her face as we passed the airport security.

"This way." She took my arm, her nails digging into my flesh.

I gritted my teeth, forcing a smile as well.

Sookie sauntered up to the airport guard. "We so excited to visit this, the beautiful state of Hawai'i," Sookie said, rattling on in English as the guard, startled at her approach, stared at her. "I plan to feed fish at Hanauma Bay, climb Diamond Head, see Pearl Harbor. And, of course, shop, shop, shop at Ala Moana Center."

Yoon turned on Sookie. "Shut up," she said, shaking her arm. "There's no official here."

Sookie pouted. "But I wanted to give my speech. I thought I would be asked questions; all they did was stamp here, stamp there. I memorized for nothing."

Yoon shook her head and stomped away.

I looked at Sookie. She grinned and winked. We scrambled to keep up with Yoon's militant strides.

"And you," Yoon hissed at me. "I don't know what game you're playing. How could you bring that . . . that child. You don't know how much trouble they cause—food, clothing, rent, school, doctors. It'll be a big problem."

"I'll pay," I said grimly.

"I'll make sure you do."

Sliding doors opened and we stepped into sunlight, raw and bright. Bursts of color shot across my lids when I blinked. My eyes felt heavy, but I forced them open, wide as I could. I had expected to see the ocean, trees loaded with flowers, hula dancers. What I saw was gray asphalt that steamed with heat, concrete blocks and red dirt, chicken wire and tractors.

"Construction," Yoon said, leading us into a fenced parking lot. "America is always getting better." She stopped in front of a long blue car. "Nice, isn't it," she boasted. "Cadillac."

"Cad-o-lac," I repeated, liking the way the word slid across my tongue. I liked as well the seats, soft and sleek, like the fur of a cat. I never before felt material soft as a baby's skin.

We fell silent during the ride, Sookie and I looking out the windows. Myu Myu played with a button on the door that made my window whir down and up. Each time the window slid down, the blaring noise of tires blasted in with hot air. Yoon grumbled and pushed a lever on her door that paralyzed my window. Houses, fat and white as lice eggs, dotted the dry, brown hills that rose above us; below, sprawled under the archway of traffic, squatted a series of buildings with laundry strung out on the balconies.

"This is U.S.?" Sookie whispered to me. "This is Hawai'i? Looks like another America Town to me."

Yoon heard and said, "This is America, not America Town. Here, without me, you're nothing. You could disappear, you could die, and no one would know. Officially, you don't exist."

"What's new?" I said bitterly.

"What's new is me." Yoon braked at a light and looked at us over her shoulder. "Listen to me, do as I say, and we can all make a lot of money." "If I can get a car like this," Sookie said, "I'm in."

Lips tight, Yoon smiled. "You're in already—for about fifteen hundred, American. That's the beginning of what you owe me. But don't worry," she added in supposed encouragement.

"Work hard and in another ten, fifteen years, you could have what I have." She turned and pressed the gas. The Cadillac lurched forward.

After turning down several narrow lanes, we pulled to the curb alongside a squat two-story building. Its brown paint was chipped in places, revealing the concrete block walls underneath. Yoon unfolded herself from the car, adjusted her skirt, and motioned us to follow her.

Reaching the door at the end of the walkway, Yoon inserted a key in the lock and pushed. Something blocked her way. Yoon placed her shoulder against the door and pushed harder.

"Hey, hey!" a voice called from inside. "Wait just a minute, will you?"

Giving suddenly, the door swung open onto a darkened room. Yoon flicked on the light and snorted in disgust. "It's past noon," she said.

Sookie and I crowded against Yoon in the only open space in the apartment, the floor of which was covered wall to wall with futons. Most of the sleeping mats were occupied by girls. The girl who answered the door rubbed the sleep from her eyes. "Mrs. Yoon," she gasped, stretching her large T-shirt over her knees. "We didn't expect you."

"I told Lulu I was coming with two new girls," Yoon griped, eyes flicking over the sleeping bodies.

The girl said, "Lulu never came home last night." The girl spoke to Yoon, but spotting Myu Myu, couldn't stop staring. When her eyes jumped to my face she screamed: "*Aiigu!*" Yoon pursed her lips. "She didn't go home with one of my customers, did she?"

The girl shook her head, forcing her eyes back to Yoon. "No, no. She went to see a girlfriend, and then, and then went to get doughnuts."

Yoon exhaled, long and slow, and eyed the girl. "That's . . . nice," she said. "I don't like it when one of my girls breaks my rules about socializing outside the club."

The girl bobbed her head, offered a hesitant smile.

"And I don't like it when my girls lie to me."

The girl's smile fell. She glanced around the room, then gestured to one corner, where there was a sink and a small refrigerator. "Can I make you some tea? Coffee?" she asked, keeping her head down.

"No, thanks, Chinke." Yoon wrinkled her nose. "I'll just leave the new girls with you," she said, backing out the door. "Fix up that ugly one as much as you can and bring them to the club early."

When the door shut behind us, Sookie and I followed the girl Yoon called Chinke, stepping over the bodies, to the kitchen area. Chinke poked at the girls sprawled in front of the sink and refrigerator. "Get up," she said to them, "we need this space."

"I heard," moaned one, without opening her eyes. "I just didn't want to get up and face Yoon."

"What's she thinking," the other yawned, "bringing in more girls, packing us in like Vienna sausages?" This girl sat up, quickly folding her blankets and futon, then glanced up. "I'm Minnie—holy shit. You are fucked up! Double fucked," she giggled, "your face and a baby!"

I hugged Myu to my chest, letting the curtain of my hair fall across our faces. Myu grabbed a handful of hair and twisted it in her fist. Eyes watering, I struggled to loosen her grip.

The girl next to Minnie sat up. She looked into and away from my face, too polite to comment. Instead she held up her arms and waved both hands. "Here, let me hold her," she urged. "I left two of these at home."

As I leaned past Sookie to hand over Myu Myu, Sookie looked at Chinke. "You from China?" she asked. "That why they call you Chinke?"

Chinke narrowed her small eyes. "No," she said.

"We just call her that because of her eyes." The girl laughed and, balancing Myu in her lap, pulled her eyes into thin slits.

"Shut your rubber-lip mouth, Froggie," Chinke shot back. "We call her Froggie because of her big mouth."

A girl lying on a mat in the back of the room near the bathroom called out: "No, we call her Froggie because when she drinks too much beer, she begins to belch like a love-sick bullfrog!" The girl let out a long burp.

Chinke laughed with the other girls, Froggie included, and opened a cabinet to pull out a teapot. "I bet Yoon shit when she saw the baby."

I shrugged, trying to hide my nervousness. "Yoon said it was my problem."

"My turn to hold the toy," Minnie said, stroking Myu Myu on the back.

"Just be sure it doesn't become Yoon's problem," Chinke said. "You won't like the way she deals with problems."

Sookie eyed the crowded room. "Where do we unpack?" she asked.

Froggie jumped up, leaving her sleeping mat in the middle of the kitchen space. "Here," she said, hopping over a girl behind her. "Next to Ari." She prodded Ari to scoot over. "You're going to have to get your own futon and blankets. You have cash?" She rattled on without waiting for an answer.

"If not, ask Yoon. She'll add it to what you already owe her." She watched Sookie dump her bag onto Ari's futon and shook her head. "And you'll need new clothes," she sighed.

Sookie held up a floral halter top and orange short shorts. "What's wrong with my clothes?" she glowered. Ari sat up and snorted. "Country bumpkins." Froggie giggled, patting Sookie on the arm before she could retort. "Ari!" she scolded. "We were all like that when we first got here." To Sookie and me, she explained, "You don't want to look like cheap country girls from Waimanalo. We're *hostesses*." Trying to sound disinterested, I forced a yawn, then asked: "Waimanalo? Where's that?"

Ari got to her feet and stretched, arms overhead, her back an arc of muscle and grace. "Nowhere."

"It's nowhere you want to be," Froggie added, tapping her chin. "I don't even think it's on this island, is it?"

Ari snorted. "Who cares. Low-class dirt farms. That's what I ran away from in Korea."

Sookie, Myu Myu, and I dozed, resting during the next couple of hours, as the other girls got up to have a cup of tea and get ready for work. They seemed to have a schedule already in place; there weren't many arguments over the bathroom. One girl, who I later found out was Lulu, ran into the apartment after her turn had passed. She hurried to the bathroom and pounded on the locked door. "Let me in," she begged. Then, turning to the other girls in the room, asked, "Who's in there? Chinke, Chinke, let me come in, too!" After a muffled answer, Lulu cupped her hand to the door and shouted, "Shit! Yoon was here? Thanks for covering for me about Stevenson. I owe you, I owe you! When Stevenson marries me, I'll pay you back for everything!"

"*If* Stevenson marries her," said a girl, someone I hadn't met yet, sponging herself from the sink. "As if that will ever happen."

"You're just jealous," Minnie said, "because Lulu found someone serious." She fluttered her eyes at the sink girl, waiting for her false lashes to dry.

Sookie and I sat next to Minnie, cross-legged on her sleeping mat, watching her put on her makeup. "Remember when Duk Hee put lipstick on us?" I asked. "She said that makeup would hide our true faces from American eyes."

Sookie stared at me, frowning. "No," she said. She poked a long finger into Minnie's cosmetics bag. "Can I use this?" she asked, pointing to a frosty blue shadow.

Minnie nodded, but groused, "Next time, get your own."

After I covered as much of my birthmark as I could, I lay back down, letting Myu Myu crawl over my stomach. When the girls called a taxi and began filing out the door, I got to my feet, lifting the baby to my hip.

"What are you doing?" Chinke demanded.

"What do you mean?" I asked.

"You can't bring a kid to the club," she said. "It's against the law."

"I told you: trouble," Sookie sang out as she brushed past me and out the door with Minnie.

"But, but . . . " I bit my lip, not knowing what else to say.

"Don't do that," Chinke scolded. "You'll get lipstick on your teeth."

I smiled despite the knot in my stomach, remembering that Duk Hee had told me the same thing when Sookie and I were children playing with her makeup. "Your father eats his lips, too," she had laughed at me. "But it doesn't matter so much if a man has no lips."

"I don't know why you're smiling," Chinke complained. "This is a problem."

I stopped smiling. "I don't know what to do," I wailed. "I have to bring her."

"Wait," Chinke ordered, then stuck her head out the door. "Froggie, come here a second."

Froggie clomped to the door on pencil-spiked shoes. "What?" she said. "I'm ready to leave."

"You're a mother," said Chinke. "You know about these things."

Chinke and Froggie frowned down at Myu Myu, who had eaten a small bowl of rice and was happily gumming the collar of my dress.

"Well," she drawled, "I left mine in Itaewon." She tapped her foot, then said, "I know." She rushed into the bathroom and came out with a small green bottle.

"NyQuil?" Chinke said, squinting at the bottle.

"It works," Froggie said. "Give her a spoonful, maybe two, and she'll sleep through the night. No problem."

My hand shook as I took the bottle. "Do I have to leave her?" I rasped. "Alone?"

"What else can you do?" Froggie shrugged, and stomped outside.

Chinke patted my arm. "She'll be all right," she said, but her voice wavered.

I nodded. Twisting open the cap, I sniffed the bottle and recoiled from the fumes. "Look," Chinke coaxed, "just do it for now, and I'll ask around, see if maybe I can find some girl who married out that can watch your kid for some extra spending money."

She lent me her futon, which I unfolded in a corner. Laying Myu Myu in the center, I forced some of the green medicine into her mouth. She cried and I rocked her until Chinke pulled me up.

"We have to go," she said. "We're already late; we'll be the last ones there."

I pushed some pillows and bags around the futon, blocking Myu Myu in. She whimpered when I stood and I squatted back down to kiss her tears. She blinked. I kissed her eyes closed and this time they stayed shut when I stood.

"Come on, come on," Chinke said, urging me up. "You can visit her during your break."

Yoon's club was only a few blocks away, but not wanting to sweat in our makeup and dresses, we took a taxicab. "They call this 'Korea-moku' Street," Chinke said as the cab stopped in front of a small corner bar.

I could see why. "Korea-moku" Street was comprised of a string of dingy-looking bars and Korean restaurants. Signs announcing naked girls and *kalbi* glittered in English and Korean. Across the street, between a club called Rose and a *pornu* shop, I saw a market advertising kimchee and hair perms.

Yoon's bar was modeled on the Korean Club Foxa. "Same same, only mine's bigger. Better. American," Yoon liked to boast. Chinke led me through the curtained door and into the dark, windowless room. I recognized a song that hit the Korea Foxa just before I left—"Spinning Wheel"—and for a moment I was spinning in time and place, unsure of where I was. I panicked, my heart pumping in time to the music, looking around, expecting to see Bar Mama and Kitchen Auntie, and the uniformed *gomshi* GIs bellying up to the stage with bills in their fists. Chinke hustled me past the bar, where she waved a greeting to the bartender, past the stage where Froggie was already rubbing her bared breasts against the pole, and toward the booths.

Instead of a blur of khaki uniforms, the men lounging at the bar and in the booths wore flowered shirts and jeans, T-shirts and shorts, soft-colored pullovers and slacks. In the dim and smoky light, I made out varying degrees of brown skin. Some of the men looked Korean. Or Chinese. Or Japanese. Or some combination with too much mixture of features for my eyes to focus on, to identify. Men who looked like Lobetto.

I spotted Sookie sipping a drink in a booth, squeezed against an enormously large man with pale skin, black hair, slanted eyes. He could have been Japanese or Chinese or white; it was hard to tell because his face was obscured by fat.

Chinke saw where I was looking and said something under her breath.

I shook my head, pointing to my ears. Leaning closer, I asked, "What?" I could barely hear my own voice above the music.

"I said," Chinke yelled, cupping a hand to her mouth, "your friend works fast. She's already latched on to one of our regulars." She shook her head and when the music stopped for a change of dancers, she explained: "Fat Danny's been looking for a girlfriend, but most of us can't stand him because he's so fat. You have to balance on that stomach mountain, bouncing up and down on a little pinkie penis—scary! I always think I'm going to slip off and crack my head." "A shy ugly," I said, but Chinke didn't hear; she was hurrying to the last booth, where Yoon was bent over an opened notebook.

"We're here," Chinke panted.

"You're late," Yoon said without looking up. She scribbled something in her book. "You both owe me forty-five minutes." She snapped her book shut and stood.

"It's almost my time on stage," Chinke said, backing away. "I'm going to go now, get ready . . . "

Yoon ignored Chinke. "I hope you're not late because of that *tweggi* bastard," she sneered.

I bit my lip to silence my retort. Eyes narrowed, I shook my head.

"That's good," Yoon drawled. "I brought you here. I can send you back."

"Yes," I said through gritted teeth.

Yoon stared at me for a few more minutes, then, apparently satisfied, she nodded and jerked her head, beckoning me to follow. We walked past the restrooms and the out-of-order video game, to two doors. "These are the backrooms," she said, "where we take any customers asking for special attention."

"How much?" I asked.

"You broke the first rule," Yoon said. "Never be the first to mention money. If he asks, you say, 'You tell me' and play hard to get until they name the right price."

"Which is?" I prompted.

Yoon pursed her lips. "You need manners," she said. "Tell them they can use the rooms for fifty dollars for half an hour. That's rent to me," she stressed. "Anything extra between you and the customer is between you and the customer."

The first night, I wasn't able to get anyone into the backroom. "Too bad," said Minnie. "That's where the real money is—make them order champagne, *pupus*, stretch out the time with eating and drinking, rack up the commission before you even get on your back."

Sookie had better luck. Fat Danny couldn't stop looking at her, and she stared at him as if he was the most fascinating man she had ever met. At the beginning of the night, I had tried to join them, but Sookie glared at me. "He's mine," she said. Her voice was light, and she laughed as if she were teasing both me and him, but her eyes were hard and I knew that she was warning me off.

Fat Danny had chuckled, his jowls slapping his neck. "Who's your friend,

Sookie?" he asked, his English spiced with an accent I came to identify as local to Hawai'i. "You know, there's plenny of me for go around."

Sookie introduced us, and we taught him a few Korean folk songs that we sang in high, girlish voices. He told us a few jokes that I didn't understand, but laughed at anyway. And then I left. I knew Sookie wasn't joking when she had marked him as her own.

I worked the way I always worked, the way Lobetto and Sookie had taught me; I cruised the room, targeting the men who were alone and nursing their drinks. I got them to laugh at my mangled English, giggling over my own stumbling tongue. I let my hands wander, stroking their muscles— or lack of muscles—telling them they were big men but treating them like babies. I even cut up their meat for them, popping the tiny morsels into their mouths. And all the time, I encouraged them to drink, knowing that each beer or vodka tonic or tequila lessened my debt by a few pennies.

After a few hours, when Yoon disappeared into one of the backrooms with a regular, I left the booths and cornered Chinke in the bathroom. "I'm taking my break," I told her. "How do I get home?"

Chinke's eyes drooped so that they were almost closed. "Don't be stupid," she said, slurring her words slightly; she had spent the last hours bouncing quarters and drinking.

"Come on, Chinke," I said.

She shrugged, then swayed to the sink to fix her makeup. She opened her eyes wide, and with exaggerated care applied her lipstick.

"Chinke," I growled.

"All right, all right." She dug through her purse for a napkin, blotted her mouth, then sketched a quick map on the flip side of the napkin.

I rushed back to the apartment, taking off my shoes to jog most of the way, and found Myu Myu motionless, curled into herself, butt in the air. I tiptoed into the room, bent over her inert form, and waited for her breath. She snuffled, exhaling a long breath, and I released my own. Once I knew she was still alive, that she hadn't been killed off by the NyQuil, I backed away and silently shut the door behind me.

In my scramble to get back to the club before Yoon noticed and penalized me for my absence, I left the map next to the baby. After several minutes of walking, I looked around and realized I didn't know where I was. I slowed, continuing for several blocks—past girls dressed like I was, girls who hooted at me, glared at me, warned me away from their sections of the street—arid came to the ocean. I circled back, trying not to panic. I couldn't even remember the name of Yoon's club. I backtracked, turning circles, until I finally recognized a Korean market near Yoon's bar. "Where were you?" Sookie screeched when I ran in. "The place is closing—are you trying to get us both in trouble?"

"I got lost," I panted, bending down to adjust the straps on my shoes.

Sookie held up her hand. "Don't tell me," she said. "You went back to check on that kid." She shook her head. "I told you she'd mess you up."

I glared at her. "And I told you, I'd deal with it."

"So deal with it," Sookie said.

Chinke hurried over. "Yoon's been asking about you," she warned. "Don't tell her I know where you went, okay?"

Though I expected her to, Yoon never asked where I was. She just glared at me, opened her notebook and scribbled something next to my name.

Despite warnings from the other girls, I continued to use my breaks to check on Myu Myu. Most nights, the NyQuil kept her in deep sleep, and I was able to get back to the club before Yoon started docking my time. Twice, however, Myu Myu was awake and crying so loud I could hear her from the sidewalk outside the apartment building. I comforted her as best as I could, pacing the room while marking the minutes on the clock, then gave her another dose of NyQuil. After a few weeks, I had to start the night with a double dose of NyQuil, though some nights not even that much of the drug would be enough to keep her from crawling around and crying for my return.

One night when I went to check on her, I didn't hear crying as I unlocked the door. At first I was relieved, thinking that Myu Myu had slept since I left her. As I walked toward our corner of the room, however, I heard gagging. I rushed over, stumbling on the pillows I used to confine her. Myu Myu was tangled in the blanket, facedown in the futon and choking. I flipped her over. Eyes rolling up into her head, her body spasmed, limbs clenched and jerking. She heaved, bile bubbling from her throat, suffocating in her own vomit. I cleared out her mouth, placed her over my knees and slapped her back. She coughed, then after a brief moment of quiet, cried. I held her against me, cheek to cheek, crooning.

I refused to leave Myu Myu behind again that night, and brought her with me when I returned to Foxa Hawai'i. Carrying her in a cardboard box cushioned with my clothes, I tried to smuggle her into the kitchen. But Yoon was waiting for me. "Where have you been?" she screeched. I ducked my head. "I'm sorry, Mrs. Yoon. This won't happen again."

"Damn right it won't!" She pulled me into one of the backrooms. "Don't think I don't know. You've been disappearing every night! You're working the streets for extra money, aren't you?"

I jiggled the box, hoping Myu would remain quiet despite Yoon's yelling. "No, no, that's not it," I whispered.

"I don't like liars and I don't like cheaters," Yoon screamed, flecking spittle into my face. "You're both. In Korea, I thought you were something special. Here, when you do show up for work, you dance like a robot, nothing like you did in Foxa Korea."

"Half the things I did in Korea are against the law in America," I retorted. But I realized that that might be the only difference; though I was three thousand miles away from Korea, I was still trapped in America Town.

"Phah!" Yoon spat. "Only if you get caught." She eyed the box I carried, distracted from her tirade. "What is that?"

"Just some clothes," I stammered, trying to back away from her.

"This bar is not one storage closet," she scolded, yanking my arm so that I almost dropped the box. "And don't you dare walk away from me. I'm not—"

Startled by the sudden violent motion of her cradle, Myu Myu cried out.

"Don't tell me you brought that fucking *tweggi* to my club! How dare you!" Yoon yelled. "What did I tell you about handling this problem?"

Myu Myu pushed the top of the carton, popping her head out. She whimpered, grasping at my chest.

"I'll handle it," I said.

"Now you've made it my problem." Yoon shoved me toward the door. "And that's it. I've had it with you. Get out. Get out of my club."

I clucked to Myu Myu as Yoon propelled us from the backroom. The other girls and their customers looked up, gawking at me carrying a baby in a box. I caught Sookie's eyes—black and empty, unreadable in the dark—only for a moment before she turned her back on me. "I'll get a baby-sitter for her, Mrs.—"

"Don't bother," Yoon said, shaking her head. "You're not coming back here. You can pay off your debt to me from Korea."

NORA OKJA KELLER *lives in Hawai'i with her husband and two daughters. She is the author of two novels,* Comfort Woman, *which won a 1998 American Book Award; and* Fox Girl. *She has a Pushcart Prize for her short fiction.*

Chris McKinney

from THE TATTOO

Honolulu. Town. It was the place I took refuge in when I was eighteen years old. The day I left, I took the uphill drive with my suped-up eighty-three Toyota Celica. It was designed with oxidized black paint, bondo patches, and surface rust corroding the bottom of both doors. I drove up the Pali with an old twin mattress and a surfboard, a Town and Country gun strapped to the roof. Boxes of clothes and books were stuffed into the back seat, oozing socks, long flannel sleeves and denim pant legs. My diving equipment, thirty-thirty and twenty-inch television were riding shotgun. I had nine thousand dollars folded in my pocket. Connected to the rear view mirror dangled my Bronze Star, the one my father had given me. Every time I looked in back of me, I saw it there. It was dark compared to the light which shined through the windshield.

I looked ahead and saw the winding asphalt in front of me. It looked almost like the road was poured down from the top of the mountain, winding down like a cooled stream of lava. As I drove, one hand was on the vibrating wheel, the other was holding a greasy roast pork sandwich. I listened to the whine of my engine in fourth gear. My exhaust system was letting out a loud, sputtering sound as I climbed the mountain range.

My great escape was a half-an-hour drive through the Koolau Mountains. The climb started with a steep, uphill drive on the Pali Highway. I took the hairpin turn. I saw the green mountains on the left, the cliff on the right. Looking over the cliff, I saw all of Kaneohe and its Bay. The suburbia spread under overcast skies. The atmosphere bled shades of gray. Looking down into the Bay, I saw the breaking waves, which looked like suspended white brush strokes on a blue canvas.

These were the cliffs where King Kamehameha the First drove his enemies into free fall. He pushed the ali'i, the chiefs of Oahu, into oblivion. Using guns and cannons brought from the West, conquering, killing. I thought about the blood that must've run down the mountains that day. The people, the blood, pouring down the cliffs like waterfalls, emptying into a pool of death below, perhaps running so far, perhaps reaching the Bay itself. But it was all gone. In that place where the pool was, instead sat a golf course. The path of the river of blood was covered with houses and asphalt roads. History dried up, and in its place rose an imported way of life. A new history, a foreign one. I never fooled myself, my ancestry was a part of this new history, too. I looked over the short cement railing and waved goodbye, taking a bite from my roast pork sandwich before I entered the first tunnel through the mountain.

After I passed through the second tunnel and began my gentle descent down the mountains, I was greeted with rain. Heavy showers, which the Koolaus are known for. I turned on my wipers and the blades squeaked against the windshield, the sound of children jumping on a box-spring mattress. The rain was really falling and, although my wipers were at max, visibility was becoming a problem. I scooted my face closer to the windshield, squinted my eyes, and saw the brake lights of a car rapidly approach in front of me. I down-shifted, then pressed down on my brake with a nervous foot. The car hydroplaned for a couple of seconds and my hands, dropping the pork sandwich, worked on the wheel. Finally the tires grabbed the asphalt, jerking my body forward. The gun was fired. I saw the surfboard fly ahead of me, almost hitting the car ahead. It cracked on the road. Regaining control of the car, I sped up and ran over it. I felt the tires leap. Well, I thought, since I'm going to town, a gun's no good anyway. I needed a longboard to surf the small waves in town. Then I wondered if this was a warning from my mother. Waving away the absurd, child-notion that my mother's spirit drifted in these mountains, I picked up the sandwich from the floorboard. My eyes remained squinted until I reached the bottom of the gentle downhill ride.

I found myself in Makiki, home of the high-rise condominiums and ugly three-story apartment complexes. My crummy studio apartment was directly north of Ala Moana Shopping Center and Keeaumoku Street. It was close enough to the mountains so that vegetation blossomed, close enough to the Ala Moana district so that the green looked out of place. For almost two years I had bled my nine grand, paying for tuition at Kapiolani Community College, paying six hundred dollars a month in rent for my studio in one of those crummy three-story apartment complexes. When I first got to town, the only two costly things I ended up spending my money on were my paulowina tattoo and this framed Otsuka print of Miyamoto Musashi, the most legendary samurai of feudal Japan.

I found him in some gallery at Ala Moana Shopping Center. There he was, covered with a glass sheet, hanging on the wall, looking like he was about to shatter the glass. The lights were on him. The glass absorbed the fluorescent glow of the bulb which hung above it. This gave the glass a mirror effect, and when I looked at Musashi I saw my reflection. I recognized Musashi immediately, his messy, long black hair, his shaven angular face. I looked into his dark slanty eyes, which somehow coupled both serenity and rage. He had that look, that "I'm going to kick your ass and there's nothing you can do about it" look. The print had this animated, cartoon quality to it. I had read about him before, read his *A Book of Five Rings*. I liked it even though, at the time, I didn't understand much of it. He was the ronin, who, by the age of thirty won over sixty duels. Shit, the crazy mother-fucker sometimes fought with sticks while his opponents had swords. He'd still kill them. He was the fucking man. I looked up to him, hanging there in the gallery. I had to have him. I walked up to the lady who was working there that day. She was a Chinese-looking lady dressed in a smart-looking lady's suit. I asked her how much. She looked at me skeptically and said, "Framed, five hundred and fifty dollars." I pulled out my wad of cash. "Well," I said, "take it down, I don't have all day."

I loved the print and the tattoo, but together they cost me about seven hundred dollars. Out of fear and guilt, I immediately got a library job at K.C.C., shelving books. Got paid five-something an hour, pulling twenty-hour weeks. I spent hours in that library, hiding in the cubicles, reading novels instead of my assigned textbooks. Slowly what was left of the nine grand bled, and through those two years I attended classes which I hated. But I was determined to make it to the University of Hawai'i at Manoa, determined to do it without any help or returning home.

Sitting in those one hundred level courses is what killed me. No, paying to sit in those one hundred level courses is what killed me. I took courses on subjects I had no interest in, courses which I was forced to take in order to meet requirements. Classes like logic, classes which were a pain to sit through, classes which forced your eyes on the clock above the professor's head. It seemed every time I eyed the clock, I'd think, I can't fucking believe I'm paying for this.

Suddenly, I found my life very boring and tedious. Besides, I was sitting side by side with some of the most uninteresting people in the world—college students. I began to long for something real, something threatening, something that made me feel alive again. I longed to make stories, do things that were interesting, new things I could tell the people back home. Every time I got back to my shitty apartment and saw the ronin Musashi look at me, I'd say to him, "Yeah, I'd like to roam the country and look for trouble like you did, make my life legendary, but I gotta do this college thing." For almost two years I didn't roam, though, I just did what I thought I was supposed to do. I managed to muddle through two years of school, two years I'll never get back. I might have made it to U.H. Majoring in what or doing what, I have no idea. But two months before my fourth semester ended, opportunity knocked. At first, I thought of it as a way to continue my education, but some of the things you get yourself into, they're not only jobs, they're lifestyles. Sometimes when you open the knocking door, you have to step through it, too. This doorway led to Keeaumoku Street, the main road which led to the heart of Ala Moana Shopping Center, the road peppered with hostess bars, massage parlors, and strip bars. These were places owned by first-generation Koreans and Vietnamese immigrants, bars which were always changing their names.

I was nineteen, having beers one night by myself at Club Mirage. Over those two years I was in school, it had changed names three times. First it was Club Oasis, then Club Fancy Dream. Finally, Mama-san settled on Club Mirage. It sounded French to her, and she thought anything French or Italian was just the shit. She was an amazing old Korean lady, all four-ten of her. She was smart and tough as hell. Every night she crammed her one hundred and fifty some-odd pounds into a gaudy, tight, sequined dress. She didn't shop with an eye for style, brand names and price tags determined what she wore. Her thinning hair was always permed, displaying an ineffective attempt at thickness. Her face was always painted heavily, false eyelashes and all. She wore a huge two-carat diamond ring on her left hand, while gold and jade bracelets crawled up both forearms. When I first saw her, oddly enough, she kind of reminded me of my father. It was the angry look she always wore, the look like one wrong word would send her into a frenzy. She was a genius at running that bar, though. Despite all of the neighboring competition, a river of cash flowed through Club Mirage for years. It became the most famous strip bar in the state of Hawai'i. Hell, guys on Kauai, Maui, and the Big Island knew about Club Mirage, and often on weekends we'd get patrons who'd fly over just to see the show.

So there I was one night, having beers and checking out naked women. The black lights were low, and Prince's *Erotic City* was pulsing in the cheap perfumed air. I was hiding out in one of the booths, nursing a Budweiser. I was watching a Japanese tourist stick his nose in between the naked legs of a tall haole dancer. After every move, she pulled on her garter, signaling her audience to deposit a tip. The tourist folded a bill and added it to the dozens of bills which wrapped around her upper thigh. I smiled as the tourist ran his hand down her leg after depositing the tip. No touching, I thought. I watched for the next two songs, watched the stripper soak the tourist for at least thirty dollars in ones. She made thirty dollars for about seven or eight minutes of work. But work it was. She contorted her body into all sorts of positions, always thrusting her naked crotch a mere inch or two away from the foreign spectator. I wondered if I could ever do it. Then I remembered that I was a guy and laughed at the mental image of me showing some tourist my hairy balls. After thinking about this, I decided it looked like some of the hardest work I ever saw.

As Guns and Roses' *Appetite for Destruction* began, I stepped out of the booth and watched as the stripper gathered her string stars-and-stripes bikini. She walked naked off the stage. A local girl took her place. She took off her panties before Axel Rose even started singing. The tourist sat still with a big wad of bills clenched in his fist.

Just as I was about to walk out, I heard yelling. I looked back and saw a naked Korean girl screaming on stage. She was being stalked by a big Samoan. He wore a white, v-neck t-shirt, which must have been a double-extra large. His arms filled the sleeves. One of these huge arms shot out. He grabbed her ankle, yanking her off the stage. Her body knocked over a row of chairs, and she hit the thin, gaudy red carpet. Her naked body was still. The Samoan turned around, seemingly expecting what was coming next. Two bouncers pounced on him, while a skinny Korean waiter shot a kick up toward the Samoan's face. The kick hit one of the bouncers instead. On impact both the Korean and the haole bouncer lost their balance and fell to the floor. The last bouncer, an out-of-shape Hawaiian, didn't stand a chance. He took two giant hits to the face and fell to the floor. At this point both the bouncers and the waiter were scrambling on hands and knees, away from the Samoan. They almost looked like a school of fish darting away from a three-pronged spear. I heard Mama-san scream from behind the bar. "I call police! You go now!" The Samoan smiled and strode toward her.

I don't know why I did what I did. I must've been fucking nuts. This solé was huge. But action, for me, was a magnet. Since King Zoo, I guess it always was. I couldn't stay out of it. There I was, acting on instinct while my brain was probably screaming, "Get the fuck out of here!" But once that instinct kicks in, all is quiet. Void. I didn't hear my brain, the music, or Mama-san, who was probably screaming her head off, not showing fear, but showing anger. I ran behind the Samoan and kicked the side of his knee. When his knee buckled, I wrapped my left forearm around the front of his neck and locked on. That's when my ride began. He lifted me off my feet and began swinging. My legs were swinging violently back and forth while he grabbed for my head. He pulled and scratched, but I didn't let go. I hid my face in his hair. It smelled like smoke and cheap shampoo. I almost gagged. Once in a while, I'd release the lock for a second and hit him with my right hand. I don't know how much good it did, every time I hit him, it seemed like his strength intensified. I knew I couldn't let go, though. If I had let go, this guy would've killed me. Finally, I felt him tire. In a last-ditch effort, he grabbed a beer bottle off the bar and blindly swung it down at my head. He missed and the bottle shattered on his head. This killed more of the fight in him and, finally, while the nearing police sirens blared, I was able to drag him out.

The lights were on when I stepped back inside. Suddenly, I saw a collage of stretch marks and shy men. The men began leaving while the dancers put on their clothes. Mama-san was talking to a couple of cops at the bar. One was short, about five-five, and Japanese. The other was much bigger, Portuguese-looking. He put his big arm around Mama-san, looking like he was trying to calm her down. I looked at his big gut and wondered what kind of physical qualifications the Honolulu Police Department had set for its officers. He looked funny there, with his arm around Mama-san. She almost looked like a child next to him. The Japanese cop whispered something in her ear. She pointed at me. I waited, expecting to get busted or something, but instead the cops walked up to me and said, "You one crazy fucka." They patted me on the back and laughed. When Mama-san approached them, they both went up to her and gave her a polite kiss on the cheek. After spending a moment catching glimpses at the dressing strippers, the cops began walking out. Just as I was about to follow them outside, I heard Mama-san's voice. "You wait! What yaw name?"

I turned around. "Ken, my name's Ken."

She stepped toward me with that angry look on her face. She reached up, grabbed my chin, and turned my head. "You Japanee boy?"

"Yup."

"Japanee boy, you like job? You come tomorrow night, I give you job, okay? You come back."

With that said, she walked away. I headed home and waited for the adrenaline rush to fade. I couldn't believe it, I was going to get to work in a strip bar. When I got home and turned on the light, I gave Musashi a wink as I threw my keys on my table.

I worked for Mama-san for about five years. For five years I had a wad of hundred dollar bills lining my pocket. For five years, I slept with painted and plastic women. I mean, sex with some of those strippers, for them it was like shaking hands or something. If they thought you were cute enough on a given night, they'd want to shake your hand. For five years, the poverty in my life evaporated. I stopped going to Ka'a'awa and Kahaluu. Once in a while I'd talk to my father, Koa, Freddie, or Kahala on the phone, but I never heard shit. I was too wrapped up in my bliss to really listen to any of them. School was no longer on my agenda. I figured, why should I go to school for a few more years, work hard, and end up with a job which paid less than the one I had? For a while, I figured this life was my calling. It was like an epiphany. I wrapped the shroud of the Club tightly over my head, and rolled around happy in it. I felt like the luckiest guy in the world.

I started as a bouncer at Club Mirage. I worked six nights a week, from about nine at night till two in the morning. Mama-san paid me cash. With that, and what the bartenders and strippers tipped me, I walked home with about two hundred and fifty dollars a night. As the months rolled by, Mama-san began giving me more and more responsibilities. Within a year I was running the place when she wasn't around. I couldn't believe it. I was twenty years old, not even old enough to drink, but there I was, helping run the most popular strip bar in the state. And if that wasn't enough, there was the partying I did with the dancers after work. Sex, drugs, and rock and roll! Twosomes, threesomes, drinks till eight in the morning, and always, the music played. I figured I had found my religion, hedonism, and it was led by a god who didn't answer dreams, but instead drowned them out in a pleasant way.

I remember my first night at work, after the last set, I helped Iris, whose real name I never knew, off the stage. She was one of the prettiest. She was young, about nineteen, local. She was from the suburbs of Moanalua, I think. Her skin was still tight, unscarred. She had this funny streak of white running through her black hair. She smiled and stepped off the stage naked and tired. I looked down at her garter, and saw all sorts of bills hugging against her leg. I remember asking her, "Why do you do this?"

She laughed. "It's all for the money, honey, it's all for the money."

For me, that summed it up nicely.

Mama-san, I came to find out, was into more than the bar business. Besides the two bars she owned, she had a hostess bar a block away on Kapiolani called Club Nouveau. She was into prostitution, loan-sharking, and gambling. She and a partner owned a massage parlor called Happy Hands, where you'd pay fifty at the door, and "tip" your masseuse for any other services rendered. In her loan-sharking, she had lent out money to dozens of Korean immigrants who were starting their own businesses in town, whether they were jewelry and apparel shops in Waikiki or bars along Keeaumoku or Kapiolani. She had two sisters—one ran an illegal casino in downtown, the other ran Club Nouveau. Her partner ran Happy Hands, while she took care of Club Mirage and the loan-sharking, the two most profitable businesses. There she was, this little lady from God-knows-where in Korea, running her own little empire. A real rags-to-riches story. And once again I found myself riding on the coattails of someone bigger than me. Again I was knighted into a kingdom which I was not born into.

It was great for the first several years. Mama-san kept paying me more and more. Besides staying at the bar, sometimes I'd pick up money for her. The loan-sharking thing, which they called the "Tanomoshi," was great. She did what no bank would, she lent out tens of thousands of dollars to the new-comers who had no credit or collateral, and charged them outrageous interest. Koreans, for some reason, always seemed to want to open their own business, unlike Filipinos who always seemed to work for somebody. The thought of enormous debt seemed something that the Koreans thought of as necessity rather than hardship.

Of course Mama-san, with her Tanomoshi, ran the risk of people not making money and skipping on their loans, and sometimes it got ugly. Sometimes I had to collect for her. After all, new businesses go bankrupt everyday, and sometimes these people had no way of paying. Mama-san was always squeamish about resorting to violence, but you can only reconsolidate a loan so many times. Some of these Koreans would be like a hundred grand in the hole, and sometimes because of this another hole had to be dug. She didn't like to do it, besides she'd rather get at least some money back. But she couldn't survive with the reputation of being somebody that's soft. Who can? Only those who can bear being the jackass among the strong. That sure wasn't her.

So, yeah, I collected, but I left the hole digging to the others, the evil-looking Koreans Mama-san owned. They were the ones way too young to remember the Korean War, but they looked like they remembered anyway. I left the killing to them, while I beat people, people who Mama-san thought would be scared of my violent Japanese looks. She thought I'd remind some, who were old enough, of the Japanese occupation of Korea. These people were usually honorable enough to attempt to fulfill their debts, but nevertheless, these people were sometimes guilty of a heinous crime in this world. They weren't making money. Immigrants from Asia looking for something better, just like my ancestors, instead finding the same damn thing. Embarrassingly, it wasn't a time in my life when I got tangled up into moral dilemmas. Coke never got me, but money did for a while. It seemed the more I got, the more I wanted. It was my narcotic, my passion, my reason for living. It was my fairy godmother.

I was a sight back then, wearing thick, gaudy gold chains around my neck and wrist, wearing designer shirts which were a size too small on my weight training-induced two-hundred-pound body. I remember this one rope chain I had, half an inch in diameter, which I wore every day. I wore it so much that a pale ring began to form around my neck. It wound tight around my jugular, almost like a dog collar. It screamed, "Hey, look at me, I get my money illegally!" It's kind of scary when I think about it, the first time I saw Mama-san, I wanted to laugh at her gaudy appearance, her jewelry, her overly-painted face. But after a while I became what she was, I became a son who worshiped the same idol.

After a while, after partying with the strippers, I noticed that they did an extraordinary amount of drugs. I didn't ask why, I was just interested in capitalizing. I dug Freddie up and he'd come to town to drop off coke, weed, and the up-and-coming drug of choice, crystal methamphetamine. Freddie, he'd drive anywhere to get his hands on more blue cats.

Sometimes, when I did collections, I'd skim some, telling Mama-san that the portion I gave her was all they had.

I dabbled in sports gambling with a buddy of mine, a silent partner, making about fifteen grand every football season.

I still collected cash from Mama-san, from the regular bouncing and collecting.

Altogether, I must've been making a hundred grand a year, tax free. My crummy one bedroom turned into a two-bedroom condo on the thirtieth floor of the Marco Polo building right outside of Waikiki. It was a real high-class place, with security cameras and a guard at the door. It even had tinted revolving doors, the kind I'd see on T.V., the kind in places like New York City. I remember the first time I saw the night guy standing by the door. He was this middle-aged Korean guy, his broad face sagged like a bulldog's. His belly hung over his tightly cinched belt. I tried to give him a twenty-dollar tip. For some reason I figured that's what people did. He thanked me, but refused. So every Christmas I gave him a bottle of soju instead. He'd smile, take the bottle and say, "Tank you." He'd bow slightly several times, looking a bit too happy in receiving his gift.

My twenty-inch television grew about forty inches. Leather sofa, glass tables, plush burgundy carpets, my Otsuka framed print of Miyamoto Musashi hung from a cement, not wooden, wall. My piece of shit Celica became a brand new black Porsche Sportster. I kept my money out of the bank, and put it in my books at home. Between the pages of pieces like Macbeth, The Odyssey, and Native Son, thousands of dollars served as hidden bookmarks. I marked my very favorite pages with thousand dollar bills, other good pages I marked with hundreds. It seemed safe at the time, I figured books were like kryptonite to thieves. I thought I was an original, one of a kind. Besides, my thirty-thirty turned into a Glock and a sawed-off shotgun. The shotgun was under my bed, and the Glock was in a case under the seat of my car. So I was confident. I was living large, and my fairy godmother never told me that the clock would strike twelve.

The life was more than entertaining during those years, especially at Mirage. Of course there were the strippers. Iris. Did her. Epiphany. Did her. Crystal. Did her. One time Crystal took me home with Chanel and I did both of them next to a glass table covered with glasses of margaritas, weed, glass pipes, and little plastic bags of crystal meth. The threesome. Everyman's dream. Didn't officially date any of them. Most of them had on-again, off-again boyfriends who were either dealers, surfers, or musicians. These were guys they usually met at work.

Watching the customers was also very entertaining. We had all types walk through the red velvet curtain. College students on a limited income. Japanese tourists brought in by limo from Waikiki. Blue-collar guys dressed in t-shirts and jeans. Drug dealers, with their tight shirts, huge gold necklaces, and wads of hundred dollar bills. Haoles walking in with that "surfer" look; shorts, t-shirts and slippers. Huge Hawaiian strong-arms who collected protection money from all the bars, including ours. Businessmen wearing slacks and aloha shirts. Most were either boyfriends or husbands. A few were of that lonely I-never-get-laid breed. On any given night, every type of thirsty man came crawling to the Mirage.

It's funny, you'd figure that the dealers or strong-arms would give us the most trouble. But the cops were often worse. At least the dealers and strong-arms were big spenders, sometimes dishing out hundreds per night. But some of the cops? They figured once they'd gotten their badges, it was discount city wherever they went. And they were right. Nobody, especially a woman like Mama-san, wanted the cops on her. Even if Mirage was a legitimate business, she had the whorehouse disguised as a massage parlor, the loan-sharking, and the casino. Besides, in the Club itself, drugs flowed in and out every night.

Those two cops who came that night Mama-san offered me the job were always there. The Portagee and the Japanee. It didn't matter, on or off-duty. Both were married. Both were alcoholics. Both were dirty. They weren't dirty in the sense that they stole, murdered, dealt drugs, or even used drugs, instead they were the type of cops who abused power. Everything in Mama-san's kingdom was free to them. Drinks were free, "massages" at the whorehouse were on the house. And in return, they turned their backs on any criminal activities Mama-san was involved with and they served as protection for her. I should've been happy to have them, but something about the whole arrangement bothered me. Maybe it was because they had too much power and they knew it, or maybe it was just that I didn't like the fact that they were hired to do a job which they didn't really do. I mean, if you're hired on as a strong-arm, kick ass, if you're employed as a cop, catch criminals. Do what you get paid to do.

Cops . . . It's hard to blame them, though. Their job is to deal with shitty things that happen. If you see enough shit, you want to have some beers and relax. And when bar owners start kissing your ass, what's a man to do? The bar becomes his favorite place. These two, the Portagee and Japanee, loved Club Mirage.

And I loved it, too. We moved with the times. I had an ATM machine brought in. I told Mama-san that she should hire a D.J. During football season, we had Monday Night specials. Cheap beer, free pupus, and a satellite dish bringing in the game live. Other sporting events. Every time Tyson fought, we made a bundle. A lot of customers would step into the trap and stay well after the satellite spectacle was over, even when beers went back up to five dollars. We ran things smart and professionally. And just as business was hitting its heights, and I was making more money that I ever did before, the clock struck twelve and in came Claudia Choy.

Christine Joy Lee

"KIMCHEE COWGIRL"

Only if you could see beyond
kimchee, rice, and skin . . .

Does my yellow
not mix
with your red
neck?

Why must
you try
to scare the color
out of me?

Stare
and shout
your "Hyee . . . YA,"
kung-fu sounds
behind my back,
while I shop
at your *esteemed*,
top-notch
Super Wal-Mart.

Drive by
our house
late at night,
honk your horns and yell
undistinguishable obscenities,
so I can be reminded
of how *smart*
country folk
can be.

Wham
your trucks
into our gate and
run over
our defenseless mailbox

to showcase your
artistic
landscaping skills.

And
as I walk
along the narrow dirt road,
race past me
in your 4X4's,
speed up, kick dust,
and fire
your hunting guns
in the air
to demonstrate
your *superb*
marksmanship abilities—
I'm confident the air is now dead.

CHRISTINE JOY LEE *was born in 1978 in Honolulu. When she was twelve, her family moved to North Carolina where she attended boarding school in Lenoir. At nineteen, she relocated to Tennessee with her family and spent years volunteering as a teacher's assistant and a missionary/translator in various states and foreign countries such as the Philippines, Kyrgyzstan, and Korea. She now resides in Honolulu, where she works as a registered nurse.*

Steven T. Wall

"STREET RACING"

In the dead of night when the streets are
silent,
There comes a new breed of cars, trucks and people.
The aren't like us;
They aren't normal.

Their cars are quick, fast, agile.
They race to unfathomable speeds
And stop unusually fast.
They turn corners by drifting

And shake towns with their engine
sounds.

Sometimes they race during rush hour
And go on the wrong side of the road to
speed around traffic.
They think life is a video game,
But it's not;
There's no restart button.

STEVEN T. WALL *was born in 1990. He attends 'Iolani School in Honolulu and is in the eleventh grade. In his spare time, he plays water polo and enjoys surfing with his dad and friends. He lives with his parents and sister.*

Joe Balaz

"KIMOTHERAPY"

Eh, you heard da news?
Daniel in bad shape,
he wen get Kimotherapy.

Yeah, I know,
kindah sad, but—

GOOD FOA HIM!
Da buggah deserves it.

Freaking rip-off artist,
probably lippin to wun nurse
right now,
but no need feel sorry foa him, brah,
da moa he suffah da bettah.

I tell you, cuz,
bad luck wen grab him by da neck.

Danny Boy
taught he wuz happening
wen he wen steal
dat surfboard

from dat car down Sunset.
I heard he wuz all mouth
wen he wen try 'um out at Ehukai.

But wen he wen
swipe dat board
from dat parked car
next to dat beach house,

too bad he nevah see
da small haole kid
dat was looking through
da hibiscus hedge.

And moa worse,
too bad Daniel nevah know
dat da kid's oldah braddah
wen just finish surfing
with da guys dat wuz driving da car—

You know dem, eh?
Alika, Roland
and Kimo,
da guys from Hauula.

Dey wen stop by Sunset
to visit dere haole friend
foa talk story
little while.

Wen da small kid
wen run into da house
foa tell dem wat happened,

dey all wen make it out in time
to see Daniel's blue sedan
turning da corner down da road,

wit Kimo's board
sticking outtah da window.

So now Daniel stay hospital
wit wun broken face—

Wen dey wen finally catch him
wun week latah,
he wen get dirty licking,

cause braddah Kimo
wen give 'um—therapy!

———————————————•·•———————————————

Bobby Burnett

"FRIENDS OR ENEMIES?"

I n the fifth grade, I was the biggest in my class, standing five feet five inches. Everyone thought I was huge. Nobody wanted to get in a fight with me.

One day this short kid came to our school. He looked about five feet tall. He was Hawaiian. You know, the surfer-type with a Gold's Gym kind of build. He always wore these oversized clothes like a gangster. I thought the nicest was his Oakland A's hat. It was white with a green brim and had an Oakland A's symbol on the white part. His name was Jesse. The first time he saw me he said, "Wass up? My name's Jesse, HAOLE!"

I got pissed off and though, "How can a little guy call me '*haole*' and tease me?" I was a little confused. We later talked and got better acquainted. "Hey, my name's Robby," I said.

"Wass up, man?" I heard you think you some big *haole* or sumting!" he replied.

"You thought right, buddy!" I said.

"Shppshshsh!" He made a noise like "get real."

Then I asked, "You wanna challenge me for a little arm-wrestle to see who's the real man?"

"Sure!" Jesse answered. "You think I sca'ade?"

"I didn't say that."

So we went and lay down on the field. We got our right hands clasped together, waiting for somebody to start us. I could feel his sweaty hand hooked with mine. With my left hand I felt the grass tickling. There were little beetles walking around under my hand.

"Hurry up, the lunch bell is almost going to ring!" yelled someone from the crowd.

Everyone was watching us, crowded around so tight that I couldn't even breathe. Finally one of my friends grabbed our linked right hands, and as he let go he said, "Ready, go!"

I tried and tried with all my might to make the back of his hand touch the dirt-coated ground, and I could feel him pushing with all of his might. The sweat from his forehead went into his eyes. I wasn't sweating that much. My hand started to sweat and almost slipped out, but I held in there. I had a good grip.

I could feel him getting tired, but I didn't want to show him my tiredness, so I cocked my arm back toward his side to make him think he was winning. Then I threw my arm back and made his hit the ground. I won!

A lot of dirt flew in my face. He was pretty mad about losing. We stood up face to face, nose to nose. His breath smelled like tuna, but I didn't say anything.

I said, "How about mercy?" He was psyched. I put my hands up, and he clasped them with his, interlacing every finger.

Someone said, "Again?"

"On your mark, get set, GO!" somebody else yelled. He got me in a lock, but I twisted around and got him in a lock instead. I pushed his hands up slowly and he yelled, "Mercy!"

I won at that too. I know he didn't want to yell "mercy" in front of his friends.

A couple of months passed. Jesse and I became really good friends, buddies. We weren't enemies anymore. We would back each other up. Nobody would mess with us. In every friendship there are fights along the way. There were a lot of fights in our case. I don't know why. It's just that we would always have buddy-buddy fights.

One day we were eating breakfast in the cafeteria. We played the "your Mama" game. (That's when people think of good cut-downs for your mom.) I started it with, "Your mama's so stupid she got hit by a parked car."

He countered with, "Your mama's so stupid she tried to choke herself with a cordless phone."

"Your mama's armpits are so hairy it looks like she had Bula'ia in a headlock," I replied. He tried t come back, but I said quickly, "Your mama's so fat she stood on a quarter and buggers shot out of George Washington's nose." He had a mad look on his face, but I thought he was joking, so I said, "Your mama's so stupid she thought a quarterback was a twenty-five cents refund."

He was still silent. Then, after thinking about it, he said, "Shut up!" then he pushed me and yelled, "What!"

I said, "You know you don't want to fight. I'm sorry."

"No. What? What!" he protested. I was getting madder and madder. Then he said again, "What!"

I put up my fists and said, "What!" right back. I didn't want to fight, but he overdid it. He asked for it. He put up his fists and swung but missed by a nick. I swung back. He blocked it and swung at my lip, which started bleeding. I'd been hit, and I wanted to hit him back, but right before I could Mrs. Nishiki yelled, "Robby! Jesse!"

Mrs. Nishiki was a teacher and was mean. She had as much authority as our principal. She smelled like potpourri.

We walked over to her. I knew I was in for it. She gave me a disgusted look and said, "Detention!" We were scared. Then she yelled, "Go to the office!"

At the office I felt funny with a bloody lip. I said, "I shouldn't've teased you that much. It's my fault."

"No, I shouldn't've hit you. You okay?"

"Yeah," I said as I gave him a handshake. Now we were real friends.

BOBBY BURNETT, *wrote this story in 1996, when he was an eighth-grader at the University Laboratory School in Honolulu.*

Katie Gallagher
"ESCAPING MANGO CHICKEN"

It had taken the mango all summer to get that perfect. You would almost think it was proud of itself, the way it weighed down the branch, showing off. It was ripe, rosy, beautiful. A small brown hand reached up and plucked it from the branch. It pulled back and took careful aim. A moment later, the mango whizzed past Vance Pferra's head. He screamed. I wouldn't have cared if he hadn't been on the handlebars of my bike. It unbalanced me, and in a split second I was thrown off. It was a short trip, but it was the reason for some very long ones.

Mango Chicken was considered inescapable to the cycling population of Downtown Kaimuki. Basically, it involved throwing overripe mangoes in the general direction of kids on bikes, not to hurt them, just to freak them out so they fell off of their own accord. You got points for knocking your former friends into the grass.

"I . . . hate . . . you!" I said to Vance, who lay stunned on the grass. He was not a thin kid, and in his current position he looked rather like a scared piglet. After picking myself up and checking for damages, I walked over to Vance.

"Get UP!" I yelled. He did.

"Jeez, you got one problem?" Vance muttered.

"Who did that?" I called into the bushes.

"That one counted double," came a happy voice. Brandon's head popped up.

Yes, I thought it would be Brandon.

"Vance? Laura? Are you guys okay? Looked for a second there like Vance was spread out all over the ground. How do you see around him anyway?"

Vance picked up what was left of the mango and threw it at Brandon's head. Brandon stood contentedly, licking it off his face. He wasn't very dark, but always dirty.

"Go buy a bra, Vance," he taunted. "You look like you need one!"

I didn't stay around to see this progress. I rode straight to Tricia's house, avoiding mango trees.

Tricia put her pants on one leg at a time. At least, that's what Vance's mother had told him. I didn't know where she had gotten that bit of information, but I didn't question it. I had been her slave the year before, and had just recently been promoted to friend, something I was very proud of.

We sat there in her living room, eating raw saimin and talking about mango chicken. Tricia was one year older than me, Filipino-Jewish, and rather pretty. She was tall and thin. And she didn't brake for mangoes.

"I hate Brandon," I said.

"I know what you mean," she said. "He hit my spokes a few times and counted it."

"I know this is going to sound crazy, but I wish it wasn't summer sometimes. I mean, it's bad enough to have to smell rotten mangoes, but I really don't like having them thrown at me."

"Well, what can we do about it?"

"We could get out of here."

"And go where?"

"Anywhere."

"When?"

"Now!" I was really loving the idea. "Why not now? My bike's outside, you'll fit in back." I ran out onto the sidewalk. She put on her shoes and followed after me. With a little trouble we both got on my bike.

Then it was off, off into adventure! Ha! Ha! Ha!

We were nervous about mangoes until we came to an area of fair-sized dwellings and trimmed hedges, commonly called the rich people's houses. Rich kids, naturally, didn't throw rotting fruit at each other. They had 16-bit video game systems, CD players, VHS recorders, and clothes they didn't want to get dirty. All this stuff kept them inside, and out of trouble. Lack of it kept us scummy kids out, and always in trouble.

We were in trouble now. The bike was going down a steep hill, and doing it fast. Tricia had panicked, and let her feet block my wildly spinning pedals.

"Put your feet baaaaack!" I shrieked. She did, too late. I slammed on my brakes. There was a hideous screech, and as I slowed almost to a halt, my front tire hit a rock, and popped off. The tire rolled a few more feet, gave up, and toppled over.

I slowly got up from where I had fallen. Tricia wasn't moving. I walked over to her.

"I'm dying." she moaned. "I'm bleeding to death, I can feel the blood."

"Tricia, you are not bleeding."

"Am too."

"You collided with a Big Gulp."

"You are just being nice to be because I am dying!"

"Good Lord, Tricia!"

"Yours or mine?"

This was nuts. I pulled her to her feet.

"Whoa! It was just soda!"

"Praise Jesus!"

"Hey!"

I started to laugh. She joined in, and there we were, cracking up on some guy's manicured lawn.

Then I jerked up.

"Laura, what's wrong?"

"I don't know where we are."

This sunk in, and we realized we had to make it home soon. We fixed the bike as best as we could, and rode around aimlessly as the sky darkened. We had almost given up hope as we rounded a corner. Suddenly, from out of nowhere, came a mango. It missed my head by only a few inches. I teetered, but did not fall.

"Brandon! Brandon! I almost got them that time!"

We knew that squeal, it was Vance Pferra's.

"We are in Kaimuki!" I shouted. We both screamed our cry of triumph. Dogs began to bark. We barked back. It was good to be home.

KATIE GALLAGHER *wrote this story in 1994, when she was an eighth-grader at the University Laboratory School in Honolulu.*

Abraham Sanchez

"SWEET MANGO"

I was sitting at the bus stop in Wahiawa.
The morning sunlight was hitting the ground.
I looked up and saw a blue light flashing.
My gangsta friend, Keoni, sat smoking buds.
He was all stoned and didn't say nothing.
The fat pig's eyes got big when he saw me smoking pakalolo.
He hit me in the face with his big, fat, ugly, wrinkled hands.
I heard the sirens coming for me and my friend.
The air smelled like pakalolo.
It smelled like sweet mango.
I saw my joint on the ground;
It was still smoking.

ABRAHAM SANCHEZ *wrote this poem in 1994, when he was an eighth-grader at Aiea Intermediate School on O'ahu.*

Hughie Long

"GOOD TIMES"

"Sup mann," Kalani shrugged, "howzit going?"
"Not bad bra not bad, how you?" The two shook hands as they walked across the street.
"I'm allgood you know me," Kalani replied
"Yeah I know you all right."
"Eh you goin' to the party to night?"
"Nah, gotta watch my baby bro, you know"
"Well, yo missin' a rage ah, choke hotties, boozed, buds, but hey you gotta do what you gotta do man."
"Yeah well, most parties now-a-dayz are just a bunch of sausage fests, no bush no buzz!"
"That's true, but all the sunset girls are showing, guaranteed!"
"Nah, well, gotta go, Ms. P's a bitch when we're late," the two shook hands, "don't wanna get locked out again! Kay then!"
"Shootzs!"

Kalani marched down the library sidewalk pass the Laie boyz, through the Kaaawa Krew and into the Sunset gang. Every morning him and his posse cruise around the green picnic tables between Building F and U, under the plumeria tree. As he neared the table he began a train of meet and greet by shaking hands and exchanging yo, watz up's and howzit hangings.

Suddenly a tinkled buzz gave out a shout and like controlled robots the teenage children rushed to their morning classes.

"Eh Matt . . . pisstzzz . . . Matt," Kalani whispered in class, "you going to the party tonight?"

"Shhhh . . . . "

"Pisstzzz . . . Matt." Kalani tried.

"What?"

"You going to the party tonight?"

"I don't know . . . it depends," he replied.

"Well . . . itza guaranteed rager," he insisted.

"Yeah . . . we'll see."

The conversation ended as soon as it began and Kalani continued to day dream as Mr. Sofakina dumbled on and on about safe sex and under aged drinking.

"See da problem in todayz so si o ti iz des stoopid kids tink dare so grown up and day like hump and drink all day, mom bi babies stay popping out all of a da place and aunites an uncles stay getting runned over by stupid drunk drivers. You now back when I could fit in one airplane seat the . . . . "

As the rambling of the over absorbed guidance teacher continued Kalani's state of hypnosis shattered, the bell ran, *thank god*, he thought as he sprinted for the door. Mondays are always hard but this one seemed to be worse and the only thoughts in Kalani's mind were, *last day . . . four more classes . . . summer . . . yes!!*

"Eh Kalanz wazup mann," a friendly voice shot out, "eh long time no see ah."

"Sup dogg . . . wats it been? Two, three weeks?"

"Yeah just got off suspension."

"Oh yeah you and Koa when drink before school, I remember, Koa got so drunk he palued all over the place. Ha . . . freking dumb ass."

"Good times . . . good times!" Kainoa added.

"Eh you going to the party tonight?"

"For sure mann . . . see you there?"

"Garandz ba barandz," Kalani replied, "eh gotta go man."

"Shootz," they shook hand, "see you tonight."

"Yeah," Kalani ran down the sidewalk, kicked up a tornado of red dirt while running down the track, hiked up the bleachers and took a sat next to Leilani, the hottest girl in school.

"Hey baby," Kalani pecked her cheek.

"Euill Kalani get off of me!" Leilani said as she pushed him away.

"Common gurl you know you want me," he pleaded.

"As if, everyone knows you da biggest playa in sku . . . ," she explained, "and I aint about to be dissed and dismissed. If we got out you'll probably screw around some skanky hoar like Misty or Tanya."

"Well . . . I gotta go to class. See you around this summer?"

"Probably, I'll be at the party tonight, you?"

"Great!!," he said with excitement, "yeah of course, I'll be there."

"Well bye . . . "

"Bye," he said as he ran off into the mound of buildings.

"Okay class now I know your all excited for summer but we have one last test for the year," Miss Ditsina explained as the students cheered with *huh's* and *boo's*, "every get out a writing utensil and answer the questions, there are ten multiple choice, five short answers and one essay question."

"Eh miss, I can go batchroom?" A student exclaimed.

"May! I go to the bathroom and yes you may," she replied.

"This is bullshit," Kalani softly said.

"Excuse me," Miss Ditz heard, "what did you say."

"This is brilliant, the test . . . I mean," he stuttered as the class laughed.

"Okay shush now!"

The class was petite twelve, fifteen kids at the most, an advanced class, hard to come by in a country high school. Kalani always did well with tests the problem is that he's one lazy Hawaiian, never doing homework and always slacking off. The test was taken and the bell shortly sang afterwards.

As Kalani paced down a walkway parallel to the schools parking lot a soiled brown '72 Chevy Camero pulled up, blared its horn and squeaked its window down.

"Hey K, we going beach, like go?"

"Howzit Boy, shootz we go," with that he opened the rusted door and jumped in. The car was a disaster, aged beer bottles and cigarette buts carpeted the floor, the leather interior was nicely punctured and there was hardly any room."

"Okay lets make like a tree and get the fuck out of here." Boy proclaimed.

"Cheehooooo," another shouted as the tool sped out on to Kamehameha Highway.

"Eh bra turn up the jamz I love dis song . . . hot like fire, cool like wata," Kalani sang terribly. "Ooooo Whoa Ohhhh . . . Ooooo Whoa Oh Oh . . . " the car vibrated with base and music, " . . . Lord a mercy . . . ," Kalani continued horribly.

"Check this out . . . Lord a mercy . . . Eddie Murphy . . . beef jerky . . . 7-11 slurpee." They all laughed as the car roared into Pounders.

"Mann schools shity . . . thank God its summer . . . party all night . . . go beach all day!"

"Hell yeah!" Boy agreed.

"Eh boyz, party tonight eh," Kalani pursued, "ten o'clock at Tiare's house, you know across from V land, you guys going or what?"

"For sure man, Guaranteed," they answered. The boys hopped out of the car and walked down to the beach. Pounders was rolling, nice swells were coming from two directions. The water looked dirty though rubbish and seaweed floated on the surface.

"So we goin' surf or what?" Matt said and they all rushed into the smudged ocean.

Two hours of Pounders is enough. It lives up to its name, many get pounded while barreled by the surf. The waves break so close to the beach its shallow, so once taken by a wave it can crush and beat you all it wants until it spits you out on to the sandy shore. After the surf sesh they washed and piled into the brown camero home bound.

Kalani lived in Kahuku across from the golf course with his father and little sister in a dispirited shack, just down a dirt road next to the Superette. As the chevy drove down the broken path Kalani's dad was standing on the porch.

"Thank eah," he said.

"Eh no problem," Boy replied, "see you tonight."

"I can have one ride yeah?" Kalani asked as he shook everyone's hand.

"Sure, aole pilikia."

"Shootz," and he walked across his yard up to the door.

At the door stood Kalani's father, a high, well cut man, wearing long khakis and a collared shirt. "And where'd you come from?" His father asked.

"The beach, somewhere you never go!" Kalani shot back.

"Hey, I have a life and a job so don't start with me today." His dad argued, "I thought you were going to get Kasie, I was called in from work, no one was there to pick her up!"

"I forgot, I got caught up, okay!"

"Well don't let it happen again, get ready for dinner, I made stew!" The two walked into the house and disappeared into different rooms.

Later that evening Kalani got ready for the party, he put on his baby blue Local Motion collared shirt, jeans and black Lugz. Then sprayed a large amount of Axe on and started to exit the homey shack.

"Where do you think your going?' His dad asked.

"Out . . . to a party."

"I don't think so, you have school tomorrow."

"No dad," he explained, "today was are last day, its summer, can I go now!" Just then a car pulled into the road and bright lights seeped through the living room curtains.

"Wait a minuet, where is this party and how are you going?" He asked, "when will you be home?"

"Its in V-land, and Boys giving me a ride, okay . . . bye." A horn sounded outside and he continued to walk towards the door.

"Whoa whoa slow down now, no drugs, no drinking, be home by twelve, and don't wake your sister up!" He listed.

"But dad, its nine thirty, the party won't end till around two or . . . "

"No buts, I want you home before tomorrow, you got it!" He interrupted.

"Yeah . . ."

"Good, have fun," he said as Kalani rushed out the door, "be safe . . . don't do anything stupid!" He yelled as the druggie car wisped down the dirt road leaving a cloud of smoke.

The brown piece of shit car gassed down the dirt road as Kalani tried to get comfortable, something hard to do with eight guys squeezing in a car made for five. Smoke lingered below the car top as the boys lit up a dubee, they passed it around and burned the weeded cigarettes down like an incensed Indian ritual. Kalani toked the blunt then passed it down to the next willing patient.

"Eh Tommy, pass the dutchie?" The reefer said. Just then the a song came to Kalani's mind and he started singing.

"Dis generation, rules the nation, with version . . ." his voice got louder, "music is da food of love . . . sounds to really make you rub and scrub . . ." more joined in.

"No bong bong bali bili bili bong ba bili bill bili bili bili bong . . ." now the whole car started in and it grew deafening.

"I say: . . Pass the dutchie on the left hand side . . . pass the dutchie on the left had side," the chorus continued, "its gonna burn, give me the music make me jump and dance . . . " they sustained but soon the glee club became a duet then turned into a solo act as Kalani ended the song in quietness. But not for long, in an instant the radio was blasting and booming Sublime, as the car raced past the shrimp farms.

"Eh Kalanz, like on bea?" Matt asked as bend down, opened a small buss up cooler and took out a bottled Budweiser, then shoved it in Kalani's face without waiting for an answer. Kalanz seized the beer, twisted the top open and began chugging the king down. "Whoa, whoa, whoa . . . slow down bra, you got all night to start buzzing."

"Thanks eah," Kalani said as he slipped the bottle between this legs and spread his arms out and rested them against the back of the car. "So," he shouted, "you guys ready to par-te to-night!"

"Hell yeah," they shouted, "you know."

"Suck em up guys suck em up!" Kalani barked. The transport then came to a screeching halt as they neared the teenage social gathering. Cars lined up on the side of the road and faint figures stood in cliques conversing in a nearby driveway. From a distance colorful lights spun, circled and shot out into the country sky and music echoed from the adolescent bash to congested sidelines.

"Where the hell am I going to park?" Boy complained.

"Ooo . . . right there between the telephone pole and fence," Matt helped.

"Eh stooped get one fire hydrant there, dummy."

"So who cares, where the hell else are we going to park?"

"Get room down da road," Kainoa added.

"Fuck if I'm walking my fat ass that far," Tom included.

"Fuck it," Boy said as he made a sharp turn to the side of the road bumping the car in back of him and the pole in front, "I aint walking either!" Then he quickly killed the engine got out and slammed the door.

As the boys got out of the car they headed up the driveway it was a hike but worth it. When they arrived the party seemed to be happening, the music was pounding, the DJ was kicking and people were dancing, if that's what they called it. Kalani held four beer bottles, two in each hand and stored two blunts in his front pocket, a lighter in his back and condoms in his right and left side pockets. The party was outside under a 20 by 40 lean two tarp tent, which only the bold stood under, the rest surrounded the outsides in the dark. It was a normal drink till you drop, dance till your tired, our until the cops show up kind of party, Kalani stood under the tent and walked around a little like he was looking for someone.

"Hey wats up Kalani," a voice drunkenly shouted.

"Nothing much" Kalani said as they shook hands, "how's the party?"

"Not bad, your right . . . choke hotties!"

"Eh have fun ah . . . no drink too much," the two parted as Kalani continued to look. Then in the corner of the tent, leaning against a pole stood

Leilani, wearing a short black skirt and white tang top. Kalani quickly realized it was her and began stalking his prey. He slowly walked around so he was in back of her, then nonchalantly grabbed her ass, and immediately put his hands around her eyes.

"Guess who?" He said jokingly.

"Kalani . . ." she sounded happy, "is that you?"

"Howd you know?" He jumped.

"I've been waiting for you all night," she smirked, "what took you so long?"

"You know I gotta make an appearance."

"What—ever."

"So wanna dance?" She asked.

"You know!" Kalani said as he grabbed her hand and took her out onto the grassy dance floor. The music was blasting and lights strobed across the tent. The pair danced provocatively through the night as sweat collected in their clothing. They skanked, swayed, bent, twisted and turned like one, and soon Leilani and Kalani were in the zone, as they would say. No one could disturb their connection, and the two continued to dance.

"Having fun?" Leilani shouted.

"Yeah you?"

"Yeah," she replied as a slow song sounded. The two held each other and swayed to the speakers rhythms then they kissed, a peck at first but soon it became a tonsil tongue hockey game. The set continued to dance and suck face for the rest of the night until blue lights began crowding the houses driveway.

The party was over. Today became yesterday and tomorrow became today, or tonight, as the children spilled down the dirtied driveway.

"I had a real great time tonight," Leilani said.

"Yeah . . . a . . . me too," Kalani replied, as they slowly walked down the hill.

"You wanna go to my place?" she asked, "my parents went to Las Vegas, we could hang out and stuff."

"Sure!" Kalani said. The highway swarmed with freed teenagers, and police. Some stood on the side of the street talking, some wouldn't leave and most left probably not homeward but gone nevertheless. As the two continued down, Boy, Kainoa and Mutt stood on the bottom, drunk off their asses.

"Yo, Kalanz over here!" One said.

"Eh bra we go, get cops all over the place, old V-land by the beach. Everyone is going . . . common bra we waiting for you," Boy yelled as Kalani slowly walked with his arm around Leilani.

"Nah . . . I get one ride home . . . but tanks oh," Kalani softly said to the gang. He then nodded his head left towards Leilani as she leaned her head on his shoulder.

"Ohh . . . I see . . . " Mutt said as the other to laughed, praised and celebrated in the background. Then the three were gone.

"So, you ready . . . " Leilani asked.

"Yeah . . . want me to drive?"

"Please!" She agreed.

"No problem." The two got into her car then drove down the highway into the morning night.

HUGHIE LONG, *born in 1986, grew up in Hauʻula on Oʻahu, attended Kamehameha Schools in Honolulu, graduated in 2005, and currently attends Manhattanville College in New York, where he studies creative and professional writing and photography.*

Junior Mika Togiola
"THEY SAY YOU BETTER WATCH OUT"

They say you better watch out.
I have the power to super-size myself
and grow eight feet tall, four feet wide,
and triple my weight.
Look at me wrong and I'll stomp
all over
you.

They say you better watch out.
I have the power to untie
my wicked ponytail
and unleash my
afro of destruction
that will strangle you
no matter where
you hide.
They say you better watch out.
I have the power to scale
the tallest

coconut trees in the world
and husk those coconuts
with my bare teeth,
so imagine
what I could do
to your head.

They say you better watch out.
I have the power to call
my immediate
and extended
super-family
from our headquarters
in the housing.
With a loud ChEeEEee Hu!!!,
they'll rush by my side
you cover my back,
and jump on yours.
They say you
better watch out.
They say I'm
dangerous.
That's what they
say.

I say
I am just a Samoan
who's going to school
and hopefully one day
I'll have the power
to erase
these stereotypes.

JUNIOR MIKA TOGIOLA, *born in Pago Pago, American Samoa, came to Hawai'i at a young age and settled in the public housing projects of Kalihi in Honolulu, on O'ahu. Drugs, alcohol, and gangs surrounded his family. Those disturbing events made an everlasting impact on his life. He earned a BA in political science and will receive a master's degree in organization change and development soon. An accomplished singer/performer, he founded the social services music program Hope Through Music, which targets at-risk teens.*

J. Freen

"HANK'S PLACE"

A fter dinner—beef stew, he was right—he is out the door and into the brisk night air before his mother can corner him to say whatever it is she has been working up to say for the past week or so. Jeez, a sweater would be good, but naw, he made his escape already. On his cell to Mikey—pick me up as soon as you can get that piece of shit started; yeah he'll put in one set on the bass tonight if the regular guy's girlfriend keeps him home again, but only one set, understand?

Down on the street he stands next to the parked cars, in front of the garage, thinking, shit, I should just walk down there. How far is it, anyway, like a mile, two? How long could it take? But naw, the neighbors already think the family's nuts. Me on my bike, mom walking everywhere—not the regular Hawaiian way, is it? But then, maybe we not da regular kine Hawaiians, huh. Thinking about his brother's e-mail he just read. Everything cool over here nothing big to report. Patrol tonight. But a mellow neighborhood. In the daytime, anyway. Probably be home by spring. My kids look like somebody else's already, in the pictures I get from Jade over the net. Little hapa kids. Shit I miss home. Not Vegas. Home home. Yeah, believe it or not. I miss Papakolea.

Which worries him. As long as his brother could be over there and manage to forget about where he comes from, and pretend, or whatever . . . forgetting might just be the key to the whole deal, yeah? Which brings to mind Mikey and his ancient VW Bug. The only automobile he will ride in. Ever again? There's a fucking thought. Mikey a ridiculously safe driver, even when drunk. Especially when drunk. The bug not capable of doing over thirty. Fifteen, climbing the hill into the homestead. Which might bring to mind—but no, it won't not tonight. Forgetting is the key. Or, at least reminding yourself to forget. While never forgetting. Come on Mikey!

He hears him long before he sees the canted set of weak yellow headlights wobbling up the street. With a rattle and a cough the engine dies as the Bug coasts to a stop. Mikey is struggling to clear a space for him inside, rearranging the guitar cases, waving him toward the car.

"Eli, take da bass, take da bass."

He knows this drill. Setting the guitar case on the pavement, he first squeezes into the front seat, then pulls the case in with him, then carefully closes the Bug's door by stretching his right hand under the case and feeling around blind for the handle. Fastening the seat belt is even trickier: his left hand must be freed from where it is jammed against Mikey's guitar and the belt passed over the bass and himself and snapped in place.

"That was easy."

"Eh Moke, how you bruddah? Cold like hell tonight, yeah?" Mikey yells as he turns the key and they roll down into the city.

Mikey is talking as they drive, explaining the lyrics to a new song he's written, going over the playlist for tonight and complaining about how expensive Christmas trees are this year, telling him there's this new hybrid fir tree that is "one natural albino haole tree" that is really cool but costs three hundred dollars and there's only maybe five examples in the whole world and one of them is on display at Home Depot and next to it is this other genetically modified one that is red, yeah, one ehu colored tree which is four hundred bucks, and he would buy one but he doesn't have the money and besides even these trees die, no, check that, are already dead, the needles ending up in one pile on your carpet, one brown pile like all the rest, so what's the point?

Something about an ehu Christmas tree? He's thinking about his brother's situation. Then about his own kids, then his dad—all far away. Like he pushed them there. Like maybe he's the cause of everything being as fucked up as it is. It is possible, you know. That doing something really bad, really stupid and bad and unforgivable might make a bunch of other really bad and stupid things happen. As punishment. But why should everybody else be punished, when he's the one who fucked up?

It is suddenly quiet.

"Eh, how's dat foah one parking spot?" Mikey says, craning his neck and admiring his parallel parking job, not normally one of his strengths as a driver. "Careful da bass when you get out, eh?"

"You come ovah heah an help me, fockah."

"'Kay, okay—no get your BVDs in one twiss, brah."

They are on the sidewalk, just down from the bar, Mikey arranging his triple-XL size aloha shirt and smoothing out his white pants, his guitar case leaned against the Bug. He looks up.

"Jeez, Moke, I tot you wuz gonna wear your good shirt. You look like one Filipino gangbangah in dat ting."

"Yeah? You look like one tent."

"Ha! Dass my Mokie! You wen wake up, eh? Come on, I buy you one beah."

They enter Hank's and they're early, Hank himself futzing around behind the tiny stage, just a few patrons at the bar, nobody sitting at the tables yet.

"Hide the beer, the Hawaiians heah!" Hank shouts, without raising his head.

They sit at their usual table. Hank slides into the booth, the smoke from his cigarette preceding him.

"Uh, sorry sir," Mikey says, "but you cannot smoke in heah."

"Yeah yeah yeah. We da kine, da modern day lepahs, no? Bambye dey make us go Molokai and you non smokahs no see us evah again."

"Uh-huh, dass it. You folks get one disease. An' you like spread em aroun'."

"Whoa, bruddah! You referring to secondhand smoke? Dat's pretty heavy da kine, social commentary, foah one musician."

"Eh, I nevah go Kam School foah nutting, my frien' an leadah."

"Criticism from one musician. Maybe I *should* quit already."

"Wat—your wife nevah criticize you?"

"My wife? You tink I listen to her?"

"I dunno. She stay listening to you," Mikey says, with a single, significant eyebrow lift.

Just visible behind Hank's big head bobs a single chopstick, stabbing toward the ceiling at a dynamic angle. Strong perfume invades, pushing back male cologne. As a look of terror transforms Hank's happy-go-lucky visage into something profoundly different—something familiar, but something that nobody really likes to see, especially this close up (especially this early in the evening)—a pile of damaged hair, held in place with the wooden chopstick, appears tableside. Male eyes, downcast, see two hands, manicured, nails done tonight in high gloss magenta, tented on the Formica surface. The right hand disappears from view. Fingers close on the smoking cigarette, pull it from between meaty lips, and flick it out the door onto the sidewalk, where the crazy haole homeless guy from L.A. pounces on it and begins puffing.

The clicking of heels on tiles, receding toward the bar. Male eyes, tentative at first, at last are raised; they meet, share a moment, an eyebrow or two nearly raised, but no, that would be overdoing it.

"So . . . " Hank exhales, reaching absently for the cigarette that someone else is enjoying. "Three sets tonight?"

"Four sets," Mikey says.

"I not paying for four."

"I know dat, boss."

"An' every time, you folks play four anyway."

"Sometimes five."

"How come?"

"Da firse tree sets foah da audience, an you, a course—cause you folks paying, yeah? Fourth set. Eh, you tell em, Mokie, wassup wid da fort set."

"It's for us."

"Foah you?"

"Ass right." Mikey laughs. "By da time fort set roll around we good and loose, eh? Tanks to you, cuz, and da bar tab you wen comp us. Plus, by den,

we already wen play what we know, pretty much. Fort set we play what we
don't know."

Hank looks both of them over.

"I still only paying foah tree sets."

Mikey laughs again. "No can blame us for trying, eh boss."

The night is young but he feels about fifty, going on fifty five. The beer
tastes like soapy water, the night air from the street is cold, goosebumps on
his bare arms. The image of the only sweater he owns sitting folded and
snug in his drawer back home, keeping his long johns and other mainland
gear warm, lodges in his head and won't shake loose.

Mikey starts the first set alone, since he sees that his bass player isn't
drunk enough yet and his ukulele player is late. There are still only about ten
people in the place, but for Hank's that's about half full, so it's clearly time
to begin the entertainment. Mikey's first song is always "Hi'ilawe," which he
plays as a tribute to Gabby Pahinui, to whom he is distantly related. It is the
only song all night he'll sing straight up, his guitar slack keyed, following
Gabby's chops exactly, lovingly, not changing a thing from the original, the
strings squeaking as he slides up and down the frets, his voice a full octave
higher than normal, to get where Gabby sang it, and from the opening lines
he begins to come out of his shit. "Kūmaka ka 'ikena iā Hi'ilawe, Kapapa
lohi mai a'o Maukele . . . "

Looking into Mikey's broad Hawaiian face, wrapped up so deep in the
music he is the music, Mokie's mind finally unloads, lets go, allows him
to move around the cabin freely, and the shot glass of whiskey, until now
untouched next to the beer mug, is elevated and descending, warms him
against the winter wind, warms him to the bar and the people and his friend's
clear-as-the-night-air voice which carries out onto the sidewalk where even
the homeless guy from L.A., who doesn't know shit from nothing, is standing
stock still and staring into the pool of light shining down on the musician
singing like a god come down to visit.

He claps when Mikey's pau, he and maybe a couple of other people.
The big Samoan or Tongan guy sitting at the bar with the haole chick
talked steadily through the whole song, and when he hears the clapping he
shoots him a look, but he ignores it, both men thinking: save the trouble
for later.

Their regular crowd starts showing up. In half an hour the booth is full,
with two or three other friends spilling over to the adjacent table. For a seat
with the core group you need to show up early. To show up early means
you've got nothing else going on, meaning single or divorced or just alone,
meaning, for the most part, male and semi-alcoholic, Tonight at least there's
a female present, making the whole thing look less like the Friday night los-

ers club meeting. Kaylah Dela Cruz, a thirty-something divorcee who's a friend of Mikey's cousin. Good-looking, half Filipino, showed up two weeks ago and clearly likes to drink and party with the boys, although why she is still here is a bit of a mystery, since she's made no move to choose anybody from the table. Maybe she's still trying to make up her mind. Maybe she's a lesbian. Ha, ha.

Bringing to mind Linda, the new dispatcher, and how much he wishes he could be out with her tonight, lezzie or no, rather than sitting here at Hank's wondering if he could take the big Samoan or Tongan guy, if and or when it comes to that. Because, although she certainly is part of his past, or at least her sister is, and it's not a past he's proud of, Linda has something, present in a set of dark Japanese eyes, that he needs. But exactly what is It? Disapproval? No doubt, there's plenty of that, bruddah. Combined, maybe, with an unrealistic hope—that the man she is looking at might be better than he seems to be? That he might be worth the effort. Isn't that what mothers have going on, behind their eyes? Which means . . . Jeez, a single fucking psych class at Chaminade, before he quit, before the . . . What did Mr. Edwards used to say at Roosevelt? A little knowledge is a dangerous thing . . . Damn. No shit.

"I telling you wuz nuts dis morning," Kenny is saying. Mikey has finished his first set and is over at the bar, flirting with Maya the bartender. "Heavy, dat storm. Had calls from all ovah. Powah out in Kakaako, Kaimuki, Kahala . . . "

"Eh," says Randall, leaning in, "you *breathe* on HECO too hahd, boom, da powah go out!"

"Ass right," chimes in Ray, "An' how come dey nevah offah foah pay you back foah all da time you stay sitting deah in da dahk, wondering wen da buggah going come back on, eh?"

"Ah, you guys fullashet. You try get along widout powah. You stay da kine, helpless widout us. We da front line."

"Ass true," says Mikey, drifting over from the bar. "No mo cold beah already, neva have 'lectricity. No no powah cords eiddah."

"Listen to da man," Kenny says, downing his draft. "He speaking da trut'."

"So den, buy me one beah, cuz," Mikey says, smiling with every tooth.

"Hah!" Ray yells "I knew it! He stay on da payroll already!"

And Kaylah sits and ponders, behind her makeup, thinking about her kids back home with her mother and what her mother is thinking right now, about her, and how this might be the last night for her, maybe last Friday should have been it actually, but giving it one more go-around the table, just to review, just to be sure.

Straight across is Kenny, the Hawaiian Electric guy. Nice looking, in a local Chinese kind of way. Something not quite right there though. Reminds her of her cousin Norman, who seemed, well, normal, a little wound-up was all, until the day he blew a fuse and lit the house on fire with his wife and kids inside. Luckily everybody got out, although Norman still hasn't yet, locked up as he is in Kaneohe in a rubber room and the whole family good with that.

To Kenny's right is Ray. A cop. Portagee looking. Maybe some Hawaiian too? She is not desperate enough to date a cop.

Next is Mokie. Vincent. The dark, cute one. Cutey Hawaiian-something. Man, those eyelashes. To die for. Something missing, though, something big. Something he lost; the others don't talk about it. Divorced? It's more than that. You don't get eyes like that from just a divorce. More than just the standard Hawaiian anger thing. Way too complicated for her, at this point, at thirty-three. Maybe earlier, like ten years earlier, she would have been willing to put in the time.

Moving to her left is Harold—Harry. Like her, hapa. Only the other half is Japanese. Could have been handsome, if it wasn't for the eyes too close together, but he's a lawyer so who cares, right? Only some public defender or something, but still. She can see he likes her, wants to fuck her, but anybody can tell, he does that a lot, so where would it go? He's been married, she can see that, Suspects he might he married right now—wouldn't put it past him.

There's the big guy Mikey. Happily married and not her type anyway. Wished she had a brother like him, a Hawaiian brother. As her real brother is fond of saying, too many Flips in their family. Her mom the exception. The long-suffering haole lady. What was she thinking back then? Yeah, dad was cute once, but still yet . . . Which, by the way, girl, could apply to your own marriage/divorce. And her mom always told her: Don't marry a Filipino, don't marry a Filipino, don't. So naturally . . . But he's from California, mom. San Francisco, in fact. Doesn't even take his shoes off before he comes in the house. Doesn't like Flip food. Hates the Marcos family You're gonna love him. And she did. Does.

"Hey, was that your father I saw on the evening news tonight, Mokie?" Harry asks, out of the blue.

With cold beer sliding down his throat, drinking from the mug like a man dying of thirst. Mokie stops and stares across the table. He shoots a questioning look at Mikey, who now wishes he had started his second set five minutes ago, like he was supposed to. He shrugs. Nods.

"Dey . . . wen buss up da Makapuu campahs. Dis morning."

"How long were they there, anyway," Harry asks, not really asking. "Like over a year?"

Silence around the table.

"It was only a matter of time," Harry won't leave it alone: "They didn't have a legal leg to stand on. That's a public park. It's for everyone. Not for just one particular group to live on like it was theirs."

"Eh," Mikey says, "Dat land belongs to da Department of Hawaiian Homes. Dey only leasing it to da State. Doze Hawaiians get one strong legal right to dat beach. An Mokie's dad stay standing up foah dat right."

"Hey, if you're Hawaiian—go to Kamehameha, shit, get on the homestead list if you're half, take the tuition waiver at UH—get what you can out of the system. But forget about the sovereignty shit, man. It's for beach park Hawaiians and who the fuck, Hawaiians included, wants to live in a tent anymore, brah."

"No say brah to me, you haole fockface. I not your brah, your cuz, your watevah"

"Jesusmoddahmary, speakadadevil," Ray exhales, everyone turns to look where he's looking, and sure enough, its the man himself, Mokie's Father, wild-haired, with his crazy Christian sidekick Kaipo, standing at the doorway, shyly taking in the scene, He finishes his beer, watching Hank approach the two men still hesitating at the door, Hank seeming to check them out before showing them an open table.

"Let's go, Mikey," Mokie says. "Time foah da second set already."

Mikey gives him a quick, questioning look, then sees that this is the only reasonable thing to do. Besides, it's either play music or punch out Harry. Punching out Harry has been on his to-do list for some time, but that can wait for another night.

Up on the tiny stage they group up with the uke player, a teenage nephew of Mikey's who plays in the modern, plugged-in, rip-it-up style that has transformed the instrument, bringing it up front, leaving the guitar and bass to follow. Mikey's okay with the change, the audience expects it now, though he occasionally has to whack the nephew on the head with the playlist to get him to come back to earth.

They start with a couple of Hank's favorites, "Honolulu City Lights" and "E Hihiwai." On the chorus Hank wanders up to the mike and leans in, singing as he has since small kid time, effortlessly, harmonizing with Mikey, the words he memorized long ago, without knowing exactly what each one means "E hihiwai la lae lae, E ho'i mai kaua la, i ka aina uluwehi O Wailau . . . " and, as they finish, in that mini-second of silence before the applause should begin, the big Samoan or Tonga guy at the bar belches once, loudly, a period to the song's last line.

The three musicians turn to glare at the big guy, who shrugs, smiles, and opens his hands, playing it cute. His girlfriend is giggling. Their eyes lock. Mokie mouths the words "That's two." The guy just smiles some more. Mikey catches the exchange. He steps between their line of sight, to the microphone.

"Tanks eh, folks. Dat waz da famous mele about one small mono-valve creatchah dat live in one big green valley on Molokai. Sometime you can find dese guys at Tamashiro's Fish Market—but be prepared, eh. You going pay big bucks for hihiwai dese days."

The rap works, as far as the moment goes. The big Samoan or Tongan goes back to feeling up his girlfriend, the musicians tune up, the audience orders more drinks. Mokie glances over at his dad and Kaipo, who have a single, untouched beer sitting on the table between them. His dad is looking directly at him through the tobacco smoke. He nods; his dad nods back. Shit, been what, a year since they last saw each other? He never visited the beachpark, taking his cue from his brother, who seemed to follow his father's activities much closer than he did, first from Vegas, then from Iraq, where he continued to read the *Advertiser* as often as he could on-line. His brother's advice? Don't encourage him. Leave him to make an ass of himself by himself.

Older. Grayer. That's how he looks. He wishes he had a cell phone with photo capability or a fucking camera. He suddenly knows how much a photo of his dad would mean to his brother. Whoa. This knowledge opens a closed door, just a crack—not wide enough so he can clearly see what it is through the beer and the whiskey. Something previously closed and locked, that's all. The key right here in front of him. In his father's tired eyes. And in his brother's e-mailed warnings.

"Okay, we're back and in tune. Or we all outta tune da same." Mikey is saying. "Watevah, at dis time we would like to ask foah any requests you folks like heah. We know da buggah, we going play 'em foah you. No be shy."

"Kaulana Na Pua." It's Kaipo, raising his hand like he's back in high school.

Mikey looks at him; he looks at his hand, The band shrugs.

"Uh, dat is one great song, one classic foah shuah. And we know da chords, we know da melody. But da kine, da words . . . "

"No problem." Kaipo says through the smoke. "He knows all the words . . . "

Mokie's dad looks up like somebody just pinched him awake.

"No," he and his youngest son say, simultaneously.

"Yeah, yeah," Mikey says. "I remembah now, dass right. You useted to sing at luau, li'dat. You wuz good, Mr. Awong. Come on up—join your bruddahs foah one song, eh? Folks, I tink he need one liddle bit encouragement."

Drunken shouts. His dad looking around, not thinking about it too long, standing up, walking to the stage. Thinner, but still the athlete's body evident, his long arms sinewy and muscular and brown, Hank brings him an old guitar, a wooden stool, Something about him—everything about him—quiets the noisy room. For a minute or two he tunes up with the hand, then turns to face the audience. One half turn back to the band. "In F okay?" and then they start, his voice shaky at first, his hands tentative and stiff on the instrument, but gradually thawing as the song takes him over.

As Mokie stays far in the background with the bass notes, he listens to the words and remembers his dad teaching his brother and him the song. Surprised at how much he remembers now—no problem on when to come in on the chorus. Harder, though, to remember what the words mean.

But then his dad starts on a stanza and a bunch of it comes hack. That the song was written back in the day, the year Liliuokalani was overthrown and the Hawaiian kingdom was no more. That it was a protest over what the haole had done, and that the stanza he is singing right now is saying: "We do not value the government's sums of money. We are satisfied with the stones, Astonishing food of the land," and, yeah, that it used to have other names, one of which was Mele Ai Pohaku, "The Stone-eating Song." Not hard to get it. We would rather eat stones than take the deal that's been jammed down our throats by the big money guys. But how many Hawaiians would say that today, 2006? Just forget all my bright shiny stuff, my SUV, and the tract house in Kapolei, three hours on the freeway every day to work and back a bummer, but at least there's flat screen football on Sunday afternoons. In exchange for what? The fucking Nation hack? Shit. Not many of us. But the beach rat singing his heart out in front of him. He would. Has. The King of nothing. Currently of nowhere.

Just as they're wrapping up, repeating the chorus "kaulana na pua, e, kaulana na pua, e" (harmonizing with his dad the very last thing he thought he'd be doing this night) two things happen at once. His mom walks in Hank's Place with a tall haole guy, and the Tonga or Samoan gets off his bar stool and yells. "Hey, I know what that song is about. You Hawaiians lost your Queen 'cause she no more the balls to stand up and fight back. We Tongans still got our King and he weighs four hundred pounds!"

Suddenly, no sound in the room, no new smoke exhaled into the pall for that frozen second when no one breathes, the people chessmen in their assigned positions, waiting for a hand to appear above the board and change everything with a single move. His dad stands up, carefully puts the guitar down, takes a step toward the Tongan. The Tongan takes his dad's face in his hand and pushes him backwards, head over heels into the band, which collapses in a heap of arms, legs, amps and instruments, in the corner.

Extricating himself out from under Mikey, he rushes to the bar where Kaipo has wrapped his arms around the Tongan guy's neck and is hanging on while the Tongan roars like a lion and tries to scrape the diminutive Hawaiian off by banging him repeatedly against the wall. Everyone in the bar seems to be yelling at once. He screams: "The King of Tonga is a fag!" The Tongan turns looks down, recognizes him, and smiles. Right behind his big Tongan mug floats Kaipo's face—he hasn't let go of the thick, sweaty neck. Kaipo is grinning.

Mokie doesn't think about it. He kicks the Tongan as hard as he can in the crotch. The big guy looks surprised, doubles over and kisses the floor. Everyone—the band members, his table of friends, Hank himself—piles on. At one point he looks to his left and the tall haole guy who came in with his mom (his mom!—he's forgotten about her!) is right next to him, sitting on the Tongan's head.

"Do the Tongans really have a king?" the haole guy asks.

An hour later, after the cops have left with the Tongan in tow, they play the fourth set, Mikey with a big bruise over his eye where he made contact with a guitar stand letting the Hawaiian thing go for now, cutting loose with roadhouse blues which he plays at full volume on the tinny amp, quickly leaving the ukulele and bass behind, chording, leading top, bottom, everywhere at once while the audience, back to smoking and drinking at full speed sits and stares. After he finishes they don't clap but roar, one guy falling out of his seat while holding his beer high, licking the slop-over suds and assuring the room, "No worries, no worries, no worries . . . "

Even if he can't exactly keep up with Mikey, he is glad to have the bass in his hands. Something to do, other than trying not to look at his parents. He looks at them anyway, and in some ways it's like seeing them for the first time. His mom is revealed as a pretty woman out on a date with a man who is looking only at her. And, although she should be nervous and uncomfortable with both her former husband and her son sneaking looks at her, she is obviously enjoying herself and seems to be mostly concerned with overcoming first date jitters.

His father is still sitting with Kaipo (who is being supplied with free beer by Hank, for taking the initiative with the Tongan). Kaipo now has a bandage wrapped around his head—reminds him of photos he's seen of refugees from a war tone. He's getting old, Pops is, so old so fast, no doubt about it, but there is something nevertheless new about him. He is sitting straight and tail in his seat, his hand wrapped around a glass of water almost like the water is holding him up, but no, he is holding himself up now, isn't he, his gray eyes watchful and calm through the smoke and the noise, even when he turns his head slightly to look at his ex. It's the calmness, the confidence, that is new. Sometime during the last year his dad has finally found something, he sees, that has moved him to some kind of shelter, where the storm of rage and guilt and dispossession can't reach. The only feeling that accompanies this realization is a deep envy that brings heat to his face and surprises the hell out of him.

They finish the last set, pack up the instruments. Hank announces last call. Mokie sits with Mikey drinking the last drink, without a thought in his head. Out of the corner of his eye he sees his dad standing next to his mom's table, talking to her about something. This should catch his attention, but he is suddenly tired with this day (now bleeding into the next) and just wants to go home. Out on the sidewalk they are loading up the car. The haole bum from L.A. asks him for two dollars and fifty cents.

"What? Beat it," he says sleepily.

But Mikey is curious. "Eh why you want dat specific amount, eh? You get some particular da kine, purchase, in mind bruddah?"

"Maybe—but I don't want the money from you. I want it from him."

Mikey ponders this.

"Give him the money."

"Huh? No way. I doan give bums money. No way."

"Eh, how you know dis one bum?"

"Wha? Look at him, Smell him."

"Eh, your faddah doan smell too good right now eiddah. He one bum?"

"Fock you."

"Wat, you nevah wen read your Bible, li'dat?"

"I wen read da Bible."

"Yeah, den you stay familiah wid da story of da kine, da good Samaritan, no?"

"Aw shit, I give up already. Here ya go. One dollah, two dollah. Nuff."

"I need fifty cents more."

"Eh, no push it already."

The others stand in the cool night air, with arms crossed, looking at him. He has never been able to take people looking at him.

"Shit," he says finally. "Heah."

"Thanks," says the haole bum. He turns to Mikey and puts the money in his hand. "This is for you. You are a great musician. Merry Christmas." He turns and shuffles down the sidewalk, headed toward the harbor.

Mikey is shaking, struggling to keep it to himself.

"You," Mokie says, taking in the quivering mass of Hawaiian flesh.

"You gonna give that back?"

"Hell no."

"You give me dat back, right now you buggah."

"Hey, that was one tip from one fan. I stay one poor musician an I keeping em, okay?"

"You stay drunk!"

"Maybe small kine."

"Small kine bullshet! I not driving anywhere wid you."

"Fine, bruddah, great. Wunnerful. Watchew going do? Walk home?"

"I crawl befoah I drive wid one drunk."

"Eh fock you. You da drunk."

Mikey makes an attempt at jumping quickly into the VW but this proves difficult to pull off. He hits his head a couple a times, makes it on the third try, and does his best to speed off in a huff. It all takes too much time to be a really effective display of anger.

He is left on the sidewalk, with the taste of the Bug's exhaust in his mouth. He looks down the street at the retreating form of the haole bum, and, just ahead of him, Mikey's Bug turning left. The night is clearer and colder, the wind fresher.

"Shet," he says, turning around, starting off in the general direction of the invisible mountains and home.

He has only gone half a block when an old van pulls up slow on his right. His dad sticks his head out, "Hey, sonny boy."

He looks over at him. Bottom line. That's dad and this is me, sonny boy. "You drunk?"

The old man shakes his head. "Two years, tree months, seven days, an', uh . . . " (glancing at his watch) hour twenty minutes sober."

From inside the van, he hears Kaipo singing. The passenger door slams. Kaipo weaves up to him.

"Eh, he da designated drivah. Foah everybody."

He surrenders. Kaipo opens the rear door of the van and they find themselves staring at two of the dirtiest bare feet he's ever seen.

"It's okay. He's alive. I tink."

He climbs in, Kaipo goes around to the front, the door slams and his dad steers them down Maunakea, left on King, left again on Alakea, the turnings true and familiar to him in the darkness of the van's interior, the way home, and before they cross the freeway and begin to wind around the back of Punchbowl he falls into a dreamless sleep and is for the first time in a long time at ease with himself.

J. FREEN (KEVIN O'LEARY) *was born in 1951. For the past thirty-six years he has called Hawai'i home. The author of ten plays (two mounted in Honolulu by Kumu Kahua), two novels, numerous short stories (several of which have appeared in* Bamboo Ridge*), and feature articles published over the last ten years in the* Honolulu Weekly, *Freen currently lives in Kalihi, Honolulu, with his wife.*

Vita Tanielu

O lenei fa'aaliga tausala,
ua fiafia tele ai le agaga.
Manaia ana mata'upu,
fa'ataua ai tu ma aganu'u.
Fa'aolaola i mafaufau,
le Fa'asamoa i ta fanau.
O tiute moni o lo ta sao,
saunia fanau mo a taeao.

'Anusa ia fa'aaliga masani,
fa'amoemoe mo teine palagi.
Sa tauva ai teine Samoa,
i tu palagi a le 'au mau'oa.
Ofu ta'ele o teine palagi,
se'e-muli'umi ma ofu-fe'ilafi.
I'i mai lava le tama'i moa,
e le'o ni tu na Fa'asamoa.

A'o le Misi Samoa e fa'ataua,
tu ma aganu'u mai i le Atua.
Leai ni se'evae ae savali fua,
sulu'ao'ao ma la'ei anamua.
Fesili-ma-Tali i gagana e lua,
gagana palagi ma la ta'ua.
A'o le taleni le siva taualuga,
o le tiute lea a tausala uma.

O nisi tausala e Fa'asamoa,
a'o nisi fo'i e misi atoa.
O nei fanau e leai ni sese,
ae peita'i o matua pe.
A le-iloa ona tautala,
e nai ou alo i le ta gagana.
Le tamaloa Toga faimai Tae,
"Oute nofo atu fua o a'u o 'Ae."

A 'e alofa i si au fanau,
fa'asa'osa'o lou mafaufau.
Ia le taotasi a'o mea e lua,

tu a palagi ma tu a matua.
Po o fea lava 'e te alu i ai,
e manino lava le mata o le vai.
Soia ia 'e te fia palagi,
ae 'apo'apo au tu masani.

Tausaga mua o le Misi Samoa,
Teine o Teresa na sili atoa.
Tauva fo'i i le Miss South Pacific,
she was awesome simply terrific.
Miss Samoa fo'i mai ma le ute,
malo fo'i i le Pasefika i Saute.
'E te taufa'aleaga ma faipona mai,
a 'o le Samoa Pageant ua iai lona 'ai.

1988 tausaga muamua,
Iona i le UHM le faufautua.
Fa'ailoa i Samoa o i tua,
a matou tiute-fai i le laumua.
i le a'oa'oina o le Fa'asamoa,
e si'itia ai si o ta igoa.
Sau se'i tepa se'i 'e maimoa,
Polokalame Samoa alu i le atoa.

Samoa uma ia tautuana,
a leai se gagana ua leai se aoga.
'Aua o le gagana na te fa'atinoa,
la ta aganu'u Fa'asamoa.
E le mafai e le gagana palagi,
fa'asoa se 'ava po o lou lagi.
Lona uiga fuli mai atoa,
e sapasapaia le Misi Samoa.

This cultural pageant of the tausala,
enlightens and uplifts my soul.
Lofty are its criterias,
perpetuating culture and traditions.
To honor in the spirit,
the Samoan Way for our children.

Our true responsibilities and contributions,
preparing youth for the future.

In local contemporary pageants,
designed for teine palagi.
Samoan girls competed in them,
based on the palagi culture of the affluent.
Swim wear of teine palagi,
high heels and fancy evening gowns.
The desperate cry of the lost little chicken,
such topics are not Fa'asamoa.

But this Samoan Pageant honors,
true traditions that are God given.
No high heels but walk barefeet,
sulu'ao'ao and traditional wear.
The interview is in two languages,
Fa'apalagi and Fa'asamoa.
Talent portion is the siva taualuga,
a cultural duty of every teine Samoa.

Some contestants speak Samoan,
while others—speak no more.
This shortcoming is not their fault,
but visionless parents with no plans.
If your child can't speak Samoan,
it is you who are shortsighted.
As the Tongan noble's ancient confession,
"I am Ae, sitting guilty and defeated."

If you truly love your children,
initiate a new cause for tomorrow.
Teach not one but two ways,
Fa'apalagi and your Fa'asamoa.
Wherever in the world you may go,
the spring's eye is always clear.
Please stop your fia palagi,
but support your usual ways.

First year of the Samoa-Hawai'i pageant,
Teine o Teresa won the crown.
Competed in the Miss South Pacific Pageant,
she was awesome and surely renowned

A conqueror she returned to Honolulu,
with a new title of Miss South Pacific.
You ridiculed and badmouthed our pageant,
but we're counted, recognized and praised.

Our inaugural year of 1988,
UHM's Iona is the advisor.
We encouraged the Samoan community
with our in-campus Samoan Program.
In teaching the language and culture,
to uplift our local identity.
To come and witness and to learn,
the Samoan program is flying high.

Samoan people please be aware,
You lose your language you lose your culture.
Because the language embodies,
our Samoa way—our Fa'asamoa.
It is impossible for the palagi language,
to fulfill the 'ava ceremony or your funeral.
Simply put please join our cause,
support the Samoan Cultural pageant.

VITA TANIELU *is a University of Hawaiʻi at Mānoa Samoan community liaison who found-*
ed the Miss Samoa-Hawaiʻi Cultural Pageant in 1988 and produced it until 2000. He also
founded the Miss South Pacific Beauty Pageant in 1987. These two pageants share the same
goal: to honor and perpetuate Polynesian language and traditions among the Islands' youth. Ta-
nielu holds two historical and royalty high chief titles (Leiataua-Lesā and Fepuleai) in Samoa.
He is an instructor of the Samoan language and culture at UH Mānoa.

Emelihter Kihleng
"THE MICRONESIAN QUESTION"

For those who
Think they know
Wonder
Don't care
Or haven't given thought to . . .

WHAT IS A MICRONESIAN?
No, not a POLYNESIAN
Not a MELANESIAN
MICRONESIAN
MICRONESIAN
MICRO-NESIAN

Micro
Small
Miniscule
Invisible
Ignored
Isolated
Distant, "tiny islands"

MICRONESIANS
Migrating
Moving
Island hopping
On Continental Air Mike
Departing from our islands
Descending upon the U.S.
who gave us
permission
back in '86
slowly getting noticed
across Honolulu
FOB MICRONESIANS
women wearing
colorful,
bright,
long skirts
Pink combs in long hair
Walking by the road
On The Bus
With babies
Accompanied by
other women
With babies
Dangling gold earrings
Crammed into apartments
Movin' on up
Stereotyped

Misrepresented
Speaking "MICRONESIAN"
If you read the news
You'd think we were
Invading legal aliens

Newspaper Headlines Read:

**"MICRONESIAN BILL TOO LONG OVERDUE; THE
ISSUE: THE FEDERAL GOVERNMENT OWES
HAWAII NEARLY $100 MILLION FOR SERVICES
PROVIDED TO IMMIGRANTS FROM MICRONESIA"**

"MICRONESIANS: THE INVISIBLE MALIHINI"

**"HAWAII MAY GET HELP IN HELPING
    MICRONESIANS"**

we are a **"BURDENSOME"** group
of more than 10,000
50% living below
federal poverty level,
relying **"not only on educational services but on social-
welfare services, health care and safety net programs"**

CAYETANO CLAIMS:

**"WE SIMPLY CANNOT ABSORB THE EXTRA COSTS
OF PROVIDING SOCIAL SERVICES AND MEDICAL
AND FINANCIAL ASSISTANCE NEEDED BY SUCH
POOR MIGRANTS"**

Are MICRONESIANS the only **"POOR MIGRANTS"**
    coming here?
Are MICRONESIANS guilty of consuming all
food stamps

invading all
KPTs,
Mayor Wrights,
and Palolo housings

Using up all
QUEST,
WIC,
MEDICAID
and welfare on island???

I DON'T THINK SO.

So where are all these "MICRONESIANS" coming from?
Who are we?
What are we?

MICRONESIA
POLYNESIA
MELANESIA
colonial constructions
colonial creations
imaginations
configurations
divisions of Pacific Islands

MICRONESIA in the Western Pacific
between Hawaii and the Philippines
And YES, Guam, the U.S. Territory,
is located in MICRONESIA
And the people there, Chamorros,
are MICRONESIANS in denial

the term "MICRONESIAN"
Was first coined on Guam
To distinguish Guamanians from
Their non U.S. citizen, inferior neighbors
migrating to Guam
MICRONESIAN became a means to
Discriminate and target a vulnerable population

At George Washington High School
On Guam
MICRONESIANS
Are discussed on a daily basis

Those fucken MICRONESIANS

I'm not sitting by stupid Trukese

I would never go out with a fucken Trukese, I'd shoot her if she tried to kiss me

my school
segregated
MICRONESIANS in A and B wings
in the cafeteria eating free lunch
Filipinos in C and D wings
Chamorros in E and F wings
And everyone else around someplace
Chuukese, AKA Trukese
not allowed
To wear red
The school
Said that was
The Chuukese gang color

MICRONESIANS don't identify as MICRONESIANS
We were given that identification after leaving home
Upon coming to Guam and Hawaii
Each of us unique like
Tongans,
Samoans, and
Hawaiians
Who do not merely identify as Polynesians

WE ARE:
Pohnpeians
Palauans
Chuukese
Chamorros
Kosraeans
Nauruans
Yapese
Gilbertese
Marshallese
and More

WE SAY:
Kaselehlie
Aiii
Ran Annim
Hafa Adai
Lenwo
Mogethin
Yokwe

So what is a **MICRONESIAN?**

Can you tell me what is a **MICRONESIAN?**

An outside invention?
A misconception?
A location?
A population?

MICRONESIAN lacks concrete definition
An inadequate
Insufficient
Identity
Misplaced
Bestowed wrongly
Upon a large and diverse
Pacific Island population
Who are not under one flag
Who do not speak one tongue
Who do not eat the same food
And most of all who
Do not want to be recognized as one

EMELIHTER KIHLENG *lives on Pohnpei Island in Micronesia, where she teaches English as a Second Language at the College of Micronesia. She grew up in Honolulu. "The Micronesian Question" is one of the first poems she ever wrote. She is working on her first collection of poetry.*

David Hsin Shan Lee
"THE BOILING POT"

One tourist tells me
very proudly
that he
is what they
all refer to now in California
as hapa
(a Japanese (?!) word
for bi-racial he explains)
because he's half Spanish
and half Caucasian.

Looking at me
perplexed, he says,
"I can't quite place
your race.
Can you please tell me
what
you are?"
Tourists always ask
that question,
but I take a slow breath for the haole
and I tell 'em,

"Hachikoraihiti'ijigermolofrenkinawanese,"

Of course da buggah gasps and says,
"What on Earth is that?"

"Hachikoraihiti'ijigermolofrenkinawanese,"
I repeat for him
before I break it down.
"Braddah, no get confuse.
One ninth I stay German,
a fifth Hawaiian
a quarter Popolo,
a twentieth of Okinawan
which is not included in the
one seventh of Japanese.

I get Chinese and Tahitian,
but no confuse that
with the Fijian.
And Korean is tricky
cuz my grandpa had quarter
but my maddah nevah have.
No ask me how that works.
But one fifth had my faddah
who also had Thai,
one fraction of French
and oh try wait, try wait . . . "
"Whoa, whoa, whoa, WHOA!"
the tourist interrupts.
"I asked for your race
not for a lesson in Algebra III."
The tourist grabs all of his stuff
and heads back
to the hotel.

"Pfff . . . he wen ask."

DAVID HSIN SHAN LEE *is Asian–American, born in Honolulu in 1984. As of 2007, he is earning a living as an agency nurse, floating from one point of care to another throughout O'ahu. In his spare time, he enjoys playing his guitar and participating in creative projects that include drawing, writing, graphic arts, and filmmaking. Although he appreciates all forms of art, he hopes to one day gain notice in the world of cinema.*

Dante Kapea Hirata-Epstein

"JEWPANESE"

From Mom I got a disliking of sakana,
or fish because of the awful smell!

From Dad I got my height and big eyes,
which makes me the tallest boy in class,
with one of the best eyesight.

From Grandma Janet Hirata I got my love
of Japanese game shows such as "Challengers of Fire."

From Grandpa Eddie Hirata I got my respect for Koboji Shingon,
a temple that we visit every new year and obon season.

From Uncle Scott I got all of his gelt
or chocolate money when I beat him in Dredel.

From Aunt Pam I got my love for Challah,
braided bread for Shabat, the Sabbath.

So I am Dante Kapea Hirata-Epstein,
and I am a Jewish-Japanese boy
who loves the Matzah of obon.

DANTE KAPEA HIRATA-EPSTEIN *was born in 1998. He is a fourth grader at 'Iolani School in Honolulu and also studies writing at Na'au: A Place for Learning. He has a twin sister named Taja who likes to sing, an irritating little brother named Rysen, an obese poi dog named Rayni, and a paralyzed rabbit named Chaco Bunny. His dream is to be the richest person in the world like Bill Gates and drive a Maybach car. Shalom and Sayonara!!!*

Amalia B. Bueno

"THE CHICHARON WIDOWS"

Everybody knows Margarita Corpuz and Estrelita Salvador. They always come on Sundays. They wake up at five a.m. when it's still dark to bake popular desserts like bibingka, tupig and puto. Then they pick and pack their homegrown vegetables. They fry pork rinds just before loading up their big, baby blue Ford truck. By the time they pull inside the yellow gates with its FRESH SHRIMP sign, it's already 7:15, when most of the breeders and cockfighters have already unloaded set up for the day.

Margarita and Estrelita, also called the chicharon widows, and also known as The RitaLitas, have been coming to the cockfights for two years now. Rita told me once the House considers them regulars. But they were not regular long enough, she said, to be on the "guarantee same spot list." She had added with a shrug, "Our spot could be better, but dis good enough.

Going get plenny people who see us," was her philosophy. Today the widows are set up three lanes away from the main cockpit, a coveted spot that is guaranteed to bring in lots of foot traffic.

I greet them in their booth, where a sign advertising RitaLita's Famous Chicharon is prominent. The white script lettering and comic rendering of dancing chicharon in browns and yellows hangs sturdy just inside the food booth's blue tarp covering. You would have to be blind to miss the sign's animated smiling pork rinds, hands joined with alternating yellow plumeria and red hibiscus flowers. The dancing legs of the happy chicharon and aloha print clad tropical flowers point to the letters in the middle. Their appendages surround the words RitaLita's Famous Chicharon like a lei. It was almost tacky, save for the feelings it evoked of warm kitchens, pleasant fragrances and happy childhoods.

Rita, the primary namesake, is dressed in a long sleeved blue chambray work shirt and milling around under the sign. Her sleeves are rolled up to her elbows and expose strong arms and calloused, veined hands. Her hands are Ilokano hands—big and strong. Her fingers knobby, the kind that are accustomed to digging into the fertile earth of Laoag, Ilocos Norte, where her family is from. Her business partner, Lita, is helping a slightly plump teenage girl pick out some desserts from a wooden display rack. Lita wears a calabash gourd hard hat. Her Army green fatigues are tucked into black rubber boots splashed with just-as-famous, red Waialua mud. I wave to both of the widows.

Their vegetable bounty is piled on three tables pushed together in a U and arrayed like a harvest cornucopia. The bright colors of the vegetables compete with the intense hues of the tablecloth, dyed with characteristic vivid stripes and patterns of native ikat weavers. Karabasa, or kabocha as the Hapons call it, take up most of the space. The mottled green and yellow-streaked pumpkins are tight-skinned and fecund, like pregnant globes. Long, dark green, snake beans are bunched together by the pound and tied with raffia. Their slender bean bodies form graceful curves, nestled and piled on top of each other. Next to them are patani, wing beans large and small that are neatly sorted by size and fitted into quart ZipLoc bags. Eggplant, singkamas, sweet potatoes, green chili peppers for dinuguan, squash for sari-sari. Kamatis, laya, bawang, sibuyas—tomatoes, ginger, garlic, onions. It is a vegetable stew on the tables.

Then there are the leaves. Paria shoots with small yellow flowers, saluyot greens bereft of their slimy okra fruit. Camote, sayote and marunggay with its splayed canopy of foliage. Lush kangkong propped up on its hollow reed stems.

Then there are the flowers, carefully placed in the shady area of the table so they won't wilt. There are beautiful, still closed tabungao flower buds, nowadays filled with fancy items and fried by gourmet chefs to be called something high makamaka like sautéed squash blossoms stuffed with crumbled feta and pine nuts. I move past three women who are picking through a stack of white, curved, beak-shaped flowers and putting the choice ones in their plastic bags. The Filipino name of this flower eludes me, but I visualize a white flower salad with tomatoes and patis.

My favorite vegetable, kabatiti, is stacked in a tall woven basket. I can never remember what this vegetable is called in English. When I first saw kabatiti as a child they reminded me of dinosaurs. They still do today as I pick one up and see a brontosaurus with its slim neck and elongated, fleshy body. I run my pointer along the hard, green ridges that run the entire length of its back. I smile at the two, good-sized ones I have captured in my hand and make them face each other. Looking around to see if anyone is watching, I bring the dinosaurs into mock battle. Gently though, so their small-tipped heads don't get knocked off like my brother and I used to do as children with on my lola's kitchen table. When one head got toppled, it signaled the end of the fight.

Then I see something new. I cannot believe it. It is ingenious entrepreneurship at its best. I marvel at how the chicharon widows are always looking out for their customers. I pick up a bag of the new item.

"Dass for young ladies like you. I make es-pe-shall for your kind," says Rita, walking over toward me and her creation. "Nowadays people no more time for cook. Always go outside and eat. Go out, go out, all the time go outside to eat. Like my son and his family. I don't know why his wife no like cook."

Maybe she's tired like me after a long day at work, I silently respond in my head. But I just smile. Rita looks me straight in the eye. "Dat one in your hands. Dat going help you make good Filipino food for your family."

We both look at the plastic ZipLoc bag filled with all of the pre-cut, pre-sorted, pre-layered fixings you would ever need to make pinakbet. You would have to just simply unzip the bag and pour. This is exactly what my generation needs. Pinakbet 101. Pinakbet Helper. Easy Stovetop Pinakbet.

"How old you now? Around 32, yeah? You no more children, hah?" she asks, slightly accusatory and sounding like a social commentary on the sad state of small nuclear family units.

"No, nana. But I have plenty nieces and nephews, so the bloodline will continue," I reply. I count on her to not notice my accompanying smirk, as it would definitely be a sign of disrespect.

"Dass good, dass good. Your younger sister is good she has her own family. How many kids now? Four? Her husband come from big family, too. The children can help. They can all help each other."

"You know how to make dis?" she asks about the bag I am holding in my hands. I give her a tentative facial expression, a cross between discomfort and eagerness. I try to nod a yes, but she senses my hesitation and takes the bag from my fingers.

"I show you how. First, like dis." She pulls the top open and fishes out the first layer. She retrieves a large pot from under the table. I am amazed again at how ready the widows are for anything. They could probably feed a crowd at a moment's notice with nothing but a five-pound box of chicken thighs in their freezer.

"Cook the ginger and tomato with water. See the ginger? Already smashed, so no need do that. Next layer is the big cherry tomatoes I put inside. So no need chop. Here's the onions next. Stay in big pieces already, so no need cut. Then add the water and the bugguong and then you boil. You get bugguong at home? Every house get. You get some, hah?"

I furnish her with a definitive nod, but it is a lie. I don't have any bugguong. I have imported patis in a bottle I bought from 99 Ranch in . . . I think it was in 1999. I keep it in the refrigerator. The expiration date has probably passed. I wonder if patis even has an expiration date. It's already fermented, so how can it rot some more?

"How much water do I put inside, Nana?" I ask.

Rita pauses. "You don't know?" She responds wide-eyed, incredulous at such an innocent question. "How come you don't know how to cook dis one? What kind Filipina you?"

I answer her in my head, the kind that don't know how to cook pinakbet.

"How come you don't know how? Aye, every Filipina should know. You watch your mama and your lola make pinakbet, hah?"

There's nothing I can do but shrug. I am guilty of not watching my elders cook. I know Rita means well, but I am feeling more and more intimidated the longer I remain in her presence. Her three daughters—Perla, Myrna and Rona—must have had it tough growing up female in her household. Her eldest, Perla, was my classmate at Haleiwa Elementary School. Perla was not someone teachers would remember as a happy-go-lucky child. With a mother like Nana Rita, I now understand why Perla was a quiet, serious, straight A student who seldom smiled.

Rita sighs as she answers my question about how much water to use. "You put enough water to cover the tomatoes. This much," she says as she pours water into the pot. The woman has made water appear out of nowhere.

"Just enough water, but not too much. Or else going get lug-lug. And don't stir. Don't do dis." She makes an exaggerated stirring motion with a ladle, which she has also magically produced from air, to demonstrate. "Just keep putting everything on top. Every kind stay inside the bag already. Next comes this."

She pours out cubed, bite-sized pumpkin squares. "Next comes this one." Out tumble three-inch pieces of shiny, purple eggplant. "But you have to soak first. No forget now. Soak the tarong to get the bitterness out. You soak in water for five minutes."

I am terrified to ask how much water I need to soak the eggplant.

Rita continues to demonstrate with each layer, diminishing the contents of the ZipLoc bag. Long beans, ends trimmed and snapped in even lengths. Wing beans, the small ones cut and the larger ones shelled for their spotted, flat fruit, which are added as another layer. I can almost smell it cooking. Next is the okra, then the kabatiti. There is a deep slit in each rectangle piece. Sequa, that's what it's called in English, I remember. And silk squash. And Chinese okra. Of all the stupid things to liken kabatiti to is okra. It's like the kiwi being called a Chinese gooseberry.

"See dis? You cut kabatiti like dis so all the flavors can go inside. I saw you looking at the kabatiti over there. You can make good soup with dis, too. You take some chicken or pork with dis one here. Aysus, broke da mouth. I no understand why you young people go eat outside alla time.

"You can cut like dis, too. Into stars, see? Thick like dis." Rita demonstrates with a small paring knife she makes appear, again out of nowhere. The sliced medallions look like flat suns with multi-pointed sunbeams. I guess it could look like stars.

"And if you no more meat, you just stir fry dis one only and stay ono by itself. Dis is good, stay easy and stay fast. Dis one good vegetable." She pronounces vegetable in four syllables. Ve-je-tah-bull. Just like my mom used to. Ve-je-tah-bull.

"You cover everything. And you cook until finish." I prepare for the worst, but decide to ask anyway.

"And for how long you cook, Nana?"

She shakes her head. "You can see, hah? You open the pot and look. You cook until it's pau! You taste, then you look inside again." She retrieves a pot cover from beneath the tablecloth and fits it on the pot. "Then you taste again. Don't overcook. You cover and toss all the ve-je-tah-bulls. You just toss like this so the bottom layer come to the top. You wait leelah bit, then you toss again," she instructs, pantomiming a gentle tossing motion using the pot's side handles.

The lesson is over because the pinakbet is done. Rita wipes her hands on her pants, and then places them on her hips. She wags a pointer near my face. "Remember the secret. Don't stir. It's easy once you know how." Finally, she smiles at me. I am encouraged. I feel like I could actually make pinakbet like she did.

"You make it look really easy, Nana," I say as I help her retrieve the contents from the pot and return them to the bag that I am going to buy. "Dios ti agngina, Nana." I can still remember the phrases that leave an impression of a decent Ilokano upbringing. She seems pleased at this.

"Wait, wait, wait. Don't forget the chicharon. Put the chicharon last. And wait leelah while before you eat. So dat all the flavors go inside the meat." I nod and spy their famous product on the table to my left, where Lita is arranging the bags on three tiered planks supported by decorative cement blocks.

"Hoy, Bolo! Whatchoo doin' hea so early? Plenny fish today?" Rita calls out to the bolohead man driving his black SUV past their booth. The man slows down, pulls over, gets out and starts walking toward us. Bob usually comes around lunchtime to sell poke. It's no secret that his poke is the best because of the freshness of his fish. The raw flesh is always shiny and creamy.

"I helping my friend with his chicken today, manang. My wife going come bring the poke bumbye," Bolo explains to Rita.

I walk toward the chicharon and Lita, who greets me with "Kumusta, balasang ko." I respond properly. She offers to take my pinakbet ingredients, kabatiti brontosauruses and sweet potato tops while I look over the desserts and pork rinds.

Lita is the behind-the-scenes person of their successful operation. Rita and Lita lived together and acted like they were sisters, but they were actually sisters-in-law. Rita had the green thumb, but it was Lita who made the pork rinds. I wonder why Rita's name came first on the label. Maybe it was because Rita was the older one. Maybe it was Rita's idea. Then I remembered why.

When my mother was still alive, she was known for keeping up with the latest tsismis, and was a popular resource for all of the juicy Waialua Town gossip. It was common knowledge that Rita's parents had been trying very hard to get her married off, but Rita refused their suggestions for a potential husband. It was local folklore that Rita was nearly 30 years old when she married her cousin's cousin, Danilo Corpuz, from her clan's neighboring village of Isabela. Danilo became a truck driver for Dole Pineapple Company by day. During his free time he raised fighting cocks as a hobby. Rita sold vegetables and desserts as a side business on cockfight days. I heard my mom tell my dad that the Corpuz family was getting rich on Danilo's chickens and Rita's bibingka.

At the height of their success Mr. Corpuz died unexpectedly of a stroke. Rita was left with five young children—three girls and two boys—to raise on her own. At the funeral mass Padre Pinacate said that Danilo was a hardworking man, a decent man, a good man who did not mind having a strongheaded wife. I never forgot that because the congregation laughed after he said it. To make a long story short, Rita ended up marrying her husband's younger brother, Lito, who volunteered to step in for his brother, according to traditional custom. Rita's children needed a father and Lito wanted to come to Hawaii and become an American.

Years later Lito was eventually able to bring his mother, father, three sisters, two brothers in law, four nieces and six nephews from the Philippines. Their household grew into an extended family, which needed an expanded houselot. There are five homes now on the Corpuz family compound. Lito's youngest sister, Lita, was the last to arrive from the Philippines.

Here's the part that gets interesting. Rita's brother, Perfecto, ended up marrying Lita, her husband's sister. This was because Perfecto's wife had died of breast cancer a couple of years after Lita arrived. Perfecto was left a widower with seven children. Lita stepped in to marry him, just as her brother Lito had done for Rita 10 years earlier. Lita was 20. Perfecto was 45. The gossip was that the Corpuz family wanted to pay Rita's family back for helping to bring them to America. They wanted to show gratitude for ending up with a better life in Hawaii. The arrangement was a bit chaotic and strange, but in the end it worked out. Rita and Lita are both widows now, with all their children and stepchildren grown.

Lita's husband, Apo Perfecto, as we children called him back then, didn't get involved with raising chickens. But he was a regular at cockfights and knew what he was doing as a gambler. He would follow the progress of all the breeders and the fighting cocks and was personable to all. He did not like it when the newer breeders began using steroids. This seemed unfair to him, so he made a big stink about it. He knew which breeders were shooting up the cocks right before a big fight. As a respected elder, he tried talking to the younger breeders and hoped they would understand the older, traditional ways of the sport and its protocol. At first the young breeders demurred and were semi-committed to fighting clean, but eventually they ignored him altogether. The practice of using steroids continued to spread and it greatly bothered him.

Apo Perfecto took the issue to the House and asked them to intervene by banning the use of steroids; they did not. The House leadership did not consider this touchy subject a part of their kuleana, so they let it go on. Apo Perfecto tried to convince them that the sport was not only about making money. But it was to no avail. In his frustration, he gave up cockfighting and concentrated on drinking.

With Lita' s husband's new pastime making him a bitter and crotchety old man, she found herself raising his children alone. There were rumors of him being an abusive father, so Lita took to his children as if they were her own blood relations. After her husband died of liver failure, Lita began selling chicharon out of her home on Sundays. Shortly after that, RitaLita's Famous Chicharon was born and they took it to the Sunday cockfights instead. It is now a best best seller at cockfights in Waialua, Waianae and Waipahu. Southern Cross Stores in Kalihi sells it exclusively.

"You don't have any of the hard kind today," I point out to Lita, who was straightening out a row of bags on the other end of the planks.

"No more already. I just sell the last five bags to Bob. Everybody like the old fashioned way, with the fat on the inside. I save some for you next week it you like," Lita says brusque and efficient.

"And these soft, fluffy ones. How you make them so light, nana?"

"Ah, you have to dry that one in the sun. And you poke holes on the hard side of the skin. The Puerto Ricans and the haoles like that kind. You use pork belly, not pork back. And you use hot, hot oil to fry in. Use only the skin. No meat. No fat."

"And what about these ones?" I pick up a bag that contained tender meat and moist fat topped off by a blistered, crackling thin layer of skin. It was mostly meat like Chinese roast pork but drier. I hadn't quite noticed the subtle differences among the contents of the bags before. I did notice they were sealed with twist ties of different colors. ZipLock bags would make them lose their crunchiness, I presumed.

"That's our new one. Meed-jum. Soft for the haoles. Hard for the Filipinos. And meed-jum for everybody else," Lita explained. Now I know why the RitaLitas were so successful. They adapted to changing needs. They worked hard. They gave from the heart all the time.

"How you make them hard, Nana?"

"You dry in the sun inside the screen box. Or hang up on the clothesline. Or on top the tray inside the oven. Then you fry slow, not so fast and noisy. So the skin no break up. You use pork back, not pork belly."

For all of the RitaLitas' culinary secrets, they sure were easy about sharing them. I did not expect tough, enterprising widows to be so generous. It seemed easy enough to make these famous pork rinds. I am going to ask Mrs. Bautista to try to copy it. An old, authentic hand like Mrs. Bautista would be able to duplicate the soft, medium and hard varieties with the information I had already gleaned from the widows. I could then trade what I knew about the LitaRitas' recipe for Mrs. Bautista's dinuguan recipe. The one she makes with the mild peppers in her version of pork blood stew. The Bautistas might want to add pork rinds to their repertoire of Filipino plate lunch offerings, fresh hot corn, and fried lumpia they offered at the Bautista's' Best food booth.

I could propose different flavored pork rinds to Mrs. Bautista. Barbecue flavor. Ranch dressing flavor. Basalmic vinegar flavor. Maybe sprinkle some li hing powder. Li hing pork rinds. Interesting. Or chili powder. Rinds fried in extra virgin olive oil. Pizza flavor. Taco flavor. The marketing possibilities were endless.

"Do you have a secret recipe, nana?"

"And what you like know all that for? How come you asking all these kind questions?" a sharp voice behind me cuts into my reverie. Rita had been standing there all this time. She is sticking labels on bags of chicharon she pulls out from a large box. She looks at Lita and they exchange mysterious glances.

"Recipe? You like one recipe," Rita spits the word like it is a disgusting taste in her mouth. "Maria Conchita Peralta, for all the years I know you and your family, you never, ever been interested in the Filipino culture. And es-pe-shally the Filipino food. Why you like know now about this kind for?"

Rita is now is directly in front of me, her face close to mine. "What you doing, Conchita? Spying on us? Or you all of a sudden became one born-again Filipina?"

She and Lita laugh heartily at this. I have to laugh, too. It is Lita who laughs so hard tears start rolling down her cheeks. She seems to be enjoying a really good inside joke.

"I want to collect authentic Filipino recipes, nana. I want to put them together in a cookbook. I cannot find any cookbooks in Hawaii about Filipino food."

"Chita, you joking, hah?" Lita catches her breath from laughing and leans in toward me. "What I need one recipe for? I know how to make already!" It is Lita's turn to make fun of me.

"I no give out my recipe to anybody. Not even my children know how to make chicharon like me. They ask me alla time to write it down. I tell them you come watch and learn. But they no like. They only like me make more money. They tell me to sell my recipe. Santa Maria! I not gonna do dat. I gonna take this recipe with me to my grave."

"This is something we no share," Lita concludes. "You young people better watch out. Nobody going know how to make this kind food any more."

Rita nods. "I tell you this if you really like do something about keeping the tradition. I give you one hint. We use red Hawaiian salt. The kind from Kauai in the salt ponds. Another important secret is when you fry, you fry with the cover on."

"Here, take this. This is the hard kind we save for es-pe-shall people," Rita continues and hands a bag of her backup stash to me.

"Now, with all that we told you, you can try to make your chicharon like this. You can try make it better than ours. You can try real hard, but it's RitaLita's secret. I can guarantee you that yours not going taste like ours."

That was the most I could get out of the chicharon widows.

Armed with a bag each of soft, medium and hard chicharon, I go to find Bino Bautista at the payut tent. I have my heart set on impressing him.

Dori-Lei Chee

"CHOW FUN CHILD"

Samurai shaved ice sweetheart
licking the shredded ice
and strawberry syrup
off the bottom
of the little cup.

Yu-gi-oh youngster
dueling my friend May
with the Red Eye Dragon card.

Look fun lunatic
slurping up the fat noodle
after dipping it in the special soy sauce.

Bento brat eating
the rice, noodles, and chicken.

Jackie Chan kung fu chopper
loving his TV commercial
when he jumps
on the bad guy's head.

DORI-LEI CHEE *is a sixth grader at Maryknoll School in Honolulu. Her hobbies include reading, eating, shopping, and traveling. She enjoys experiencing new and different places and cultures, and hopes to visit as many states and countries as she possibly can.*

Kelsie Julia Chong
"GRANDMA'S HANDS"

People's hands feel different
My grandma's hands are special
If my hands are cold
Her hands keep my hands warm
They're soft and cozy
When I hold my grandma's hands, I can
feel the wrinkles
I can tell her hands have done a whole lot
She has combed my hair
Cooked for me
Tucked me into bed
And played with me
She has done so many things
When I have a tough day, I just hold her hands
They make me happy again
My grandma's hands.

KELSIE JULIA CHONG *was born in 1994. She grew up living in Kahului, Maui, with a family consisting of a mother, father, sister, and brothers. She now attends Kamehameha Schools in Honolulu. She was inspired in writing poetry by her older sister and brother. In her poem, she wanted to explain to the reader how much she appreciates her grandma and everything she has done for her.*

Courtney Sen
"MY GRANDPA"

I remember the old Grandpa
who took care of me.
Who smiled,
And picked me up from school.
Always there,
Watching out for me.
He was almost as kind as God's angel.

The perfect Grandpa, until
he went to the hospital.

Now he's as quiet as a mouse
And never smiles.
Never talking to me,
Or calling my name.
I doubt he even remembers it.
I know it's him when I hear his
walker's wheel
Softly screeching.
The joy of his heart seems
to have disappeared,
Leaving sadness.
I miss the old Grandpa.

COURTNEY SEN *was born in 1992 in Honolulu. She is currently in ninth grade at 'Iolani School. She has loving parents and three sisters named Cherisse, Chelsie, and Christina. She also lives with her grandpa Clarence, a dog named Patches, and a cat named Benny. When she has free time, she enjoys playing volleyball, going to the beach, reading, and spending time with her friends and family.*

Samuel Peter Lenzi
"THE RAIN AT ALA WAI PARK"

Remember the ocean of the North Shore
basking in the moonlight
illuminated everything around us?

Remember the rain at Ala Wai Park
pouring so hard
it was all I could see,
all I could hear,
and all I could feel?

Remember how hard I work,
how I always try my best
to make myself better.

Remember the trees at Mount Kalaepohaku
and how the trees can tell a good day
from a bad one and how they just want
to make you feel comfortable?
Such a good place to sit.

Remember your dad
and no matter how far you fell down,
he could always pick you up?

Remember your mother
and how when you were sad
she was sad,
and she was happy,
to see you happy,
and if something was wrong,
she always tried to make it right?

Remember your birth
and how your mother tried so hard
to bring a late Christmas present
into the world?

Remember the early morning out at Hawai'i Kai,
and how it's just like a backwards sunset,
the darkness slowly creeping away?

Remember your childhood
and how learning the smallest things
such as riding a bike
making you feel so accomplished?

Remember when the power went out
on Kapiolani Boulevard
and how we figured
out natural light was the best?
The Moon!

Remember your words
and how which ever way you choose them,
they mean much more when written?

Remember your grandparents
and how they loved to spend time with you,
and before you know it they are gone,
and it's the other way around?

Remember your pet fishes
and how they were so interested in your homework
they jumped out to see it?

Remember the darkness of night
in the building of Marco Polo
and how no matter how many
horror movies you watched
nothing's really there?

Remember that Jimmy Hendrix is left-handed.

Remember that the powdery stuff
on mochi is corn starch?

And remember the sunsets at Waikiki,
and how they remind you
that the world must always try its best to operate
even between the darkness and the light?

SAMUEL PETER LENZI *was born in 1991 and raised in Honolulu. He is half Korean and Italian-American. He is a WEBCO Scholar at Saint Louis School in Honolulu, and a National Honor Society member. He enjoys fishing, wrestling, judo, and going to the beach. He was inspired to write this poem by his beautiful Island home and the people who helped him realize he would one day come to miss it.*

Tyler Shimizu
"THE SONG OF TYLER SHIMIZU"

I sing of Waialae Iki, Edith and Harry Ezuka
who always grow cherry tomatoes
in the garden next to the garage;

I sing of grapefruit trees, pinkish yellow,
and Kiwi, the Japanese dog who died of fleas;

I sing of sapphire the color of neon
and crimson the color of dragons;

I sing of chicken teriyaki that we eat
at Gyotaku Japanese Restaurant when my parents
are too tired to cook,
mochi ice cream in flavors of chocolate,
strawberry, and vanilla;

I sing of my Gameboy Advance SP
which is in a case and hidden;

I sing of my fear of heights and being grounded,
my love of basketball and my love of my family;

I sing of sometimes being grumpy
and of being a trusted friend;

I sing of the ocean—
the restless waves that scintillate
the faded sand blending into the water,
the shimmering sun creating heatful rays—
I see the luminous, enchanted moon gleaming
over the whispering ocean.

TYLER SHIMIZU *is currently a ninth grader at Punahou School in Honolulu. He loves to play basketball for his school and clubs. He enjoys spending time with his family, laughing with friends, NBA and Madden video games, instant messaging his friends until 2 AM, and body surfing at Waimānalo Beach with friends and cousins. He has a very loving and supportive family: a father, Curt, a mother, Gayle, and a younger sister Darcy.*

Carlee M. K. Matsunaga

"THERE ARE STARS ABOVE KELEWAA STREET IN MILILANI"

There are stars that smell
of burning fire
in a fire place.

There are stars
that taste like sugar
in a slate cup.
There are stars that sound like
jingling chimes
at Christmas.

There are stars that feel
like a smooth carpet
at Grandma's house.

Some stars sparkle in the night
sky over Diamond Head.

Other stars help
each other clean up
by brushing on their back with sponges.

Among the stars are those
who are xanthic.

There are stars
above Kelewaa Street in Mililani.

There are stars
that smell like strawberry Otter Pops,
taste like icicles,
sound like jingling bells,
and feel like a soft
dog named Buster.

CARLEE M. K. MATSUNAGA *was born in 1999. She is a third grader who attends Manana Elementary School in Pearl City, Oʻahu, and Naʻau: A Place for Learning. She enjoys her learning time with Aunty Lois, Uncle Mel, Aunty Katie, and Aunty Lindsay at Naʻau. She is a member of the Manana Children's Choir and enjoys singing in groups. She also likes to sketch clothes and fashions in her spare time.*

Trey Saito

"RADIANT JAPANESE MAPLE TREE"

I am from a washing dishes,
cleaning my room,
and picking up weeds family.

I am from a big pick,
a small weeder,
and a sharp knife family.

I am a radiant Japanese maple tree
that breathes in soft clouds.
A delicate pung su tree
that flickers
when under the sunlight.

I am from sweet azuki beans
and obi which is a wrap
that ties around a woman's waist.

From Frances Lee
and Makoto Saito.
From don't put your elbows on the table
and wash your hands before you eat.

I'm from Kwanju
and Shizuoka.

From disgusting natto
and nasty taegu.

I'm from a slurping drink family
and sucking noodles through their nose.

In the basement
there is a photograph
of Grandma Franny in a jeweled dress
out with her mom
and having a good time
at Sekiya's restaurant.

TREY SAITO *was born in 1995 and is the youngest of three children. He is an active child and loves to play! He enjoys playing baseball and basketball. He also enjoys writing because he can express himself. He writes it just like it is in his mind and thoughts.*

Karri Leilani Villanueva
"HANA PAʻA?"

Sittin down wit mah Papa insai his boat,
I stay holdin out mah bamboo pole
Ova da watahs of Kalihi.
I am mad ah, cuz I stay wait long time.
T h i r t y m i n u t e s alredeh . . . And da fish no bite!
No even nibble—
Nottin
I look ova to mah Papa and
             Ho! Papa stay catchin choke!

He stay reelin in fish afta fish!
How come me, no moa nottin?
right deah I wen give up.
All futless alredeh, I wen jerk mah pole
Out of da watah!
Then,   Ay!
Mah Papa stay pointing at mah line, "Eh, look!"
Gazin at mah pole,
I stay tinkin to mah self,

Da first rule of fishin:
Put bait on da hook!

Zackary Kaneshiro
"DINNER AT A SUSHI STAND"

They say of my father:
Bryan is awesome at putting
at Pearlridge Golf Course.

They say of my mother:
Lesley is awesome
at making sushi like natto.

Some say of my grandfather Shiro:
he is marvelous at chipping
out of the sand traps.

Some say of my grandmother Shiro:
she is super at sewing towels
for the bathroom.

They say of my uncle:
Curt is always buying his dinner
at a sushi stand.

They say of my aunty:
Raynee is wonder at making dinner
like brown rice and chicken.

This is what they say about me:
I am COOL at chess.

ZACKARY KANESHIRO *was born in 1999 and lives in ʻAiea, Oʻahu. He attends Maryknoll School and Naʻau: a Place for Learning. In his free time, Zackary enjoys golfing, swimming, and playing the guitar. He is also a huge football and baseball fan and enjoys rooting for the University of Hawaiʻi Warriors! Zackary especially looks forward to his weekly class at Naʻau.*

Kimberly Hiʻilei Coleman
"TIDE POOL"

You took me to the shores one day,
And sat me on the lava rocks that had been worn smooth
By the pounding, thunderous, waves.
I watched as you prowled around:
A giant, ankle-deep in the salty water.
You lifted a rock
Covered in a small forest of limu,
And with more quickness than a shark
Caught something—I couldn't see what.

You made your way back to me,
And though you almost slipped on the rocks,
I was too interested in what was hidden
In the palm of your hand to care.
You gave your treasure to me: a tiny brittle star.
I was enchanted by the watery movements
Of that strange, black creature.
I made sure that you took it back to its home
And replaced the limu forest on top of it.

We came another day; you were still a giant,
But perhaps not so tall this time around.
We came armed with nets like swords,
And buckets to collect the spoils.
Now I could wade in the pools, ankle deep in the cold water.
I climbed over the rocks to the pools with my net,
And swung my net
At clouds of silver darts below the surface.
I showed you a tiger-striped fish (a manini, you said)

I climbed out toward the sea,
To where the pools were deeper,
And filled with seaweed that grew
In purple and red, instead of the usual green.
Then you called out to me, holding something up in your hand,
And I scampered back.
You put in my hand
A sea slug; its pink and yellow frills
Waving like the ruffles on a gypsy's dress.

KIMBERLY HIʻILEI COLEMAN, *born in 1985, was raised in Honolulu. She wrote "Tide Pool" while attending Kamehameha Schools, to commemorate a favorite childhood memory. She recently graduated with honors from Chapman University with a BA in English literature. She also majored in art and is now an artist working on Oʻahu.*

Wing Tek Lum

"A MOON FESTIVAL PICNIC AT KAHALA BEACH PARK"

"But why is it always full
just when people are parted?"
—Su Tung P'o

I am sitting on a bench near the beach
with Rolanse and Irene
who like my wife are from Hong Kong.
And each of us has our one kid
on our respective laps
and we are all reciting
a Cantonese nursery rhyme
that starts off celebrating
the brightness of the moon.
And it's just gotten dark and cool
with the full moon
rising off the water from the east,
lemon-hued, and fat and sassy,
like the cheerful face of a child
playing peek-a-boo among the clouds.
And I am content
to just sit and relax on this bench
having just stuffed myself
with fresh clams from Tamashiro's
and some barbeque chicken
and a lot of potato salad.
And I recall from my experience
living in Hong Kong
that each year on this eighth moon
families always gathered together
for a special dinner
—like my wife's folks
who without fail
served a whole chicken and shrimp
and a soup made from pork and lotus root.
And even now my wife reminisces
about how her father
always made a big deal
about having to buy

a certain kind of vegetarian mooncake
only made at this time of the year.
And then I begin to think
about these sentiments
and how they've been
in this culture of ours for generations.
It reminds me of something
that my wife once did—suddenly—
when we were on a date one night
near the Star Ferry
walking outdoors under the moon.
She recited for me from memory
 a poem by Tu Fu, in exile,
wanting to be with his family
on this same festival night.
He had looked up at the moon
and found solace that his brothers too,
though far away,
were somehow viewing
his same moon at the same time.
It is as if even then
custom had already been imprinted
within our race
—the desire of families
to be with each other
coursing through our blood
at this moon's first waxing.
And I think of asking Rolanse and Irene
about their own families
and about what family traditions
they would be observing
in Hong Kong right about now.
But maybe it's because before dinner
I was listening to Sam
who programs the computer
for the Planetarium's show
talk about the moon
and how it spins around the earth
in the same clockwise direction
as our planet's own rotation.
For it suddenly dawns on me

that this levitating ball in the sky,
growing paler and smaller
as we sit here,
is not yet in the heavens over
Hong Kong or for that matter
over anywhere in all of China,
separated as we are
by some half an ocean
following in the flightpath of the moon.
In fact because of the dateline
they've already celebrated
this festival our time yesterday.
It's just one more difference
to our overseas Chinese lives, I decide,
thinking now of the moon's path
as some discarded umbilical cord
or a lifeline unravelling.
And I look at these three little ones here,
their round heads bobbing up and down
in time to our chanting,
to a cadence even now
they do not hear in their preschools.
Each of them was born here
in this new land,
young settlers for whom
the changes of the moon
will merely mean a cold astronomy,
for whom a grandparent
will just bring to mind
a small voice across a long distance line.
And I wonder what new traditions
will be passed down
to their own children
years from now on this night.
And as they look out
at the expanse of this dark ocean
I can see their wide open eyes
sparkling from the brilliance in the sky
like the candied squash and apricots
that we will pass out later.
It is from the excitement of the hour,

of all of us together,
that fills their voices,
a sense of a new family,
of these children and their parents
and their parents' friends.
I hold on to my daughter tightly
resolving next year to return
with her and with these others
for another picnic by this beach
to marvel once again
at this same full-flowering of the moon.

Ian MacMillan

from THE RED WIND

T here were around thirty people at the lū'au at first. George and a cousin . . . dug a pit and roasted a small pig wrapped in chicken wire in
it for a day and a half before Christmas . . . Dennis was impressed by the
gathering—the people did seem all of one family, huge men who shook his
hand with their large, soft hands, huge women in muumuus who sat around
in the shade fanning themselves and talking story with the aroma of pork
escaped from the ground, and they all talked with the familiarity of a family
even though, as he understood, they hadn't seen one another in a year.

The cars parked in front of the Maunawili house went right out of sight in
both directions . . . and both the front and back porches had an absurd profusion of slippers, shoes and high heels piled up by those who went into the
house. One Waianae cousin came in a suit with a vest and gold watch chain,
and Kenika found him sitting in the grass taking off his shoes before going
into the house, and told the man that he really didn't have to do that, but he
said, nah nah, s'okay. His hand was shaken by the meaty hands of dozens of
uncles and cousins and friends, and he was mauled by huge women wearing
startlingly bright muumuus, who planted kisses on his cheeks and put leis
over his head until they rose all the way to his nose.
    A three-man guitar and ukulele band showed up just after noon, and
played Hawaiian songs as the people chattered. George and his friends drew

the chicken wire-wrapped pig out of the pit in the backyard at two, but Kenika thought it surely had to be superfluous because there was so much food everywhere, heaps of little crabs, shrimp, various kinds of fish and octopus chunks, Japanese and Chinese and Filipino delicacies, little squares of coconut cake, beer, juice for the kids. But with the pig came the sweet potato, poi, lomi salmon, fried chicken, and more obscure vegetables and meats and desserts from the aunties and uncles and calabash cousins of different backgrounds and mixes of races . . .

Each time Honolulu city lights
Stir up memories in me
Each time Honolulu city lights
Will bring me back again

Epilogue

Epilogue

Keola Beamer

"HONOLULU CITY LIGHTS"

Looking out upon the city lights
And the stars above the ocean
Got my tickets for the midnight plane
And it's not easy to leave again

Took my clothes and put them in my bag
Try not to think just yet of leaving
Looking out into the city night
It not easy to leave again

> *Each time Honolulu city lights*
> *Stir up memories in me*
> *Each time Honolulu city lights*
> *Will bring me back again*

You are my island sunset
And you are my island rain

Put on my shoes and light a cigarette
Wondering which of my friends will be there
Standing with their leis around my neck
It's not easy to leave again

> *Each time Honolulu city lights*
> *Stir up memories in me*
> *Each time Honolulu city lights*
> *Will bring me back again*

> *Bring me back again*
> *Bring me back again . . .*

Sources and Acknowledgments

Great care has been taken to trace all sources as well as owners of copyright material included in this book and to make full acknowledgment. If any have been inadvertently omitted or overlooked, please bring to the publisher's attention to include in future editions.

Agawa, Hiroyuki and James Araki, trans. "Hanauma Bay." *KAIMANA* (Winter-Spring 1990).

Akana, Kalani. "Da 23rd Psalm." *Tinfish* 14 (2004).

Altizer, Nell. "Haleiwa Churchyard," in *Poetry in Hawaii*, edited by Frank Stewart and John Unterecker. Honolulu: University of Hawai'i Press, 1979.

Among, Michael Darnay. "Near My Home in the Valley," in *YOBO*, edited by Nora Okja Keller, et al. Honolulu: Bamboo Ridge Press, 2003.

Anderson, Jane. Untitled. *Seaweeds and Constructions* 4 (December 1977).

Ariyoshi, Rita. "Jamming Traffic," in *The 1998 Pushcart Prize XXII*, edited by Bill Henderson and the Pushcart Prize editors. New York: Pushcart Press, 1997.

Armitage, Kimo. "Awawa o Waimea, Oahu." *'Ōiwi* 2 (2002).

Ayento, Carol. "King Kong Ants," in *Timek Dagiti Agtutubo: Voices of the Youth*. Honolulu: Filipino Association of University Women, 1990.

Baker, Ray Jerome. "Rusty's Early Life at Taki's." *Honolulu Advertiser*, May 16, 1943.

Balaz, Joe. "Kimotherapy." *KAIMANA* (Summer-Fall 1991).

———. "Moe'uhane," in *After the Drought*. Honolulu: Topgallant Publishing Co., Ltd., 1985.

———. "Waikīkī Street Women," in *Paper Rain*. Wahiawā: Honolulu Bench Press, 1982.

Ball, Pamela. From *The Floating City*. New York: Viking Penguin, 2002. From THE FLOATING CITY by Pamela Ball, copyright © 2002 by Pamela Ball. Used by permission of Viking Penguin, a division of Penguin Group (USA) Inc.

Banggo, Kathy Dee Kaleokealoha Kaloloahilani. "No Mindless Digging," in *Growing Up Local*, edited by Eric Chock, et al. Honolulu: Bamboo Ridge Press, 1998.

Baptista, Andrea Castillo Simeon. "Love, Fil-Amer Style," in *Bullalayaw: Antolohia Dagiti Nangab–Abak Iti Salip Iti Sarita Iti*, edited by Pacita Cabulera Saludes and Mario A. Albalos. Honolulu: GUMIL-Hawaii, 1978.

Beamer, Kapono, Keola Beamer, and Bob Magoon. "Mr. Sun Cho Lee." *Hawaii's Keola and Kapono Beamer*. 1994. "Mr. Sun Cho Lee." Music and lyrics by Bob Magoon, Kapono Beamer, Keola Beamer.

Beamer, Keola. "Honolulu City Lights." *Honolulu City Lights*. Honolulu: Niniko Music, 1987.

———. "Stalking Haunani," in *The Shimmering*. Lahaina: Ohe Books, 2002.

Berlin, Irving. *Stop!Look!Listen!* Typescript libretto. New York Public Library for the Performing Arts.

Blanding, Don. "Baby Street (Down Palama Way)," in *Paradise Loot*. Honolulu: Patten Company, 1925.

———. "Camera Angle, Waikiki Beach," in *Hawaii Says Aloha*. New York: Dodd, Mead & Co., 1955.

————. "Waikiki Skin-Game," in *Hawaii Says Aloha*. New York: Dodd, Mead & Co., 1955.

Blitzstein, Marc. *The Cradle Will Rock*. New York: Random House, 1938. THE CRADLE WILL ROCK By MARC BLITZSTEIN © 1938 (Renewed) CHAPPELL & CO., INC. All Rights Reserved. used by Permission of ALFRED PUBLISHING CO., INC.

Bowman, Sally-Jo Keala-o-Ānuenue. "Chapter 17, *Nā Koa*." *ʻOiwi* 2 (2002).

Breckons, Evelyn. "Cowboy Tony." *Oahuan* March 1915.

Broadbent, Dora. "The Thrift Stamp Buyer." *Oahuan* April 1918.

Brooke, Rupert. "Waikiki," in *The Collected Poems of Rupert Brooke*. New York: Dodd, Mead & Co., 1915.

Buckingham, Dorothea N. *Staring Down the Dragon*. Kailua: Sydney Press, 2003.

Bueno, Amalia B. "The Chicharon Widows." *Bamboo Ridge* 89 (2006).

————. "Whea You From." Unpublished.

Burgess, Puanani. "ʻAwapuhi," in *Hoʻomānoa*, edited by Joseph P. Balaz. Honolulu: Ku Paʻa, Inc., 1989.

Burnett, Bobby. "Friends or Enemies?" *Write On, HEA!* (1996).

Bushnell, O. A. *Kaʻaʻawa*. Honolulu: University of Hawaiʻi Press, 1972.

————. *Molokai*. Cleveland and New York: The World Publishing Company, 1963.

Cabacungan, Darryl Keola. "Ka Loke Hākea A Ka Mahina." *Hanai* (1977).

Cabral, Elma T. "The Irresistible Henrique." *Paradise of the Pacific* 66 (1954).

Calhoun, Alfred R. *Kohala of Hawaii*. New York: Peter Fenelon Collier, 1893.

Calixto, Jeremias A. "Maysa A Malem Iti Aala Park," in *GUMIL Hawaii Iti Dua A Dekada 1971-1991*, edited by Pacita C. Saludes, et al. Honolulu: Gumil Hawaii, 1991.

Callejo, Emily. "An Etching." *Star Poets Journal* (2003).

Canham, Ruth B. "Little ʻAmakihi," in *Bamboo Shoots*, edited by Dennis Kawaharada. Honolulu: Bamboo Ridge Press, 1982.

Cardwell, Guy. "Odalisque." *Hawaii Quill Magazine* 1, no. 1 (January 1928).

Chang, Gary. "Three Mammals Indigenous to Hawaiʻi Before Man's Arrival: The Hawaiian Monk Seal, the Hawaiian Bat and Captian Aloha," in *Nowhere Near Molokaʻi*. Cohasset: Bear Star Press, 2004. *Nowhere Near Molokaʻi* © 2004 by Gary Chang (Bear Star Press).

Chee, Dori-Lei. "Chow Fun Child." Unpublished.

Chin, Frank. *Gunga Din Highway*. Minneapolis: Coffee House Press, 1995.

"Ching Chong and His Hana." *Ka Leo O Ka Lahui*, September 25, 1891.

Cho, Byung Hwa. "One Scene at Waikiki," in *Hawai Sisim 100-yon: 100 Years of Korean Poetry in Hawaii*, edited by the Korean Literary Club in Hawaii. Seoul: Kwanak Publishing Co., 2003.

Chock, Eric. "Making Da Scene," in *Last Days Here*. Honolulu: Bamboo Ridge Press, 1989.

————. "Manoa Cemetery," in *Talk Story*, edited by Eric Chock, et al. Honolulu: Petronium Press, 1978.

————. "Waolani Stream, 1955/1975," in *Poetry in Hawaii*, edited by Frank Stewart and John Unterecker. Honolulu: University of Hawaiʻi Press, 1979.

Chong, Kelsie Julia. "Grandma's Hands." *Star Poets Journal* (2004).

Chun, Henry. *Kindness to Cobras*, in *College Plays*. Honolulu: University of Hawai'i English Department, 1937.

Chun, Herbert K. K. "Pa-ke." *Bamboo Ridge* 2 (1979).

Chun, Pam. *The Money Dragon*. Naperville: Sourcebooks, Inc., 2002. From *The Money Dragon*, copyright 2002 by Pam Chun. Excerpted by permission of the publisher, Sourcebooks Landmark.

Chun, Wai Chee. *For You A Lei*, in *College Plays*. Honolulu: University of Hawai'i English Department, 1937.

Coito, Manuel Jesus. "A Desgraça." Unpublished.

———. "Jogo—Messinha." Unpublished.

———. "O Fado De Honolulu." Unpublished.

———. "Tasca Do Monte, Kalihi." Unpublished.

Coleman, Kimberly Hi'ilei. "Tide Pool." *Ho'okumu* (2002).

Cottell, Roxanne Mapuana. "Treasures." *'Ōiwi* 3 (2003).

Cowing, Sue. "At the Honolulu Aquarium, with Camera." *Bamboo Ridge* 69 (Spring 1996).

———. "Lion Dancer," in *My Dog Has Flies*. 'Ewa Beach: BeachHouse Publishing, 2005.

Dalton, Helen E. Untitled. In *Haiku of Hawaii Nei*. Hilo: Marble-Us, Inc., 1978.

Davenport, Kiana. *House of Many Gods*. New York: Ballantine, 2006. From HOUSE OF MANY GODS by Kiana Davenport, copyright © 2006 by Kiana Davenport. Map copyright © 2006 by David Lindrith, Inc. Used by permisison of Ballantine Books, a division of Random House, Inc.

———. *Shark Dialogues*. New York: Scribner, 1995. Reprinted with the permission of Scribner, an imprint of Simon & Schuster Adult Publishing Group, from SHARK DIALOGUES by Kiana Davenport. Copyright © 1994 by Kiana Davenport. All rights reserved.

Davis, Frank Marshall. "Horizontal Cameo: Lani," in *Black Moods*, edited by John Edgar Tidwell. Champaign: University of Illinois Press, 2002.

———. "Horizontal Cameo: Rita." Ibid.

———. "This Is Paradise." Ibid.

Day, Emily. "Midnight." *Star Poets Journal* (2003).

De Lima, Frank. "Caucasians Are Strange People," in *The Da Lima Code*. Honolulu: Bess Press, 2006.

———. "Da Blallah." Ibid.

Didion, Joan. *Democracy*. New York: Simon & Schuster, 1984. Excerpt of DEMOCRACY by Joan Didion. Copyright © 1984 by Joan Didion. Originally published in *DEMOCRACY*. Reprinted by permission of the author.

Donnelly, Milly Lou. "The Bard in Pidgin," in *Me Spik English*. Honolulu: Honolulu Star-Bulletin, Ltd., 1938.

———. "Part-Sojer." Ibid.

Edel, Marjorie. "Kimi." *The Paper* 3, no. 2 (1984).

Egami, Corey. "Cascaron." *Katipunan* 1, no. 1 (Spring 1998).

Felipe, Virgilio Menor. *Hawai'i: A Pilipino Dream*. Honolulu: Mutual Publishing, 2002.

———. "Love Letter from Laoag to Waipahu." Unpublished.

Fraticelli, Carlo Mario. "La Escula No Es Suficiente," in *A Puerto Rican Poet on the Sugar Plantations of Hawaii*, edited by Austin Dias and Blase Camacho Souza. Honolulu: Puerto Rican Heritage Society of Hawaii, 2000.

———. "La Hora Suprema." Ibid.

———. "Yo Me Voy De Este Lugar." Ibid.

Freen, J. "Hank's Place." *Bamboo Ridge* 89 (Spring 2006).

Frumkin, Gene. "Haole in Honolulu." Unpublished.

———. "Hotel Street." Unpublished.

Fukushima, Howie. "Surfscape with Cruel Action, 1966." Unpublished.

Furuya, Kathlyn "Kiki." "White Cotton Socks." Unpublished.

Gallagher, Katie. "Escaping Mango Chicken." *Write On, HEA!* (1994).

Goodman, Allegra. *Paradise Park*. New York: The Dial Press/Dell Publishing, 2001. From PARADISE PARK by Allegra Goodman, copyright © 2001 by Allegra Goodman. Used by permission of The Dial Press/Dell Publishing, a division of Random House, Inc.

Hamada, James T. *Don't Give Up the Ship*. Boston: Meador Publishing Co., 1933.

Hamasaki, Richard. "Da Mento Hospito," in *From the Spider Bone Diaries*. Honolulu: University of Hawai'i Press, 2001.

———. "Does the Temple Bell Still Toll at the Mō'ili'ili Hongwanji." Ibid.

———. "Kapahulu Girl." Ibid.

———. "Mō'ili'ili." Ibid.

———. Untitled. Ibid.

Hara, Marie M. "Fourth Grade Ukus," in *Bananaheart and Other Stories*. *Bamboo Ridge* 61 and 62 (1994).

———. "The Honeymoon Hotel, 1895." Ibid.

Hara, Mavis. "An Offering of Rice," in *Home to Stay*, edited by Sylvia Watanabe and Carol Bruchac. Greenfield Center: Greenfield Review Press, 1990.

———. "Visiting Hickam Air Force Base, 1956." *Bamboo Ridge* 41 (Winter 1989).

Harada, Margaret N. *The Sun Shines on the Immigrant*. New York: Vantage Press, 1960.

Hartman, Lee. "Museum Tour: Honolulu Academy of Arts." *HAPA* 1 (Spring 1981).

Hemmings, Kaui Hart. "House of Thieves" and "Secret Clutch," in *House of Thieves*. New York: Penguin Books, 2005.

"Henehene Kou 'Aka," in *He Mele Aloha*, edited by Carol Wilcox, et al. Honolulu: 'Oli'Oli Productions, 2003.

Heroy, Susan. "Le Chinois, Honolulu." Unpublished.

———. "Japanese Cemetery, Nuuanu, Hawaii." *Bamboo Ridge* (June-August 1981).

Hewitt, Geof. "Letter," in *Poetry in Hawaii*, edited by Frank Stewart and John Unterecker. Honolulu: University of Hawai'i Press, 1979.

Higa, Jeffrey. "Christmas Stories." *Bamboo Ridge* (Spring 1999).

Hirata-Epstein, Dante Kapea. "Jewpanese." Unpublished.

Holt, John Dominis. "Hapa." *Ramrod* 6 (1985).

———. "Princess of the Night Rides," in *Princess of the Night Rides and Other Tales*. Honolulu: Topgallant Publishing Co., Ltd., 1977.

———. "Remembering Kaka'ako." *Ramrod* 6 (1991).

Hopkins, Seward W. *Two Gentlemen of Hawaii*. New York: Robert Bonner's Sons, 1894.

Hui, Jason. "The New Chinese Boy in School," in *Buss Laugh*, edited by Lee A. Tonouchi. Aiea: Major Danger Press, 2004.

Huie, William Bradford. *The Revolt of Mamie Stover*. New York: Duell, Sloan and Pearce, 1951.

Ige, Philip K. "The Forgotten Flea Powder." *Paradise of the Pacific* (November 1946).

Ikehara, Kate. "The Ignored Storyteller." *Star Poets Journal* (2006).

Illerbrun, W. J. "Still Iz." Unpublished.

———. Untitled. Unpublished.

Inouye, Lisa Toishigawa. *Reunion*, in *Kumu Kahua Plays*, edited by Dennis Carroll. Honolulu: University of Hawai'i Press, 1983.

Isokane, Sam. "Waves of Waikiki."

Izumi, Sadao. Untitled. *Cho-on Shisha* (1923).

Johnson, Denis. *Tree of Smoke*. New York: Farrar, Straus and Giroux, 2007. Excerpts from '1966' from TREE OF SMOKE by Denis Johnson. Copyright © 2007 by Denis Johnson.

Jones, James. *From Here to Eternity*. New York: Dell Publishing, 1951. FROM HERE TO ETERNITY by James Jones, copyright 1951 by James Jones. Copyright renewed 1979 by Gloria Jones, James Anthony Phillipe Jones and Kaylie Anne Jones. Used by permission of Dell Publishing, a division of Random House, Inc.

"Ka Ulu Lā'au O Kai," in *The Echo of Our Song*, translated and edited by Mary K. Pukui and Alfons L. Korn. Honolulu: University of Hawai'i Press, 1973.

Ka-'ehu. "Mele a Ka-'ehu ka Haku Mele," in *The Echo of Our Song*, translated and edited by Mary K. Pukui and Alfons L. Korn. Honolulu: University of Hawai'i Press, 1973.

Kahanu, Hina. "When I was Young On an Island," in *Growing Up Local*, edited by Eric Chock, et al. Honolulu: Bamboo Ridge Press, 1998.

Kaiwi, Monica A. K. "Hey, Haole Lady . . . ," in *Whetu Moana*, edited by Albert Wendt, Reina Whaitiri, and Robert Sullivan. Honolulu: University of Hawai'i Press, 2003.

Kalahele, Imaikalani. "Hui Kau." Unpublished.

———. "Ode to Fort Street," in *Kalahele*. Honolulu: Kalamakū Press, 2002.

———. "A Poem for Chinatown." *'Ōiwi* 2 (2002).

———. "Waikīkī Samatime," in *Kalahele*. Honolulu: Kalamakū Press, 2002.

Kamakau, Samuel Mānaiakalani. Untitled, in *Tales and Traditions of the People of Old*. Honolulu: Bishop Museum Press, 1991.

Kanae, Lisa Linn. "Island Girl." www.downwindproductions.com.

———. "Ola's Son." *Tinfish* 9 (1999).

Kaneshiro, Zackary. "Dinner at a Sushi Stand." Unpublished.

Kaopio, Matthew. *Written in the Sky.* Honolulu: Mutual Publishing, 2005.

"Kau a Hi'i-aka i Ka-'ena," in *The Echo of Our Song*, translated and edited by Mary K. Pukui and Alfons L. Korn. Honolulu: University of Hawai'i Press, 1973.

Kelekona, Kahikina (John Graves Munn Sheldon), translated by Puakea Nogelmeier. "He Haawina Pahaohao," in *The True Story of Kaluaikoolau, as Told by his Wife Piilani.* Honolulu: University of Hawai'i Press, 2001.

Keller, Nora Okja. *Fox Girl.* New York: Viking, 2002. Copyright © 2002 by Nora Okja Keller. From FOX GIRL, published by Penguin Books in 2003 and originally in hardcover by Viking. Reprinted by permission of Susan Bergholz Literary Services, New York, NY and Lamy, NM. All rights reserved.

Keohokālole, Emalia, Fred Kalani Meinecke, and Earl Pāmai Tenn. "Windward Community College Hula." *Rain Bird* 6 (1995).

Kern, Jerome. *Very Good Eddie.* Typescript libretto. New York Public Library for the Performing Arts.

Khim, Charles K. Y., and Wayne Takazono, ill. *He's a Nice Boy, But . . .* Honolulu: The General Assistance Center for the Pacific, College of Education, Department of Educational Foundations, University of Hawai'i, 1976. Written by Charles K. Y. Khim, illustrated by Wayne Y. Takazono, produced and printed by The General Assistance Center for the Pacific, College of Education, Department of Educational Foundations, University of Hawaii, Honolulu Hawaii, 1976, Director Melvin Ezer.

Kicknosway, Faye. "The Other Shoe." Unpublished.

———. "Short Take 16," in *Mixed Plate.* Middletown: Wesleyan University Press, 2003.

Kihleng, Emelihter. "The Micronesian Question." *Bamboo Ridge* 87 (Spring 2005).

Kim, Willyce. "Migrations," in *YOBO,* edited by Nora Okja Keller, et al. Honolulu: Bamboo Ridge Press, 2003.

Kim, Yong Ho. "Hawai Sat'angsusu Pat," in *Hawai Sisim 100-yon: 100 Years of Korean Poetry in Hawaii,* edited by the Korean Literary Club in Hawaii. Seoul: Kwanak Publishing Co., 2003.

Kingston, Maxine Hong. *China Men.* New York: Alfred A. Knopf, 1980. From CHINA MEN by Maxine Hong Kingston, copyright © 1977, 1978, 1979, 1980 by Maxine Hong Kingston. Used by permission of Alfred A. Knopf, a division of Random House, Inc.

Kokolia, J. and Solomon Hiram. "Sassy," in *He Mele Aloha*, edited by Carol Wilcox, et al. Honolulu: 'Oli'Oli Productions, 2003.

Kong, Abbie and Johnny Noble. "Kāne'ohe," in *He Mele Aloha*, edited by Carol Wilcox, et al. Honolulu: 'Oli'Oli Productions, 2003.

Kong, Charles. "Well, Then," in *Hawaiian Legacy.* Honolulu: Konch Corp., 1981.

Kono, Juliet S. "Missing Person All Points Bulletin," in *Tsunami Years.* Honolulu: Bamboo Ridge Press, 1995.

Kubota, Davin. "Boyfurendo/Garufurendo," in *Buss Laugh*, edited by Lee A. Tonouchi. Aiea: Major Danger Press, 2004.

LaGory, Michael. "Double Rondeau." *KAIMANA* (Summer-Fall 1991).

Lamadrid, Kyleena. "Mother Dearest." *Star Poets Journal* (2006).

Landgraf, Kapulani. "He Au Koʻolau Lā." *Ramrod* 9 (1991).

Lanzilotti, Leona Nāwahineokalaʻi. "Kealiʻiloma." *Star Poets Journal* (2003).

Lea, Fanny Heaslip. "Moon of Nanakuli." *Collier's* (February 8, 1919).

Lee, Christine Joy. "Kimchee Cowgirl," in *Buss Laugh*, edited by Lee A. Tonouchi. Aiea: Major Danger Press, 2004.

Lee, David Hsin Shan. "The Boiling Pot." *Ka Nani* 23 (2006).

Lee, Tracee. "Mānoa Paranoia." *Bamboo Ridge* 25th Anniversary Issue (2003).

———. "Rocks." *Bamboo Ridge* 75 (Spring 1999).

Lei-Lanilau, Carolyn. "Carolyn and the Cop," in *Ono Ono Girl's Hula*. Madison: University of Wisconsin Press, 1997. Lei-lanilau, Carolyn. ONO ONO GIRL'S HULA. © 1997. Reprinted by permission of The University of Wisconsin Press.

Lenzi, Samuel Peter. "The Rain at Ala Wai Park." Unpublished.

Leong, Lucretia. "Manna from Heaven," in *YOBO*, edited by Nora Okja Keller, et. al. Honolulu: Bamboo Ridge Press, 2003.

Lew, Walter K. "Mānoa Run." *Bamboo Ridge* 75 (Spring 1999).

Li, Peter C. T. "A Fire in the Fields." *Bamboo Ridge* 69 (Spring 1996).

———. "Tai Chi Masters of Dim Sum Checks," in *Growing Up Local*, edited by Eric Chock, et al. Honolulu: Bamboo Ridge Press, 1998.

Liliʻuokalani, Lydia Kamakaʻeha Kaʻōlalanialiʻi Neweweliʻi. "Queen's Prayer," in *He Mele Aloha*, edited by Carol Wilcox, et al. Honolulu: ʻOliʻOli Productions, 2003.

———. "Ka Wiliwiliwai." Ibid.

Lim, Genny. *Bitter Cane*, in *Paper Angels and Bitter Cane*. Honolulu: Kalamakū Press, 1991.

Lodge, David. *Paradise News*. New York: Penguin, 1993. From PARADISE NEWS by David Lodge, copyright © 1992 by David Lodge. Used by permission of Viking Penguin, a division of Penguin Group (USA) Inc.

Logan, John. "Middle Aged Midwesterner at Waikiki Again," in *Poetry in Hawaii*, edited by Frank Stewart and John Unterecker. Honolulu: University of Hawaiʻi Press, 1979.

London, Jack. "The House of Pride," in *House of Pride and Other Tales of Hawaii*. New York: Turtle Point Press, 2005.

———. "The Kanaka Surf," in *On The Makaloa Mat*. New York: McMillan, 1919.

Long, Hughie. "Good Times." Unpublished.

Loomis, Albertine. *Grapes of Canaan*. Honolulu: Hawaiian Mission Children's Society, 1951.

Losch, Naomi Clarke. "Blood Quantum," in *Whetu Moana*, edited by Albert Wendt, Reina Whaitiri, and Robert Sullivan. Honolulu: University of Hawaiʻi Press, 2003.

Lum, Darrell. "Marbles," in *Sun*. Honolulu: Bamboo Ridge Press, 1980

———. "The Moiliili Bag Man," in *Pass On, No Pass Back*. Honolulu: Bamboo Ridge Press, 1990.

———. "Paint." Ibid.

Lum, Wing Tek. "The Butcher." *Bamboo Ridge* 52 (Fall 1991).

———. "A Moon Festival Picnic at Kahala Beach Park," in *Expounding the Doubtful Points*. Honolulu: Bamboo Ridge Press, 1987.

————. "To Live and Let Live." Ibid.

Lunalilo, William Charles. "Ka ʻŌlelo a ke Aliʻi Kāne i ke Aliʻi Wahine," in *The Echo of Our Song*, translated and edited by Mary K. Pukui and Alfons L. Korn. Honolulu: University of Hawaiʻi Press, 1973.

MacFarlane, Kathryn Jean. "Flapper's Acre." *Hawaii Quill Magazine* 6, no. 12 (1933).

MacMillan Ian. *The Red Wind*. Honolulu: Mutual Publishing, 1998.

————. "ʻUhu," in *Exiles From Time*. Honolulu: Anoai Press, 1998.

"Makalapua," in *He Mele Aloha*, edited by Carol Wilcox, et al. Honolulu: ʻOliʻOli Productions, 2003.

Malo, David. "He Inoa Ahi nō Ka-lā-kaua," in *The Echo of Our Song*, translated and edited by Mary K. Pukui and Alfons L. Korn. Honolulu: University of Hawaiʻi Press, 1973.

Mark. Untitled, in *Small Kid Time Hawaii*, edited by Eric Chock. Honolulu: Bamboo Ridge Press, 1981.

Maruyama, Sojin. Untitled. *So-un Sha* (1941).

Matsuda, Yoshiko. Untitled. *KAIMANA* (1990).

Matsueda, Pat. "Inflamed." *Hawaiʻi Review* (Fall 1984).

Matsunaga, Carlee M. K. "There Are Stars Above Kelewaa Street in Mililani." Unpublished.

Maugham, W. Somerset. "Honolulu," in *Collected Short Stories* vol. 1. New York: Penguin Books, 1977.

————. "Rain." Ibid.

Maxwell, Ellen Blackmar. *Three Old Maids in Hawaii*. New York: Eaton and Mains, 1896.

McKee, Ruth Eleanor. *After a Hundred Years*. New York: Doubleday, 1935. From AFTER A HUNDRED YEARS by Ruth Eleanor McKee, copyright 1935 by Ruth Eleanor McKee. Used by permission of Doubleday, a division of Random House, Inc.

————. *The Lord's Anointed*. New York: Doubleday, Doran & Company, 1957.

McKinney, Chris. *Bolohead Row*. Honolulu: Mutual Publishing, 2005.

————. *Hawaiiamerica*. Unpublished.

————. *The Tattoo*. Honolulu: Mutual Publishing, 1999.

McMullin, Dan Taulapapa. Untitled. www.downwindproductions.com/poem.html.

McPherson, Michael. "Auntie Kina On the King Street Tram," in *Singing With the Owls*. Honolulu: Petronium Press, 1982.

————. "The Long Swim." Ibid.

————. "My Uncles Surfing at Waikiki, Circa 1935." Ibid.

————. "Zero Break." Ibid.

————. "Kaimuki." *All Those Summers*. Honolulu: Watermark Publishing, 2004

Medrano, Kaʻimi. "Maikaʻi Nō! Very Good Indeed!" *Rain Bird* 6 (1989).

Melville, Herman. *Omoo*. New York: Viking Press, 1982.

————. *Typee*. New York: Viking Press, 1982.

Michener, James. *Hawaii*. New York: Random House, 1959. From HAWAII by James Michener, copyright © 1959 and renewed 1987 by James A. Michener. Used by permission of Random House, Inc.

Miyake, Wendy. "GetMyMoi.Com," in *Beads, Boys and the Buddha*. Mililani: Lotus Moon In Love, 2006.

Moore, Susanna. *Sleeping Beauties*. New York: Vintage Books, 1993. From SLEEPING BEAUTIES by Susanna Moore, copyright © 1993 by Susanna Moore. Used by permission of Vintage Books, a division of Random House, Inc.

Morales, Rodney. "Clear Acrylic Enamel," in *The Speed of Darkness*. Honolulu: Bamboo Ridge Press, 1988.

———. *When the Shark Bites*. Honolulu: University of Hawai'i Press, 2002.

Moriyama, Hiroko. Untitled. *Bussouge* 2 (1995).

———. Untitled. *Bussouge* 3 (1996).

Murayama, Milton. *Plantation Boy*. Honolulu: University of Hawai'i Press, 1998.

Nakashima, Ali S. Y. "Kuhio Vines Are Peaceful." Unpublished.

Nakashima, Naoto. *Hawaii Monogatari*. Tokyo: Sunagoya Shobo, Showa, 1936.

Nelson, Paul. "West of Waimea." *KAIMANA* (2002-2006).

Newell, Charles Martin. *Kalani of Oahu*. 1881.

Novak, Walt. *The Haole Substitute*. Fort Bragg: Cypress House, 1994. *The Haole Substitute*, copyright © 1994 by Walt Novak.

Oliveira, Paul. "Ho'omalimali." *Seaweeds and Constructions* 1 (April 1976).

Omura, Sarah. "Beware of the Ala Wai." *Star Poets Journal* (2005).

Ondaatje, Michael. Untitled selections, in *Secular Love*. Toronto: The Coach House Press, 1984. Copyright © 1984 by Michael Ondaatje. Reprinted by permission of Ellen Levine Literary Agency / Trident Media Group.

Ota, Shelley Ayame Nishimura. *Upon Their Shoulders*. New York: Exposition Press, 1951.

Owen, J. A. *Our Honolulu Boys*. London: The Religious Tract Society, 1881.

Pak, Gary. *Children of a Fireland*. Honolulu: University of Hawai'i Press, 2004.

———. "The Garden of Jiro Tanaka." *Bamboo Ridge* 41 (Winter 1989) and *Watcher of Waipuna and Other Stories*. Honolulu: Bamboo Ridge Press, 1992.

Pak, Ty. "Exile," in *Guilt Payment*. Honolulu: Bamboo Ridge Press, 1983.

Park, Chan E. *In 1903, Pak Hŭngbo Went to Hawai'i*, in *YOBO*, edited by Nora Okja Keller, et al. Honolulu: Bamboo Ridge Press, 2003.

Park, Sandra. "My Dad's Girlfriend." Unpublished.

Pasch, Emily. "The Diamond Head Hike." *Write On, HEA!* (2007).

Pascua, William. "Miles from Normal." *Star Poets Journal* (2006).

Passion, Christy Anne. "What We Are (Father to Daughter)." Unpublished.

———. "Sand Island." *Bamboo Ridge* 87 (Spring 2005).

Perez-Wendt, Mahealani. "Host Culture (Guava Juice on a Tray)." *'Ōiwi* (1998).

———. "Kalua." Unpublished.

————. "My Bus Is Two Hours Late." *'Ōiwi* (1998).

Perkins, Leialoha Apo. *Kamaka of Mamala Bay*. Honolulu: Kamaluʻuluolele Publishers, 1980.

Pinao, S. "Hoohuiaina Pala Ka Maia," in *He Buke Mele Lahui*. F. Testa, 1895 and Hawaiian Historical Society, 2003.

Pizo, Elmer Omar "Hammurabi." "Black Dog (Pinoy Style)." *Bamboo Ridge* 75 (Spring 1999).

Pritchett, John S. "Kids at the Bus Stop."

"Pua Mana Nō," in *The Echo of Our Song*, translated and edited by Mary K. Pukui and Alfons L. Korn. Honolulu: University of Hawaiʻi Press, 1973.

Pughe, Debbi. "Miyazawa No Yomu Toki." *Seaweeds and Constructions* 4 (December 1977).

————. "Sitting Vigil with Pablo Carlos." Ibid.

Quagliano, Tony. "Man Alone the Beast." *HAPA* 2 (Spring 1982).

————. "Poetry on the Bus." *Literary Arts Hawaii* 86 (Fall 1987).

Ramirez, Tino. "Shorebreak." *Hawaiʻi Review* 9 (Fall 1979). Reprinted with permission of Tino Ramirez and the Hawaiʻi Review, the literary journal of the Board of Publications at the University of Hawaiʻi at Mānoa.

Reiplinger, Rap. "Room Service." *Poi Dog With Crabs*. The Mountain Apple Company, 1995. Room Service authored and created by James K. "Rap" Reiplinger. Used with the permission of the Mountain Apple Company. Copyright 1978, All Rights Reserved.

Reynolds, Carol. Untitled, in *Haiku of Hawaii Nei*. Hilo: Marble-Us, Inc., 1978.

Rogerson, Helen. Untitled. Ibid.

"A Romance." *Ka Leo O Ka Lahui*. May 15, 1891.

Ross, Albert. *A Sugar Princess*. London: Chatto and Windus, 1900.

Sabal, Sean. *The Return of Braddha B*, in *College Plays*. Honolulu: Drama Department, University of Hawaiʻi, 2001.

Sadorra, Efren Baylon. "Hawaii," in *GUMIL Hawaii Iti Dua A Dekada 1971-1991*, edited by Pacita C. Saludes, et. al. Honolulu: Gumil Hawaii, 1991.

Sadorra, Perlita Tapec. "Biag Ditoy Hawaii," in *GUMIL Hawaii Iti Dua A Dekada 1971-1991*, edited by Pacita C. Saludes, et al. Honolulu: Gumil Hawaii, 1991.

Saiki, Jessica Kawasuna. "Learning," in *From the Lanai and Other Hawaii Stories*. Minneapolis: New Rivers Press, 1991.

Saiki, Patsy. "Communion," in *Passages to the Dream Shore*, edited by Frank Stewart. Honolulu: University of Hawaiʻi Press, 1987.

Saito, Ryan Shinichi. "The Man on the Corner." *Star Poets Journal* (2005).

Saito, Trey. "Radiant Japanese Maple Tree." Unpublished.

Sakai, Edward. *And Never the Twain Shall Meet?*, in *College Plays*. Honolulu: University of Hawaiʻi English Department, 1937.

Sakamoto, Edward. *Aʻala Park*, in *Aloha Las Vegas and Other Plays*. Honolulu: University of Hawaiʻi Press, 2000.

Sakumoto, Matthew Rikio Nihei. "GurlStar's Reply." *Star Poets Journal* (2006).

Salisbury, Graham. *Under the Blood-Red Sun*. New York: Dell Publishing, 1994. From UNDER

THE BLOOD-RED SUN by Graham Salisbury, copyright © 1994 by Graham Salisbury. Used by permission of Dell Publishing, a division of Random House, Inc.

Salt. "Kalihi Hypocrite." *Bamboo Ridge* 73 (Spring 1998).

Salvador, Normie. "Big Shuga Daddy." *Hawai'i Review* 57 (Summer 2001).

———. "Named by Numbers." *Bamboo Ridge* 79 (Spring 2001).

Sanchez, Abraham. "Sweet Mango." *Write On, HEA!* (1994).

Santos, Jerry. "Ku'u Home o Kahaluu." Olomana Publishing Co., 1976.

Sasaki, Cameron. "The Song of Cameron Sasaki." *Star Poets Journal* (2004).

Sato, Courtney. "Mariner's Ridge." Unpublished.

———. "Wishes." Unpublished.

Schultz, Susan M. "Local Politician," in *Portraits*. Kāne'ohe: Tinfish Press, 2005.

Sen, Courtney. "My Grandpa." *Star Poets Journal* (2005).

Shimizu, Tyler. "The Song of Tyler Shimizu." *Star Poets Journal* (2004).

Shirota, Jon. *Lucky Come Hawaii*. New York: Bantam Books, 1965.

Sledge, Linda Ching. *A Map of Paradise*. New York: Bantam Doubleday Dell, 1997. From A MAP OF PARADISE by Linda Ching Sledge, copyright © 1997 by Linda Ching Sledge. Used by permission of Bantam Books, a division of Random House, Inc.

Snyder, Gary. "Waikiki." *Chaminade Literary Review* 1 (Fall 1987) and *Left Out in the Rain*. San Francisco: Shoemaker and Hoard, 2005.

Soares, Rae. "A Deal in Opium," in *Cupid and the Law*.

Song, Cathy. "A Conservative View," in *Growing Up Local*, edited by Eric Chock, et al. Honolulu: Bamboo Ridge Press, 1998.

———. "A Grammar of Silk." Ibid.

———. "Picture Bride," in *Picture Bride*. New Haven: Yale University Press, 1983.

Souther, Sherman. "Buffo Nights," in *Surgical 'Brū-Ez*. Kāne'ohe: Tinfish Press, 2005.

Spahr, Juliana. "Gathering Palolo Stream," in *Fuck You-Aloha-I Love You*. Middletown: Wesleyan University Press, 2001.

Spalding, Linda. *Daughters of Captain Cook*. New York: Carol Publishing Group, 1988.

Spring, Noelle Elizabeth. "The White Mailbox." *Star Poets Journal* (2005).

St. John, Susan Lee. "Getting Groceries," in *Paké*, edited by Eric Chock and Darrell H. Y. Lum. Honolulu: Bamboo Ridge Press, 1989.

Stafford, William. "Customs Declaration: Honolulu." Unpublished.

———. "The R. L. Stevenson Tree on Oahu," in *Poems for Tennessee*. Martin: Tennessee Poetry Press, 1971. "The R. L. Stevenson Tree on O'ahu" © 1971 by William Stafford in *Poems for Tennessee* (Tennessee Poetry Press). Reprinted by permission of The Estate of William Stafford

Stanton, Joseph. "Driving Through Late-Night Downtown Honolulu," in *A Field Guide to the Wildlife of Suburban Oahu*. St. Louis: Time Being Books, 2006.

Steinhoff, William D. "Honolulu Hand Grenade R & R," in *The Best of Honolulu Fiction*, edited by Eric Chock and Darrell Lum. Honolulu: Bamboo Ridge Press, 1999.

Stevenson, Robert Louis. "To Princess Kaiulani," in *Ballads and Other Poems*. New York: Scribner, 1897.

Stewart, Frank. "Chinatown." *Bamboo Ridge* 1 (1978) and *The Open Water*. Point Reyes Station: Floating Island Publications, 1982.

———. "Honolulu: Waikiki Nights." *The Paper* 1, no. 4-5, (May-July 1981).

———. "Honolulu, Winter Morning," in *Reunion*. Honolulu: The Paper Press, 1986.

Stone, Lloyd. "Chinese Grandmother," in *Poems to Be Served With a Poi Cocktail*. Honolulu: Keith Stone, 1940.

———. "Kobe." Ibid.

———. "Picture of a Chinese Gardener Driving a Model 'T' Ford Through Heavy Traffic." Ibid.

Stover, G. H., and Henry Kailimai. "On the Beach at Waikiki," in *Noble's Hawaiian Favorites*. 1915.

Sueoka, Dawn. "Captions for an Imaginary Book about Honolulu." Unpublished.

Svoboda, Terese. "The Little Grass Shack." *Boundary* 2 (1994).

Taggard, Genevieve. "The Luau," in *Origin*. Honolulu: Donald Angus, 1947.

———. "The Tourist." Ibid.

Takahata, Carrie Y. "What I Carry." *Hawai'i Review* (Winter 2003). Reprinted with permission of Carrie Takahata and the Hawai'i Review, the literary journal of the Board of Publications at the University of Hawai'i at Mānoa

Takara, Kathryn Waddell. "Isis the Cat: Elegy." Unpublished.

———. "Plantation Compound." Unpublished.

Takushi, Puahaulani. "Conversations on Route 51." *Westwinds* (1997).

Talwar, Kalei. "Walmart is the Superstore of the Universe." *Ka Wai Ola*.

Tanielu, Vita. "Miss Sāmoa-Hawaii Cultural Pageant." *Tātou Tusi Tala* 1, no. 1, (Spring 1999).

Tavares, Kaci X. "The Mānoa Rain." *Star Poets Journal* (2006).

Teraoka, Tatsuo. Untitled. *Cho-on Shisha*. Tokyo: Bunkyo-sha, 1978

Theroux, Paul. *Hotel Honolulu*. Boston: Houghton Mifflin Company, 2001. © 2001 by Paul Theroux, reprinted with the permission of the Wylie Agency.

Thomas, Debra. "Rainbow Falls A Stair." *Seaweeds and Constructions* 4 (December 1977).

Thomes, William H. *A Whaleman's Adventures in the Sandwich Islands and California*. Boston: Lee & Shepard Publishers, 1876.

Thompson, Hunter S. *The Curse of Lono*. New York: Random House, 1983. Reprinted by permission of International Creative Management, Inc. Copyright © 1983 by Hunter S. Thompson.

Thon, Lynelle. "My Roommates." *Ka Nani* X (1992).

Togiola, Junior Mika. "They Say You Better Watch Out," in *Buss Laugh*, edited by Lee A. Tonouchi. Aiea: Major Danger Press, 2004.

Tolentino, Janet Ulep. "Grandpa Juan," in *Timek Dagiti Agtutubo: Voices of the Youth*. Honolulu: Filipino Association of University Women, 1990.

Tomisato, Alison. "Hale'iwa Fisherman." *Star Poets Journal* (2003).

Tonouchi, Lee A. "Da House of Liberty." *Tinfish* 8 (1999) and *Da Word*. Honolulu: Bamboo Ridge Press, 2001.

———. "Da Word." *ZYZZYVA* 53 (Fall 1998) and *Da Word*. Honolulu: Bamboo Ridge Press, 2001.

———. "Wot Village You From?" *Tinfish* 13 (2003).

Tonouchi, Lee A. and Da Fall 2001 PCC Classes at KCC. "Dey Say if You Talk Pidgin You NO CAN," in *Living Pidgin*. Kāne'ohe: Tinfish Press, 2002.

Toyama, Jean. "Sarumata." Unpublished.

———. "Special." Unpublished.

Trask, Haunani-Kay. "Into Our Light I Will Go Forever." *Bamboo Ridge* 44 (Fall 1989).

———. "Pūowaina: Flag Day," in *Night Is a Sharkskin Drum*. Honolulu: University of Hawai'i Press, 2002.

———. "Racist White Woman," in *Light in the Crevice Never Seen*. Corvallis: Calyx Books, 1994.

———. "Returning to Waimānalo," in *Ho'omānoa*, edited by Joseph P. Balaz. Honolulu: Ku Pa'a, Inc., 1989.

———. "Waikīkī," in *Light in the Crevice Never Seen*. Corvallis: Calyx Books, 1994.

Troy, Mary. "Island Entertainment," in *Cookie Lily*. Dallas: Southern Methodist University Press, 2004.

Tumpap, Alecia M. "The Bus Driver." *Star Poets Journal* (2004).

Twain, Mark. Microfilm Edition of Mark Twain's Literary Manuscripts Available in the Mark Twain Papers. 42 vols. Berkeley: The Bancroft Library, 2001. Reel #17. Courtesy of the Mark Twain Project Bancroft Library University of California, Berkeley.

Tyau, Kathleen. *Makai*. New York: Farrar, Straus and Giroux, 1999. Excerpts from 'Puka Nights' and 'Keeping the Beat' from MAKAI by Kathleen Tyau. Copyright © 1999 by Kathleen Tyau.

Uyeno, Joy Hiromi. "Treetops Flying." *Write On, HEA!* (2001).

Van Dyke, Peter. "Wordsworth and Dr. Wang," in *The Best of Honolulu Fiction*, edited by Eric Chock and Darrell Lum. Honolulu: Bamboo Ridge Press, 1999.

Villanueva, Karri Leilani. "Hana Pa'a?" *Star Poets Journal* (2006).

———. "Rubbah Slippas." *Star Poets Journal* (2005).

Wall, Steven T. "Street Racing." *Star Poets Journal* (2005).

Walter, Jeremy. "If I Were the Ko'olau Mountains." Unpublished.

Wang, Zoe. "Dance to the Rhythm of Chinatown." *Star Poets Journal* (2005).

Westlake, Wayne Kaumualii. "Native Hawaiian." *Ramrod* 1 (1980).

Wouk, Herman. *The Winds of War*. New York: Little Brown & Company, 1971. From THE WINDS OF WAR by HERMAN WOUK. Copyright © 1971 by Herman Wouk; copyright renewed © 1999 by Herman Wouk. By permission of LITTLE BROWN & COMPANY.

Yamanaka, Cedric. "The Lemon Tree Billiards House," in *In Good Company*. Honolulu: University of Hawai'i Press, 2002.

Yamanaka, Lois-Ann. *Behold the Many*. New York: Farrar, Straus and Giroux, 2006. Excerpts from 'Kalihi Valley' and 'Little Leah's Lament' from BEHOLD THE MANY by Lois-Ann Yamanaka. Copyright © 2006 by Lois-Ann Yamanaka.

———. "Boy Wen' Flunk Eight Grade English Again." *Hawai'i Review* 53 (Summer 1999).

Yi, Hong-gi. "The Attack on Pearl Harbor," translated by Hyeran Seo. Unpublished.

———. "The First Impression of Honolulu," translated by Hyeran Seo. Unpublished.

York, Y. *Nothing is the Same*. Woodstock: Dramatic Publishing, 2004. Copyright MMVI by Y York. Printed in the United States of America. *All Rights Reserved. All inquiries regarding performance rights should be addressed to Dramatic Publishing, 311 Washington St., Woodstock, IL 60098. Phone: (815)338-7170. Fax: (815)338-8981.*

Yoshinaga, Ida. "Uyesugi Gumi: Sonnets from the Non-Samurai Sansei Boys' Club." *Tinfish* 13 (September 2002).

Author Index

ABOUT THE EDITORS

GAVAN DAWS first came to Hawai'i in 1958. He has written thirteen books, published worldwide, in a life that has taken him back and forth between the United States and Australia, with stints in Europe and Asia. His books about the islands include *Shoal of Time; Holy Man: Father Damien of Molokai;* and *Land and Power in Hawaii.* He is the recipient of the Hawaii Award for Literature, and has been named a Distinguished Historian by the Hawaiian Historical Society, and a Distinguished Alumnus by the University of Hawai'i. Beyond Hawai'i, in the Institute of Advanced Studies at the Australian National University, Daws headed historical research on the Pacific and Southeast Asia for fifteen years. He was elected a Fellow of the Academy of Humanities in Australia, and served as the Pacific member of the UNESCO Commission on the Scientific and Cultural History of Humankind. He has been Senior Fellow at the Center for Cultural and Technical Interchange between East and West. He has received grants from, among others, the National Endowment for the Humanities, the National Endowment for the Arts, the American Philosophical Society, and the Australian Film Commission. His documentary films have won awards internationally, including Best Documentary at the Hawai'i International Film Festival, the gold medal at the leading European documentary festival, and the Australian Film Institute Award, the national Oscar-equivalent. He has written screenplays, a stage play with music and choreography, and his songs have been performed at the Waikīkī Shell and the Hollywood Bowl, and in clubs from San Francisco to Greenwich Village. Daws and his Hawai'i-born wife live in Honolulu.

BENNETT HYMER has lived in Honolulu for almost forty years. Since founding Mutual Publishing in 1976, he has helped produce close to five hundred books about Hawai'i, in almost every genre. A love of the islands, and a love of stories and writing about the place, continue to inspire his work. In 2001, he co-authored, with Glen Grant, *Hawai'i Looking Back: An Illustrated History of the Islands.* He is a graduate of McGill University (BA) and Northwestern University (PhD). He has taught at Northwestern University and the University of Wisconsin-Milwaukee, and has been an urban researcher for the Chicago Urban League and an economist for the state of Hawai'i. He travels extensively to Asia, and to Germany, where family members reside.